DATE DUE			
Apr 15 '72			
Oct 21 '76			
Nov 3 '76			
Nov 18 '76			
Dec 2 '76			
Dec 10 80			
Apr 24 '81			

THE LABOR SECTOR

THE LABOR SECTOR

SECOND EDITION

NEIL W. CHAMBERLAIN

Graduate School of Business
Columbia University

DONALD E. CULLEN

New York State School
of Industrial and Labor Relations
Cornell University

McGraw-Hill Book Company

New York   St. Louis   San Francisco   Düsseldorf   Johannesburg
Kuala Lumpur   London   Mexico   Montreal   New Delhi   Panama
Rio de Janeiro   Singapore   Sydney   Toronto

This book was set in Times Roman by Monotype Composition Company, Inc., and printed and bound by Von Hoffmann Press, Inc. The designer was J. E. O'Connor; the drawings were done by John Cordes, J. & R. Technical Services, Inc. The editors were Jack R. Crutchfield and James R. Belser. Les Kaplan supervised production.

THE LABOR SECTOR

Copyright © 1965, 1971 by McGraw-Hill, Inc. All rights reserved. Printed in the United States of America. No part of this publication may be reproduced, stored in a retrieval system, or transmitted, in any form or by any means, electronic, mechanical, photocopying, recording, or otherwise, without the prior written permission of the publisher.

Library of Congress Catalog Card Number 77–154220

07–010428–X

1234567890 VHVH 7987654321

CONTENTS

PREFACE

In preparing this revision of *The Labor Sector*, we attempted particularly to cope with the problem of fragmentation that plagues the study of industrial relations. It is true that much of the fascination of this subject stems from the fact that there is no all-embracing "theory of industrial relations." Instead, both the scholar and practitioner in this field must draw upon the insights of all the social sciences—history, economics, political science, sociology, psychology—and frequently upon the pages of the daily newspaper as well. Yet, to the reader of a survey text, this rich diversity can also be a source of confusion if he sees no relationship among such subjects as occupational mobility, personnel management, and the Taft-Hartley Act.

To provide this needed integration, we have adopted several devices. First, a new opening chapter presents an overview of the labor sector to help students see, from the outset, the general shape of the terrain they will be exploring. Second, we have retained the stress of the first edition upon the household as a decision-making unit, a fact which is crucial to an understanding of both the causes and effects of nearly every labor problem in our society. Third, we have argued that most of the controversial issues in the labor field are variations on one or more of the following themes: the debate over how a modern society should resolve the clash of consumer and producer interests; the search for the ideal mixture of security and incentives in the labor sector; and the question of whether a modern economy can simultaneously enjoy full employment, stable prices, and a minimum of government controls. These themes are neither original nor mutually exclusive ideas, but we believe they pose the questions of primary interest to most students of industrial relations and will, therefore, provide a useful frame of reference.

This edition also includes, of course, the significant developments in the labor sector since the early 1960s, when the first edition was written. In reviewing those eventful years, we were struck by the importance—but also the difficulty—of portraying the labor sector as having reached a stage in which, in certain basic respects, it is now poised between the worlds of the known and the unknown, the old and the new. In a general sense, the same can be said of any segment of society at any point in time, but seldom have the forces of continuity and change been so evenly balanced in the labor sector as they are today.

Consider, as a prime example, that in 1970 one of every two American workers held a white-collar job, and that those workers producing services actually outnumbered those producing goods. Economists and others have known for some time that this was the direction in which the economy and the labor force were moving, and yet we know surprisingly little about what these developments mean for the future. In this respect, the study of industrial relations has suffered from a kind of cultural lag: We have devoted a great deal of research effort to the one-half of the labor force typified by the worker on a General Motors assembly line—how he searches for a job, how he reacts to a factory setting, why he may join a union, and so on—but (with some notable exceptions) we have only recently begun to study that other half of the world of work found in offices, stores, hospitals, schools, government agencies, and similar settings.

We therefore found it impossible to break away completely from the traditional emphasis of labor textbooks upon the factory worker, but we have broadened our focus whenever possible. In describing the labor force in Chapter 2, for example, we have stressed Eli Ginzberg's useful concept of the pluralistic economy and also drawn upon Victor Fuchs' recent research on the service industries, and in later chapters we have incorporated the results of the few other studies now available on the white-collar worker and the service sector. (On this, as on other subjects, we may have missed some important studies in our review of the literature, and we duly apologize for any such oversights.)

On the policy front, too, we believe that the labor sector has reached a significant crossroad today. When one recalls the great debates of the 1930s over the remedies needed to cope with the grievous labor problems of that day, it can be seen that our society has subsequently given a fair trial to the solutions proposed by both sides to those debates. Liberals have won the adoption of nearly every element of the welfare state that appeared so radical a generation ago, and conservatives have seen the economy operate relatively unfettered (except in war time) and at nearly full capacity for an unprecedented stretch of thirty years. Most American workers have profited enormously from this economic growth and from the adoption of the welfare state as well, and yet the turbulent events of the 1960s demonstrated that labor problems—some old, some new—still abound in our society. Few people believe that yesterday's remedies should be scrapped, but many believe that additional ones are now needed.

Many developments in the 1960s illustrate this point: Public assistance (welfare) programs did not dwindle away as once expected, but instead became so costly and ineffective that the demand for radical reforms, such as a negative income tax, now comes from every political quarter; the Civil Rights Act of 1964 outlawed the old-style forms of discrimination in the job market, only to reveal the need for some new kind of "affirmative action"; manpower training programs proliferated, but the problems of the hard-core unemployed proved to be even more severe than anticipated; millions of government workers finally won the right to bargain collectively, only to raise the issue of whether that right is meaningful when coupled with a ban on strikes; and the unemployment–inflation dilemma baffled both Democratic and Republican administrations.

Needless to say, this edition does not unveil "the answers" to these and similar policy problems, but we have deliberately presented many issues from this perspective of the 1960s as marking a period during which there was growing dissatisfaction with the solutions tried since the 1930s—and the 1970s as promising to be a period during which new labor policies will be sought by conservatives and liberals alike.

Finally, as must already be evident, we have followed the lead of the first edition in permitting ourselves the luxury of stating our own views on several controversial matters. We hope that these opinions will give the student a target against which to test his own convictions, and that they will also alert him to the bias that, despite our best efforts, has probably crept into our presentation of other people's views. Certainly the least of our worries is that many students today will unquestioningly accept our opinions as the revealed truth—and that is all to the good.

Neil W. Chamberlain
Donald E. Cullen

PART ONE

THE LABOR SECTOR: AN OVERVIEW

In appraising the labor sector of the economy, there is always a temptation to think in terms of the typical worker. For those interested in the practical problems of running a business or an economy, "labor" often means the worker in General Motors or United States Steel who tries to solve his job problems by joining a union and by pushing for certain types of labor laws—actions which in turn are seen as creating problems for the worker's employer and for the rest of us who are consumers. For those observers with a theoretical bent, the labor sector is essentially the same as any other market in which buyers and sellers compete, and for purposes of abstraction one worker or unit of labor supply may often be taken as typical of all others.

Both of these views of labor have their uses, as we shall see in later chapters, but neither adequately portrays the labor sector as a whole. For that purpose, it is best to begin not with the individual worker, either on a real job or as a unit on a supply curve, but to consider labor as it is organized into family households. The fact is that 94 percent of our population is attached to a household, so that it is the family unit—not the individual worker, typical or not—which acts as the primary supplier of labor services and is the ultimate consumer of nearly all that is produced.

The household as an organizer of economic activity was a more readily recognized institution in earlier days, when the average farm was almost a little subsistence economy of its own. Although households today are far less self-sufficient, selling the services of their members in order to purchase from others the goods which are consumed, it remains true that our society's structure of wants is chiefly a product of family decisions, and the type and quantity of labor made available to the economy is also principally a result of family decisions.

By focusing on the household as an economic unit, this first section also introduces certain themes that will be helpful in later chapters when we tackle the more exciting aspects of the labor sector, such as poverty and management rights and union monopoly and the welfare state. For example, most of these fighting issues pit *producer interests* against *consumer interests,* in that worker-producers strive to improve their income and working conditions in ways (such as strikes and featherbedding and minimum-wage laws) that may threaten consumers' interests in lower prices and in more and better products. By the economist's scale of values, the choice is obvious: Consumers' interests are nearly always to be preferred over those of any group of producers, whether they be oil companies lobbying for a depletion allowance or carpenters striking for a closed shop.

We shall argue that the choice is seldom this simple on labor issues, for reasons suggested by the dual role of most families as both consumers *and* producers of income. As consumers, we all are in favor of maximum competition and efficiency; on the job, however, most of us want more income and security and control over our fate than the "free market" normally provides. Thus the difficult task of national labor policy is not to choose between one group labeled "workers" and another labeled "consumers," but rather to strike some balance between the producer and consumer interests that exist together in nearly every household.

Essentially the same issues underlie the controversy over the mixture of *security and incentives* that should prevail in the labor sector, a controversy that many thought was settled in the 1930s but which continues unabated today. We shall see that it is too easy to dismiss this as a problem created by some individuals who want a free ride from the government or their employer, at the expense of the rest of us who realize that a dynamic economy requires incentives for achievement and penalties for failure. Or, if one's sympathies run in the other direction, it is equally misleading to attribute worker insecurity to profit-minded employers who automate jobs and underpay workers with no thought of the human values at stake.

Again the household offers a better clue to the complexity of this issue. The typical family very much wants the benefits of a risk-taking economy, with its rising standard of living and the opportunity for children to do better than their parents. At the same time, however, the family dreads the risk that its income may abruptly be shut off through no fault of its breadwinner, if his plant moves south or he is sick or injured or the economy sags or the new boss just doesn't like his personality or the color of his skin. Thus, while the poor most urgently challenge our society to find a way of providing security without destroying incentives, we shall argue that this dilemma exists at every level of the labor sector— from the union member cherishing his seniority rights to the professor striving for tenure and the executive dickering for a handsome pension at company expense.

Finally, a view of the household as an economic unit also serves to introduce the critical issue of whether a modern economy can simultaneously enjoy *full employment, stable prices,* and *minimum government control over wage and price decisions.* No industrial society has yet achieved that trilogy of goals for any sustained period, and both the causes and consequences of that failure will occupy our attention in several later chapters. At this point, it is enough to suggest the dimensions of the problem by noting how certain remedies may affect the average family.

As the economy approaches full employment, a number of forces may trigger a wage-price spiral which no one wants. An obvious solution is to cool off the economy with orthodox fiscal and monetary measures, which simply translated means that some families may have to suffer a jolt of unemployment in order that all families may benefit from stable prices, a trade which understandably appeals more to the winners than to the losers. A second policy option is to permit full employment to continue and to choke off any inflationary pressures by means of wage and price controls, a solution which might work for a brief time but over the long haul can pose severe problems for a family in satisfying either its producer or consumer needs. Or a society might even decide to accept inflation as the necessary cost of full employment and free markets, but apparently few American families care to gamble that their wage or salary income can consistently stay ahead of escalating prices.

No one has yet devised a painless solution to these or the other conflicts that run throughout the labor sector, nor are any panaceas about to be unveiled in this text. Enough should now have been said, however, to suggest some of the reasons why labor problems persist in even the richest of all countries, and why a first step toward understanding these problems is to examine the household as both a producer and a consumer of income.

CHAPTER 1

**LABOR AS A PRODUCER
AND CONSUMER OF
INCOME**

As any family makes its daily decisions about working and spending, it is participating in an extraordinarily complex process. Within every household in a market economy, some portion of its time is sold to someone else for money. The more appetite a household acquires for goods and services which must be purchased with money, obviously the more time it is likely to sell in the labor market. Thus the supply of labor available to the economy ultimately depends upon the strength of every family's demand for goods and services.

At the same time, it is this demand from household consumers which creates a market for sellers to supply. Business firms and universities and government agencies and a host of other institutions spring up to meet this consumer demand, and in so doing they provide employment opportunities for the members of households who want income. Thus a circular flow is created. Households provide labor in order to buy goods from others who in turn buy labor in order to supply the goods that the households want.

That, of course, is far from a complete picture of a modern economy, but it accurately points up the interaction of the supply of labor and the demand for goods and services—or, more simply, the economic role of the household as both a source and a consumer of income. Elementary as that concept may appear, it is surprisingly difficult to illustrate or apply. Most labor statistics describe either "the worker" or "the consumer" at

a point in time, and it is much easier to deal with labor issues in those partial terms than to grapple with the idea of a continuous and circular flow of interlocking decisions binding together the family, the labor market, and the product market. In fact, most of the chapters that follow will focus on just one or another of the household's many activities in the labor sector—choosing an occupation, searching for a job, joining a union, and so on.

It is nevertheless possible, and important, for this opening chapter to sketch in the current status of the American household as both a producer and a consumer of income. Within the typical household, who works and why? How much income does the family receive for selling part of its time in the labor market? What are some of the major trends in the world of work that have altered the household's economic status? Some preliminary answers to these questions will delineate the boundaries of the labor sector of the economy, and will also introduce most of the issues to be explored in later chapters.

The supply of labor

In 1970, when the population of the United States reached 205 million, only 86 million individuals were working or looking for work. What distinguishes the 40 percent who work from the 60 percent whom they support?

There is no mystery about many of those in the

60 percent group: children under sixteen years of age and inmates of institutions are clearly not candidates for the labor force, and those two sub-groups form just over one-half of the "non-workers" today. Most of the other half are house-wives and students, as one would expect, and yet that generalization masks most of the interesting questions about who works and why. Table 1-1 shows, for example, that among all those who might conceivably have looked for a job in 1968 —the "civilian noninstitutional population 16 years and over"—the proportion actually in the labor market varied sharply by age and sex and to some extent by color.

These varying participation rates carry several implications. First, the trend among age groups, particularly for whites, reflects what has been termed the life cycle of the typical household. In the United States, marriage usually occurs in the late teens or early twenties and frequently both husband and wife work for the first few years in order to buy furniture and appliances and per-haps save for a down payment on a house. With

Table 1-1 *Civilian Labor Force Participation Rates,* by Age, Sex, and Color, 1968, percent*

	Male		Female	
Age	White	Non-white	White	Non-white
Total, 16 years and over	80.4	77.6	40.7	49.3
16 and 17 years	47.7	37.9	33.0	22.3
18 and 19 years	65.7	63.3	53.3	46.9
20–24 years	82.4	85.0	54.0	58.4
25–34 years	97.2	95.0	40.6	56.6
35–44 years	97.6	93.4	47.5	59.3
45–54 years	95.4	90.1	51.5	59.8
55–64 years	84.7	79.6	42.0	47.0
65 years and over	27.3	27.6	9.4	11.9

* The percent of the civilian noninstitutional population 16 years and over who are in the civilian labor force. The latter term refers to those who are unemployed and look-ing for work as well as to those who are actually working. It excludes members of the armed forces, who numbered 3.5 million in 1968.

SOURCE: *Statistics on Manpower, A Supplement to the Manpower Report of the President, 1969*, p. 5.

the arrival of the first child, the wife usually quits her job, earnings of the household drop, and there is a consequent adjustment in expenditures. Be-fore long, and particularly if there is a second child in the interim, the chances are 50-50 that the young couple will move into a home of its own, incurring a long-term debt to be paid off in installments out of current income. Then it has become increasingly common for the wife to re-turn to work sometime in her mid-thirties, when her children are occupied with school. In time, the younger members of the household may add to family income by summer jobs or part-time work during the school year, before leaving to start households of their own. Finally, when retirement arrives, incomes drop precipitously for most older people and outlays are scaled down to necessitous goods and services.

Because of these familiar facts, no one wastes much time wondering why four out of five males of working age are employed or actively looking for work (the participation rate includes both groups). Nor is it surprising that this proportion rises to nearly 100 percent in the prime working ages of twenty-five to fifty-four years—after the completion of education and before the appear-ance of the disabilities of old age. Not only does our culture expect the male head of the family to be at work, but the economic pressures for him to be there can appear nearly as unrelenting to the father in Scarsdale, facing his children's Ivy League tuition rates and the monthly payments on a $100,000 home, as to the Alabama sharecrop-per struggling to meet food and clothing bills. It is nevertheless significant that among moon-lighters—the 5 percent of employed persons who hold two or more jobs—there is a predominance of young fathers with low earnings.[1]

But if males enter the job market primarily because of economic pressures, and sometimes take on two or three jobs to make ends meet, why are the participation rates of Negro males gen-erally lower than those of white males?[2] In view of the low income of the average Negro family, one might expect its adult males to show, if any-thing, even higher rates than their white counter-parts, as Negro females so clearly do in most age groups. Notice, in fact, that when many white females drop out of the labor force to have children between the ages of twenty-five and thirty-four, the participation rate of Negro females dips only slightly before continuing toward its peak of 60 percent.

There is no simple economic explanation for this behavior of Negro participation rates. Many men just give up the search for work (and hence drop out of the labor force) after bitter experience teaches them that they do not have the "right" education, training, contacts, or color to land a decent job. But even when Negro men stay in the job market (as most obviously do), their employment experience is often so unstable and low-paying that there is far more need for the Negro wife to work than for the white wife to do so. For other Negro women, the key fact is that the Negro family itself tends to be more unstable than the white, for a variety of reasons, so that the mother is more likely to be the only bread-winner in the household. And through all these considerations run questions about the role of social legislation as either a cause or a cure. For example, what would happen to the participation rates of both Negroes and whites if relief payments were slashed tomorrow—or if, on the other hand, we guaranteed every American family an income of $3,000 a year? In short, Table 1-1 clearly raises many issues that need to be explored in later chapters.

Working wives

Two more of these issues deserve mention in this sketch of labor supply. Quite apart from Negro–white differences, the extent to which married women in general enter the job market is a subject of prime importance today.

The continuing change of greatest effect, as well as greatest magnitude, in labor force participation is among married women. The twentieth century ushered in the change, but it continues at an accelerated rate through post-World War II years. In 1947, 1 out of 5 married women worked; today [in 1967], . . . more than 1 out of 3 is in the labor force.

As a result . . . , married women now constitute 20 percent of all civilian workers 14 years and over, compared with 11 percent in 1947.[3]

It is easy to understand why nearly every male sooner or later enters the labor force, but it is not at all obvious why some women work and some do not when they have husbands to support them, or why those working have been increasing in number so much faster than those not working. A century ago, for example, when only a few married women from the poorest families worked outside the home, it would have taken a rare economist to predict that as the average family's income soared over the years, so would the number of working wives.

We shall examine the reasons for this long-term trend in the next chapter, and focus here on the working wife as of March, 1967, the date of a nationwide survey.[4] The focus, however, is a trifle fuzzy. On the one hand, the impact of the *family life cycle* was much as one would expect from Table 1-1: the participation rate for married women dropped sharply during the prime child-bearing ages of twenty-five to thirty-four years, and the rate was lowest for women with pre-school-age children and highest for those with no children under eighteen years old. On the other hand, the role of *education* was quite surprising: the more years of education, the more likely that the wife would seek a job outside her home, and this relationship existed within every category such as age, color, and presence of children. In fact, among all married women whose husbands were present in the household, those with fewer than five years of schooling showed a participation rate of only 19 percent, compared to 40 percent for high school graduates and 50 percent for college graduates.

As a result, the influence of the *husband's income* on the wife's decision to work is less significant today than it once was. In 1967, the participation rates of married women were about 40 percent for those whose husband's income was $3,000 to $6,999, and about 33 percent for wives of men in both lower- and higher-income groups.

On balance, the most substantial postwar increases in labor force participation of married women have been among those whose husband's income is above the average. More and more wives are going to work not because the basic necessities are lacking, but to afford a higher standard of living, to satisfy personal nonmonetary aspirations, and, very probably, to assert a measure of economic self-sufficiency.[5]

The unemployed and underemployed

Finally, from the viewpoint of too many households, the only important question about labor supply is why it is usually underutilized. The participation rates in Table 1-1 draw no distinction between the employed and the unemployed members of the labor force, or between those working full time and those on short time, but obviously these differences can be crucial to the worker and his family and indeed to the entire society.

Table 1-2 describes the incidence of unemployment in 1969, one of the best employment years since the end of World War II. Total employment reached an all-time high of 78 million in that year, and the overall unemployment rate (3.5 percent) was at its lowest level since 1953. Also, the rate of 1.5 percent for married men, in many ways the most critical index of unemployment, was at its lowest point since 1955, the year when annual rates for that group were first collected.

Yet a rate of 3.5 percent means that in an average month in 1969 there were *2.8 million* individuals in the job market but out of work. Over 40 percent of these individuals had been unemployed for more than 4 weeks, and 1 out of 8 for more than 14 weeks. Also, because there is turnover within this group over the year, as some land jobs and are replaced by others losing jobs or looking for their first job, a total of about *11 million* individuals were unemployed at one time or another even in the prosperous year of 1969.

Also, Table 1-2 demonstrates the extent to which the burden of unemployment falls disproportionately on the Negro, the young, and the unskilled. As a standard for comparison, if *total* unemployment rose to 6.5 percent, roughly equal to the 1969 rates for Negroes and for unskilled workers, economists would declare the existence of a recession; if the overall rate rose to the astronomical level shown by Negro teen-agers in 1969, the economy would be in a depression on the scale of the 1930s.

As for the *under*employment of the labor force, there is no adequate measure of workers with jobs below their educational or skill level, although there certainly are many who find themselves in that situation. Part-time employment can be measured, however, and while most part-timers prefer a short workweek (because they are students, housewives, and the like), others would prefer a full-time job but are subject to partial layoff or for other reasons cannot find full-time work. In an average week of 1969, there were about 2 million workers in this category of involuntary part-time employment—or part-time unemployment.[6]

Which view of the labor market is correct? Was 1969 a year of full employment, in the sense that most workers, and particularly nearly every married man, had a job who wanted one, and that some unemployment must always exist in a dynamic economy? Or was 1969 further proof of the exorbitant cost of an unregulated economy, as literally millions of families suffered a loss of income for reasons usually beyond their control, and most of the losers were, as always, those already at the bottom of society? The easy answer

Table 1-2 *Selected Unemployment Rates in 1969, percent*

Total, 16 years of age and over	3.5
White	3.1
Nonwhite	6.4
Total, 16–19 years of age	12.2
Nonwhite	24.0*
Total, males 20–44 years of age	2.4
Nonwhite	4.2
Total, experienced workers†	3.3
Managers, officials, and proprietors	1.0*
Craftsmen and foremen	2.2
Nonfarm laborers	6.7
Married males, wife present	1.5

* Estimated.
† As distinguished from unemployed persons who never held a full-time civilian job.

SOURCE: *Economic Report of the President, 1970*, pp. 48, 152, and 205.

is that the truth lies somewhere between those extremes, but just where—and what to do about it—are questions that will occupy a good many of the chapters to follow.

Family income

In exchanging its labor for money, how well is the average family doing? That, after all, is the first (though not the only) test of any economy. Unemployment and participation rates and the activities of employers and unions—these and similar subjects are of concern primarily because of their implications for family income. At the time of writing, income data were not available for 1969 to offer a direct parallel to the preceding employment data, but the 1968 figures provide a reasonably accurate picture of the current income of American families.

In the mountain of statistics available on income, perhaps the most important is that *the median income of all families in 1968 was $8,600.* That single fact suggests both how well off we are as a society and the vast resources available to correct our remaining problems.

To most Americans, of course, $8,600 is not particularly overwhelming as an annual income. By definition, half of all families earned more than that in 1968, and those around the average found that a pretax income of about $165 a week hardly permits lavish living by today's standards. By any other standards, however, that is a staggeringly high figure for the average income of an entire society. Only two decades earlier in this country, in the boom year of 1947, the median family's income was $3,000 or, when translated into 1968 dollars (to correct for price increases), still only $4,700 as compared to $8,600 in 1968.[7] Precisely comparable figures are not available for earlier years, but they would undoubtedly be much lower. In short, even by American standards of a generation ago, the typical household today is extremely well off.

And by the standards of other countries, income in the United States appears almost indecently high in this age of concern for the impoverished nations of the world. Cross-country comparisons of income and living standards are notoriously difficult to make, but Table 1-3 pro-

Table 1-3 *Gross Domestic Product Per Capita in Selected Countries, 1964*

Country	GDP per capita* (U.S. dollars)
United States	$3,002
Sweden	2,013
Canada	1,987
France	1,523
Great Britain	1,472
Japan	671
Mexico	442
South Vietnam	105
Kenya	85
India†	82
Congo	68

* Gross domestic product (GDP) at factor cost converted to U.S. dollars at official exchange rates. The GDP differs from gross national product only by the exclusion of net factor incomes received from abroad and of the excess of indirect taxes over subsidies.
† Data are for 1963.
SOURCE: United Nations, *Yearbook of National Accounts Statistics, 1965,* New York, 1966, pp. 493–496.

vides a rough indication of why, in the eyes of the world, we have all the lovely and unlovely attributes of the richest family in town.

It is both fashionable and justifiable to criticize many aspects of this country's "materialistic culture," such as our penchant for spending billions on comic books and cigarettes and color television while watching our cities crumble about us. Yet, note that most of these criticisms are aimed not at the high levels of income generated by our economy, but rather at the ways in which we choose to spend that income. Or, stated differently, there are few if any countries that would not leap at the opportunity to exchange average income levels with the United States. We shall frequently discover, however, that these facts settle few arguments among ourselves. Critics of the welfare state, for example, have long argued that the government should cease tampering with a system that obviously works better than any other one around. The defense retorts that the government has been "tampering" in the labor sector for over thirty years now and obviously our system has never worked better.

Poverty

But the burning issue regarding family income today is not how fast the average is increasing, but how equitably other families are distributed around that average. Consider Table 1-4. Two-fifths of all white families were over the $10,000 mark in 1968, compared to only one-fifth of non-white. Also, 23 percent of all Negro families had under $3,000, compared to 9 percent of white—and for both groups this counts money income for every member of the family and from *every* source, including welfare payments and unemployment insurance as well as wages, interest, dividends, and the like. On the other hand, note that Negroes have no monopoly on poverty, for in absolute numbers there are many more white families than Negro in the under-$3,000 category.

What is so significant, however, about the $3,000 figure? After all, that was the median income of *all* American families as late as 1947, and it is still miles above the average income of most of the world's population. This is another important question to which we shall return later, for both the concept and the measurement of poverty are crucial matters today. At this point, just note that if a worker were receiving only the legal minimum of $1.60 per hour today, and if he were lucky enough to work full-time the year

Table 1-4 *Families by Total Money Income and Color, 1968*

Total money income	All families	White families	Nonwhite families
Number (thousands)	50,510	45,437	5,074
Percent	100.0	100.0	100.0
Under $3,000	10.3	8.9	22.8
$3,000–$4,999	12.1	11.0	22.0
$5,000–$6,999	14.5	14.3	16.5
$7,000–$9,999	23.4	24.0	17.6
$10,000–$14,999	25.0	26.2	14.7
$15,000 and over	14.7	15.7	6.3
Median income	$8,632	$8,937	$5,590

SOURCE: U.S. Bureau of the Census, *Current Population Reports*, ser. P-60, no. 66, "Income in 1968 of Families and Persons in the United States," 1969, p. 19.

Table 1-5 *Percentage Share of Aggregate Income Received by Each Fifth of Families, Ranked by Income, 1968*

Income rank	Share of aggregate income received
Total	100.0
Lowest fifth	5.7
Second fifth	12.4
Middle fifth	17.7
Fourth fifth	23.7
Highest fifth	40.6
Top 5 percent	14.0

SOURCE: U.S. Bureau of the Census, *Current Population Reports*, ser. P-60, no. 66, "Income in 1968 of Families and Persons in the United States," 1969, p. 22.

around, he would earn $3,300. In 1968, there were over 5 million families receiving *less* than that meager sum. No one can mathematically prove that most of those families were poor, but who would care to argue that—by today's standards in the United States—most were not poor?

Table 1-5 presents an even more pointed definition of the same problem. No one expects income to be divided equally among all families, and certainly no major society of any ideology has ever approached a literal equality of income. But neither are there any immutable laws of nature or economic theory which dictate that the "best" pattern of inequality is one in which one-fifth of all families win 40 percent of the income pie while another fifth win only 6 percent.

None of these statistics, however, sheds any light on the causes of income inequality or the cure for poverty. To take an extreme example, why did male farm workers earn an average wage income of only $2,073 in 1968, a year when the president of Seagrams Distillers drew a salary of $331,475 (a tidy $908 a day) and the chairman of General Motors received a salary of $225,000 plus a bonus of $427,500? Or if that is too extreme, why did the weekly wages of factory workers in June, 1969 range from $70 for workers in one branch of the clothing industry to $170 for those in the auto industry? Or for that matter, in the academic year of 1966–1967, why did the average faculty member receive a salary and fringe benefits totaling $18,700 at Harvard, but only $11,048 at Antioch College and $8,336 at Tuskegee Institute?[8] We shall be wrestling with these questions at several points in the text, and shall also examine the major proposals for eliminating poverty, a problem which frequently has little to do with low wages.

Inflation

Everyone knows why consumers dislike inflation, but not everyone appreciates how subtle the inflation problem has become in recent years. There is a widespread impression, for example, that most or all of the postwar increase in money wages and salaries has been eaten up by offsetting price increases. That is simply not true. As indicated above, the rise in family income has far outstripped price increases over the postwar period as a whole. Nor have we experienced anything like the inflations that have ripped through several underdeveloped countries, with prices jumping 200 or 300 percent in a single year.

Our very different inflation problem can be illustrated by the chain of events triggered by the modest price increase of 3 percent that occurred from 1965 to 1966, primarily as a result of government spending for the rapid military buildup in Vietnam. Over the same period, take-home pay —earnings minus social security and income taxes —for the average factory worker with three dependents rose a respectable $2.62 a week, from $96.83 to $99.45.[9] Unfortunately, however, that was only a 2.3 percent rise in take-home pay, not enough to match the 3 percent increase in prices. The result: Workers understandably pressed for catch-up wage increases, employers understandably tried to pass along increased wage costs, and for these (and other) reasons prices continued to rise in 1967 and 1968; to cool off the economy, taxes were raised and unemployment rates remained higher than most people desired.

Needless to say, that is a much oversimplified description of the tangled events of 1965 to 1968, but there is enough truth in it to illustrate again the unique problems of the American labor sector. At a time when much of the world's population is on the razor's edge of starvation, it can appear absurd to worry about our 3 percent price creep, or 4 percent unemployment, or even the bottom 15 percent of our lush income structure. Yet, it is precisely *because* we are the epitome of "the affluent society," in Galbraith's apt phrase,[10] that some of these remaining problems so aggravate our social conscience. In a country as desperately poor as India, there is absolutely no way for either the government or the private economy to eliminate poverty in this generation. In the United States, however, the sum required to bring all families above the poverty line would represent *less than 2 percent of national income*,[11] and yet we are unable to agree on how to effect this transfer from the haves to the have-nots.

As for the majority of American families above the poverty line, the relevant income comparison is not a family in Bombay or even American families of a generation ago, but rather the norms of our own society here and now. Using just that relative standard, the United States Department of Labor recently estimated the annual cost for an urban family of four persons (wife not employed outside the home) to live at a "moderate standard"—not on a welfare or a luxury budget, but consuming "what people commonly enjoy and see others enjoy."[12] The budget required for that family was estimated to have been $9,191 in 1966, when the median family income in the United States was $7,436. *That* is the way the economic world really looks to whatever one means by the typical American household.

Change and stability

In the labor sector as a whole, two trends particularly dominate the shifting fortunes of the family: ceaseless technological change and a growing security of job and income. Everyone knows that these trends can bring enormous benefits to the family as both workers and consumers, just as everyone knows that each trend can be costly in terms of the other. Yet, an astonishing amount of time is still spent in arguing that there is no conflict between change and security in the labor market, or that the conflict is so irreconcilable that we must choose one over the other. When the speeches are over and a decision has to be made, of course, most union and management officials and most legislators do exactly what the rest of us do nearly every day, namely, strike some sort of compromise between the advantages of change and progress on the one hand and the advantages of stability and security on the other.

But just what the terms of that compromise should be is a subject of endless and legitimate dispute—on the picket line and in the halls of Congress and concerning every type of labor issue —so it behooves us to conclude this overview of the labor sector with a quick look at these trends of such importance.

Technological change

Howard R. Bowen has succinctly placed this subject in its proper perspective:

> It is easy to oversimplify the course of history; yet if there is one predominant factor underlying current social change, it is surely the advancement of technology. . . .
>
> The vast majority of people quite rightly have accepted technological change as beneficial. They recognize that it has led to better working conditions by eliminating many, perhaps most, dirty, menial, and servile jobs; that

it has made possible the shortening of working hours and the increase in leisure; that it has provided a growing abundance of goods and a continuous flow of improved and new products; that it has provided new interests and new experiences for people and thus added to the zest for life.

> On the other hand, technological progress has . . . raised fears and concerns which have led to some questioning of its benefits. One of these concerns has been the fear of annihilation by "the bomb." Another concern has been the apparently harmful influences of modern technology on the physical and community environment. . . . Another has been the apparently harmful influence of urban, industrial, and technical civilization upon the personality of individual human beings—leading to rootlessness, anonymity, insecurity, monotony, and mental disorder. Still another concern . . . has arisen from the belief that technological change is a major source of unemployment. . . .
>
> *As a nation we have willingly accepted technological change because of its many benefits, but we have never been fully successful in dealing with its problems, even when the pace of technological change and the growth of the labor force were less rapid than today.*[13]

But what is the pace of technological change today? Figure 1-1 should lay to rest two contra-

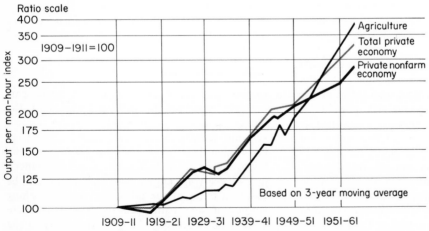

Fig. 1-1. *Indexes of output per man-hour, 1909–1965.*

SOURCE: Technology and the American Economy, *National Commission on Technology, Automation, and Economic Progress, 1966, vol. 1, p. 3.*

dictory but pervasive myths on this score. One is the belief that there has been a second Industrial Revolution in the last decade or two, and that something new called automation has been devouring jobs and sending productivity shooting up at a rate never before seen. The fact is that output per man-hour (the most common measure of productivity or efficiency) has indeed been increasing more rapidly in the private economy since 1947 than it did over the 1909–1947 period as a whole. Note in Figure 1-1, however, that the increase in the trend rate is not huge; that the recent rate of increase was matched in the 1920s; that the 1909–1947 trend is dragged down by the depression decade of the 1930s; and that the most startling gains in productivity since World War II have been registered in agriculture, not in the nonfarm sector associated with the age of automation. Also, though not shown in Figure 1-1, it is common knowledge that employment levels have been far higher since World War II than ever before, belying the belief that more machines mean fewer jobs.

At the other extreme is the myth that efficiency gains have practically ground to a halt in recent years, as unions handcuffed employers with featherbedding rules, the welfare state robbed workers of their incentive to work, and the graduated income tax robbed millionaires of their incentive to invest. Again, the facts present quite a different picture. Whatever the reason, productivity *has* been increasing at a higher rate in recent years: over the period from 1909 to 1947, the trend rate in the private economy was 2 percent a year, and it rose to 3.2 percent from 1947 to 1965.

As the National Commission on Technology, Automation, and Economic Progress summed up the evidence on this question in 1966:

> Our broad conclusion is that the pace of technological change has increased in recent decades and may increase in the future, but a sharp break in the continuity of technical progress has not occurred, nor is it likely to occur in the next decade. . . .
>
> If this increase in the rate of productivity growth [from 2 to 3 percent a year] does not square with the assumption that a veritable technological revolution has occurred, the increase

is nevertheless substantial. Growth at 2 percent a year doubles in 36 years; . . . growth at 3 percent a year doubles in about 24 years. The notion that the product of an hour of work can double in 24 years—not much more than half a working lifetime—is quite enough to justify the feeling of continuous change that is so much a part of the contemporary environment. The time scale has indeed shrunk visibly.[14]

The quest for security

Although technological change has not created mass unemployment, its effects on particular families at particular times have been absolutely devastating. The spectacular increase in farming efficiency has made us, in some wag's description, the first nation in which more people worry about becoming fat than about starving to death. For the farmers themselves, this productivity increase has been a mixed blessing: after remaining roughly constant from 1920 to 1940, the farm population has fallen by almost *two-thirds*, from 30.5 million in 1940 to 11.6 million in 1966.[15] Many left the land voluntarily and are far better off in other occupations, but many others were driven to move by their inability to make a living on the farm and are now huddled in urban ghettos with the "wrong" skills and the "wrong" education and often the "wrong" color to make a living there either.

Such examples could be multiplied endlessly. American bituminous mines are by far the most efficient in the world, but (and in large part, consequently) the number of coal miners has plummeted from 420,000 in 1948 to about 110,000 in 1970, and the resulting misery in Appalachia refuses to go away. In railroading, where many assume the unions permit no one to be laid off for less than first-degree murder, total employment actually fell by more than 50 percent from 1948 to 1970.[16] And in manufacturing, of course, the disruptive effects of change are everywhere: plants must be opened in one state and closed down in another; workers are hired in busy months and laid off in slack months; today's methods and machines undermine yesterday's incentive rates and job skills and informal work groups; some men are promoted as others are fired; and so on and on.

In the face of this ceaseless turbulence in the job market, the most surprising aspect of labor's drive for security is that it still surprises anyone —such as the economist on tenure or the senator with a six-year contract and impregnable seniority privileges, both of whom have been known to bewail labor's demand for more security than the free market voluntarily supplies. In any event, most workers and their families obviously have more income security today than ever before, because of developments on three fronts.

First, there is much truth to the cliché that a healthy economy is the best guarantee of income security, and the American economy has never been healthier than in the years since 1940. Utopia has not yet arrived, but there are reasonable grounds for believing that we need never again suffer a major depression, which has been the principal destroyer of income security in this country since the advent of the Industrial Revolution.

Second, on the legislative front, the welfare state is clearly here to stay. It was not all that long ago that a worker could be hired or fired solely on the basis of his religion or color or union membership, and if he were injured or too sick or too old to work, his family could expect outside help only when its members were destitute enough to qualify for charity. It is inconceivable that we shall ever return to those days, regardless of who wins future elections.

Finally, the gains won through collective bargaining extend to many others besides the minority of the labor force who are union members. For a variety of reasons interesting to speculate upon, the nonunion organization of any size today is likely to have adopted many (though certainly not all) of the policies and benefits found in unionized companies: they place restrictions on the supervisor's former authority to hire and fire and to set wages and discipline for any reason that suited him, as well as provide the lower ranks with the paid vacations and holidays and sick leave and health insurance and pensions that were once the exclusive prerogative of top management or, at most, of white-collar workers. In addition, many union contracts ease the impact of technological change in a number of ways, from seniority clauses to those providing retrain-

ing at company expense and, in a few cases, a guaranteed annual wage.

Notice, however, that *most of these income props are designed for those who have a job more or less regularly, not for those outside of the labor force.* In the 1930s, the prime problems were to provide jobs for those who needed them, to protect workers from arbitrary treatment while on the job, and to help them over the period between jobs and when they had to retire from their jobs. But after thirty years of nearly full employment and the welfare state and collective bargaining gains, we find many people were left behind because they are cut off from the labor force. Thus about *one-half* of all poor families in 1968 were headed by someone not even in the job market, such as a woman with children to care for or a man too old or sick or discouraged to seek work.[17] Is there any way of providing income security for these families except by keeping them on the dole?

Conclusions

In this introductory survey of the labor sector, we have concentrated on the household as an economic unit partly because of its sheer numerical importance as the locus of decisions and aspirations for 94 percent of the population. But equally important, viewing the world of work through the eyes of the family should have demonstrated the complexity of labor issues better than if we had begun with the individual on the job.

The fascination and challenge of most labor problems lie not just in the clash of labor versus management or poor versus rich or progress versus security, but in the fact that most people are really on both sides of the important issues. They want the numerous benefits that a dynamic economy bestows on workers and consumers, but also they understandably want some protection from the threats that such an economy constantly poses to job and income and simple peace of mind. All of these ambivalent desires are mirrored in the dual role of the household as simultaneously a source of labor and a consumer of income.

Also, even this cursory sketch should have revealed the enormous diversity that characterizes the labor sector. It is useless to talk about "the unemployed worker" or "the poor family" or "the working wife" if there is no awareness of the infinite variety hidden under those labels, and we shall see the same is true of the union member, the employer, and many others. Yet, neither the scholar nor the policy maker can function without trends and averages and models, such as "the typical family" to which we have referred as if such a family actually existed somewhere. There is no adequate solution to this dilemma—no way to count all the trees and describe the forest with equal accuracy—except to warn the unwary against both the sweeping generalization and the despairing assumption that no patterns whatever exist in the labor sector.

Finally, this chapter has introduced a puzzle to which we shall return again and again: In their behavior in the labor market, families and individuals and institutions obviously act out of a mixture of economic and noneconomic motives, but under what circumstances one or the other of these will dominate—and even what is meant by "economic" and "noneconomic" behavior— are subjects of endless debate. In examining the supply of labor, for instance, we saw that the participation rates for most groups can be explained by the simplest of economic analysis, but that the rates for married women and Negro males reflect cultural forces that are not found in the usual supply and demand chart. The same problem will confront us when we examine the way in which people select occupations, hunt for jobs, negotiate a union contract, and in other ways behave like real people instead of a homogeneous mass called "labor."

ADDITIONAL READINGS

Bowen, Howard R., and Garth L. Mangum (eds.): *Automation and Economic Progress,* Prentice-Hall, Englewood Cliffs, N.J., 1966.
Economic Report of the President, issued annually.
Friedman, Milton: *Capitalism and Freedom,* The University of Chicago Press, Chicago, 1962, chaps. 1, 2, and 10–12.
Galbraith, John Kenneth: *The New Industrial State,* Houghton Mifflin, Boston, 1967, chaps. 1, 2, 12, 21, and 22.
Manpower Report of the President, issued annually.

FOR ANALYSIS AND DISCUSSION

1. Compare the decision to enter the labor market with the decision to enter college. In your own case, was the decision made principally by you or by your parents? Was the decision motivated by economic considerations (college graduates earn more money, for example) or noneconomic (such as the desire to make new friends)? In your high school graduating class, were differences in intellectual ability the only distinction between those who went to college and those who did not? Estimate the "college participation rate" of your high school class and explain why it differs from the rates for some of your college classmates' high schools. On balance, is the decision-making process regarding college entry basically similar to or different from the decision to enter the labor force?

2. In most colleges, the student faces a system of rewards and penalties similar in some respects to that faced by the worker on his job: Ability plus hard work should yield top grades, the absence of either or both brings failure, and most of the "population" get grades somewhere between. How effective is this system in motivating you to perform well as a student? Would you study more, less, or not at all if you were guaranteed a *C* grade in every course? Or an *A* grade? Are workers any different from students in their response to the carrot and the stick?

3. If you could redesign American society to your own specifications, how would you redistribute income among the fifths and the top 5 percent of families shown in Table 1-5, being both "fair" and "practical"? Defend your decisions.

4. When unions pressed for higher wage increases after 1965, partly because the real *take-home* pay of their members had fallen, some economists argued that a better wage criterion would have been real *total* weekly pay. When would these two measures show different rates of change, and why would anyone care if they did?

5. In certain Eastern cultures, highly sophisticated individuals have cultivated abstinence in the belief that they are richer spiritually if they

require few of this world's goods. Thoreau in his Walden retreat came close to such a philosophy and echoes of it also appear among those today who wish to "drop out of the middle-class rat race." Discuss (*a*) the desirability of such a philosophy purely from the individual's perspective, and (*b*) its desirability from the viewpoint of society as a whole.

NOTES

1. Among married men twenty-five to fifty-four years old in 1966, the moonlighting rate (the percent of those holding two or more jobs) was 12.5 percent for those earning less than $60 a week, more than twice as high as the 5.3 percent for men earning $200 or more a week. Also, the rate for men with at least five children was nearly twice that for men with no young children. Harvey R. Hamel, "Moonlighting— An Economic Phenomenon," *Monthly Labor Review,* October, 1967, p. 18.

2. Data for nonwhites will frequently be referred to as data for Negroes, for the latter constitute about 92 percent of all nonwhites in the United States. Only limited data are available for Negroes alone.

3. Vera C. Perrella, "Women and the Labor Force," *Monthly Labor Review,* February, 1968, p. 1.

4. The same, pp. 1–12.

5. The same, p. 5. Compare the results of this study with Clarence Long's conclusion, based on a study of census data for 1940 and 1950, that there was then a pronounced, inverse relationship between a wife's tendency to work and her husband's income. Clarence D. Long, *The Labor Force under Changing Income and Employment,* Princeton University Press, Princeton, N.J., 1958, p. 82.

6. *Monthly Labor Review,* January, 1970, p. 92. Part-time workers are defined as those who worked fewer than 35 hours during the week in which they were surveyed. An average of 10 million workers were on "voluntary part time" in 1969.

7. U.S. Bureau of the Census, *Current Population Reports,* ser. P-60, no. 66, "Income in 1968 of Fam-

ilies and Persons in the United States," 1969, p. 20. For the 6 percent of the population classified as "unrelated individuals" (those not living with any relatives), income averaged $2,786 in 1968.

8. The same, p. 102, for the wage income of farm workers. Executives' salaries from "Top Men Fatten Their Pay," *Business Week,* June 7, 1969, pp. 84–106. Factory wages from U.S. Bureau of Labor Statistics, *Employment and Earnings,* August, 1969, Table C-2. Faculty salaries from "Further Progress: The Economic Status of the Profession," *AAUP Bulletin,* Summer Issue, June, 1967, pp. 160, 171, and 181.

9. U.S. Bureau of Labor Statistics, *Employment and Earnings Statistics for the United States, 1909–67,* Bulletin 1312-5, 1967, p. xxx.

10. J. K. Galbraith, *The Affluent Society,* Houghton Mifflin, Boston, 1958.

11. This statistic needs careful interpretation. It has been estimated that the "poverty income gap"— the difference between the actual income of those classified as poor and the income they would have received if they had been just over the poverty line— was $10 billion in 1968, which is equivalent to 1.4 percent of that year's national income of $714 billion. That does not necessarily mean that giving the poor $10 billion in 1968 would have eliminated poverty. For example, if some of the poor worked less as they were given more, the gap would conceivably remain the same or even widen. For definitions and measures of both the poverty line and the income gap, see *Current Population Reports,* ser. P-60, no. 66. pp. 1–12.

12. U.S. Bureau of Labor Statistics, *City Worker's Family Budget,* Bulletin 1570-1, 1967, pp. 1–3.

13. *Technology and the American Economy,* Report of the National Commission on Technology, Automation, and Economic Progress, vol. 1, 1966, p. xi. Emphasis added.

14. The same, pp. 1–2.

15. *Economic Report of the President, 1968,* p. 131.

16. U.S. Bureau of Labor Statistics, *Employment and Earnings Statistics for the United States, 1909–69,* and *Monthly Labor Review,* various issues.

17. U.S. Bureau of the Census, *Current Population Reports,* ser. P-60, no. 68, "Poverty in the United States: 1959 to 1968," 1969, p. 44.

PART TWO

LABOR AS A SELLER OF SERVICES

In presenting an overview of the labor sector in Part One, we stressed the difficulty of viewing labor "in the round," of always keeping in mind its simultaneous activities as both a producer and a consumer of income. On closer examination, this problem is even more difficult, for "labor" can also be viewed as a seller of services, a union movement, a factor of production, a political pressure group, and a power in other important areas. Each of these roles is related to all the others, of course, but the mind boggles at the prospect of trying to discuss all of them simultaneously.

Part Two therefore focuses primarily on labor as a seller of services, a role not only important in itself but one which critically affects all of labor's other functions that will be described in later sections of the text. Before one can intelligently appraise the practice of collective bargaining or the theory of the labor market, for example, it is necessary to know more about what the labor sector actually looks like today and how it operates to distribute workers among jobs and occupations.

The best way to begin this task is to take a closer look at those 85 to 90 million people called "the labor force." Part One described why some people choose to participate in the labor force—that is, to sell their time and services for money—and why others do not. Everyone knows, moreover, about such general trends in the labor force as the dwindling of farm employment and the increase in white-collar jobs. But that is hardly enough. Precisely where and how do most people make a living these days—in which industries and occupations? How important numerically is that stereotype of the worker and backbone of the labor movement, the blue-collar factory employee? How important are the professional and managerial occupations toward which most readers are heading? And regarding these and other aspects of the labor force, what are the major trends of the recent past and thus the likely outlook for tomorrow's labor force—which in turn will largely shape tomorrow's labor problems?

Once we have located where most people are within the labor force at any given time, we can tackle the fascinating questions of how and why people move about as they do within its boundaries. These are among the most basic and difficult questions in the entire labor field. On the one hand, there is the picture of labor selling its services in a reasonably rational manner: not in as calculating a fashion as the stock-market operator buys and sells, but attempting generally to maximize returns on its investment of time and effort and, on the whole, moving predictably from low-wage to high-wage jobs and occupations, from stagnant to expanding regions and industries. Most workers, after all, have moved from the farm to the factory and from the South to the North, not in the reverse directions. This is also the view of the labor sector that emphasizes the necessity of constant change if workers are to have opportunities to improve their lot and consumers are to gain the benefits of an expanding national product.

On the other hand, there is the view of the labor market as being rational and predictable only within limits so broad as to have significance solely to the defender of the status quo. The worker on a $1.60-an-hour job would certainly prefer a job at $3 an hour, but he may not know such a job opening exists a hundred miles away, or he cannot afford to move his family; or perhaps he doesn't have the right connections or age or color to suit the employer or the union; or he has not had an equal chance for the education and training necessary to hold a better job. Other workers move only because they are driven to do so—such as the "obsolescent," fifty-year-old engineer laid off because of the cancellation of a defense contract. For these workers the only rational decision after several months of unemployment is to take anything that is offered. In these and other ways, the free market can appear to be an exceedingly crude method of selling one's services. In this view, economic change is more often to be feared than welcomed, and the most predictable feature of the labor market is that those at the top will always wonder why those at the bottom don't bestir themselves and get a decent job.

This debate has many implications, from understanding why workers do or do not join unions to judging the usefulness of the competitive model of the economy. Thus some facts are badly needed on just where and how labor sells its services today.

CHAPTER 2

THE LABOR FORCE

For some purposes, shorthand phrases can often capture the essence of a society better than a lengthy treatise. Thus there is an important element of truth in variously describing the United States as a free society, an affluent society, a mixed economy, a welfare state, or the stronghold of capitalism. In characterizing the American labor force today, however, perhaps the most apt phrase is one recently coined by Eli Ginzberg and two of his associates: the "pluralistic economy."[1]

Those authors use the term to point up the significance of two sectors of the economy—one, the government; the other, private, nonprofit organizations (such as many hospitals and universities)—which theorists frequently overlook in their absorption with competitive and profit-oriented markets. These two "not-for-profit" sectors employ millions of persons directly and millions more indirectly, such as those working for defense firms (which operate for profit but not in a normal competitive market). Ginzberg and his colleagues concluded that "the number of persons employed directly in and indirectly for the not-for-profit sector(s) in 1963 comprised *at least one-third of the entire employed population;* and the correct total may approximate two-fifths."[2]

Among other things, that development suggests that many readers of this book will never become the small entrepreneur of classical economic theory or even work for a corporation that competes exclusively in private markets. They will instead be on a payroll dependent in whole or in part on the government or a nonprofit organiza-tion, for that is where nearly two out of every three professional and technical workers are now employed in this country.[3]

But the term "pluralistic economy" also fits many other developments in our kaleidoscopic labor force. Within this generation, for example, the United States became the first nation in history in which white-collar workers outnumber blue-collar workers and in which those producing intangible services outnumber those producing physical goods. The social and economic implications of those two facts alone are almost impossible to exaggerate. Yet, there have been other manpower developments nearly as significant, as shifts continue to occur in the age, sex, education, and color composition of the labor force.

As an epitome of the labor force, the farmer was of course displaced years ago by the picture of an assembly-line worker in a large factory. But what figure epitomizes a work force composed nearly equally of blue-collar and white-collar workers, with most producing services which no one can see or measure and a sizable minority not even working for a profit-making concern? Or who typifies a work force in which two-thirds are men and one-third are women? Or 60 percent have a high school diploma or better, and 40 percent do not?

Clearly we are between economic worlds. No one is comfortable with the old stereotypes of the labor sector, but neither can anyone confidently predict the shape of the future. It would be soothing to believe that we are entering a new era in which all work is ennobling, poverty and discrimination are relics of the past, and harmony reigns between boss and worker. Unfortunately, miracles appear to be in short supply these days.

But if we cannot discern where this pluralistic labor force is heading, we can at least see where it is today and how it got there. We start with the following reminders:

1. The *total* labor force includes all those sixteen years and over who are working, plus those who are unemployed and looking for

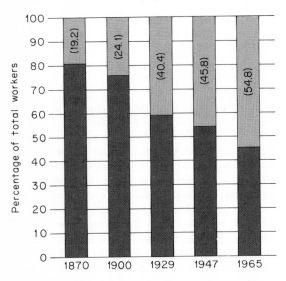

= Services which are comprised of wholesale and retail trade, finance and insurance, real estate, services, and general government (including Armed Forces).

= Goods which are comprised of agriculture, mining, construction, manufacturing, transportation, communications and public utilities, and government enterprise.

Fig. 2-1. *Distribution of employment by goods-producing and service-producing sectors, selected years, 1870–1965. Data on percentage of total workers for 1870 and 1900 include unpaid family workers and the unemployed. Data for later years are for self-employed persons plus wage and salary employees reduced to full-time equivalents; unpaid family workers and unemployed are not included.*

SOURCE: *Victor R. Fuchs, The Service Economy, National Bureau of Economic Research and Columbia, New York, 1968, pp. 19 and 24.*

work, plus those in the armed forces. The *civilian* labor force excludes members of the armed forces.

2. About 40 percent of the population is in the total labor force today.

From there on, things become more complicated.

The shift to services

Figure 2-1 portrays the dramatic transformation of the American labor force over the past century, from one in which four of every five workers were engaged in goods-producing industries to one in which fewer than one-half are so engaged today. Using somewhat different data, Table 2-1 narrows the focus to the past half-century and shows the actual employment in each sector as well as its relative share.

Before discussing the implications of this "shift to services," we must first pin down that elusive term. It is actually a contradiction in terms in one sense, as suggested by the theme of Chapters 2 to 4 that *every* member of the labor force is selling his services in exchange for money. Even in a narrower sense, however, it is necessary to disentangle the service sector, the services industry, and the service-worker occupation.

The *service sector* consists of all the individual industries that produce something intangible like health care or education, in contrast to industries turning out physical goods such as food, clothing, and cars. When this definition is applied conventionally, as in Table 2-1, data for the intervening years show that service employment broke ahead of goods employment in the middle 1940s. But Victor Fuchs, the leading authority on the service sector, excludes from that sector the group of industries called "transportation, communications, and public utilities," on the grounds that "in their use of physical capital and the nature of their production processes," those industries more nearly approximate manufacturing and other goods industries. By that classification, which is used in Figure 2-1, the data show service employment did not surpass goods employment until the middle 1950s. The issue is debatable, but we shall use the grouping in Table 2-1 unless noted otherwise.[4]

Table 2-1 *Distribution of Employment by Goods-producing and Service-producing Industries, 1919 and 1969*

Industry division	Employment (thousands)	Percentage of U.S. total	Employment (thousands)	Percentage of U.S. total
	1919		1969	
Total employment*	37,837	100.0	73,745	100.0
Goods-producing industries	23,562	62.3	27,765	37.7
Agriculture	10,749	28.4	3,606	4.9
Mining	1,133	3.0	628	0.9
Manufacturing	10,659	28.2	20,121	27.3
Construction	1,021	2.7	3,410	4.6
Service-producing industries	14,275	37.7	45,980	62.4
Transportation, communications, and public utilities	3,711	9.8	4,449	6.0
Wholesale and retail trade	4,514	11.9	14,644	19.9
Finance, insurance, real estate	1,111	2.9	3,558	4.8
Services	2,263	6.0	11,102	15.1
Government	2,676	7.1	12,227	16.6

* Excludes military personnel and the unemployed. Data for agriculture include self-employed and unpaid family workers; data for all other industries exclude the self-employed and domestic servants.

SOURCES: Agriculture for 1919 from John P. Henderson, *Changes in the Industrial Distribution of Employment, 1919–59*, University of Illinois, Urbana, 1961, p. 12. All other data from U.S. Bureau of Labor Statistics, *Employment and Earnings*, January, 1970, pp. 15 and 43.

That table also shows that within the service sector only a minority of workers are in the *services industry* as such. There is no simple definition of this industry, for it is a catchall grouping of all the service activities that do not fit in any of the other industries in that sector. More specifically, it includes the following:

Business and repair services—from advertising and modeling agencies to the repair of cars and TV sets

Personal services—housework for pay; hotels and motels; laundries and dry cleaning and barber and beauty shops; reducing salons; and many others (including brothels and funeral homes, both solemnly classified by the Census Bureau under "miscellaneous personal services")

Entertainment and recreation services—from professional wrestling and animated cartoons to bowling alleys and ballet companies

Professional and related services—nongovernmental medical, legal, educational, welfare, religious, engineering, accounting, and related services

The fuzziness and breadth of this industry's definition may well reflect our cultural lag in adjusting to the new shape of the American economy. Other industry titles also span a large variety of activities, of course, but everyone has a fairly workable notion of what is meant by titles like agriculture, mining, and construction. Yet, the services industry—which Table 2-1 shows to be larger than those three goods industries taken together, and to have grown in payroll employment more rapidly than any other private industry over the past fifty years—has not achieved any identity outside of statistical tables. Who has ever described himself or others as working "in services," although there are over 10 million there right now?

Finally, to compound the confusion, there is a *service-workers occupation* and not all service workers are found in the services industry or even the service sector. This too is a catchall category, this time for jobs that do not neatly fit any other occupational pigeonhole. For example, policemen are not exactly "craftsmen" or "semiskilled operatives" or "laborers," so they are termed protective service workers and may be found not only in government but also in manufacturing (plant guard), transportation (railroad detective), and retailing (store detective). Other occupations under the service-worker heading include firemen, hospital attendants, barbers, bartenders, waiters, cooks, and domestic servants. Most do in fact fall in the service sector, but this occupation as a whole has no more public identity than the services industry.

To recapitulate, it is most important to specify one's terms in discussing the shift to services. If "services" is taken in its generic sense, there has not been any shift at all, because all of labor has always sold its services. Also, we shall see shortly that the growth of the service *occupation* has been of only minor significance. It is the growth in the service *industry* and *sector* that is transforming the character of the American labor force.

Some qualifications

And even that statement must be interpreted carefully. For one thing, note in Table 2-1 that the growth in the service sector has been entirely at the expense of agriculture and mining, not of manufacturing and construction. Thus any obituary notices for the factory worker or the building trades are decidedly premature. For another thing, economic power does not necessarily flow to where the work force is largest. Galbraith, for example, argues that the economy is essentially bifurcated into "the world of the few hundred technically dynamic, massively capitalized and highly organized corporations on the one hand and of the thousands of small and traditional proprietors on the other," and that "the heartland of the modern economy" is still the world of the large corporation—"that part which is most subject to change and which, accordingly, is most changing our lives."[5]

Then what has really changed, if the giant manufacturing corporation still holds sway in the economy? Here we are stumbling over stereotypes again. In his brilliantly provocative writings, Galbraith often seems to imply that General Motors is indeed synonymous with the modern economy, but at one point he describes the province of the corporation as follows:

Nearly all communications, nearly all production and distribution of electric power, much transportation, most manufacturing and mining, a substantial share of retail trade, and a considerable amount of entertainment are conducted or provided by large firms. The numbers are not great; we may think without error of most work being done by five or six hundred firms.

This is the part of the economy which, automatically, we identify with the modern industrial society.[6]

Since five of the seven industries he cites are usually considered service-producing, the point is again clear: The essence of the "modern industrial society" is something more than a General Motors assembly line. Whether that something more is the large corporation, regardless of industry, is a question beyond the purview of this text, although Galbraith surely overstates his case when he asserts that "to understand the rest of the economy is to understand only that part which is diminishing in relative extent and which is most nearly static."[7]

The continuing importance of construction and particularly manufacturing should not be minimized, however. It is true that factory jobs have dwindled as a share of *nonfarm* employment over the past fifty years, but their share of *total* employment has remained roughly stable over that period.[8] Also, among the major industry groupings, manufacturing remains by far the single largest employer in the economy and a key to economic growth.

With all of these qualifications, the fact persists that a quiet revolution has occurred in the American labor force. In the underdeveloped countries, most of the world's population are still struggling with the massive problem of how to shift resources from agriculture to manufacturing within the goods sector. It is another index of our wealth that we now require fewer than half of our work force to produce not only the basic necessities of food, shelter, and clothing, but also the cars and television sets and indoor plumbing and freeways and guns and Coca-Cola that typify the American way of life to many friends and critics alike. At least in terms of employment growth, that is not where the action is these days, but instead it is in the still-expanding service sector.

To quickly illustrate the point: from 1947 to 1967, nearly four out of every five new jobs added to the nonfarm economy were in the service sector; more people now work in hospitals than in the entire automobile and basic steel industries put together; more people work for the Post Office Department than in all of mining; and twice as many work in education as in construction.[9]

Government employment

Within the service sector, the mushrooming of government employment is particularly interesting for several reasons. Probably few people realize that employment has grown more rapidly in government than in any of the major private industries (except services) over the past fifty years, and even fewer realize that *in 1969 one out of every six wage and salary workers was on a government payroll.* (Also notice that these figures from Table 2-1 do not include members of the armed forces.) By way of comparison, the public sector in Sweden, often considered the epitome of the welfare state, employs one of every four persons in that country's labor force.[10]

Although no one today expects the government to restrict itself to printing money and delivering the mail, these figures are surely surprising. Are there really 12 million bureaucrats somewhere in this country?

Table 2-2 should clarify matters considerably. Although federal civilian employment quintupled from 1929 to 1969, most of that increase occurred during the three wars in that period, particularly World War II. The number of federal civilian employees doubled during the New Deal era of the 1930s but did not pass the million mark until August, 1940, and increased by less than one million from 1947 to 1969. State and

Table 2-2 *Government Employment, 1929, 1947, and 1969*

Government level	All employees* (in thousands)		
	1929	*1947*	*1969†*
Government, total	3,065	5,474	12,514
Federal, total	533‡	1,892	2,705
Executive		1,864	2,669
Dept. of Defense		689	1,091
Post Office Dept.		467	726
Other agencies		708	852
Legislative		25	29
Judicial		3	7
State and local, total	2,532	3,582	9,809
Education	1,143	1,499	5,257
Other	1,389	2,083	4,551

* At the federal level, data exclude members of the armed forces and employees of the Central Intelligence and National Security Agencies. At the state and local levels, data exclude paid volunteer firemen and elected officials of small local units.
† Data are for November, 1969.
‡ The distribution of federal employment is not available for 1929 in a form comparable to that for the other years.
SOURCES: U.S. Bureau of Labor Statistics, *Employment and Earnings Statistics for the United States, 1909–67,* 1967, pp. 749–755, and *Employment and Earnings,* January, 1970, p. 51.

local public employment, on the other hand, rose by a phenomenal 6 million jobs over the 1947–1969 period—or by enough to have doubled government employment since 1947 even if the federal total had not changed at all.

If socialism is creeping in at the Washington level, these figures suggest it is in a mad gallop at the state and local levels. Obviously such issues are a trifle more complicated than counting noses on the public payroll. Another reminder to the same effect is that more than half of all civilian workers in the government "industry" are engaged in defense, postal, or educational activities, areas seldom claimed by private industry.

But Table 2-2 presents only the narrowest measure of government-related employment. In 1968, when public employees numbered 11.8 million, all levels of government purchased about $100 billion of goods and services from private industry, a sum which generated another 8 million jobs outside of government. There were also 3.5 million members of the armed forces who were part of the total labor force in that year. Adding all these up—direct civilian and military employment plus indirect employment—yields the staggering total of 23 million jobs, or more than one out of every four in the economy, that were underwritten by some government unit in 1968.[11]

The employment effect of any industry can be magnified by adding the employment it generates in other industries, of course, for every industry is always buying goods and services from others. Government-generated employment is nevertheless unique in certain respects. The decision to build a school or highway or guided missile is not made on the same grounds used by a private firm in planning its output and manpower needs. In fact, government spending may run directly counter to market trends, as when public spending is increased to offset a slump in profits and employment in the private sector.

This does not mean that government employment is unique in all respects. As the study by Ginzberg, Hiestand, and Reubens emphasizes, government employers compete in the labor market just as private firms do (in hiring college graduates, for example); government employees often perform precisely the same tasks as their private counterparts (secretaries, teachers, doctors, and most others); and many government activities directly support or complement those of private industry (imagine what the demand for autos would be without the billions spent on public highways, or what farm output would be without the research done in state agricultural colleges).[12]

Thus it is equally misleading to think of the labor sector as composed exclusively of employees in profit-seeking firms, or of free enterprisers versus a unique and hostile tribe of bureaucrats. In short, the work force accurately reflects the pluralistic nature of the American economy as a whole.

The shift to white collars

The emergence of the white-collar worker as the dominant figure in the labor force is a familiar story by now, and yet the full significance of this occupational shift is not always recognized. In diagrams such as Figure 2-2, there is an appearance of historical inevitability about this trend, for white-collar employment expanded almost without pause throughout this century, overtook blue-collar employment in the mid-1950s, and is still expanding today. Until recently, however, few people saw anything inevitable about this trend, so firmly rooted was the conditioning of centuries that nonmanual occupations were reserved for a fortunate few. Even those who waxed most lyrical about the glories of the machine age usually stressed its advantages for the blue-collar worker, in making his job easier and safer and better-paying, while critics were concerned that the independent farmer and craftsman would be displaced by the robotlike assembler.

Certainly in the 1860s, when the Industrial Revolution took off in this country, no one could have predicted that it would take only a century to produce a work force nearly evenly split between white-collar and other workers. And only a generation ago, no one would have believed that *one out of every four workers* would soon be a professional or technical worker (14 percent in 1969) or a "manager, official, or nonfarm proprietor" (10 percent).

Again a pause is necessary to straighten out definitions. Just as the grouping of the service and goods industries is partly arbitrary, so too is the boundary between white-collar and blue-collar occupations. If these terms had not taken on different connotations in the past, we would surely consider farm workers to be in the blue-collar category today, and probably such manual service workers as cooks, porters, and janitors. On the other hand, should farm owners be grouped with farm foremen and laborers (as in Figure 2-2) or together with proprietors of drug stores and the like under the white-collar label? And where do you slot hospital attendants and policemen and waitresses and hairdressers, if not under something vague called "service workers" that is neither blue nor white in collar color? Clearly, these occupational groupings are as much in the province of the sociologist as the economist or statistician.

Figure 2-2 also shows that several interesting

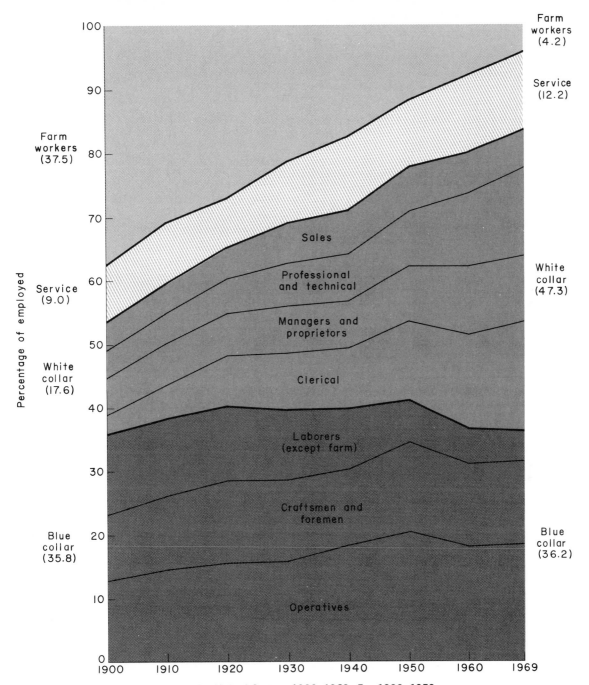

Fig. 2-2. *Occupational trends in the United States, 1900–1969. For 1900–1950, data are for persons fourteen years and over; for 1960 and 1969, for persons sixteen years and over.*

SOURCES: *U.S. Bureau of the Census, Occupational Trends in the United States, 1900 to 1950, 1959, Table 1; Manpower Report of the President, 1968, Table A-9; and Employment and Earnings, January, 1970, p. 115.*

shifts have occurred within each of the major categories. In the blue-collar field, for example, the drop in the proportion of unskilled laborers must surely be chalked up as a major dividend of technology. It is tempting to romanticize those nineteenth-century stalwarts who carved a civilization out of a wilderness, but in fact much of the work in factories, mines, and construction of that period was incredibly dangerous and just plain brutish by today's standards. (Much the same argument could be made about a great number of the unskilled farm jobs that have vanished, but the nonwork values of farm life are so intertwined with this question that one generalizes at his peril.)

The fact that skilled craftsmen have apparently held their own since 1900, and actually increased from 10 to 13 percent of the employed, has not settled the arguments over the net effect of technology on manual skills. For example, skeptics question whether a carpenter wielding a power saw and hammering together prefabricated forms today is the equivalent of yesterday's cabinet-maker, either in skills or job satisfaction. On the other hand, the electrician of today undoubtedly knows more than his predecessors. And how does one appraise the net effects of something like numerical-control technology, a type of automation that reduces the skill required of machinists and increases that required of machine repairmen? In any event, by the only measures we have of manual skill, the proportion of craftsmen has increased over the last seventy years.

These and other occupational trends could be explored further, but for our purposes the most significant pattern that emerges from Figure 2-2 is the close link between the occupational and industry makeup of the labor force. The growth in the service-industry sector is mirrored in the growth of the white-collar occupations; the relative stability of the employment shares of manufacturing and construction is paralleled by the stability of the blue-collar occupations; and of course the declines in farming and in farm occupations are one and the same in employment terms. Obviously there is a close interplay of cause and effect here: beyond some point the education "industry" cannot expand without an increasing supply of professional teachers, nor

can the number of teachers increase appreciably without a growing demand for educational services. We shall return to this point and examine more closely how the various occupations are now distributed between the service and goods sectors, but first it is necessary to survey certain other developments before attempting to present a coherent picture of the labor force as a whole.

Other trends in the labor force

Three other changes that have occurred in the labor force—in the educational attainment of workers and in their distribution by age and sex —deserve at least a chapter or two apiece but must instead be summarized in a few paragraphs.

Concerning the *educational attainment* of workers, it is hardly news that this has increased tremendously since 1870, a year when a grand total of 16,000 students graduated from American high schools and exactly one Ph.D. was conferred in the entire country. But the changes only in recent years have also been dramatic: just since 1940, the proportion of workers with a high school diploma or better has doubled (to 62 percent in 1968), as has the proportion with a college degree (12 percent in the same year).[13] Although we certainly have not solved all of our educational problems in this country—such as the dropout, school integration, and the inferior quality of much vocational education, to name a few—the average educational level of the work force will undoubtedly continue to climb for years to come.

In terms of its *age distribution,* the labor force has changed in a complex fashion.[14] One would expect the proportion of young people in the job market to have dropped sharply since the turn of the century, in light of the extension of child-labor laws, the movement from farm to city, and particularly the much longer time now spent in school by the average youth. The proportion of young workers has indeed dropped, but not spectacularly: in 1900 about 30 percent of the labor force were 14 to 24 years old, compared to 20 percent in 1966. And some of this decline simply reflects the decrease of that age group in the population as a whole, from 22 to 18 percent.

These figures suggest that, contrary to all parents' firm belief, nearly as high a proportion of youth works today (or is actively seeking work) as in the past. The participation rate of fourteen to twenty-four-year-olds (the proportion of that age group that is in the labor force) dropped only from 52 percent in 1900 to 46 percent in 1966. Within that group, participation rates fell significantly only among male teen-agers, rose sharply among females twenty to twenty-four years old, and remained about the same among female teen-agers and males twenty to twenty-four years of age. Even among full-time college students, 35 percent held some kind of job in October 1968, and the rate among part-time students was 87 percent.

At the other end of the age scale, all kinds of crosscurrents have been at work. The pattern was neat and orderly in 1900: Those sixty-five and over made up 4 percent of both the population and the labor force, and well over half the men of that age (63 percent) still had to work for a living. Since that time, of course, life expectancy has soared and aged people now constitute nearly 10 percent of the population—a development tending to push up their share of the labor force. On the other hand, several developments have been working in the opposite direction, such as the rise of private and public pension plans and, again, the shift from farm to city (for it was easier for the aged to cut back their work load gradually on a farm, with other generations present to take up the slack). By 1968 these offsetting forces had struck such an even balance that the aged constituted nearly the same share of the labor force as in 1900—3.8 compared to 4.0 percent. The *participation rate* for aged men, however, had plummeted from 63 to 27 percent over that period.

The important role of *women in the labor force* today was discussed in the previous chapter. An historical perspective can be quickly added by noting that the key statistical values have conveniently doubled. From 1900 to 1969, the participation rate of women fourteen years and older jumped from 20 to 42 percent, and their share of the total labor force also doubled, from 18 to 37 percent.[15]

What influences led to this remarkable redeployment of women in our society and economy?

As family income went up, why did more instead of fewer women seek jobs? Certainly one reason was the impact of technology, both at home and on the job. As household maintenance was requiring fewer hours, outside jobs were requiring less physical strength—illustrating again the fusing of consumer and producer interests within the household. Also, the shift from rural to urban locations, that enormously important phenomenon that we encounter at every turn, had a double effect on women. Since the urban home was less often a "homestead" embracing three generations, women had smaller families to care for and could turn their attention outward from the home. Also, urban locations offered many more opportunities for paid employment, either on a full-time or part-time basis.

In addition, as the feminist movement gathered strength, women began to regard themselves as participants in social and economic affairs, and not simply as observers. The notion of a "working girl" as some underprivileged soul whom heaven would (perhaps) protect, or else as someone little better than a streetwalker, gave way to the idea that respectable women too could choose to smoke, drink, work, and even vote. They also chose to continue their education for longer periods, making them more valuable to employers and often less satisfied with a life of nothing but domesticity.

Finally, two world wars that drained off millions of young men who otherwise would have been in the job market, and at the same time placed heavy demands on the economy for expanded output, provided many women with their first work experience.

The labor force today

What does this maze of trends in the labor force add up to—the shift toward service industries and white-collar occupations, the rising educational level of the work force, the continued importance of the young worker, the precipitous decline in the participation rate of older men, and the equally precipitous rise in the participation of women in the labor force? Simply listing these trends makes apparent that they are not random developments in various corners of the labor market, but are mutually reinforcing elements in a common pattern.

The dynamics of that pattern are far too intricate to be captured in any diagram or theorem, for we have seen that the labor force is shaped not only by the changing needs of the economy but also by many of the cultural pressures that have reshaped society as a whole. Table 2-3 nevertheless offers a hint of how these many trends have interacted over the years by showing the merger of two of the most significant: the shifts toward service industries and white-collar occupations. (Farm owners and workers have been distributed among the other appropriate occupations in this table, since it would not be very illuminating to show that all farm workers are employed in agriculture.)

Detailed data like these are available only from the decennial census, but the occupation-by-industry pattern shown for 1960 has, if anything, become more pronounced in subsequent years. It should be no surprise by now to see that the expanding occupations are concentrated primarily in the expanding service sector, but the extent of that concentration is still impressive, particularly in trade, services, and government. On the other hand, note that the transportation group does not fit the service mold in this as in other respects; that manufacturing remains well represented in every occupation; and that construction, with only 5 percent of total employment, nevertheless accounts for nearly one-quarter of all craftsmen.

Victor Fuchs has used his slightly different definition of the service sector (excluding the transportation group) to show further the interrelationships of the basic trends in the labor force. Fuchs estimates that in 1960 the service sector employed:

71 percent of working women;

68 percent of workers with more than twelve years of school;

37 percent of those with fewer than nine years of school;

59 percent of workers over sixty-five years of age; and

15 percent of union members.[16]

The pattern again comes through. Since the work in many service industries requires less physical strength and often less regular scheduling than in goods industries, it offers more job opportunities for women, students, and older workers on either a full-time or part-time basis. And as the major employer of professional and managerial talent, the service sector naturally boasts the lion's share of workers with a college education.

The proportion of union members in this sector would be somewhat higher than 15 percent if the transportation group were included, for those industries are strongly organized. Under any reasonable definition, however, the service sector is far less organized than the goods sector, and it is tempting to attribute this to the belief that women and professionals and other white-collar types just don't like unions. There is something to that, but it is an explanation that raises more questions than it answers. After all, women have been staunch union members in industries such as clothing; professional entertainers are strongly organized; and the American Medical Association has often been described by critics as one of the strongest unions in the country.

More meaningful explanations can be found in the high proportion of part-timers and self-employed persons in retailing and the services industry; the exclusion until recently of government and some other service workers from the laws protecting union activity; the small size and scattered locations of many service firms; the preferred treatment in salaries, fringes, and job security often accorded white-collar workers (again, until recently); and the simple fact that white-collar work is less apt to be as routine, closely supervised, and stultifying as much blue-collar work.

Whatever the reason, unions have not penetrated far beyond the perimeter of the service sector. After their explosive membership gains in the goods industries during the 1930s and early 1940s, 36 percent of nonfarm employees were union members in 1945, but that peak has never been reached since. By 1966, in fact, union members formed only 28 percent of nonfarm employment, about the same as in 1939, and the primary reason for this slippage has been the rapid growth of the service sector. It is therefore no

Table 2-3 *Distribution of Employment by Industry and Occupation, 1960, percent*

Industry division	White-collar				Blue-collar			Service workers
	Professional and technical	Managers, officials, and proprietors	Sales	Clerical	Craftsmen and foremen	Operatives	Laborers	
Total in occupation	100.0	100.0	100.0	100.0	100.0	100.0	100.0	100.0
Goods-producing industries	22.3	48.4	14.8	25.2	63.2	69.5	71.7	4.6
Agriculture	0.8	32.0	0.2	0.3	0.3	0.9	34.6	0.2
Mining	0.7	0.5	0.1	0.5	0.2	3.0	*	0.1
Manufacturing	18.4	11.2	14.2	22.5	39.3	62.8	22.8	4.0
Construction	2.4	4.7	0.3	1.9	23.4	2.8	14.3	0.3
Service-producing industries	77.5	51.3	84.9	74.5	35.1	30.3	27.3	95.2
Transportation, communications, and public utilities	3.2	4.3	0.9	11.5	10.9	10.5	8.9	1.7
Wholesale and retail trade	3.1	28.3	68.9	17.4	10.0	1.2	9.6	22.8
Finance, insurance, and real estate	1.2	6.0	12.8	13.5	0.6	0.1	0.8	2.1
Services	39.7	8.1	2.2	15.1	9.8	18.1	5.2	55.6
Government	30.3	4.6	0.1	17.0	3.8	0.4	2.8	13.0
Industry not reported	0.2	0.3	0.3	0.3	1.7	0.2	1.0	0.2

* None reported.

SOURCE: U.S. Bureau of the Census, *1960 Census of Population*, vol. I, *Characteristics of the Population*, part 1, *U.S. Summary*, 1961, pp. 557–562.

accident that today's counterpart of the great organizing drives of the 1930s—complete with violence, jail sentences for union leaders, shocked editorials, and a spate of new labor laws—is to be found in the fastest-growing industry around, that of state and local government, where it is getting harder every day to remember that professionals such as teachers really don't like unions.

Other implications

As previously noted, the pioneering work in exploring the dimensions of the service sector has been done under the direction of Victor Fuchs at the National Bureau of Economic Research. In one of his papers,[17] Fuchs has speculated upon the possible implications of a service-dominated economy, and though we cannot do full justice here to his insights, their general tenor can be indicated.

First, Fuchs raises the intriguing possibility that the shift to services may partly alleviate the worker alienation that many observers have felt to be a major cost of mass-production techniques. Innumerable qualifications spring to mind: The hospital attendant hustling dirty laundry can hardly feel the job satisfaction of a skilled tool- and diemaker, the factory worker is far from fading into oblivion, and so on. On balance, however, it is worth stressing that many workers in the service sector are not tied to a single work station and to repetitive operations on a small part of a product destined for an unknown consumer. Many deal directly with customers, do not need to maintain a uniform work pace, and work in safe and pleasant surroundings in small firms or offices. No one yet knows how to guarantee employee satisfaction, but these changes might well help.

In the same vein, the shift to services may blunt the trend toward giantism in our society that has concerned liberals and conservatives alike. All other things equal, few people actually prefer the huge corporation or union or government agency to their smaller predecessors, but until recently the benefits of large organizations have appeared to outweigh their costs. Now, with their smaller need for machinery and equipment, many trades and services offer greater opportuni-

ties for self-employment and small firms. Even within government, Fuchs reminds us, there are more employees at the local level than at the federal (civilian) and state levels combined. This does not mean that the mom-and-pop store is about to knock General Motors out of business, or that the problems of the giant university are any less serious than those of IBM. Nevertheless, small-scale operations are far more dominant in the expanding service sector than in manufacturing, and Fuchs considers it significant that the share of national income originating in corporations—which grew steadily throughout this century to a peak of nearly 60 percent in 1956—has subsequently remained stable or even declined slightly.

Perhaps even more important is the evidence suggesting that a service-oriented economy may provide more security and stability to both the individual worker and the economy as a whole. A simple illustration of this point is that a union demand for a guaranteed annual wage for blue-collar workers is still considered fairly radical nonsense, while no one thinks twice about the propriety of an annual salary for the engineer or high school teacher or government economist or professional quarterback. Further, many service industries are less vulnerable than goods industries to inventory and seasonal swings in activity. As a result, Fuchs shows, unemployment in the service sector averaged only 3.8 percent over the years 1948 to 1963, compared to 5.8 percent in the goods sector.

The other side of the coin

Before anyone concludes that utopia is just around the corner, however, he should consider some of the other implications of the employment shift toward the service sector. The primary focus in the studies conducted by the National Bureau of Economic Research has been on productivity because economists have long believed that output per man-hour increases at a slower rate in services than in goods. After all, you can greatly increase the efficiency of a miner or farmer by giving him more capital equipment with which to work, but how do you help a barber trim more heads per hour? If this is true, a shift to services could mean not only a slower rate of increase in our standard of living, but also severe price pressures if added wage and other costs could not be offset by added efficiency. The significance of this threat is illustrated by the fact that service prices accounted for nearly half the total rise in consumer prices in 1966 and 1967.[18]

But the fact is that no one knows what the productivity rate is in the service sector. It is hard enough to measure output per man-hour in the goods industries, where the output of cars and medicines and houses today is not of the same type and quality as ten or twenty years ago. Imagine, then, the difficulty of estimating the efficiency of a surgeon or a Secretary of Commerce or a policeman or a civil engineer at two points in time. It simply cannot be done, and therefore the conventional practice in estimating national productivity averages is to assume a zero rate of increase for the government and certain other service industries—which is to assume that 20 percent or more of the labor force, including a large share of the most highly educated, are contributing no more with an hour's work today than their counterparts did fifty or a hundred years ago.

In a study of several service industries for which productivity measures could be devised, Fuchs and Jean Wilburn singled out two for intensive analysis—beauty shops and barber shops, which together provide jobs (including self-employment) for nearly as many people as does the basic steel industry, and which also are fascinating examples of the difference between the worlds of goods and service producers.[19] Instead of the usual study showing the impact of mammoth machines and electronic brains, this study focuses on the drastic employment effects of the lowly safety razor and the cold-wave permanent. As late as the 1920s, shaving was the main task of barbers and they formed the largest group in the services industry; by 1960, after men had switched to safety and electric razors at home, the number of barbers had fallen by 30 percent in thirty years and their productivity was largely determined not by technology but by the uneven flow of customers into their shops. On the other hand, before 1920 beauty shops were for rich women, but then the bobbed-hair fashion led to

the need for permanent waves and the adoption and improvement of the permanent-wave machine, followed by the cold-wave permanent, hair coloring, wig service—and a tripling in the number of beauticians from 1930 to 1960.

Altogether, this study examined productivity trends in eighteen retailing and personal-service industries and found that efficiency did increase in sixteen of the eighteen during the period from 1939 to 1963—in some cases quite rapidly but on the average only half as fast as productivity increased in the goods sector.[20] Thus there remain grounds for concern over the implications for productivity of a further shift to services.

Also, it must be remembered that not everyone in the service sector is a brain surgeon or a banker. In 1960, 44 percent of this sector's employment was in the blue-collar and service-worker categories, and for many of these workers this sector is a low-wage area to be entered only if they cannot break into the goods sector. In November, 1969, for example, hourly earnings of nonsupervisory workers averaged $2.36 in retailing, $2.06 in laundries and dry cleaning plants, and $1.89 in hotels —compared to $3.26 in manufacturing, $3.69 in mining, and $4.95 in construction.[21] Wage data are lacking for much of the service sector, particularly for the services *industry* (aside from laundries and hotels), but no one doubts that hourly wages are also miserably low in domestic service, in many hospitals and other nonprofit organizations, and in many state and local government activities. Add to this the absence of union protection against arbitrary supervision and you have an idea of why the shift into services may look like something less than progress to the manual worker.

These facts also have important implications for the Negro worker and his family. Why do civil rights organizations spend far more time attacking racial barriers in the relatively small construction industry than in the large and expanding service sector? Because, of course, Negroes already have more than their share of low-wage jobs and would like to try the other kind for a change.

More specifically, in 1960 the high-wage sector of mining, manufacturing, and construction employed 35 percent of all white workers but only

24 percent of all Negro workers. In the same year, 31 percent of Negro workers were concentrated in the low-wage services industry (hotels, laundries, domestic service, etc.), where only 16 percent of white workers were employed.[22]

Comparable industry data are not available for later years, but the occupational data in Table 2-4 are equally revealing. It is true that Negroes made some appreciable gains from 1960 to 1967, not the least of which is that they are no longer overrepresented in farm employment. But some of these occupational gains in recent years are probably temporary, reflecting the upsurge in manufacturing employment during the Vietnam conflict; if cutbacks should occur, Negroes, being among the last to be hired, will be among the first to go.

Thus, in a sense the shift of the labor force toward the service sector has come too fast and too soon for many Negro workers. Since the 1930s, racial barriers have been considerably whittled away in manufacturing, and they are now beginning to crumble in construction—but these high-wage areas are no longer where most of the new jobs are opening up for either whites or Negroes. On the other hand, there are many Negroes in the expanding service industries, but there they are largely in the wrong occupations to earn a decent income.

How much of the occupational differences be-

tween Negroes and whites can be explained by differences in education and how much is due to discrimination? Such questions can never be answered precisely, of course, but Harvey R. Hamel has made a provocative estimate from data for March, 1967. At that time, only 37 percent of employed Negro men had at least a high school education, compared with 61 percent of employed white men, but statistics like that do not reveal how Negro and white workers at the *same* educational level make out in the job market.

To estimate this, Hamel standardized "the opportunity for employment" by applying the occupational distribution of employed white men to the total number of employed Negro men at each level of education. For example, of the 8.6 million employed white men with eight years or less of schooling in March, 1967, 25 percent were employed as craftsmen, 7 percent were managers and proprietors, 3 percent were clerical workers, and so on. Hamel applied these percentages to the 1.8 million employed Negro men who also had eight years or less of schooling on that date, to arrive at the "expected" occupational distribution of that group of Negro workers if they had "full equality of employment opportunity." This process was then repeated for workers at all levels of education and for all the white-collar occupations plus craftsmen.

The problem was to explain the fact that 63.6

Table 2-4 *Employed Persons by Occupation and Color, 1967*

Occupation	Percent distribution of employment, 1967		Percent change in employment, 1960–67	
	Nonwhite	White	Nonwhite	White
Total	100.0	100.0	15.6	12.8
Professional, technical, and managerial workers	10.0	25.0	58.0	17.8
Clerical workers	11.0	17.2	78.7	23.6
Sales workers	1.7	6.6	39.4	4.6
Craftsmen and foremen	7.7	13.9	48.7	12.9
Operatives	23.5	18.1	33.4	14.3
Service workers, except private household	19.0	9.1	25.4	27.2
Private household workers	10.4	1.4	−15.8	−13.9
Nonfarm laborers	11.2	4.0	−5.4	4.1
Farmers and farmworkers	5.4	4.7	−49.6	−27.1

SOURCE: *Manpower Report of the President, 1968*, p. 63.

percent of white male workers were in white-collar and skilled manual jobs in 1967, compared with only 31.8 percent of Negro male workers. The results:

> Comparing the "expected" occupational distribution of Negro men to that of white men . . . reveals that the difference in the proportion of white and Negro men with white-collar and craftsmen jobs would have been only *9.1 percentage points* if the difference was due solely to the lower levels of education attainment of Negroes. In actuality, there was a difference of 31.8 percentage points. . . . This suggests that the variation between them (22.7 percentage points) might be attributed not to an education effect but to other factors such as employment discrimination, inferior quality of education, residence, lack of capital to enter business, or inability of Negro workingmen to obtain jobs commensurate with their education levels.[23]

Although both Negroes and whites will need more education to cope with the shift to services and white collars, clearly that is far from being the only barrier facing the Negro worker.

Conclusions

After that avalanche of statistics, it may be difficult to believe that this chapter has described only a few of the changes that are occurring daily within the American labor force. Nothing has been said, for example, about the ceaseless flow of people in and out of the labor force, so that the total number in the job market for some period during any year is considerably higher than the annual averages used in this chapter, and attachment to the labor force varies among workers far more than we have indicated. Nor have we explored the seasonal and cyclical swings that occur in the labor force as a proportion of the working-age population, or the mystery of why that proportion has nevertheless been remarkably stable since the turn of the century. Or the research being done on the "discouraged worker" and others who want a job but have dropped out of even the unemployed portion of the labor force during these prosperous years.[24]

But even without those complications, it should be amply clear why this labor force deserves to be termed "pluralistic." In cold figures, the serv-

ice sector is now larger than the goods sector, the "for-profit" sector is larger than the "not-for-profit" sector, men workers outnumber women, whites outnumber Negroes, and so on. Yet, to picture the "average worker" today as a white male working for Sears Roebuck would conceal as much as it would illuminate the major trends and problems within the labor force. And what job should that average worker be holding, when the labor force is split evenly between those with white-collar jobs and those with blue-collar or service jobs?

It should also be clear why no one knows what the labor force will look like in 1990 or the year 2000. It is easy to predict that factory and farm jobs will still be in the minority and workers will be far better educated, but how far will the shifts to services and white collars go? The Labor Department predicts that both trends will continue through 1980,[25] but there is no law of economic development that dictates the continuation of these trends until everyone has a Ph.D. and a white-collar job.

In particular, remember that the service industries and white-collar occupations have grown almost entirely within the labor force "space" vacated by agriculture and mining. Since both of these industries have nearly reached the vanishing point in employment terms, any further growth in service and white-collar jobs will soon have to be at the expense of the manufacturing and construction industries and of nonfarm blue-collar jobs in general. This may well happen, of course, if government employment continues to grow, the long-heralded day of the automatic factory and prefabricated house finally arrives, and similar possibilities develop. It is also quite possible, however, that these shifts in employment will continue but at a far slower pace than in the past, in which event we may remain for some years as a baffling mixture of a blue-collar, industrial society and a white-collar, service-oriented society.

ADDITIONAL READINGS

Employment and Earnings, monthly publication of the U.S. Bureau of Labor Statistics.

Fuchs, Victor R.: *The Service Economy,* National Bureau of Economic Research and Columbia University Press, New York, 1968.

Gordon, Robert Aaron, and Margaret S. Gordon (eds.): *Prosperity and Unemployment,* Wiley, New York, 1966.

Henderson, John P.: *Changes in the Industrial Distribution of Employment, 1919–59,* University of Illinois, Bureau of Economic and Business Research, Urbana, 1961.

Manpower Report of the President, an annual report.

Ross, Arthur M. (ed.): *Employment Policy and the Labor Market,* University of California Press, Berkeley, 1965.

Special Labor Force Reports, published by the U.S. Bureau of Labor Statistics as a series, and also as occasional articles in the *Monthly Labor Review.*

FOR ANALYSIS AND DISCUSSION

1. Assume that in the near future we magically solve most of our racial, educational, and productivity problems and that the entire labor force is employed in white-collar jobs. What labor problems might still remain?

2. If the move is to services, why are domestic servants (private household workers) rapidly declining in numbers, as shown in Table 2-4?

3. Within manufacturing, the ratio of nonproduction to production workers (essentially white-collar and blue-collar workers) has exhibited an interesting pattern over the years. From 1919 to 1929, the proportion of nonproduction workers remained stable at about 20 percent; rose a few percentage points between 1930 and 1932; returned to the 20 percent level from 1933 to 1940; slumped sharply during World War II; and then steadily increased from 16 percent in 1947 to 26 percent in 1967. What factors might have influenced this pattern?

4. Senator Proxmire has suggested that a useful way of reducing unemployment would be to raise the legal school-leaving age, now sixteen in most states, to seventeen years, and to couple this with a provision of better vocational education for those who do not wish to go to college. "It seems to me," he said, "while this means the labor force is less, less employment perhaps, nevertheless society is moving ahead and unemployment

would be sharply reduced." Do you agree with the Senator?

5. What practical difference does it make how we measure the labor force? Isn't one measure as good as another?

6. Making use of the appropriate statistical sources of the U.S. Department of Labor and Bureau of the Census, estimate how many competitors you are likely to have in your chosen field upon graduation, as compared with your counterpart of ten years ago and ten years hence. Identify whom you include in your "competing category."

NOTES

1. Eli Ginzberg, Dale L. Hiestand, and Beatrice G. Reubens, *The Pluralistic Economy,* McGraw-Hill, New York, 1965.

2. The same, pp. 203–204. Emphasis added.

3. The same, p. 207.

4. In all of his writings on this subject, Fuchs correctly insists that any definition of the boundary between goods and service sectors must be partly arbitrary. For the quotation concerning his exclusion of the transportation and utilities group, see Victor R. Fuchs, *Productivity Trends in the Goods and Service Sectors, 1929–61,* Occasional Paper no. 89, National Bureau of Economic Research, New York, 1964, p. 2, n. 2. The U.S. Department of Labor has used both classifications. (In *Manpower Report of the President, 1968,* compare pp. 174–177 and p. 304.) Also note the other important differences between the data in Figure 2-1 and Table 2-1, as described in their respective footnotes.

5. John Kenneth Galbraith, *The New Industrial State,* Houghton Mifflin, Boston, 1967, p. 9.

6. The same.

7. The same. Galbraith nevertheless provides great insight into that part of the economy on which he concentrates his analysis. Also, note that it is for reasons similar to Galbraith's that Victor Fuchs prefers to exclude transportation, communications, and public utilities from the service sector.

8. In his excellent study, *Changes in the Industrial Distribution of Employment, 1919–59* (University of Illinois, Urbana, 1961, Bureau of Economic and Business Research Bulletin 87, pp. 14–15, 46–59), John P. Henderson describes the contradictory nature of employment trends in manufacturing. On the one hand, that sector has shown more short-run employment fluctuations than any other, and it has not had any consistent long-run growth since 1919 but instead has recorded two rough plateaus of employment linked by the wartime jump in jobs during the period from 1940

to 1943. On the other hand, except for the abnormal years of 1931 to 1933 and 1943 to 1944, manufacturing consistently accounted for 20 to 30 percent of all employment (including self-employment, which is excluded from Table 2-1 above) in every year from 1919 (25.5 percent) to 1959 (25.4 percent).

9. U.S. Bureau of Labor Statistics, *Employment and Earnings,* May, 1968, pp. 45–52. "New jobs added" is an artificial but useful statistic, computed in this case by dividing the increase in service employment from 1947 to 1967 (17.4 million) by the increase in total nonfarm employment (22.2 million) over the same period. In excluding the self-employed and domestic workers (as well as military personnel), the data here and in Table 2-1 probably understate the shift to services. Domestic servants are declining in number, but for a measure of the high incidence of self-employment in the service sector, see Henderson, pp. 64–67.

10. Contrary to popular impression, more than 90 percent of Swedish industry is privately owned (measured by value of production). A recent manpower survey classified 950,000 employees in the public sector in Sweden in August, 1968, a number equal to 26 percent of the total labor force (3.7 million) that month and 30 percent of all wage and salary employees (3.2 million). We are grateful to Mr. Ivar Norén, Labour Attaché of the Royal Swedish Embassy in Washington, for providing these data.

11. Specifically, 29 percent of military and civilian employment (including the self-employed), which totaled 79.4 million in 1968. The estimate of indirect employment includes only those jobs generated in supplier industries, and not those generated by individuals spending income derived from government. *Statistics on Manpower, A Supplement to the Manpower Report of the President, 1969,* pp. 106–107.

12. Ginzberg, Hiestand, and Reubens, *The Pluralistic Economy,* chaps. 2–4 and 9.

13. Data for 1870 from U.S. Bureau of the Census, *Historical Statistics of the United States, Colonial Times to 1957,* 1960, pp. 207 and 212. Data for 1940 and 1968 from Harvey R. Hamel, "Educational Attainment of Workers," *Special Labor Force Report* no. 92, U.S. Bureau of Labor Statistics, 1968, p. A-6, and *Statistics on Manpower . . . , 1969,* p. 37.

14. Age data in this section are from U.S. Bureau of the Census, *Historical Statistics of the United States,* pp. 8 and 71, and *Historical Statistics . . . , Continuation to 1962,* p. 13. Also, Elizabeth Waldman, "Employment Status of School Age Youth," *Monthly Labor Review,* August, 1969, p. 30; and *Statistics on Manpower . . . , 1969,* pp. 2–3.

15. *Historical Statistics of the United States,* p. 71, and *Employment and Earnings,* January, 1970, pp. 105 and 123.

16. Victor R. Fuchs, *The Growing Importance of the Service Industries,* Occasional Paper no. 96, National Bureau of Economic Research, New York, 1965, p. 15.

17. The same, pp. 14–29.

18. *Economic Report of the President, 1967,* p. 76, and the same, *1968,* p. 106.

19. Victor R. Fuchs and Jean Alexander Wilburn, *Productivity Differences Within the Service Sector,* Occasional Paper no. 102, National Bureau of Economic Research, New York, 1967, pp. 55–109.

20. The same, pp. 14–16. Also see Fuchs, *The Service Economy,* National Bureau of Economic Research and Columbia University Press, New York, 1968, for a summary of this author's studies of the service sector.

21. *Employment and Earnings,* January, 1970, Table C-2.

22. U.S. Bureau of the Census, *1960 Census of Population,* Vol. I, *Characteristics of the Population,* Part 1, "U.S. Summary," pp. 221–222.

23. Harvey R. Hamel, "Educational Attainment of Workers," *Special Labor Force Report* no. 92, U.S. Bureau of Labor Statistics, 1968, p. 34. Emphasis added.

24. We shall discuss several of these issues in Chapter 17.

25. U.S. Department of Labor, *U.S. Manpower in the 1970's: Opportunity and Challenge,* 1970.

Suppose that a family decides to play the labor market as coolly as it might play the stock market. A son is graduating from high school and his parents are willing to support him through college, but the family wants to earn the best return possible on the huge investment it is about to make. Which occupation should the son shoot for?

That is the problem two economists, Arthur Carol and Samuel Parry, recently set out to explore, with highly interesting results. They suggested that such a family would consider the following option: Instead of going to college, the son will go to work immediately and his family will support him for as many years as they would have supported him in college; in return, the family will take his wages for that period, plus the money that would have gone for tuition, and place this sum in bonds or a savings bank or some other investment yielding a 5 percent return a year. After the college-equivalency period, this option will continue to yield the 5 percent income plus whatever wages the son may expect to earn during the rest of his life with a high school education. The family would then compare that total sum to the lifetime earnings the son may expect with a college degree, and decide whether it would really pay for him to go to college.

The answer, the family would discover, is that it might or might not pay, depending principally on which pair of occupations the son was choosing between. Carol and Parry calculated that if a family had to pay (or save) $2,000 for each year

of college attendance, its "investment" would yield a top return if the student became a doctor, dentist, mechanical or electrical engineer, or a management official in manufacturing or finance —regardless of which other occupation he might have considered entering after high school. On the other hand, if the son moved directly from high school into learning the trade of tool- and diemaking, he would probably earn a higher lifetime "return on investment" than if he became a lawyer; he would do better as a plumber than as a chemist; and he would do better as a truck driver or a postal clerk than as a teacher in elementary or secondary school.[1]

No economist has been known to urge his son to forget law school and take up toolmaking, nor do Carol and Parry suggest that anyone should make college and career decisions solely on the basis of expected cash yield. They argue, however, that if a family knew the economic value of various occupational options as well as it knows the individual's noneconomic preferences, better decisions might be made for all concerned. But where would a family turn for such information? To arrive at their estimates of net lifetime earnings by occupation, Carol and Parry utilized sophisticated formulas, computer analysis of census data, and a research grant, and at that the authors make no claim that their results are timeless and precise.

Then how are occupational choices made, if not through careful economic calculus? One view may be summed up in the aphorism that the rich get richer and the poor get poorer. The children of well-to-do and well-educated parents have everything going for them—home environment, money for college, contacts in the father's firm or profession—to ensure that they too will end up in a high-paying occupation, while the equally intelligent child from the family of an unskilled laborer is more likely to wear a blue collar for life, through no fault of his own. The other view is that there are both opportunity and rationality in the labor market, for we are not a caste society, education does pay off far more often than it does not, and as proof, millions of workers today are on a higher rung of the occupational ladder than their fathers occupied.

The implications of this issue are obviously far-reaching. Our economy has always had shifting occupational needs, of course, but never before has it required such a huge and growing number of professional and other white-collar workers. And beyond our economic needs, the extent of occupational mobility provides a significant test of our attempt to be a society in which individual merit counts for more than family antecedents.

The nature of occupational choice

The phrase "occupational choice," despite its general currency, is grossly misleading. It has about it the connotation of a process of rational reflection which ultimately leads a person to a conscious decision to follow a clearly identified career, usually of a skilled or professional nature. Perhaps such a process does occasionally occur, but it is the exception.

First of all, we should recognize that the word "occupation" has several operational meanings. Those who come from middle- or upper-class backgrounds tend to identify it with a "calling" or "vocation," an activity which is readily identifiable, which offers those who pursue it certain sources of satisfaction, which usually requires special training or skill or years of experience. Vocational choice in this sense is epitomized by the young acolyte who has been "called" to a lifetime of religious practice, but on a more mundane level it applies as well to the youngster who has

"always liked to fool with machines" and who becomes a mechanic or an engineer; it covers all the professions and the licensed trades. About "occupations" in this sense, there is always supposed to be some reason, some special attraction, which draws the individual to that line of work or holds him there once he is in it.

But "occupation" is often used too as virtually synonymous with "job." It refers to a particular bundle of activities, to be sure—typing, filing, assembling, cleaning, clerking, digging, grinding, and so on—all of which may be necessary to the world's productive activity, most of which are perfectly respectable, at least some of which may even carry with them their own minor satisfactions (though these are more commonly associated with the workplace than with the work itself), but a bundle of activities whose chief attribute is that they provide an income. If the individual performing such tasks were to be offered a transfer to some other type of work paying more, with all other considerations remaining equal (pleasantness of physical surroundings and social contacts, for example), he would have little hesitancy in making the switch. He would not be concerned that he was thereby abandoning some important part of his past self or becoming a different person. He would consider only that he was improving his financial position, a net gain.

These two conceptions of occupation have been presented as antithetical. Actually, however, they represent polar positions of a spectrum, along which all jobs can be spotted. There are few people so dedicated to a profession that they will pursue it regardless of the income they earn from it. On the other hand, even the person in a routine job calling for little skill can develop a feeling of pride in the dexterity with which he accomplishes his set task and will be reluctant to forfeit this claim to distinction by taking up some other equally unskilled job even though it pays more.

Nevertheless, although the distinction between a vocation and a livelihood is not one of black and white, the distinction does exist, and it is important in understanding the process which we label "occupational choice."

The second word in that label, "choice," is also misleading. We would do better to substitute the word "commitment," and to consider the process whereby a person became committed to a career line. It is a process extending over many years of a person's life. It is part and parcel of the process of self-conception in which we are all engaged—the building of a mental picture of the kind of person we believe we now are (with our heritage of the past, as we conceive that to be), the kind of person we believe we are in the process of becoming, and the kind of person we want to become. For every male, that self-conception necessarily involves some kind of occupation. If we also include the unpaid occupation of housewife in our spectrum, the same is true for every girl—whether or not expecting to follow any career in addition to or instead of that of marriage. For some people the self-conception is a little cloudy; for others it is very clear.

As an individual moves through time, his picture of his present and future self undergoes change. As he matures, the concept he holds of his future adjusts to the realities of which he is increasingly a better judge. He is a better judge not simply because his intellectual powers are improving but because there is more and more of his past on which to base his projections to the future. The passage of time involves him necessarily in a series of decisions or actions—whether to take an academic or vocational curriculum in high school, whether to get married, whether to go on to college, whether to work summers and if so at what jobs, what major course of study to pursue if he goes to college, and so on.

Each of these decisions closes off certain lines of possible occupational activity and opens up others. If he elects vocational training in high school, he closes off the opportunity to go to college, with the attending occupational choices which college would make possible. On the other hand, he opens up the possibility of a career in carpentry or machining, which the election of an academic curriculum would probably have foreclosed. Thus act by act and decision by decision he sets himself along certain paths from which he cannot readily turn back.

This continuing process of occupational self-conception starts at an early age with the typical fantasy pictures of the child: he intends to be a fireman when he grows up, or a spaceman, or a

cowboy. But fantasies are not typical only of the very young. Even in high school, many boys and girls imagine themselves following a career for which they are unfitted by reason of intellectual or physical capability or willingness to invest the time and effort it would require.

At some point, however, such fantasies usually retreat before inescapable realities. The early ambitions have proved—in the event—to be excessive and they are scaled downward. Sometimes exposure to a new influence may open up potentialities not before seen or appreciated, but as time unrolls, the pattern becomes more and more determined. "Somehow or other, the person becomes committed to a line of action in such a way that he finds he must continue it because all other alternatives carry penalties and costs he does not wish to incur. . . . What happens is that many small steps are taken whose consequences are not foreseen. Each step tends to limit the alternatives available at the next step until the individual suddenly finds himself at a decision point with only one 'alternative' to choose from."[2]

These steps are not always the product of conscious decisions, and certainly not always the product of decisions consciously directed toward the choice of a career. A variety of influences stemming from school, family, friends, the chance exposure to fresh ideas, or repeated contact with familiar ideas may mold the person without his awareness of what is shaping his occupational destiny. Personality characteristics may mean that he is more of a reactor to stimuli than an initiator; inertia, fear of error, reluctance to face decisions may mean that his future is affected by forces which he makes little effort to mold or control. One writer has termed this process "default."[3] Default is characteristic of all people in varying degrees, just as is decision making. It is evidenced in some cases by absence of any conscious or sustained thought to occupational choice—something which appears to be true of a large proportion of high school students.

We can thus say that a person's choice of occupation is something occurring over a period of time, as a result of many decisions, many social pressures, and many defaults, the cumulative effect being to mark out a path of probable occupational activity, the path being at first shadowy and more permissive but increasingly clear and determining.

The case of the physiology students

How this process of choice operates is indicated in a field study of graduate students in physiology at a large state university.[4] The first-year postgraduates were generally uncommitted to this particular discipline of study. Most were students whose applications for admission to medical school had been rejected. Here, then, was a group of individuals who had already invested a substantial amount of time and money in career preparation and who were seeking an interim activity which would not jeopardize that investment. Even those who had a deep interest in science did not have a strong identification with physiology as a field, however.

During this first graduate year, the new experience began to have its effect. The students discovered that some of what physiology they had been taught as undergraduates was still in the realm of doubt and that the research needs of the field were great. As they acquired more technical competence, they began to entertain ideas of making research contributions of their own.

At the end of the first year of graduate study, some of the group reapplied for admission to medical school. Those who were again unsuccessful decided to continue with their work in physiology, with a master's degree as immediate objective. But in this second year, partly as a result of a growing interest in the subject and partly with the realization of their diminishing likelihood of being admitted to a medical school, they now began to think seriously of physiology as an alternative career. More frequent laboratory assignments and closer association with professors on research projects increased the sense of a growing identification with the field.

Nevertheless, at the end of the second year of graduate study there were still those who sought admission to a medical school, but even for these the effort was now more perfunctory. A double realization was beginning to have its effect—one, that they now had an investment in this field which would be largely lost if they were to leave it, and second, that the field was an absorbing one

with high potential for satisfying life work. In some there even began to emerge a sense of superiority of the scientist over the medical practitioner. Sponsorship by a professor for one's doctoral dissertation and first job usually completed the occupational identification.

In this example we have a number of individuals whose decisions, social pressures, and defaults have already led them through an undergraduate premedical curriculum, with a growing commitment to the field of medicine. The insurmountable obstacle of nonadmission to professional instruction prevents immediate accomplishment of the original design. A substitute but related activity is chosen as a temporary expedient while the original commitment remains effective. But inability to remove the impediment leads to adoption of the temporary substitute as a new and permanent commitment, preserving the value of the original investment. What other reasonable alternative remained?

The nature of occupational mobility

Although that is a reasonably accurate description of how most individuals choose a career—or how a career chooses them, it does not tell us much about the extent of occupational mobility in the labor sector as a whole. In conceptual terms, the same process of decision making undoubtedly does occur in rich families as in poor ones or in depression periods as in prosperous years, but surely with very different results. It is therefore necessary to dig deeper to discover how these individual decisions are translated into the sweeping changes in the occupational structure described in the previous chapter.

We begin with a single year. In January, 1966, there were about 70 million Americans eighteen years of age and over employed in civilian jobs. Of that total, *about 5½ million—or 8 percent— were then working in an occupation different from the one they were in a year earlier.* This would be astounding if "occupation" here meant one of the nine broad groups used in the previous chapter, such as professional, clerical, and laborers, but it instead refers to the 296 detailed occupations into which the Census Bureau divides those nine large groups. (Under "professional, technical, and kindred workers," for example, mechanical and electrical engineers represent separate occupations, just as semiskilled "operatives" are divided into bus drivers, taxi drivers, assemblers, and so on.) Even among the nine major groups, however, the volume of mobility was impressive: 3.7 million individuals—or better than one of every twenty workers in January, 1966—had shifted from one major occupational group to another during 1965.[5]

But a large *volume* of occupational shifts does not necessarily serve either economic or social ends, for the *pattern* of those shifts may be perverse by one standard or another. Table 3-1 therefore presents one measure of the direction those shifts took in 1965. The second row in this table

shows, for example, that of those men who changed detailed occupations during 1965 and ended up in the professional group in 1966, 32.8 percent came from within the same group (that is, shifted from one detailed professional occupation to another, such as from professor to dean, mechanical engineer to sales engineer, reporter to public relations man); 16.9 percent came from the managers group; 13.1 percent from the clerical group; and so on. For each occupation group, the major origin of the shifters is underlined.

Note three patterns. First, most shifts tend to be for a short "distance," either within the same major group or to an adjacent group. In the absence of any standards, it is difficult to characterize this as good or bad, for no one would

Table 3-1 *Major Occupation Group in January, 1966, of Men Who Changed Their Occupations during 1965, by Major Occupation Group in January, 1965, percent distribution*

| | | Occupation in January, 1965 | | | | | | | | |
| | Total employed | White-collar | | | | Blue-collar | | | Service and farm | |
Occupation in January, 1966		1	2	3	4	5	6	7	8	9
Total, 18 years and over	100.0	6.8	8.2	9.2	7.0	16.8	27.9	10.5	7.7	5.8
White-collar										
1. Professional, technical, and kindred workers	100.0	32.8*	16.9	13.1	3.8	14.0	8.7	5.2	4.9	0.6
2. Managers, officials, and proprietors, except farm	100.0	13.9	8.7	8.7	25.1	18.7	13.9	2.5	5.3	3.2
3. Clerical workers	100.0	9.2	10.1	27.2	8.9	9.2	23.8	5.4	5.0	1.2
4. Sales workers	100.0	9.8	23.4	8.3	13.2	13.2	14.6	6.8	7.3	3.4
Blue-collar										
5. Craftsmen, foremen, and kindred workers	100.0	2.8	6.7	6.5	4.3	24.6	33.8	12.0	5.5	3.9
6. Operatives	100.0	1.1	5.6	5.7	4.0	17.4	35.9	16.4	8.3	5.7
7. Laborers, except farm and mine	100.0	1.0	3.3	5.7	1.7	13.1	38.0	9.3	12.1	15.9
Service and farm										
8. Service workers, including private household	100.0	2.5	5.6	6.9	4.0	12.5	29.3	13.7	17.1	8.4
9. Farmers and farm workers	†									

* For each occupation in 1966, the single largest proportion of changers is underlined.
† Percent not shown where base is less than 100,000.
SOURCE: Samuel Saben, "Occupational Mobility of Employed Workers," *Special Labor Force Report* no. 84, U.S. Bureau of Labor Statistics, 1967, p. 36.

expect the proportion of long moves (such as laborer to professional) to equal the proportion of short moves during the course of a single year. Just what the mix should be in an ideal society, however, is anybody's guess. Second, note the large amount of *both* upward and downward mobility that occurred during 1965. Needless to say, "up" and "down" are subjective terms here, but most people would agree that an upward move was made by those men who were craftsmen one year and managers or proprietors the next year (19 percent of those shifting into or within the managers group in 1965), just as most would agree that the reverse was a downward move (7 percent of those shifting into a skilled manual occupation had been in the managers group a year earlier).

For our purposes, however, the most interesting question is what the chances are for blue-collar workers to move into the expanding white-collar occupations. The author of the report from which Table 3-1 is taken concluded that "shifts from blue-collar to white-collar occupations were relatively uncommon," numbering only 12 percent of all shifts by men in 1965.[6] But even that cautious statement is quite misleading, for Table 3-1 shows that of all men who moved into a professional occupation that year, *one-third came from outside the white-collar sector:* 28 percent from the blue-collar group and another 5.5 percent from the service and farm groups. For each of the other white-collar occupations (managers, sales, and clerical), the proportion of changers is even higher—about 45 percent—from outside the white-collar field. These figures hardly suggest an "uncommon" occurrence.

How can the rate of blue-to-white-collar mobility be both high and low in the same year? Because, of course, mobility can be measured in different ways. Most men (unlike women workers) are still employed outside of the white-collar sector, and for fairly obvious reasons the manual or service worker changes jobs, voluntarily or involuntarily, more often than the white-collar worker. Also, a job change can more easily involve an occupational change for this worker— from bus driver to taxi driver, for example—than for the chemist or physicist. For all these reasons, it is true that of all occupational shifts by men

in a given year, most occur within the blue-collar, farm, and service-worker categories. On the other hand, when openings *do* occur in the smaller (for men) and more stable white-collar sector, a surprisingly high proportion are filled from "below" —from one-third to nearly one-half as measured in Table 3-1.

A broader view

Clearly an analysis of occupational mobility in a single year has severe limitations. No one, for example, expects a fifty-year-old laborer with an eighth-grade education to have an "equal chance" to become a doctor next year, but ideally his children should have that equal chance, or at least a better chance than he had. For information on mobility between generations, the best source is an exhaustive study directed by Peter Blau and Otis Duncan, who used the same national sample of households that is the basis for most of the labor force data published by the Federal government. This is another study to which we cannot do full justice, but some of its highlights can be described.[7]

When the Bureau of the Census conducted its monthly Current Population Survey among 35,000 households in March, 1962, information was collected from men twenty to sixty-four years of age on items such as the birthplace, education, occupation, and industry of both the respondents and their fathers. This information provided the basis for several measures of intergenerational mobility, one of which is presented in Table 3-2.

Several patterns emerge from the data in that table. First, there is more than a trace of "occupational inheritance" in American society. This can be seen most clearly among the 90 percent of men who are non-Negro (primarily whites, of course). Of the white men whose fathers were in higher white-collar occupations, 54.3 percent were also at that choice occupational level in 1962, and only 11.9 percent of these sons were in the "lower manual" category. By contrast, of those whites whose fathers were in "lower manual," only 21.3 percent were at the higher white-collar level in 1962 and 36 percent were still at their father's occupational level.

Second, there is nevertheless a great deal of

Table 3-2 *Mobility from Father's Occupation to 1962 Occupation (percentage distributions) by Race, for Civilian Men 25 to 64 Years Old, March, 1962*

Race and father's occupation	1962 Occupation*						Total	
	Higher white-collar	Lower white-collar	Higher manual	Lower manual	Farm	Not in experienced civilian labor force	Percent	Number (000)
Negro:								
Higher white-collar	10.4	9.7	19.4	53.0	0.0	7.5	100.0	134
Lower white-collar	14.5	9.1	6.0	69.1	0.0	7.3	100.0	55
Higher manual	8.8	6.8	11.2	64.1	2.8	6.4	100.0	251
Lower manual	8.0	7.0	11.5	63.2	1.8	8.4	100.0	973
Farm	3.1	3.0	6.4	59.8	16.2	11.6	100.0	1,389
Not reported	2.4	6.5	11.1	65.9	3.1	11.1	100.0	712
Total, percent	5.2	5.4	9.5	62.2	7.7	10.0	100.0	
Total, number	182	190	334	2,184	272	352		3,514
Non-Negro:								
Higher white-collar	54.3	15.3	11.5	11.9	1.3	5.6	100.0	5,836
Lower white-collar	45.1	18.3	13.5	14.6	1.5	7.1	100.0	2,652
Higher manual	28.1	11.8	27.9	24.0	1.0	7.3	100.0	6,512
Lower manual	21.3	11.5	22.5	36.0	1.7	6.9	100.0	8,798
Farm	16.5	7.0	19.8	28.8	20.4	7.5	100.0	9,991
Not reported	26.0	10.3	21.0	32.5	3.9	6.4	100.0	2,666
Total, percent	28.6	11.3	20.2	26.2	6.8	6.9	100.0	
Total, number	10,414	4,130	7,359	9,560	2,475	2,517		36,455

* Combinations of census major occupation groups. *Higher white-collar:* professional and kindred workers, and managers, officials, and proprietors, except farm. *Lower white-collar:* sales, clerical, and kindred workers. *Higher manual:* craftsmen, foremen, and kindred workers. *Lower manual:* operatives and kindred workers, service workers, and laborers, except farm. *Farm:* farmers and farm managers, farm laborers and foremen. Classification by "father's occupation" includes some men reporting on the occupation of a family head other than the father.

SOURCE: *Toward A Social Report*, U.S. Department of Health, Education, and Welfare, 1969, p. 24.

mobility which cannot be explained by occupational inheritance. Turning around the above examples, nearly half of those with fathers from higher white-collar backgrounds were in "lower" occupations in 1962, and more than half of those from "lower manual" backgrounds were in "higher" occupations than their fathers'. On balance, there has been more upward than downward mobility among white males.

Third, there is far less upward mobility among Negroes than among whites.

Most Negro men, *regardless of their fathers' occupations*, were working at unskilled or semi-skilled jobs. Even if their fathers were in professional, managerial, or proprietary positions, they were usually operatives, service workers, or laborers. . . .

The Negro man originating at the lower [occupational] levels is likely to stay there, the white man to move up. The Negro originating at the higher levels is likely to move down; the white man seldom does. The contrast is stark.[8]

Determinants of occupational achievement

Although an individual's occupational success is clearly influenced by his race and his father's occupation, just as clearly those factors are not the whole story. Everyone knows that educational achievement has enabled many persons to climb higher than their fathers in the occupational hierarchy. In addition, a person's family background can be important not only because of his father's race and occupation but also for reasons such as place of residence (for example, there are more economic opportunities in Northern cities than in Southern rural areas) and the size of his family (the number of a boy's siblings and his position among them may affect the amount of money his parents can spend on his education). And to further complicate matters, education and family background may reinforce one another—the father in a well-paid profession and with a small family is often in the best position to provide the college education his sons need to enter his own or another top-rated occupation.

Blau and Duncan have gone further than anyone else in disentangling these several influences on occupational mobility. Their statistical techniques are too complex to be reproduced here, but Figure 3-1 presents their principal findings on the extent to which the distribution of men among more or less prestigious occupations can be explained by their education, their family background (broadly defined), or some combination of those two factors.[9]

These findings should give pause to both sides in that ancient debate over whether economic success is determined by "who you know" or "what you know." The truth seems to be that education has an edge over family background but that both factors are certainly important to occupational achievement, and there are others just as decisive which no one has yet pinned down.

It is highly encouraging to note, as a measure of equality of opportunity, that the independent influence of education far outweighs the independent influence of family background in determining occupational achievement. This does not mean that life is an old MGM movie in which the poor-but-honest lad always wins out over the rich young wastrel, but Figure 3-1 does show that, "all other things being equal," social origin is decidedly less influential in the labor market than education.

Unfortunately, as we shall note frequently in this book, all other things are seldom equal in

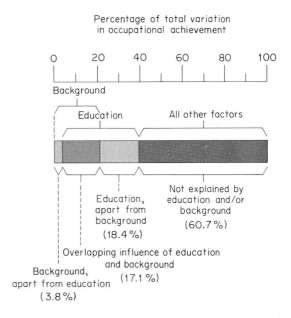

Percentage of total variation in occupational achievement

Fig. 3-1. *Sources of variation in occupational achievement, for men 20–64 years old in the experienced civilian labor force, March, 1962. Background factors included: occupation and education of father, color, number of siblings and sibling position, parentage (native or foreign), birthplace and region of residence.*

SOURCE: *P. M. Blau and O. D. Duncan,* The American Occupational Structure, *Wiley, New York, 1967, Appendix H, as presented in* Toward A Social Report, *U.S. Department of Health, Education, and Welfare, 1969, p. 23.*

the labor market. It is true that the laborer's son who gains an M.D. will usually do better than the doctor's son who drops out of high school, but it is also true that it is the doctor's son who is more likely to get a good education.

This is true even after differences in academic ability have been taken into account, as can be shown by considering only those high school graduates who rank in the top one-fifth of [a national] sample in academic aptitude. If the parents of these relatively able youth are from the top socioeconomic quartile, 82 percent of them will go on to college in the first year after high school graduation. But, if their parents come from the bottom socioeconomic quartile, *only 37 percent* will go on to college in the first year.... Even 5 years after high school graduation, by which time almost everyone who will ever enter college has done so, only 50 percent of these high ability but low status youth will have entered college, and by this time 95 percent of the comparable students from high status families will have entered college....

Differences in attendance at graduate or professional schools are even more striking. Five years after ... graduation, those high school graduates in the top fifth by ability are *five times more likely to be in a graduate or professional school* if their parents were in the top socioeconomic quartile than if their parents were in the bottom quartile.[10]

It is facts such as those which underlie the tendency toward "occupational inheritance" shown in Table 3-2 and the data in Figure 3-1 which show that the overlapping influence of education and family background accounted for 17 percent of the variation in occupational achievement of American men in the 1960s.

A major reason for this pattern is simply that high-income families can best afford to provide their children with the college education needed to enter most high-status (and high-income) occupations today, but there are other, less obvious reasons. For instance, in a home where the parents have college degrees, expectations for (and pressures on) the children to go to college are probably higher than in many other families; these children are often attending high schools in which "everyone else" is going to college; their fathers present a successful model to emulate; and, finally, a son may well develop a genuine interest in his father's occupation through seeing it at first hand, whether that occupation is medicine or farming.

In short, occupational inheritance is not always evidence of unequal opportunity and some father-to-son job relationships would persist even if education were freely available to everyone through the graduate level. Yet, the evidence above demonstrates that we are far short of that point, and educational achievement—though it has provided upward mobility for millions of Americans—has been denied to millions of others because of the accident of their family background.

In addition, this study provided further proof that the income differential between whites and blacks cannot be explained away by differences in education alone. When a comparison was made between Negro and white men with the same years of education and from the same family background (such as family size, area of residence, and father's occupation) and even working in the same occupation in 1962, the annual income of whites in 1961 was still $1,430 higher than that of Negroes.[11] In fact, the better-educated Negro appears to suffer most from job discrimination:

The difference in occupational status between Negroes and whites is twice as great for men who have graduated from high school or gone to college as for those who have completed no more than eight years of schooling. ...

Here we see how cumulative disadvantages create a vicious circle. Since acquiring an education is not very profitable for Negroes they are inclined to drop out of school relatively early. The consequent low level of education of most Negroes reinforces the stereotype of the uneducated Negro that helps to justify occupational discrimination against the entire group, thus further depressing the returns Negroes get for the education investments they do make, which again lessens their incentives to make such investments.[12]

Finally, note that Figure 3-1 shows that 60 percent of the variation in men's occupational achievement cannot be explained statistically by *either* education or family background (including color). This category presumably includes such intangibles as personality, motivation, mental health, "native intelligence," a "natural aptitude" for composing music or fixing motors or leading other men—traits which everyone acknowledges to be important determinants of success in the labor market (and many of which are doubtlessly linked to family background), but which no one can yet measure with any precision.

Some appraisals

No matter how many statistics we amass on this subject, we keep returning to the problem of how to rate them. On balance, are the volume and patterns of occupational mobility in the United States pretty good or pretty bad?

One test is to ask whether such mobility has met the changing needs of the economy. Unfortunately, this kind of question is difficult to answer with any precision or without becoming trapped in circular reasoning. At the most general level, our economy has been so successful over the long run that one can justify anything and everything in it—from monopoly to poverty—on the grounds that "it works." As for occupational mobility itself, clearly we have had enough to alter the entire structure of the labor force within a few decades, from goods toward service producers and from manual toward white-collar jobs. But how do you measure what might have happened if over the past fifty years everyone had had an equal chance for adequate housing and medical attention, a good education, and employment opportunities based on merit instead of racial, religious, or similar grounds? Would the economy have performed about the same, except that the fruits of progress would have been distributed more fairly? Or would the economy actually have performed far better, with more for everyone, if the quality of the labor force and the chances for upward mobility had been even better than they were?

As we have noted before, demand and supply interact in such a complex fashion in the labor sector (as elsewhere) that it is difficult to disentangle the effects of one or the other. At the very least, however, one must beware of assuming that whatever occupational mobility we have at the moment must be just right because the numbers of workers and jobs come out about even. They did in the Middle Ages, too.

Since economic criteria are difficult to come by, one might appraise the equity of our mobility patterns against a statistical measure of "perfect mobility." This is the standard implicit in Table 3-2. If occupational achievement were solely related to ability (and ability is randomly distributed through the population), and if there were complete equality of opportunity, then one would expect the data in Table 3-2 to show no relationship between occupation and family background. That is, each horizontal row of data would contain approximately the same figures, showing the occupational distribution in 1962 to be identical within each group of men, regardless of their fathers' color and occupation. By that test, there is no question that our mobility patterns are inequitable today, and the barriers to Negro mobility are only the most egregious examples of this inequity.

But how realistic is that test? As we observed earlier, there are many reasons other than inequality of opportunity why the sons of farmers might "disproportionately" prefer farming and why many sons of doctors choose medicine as a career. Unless one assumes a Plato-like community in which all children are removed from their parents at birth, it is obvious that a family must have *some* influence on its members' choices and this influence need not be socially pernicious. That fact certainly does not explain all (or perhaps even very much) of the occupational inheritance that exists in our society, but it does explain some unknown portion and therefore it reduces the utility of "perfect mobility" as a test of equity.

Also, there has never been a major society that remotely approached a passing grade by the test of perfect mobility, so perhaps it would be more realistic to mark on a curve—that is, to compare mobility today with mobility in the American past or with mobility in other countries today.

Concerning historical trends within this country, two stereotypes prevail: One, that because of the increase in educational opportunities, Horatio Alger could rise even farther and faster today than in the past; the other, that the closing of the frontier and the growth of the modern corporation have choked off opportunities for the enterprising individual to rise from rags to riches. Neither stereotype is supported by the available evidence, which indicates instead that there has been little change in the influence of social origins on occupational mobility since about 1910, which is as far back as the data permit comparisons. More precisely, workers from farm backgrounds naturally tend to move out of farming today more frequently than in the past, and there may have been a slight increase in upward mobility during the years since World War II, but for most nonfarm workers and for most years since 1910, father-son measures do not show that occupational mobility has either increased or decreased to any extent.[13]

Finally, how does occupational mobility in the United States compare to that in other countries? Are we more of an "open society," as we have long claimed to be? There is a fascinating literature on this subject, and the most recent and comprehensive studies agree on two significant points: *The rate of mobility from blue-collar to white-collar occupations is about the same in most industrialized countries, including the United States, but the rate of movement into "elite" occupations from manual backgrounds is higher in this country than in others.*

The startling conclusion that blue-to-white-collar mobility is about the same in this as in other countries had been suggested by several scholars through the years, but the evidence to support this conclusion was first presented systematically by Lipset, Bendix, and Zetterberg in 1959 and later confirmed by S. M. Miller and by the Blau and Duncan study.[14] The principal explanation for this fact is apparently that no country, regardless of its political ideology or class traditions, can transform its economy from an agricultural to an industrial base by keeping the lower classes down on the farm or in other manual occupations. Industrialization everywhere creates a growing need for professionals, managers, and sales and clerical personnel, and this need simply cannot be met by the favored few at the top when this revolutionary process is first touched off.

In the face of these similar experiences, why do many Europeans as well as Americans continue to believe that we have fewer barriers to occupational mobility? Lipset has suggested two reasons. Because income in all classes is so much higher in the United States than in Europe, the gap in living standards between workers and managers is not so noticeable in this country, where the proportion of workers who own homes and cars and so on is higher than in Europe.

But divergent value systems also play a role here, since the American and European upper classes differ sharply in their conceptions of egalitarianism. The rags-to-riches myth is proudly propagated by the successful American businessman. Actual differences in rank and authority are justified as rewards for demonstrated ability. In Europe aristocratic values and patterns of inherited privilege and position are still upheld by many of the upper class, and therefore the European conservative wishes to minimize the extent of social mobility.[15]

Yet, another reason why the belief persists in our superior opportunities is that they *are* superior when measured by access to the "elite" occupations, instead of to all white-collar occupations. It can be argued that upward mobility from a blue-collar family to a job as salesclerk is no longer regarded as a great achievement, and that the prime test of opportunity is whether the upper classes have a monopoly on the professional and managerial occupations that rank highest in income, prestige, and often in several varieties of power.

Table 3-3 shows that in this important respect the United States ranks at the top. The concept of an elite occupation is obviously a slippery one, and can mean different occupations (including royalty) in different countries. In all industrialized countries, however, professionals and managers usually form the bulk of the elite, and although Table 3-3 uses only professionals to represent the American elite, Miller's study shows much the same results when American managers are included.[16] To illustrate the meaning of the mobility ratios in this table: Column 2 shows the proportion of sons from blue-collar families who were employed in elite occupations in recent years (the dates vary) and column 3 corrects for differences in the size of these elites (partly caused by differences in definition) by dividing the values in column 2 by those in column 1. The ratios for both working-class and manual-class mobility in this country are well above those for other countries, and the United States ratio for middle-class mobility is high but, being partly depressed by the high manual ratio, is exceeded by those for Sweden, Italy, and West Germany.

Conclusions

Like all aspects of the labor sector, occupational mobility exhibits a bewildering mixture of rational and seemingly irrational elements, of predictable and unpredictable behavior. We know

Table 3-3 *Mobility into Elite Occupations: International Comparisons*

Country	Percent of all men in elite* (1)	Working class† into elite		Manual class‡ into elite		Middle-class§ into elite	
		Percent (2)	Mobility ratio ¶ (3)	Percent (4)	Mobility ratio ¶ (5)	Percent (6)	Mobility ratio ¶ (7)
Denmark	3.30			1.07	.32	4.58	1.39
France I (Study I)	8.53	4.16	.49	3.52	.41	12.50	1.46
France II (Study II)	6.12	1.99	.33	1.56	.25	10.48	1.71
Great Britain	7.49			2.23	.30	8.64	1.15
Italy	2.77	.48	.17	.35	.13	5.76	2.08
Japan	11.74			6.95	.59	15.12	1.29
Netherlands	11.08			6.61	.60	11.55	1.04
Puerto Rico	13.79	11.42	.83	8.60	.62	23.17	1.68
Sweden	6.66	4.43	.67	3.50	.53	18.09	2.72
U.S.A.	11.60	10.41	.90	9.91	.85	20.90	1.80
West Germany	4.58	1.55	.34	1.46	.32	8.28	1.81

* For the United States, elite is equivalent to professional, technical, and kindred workers. For other countries, see definition in source below.
† Blue-collar occupations.
‡ Blue-collar plus farm laborers.
§ White-collar occupations excluding the elite.
¶ For column 3, ratio equals column 2 divided by column 1; for column 5, column 4 divided by column 1; and for column 7, column 6 divided by column 1.
SOURCE: Peter M. Blau and Otis Duncan, *The American Occupational Structure*, Wiley, New York, 1967, p. 434.

that few people choose an occupation in a fashion as rational or calculating as the one they would employ in investing money, but instead, most of us arrive at that decision by a series of small steps and as a result of innumerable influences of which we are only dimly aware. We know also that there has been and continues to be a tremendous volume of movement among occupations even during the course of a single year, and we can predict some of the basic patterns those moves will describe in the near future. Finally, we have some idea of the influence exerted on a man's career by his family background and his education.

Yet, no one pretends that we really know very much about this critical process. We certainly cannot predict the achievements of a particular individual who is just beginning his career, and the linkage is obscure between the mobility measures discussed in this chapter and the labor force changes described in the previous chapter. Most important, we have no generally accepted yardstick by which to gauge whether occupational

mobility in the United States is near to or far from the feasible optimum needed to realize both our economic and social goals.

ADDITIONAL READINGS

Becker, Howard S.: "The Implications of Research on Occupational Careers for a Model of Household Decision-making," in Nelson N. Foote (ed.), *Household Decision-making,* New York University Press, New York, 1961, pp. 239–254 (with bibliography on p. 254).

Blau, Peter M., and Otis Dudley Duncan, with the collaboration of Andrea Tyree: *The American Occupational Structure,* Wiley, New York, 1967.

Jackson, Elton F., and Harry J. Crockett, Jr.: "Occupational Mobility in the United States," *American Sociological Review,* vol. 29, 1964, pp. 5–15.

Jaffe, A. J., and R. O. Carleton: *Occupational Mobility in the United States, 1930–1960,* King's Crown, New York, 1954.

Lipset, Seymour Martin, and Reinhard Bendix: *Social Mobility in Industrial Society,* University of California Press, Berkeley, 1959.

Miller, S. M.: "Comparative Social Mobility, A Trend Report and Bibliography," *Current Sociology,* vol. IX, 1960, pp. 1–89 (with annotated bibliography on pp. 81–89).

FOR ANALYSIS AND DISCUSSION

1. In view of the importance of education to occupational achievement, what do you consider the principal weaknesses of our present educational system, and what remedies do you think we ought to consider adopting?

2. What is the case for compulsory education? Do you find it convincing?

3. Appraise the relative merits of three approaches to eliminating employment discrimination against Negroes: outlawing school segregation, as a long line of Supreme Court decisions has done since 1954; outlawing discrimination by employers and unions in all phases of employment—hiring, promotion, discharge, etc.—as done in the Civil Rights Act of 1964; and pressing for a quota system of hiring, under which employers would be required or induced to hire a certain proportion of Negroes (perhaps 11 percent, the proportion of Negroes in the population as a whole) at each occupational level in their companies.

4. The following are some of the questions asked of a sample of college students in a study reported by Morris Rosenberg in *Occupations and Values* (Free Press, New York, 1957), pp. 137–148. How would you answer them for yourself?

a. What three things or activities in your life do you expect to give you the most satisfaction? (Indicate order by 1, 2, 3.)

Career or occupation

Family relationships

Leisure-time recreational activities

Religious beliefs or activities

Participation as citizen in affairs of your community

Participation in activities directed toward national or international betterment

b. What business or profession would you *most like* to go into? What business or profession do you realistically think you are *most apt* to go into?

c. What did your father do for a living at the time you were born? What does he now do for a living?

d. If you could have your own choice in the matter, what kind of *firm* or *outfit* would you like best to work in after you finish your schooling?

Own business or own farm

Own professional office

Educational institution

Social agency

Other nonprofit organization

Government bureau or agency

Military service

Family business or enterprise

Private firm, organization, factory

Other (specify)

Now, aside from your own preference in the matter, what kind of firm or outfit do you think you are realistically most likely to wind up working in?

e. The ideal job for you would have to ... (indicate high, medium, and low importance)

(1) Provide an opportunity to use your special abilities or aptitudes.
(2) Provide you with a chance to earn a good deal of money.
(3) Permit you to be creative and original.
(4) Give you social status and prestige.
(5) Give you an opportunity to work with people rather than things.
(6) Enable you to look forward to a stable, secure future.
(7) Leave you relatively free of supervision by others.
(8) Give you a chance to exercise leadership.
(9) Provide you with adventure.
(10) Give you an opportunity to be helpful to others.

f. College students have different ideas about the *main purposes of college education.* Some of their ideas are listed below. As you read this list, consider what educational goals you think the *ideal* college or university *ought to emphasize.* Indicate your opinion by writing H (high) next to the goals you consider highly important in a university; M (medium) next to the goals you consider of medium importance; and L (low) next to the goals you consider of little importance, irrelevant, or even distasteful to you.

(1) "Provide vocational training; develop skills and techniques directly applicable to your career."

(2) "Develop your ability to get along with different kinds of people."

(3) "Provide a basic general education and appreciation of ideas."

(4) "Develop your knowledge and interest in community and world problems."

(5) "Help develop your moral capacities, ethical standards and values."

(6) "'Prepare you for a happy marriage and family life."

NOTES

1. Arthur Carol and Samuel Parry, "The Economic Rationale of Occupational Choice," *Industrial and Labor Relations Review,* vol. 21, pp. 183–196, January, 1968, particularly Table 2, col. 2. Expected lifetime earnings were estimated from 1959 median annual earnings of males by occupation, age, and years of school completed. Although there may have been some subsequent shifting in income patterns among occupations, there will still be some blue-collar occupations that outrank some professional occupations by the authors' measure of net lifetime earnings.

2. Howard S. Becker, "The Implications of Research on Occupational Careers for a Model of Household Decision-making," in Nelson N. Foote (ed.), *Household Decision-making,* New York University Press, New York, 1961, p. 245.

3. The same.

4. Reported by Howard S. Becker and James W. Carper, "The Development of Identification with an Occupation," *American Journal of Sociology,* January, 1956, pp. 289–298.

5. Samuel Saben, "Occupational Mobility of Employed Workers," *Special Labor Force Report* no. 84, U.S. Bureau of Labor Statistics, 1967, pp. 31–35.

If occupation changers are measured as a proportion of only those employed in both January, 1965, and January, 1966, the mobility rates are about one point higher than the percentages cited in the text, which are based on everyone employed on the later date (including new entrants and reentrants). Unfortunately, there are no year-by-year data available by which to judge whether 1965 was a typical year in terms of occupational mobility. The only other comparable study of a national sample covered those age fourteen and over during the reconversion period of August, 1945 to August, 1946, and understandably showed mobility rates one and a half to two times as high as the 1965 rates for those eighteen and over (see Saben, p. 37).

6. The same, pp. 31 and 55.

7. For a complete description of this definitive study, see Peter M. Blau and Otis Dudley Duncan, with the collaboration of Andrea Tyree, *The American Occupational Structure,* Wiley, New York, 1967. For a condensation of some of the major findings, see *Toward A Social Report,* U.S. Department of Health, Education, and Welfare, 1969, chap. II. To minimize the technical complexities of the original study, our description is based primarily on the latter source.

8. *Toward A Social Report,* pp. 22–24.

9. See Blau and Duncan, chap. 4, for a description of how this study ranked occupations for comparison with men's education and family background. In brief, the authors used a 1947 survey which asked a cross section of the American public the degree of status they thought attached to each of forty-five occupations, and these prestige ratings were extrapolated to provide a numerical status "score" (ranging from 0 to 96) for each of 446 detailed Census occupations. The resultant rankings are generally what one would expect (most managerial and professional occupations have a high ranking, most unskilled a low ranking), although there were numerous exceptions. Also as one might expect, the prestige ratings for the basic forty-five occupations correlated very strongly with the average income and educational attainment of workers in each occupation.

10. *Toward A Social Report,* p. 20.

11. The same, pp. 24–26.

12. Blau and Duncan, *The American Occupational Structure,* pp. 405–406. The authors show, however, that the "vicious circle" of cumulative disadvantages does not operate as severely among white "minorities" such as the sons of immigrants and Southern whites, groups whose members also tend to have fathers with below-average education and low-ranking occupations, to have less education themselves than the majority group of non-Southern whites with native parentage, and to start their job careers on relatively low levels. Sons of immigrants overcome these handicaps and do as well on the average as the majority group of northern whites. Southern whites fit the model, so to speak: They do not (on the average) achieve the

same occupational success as non-Southern whites, but the difference can be explained almost entirely by their disadvantages in social origins, education, and career beginnings. But for Negroes, these handicaps (being reinforced by discrimination) are cumulative in their effect, rather than partially offsetting or overlapping.

13. Blau and Duncan, chap. 3 and pp. 424–425.

14. Seymour Martin Lipset and Reinhard Bendix, *Social Mobility in Industrial Society,* University of California Press, Berkeley, 1959, chap. II (written by Lipset and Hans L. Zetterberg); S. M. Miller, "Comparative Social Mobility," *Current Sociology,* vol. 9, 1960, pp. 30–31 and p. 58; and Blau and Duncan, pp. 432–433.

15. Seymour Martin Lipset, *Political Man,* Doubleday, Anchor Books, Garden City, N.Y., pp. 268–269.

16. Miller, pp. 36–46 and 58.

Having investigated the major employment trends among industries and occupations, we now need to focus on the most frequently occurring of all employment shifts: the movement of workers from job to job, sometimes within the same occupation and industry and sometimes not. A man can obviously pursue the occupation of a truck driver or an electrician or a personnel director for any one of a number of companies or government agencies and in a variety of locations. Thus the distinguishing characteristic of "job mobility" is usually a *movement from one employer to another,* whether or not the worker also changes occupation, industry, or geographic location. (Strictly speaking, job mobility also encompasses movement among jobs within the same firm, but this "internal mobility" has not been studied as extensively as the moves among employers.)

The practical implications of job mobility are far-reaching. For example, if American families want more and better medical care or highways or schools, workers must be attracted into these activities and away from areas of declining or lower priority employment. And if workers within each industry move easily from marginal, high-cost firms to the expanding, low-cost firms, this too serves the interests of consumers. In addition, such movement can serve the interests of the worker himself, for the efficient and expanding firm usually provides steadier employment

and often higher wage rates and better working conditions than the marginal firm.

On the other hand, "job mobility" can be a euphemism for disaster in the lives of many workers. It is one thing for a recent high school or college graduate to shop around from job to job, but it is quite another matter for the fifty-year-old coal miner with an eighth-grade education, his family and roots in a West Virginia town, and his seniority and pension rights concentrated in a fading job that provides him with fewer days of work each year. Who would care to tell this worker that mobility is good for the economy and that he should welcome the opportunity to uproot his family and take his chances in the Chicago or Los Angeles labor market? And should society subsidize his search for another job, or will market forces match workers and jobs far better than any government agency can?

These and similar questions have long divided professional economists as well as politicians. Several studies have shown that the average factory worker has only a foggy notion of the job alternatives available in his own labor market, let alone in other areas; that he prizes many things about a job besides its wage rate (such as the nature of supervision, steadiness of employment, and congeniality of the work group); that he is reluctant to change jobs and particularly geographic areas; and that when forced to move, he often takes the first decent job he finds, rather than shopping around to "maximize returns" on his labor. Reasoning from facts such as these, one school of economists argues that the orthodox model of competitive behavior is a poor guide to understanding how labor markets actually operate.

Defenders of the competitive model retort that its critics have misread both the theory and the evidence. They argue that the theory calls for only some workers, not all, to be willing to move at any given time; that the competitive theory is valid if workers tend to move as predicted, that is, *as if* they were indeed economic men; and that the evidence shows this is how workers do in fact move: from other countries to the United States, from our South to the North, from farms to cities.

In short, how competitive and predictable is the labor market? As a partial answer to that question, this chapter surveys the evidence on how much job mobility takes place in the American economy and how purposeful or predictable that mobility appears to be.

The anatomy of job mobility

Although several studies have been made of mobility in local labor markets, particularly among factory workers, there have been only two surveys of all the job changes made within the entire labor force, one for the year 1955 and the other for 1961.[1] These two surveys showed surprisingly similar results, considering that both were based on a sample of household interviews and that employment conditions were quite different in the years studied. In 1955, a good employment year, 11.1 percent of those who worked changed employers one or more times; in the recession year of 1961, Table 4-1 shows that the job mobility rate was nearly identical—10.1 percent.

As with most such statistics, these figures prove nothing by themselves. To those who believe that labor is basically immobile, the significant point is that 90 percent of all workers do not change jobs during the course of a year, in spite of the fact that a dynamic economy is constantly forcing some people to move involuntarily and providing job openings for others who might want to move voluntarily. As further ammunition for this point of view, a recent study of job tenure

has shown that of all men employed in January, 1966, one-half had been with their current employer slightly over 5 years, one-third over 10 years, and nearly 8 percent over 25 years.[2] On the other hand, those who stress the flexibility of the labor force would be impressed that 1 out of every 10 workers changes jobs every year, in spite of the major wrench that such a move represents to most people, and that half of all men have been on their current jobs for only about five years or less. The competitive model can be easily satisfied with that much worker movement.

Clearly, we need more facts and some criteria in order to evaluate these conflicting claims. Table 4-1 shows, for example, that the overall mobility rate of 10 percent is a compound of quite different rates among various groups within the labor force, each of which requires some explanation.

The fact that men change jobs more frequently than women may partially reflect the greater concentration of women in white-collar occupations, in which mobility rates tend to be lower than in blue-collar occupations. Perhaps more important, however, is that when women lose or quit their jobs for any reason, they are more likely to drop out of the labor force for a time than are men, who usually are heads of families and therefore must land another job fairly quickly. A survey of mobility in any one year would not count those dropping out or reentering the labor force as job changers, and in that sense would understate the mobility rate of women.[3]

In view of the concentration of Negroes in the least desirable and most unstable occupations, it is surprising that their job-changing rate is not considerably higher than that of whites. In fact, among women the whites' rate in 1961 was higher than Negroes' (8.8 percent compared with 7.0 percent), so that there was very little difference between the overall mobility rates of the two groups. One reason for this similarity is that Negroes are more likely than whites to be unemployed between jobs, and they are unemployed for a longer period than are whites who also lose time between jobs.[4] Again, in a survey limited to job changes completed in one year, this pattern works to understate Negro mobility.

Also, note in Table 4-1 the marked reversal of percentage rates by color when the comparison is

Table 4-1 *Rates of Mobility for Selected Groups and Years*

Type of job change, by year and group	Mobility rate	
	Percent of all persons who worked in specified group in 1961	*Percent of men 18 to 64 years old in specified group, 1962–1963*
Changed employers in 1961:		
All workers, 14 years and over	*10.1*	
Males	11.0	
Females	8.6	
White males	10.9	
Nonwhite males	12.8	
Males, 18–24 years old	24.2	
Males, 45–64 years old	5.8	
Changed major occupation group in 1961:		
All workers, 14 years and over	*4.7**	
Changed major industry group in 1961:		
All workers, 14 years and over	*5.7**	
Changed county of residence between March, 1962, and March, 1963:†		
Total population		*6.9*
White		7.2
Nonwhite		4.7
18–24 years old		12.4
45–64 years old		3.5
Civilian labor force		6.0
Employed		5.7
Unemployed		10.9
Family heads		6.3

* Data in the original source, showing total *shifts* among occupations and industries, have been adjusted downward to estimate the number of *persons* making one or more such shifts.
† Population and age as of March, 1963; labor force status as of March, 1962.
SOURCES: Gertrude Bancroft and Stuart Garfinkle, "Job Mobility in 1961," *Special Labor Force Report* no. 35, U.S. Bureau of Labor Statistics, 1963, pp. 1–10. Samuel Saben, "Geographic Mobility and Employment Status, March 1962–March 1963," *Special Labor Force Report* no. 44, U.S. Bureau of Labor Statistics, 1964, p. 875.

limited to *geographic* mobility (7.2 for white males compared to 4.7 for nonwhite males). In other words, in spite of the substantial shift of Negroes from rural to urban areas, the average white worker is even more likely to change location during the course of a year—which in turn means that Negro men must change jobs far more often than whites within *local* labor markets in order to bring their total change rate above that of white males (12.8, in contrast to 10.9). That makes sense because—to put it in extreme terms —the white professional is less likely to lose his job than the Negro laborer, but when the former does switch employers, he is better able to afford a long-distance move and the effective market for his skills is more national in scope.

But of all worker characteristics, *age is by far the most dependable predictor of job mobility.* Study after study has shown that as age increases, there is a steady decrease in the propensity to change employer, occupation, or area. Stated differently, young workers form a disproportionate share of job changers: in 1961, only 21 percent of all who worked were between fourteen and twenty-four years old, but 36 percent of job changers were in that age group. Again that makes sense, for the young person just entering the labor force often has a difficult time adjusting to the discipline of working life; he does not know what to look for or expect in selecting his first job or two; and he is sometimes moving among temporary jobs while still in school. In addition, the young worker is less encumbered with family responsibilities such as mortgage payments and the desire to be near good schools for one's children; or with long-term ties to friends and community; or with seniority and pension rights and specialized skills invested in a particular job. All this adds up to the fact that young workers have both the desire and the ability to shop around among jobs much more frequently than older workers do.

Types of job mobility

Up to this point we have been concentrating primarily on moves among employers, regardless of whether these moves also involve a change of occupation, industry, or area. Table 4-1 shows that at least one-half of all job moves include a change along one or more of these other dimensions of mobility. The 4.7 rate of change in 1961 among major occupation groups (such as professional, clerical, and craftsmen) is roughly consistent with the rate of 5.5 percent for 1965 shown by the study cited in the previous chapter.[5] The somewhat higher rate of shifts among major industries (manufacturing, construction, and the like) confirms the findings of other studies that workers are less firmly attached to an industry than to an occupation.

The extent of geographic mobility shown in Table 4-1 is particularly interesting, for in many ways this is the ultimate test of the propensity to move, and it is also the type of job shift that, according to earlier studies of local labor markets, is most resisted by workers. Why, then, do the data suggest that geographic mobility is even greater than occupational and interindustry mobility?

Part of the reason lies in the measure of geographic mobility used in Table 4-1. A move of residence across county lines does not necessarily mean a change of jobs, and if the basis of comparison is limited to residence moves between *states,* the geographic mobility rate of men in the labor force in 1962 drops from 6 to 3 percent. That is an extremely conservative measure, however, for many moves within a state surely represent a major shift in job and home location, and indeed the same can even be true of some moves within a single large county. There is no ideal solution to this measurement problem, but a recent study by John Lansing and Eva Mueller offers a good compromise: the movement of residence by heads of families from one *labor market* to another, regardless of state or county lines. By that measure, the geographic mobility rate was 5.0 percent between the fall of 1962 and the fall of 1963, compared to the 6.3 rate shown in Table 4-1 for male family heads moving across *county* lines in roughly the same period.[6]

But another reason why the geographic change rates in Table 4-1 appear surprisingly high is that the early mobility studies, because of limited time and money, focused on blue-collar workers in New England.[7] Subsequent samples of the entire labor force have shown that geographic mobility increases with education, that professionals alone account for nearly one-fifth of all intercounty migrants, and that the Northeast exhibits the lowest rates of any region in all types of geographic mobility.[8]

On balance, then, the best evidence indicates that geographic mobility is as common as worker shifts among occupations and industries—*about 5 percent of all workers make one or more of these types of job changes each year.* The qualification of "one or more" is important, for obviously there is overlapping among these changes or the three groups just described would themselves add up to more than the total of 10 percent of workers we know make *all* types of job changes during a single year. In fact, note that Table 4-1 contains no estimate (because none is available) of the proportion of that 10 percent who make the fourth and narrowest type of employer shift, that within the same labor market, industry, and occupation.

An equally important qualification is that some workers make repeated job shifts, so that none of the annual rates in Table 4-1 is fully cumulative over the years. For example, if each migrant moved across county lines only once in his lifetime, in five years nearly 35 percent of the population would have changed county residence (five times the annual rate of about 7 percent). Yet only about 18 percent actually make such moves over a five-year period, indicating that many of this year's migrants also moved last year and may move again next year (some back to where they started from).[9] In spite of this, lifetime migration rates are impressively high and surprisingly stable:

> Estimates have been prepared of the proportion of the native population born in one state and living in another at the date of the [decennial] Census. In 1850 it was 24.0 percent and in 1960 25.5 percent. The impression of stability in the rate is confirmed by data for the other decades.
> [In] areas smaller than states, lifetime mobility is much higher. . . . Of all heads of families [in 1962–1963] 68 percent are living in a labor market area other than that in which they were born. Of the remainder 5 percent report that at one time they lived elsewhere, *leaving only 27 percent who never have lived outside their present area of residence.*[10]

Finally, note the higher migration rate of the unemployed compared to the employed, suggesting that the jobless are not quite as lazy as sometimes pictured.

Those, in brief, are the major dimensions of job mobility in the United States, but it can be seen that the data have at least two glaring deficiencies. First, we have no national samples of job movement *within* private firms and public agencies. Many employers are known to hire blue-collar workers primarily at the bottom of the skill ladder and then to promote from within, at least below the level of apprenticeable crafts, and the same pattern is followed in some white-collar occupations. Yet we do not know the rate of such internal mobility, which can often be as important to the worker, the employer, and the economy as the various types of external mobility.

Second, mobility rates are relatively meaningless without some standard of evaluation. Most economists would agree that a job-change rate of 10 percent a year is perfectly adequate to meet the shifting needs of the economy and the expectations of competitive theory—but *only* if most of those changing jobs are the "right" workers moving at the "right" time and in the "right" direction. The rates in Table 4-1 show only that some workers are more likely than others to change employers, leaving unanswered the question to which we now turn: "How purposeful are all these job shifts?"

The determinants of job mobility

In evaluating the adequacy of job mobility in this country, we do not have extensive cross-country comparisons such as those used to appraise occupational mobility in the previous chapter.[11] We shall therefore concentrate on four other measures of attitudes and behavior: What workers say they look for in a job; why they leave one job for another; how they find and select another job; and whether their moves are predictably toward higher-paying jobs.

Worker opinions

Orthodox economic analysis has tended to stress the rate of remuneration as the major factor affecting job choice. If one job pays more than another, it is for that reason a better job and will be preferred. To this generalization is added the major qualification of *ceteris paribus,* meaning "all other things being equal" about two jobs, workers will take the one paying the higher wage. Or much the same thing, the basic proposition may be broadened to state that workers will choose jobs in terms of their total net advantages, meaning that workers will compare jobs not only for their wage rates but also for their stability, safety, cleanliness, opportunities for advancement, and so on, and that each worker will pick the job maximizing the various features important to him.

This approach has been challenged over the years by the so-called "institutional economists," who have reasoned not so much from general principles as from empirical observations. As previously noted, almost every study of worker attitudes concludes that workers value several aspects of a job in addition to its pay rate. First, there is a cluster of satisfactions related to the intrinsic nature of the work itself: Some jobs are boring and some fascinating; some provide the worker with a great deal of independence and some are closely controlled by a supervisor or a machine; some are dirty and hazardous, some clean and safe. Second, there is a cluster of satisfactions which involve the social setting of the job: Whether it permits frequent and pleasant interpersonal relations; the congeniality and stability of the immediate work group; whether supervision is fair and values workers' opinions. These and similar nonwage matters are the things that other economists have impounded in the phrase *ceteris paribus,* but the institutionalists argue that these factors are too important to dismiss as a mere qualification in describing worker values and behavior.

This argument cannot be settled by abstract logic alone. On the one hand, when the orthodox theory of worker behavior is stated with its proper qualifications, it is correct but uninteresting. Who is surprised to learn that a worker will choose the higher-paying of two jobs that are identical in all other respects? The institutionalists argue that a worker seldom has that choice in the real world and that his actual choices are not illuminated by restating the theory to mean: "Depending upon circumstances, workers may maximize net advantage by moving to a new occupation which pays more, less, or the same rate [as their previous occupations], and any one of the three can be consistent with the classical doctrine."[12] By that test, anyone could explain any mobility pattern after the fact, but would be hard-pressed to predict a pattern before the fact.

On the other hand, the institutionalists' attitude surveys are not necessarily any better as predic-

tors of human behavior. The worker who says that a fair supervisor is more important than wages in his scale of job satisfaction may only be saying that his current wages are closer than his current foreman to his expectations of what is normal and right; he might (or might not) move to a better-paying job with an unknown supervisor tomorrow. In other words, if the institutionalist approach is pushed too far, it strains credulity by implying that there is no observable pattern whatever to worker mobility—there are only individuals, each unique to some extent in his noneconomic preferences, choosing unpredictably among workplaces, each unique in its noneconomic characteristics.

In summary, if job changes are so unpredictable that they can only be explained by depth interviews with each individual after he has moved, it matters little whether one says that mobility is determined primarily by "institutional" factors or by "total net advantages"—each theory is correct but neither is useful as a basis for prediction or policy making. If there is a meaningful difference between these theories, it emerges only when their qualifications are largely ignored. The classicist really does expect mobility to be primarily from lower- to higher-income jobs, in spite of his bows to *ceteris paribus.* And the institutionalist really does expect mobility to be only loosely related to wage differences, in spite of his acknowledgment that workers naturally prefer high to low wages. It is this difference in emphasis and expectation that has divided labor economists, and it cannot be resolved by more elegant models or better attitude surveys. The decisive test of mobility theory is what workers *do,* not what they say or what theorists assume.

Why workers change jobs

Table 4-2 reminds us that job changing can mean different things to different groups of workers. Generally speaking, white-collar workers change employers less frequently than blue-collar and service workers do; they are less likely to be unemployed between jobs; and *they are less likely to move because they have to* (that is, because of layoffs due to lack of work) *and more likely to move to improve their status* (that is, to quit to

Table 4-2 *Mobility Rates and Reasons for Job Changes by Men, by Occupation, 1961*

Occupation of job held longest in 1961	Job changers*		Job shifts†			
	As percent of persons who worked in 1961	Percent of changers unemployed between jobs	Total	Reason for job shift (percent distribution)		
				Lost job	Improvement in status	Other‡
All men	*11.0*	*47.2*	100.0	*37.5*	*33.7*	*28.9*
Professional and technical workers	8.5	29.3	100.0	25.0	42.4	32.6
Managers and proprietors, except farm	4.7	34.7	100.0	34.5	39.6	25.8
Clerical	9.1	47.6	100.0	18.1	43.8	38.1
Sales	13.0	43.7	100.0	17.2	54.8	28.0
Craftsmen and foremen	13.3	51.0	100.0	56.9	28.3	14.8
Operatives	13.8	52.7	100.0	39.4	37.0	23.6
Laborers, except farm	16.4	54.3	100.0	47.3	23.8	28.8
Service workers	12.1	52.4	100.0	21.8	36.7	41.5
Farmers and farm managers	1.9	n.a.	n.a.			
Farm laborers and foremen	15.2	35.3	100.0	15.0	21.0	64.0

* Persons who changed employers at least once during 1961.
† All changes from one employer to another during 1961. Since some persons changed employers more than once, the number of job shifts is larger than the number of job changers.
‡ Includes termination of temporary job (10.9 percent of all shifts), school responsibilities (4.7), illness (2.3), and other reasons (11.0) such as fired, retired, household responsibilities, or not reported.
SOURCE: Gertrude Bancroft and Stuart Garfinkle, "Job Mobility in 1961," *Special Labor Force Report* no. 35, U.S. Bureau of Labor Statistics, 1963, pp. 7, A-12.

take a "better" job or to leave a job with which they are dissatisfied).

All of this suggests that mobility may be more purposeful in white-collar than in blue-collar markets. If a worker can control his job shifts, in the sense of having a better job lined up before or shortly after he quits his old job, he might be expected to behave more like a calculating "economic man" than the worker who is buffeted by forces beyond his control. The latter—laid off with little advance notice, uncertain whether or when he will be recalled to his old job, his debts increasing as he remains unemployed—is hardly in a position to hold out for a job that will be an "improvement in status." By the same reasoning, one would expect the classical model of market behavior to give better predictions during periods of full employment, when job openings are plen-

tiful, than during recessions or depressions. It is no accident, for example, that the quit rate closely follows the ups and downs of the business cycle.[13]

Yet all of this is at best indirect evidence of the directions in which workers move. The voluntary job changer may quit to get more money, but he may also consider another job to be better because it is more interesting or steadier or has a better boss, even if it does not pay more than his previous job. And the involuntary job changer may end up in a higher-paying job almost in spite of himself, as when he is forced to leave a dying firm or area and look for work elsewhere for perhaps the first time in years. Finally, note that over one-quarter of all job shifts in 1961 were for a hodgepodge of reasons—such as illness, school responsibilities, and the termination of a seasonal job known to be temporary when it was taken—from which it is difficult to infer anything useful about mobility patterns.

Table 4-2 therefore does not settle the debate over mobility theory, but it further illustrates why the debate began and why it continues. In the real world, workers change jobs for many reasons—only one of which is the desire to make more money—and many workers, particularly in the blue-collar ranks, change jobs only because they have to, not because they want to.

How workers find jobs

When workers do leave their jobs, either voluntarily or involuntarily, how efficient is their search for the next job? The answer to this question is important not only to those seeking jobs but also to consumers, who at any given time "need" workers more in some jobs than in others. As Lansing and Mueller have observed of geographic mobility:

> It is only necessary that comparatively few workers move to areas where there is greater demand for their services, as indicated by more job openings and/or better pay. However, when moving decisions are made in a haphazard fashion without sufficient information . . . , mobility is bound to be inefficient economically. Inefficiency means that many more moves occur than are needed to bring about the required reallocation of the labor force.[14]

Regarding blue-collar workers, the evidence has long been clear that they typically have only sketchy information about job alternatives even within their local labor markets, and that they rely primarily on informal sources for job information. More specifically, friends and relatives are the principal source of information that blue-collar workers use in finding out about possible job openings. *It is "contacts" that count.* The direct application to a plant is also important, though primarily with respect to companies located in the worker's immediate neighborhood, where he can easily drop in to inquire about hiring prospects, and to the large and well-known firms, whose very size guarantees enough turnover to give some expectation that they might

always have some openings. Public and private employment agencies are not extensively used, although their purpose is to provide a maximum of choice to both the employer and the job seeker.[15]

Until recently, little has been known about the job-search methods of white-collar workers, but the Lansing and Mueller study of geographic mobility has now provided this information from a national sample of households. Figure 4-1, drawn from that study, shows that blue- and white-collar workers use essentially the same search methods, in that both groups rely more on friends and relatives for job information than on formal sources such as employment agencies and newspaper ads. Yet, white-collar workers do exhibit a more "rational" search pattern, relying less than blue-collar workers on the grapevine of friends and relatives and making greater use of private agencies, ads, information from a prospective employer, and scouting trips to the new area. This difference is consistent with our knowledge that white-collar workers tend to be in a better market position than many blue-collar workers—more in demand, better able to afford scouting trips, and more likely to move because of the pull of a better offer than the push of unemployment.

Much the same pattern emerged when the authors investigated the deliberation with which workers make their decision to move between areas and jobs. Only about one-third of all movers considered alternative places to which they might move, but 44 percent of professional workers did so, compared with only 22 percent of blue-collar workers. Similarly, fewer than one-half of all movers used more than one source of job information, but the percentages by occupation ranged from 52 for professionals to 36 for blue-collar workers.[16] Thus neither group of workers approaches the theoretical ideal of an economic man, utilizing all available sources of information and then weighing a large number of job alternatives, but white-collar workers come closer to this ideal than do blue-collar workers.

These similarities and differences have been pointed up by studies of particular groups of white-collar workers. For example, when 1,200 engineers and scientists were laid off in the San Francisco area during a cutback in defense contracts, their experiences paralleled those of unem-

Sources of information

Percent of movers who used each source

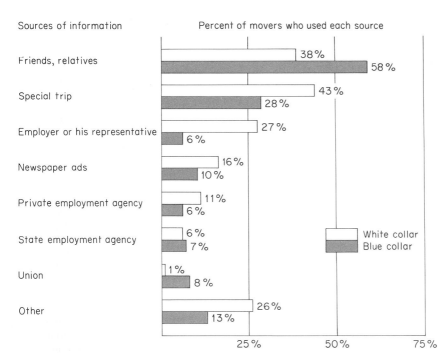

Friends, relatives — 38%, 58%

Special trip — 43%, 28%

Employer or his representative — 27%, 6%

Newspaper ads — 16%, 10%

Private employment agency — 11%, 6%

State employment agency — 6%, 7%

White collar
Blue collar

Union — 1%, 8%

Other — 26%, 13%

25%   50%   75%

Fig. 4-1. *Sources of job information used in geographic moves, 1957–1963. "Movers" are heads of families who changed residence from one to another labor market between 1957 and 1962 or between 1958 and 1963 (depending on interview date), excluding those transferred by their employers or not in the labor force. Percentages total more than 100 because some movers used more than one information source.*

SOURCE: *John B. Lansing and Eva Mueller,* The Geographic Mobility of Labor, *University of Michigan, Institute for Social Research, Ann Arbor, 1967, p. 225.*

ployed blue-collar workers in several respects: the older workers were unemployed longer than the younger; those who migrated to other states were younger and had a higher level of education than those who stayed behind; and these scientists and engineers landed their next job more often through "friends and personal contacts" than by any other method. On the other hand, these professionals made more extensive use of direct applications (the average man applied to about twenty-five companies), newspaper ads, and private employment agencies than blue-collar workers tend to do, and over one-third proved willing to leave San Francisco to obtain another job.[17]

Or consider the academic labor market in which demand is high, the average professor is willing and sometimes anxious to move, and both employers and employees are trained to tackle problems systematically. In this seemingly ideal market, faculty members behave very much like other workers. The new Ph.D. may land a teaching job through a formal market channel—such as blind letters to various colleges, or the "slave market" at the annual meeting of his professional association, or through his college's placement office—but his best bet, particularly for a job at a prestige university, is his thesis adviser. "Through personal contact, graduate school mentors learn where the vacancies are and refer their protégés to them."[18]

For the established faculty member who wishes to move, the search problem is even more complex because of a lingering academic tradition that overt job seeking is somehow unprofessional.

There are certain jobs such as those at tenured ranks in the more prestigious institutions that will not be sought. The man who gets caught chasing such jobs is almost automatically eliminated from consideration. . . .

Professors, hoping to remain inconspicuous, approach the academic market place sequentially. At first the prospective job changer privately and silently hopes to be tendered an excellent offer out of the blue. This failing, the strategy evolves from casually intimating unhappiness to close friends to informing systematically all acquaintances by all means. . . . *Formal methods are used only after informal contacts have failed to yield a good job.*[19]

Finally, when faculty members do change jobs, they typically have investigated no more than two openings.[20]

This reliance of most workers upon personal contacts does not mean that workers are irrational in their job-search methods. For reasons to be explored later, neither public nor private employment agencies list more than a fraction of the jobs open in the economy at any given time, and they are particularly weak in covering the choicest jobs. Given this and other deficiencies in the formal sources of job information, it is perfectly sensible for workers to turn to informal sources. The fact remains, however, that most job chang-

ers are unable or unwilling to explore alternative opportunities as systematically as the competitive theory implies, which in turn means that many job moves are probably inefficient from the viewpoint of both the worker and the consumer.

Mobility and income

Do workers move predictably from lower- to higher-income jobs? Or because of the inefficiency of search methods, the importance of the non-wage aspects of jobs, and the involuntary nature of many moves, is mobility largely independent of wage differences?

Table 4-3 presents the results of the only study that has come close to answering these questions with respect to all types of mobility occurring throughout the labor force in a given year. Although the data were gathered from a national sample of households, it can be seen that the earnings comparisons were limited to male job changers who worked full time on their first and second jobs in 1961 (because women and part-timers probably change jobs more often for family or other "noneconomic" reasons) and to those who earned between $40 and $150 a week on their first jobs—about 80 percent of the full-time group of male changers.

It can also be seen that the results of this study

Table 4-3 *Earnings of Male Job Changers, 1961, percent distribution*

Average weekly earnings on first job, and employment status between jobs	Total	Earnings on second job		
		Lower earnings group	*Same earnings group*	*Higher earnings group*
All job changers*	100.0	18.2	48.5	33.3
$40 to $59	100.0	8.7	44.6	46.7
$60 to $79	100.0	16.3	41.4	42.3
$80 to $99	100.0	24.8	41.1	34.1
$100 to $149	100.0	23.6	63.0	13.4
Changers with no unemployment between jobs	100.0	13.7	46.4	39.9
Changers with some unemployment between jobs	100.0	23.3	50.9	25.8

* Men who changed employers at least once in 1961, who worked full time on their first and second jobs, and who earned between $40 and $150 a week on their first job.

SOURCE: Gertrude Bancroft and Stuart Garfinkle, "Job Mobility in 1961," *Special Labor Force Report* no. 35, U.S. Bureau of Labor Statistics, 1963, pp. 7, A-12.

are most ambiguous. In support of the competitive model, far more workers moved to higher-paying jobs than in the reverse direction, even though unemployment was high in 1961 and job choice therefore was more limited than in most recent years. Also, low-to-high moves were more pronounced among those who suffered no unemployment, implying that workers with an effective choice may indeed tend to behave as if they were economic men. On the other hand, it is plain that *most* of the job changes described in Table 4-3 were not from a lower- to a higher-paying job, even among those workers who lost no time in shifting. Finally, the surprising fact that low-wage workers were most likely to improve their earnings status through a job change would probably not have been predicted by either mobility model.

Other studies have shown that the relationship between earnings and mobility varies with the type of move and the mover. This relationship is perhaps strongest among workers who make geographic moves. Migration among countries has been predominantly from lower- to higher-income areas, of course, as have the massive shifts from rural to urban jobs within all industrialized countries. As for long-range mobility within this country, Robert L. Raimon has demonstrated that net migration is primarily from lower- to higher-income states, and Lansing and Mueller found that 65 percent of geographic movers earned more after their move than before, while only 24 percent earned less and 11 percent earned the same.[21]

There also may be differences between blue-collar and white-collar workers in this respect. The early studies of manual workers in local labor markets suggest that little more than half of all voluntary job shifts, and far less than half of all involuntary shifts (those resulting from layoffs or discharges), result in wage improvement for these workers.[22] The few studies of white-collar workers present a mixed picture: Among clerical workers in Boston in the mid-1950s, three-fourths of job shifts were to higher-paying jobs when the changers stayed in the labor market; among college professors who changed jobs in 1963–1964, 69 percent moved up in income; but among scientists and engineers laid off in the San Francisco area during the early 1960s, job shifts resembled those made by blue-collar workers—about half were to higher-salaried jobs before the layoff, but only one-fifth after the layoff.[23]

Given the importance of this question, it is surprising that so few economists have investigated it systematically. On the basis of the scattered evidence now available, it can only be predicted that moves from lower- to higher-paying jobs will be more frequent among voluntary than involuntary shifts, among long-range rather than local shifts, in tight labor markets rather than in those with high unemployment, and perhaps among white-collar rather than blue-collar workers. Among all job shifts occurring at any given time, however, there is only a weak trend toward low-to-high movement.

Conclusions

What does this welter of mobility studies add up to, beyond the obvious fact that we need more and better studies, particularly of white-collar workers, than we now have?

On the theoretical front, the facts suggest that the labor force is much more flexible and mobile than the institutionalist approach implies, but this extensive mobility is far less efficient and predictable than the competitive model indicates. More specifically, about 10 percent of all American workers will change their jobs next year, about half of these will also move their families to a different labor market, and most will move to a job paying as much as, or more than, the job they have left—all of which suggests a fairly competitive labor market. Yet, much of this movement will be involuntary, few of even the voluntary movers will be efficient in their job search, and the safest prediction of income change is that the average mover will end up neither gaining nor losing very much on his new job.

That may seem to be a woefully inconclusive picture of labor mobility, but worker behavior simply refuses to support any more definitive generalization. As noted in earlier chapters, most controversial issues in the labor sector pit producer interests against consumer interests, and mobility is no exception. In their role as consumers, most families would benefit by a high level of "rational" mobility, and they pay a price for anything that impedes the efficient allocation of labor. In their role as worker-producers, however, family heads value their jobs and areas of residence for both economic and noneconomic reasons, and they seldom have the luxury of choosing between jobs equal in all respects except income. The result is this blurred picture of a labor market in which mobility partially serves both consumer and producer interests, without maximizing either in a neatly predictable fashion.

The same can be said with reference to the controversy over the mixture of security and incentives that should prevail in the labor sector. It is true that the overwhelming majority of American workers do not change jobs in any given year, and the growth of seniority clauses, featherbedding practices, welfare legislation, and the like appear to favor the worker's desire for security over the economy's need for change and risk taking. Yet, there is no evidence that workers are much less mobile today than before the spread of collective bargaining and the welfare state. It will be recalled, in fact, that Lansing and Mueller found that lifetime migration rates among states are about the same today as in 1850. Also, we have seen that a tremendous volume of job changing occurs constantly throughout the labor force, both by workers quitting to look for something better and by those who are forced out of their old jobs in spite of union contracts or other protection. Finally, Lansing and Mueller found that geographic mobility is retarded only slightly, if at all, by private pensions, unemployment insurance, or welfare assistance—much less than by home ownership, age, race, or lack of education.[24]

But even if the *volume* of labor mobility is probably adequate for most purposes within the American economy, few experts would deny the need to increase the *efficiency* of that mobility. On this point, there is no disagreement between the institutional and the classical theorists. Both schools recognize that reducing certain market frictions—such as racial barriers and inadequate market knowledge—would improve the chances for mobility to benefit both the worker and the consumer. As the economy approaches full employment, for example, inflationary pressures gather force not only because of union-wage pressures and employers' pricing practices but also because bottlenecks develop in the labor market.

Some of these bottlenecks are unavoidable, such as a sudden need for a particular skill requiring years of training, but others result from the inability of our present market mechanisms to match available workers and jobs as quickly as desirable. Workers who might welcome a move to expanding firms do not easily learn about the jobs they could fill, and employers accustomed to tapping the pool of unemployed may have to resort to expensive overtime work, or belatedly initiate recruiting programs, or finally institute large wage increases.

In the same way, the labor market can unwittingly discriminate against Negroes even in the absence of formal color bars. So long as workers must depend primarily on friends and relatives for job leads, those in urban ghettos are severely handicapped by knowing few workers in good jobs outside the ghetto, which is one of several reasons why unemployment is high in slum neighborhoods even when job openings are plentiful in the surrounding city and suburbs. And in depressed areas such as Appalachia, a vicious cycle can be triggered: Many workers in these areas do not know that better jobs exist elsewhere or how to find them; those who do move out are the younger, better-educated, and more skilled; relatively few workers of comparable quality are attracted into these areas; and the net result can be a steady deterioration in the quality of an area's labor force, making it unattractive to the new industry needed to revive that area.[25]

Most of these facts have been known for some time, but we have made little headway in improving the efficiency of labor mobility. The obvious policy would seem to be to improve the public employment service, a joint federal and state operation that maintains offices in every important labor market throughout the country. Unfortunately this employment service is also a victim of the grapevine: experience teaches the best workers that good jobs are landed primarily through personal contact, so they seldom register at the public employment office unless they are unemployed or have had no luck through the grapevine; employers know this and often do not register their best job openings unless they fail to find good workers through informal channels. Each party thus reinforces the other's expectations and the employment service is left with a disproportionate share of poor workers and poor jobs, which further reinforces its image as a job source of last resort.

Nor do these difficulties occur only in blue-collar markets. In Europe there is a tradition of publicly advertising all openings for college teachers, but no such tradition exists in this country. Even during the years of most severe teacher shortage, relatively few academic employers and teachers used advertisements in professional journals or private or public employment agencies, and those who did were usually not the top institutions or the sought-after teachers.[26] As we have seen, personal contacts are as often the key to good jobs for Ph.D.'s as for machinists and welders.

None of this means that the labor market is hopelessly irrational. Informal search methods work quite well for many workers and employers, and formal channels are used more extensively than the above criticisms imply. Each year the public employment service fills many thousands of jobs, often for the workers and employers who most need such help, and it is attempting to improve its usefulness to both the disadvantaged and the white-collar groups. In addition, private employment agencies, college placement offices, and newspaper advertising are obviously used by many job seekers, while on the policy front we have been cautiously following the lead of other countries and experimenting with subsidies to aid workers to move out of depressed areas, to train those left behind, and to entice new industry into such areas.

On balance, however, the evidence strongly indicates that the impressive mobility of the American work force is too often inefficient from the viewpoint of consumers and needlessly painful and unproductive for many workers. This fact is central to an understanding of most other issues in the labor sector. If all workers could move from job to job as easily and purposefully as some now can, there would certainly be less need for labor unions and many types of social legislation now on the books. For millions of workers, the right to quit and seek a better job has provided great opportunities for advancement. But for millions of others, mobility often means the right to be fired or laid off from a much-needed job and to join the unemployed for whom no better job may exist or, if it exists, may never be discovered. To workers such as these, advancement may appear to lie not in job mobility but in concerted action to protect and improve the jobs they already have. It is to this group of workers who join unions that we turn in the following chapters.

ADDITIONAL READINGS

Brown, David G.: *The Mobile Professors,* American Council on Education, Washington, 1967.

Foltman, Felician F.: *White- and Blue-collars in a Mill Shutdown,* Cornell University, New York State School of Industrial and Labor Relations, Ithaca, N.Y., 1968.

Lansing, John B., and Eva Mueller: *The Geographic Mobility of Labor,* The University of Michigan, Survey Research Center, Ann Arbor, 1967.

Palmer, Gladys L., and others: *The Reluctant Job Changer,* University of Pennsylvania Press, Philadelphia, 1962.

Parnes, Herbert: *Research on Labor Mobility,* Social Science Research Council, New York, 1954.

FOR ANALYSIS AND DISCUSSION

1. There is no reason to expect that workers "like" work or are ever "satisfied" with a job. By its very nature, a job differs from a pastime in that it exercises a certain compulsion over a person to which, without remuneration, he would be unwilling to submit. But jobs vary in the degree to which a worker accepts and adjusts to the requirements made on him. What are some of the factors which hold a person to an unliked job? To what extent do these give an employer (or supervisor) power over the employee? Is it to society's advantage to try to reduce this power? Why? How much "compulsion to work" is desirable in a society, if any?

2. Draft your own set of specifications for a "good" job. Try to rank the job characteristics which you consider important. Is pay your prime consideration? If not, what is? Under what circumstances would you expect that the amount of remuneration *might* become your foremost concern?

3. Reconstruct the job path by which your father reached his present position (this will probably have to wait until your next trip home!). See if you can extract from him the reasons for such job changes as he made. To what extent would you say he was influenced by economic or noneconomic considerations?

4. For whatever occupation or profession you expect to follow (or for one which is at least among your likely alternatives), draft a career timetable.

5. For what kind of person do you believe that nonadvancement in a career line would be equivalent to failure?

6. Presumably, as a student you have some option to move around among colleges and universities, selecting the one which gives you greatest satisfaction. What factors induce or inhibit your "student mobility"? To what extent are these comparable to the considerations influencing the job mobility of a worker? Do you think it is desirable to increase the effective mobility in both cases?

NOTES

1. Gertrude Bancroft and Stuart Garfinkle, "Job Mobility in 1961," *Special Labor Force Report* no. 35, U.S. Bureau of Labor Statistics, 1963; and "Job Mobility of Workers in 1955," *Current Population Reports,* Series P-50, no. 70, U.S. Bureau of the Census, 1957.

2. Harvey R. Hamel, "Job Tenure of Workers, January 1966," *Special Labor Force Report* no. 77, U.S. Bureau of Labor Statistics, 1967, pp. 31–32. As would be expected, the job tenure of women was much lower than that of men: a median of 2.8 years compared to 5.2 years for men.

3. Bancroft and Garfinkle, p. 7.

4. The same, pp. 3–4.

5. Computed from data in Samuel Saben, "Occupational Mobility of Employed Workers," *Special Labor Force Report* no. 84, pp. 31–38. The 1965 rate of 5.5 is the percentage of those eighteen years and over employed in January, 1966, who changed occupations during the previous year; the 1961 rate of 4.7 is based on all those fourteen and over who worked during that year, a measure expected to yield a lower rate even if the years were the same.

6. John B. Lansing and Eva Mueller, *The Geographic Mobility of Labor,* University of Michigan, Survey Research Center, Institute for Social Research, Ann Arbor, 1967, p. 16. "In general the boundaries of labor markets coincide with the boundaries of metro-

politan areas," with county boundaries used for areas where the U.S. Department of Labor has not yet defined labor market lines. See the same, pp. 12–14.

7. For the classic study of this nature, see Lloyd G. Reynolds, *The Structure of Labor Markets,* Harper, New York, 1951.

8. Lansing and Mueller, pp. 43–44 and 113–118, and Samuel Saben, "Geographic Mobility and Employment Status, March 1962–March 1963," *Special Labor Force Report* no. 44, U.S. Bureau of Labor Statistics, 1964, p. 876.

9. Lansing and Mueller, pp. 14–17 and 29–33.

10. The same, p. 17. Emphasis added.

11. The evidence available—two studies of job changes in West Germany, plus the indirect evidence afforded by the similarity of occupational mobility in industrialized countries—suggests that job changing may be as frequent in Western Europe as in the United States, but this is flimsy evidence on which to base any generalizations. See *Wages and Labour Mobility,* Organisation for Economic Cooperation and Development, Paris, 1965, p. 55.

12. Simon Rottenberg, "On Choice in Labor Markets," *Industrial and Labor Relations Review,* vol. 9, p. 198, January, 1956.

13. For quit rates of manufacturing employees since 1930, see U.S. Bureau of Labor Statistics, *Employment and Earnings Statistics for the United States, 1909–67,* Bulletin 1312-5, 1967, p. xxx. For quits within the entire labor force in 1955 and 1961, see Bancroft and Garfinkle, "Job Mobility of Workers in 1961," p. 2.

14. Lansing and Mueller, p. 198.

15. For example, see Reynolds, chaps. 3–5.

16. Lansing and Mueller, pp. 208–224.

17. R. P. Loomba, *A Study of the Re-employment and Unemployment Experiences of Scientists and Engineers Laid Off from 62 Aerospace and Electronics Firms in the San Francisco Bay Area During 1963–65,* San Jose State College, Center for Interdisciplinary Studies, Calif., 1967, pp. 48–80.

18. David G. Brown, *The Mobile Professors,* American Council on Education, Washington, 1967, p. 119.

19. The same, p. 117.

20. The same, p. 55.

21. Robert L. Raimon, "Interstate Migration and Wage Theory," *The Review of Economics and Statistics,* vol. 44, November, 1962, pp. 428–438; and Lansing and Mueller, pp. 247–249.

22. Herbert S. Parnes, *Research on Labor Mobility,* Social Science Research Council, New York, 1954, pp. 174–190.

23. George P. Shultz, "A Nonunion Market for White Collar Labor," in National Bureau of Economic Research, *Aspects of Labor Economics,* Princeton University Press, Princeton, N.J., 1962, p. 134; Brown, p. 36; and Loomba, pp. 85–86.

24. Lansing and Mueller, chaps. 6 and 12.

25. The same, chap. 11.

26. Brown, pp. 130–134.

PART THREE

LABOR AS A MOVEMENT

A major aspect of the so-called "labor problem" consists of programs that are designed to meet economic adversity when it strikes the household. We shall examine a number of such programs in the chapters to come. Some are governmental in nature, such as unemployment insurance. Others, like health insurance, are provided by employers or by the households themselves, sometimes with a difference of opinion prevailing as to whether these should remain private or be taken over by the government.

Over the centuries the multitude of families which constitute a society have struggled to achieve a greater measure of protection against the forces of disaster. They have sought to make themselves "secure" against ills over which they believed they had little control or against the effects of which they believed they could not adequately provide in view of their needs of the moment. Households individually can do little to bring about the kinds of "reforms" they believe desirable. They are effective only if they act in concert. Thus political action, rebellion, and threat of insurrection have been weapons sometimes employed to bring about social innovations—mass protests against adversity, leaving the remedy to be devised by others (sometimes people of similar persuasion, sometimes people not in sympathy with the masses but attempting to pacify them). With the rise of democratic governments and mass politics, would-be leaders have tried to win votes by promising additional benefits, sometimes in anticipation of people's wants rather than in specific answer to vocal demands.

But households have also made use of one other instrument in their struggle for security and advancement—the labor union. The labor union came into being as the agent of the worker and his family. It performed, and still performs, a dual function: One (and the one that has perhaps been most publicized) has been to try to achieve some redistribution of a nation's wealth by raising the wages and earnings of its members. The effect would be to permit each household, on its own, to improve its living standards and in the process become better able to provide against involuntary changes in its economic position; it is no secret that upper-income families are in a better position to provide against unexpected expenditures or temporary losses of income than families on the edge of subsistence and are in a better position to secure for their children the advantages of education which will enhance their occupational status. Thus the objective of redistributing income has the advantage, for those who benefit from it, of giving them improved living circumstances in the present and greater security for the future.

The second union objective is, however, more directly related to the security role in the here and now. Through various types of union welfare funds and later through pressures for employer welfare programs and governmental social security measures, unions have sought to obtain for their principals, the households whom they represent, a greater measure of protection against the major economic hazards to which they are subject. And they have also attempted to foster the security of their principals in another and more controversial way—by demanding a voice in management decisions that may threaten worker security. Only a generation or two ago, many employers considered unions to be downright subversive for daring to ask for an equal role in determining wage rates and the length of the workday. Today, unions take for granted that they will also bargain about the terms of discipline, layoff, promotion, and other personnel policies—indeed, their right to do so is proclaimed and protected by law—and in addition, many unions negotiate the size of work crews, the speed of the production line, and the terms upon which employers may introduce new machinery or subcontract work to other employers or shift the location of their plants.

All of these union activities have been vigorously challenged, of course, and not only by employers. Many economists, for example, have considered at least some union behavior as a classic illustration of a group of producers pursuing their parochial interests at the expense of consumers and of unorganized workers. For many years it was argued that unions could indeed win wage increases, but that these increases would redistribute income not from the rich to the poor but only from the unorganized to the organized within the labor sector; today the argument has shifted to the charge that union-wage pressure is a major cause of price increases that harm worker and nonworker alike. As for the unions' drive for a greater voice in nonwage decisions within the firm, the clash of "management rights" versus "industrial democracy" is at the heart of nearly every controversy that swirls about the practice of collective bargaining. Whether the subject is the closed shop, featherbedding, seniority, or jurisdictional strikes, most critics of union behavior are basically charging that labor's drive for security has undermined the system of incentives needed to keep the economy efficient.

To evaluate these conflicting claims, it is first necessary to understand the dual nature of labor unions. It is true that unions came into existence as agents for households. They were designed as the spokesmen for men who were heads of families and who felt it necessary to band together to protect their families' welfare. We are still justified in regarding them in that original light. But over the years institutional change has been at work. Labor unions have grown into mass organizations, some with hundreds of thousands of members. Their officials have acquired power and authority over the security and welfare of the members whom they represent—power and authority which usually are exercised on behalf of the members, but not necessarily and not always. They have become organizations wielding certain political influence in their own right, even though many of their members may have differing political opinions. Like all organizations, they develop interests which are sometimes independent of their original functions, and they acquire an urge for survival, and sometimes expansion, which does not spring so much from their primary agency role as from the institutional will to perpetuate the organization and its attached bureaucracy.

These remarks are not made in criticism or derogation of labor unions, but simply as matters of fact. Unions still perform their principal purpose of acting as agents for millions of households, providing those households with a degree of economic security which they would not otherwise enjoy. But in the process they (the organization personified in the form of those who constitute its officialdom) have developed the same wish for institutional and occupational survival that characterizes virtually any organization. They are neither better nor worse in this respect than most churches, most colleges, most forms of government, most businesses.

Labor unions have often sought to portray themselves as identical with the labor force. Of course they are not—not even for that portion of the labor force which constitutes their membership. At one and the same time they serve that membership and are independent of it; they will not serve it so completely as to ignore their own institutional interests and survival, nor can they be so independent of it that they lose its support. In looking at the labor unions, then, we must examine both their functions—the security which they provide to their members and their households, which is their rationale for existence, and their own organizational needs, activities, and effects.

In a previous chapter we observed that a number of reasons determine whether a worker is satisfied to remain with a job or decides to try his luck elsewhere. A segment of the labor force tends to be opportunity-conscious and mobile, ready to shift from one employer to another (indeed, from one region to another) if this seems to offer possibilities of self-advancement. On the whole, however, a high proportion of workers—particularly adult males—tend to settle into employments from which, if they move at all, they are pushed by adverse circumstance or some aspect of the job which becomes increasingly unsatisfactory, rather than by being pulled by the prospect of a better job elsewhere.

Many studies have been made of the elements of a job which are important to workers—the factors on the basis of which they judge whether a job is satisfactory or unsatisfactory. The results of such surveys show considerable similarity. We may take one[1] as typical. Seven criteria by which jobs were judged were identified in interviews with a number of manual workers: (1) the acceptability of the wage level; (2) physical characteristics of the job (cleanliness, state of the machinery, etc.); (3) degree of independence and quality of direction on the job; (4) the interest attaching to the work itself; (5) the fairness of treatment by management; (6) relations with fellow workers; and (7) the steadiness of work.

It is not possible to list these factors in job satisfaction in any order of priority. Their im-

portance varies from situation to situation. In general, we may expect that their order of significance follows the law of diminishing marginal importance: those factors which are *least* satisfactory are regarded as most important. If a worker with relatively good wages felt that his foreman was unendurable, he would be likely to tell any interviewer that fairness of treatment by management was more important than wages, and vice versa.

If workers become greatly dissatisfied with a job because it fails in one or more of the factors listed above, they may be impelled to look for another job elsewhere. They may be stimulated to become one of the mobile segment of workers. But there is another possibility. They may seek to change the unsatisfactory situation—to raise wages, to force management to be fairer, to improve sanitary and safety conditions, and so on. To obtain such changes usually requires more power than a single unsatisfied worker can muster, however. The answer? A union.

Worker objectives

Whether the elements of job satisfaction are seven (as in the study mentioned above) or forty-some (as in other studies which have been made), most if not all of them can be subsumed under certain main categories, and it is with respect to these that workers may come to believe that a union can benefit them. As far as the individual employee is concerned, the union exists only to obtain some improvement for him in one or more of these particulars. The union is his representative, his spokesman, his agent in dealings with his employer. It is his agent (and the agent of his fellow workers) in his capacity both as an individual who has certain personal interests and satisfactions deriving from his job and as a member of a household whose income depends in part on the terms of sale of his time and effort. Thus the labor union is not simply a representative of a collection of individual workers; it is at least as much a bargaining agent for all those households represented by its members. In a perfectly valid sense, the union is the creature of the household, a means of strengthening its position in the sale of the time it allocates to the market.

This agency function of the union is most clearly seen when we remind ourselves that, unlike the households which it represents and the business firms with which it deals, it derives its income not from those *with* whom it negotiates but only from those *for* whom it negotiates. The union does not bargain with an employer for income for itself; it gets its income only from its members for whom it bargains, in the form of initiation fees, dues, or special assessments.

What are the job elements about which workers are most concerned and in the improvement of which they sometimes turn to unions? We may summarize the objectives which workers seek through their unions as follows:

1 Steady employment providing an adequate income By "adequate," workers do not mean subsistence but a progressive, if modest, improvement in their standard of living. But steady employment is something which their employer by himself may be unable to guarantee; his ability to provide it is limited by the state of the market, which is in large part beyond his control. Achievement of this aspiration may thus involve workers, through their unions, in political action for the maintenance of full employment. This broad economic objective of unions—enough jobs at good pay—is the one the public knows best. But there are others.

2 The rationalization of personnel policies The economic security of an employee is bound up not only in the wage level of his company and the duration of his employment but also in management's personnel actions—in its selection of employees for layoff, rehire, and promotion, in the assignment of employees to jobs, in their transfer, in the disciplining of employees. If decisions of this order are the result of subjective evaluation or capriciousness, there is no security for the worker. If such decisions are, however, governed by stated rules which are enforceable by the employee or his representative, there is greater assurance of fair treatment and equal justice. It is difficult to overstate the importance workers attach to union controls of this nature.

3 A voice in decisions affecting his welfare The worker may successfully pressure for higher wages. He may achieve a satisfactory rationalization of personnel policies. But if the vital decisions as to the scale and schedule of production, the introduction of laborsaving devices which may rob him of further chance to use his skills, the closing or relocation of a plant—if decisions of this type remain outside his effective influence, there is no real security for him. He experiences a cold reaction to such management statements as: "It is axiomatic, of course, that the ultimate success of any given employee comes only through the success of the company." He wants to know what his chances are for success *within* the company: Will new machinery reduce him from a skilled operative to a machine tender or a member of the custodial force? He wants to know what his chances are for continued attachment *to* the company. What is "the success of the company" to him if, when its operations are transferred from New Bedford to Charlotte, he is severed from the payroll? The intervention of the union in such management decisions is the only method by which the worker is able to achieve any degree of control over the affairs that concern him.

4 Protection from economic hazards beyond his control There are some conditions which may not lend themselves to effective family planning and protection—an accident or ill health, for example. There are other circumstances whose adverse effect a family might hope to mitigate, but its resources are not always adequate to the task

—tiding itself over a period of unemployment, financing old age, etc. For these purposes a union may prove an effective bargaining agent—either through political pressure for public benefit programs or through economic pressure on employers for private benefit programs.

5 Recognition and participation The assertion of one CIO union in the stormy days of the thirties still holds good:[2]

> Underlying its aspirations for full participation in the job of production is labor's basic position of equality. This is more than equality at the bargaining table. It is intellectual equality. This contemplates abandoning the illusion, all too prevalent in industrial circles, that the human beings on management's side are possessed of greater intellectual faculties than are those among the working force. The idea that workers are intellectually inferior to management is the source of many of our difficulties. Years ago we used to believe that a woman was intellectually inferior to a man. Today we have admitted that we were wrong. The intellectual equality of management and labor is a prerequisite to the development of industrial relations along constructive lines.

A notable characteristic of these five worker-household-union objectives is that not one of them is revolutionary. While the attempt to realize these goals often involves demands which managements vigorously oppose and only reluctantly concede, they do not require modification of our social and economic system along lines representing a sharp break with basic traditions.

Why workers joins unions

There is a difference, however, between the functions which unions can perform on behalf of members and which therefore constitute the *rationale* for membership, and the actual reason which—at some moment, on some occasion—may prompt individuals to organize or join a union. We are sometimes misled into thinking of the rationale for the union's functions as the members' reasons for joining; it *may* be that, but there are other explanations why some individuals take out membership.

To be sure, a specific grievance against man-

agement may cause a worker to "sign up." Many successful organizing drives by unions have been based on some general employee unrest triggered by a management action. These are the dissatisfactions experienced by workers which might, if unresolved, push them to look for another job elsewhere, or at a minimum, leave them disgruntled and resentful employees. One study, made of a representative sample of union members in a large basic steel mill in Chicago,[3] disclosed that 39 percent of the local union's leaders, 21 percent of its active rank-and-file members, and 15 percent of its inactive members had joined the union because of some unhappy experience in the plant. The authors of this study concluded that personal matters, such as discipline for minor offenses, the feeling that they were being "pushed around" too much, and inequitable treatment with respect to wage rates or opportunities to work, play a large part in the thinking of workers. "An unpleasant personal experience becomes a powerful motivation that turns workers toward a union and may get them to become active and accept leadership positions in it."

But other reasons were also influential. Some workers in this steel plant had joined the union because their fathers had implanted the seeds of unionism in them. In the words of one, "I attended union meetings with my father before I was ever inside a church." From another, "My dad was a great union man and that's where I got it—if it wasn't union, it wasn't no good." As the authors of this study note, the spread of union membership in the United States in the last quarter-century suggests that a greater number of workers will be brought up in families where union membership is taken for granted, perhaps endowing the movement with a stability that it has not been able to count on in the past.

Other members of the local were persuaded by the logic of union organizers. Without previous union experience and without prior conviction, they were led to join by the force of argument. "I heard the fellows talk about it in the mill. They were all saying that you can't get any place by yourself but that you have to get the guys together and then maybe you can do something." Another told of a meeting with a union organizer. "We got to talking about it and he convinced me it was a good idea."

For others, however, membership in the union came not out of conviction—whether induced by personal experience, by family influence, or by persuasion by others—but out of pressure. For some, the subtle effects of social conformance were responsible; they responded to group feeling. "I was fresh out of school and didn't know anything about unions. Other fellows were joining and I joined." Said another, "I suppose I joined in order to jump in line with the majority to say I was a union member." And from another, "I can't think of a good reason except everybody else was in it."

For those who fail to respond to such social pressure, there may be more overt coercion. "They approached you, kept after you, hounded you. To get them off my neck, I joined." And finally, there may be actual compulsion, a requirement negotiated by union and management that workers must belong to or remain in the union in order to hold their jobs. This normally takes the form of a union-shop or maintenance-of-membership provision, and involves issues which we shall examine later.

It is significant, however, that even many of those workers who join the union not because of conviction but under some sort of social or institutional duress come in time to accept the union as desirable. Such workers may never evidence any actual enthusiasm for it, but if asked whether they want the union, they will reply "yes" and, if asked why, will frequently answer that they consider it like an insurance policy. The union gives them a measure of independence and control over their own affairs. Management's word is not necessarily final. The individual who feels he is unfairly dealt with can have a hearing. The union is prized not so much because of a belief that it will win them higher wages as because of a desire to be able to stand up against management decisions which are regarded as unfair.

There is one other reason why a substantial number of workers are to be found on the union rolls, a reason which a survey conducted in a steel plant or any other manufacturing establishment would be unlikely to disclose. There are some types of employments which are "casual" in nature. They do not consist of working for the same company week in and week out, as part of a fairly stable work group. They involve a series of short-run jobs with different employers—not because of bad times or instability in the industry but simply because the industry is organized that way. In the building trades, for example, a carpenter or a plumber or an electrician may work for one contractor on a particular job, and when that job is finished he will look for work with some other contractor. This casual quality also characterizes many of the jobs connected with the maritime industry—when seamen sign on for a voyage, for example, or longshoremen unload the cargo of a particular vessel.

In such industries, where there is not steady employment but a succession of short-run jobs, workers must be able to move easily from one employer to another if they are to avoid loss of income. This suggests the need for some form of central employment office or hiring hall where workers who have just finished with one job can be assigned to another and where employers who need a crew for a short-run contract can find a "pick-up" gang of men. Unions in these industries typically perform this function.

An official of one union in the construction industry thus commented: "Above all we are an employment agency. If we couldn't supply jobs for our members and competent craftsmen for our employers, we might as well go out of business." How this operates was illustrated by a paid officer of another building-trades union, who might tell a member at work on a job: "It looks like you'll be finished next Monday. Stevenson is opening a big job next Friday and if you want, Thatcher and Sons has a small alteration that will take you two or three days which you can sandwich in between. If you want that, I'll have them both save places for you."[4]

Besides acting as a clearinghouse for jobs, such unions usually seek to perform the other more typical functions of making sure that employment conditions are satisfactory, though their methods of accomplishing this objective may differ from those of unions representing stable work forces.

How unions represent workers

There are two principal arenas—public politics and private economics—in which organized workers seek the achievement of their objectives. Although in most other countries political action has tended to assume greater importance than private economic bargaining, historically in the United States labor's effort has emphasized union–management negotiations over the terms of employment. We probably tend to exaggerate the extent to which this has been the case. Political pressure has probably had, even in the past, a greater impact on the field of industrial relations than we have been willing to recognize. Nevertheless, in contrast with the absorption of labor movements of other countries in political activity, our unions have traditionally pursued a policy of what has been termed "job-conscious activity"— the attempt to effect an improvement in wages, hours, and working conditions at the level of the individual plant. This has meant bargaining with the employer—*collective* bargaining, a process which we shall examine in some detail in later chapters.

An individual worker bargaining for himself is often at a disadvantage relative to the employer. The only commodity he has to sell, his own labor, is perishable. Since it cannot be stocked, what is not sold today cannot be sold tomorrow. Unlike physical commodities, it cannot be stored until a better price is offered. Even though the worker may consider the price for his labor inadequate, refusing to sell it is likely to cause him greater financial loss than selling it cheap. Work at a low wage rate is better than no work at all; moreover, the individual worker seldom has a backlog of savings to sustain him if he holds out for a higher wage rate. Because he often lacks capital, his immediate need for continued income can be satisfied only by a daily wage. He cannot afford to refuse work, even at a low wage rate, when he and his family depend on wage income, day by day, to finance their normal living expenses. Thus the perishability of his labor and the need for continuing income both operate to create a high cost to the worker of refusing an employer's terms.

Added to this disability is the fact that recurringly in our history, with the swings of the business cycle, there has been some surplus of labor. Even when work has been generally available, particular jobs have not always been easy to come

by, especially jobs commensurate with a worker's skills and past experience. Hence a job has come to be viewed as something to be prized, not to be cast aside lightly. If the employer's terms were not so favorable as the worker would like or had reason to expect, or if an employer seemed to take advantage of the individual, any complaint could often be met with the employer's assertion that if the worker didn't like it, there were others who would be only too glad to have such a job. One of the most respected students of the labor movement, Prof. Selig Perlman, based his theory concerning the reasons for the rise and direction of unionism in part on a "scarcity consciousness" which he thought was characteristic of workers— a realization that jobs are the key to scarce resources (food, clothing, and shelter) and a sense that workers are always more plentiful than jobs.[5]

This scarcity consciousness on the part of workers contrasts with the previously noted conclusion of economists that over the long haul labor has been the scarce factor in the United States, thus contributing to high wages. The difference in these two points of view arises from the fact that typically an employer wants not just "a worker" but a worker with particular skills, good health, a reasonably stable work record, and so on. Such a person is not always easy to find even if there are a dozen applicants for a job. But to a worker who is one of the dozen applicants, the picture is one of too many workers competing for too few jobs.

In the bargaining relationship between individual worker and employer, there thus seemed usually to be a considerable advantage in the latter's favor. How redress that imbalance? Little could be done to reduce the perishability of labor, and there was no apparent way in which the worker's capital could be increased sufficiently to lessen his dependence on current income. But the organization of workers into a union could reduce the competition of workers for jobs. If not one but all of an employer's employees were to seek an improvement in their terms, it would not be so easy for that employer to replace the entire work force with others willing to work at the old terms. Unionization meant that workers ceased to compete with one another for jobs on the basis of who was willing to accept whatever terms the employer offered. They thus increased their group bargaining power. And this was a result which, within limits, drew public approval because of the widespread belief that an individual workman was no match for an employer in a contest of economic strength.[6]

The extent of unionism

The function of unions, then, is to act as representative and agent for the employee, both as an individual who has his own personal interests in the way he is treated on the job and as a member of a household which relies on him for part of its income. This would seem to constitute an enormously important function—so important that we

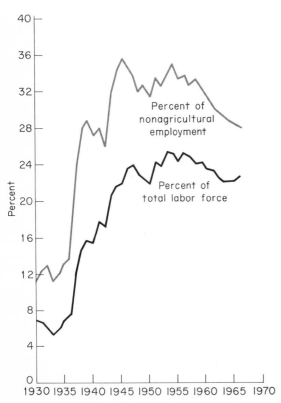

Fig. 5-1. *Union membership as a percent of the labor force and of nonagricultural employment, 1930–1966.*

SOURCE: *U.S. Bureau of Labor Statistics,* Bulletin *1596, p. 57.*

would expect most workers to join unions as a matter of course. What, in fact, has happened? How many workers have taken out membership in unions?

Figure 5-1 shows that, in relative terms, unions reached their high-water mark in the mid-1940s, when membership equaled about one-quarter of the total labor force and over one-third of non-agricultural employees. (The latter is a better measure of organizing accomplishment, since it excludes the armed forces, the self-employed, farmers, family and domestic workers, and the unemployed. It nevertheless includes many people, particularly executives and managers, who are obviously not targets for organization.) Then, following a period of stability in the early 1950s, the organized portion of the labor sector shrank for several reasons, including the continuing employment shift into service industries and white-collar occupations and the severe impact of two recessions on employment in union bastions such as autos, steel, construction, and mining.

In absolute numbers, union membership rose from a low of about 3 million in 1933 to nearly 15 million by the mid-1940s, and then climbed more slowly to a peak of 17.5 million in 1956. Membership then sagged for the reasons described above and did not regain its 1956 level until ten years later, when employment expanded rapidly (especially in manufacturing) during the Vietnam war years and also when the organization of government employees had gained momentum. In 1966 a total of 17.9 million members were claimed within the United States by 190 national and international unions. (Unions classified as "internationals" also had 1.4 million members outside of the United States, primarily in Canada.) In addition, there were then about 500,000 members claimed by small unions limited to a single state or firm and not affiliated with any national union.[7]

Organization of a little over one-quarter of the "organizable" employees into unions may be considered a remarkable development, since as recently as the early 1930s only one in eight was a unionist. From another point of view, however, this result is surprisingly modest. In light of the important agency function which unions perform for their members, why have only a minority of

American workers chosen to join them? Where have the unions met with success, and where with failure?

Table 5-1 indicates that union members are distributed almost equally between the manufacturing and nonmanufacturing sectors of private industry, but they are distributed very unevenly within each of those sectors. Note, for example, that nearly one-half of all union members are in four industry groups: metals (including basic steel, fabricated metals, machinery, and electrical equipment), transportation equipment (autos and aircraft), construction, and transportation (trucking, railroads, airlines, and shipping). In contrast,

Table 5-1 *Distribution of National and International Unions by Industry Group, 1966*

| | All unions | | |
| | | Members† | |
Industry group	Number*	Number (thousands)	Percent
All unions‡	190	19,125	100.0
Manufacturing:	103	8,769	45.8
Food, beverages, and tobacco	26	1,084	5.7
Clothing, textiles, and leather products	21	1,194	6.2
Furniture, lumber, wood products, and paper	22	829	4.3
Printing and publishing	15	357	1.9
Petroleum, chemicals, and rubber	20	570	3.0
Stone, clay, and glass	20	295	1.5
Metals, machinery, and equipment (except transportation equipment)	36	2,874	15.0
Transportation equipment	19	1,297	6.8
Manufacturing (not classifiable)	36	269	1.4
Nonmanufacturing:	101	8,640	45.2
Mining and quarrying	13	324	1.7
Contract construction	26	2,463	12.9
Transportation	43	2,535	13.3
Telephone and telegraph	10	505	2.6
Electric and gas utilities	14	324	1.7
Trade	20	1,353	7.1
Finance and insurance	6	62	§
Service industries	28	1,002	5.2
Agriculture and fishing	6	35	§
Nonmanufacturing (not classifiable)	9	37	§
Government:	58	1,717	9.0
Federal	57	1,073	5.6
State and local	17	644	3.4

* This column is nonadditive; many unions have membership in more than one industrial classification.
† Number of members computed by applying reported percentage figures to total membership, including membership outside the United States.
‡ Of these, 169 unions reported an estimated distribution by industry; for 21 unions, the Bureau estimated industrial composition.
§ Less than 0.05 percent.
SOURCE: U.S. Bureau of Labor Statistics, Bulletin 1596, p. 62.

union members are thinly distributed throughout most of the service sector, although the percentage representing government employees is higher than many people would expect and has been steadily growing for some years.

But Table 5-1 can be misleading, for there may be fewer union members in a well-organized but small industry, such as mining, than in a weakly organized but very large industry, such as retailing. Table 5-2 therefore presents two measures of union strength which attempt to correct for differences in industry size. Although many of the estimates in that table are very rough, the *rank order* of industries by union organization or contract coverage is believed to be fairly accurate. In general, this table confirms the concentration of union strength in transportation, construction, and certain durable-good manufacturing industries, and shows unions to be even weaker in the service sector than Table 5-1 indicated.

The same problem exists in measuring the geographical pattern of union membership. For example, in 1966 nearly one-half of all union members were concentrated in just five states—New York, California, Pennsylvania, Illinois, and Ohio —but these are obviously states which rank at or near the top in total population. When the comparison is made of union membership as a percentage of nonfarm employees, the most strongly organized states in 1966 were (in order) West Virginia, Michigan, Washington, Pennsylvania, and New York. Organization was weakest by this measure in South Carolina, North Carolina, South Dakota, Mississippi, and Florida. Unions are not uniformly weak in the South, however. In industries such as autos and steel, the Southern plants of national corporations are usually organized, as is longshoring in most Southern ports and even construction in many Southern cities. But in four industries particularly important in the South— textiles, clothing, lumber, and furniture—unions are decidedly weaker in that region than elsewhere in the country.[8]

In view of the industries in which unions are concentrated, it is not surprising that relatively few office workers and other white-collar groups are organized. In 1966 about 2.7 million of these workers were union members, representing only 14 percent of total membership and an even smaller proportion of total white-collar employment. Nor is the number of women in unions proportional to their strength in the labor force; about one-fifth of union members were women in 1966, when women formed over one-third of the labor force. Finally, unions have made their greatest headway in the largest companies, have had a somewhat lesser success in the medium-sized establishments, and have had their least success in the small shops and plants.

Reasons for the distribution of unionism

What reasons lie behind these statistics? The regional differences may be attributed to the fact that Southern employers exhibit a more intense and unyielding opposition to unionization than employers in other regions exhibit today. This opposition springs in part from the more recent industrialization of the South, from a belief that union organizers are primarily "outsiders" intent on stirring up trouble where none exists, and probably from lingering attachment to a philosophy of paternalism, particularly in the smaller communities; a philosophy of professional managerialism is more likely to be found in the plants of national corporations in major Southern cities.

The notable inability of unions to attract white-collar workers also has a complex explanation. In part, it is due to the fact that office employees often work more closely with managers and come to associate themselves more intimately with them. White-collar workers tend to be more highly educated than manualists, which not only creates some social barrier between white-collar and blue-collar workers but also provides the former with an indispensable prerequisite to advancement into management ranks themselves, a prospect which the manualist typically cannot realistically entertain. White-collar employees also tend to shrink from some of the traditional union tactics, such as strikes and picket lines.

But unions have recently made some significant breakthroughs on the white-collar front. For many years, union strength in this sector was concentrated in occupations such as those of actors, pilots, postal clerks, musicians, and newspaper reporters, with only scattered pockets of organization among occupations like those of engineers,

Table 5-2 *Estimated Union Organization or Contract Coverage, by Industry, 1960–1964 Period*

Industry	Percent of production workers covered by union contracts*	Union members as a percent of all employees†
Manufacturing:	62	50
Transportation equipment	83	
Primary metal (basic steel, etc.)	82	
Paper and allied products	81	
Stone, clay, and glass	74	
Rubber products	72	
Ordnance	65–75	
Electrical equipment	69	
Fabricated metal	66	
Tobacco manufactures	66	
Food and kindred products	61	
Printing and publishing	59	
Petroleum refining		50–75
Leather products	56	
Machinery	52	
Apparel	50	
Furniture	46	
Miscellaneous manufacturing	42	
Instruments	41	
Chemicals		25–50
Lumber	37	
Textile	27	
Nonmanufacturing:		25
Transportation		85–95
Construction		65–75
Telephone and telegraph		45–55
Mining		40–50
Electric and gas utilities		40–50
Service industries		5–15
Retail and wholesale trade		5–15
Finance and insurance		0–15
Agriculture and fishing		0–5
Government		15

* More precisely, the percentage of production workers employed in establishments in which a majority of such workers were covered by union contracts, primarily in 1962. Production workers are largely blue-collar, nonsupervisory employees. Not all workers in plants where a majority are covered by contracts are union members, and not all union members are employed in such plants.

† Union membership in 1964 by industry, divided by industry employment in 1964. Estimates are not precise because union data include members in areas outside the United States and some members not in the labor force in 1964. Also note that "all employees" include managers, professionals (except self-employed), and salesmen as well as clerical and blue-collar workers. In 1964 nonproduction or supervisory workers formed 17 percent of total employment in private industry, ranging from 9 percent in retailing to 26 percent in manufacturing.

SOURCES: Manufacturing data primarily from Arnold Strasser, "Factory Workers Under Bargaining Agreements," *Monthly Labor Review*, February, 1965, pp. 164–167; U.S. Bureau of Labor Statistics, *Major Union Contracts in the United States, 1961*, Bulletin 1353 (1962); and Harold J. Levinson, *Postwar Movement of Prices and Wages in Manufacturing Industries*, Joint Economic Committee Study Paper No. 21 (Washington, 1960). Other data from U.S. Bureau of Labor Statistics, Bulletin 1493, pp. 55–56.

retail clerks, and general office workers. Within the last decade, however, union organization has mushroomed among three groups—teachers, nurses, and civil service employees at all levels of government—all of whom have high visibility and prestige and were once considered the epitome of antiunion, white-collar workers.

There are many reasons for this sudden union success: the belief (often justified) that unionized blue-collar workers had narrowed or eliminated the gap in wages, fringe benefits, and working conditions that once favored the white-collar worker; the realization that teachers and nurses were in short supply and thus in an excellent bargaining position; the growing number of male family heads who entered public school teaching, once a predominantly feminine province; the recent extension to many employees of government and nonprofit institutions of the same legal protection for union activity which the Wagner Act long ago gave to workers in private industry; and yet other reasons. What remains unclear at this time, however, is whether these particular breakthroughs presage a wave of organization among other white-collar groups, such as the army of clerical workers scattered in offices throughout the country, or whether future membership gains will be largely limited to garnering more teachers, nurses, and public employees. Even the latter would represent a significant gain for organized labor.

We should note, however, that women have traditionally shown sales resistance with respect to taking out membership in a union. This resistance probably springs from the fact that many of them are in the labor force on only a part-time basis, as we have seen, and probably feel less firmly attached to the labor force than their more career-oriented husbands. Moreover, unions have themselves been run by men and are part of a labor movement which is presided over by men, conveying an impression that women members are accorded less than full representation.

Weaknesses in union organization and public exposure of certain union malpractices have tended to turn some potential members away, at the same time that management practices have often become more enlightened, partly in response to the threat of unionization.

The expense of carrying on an organizing campaign in a small establishment, relative to the small revenue which would be derived from dues even if the campaign were successful, makes it excessively costly for unions to concentrate on the fringe of small enterprises, even in the manufacturing sector.

What are the prospects that unions can surmount the difficulties which so far have impeded their enrolling more than one-third of those eligible? The future is always an unknown, but two labor force trends, noted in the previous section, appear to be running against the unions. The proportion of the labor force employed in the service industries and at white-collar occupations has been steadily increasing and will probably continue to increase, but these are groups, as we have just seen, with which the unions have had distinctly limited success. The proportion of women in the labor force has likewise been steadily rising and, as we have noted, the union has been less attractive to them than to male workers. To some extent these two effects overlap—it is women who are going into service and white-collar occupations—but if this reduces the extent of the impact of these two labor force trends, it increases the intensity of resistance to union organizing efforts.

With the growth of the population and of the gross national product, the absolute size of establishments can be expected to increase, and this effect will be favorable to the unions. It may also be expected that as time passes, some of the resistance to unionism in sections of the South will be lessened. There is little question, however, that unions will be waging an uphill fight for new members from here on. Whether or not the expansion phase of the American labor movement is at an end is a question that has been argued with great vigor but to no resolution.

Differential union growth and size

The growth of individual unions may of course differ from that of the labor movement as a whole. Some have become gigantic, while others have dwindled away. The reasons for disparate size among the unions are several. To some extent the changing industrial pattern is responsible. The rise of the automobile industry has given birth to one of the largest unions in the United States, which was nonexistent at the turn of the century. On the other hand, the cigar makers' union has fallen off in membership as the cigar industry has declined in importance. To some extent the size differentials reflect the size of the groups in the economy over which the unions have jurisdiction. There will always be more steelworkers than diamond cutters. And to some extent the varying size of unions reflects differences in the kinds of leadership. A dynamic and ruthless leadership will seek a larger and larger empire. Smaller unions may be swallowed up and other unions' jurisdictions invaded. Mergers may occur.

For these and perhaps other reasons, while the labor movement has tended to show a relative stability in recent years, there have been some fairly major changes in the size of the constituent unions. Thus, during the period from 1951 to 1966, four out of every five unions either grew or declined by 10 percent or more from their 1951 base. The major gainers during this period were the unions in government service, printing, retail trade, construction, and trucking. Among unions losing members were those in railroading, mining, textiles, marine transportation, and shoe-making.[9]

Three unions in 1966 had over a million members each: the Brotherhood of Teamsters, the United Automobile Workers, and the United Steelworkers. The membership changes of these and the next three largest unions between 1951 and 1966 are shown in Figure 5-2.

The three largest unions—constituting only 2 percent of the total number of unions—accounted for about 20 percent of all union membership in 1966. The top 10 unions, representing only 6 percent of the number of national unions, contained 45 percent of total union membership. On the other hand, there were 91 national unions with fewer than 25,000 members each; these accounted for nearly 50 percent of the number of unions but

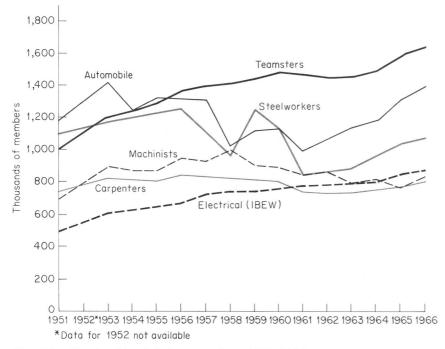

Fig. 5-2. *Membership of six largest unions, 1951–1966.*

SOURCE: *U.S. Bureau of Labor Statistics,* Bulletin 1596, *p. 58.*

less than 4 percent of total membership. Thus, reminiscent of the size distribution of business firms, there is a high degree of concentration in the labor movement.

Unions as institutions with interests of their own

The only function of a union is to act as agent or representative for its members. But once a union comes into existence, it becomes an ongoing institution which of necessity develops its own organizational interests and requirements, and these in some respects differ from the interests and objectives of its members. Apparent conflicts between the preferences or welfare of members and that of the organization are sometimes seized on to demonstrate that union leaders are really out to feather their own nests rather than to aid the individual worker. The leaders are accused of pursuing policies contrary to, or regardless of, the interests of the members. The high degree of union concentration on such matters as amending Federal and state legislation to remove restraints on union organizing, and achieving compulsory union membership through union or closed shops, and cementing political alliances, and conducting jurisdictional disputes or rival-union warfare is often said to reveal official preoccupation with the welfare of the union rather than of the members. These matters, it is argued, are of little importance to the rank and file but strongly affect the power and prestige of an officeholding clique.

There is an element of truth in such charges, to be sure. The leader of the union is more immediately concerned in such matters because they affect his own career more directly and more immediately than they do the fortunes of the membership. But there are more impersonal motives. That the interests of an organization and its members sometimes in fact differ is not confined to unions; it is a characteristic of institutionalized society.

There are several reasons why the organization (that is, the official hierarchy) must take stands which appear to have little relevance to the membership's immediate advantage. For the moment, let us distinguish the organizational interests from the personal interests of those who are in charge of the union. We can readily admit that a union official may have his own ax to grind and may be seeking some personal gains from his office, and at the same time recognize that he may be—indeed, almost certainly is—motivated in some of his actions by a genuine concern for the organization as such. And further, that these latter, organizationally directed actions may at times cause him to override the expressed preferences of his members or, at a minimum, to involve them in activities and expenses which they would not necessarily have undertaken on their own. Let us explore some of these reasons.

First, when a person is elected to office in a union, he inherits a responsibility to pass on the organization to his successors in at least as good a shape as it came to him—perhaps even in better shape. Any manager can readily understand that compulsion. Any institution has not only a past and a present but also a future. It lives not only for the benefit of its present members but also for its future members, and that is true whether the members are stockholders in a corporation, students in a university, citizens of a state, or workers in a union. The official of an organization cannot act solely for the benefit of those who happen to be on the membership roll at the moment. At times he may have to call for present sacrifices in order to keep an organization alive and vital for those who are to come after, but always he must keep in mind the balance between satisfying the legitimate wants and aspirations of those who now compose the organization and whose adherence to it is necessary for its survival, and adopting policies which may have little direct benefit to present members but which help to ensure the future of the organization.

Just as the present membership is the beneficiary of similar past policies aimed at continuity and survival, so may the future membership—now nonexistent—impose obligations on the present generation to preserve the vitality of the organization for its benefit. The sacrifices of those unionists who fought for the right to organize and to bargain with employers, in an earlier and more difficult day, were not intended to result in benefits terminating with the present union membership but to continue on into an indefinite future. The union leader cannot forget that responsibility, even though it may involve him in policies and actions unpopular with both his members and the public.

There is a second reason why the union official must be concerned with organizational interests. From the vantage point which he occupies, he has a clearer perception that whatever gains unions can win for their members come through the union's bargaining strength, both within industry and within the legislatures. It makes sense, then, to be concerned with matters which do not relate to the immediate job interests of the rank and file, which do not deal directly with wages or relations with supervisors or job security or the physical characteristics of employment, but which are frankly concerned with union power. For it is only through union power that the aspirations of the membership can be enforced. A management today may, it is true, be sympathetic to its workers' wants, but unless those workers are willing to rely on management's conception of their wants, that is, rely on the goodness of business authority, it takes power to make effective their own conception of what they are entitled to. Union leaders, in seeking power for their organizations, are thus creating instrumentalities for the pursuit of worker objectives. They are concerned not only with ends, the matters which preoccupy the worker on his job, but also with means, about which the worker has less direct interest and competence. This is one of the necessary functions of leadership in an organization.

As a third consideration, when an institution serves as agent for a large number of people, the interests of one group or segment may diverge from the interests of other component groups. How should the common agent resolve such a conflict between its principals, who presumably are entitled to equal representation? Whatever the course taken, we can be sure that it will be justified as being "in the interests of the organization as a whole." Such a rationalization quite frankly accepts that the advantages of individual members are not always coincident with the welfare of that amorphous entity, "the organization."

The fact that union officials must necessarily be concerned with organizational as well as membership interests does not, of course, justify all their actions. Measures may be taken in a genuine

belief that they are for the good of the union, but the belief may be mistaken or at least arguable. Even though rank-and-file members may tend to be more shortsighted than officials, or at least more oriented to their own immediate interests, viewing the union as their agent and representative in terms of their present needs, the rank and file are not always wrong. There are grounds for differences in views, and usually there is no objective basis for asserting who is right and who is wrong.

Keeping this in mind, we may now examine some of the respects in which the organizational point of view of union officials may lead to policies which appear to be in conflict with the interests of a member or at least to be of no direct advantage to him.

Centralization of authority

We shall examine in a later chapter the governmental processes of labor unions. Here, however, we may note that at times labor officials are led to take a "poppa knows best" attitude toward members, denying them privileges of participation in the operation of the union on the ground that "the good of the organization" demands control by experienced and wiser heads. This is particularly likely to be true in those unions founded by professional organizers or long-time unionists. A classic case was the manner in which Philip Murray, a principal organizer and first president of the Steelworkers Union (coming out of the Mine Workers Union to take on that function), insisted on a very personal control of the union in its early days and took offense at the efforts of some of the more restive members to assume such rights as the election of the field staff which then was influential in the affairs of all the newly formed local unions.[10]

It would be a mistake, he said, for the delegates to assume "that the functions of your organization have been so stabilized that we can run the gamut of every known kind of democratic procedure, even to the point of license in the operation of our affairs.

"I don't mind telling you ... that your interest still needs some safeguarding in this man's country. My personal judgment is that your situations are not sufficiently well-stabilized [to elect] all your representatives."

The Mine Workers, from which Murray had come, itself has had a long tradition of national officials imposing on many of the district units officers appointed by them rather than locally elected. To repeated membership protests, former President John L. Lewis often thundered the reply that he was only acting in the best interests of the organization, rescuing the trusteed districts from their own incompetence.

Students of the subject may have legitimate differences of opinion as to whether centralization of authority in the hands of experienced leaders, or rank-and-file control of affairs, even though less effective, is preferable. There is no dispute, however, over the fact that union officers have often sought greater authority in the genuine belief that they could do a better job for the organization—in terms of increasing both its present bargaining power and its potential survival power and regardless of the preference of the membership.

Jurisdictional rights

Few concepts have been so significant in the historical development of the American labor movement as that of jurisdiction. Traditionally, jurisdiction has been as important to a union as territory has been to a nation; it constitutes the job boundary line within which, or the work territory over which, the union has "sovereign" rights. As long as other unions recognize and respect its jurisdiction, a union possesses a monopoly on organizing and administering the work and workers defined by that jurisdiction. It has posted "no poaching" signs over certain kinds of work or clusters of jobs, and other unions have observed its exclusive rights. If another union contests its job boundaries and invades its work territory by organizing workers of the given characteristics, it is as though a nation had invaded the territory of a neighboring state. Jurisdictional conflict ensues. In the annals of American labor history, some jurisdictional struggles have run on for decades and have involved deep animosities and even violence. This has been true, for exam-

ple, in the jurisdictional contest between the Brewery Workers and the Teamsters over the right to organize the drivers of beer trucks.

It is understandable enough that most unions seek to define their jurisdiction broadly enough to give themselves plenty of room for survival, if not expansion, and that in the process they can scarcely avoid overlapping the vague or shadowy claim of some other union also bent on survival and expansion. The processes of technological change almost guarantee that result. The Brotherhood of Carpenters has been one of the most beleaguered of unions, since new building materials have steadily been replacing wood in the construction industry. In order to put a stop to the gradual erosion of its jurisdiction, this union asserted a claim to work involving everything "once made of wood." It was predictable that this sweeping claim would embroil it with numbers of other unions—with the Ironworkers, for example, in the installation of a metal trim which took the place of a wood trim.[11] A maneuver such as this, or the early staking of a claim to some entirely new area of work, may seem necessary if a union is to survive, or survive with strength. Thus, when glass fiber became a commercially successful product, control over it was sought by the Textile Workers, the Glass Workers, the Chemical Workers, and a few other unions, all of which viewed this annexation of job territory as important to their organizational position. The examples could be multiplied almost indefinitely.

In some situations the personal interests of an individual member may be very much bound up in his union's jurisdiction. To the extent that his union manages to stake out a claim to a larger work territory, then presumably there are more jobs for which he can apply. If the Carpenters, for example, were unsuccessful in claiming the installation of metal trim or the construction of metal forms for concrete, then there would be fewer jobs for carpenters. One student has observed that "the primary historical function allotted their national union by the carpenters has not been wage determination but work preservation."[12] As one business agent of a building-trades union told his members at a local meeting: "The men should be willing to lose a few days' work [due to strikes designed to force an employer to recognize their jurisdiction over certain work] in order to save jobs for everybody. Jobs are going to be more scarce in the next two years and we ought to think of this."[13]

Such an identity or near identity of interests is most likely to occur where a worker's employment consists of a succession of short jobs and his continuity of employment therefore depends on there being enough short-run jobs to lay end to end, or where workers whose output is directly competitive with his own are brought under comparable terms and conditions of employment so that they do not compete with him on the basis of lower standards. But when the organizational drive is in fields not related to his own occupation or to the product he is producing, any advantages are more likely to be long-term and institutional rather than immediate and personal. The automobile worker is much less involved in the issue of whether his union is able to extend its organizing claims to the aerospace industry, for example, than are the Auto Workers officials. The union, with a life expectancy greater than its present membership and with its concern for preserving or expanding its organizational power, can be expected to regard its jurisdiction from a different perspective than simply that of agent for its members. It has longer-run interests of its own.

Union security

The obligation of all workers in an already-unionized establishment to become dues-paying members, which goes by the generic name of "union security," may be enforced by union members directly through the sanction which the early unionists adopted—refusing to work alongside a nonunion man—or by an understanding with the employer that he will not hire a worker who is not already a member of the union or will discharge a worker who does not join the union within some brief period of time following his hiring. Legal attitudes toward these provisions have a long and colorful history, which we cannot go into here but shall examine later.

Here—as in the case of jurisdiction—the interests of an individual union member and the union as an organization may be different and sometimes conflicting. Union-security provisions

are primarily of benefit to the union as an organization—even though, by contributing to union strength, they may indirectly benefit the individual worker. It is true that a great many workers appear to have no objection to compulsory union membership, at least in the industrial sectors where unionism has its greatest strength,[14] but there is a difference between a worker's willingness to be bound by a union-security provision and his perception of such a provision as of direct benefit to him. If given a choice by the employer as to whether they would prefer a 10-cents-an-hour wage increase or a compulsory-membership clause in the collective agreement, a kind of choice which some employers have in effect offered union negotiators, probably many workers would choose the former, whereas virtually all union officials would quickly accept the latter. Where a union shop already exists, there are almost certain to be some workers who have joined the union involuntarily, and they, at least, do not consider—whether rightly or wrongly—that their interests are the same as the organization's.

Organization discipline

In the matter of organizational discipline, the two roles of union as agent for its members (and their households) and as an organization with interests of its own again sometimes diverge. If the union were only a representative of its current membership, it would presumably take its instructions from them and respond to their bidding. But since it is also an organization whose long-run survival depends on its public standing and its acceptance by employers and government as well as members, it is sometimes driven to take disciplinary action against its members for behavior which is considered contrary to the union's best interests.

The union's concern for its reputation may lead it to countenance employer discipline against its members for wildcat strikes or insubordination even though their actions were precipitated by a company agent such as an overbearing foreman. Here the refusal to defend its *members'* "irresponsible" behavior would be justified as *organizational* "responsibility."

It was in this light that former Supreme Court

Justice Arthur Goldberg, when legal counsel for the Steelworkers and the AFL-CIO, once remarked:

> Under [the] system of industrial government, the employer has a right to expect from the union that (1) it will live up to and observe the rules so far as the union, *qua* union, is concerned and (2) equally important, that the union will see to it that every employee who is part of the bargaining unit will abide by these rules. So that if an employee objects to the settlement of a grievance made by the union in his behalf with the employer, then the employer can appropriately insist that a final determination of the issue has been made and that it is up to the union to secure compliance from the individual employee.[15]

An even more apparent case of the opposition of personal and organizational interest is presented in those situations where the union fights the secession of a dissident group of members. In some situations a whole local union has voted to disaffiliate from its parent, sometimes in order to operate as an independent organization and sometimes in order to affiliate with another national union from which it expects better performance. In such situations the parent organization can be counted on to fight the attempted withdrawal, just as it would in schisms in religious bodies, professional associations, and civil governments. The effort on the part of the local group to secure representation of its own choice, to name its own agent, will be opposed by the organization as a threat to the larger (national) membership. A conflict is posed between the principles of self-determination (at the local level) and self-preservation (at the national level).

The need for compromise

In a number of respects, then, the union shows itself to be more than the agent of its members. It regards itself as an institution with a life and interests of its own. It has commitments to a past and future which require it to think and act within a broader frame of reference than the member would do if only his own interests were at stake. It has commitments to a larger, often ill-defined constituency which oblige it to subordi-

nate divergent interests to some mystic "whole." This divergence of objectives should not be taken as indicating its failure to perform a representative role. Like any organization which sees itself as operating in perpetuity, it must seek workable compromises between the needs of its present members and its "own" needs, and compromises among competing interests of its component parts based on the interests of the "organization."

One illustration of the necessity for such compromises is provided by the experience of the UAW at North American Aviation, where, over a period of less than seven years (1956 to 1962), 70,000 members passed in and out of the organization, while the organization remained essentially the same size. Should the UAW govern its policies solely with regard to the immediate interests of such a transient membership, or must it be aware of the fact that, after the 70,000 have come and gone, it will still be there seeking to take care of the needs of another group of employees who constitute its then "present" membership—and taking care of the needs of other groups elsewhere as well? That is more than a rhetorical question, since if the union *fails* to take care of present interests adequately, this may be the surest way of guaranteeing that it will *not* be there after the 70,000 have come and gone. Clearly, then, it must effect some pragmatic compromise between its own organizational aims and its members' personal goals. Its leaders must perform not only like lawyers on behalf of members who are its clients but also like politicians who seek to put together a continuing majority out of a shifting constituency.

Leadership interests

We have seen that the interests of the organization must in some respects differ from those of the members. It is also true that the interests of the leadership usually differ in significant ways from those of both organization and membership. Once a union has come into existence and acquired a set of functionaries, it becomes the tool or instrument by which the officials attempt to obtain their personal objectives. Again we note that this is not a condition peculiar to unions but a characteristic of any organization. The drives of the membership and the leaders, in a democratic organization, must coincide in important respects, since the leaders can achieve security, recognition, and self-expression only insofar as they satisfy their constituency, when their tenure is actually at its pleasure. In subtle ways the drives may differ, however. The membership, for example, may regard the union as a means of easing tensions created by unsatisfactory working conditions. Officials may regard the union as the means not only of easing tensions but of creating them, if they are to demonstrate to the membership its continuing need for the organization and for their own official services.

While union offices sometimes go begging, these are usually the unpaid local offices, such as those of shop steward, local committeeman, and even local president. Understandably enough, such positions are often looked upon as requiring considerable personal sacrifice in time and effort, with little reward except possibly a satisfied sense of duty. But even in these local offices, especially in large plants with thousands of employees, the prestige of office may bring out numbers of candidates in fiercely waged political contests. Where the union office is a full-time paid position, the prize is all the more eagerly sought. This is particularly true of national offices. And a political contest is popularly—and validly—associated with deals, promises, cajolery, and compromised principles, all designed to win office.

The political contest in labor unions is much more exposed than it is in most private organizations, and has generally been more sharply criticized. The vigor of the denunciation probably has something to do with the belief that unions should be idealistic and selfless organizations in their chosen mission of remedying the "hard lot" of the workingman, and a consequent sense of disillusionment in learning that they are the same object of "dirty politics" as, say, most big-city governments. It is a little as though we were to discover some morning that a self-serving clique had entered into a series of questionable deals designed to capture the Red Cross or the First Presbyterian Church of Pittsburgh or the Salvation Army.

Thus, although the once-popular stereotype of the union leader as a foreign agitator has largely faded, there still appears to exist a widespread belief that unions, particularly at the national level, are run by ruthless, power-hungry bosses whose primary motivation is the exploitation of workers for personal benefit. Editorial writers are sometimes led to express their sympathy with the rank and file of the union membership, who are the objects of such exploitation. A sharp distinction is made between the union which ought to be run for the benefit of its members (good) and the union which in fact is run for the benefit of its officers (bad).[16]

Since progress within the union hierarchy is dependent not simply on ability but on votes as well, many if not most union officials are driven to the same types of political conduct that characterize our civil life. They become part of "machines" or "cliques," secure preferment from those in positions of power, and work themselves up to inherit those positions.

Selfless and self-serving

Why is it that union leaders resort to these devices to maintain themselves in office? Before we leap too quickly to the conclusion that it is only to satisfy themselves with the spoils of office, we ought to recognize the existence of another, more unselfish motive. Unions often view themselves as militant organizations, geared to win improved conditions of employment for their memberships and survival power for themselves only over the opposition of management. There may be lulls in the conflict, signified by the signing of an agreement with the company, but these are at best only truces in a protracted contest. The lore of union history is for the most part military in character —battles won or lost in the continuing struggle for survival and gain. Under such circumstances, it is easy for union leaders to convince themselves —in good conscience—that their control of the union's political machinery removes the danger of factional fights within the organization which would divide and weaken it. Their tight rein on the union's government prevents dissident and insurgent groups from sowing the seeds of disunity that would turn the organization from a disciplined fighting force into a debating society. The literature of labor is filled with excoriation of "dual unionists" and "secessionists" and "splinter groups" as unwitting tools of the employers. We can safely assume that to some extent this criticism is a useful device which labor leaders employ to eliminate opposition to their perpetuation in office, but it is also an article of genuine faith. They often truly believe that to allow a contest over reelection would be contrary to the best interests of the membership, by encouraging rival camps when the good of all demands unity. The appropriate slogan is "close ranks" rather than "form factions."

But along with this "organization-mindedness" goes the more personal side as well, the self-interest which even a conscientious official must feel even though he seeks to mask it in terms of the good of the cause. It is an understandable attitude, which those who have climbed to the top of any pyramid can share.

Union leaders, it must be remembered, are workers who have come up through the ranks. They have established themselves in positions of influence and even some affluence. At least in the national organization, the salaries of union leaders are now a good deal higher than the annual wages of the men they represent. The larger unions grant up to $75,000 a year to their presidents, and even the smaller unions are likely to provide for salaries higher than could be gained working in the industry with which the union is connected. Even more important are the prestige and power associated with position.

Once the union leader has been in office for a few years, the prospect of a return to overalls is not pleasing. In the nature of union politics and sentiments, there is only a very limited opportunity for the union leader, should he fail of reelection, to return to a previously held office of international representative or to transfer to an operating or staff position with another union, as a vice-president of one business might transfer to another. Nor has he another profession to fall back on, as does the unsuccessful congressman who can return to the practice of law. His future looks bleak indeed if he cannot muster the necessary votes to remain in office. There are few positions of authority in our society which so expose the ex-incumbent to insecurity. The inevitable consequence is the buildup of the political ma-

chine for one-party government within the union. Only in this fashion can union officials gain security. But the consequence is the curtailment of the contests and disputations which are the life-blood of a democratic organization.

Bureaucratic growth

Along with the machine politics of the national organization, there must also be put into the picture a measure of the idealism of many of its officials. Just as the business executive who has created his own proxy machinery to ensure his continuity in office maintains a sense of responsibility to the business which he heads, despite the occasional exception who is out to milk the company in his own interests, so the union official who has sought to set up the counterpart of proxy control brings to his job a loyalty to the membership and a feeling of responsibility for the welfare of the workers, despite the much-publicized exceptions who are seeking simply to line their own pockets. Among the union hierarchy there is an attachment to a cause as well as a desire for personal advancement; there is a belief in the rightness of the labor movement as well as in the soundness of one's own leadership.

Moreover, it would be erroneous to overestimate the power of union officials to manipulate election results. No leader is so powerful that he is able to ignore the interests and sentiments of his constituency. He must always be conscious of the areas of potential opposition. Even the entrenched official cannot forget the occasions on which seemingly secure leadership had been overturned by a rebellious faction, just as the entrenched business official cannot overlook the lessons to be gained from proxy fights in which a dissident stockholder group has turned out the incumbents. Many local union officials have lost their bids for reelection, and even at the national level, where challenges to an incumbent are far more difficult to mount, "rebels" have captured the presidency, in recent years, in the Steelworkers, the Rubber Workers, the International Union of Electrical Workers, and the American Federation of State, County, and Municipal Employees, as well as in some smaller unions.

Nevertheless, we are justified in noting that

the interests of the union leadership are not identical with those of the membership, any more than the objectives of the union as an ongoing organization are always congruent with the objectives of the present membership. This is not said in any spirit of criticism, since the same is true of any organization with an indefinite life span. It helps us view the union objectively and realistically, however, once we take explicit note of these organizational facts of life.

As we shall see in a subsequent chapter, the current period is one of disillusionment for many former friends of labor, as they look around and observe that the missionary zeal and sense of dedication seem to have gone out of the labor movement. But the cause of their disillusionment lies as much—not wholly, but as much—in their own illusions as in any weakness inherent in the unions themselves. A missionary fervor cannot survive bureaucracy, and bureaucracy is essential to organizational continuity. Sooner or later, dedication gives way to routine. The functions may still be served, but they are served as a matter of course. The interests of the impersonal bureaucracy and of the very personal bureaucrats acquire their own rationale, independent of (that is, alongside) the interests of the membership.

Summary

Labor unions have their reason for existence in the representational function which they perform for their members. This agency relation covers the need of the individual worker for fair treatment on his job and the need of his household for protection and enhancement of the income stream on which it relies. Performance of this representational function may get the union into political action, but in the United States collective bargaining has been a more important instrumentality. The public has come to accept collective bargaining out of a belief that the individual employee is no match for the employer and that a fair balance of power between the two can in many instances be achieved only when workers act together.

In view of the useful agency function which unions perform and the various kinds of pressures on workers to join, one may wonder why only one-third of the potentially organizable employees have become unionized. The reasons are numerous, involving differential appeals to workers based on regional, occupational, and sex differences, and the dispersion of a sizable proportion of the labor force among small business firms. The fact that labor unions as a whole have found it difficult to add to their total membership in recent years does not mean, however, that individual unions have not grown. Many have. One of the interesting but scarcely surprising facets of unionism in the United States is that a few large unions have a high proportion of all members.

Once a labor union has come into existence, it acquires organizational interests of its own which differ in some respects from the interests of the individual member who looks to it as his agent. This is due to the fact that the union regards itself as an ongoing institution, whose interests therefore require it to consider a potential future membership as well as its present constituents. Moreover, as a collective representative it encounters conflicts *within* its own membership, and it can scarcely act as an agent for conflicting interests except by rationalizing its actions in terms of organizational welfare.

The fact that a union has institutional objectives of its own, which sometimes diverge from those of its members, does not distinguish it from other representative organizations in our society —it is no different in this respect from corporations or mutual life insurance companies or churches. Sometimes unions are criticized for taking actions which are of little interest or value to their members but which involve only a "grab for power." Without attempting to condone all their actions, we can see that concern for their survival ability over time is a perfectly understandable organizational attitude, and not itself the basis for criticism. That recognition will help us later in understanding some present-day aspects of the labor movement.

ADDITIONAL READINGS

Bakke, E. Wight, Clark Kerr, and Charles Anrod: *Unions, Management, and the Public,* 2d ed., Harcourt, Brace & World, New York, 1960. chap. 4.

Barbash, Jack: *Labor's Grass Roots,* Harper, New York, 1961.

Chamberlain, Neil W.: *Sourcebook on Labor,* McGraw-Hill, New York, 1958, chap. 4.

Harrington, Michael, and Paul Jacobs (eds.): *Labor in a Free Society,* University of California Press, Berkeley, 1959.

Marshall, F. Ray: *Labor in the South,* Harvard University Press, Cambridge, Mass., 1967.

Purcell, Theodore V.: *The Worker Speaks His Mind on Company and Union,* Harvard University Press, Cambridge, Mass., 1953.

Rees, Albert: *The Economics of Trade Unions,* The University of Chicago Press, Chicago, 1962, chaps. 1, 10.

Seidman, Joel, and others: *The Worker Views His Union,* The University of Chicago Press, Chicago, 1958.

FOR ANALYSIS AND DISCUSSION

1. Some people take exception to the unions' organizing efforts, arguing that if workers want unions, they should be allowed to join but that there is no reason why troublemakers (union organizers) should be permitted or encouraged to go around stirring up discontent where none previously existed. These people believe that the spark for unionization should come from the workers themselves, not from an outsider who may be simply trying to reap a personal advantage by inducing workers to sign up with the union who would not have done so on their own.

Two answers have been given to this criticism: (*a*) The "missionary" answer: The unorganized have not had the facts presented to them so that they can make an intelligent decision; unions are contributing to the welfare of workers by acquainting them with the advantages of unions. The organizing union may reap some financial advantage from the additional membership, but this is incidental to the basic task of spreading the union doctrine. Just as religious faiths have propagated among the unknowing, to the glory of their church as well as to the presumed advantage of the unenlightened, so too do unions spread enlightenment among the workers. (*b*) The "mutual dependency" answer: The welfare of workers already organized can be properly secured only if workers now unorganized are also brought into the union. The union cannot gain advantages for those already members if there are some employees outside the organization who are willing to work on less advantageous terms. Decent standards cannot be preserved by one employer if he has "sweatshop" competitors. Thus the union cannot rest until it has signed up all those who could act as a threat to the maintenance of the standards it seeks to preserve.

Think through the assumptions behind both the criticism and the replies. Draft a statement setting forth your views on whether it is socially desirable for unions to carry on organizing campaigns, supporting your conclusion with logic.

2. There has been considerable argument in recent years over whether the labor movement has reached its point of greatest growth. Prof. Daniel Bell of Columbia University has said (*Proceedings of the Industrial Relations Research Association,* 1954, pp. 231–236) that union organization in the United States proceeds by *eruption* (a massive "breakthrough," as in the thirties), *extension* (the mopping-up operations), and *enforcement* (compulsory acceptance of membership by employees under union-shop agreements). Bell believes that because of the inability of unions to adjust and appeal to white-collar attitudes, and because of management's own modification of its ways, further *eruptions* cannot be expected. *Extensions* from now on will be difficult and unrewarding. *Enforcement* will run into resistance based on public opinion and in any event would not yield many more members. Bell therefore concludes "that the tide of unionism has reached a high-water mark."

Would you go along with this analysis? Or would you be more inclined to agree with some employers who have themselves predicted that it is only a matter of time before such nonunion areas as the South and white-collar workers are under the union banner? What factors will decide which of these predictions is right?

3. Suppose you were an official of the AFL-CIO and were concerned with how organized labor could best overcome the blocks to further expansion of union membership. Draft a set of recommendations.

4. Do you think it would be in society's best interests if more employees found their way into labor unions?

5. Should teachers join unions?

6. Do you think it possible for a union leader to develop a code of conduct or statement of principle which would strike an appropriate balance between the objectives of the present membership and the needs of the ongoing organization?

7. If you were a member of a union, under what circumstances, if any, would you want your national officers to fight for, and spend union money on, an extension of your organization's jurisdiction? Under what circumstances, if any, would you want them to defend your union's existing jurisdiction? Is there any difference between the causes for extension and the defense of jurisdiction?

8. Would you agree that the same standards which might apply to the professional behavior of a business manager should also apply to the behavior of a union official? Is there any difference in their functions or responsibilities which makes a different standard necessary or desirable?

9. Some argue that whenever a worker is disciplined by management and protests the discipline as excessive or unwarranted, the union should act as a lawyer and make the best case possible in its "client's" interests. Do you agree? If not, what should guide its judgment in such matters?

NOTES

1. Lloyd G. Reynolds, *The Structure of Labor Markets,* Harper, New York, 1957, p. 93.

2. *Organized Labor and Management,* Steelworkers' Organizing Committee, p. 13.

3. Joel Seidman, Jack London, and Bernard Karsh, "Why Workers Join Unions," *Annals of the American Academy of Political and Social Science,* vol. 274, pp. 75–84, March, 1951.

4. Both quotations come from George Strauss, *Unions in the Building Trades,* University of Buffalo Studies, vol. 24, no. 2, pp. 89–90, June, 1958.

5. Selig Perlman, *A Theory of the Labor Movement,* Macmillan, New York, 1928.

6. One early expression of this sentiment came from the pen of Horace Greeley, who, as editor of the *New York Daily Tribune,* in the issue of April 13,

1853, wrote a strong statement in support of collective bargaining, in the course of which he remarked:

We believe that unregulated, unrestricted competition—the free trade principle of "every man for himself" and "buy where you can the cheapest"—tends everywhere and necessarily to the depression of wages and the concentration of wealth. Capital can wait—Labor cannot—but must earn or famish. Without organization, concert and mutual support, among those who live by selling their labor, its price will get lower and lower as naturally as water runs down hill.

7. U.S. Bureau of Labor Statistics, *Directory of National and International Unions in the United States, 1967,* Bulletin 1596, pp. 54–57.

8. The same, pp. 59–65, and Arnold Strasser, "Factory Workers Under Bargaining Agreements," *Monthly Labor Review,* February, 1965, p. 165. The former is also the source for the data to follow on membership by sex and occupation.

9. U.S. Bureau of Labor Statistics, Bulletin 1596, pp. 56–59. This is also the source for the data to follow on the concentration of membership.

10. *Collective Bargaining in the Basic Steel Industry,* a study directed by E. Robert Livernash, U.S. Department of Labor, January, 1961, pp. 81, 82–83. The quotation is from the Convention Proceedings of the Steelworkers Union.

11. Strauss, *Unions in the Building Trades,* p. 119. Strauss estimates that only about 25 percent of the carpenters involved in his study did work which required their traditional skill. Many engaged in such operations as assembling metal forms for concrete, forms once made of wood.

12. Robert Christie, *Empire in Wood,* Cornell University, New York State School of Industrial and Labor Relations, Ithaca, N.Y., 1956, p. 328.

13. Strauss, *Unions in the Building Trades,* p. 120.

14. That sometimes even unionists may be opposed to union-security provisions was suggested in three aerospace companies in Southern California in the fall of 1962, when the vote on behalf of such a clause was smaller than the total union membership.

15. Arthur J. Goldberg, "A Trade-union Point of View," in Michael Harrington and Paul Jacobs (eds.), *Labor in a Free Society,* University of California Press, Berkeley, 1959, pp. 110–111.

16. No recent general survey of the personal characteristics of union leaders has been made, but the one published by Prof. C. Wright Mills in 1948 (*The New Men of Power,* Harcourt, Brace & World, New York) probably still holds good in broad outline. Based on questionnaire replies from 410 national, state, and city officials of labor unions (thus excluding the officers of local unions), it showed:

Nine-tenths of these labor leaders were born in the United States, and three-fifths had fathers who were also born in the United States.

Almost one-third of their fathers were small-farm or business proprietors, but three-fifths of their fathers came from the ranks of wage earners. Theirs has been predominantly a worker-oriented home environment. To a much larger extent than characterizes the male population at large (one-third as opposed to one-seventh), however, their fathers were skilled workers or foremen rather than semiskilled, unskilled, or farm workers.

Three-fourths of the leaders themselves were likewise wage earners before taking union office (the other fourth came from middle-class occupations or business proprietorships). More than half had been in the skilled categories or served as foremen.

Almost nine out of ten had worked themselves up to their present union positions by holding office in local unions or serving as field organizers. They had made good within the union hierarchy.

CHAPTER 6

The union is something more than an agent for its membership and an ongoing institution with interests of its own. It is part of something larger than itself which is called "the labor movement."

It is not easy to define the labor movement. For present purposes, we shall think of it as consisting of the numerous worker efforts, taking many forms, to defend and advance working-class interests. It is thus rooted in a sense of identification with a particular segment of society which is defined by its function or by its social status. It also involves, as the very word "movement" implies, a sense of continuity over time, a sense of unfolding history, a sense of direction. The union is the instrument of the labor movement, and as such considers itself part of a sweep of history in which its members are the contributors, not necessarily the beneficiaries, in an almost Tolstoyan sense. Indeed, we shall find that some of the pulling and hauling, the backing and filling, the advances and retreats which have characterized unionism in the United States are due to the difficulty of resolving the question of which is more important—the interests of a particular union's own members, or the longer-run interests of the worker class as a whole.

The first emphasis suggests a matter-of-fact, bread-and-butter, businesslike kind of approach to relations with employers. The second suggests a more idealistic and missionary spirit, which accepts present sacrifices for the good of the future, a future in which the present generation may not even share. One emphasizes, in the familiar culinary language of the movement, "pork chops now," the other "pie in the sky bye and bye." Both of these philosophies have been evident over the years, at times one being stressed more than the other. It is the interplay of these basic themes in the light of changing circumstances which endows the study of labor history with its real drama, not the occasional episodes of violence or the intricacies of legal judgments.

In trying to condense into short space 150 years of such complex social history, we shall necessarily have to simplify. This is not without its advantages, however, as sometimes the stripping away of detail and the singling out of particular developments serve to highlight the significance of a period in a way which a more accurate and complete account could not do.

Nineteenth-century beginnings

The existence of craftsmen's guilds can be traced back for many centuries, but the modern labor union did not come into existence in the United States until shortly before 1800. The early unions were composed of skilled craftsmen who had served their apprenticeship according to time-honored custom, and many of whom looked forward to establishing themselves as their own masters in the course of time. The distinction between employee and employer was not one of social class, since both were producers, both were workers. The employer—the master—was simply a journeyman who had made good.

These early unions were not concerned with the welfare of unskilled laborers, who were indeed a class apart. They were organized because economic change was beginning to threaten the social status as well as the material welfare of the skilled artisans who formed them. They were seeking to protect their position in the economic community. The threat came from several sources: One was the growing development, in the early decades of the nineteenth century, of production for a widening wholesale market, which pitted one producer against another in a more intense kind of competition than had previously been experienced in local markets, thus putting pressure on the master to restrain wages or to find other means of cutting costs. One of these "other means" was to encourage a greater degree of specialization in the work process, but this carried with it a threat to the craftsman who saw himself not as someone who performed only a part of a job but as one who had earned his status precisely because he could do the whole job. Shoemakers and weavers were among the craftsmen most subject to these pressures.

It also seems clear that some early unionization was directed less at a master employer than at the public. If all the journeymen of a particular skill—carpenters, say—could band together and agree that none of them would work for less than a specified rate, they all stood to benefit. As long as they were not involved in competition with workers of similar skills in other communities, such a combination might be quite effective. This would be true of the construction industry, for example, and perhaps of the bakery industry (though in the latter, housewives always stood as potential "competitors"). This kind of action was usually precipitated in a time of rising prices, when workers who felt their standard of living slipping might seek remedy in this form of association.

If these early unions were not composed of the most oppressed and least fortunate workers, even the skilled workers who were their members operated under serious social and economic disabilities, compared with the more privileged propertied groups. Ownership of property was usually made a requirement for voting. Education was frequently beyond the means of those who lived only on what they could earn. Justice was not applied equally between the manual worker, however skilled, and the well-born. Thus workers could legitimately view themselves as underprivileged in comparison with the propertied ("nonworker") minority in society, who toiled not but seemed to reap most of the benefits that workers spun.

Out of this set of circumstances arose quite naturally—one might also say inevitably—the ambivalence of the labor movement which we earlier noted. Economic pressures (from competition, fractionization of skills, rising prices) drove workers to try to improve their lot "here and now." To achieve that immediate objective, they formed unions and sought to obtain an increase in their wages, an effort which was at times successful in view of the strategic skills they possessed. But more basic disadvantages imposed on them by a social system which seemed to favor those with property could not be so easily remedied; no bargain with a master of the shop in which they were employed was likely to increase their wages enough to enable them to send their children to tuition schools or to buy the property that would qualify them for the vote. To meet these social disabilities, political action rather than collective bargaining was the more appropriate instrument. Even if there was little expectation that success could be achieved on this much broader front within the space of a few years, one could always seek to make progress in the general direction of reforming society along lines more conducive to producers' interests (producers in this case not even—or at least not always—excluding the master who worked alongside them).

Idealism and reform

Throughout the whole of the nineteenth century, workers—skilled workers—alternated between these two approaches to their problems. On the political front, they were sometimes joined by unskilled laborers, at least after the fight for suffrage had been won. By and large, the pattern which dominated the century was for craftsmen in the principal urban settlements to join in broad political reform movements when times were bad and their bargaining power was weak, and then to band together in unions to exercise their economic strength during periods of prosperity, when a rising cost of living had made itself felt and when the demand for their services was brisk enough to give some likelihood of success.

These first unions tended to be short-lived. Workers often organized for a particular occasion, meeting at one another's homes or at the local taverns and coming to some agreement on the demands they would make of the masters who employed them. After the effort had met with success or failure, the group would tend to disintegrate. In the early years of the century, refusal of the group's demands on the part of the masters would at once precipitate a strike, with the men "standing out" until one of the two embattled groups gave in and agreed to the other's terms. As the years passed, however, the practice of negotiating the men's demands became somewhat more common. By the end of the century, in some trades, the art and procedures of collective bargaining had advanced almost to the stage where they are today.

It was not the development of wage bargaining in periods of prosperity which characterized the nineteenth century, however. We distinguish that phase of the labor movement's history from its later years by the ways in which it differed from the present movement. The most striking difference was the readiness with which workers would abandon their unions and their economic pressures in the face of recurring depressions and unemployment and would turn to political pressures and panaceas as they sought amelioration of their lot as a class.

Indeed, the labor movement of this period can best be viewed not as workers organized for economic and political gain as much as a broad humanitarian movement which divided society into two classes—the rich against the poor (rather than employer against employee), the exploited producers against the idle and propertied nonproducers. The organizations of the period were,

with few exceptions, relatively formless and unstructured, unbusinesslike in their methods, impermanent, faction-ridden along ideological lines. The principal object of attack was the wage system itself, which was regarded as the underlying evil reducing workers to an unnatural state of dependency.

For skilled workers, the nineteenth century was one of gradual deterioration of their social status and economic condition. It was not simply that competition which spread out from other urban areas pressed down on their rates, or that their skills tended to become more and more fragmented so that they could be parceled out among immigrants, women, and apprentices, though these were elements of their dissatisfaction. It was also that they were being converted from a dignified status of "producer" to one of "hired hand."

The fierce resentment expressed again and again against the "wages system," for example, can only be understood in light of this shift from the sale of their product to the sale of their time. In earlier years the artisan had received a "price" for his work, not a wage, and the price represented the product he produced, not the time he put in on a job. The resentment at the wages system, then, was directed at a system which was regarded as requiring the worker to sell himself rather than his product, and hence constituted a species of slavery. The recurrence of the notion of producers' cooperatives throughout the century was an expression of a desire to return to a system where the craftsman was recognized for his true worth as a producer rather than for the pecuniary profit which he might create for some capitalist nonproducer. Many of the reform movements were based on this theme.

The notion of a producers' workshop was a dream turned to the past, however, rather than a reform project suited to the country's future. The small establishment which a number of craftsmen might operate on their own became increasingly illusionary. With expanding markets and larger and larger industrial establishments, the amount of capital required to establish a successful enterprise was more than a group of workers could hope to muster among themselves. But it was hard for many of the more idealistic among the skilled-worker class to accept that fact, to face the reality of the age of industrialization which required the massing of capital and men and which rested on a system of payment for time rather than for a whole product.

Internal conflict

The last half of the century thus witnessed a contest between two schools of thought within the labor movement itself—the utopian reformist group, which sought to recapture a "golden age," and the realist group, which was ready to come to terms with the developing industrial system as long as the workers could get their share of its benefits. Members of the former group relied more heavily on political action to achieve their objectives. They looked on labor as a class; crafts and skills became so diluted that relatively untrained and "inferior" groups, such as women, Negroes, and children, became competitors for their jobs, and there was even some willingness to admit these people to the ranks of the movement.

The latter group, the realists, relied on their own economic strength in bargaining for benefits, ready to strike for advantages for their own trade group whenever circumstances seemed propitious, and on the whole holding aloof from mass movements and reformist programs. But the distinction was never clean-cut. The utopians were not above resorting to direct economic action for immediate gains, and the realists could not refrain from some degree of political involvement, but in each case these actions were viewed as diversions from their main thrust. The difference in philosophy was clear, even though in practice it was sometimes blurred.

This dramatic conflict within the ranks of labor reached its zenith in the contest between the Knights of Labor, the utopian champions, and the American Federation of Labor, which ultimately formulated the realist creed. The full story is a long one, but it is important enough to recount briefly.

The rise of national trades unions

As we have already seen, the gradual extension of product-market competition from the locality to the nation also brought workers into competition with one another. The "traveling product" was a threat to local wage rates; if it was made cheaper elsewhere, it could undersell the local manufacturers and bring pressure on local masters to cut their costs. If local masters (or financial interests which supported them) wished to send their products to other markets for sale, they had to produce cheaply in order to compete effectively. Again there was pressure on wage rates and methods of production, which, as we have seen, led to the formation of local unions.

Before long, however, it became evident that local unions were relatively ineffective operating on their own. They lacked the power to exclude from their communities goods which were produced more cheaply elsewhere. Hence, local craft groups felt a need to federate—to form a national union representing their craft, which would support all the locals in the attainment and enforcement of common standards.

Not only traveling products but traveling workers underscored this need. If a group of shoemakers in Philadelphia went on strike for improved terms, they did not relish having their jobs taken and their strike broken by itinerant shoemakers from New York or New Haven or Pittsburgh, recruited by advertisements placed in those cities by the struck Philadelphia shops. Organization of workers into a national union seemed the only solution, so that wherever they moved, they remained members of the union and conformed to its standards—and could be blacklisted if they did not. Thus traveling products and traveling workers both helped to create the conditions which made national trade organization sensible if not indeed essential.[1]

The first true national trade unions were formed in the decade of 1850, when six came into existence. These and others which soon joined them tended to eschew political reform and to concentrate on economic action. They moved increasingly toward organizational behavior (bargaining and strike action) which rationalized their existence. If that meant accepting the wage system and living within it, so be it.

But other elements in the labor movement were reluctant to give up the bright dream of a producers' society which they had pursued in their youth in the reform wave of the 1840s, and which itself came out of a homespun Jacksonian philosophy of the independent artisan. They were still protesting the system which made them "wage slaves." The struggle between these two philosophies within the labor movement was approaching its climax.[2]

The National Labor Union

The clash of these two approaches was perhaps first dramatized in the founding—and foundering—of the National Labor Union. Organized in 1866, it represented the outcome of an ambition which had frequently been voiced to bring together into one national organization all the diverse labor organizations of the country. Its inspiration and first president was William H. Sylvis, president of the Iron Molders International Union, who had inherited the fervor of the pre-Civil War reformist movements and was dedicated to the abolition of the wage system and the establishment of a cooperative society.

The National Labor Union opened its doors not only to local trade unions, city centrals, and national trades unions but also to a variety of reform groups—Eight Hour Leagues, suffragettes, land reformers, antimonopoly groups, and utopians of several other persuasions. The local trades councils (city centrals) and reformist groups, under Sylvis's leadership, soon won control of the organization. The national trades unions, sensing clearly enough that their program of practical, short-run wage-and-hour objectives was being swamped by longer-term goals directed at reforming economic society, began to withdraw. In 1872, after six short years, it came to an end, its final congress attended by only seven delegates. Its brief existence would hardly be worthy of note except that it brought sharply into focus the fact that the two philosophies of the labor movement, which had alternated over the years, were now diverging, perhaps irreconcilably.

The Knights of Labor

The Panic of 1873 played into the hands of the reform group for a time. The national trades unions, who regarded their function as one of extracting bread-and-butter gains for their members, found themselves reduced to impotence during a period of severe depression. Many went under. Of the approximately thirty such organizations which had been in existence in 1873, only eight or nine remained a few years later. The Cigar Makers lost five-sixths of its membership, the machinists, two-thirds; the Typographical Union (oldest and one of the strongest) was cut in half.

In contrast, the panic was a stimulus to the growth of a new reform group, which had been founded in 1869, even while the old National Labor Union was still alive. Led by Uriah Stephens, another of the evangelist breed of labor leaders, a group of nine garment makers in Philadelphia had formed a secret society which they named the Order of the Knights of Labor. They added recruits slowly. The second local assembly came only in 1872. But the depression which had been death to many of the national trades unions proved the making of the new reform movement: eighty chapters were added in 1873. The same year, the first district assembly, bringing together the local assemblies, was organized, and in 1878 the first national congress was held. The following year, Stephens retired as Grand Master Workman of the Order and was succeeded by Terence V. Powderly, who held that position until 1893. Secrecy was dropped with Powderly's advent.

The Order of the Knights was a direct descendant in the line of reform organizations which looked to the establishment of a producers' commonwealth, its most recent predecessor in that respect having been the National Labor Union. It played a substantial role in helping to organize a number of small producers' cooperatives and played a large role in propagandizing to that end. Powderly asserted that the aim of the organization was to make each man his own employer. A member of the General Executive Board spoke for the dominant view within the Knights when he asserted that the emancipation of labor would not come with increased wages and a reduction in the hours of labor: "We must go deeper than that, and this matter will not be settled until the wage system is abolished."[3]

Along with this idealistic drive toward the

establishment of cooperative producing units which would again make workers their own masters went an uncompromising attitude toward the economic program of the national trades unions, which by 1880 had begun to recover from the preceding depression and were asserting their members' claims to better wages for shorter hours, backed by strikes where necessary. To Powderly and those who thought like him, this bread-and-butter program was shortsighted and misguided. It emphasized the symptoms—unsatisfactory conditions of employment—rather than attempting to get at the cause, which was the wage system itself. Why bother raising wages by a few cents an hour when the real remedy lay in restoring to each craftsman his right to the whole price of the fruits of his labor? As for the strike, this was a weapon which Powderly quite freely denounced as a "relic of barbarism." Throughout his tenure in office, he did his best to eliminate its practice and to substitute for it reason, persuasion, and arbitration.

The mounting antagonism between the utopian and realistic wings of the labor movement was clearly demonstrated in the structure and the policy of the Knights. Its organization was based on the local assembly, of which there were two kinds: One was the mixed assembly, which the national leadership preferred and encouraged, which enrolled "producers" of any and all skills and professions, including working employers. The only categories excluded were professional gamblers, stockbrokers, lawyers, bankers, and purveyors of liquor—all people who were viewed as social parasites, profiting by financial manipulation or exploitation rather than as contributors to social well-being. The other type of local assembly was the trade local, composed solely of members of a given skill or craft. Thus the two kinds of locals reflected the basic cleavage in labor philosophy.

Above the local assembly stood the district assembly, which had jurisdiction over all the locals in its geographical area, mixed and trade locals alike. The district assemblies elected delegates to the General Assembly, which was the supreme national body. In this organizational structure there was at first no place for a national gathering of the local trade assemblies of a given craft, though at a later date Powderly grudgingly made room for "national trade assemblies" as a means of combating the attraction of those national trades unions which remained outside the Order. But the national trade assembly had little function other than an organizing one. It was helpful in enrolling new members, but it performed no meaningful role on behalf of its local trade assemblies, once they were organized. The district assembly, inclusive of mixed and trade locals both, was more influential, and it was ill suited to a collective-bargaining function, composed as it was of a regional and heterogeneous collection of manual and professional workers. The national trade assembly could seek to coordinate the activities of its locals on a national basis, but only in so far as this did not conflict with the policies of the district assemblies or of the General Assembly. Small wonder, then, that the trade-oriented unionists chafed under a form of organization which denied their major premise—that the interests of their members were best served by economic action in the here and now, directed against their employers, and coordinated on a national basis since their traveling members and the traveling products which they produced were in competition with one another.

Frustration was increased by a principal policy decision of the Knights. As we have seen, the Order's leadership was strongly inclined toward propagation of, and propagandizing on behalf of, producers' cooperatives and ultimately a producers' "commonwealth." The national trades unions (which again numbered twenty-nine by 1880) were more concerned with bargaining for improved terms, relying on strike action where necessary. They therefore pressured for the establishment of a common strike fund, and were successful in bringing into existence a "resistance fund" in 1878. The use to be made of the money accumulated was left undecided, however. The Powderly faction wished to apply it to the support of producers' cooperatives rather than to strikes. Eventually, an uneasy compromise was worked out, which parceled the rather meager pool of resources three ways—60 percent to cooperation, 10 percent to education (propaganda), and 30 percent to strike assistance. The dissatisfaction of the trades bloc with this solution scarcely requires comment, particularly when the General Assembly, in the process of creating the "defense fund," went on to assert that strikes "are, as a rule, productive of more injury than benefit to working people, consequently all attempts to foment strikes will be discouraged."[4]

The ideological conflict between the utopians and the realists smoldered for some time before it broke into flame. With the return of prosperity, the old pattern of workers coming together into unions to pressure for wage increases reasserted itself, and both the Knights and the independent national trades unions were the beneficiaries. Despite its reform orientation, the Order was a natural home for numerous local groups of craftsmen for whom no national union existed. As a matter of fact, a count in 1882 showed that the Knights had many more trade assemblies than mixed assemblies, even though the latter were preferred.

The national trades unions themselves had no mutual organization of their own until 1881, when they organized the Federation of Organized Trades and Labor Unions. The clear intent of this new federation was to assert the realist position (accepting the new industrial order but seeking benefits from it) as against the idealism of the Knights, but the state of ideological confusion of the times is indicated by the fact that almost half the delegates at this founding convention were members in good standing of the Knights. Some were there at the instigation of Powderly, in the hope of capturing the new organization, but others were trade-oriented unionists who welcomed a new federation based on trade lines.

The two organizations were wary of each other but avoided open conflict for some time. Dual membership was not uncommon among individual workers and local unions. The Knights were hopeful of swallowing up the new federation, and made concessions to the trade-union philosophy by authorizing at this time the formation of national trade assemblies *within* the Order, though Powderly made no secret of his dislike for this form of organization. No effort was made to establish national trade assemblies for crafts

where national unions already existed, *outside* the Order, in the new federation, so that direct competition between the two groups was largely averted. The situation was uneasy but not serious.

The ironic consequence of the Wabash victory

Despite the Knights' opposition to the use of the strike, the militancy of many of the trades locals could not be easily contained, however, and to Powderly's embarrassment, numerous locals subsequent to 1880 became embroiled in strike actions. These strikes were all quite local affairs; only their number aroused any public interest. But in 1885 the Knights on Jay Gould's Wabash Railroad went on strike in protest against wage reductions and layoffs. This was something to focus national attention. The climax came when Gould, the public image of the business titan, "surrendered" to the Knights. The reason for this accommodation appears to have been that Gould was concerned with financial operations involving the Wabash at the time, and preferred not to jeopardize them with a strike. But all that the public saw was that the Knights had triumphed over a giant foe.

The year 1886 marked the great divide. In that year a number of things happened. Workers who had been hesitant and cautious now swarmed to the Order. In the single year of 1886, its membership expanded from 100,000 to 700,000. For the most part, these were workers who expected a similar resolution of their own discontents and counted on the Knights to display its amazing strength on their behalf as it had on behalf of the Wabash workers.

The irony of this situation is almost without parallel in union annals. Powderly, the idealist who abhorred strikes, and whose role in the Wabash difficulty had been to try to end the strike as soon as possible, and who had found Jay Gould of a similar mind (though for quite a different reason), now found his Order being swamped with fair-weather unionists demanding prompt action for immediate gains. He who regarded wage-and-hour objectives as delusory and put his faith in long-term reform, who had an almost pathological distaste for the strike and would have relied solely on education and persuasion, now found himself presiding over a swollen organization whose new members were crying for direct action with quick results. He and his fellows on the General Executive Board became alarmed. They issued orders that workingmen already on strike should not be admitted to membership, and in March ruled that all organizing activity should be suspended for forty days since too many new members were rushing headlong into strikes without an understanding of the more basic issues involved.

The national trades unions also expanded in this period, but it was the Knights who flourished, so greatly had the Wabash victory added to their luster. Disillusionment set in quickly among the new recruits. Two more major strikes, attracting national attention, took place in 1885, but without the peculiar circumstances which had led to the favorable Wabash outcome. Powderly's true feelings toward strikes for higher wages made themselves evident. In a dispute involving Gould's Southwest railroad system, principally the Texas Pacific and the Missouri Pacific, as well as a strike at the Chicago stockyards, messages from Powderly (which quickly became public) undermined the position of the strikers and led to their abject defeat. "You must submit to injustice at the hands of the employer in patience for a while longer," he had written in one circular. ". . . Do not strike, but study not only your own condition but that of your employer. Find out how much you are justly entitled to, and the tribunal of arbitration will settle the rest." In the stockyards case, he ordered the strikers back to their jobs until the Knights had itself reached some decision with respect to the 8-hour day, for which the men had walked out.

The Knights' position on the 8-hour movement, largely under the impetus of the national trades unions but with the strong support of trade groups within the Knights as well, was another source of irritation. Powderly regarded this crusade as a diversion from more fundamental reforms. He was not opposed to a shorter working day in principle any more than he was opposed to higher wages, but he would not have made these issues the objectives of major worker efforts. Producers'

cooperatives were a more fundamental answer to these needs than the attempt to wring concessions from employers. The lack of success attending the 8-hour program in 1886 was attributed by many to Powderly's aloofness from the movement, earning him a resentment from the trade unionists both within the Knights and outside the Order.

Decline of the Knights

The Haymarket affair in Chicago, in which a worker-protest meeting ended in the throwing of a bomb among a group of policemen, has often been said to have turned public opinion against the Knights—not because the members were directly involved (indeed, it is now generally conceded that the crime was falsely attributed to them) but because the preceding wave of strikes was somehow connected with a state of anarchy of which the bomb-throwing episode was another symptom. A more valid reason for the quick decline of the Knights (from a membership of 700,000 in 1886 to 500,000 the following year, half that number in 1888, and less than 100,000 by 1890) was the disillusionment of the members with the Knights' lack of support of their strikes and its attitude toward the 8-hour day.

Before that disillusionment set in, however, the contest between the realist and utopian philosophies became intensified. The focus of the struggle now shifted from the tug-of-war between two camps which had gone on largely *within* the Knights, to a sterner conflict between the Knights and the independent national trades unions, with which the Order had previously maintained an uneasy truce. As the Knights' numbers swelled, these newly assimilated workers—many from crafts also represented by national trade unions —sometimes worked on terms and conditions which undercut the trade unions. Moreover, while the trade unions did not agree with the Knights' exclusive emphasis on political reform at a future date, they could afford to be more or less neutral toward such a policy as long as it did not interfere with their own preference for direct action for immediate gains. The Knights' ascendancy in 1886 posed such a threat to the unionists' collective-bargaining programs. Powderly's public derogation of the strike had been, in their view, an important cause of their defeats. His refusal to cooperate on the 8-hour day had lost them that objective. The truce could no longer be maintained. The two ideologies no longer could live side by side, with shifting emphasis from time to time; they were coming into direct conflict, and the issue must be resolved.

The fateful year of 1886 saw the step which led to that resolution. In that year the representatives of approximately twenty national trade unions met as a committee and agreed to the terms of a "treaty" which they offered to the Knights. Its principal provision was that the latter would abstain from organizing any trade where a national union already existed and would withdraw the charter of any local trade assembly for which a national union existed. The intent was clear: The trade unions wished to have exclusive jurisdiction over all organizations formed on a trade basis and to make these the instrument for negotiating terms with employers. To that end they also specified that no assembly of the Knights should interfere with their bargaining efforts. On the other hand, the trade unions would leave to the Knights the reform functions of the mixed assemblies. Thus a line of demarcation would be drawn between their respective spheres of activity.

The Knights (which at this time were still riding the crest of the Wabash-born enthusiasm) refused the terms of this treaty but indicated their willingness to continue discussions. For a time there was some optimism that the issue could be amicably resolved. Then, at a meeting of the Knights' General Assembly in the fall of that year, one of the more belligerent district assemblies introduced a resolution requiring that all workers holding membership in both the Knights and the Cigar Makers International Union (a trade union with which there had been considerable conflict) must resign their membership in the latter. The adoption of this resolution was the fateful act which opened the breach too wide for any subsequent efforts to close. The trades unions, now concerned for their own survival, assembled in Columbus, Ohio, a month later and established their own organization, the American Federation of Labor.

Rise of the AFL philosophy

In the next eight years the two organizations attempted repeatedly to arrive at some common understanding, but with no success. As the AFL prospered, so did the Knights decline. By the end of the century, the Order had virtually ceased to function.

Understandably enough, we tend to place primary emphasis on those institutions and individuals that manage to stand the test of history, the ones that the ensuing turn of events somehow "proves right." From this standpoint, it is the American Federation of Labor which customarily gains the spotlight over the Knights of Labor, as the challenger which displaced the champ, as the organization which read the times rightly and adapted accordingly. But as students of the *labor movement*—that "fraternity" of the workers which has its own peculiar ethos which is so difficult to define—we must recognize that the demise of the Knights of Labor is just as important as the rise of the American Federation of Labor. Its passing marks the end of an epoch. It constitutes institutional recognition that the economic system had passed beyond the stage when any simplistic notion of its organization along cooperative or associational lines could have held any appeal to most workers. Restless individuals have never ceased to aspire to "own their own business," but the illusion that the economy can be organized on such a principle is no longer viewed seriously.

The passing of the Knights of Labor marked the emergence of worker acceptance that the wage relationship had come to stay, that production would be organized not by the single artisan but by professional managers, that the small workshop was rapidly being replaced by aggregations of capital. In short, the passing of the Knights of Labor marked the triumph of the system of private, capitalistic enterprise. The American Federation of Labor survived and grew because it came to terms with that system, adapting to it rather than seeking to destroy it.

Labor reform movements

The reformist element within the labor movement did not wholly disappear with the Knights and the rise of the AFL, however. If there were more space we might detail, at considerable length, the new reform themes which replaced the old. Socialism, particularly of the Marxist persuasion, became an increasingly important reform movement —less so in the United States than abroad, but even here one which has had its powerful spokesmen within the labor movement. It sought the overthrow of private capitalism but differed from the reform movements we have examined in recognizing that large-scale industrial enterprise demands new forms of organization, so that idyllic dreams of the small cooperative workshop are out of place. It retains, however, the belief or credo that labor is the only source of wealth, that property is a source of exploitation, permitting those who contribute nothing of themselves to the production process to reap its richest rewards simply by virtue of ownership claims sanctioned by laws which they themselves have been instrumental in devising and imposing. It would therefore do away with private ownership of the means of production, placing these in the control of the state as trustee for society.

In addition to American branches of the several international Socialist (Communist) parties which have existed for close to a hundred years, one major homespun anarcho-syndicalist movement, the Industrial Workers of the World, came into existence in 1905 in protest against not only the evils of the capitalist system but also the conservatism of the AFL, which it regarded as a lackey of the capitalist order. The IWW had a brief period of notoriety, winning several important strikes, capitalizing on the unrest of casual laborers whose conditions were truly miserable, and becoming branded during the patriotic fervor of World War I and its hysterical aftermath as a dangerous, subversive organization. Its members were hounded in police raids. Like the Knights of Labor before it, the IWW eventually faded into insignificance, although it still formally survives.

These remarks come out of our chronological order and have been placed here only because, in a brief history of the labor movement, they cannot be explored in greater detail in their proper sequence and because it is important for us to appreciate that, despite the rise to dominance in the labor movement of the AFL, which is not in the reformist tradition, a reformist element has nevertheless almost always been present somewhere in the labor movement, constituting a nucleus of protest to existing economic society. Discontent could presumably rally around this nucleus if circumstances warranted. As we shall see later, it is the almost total absence of any such reformist element in the American labor movement today which probably most distinguishes it from the past.

Business unionism

In any event, the labor movement which was taking shape in the closing years of the nineteenth century under the direction of the American Federation of Labor, whose chief architect was Samuel Gompers of the Cigar Makers Union, has generally been labeled "business unionism," a term intended to convey that it is both businesslike in its operations and business-oriented in its dealings. Its underlying conviction was then, as it is now, that it is preferable to eschew long-range reforms and concentrate upon immediate gains. It thus committed itself to an acceptance of the wage system, in contrast to its forebears, and sought only to improve the lot of its members within that system. It prided itself upon an absence of ideology and broad social objectives. Its philosophy was typified by the responses of its two early leaders, Adolph Strasser and Samuel Gompers, to questions addressed to them during testimony before congressional committees, in two different inquiries separated by a number of years. In 1883 Strasser had asserted: "We have no ultimate ends. We are going on from day to day. We are fighting only for immediate objects— objects that can be realized in a few years." Some years later, Gompers replied to a question as to the objectives of unions by declaring: "More. More. More." Here is evident the shift in philosophy from earlier days when labor leaders like Sylvis and Powderly had regarded the basic objective of the labor movement to be the overthrow of the wage system.

The AFL philosophy cast unionism in the role of agent for one interest group, labor, within a contractual, business system. In recognition of this new emphasis, an eminent student of industrial relations, Prof. Robert F. Hoxie of the University of Chicago, commented in 1916:[5]

> The outlook and ideals of this dominant type of unionism are those very largely of a business organization. Its successful leaders are essentially business men and its unions are organized primarily to do business with employers—to bargain for the sale of the product which it controls.... Its position and experience have been very much like that of a new and rising business concern attempting to force its way into a field already occupied by old established organizations in control of the market. Like the new business concern, it has had to fight to obtain a foothold.

Expressive of this new realism, which accepted the spreading industrial system, was the institutionalization of the "trade agreement"—a contract negotiated between union and management, setting forth the terms and conditions under which workers would be employed. The negotiation of terms can be traced back to the beginning of the nineteenth century, and the reduction of terms to informal written agreements to at least the middle of that century, but these activities had always been local and ephemeral. A national agreement had been negotiated in the iron and steel industry as early as 1865, it is true, and stable local agreements could be found in a few instances, such as the Chicago bricklayers, but these were exceptions. It was with the negotiation of a national agreement in the stove foundry industry in 1891, bringing to an end some thirty years of union–management conflict, that the system of modern collective-bargaining contracts can be said to begin. Under that agreement, committees of three each from the union and the employers were to meet annually to draft terms covering the organized portion of the industry. Local disputes, affecting only a single plant and its workers, were to be settled by the local parties if possible; failing resolution there, they were to be referred to the national presidents of the workers' and employers' organizations, and ultimately, if necessary, to a joint conference similar to the six-man negotiating group. This system proved successful both in solving the industry's union–management problems and in maintaining its continuity over the years.

When the Industrial Commission appointed by Congress in 1898 came to examine the state of industrial relations at the turn of the century, it could report that such agreement procedures, while of quite recent origin, were no longer novel. National agreements were to be found in almost a dozen industries and local agreements in many towns and cities. Prof. Selig Perlman, one of the foremost historians of American unionism, once commented: "Without the trade agreement the labor movement could hardly come to eschew 'panaceas' and to reconstitute itself upon the basis of opportunism."[6]

The trade agreement is perhaps more symbolic than any other single thing of the accommodation of the labor movement to the system of private capitalism. It constituted a formal acceptance of the wage relationship, seeking only to reduce that relationship to agreed-upon terms in the form of a business contract.

ADDITIONAL READINGS

Chamberlain, Neil W.: *Sourcebook on Labor,* McGraw-Hill, New York, 1958, chap. 2.

Grob, Gerald N.: *Workers and Utopia,* Northwestern University Press, Evanston, Ill., 1961.

Perlman, Selig: *A History of Trade Unionism in the United States,* Macmillan, New York, 1922, part 1.

Ulman, Lloyd: *The Rise of the National Trade Union,* Harvard University Press, Cambridge, Mass., 1955.

Ware, Norman J.: *The Labor Movement in the United States, 1860–1895,* Appleton-Century-Crofts, New York, 1929.

FOR ANALYSIS AND DISCUSSION

1. One of the most interesting of the numerous reform movements of the nineteenth century, and one among those which had particular appeal to workingmen, was an imported scheme known as "Associationism." The French philosopher Charles Fourier developed a "scientific" theory of the

basis for social organization, translating it into a program which called for the joint efforts of capital, labor, and intellect in a cooperative community or "phalanx" which, while not seeking to eliminate inequality, would ensure to each a full measure of its just deserts.

More romantic than scientific, this philosophy of association was retailed in the United States by a Fourier disciple, Albert Brisbane, a wealthy intellectual. The idea gained wide currency and considerable acceptance, winning favorable editorial comment from some of the leading newspapers of the day and enlisting in its cause many influential writers and speakers. By the early forties a number of workers, suffering misfortunes following the Depression of 1837, had joined the ranks of these intellectual reformers. In 1842 subscriptions were invited for capital stock in the first Associationist experiment, known as the North American phalanx, to be located near New York City. The slow response to this invitation aroused the impatience of a group of mechanics who, on their own except for the help of a few friends, founded a phalanx in Sylvania, Pennsylvania. Others followed suit, and before long some forty phalanxes were scattered throughout the East and Middle West. The North American phalanx, intended as a showpiece of Associationism, began operations in 1843 and actually remained in existence until 1856. Long before then, however, the spark of worker enthusiasm had died down. With returning prosperity, further fed by the influx of gold from the California discoveries, the attention of action-minded workers had switched from efforts to find a substitute for the wage system to efforts to improve their immediate position within the wage system.

Investigate and outline the tenets and philosophy of Fourier's Associationism. Wherein lay their appeal to workers of the mid-nineteenth century?

2. Of the union-sponsored ventures in producers' cooperatives, one of the best organized was that of the Molders, who resorted to cooperation as a consequence of the heavy unemployment of their members in the years following the Civil War and a disastrous strike against the employers' association in 1867. William H. Sylvis, who was president of the Molders' Union, was also re-garded as the most influential figure in the labor movement of that day. The misfortunes of his union led this already reform-minded leader to urge upon his membership that, after all, the principal goal of the labor movement must be to find some means of escaping from the tyranny of the wage system. The most likely escape hatch appeared to be producers' cooperative societies.

In the summer of 1866, the Molders established at Troy, New York, the first of a number of cooperative foundries. Within little more than a year, eleven more had been added. The enthusiastic Sylvis was able to persuade his members, in the convention of September, 1868, to change the name of their organization from the Molders' International Union to the Iron Molders' International Co-operative and Protective Union. In his presidential report, Sylvis wrote:

> Combination, as we have been using or applying it, makes war upon the effects, leaving the cause undisturbed, to produce, continually, like effects. . . . The cause of all these evils is the WAGES SYSTEM. . . . We must adopt a system which will divide the *profits* of labor among those who produce them.

Although the Molders' cooperative venture gave early indication of success, it was soon found that the managements of the cooperative foundries exhibited most of the same qualities as the managements of the foundries which they were intended to replace. Price cutting and wage restraints by union-sponsored cooperative shops, to maintain position in a competitive market, led many an old-line unionist to comment sadly on the curious change in the Molders' organization, once considered the leading trade union of its time. Nevertheless, the virus of producers' cooperatives as a panacea for the ills of wage dependency remained alive. For example, the unionized coopers of Minneapolis turned to cooperation about 1870 and established a total of seven shops based on this principle, which proved relatively successful.

Perhaps the greatest ascendancy of the cooperative movement was reached in the eighties, when the Order of the Knights of Labor, predecessor to the American Federation of Labor as the principal organization of the labor movement, sponsored such societies in response to membership demands. So enthusiastic were unionists in the assemblies affiliated with the Knights that, in 1885, Grand Master Workman Terence V. Powderly complained that "many of our members grow impatient and unreasonable because every avenue of the Order does not lead to cooperation." Within a period of four or five years, some 135 cooperative ventures in 39 industries (most of them small-scale) had been undertaken. The high-water mark for cooperation came in 1886. From then on, the cause declined because of inefficient management, internal dissension, lack of capital, the discriminatory tactics of other businesses, and the decline of the Knights of Labor itself.

What tentative hypotheses about the requirements of an effective industrial organization can you suggest on the basis of the experience of producers' cooperatives such as those sponsored by the Molders' Union and the Knights of Labor in the 1870s and 1880s?

3. Can you think of other organizations or movements which have gone through alternating periods of realism and idealism, or periods in which these two philosophical approaches have contended with each other? If so, do you discern any similarities between such institutions and the labor movement?

4. Prepare brief biographical sketches of William H. Sylvis or Terence V. Powderly, on the one hand, and of Adolph Strasser or Samuel Gompers, on the other. As a citizen of American society, are you just as happy that the philosophy represented by the latter pair of labor leaders prevailed?

5. Why should unions of the nineteenth century have had such a difficult time surviving depressions, and why should periods of prosperity have been favorable to their expansion?

NOTES

1. On the rise of national unions, the most exhaustive treatment has been provided by Lloyd Ulman in *The Rise of the National Trade Union,* Harvard University Press, Cambridge, Mass., 1955.
2. Material on the National Labor Union, and much of the discussion of the Knights of Labor contest with the AFL, is drawn from Gerald N. Grob's absorbing study, *Workers and Utopia,* Northwestern University Press, Evanston, Ill., 1961.
3. Grob, *Workers and Utopia,* p. 38.
4. Quoted in Grob, *Workers and Utopia,* p. 49.
5. Robert F. Hoxie, *Trade Unionism in the United States,* Appleton-Century-Crofts, New York, 1921, pp. 336–337. This book was published by Hoxie's students after his death. The remark quoted was actually written in 1916.
6. Selig Perlman, *A History of Trade Unionism in the United States,* Macmillan, New York, 1922, p. 145.

If the mainstream of the American labor movement had by the turn of the century accepted the system of private capitalistic enterprise and sought only to make a place for itself within that system, there was no reciprocal acceptance by managers of the role of the unions. Ironically, this very disavowal of reformism by the AFL sharpened the union–management conflict. The utopian dreams of a producers' commonwealth had never appeared as any threat to private industry. Such reform movements were too far removed from practicality to be menacing. But when the AFL turned its back on these panaceas and took as its objective the mobilization of the power of workers to wrest more favorable terms from an economic system with which it professed no fundamental quarrel, it posed a much more realistic threat to business interests. Thus, at precisely the period when American labor accepted a wage and profit system such as the dominant business groups represented, it found itself more than ever rejected.

Property rights versus human rights

The clash centered on differing conceptions of the role of private property in economic society. At some risk of simplification, it helps to understand the nature of the conflict if we think of business as insisting on its right to use its property—its plants and capital equipment—as it saw fit. This meant a freedom to modify industrial processes,

to take equipment out of production, or to change the location of production as it deemed desirable and profitable. But of what value is a plant without the men to run it, or tools without men to put them to use? Freedom to use property as the owner wishes in fact depends on the acceptance by workers of rules, regulations, and instructions concerning the operation of the machines and equipment. But this goes beyond a mere right of property and extends into a right of power and authority. A manager can decide that he will allow his plant to be operated in only a certain way, in the sense that he can permit it to stand idle if he finds no workers willing to conform to his wishes; that is his property right. But such a property right does not allow him to insist that workers must in fact operate his plant in that way; that requires an authority over men which ownership of things does not confer.

Many managers, however, failed or were unwilling to see this distinction. To them, the effort by workers through their unions to impose "working rules" on management constituted an interference with the rights of property. Refusal of organized workers to work at the pace or under the conditions which management sought to impose was branded not only as a restriction on output but as a violation of an authority legally grounded in ownership of the means of production. In this sense there was indeed some tendency, as labor leaders claimed, for management to look on workers as mere extensions of their machines, whose actions should be controlled by or made responsive to the speed and operations the machines (property) dictated.

The worker claimed jurisdiction over his own performance. If he sought to protect himself against a foreman's authority to hire and fire by joining with his fellows in a concerted agreement that they would work only at a given pace or produce only so much within a given time, or would operate only so many machines, this was simply an exercise, as he saw it, of *his* "property" right in his own labor. The fact that such decisions on his and his union's part could affect the capital values (property rights) of owners and managers was of no concern to him. A struck plant may lose capital value; a plant with poor morale can earn less profit, with a resulting lower capitalized value; a plant which produces only half the product which technically it is capable of producing has its capital value halved. These considerations did not disturb workers and unions, since they involved (as they saw it) not property rights but human rights, not an authority which the employer had a right to assert but a performance which the worker had a right to withhold. Thus there was a collision of rights—rights of property and performance—which was resolvable only through some form of compromise. Workers sought to arrive at compromises by bargaining through their unions. Managements sought compromise by attempting to come to terms directly with their own employees, either individually or collectively, free of union intervention. In general they regarded the unions as superfluous, and with occasional exceptions they tried to rid themselves of these organizations.

Opposition to the AFL

One organization, the National Civic Federation, formed in 1900 and including a number of distinguished public figures, did seek to propagate the view that accommodation between unions and managements through discussion and agreement was preferable to industrial conflict. Its views made little headway, however, against the organized opposition of such groups as the National Association of Manufacturers (NAM), founded in 1895 and becoming involved in industrial rela-

tions policy a few years later; the National Metal Trades Association (NMTA), organized in 1899 and changing swiftly from a policy of negotiating with the International Association of Machinists to one of belligerent opposition; and the American Anti-Boycott Association, an association of manufacturers organized secretly in 1902. In addition to these national groups, there were numerous local employers associations, associated industries, and citizens alliances, the latter taking into their membership any citizen opposed to unionism.

The philosophy of these groups was expressed in the NMTA's declaration of principles, which included these among other propositions:

(5) We will not permit employees to place any restriction on the management, methods or production of our shops, and will require a fair day's work for a fair day's pay. Employees will be paid by the hourly rate, by premium system, piece work or contract, as the employers may elect. (6) It is a privilege of the employee to leave our employ whenever he sees fit and it is the privilege of the employer to discharge any workman when he sees fit. (7) The above principles being absolutely essential to the successful conduct of our business, we cannot permit the operation of our business thereunder to be interfered with. In case of disagreement concerning matters not covered by the foregoing declaration, and not affecting the economic integrity of the industry, we advise our members to meet such of their employees who may be affected by such disagreement and endeavor to adjust the difficulty on a fair and equitable basis.

Imbued with this philosophy, many employers felt justified in using every available weapon to prevent unions from gaining a foothold in their firms. Until the passage of the Wagner Act in 1935 (to be described in the next chapter), the basic weapon of the antiunion employer was his legal right to hire and fire for any reason whatever, including a worker's real or suspected sympathies for the union cause. Nothing will cool off a union-organizing drive faster than the discharge of the "ringleaders" within a plant, and many employers wielded this weapon with enthusiasm and effectiveness. Two variations on this technique were the blacklist, an agreement among employers to circulate the names of union sympathizers to prevent their being hired, and the "yellow-dog contract," a written pledge required of new employees that they would not join any union.

If those weapons failed to smash a budding union, the determined employer could still mount an attack on several other fronts. First, he was under no legal compulsion to meet with union officials, even if they had the support of every worker in the shop. Thus many strikes were not directly over wages and similar issues but were "recognition strikes" over the basic question of whether the employer could be forced to meet with union officials to discuss anything; if the union could not win such a strike through sheer power, the employer was free to ignore its demands. Also, he could legally defeat such a strike by planting spies within the union, bribing union officials, securing sweeping court orders that prohibited most union activities, and hiring strike replacements—who might be either legitimate nonunion workers or armed thugs and private detectives with an aptitude for beating up pickets. Finally, in the "company towns" that were once quite numerous, the local police force often performed yeoman service for the employer in evicting strikers from company housing, breaking up picket lines, and helping "outside agitators" catch the next train out of town.

But all was not blood and thunder on the labor front during these early years of the 1900s. Some employers accepted unions and some fought them with weapons more subtle than the blacklist and the billy club. As we noted in the previous chapter, in a few industries the practice of collective bargaining had become established by the turn of the century, and in these cases (such as, locally, in printing and construction and, nationally, in coal) unionism was at least tolerated. Moreover, the AFL, having bested the Knights of Labor in the conflict within the labor movement, attracted substantial numbers of workers to its fold in the period up to 1904. The number of unionists in the United States in that year has been estimated at over two million, of whom more than four-fifths were in the AFL. But this was to be the high-water mark until World War I provided a boost. Beginning in 1904, the unions

found it increasingly difficult just to hold their own.

One example of the AFL's struggle for acceptance in this period is provided by a brief account of its contests with management over scientific management and employee representation.

Scientific management

The scientific-management movement had come into being in the closing years of the nineteenth century, fathered by Frederick W. Taylor. Indeed, "Taylorism" and scientific management for many years were synonymous. One economic historian has provided a neat thumbnail description of this progenitor of the movement. "Taylor was an aggressive, self-confident individual, seldom at a loss for words and with no small opinion of his own importance. When he expounded the meaning of scientific management, he was capable of making it sound like a turning point in the history of the human race."[1]

From such a personal beginning, the cause gained sufficient momentum in the period immediately prior to World War I to arouse labor's wrath, stimulate a congressional inquiry into its practices, and provoke federal legislation limiting its application in government military establishments. Since then, at least certain of its forms have taken hold in virtually every American business sizable enough to support a professional management.

A good working definition of scientific management is that it consists of any of a number of systems of shop and office management which seek to secure greater productive efficiency through the systematic standardization of the elements of production. These systems include the planning of the work by specialists so that it may be most economically handled and routed through the unit; the time-and-motion study of all mechanical and manual movements, so that the machines' potentialities and the workers' performance can be analyzed in their elements, from which tasks can be defined and fixed; the payment of workers according to their objectively measured contributions as determined under job evaluation or incentive systems, the latter presumably having the advantage of motivating workers to improved performance.

To appreciate the intensity of the controversy, one must think back to a period when scientific management and the new unionism were both in their infancy, when the practitioners of each were struggling for a foothold, and when each regarded the other as its complete antithesis. The contemporary argument between the two movements can be succinctly stated about as follows:

Claim by scientific management   Scientific management has discovered the means by which all production processes and all relations between managers and workers can be reduced to a scientific basis of objective fact and law. It substitutes exact knowledge for guesswork and force in determining all the conditions of work and pay. It ensures just treatment of individual workers by replacing the arbitrary decisions of employers and unions with a rule of law; it gives workers an equal voice with employers, in effect, since both can refer only to the arbitrament of science and fact. In working out scientific laws governing the performance of tasks and the payment of wages, scientific management rules out not only force and opinion but bargaining as well. There can be no legitimate bargaining, individual or collective, where the facts have been properly established. In the words of Tayor, "As reasonably might we insist on bargaining about the time and place of the rising and setting of the sun." "The laws of the workplace, scientifically based, are no more subject to bargaining than the tensile strength of steel."[2]

Rejoinder by labor   The claims of scientific infallibility are fallacious. There are no "laws" which objectively establish norms of human effort for classes of workers or which dictate their appropriate remuneration. These remain matters of judgment. At best, such devices as time-and-motion study provide data on which opinions as to a fair rate of work may be based. But the college-trained man with the stopwatch is incapable of determining with any scientific authority what allowance for fatigue must be made on one job in contrast to another, what psychological factors may affect one operation in a manner

quite distinct from their effect on another, how the variable quality of materials may alter the rate of output, how many observations of how many individuals must be made before one can properly speak of an "optimum" or "average" performance, and even what the significance of such measures might be. Even among experts on physiology, psychology, technology, and statistics, differences of opinion arise on such issues. Scientific management should be exposed as a shameless effort by management to cloak opinions and estimates favorable to it, based on the logic of efficiency and profit, with the respectability of "scientific laws." It is an attempt to provide validation for biased judgments. Actually, decisions relating to all such matters affecting labor should be made not by management alone but jointly, through collective bargaining.

Claim by scientific management   Industry should be encouraged to adopt all methods which replace inaccuracy with accurate knowledge and which systematically operate to improve productive methods and eliminate economic waste. Just so, scientific management seeks to discover the best character, combination, and arrangement of tools, materials, machinery, and workmen, resulting in greatest output or lowest cost. The increased productivity will redound to the benefit of workers, as it will to the benefit of all others, by providing a rising standard of living. At the same time, the welfare of workers on the job will be protected since, under scientific management, they will be trained in the best and easiest methods, they will be asked to perform only at rates of speed which have been found to be normal and beyond which they cannot be driven by a domineering foreman, and their pay rates will attach to their operations and hence will be safeguarded from arbitrary reduction.

Rejoinder by labor   We do not trust management to look after the worker's interests. Time-and-motion study will be used to build speedups into industry by holding workers to a "norm" which has been established by timing some management-chosen, pacesetting worker. Moreover, the study of all the elements of each operation is designed to permit the breaking down of skilled jobs into their component parts, each of which may be assigned to some unskilled or semiskilled worker. By fractionalizing the skilled worker's job through motion study, scientific management seeks to transfer ownership and control of the craftsman's skill to management. The skilled worker will be reduced to the level of a semiskilled operator on some routinized phase of his present total job, to be repetitively performed. The result must be to reduce the bargaining power of labor by making all labor more and more interchangeable on operations which require less and less skill. Workers thus cannot rely on management systems for their protection but must depend upon unions.

With the passage of time, the extreme views of the two sets of partisans have become somewhat muted although the basic difference in their viewpoints persists. What is most significant about the controversy in the years prior to World War I, however, is that unions fought the scientific-management movement not because it was part of the business system but because it denied them a place in the business system.

World War I

World War I brought what the unions had not been able to win for themselves—acceptance and growth. Both proved to be temporary, but for a time labor leaders found themselves the recipients of government commissions, and unions were able to achieve gains that had been denied them for years. These results followed from two causes: One was the natural economic consequence of a sudden increase in the demand for labor, putting workers and unions into a better bargaining position than they had ever known until that time. The other was the discovery, at the beginning of American involvement in the war, that the production of vitally needed goods was being impeded by industrial conflict. With the government assuming control of economic organization for military purposes, federal officials found themselves increasingly involved in the internal processes of management. Their concern was less with the rights of owners than with the need for output. If that required concessions to the unions, concessions were made.

Army and Navy procurement contracts had written into them stipulations that the normal working day should be 8 hours—an objective which organized labor had been seeking without much success since 1886—with overtime pay for extra work. Union recognition, collective bargaining, and the resolution of grievances were provided for. Samuel Gompers, still AFL president, was appointed a member of the high-level Advisory Commission to the Council of National Defense, and was influential in that position in helping to secure the staffing of the National War Labor Board, a tripartite agency, with bona fide representatives of organized labor. The board was authorized not only to define the terms on which labor–management disputes were resolved (though it had no formal powers of enforcement) but also to ensure the rights of workers to organize and bargain with their employers. Its policies included the then bold declaration that "the right of workers to organize in trade unions and to bargain collectively through chosen representatives is recognized and affirmed. This right shall not be denied, abridged, or interfered with by the employers in any manner whatsoever." Between 1915 and 1920, union membership doubled, passing the five-million mark for the first time, with more than four million in the AFL alone.

The employee-representation challenge

The period of glory was brief. The reaction was foreshadowed in the National Industrial Conference convened by President Wilson in 1919, composed of representatives of management, labor, and the public, to attempt to work out a set of principles which would smooth the process of readjustment to a peacetime economy. The conference broke up without agreement, foundering on the unwillingness of the industry delegates to concede the right of workers to be represented by "outside" unions such as those in the AFL. If their own employees chose to form a union, electing representatives from among their own number, management was prepared to deal with them. This was progress—a recognition by the employers that in the evolution of industry, many firms had become so large that any notion of reaching terms with employees individually was impractical. Personnel policy had to be made on a collective basis, in ways in which the views of the employees were given consideration. But employers still sought to avoid recognition of unions which were organized on a national basis and led by professionals. If they had been compelled to grant that recognition in wartime, peace brought their escape from the obligation. Thus they countered the union demand for recognition not simply by refusal but by offering their employees a direct substitute for unionism—"employee-representation plans," as they termed them, or "company unions," in the labor vernacular.

An NAM subcommittee of 1919 thus advised employer-members:

> Such a plan of representation in establishments where the number of employees is so great that individual contact by the employer with each employee is impracticable, would appear to be a valuable and necessary channel of communication between the employer and the employees, whereby they may be able to avoid misunderstandings, to determine in a reasonable manner upon modifications of wages or working conditions, and in general to establish such friendly relationships as will be beneficial to the interest of both employer and the employees.

Although there were numerous varieties of representation plans, the basic elements were the same. It was a "constitutional" system under which the employees in an individual company or plant, shop by shop or department by department, selected representatives to a "legislature," in which management, too, was represented. There were generally no separate meetings of the parties—indeed, the concept of parties was sometimes disavowed by substituting for it the concept of workers and management as being, together, the citizens of an industrial community. Nevertheless, while workers' representatives were permitted to raise questions concerning wages and working conditions in assembly, final decision rested with management.

The whole plan thus resembled a large grievance committee through which management was enabled to learn some of the complaints held by the workers, and through which it could in turn convey to the workers what was being done on their behalf by the company. It was more a part of the company's communication system than a means of joint decision making. The latter aspect was, however, stressed by leaders in the movement, and employee representation was made to appear preferable to collective bargaining, with which strikes, lockouts, violence, picketing, and similar unsavory activities were associated. In this respect, employee representation seemed to union leaders to constitute a more effective if less direct threat to collective bargaining than the espionage, blacklisting, and strikebreaking pools of the period, since it promised the same benefits.

Here again the unions were fighting for a place in the *business* system. Although occasionally the bitter resistance of employers drove segments of the labor movement to espouse socialization of their industries (as, very briefly, the railroad brotherhoods and the coal miners' union did in the twenties), and provided the radical fringes of the labor movement with fuel for their propaganda fires, the main body of organized labor was not diverted into the old paths of reformist attempts to find a substitute for the wage system. Although the employee-representation movement gained great headway and by 1932 embraced almost as many employees as the AFL, the latter remained firm in its resolution to win a place for itself within the existing system. It was a stepchild that sought acceptance.

"The American Plan"

Thus the unions were faced in the 1920s with a double challenge—an employer assault on their own institutions very reminiscent of the concerted drive at the turn of the century, coupled with an employer threat to replace them with other institutions of the employers' own creation, the company unions. The assault took several forms. One was an intransigence in negotiations at war's end that led to bitter strikes that "broke" union strength in a number of industries, notably steel. The other was a propaganda drive that took shape under the term "the American Plan," which attempted to profit from a postwar xenophobia by linking unions with subversive foreigners seeking to dominate native-born American workers and to force them into union membership against their will. It was not an accidental choice of words that led Charles M. Schwab, former president of United States Steel and then chairman of the board of Bethlehem Steel, to assert before a Chamber of Commerce audience in 1918, in an otherwise folksy speech:[3]

> I believe that labor should organize in individual plants or amongst themselves for the better negotiation of labor and the protection of their own rights; but the organization and control of labor in individual plants and manufactures, to my mind, ought to be made representative of the people in those plants who know the conditions; that they ought not to be controlled by somebody from Kamchatka who knows nothing about what their conditions are.

In similar vein, Associated Industries of Seattle, in describing its version of the American Plan, commented:

> The feeling on the part of the more ignorant of our foreign-born workers is that their opportunity has come to seize property and control in the United States as the revolutionists did in Russia. The feeling has been assiduously cultivated by radicals in the ranks and particularly the leadership of labor, and finds expression in sabotage and strikes in an effort to bring about "revolution."

One need not impute to employers of this period (or at least to all employers) any motive of trying to undermine the unions in order to exploit workers the more readily. Many prominent industrialists were genuinely interested in the welfare of their workers. They were simply opposed to being told by "outsiders" what they should do in their "own" plants. Some, on their own initiative, introduced pension plans and, under the prodding of public opinion, reduced the number of days and hours of work per week. In other instances they maintained wage rates even in the face of falling demand.[4]

The union plea for acceptance

This double-barreled attack on unionism had its effect on AFL membership. Traditionally, union-

ism had always made gains in prosperous times, but it not only failed to do so during the relatively plush years of the 1920s, but, between 1920 and 1925, it lost more than a million in membership strength. At the same time, the number of employees enrolled in company-representation plans increased. The AFL, more than ever on the defensive, sought to meet this threat by an affirmative response of its own.

Following the disastrous strike of the railroad shopmen in 1922, the AFL had joined with a leading exponent of the Taylor scientific-management school in establishing, on the B & O Railroad, a union–management cooperation program which was designed to improve efficiency and increase productivity and profits by tapping the accumulated experience of the workers at the same time that the railroad management agreed to share some of the gains from this cooperation with the organized workers. The program was initially undertaken with mixed skepticism and hope, but success and favorable publicity led the AFL leadership to see in this type of program a possible answer to company unions. The AFL sought to represent itself as holding out a hand of cooperation rather than a hand of importancy. Its pronouncements took on an evangelical fervor: "It is more than collective bargaining that is required. In sending up its voice for a great constructive democratization of industry Labor is not asking for a chance to get. Labor is asking for a chance to *give*. There will be enough for *all* when it comes to getting."[5]

The AFL leadership was hopeful that its proffer of cooperation would soften employer resistance to its organizing efforts. By reassuring business that organized labor was concerned not with restriction of output but actually with greater productive efficiency, it hoped to win business acceptance of labor's representative role. Its aim was to induce managements to deal with it rather than establish their own representation plans, and to do this by convincing managements that such a policy was "better business."[6]

> Certain employers claim that the company-union makes possible cooperation between management and workers in production problems. Such cooperation with unions they claim is im-

possible, because, as they say, unions are organized for militant purposes only. There is no justification for this declaration, for employers themselves have made it necessary for unions to employ defensive and militant purposes and methods.... There are convincing proofs of the economic value of union-management cooperation, which demonstrate that the cooperation between company unions and management is most superficial.

These words of President William Green, who had succeeded Samuel Gompers in 1924, were echoed in the 1927 AFL convention. Officers asserted: "The establishment of collective bargaining opens the way for sustained cooperative relations between management and workers.... These constructive activities are based upon a conception of the interdependence of all interests. ... Workers cannot help themselves by injuring other legitimate interests in industry."

The AFL's effort at appeasing business was strikingly unsuccessful. Few managers accepted its proffered aid or lessened their resistance to it. If the AFL's philosophy of accepting the prevailing economic order and seeking only a place within it and benefits from it had been proved more successful than the reformist philosophy of the Knights of Labor, it was only in the sense that the AFL had managed to stay alive over a forty-year period, through several depressions and against employer opposition. But by 1932 its membership numbered only 750,000 more than in 1904, and it had barely held its own through the last prosperous decade; with the onslaught of the Great Depression in 1929, its numbers began to melt away distressingly. By 1933 it had only slightly more than two million members, hardly as many as were to be found in the company unions created by the employers themselves.

Depression and governmental intervention

The period from 1935 through World War II saw labor's greatest triumphs. At its start, unionism was fighting for survival. Five years later, it had achieved a position of influence in the business sector and in the economy at large that some managers had exaggerated into a fear that labor would "take over."

One cannot understand the events of this period aside from their social setting. In 1932 a depression was on the land, the enormity of which dwarfed any previous depression. Not until the defense buildup almost ten years later did the heavy unemployment rolls finally disappear. At its worst, as many as one-third of the residents of industrialized areas were on public relief.

Only in the light of this economic catastrophe can one appreciate the powerful appeal of Franklin D. Roosevelt and his New Deal program to the masses of workers. Although Roosevelt admitted that he did not know what needed to be done to meet the disaster which had befallen the nation, he argued that *something* had to be done, and he was willing to engage in social and economic experiments in an effort to achieve recovery. The man in the street had even less of an inkling of how employment might be stimulated, but he responded positively to a leadership that was willing to act.

Among the policies adopted by this administration was legal protection for workers to organize into unions of their own choosing. In part, this action was based on an economic belief (disputed then and disputed still) that the business community had failed to distribute enough of its earnings as wages to workers, resulting in a lack of purchasing power in the hands of consumers, making investment less profitable since there were not enough buyers to warrant additional production, with a consequent slackening of both household and business expenditures, bringing on the depression. Stronger unions were considered a corrective for this kind of situation because they would increase labor's bargaining power to win higher wages and a greater share of the national income.

The National Labor Relations Act, passed in 1935 and commonly referred to as the Wagner Act after the senator from New York who fathered it, gave enforceable rights to workers to form unions, unmolested by employer opposition. It provided for elections supervised by the Federal government to determine whether a majority of workers in a defined bargaining unit wished to be represented by a union, and if so, what union. It required employers to recognize and bargain in good faith with unions which won such elections. These provisions remain on the statute books today, and we shall examine them in greater detail later.

The protection afforded by the act provided the unions with an unparalleled opportunity to expand their memberships. The challenge was thrown squarely to the labor movement: now granted government protection from employer opposition, how should the unions go about seeking new members? In the vast mass-production industries where unionism had barely a toehold, how should the AFL set about bringing workers into unions?

Craft versus industry philosophy

The AFL, controlled at the top by the presidents of the powerful craft unions in the building and metal trades, insisted that workers possessing the skills and training which had been traditionally represented by their unions should be enrolled in these unions, regardless of the industry in which they were working. This was known as the craft doctrine. It meant that machinists, whether in steel or rubber or electrical appliances or automobile manufacture or other industry, should be organized into the machinists' union, that carpenters in all industries would be assigned to the carpenters' brotherhood, and so on. Because it was espoused by the politically most powerful leaders in the federation, it was this policy that was adopted in the new organizing effort that the New Deal set in motion. Although organizing committees were set up for specific industries, such as the automobile and the rubber industries, it was expected that these committees would act only as a holding device. Once having enlisted the support of the workers in such "federal" unions, as they are known, in time the various crafts would be parceled out to the appropriate craft unions. The federal union or organizing committee would then cease to exist.

There was a significant opposition to this policy within the AFL. Other powerful leaders of national unions, although outnumbered by the craft exponents, advocated the formation of unions on an industry basis, without regard to craft. With this approach there would be one union for the automobile industry, and all automobile workers, regardless of craft or skill or training, would belong to the union for that industry. The thinking behind this approach was that modern technology had made craft jurisdictions obsolete. To what craft did workers on an automobile assembly line belong? What craft affiliation could semiskilled operators of simple industrial equipment be said to have? It was the belief of these industry-oriented labor leaders that a craft approach would mean that the labor movement would forever remain a small body of the aristocracy of skilled workers, having no interest in, and holding out no promise to, the larger segment of American workmen who failed to fit within the traditional craft definitions. In the desire to expand the union movement to embrace all labor, they advocated the all-encompassing industry approach in opposition to the more selective craft approach.

CIO versus AFL

Finding no support in official AFL policy, the small group of union leaders who held to the industrial-union philosophy, with John L. Lewis of the United Mine Workers acting as their spokesman, set up an unofficial committee to promote industrial organization. Their action was held by the AFL executive committee to constitute a violation of official federation policy, and they were ordered to disband the committee. When they refused to conform, they and their unions were expelled from the AFL. Thus was born the Congress of Industrial Organizations (CIO).

Both federations then set about their organizing efforts. In the mass-production industries it quickly became evident that the industrial philosophy was more appropriate than the craft philosophy. The United Automobile Workers, the United Rubber Workers, the United Steelworkers, the United Electrical Workers, and other similarly industrially oriented groups flourished. The two in automobiles and steel in time grew to become organizations of over a million members, a size which few craft unions could boast.

The CIO never surpassed the AFL in number of members, but it was nevertheless much more broadly based. Potentially, it appealed to the whole of the nonmanagement labor force. That its organizing efforts fell far short of this potential, and even short of the membership of its older rival, did not prevent it from being a mass movement in a way that the AFL never had been.

Moreover, in the same way that the New Deal had appealed to workers in the industrialized areas, hard hit as they were by unemployment, so did the CIO carry an enormous appeal. It was willing to take bold and dramatic action. Its leadership had the support of government. Its president, Lewis, was for a time perhaps the most talked-about man in the nation except for the nation's own President. The workers themselves sensed possession of a new economic and political power. The result was a virtual uprising of worker protest across the nation, reaching its peak about 1937, with a militancy that bred in defenders of the established order a fear that the society which they knew and prized was breaking up around them.

Days of union glory

It is difficult for one who did not live through this period to appreciate its electric quality, but Murray Kempton has captured its essence in his description of the battle for union recognition within the General Motors plants in Flint, Michigan:[7]

> The war for Flint began on December 30, 1936, when 3,000 men sat down in Fischer [Body Plant] Number One. They started in a carnival mood. On New Year's Eve, a foreman brought in liquor; two prostitutes came across the lines; the casual and the neutral began drifting out; by dawn fewer than a hundred men remained. The dedicated thereafter threw out their guests, sent for reinforcements, banned all whisky, and settled down to the sit-down strike's unaccustomed discipline for the next six weeks. . . .
>
> Hour after hour, in groups, they practiced throwing car hinges at a piece of beaverboard to train themselves to repel invaders. But when they walked out, they left the company's property otherwise intact, except for the gougings of someone's file on a few car bodies, an act which Bud Simons, a Communist activist inside the plant, described in terms of the outraged morality of these incendiaries: "Only a stoolie would have done such a disgusting thing.". . .

> Chevrolet Plant Number Four, where the engines were made, was the only [other] operation worth stopping; the UAW's resources there were terribly small; there were, in fact, only fifty trustworthy men in all Flint Chevrolet. . . . Their only chance, said Roy Reuther, was in a diversion. The union would call in its noncoms and announce a plan to capture Chevrolet Number Nine, just across the way from Number Four. The Pinkertons (company spies) could be expected to inform the company of this schedule and GM would strip its other plants of guards to protect the threatened point. . . . On January 29th, Chevrolet Works Manager Arnold Lenz, alerted as expected, showed up with all his guards to meet the decoy invasion as it came. They fought in clouds of gas, the guards with blackjacks, the strikers with oil pumps. . . .

> But, by now, a skeleton crew of foremen was all that was left to fight for General Motors inside Chevrolet Four. . . . Roy Reuther's squad subdued it quickly, marching through with their wrenches, calling out their friends, cowing the undecided. As the battle for Chevrolet Nine swirled toward its predestined end, there was a sudden silence from Chevrolet Four; and the pickets outside understood that GM's main engine plant had been halted. . . .

> The seizure of Chevrolet Four meant the end of the GM strike; the company recognized that it had lost the ascendancy; John Lewis came in to invest the men in its plants with his own heroic effrontery, to strut and fret and wangle a settlement. The union had won very little on paper. Outsiders wondered if it had won anything at all. But the men in the plants knew that this was a victory; it was summed up for them in the words of a striker who announced that he would slug the first foreman who looked cockeyed at him.

> On February 11, 1937, they marched out in the twilight, down Chevrolet Avenue, the beards still on many of their faces, the cigars in their mouths, the confetti sifting down from the gates of Chevrolet Four, on into the center of Flint, and no one who watched them could doubt who the winners were.

The similarities of such organization campaigns to the civil rights campaigns of a generation later are apparent: the willingness of a dedicated few to risk beatings and jail sentences and even death in the name of "the cause"; the apathy or fear of the uncommitted majority; the clash of "property rights versus human rights" and of "law and order versus justice." The events of that era also help to explain why labor leaders today sometimes talk and act as if their unions must be maintained in a state of combat readiness if they are to survive in a world of hostile employers. Some of this is just empty rhetoric, of course, but some of today's union leaders were actively involved in the great organizing battles of the 1930s and may honestly suspect that employers never change their spots.

These were times when one sensed that a new society was stirring in the womb of the old. For the first time, the labor movement was seriously challenging the business community for leadership in society at large. When the desperate economic conditions, the widespread willingness to experiment with anything that promised a way out, and the violence of the struggle for leadership by imaginative and determined men are recalled, one can realize that all the ingredients for radical social change were present.

And it is true, to be sure, that very significant social changes were made. The government assumed a new role as an active economic agent, in contrast to its previous passive role of umpire. Social security, minimum-wage laws, banking and stock-market reforms, the breakup of public-utility holding companies, agricultural-production controls, enforcement of collective bargaining— these and other measures were passed within a very few years. But while the new leaders in the bifurcated labor movement supported most of these reforms and fought for still others, while they were concerned with political reform to a degree that had not been characteristic of unionism since before the turn of the century, it is significant that their interest still lay only in a remaking of society within its existing framework. The radicalism for which the times were propitious gained little support within the labor movement despite the charges of radicalism directed against its leaders. What the new labor leadership sought was a larger measure of control over the economic system, permitting its modification but preserving its essential characteristics. *It never abandoned its primary concern with building unions rather than reform movements,* and though

it achieved notable political gains, its greatest successes were in the realm of private collective bargaining.

This was what might well be called "the golden age" of American unionism. It lasted for but a short spell, but in that time it developed a group of bold and able leaders who left their indelible impress not only on the labor movement but on society as a whole. It turned American unionism from a narrowly centered, craft-conscious nucleus into a broadly based movement. It demonstrated the importance of power in achieving social ends. It taught the labor movement that its interests were involved in virtually all social action and social legislation.

Within this brief period it racked up important successes. For the only time in its history, it came close to seizing initiative and leadership in society from the business groups. But the pace could not be sustained. By 1940 internal dissension had divided Lewis from his former lieutenants. Then the war years intervened to put a damper on labor activity.

World War II

Whether the unions would have expanded faster and on a larger scale if World War II had not intruded is a speculative question which labor leaders were inclined to answer in the affirmative and business leaders in the negative. As in World War I, a tripartite National War Labor Board was established to rule on labor disputes and to curb strikes. Strikes were not formally outlawed but labor participation on the board was a tacit recognition that it intended to forgo use of this weapon except in extraordinary situations. This voluntary limitation (in some respects one might more realistically term it a negotiated arrangement) on the use of traditional union weapons is what left some labor leaders believing that wartime compromise had arrested the organizing momentum of the previous years. There is at least as much ground for believing, however, that this momentum had already reached its peak. In any event, by war's end the labor movement which had been struggling for survival in the early thirties had reached a membership of 15 million.

Restraint of union power

In this and the preceding chapter we have sought to emphasize the major currents of American economic society as they have influenced the shape and spirit of the labor movement. In doing so, we have purposely sought to abstract from legislative and judicial developments as far as possible, since these in large measure—important as they are—reflect forces at work in society rather than independent influences. This is not to deny the importance of the law as an instrument for rationalizing and systematizing and extending social pressures, but to try to place the law in proper perspective. In the chapters which follow we shall insert the legal landmarks which have here been omitted in order to emphasize the social forces at work.

This is simply by way of explaining that if one takes the date of 1947, the year in which the Taft-Hartley Act was passed, as the year which brought to a close the golden age of the American labor movement, we should not construe the act as the cause but only the symbol. The fact was that unions were in trouble with the public. In moving to put some restrictions on their power and influence, Congress was reflective of both an immediate impatience with unions for the spate of postwar strikes in which they engaged and an uneasiness at the internal characteristics of particular unions. Ironically, this action came at a time when unionism had already reached, if not passed, the peak of its greatness and was engaged in a struggle to save its own soul.

Passage of the Taft-Hartley Act had as one of its major consequences a rekindling of the urge to unify the two wings of the labor movement, pooling their resources the more effectively to combat what was regarded as the forces of reaction. Unity efforts had seldom ceased since the withdrawal of the CIO unions from the AFL, but they had met with seemingly insurmountable obstacles. These obstacles now began to drop away.

The AFL-CIO merger

The old AFL craft orientation had been very much watered down under the spur of CIO competition. AFL unions, finding themselves in organizational contests with CIO unions, were driven to make room for workers with little or no skill, in whom they had previously manifested little interest. Old, established craft groups like the Flint Glass Workers, the Machinists, the Electrical Workers, and the Teamsters, in their rivalry with the CIO industry-based unions, themselves began to pull in larger and more comprehensive groups of employees, regardless of craft. Crafts sometimes served as a nucleus for organizing, but they ceased to constitute limits to organization. There thus grew up within the AFL an industry-mindedness different from that of the CIO only in degree. It was primarily in the building-trades jurisdictions that craft orientation retained much of its old vigor. While overlapping jurisdictions of AFL and CIO unions remained a problem requiring solution, at least the "craft-versus-industry" issue ceased to distinguish one federation from the other in the way that it formerly had.

The fact that workers, through governmentally conducted elections, could decide for themselves what union, if any, they wished to represent them was a major factor in breaking down old jurisdictional lines. Unions which had once considered themselves "craft" might find that in order to participate in such an election, they had to consent to the inclusion of relatively unskilled workers. Jurisdictional lines between unions became more and more blurred even within the AFL, let alone between its unions and those of the CIO. The old problem of jurisdictional disputes which had plagued unions over the years became more intense. Within both federations, special provisions for deciding jurisdictional issues were formulated, and in 1953 a number of unions from both federations entered into a voluntary "no-raiding" agreement, appointing an umpire to decide cases which could not be resolved by discussion. Ultimately it was a very similar formula which served to make merger possible. Instead of seeking to rationalize jurisdictional lines *before* merger took place, it was agreed that unions should refrain from raiding one another's existing organized groups, submitting to an umpire charges of violation of this agreement. Competition for unorganized workers would be left wide open, though with an expectation that unions would tend to follow familiar jurisdictional paths. Thus trial and error served to remove what had been a major impediment to unity.

A second barrier which fell by the wayside was the stereotype which each of the two labor groups had built up of the other over the years. To the AFL, the CIO unions were for a long time regarded as Communist-infiltrated. To the CIO, the AFL old-line unions were viewed as racket-ridden. These charges were in some measure justified. Their converses were equally true. The AFL had by and large preserved itself immune from Communist borings. The CIO had largely kept free of the taint of labor racketeering.

By 1955, however, the two federations had gained a new respect for each other. For in 1949 and 1950 the CIO had firmly set about to clean its house of Communist sympathies by expelling eleven unions which, as a result of lengthy hearings conducted by its own specially established committee, were found to be Communist-dominated. And the AFL in 1953 similarly expelled the International Longshoremen's Association on charges that it had failed to rid its ranks of gangsters and criminal elements who were using the union as a device for self-enrichment. Thus each of the federations took decisive actions which helped to dispel the stereotype each had built of the other.

It took more than a removal of previous deterrents to unity to bring about eventual merger, however. Some positive incentive was necessary.

Late in 1952, William Green, president of the AFL, and Philip Murray, president of the CIO, died within two weeks of each other. The former was succeeded by George Meany, who had previously served as secretary-treasurer of the federation, and the latter by Walter Reuther, president of the United Automobile Workers. But as frequently happens at the time of such successions, there was some stirring among other union officials who held personal aspirations. With each federation president thus faced with internal problems, it seemed natural that the thoughts of each should have turned more and more to merger. With a pooling of the strength of both groups, the merged organization could better withstand whatever divisive action might be taken by dissident member unions.

Complacency and astigmatism

The merger which came in 1955, combining the two groups under the compound name of the American Federation of Labor and Congress of Industrial Organizations (AFL-CIO), gave rise to hopes in union circles of a fresh impetus to organizing the increasing numbers of the unorganized. It stimulated an optimism that the conflict between unions would now be laid to rest and that all unions could unite in a push to even greater power and influence. The hope and the optimism, however, went largely unfulfilled. Instead, the bloom on the merger faded rather quickly, and bickering again broke out among the factions which composed it. The reasons for this development are complex, but they can perhaps be summarized, for present purposes, under the three headings of complacency, disillusionment, and astigmatism.

It may be hard to see how a movement which has been unsuccessful in enrolling important bodies of workers, as we noted in Chapter 5, can afford to be complacent. White-collar workers have been largely unresponsive, the South is still less organized than the rest of the country, women have not joined in the same proportion in which they are represented in the labor force, and the numerous employees of small firms are still largely outside the labor movement. These failures, of which the unions are tired of being reminded, do not disturb the complacent attitude of American labor, however, because of the limited identification of individual unions with the labor movement as a whole. By and large, the major unions feel relatively secure in the strongholds they now occupy; like the monopolist in business, one of whose chief advantages is that he can afford to be lazy since he is under no competitive pressure, many of the major unions have been under no compulsion to organize the difficult areas outside the ripe fields which they have already harvested. As Reuther warned the AFL-CIO Industrial Union Department in 1959, labor has "grown a little bit flabby . . . a little bit soft in the middle."

Also contributing to this sense of satisfaction was the fact that the labor movement had largely accomplished its avowed purpose of fifty years' standing—to win acceptance in the system of private capitalistic enterprise, to be recognized by business and accorded a role to play in the business system. Even if managers have not embraced unionism with enthusiasm, there are few who believe that it can ever be eliminated, and many who concede that it plays, or can play, a constructive role. Thus for the American labor movement the game has largely been won. It has won and is winning "more, more, more," in the Gompers tradition. Only a feeling that unionism is under attack, that it again has to fight for survival, seems able to shake this complacency that comes from being accepted in the community where it has sought acceptance.[8] Having arrived at membership in the club, unions have no real mission, no big objective, that spurs them on. This statement contains exaggeration, but it expresses the essence of the matter.

That some union leaders themselves have felt this change in the labor movement's character is attested by the following unofficial remarks from one national leader:

> The American trade union leader is not the great moral figure that he has been in the past. The union movement has lost a great deal of its idealism, and consequently the union leader carries little of this old prestige.
>
> The American trade union movement is decentralized, and the smugness of each part is so pervasive that it is very difficult to carry on and maintain anyone's interest when one union is suffering from adverse conditions. The old messianic character of the movement is completely absent and, as a result, there is very little help to be obtained by one union from others. How much help can you expect from a Teamsters Union?
>
> Furthermore, there is an aversion to bringing new tools to old problems.
>
> I think this failure represents a pitiful abdication of leadership in the American trade-union movement, both at the top and at the bottom levels. The commitments of the trade-union movement to modern industry are necessarily pretty sweeping, yet the trade-union movement lacks a philosophical commitment to doing its share, and that is why management has assumed more and more responsibility. Formerly unionism created a spark of new

status and personal participation which extended to all the aspects of the workers' lives. But when you look at the American trade-union scene today you see that the workers have rejected the union in all areas except the shop. In other local activity the union is not the agent of the worker. Perhaps it is because of the fluid nature of our society, but it is a fact that the trade-union movement has become more restricted in its function and more modest in its purpose. These changes are having important effects on the fate of the union movement.

Morality under the microscope

A cause or a consequence—it is hard to say which—of this sense of loss of mission or purpose has been some loss of moral tone in the movement. To be sure, certain industries—principally those characterized by small businesses in metropolitan areas—have always been subject to a certain amount of unionized racketeering; gangster elements have seized control of strategic locals and used their power to threaten slowdowns, strikes, and boycotts as a means of extorting bribes. Periodically, municipal and state investigations have disclosed such unsavory practices, which tend to reflect on the labor movement as a whole.[9] But beginning in 1955, about the time of the merger, there occurred a series of congressional exposés of union corruption which suggested that the disease was more widespread than had been supposed. Subcommittees, under such distinguished and liberal chairmen as Senators Ives, Douglas, and Kennedy, examined the management (or mismanagement) of union health, welfare, and pension trusts, and in doing so disclosed such malpractices as:[10]

> . . . excessive salaries paid to union officials running health and welfare funds, the splitting of commissions by insurance agents with the union trustees of such funds, the organization of brokerage businesses by trustees to increase their take, some direct stealing of trust monies, and the connection of notorious criminals with a few of the funds.

There followed, in 1957, the disclosures of the Select Committee on Improper Activities in the

Labor or Management Field, under the chairman-ship of Senator McClellan, the final report being issued in 1960. Initially, the testimony under oath of officials of the Teamsters, Bakery, Laundry Workers, Distillery Workers, and Operating En-gineers unions rocked even the "house of labor." President Meany of the AFL-CIO, speaking be-fore the Industrial Union Department convention in November of 1957, commented:[11]

> We thought we knew a few things about trade union corruption, but we didn't know the half of it, one-tenth of it, or the one-hundredth part of it.
> We didn't know, for instance, that we had unions where a criminal record was almost a prerequisite to holding office under the na-tional union.
> We didn't know that we had top trade union leaders who made it a practice to secretly borrow the funds of their union.
> We didn't know that there were top trade union leaders who used the funds for phony real estate deals in which the victims of the fraud were their own members.
> And we didn't know that there were trade union leaders who charged to the union treas-ury such items as speed boats, perfume, silk stockings, brassieres, color TV, refrigerators, and everything else under the sun.

Meeting the challenge head on, the AFL-CIO conducted its own hearings of the offending unions before the Ethical Practices Committee which had been provided for in the founding convention of the merged movement in 1955. Several unions were suspended indefinitely or ex-pelled. As the work of this committee ground on under the relentless prodding of its counsel, Ar-thur Goldberg (later to be a justice of the Su-preme Court), a reaction began to set in among old-line labor leaders, particularly in the building-trades unions and in some others which had been part of the premerger AFL. A sour joke began to make the rounds that if Goldberg were allowed to continue, Meany would be left president of the CIO, which is to say, president of the premerger CIO unions whose record was remarkably clean in contrast. The attitude of the unions toward the McClellan Committee, originally favorable, turned critical; he and several of his committeemen were said to be out to "get" the unions. Important

unions within the federation began to evince sympathy for some of those against whom puni-tive action had been taken. Although they had been forbidden by the Executive Committee to maintain relations with the expelled Teamsters Union, which was the principal target of both the McClellan Committee and the AFL-CIO, even some members of the Executive Committee re-fused to comply with the instruction. The original mood of outraged righteousness began to subside. The labor movement, it was said, was no better and no worse than other segments of American society.

The widening rifts

Hardly had the dust begun to settle over the cor-ruption issue when the labor movement came un-der strong attack from the new civil rights move-ment. Through the 1950s the drive for racial equality had centered on institutions such as pub-lic schools and transportation facilities, but Ne-gro leaders increasingly warned that equality under the law was relatively meaningless without equality in the labor market. Their concern was spurred by two developments discussed in previ-ous chapters: the relative decline, over the post-war period, in blue-collar jobs open to Negroes in high-wage manufacturing industries such as auto and steel, and the drastic impact on Negro unem-ployment of the recession period stretching from 1958 to the early 1960s. One solution to these problems, it was argued, was to open up the often lily-white ranks of the high-wage construction crafts.

Why did this demand create further dissension within the AFL-CIO, whose constitution explicitly barred racial discrimination and whose leaders had officially supported the civil rights movement? Part of the answer lies in the realm of principle or ideology. Leaders of many of the "CIO unions" were sincerely committed to the goal of racial equality; their organizations had a high propor-tion of Negro members and the national leaders sometimes fought both employers and their own white members who wished to discriminate. Many leaders of craft unions, on the other hand, have a reputation for political conservatism on issues not directly involving union welfare. But there are other differences. An industrial union has little need or opportunity to influence the hiring decisions made by a factory management, but in a casual labor market such as construction, in which most workers move from employer to employer, the unions have long felt it necessary to be deeply involved in the hiring process. Thus, if discrimination is attacked in a factory setting, the employer is usually the primary target of government or private action, but in construction the unions and their hiring halls become the target.

Further, the high skill content of construction work can be used as a cloak for racist attitudes *or* as a legitimate explanation for some of the differences in the racial composition of unions. In a factory hiring a majority of unskilled and semiskilled workers, white managers and workers may not object strenuously to Negroes in low-level jobs (just as there are many Negroes in the Laborers Union in construction), and these are jobs for which Negroes can easily qualify even if they are handicapped by poor education and training. In a construction craft, on the other hand, the union's fight to maintain skill standards—through such devices as limiting the number of apprentices and specifying their initial qualifications and the nature of their training programs—long antedates the civil rights revolution. Also, nepotism is an honorable practice in some crafts in which fathers are genuinely proud of their skill and, unlike many factory workers, want their sons to have first chance at any openings in their trade. In short, a Negro may be denied admission to a construction union because he really does not meet educational or training standards, or because nepotism perpetuates any exclusionary practices adopted in the dim past, or simply because the present members don't like Negroes and will use any excuse to bar them. Much of the controversy over this issue revolves about which of these reasons is the major explanation for the small proportion of Negroes in the skilled building trades.

It can easily be seen why this controversy further split the ranks of the AFL-CIO. To those leaders who wished organized labor to be in the vanguard of progressive social action, as in the 1930s, it was humiliating for the AFL-CIO to be attacked as part of "the racist establishment," and they urged the federation to take action

against racial discrimination in the labor movement as vigorously as it had attacked corruption in the 1950s. To these critics, the symbol of this policy dispute was the dramatic March on Washington in 1963, in which Walter Reuther participated but George Meany (who had risen from the ranks of the Plumbers Union) did not. President Meany's supporters argued that his critics did not appreciate the special problems of the building trades; these unions were changing their admission policies but could not single-handedly rectify society's failure to provide full employment and a decent education for Negroes; and it would accomplish little to expel unions whose membership reflected community attitudes on racial matters. To these defenders of Meany, it was less important that he failed to participate in the March on Washington than that he pressed vigorously for the passage of the Civil Rights Act of 1964, including the provisions that forbid discrimination by unions in their admission policies.

And yet other differences boiled to the surface. Critics of Meany, among whom Reuther was the most vocal and important, charged that the AFL-CIO had failed to press organizing drives in the South and among farm and white-collar workers; that Meany committed the federation to a "hard-line" position on many issues of foreign policy, including the Vietnam war; and that Meany was in general running the federation in a peremptory and undemocratic fashion. Meany's supporters suggested Reuther was simply a poor loser: in every policy showdown, the majority of the AFL-CIO Executive Council voted to support Meany over Reuther, and in organizing the unorganized, Reuther had little more success than anyone else in recent years, although he was chairman of the AFL-CIO's Organization Committee and president of its Industrial Union Department as well as of the United Automobile Workers (which itself dwindled in size through most of the postmerger years). Finally, as might be expected, this internal battle was strongly colored by the personal antagonism that developed between the two major leaders of the federation.

All of these differences culminated in the Auto Workers' decision in 1968 to refuse to pay dues to the AFL-CIO, knowing this meant suspension and eventual expulsion from the federation. This was the most shattering blow to labor unity since the Teamsters Union was expelled from the federation in 1957, an action then strongly supported by Mr. Reuther. There was thus considerable surprise when, in 1968, the UAW followed up its secession from the AFL-CIO by joining with the Teamsters to establish the Alliance for Labor Action, an organization to promote cooperation on labor and political matters between these unions, the two largest in the country, as well as with any other unions that cared to join. The AFL-CIO Executive Council promptly warned its remaining affiliates that membership in the new Alliance would be ground for suspension from the federation, and those who had had high hopes for the merger in 1955 now feared a return to the fratricidal warfare of 1935.

A reevaluation of the labor movement?

As a result of these several frustrations and failures, many people inside and outside of the labor movement have come to agree with the criticisms described previously—that most American unions today have succumbed to success and are more interested in preserving what they have won than in helping those who have yet to win much of anything. In this view, yesterday's union rebel has become a staunch pillar of today's middle-class establishment, as suggested by the fact that 46 percent of all union families were in an annual-income bracket of $7,500 to $15,000 in 1967.[12] But even more suggestive, it is argued, is the response of some union leaders and members to charges of corruption and racial discrimination within unions: "Everybody else does it."

With this loss of a sense of "mission" has gone a lessened feeling of unity in the labor movement, of one union's identity with all unions. Such a feeling of oneness has existed in varying degree in the past, but it is ironic that the insularity of individual unions has seldom been greater than it is today, following a merger which was designed to create a single "house of labor." And the final count in this indictment is that the labor movement has betrayed a reluctance or an inability to meet the challenge of new problems in new ways, such as organizing migrant farm workers or white-collar employees, meeting the legitimate aspirations of Negro workers, or coping with the inflationary potential of rapid wage increases during periods of full employment.

But other observers argue that such criticism is too harsh. If we recall the more than 150 years of union history in this country, we will remember that there has tended to be a continuing interplay between two credos—one the realistic, bread-and-butter, here-and-now philosophy, the other a more utopian, reform-minded, future-oriented philosophy. Generally one theme has been given greater emphasis than the other at a particular point in time, but the other theme, even though muted, has never been wholly absent. It is possible, though by no means certain, that today the labor movement is simply going through one of its recurring phases of realism, and will be metamorphosed into a more idealistic, goal-seeking institution under appropriate future conditions.

It is also possible that in suggesting that the unions should somehow be more moral than the society of which they are a part, more idealistic than other institutions to which their own members belong, more impatient with economic distress wherever it may be found in society, we are expecting more of the labor movement than we should. We may be misled by the colorfulness of its origins, which gave to it a crusading zeal and missionary fervor in the days when it had to operate covertly or before industrial society had settled into its present mold. We may be confusing an historical epoch with a continuing quest. When it is said that union leadership has fallen victim to business standards of morality and has lost its idealism, when it is urged that the labor movement must search for new goals and a new mission,[13] this may be sheer nostalgia. It may be much nearer reality to believe that the unions have certain limited functions to perform in a business society, that they should perform them as efficiently as any business performs its functions, and that this is all we should expect of them. From this point of view, "labor" would constitute a movement in the same sense as "business" or "medicine" would constitute movements, and the AFL-CIO would represent such a movement in the same sense as the United States Chamber of Commerce and the American Medical Association represent movements. Such a conclusion would, however, radically change our present conception of what the labor movement is all about. We shall return to this matter in a later chapter.

Meanwhile, it is enough to remember that the labor union in the United States is fundamentally an agent for the individual worker and his household. But in addition, it has certain interests of its own, owing to its ongoing nature as an institution. And beyond its own institutional interests it has also had, traditionally, ties to other unions which unite them and their members into some entity—not clearly defined, not often, and certainly not now, very unified—which we call the labor movement, which purports to have broader conceptions of how society should be organized in the interests of all working people.

ADDITIONAL READINGS

Aitken, Hugh G. J.: *Taylorism at Watertown Arsenal,* Harvard University Press, Cambridge, Mass., 1960.

Bernstein, Irving: *The Lean Years,* Houghton Mifflin, Boston, 1960.

Kennedy, Robert: *The Enemy Within,* Harper, New York, 1960.

Ozanne, Robert: *A Century of Labor-Management Relations at McCormick and International Harvester,* The University of Wisconsin Press, Madison, 1967.

Perlman, Selig: *History of Trade Unionism in the United States,* Macmillan, New York, part II.

Taft, Philip: *The AFL in the Time of Gompers,* Harper, New York, 1957; also *The AFL from the Death of Gompers to the Merger,* Harper, New York, 1959.

Taft, Philip: *Organized Labor in American History,* Harper & Row, New York, 1964.

FOR ANALYSIS AND DISCUSSION

1. The formative years of the scientific-management movement make a fascinating story. Prepare a brief bibliography of writings which bear on these early years. Examine the references you have compiled to discover what managerial practices generally accepted today were introduced by the scientific-management pioneers, why

there was early resistance to such practices by either old-line managements or unions, whether or not any of these early objections are still valid today, and why such practices, which once were regarded with suspicion, have been widely adopted today.

2. Although scientific management and unionism are still regarded by many people as basically antithetical, the typical manufacturing plant today accommodates both. What compromises or shifts in the conception of the role of each have been necessary on the part of both management and union people to permit these two philosophies and movements to exist side by side?

3. Many intellectuals and labor observers of the 1930s regarded the CIO as labor's salvation, the wave of the future, a mighty force for good in a society which had become encrusted with the barnacles of conservatism and special privilege. What grounds were there for this view?

4. Prepare brief biographical sketches of John L. Lewis, Sidney Hillman, Philip Murray, and Walter Reuther. If you were a member of management, with which of these would you prefer to deal, and why?

5. If a depression of some severity were to persist for more than five years, would you expect the leaders of labor or of business to show the greater initiative and leadership qualities in meeting the emergency?

6. If you were a forward-thinking labor leader, what social philosophy would you think should motivate the labor movement today?

7. Is there any good reason for imposing a "double standard" of morality on labor unions—that is, expecting them to be more moral than business?

8. On the basis of our brief historical review and any additional reading for which you find time, can you identify the labor movement in the United States with some "mission," first with respect to the past, then with respect to the present?

NOTES

1. Hugh G. J. Aitken, *Taylorism at Watertown Arsenal,* Harvard University Press, Cambridge, Mass., 1960, p. 16. This is a fascinating study of events surrounding the attempted introduction of scientific-management methods into a government arsenal, with

a perceptive delineation of their economic and historical significance.

2. These claims were collected by Prof. Robert Hoxie in the course of his study for the 1915 congressional committee and are cited in *Trade Unionism in the United States,* Appleton-Century-Crofts, New York, 1921, pp. 299–301.

3. Charles M. Schwab, "Capital and Labor," in *A Reconstruction Labor Policy,* Annals of the American Academy of Political and Social Science, January, 1919, p. 158.

4. John A. Garraty describes some of the "benevolences" of the Morgan group that was in control of United States Steel (in contrast to the "steel men" themselves, as typified by Schwab) in "The United States Steel Corporation Versus Labor: The Early Years," *Labor History,* vol. 1, winter, 1960.

5. *American Federationist,* May, 1924, p. 401. The best account of the AFL's cooperation crusade is contained in Jean Trepp McKelvey's *AFL Attitudes toward Production: 1900–1932,* Cornell University New York State School of Industrial and Labor Relations, Ithaca, N.Y., 1952.

6. *American Federationist,* October, 1925, pp. 873–874.

7. Murray Kempton, *Part of Our Time,* Simon & Shuster, New York, 1955, pp. 284–287.

8. As in the 1959 steel strike, which came to be interpreted by the union and its sympathizers as an attack on the union itself. At the point when that conviction settled in on the membership, what had been an apathetic strike which the union could not seemingly win was converted into a determined struggle "for existence," leading to a settlement extremely favorable to the union.

9. Professor Taft comments on some of these instances in *The AFL from the Death of Gompers to the Merger,* Harper, New York, 1959, pp. 421–427.

10. E. E. Witte, "The Crisis in American Unionism," in *The Arbitrator and the Parties,* Bureau of National Affairs, Washington, 1958, p. 178.

11. *New York Times,* Nov. 2, 1957.

12. Alexander E. Barkan, "The Union Member: Profile and Attitudes," *AFL-CIO American Federationist,* August, 1967, p. 1.

13. The position of one unionist, Sidney Lens, in his popular book, *The Crisis of American Labor,* Sagamore Press, New York, 1959, and of the late Professor Slichter in *Labor in a Free Society,* University of California Press, Berkeley, 1959.

Labor unions have not always been accepted in the United States. For some years they had the character of unwanted institutions. Even today, when legislation protects their right to existence, they are often accepted with reservations about certain functions they perform or certain practices in which they engage. Unions still are not accorded the same matter-of-fact acceptance that business organizations enjoy, and the right of an individual to join or form a union is still, in some areas, not exercised with the same freedom as an individual's right to go into business for himself.

Public concern with the uses of power

Why should this attitude prevail? Is it simply lack of public understanding or tolerance, or is it the ability of business interests to mold public thinking to their own benefit? These are hardly sufficient explanations. More important is the fact that labor unions represent a pooling of private power which is capable of being directed, on the one hand, against the public, and on the other hand, against the very individuals whom they represent or seek to represent. As a result, the government, in the person of its legislatures and its courts, is always concerned with the question of how much pooled power is being used in what ways for what purposes.

It is true, of course, that businesses also often represent power combinations which can be misused with respect to public and private interests.

In particular, concern is often voiced at the power potential of the large corporation. We are fearful that business cartels or trade associations or "big business" can sometimes control product markets and thus "milk" the public by charging excessive prices. We also express suspicions that corporate bureaucracies may dominate the employees who compose them, forcing them into patterns of conformance which rob individuals of their individuality, subjecting them to imposed decisions and authoritarian methods of decision making. But these doubts, while real, are probably not so strong as the doubts society has tended to have about unions, for several reasons.

First, business combinations are seldom able to dominate a community or a nation, an industry or a trade, so completely as to deprive either customers or employees of choice. If prices are too high, there are often competitors to which the buyer can turn for the goods or services wanted. If an employer is too domineering, there are usually other employers to whom the worker can presumably apply for a job. Thus a society which is populated by a number of competing business firms—an "open" society, a society of private enterprises—limits the power any single business or business combination can exercise.

But second, to the extent that businesses do exploit the public at large or their own employees, society has tended to take corrective action. Even before the passage of the Sherman Antitrust Act in 1890, there had for several years been common-law doctrines, brought to this country from England, against monopoly practices. In certain fields where competition seemed impractical or was deemed ineffective, as in local utilities or national railroads, public regulation was substituted. Thus there was a continuing attempt either to enforce competition or to prevent monopolistic exploitation of the public.

Employees were less well protected from business domination. Immobility of labor and recurring depressions often made jobs scarce and alternative employments nonexistent. Skilled craftsmen were in a more favorable position than the unskilled, to be sure. They might look forward to going into business on their own (becoming a master craftsman, in an earlier day), and even aside from some such eventual escape from employee status, they could be relatively more certain that if they chose to move on to another community, there would be a place for them. Particularly in a developing economy such as the United States of the nineteenth century, skilled workers tended to be in short supply. But even for skilled workers there were frequent periods of business slack when they found themselves forced to "knuckle under" to the employer, to recognize that the man who paid them their wages was the boss; in periods of prosperity prices often outran their wages, pressing on standards of living. For unskilled men the power of the employer over their conditions was great indeed.

It was precisely for these reasons that society gradually came to accept the labor union as a legitimate institution, insofar as it protected workers against exploitation by employers. A union could then be viewed as a protector of individual rights. As recently as post-World War II, a highly respected economist could refer to unions in such strong words as the workers' "alternative to serfdom."[1]

The difficulty was that unions brought with them problems of their own, of an identical nature. A union which included all the workers of a given occupation in a locality could dictate the terms on which they would sell their services to the community, either directly (as carpenters might) or to employers who would then have to raise the prices they charged their customers. Was

this any less a monopoly than a business monopoly? Could not workers, by joining together, achieve an excessive degree of power against the rest of the community? Did not the public and employers have to be protected against such pooled power in order to keep the prices of services and products reasonable, that is, competitive?

Moreover, since a union could achieve effective power only to the extent it was able to enroll in its organization *all* the workers of a particular skill or trade (since any outside the organization could undercut the terms it sought to impose), it often had to resort to actions which compelled unwilling individuals to join its ranks. As unions grew, unscrupulous union officials sometimes engaged in measures inimical to the interests of particular members, such as blacklisting them and thereby making employment difficult, if they resisted policies or actions the officials sought to undertake. Was such domination of workers by unions any better than their domination by employers? Was it not the responsibility of the community to protect the individual against being forced into organizations which could engage in such compulsive or exploitative tactics?

Thus from the very beginning, labor unions had to contend with a peculiar dilemma. If they were to be effective, they had to organize all the workers who might otherwise compete against one another and undermine the improved terms which the group as a whole was seeking. But if they were effective, they were likely to incur the opposition of society and the courts, which would charge them with using undue power first to force reluctant workers into the organization and then to raise wages and thereby the price of their services and products. To achieve the objectives society approved, they had to engage in tactics which society condemned or at least questioned.

Throughout the history of legal regulation of labor unions in this country, these same two themes recur: (1) What is the appropriate relationship of the organized group to society at large and to the employer who, as a producer of goods and services, may in this capacity be regarded as society's agent? (2) What is the appropriate relationship of an organization of workers to the individual worker?

Unions as conspiracies

The first legal doctrine applying to labor unions in this country, in which these two themes are interwoven, was the common-law doctrine of criminal conspiracy. Common law, of course, is judge-made law rather than legislative statute—an interpretation of lawful conduct rendered by the courts in the light of precedents and with regard for what Justice Holmes called, in an enduring phrase, "the felt necessities" of the times.

The doctrine of criminal conspiracy has been variously interpreted. In its most rigid form, it held that labor unions themselves were illegal, that although an individual employee might attempt to secure wage increases and improved working conditions, a number of workers who came together to do the same thing constituted an illegal conspiracy. What one could do legally, people joined together could not legally do. The union itself, under this rigid interpretation, became an illegal organization. Perhaps the more general application of this doctrine, however, was directed to the means these organizations employed.

One of the practices the courts were particularly concerned with at this time was the closed shop, which is still very much a live issue. Their concern grew out of the second theme mentioned above, the relationship of the union to the individual. They did not believe that any organized group of workers should have the right to insist that other workers would not be allowed to work at their trade unless they too were members of the same organization. They could not see any legal basis for permitting a private group to determine that only its own members would be allowed to follow a given occupation.

The courts reasoned thus: If our elected state legislature were to pass laws saying that only members of a particular organization would be allowed to work in a particular trade, we would rise in protest. We would consider this a discriminatory exercise of legislative power, a power which the state legislature could not therefore legally exercise. If we do not delegate such authority even to our elected legislators, how can we possibly allow it to rest in the hands of a private group?

With this line of logic the courts held that the attempt of unions to impose a closed shop constituted a deprivation of personal liberty. It was an unacceptable action by an organized group against individuals. With respect to the second of the two themes, the relationship of the group to the individual, then, the courts of the early nineteenth century found that organized labor constituted a conspiracy to injure any worker who sought to exercise his independence.

There was also the first theme—the relationship between the organized group and society. The early unions, growing up in metropolitan centers primarily along the Eastern seaboard, were composed of workers in particular trades. All the carpenters in the area of New York City, or Baltimore, or Philadelphia, or Boston would be organized into a carpenters' union. All the masons, the tailors, the shoemakers would be similarly organized, and each group would negotiate an agreement covering all the shops in its particular trade. "Negotiate an agreement" is perhaps too formal a way to put it, since the type of collective bargaining that we now know had not yet developed, but workers did take organized action directed to obtaining common terms over all similar establishments in an area.

The courts felt that this was an exercise of monopoly power which English common-law precedents, followed in this country, had declared unlawful. On the strength of these precedents, they reasoned thus (as in a conspiracy trial in 1815, involving a group of shoemakers in Albany): Suppose that all the bakers in the city were to come together and agree not to sell bread to anyone in Albany except at a certain price. This would be an illegal exercise of monopoly power. Now, the court argued, what is the action of this union but a comparable form of monopoly power? In this instance, all the shoemakers in the community joined together in agreeing not to work except for a particular wage rate; in so doing, they are exposing the community to their arbitrary authority, since the price of shoes is dictated by their conspiracy. We cannot, the court said, allow this kind of economic power to be exercised by private groups in our community.

Thus in the first legal doctrine applying to

unions in this country, the courts held that such organizations used their powers to deprive other individuals of certain of their liberties and to benefit themselves at the expense of the community. As one court official commented in the Philadelphia Cordwainers (shoemakers) Case of 1806, "A combination of workmen to raise their wages may be considered in a twofold point of view: One is to benefit themselves. . . . The other is to injure those who do not join their society. The rule of law condemns both."

Good combinations as well as bad

The doctrine of criminal conspiracy was invoked in at least sixteen cases. There may have been more, of which we have no record. In any event, we do know it was applied in this manner until 1842. In that year there occurred the landmark case of *Commonwealth v. Hunt,* in Massachusetts. In this decision Chief Justice Lemuel Shaw, on rather technical grounds, refused to apply the criminal-conspiracy doctrine to the Boston shoemakers, who had been enforcing a closed shop.

The prosecutor arguing the case knew that the facts were consistent with all previous conspiracy trials. He had evidence that this union had sought a closed shop, and he had every reason to expect that this would be sufficient to establish criminal conspiracy. Chief Justice Shaw, however, held that the evidence was insufficient. A closed shop could be established for good purposes as well as for bad ones.

Shaw reasoned in this fashion: Suppose that the shoemakers of Boston had come to the conclusion that the use of strong alcoholic beverages by certain of their numbers was deteriorating the standards of their craft, so that the quality of workmanship which had been protected by apprenticeship regulations over the years was being threatened. If they had agreed among themselves that they would not work alongside any shoemaker who took strong drink, the community would have applauded this action. Citizens would have said, "What a fine lot of journeyman shoemakers we have here, who take these steps to maintain their profession at its high level." But, said Chief Justice Shaw, what would this be but another form of the closed shop? These workers would be refusing to work alongside other workers who did not conform to certain standards of sobriety which they had imposed. This clearly shows that it is not the closed shop itself which is unlawful, but the purposes to which it is directed. The prosecutor had not established that the purposes sought by the closed shop in this instance were unlawful, and on this technicality Chief Justice Shaw threw out the case.

Because the criminal-conspiracy doctrine was common law, there was no legislation to be overturned. But because Chief Justice Shaw enjoyed a reputation as a legal authority in other states, many other courts followed his lead. Since then the doctrine of criminal conspiracy has ceased to be a threat to the labor movement.

The doctrine of illegal purpose

However, the two central problems remained. Society and the courts were still uncertain how to deal with groups of workers who had come together to advance their own working conditions. A growing number of people felt that some kind of workingman's organization was necessary, but however much one might subscribe to that belief, those same two problems which we initially identified could not be dismissed. How much authority should a group be permitted to exercise over an individual? What should be the role of the group as it affected society at large? The courts, understandably enough, felt that the law must provide *some* means of controlling pooled power.

After the lapse of the doctrine of criminal conspiracy, a new doctrine rose to meet these continuing problems. This doctrine goes by various names, such as "the doctrine of civil conspiracy" and "the doctrine of illegal purpose." The latter title suggests its genesis: It follows from the argument of Chief Justice Shaw in *Commonwealth v. Hunt* that the purpose of the action complained of must be considered along with the action. Whereas under the criminal-conspiracy doctrine it had been the public prosecutor who brought the charge and the penalty had involved fine and imprisonment, under the doctrine of civil conspiracy the aggrieved party, usually an employer, took the initiative and the penalty usually came in the form of money damages.

The courts continued to examine labor unions with an eye to the impact on the individual and on the community, but no longer to inquire whether the labor union was illegal per se. Shaw had taught them that at least some organized actions were to be tolerated if not approved. The question was to distinguish the permissible from the nonpermissible or, as the judges tended to put it, the licit from the illicit.

The application of the civil-conspiracy doctrine was by state courts, and their judgments differed. If generalization can be made, unions were permitted to carry on their activities as long as injury to others (an employer or other workers) was purely incidental to the achievement of legitimate objectives of their own. Applying such a principle was not a simple matter, however. What was "incidental"? What was "legitimate"? Ceasing work in order to pressure an employer into paying higher wages was generally, though not always, tolerated; actions to make a strike effective, however, were very often construed as having specifically intended harmful consequences to society and individuals.

In Shaw's own Massachusetts, the courts tended to pay particular attention to the motivation behind union behavior. They were especially hostile toward the closed shop, arguing that unionists did not enjoy any rights or privileges of association which would justify their denying employment to a worker who was not a union member—the harm to the individual was direct and not incidental, and the union objective of monopolizing control of employment was not legitimate.

The New York courts, by the turn of the century, had begun to move away from this restrictive view. If unions could be taken as themselves lawful, and if the means they employed were legitimate (as a strike, by itself, was considered to be), then it made no difference to the courts what they were striking to achieve. But it was difficult always to adhere to this more liberal approach, and the New York courts, too, found themselves weighing ends as well as means. Was it permissible, for example, to conduct a strike to force an employer to hire workers whom he did not want, or to forgo the benefits of tech-nological improvements because they would mean a loss of jobs to union members, or, for the sake of argument, to force him to engage in some *illegitimate* activity? Such actions, at some point, ran contrary to society's best interests or to the freedom of the individual. At some point even the most liberal judges felt compelled to examine whether means and ends, both, were "good" or "bad," permissible or nonpermissible.

The labor injunction

The doctrine of civil conspiracy was given a substantial lift and its application considerably aided by the use, beginning about 1877, of the labor injunction. This device came into effect by a rather devious path. In its historical usage, the injunction had been a weapon which courts had used, in any kind of court proceeding, to uphold their own authority. When a number of financially weak railroads went into bankruptcy after the depression of 1873, they were operated by court-appointed receivers. Strikes on these railway lines were subsequently construed as interference with the courts' agents and procedures and hence subject to being enjoined.

Within a few years, however, the question was raised as to why bankrupt railroads were thus immunized from strikes, but sound railroads were not; the public interest was equally involved in both. By a process of extension, the injunction was applied to all railroads, and then to business firms generally. The "labor injunction" had thus been created.[2] This meant that, instead of the employer's having to wait for the union to commit an act which damaged him before entering a suit for the recovery of damages, he could petition the court to stop the action of the union before it was undertaken. He could ask the court to enter an order restraining the union from undertaking a threatened action if it could be argued that that action might irreparably damage his business. Coupled with the doctrine of civil conspiracy, the injunction placed in the hands of the courts very strong controls over the labor unions. Even outside the unions, some people felt that the injunction was being misused or abused to make the efforts of labor unions totally ineffective. In any event, society had "protection."

The employer as public defender

It might seem that this approach to legal regulation of labor unions was designed to defend business interests more than those of the community, but in fact they were believed to be closely identified. As we have seen, the community's interests were conceived to lie in the avoidance of monopoly powers and the maintenance of personal liberties. Admittedly, any employer had a stake in the outcome, too: if union activity could be restrained, he benefited. But an employer, when confronted by a union, could be expected to fall back on arguments that the labor organization sought to exploit not him but the community (by raising costs and therefore prices, and by lessening competition); or that the union deprived not him but his workers of freedom (by seeking to impose its conditions on them). The employer, if persuasive in pressing such arguments, could be presumed to be defending other interests than his own. The two themes of the proper role for organized labor activity vis-à-vis both the public and the individual employee continued to be played in counterpoint before the courts, even when the most deeply involved antagonist was an employer with private interests of his own.

We might take specific note here, too, of the courts' attitude toward picketing as a form of organized union activity. Under the doctrine of civil conspiracy the courts would, as we have seen, entertain arguments that the means employed by the unions were inimical to the rights of the community at large or of individuals. They would sometimes adopt the view that the end sought was not so vital or so equitable as to justify the use of certain forms of union pressure (in some instances, even the strike). Ends and means seemed inextricably entwined. Picketing was one of the instruments employed by the unions which the courts particularly frowned upon.

Even down through the 1920s, courts made such sweeping statements as "Peaceful picketing is a contradiction in terms." The view was that whenever a union undertook to picket, its purpose was not simply to advertise the dispute but also to make an implicit threat of violence against those who undertook to cross the picket line.

In consequence, the courts had adopted the view that picketing itself was something which could not be condoned, since it carried seeds of violence, a threat to the person and rights of others. When Chief Justice Taft, in a decision in 1921, allowed a union to post a "missionary" at each plant entrance and exit, his decision was construed by some as a liberal one.

Unions as restraints on trade

We have been talking about the common law as a form of control over the actions of labor unions. It is time for us now to turn to the statutory law, which also was used to control the conduct of labor unions.

The first piece of legislation which had any major impact upon unions was the Sherman Act, passed in 1890. There has been considerable controversy over whether the Sherman Act was ever intended to apply to labor unions. There are those who believe that it was designed to apply only to business organizations as an antitrust measure growing out of the heated agitation of the seventies and eighties against the growth of large-scale business enterprises which were restricting competition. Whether or not it was intended to affect labor unions, however, it was so interpreted very soon after its passage.

The principal application of the Sherman Act to labor unions took two forms. First, it affected their use of the boycott. The purport of the Danbury Hatters' case, heard first in 1908 and again in 1915, was that the boycott was an unlawful union weapon whenever it tended to inhibit the flow of interstate commerce.

In this case the organized hatters in Danbury, Connecticut, had been unable to secure recognition from one employer. They had struck and had also organized a nationwide boycott against his products. The AFL had circulated a "we do not patronize" list which included the name of the struck employer. Sympathetic groups were urged not to patronize stores in which the hats of this manufacturer were sold. On his complaint, the Supreme Court held that by its actions, the union had impeded the flow of the company's hats across state lines and therefore had subjected itself and its members to the terms of the Sherman

Antitrust Act. They were found guilty and a fine of $210,000 plus costs was assessed them. For a time it looked as though the homes of members would have to be sold to satisfy the judgment, but the AFL appealed for contributions, and the fine was finally satisfied without such a dire consequence. This decision and others like it limited the use by unions of the technique of the organized boycott.

The second way in which the Sherman Act restricted the labor unions was with respect to strikes. Here the key case—again it was argued twice—was the Coronado case. The United Mine Workers had engaged in an organizational strike against the Coronado Coal Company of Arkansas. The company had stocks of coal already mined and at the pit heads, but the union's picketing operations prevented the movement of the coal into the normal channels of trade. The company sued the mine workers' union on the ground that this was a prevention of, or a restraint upon, interstate commerce.

In the first case, the court refused to hold that the union was guilty. It concluded that the union did not *intend*, as its prime objective, to prevent the movement of a nonunion product into interstate commerce, as had been the intent in the case of the hat boycott, but that any interruption to trade was simply an incidental effect of a strike for recognition.

A second case was brought two years later, however, in which new evidence was obtained from a disgruntled official of the United Mine Workers, who had himself been active in conducting the strike. He testified before the court that in strike councils which he had attended, union officials had said their *purpose* was to prevent the coal which was already mined from moving out into the channels of trade. On the strength of this additional evidence, the court found the union guilty.

Unions could not, realistically, appreciate the distinction which the court so carefully made in the two cases. A strike and its attendant picketing operations were of course intended to prevent a company's normal operations and its trade relations. If this constituted a violation of statutory law, then any strike affecting a company whose products moved across state lines would seem open to challenge and strike leaders would seem liable to punishment.

These, then, were the applications of the Sherman Act to two major union weapons—the boycott and the strike—as they affected interstate activity. There is little need to speak of the Clayton Act, which was passed in 1914 and which the unions at that time believed would free them from the weight of the Sherman Act, but which judicial interpretation rendered ineffective. The Coronado cases came in 1922 and 1925, subsequent to the Clayton Act, indicating its failure to lighten the burden of the Sherman Act on the labor unions.

Thus down through the 1920s a rather imposing structure of labor law, both common law and statute law, was erected to regulate and control the labor unions. By 1930 many people were convinced that the controls were too sweeping and were preventing the exercise by labor unions of rights and privileges which should be allowed. But whether one argues that the controls so established were only adequate to the need for them or that they were excessive, the controls did exist. If labor unions could have potentially harmful effects upon individuals or society through the exercise of their organized power, that power was effectively curbed by legislative and common-law devices.

Unions as instruments of democracy

Beginning about the time of World War I, a new current of thought toward the organized activities of labor unions became apparent. There were at least two important causes for this change in attitude, which we shall note only briefly since we have encountered them before.

One was the expansion in size of business organizations themselves, the growth of large corporations which massed together thousands of employees. People began to appreciate that the old notion that the employer-employee relationship should be an individual one was no longer applicable when so many workers were joined together in a single operation. Here the individual was virtually powerless against his employer. He had nothing to say about the terms of the private labor contract under which he worked. The terms were set; he accepted or rejected, but could not modify, them. Because of lack of employment openings in particular communities or because of business depression, there was often very little opportunity even to reject them. In the large corporation, then, individual employees became relatively helpless as bargaining agents. People began to see more clearly the function of a labor union which did not deny liberty to the individual but acted as his representative.

One of the evidences of this changing attitude came from the employers themselves. At the close of World War I, a National Labor-Management Conference was assembled by President Wilson to attempt to establish some kind of workable principles to guide union–management relations. No agreement could be reached between the labor and management groups. The unions insisted upon free collective bargaining, with the workers represented by unions of their own choosing. The position of the employers was not that there should be no union but that the union should be confined to employees of a particular company. This became the basis of the company-union movement of the twenties, which we examined in the previous chapter. But this acceptance of the company union was itself evidence that employers themselves were coming to appreciate that relations between employer and employee could no longer be continued on an individual basis; some kind of representation was necessary. The argument now turned on the *method* of representation. The question of the relationship between the individual and the group was receiving a different answer, with increasing acceptance of the group as the agent or representative of the individual, not depriving him of liberty but making his liberty real.

The second major cause of a change in attitude toward unions was the Great Depression of the thirties. The unemployment of millions of workers provided clear evidence of the impotence of the individual in the face of an economic catastrophe. The preamble of the National Labor Relations Act, passed in 1935, included a statement to the effect that the Depression was largely brought about by maldistribution of income and that only through the organized efforts of employees to secure a fairer distribution of income could pur-

chasing power be sustained and the economy kept on an even keel. Regardless of the economic soundness of the argument, this was recognition that the organized group, the labor union, had a role to play in society, protective not only of the individual but also of the community welfare, of its economic prosperity.

Congressional and judicial change of view

As a consequence, there occurred during the thirties a rather startling shift in the legal attitude toward labor unions. Sometimes we identify the new philosophy with the New Deal, and to a large extent the New Deal did act as the agent of this change, promoting legislation which we shall consider shortly. But the first major piece of legislation evidencing the new trend—the Norris-LaGuardia Act—came in the closing days of the administration of President Herbert Hoover. We cannot say, then, that the changed outlook must be identified wholly with the Democratic New Deal administration. The recognition was far more general. There was arising in many quarters of society a new viewpoint with respect to union–management relations.

The Norris-LaGuardia Act, passed in 1932, is known as the Anti-injunction Act. Actually, it did not forbid or ban injunctions but curbed their issuance by the federal courts. It laid down sweeping restrictions on the circumstances and conditions under which they might be granted and then further provided that only after the employer had made "every reasonable effort" to settle a labor dispute, "either by negotiation or with the aid of any available governmental machinery of mediation or voluntary arbitration," could an injunction finally be entered by the court.

This act applied to the federal courts only, but it was followed by a series of "baby Norris-LaGuardia state anti-injunction acts." They were not adopted in all the states, but the twenty-four states which passed such acts over the next decade included most of the principal industrial centers.

The consequence of the anti-injunction acts, both federal and state, was a substantial limitation upon the use of the injunction to support the doctrine of civil conspiracy. Injunctions were still granted, to be sure. The restrictions proved to be most potent in the federal courts and less so in the state courts. But passage of this legislation markedly blunted the teeth of the injunction in its support of the doctrine of civil conspiracy.

Decisions were beginning to come from the Supreme Court that also modified the structure of earlier controls. With respect to picketing, the Supreme Court adopted a radically different view in *Thornhill v. Alabama,* in 1940. In a labor dispute, it said, management has numerous methods of having its views made public. It can purchase advertising in the newspapers. It can buy radio time. It can distribute leaflets broadside. But the labor union does not have equal means of making its viewpoint known to the community because it usually lacks the financial resources to do so. It must therefore fall back on simpler means of publishing its position. Picketing is the principal alternative method—the sandwich signs carried by pickets in front of the plant gates advertising the fact of a labor dispute to the employees and to the public. This, said the Court, is a form of communication, a form of speech, and as such is entitled to all the constitutional protection of the First Amendment.

Instead of the courts frowning so hard on picketing that peaceful picketing was regarded as a contradiction in terms, now the law provided constitutional protection for the conduct of picketing. This protection was watered down if not washed away by subsequent cases, but at the time it represented a major break with the past.

The Sherman Act reconsidered

At about the same time, the application of the Sherman Antitrust Act to labor underwent a major reinterpretation in a series of Supreme Court decisions. The first of these came in 1940 with the case of *Apex v. Leader.* The issue was remarkably similar to that in the Coronado case, under which the doctrine had been established that strikes designed to inhibit the flow of interstate commerce were illegal under the Sherman Act.

There had been a sit-down strike in the plant of the Apex Hosiery Company in Philadelphia. Local 1 of the American Federation of Hosiery Workers, under the presidency of William Leader, conducted the strike, during the course of which damage done to the equipment in the plant amounted to several hundred thousand dollars.

The strike also prevented the shipment of accumulated stocks of hosiery, just as in the Coronado case strikers had prevented stocks of coal from moving into interstate commerce. Inventories of hosiery were available, orders were on the books, and customers were waiting for deliveries, but the stock couldn't move.

Now, however, the Court in effect reversed its Coronado ruling, even though it sought to distinguish the two cases, and held that this strike could not be touched by the Sherman Act. Justice Stone, speaking for the Court, argued that it had not been the intent of the union either to affect the price of the product or to limit the production of hosiery in the plant, except incidentally to the strike; there had thus been no conspiracy or design to exercise monopolistic power. If it were to be held that the union, by preventing the flow of hosiery into interstate commerce, was monopolistically exercising its economic power, such a ruling would in effect render any strike illegal under the Sherman Act, said the Court, because virtually every strike affects interstate commerce in some degree. And surely it was not the intent of Congress to outlaw all strikes.[3]

This decision revealed that the Court's view of what constituted illegal union activities under the Sherman Act was undergoing a change, but how far that change would go was still uncertain. The Court put doubts to rest by a subsequent decision in 1944 in the Allen-Bradley case. This was a matter involving Local 3 of the International Brotherhood of Electrical Workers of New York City, which had effected an ingenious arrangement with the manufacturers' and contractors' associations producing and installing electrical fixtures in New York City. In a three-cornered agreement, the local union affirmed that it would not furnish any electricians to any contractor who installed fixtures made outside New York City, and in return it secured the promise of both the contractors' and the manufacturers' associations to employ only union labor.

The effect of this three-way agreement was to erect a virtual embargo on fixtures made outside the city. The wages of union labor could be raised and the increase in cost could be passed along in the form of price increases to the consumer, for both the manufacture and the installation of fixtures, since the consumer had no other place to go. This was the case which was being tested by Allen-Bradley and other companies, outside firms that wanted to enter the New York market.

The Supreme Court held that the action of the union was illegal under the Sherman Act. This finding itself was less important than the rationale which supported it. The Court said the union was guilty because it had entered into a specific agreement with the employers' association and that it was this relationship to the employers which had "tainted" it. If the union had itself undertaken to police this arrangement without formal agreement, the Sherman Act would not have touched the union. This constituted a reversion to an interpretation of the Sherman Act which had frequently been urged on the Court but never previously accepted by it, namely, that the act had been designed to prevent only *business* practices from restricting competition. For all practical purposes, this decision released labor unions from effective control by means of the Sherman Act.

Consider now what had happened. Within the rather short period from 1932 to 1944, there had been struck down virtually the whole of the imposing structure of controls which had been erected to limit the power of labor unions with respect to the interests of society at large and of individuals who might be injured by union policies or practices. Use of the injunction, supporting the illegal-purpose doctrine, had been sharply limited. Picketing had become constitutionally immune from attack. The Sherman Act had been rendered virtually inapplicable to unions. There were now very few specific restraints operating, only those which were applicable under the general police powers of the several states or under emergency federal provisions.

This summary statement admittedly exaggerates the state of affairs. In many communities, employer opposition to unions, still adamant and free to express itself, found judicial support. Entrenched attitudes and deeply held convictions, both private and judicial, could not be set aside overnight. Labor unions were more often than not still on the defensive. Nevertheless, the general trend of events was unmistakable. There had been a marked lessening of the legal controls over the operations of labor unions. It was still no picnic for workers to form a union—sometimes it was a dangerous and risky gamble indeed; but where labor unions *were* able to organize and assert their power, legal restraints on the exercise of that power had become notably weaker.

The Wagner Act

During the period in which the earlier structure of limitations on labor unions was being substantially dismantled, the power of the Federal government was, for the first time, used to support and encourage unionization. It was true, of course, that during World War I there had been a temporary accord between unions and the Federal government as part of the war effort, but this was an accommodation forced on the government as a matter of necessity and it did not outlast the Wilson administration. And it was also true that, in 1926, the Railway Labor Act had given the politically effective railroad brotherhoods certain protections and advantages which were not extended to organized labor generally. But the first general legal protection of the right of workers to join unions came with Section 7(a) of the National Industrial Recovery Act in 1933, superseded in 1935 by the much more sweeping terms of the National Labor Relations Act, popularly dubbed the Wagner Act. Supreme Court validation came in 1937.

The significance of this act can only be judged against its background. Prior to its passage, as noted in the previous chapter, employers were completely at liberty to refuse to hire union members, to discriminate against them on the job, or simply to fire workers for no reason other than their joining a union. (Since the Norris-LaGuardia Act of 1932, just three years earlier, employers could no longer, however, enforce a contract specifying that as a condition of a worker's employment, he would never join a union.) Employers were under no compulsion to recognize a union representing their employees if they had the fortitude to form one. They could ignore its existence, or hire *agents provocateurs* and industrial spies to disrupt it, or bribe its officers to sell it out. They could fight it with company unions of their own creation. If a union called a strike, there was no law that forbade their using every device to break it, including the use of armed Pinkertons for "protection."

The Wagner Act deprived employers of all these rights. It enunciated a new policy—namely, that the Federal government encouraged the practice of collective bargaining. To implement that policy the act created a National Labor Relations Board (NLRB), first consisting of three presidential appointees, later enlarged to five. Whenever a significant number of workers in a plant or shop or area had formed a union, they could petition the Board to conduct a "representation election." If a majority of the eligible employees voting declared themselves in favor of one union or another, the Board could "certify" that the union chosen was the legal representative of all the employees. The employer was required to recognize it as such and to negotiate with it in a good-faith effort to arrive at a collective agreement, which was binding on him. If he attempted to penalize or discriminate against any workers for joining a union or engaging in union activity, he could be charged with "unfair labor practices" and subjected to legal proceedings. The same was true if he tried to interfere with the efforts either of his employees to form a union or of outside union organizers to try to enlist workers in their unions. He was forbidden to create his own company union or to try to dominate or control a union formed by his employees.

All these provisions were spelled out in a rather lengthy piece of legislation, which we shall not attempt to examine section by section. As we shall have occasion to note shortly, the Wagner Act was followed in 1947 by the Taft-Hartley Act, which modified it in a few particulars but primarily made additions to it. The Taft-Hartley Act in turn was followed by the Landrum-Griffin Act of 1959, which also modified the Taft-Hartley Act in only minor particulars but principally added to it. These later acts are mentioned here only to emphasize that their passage did not substantially alter the legislative provisions of the Wagner Act as described in the preceding paragraph. The obligation on an employer not to in-terfere with his employees' union activities and to deal in good faith with any union which a majority of them may choose is still federal law, despite all subsequent legislation.

The National Labor Relations Board

The meaning of the law is, to be sure, what the National Labor Relations Board and the courts which pass on the Board's rulings say it is. Because it has many provisions which permit considerable discretion in interpretation, the actual content of the law changes over time with the composition of the Board. There was a tendency for the first Board to move gingerly until the Supreme Court ruled that the act was constitutional. Through the Democratic administrations of Franklin D. Roosevelt and Harry Truman, Board interpretations at first appeared to lean more in favor of the unions than of employers, and more to the CIO than to the AFL. In the last several years of the Truman Board, there was evidence of some "tightening up"; some earlier precedents favorable to the unions were modified or reversed. This was largely but not wholly a reaction to the evident congressional intent, expressed in the Taft-Hartley legislation, to be stricter with organized labor. The real shift, however, came during the Eisenhower administration, when the direction of the Board's "lean" appeared to favor management. The pendulum of administrative interpretations swung noticeably back toward labor with the first Kennedy appointments to the NLRB. These shifts in Board policy in response to the direction of political winds should not be taken as indicating capriciousness or blind partisanship, however. The fact is that the act is susceptible to variant interpretations, and it is only natural that changing membership on the Board should introduce honest changes in interpretation.

Because the act is detailed and because over a period of years NLRB doctrines have been modified, as noted above, only a legal treatise could adequately deal with labor law. Instead of concentrating on the detail, however, we shall here concern ourselves with the major respects in which the three principal pieces of labor legislation—the Wagner Act, the Taft-Hartley Act, and the Landrum-Griffin Act—deal with the two themes which we have traced down from the early nineteenth century. These are (1) the relationship of the pooled power of unions to society at large (and especially toward one component of society, the business sector which provides for society's material wants), and (2) the authority of organized labor over the individual employees whom it purports to represent and who presumably have called it into existence.

The legitimate exercise of union power

We shall approach the first of these themes by inquiring how the Wagner Act affected the permissible exercise of union power. To what ends, and with what means, could organized labor exert its strength?

The objective which the new legislation envisaged was purely and simply the encouragement of collective bargaining, that procedure for arriving at an agreement between employer and employees as to the mutually acceptable terms and conditions of employment which we examined briefly in an earlier chapter and shall explore in greater detail in a later one. In 1947 the legislative intent was made more explicit when Congress defined the process:[4]

> To bargain collectively is the performance of the mutual obligation of the employer and the representative of the employees to meet at reasonable times and confer in good faith with respect to wages, hours, and other terms and conditions of employment, or the negotiation of an agreement, or any questions arising thereunder, and the execution of a written contract incorporating any agreement reached if requested by either party. . . .

But this objective of the law is not quite so clear as it might appear on first encounter. It involves a number of subsidiary questions, some of which relate to means and others to ends. For example, the obligation to "confer in good faith" is something which the NLRB has been spelling out in quite a number of specific cases throughout the years of its existence; its decisions on this point concern the *procedures and methods* of achieving the objective—a mutual agreement on wages, hours, and other terms and conditions of employment. Good-faith bargaining is something which is desired not for its own sake, but only because it is believed to lead to joint understanding. But a joint understanding as to what? Wages and hours may seem like perfectly straightforward subjects for discussion, although we find that even these apparently simple terms have their complexities if we explore them in depth. But what is included in the catchall phrase, "other terms and conditions of employment"?

This is a question which the NLRB must decide in specific cases brought to it by unions and employers. (Ultimately, the matter may be referred to the federal courts for review of whether the NLRB's construction of the term is reasonable.) It is a question, of course, which goes to the heart of the issue of the permissible *objectives* of unions. What are the ends that society will allow labor unions to pursue through use of their pooled power?

Appropriate subjects for bargaining

The Board has sought to answer this question by dividing the subject matter of collective bargaining into three categories: mandatory, permissible, and prohibited. The first of these includes subjects which must be discussed and on which agreement must be sought if either party (normally the union, as the party which customarily opens the bargaining) so desires. Among matters which have been included in this category are group insurance, company housing, wage incentives and bonus systems, pensions, the price of company-provided meals, work loads and standards, stock-purchase plans, and the subcontracting of work which normally has been done by the employees in the bargaining unit.

This last issue can be taken as one illustrating, first, how Board opinions on what the act requires may change, and second, that although the parties may be required to bargain about certain subjects in an effort to reach agreement, they cannot be compelled actually to reach agreement. If there is no meeting of the minds, either party is free to exert additional pressures on the other in an effort to induce it to give in, but if such pressures are resisted the matter may go to an impasse. The *intent* of the act is that the union and management effect an understanding, but there is no way of forcing that result.

In the subcontracting case, a Board majority in 1961 ruled that a company which had decided to cease one phase of its operations, farming it out to another firm, did not first have to bargain with the union concerning its decision. Although the company's action might mean a loss of jobs for union members, this was a simple business decision taken for economic reasons, and it was not mandatory for management to negotiate with the union regarding such a modification of corporate practice and structure.[5] But the issue was again raised a year later, and this time a majority of the Board reversed the previous finding. It ruled that while the employer was not required to modify or retract its decision to subcontract certain phases of its operations, it was obligated to discuss its decision with the union before putting the decision into effect. The company did not have to yield to the union's plea not to subcontract the work, but it was "the very essence of the Act" that company and union engage in joint discussion concerning a matter so importantly affecting employment before any unilateral action was taken.[6]

Permissible (but nonmandatory) bargaining areas, as the name implies, relate to matters which the law, as interpreted by the Board and the courts, does not obligate management to discuss with the union, but which it may discuss at its own discretion. These matters presumably deal with topics which are not considered "terms and conditions of employment." In the Mill Flooring case, for example, the union demanded that a company make a contribution to an industry promotion fund. The idea was that through the promotional program which such a fund would make possible, the industry's sales would expand, and jobs along with them. But the company, which was not a member of the trade association operating the fund, refused to make the requested contribution. The NLRB ruled that its refusal to bargain on such an issue was entirely within its discretion; society laid no obligation on it to do so. In effect, the Board is saying that a union may ask for concessions on such an issue but it can neither strike nor secure a Board order to force an employer to bargain on that issue if he

does not want to. Actually, only a handful of rather trivial subjects has been ruled to fall in this peculiar area of nonmandatory bargaining.[7]

There is a third category of subject matter about which it is considered unlawful to bargain. In brief, union power cannot be used to try to compel an employer to engage in an illegal activity, such as entering into a collusive agreement with other employers, which would be a violation of the Sherman Antitrust Act, as in the Allen-Bradley case previously noted. Nor may an employer enter into such an agreement, even if he is willing to: The subject matter is excluded by law from union–management negotiation. As we shall see, the Taft-Hartley Act expanded this category to include the closed shop and some kinds of actions which an employer would himself normally be free to engage in (such as deciding with what customers he will do business) but concerning which a union may not negotiate. In this class of cases, society has ruled that it will not countenance the use of union power to secure the specified objectives. In these particular instances, the use of private pooled strength to obtain advantages which are likely to discriminate against the reasonable interests of others is out of bounds.

Unfair labor practices

We noted earlier that the Great Depression helped to spread the notion that labor unions could be socially useful devices to ensure a greater degree of democracy (self-determination) in industry and to secure a more favorable distribution of income which would help to keep the economy in balance—both rather poorly defined conceptions but both having a strong and widespread appeal. The emphasis throughout the decade was thus understandably on an enlargement of union powers to enable organized labor the better to achieve these objectives. We have also noted how some of the limitations of earlier years were removed during this period. The Wagner Act went still further in this direction by giving organized labor new powers. It did this by creating several categories of employer actions which it branded as "unfair labor practices." When an employer engaged in such practices, a union could initiate legal proceedings before the NLRB.

The basic purpose of the new line of federal labor legislation which began in 1932 is to facilitate the smooth functioning of collective bargaining. It is considered socially advantageous for employer and employee to reach a mutual decision, a joint understanding, a voluntary agreement, on "wages, hours, and other terms and conditions of employment." Unfair labor practices are acts which, if committed, are likely to imperil that result. Charges of unfair activity are initiated by the party offended, employer or union, which files a complaint with the regional office of the Board. It is the function of the agency's general counsel to determine whether there is merit in the charge and whether it should be prosecuted. If his decision is in the affirmative, one of his attorneys presents the evidence before a trial examiner who is appointed by the five-man Board to hear the case. Witnesses are called, and the defendant has full opportunity to present his side of the matter. Subsequently, the trial examiner issues what is known as an intermediate report, which constitutes his findings and judgment. This report goes to the Board (any three of its members being empowered to exercise its judicial powers), which reviews it. If neither party enters an objection to the examiner's report, that report is made final by the Board. If either party objects, the Board will accept new evidence and may even hold further hearings, if this is thought necessary. It may confirm the decision of the trial examiner, or modify his opinion in some respects, or reject his judgment altogether and substitute its own. Its decision is final within the agency.

If it is found that an unfair labor practice has been committed, the Board is empowered to determine the appropriate remedy. It also issues a "cease and desist order," which instructs the offender to discontinue the practice complained of. If the party ignores the order, the Board may then apply to a federal circuit court of appeals for enforcement of its ruling. Failure of the party to conform to the court's order renders it liable to penalties for contempt of court. On the other hand, a union or an employer may appeal the Board's decision before the federal courts, which will hear the case to determine whether it should be upheld.

Illegal employer practices

The unfair labor practices with which the Wagner Act was concerned were all actions in which an employer might engage if he were out to disrupt or destroy a union. The legislation, then, was designed to protect a labor union's exercise of its traditional weapons of (1) organizing employees into a cohesive force, (2) making demands on an employer which he was expected to negotiate with it, and (3) putting pressure on him by such devices as striking, picketing, boycotting his product, or other forms of harassment in the event of his refusal to deal with the union or to make satisfactory concessions. The legal protection of these devices, however crude they may sound, seemed essential in 1935, and still seems essential today although with important modifications introduced in later legislation. The reason is that only when organized workers have in their hands some means of bringing pressure on management can they counterbalance the pressures which management can bring to bear on them through its control over their jobs; with each party thus holding some power over the other, there is a positive inducement for them to discuss differences and try to reach agreement. And that was (and is) the objective of the whole process—the drafting of a *mutual* understanding as to the terms and conditions of employment, giving employees something to say about the circumstances under which they worked, introducing what was (and is) popularly called "industrial democracy."

How did the Wagner Act go about protecting the employees who wanted this kind of "industrial democracy" for themselves? First, it decreed that any actions by an employer which were designed to interfere with the efforts of his employees to organize a union were "unfair," meaning illegal. Second, it made this general proscription more concrete by specifying that an employer could not attempt to create or dominate a union in order to avoid dealing with an independent union, he could not discriminate against an employee because of the latter's union activity, and he could not make reprisals against an employee who brought charges against him before the NLRB. Third, the law established election machinery by which employees could indicate whether they wanted a union to represent them, and if so, which union. If they indicated a desire for union representation, then the employer was obligated by law to bargain with the union they chose. Fourth, any interference by the employer with the bargaining process was branded unfair, again meaning illegal.

Over the years, thousands of decisions by the Board have given life to these provisions, building up a body of precedents which instruct employers and managers in what they may or may not do. It is impossible to do more than give a general idea of the nature of the unfair labor practices chargeable to an employer. "For the most part," to quote the Board, they involve "such clearly coercive conduct as reprisals, and express or implied threats of reprisals, for participating in union or other protected concerted activities, and promises or grants of economic advantages to discourage such activities."[8]

Among the specific instances of reprisals which the Board has found to be illegal have been such actions as the following: The eviction of strikers from company living quarters; the discharge of an employee for presenting a grievance on behalf of herself and fellow employees; threats of plant shutdown and discharge, loss of overtime, reduced hours of work, loss of promotion if employees persisted in their union activity; threats to rescind wage increases or to cut wages or to go out of business; an offer to discharged workers that they could have their jobs back if they forgot the union; interrogation of employees about union activities as part of a coercive pattern of conduct; prohibiting employees from distributing union literature on company premises when no similar ban applied to any other kind of pamphlet distribution; and other such forms of harassment.

If an employer takes discriminatory action against any of his employees because of their union activity, the Board, in addition to ordering him to cease such activity, customarily orders restoration of the employee to his former job (if he has been fired or reassigned) or to his former job rights, with reimbursement for any lost wages or other benefits.

But the Board faces a difficult problem in as-

certaining an employer's motivation. Suppose a worker is fired. He happens to have been active in helping to organize a union at his company. It would appear that his employer has taken punitive action against him for his union activity, in violation of the act. But then the employer asserts that his union interest was not at all the basis for the discharge; the man was fired because he had not been doing a good job. And the employer cites several reasons for the action: The employee had been late again the previous week; his foreman had had to speak to him about the quality of his work; he hadn't shown the kind of initiative that was wanted. If these were the real reasons for the discharge, the employer's action is perfectly legal. The law still permits an employer to fire a union member for incompetence or any other reason, good or bad—*if* the employer's purpose is not to punish the worker for his union activity.[9] Hence the Board must sift the employer's intent. Had he really fired the man for the causes he cited, or were these simply trumped-up reasons of a kind that could be marshaled against almost any employee, with his union activity being the real motive for the discharge?

In order to establish motivation, the Board falls back on the device of seeking what it calls objective indicia of the employer's intent. That is, it seeks objective, factual evidence suggesting the reason for the action. Thus, in the case above, if the Board had found that other employees who were not active in the organization effort had been late more frequently, had had poor quality of work, and had shown even less initiative, these facts would indicate that the reasons given by the employer were not the real reasons motivating him. In the light of this evasiveness and the employee's known organizational activity, it would seem likely that it was an antiunion animus that had prompted the discharge. The employer would have a chance to rebut this presumption but, failing rebuttal, he would be charged with violation of the act and would be required to restore the employee to his job and make good the wages he had lost.

Among the objective indicia which the Board has found to suggest discriminatory treatment of employees for union activity have been such things as discharge shortly after a man becomes active in union work although he has had a good employment record; unequal treatment of union and nonunion personnel in layoffs, job assignments, promotions, and discipline; disregard of established practices in such matters as the application of seniority or the recall of laid-off employees.

Although the most common form of discriminatory action is probably outright discharge for union activity, sometimes an employer will resort to what has been termed a "constructive discharge." This is where an employer drives a worker to resign by such a device as assigning him to undesirable work. In one instance, because he filed a grievance an employee who was going to college was transferred from the night shift to the day shift, making it impossible for him to complete his studies if he remained, so he resigned. Similarly, an employee with twenty years' service, on becoming active in union work, was compelled to quit because he was transferred to heavy work for which he was physically unfit because of a hernia condition. These actions were held to violate the law.

Representation elections

The basic intent of the federal labor policy is, as we have seen, that workers shall be represented, when they so wish, by unions of their own choosing for purposes of negotiating terms with an employer. This objective—so commonplace now, so radical in 1935—raises a number of difficult questions. What workers shall be represented? By whom can they be represented? Under what circumstances can they change representatives? What are the rights and obligations of representatives in the bargaining process?

Representation could conceivably take several forms. For example, plant workers who wished to have a particular union act as their agent could nominate it for that purpose. As many different unions as were nominated would then seek to negotiate with the employer on behalf of those who had named them. This is known as "members only" representation. Or joint representation is another possibility: instead of such representatives negotiating individually for their own members, all representatives could get together and agree among themselves on the demands they would make on the employer, and negotiate jointly. Both these approaches were in fact tried under the federal labor policies of the National Industrial Recovery Administration in the two years preceding passage of the Wagner Act. Both were found to have serious limitations. In the "members only" kind of representation, a union would be precluded from bargaining on some matters which affected all employees. Seniority, for example, was something which workers were anxious to establish, but one union representative could not ask for plantwide seniority for its members if another representative sought departmental seniority for its members. Moreover, an employer could frustrate efforts to organize by giving unrepresented workers terms or conditions superior to those represented by a union. In the case of joint representation, to ask conservative unions, Communist unions, Socialist unions, and unions whose leaders had conflicting personal motivations—all of which might have some constituency within a plant—to agree among themselves on the demands to make or the offers to accept was asking for cats and dogs to agree. Parenthetically, it might be noted that both these approaches have worked—though not always well—in other countries where unions were more wholeheartedly accepted, but they have been found quite impractical in this country, with its heritage of industrial strife.

The solution adopted here was "exclusive representation." Whenever a number of employees in a unit—a minimum of 30 percent—indicate their desire to be represented by some union, they may petition the Board to conduct an election. The name of the union—known as the petitioner—is placed on a ballot, along with a space where employees may vote for no union. If another union likewise seeks representation rights within the same unit, it too may be listed on the ballot, upon a showing of interest. (Such a union is known as an intervenor, and it need not show authorization cards for more than 10 percent in order to gain a place on the ballot.) The director of the Board's regional office then conducts an election at a specified time, usually on the company premises, in which all the employees in the unit may vote.

If a majority voting cast their ballots for a particular union, that union is certified as the exclusive bargaining representative for all the employees in the unit. It and it only is qualified to negotiate terms with the employer, *and the terms so negotiated apply to all employees in the unit, whether they are members of the union or not.*[10]

It is difficult to exaggerate the significance of this ingenious solution to the representation problem. First, the election machinery provides a peaceful and democratic method of determining whether particular workers really want a union, a question always in dispute and previously settled by sheer power rather than by ballots. Second, by preventing the employer from negotiating with individual workers or a rival union, the principle of exclusive representation grants a certified union far more institutional security than most unions ever had in the past. Although it may appear to be undemocratic to deprive those who voted against the union of any right to negotiate their own terms of employment, our political system follows the same principle in declaring the winning candidate the "exclusive representative" of all the people in his election district, whether or not they voted for him, and in requiring everyone to observe the laws agreed upon by the majority. This same principle also requires, however, that all contract gains must be extended to union members *and* nonmembers alike in the bargaining unit, a provision which reduces the incentive of workers to join the union and in turn stimulates union pressure for compulsory-membership clauses. We shall return to this right-to-work issue in the next chapter.

Limitations on campaign behavior

Representation elections are usually the occasion for intensive campaigning on the part of the rival union groups, as well as of employee groups which wish to remain unrepresented. Unions attempt to whip up enthusiasm for their cause by vilifying the employer and reminding employees of what they can do for their members, in typical political-campaign fashion. If two unions are running against each other, there is likely to be a good deal of mudslinging, with each telling "the worst" about the other. The employer, however,

is supposed to play a more discreet role. On the theory that the purpose of the election is to allow the employees to decide for themselves, the law forbids employers to attempt to influence the election by threat or promise. They cannot say to their employees, for example, "If you vote for the union we will close down the plant or move to another location"; nor can they say, "If you vote against the union we will grant a 10 percent wage increase." These are considered unwarranted interventions in the employees' own right of self-determination.

In the early years of the NLRB, an employer was likewise forbidden to speak for or against a union but was supposed to remain silent on the sidelines. In answer to employer protests, however, the so-called "free-speech" provision of the Taft-Hartley Act permits an employer to make any statement concerning the election which does not carry a threat or promise of reward. Thus an employer may now speak disparagingly of the union on the ballot, comment on its record in other bargaining situations, and state his opinion of unions in general.[11]

But why should the Board be permitted even limited powers of censorship? After all, many candidates for political office promise paradise if they are elected and disaster if their rivals should win, and we trust the voters to judge this propaganda with no help from a government agency. The difference in a representation election is that one party—the employer—often has the power to carry out his threats and promises. It is one thing for a voter to hear a presidential candidate promise prosperity if elected; it is quite another to hear your employer promise to raise wages if the union loses a representation election and to fire you or move his plant if the union wins. It is this element of possible coercion in the employer-employee relationship that justifies most restrictions placed upon an employer's campaign behavior.

Much more debatable, however, is the Board's broader aim that representation elections should "provide a laboratory in which an experiment may be conducted, under conditions as nearly ideal as possible, to determine the uninhibited desires of employees." The ambiguity of this criterion is illustrated by two cases involving racial propaganda. In one, the union had lost an election in rural Georgia following a campaign in which the employer distributed several issues of a tabloid attacking the racial views of "the Communist Party, the NAACP, the labor unions, the National Council of Churches, the Kennedy Administration and their ilk"; mailed employees a picture of a Negro man dancing with a white woman (captioned "The C.I.O. Strongly Pushes and Endorses the F.E.P.C.") and a picture of a white man dancing with a Negro woman ("Union Leader James B. Carey Dances With a Lady Friend"—although Carey was president of a different union than that involved in the election); and distributed similar propaganda. Although the employer had not directly threatened his workers or promised any rewards for voting against the union, the Board set aside the first election and ordered that another be held, arguing that the employer's propaganda was so irrelevant and inflammatory that it prevented a "reasoned basis for choosing or rejecting a bargaining representative."

In the second case, decided on the same day, the Board refused to set aside an election lost by the Textile Workers after the employer sent a letter to all employees stating that the position of the AFL-CIO, to which the Textile Workers belong, was one of favoring integration in "schools, plants, and elsewhere"; that the AFL-CIO had contributed $75,000 to the National Association for the Advancement of Colored People; and that the Textile Workers had taken over one of its locals to prevent it from using union funds to finance a private white academy set up to thwart a school integration order. The Board judged this letter to be "temperate in tone, germane and correct factually," and thus to be permissible campaigning by the employer.

Clearly the Board has an unenviable task in balancing the employer's right to free speech against the worker's right of free choice in representation elections. Few would quarrel with the principle that employers should not threaten or bribe worker-voters, but many observers are uneasy over the Board's attempt to go further and assess campaign propaganda which is repugnant but noncoercive. Rather surprisingly, the Board's position on racial propaganda, first enunciated in

1962, had still not been tested before the Supreme Court by 1970.

The bargaining unit

Before an election of any sort can be held, it is necessary to determine the voting constituency. The law empowers the Board to determine the "appropriate bargaining unit." Generally, if the union and the management agree on the bargaining unit, the Board will honor their preference. But if the union and management are at odds on which employees are to be covered, or if two or more unions seek conflicting determinations, then the issue must be resolved by the Board's exercise of its own discretion. In general, it seeks to group together in the same unit employees whose interests are sufficiently homogeneous to give grounds for expecting the relationship to be a stable one.

This may appear to be an innocuous administrative task, but a brief description of two problems—craft severance and industrywide bargaining—will illustrate that serious policy issues are also at stake. More specifically, these problems illustrate how difficult it is to define the appropriate scale of union power in our society, for, contrary to expectations, employers do not always want small bargaining units nor do workers invariably prefer large units.

"Craft severance" refers to the question of whether a group of skilled workers may opt out of a larger unit in order to bargain for themselves. Suppose, for example, that the tool- and diemakers in an auto plant become convinced that the UAW is neglecting their special interests and favoring its more numerous semiskilled members. Should the NLRB permit a new election in which only these toolmakers could vote, choosing between the UAW and a craft union? Such a petition will be opposed not only by the UAW but also by the employer, who has no desire to add to his bargaining problems by having to negotiate with the UAW *plus* a series of splinter groups, each with the power to shut down production in the event of disagreement.

Here the Board is confronted with a dilemma —a dilemma which has characterized many of its deliberations in connection with representation elections. There are two principles which it considers to guide it in its election decisions, both equally valid. It must seek to honor the wishes of the employees involved, in line with the general intent to encourage unions of their own choosing. It must also seek to create stability in bargaining relations, for the whole representation machinery is geared to facilitate effective collective bargaining. If it allows employees to change their minds from contract to contract about the kind of unit and the kind of representation they want—a policy which admittedly would give greatest weight to the employees' own wishes—this would create an instability in bargaining relationships, thus sacrificing the other objective. An employer and a union can never learn how best to get on with each other if the bargaining unit is always subject to change as craft groups move into and out of comprehensive groups as suits their mood and interests. Moreover, even if the wishes of employees were the sole criterion, the question would persist of *which* employees should decide this issue—the minority of a plant's workers with craft interests or the majority who prefer plantwide bargaining?

In resolving this dilemma, the NLRB has vacillated over the years. Its rulings under the Wagner Act tended to militate against allowing a separation of craft groups from established plantwide units, much to the distress of AFL unions. After passage of the Taft-Hartley Act in 1947, Board policy veered toward permitting the severance of nearly any craft group that met a few general standards, a policy which displeased many employers and industrial unions.[12] Then in 1967, the Board sought a middle ground in the Mallinckrodt doctrine (taken from the decision in the Mallinckrodt Chemical Works case) which declares that the Board will examine petitions for craft units on a case-by-case basis, weighing all the relevant factors in each case instead of applying any general "mechanistic" rules to all situations. For example, the Board now asks whether the proposed unit consists of a homogeneous group of truly skilled journeymen; whether the existing pattern of bargaining in the plant and industry involved has produced stable labor relations and whether such stability will be "unduly disrupted"

by a new craft unit; and whether the craft group is extensively integrated in the employer's production process and could easily disrupt normal operations.

Clearly, there is no easy way to decide whether a group of workers should be permitted to splinter an established bargaining unit, but to many people the more important question is whether workers should be permitted to *expand* a bargaining unit to cover an entire industry. More precisely, what does the law say about a union which attempts to organize all the workers in an industry, whether it then bargains with each employer separately (as in the auto industry) or with all or many employers simultaneously (as in coal and railroading)? And what about a union that organizes workers in several industries—in labor "conglomerates" such as the Teamsters? Are there no limits to union expansion?

The short answer to these questions is that our labor laws say almost nothing on this subject. In framing the Wagner Act in 1935, Congress thought in terms of helping workers to stand up to giant corporations such as United States Steel and General Motors, and any proposal to limit each union to the workers of one employer would have been dismissed as an attempt to perpetuate the tame "company union." In the 1947 Congress, on the other hand, the mood was very different and a determined effort was made to include the following provision in the Taft-Hartley Act: A union could represent employees of competing employers only if (1) the union represented fewer than 100 employees of each employer and (2) the plants of the competing employers were less than 50 miles apart. Stated differently, unions and bargaining units would be limited to single companies in basic industries like steel and autos, but multiemployer bargaining would be permitted within a 50-mile radius in small-firm industries like clothing and construction. This proposal actually passed the House in 1947 but a similar bill was defeated by one vote in the Senate.

The curious result is that, with few exceptions, the law and the NLRB now determine only the *election unit,* which may or may not be the same thing as the *bargaining unit* (the workers covered by a labor contract) and is almost never the same as the *organizing jurisdiction* of any union. For example, if General Electric opens a new plant in Kentucky tomorrow, any union, regardless of its normal jurisdiction, can secure a place on the NLRB ballot—the Longshoremen or Miners or Teamsters or any of the three electrical workers unions—provided only that it can demonstrate the support of 30 percent of the plant's workers (or 10 percent for an intervenor union). If a union wins the election, the law permits the parties to negotiate a contract covering only that plant, *or* to include the plant under a master contract covering all the GE plants organized by the same union, *or* even to include it under a contract covering GE, Westinghouse, and all other electrical manufacturers in the country organized by the same union.[13] The major exception to this rule is that unions may not force unwilling employers to bargain simultaneously for several election units, but if employers are willing to do so, the law permits the parties to broaden the bargaining unit to any size they desire.

Organized labor naturally approves of this hands-off policy, arguing that a union limited to a single company or area could seldom match employer strength nor could it pursue the primary mission of unions to "take labor out of competition" throughout an industry.[14] Many employers, on the other hand, argue that if the law were changed to limit the scope of union organizing and particularly the size of bargaining units, we could eliminate the primary cause of large-scale strikes and inflationary wage pressures. But other employers are wary of this proposal, each fearing the competitive consequences if his company should happen to end up with the strongest, or the only, union in his industry. An employer may deplore industrywide unions or bargaining in principle, but if in practice his own workers organize and win a higher wage scale, he may well share their desire to extend the same scale to all of his competitors.

We shall return to the problems of bargaining structure in later chapters, but at this point it should be stressed that the political power of organized labor is not the only reason why the law places no ceiling on the size of bargaining units. In both the Wagner and Taft-Hartley Acts, Congress tried to promote an equality of power

between labor and management, and it is true that the scope of the bargaining unit can affect this power relationship. Unfortunately it is also true, for reasons described later, that bargaining power is a very elusive concept that resists accurate measurement; at any given time, the distribution of power varies greatly among the thousands of diverse union–management relationships in this country and can even fluctuate over time within the same relationship; and therefore no one can predict the net effects of imposing a uniform structure upon every union and every contract negotiation. It is easy to criticize the present law for failing to produce an equality of power in every bargaining relationship but much harder to devise a new structure that can guarantee any better results in this respect.

Finally, note again the ambivalence of both labor and management on this crucial question of the appropriate size of bargaining units. When unions can be found on both sides of the craft-severance issue and employers on both sides of the industrywide bargaining debate, it is hardly surprising that Congress and the NLRB have also failed to discover that ideal structure which would permit each union to exercise "enough but not too much" power.

Compulsory bargaining

Thus the labor legislation introduced in 1935, and still effective today, forbids the employer to interfere with the organizing activities of his employees and lays down a variety of specific kinds of union activity—all looking toward collective bargaining—in which they are privileged to engage without fear of reprisal from him. It establishes an election machinery which allows the organized employees, when they believe they have sufficient strength, to seek the certification of their union as the official agent in the particular unit which the Board has defined. If their union wins a majority of votes cast, it has the exclusive right to represent all the employees. And the employer has a legal duty to recognize it, bargain with it, and attempt to reach an agreement with it. It is an unfair (illegal) practice for him to engage in any action which interferes with that intended result. (The 1947 amendments placed a similar obligation on unions, in view of the occasional practice of a strong union to adopt a "take-it-or-leave-it" attitude toward a small business, as the Teamsters have sometimes been charged with doing.) The law specifies, however, that the duty to bargain in good faith "does not compel either party to agree to a proposal or require the making of a concession." The question of agreement or concessions is left to the bargaining process itself.

Once a union has been designated as a majority representative, the employer is obliged not only to bargain with that union but also *not* to bargain with any individual or groups of employees concerning the matters coming under the union's purview. He is also precluded from voluntarily offering his employees any improvement in their terms —an increase in wages or an additional holiday, for example. It may seem strange that an employer's unilateral granting of an employee benefit should be construed as "unfair," but the thought is simply that an employer, by such an action, engages in a kind of benevolent paternalism in which he dispenses benefits as he sees fit, without consulting the union which his employees have chosen as their agent. He thus acts counter to the philosophy of the law that such "conditions of employment" should be determined by *mutual* agreement, with the participation of his employee's agent rather than by his own fiat.

An employer's duty to bargain includes the obligation to furnish the union with sufficient information to enable it to bargain intelligently. He must on request furnish the union, for example, with a list of employees in the bargaining unit, showing their individual wage rates and job classifications and any merit increases obtained within a recent period. In one instance, the Board ruled that an employer was bound to disclose information contained in a survey on which it based its assertion that its present rates equaled or exceeded rates paid for similar work by other employers. The Board has also held that an employer could not lawfully refuse to furnish information substantiating its claim that it was financially unable to grant the wage increase the union was asking.

The employer's duty to bargain is not satisfied merely by meeting with union representatives and discussing terms with them. As the Board has

said, "The real question is whether or not the [company] was dealing in good faith, or engaged in mere surface bargaining without any intent of concluding an agreement on a give-and-take basis." Here again the Board faces the question of motivation, and, as in the case of discriminatory treatment, it seeks objective indicia on which to found its judgment. Its determination of the employer's good faith usually is the result of an appraisal of the employer's entire dealings with the union.

Thus in one case the Board held that the employer's bad faith was clearly demonstrated where the negotiations were characterized by dilatory tactics such as repeated postponement of bargaining conferences, the employer's failure to make concrete proposals, his granting of individual merit increases while at the same time refusing to negotiate a general wage increase or a vacation plan in lieu thereof on the ground that no increase in expenses was possible at the time, and by his refusal to continue negotiations after the union had filed charges of unfair labor practice.

If an employer negotiates with a union and the two parties reach an impasse so that no agreement is in existence or in prospect, the employer is then free to take independent action, as long as he does so in a manner which does not undermine the union's status and authority. At the same time, his employees are free to take independent action as well, in the form of a strike, accompanied by picketing as long as it is nonviolent. Striking is considered a legitimate form of union activity, and an employer would be committing an unfair (illegal) practice if he penalized or disciplined employees for engaging in a strike. Strikers may be replaced but they cannot be discharged. The possibility of being replaced by a new hire is a risk which a striker voluntarily assumes, but discharge for having gone on strike constitutes a penalty for having exercised his right to strike. A strike may, however, lose the protection of the act because of the manner in which it is conducted (plant seizure or sit-down, for example) or because its objective conflicts with law or public policy (such as a strike to force an employer to ignore the certified bargaining representative and deal with an independent group, or a strike in breach of a no-strike agreement). In these cases, employees may be discharged without re-course. Individual strikers may likewise be discharged for engaging in violence.

If strikers abandon their demands and agree to return to work unconditionally, the employer must take back all those who have not been permanently replaced. But a strike which has been provoked by the employer's violation of rights guaranteed by the act is known as an unfair-labor-practice strike, and employees who engage in it are not only granted the protection of the act but, if they have meanwhile been replaced, the employer must usually discharge the replacements to make room for them on their return.

This is a very summary version of the way in which the Wagner Act of 1935, only slightly modified by later legislation with respect to the matters touched on above, changed the status of labor unions in society in answer to that persisting question which has come down through the years: What is the appropriate role for labor unions to play? Or to phrase it another way: What is the legitimate use of the private pooled power of organized labor, taking into account the broader interests of society as a whole and the rights and interests of other segments of society? In the mid-thirties, it was decided that unions not only had a legitimate role to play in representing the interests of their members but that this role was sufficiently important to the preservation and pursuit of the democratic values of our society to warrant strong legal protection.

The Taft-Hartley Act

Let us pause to take stock of the legal developments down to the end of World War II. We saw in an earlier section that changing social attitudes toward labor unions during the years of the Great Depression had been reflected in the removal of legal difficulties which organized workers had suffered for many years. The use of the injunction had been curtailed. Picketing was viewed more favorably by the courts. The Sherman Antitrust Act had, for all practical purposes, ceased to apply to unions. But in addition to these sweeping changes, new legislation had placed added powers in the hands of labor unions. These unions were now regarded as something which had been made

necessary by concentrated industrial power, and thus were entitled to exercise what an economist, Prof. J. K. Galbraith, was later to call "counter-vailing power." The organized business–organized labor conflict was looked upon not just as a private quarrel but as something involving the rights and welfare of a large segment of society. In supporting unions, society was thus supporting its own best interests. Moreover, since unions were organized to represent workers, one need not be much concerned about a possible conflict of interest between unions and their members.

The decade and a half from 1930 to 1945 was a period in which unions enjoyed legal favor and, on the whole, popular support. It was also a period during which they more than quadrupled their strength. The rise of the CIO had succeeded in accomplishing what the older craft-oriented unions had never been able to do, namely, organize the major mass-production industries, in the process shaking the AFL out of its lethargy. Thus the war ended with labor unions stronger than ever before in the history of this country, both absolutely and in relation to industry's strength.

National defense preparations and World War II, during which unions had voluntarily limited the exercise of their power in the national interest, obscured from the public the full extent of the increase in union strength. But at the war's end the manifestation came in a wave of strikes that touched every major industry. Oil, coal, lumber, glass, automobiles, electrical appliances, steel, farm equipment, and the railroads—all these and other industries were closed down by a seemingly never-ending succession of strikes, some five thousand of them in the year following victory over Japan. This strike activity coincided with the period when consumers were impatiently awaiting the promised flow of goods, particularly of consumer durables such as automobiles, refrigerators, kitchen ranges, washing machines, radios, television sets, and especially housing. Here was a demonstration of the power of labor unions in the economy, power to affect the welfare of society at large, and at the same time a demonstration of the relative lack of controls or limitations over such organizations. Arguments that large-scale unionism constituted monopoly power which could be directed against public interests gained a more sympathetic hearing. It was also argued that the government itself was responsible for creating these pools of excessive private power by granting unions exclusive jurisdiction in bargaining units and permitting them to force workers into their organizations through the closed shop and the union shop.

Only in the light of this development in social and legal history can one understand passage of the Taft-Hartley Act. That act was supported and partly written by employers, it is true, who had much to gain by securing controls over labor unions. But this was not a sufficient condition for the law's passage. The Taft-Hartley Act came in response to a reassessment of the role of the labor union relative to the individual and to society at large, resulting in a considerable popular acceptance of the need for some types of controls to be imposed on the unions.

Limitations on union power

If one reads through the Taft-Hartley Act, it is clear that much of the new emphasis is upon protecting the individual as opposed to the group, upon balancing the power of the organization by encouraging the privileges and the liberties of the worker who does not want to conform to the labor union. There was thus an effort to reduce the power of the union over the individual—but at the same time no denial of the fact that the labor union still is the only effective means by which the workingman can be represented in industrial decision making.

The 1935 Wagner Act had made no provision for employers to bring charges of "unfair" practices against the labor unions, on the assumption that it was the weakling labor movement, which had for years been pushed around by more powerful managements, that required special protection. There was at that time no intent to pass a piece of "balanced" legislation, since it was thought that balance in the relations between unions and management could only be obtained by special and one-sided protection for the unions. By 1947 the labor movement was no longer weak, and the possibilities of abuse of its power—against society, against workers and members—had become

recognized. The balance of power which labor legislation had sought could be achieved, it was thought, only by limiting certain union excesses. Thus the Taft-Hartley Act identified unfair labor practices on the part of unions, to be laid alongside those which the Wagner Act had charged to employers.

Like its predecessor, the Wagner Act, which it in fact incorporates with only a few amendments, the Taft-Hartley Act is a complex piece of legislation and has been subject to continuing interpretation by the NLRB and the Federal courts. It would be quite impossible to examine all its provisions here. We shall therefore select for emphasis those aspects which bear most directly on the congressional effort to define the proper exercise of the union's private power against other segments of society and also against individual workers whom it seeks to represent.

Since the strike wave of 1946 was largely responsible for turning public opinion against the union, it could be expected that special provisions would be made to control labor's use of the strike weapon. We shall only note that fact here and defer consideration of it until a later chapter, when we shall examine the strike issue in greater detail. The most important respect in which Congress sought to limit the coercive power of unions was in their use of secondary boycotts. The Taft-Hartley Act went a long way toward making such boycotts illegal, and the few loopholes it left were later closed by the Landrum-Griffin Act.

The protection of neutrals

A secondary boycott (or strike) is a device by which a union which has a dispute with one employer (designated the primary employer) seeks to enlist support for its cause. Firms which act as suppliers to or customers of the primary employer, which are not involved in the dispute, and which may in fact be enjoying good relations with their own union, are designated as neutrals or secondary employers. The union which has the dispute with the primary employer can increase the pressure on him if it can get the workers of a neutral employer to support it either by going out on sympathetic strike or by refusing to handle materials coming from or destined for the pri-

mary firm. The neutral employer, anxious to restore his own good relations and aware that he cannot do so until the primary dispute is resolved, can be expected to bring pressure on the primary employer to settle. Moreover, the primary employer will be subject to greater inducement to settle if his suppliers or customers refuse to do business with him as long as he is at odds with his union.

In the Taft-Hartley Act, Congress ruled that this involvement of neutral employers was an unwarranted exercise of union power—an antisocial means which could not be justified by the end. Unionists have objected to this blanket restriction, claiming that if a nonunion firm is maintaining below-standard conditions, it threatens all the gains which unions have won elsewhere by dint of long struggle and personal sacrifice, and that any pressures which can be brought to bear on such a firm, including the secondary boycott, are warranted. The employer who aligns himself with such nonunion firms by supplying or buying from them is not really neutral, from the union's point of view.

Enforcement of the provisions banning secondary boycotts has involved many complicated constructions by the Board. The law forbids a union to induce employees of a neutral employer to engage in a secondary strike or boycott the purpose of which is to force the neutral employer to stop doing business with another (the primary) employer. But when is an employer neutral and when is he primary? In some instances, two firms may be under the same ownership. If a union strikes one of them, the owner diverts business to the other, continuing to supply customers as usual. Is the second firm then a neutral? Here the Board has ruled in the negative, saying that there is a community of interests or an alliance which makes them both primary disputants.

Or consider this question: A union has a dispute with an employer, calls a strike, and establishes a picket line. Some truck drivers have deliveries and others have pickups to make in the struck plant. If the pickets, marching up and down before the gates with signs saying, "We are on strike—help our cause," induce the truck drivers to turn away, is this a violation of the law? For the union has induced employees of

neutral employers to cease doing business with the primary firm.

The Board recognized that such a construction would outlaw virtually all picketing, an outcome which the proviso to this section excludes. Hence it has held such action to be lawful. The rule it generally follows is that a union's conduct is secondary and prohibited if it occurs at the premises of a secondary employer—away from the primary dispute. But picketing confined to the primary employer's premises is lawful even though it has the traditional objective of inducing neutral persons not to enter the premises for business reasons.

Efforts to get employees of neutral companies to refuse to work on the product of a primary firm (the so-called product boycott) are unlawful. As the Board said in one case, the act's prohibition on secondary boycotts applies to all cases in which "a union causes employees to refuse to work on the product of any producer *other than their own employer* because that product is . . . nonunion, and it does so with the object of causing their employer to cease using the product of, or doing business with, the other producer."

What of traditional consumer boycotts, such as the "We do not patronize" lists on which unions post the names of nonunion firms? If consumers are thereby induced not to purchase nonunion retail products and even to stay away from stores which handle them, will not the retail stores cease carrying the nonunion goods simply to retain their customers? And would this not constitute the involvement of neutrals in a dispute which does not concern them? The 1959 Landrum-Griffin law makes clear that while the picketing of stores to achieve this result is unlawful (since picketing would affect deliveries and services to the neutral store), other forms of truthful publicity about the nonunion nature of particular products is permissible—as long as it does not have the effect of inducing the store's employees to refuse to handle the product or cause other workers to refuse to perform their usual services for it.

After passage of the Taft-Hartley Act, some unions (notably the Teamsters) sought to get around the secondary-boycott provisions by demanding that employers include in their collective agreements a so-called "hot-cargo" clause. This clause specified that the firm's employees could, if they wished, refuse to handle struck or "unfair" (that is, "hot") goods. Thus a neutral employer whom the act was seeking to protect in effect was forced to waive his neutrality and agree that if his employees preferred not to work on products or handle shipments made by an employer with whom their own or another union was having a dispute, he would not bring any charges under the act.

For a time the doctrine was that it was lawful for a union to seek such a clause in its collective agreement, but it was against the law for it to enforce the clause. This ambiguity was resolved by the Landrum-Griffin Act, however, which provided that it is an unfair labor practice even to make such an agreement. The hot-cargo clause is thus now illegal—with two specific exceptions. Because of longstanding practices and the peculiar characteristics of the clothing industry, with its manufacturers, contractors, and jobbers all tied together in an intricate system of relationships, a broad exemption from the anti-hot-cargo provision has been granted. In the case of the building and construction industry, agreements relating to the contracting and subcontracting of work to be done at the building site are also excepted from the ban, for it is difficult to identify a neutral employer in this industry in which, unlike manufacturing or trucking, several companies are usually operating together on the same site.[15]

One other limitation on union power may be briefly noted. The Taft-Hartley Act provides that a union cannot engage in a strike to force an employer to assign work to it rather than to some other union—the jurisdictional strike which, aside from the fact that it plagues employers, is offset by no real social benefit. It does not involve industrial democracy, it is not a question of giving employees a say about their terms of employment —usually an employer would be glad to deal with either of the two contending unions. It is simply a contest between two unions, each trying to stake out a claim for itself and its members. If an employer protests such a strike to the Board, the parties are given ten days to adjust their dispute, after which the Board is empowered to make a determination. In general, the Board has maintained the right of an employer to assign work

free of pressure from a union with which he has no collective agreement, which has no members among his employees, and which enjoys no representational rights touching on the disputed work as a result of some previous Board certification. At one time, the Board was content to rule that a union could not strike to enforce a jurisdictional claim, but as a consequence of a Supreme Court decision it has, since 1962, made specific awards as to which of two or more contending unions was entitled to claim jurisdiction over the disputed jobs. In doing so, it considers such relevant factors as the skills and work involved, company and union practice, agreements touching on the subject (including jurisdictional understandings between unions), arbitration awards, and "the efficient operation of the employer's business."

The Taft-Hartley Act thus sought to limit certain instruments of union power (notably the secondary boycott, and to a lesser extent, the strike) and certain ends to which these might be directed (notably to force an employer to recognize a union over the opposition of his employees, or to cease doing business with other employers who found themselves on a union's "proscribed" list, or to do business with one union rather than another).

Again the Sherman Act

As a final illustration of the legal problems posed by union power in a competitive economy, no better examples can be found than two controversial decisions handed down by the Supreme Court in June, 1965.

One case (*United Mine Workers v. Pennington*) involved the charge that the Mine Workers union and the major employers' association in bituminous coal had embarked in 1950 upon a long-term conspiracy to eliminate marginal producers as a solution to the problems of strikes and overproduction which had plagued this industry throughout the 1940s. More specifically, it was alleged that the major companies agreed to grant liberal wages and fringe benefits in return for the union's pledge to permit rapid mechanization *and* to impose the same wage-and-benefit scale on small producers whose mines were not mechanized, thus driving these companies out of business. In a suit filed by one of these small companies, a jury found the union guilty of violating the Sherman Act and ordered it to pay the company a triple-damage penalty of $270,000. Not surprisingly, the union appealed this conviction.

The other case (*Local 189, Amalgamated Meat Cutters v. Jewel Tea Co.*) involved a multi-employer contract with a clause prohibiting unionized food stores in the Chicago area to sell meat after 6 P.M. on any day. All employers agreed to this contract except the Jewel Tea Company, which finally signed under pressure of a strike threat but then brought suit for violation of the Sherman Act against both the union and the employers' association. Jewel Tea asserted that the contract served no legitimate labor objective in banning night work by butchers on any terms and particularly in banning the night operation of self-service meat departments which required no butchers; instead, this clause illegally restrained competition by depriving both the company and consumers of the advantages of night service. The union replied that its members strongly opposed night work; even self-service departments required tasks, such as replenishing meat cases, which were butchers' work; if self-service stores were permitted to sell meat at night, other stores would be forced to do the same; and therefore the clause was a legitimate bargaining issue. One lower court agreed with the union, another agreed with the company, and the case went to the Supreme Court.

How should the highest court have ruled in these cases, which were considered and decided together? Were these unions only exercising the power they must have to restrain competition in the labor market in order to win improved wages, hours, and working conditions? Or did these unions (and several employers) also restrain competition in the product market and thereby damage consumer interests? And is there a difference?

Almost regardless of your opinion, you have the impressive backing of at least three Supreme Court justices, for three found an antitrust violation in both cases, three found no violation in either case, and three found a violation in the first case but not in the second! In the Pennington coal case, the majority followed the Allen-Bradley precedent set in 1944, holding that a union may independently seek the same contract terms from different employers but it cannot do so as part of

an agreement with one group of employers who wish to drive another group out of business. The minority argued that this decision arbitrarily favored one bargaining method over another—securing uniform labor standards through a single, industrywide contract would now be safer than pursuing the same objective through pattern bargaining—and in any event labor's drive for uniform wages is a protected activity very different from union participation in an Allen-Bradley type of conspiracy to fix prices or divide markets.[16]

In the Jewel Tea case, a different majority found no antitrust violation because all of the employers involved were in the same bargaining unit and thus there was no conspiracy to force one unit's contract upon another unit; also, the clause restricting marketing hours was sufficiently related to labor's legitimate interest in regulating working hours to qualify as a mandatory bargaining subject. A different minority, of course, saw no essential difference between these cases; in Jewel Tea as in Pennington, they argued, a union conspired with one group of employers (those who did not want to operate at night because they had no self-service system or for some other reason) to restrain product competition by another group of employers.

In short, we are still agonizing today over essentially the same issues as were raised in the first labor-law cases in the early 1800s. It is true that we no longer label every union activity as a criminal conspiracy, and in fact society now protects union activity to an extent that nineteenth-century judges would find incredible. And yet the bewildering divisions of opinion in Jewel Tea and Pennington demonstrate that the Supreme Court, like Congress and the rest of us, has still not found a clear and final answer to the question posed in those first conspiracy trials: What are the appropriate limits to union power in a competitive economy? That, we have seen, is one of the two themes recurring throughout the history of legal regulation of labor unions in this country, themes which can never be finally resolved but must be faced continuously.

Union activity among government workers

The evolution of labor law covering the private sector of the economy is now being repeated within the public sector, although with some important differences. Until the mid-1950s, unions of government employees were in much the same legal status as that of unions in private industry in the early 1800s. Both the Wagner and Taft-Hartley Acts explicitly *excluded* government workers from their protection, and there were almost no other statutes at any level of government that declared public employees had any right to participate in union activity or that public employers had any obligation to recognize unions formed by their employees. Further, common-law precedents could be found for prohibiting exclusive representation, the dues checkoff, and compulsory-membership clauses within the public sector, or for prohibiting any contract at all between a government agency and a labor organization, or even for prohibiting public workers from joining any union. As for the strike, the Taft-Hartley Act explicitly forbade the use of this weapon by federal workers and a few states had similar bans, but in a sense these statutes were unnecessary because common law in every jurisdiction prohibited such strikes and courts were always willing to issue injunctions against them.

In recent years, this legal structure has been shaken to its foundation by the growing size and militancy of unions within the public sector. Organizations of government workers have long existed, of course, but for the most part they were professionally oriented, such as the National Education Association, or they were civil service groups which engaged in gentlemanly lobbying to achieve their ends. Today, however, the American Federation of Teachers, an AFL-CIO affiliate, has organized teachers and conducted strikes in several school systems, forcing the NEA itself to become more militant. Another AFL-CIO affiliate, the American Federation of State, County, and Municipal Employees, has become one of the fastest-growing unions in the country; government hospital, welfare, and sanitation workers have engaged in strikes; and even firemen's unions and police "benevolent associations" have been growing decidedly less benevolent.

The response of public policy has been similar to that which occurred in the 1930s with respect to unions in the private sector: for the first time, many government jurisdictions have now guaranteed the right of their employees to engage in union activity and have directed public employers to bargain with unions chosen by their employees. As with the Wagner Act, a primary impetus behind these laws has been the hope that strikes and other forms of worker unrest can be allayed by providing a peaceful method of resolving the representation issue and by establishing orderly bargaining procedures.

On the other hand, the current wave of policy changes in the public sector falls short of the Wagner Act revolution of the 1930s in two crucial respects. First, the Federal government has been reluctant to impose its authority over state and local governments—both for political reasons and because of doubts of the constitutionality of such a move. As a result, *there is no "national labor policy" governing unionism in the public sector* but, instead, a bewildering patchwork of statutes, executive orders, common-law doctrines, and civil service and other personnel regulations—all of which vary widely among the hundreds of thousands of federal, state, county, and municipal jurisdictions throughout the country. Some government workers have now won nearly all of the organizational rights enjoyed by workers in private industry since 1935, but others have gained only a few of these rights and yet others can still be fired for any union activity whatever.

The second major difference from the 1930s is in the legality of the strike. In the Norris-LaGuardia and the Wagner Acts, Congress legalized nearly every strike in the private sector. In contrast, no legislative body in this country had legalized strikes by any government workers for any reason prior to 1970, when Hawaii and Pennsylvania became the first states to adopt laws permitting certain public employees to engage in strikes that do not endanger the "health, safety, or welfare of the public."

The new laws in the public sector

In spite of these major qualifications, *the trend is clearly toward enhancing the legal status of union activity in public employment.* The initial breakthroughs occurred mainly at the municipal level in "union towns" such as Philadelphia and New York City. In the latter, for example, Mayor Robert Wagner issued an Executive order in 1954 that guaranteed the right of city employees to organize, and another order in 1958 that provided election machinery for resolving representation disputes and pledged city authorities to bargain with unions chosen by their employees. In 1967, during Mayor John Lindsay's first administration, these rights were incorporated in a New York City Collective Bargaining Law, which also defined mediation procedures for deadlocked disputes and established a unique administrative agency, the Office of Collective Bargaining, headed by a board composed of two union designees, two members appointed by the Mayor, and three impartial persons chosen by the four partisan members.

The Executive order was also the instrument of change at the federal level. In an order issued in 1962, President Kennedy proclaimed the right of federal employees to organize and bargain and directed each agency to establish procedures for resolving representation questions. This order was supplemented in 1963 when the President issued the Code of Fair Labor Practices which, in effect, prohibited within the Federal government many of the unfair labor practices prohibited in private industry by the Taft-Hartley Act. In a new Executive order effective January 1, 1970, President Nixon reaffirmed the employee rights granted by the Kennedy order, improved the administration of this program in several respects, and established new procedures for resolving impasses in negotiations. Strikes by federal employees remain illegal, and their contracts may not contain a union-shop clause. Union membership has nevertheless expanded significantly in the federal sector since the issuance of the Kennedy Executive order. Only one strike of any consequence had occurred by 1971 (the one-week walkout by about 200,000 postal workers in 1970), and both presidential orders probably influenced, through example, the labor policies of many state and local governments.

At the state level, diversity and change are the keynotes of public policy on this subject.

At one end of the spectrum are such states as Alabama and North Carolina. Alabama, for instance, prohibits all but a few categories of public employees whose compensation comes in whole or part from the state . . . from joining or participating in any labor organization at pain of forfeiting all their rights of public employment and reemployment. Correspondingly, agencies and subdivisions of the state (such as cities, counties, and boards of education) have been held . . . to be without authority to recognize or make contracts with labor organizations. The North Carolina statute prohibits membership of policemen and firemen in a labor union and invalidates agreements between governmental units and labor unions covering such employees. Violation of the North Carolina statute is punishable as a crime.

On the other hand, there is an increasing number of states with statutes either authorizing or mandating (when certain conditions are met) collective dealing between government and some or all public employees. These are Alaska, California, Connecticut, Delaware, Florida, Maine, Massachusetts, Michigan, Minnesota, Missouri, New Hampshire, New York, Oregon, Rhode Island, Washington, Wisconsin, and Wyoming. Indicative of the intensity of recent activity is that twelve of these seventeen states either enacted or amended their statutes in 1965.[17]

The double standard

The basic policy question in this area of labor relations is whether all workers should have the same legal rights to engage in union activity regardless of whether they work for a private or public employer. Consider, for example, the curious status of a worker on an Alabama highway project that might be done by either a private construction firm on bid or by the state highway department. If the work is done by a private contractor, the employee's rights to organize and bargain and strike are guaranteed by law, but if the state highway department is his employer, the same worker doing the same job can legally be fired for even joining a union. Where is the logic or equity in such a double standard?

One explanation of these differences is that public employers are no more eager than private employers to deal with a union if they can possibly avoid it, and as makers and administrators of the law, they simply have been in a better position than private employers to protect their managerial interests. In addition, however, there are three justifications given for this double standard which go to the heart of the problems posed by union power in the public sector.

First is the claim to *sovereignty,* the argument that in any orderly society the government must be supreme in its authority. In a free society, of course, that authority is derived from the electorate and subject to many checks and balances, but the principle remains that a viable government cannot be coerced into negotiating with a group of its own citizens as if the latter were also a sovereign entity with equal powers. Whether the government is setting a tax rate for everyone or a wage rate for its own employees, it is assumed to be acting in the interests of the entire society. If certain taxpayers or employees dislike these decisions, they can lobby for a change or vote for those who promise a change, but they cannot force the legislature to meet with them as equals for the purpose of jointly determining public policy. In fact, in its purest form, the sovereignty doctrine holds that a government cannot negotiate a labor contract even if it wants to because that would be an improper delegation of governmental authority.

That is the traditional argument for prohibiting union activity in government employment. "Its difficulty lies in the circumstance that life has a way of running ahead of logic and that history tends to be more complex than political theory."[18] Government agencies regularly negotiate a huge number of contracts with private organizations to supply everything from missiles to paper clips, and no one suggests that these suppliers must accept whatever terms the government dictates or that these contracts represent an invasion of sovereignty. Also, although the government was long held to be immune from suit, the Federal government and several states have voluntarily limited their sovereignty in this respect by establishing special courts in which citizens may sue the government for alleged contract violations or on other grounds. And indeed that appears to be the direction in which the law is now headed with respect to unions of public employees: *A government cannot legally be forced to bargain collectively with its own employees, but the sovereignty doctrine does not prohibit the government from authorizing or engaging in such bargaining if it chooses to do so.*

As the sovereignty defense has crumbled, there has been increased emphasis upon the *essential nature of government services* as the reason for restricting union activity in the public sector. At its most extreme, this argument assumes that every government activity is so vital to the functioning of society that work stoppages by any group of public employees would constitute an emergency. Most people would agree with this argument when applied to the armed forces or to policemen and firemen, but "there are innumerable government services which can by no stretch of the imagination be considered so essential that they cannot be interrupted even for short periods: state-owned liquor stores, city botanical gardens, recreation centers, government cafeterias, automobile license bureaus; the list is almost endless."[19] And if essentiality is to be the policy criterion, why are unions and strikes permitted in privately owned "public utilities" such as gas and electricity and telephone companies?

To meet these criticisms, this argument is often modified to state that government services do indeed range from the essential to the inessential, but endless disputes would arise if legislators or administrators tried to draw a sharp line between those public workers who should have the right to strike and those who should not. Even in its modified form, however, this argument is directed solely at the right to strike and offers little basis for also prohibiting government workers from joining unions and negotiating contracts by means other than the strike.

The latest and most sophisticated justification for the double standard in labor law is *the lack of countervailing economic power* in the public sector. In private industry, runs this argument, union power is usually kept in check by the employer's limited ability to pay and the threat that competition will wipe out jobs if the union pushes too hard on costs and prices. In the public sector, on the other hand, the power to tax gives the employer almost an unlimited ability to pay; a particular governmental unit does not lose "sales" or jobs if it pays higher wages than anyone else; in a union town, the public employer may even gain political support by settling generously with his employees; and the management personnel in a public agency may directly profit from granting high wages since their own salaries may then be pushed up to maintain normal differentials. For these reasons, it is argued, union power is more likely to be abused in the public than the private sector.

Critics contend that this argument underestimates the potency of political forces as a substitute for market forces. Few things, they say, stir up voters more than a tax increase, so a political leader negotiating a wage increase must be as conscious of irate taxpayers and his political opponents as the private employer must be of his customers and competitors.

Other problems in the public sector

As we have seen, the current trend in many jurisdictions is toward admitting that the above justifications for the double standard in labor law are less persuasive than they were once thought to be. In particular, there is growing acceptance of the idea that public employees should have the same rights as private employees to organize in unions of their own choosing, to negotiate written contracts with their employers, and to be protected from employer discrimination for engaging in such union activity. But this does not mean that the day of the single standard is just around the corner, for the strike is still illegal in most of the public sector and this prohibition poses many problems.

We shall discuss the function of the strike in later chapters, but here it is sufficient to note that in the private sector, the right to strike, even if seldom exercised, is generally assumed to be absolutely necessary for effective collective bargaining. Why should an employer agree to any union demand if the union is powerless to make disagreement costly? But if that is true, how can bargaining be effective in the public sector without the strike weapon? It is obviously not enough just to pass laws against strikes by government workers. Their unions have been fined for striking, their leaders have been jailed, the strikers themselves have been discharged, and still strikes occur because government workers, like those in private industry, are often convinced that striking is the best or only way to get action from their employers.

Thus the most critical labor problem in the public sector today is how to devise an effective substitute for the strike, to apply either to all public employees or to those considered most essential. One approach is to provide that in the event of an impasse, skilled neutrals will mediate the dispute and, if necessary, make public their recommendations for a fair settlement, thereby substituting an appeal to reason and public opinion for the strike. Another proposal is to submit deadlocked disputes to binding arbitration by neutrals, a method increasingly used in the public sector to settle minor grievances and the method employed to settle the 1968 sanitation strike in New York City.[20] Also, unions may still use lobbying and similar political tactics to press their demands. The fact is, however, that no one yet knows whether these alternatives will produce effective bargaining, and indeed few experts believe that strikes can be entirely eliminated from the public sector either by punitive legislation or by providing alternatives such as mediation and arbitration.

Even if that hurdle is surmounted, there remains the question of just what the parties can bargain about. We have seen that the Taft-Hartley Act explicitly requires bargaining over wages and hours, and private employers only question whether issues like subcontracting are also negotiable. But in the public sector, even wages may be declared out of bounds. The problem is that most government employees work in the executive branch while the power to raise and appropriate public funds is a prerogative of the legislature. For example, Congress determines the salary schedule covering most federal employees, and no executive agency can negotiate a 10 percent increase when Congress will only appropriate funds for a 5 percent increase. The result is that most unions of federal employees can only lobby before Congress on the crucial issue of salaries (and fringe benefits) and must restrict their collective bargaining with agency heads to other issues.[21]

This is sometimes less of a problem at the city level, where the legislative and executive branches are not so sharply separated in practice and where many unions, being stronger than those at the federal level, have simply forced bargaining on wages and most other issues. The problem nevertheless exists to some extent at every level of government: *The public employer at the bargaining table seldom has the authority of the private employer to commit his organization to major expenditures.* This is particularly troublesome if bargaining occurs after the legislature has fixed the budget and tax rates for that year. Some of the recent laws (in New York and Connecticut, for example) therefore encourage or require bargaining to be completed before the date a mayor or governor must submit his budget requests to the legislature, a procedure which allows executive discretion in negotiating a tentative agreement while preserving the final authority of the legislature in fiscal affairs.

In summary, unions in the public sector pose serious policy problems, but not all of them are as unique as most people assumed only a generation ago. It is easy to predict that, eventually, most government employees will be guaranteed the right to form or join a union without fear of punishment and that most public employers will assume the obligation to negotiate with unions of their employees—two vital rights which society has granted most workers in private industry since 1935. In those matters, the argument for a single standard of labor law appears to be unassailable. But in other respects public-sector unionism does indeed pose unique problems: the need to ban strikes by at least some government workers and in turn the need to find an effective substitute for the strike; the negotiating difficulties created by the separation of legislative and executive powers; and the uncertain effects of basing bargaining power upon political rather than market forces. To cope with those problems, society will undoubtedly continue for many years to apply more stringent standards to unions in the public sector than to those in private industry—although no one can yet predict the shape of this new double standard emerging in labor law.

Thus the issue of union power runs deeper than has sometimes been assumed. The question of labor's power relates not only to its appropriate exercise against other private powers like individual employers and corporations. It also concerns the much broader issue of how much power society—viewed as a social *system,* as a complex

if often ragged ordering of its myriad relationships —can afford to leave in the hands of any of its component parts. Too much power spells disruption and chaos, or dictation and surrender. Too little power spells impotence, alienation, and frustration. The issue of union power is, in this respect, an early manifestation of such more recent phenomena as "black power" and "student power."

ADDITIONAL READINGS

Chamberlain, Neil W.: *Sourcebook on Labor,* chaps. 8–10, McGraw-Hill, New York, 1958.

Gregory, C. O.: *Labor and the Law,* Norton, New York, 1961.

Hanslowe, Kurt L.: *The Emerging Law of Labor Relations in Public Employment,* Cornell University, New York State School of Industrial and Labor Relations, Ithaca, N.Y., 1967.

Northrup, Herbert R., and Gordon F. Bloom: *Government and Labor,* Irwin, Homewood, Ill., 1963.

Ross, Philip: *The Government as a Source of Union Power,* Brown University Press, Providence, R.I., 1965.

FOR ANALYSIS AND DISCUSSION

1. Early judicial disapproval of union activity was based in part on the doctrine that what one person may lawfully do, a number of people in concert may not do. Thus in the first judicial trial of a labor union, in 1806, in which an association of shoemakers was found guilty of criminal conspiracy, the recorder who rendered the decision quoted the rule "adopted by Blackstone, and laid down as the law by Lord Mansfield in 1793, that an act innocent in an individual, is rendered criminal by a confederacy to effect it."

In later cases, however, the courts moved toward the view that what one may do legally, a number acting together might legally do. As another judge commented in a later case, "If they had the right individually, I can see no reason why the same right might not be exercised by them collectively and simultaneously. . . ."

What are some of the practical and philosophical difficulties involved in affirming either of these views?

2. Compare the two Sherman Act cases in which activities of the United Mine Workers were held to be subject to antitrust prosecution—the 1925 Coronado case and the 1965 Pennington case. What are the chief differences *and* similarities in the Supreme Court's decisions in these two cases?

3. Under the law, management must consult or negotiate with the union before taking action in the areas of wages, hours, and conditions of employment. This principle forces management to share with the union any "credit" for an improvement in terms which management might have been quite willing to grant on its own. If a managerial decision, such as a wage increase, is of benefit to the workers, why should consultation with the union be necessary? Is the requirement that management deal with the union before undertaking actions favorable to its employees a reflection of some belief that management-given benefits are only a form of "bread and circuses" to delude the workers and that only through union intervention can workers gain any lasting benefits?

4. A comprehensive or industrial bargaining unit contains diverse groups—some workers more skilled than others, or occupationally differentiated, or even spatially distinct from the others. Such groups may splinter a large bargaining unit by seeking to establish their own separate bargaining unit. What considerations might affect the decisions of such a group either to remain in the comprehensive unit or to seek to leave it? What considerations of public policy might be involved?

5. State and defend your opinion as to whether public school teachers should be granted the right to strike. Would you draw any distinction between the members of a state university faculty and teachers in elementary and high schools?

NOTES

1. J. M. Clark, *Alternative to Serfdom,* Harper, New York, 1948. At the same time, Professor Clark recognized the limitations of union power referred to in the next paragraph of the text.

2. For a detailed account of the origin and extension of labor injunctions, see Donald L. McMurray, "The Legal Ancestry of the Pullman Strike Injunctions," *Industrial and Labor Relations Review,* vol. 14, pp. 235–256, January, 1961. The classic treatment is by Felix Frankfurter and N. Greene, *The Labor Injunction,* Macmillan, New York, 1930.

3. Note that the *Apex* decision did not declare the sit-down strike legal in every respect. For occupying the employer's plant and damaging his equipment, the Apex workers were still liable to discharge and to prosecution under the usual local laws prohibiting trespass or other damage to private property. The Supreme Court's decision only said that these activities were not a violation of the Sherman Act.

4. Labor Management Relations (Taft-Hartley) Act of 1947, sec. 8(d).

5. This decision was reached in *Fibreboard Paper Products Corp.,* 130 NLRB 1958 (1961). Hereafter, no specific citations will be given, to avoid excessive annotation. The interested reader is referred to the NLRB's annual reports, or any of the standard labor-law reporting services, for fuller discussion of all the cases and issues discussed in the remainder of the chapter.

6. The divergent points of view of these two Fibreboard decisions are analyzed by John H. Fanning in "The Duty to Bargain in 1962," *Labor Law Journal,* January, 1963, pp. 18–27.

7. For a criticism of the rulings establishing this category of bargaining subjects, see Robben W. Fleming, "The Obligation to Bargain in Good Faith," in J. Shister, B. Aaron, and C. W. Summers (eds.), *Public Policy and Collective Bargaining,* Harper, New York, 1962, pp. 66–68, 84.

8. *Twenty-Sixth Annual Report of the National Labor Relations Board,* 1961, p. 77.

9. The Civil Rights Act of 1964 has further—and substantially—modified an employer's rights in this respect, however. It remains true that the four principal pieces of general labor legislation (Norris-LaGuardia, Wagner, Taft-Hartley, and Landrum-Griffin) and the powers of the National Labor Relations Board do not extend to any form of employer discrimination except that for union activity. The Civil Rights Act, in addition, specifies that employers may not discriminate against employees or job applicants for reasons based on race, color, religion, sex, or national origin. Its provisions are enforceable, at the federal level, by an Equal Employment Opportunity Commission created by the act.

10. If there are three or more choices on a ballot (say, for example, the Auto Workers, the Machinists, and no union), and none wins a majority, then a runoff election is conducted between the two choices which have polled the highest number of votes.

If a union claims to represent a group of employees and seeks to bargain on their behalf without petitioning for an election, the employer is free to recognize and bargain with the union or, if he doubts that the union really represents a majority of workers, he himself (under a Taft-Hartley provision) may petition the Board for an election. And if employees who have once voted in a union subsequently change their minds and decide they don't want a union after all, they can (again under a Taft-Hartley provision) petition for a decertification action, in which a majority vote against the union deprives it of its bargaining rights. In no case, however, can more than one election of any kind be held within a year.

Further, if a certified union negotiates a contract with a term longer than a year, under Board rules that contract will generally bar another election during its lifetime—for a period up to three years in any case, and up to five years if such contract periods are common in the particular industry. Thus, in most bargaining units a new election can be held only upon the expiration of a current contract.

11. Just how far an employer may go in his comments during a representation election has remained a hotly debated issue. Depending on its composition and outlook, the Board has been very rigid in circumscribing employer statements (as under the Roosevelt Board), very permissive (as under the Eisenhower Board), and middle-of-the-road (as under the Kennedy Board). A good discussion of this issue is contained in Benjamin Aaron's "Employer Free Speech: The Search for a Policy," in Shister, Aaron, and Summers (eds.), *Public Policy and Collective Bargaining*, pp. 28–59.

12. The Taft-Hartley Act stipulated that the NLRB shall not decide that a craft unit is inappropriate "on the ground that a different unit has been established by prior Board determination, unless a majority of the employees in the proposed craft unit vote against separate unit representation." The Board thereafter placed less emphasis upon bargaining history and eventually adopted the American Potash doctrine in 1954 under which a craft group's petition for an election would be honored if the workers formed a true craft group, if the petitioning union had traditionally represented that craft, and if the workers were not in any of four industries (steel, aluminum, lumbering, and wet milling) that the Board had decided were too integrated in their production processes to permit craft severance.

13. There actually is no multiemployer contract in the electrical-manufacturing industry, but the point is that such a contract would be perfectly legal if the parties should want one.

14. Labor does not approve, however, of the policy exception that forbids unions to coerce employers to combine election units. Surprisingly few employers challenged unions before the NLRB on this point until recent years, presumably because most employers faced with a demand to broaden the bargaining unit either agreed on its desirability (to promote stability) or were strong enough to reject the demand with no help from the Board. But the rise of "coalition bargaining" in the mid-1960s—in which several different unions, each with representation rights in different plants of the same company, attempted to form a common front in bargaining with that company—led to several NLRB cases. See George H. Hildebrand, "Cloudy Future for Coalition Bargaining," *Harvard Business Review*, November–December, 1968, pp. 114–128.

15. Although the hot-cargo exemption for the construction industry is limited to agreements concerning work done at the building site, this has not prevented some construction unions from barring materials prefabricated off the building site. In a controversial case in 1967, the Supreme Court upheld an NLRB ruling that "will not handle" clauses are legal when the union intent is to preserve jobs traditionally performed by its members rather than to disrupt relations between a primary employer and his suppliers. In this case a carpenters' local, citing such a provision in its contract, refused to handle prefitted doors; the employer returned the doors to the manufacturer and obtained unfitted doors which the carpenters fitted at the site; and the manufacturers' association charged, among other things, that the union had violated the hot-cargo ban. In a 5 to 4 decision, the Court rejected that charge.

16. Actually the Supreme Court remanded the coal case for a new trial because the trial court had admitted evidence concerning the joint efforts of the union and the major companies to persuade the Secretary of Labor to set a high Walsh-Healey minimum wage in government coal contracts. The Court held that such lobbying with a government agency was legitimate activity which could not be considered evidence of an illegal conspiracy. In the new trial, the federal district court decided that the union did not violate the Sherman Act, but the principle enunciated by the Supreme Court still stands: if the evidence had supported the existence of the alleged agreement between the union and the major companies, the union would have forfeited its usual exemption from antitrust prosecution.

17. Kurt L. Hanslowe, *The Emerging Law of Labor Relations in Public Employment*, Cornell University, N. Y. State School of Industrial and Labor Relations, Ithaca, N.Y., 1967, pp. 49–50. This section draws heavily upon this excellent source.

18. The same, p. 15.

19. Jack Stieber, "Collective Bargaining in the Public Sector," in Lloyd Ulman (ed.), *Challenges to Collective Bargaining*, Prentice-Hall, Englewood Cliffs, N.J., 1967, p. 82.

20. Another unresolved question is whether the government may legally agree to be bound by the decision of an arbitrator. On the one hand, a court might well rule that this would be an improper delegation of legislative or executive authority. On the other hand, it might be held that the arbitration of a new contract is in principle no different from the current practice of arbitration by private neutrals of minor grievances or, if the arbitrators were specially

designated judges instead of private citizens, such a "labor court" might be accepted as the equivalent of a court of claims in which private citizens can now receive awards binding upon the government.

21. There are some exceptions, such as employees of TVA and the Government Printing Office, who have long bargained over wages, and a large group of blue-collar workers whose wages must by law equal those paid for comparable private work in their area, a principle permitting some limited negotiation. On the other hand, the Kennedy Executive order of 1962 severely limited even those nonwage issues which could be negotiated at the agency level, declaring that agency heads retain the right to direct, hire, fire, discipline, or lay off employees, to maintain efficiency of operations, and to make many similar decisions "in accordance with applicable laws and regulations"—a sweeping management-rights clause that many private employers would envy.

CHAPTER 9

THE ROLE OF LAW IN
UNION–MEMBERSHIP
RELATIONS

The creation of organized pockets of private power raises a second issue, it will be recalled— the question of the relation of these private "governments" to the people whom they govern or over whom they exercise control, in this case, the workers whom they represent or claim to represent. On this issue the 1935 Wagner Act had little to say explicitly, and what it did say on the whole strengthened the power of union governments in their own jurisdictions. Thus it specifically made legal, for the first time in statutory law, the closed shop and the union shop—those devices which obligate an employer to hire only members of the union or which require workers, once hired, to join the union. These forms of "union security," as they are known, place considerable power in the hands of union administrations since, under their terms, the holding of a job becomes dependent on obtaining and retaining union membership. (As we shall note, limitations on this power were imposed by law in 1947.)

Compulsory representation

At the same time that the Wagner Act strengthened internal union governments in this manner, it did impose on them one major obligation once they were chosen as the exclusive representative in an NLRB-conducted election—that they represent fairly and impartially all the employees in the bargaining unit without respect to whether they were members of the union; or if a union-security provision was subsequently negotiated requiring union membership, that it represent fairly all employees without respect to their past preference for another union and also those employees to whom, for whatever reasons, it might refuse to accord membership rights.

As the Supreme Court declared in one instance, "The duties of a bargaining agent selected under the terms of the Act extend beyond the mere representation of the interests of its own group members. By its selection as bargaining representative, it has become the agent of all the employees, charged with the responsibility of representing their interests fairly and impartially."[1]

If the act had little to say explicitly on the subject of the relation of the union to its membership, there was, however, a great deal said by implication. First, the whole machinery by which workers could choose what union they wished to represent them, if any, was not simply a device protecting union organizers against the opposition of employers; it was equally a device for giving workers their free expression of union preference without respect to what jurisdictions had been "awarded" to particular unions by the labor federations. If a group of electricians wished to be represented by the machinists union, it was for them to say, not the AFL which sought to define nonconflicting jurisdictions.

This freedom of employee choice was watered down in two ways, however:

1. By the Board's contract-bar rule which we

encountered in discussing representative elections —a union which is certified and which negotiates a valid contract for a period of up to three years can retain its agency role for that length of time without being subject to challenge by another union which the employees might later decide they prefer. The Board's rationale here is that freedom of employee choice must be balanced against stability of the bargaining relationship.

2. By agreement among themselves, unions affiliated with the AFL-CIO now will not challenge a sister union which is already certified. Thus if a group of electricians who are represented by the IBEW decide that they prefer to be represented by the Machinists, and the present contract is on the point of expiring so that no contract-bar rule applies, the Machinists union would refuse to allow itself to be chosen. The employees would then have to remain with the union with which they are dissatisfied, or seek its decertification, leaving them without any representation, or form an independent union of their own (which would probably reduce their bargaining power), or turn to a union unaffiliated with the AFL-CIO, such as the Teamsters or District 50 of the Mine Workers.

A third respect in which unions might frustrate freedom of employee choice was subsequently removed by the Taft-Hartley and Landrum-Griffin pieces of legislation. Before these new provisions were in effect, however, it was legally possible for a union to picket an employer to force his recognition of that union even if his employees had voted in favor of another union or had voted not to be represented at all. This is no longer permissible.

The Taft-Hartley legislation dealt with the second theme—the relationship of the union to those whom it represents or seeks to represent— in a number of additional ways, among other things providing an opportunity for workers to petition for an election to *decertify* a union which previously they have voted in but with which they have subsequently become dissatisfied. But perhaps the most important respect in which the law modified the power of the union vis-à-vis members and workers was to limit the use of the closed shop and union shop.

Union security

For approximately 150 years one of the thorniest issues in labor relations has been the insistence by unions that, in organized shops, all workers must join the union. Judicial disfavor blocked the spread of this practice for many years, as we saw in the previous chapter. Employer opposition sometimes took the form of yellow-dog contracts —a type of work contract between the employer and individual employee under which the latter agreed that, as a condition of employment, he would not join a labor union. The use of such contracts expanded, and when Congress made some effort to outlaw them on the railroads, the Supreme Court ruled in 1908 that it could not impair an employer's freedom of contract in this respect, invoking the "due-process" clause of the Fifth Amendment to strike down the legislation. Seven years later, the Court added that the Fourteenth Amendment precluded state legislative action designed to curb the use of yellow-dog contracts.

Despite these legal handicaps, in some industries—notably those characterized by small firms —some form of closed-shop or preferential agreement took root. This was true in printing, construction, and after 1910 in clothing, for example. In general, however, the open-shop campaign and the yellow-dog contract proved effective deterrents to the principle of union security.

The tide turned in 1932 when the Norris-LaGuardia Act made yellow-dog contracts unenforceable—an action which was not this time struck down by the Supreme Court. And in 1935 the Wagner Act specifically recognized the legitimacy of closed-shop agreements entered into by unions certified to be exclusive representatives. The increase in union strength during this period, coupled with such legal assistance, led the unions to initiate widespread demands for either the closed shop (under which a man, in order to be hired, must already be a member of the union and usually is referred to the employer by the union) or the union shop (under which an employer may hire anyone he pleases, whether a member of the union or not, but within some specified period, usually thirty days, the new hire must join the union). Employers generally continued to oppose union-security provisions, however, and the new law did not oblige them to grant what the unions requested.

By the time of World War II, many observers felt that the issue of union security was perhaps the most pressing problem in industrial relations. With the advent of war and the necessity of curbing strikes so that vital war production would not be lost, some formula had to be devised by which the unions, pressing for closed shops or union shops, and employers, equally strong in their resistance, could be reconciled. To meet this need, there came into being the "maintenance-of-membership" shop.

Under this arrangement, a nice piece of improvisation called into existence by necessity, the unions were given the guarantee that those who were members at the time they signed an agreement would remain members for the lifetime of the contract, as a condition of their continued employment. An exception was made, however: A short period, usually fifteen or thirty days, was provided, during which any unionist who wished to resign from the union might do so; but after that escape period, all union members were frozen in their union membership as long as they continued to work at the company. New hires and employees who were not union members were not, however, compelled to join. Unions were thus released from the necessity of having to maintain the adherence of their members during a period when their activity in gaining benefits was necessarily curbed by wartime controls. This maintenance of membership was granted to a union by the War Labor Board virtually for the asking.

With the end of the war, unions embarked upon a campaign to convert maintenance-of-membership provisions into standard closed- or union-shop agreements, while employers, with equal determination, sought to remove even this vestige of compulsory union membership which had been forced upon them as a wartime expedient. The battle lines were drawn.

Restrictions on union security

Precisely at this juncture, however, came the passage of the Taft-Hartley Act, by which the legal right of unions to seek security provisions was sharply curtailed. Four limitations were imposed.

1. The closed shop was outlawed altogether in interstate commerce. No longer could a union lawfully seek to make union membership a previous condition of employment, within the federal jurisdiction.

2. A union-shop agreement was still permissible, but a union could not negotiate such an agreement until a majority of all employees in the appropriate bargaining unit had, in secret balloting conducted by the NLRB, specifically authorized the union to negotiate such an agreement. This authorization did not, however, compel the employer to grant a union shop if a majority expressed approval. The balloting simply authorized the union to make the demand in collective bargaining, but whether the demand was granted depended on the normal play of relative bargaining powers.

3. Even if an employer conceded the union shop, requiring membership as a condition of continuing employment after an initial waiting period of thirty days, the union's rights under such a provision were restricted. Previously, if a man lost his union membership for any reason (because he failed to keep up with his dues, or because he was expelled for crossing a picket line, or because he supported a rival union, and so on), the union could demand his discharge. Continued union membership was a necessary condition for continued employment. But the Taft-Hartley Act specifies that the only reason a union can ask for a man's discharge, under a union-shop provision, is that he has failed to pay the normal initiation fee or the regular dues. If he is expelled from the union for any other reason, the loss of his union membership does not mean loss of job. As long as he pays his dues, he conforms to his obligation to the union as far as the law is concerned. Basically, this provision means that a worker must help to support the union financially but cannot be forced to assist it or comply with its rulings in any other way.

4. Recognizing that there were employers in some states who objected strenuously to even this watered-down form of union security, the legislators provided that if any state passed a more

restrictive law on this point, it would supersede the federal law. States' rights were to take precedence over federal action in those states which chose to deal more harshly with the unions, but only in those states.

This last provision led to intensified political activity in the area of labor relations. In virtually every state, employers organized to put across legislation outlawing all forms of union security. These measures were popularized under the term of "right-to-work" laws, a name which the unions found particularly offensive because, they claimed, it gained support for such legislation from some individuals who mistakenly thought it guaranteed employment. It was, of course, the right to work without the necessity of joining a union holding representation rights that employers really had in mind. Bills introduced into state legislatures commonly included three central provisions, to which others were frequently added: (1) No employee could be required to become or to remain a member of a labor union as a condition of employment; (2) no employee could be required to pay dues or their equivalent to a union as a condition of employment; and (3) any collective agreement containing such provisions was unlawful. Penalties were usually provided. Laws of this nature have been passed in a number of states—twenty by 1968, most of them in the Southern, Plains, and Mountain areas.[2]

At times, however, despite federal and state law, employers have interposed no objection to continuing traditional closed-shop hiring practices, even though any provision to that effect has necessarily been dropped from the agreement. The only way in which such evasion of the law is likely to come to light is in the event that a nonunion employee files a charge with the Board that he has been discriminated against because of nonmembership in a union. It seems fairly certain that such bootleg closed-shop arrangements must occur frequently.

In states which have banned all forms of union security, such bootlegging extends to the union shop as well as the closed shop. Although formerly a company may have operated under a contractual arrangement that every employee hired had to join the union within thirty days,

when such an arrangement is no longer permissible a more informal approach may be adopted. A new employee is not advised that he will be required to join the union, but at the time of his hiring the personnel office may give him a union application card and point out that virtually all the employees are members, or that employees "customarily" join.

The Taft-Hartley Act, as we have just noted, required employees to authorize a certified union to negotiate a union shop before it could even present such a demand to the employer. The obvious reason for this provision was a legislative belief that most employees did not want compulsory union membership, that union-security clauses were inserted into collective agreements only for the benefit of union bosses, and that the latter's autocratic power could be curbed if greater control were given to the union membership itself.

Over a four-year period, more than 46,000 union-shop authorization elections were conducted by the NLRB. To the surprise of sponsors of these election procedures, in almost 45,000 cases employees authorized their unions to negotiate compulsory-membership agreements. The elections, in total, drew a surprisingly high participation of about 85 percent of those eligible to vote, and of these, 91 percent cast their ballots for a union shop. Employers opposed to compulsory union membership found themselves embarrassed. Such overwhelming expressions of worker support for the union shop made it more difficult to reject the union's demand for it. During this period the number of union-shop agreements in the United States rose considerably, and some experts attribute their spread in part to this demonstration that rank-and-file workers as well as union leadership often favored such provisions.

The time of Board personnel was being occupied with the conduct of elections which seemed to have little point in view of the almost predictable response, and the expense involved seemed wasted money. In consequence, a 1951 amendment to the act eliminated elections held for the purpose of authorizing unions to negotiate union-shop agreements; however, it retained elections to *de*authorize union-shop agreements, which may be petitioned for by dissatisfied employees within a unit.

As one might expect, neither unions nor employers are satisfied with the present legal status of union-security provisions. Their arguments—which are detailed in the appendix to this chapter—still tend to run in the extreme terms usually reserved for matters of principle. Unions stress that, as the duly elected representative of all the employees in a unit, they are owed the support of all those in the unit and should be able to expect their reasonable compliance with majority-determined rules. This is possible only through some form of compulsory relationship which, they maintain, does not differ from the compulsory support which Democrats give Republican governments, and vice versa, in the form of tax payments and conformance to majority-determined laws. Employers emphasize the impropriety of compelling an individual to join or support private organizations of which he may disapprove.

We can easily recognize here the same basic arguments about the relationship of the organization to the individual members who compose it which we have continually encountered since the Cordwainers' case of 1806. It appears, however, that the working out of this problem will not come by accepting or rejecting a "fundamental" principle but by effecting a compromise which recognizes some validity in both points of view. The Taft-Hartley Act has moved in this direction by permitting the union shop but guarding against its possible abuse.

Nevertheless, some neutral observers have questioned whether the Taft-Hartley limitation on the union's right to discipline a member by restricting its right to secure his discharge to the single case of nonpayment of dues, under a union-security provision, may prove to be adequate protection to the individual worker. Although the union may have no legal right to insist on a member's discharge for other cause, an employer seeking to maintain good relations with the union may be willing to comply with its demand for the firing of a worker who has "made trouble" for the incumbent administration. It is not difficult for an employer to find *some* reason for dissatisfaction with employee performance or to make the same kind of "constructive discharge" which we encountered in discussing unfair labor practices—only in this instance the union does not

plead the worker's case but is, on the contrary, responsible for his misfortune. We shall have occasion to return to this matter after we have examined the next piece of labor legislation, the Landrum-Griffin Act, which came in 1959.

The Landrum-Griffin Act

For many years prior to passage of the Landrum-Griffin Act, it was known that, in some labor unions, the membership was prey to both gross and subtle forms of exploitation by entrenched officials, that democratic procedures for calling the exploiters to task were often deficient or lacking at both the local and national levels, and that civil judicial remedies for such malpractices were uncertain and not without their own dangers of retaliation when employed. Periodically, some particularly malodorous situation would be exposed and would evoke public protest. Even those favorably disposed toward labor unions, such as the American Civil Liberties Union, had remarked at some length and for some time on the need for greater democracy within labor-union governments. It was not, however, until the two-year hearings of the McClellan Committee had paraded across the congressional stage a collection of unsavory union officials, most of whom had been handpicked to make the Committee's point, that sufficient steam was generated to ensure passage of a bill designed to curb internal union excesses. If the public tended to lump all unions together and conclude that a general housecleaning was in order despite the relatively small number of unions directly involved in the Senate hearings, even among the experts there was a widespread belief that some controls over internal union practices were called for. Indeed, that belief was shared, up to a point, by officials of the AFL-CIO.

Out of the number of bills which were introduced to meet the felt need, the one which was finally translated into legislation was the Landrum-Griffin Act. Like the Taft-Hartley Act, it did not so much modify the labor legislation which had preceded it as add to that body of law. Its provisions did tighten up on secondary boycotts, as we have already seen, and they clarified the boundary lines between federal and state administration of the subject matter coming under the NLRB and provided that striking employees would be qualified within certain limitations to vote in representation elections. But the main thrust of the new act was to provide a rather sweeping set of rules governing the relationship between union governments and their constituencies. It was concerned with the use of private pooled power vis-à-vis the people on whose behalf it was presumed to be exercised.

The official title of the new piece of legislation was the Labor-Management Reporting and Disclosure Act of 1959, which might suggest that it is chiefly directed to data collection. One might be justified in believing, however, that it had been so named only in a rather heavy-handed attempt at irony. The fact is that only one of its seven sections deals with reporting requirements. The importance of this one section is not to be minimized. It obligates every labor union, local and national alike, to file annual financial reports disclosing not only income and balance-sheet data but also specific information on officer salaries, reimbursed expenses, and loans, and to make this information available to union members, who are also assured access to books and records to the extent necessary to verify such reports. "Conflict-of-interest" transactions must also be reported to the Secretary of Labor, whose office (not the NLRB) is the administrative and enforcement agency for purposes of the act. Information concerning dues, initiation fees, and special assessments must be provided.

The body of the law, however, relates to internal union affairs. There are four main sections: (1) a "bill of rights" for union members; (2) provisions for the conduct of union elections; (3) limitation on national union "trusteeships" over local unions; and (4) the spelling out of fiduciary responsibilities of union officers. Like the other legislation which we have examined, the detail here is too great to permit extended discussion. The most we can do is to get a general comprehension of the purpose of these four sections and why they were believed to be needed.

The bill of rights

The bill of rights specifies that every member of a union shall have an equal right to participate in union meetings and elections. He is entitled to freedom of speech and association with other members in discussions involving union affairs, both in and out of union meetings. Dues and initiation fees can be increased and special assessments can be levied only by majority consent. Individuals may bring suit against their union, after having first exhausted any internal remedies available to them, providing that the process does not require longer than four months. Perhaps most important, "No member of any labor organization may be fined, suspended, expelled, or otherwise disciplined [by a union] except for nonpayment of dues ... unless such member has been (A) served with written specific charges; (B) given a reasonable time to prepare his defense; (C) afforded a full and fair hearing."

These may sound like elementary privileges. Why is it necessary for federal legislation to provide for them?

The answer is twofold. First, although many union constitutions provide for most of the liberties listed, the provision is frequently couched in general and ambiguous terms or subject to additional provisions which weaken the effect. Particularly relevant is the customary constitutional injunction against any resort to the civil courts until all appeals procedures within the union are exhausted—without any limit as to time. Since the final appeals body is customarily the convention, and many conventions meet only every four years, a disciplined member might have to wait that long before he would be—constitutionally—privileged to have his case reviewed by an outside authority.

Moreover, courts have frequently upheld such provisions in union constitutions. By and large, they have tended to look on labor unions as voluntary associations and to limit their own judicial function to interpreting the constitution which the member presumably accepted when he voluntarily joined.[3]

One New York court stated that "the general policy of the courts is one of non-intervention with the internal affairs of labor organizations." As reasoned by the Oregon Supreme Court [in a suit brought by a member], there was no need for intervention, since "a union may, by its constitution, provide an exclusive and final method of resolving all internal disputes, including questions of constitutional interpretation." A Michigan court made the following unusually strong statement in declining jurisdiction over an election complaint: "It is not the business of an equity court to assure union members that their union affairs shall be conducted in a thoroughly democratic manner."

The reason for this judicial attitude lay in the fact that, once a court moved outside the framework of the union's own constitution, it lacked any specific standards, derivable from any relevant body of precedents, which it could apply. Nevertheless, in particularly flagrant cases of miscarriage of justice or abuse of power, the courts would sometimes intervene. Occasionally they would do so under the pretext of having found some procedural defect in the union's action. Occasionally they would look behind the surface facts at the reality of the situation, noting in some instances that further compliance with internal union remedies would be pointless since the result would be predictable.

That civil law did not provide a satisfactory protection for the rights of individual members had already been recognized by the AFL-CIO when, in 1957, it adopted its own Ethical Practice Code on Union Democratic Processes. While expressing pride in the record of the labor movement generally in this respect, it admitted that "a few unions do not adequately provide for these basic elements of democratic practice," and went on to specify most of the provisions which the Landrum-Griffin Act was later to write into law. The most notable omission was the four-month limitation on exhaustion of internal remedy. The AFL-CIO code concluded: "When constitutional amendments or changes in internal administrative procedures are necessary to comply with the standards herein set forth, such amendments and changes should be undertaken at the earliest practicable time."

Despite the agreement in principle between the labor federation and the new law, AFL-CIO officials were unhappy with some aspects of its bill of rights. Their chief objection centered on the right of members to enter civil suit against the union for alleged infringement of their freedoms. This, it was feared, constituted "an invitation to litigation" by dissident members, of whom there are some in every organization, which would be a source of harassment to officers even when engaged in entirely legitimate union activity. So far, these fears do not seem to have been borne out.

In the first seven years under the new law, about 725 private suits were filed by union members against their unions or union officers, and a majority of them charged violations of the law's bill of rights.[4] For example, union members have brought suit when disciplined for the following offenses:

> . . . "noncooperation"; display of religious articles in offices of the union; libel and slander; creating "dissension among the members"; . . . filing charges with the National Labor Relations Board; "treason"; working behind an authorized picket line; picketing a union hall in protest against actions of the local leadership; . . . offering a resolution vividly criticizing union leadership; and campaigning for [a right-to-work law] in California.[5]

No boxscore is available on the outcome of all the civil suits filed against unions under the Landrum-Griffin Act, but this sampling of "union crimes" shows why Congress believed it necessary to guarantee, within unions, such elementary privileges as free speech and the right of accused individuals to be served with specific charges.

On the other hand, consider the controversial case of *Salzhandler v. Caputo*,[6] in which the financial secretary of a painters' local accused the local's president of having his hand in the union till. A union trial body found this allegation to be false and decreed that Salzhandler could remain a union member but that he should be removed from his part-time position as financial secretary and not be permitted for a period of five years to attend union meetings, to vote on any union matter, or to be a candidate for any union office. When Salzhandler charged a violation of Landrum-Griffin's bill of rights, a federal district court dismissed his complaint, finding that his statements had indeed been false and that the act's guarantee of free speech does not include the right to libel union officers. Upon appeal, however, a circuit court reversed this decision, holding that the union president could sue Salzhandler for libel if he chose but the union itself could not punish any member for spreading his opinions regarding the union's officers, "regardless of whether his statements were true or false." Here we encounter again the difficulties of interpreting freedom of speech in a labor-market context. In union-organizing campaigns, we have seen, the NLRB must balance the employer's right to criticize unions against the worker's right to vote free of his employer's threats or promises. Now, in internal union affairs, the courts must balance the member's right to criticize his officers against the union's right (also explicitly set forth in Landrum-Griffin) to enforce "reasonable rules as to the responsibility of every member toward the organization as an institution." Is libel of union officials a reasonable basis for internal discipline, or is it so easily abused to smother legitimate dissent that the courts should, as in *Salzhandler,* forbid its use by unions?

Questions have also been raised about the effectiveness of the act's guarantee of a "full and fair hearing" before expulsion or other discipline can be imposed. The courts can move, and have done so, against blatant bias such as including on a trial body the very officials who brought charges against the accused member. But suppose the dispute "is one which, by its very nature, will have an impact on the entire range of membership from which a trial board may be selected," or is one in which "members of the trial board, though themselves not directly concerned, may be entirely conscious of the fact that officers holding some control over their economic lives are intimately concerned with the outcome of the dispute"?[7] In these situations it might be argued that a truly neutral jury of union members can never be found, but by that test what remedy could be ordered by a court? In the following chapter we shall see that a few unions have voluntarily sought to meet this problem by the designation of outside appeals boards, but the law itself does not require this safeguard.

Election procedures

The second major section of the Landrum-Griffin Act governing relations between union government and union constituencies deals with election procedures. Here the problem lay in the attempts of some union administrations to eliminate opposition to their reelection by such devices as

prohibiting the circulation of campaign literature without their consent, threatening discipline for "causing dissension" or "creating disharmony," preventing membership participation in nominations by inadequate notice or by control over procedures, expelling opposition candidates or their principal supporters, and manipulating or rigging the vote. In some unions, elections have been held so infrequently that memberships have been effectively disenfranchised. Moreover, the same judicial attitude which often rendered ineffective a member's protest to the civil courts concerning disciplinary actions operated with respect to complaints concerning irregular election practices.

The 1959 act seeks to meet abuses such as these in part through the protective provisions of the bill of rights but also through measures dealing specifically with union elections. It requires that national officers be elected, by secret ballot, no less frequently than every five years; the officers of intermediate bodies such as joint councils, no less than every four years; and those of local unions, every three years. A reasonable opportunity must be given to nominate candidates, and the union must comply with reasonable requests to distribute campaign literature at the candidate's expense, with all candidates receiving equal treatment as to the cost of such distribution. Notice of an election must be mailed to each member no less than fifteen days before it is scheduled to take place. Union funds may not be used to promote the candidacy of any individual. Ballots and other election records must be preserved for one year.

Complaints with respect to violation of any of these provisions may be addressed to the Secretary of Labor, who can act through the federal district courts to declare an election invalid if the complaint is sustained. In the first seven years of the act's life, approximately 1,300 election complaints were filed with the Secretary, of which about three-quarters proved to be "not actionable" upon investigation—either because no violations of the law were found or because those found did not affect the outcome of the disputed elections. In 110 cases during this period, however, the Secretary went to the courts to correct alleged violations, and in 250 other cases, he secured the voluntary compliance of unions in correcting violations, usually by holding new elections under the supervision of the Department of Labor.[8] A Department official has described some of the serious offenses which these investigations brought to light:[9]

Ballots had been printed in excess of those required in the election and some were removed from the printer's package before the time for mailing. Voted ballots were returned to the custody of one of the candidates, who had possession of them for a considerable period before the time for counting of the ballots.

Another election investigation determined that union funds derived from dues and assessments were used to pay workers for promoting the candidacy of incumbent officers seeking reelection. In this same case it was found that a number of ineligible persons were permitted to vote in the election.

In still another case, a number of members in good standing were disqualified as candidates for office. This was contrary to the provision of the union's own constitution, which also was violated in that local officials permitted the national president to endorse certain candidates in the local's newspaper. Certain incumbent candidates were permitted to distribute campaign material, while this privilege was denied to their opponents.

Violations, we have found, also sometimes are based on the ugly practice of ballot stuffing. In one of our major cases, entire batches of ballots obviously marked by the same person with the same pencil were cast for the winning candidate. From the facts, it was evident that these votes could not have been attributed to any eligible voters, since there were considerably more votes than voters. In a more sophisticated case of ballot manipulation, the investigation which led to the filing of a suit indicates that, because of the lack of adequate safeguards, ballots were substituted after the polls had closed.

Nor have these shenanigans been confined to isolated local elections. In the 1964 election for the presidency of the International Union of Electrical Workers, the official union tabulation awarded victory to the long-time incumbent, James B. Carey, by a margin of 2,193 votes, but a recount of the same ballots by the Department of Labor showed that Carey actually lost by 23,316 votes. In the 1966 election of officers in the National Maritime Union, the issues were more subtle. Prior to the passage of the Landrum-Griffin Act in 1959, the NMU constitution declared that any member was eligible to hold any office if he had been in good standing during the one year preceding the election, but beginning in 1960 a series of amendments tightened the union's constitution in a fashion hardly intended by Congress. One set of amendments introduced new eligibility rules, each plausible in itself—such as requiring five years of good standing for any candidate, sailing time in each of the five years preceding nomination (or an equivalent time ashore in holding a union office), and four years spent in a lower office before being eligible for a national office. Taken together, however, these new rules meant that fewer than 1 percent of the NMU's 47,500 members were eligible to run for national office in 1966. Yet another constitutional amendment had reduced the number of elective office positions by over one-half, permitting the NMU president to appoint a group of officials who, under Landrum-Griffin, should have been elected. For these reasons, a federal court set aside the union's 1966 election and directed the Secretary of Labor to conduct another free of those violations. (The incumbent officers won again in the new election conducted in 1969.[10])

By far the most extensive investigation of a union election was that of the bitter contest in 1969 between W. A. Boyle and Joseph Yablonski for the presidency of the United Mine Workers. Boyle defeated Yablonski but, following the murder of Yablonski three weeks after the election, the Labor Department launched an investigation of the election that involved 200 federal agents and 4,400 interviews at a cost of $500,000. On the basis of this study, the government went into court in 1970 under the Landrum-Griffin Act and moved to set aside the election results on the ground that the incumbent union administration, headed by Boyle, had violated in several ways the members' right to a fair election. (At this writing, the case was still before the courts.)

One other consequence of the act's election provisions has been to oblige numerous unions to modify their constitutions. The International

Union of Operating Engineers, one of the unions to which the McClellan Committee had paid particular attention, revised its constitution at its 1960 convention to give voting rights, for the first time, to nearly half its members, who had been enrolled in so-called "branch locals" which had not been entitled to a vote.

One of the more debatable provisions of the act affects union elections but not in a procedural way. No person who is, or within the preceding five years has been, a member of the Communist party, or who, within the preceding five years, has been convicted of one of a long list of specified crimes or of violation of the reporting or trusteeship provisions of the act itself, is permitted to serve in any official union capacity. When tested before the courts, however, the clause relating to Communist party membership was declared unconstitutional as a bill of attainder.[11]

Trusteeships

A third major respect in which the Landrum-Griffin legislation sought to reduce the power of union organizations vis-à-vis their members was in the area of trusteeships imposed on local unions. A trusteeship is an instrument for depriving the subordinate body of its autonomy and placing it under the control of agents usually appointed by the national office. It is a device which experience has shown to be necessary under certain circumstances, as when a national union must protect both its good name and its members' interests from local misgovernment or corruption, or when a local union has shown itself unwilling to live up to its collective-bargaining responsibilities. But there have also been occasions when trusteeships have been imposed to silence opposition to union officers or their policies or to make a raid on a local treasury. In some cases local unions have been deprived of the right to govern themselves for extended periods of time. The constitutions of a number of unions give the national office power to determine when a trusteeship shall be instituted and when removed, sometimes without provision for any form of hearing, or with inadequate provisions.[12]

The hearings and findings of the Senate Select Committee on Improper Activities in the Labor-Management Field (the McClellan Committee) . . . focused primarily on trusteeships in three international unions, the Teamsters (Ind.), the Bakery Workers (Ind.), and the Operating Engineers. It also treated to a lesser extent trusteeships in the Allied Industrial Workers, the Meat Cutters, and the Jewelry Workers. It was found that in the Operating Engineers, 12 locals representing 20 per cent of the membership were in trusteeship and that 7 of these had been in trusteeship for over 20 years and 2 for over 29 years. Roughly 13 per cent of all Teamster (Ind.) locals were in trusteeship, some for more than 15 years. James R. Hoffa [Teamster president and a favorite target of the Committee] was personally the trustee of 17 of these locals. Detailed investigations of a number of locals of the surveyed internationals revealed situations of impositions of trusteeship at gunpoint, looting of a local treasury by the trustees, and the placing of a dissident local under trusteeship on the pretext that such control was necessary for the conduct of an organizing drive. In one case, two local officers under indictment for extortion were appointed as business agents of the local after imposition of a trusteeship.

The Landrum-Griffin Act recognizes four legitimate purposes for establishing trusteeships: correcting corruption or financial malpractice; assuring the performance of collective-bargaining agreements; restoring democratic procedures; and "otherwise carrying out the legitimate objectives" of labor unions. (Included in the latter catchall category are caretaker trusteeships, the most numerous type, which may be installed when a local union has become inactive due to the closing of a plant or a sudden loss of leadership, as through illness or death, or because it is a new local still inexperienced in the conduct of its own affairs.)

The law provides that whenever a trusteeship is instituted for one of these reasons, the union must report the circumstances and the degree of participation which has been left to local members in the selection of delegates to conventions and other policy-making bodies. Unless delegates from trusteed locals are elected by secret balloting of the membership, their votes are not valid. No more than the normal per capita tax and legitimate assessments may be paid out of the local treasury to the national union, except upon bona fide dissolution. A trusteeship established in conformity with these provisions and the procedural requirements of the union's constitution (including authorization or ratification of the trusteeship after a fair hearing before the union's executive board) will be presumed effective for eighteen months. During that period it is not subject to challenge except upon clear proof of bad faith. After the expiration of the eighteen-month period, the trusteeship will be presumed invalid unless it can be shown by convincing proof that continuation is necessary for one of the purposes specified in the act.

These provisions have effected a drastic reduction in both the duration and number of trusteeships. Of the approximately 500 in operation when the law was enacted in 1959, only 19 were still active in 1966. All but one of the nineteen involved districts of the United Mine Workers which have been under the national union's direction since the 1930s, and the Secretary of Labor has challenged their legality in the courts. In addition, various unions have established new trusteeships under Landrum-Griffin, but in 1966 the total number in operation was only 234.[13]

Fiscal responsibility

The fourth major section regulating the relationship between the governed and the governing in labor unions deals with the fiduciary responsibilities of officers. This was an area in which four ethical practice codes of the AFL-CIO had earlier set out desirable standards to which their affiliates were expected to conform. The act first reminds union officers of their financial stewardship on behalf of the members and enjoins them to avoid any financial dealings in which there is a conflict of interest. If any officer is alleged to have violated this trust and the responsible union authorities fail to act to recover funds which have been misappropriated or misused, any member may institute a suit to that effect in either federal or state courts. Any expenses which a member in-

curs in so doing may be provided for, in the court's discretion, out of funds recovered.

Except in small unions whose annual receipts are less than $5,000, every union official must be bonded in an amount not less than 10 percent of the funds he or his predecessor handled in the preceding year, ranging from no less than $1,000 for a local officer up to no more than $500,000 for a national officer. A union cannot make loans to an officer totaling more than $2,000, nor can it undertake to pay on his behalf any fine to which he may be subject as a result of violation of the act.

In addition to the private suits which union members can institute to recover misused funds, the government can bring criminal actions for violation of these fiduciary provisions. In fiscal 1966, for example, the Justice Department secured convictions of sixty-one officers or employees of unions for embezzlement, falsifying records, and other violations of these provisions, and indictments were issued against another twenty-four officers or employees.[14]

Evaluation of internal union controls

These are the chief provisions of this first piece of legislation to deal explicitly with internal union government. Several observations may be made with respect to the effort. First, while it is true that "democracy cannot be legislated," as opponents of the act have argued, it is also true that legislation can facilitate application of and practice in the institutions of democracy. It would be equally logical for those making this statement to argue that good-faith collective bargaining cannot be legislated, but the Wagner Act went a long way toward inculcating practices which have led to rather widespread acceptance by employers of an institution to which most of them were originally opposed. It seems an entirely reasonable congressional judgment that labor unions had arrived at a stage of sufficient survival ability and power so that abuses of that power could be remedied without threatening survival. Granted that not many of the thousands of labor unions in the United States actually engage in the practices proscribed, there has been evidence of enough transgression to warrant preventive measures. While there may be legitimate objection to specific provisions, the intent of the legislation seems well founded.

Second, the act can help to check the worst internal abuses of union power, but the most effective prevention lies in the hands of the unions themselves. To the extent they recognize the legitimacy of society's concern with their exercise of power over members and other affected workers, they can take action on their own initiative to bring their own procedures into closer coincidence with the values of the society which protects their existence. We shall have occasion to examine this issue further in the next chapter. At the same time, society itself must recognize that this is by no means a simple matter; there is room for legitimate probing and questioning about the extent to which traditional procedures associated with "democratic" government are directly transferable to labor unions. Are they any more applicable to union government than to corporate government, for example?

Third, we can distinguish between two legal approaches to labor unionism. One may be called the trusteeship doctrine. This maintains that a union's responsibility runs to those whom it represents. A relationship of trust lies between it and its members, or between it and the unit of employees a majority of whom have chosen it as agent. The union's responsibilities as trustee are discharged when it faithfully represents all to whom it bears an agency relationship. This is the philosophy which the Taft-Hartley Act touched on (by its restriction of a union's use of power to compel the discharge of an employee) and the philosophy which the Landrum-Griffin Act wholly adopted.

There is a second philosophy of the relationship of labor unions to their constituencies which may be called the public-utility doctrine. This maintains not only that a union must be responsive to the wishes and welfare of its members or of those whom it represents for collective-bargaining purposes. It maintains, further, that any person whom it represents should also have the right to become a member and to participate equally in the conduct of its affairs. This more sweeping

doctrine Congress has steadfastly refused to incorporate in any labor legislation. It remained for the Civil Rights Act of 1964 to introduce this principle by providing that it shall be an "unfair employment practice for a labor organization (1) to exclude or expel from its membership, or otherwise to discriminate against, any individual because of his race, color, religion, sex, or national origin," (2) to classify its membership in any way which would have that effect, and (3) to attempt to influence an employer to discriminate against an individual on any of the proscribed grounds. Enforcement of this provision is left, first, to any existing agency in the state where the alleged offense occurs, and second, if no such agency exists or if it fails to provide relief, to a newly created national Equal Employment Opportunity Commission whose findings are enforceable in the federal courts. This provision goes considerably beyond the Landrum-Griffin legislation in requiring unions to surrender the legal fiction of being voluntary associations or clubs and to recognize that their exclusive-representation role is conferred on them by public law and that it imposes on them a corollary duty to accept as participating members all who are bound by their representative role.

The limited nature of the control over union internal authority

Finally, although the labor movement regards the Landrum-Griffin Act as a sweeping intervention in internal union affairs, the limited nature of its application should be recognized. In the next chapter we shall explore the fact that unions really tend to have two governments—one dealing with the organization's internal affairs, the other handling its collective-bargaining relationships. The legislation we have been discussing refers only to the first of these governments, that dealing with internal matters such as meetings, dues, elections, and union discipline. The individual member is protected from organizational abuse of power in those areas inside the union. But the act does not touch on the individual's rights in the second kind of union government, where bargaining officials get together with members of management to negotiate and administer a collective agreement in which important personal rights may also be involved.

Other laws do deal with this subject, but in a fashion that makes this one of the most tangled areas of labor legislation. We have seen that, under the Wagner and Taft-Hartley Acts, the doctrine of exclusive representation permits a duly chosen union to negotiate and administer the contract terms that cover *all* employees in a bargaining unit, whether or not they are members of that union. This union prerogative carries a price, however, for the NLRB and the courts have held that it implies a duty for each union to represent fairly and equally all the workers for whom it bargains, member and nonmember alike. It is well settled, for example, that a union cannot legally negotiate one wage increase for its members and a smaller or zero increase for nonmembers doing comparable work in the same bargaining unit, nor can a union refuse to handle the contract grievances of nonmembers or charge them a fee for that service, or in other ways discriminate against nonmembers in negotiating and administering contracts—with the single exception, of course, that a contract with a union-shop clause permits discharge for nonpayment of union dues and initiation fees.

But far less clear is the extent to which this duty of fair representation forbids favoritism on grounds other than union membership. It would seem, for example, that this doctrine would have banned racial discrimination in union contracts long before the passage of the Civil Rights Act. And indeed the Supreme Court took precisely this position as far back as 1944 with respect to the Railway Labor Act, which also provides for exclusive representation in the rail and air transport industries. In *Steele v. Louisville and Nashville Railroad Co.,* a union negotiated a contract with twenty-one railroads that severely restricted the seniority rights and hence employment opportunities of Negro firemen and correspondingly expanded the job rights of white firemen in the same unit. The Court overturned this contract, not because it discriminated against nonmembers of the union (although Negroes were in fact barred from joining this union) but because the union had arbitrarily favored one group over another within the bargaining unit. Stated differently, the Court plainly indicated that its decision would have been the same even if the Negro firemen had been members of the union.

> This does not mean that a statutory representative of a craft is barred from making contracts which may have unfavorable effects on some of the members of the craft represented. Variations in the terms of the contract based on differences relevant to the authorized purposes of the contract . . . , such as differences in seniority, the type of work performed, the competence and skill with which it is performed, are within the scope of the bargaining representation of a craft, all of whose members are not identical in their interest or merit. . . . Here the discriminations based on race alone are obviously irrelevant and invidious.[15]

Curiously, however, this radical precedent was almost never applied to ban racial discrimination in bargaining under either the Wagner or Taft-Hartley Acts. These laws, it will be recalled, spelled out several unfair labor practices, but under Wagner these were limited to employer activities and under Taft-Hartley none of the union unfair practices specifically referred to racial discrimination. For whatever reason, it was not until the 1960s that a divided NLRB declared such discrimination in bargaining to be a union unfair practice. By that time the Board's move in a sense only confused matters, for there now exists the possibility of attacking racial discrimination by unions under either Taft-Hartley or the Civil Rights Act of 1964—each with quite different enforcement agencies and methods and remedies.[16]

Whichever agency attacks this problem, it faces formidable problems in fashioning an adequate remedy for some types of racial discrimination. For example, suppose that a union and an employer—either by written or unwritten agreement—have systematically restricted Negro workers for several years to a seniority unit covering only the less desirable jobs in a plant. Is the appropriate remedy simply to forbid the parties to continue this practice in the future, which may mean that Negroes who now have many years of plant seniority will still need many more years to qualify for the best jobs because they have been denied the opportunity to gain experience on the middle-range jobs that lead to the top of the skill ladder? Or, to make amends for this past injustice, should a federal agency order preferential treatment in promotions for Negroes with plant experience, thereby diluting the job rights of white workers in that plant and provoking the charge of reverse discrimination? To date, no one has solved that agonizing problem to the satisfaction of all the contending interest groups.

Even aside from union discrimination against nonmembers or racial minorities within the bargaining unit, there remains a type of "unfair representation" which is very difficult to detect or remedy.

> The problem is one of policy—what rights *should* an individual have under a collective agreement? This problem is rooted in the need for reconciling the interests of the individual with the collective interests of the union and management. It is most sharply focused when the union and the employer seek to settle or adjudicate grievances without the consent or participation of the individual employees concerned.[17]

Suppose that a union is pressing five grievances at a particular time, in three of which the union believes it has a strong case and in the other two an arguable but weaker case. Both the employer and the union may prefer to avoid impartial arbitration if possible, which can be costly and time-consuming and can also produce precedents which one party or the other may not like. A deal is therefore proposed: The employer will yield on four of the grievances if the union will drop the fifth, a case about which the employer feels strongly, for some reason. If the union agrees to this trade, is it merely acting in a responsible manner by avoiding a needless drain on union funds, winning a larger share of these grievances than it might in arbitration, and cementing relations with the employer? Or is the union selling out the member whose grievance was dropped, whether his was one of the strong or weak cases?

The Taft-Hartley Act barely touches on this problem by providing that an individual employee may present a grievance to his employer without the intervention of the union, as long as any settlement reached is consistent with the terms of the agreement and a union representative is permitted to be present. But what of the situation where an individual presents his own grievance, which is rejected by the employer, and the union refuses to process the matter further? When union and management find it in their mutual interests to deny the claim of an employee, however well founded that claim may be, the individual has little chance of effective appeal. In the settlement of grievances, individuals and even groups of employees can be singled out for discriminatory treatment. "The opposition leader may find his grievance traded for one filed by a 'favorite son'; individuals who 'needle' both union officers and foremen may find themselves eased out by joint consent; and minority groups or factions may have their grievance ignored or half-heartedly argued."[18]

In a 1967 decision, *Vaca v. Sipes*,[19] the Supreme Court determined for the first time that the Taft-Hartley Act does create the right for an individual to bring action against his bargaining representative for not processing a grievance to his satisfaction—*but to win relief, the worker must prove that the union's conduct was "arbitrary, discriminatory, or in bad faith."* In this case, a worker was fired on the ground of poor health and, in the face of conflicting reports by the company's doctor and the worker's own physician, the union pressed his claim for reinstatement through four steps of the grievance procedure. At that point, the union sent the worker to a new doctor at union expense, and when the new examination did not support the worker's position, the union refused to carry his case to arbitration. The worker thereupon sued the union for failing to represent him fairly and a jury awarded him $10,300 in damages. The Supreme Court overturned this award, ruling that the worker could indeed sue his union for this type of alleged offense (or possibly could charge a union unfair practice before the NLRB), but in this case he had not proved that the union had acted in bad faith.

There are several ways of viewing that decision. Some critics would doubt that an individual worker ever has much chance of proving bad faith when his union drops a grievance or settles for less than the worker deems equitable, for grievances are frequently borderline in merit, like many law cases, and they are usually settled in meetings where few if any records are kept. Also, few workers have the will or the resources to undertake a lengthy fight in the courts or before the NLRB. For these reasons, some have suggested that every individual should have the right to have his grievance taken to the private arbitration provided under most labor contracts, perhaps at his own expense if his claim proves unjustified and at the expense of the union and the employer (who usually share these costs) if he should win. Others argue that such court decisions can be too effective, in the sense that union officers may try to avoid damage suits by pressing both good and bad grievances, which makes for poor labor relations, or that unions will face a Hobson's choice in spending their money on foolish arbitration cases or defending themselves in foolish court cases. Some experts, however, believe that the Court has fashioned a workable middle course which permits unions to screen grievances for lack of merit but not for discriminatory reasons. (It is a nice question, as yet undecided, whether it is discriminatory to trade off legitimate grievances, as in the hypothetical case above.)

A final illustration of these complexities lies in the practice of most unions to submit tentative contracts to their members for final acceptance or rejection. During the 1960s there was a marked increase in the number of cases in which members voted down contract terms that had been tentatively accepted by their union negotiators. This development troubled union officials whose judgment was repudiated, employers who thought they had gone "the last mile" in bargaining and then faced a strike for even more, and government officials who wished to minimize both strikes and costly wage settlements. Union officials often blamed the Landrum-Griffin Act for this development, implying that the act somehow reduced unions to a state of near anarchy. It is hard to take this charge seriously, for there is nothing in that law which requires membership ratification

of bargaining agreements (most unions required this long before Landrum-Griffin), and certainly nothing in the act prevents union officers from arguing the case for ratification before any contract vote is taken. On the other hand, it is possible that Landrum-Griffin has stimulated a more democratic atmosphere in many unions, so that members are more willing to challenge their officers' opinions even when, as here, there is no question involved of illegal discrimination or corruption.

Whatever the cause, the problem itself has produced an ironic counterpoint to the usual chorus of criticism concerning the lack of union democracy: On this subject, the complaint is that unions may be *too* democratic and, since officers are usually "better informed" and "more responsible" than the rank and file, perhaps we need a law forbidding ratification votes by the membership. The rationale for such a proposal is the presumed advantage of a representative over a pure democracy; in our political life we pass on the performance of our leaders in periodic elections, not by a referendum on every complex issue. Others understandably argue that it would be the height of absurdity for society to promote democracy in every phase of union government except the most important one—deciding the members' terms of employment.

Thus the individual covered by a labor contract does have several enforceable rights to fair treatment by his union representatives in the bargaining process as well as in the internal government of unions. It is most difficult to pin down the scope of the individual's rights in the bargaining process, however, for some are of recent origin (such as those created by the Civil Rights Act) and others rest only upon an implied duty of fair representation rather than upon explicit statutory language. This does not necessarily mean that we need yet another labor law to police this type of relationship between union members and officials, but neither can we pretend that no problems exist in that area. Clearly, the issue of the proper relationship of the individual to organizations possessing private powers over him has not been finally resolved—nor will it ever be, since institutions change and the problem persists in new forms.

Conclusion: the two themes involving union power

In leaving this phase of our study of labor and its institutions, we should remind ourselves that, along with the growing federal role in labor affairs, there has continued the role of the states. It is difficult to maintain any tally of the legislative provisions of fifty jurisdictions, but at least eight states operate under what have been termed "little Wagner Acts" and four more under "little Taft-Hartley Acts." More recently, a number of states have legislated Landrum-Griffin provisions, though not always accompanied by guarantees of the right to organize and bargain. These acts provide for industrial-relations matters which are purely intrastate in nature.

We have covered a great deal of territory in tracing the legal position of labor in the United States over more than a century and a half. It is less important to recall the specific doctrines which have evolved over the years, or the titles of legislation, or even their principal provisions, than it is to remember the major themes which have run through all judicial doctrines and legislative enactments. Once the right of workers to combine into organizations became recognized, there arose the possibility that the organizations so created could exercise their pooled power in ways which conflicted with basic philosophical values concerning the rights both of the individual and of society as a whole. The labor union, like the business corporation, became an instrument for which a genuine social need existed, so that eventually society came to support its unique and vital function. But the union, again like the corporation, was also an instrument which could be misused to the detriment of both the individual on whose behalf it was brought into existence and society who gave it protection. The issue of the appropriate use of private pooled power, vis-à-vis the individuals whom it governs and society to whom it constitutes a peculiar combination of both general and special interests, is one which never has a terminal resolution.

Unions, as representative of their members and workers in bargaining units, seek benefits for them which bring them into conflict with other private and usually organized interests, chiefly of business. Much of our labor legislation has seemed to be an attempt to arbitrate between, or balance, the competing rights of these private-interest groups. Organized labor and organized business each seeks limitations on the power which the other may exercise over it. (In the six months prior to passage of the Landrum-Griffin Act, business groups spent over $850,000, and the unions almost $400,000, in lobbying for their special interests in Congress, and much of the expenditure was with respect to the pending labor measures.)

But much more is involved than competing private interests. Generally speaking, private interests in labor legislation receive congressional approval only when they coincide with conceived social interests. The balance sought is one which is not simply fair to the parties but which is in the best interests of society as a whole. We can expect that unions and employers alike will take advantage of changing developments to press their own causes, but to credit them with the power to change labor legislation to their particular advantage is to credit them with too much. Changes in labor legislation are prompted by a reassessment of the relationship of the group to individuals and to society. The private power groups will, understandably enough, encourage and promote attitudes which are developing to their advantage, but they cannot create those attitudes out of whole cloth.

Starting from a period when unions had to fight for their existence and judicial decisions held them to be illegal conspiracies, we have moved into a period in which unions have won social acceptance and with it power, and the law has provided support to them along with restraints on them. But no institution—neither unions nor business—can assume a fixity of relationships. In the face of a changing social economy, new demands are made on old institutions, and new institutions seek a place for themselves. The shape of the union–management relationship today, the bundle of union and management powers and privileges which each possesses, is not likely to remain the same in the future.

APPENDIX: THE UNION-SECURITY ISSUE

The labor unions have not given up their fight to restore the right to negotiate union-security provisions in all states. They have marshaled a number of arguments in support of their cause.

1. In view of management's historical opposition to unionism, an opposition which, the unions believe, continues right down to the present, a provision requiring workers to become members once a union has been voted in by a majority of workers is almost necessary for survival. As long as employees remain free to join the union or not, or to drop out of the union after having once joined, the employer's opposition can operate in subtle ways to undermine union strength. Any temporary reversal, such as a lost strike, can be made the basis for employer pressures on workers to get rid of their union.

2. This possibility is enhanced by the high degree of turnover in industry. In the manufacturing sector, turnover rates frequently are in the neighborhood of 50 percent. This means that if the union is to maintain its representative position, some means must be found of enrolling the continuing influx of new members. One study of District 9 of the International Association of Machinists revealed that, within a thirteen-year period, the membership had increased from 4,000 to 25,000, but to achieve that net increase of 21,000 it had been necessary to take in 91,000 members. The marked discrepancy between these two figures was accounted for by turnover. Another way of putting it is to say that, for every nine members who join the union, only two will become long-run members.[20] In the seven-year period from 1956 to 1962, the UAW enrolled some 17,000 members in the North American Aviation Company, but the net gain over the period was only 700.[21] To combat this persistent gnawing away at a union's membership roster by the inflow and outflow of workers in a plant, a union may engage in a perpetual organizing campaign. Each new employee can be approached and urged to join the organization. There are many who believe that this is the most desirable method, since a worker who joins under such circumstances is more likely to do so from a genuine conviction that the union is desirable. Such an approach, however, is time-consuming and costly. It simplifies matters enormously for a union if every new employee is informed that he will be expected to join the union within thirty days.

3. Workers who choose not to belong to a union in a unionized shop gain all the benefits of union representation while accepting none of the costs. Such nonjoining members have been termed by the unions "free riders" and have been regarded with hostility and fear. Their presence constitutes a continuing reminder to paying members that they too could profit by dropping their union membership—as long as enough employees remain members to ensure its continued functioning.[22]

The nonpaying nonmember who enjoys the benefits of trade unionism is like a member of the community who refuses to pay taxes for the upkeep of the schools, parks, and police and fire departments, and who refuses to vote in the community's elections. Such a citizen is not merely antisocial; he is a threat to the continued health and safety of the community. If he is permitted to get away with it, others may well follow his example. The finances of the community could be weakened, community service could suffer, and possibly community peace and order could be supplanted by chaotic battles between taxpayers and nontaxpayers.

It is similar in industrial relations. The nonmember refuses to accept his social obligations. His fellow workers view him as a self-appointed person of special privilege. He is a threat to the union and to the continued peace and order of collective-bargaining procedures. Dues-paying union members view nonmembers as an insult. The presence of nonmembers creates a situation that is loaded with danger to peaceful relations and uninterrupted production.

4. Unions also argue that some form of security permits them to exercise a greater degree of responsibility. If they are faced with the necessity of holding onto their present membership by constant persuasion and of enrolling new members by continual organizing, they must demonstrate that they can "get something" for their members. They are driven to making excessive demands on the company in negotiations and in processing unwarranted grievances as a tactical means of holding their constituency. Similarly, they find it advantageous to disparage manage-

ment and to portray it as unmindful of employees' interests as a means of convincing workers of their need for a union. If union membership were made a simple condition of employment, the unions argue, it would be less necessary to engage in such propaganda, which admittedly has a harmful effect on the bargaining relationship.

5. In some industries—principally those in which employment is casual and of short duration —the union serves as an employment agency, supplying workers to employers as they are needed; however, the union cannot reasonably be expected to perform this function, which is sometimes quite costly, on behalf of nonmembers. This issue has been an especially difficult one in those industries where the union has operated a formal hiring-hall arrangement, as in the West Coast longshore industry and some branches of the construction industry in major metropolitan areas. When a union goes to the expense of establishing rather elaborate machinery for rotating work opportunities among its members, and for providing workers to employers who may need them for only short spells at a time, the union thinks it an inequity that it must "cut in" those workers who make no contribution to the institution which benefits them. Nevertheless, the terms of the Taft-Hartley Act require it to do so.

Further, unions in these industries argue that they have a special need for a voice in the hiring process. In the average factory, a union member with ten or twenty years of seniority is more or less assured of continued employment and income as long as he performs creditably and his employer needs workers of his type; in case of a temporary layoff, junior men go first and workers are recalled in order of their seniority. But many longshoremen and carpenters with equivalent experience have no such assurance, for they are constantly subject to layoffs and rehiring as they move from one employer to another, any one of whom in a nonunion market may hire a worker with little or no experience in preference to a man with more seniority. Not only is this unfair, unions argue, but it can lead to a flooded labor market, in which two or three workers vie for the equivalent of each full-time job, with the possible result that no worker achieves a decent annual

income. There is less danger of this in a factory setting, where the employer himself usually strives to minimize turnover, but in a casual labor market, employers profit from a surplus labor force that is available to meet occasional peak demands and at other times is simply underemployed at no cost to management. For these reasons—to assure equity in assigning the available jobs and to limit the size of the work force to the number for whom the industry can provide steady, year-round work—unions in casual labor markets assert they need more control than is provided even by the union shop, under which the employer still may hire anyone he pleases. Instead, these unions want the same control over hiring that factory unions have over layoffs and recalls.

The legal status of union hiring halls under Taft-Hartley has always been ambiguous. Senator Taft himself stated that the act did not outlaw these halls per se, and the NLRB and the courts have consistently echoed his view. Yet the opportunities for a union hiring agent to discriminate against nonunion workers are so obvious that it is widely believed that, in practice, the closed-shop ban has been violated in many labor markets since 1947. Beginning in 1956, the NLRB made an all-out effort to uproot the closed shop, particularly in construction, by laying down certain general rules to which all hiring halls had to conform and by imposing very severe penalties for violation (the refund of all dues and initiation fees paid by all local union members during the period beginning six months prior to the filing of a charge found valid by the Board). In 1961, however, the Supreme Court struck down this Board policy, ruling that Congress had given the Board the power only to remedy specific acts of union discrimination and that the Board could not invalidate an entire hiring-hall arrangement just because it discriminated against one or two individuals or because its covering contract did not contain certain hiring rules enunciated by the Board but not by Congress. Thus the test of a hall's legality was to remain as it was before 1956: If a specific individual is discriminated against, he is entitled to a back-pay award from the union, but without other evidence the hiring hall itself is presumed to be legal.

In the midst of this legal battle, Congress partially clarified matters when it devoted one part of the Landrum-Griffin Act of 1959 to amending Taft-Hartley. One of the amendments provided that in the construction industry alone, a labor contract could legally require an employer to give a union notice of all job openings and the opportunity to refer qualified applicants for such openings before they were filled in the open market; and a construction agreement could also require hiring priorities based on training or experience or length of service in an area or craft—but still not on union membership as such. In addition, Congress provided that construction contracts could require union membership after only seven instead of thirty days, to meet the criticism that a man could work for several months in construction on a succession of jobs, each lasting less than a month, and thus evade a thirty-day union shop clause.

All of these considerations are cited as evidence that the union-security issue is far more complex than Congress thought it was in 1947. Outlawing the closed shop means nothing to most unions in industries like manufacturing, for they have no need or desire for a voice in the hiring process, but the hiring hall has persisted in casual labor markets because it fills a legitimate need—a need which Congress was forced to recognize in its 1959 amendments. Critics are still skeptical that a union hiring hall in any form can be truly nondiscriminatory, but labor argues that no one has yet come up with a better substitute.

6. Finally, labor argues that if you are worried about corruption or a lack of democracy in unions, one of the worst remedies is to encourage the honest dissenters to get out or stay out of the union and thus leave policy making in the hands of corrupt or undemocratic officials. Surely it is much better to require everyone to join and then, through Landrum-Griffin or similar laws, enforce the members' rights to have a clean and democratic organization. Also, since the Taft-Hartley Act provides for both deauthorization and decertification elections (the first permitting workers to rescind a union-shop clause and the second permitting them to eject a union completely), workers have several more effective ways to re-

form a union than simply opting out and leaving the union free to do as it pleases.

Arguments against union security

As might be expected, opponents of union-security provisions reject most of the above prounion-security contentions. But in addition to denying the force or validity of the union's propositions, they counter with four primary arguments of their own.

1. Forcing a man to join an organization against his will violates the fundamental principle of voluntarism. There are some employees who do not approve of unions. Should they nevertheless be required to swallow their scruples and join an organization to which they are opposed, in order to keep their jobs? Are we to sacrifice the principle that individuals may follow the dictates of their conscience in deciding whether to associate themselves with a particular group, whether political, religious, fraternal, social, or economic? This principle, the National Association of Manufacturers has contended, is neither prounion nor antiunion; it is simply one of the morals of freedom. It may be true that by according individuals the right of free decision, union strength will be less than if workers were forced into unions. But is strengthening the unions so important an objective that we are willing to sacrifice a basic principle to it?

2. However desirable unionism may be in the abstract, there are particular unions (such as those which are Communist-dominated) and particular union leaders (such as those who are racketeers or greedy for their own gain) that are undesirable. Making employment conditional upon workers' remaining members of such unions, in the plants and shops where they are entrenched, means delivering over the work force to exploitation. If union membership is necessary for holding a job, moreover, those in control of the unions—even if not racketeers—can perpetuate themselves in office by threatening the opposition with expulsion. The price of keeping a job becomes conformity to the dictates of those who hold power in the union. (The Taft-Hartley Act

has recognized this possible abuse of power by providing that the only reason for which a union may seek an employee's discharge under a union shop is nonpayment of the regular initiation fees and dues. Expulsion from the union for any other reason therefore does not deprive a worker of his job.)

That this concern is not an idle one can be documented by reference to a 1962 case coming before the NLRB, in which it was found that officials of a local of the Operating Engineers were using their control over the union's job-referral system to discriminate against members of a reform group within the local. In view of the ruthlessness of the discrimination practiced, the Board took the extreme measure of placing the union's hiring-hall arrangements under the supervision of its regional office for the period of a year.

3. Labor's free-rider argument is vulnerable on three counts.

a. The taxpayer analogy collapses because there is a world of difference between a government and a private organization. Obviously the government has the power to levy taxes on all citizens, just as it has the power to draft them into the armed services, clap them into jail for committing crimes, and in other ways coerce them to observe various laws. But these coercive powers of a government are determined by society as a whole, and it has never been assumed that a private body can do everything a public body can do. If it could, society would indeed be in a sorry state.

b. The doctrine of exclusive representation cuts both ways. Some nonmembers admittedly may be free riders who gain the benefits of the union contract without paying their share of union costs, but other individuals are "forced riders" who could do better bargaining for themselves but are denied this opportunity. For example, in a nonunion shop a young and energetic worker may be preferred over an older and slower man when his employer is determining wage increases, promotions, or layoffs. In a union plant, however, this worker must abide by the common rules negotiated by the union for everyone. In a sense, it is a form of double taxation to require this worker not only to give up his right of individual bargaining but also to join and pay dues to the union depriving him of this right.

c. It is particularly obnoxious to force an individual to contribute money to an organization whose political views he finds objectionable. If a worker votes Republican and his union leaders are staunch Democrats, why should he support their political activities? It is true that the Taft-Hartley Act forbids union funds to be contributed directly to candidates in federal elections, but this law has many loopholes. Not all states have comparable laws regarding state and local elections; even in federal elections, a union newspaper may editorialize for various candidates and union staff members may perform unpaid "voluntary" work for a candidate; and at any time a union official may legally lobby for various measures with which a particular member may disagree.

4. Nor is the argument persuasive that unions need compulsory membership clauses to protect themselves against hostile employers. This may have been true before 1935 but if it is still valid today, then the Wagner Act was a monstrous hoax. That law's list of unfair labor practices and its doctrine of exclusive representation are still in effect and they forcefully prevent an employer from favoring nonunion over union workers in any way. After all, that was the major point of the law and its thousands of NLRB cases, and to add the union shop to these many protections of the law is to permit labor to have its cake and eat it too.

The future of union security

So run the arguments pro and con. It may appear strange that it is principally the employers who seem to be so concerned for their employees' freedom and independence from control, when only a few years ago it was they who, as a group, were seeking to deprive workers of any freedom from their own control. Is the employer's line of argument only a subterfuge for an effort to shift the balance of power further in management's favor?

One would be naive not to concede that such is indeed the case. Obviously, management is seeking to limit union power over its membership as a means of limiting union power in collective bargaining. But it would be equally naive to assume that this fact removes the basic issue or even negates management's arguments. For employers, in seeking public support for their own position to their own advantage, must couch their arguments in terms which appeal to the public's sense of morality. And it is true that the practices of union security do raise significant and unavoidable questions concerning the power or control which unions may properly assert with respect to their members and other workers affected by such provisions—questions which are not yet settled.

Nevertheless, the trend appears to be in the direction of the extension of some form of union-security devices. Prior to World War II, the union shop had scarcely a toehold in the manufacturing industry. By 1965, a national sample of union contracts showed that 85 percent then contained some type of union security: 67 percent had union-shop clauses, another 8 percent had maintenance-of-membership provisions, and 10 percent called for the agency shop (under which each member of the bargaining unit must pay the equivalent of dues to the union but no one is compelled to join the organization). Outside of the right-to-work states, over nine out of ten contracts contained one of these security provisions.[23]

But union-security provisions, even if they should become universal, are not likely to mean what they have in the past. It appears improbable that unions will regain the power to compel the discharge of workers who have lost their union membership for any reason other than nonpayment of dues. Refusal to honor a picket line, or nonattendance at meetings, or campaigning on behalf of a rival union, or seeking the deauthorization of a union shop, or "conduct unbecoming a union member" may be the cause of a member's expulsion from the union but not for his discharge from his job. This would mean that the union shop essentially has become a means of requiring every worker in a unit to support financially the union which represents him. As noted above, about 10 percent of union contracts now require only this agency-shop arrangement, and in fact this is the maximum union security which is enforceable under the Taft-Hartley Act. It is true that two-thirds of union contracts still call for "union membership" as a condition of employ-

ment, but the NLRB has ruled that, under such a contract, a worker who tenders only his dues and initiation fee has met the requirements of the law and cannot be discharged for refusing to take a membership pledge or attend union meetings or meet any other requirements of formal membership.[24] Many union officials feel that this form of security is too diluted to meet the legitimate needs of their organizations, but many other people consider it a good compromise: the worker must contribute to the cost of maintaining the union and thus is not a free rider, but neither does he have to subject himself to the internal rules and politics of a union if he prefers not to do so.

ADDITIONAL READINGS

Chamberlain, Neil W.: *Sourcebook on Labor,* McGraw-Hill, New York, 1958, chaps. 11 and 12.

Estey, Marten S., Philip Taft, and Martin Wagner (eds.): *Regulating Union Government,* Harper & Row, New York, 1964.

Kennedy, Robert F.: *The Enemy Within,* Harper, New York, 1960.

Shister, Joseph, Benjamin Aaron, and Clyde W. Summers (eds.): *Public Policy and Collective Bargaining,* Harper, New York, 1962.

Williams, Jerre S. (ed.): *Labor Relations and the Law,* Little, Brown, Boston, 1965 edition and supplements for later years.

FOR ANALYSIS AND DISCUSSION

1. Elinore Herrick, formerly personnel director for the *New York Herald Tribune* and a regional director of the NLRB, once commented: "The great problem we face—and it can only be answered by persistent effort to make unionism serve the public interest—is reconciling the preferred status of trade unions today with their claim to be voluntary associations."

Restate the problem she has posed and suggest some of the difficulties which we encounter in resolving it.

2. It has been argued that yellow-dog contracts and union-shop contracts are essentially two sides

of the same coin in labor relations, and that an even-handed public policy should treat them alike: either outlaw both or legalize both. Describe and appraise the logic of this proposal.

3. Compare the free-rider and forced-rider arguments described in the Appendix. Which do you find more persuasive? Since both rest upon the doctrine of exclusive representation, would the repeal of that doctrine resolve the endless battle over union security?

4. It has been argued that when a worker is one of many hundreds or even thousands of employees in a large enterprise, he is incapable of exercising any influence or control over that enterprise even though *it* controls *his* working life. A union of which he is a part can secure some measure of influence over his working conditions, however. Thus a union, instead of submerging the individual, actually helps him to achieve some measure of independence.

Evaluate this contention.

5. The NLRB once ruled that it was not illegal for a Florida employer to dismiss a group of Cuban workers in the belief that they were supporters of Fidel Castro—in other words, to discharge employees because of their political belief.

How much freedom do you think an employer should have in deciding the grounds for firing a person? What difference, if any, is there in the right of an employer to discipline or discharge a worker and the right of the union to discipline or expel a member?

NOTES

1. *Wallace Corporation v. NLRB,* 65 SCt. 238 (1944). This issue is discussed at greater length in Neil W. Chamberlain, "Obligations upon the Union under the National Labor Relations Act," *American Economic Review,* vol. 37, pp. 170–177, March, 1947.

2. In addition to these twenty states, Louisiana has a right-to-work law which applies only to agricultural workers.

The Railway Labor Act, passed in 1926 and amended in 1934, outlawed all forms of union security on the railroads. This ban was originally supported by "legitimate" railroad unions who feared that, otherwise, employers would use compulsory-membership clauses to strengthen company-dominated unions. This was in contrast to the Wagner Act of 1935 which, as we know, permitted union-security clauses in industry generally. Ironically enough, the

position of railroad and other unions has since then been reversed. In 1947 the Taft-Hartley Act gave states the authority to pass laws banning compulsory union membership, even though its own terms permitted the union shop. But in 1951 the Railroad Labor Act was again amended to authorize the union shop on the railroads—without conceding to states any authority to outlaw union-shop provisions as they applied to railroads.

3. Julius Rezler, "Union Elections: The Background of Title IV of LMRDA," in Ralph Slovenko (ed.), *Symposium on the Labor-Management Reporting and Disclosure Act of 1959,* 1961, p. 479, with citations.

4. U.S. Department of Labor, Labor-Management Services Administration, *Summary of Operations, 1966, Labor-Management Reporting and Disclosure Act,* 1967, p. 19. The data cited are estimates, with no breakdown given of the precise number of suits filed under the bill of rights and the number filed under other provisions of the act. Several suits span both categories.

5. Thomas G. S. Christensen, "Union Discipline under Federal Law: Institutional Dilemmas in an Industrial Democracy," *New York University Law Review,* vol. 43, pp. 240–241, April, 1968, with citations.

6. 316 F.2d 445 (2d Cir.), cert. denied, 375 U.S. 946 (1963).

7. Christensen, "Union Discipline under Federal Law," p. 250. Prof. Clyde Summers has also commented persuasively on this point in *A Labor Union "Bill of Rights,"* American Civil Liberties Union, New York, 1958, p. 20, and in "Legal Limitations on Union Discipline," *Harvard Law Review,* vol. 64, p. 1084, May, 1951.

8. "The Election Labyrinth: An Inquiry into Title IV of the LMRDA," a Note in *New York University Law Review,* vol. 43, pp. 337–338, April, 1968.

9. John L. Holcombe, "Union Democracy and the LMRDA," *Labor Law Journal,* July, 1961, p. 601.

10. For the details of the IUE election, see "The Election Labyrinth," pp. 355–359. For the NMU election, see *Wirtz v. National Maritime Union,* U.S. District Court, Southern District of New York, no. 66-4519 (1968).

11. *United States v. Brown,* 381 U.S. 437 (1965).

12. *Union Trusteeships,* a report to the Congress by the Secretary of Labor, 1962, p. 141.

13. U.S. Department of Labor, *Summary of Operations, 1966, LMRDA,* pp. 15–17.

14. The same, pp. 40–46.

15. 323 U.S. 192 (1944).

16. For NLRB policy before the 1960s, see Michael L. Sovern, "The NLRA and Racial Discrimination," *Columbia Law Review,* vol. 62, pp. 563–632, April, 1962. For the divided opinions within the Board in the 1960s, see Hughes Tool Co., 147 NLRB No. 166 (1964).

17. Clyde W. Summers, "Individual Rights in Collective Agreements: A Preliminary Analysis," *Buffalo*

Law Review, vol. 9, p. 241, Winter, 1960. This article constitutes an excellent discussion of the issue.

18. The same, p. 245.

19. 386 U.S. 171 (1967).

20. Hjalmar Rosen and R. A. Hudson Rosen, *The Union Member Speaks,* Prentice-Hall, Englewood Cliffs, N.J., 1955, p. 12.

21. *Business Week,* Nov. 10, 1962, p. 144.

22. AFL-CIO, *Labor's Economic Review,* January, 1956, p. 6.

23. More precisely, 14 of the 67 percent of union-shop contracts provided only a modified union shop, which usually required membership of all employees except those who were not members on the date the union shop was originally granted. Data are from *Basic Patterns in Union Contracts,* The Bureau of National Affairs, Washington, 1966, p. 87:1.

24. Union Starch and Refining Co., 87 NLRB 779, 1949.

The labor movement in the United States consists of a complex of organizations ranging all the way from local unions, of which there are approximately 77,000, to the principal federation, the AFL-CIO, under whose banner come more than 15 million workers. Each of the organizations has its own government, and most of these governments are linked to one another as city governments are linked to state governments and state governments to the Federal government. Unlike the analogy, however, the peak government (the AFL-CIO) is not the most influential and powerful of this complex. That distinction falls to the national unions, of which, in 1968, there were 189, each operating in some jurisdictional area vaguely bounded by occupational or industry lines. The national unions include such well-known organizations as the Teamsters (formally, the International Brotherhood of Teamsters, Chauffeurs, Warehousemen and Helpers of America), and the UAW (the International Union of United Automobile, Aerospace and Agricultural Implement Workers of America), and such lesser-known bodies as the International Alliance of Bill Posters, Billers and Distributors of the United States and Canada, and the International Brotherhood of Operative Potters.

If the national unions are the most powerful organizations in the labor movement, the local unions constitute the building blocks of which the nationals are constructed. Indeed, as we noted in an earlier chapter, historically the national trades

unions were created by a number of local unions in the particular trade which felt the need for some sort of coordinating agency. The organizations which they created were designed to systematize the conditions and relationships of the skilled workers in the trade, who might themselves travel from one local jurisdiction to another or whose products might compete against each other, hence rendering desirable the determination of minimum standards and common terms with which all locals would comply. Over time, the national unions came to dominate the local unions which had spawned them. Particularly as national unions became responsible for organizing new locals did the latter come under their influence. Nevertheless, the local union is still the "elemental" unit out of which the national unions and the labor movement as a whole are built, and it still plays an important role. It may be viewed as roughly corresponding to local government in civil life.

The structure of unions

The local union A local union is composed of members of a particular trade or craft in a community (such as a local of carpenters in the city of Scranton), or of workers in a particular plant (such as workers in a local of the Steelworkers in the South Chicago plant of Carnegie-Illinois), or of workers in a number of companies in a particular locality (such as Local 12 of the Automobile Workers, which includes people working at hundreds of shops in the city of Toledo). Thus some local unions are minuscule in size, having only a handful of members, while others number their members in the thousands.

The functions of a local union are numerous. It seeks to expand its membership until all eligible employees are enrolled. It provides many services to its members, such as assisting them in applying for workmen's compensation or unemployment benefits, securing medical assistance for them, and sponsoring social activities. It negotiates, or helps to negotiate, the collective-bargaining agreement for its plant or craft. It appoints or elects stewards who represent the members in the various shops of the plant or job sites in defending their interests in the face of adverse management action. It conducts strikes as necessary and provides legal assistance to any members who may be prosecuted for conduct on behalf of the union during a strike.

The governmental processes of local unions depend on their makeup. Obviously a steelworkers' union which is composed of a thousand members, all of whom work at the same plant, will have different needs from an electricians' union, even of the same size, made up of members who are dispersed throughout a city on a number of short-term small jobs. While it might be possible to develop a more complex typology of local unions, for our purposes these two contrasting types may be taken as the most important ones. We may call the first type a local industrial or plant union and the second type a local dispersed union, usually craft in nature and most frequently encountered in the building trades.

Both types of unions are governed by elected officials, including a president, a secretary-treasurer, and an executive board. In addition, there may be trustees, a finance committee, a negotiating committee, and other appointed or elected officers, such as shop stewards or job stewards, who are the union representatives in a division of a plant or on a particular job, for example, a construction site.

In an industrial union, the officials are not normally paid for their services. Usually they are jobholders in the plant or trade and are compensated only for such time as they have to spend away from their jobs on union business; in other instances, they receive a token salary; only in the larger local unions, where administration is a full-time job, are they paid a full salary, which is likely to be the equivalent of what they would earn in the plant or trade. The president is usually not only nominally but actually the chief executive. He works closely with his associates, and there is a large amount of committee activity. Relationships incline to be relatively formal and prescribed. With respect to both the administration of the local union itself and its varied activities, and the administration of the collective agreement which it negotiates with the employer or employers of its members, there tend to be rather definite and understood procedures and practices. The fact that most of the members have a common place of work, common eating facilities, often common recreational facilities, means that there are relatively good opportunities for direct transmission of union information, for "bull sessions" concerning union or company activities, and for contact with union officers.

In contrast, the dispersed union of the building-trades variety tends to be much more informal in its operations. With its membership scattered throughout its jurisdiction on a number of jobs, sometimes of short duration, work crews are recurringly brought together for a while, then broken up and new ones assembled with a different composition. In these circumstances some full-time agent is usually needed to make the rounds of all the job sites where members are employed to make sure that agreed-upon conditions are being observed and that the gripes of the members are paid prompt attention. Since jobs are so often short-lived, unless grievances are resolved promptly they are not likely to be resolved at all. Sometimes it is the employer—a contractor, perhaps—who has a complaint—perhaps that the men are jumping the quitting hour or that the performance of some individual is unsatisfactory—and he too must be listened to promptly by a union representative or the employer–union relationship suffers.

Except in small locals, the full-time job of representing this kind of union may be performed by a "business agent," who is elected by the membership. He, rather than the president, tends to become the majordomo of the local. The president runs the union meetings and takes care of its routine functions. He is usually an unpaid officer, just as in most industrial unions. But the business agent takes care of the administration of the collective contract with the employer or employers' association on a full-time, paid basis. Since this is the local union's most important function, he naturally is likely to become the local union's most important officer.

In his operations, he must exercise his judgment in the making of quick decisions. There is seldom the time or opportunity for committee meetings or collective judgment. He deals directly with member and employer in ironing out problems arising under the agreement; his determinations can of course be appealed to the executive board or the local-union meeting, but this happens infrequently. In a manner quite unlike the industrial-union government, then, the business agent of a dispersed union tends to personalize and centralize one major area of local-union activity. This is not a difference of philosophy but of structural necessity. It does, however, have its consequences affecting the general nature of labor-union government in that it tends to deemphasize membership participation in union affairs and to limit opportunities for members to develop leadership capacities.

A local union is chartered by the national office of that union. (The national is commonly referred to as international since most unions have members in Canada as well as the United States.) In the process of obtaining that charter, the local binds itself to conform to the international constitution of the union. The nature of the international union's constitutional authority over the local union varies from organization to organization, but in general that power is very great. It usually includes the authority to approve or disapprove locally negotiated collective-bargaining agreements; to sanction or refuse to sanction local strikes; to require payment of per capita dues for each of the local's members; to remove local officers for cause and, when considered necessary, to establish a trusteeship over the local union; to pass on the propriety of local-union disciplinary actions against its members; to supervise the conduct of local elections as deemed necessary; and to inspect the local union's financial books.

The national union Since the power of the national over the local union is so great, it is reasonable to inquire who controls the national unions. With virtually no exceptions, the final authority in the national union resides in the convention. The convention is composed of delegates chosen from the local unions, the number of delegates to which any local is entitled being determined by the number of its members, though usually not on a strictly proportional basis, to avoid domination of the convention by a few large locals. The convention usually has the power to amend the union's constitution, although sometimes such amendments must also be submitted to membership by referendum. In more than two-thirds of the national unions, the convention elects the union's national officers. In the other unions, the national officers may be nominated by the convention but elected in a general referendum, or nominations may come directly from the local unions and then be submitted to referendum; and in a few small unions, both nomination and election are by general-membership meetings. The convention also has the final voice in all union-policy matters and may in fact reverse prior actions of its officers which it disapproves. It is also the union's highest tribunal in any cases of union discipline which have been appealed by the member or local union disciplined.

How often are national conventions held? Since the Landrum-Griffin Act requires election of national-union officers no less frequently than every five years, that is now the maximum allowable period between conventions for that large majority of unions which either nominate or directly elect their national officers in convention. Most nevertheless meet more frequently than required by law. Of 190 national unions reporting one-half held conventions every one or two years —16 percent annually and 34 percent every two years. Another 13 percent met every three years, 21 percent every four years, and 11 percent every five years. Only 5 percent reported that they did not hold national conventions, and nine of these ten "national" unions were actually small organizations confined to a single area or occupational group.[1]

The interval between conventions is a matter of considerable consequence, in view of the fact that the convention constitutes the only effective check on the actions of national officers. Long delays between conventions permit the union president or executive board to carry out policies which, however well intentioned, may be thought by other members to be contrary to the best interests of the organization and which, in any event, have not been subjected to review or sanctioned by more general authority. On the other hand, the calling of a convention is an expensive undertaking, and conventions held too frequently— particularly when accompanied each time by the election of national officers—can be unsettling to the incumbent administration, requiring it to spend an undue amount of its time in political fence mending to ensure support or reelection.

Between conventions, the supreme authority of the union commonly rests with the general executive board, an elected body. There are some constitutional variations, however, in which the general president has powers which in effect subordinate the board to him, as in the American Federation of Musicians. In other national unions, the president is a man of long tenure who has gained such prestige in the eyes of his membership that few members of the executive board would contemplate opposition to his policies. In most unions, the president in fact exercises a leadership role which tends to make him the major influence in the affairs of the union. It is primarily where there is factionalism or where the president is new, inexperienced, or weak that the general executive board takes on actual as well as intended power relative to the president.

It may be clarifying to think of the union convention as similar to, but usually more effective than, a stockholders' meeting in a corporation and the union's executive board as similar to an inside board of directors in a corporation.

Local–national relations

Facilitating a closer working relationship between a national union and its local unions are a number of staff personnel including the editor of the union newspaper, who tries to act both as mouthpiece for headquarters and a reviewer of the trials, successes, and setbacks of the locals; the research director, who prepares materials to document the union's official position but who also may assist local unions in preparing their bargain-

ing presentations; and the education director, who organizes packaged materials which help to provide members with the historical background of the labor movement in the United States, the present-day role of the union, the special problems confronting the members' own union, and aids for the member who wants to play a more active role. Particularly in the industrial unions, however, the chief links between national and local organizations are the (inter)national representatives, appointed by the president as full-time field officers but lacking any formal authority. They are not part of the line but of the staff. It is their duty to transmit to local unions, and to help them to translate into action, the policy directives of the national headquarters. It is also their function (and from the standpoint of the local, their most important one) to assist in the negotiation of a collective agreement, if called upon to do so. Their influence comes in part from whatever personal abilities they may be able to exercise but also in part from their close ties with the national office. Both employer and local union treat the international representative with respect, since he constitutes the chief source from which the national union will receive its impressions and recommendations concerning their relationship.[2]

The financing of all union activity, local as well as national, stems from three primary sources: dues, initiation fees, and special assessments. In a few cases the national constitution prescribes a definite rate of dues and initiation fees, sometimes on a flat basis and occasionally on a proportion-of-earnings basis. More commonly, however, the local union is authorized to set its own rates, though in some instances with a prescribed minimum or maximum. Although there is a belief in some quarters that unions charge excessive dues and initiation fees, the evidence does not support this contention. Where rates are high, their size is commonly attributable to the fact that some portion of the figure is allocated to special insurance or benefit funds rather than all of it going into the union's general treasury.

Reports from 50,000 local unions, filed with the Secretary of Labor in response to the requirements of the Landrum-Griffin Act, revealed that more than half of them charge monthly dues of less than $4. Only one in a hundred charges $10 or more. Only five locals had monthly dues of

$25 to $35 (the highest reported), while almost 900 charged less than $1.

Initiation fees follow much the same pattern. Most unions, especially in the mass-production industries, make a nominal charge of $10 for enrolling a new member. The cost of joining a union rises in the more skilled trades, where limitation on the number of craftsmen is more jealously guarded and where special financial benefits may accrue. A few unions charge fees as high as $1,400.[3]

Special assessments are usually, but not always, provided for in the constitution. In the face of an unexpected drain on the union's treasury, such as would be caused by the conduct of a major strike, the union may be empowered to impose a special tax on its members. Usually there are restrictions on the exercise of such power, such as a stated maximum amount or a specified number of times within a year that such assessments may be levied. In some instances, these special charges can be levied only after referendum approval. In general, the assessment power is used sparingly. Also, it will be recalled that the Landrum-Griffin Act bars increases in dues or fees or the levying of special assessments except upon approval of the membership—by secret ballot at a meeting after notice, or by referendum or convention vote.

How is the money raised by these means spent by the unions? Something more than one-half of the sums paid to the local union is retained for its own expenses of maintaining a hall and servicing its members. The remainder is paid to the national union in the form of a "per capita tax," that is, a specified amount, determined by the convention or by referendum, per dues-paying member. How these receipts are used is suggested by the distribution of per capita payments by one union, the American Newspaper Guild. Approximately 35 percent was used for organizing and servicing local unions; 23 percent for administration, including executive salaries; 5½ percent as per capita tax to the parent federation; 11½ percent for publishing a union newspaper; 3 percent for collective-bargaining purposes; 8 percent each for the educational program and the research department; and 14 percent for miscellaneous other expenses, including political lobbying and strike benefits. While these proportions are subject to change over time and to variations among unions, they are roughly characteristic of the uses of per capita receipts by national unions.

Intermediate bodies The local and the national do not constitute the whole of the union organizational system, however. In addition, there are several types of intermediate structures.[4]

1. A number of locals of the same national union, located within the same community, may organize into a *joint board,* which will coordinate the activities of the locals to ensure that the actions of one do not undercut the actions of another. (They may coordinate a wage demand, for example). To take but one instance, the Joint Council of Teamsters No. 13, centered in St. Louis, is composed of numerous affiliated locals in that and adjacent communities, including separate locals of brewery drivers, laundry drivers, taxicab drivers, local and over-the-road freight drivers, and so on.

2. The local unions and joint boards within a region may be organized into or serviced by a *district* of the national union. The district or regional director of the union is commonly appointed by the national office and coordinates the bargaining and organizing activities of his union within that area.

3. The locals of the same national union which function in different plants of the same national corporation may form a *council,* for purposes of coordinated bargaining. For example, all the auto-worker locals in General Motors plants may form a GM council. (This council exercises an important role in determining the relationship with the company, but that function is also shared with a General Motors Division of the national union. Thus top national leaders combine with grass-roots representatives in determining what issues shall be raised with GM management and what shall be considered a satisfactory settlement of any demands which are made.) Similarly, all the electrical-worker locals (IUE) in General Electric plants form a GE council within the union.

Two kinds of government

Even the simplest and least complicated of trade unions is thus likely to be composed of a national office, a number of local unions, a parcel of joint boards or joint councils serving as area coordinators for collective bargaining, districts or regions serving as area coordinators for union administrative purposes, and special councils (whether organized on corporate or some other nongeographical basis, such as a skill group within the union) which also coordinate local-union bargaining activity. More complex unions introduce other divisions between the national and local bodies and also within the larger locals, since these may themselves be subdivided into shops or sections or chapels (the terminology varies).

What strikes one most forcibly about these various governmental units is that they often represent two quite discrete kinds of activity—one, the actual administration of the union as an organization, involving the enrolling of members, the collection of dues, the conduct of a variety of membership programs (recreation, education, politics), the holding of regular membership meetings, and so on; and the other, the conduct of the collective-bargaining relationship with the employer or association of employers, which involves the negotiation of an agreement, its enforcement, the processing of grievances, and related activities.

A union thus possesses not one but two governments—a government for internal affairs and a government for external relations. In those local industrial unions whose members all come from the same plant—"one union–one agreement" locals—the president and his associates typically both run the union and administer the agreement. But another system commonly operates in the craft-based "dispersed locals," in industrial unions whose members come from a number of plants (sometimes referred to as "amalgamated locals"), and in the case of joint boards which coordinate the bargaining activity of a number of geographically contiguous local unions, and of councils (such as those organized by the UAW for the major automobile producers and by the IUE for the major electrical manufacturers) which coordinate the bargaining activity of geographically scattered but corporatively integrated local unions. In all these instances, there is commonly a set of union functionaries who are concerned primarily if not solely with the external-relations aspects of union government. They leave to other bodies, such as the local unions and the district or regional offices, the internal government of the union.[5]

At the national level, the same division of union functions may occur. It is true that in those few unions which engage in industrywide bargaining, the national president figures prominently in negotiations and thus combines the internal government and external relations in his office. But in unions which bestride more than one industry or trade or which may have separate agreements with several nationwide corporations, the bargaining activity (the "government" for external relations) may find its own organizational expression in councils and divisions which have the authority to conclude and administer agreements governing their members in their working environments. The president may be active in these negotiations, in which case the two types of governmental structure again are joined, or these collective-bargaining functions may be decentralized and quite independent of internal union affairs.

The Teamsters Union exhibits this bifurcation of governmental functions very neatly. Although its local unions still frequently negotiate agreements with individual companies, in the major metropolitan areas joint councils had, by the close of World War II, largely taken over the bargaining function, dealing with associations of employers. The joint council thus had preempted the government of external relations, leaving internal governmental functions still in the hands of the local unions. The national office was not deeply involved in the large number of localized negotiations, which contributed to a substantial buildup of power within the union's larger locals and joint councils, frequently referred to as "baronies." The national office had limited powers relative to them, and such power as it exercised was largely limited to internal union operations.

Later the brotherhood established "area conferences," of which there are now four—the Western, Central, Eastern, and Southern conferences—each embracing all the states in its territory. If a majority of local unions in the defined areas vote for area negotiations, all locals in that region are bound by the decision. Thus the area conferences are now taking away from the joint councils the bargaining function which previously these councils had abstracted from the local unions. While the joint councils still conduct some specialized bargaining, this development has left them in the position of finding new functions to justify their existence, and these are likely—almost by necessity—to take the form of internal governmental functions, the coordination of local-union activity in other than bargaining matters. The further consequence is that the national president has himself taken a controlling role in the area conferences and thus centralized in his office the power which had previously been dispersed among the baronies.

But an area conference still has its limitations. For one thing, it incorporates truck drivers in a variety of industries, some with quite distinct problems who do not fit into the area cartage agreement, as well as those members of the union who do not belong in the truck-driver category—such as employees of airlines. The Teamsters has thus moved to establish "trade divisions" within the area conferences, with these becoming the nucleus for *national* trade divisions cutting across area lines. There are now some sixteen such divisions, though not all have been activated. They give promise of transcending geographical boundary lines and negotiating, through their special organizational mechanism, a national agreement for a particular trade within the overall union, as was in fact done in 1964 for over-the-road trucking. Neither area conference nor national trade division has anything to do with internal union government; both are concerned with external relations (collective bargaining). They exist side by side with the organs of the union which have been set up to carry on its internal administration. Teamster members are thus subject to two kinds, or two lines, of government: one which prescribes their duties and enlists their activity as members of a Teamster unit, the other which prescribes their conduct and defines their rights as employees of a company with which the union maintains a working relationship. Increasingly, these two distinct lines of government head up in the office of the national president, but this is always subject to change. In fact, following the imprisonment in 1967 of Jimmy Hoffa—who in his stormy tenure as union president had increasingly run the Teamsters as a one-man show—lower-level officials recaptured some of their former control from Hoffa's successor, Frank Fitzsimmons.[6]

In general, it appears that those in charge of the bargaining organization in a union constitute the union's power centers. This is not surprising in view of the fact that the principal purpose of labor unions is the conduct of collective-bargaining relationships. The decentralized power structure of the building-trades unions, in contrast to most of the industrial unions, is due to this fact: The former embrace a large number of local bargains under local control, while the latter are more likely to have some large-corporation, pattern-setting negotiation in which the national president plays the leading role. At the same time, the thorniest questions concerning a member's relation to his union have arisen with respect to the internal governmental procedures—how much of a voice a member may have in the determination of union policies, the degree of disciplinary authority which his union holds over him, the extent to which he may be led to support political activities which run counter to his own persuasion. We shall examine some of these issues shortly.

The federations

So far, we have been discussing the organizational structure within a single union, whether formed on industry or occupational lines. In addition, there are a variety of ways in which a number of different unions may pool their efforts. These federations of unions occur at all levels.

1. The locals of all unions within a community —the carpenters, the steelworkers, the plumbers, the auto workers, and so on—are organized into a "city central," or industrial council, the purpose of which is to represent labor's interests within the community and to encourage the support of each local union by all other local unions in that community. (Prior to the merger of the American Federation of Labor and the Congress of Industrial Organizations, each of these two branches of labor organized its own city centrals.) In American labor history, the city central actually preceded the national union.

2. What is done at the community level is repeated at the state level. A statewide organization of all local unions and joint boards is established, with elected officials, the chief purpose of which

is to represent the interests of organized labor in the state legislature and generally to provide mutual defense and support among the unions within that state.

3. The apex of labor organization occurs with similar federation at the national level. Formerly, there were two, the AFL and the CIO, but, as we have seen, in the fall of 1955 these two national federations merged into a single body which preserved both their names in the awkward title of American Federation of Labor and Congress of Industrial Organizations (AFL-CIO). Not all national unions belong to this top federation, however. Several railroad brotherhoods have traditionally remained aloof, and from time to time some organization which has normally been a member of the federation may withdraw for reasons of pique or principle, as the United Automobile Workers did in 1968. Other unions are not members because they are unacceptable to the federation and have been expelled, as the Teamsters were in 1957. A large majority of the national unions are affiliated with the AFL-CIO, however, and they include 75 percent or more of all union members in the United States.

4. Within the top federation, there are several trade departments. These have as members those national unions within the federation which have trade interests in common. Thus the building-trades unions have set up a building-and-construction trades department to discuss and act on their common specialized interest. Similarly, those unions connected with shipping activities have organized a maritime-employees department. Other departments are the metal-trades department, the railway-employees department, and a department of industrial organizations, the latter encompassing those unions (primarily in the mass-production industries) which seek to enroll members on an industry rather than a craft basis. These departments too sometimes have their local councils.

The principle of union autonomy

The union federations (whether at the municipal, state, or national departmental level) constitute a loose confederacy of autonomous organizations. Thus, for example, despite the fact that the public hears more frequently about the AFL-CIO than it does about most of the unions which compose it, the officers of the AFL-CIO have very limited functions and powers. They have nothing whatsoever to say about the collective-bargaining policies of the unions—what wage changes to seek, whether to go after pension improvements or guaranteed annual wages. These decisions rest with the national unions themselves or their locals. Nor can the AFL-CIO control the political policies of the constituent unions. Even should its executive board decide to support the Democratic candidate in a presidential election, there would be nothing to prevent the printers' union or the carpenters' brotherhood from actively campaigning on behalf of the Republican aspirant, and no disciplinary action could be taken against them for their failure to conform to a policy which has only the power of a recommendation.

The AFL-CIO does have the authority to make decisions as to the jurisdictional lines of its constituent unions. Moreover, its policy-determining function on issues either internal to the union movement or concerning its relations with others should not be underestimated. Its decisions and pronouncements are always treated with respect by member unions, since it speaks with the force of the united labor cause. Nevertheless, if a member union should take some action contrary to announced AFL-CIO policy or decision, the federation would have only one way of enforcing its action—by threat of expelling the union. If the International Longshoremen's Association is believed to be gangster-dominated or if the International Fur and Leather Workers' Union is believed to be Communist-led, the federation has no power to move in and compel the union involved to clean its house. The most it can do is to investigate, to expose, and then to warn the union that unless it does a good housecleaning, it will be expelled from the federation. The threat is often sufficient to secure the compliance of the dissident union, but sometimes expulsion is the only resort. Occasionally, in the premerger past, if a powerful union stood fast, it was the federation itself which backed down, with some face-saving expedient. Post-merger, the federation has shown greater resolution in dealing with such problem unions.

The government of the AFL-CIO is thus solely of the "internal" variety, since it is concerned only with the administration of the labor movement's own affairs—its policy and political positions, its public relations, the relationship of its constituent parts to one another, the operation of its several trade departments, and all the governmental apparatus which is necessary for these purposes. It has no "external" relations with employers, no function in collective-bargaining negotiations, no official voice as to the terms on which major strikes should be settled, even though its officials may exercise some "moral suasion" behind the scenes. It is the spokesman for the labor movement, but not the general-in-chief of the labor forces. There is no organization or office of the latter sort, since the "armies" of labor—the action forces—are all independent, consisting of the autonomous national unions. The presidents of these unions man the chief organs of the AFL-CIO and are most zealous in guarding their independence from any encroachments by the peak federation. Thus, in appraising the "labor monopoly" issue in this country, one may legitimately question whether the power of particular unions in collective bargaining is excessive, but it is fanciful to describe the AFL-CIO itself as a bargaining monopoly in any sense.

The supreme governing body of the federation is the convention, just as in its constituent national unions. Meeting biennially, it is composed of representatives of the national (international) unions, with voting strength determined by the number of members on whom they pay a per capita tax to the federation treasury. The convention elects the president and secretary-treasurer. Between conventions, an executive council, consisting of twenty-seven vice-presidents of the federation (all of them presidents of national unions) plus the two executive officers, wields final authority. Finally, a general board, composed of principal officers (usually the president) of all the national unions, meets upon call to act on any matter referred to it by the officers or the executive council. In voting, it follows the convention principle of casting ballots which are weighted by membership strength. Figure 10-1 diagrams the structure of the AFL-CIO.

The power of the national unions to control the federation is evident in this governmental organization. The principle of "autonomy" has been cardinal to the labor movement ever since the birth of the AFL in 1886. The constitution of the merged federation, adopted in 1955, gave an appreciably greater authority to the central federation to move against its constituent national unions but still restricted its power to investigate, recommend, suspend, and expel. The adoption of explicit codes of appropriate union conduct, conformance to which would be required of national unions, marked a decisive step toward greater federation control over member behavior, even though the national unions, particularly in the building trades, still have sufficient control over federation policy to ensure that the codes (initially applied with vigor) are now applied with greater "discretion."

Nevertheless, the desirability of national-union autonomy has been and is being subjected to a more intensive scrutiny than it has ever had to withstand before. There are voices now insisting that the federation, which stands in the public eye as the official representative of the labor movement, must have greater authority to intervene directly in the affairs of national unions which violate codes of ethical conduct. More and more frequently is it said that the power to expel a union leaves uncorrected the condition which has led to expulsion—a racket-ridden union remains racket-ridden after it is expelled and inevitably tarnishes the reputation of organized labor in general, and the same is true of a union that discriminates against racial minorities. Better to hold such a problem union within the federation, it is argued, and give the federation power to move in to clean up the undesirable conditions.

As yet, the national unions have been reluctant to cede such additional authority to the federation. Nevertheless, it would be surprising if over the years the AFL-CIO did not come to possess a greater measure of governmental power over its constituent members, even though that power were circumscribed with strict constitutional limitations on its exercise.

The evolving structure

As we have seen, there are approximately 190 national unions in the United States, of which approximately 125 are members of the AFL-CIO. Each of these has some jurisdictional area (industry or occupation) within which it tends to op-

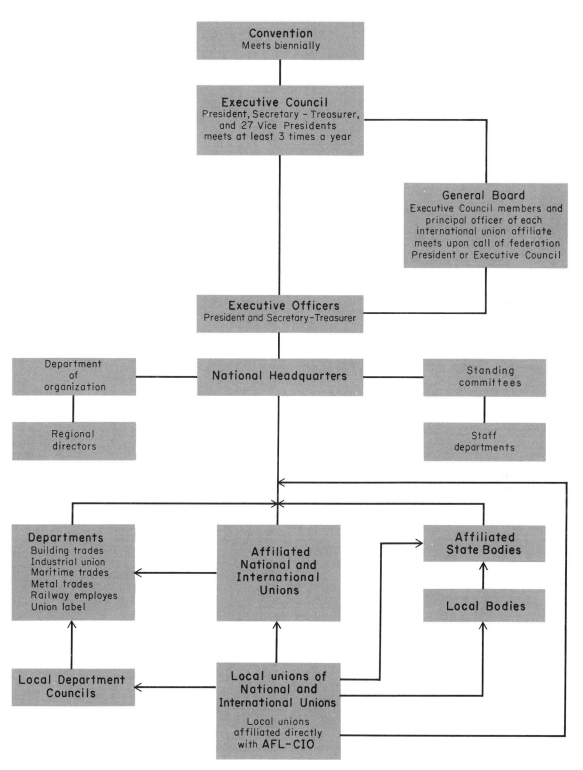

Fig. 10-1. *Structure of the AFL-CIO.*
SOURCE: *U.S. Department of Labor.*

erate, though jurisdictions have become notoriously fuzzy. The history of jurisdictional conflict in the American labor movement is so extensive that it would require several pages even to outline it. Suffice it to say that formerly the resolution of conflicting jurisdictional claims was sought chiefly through negotiation, persuasion, and political maneuvering within the tent of the AFL, though with only moderate success.

The advent of the National Labor Relations Act, which gave employees themselves the power to determine which union they wished to represent them regardless of any jurisdictional lines laid down by the unions, was an important influence in diffusing the membership composition of a great many unions. The Steelworkers might find themselves sought as representative by a group of plastics employees in a community in which the steel union was the most influential and powerful labor organization. The Electrical Workers might discover that, in order to represent their own skilled craftsmen in a plant which the NLRB had decided should be structured on a comprehensive rather than a craft basis, they would have to take in an assortment of unskilled and semiskilled workers as well. Some more opportunistic unions, like the Mine Workers and the Teamsters, stood ready to represent any group of workers which turned to them for assistance. The jurisdictional lines which had so carefully been kept discrete over the years (or had at least been the object of such an effort) now became blurred, confused, and overlapping.

The rise of the CIO, which organized competing unions in many AFL jurisdictions, further added to the complication. The result has been that, since 1950, the resolution of jurisdictional claims has tended more and more to be undertaken through special machinery established by the federation, relying, as a last resort, on an arbitral decision rendered by an outside authority —an "umpire" appointed by the federation or by one of its departments (such as the building trades)—whose decision is intended to be final and binding.

Despite the improvement which this has effected, the whole jurisdictional concept is increasingly being called into question. Even within the labor movement there are those who recognize

that jurisdictions founded on particular *skills* are too evanescent, in the face of rapid technological change, to provide the basis for an organization's sphere of operations. Is an industry any better as a basis? The industry identification of corporations in the United States is about as subject to change as the skill base of workers. A company that starts out manufacturing one line of products, say, railroad coaches and street cars, may find less and less of its business in that field and turn more and more to some other output, say, the production of heating units. Even more commonly, as companies grow they tend to become diversified, so that one company may operate in five or fifty industries. Since unions generally find that they can exercise greater bargaining leverage if they deal with a company on a company-wide basis rather than in five or fifty different industrial units, there is a tendency for an industrially based union to organize under its umbrella workers in quite different industries but employees of the same company. As that company comes into competition with numbers of other companies in a variety of product lines, the union—to preserve or achieve standards of employment—must "follow the competitive flag." The "conglomerate corporation" is thus outdating industrial unionism.[7]

The consequence of this undermining of both the craft and the industrial basis for union jurisdiction seems to be a slow but steady nudging of the existing national unions to merge and amalgamate into a smaller number of larger unions with broader jurisdictions. In some instances (the Teamsters, District 50 of the Mine Workers, to a lesser extent the Machinists), the tendency is for the organization to become a "general union," ready to enroll any group of workers which it is capable of organizing or which comes to it for assistance. Just as corporate charters have not inhibited the major corporations from moving into virtually any field of activity which suited their purposes, so may union charters cease to have much of a limiting effect on union organization. It seems likely that there will remain some central core of activity (the Automobile Workers are likely to continue to have major strength in that field even though organizing in a hundred others, just as General Motors is likely to maintain its principal strength in the automobile industry even though operating in dozens of other industries), but without that core of activity serving as a barrier to entry in other fields. One can imagine that the number of national-union organizations may thus be halved within another decade or two, or in any event that most of organized labor will be found in an ever-declining number of national unions.

Another approach to the same problem is the tactic of "coalition bargaining," which calls for several unions dealing with the same corporation or industry to form a common front during negotiations—to serve the same basic demands upon management, sometimes to negotiate as a single team, and to decide together whether to strike or accept management's last offer. This tactic has been vigorously promoted since 1961 by the Industrial Union Department of the AFL-CIO as a method for increasing union strength, without permanent mergers, in bargaining with diversified corporations or even with nondiversified companies whose employees are divided among several unions. The legality of this bargaining weapon is under challenge before the NLRB, but meanwhile it continues to be used by several unions, sometimes as a preliminary move or as an adjunct to a formal merger. The copper industry, for example, ranges from mining through smelting and refining to the fabrication of copper products, and it has many unions and companies in each branch of the industry plus some unions and corporations that span two or all three branches. To introduce some order (and bargaining strength) into this chaotic structure, the two largest unions in the industry—the United Steelworkers and the Mine, Mill, and Smelter Workers—formally merged in 1967 and also persuaded some twenty-five other unions to join in coalition bargaining for the entire industry. This move was strongly resisted by employers and the resulting contest of strength led to an industrywide shutdown lasting 8½ months in 1967 and 1968, with the unions ultimately winning major but not uniform gains in wages and other contract terms.

But along with this tendency toward a smaller number of larger organizations with diffuse jurisdictions, there appears also a reverse tendency. The skilled groups within the large unions seem to resent being swallowed up in an amorphous mass. They tend to believe that their own interests would be better served if they could exercise their own bargaining power, based on scarce skills, rather than accept terms and conditions negotiated for a whole work force which lumps together the less skilled and easily replaceable along with themselves. They seek differentiated treatment. Similarly, in those instances where collective agreements have expanded in coverage so that their terms apply to a whole industry or whole area (as in the Teamsters' area conferences mentioned previously), there is some unrest when the employees of more profitable companies find themselves being granted wage and benefit increases no greater than are received by the employees of struggling firms.

In effect, when a labor union expands to take in a larger jurisdiction or a collective agreement expands to embrace more plants, the competition which formerly went on between groups of employees (as to who should get the better terms) is internalized within the *same* organization. The problems are not resolved by expansion of the union or the bargaining unit; they are simply brought *inside* the organization. The craft workers who, previously in their own union, had sought to "top" the wage gains of a quite separate union composed of a mélange of less skilled workers, still try to top that group even though both are now within the same union or under the same collective agreement. The conflict—which is inescapable when it is a matter of allocating scarce resources among competing groups—has to be met by modifying the structure of the union to provide a mechanism for resolving competing claims.

This is already occurring within the larger unions, where special "craft councils" have been established to pay particular attention to craft needs and with some element of autonomy to bargain for themselves, as in the UAW. The Rubber Workers and the Electrical Workers have also established skilled trades departments within their comprehensive unions. Such groups may have their own conventions or may be given special representation on the executive board. Separate divisions or sections or branches may be organized to provide craft groups with special status within the mass union.

Thus the labor movement appears to be subject to both centrifugal and centripetal forces. The blurring of craft and industry lines is leading toward more comprehensive unions, approaching the "general" type. The government of the union, its bureaucratic apparatus, its drive to survive and grow can thus all be used to better advantage, since it is not circumscribed by arbitrary and shifting jurisdictional boundaries. At the same time, as jurisdictions expand and lose preciseness of definition, the clashes of interests between skilled and unskilled workers, and between workers in prosperous companies and those in marginal establishments, become incorporated within the larger structure. New ways of meeting special interests must be devised. The superior bargaining power of strategically placed groups has to be recognized, as a matter of political necessity. Thus the structure and government of the union must be modified to give expression to special interests. There is diversity within unity. This is no different from the kind of political accommodations which are necessary when a government expands to serve minority groups and regional blocs. The structure and government of the United States represent the same effort to accommodate conflicting internal elements while preserving the Union.[8]

Politics and government

No government is possible without political life. A government is composed of people, and which people become the government is usually a source of controversy. The unpaid jobs in local unions sometimes go unsought, and incumbents have to be found and persuaded to serve; there may be no one willing to make the personal sacrifice required, for example, of a president of a small local. But more generally, union offices, both at the national and local levels, are prizes which are sought. We have already encountered this phenomenon in a previous chapter, when we were dealing with unions as institutions having interests of their own and captained by leaders who likewise have interests which in some respects diverge from those of the membership. There is no need to repeat here the incentives felt by a national-

union president to build a political machine which will keep him in office.

It is, however, worth noting that, typically, a national president stands unopposed for reelection. Contests for office do occur, but they are the exception. It is quite comparable to the presidency of a corporation where the incumbent usually is confirmed in office by a board which is responsive to him, in view of his control of the proxy machinery. In the labor union, there is no proxy machinery but there is a political machine which the president has built. Although delegates to the national convention are elected by their local unions, it is the president who controls assignment to convention committees and who wields the gavel at convention sessions. It is he who has access to the pages of the union newspaper to define the issues as he sees them, who appoints international field representatives who are in constant contact with the local unions and who can be expected to maintain the interests of the administration which has appointed them.

In this kind of environment, it is extremely difficult for opposition to arise. There is little way in which a dissident can present his case to his fellow unionists. He might, it is true, "sound off" at the convention if he is a delegate, but this provides no platform from which the whole union membership can hear him, and certainly no continuing forum. At best, the convention oppositionist is likely to be remembered by a few other delegates as "that guy from Toledo who objected to a dues increase." He has no access to the union paper, and although the Landrum-Griffin Act now guarantees him an opportunity to use the membership mailing list for purposes of circulating his views, this is an expensive undertaking of which few are likely to avail themselves. (The Securities and Exchange Commission similarly permits stockholders the opportunity of circularizing other stockholders, but this privilege is seldom exercised, and is seldom effective when it is.)

The net of all this is that a person who is ambitious to rise within the union and who aspires to union office can most easily do so not by opposing the incumbent administration but by joining its political bandwagon. The individual who shows himself to be an effective local leader may be rewarded with a special position at the convention, and perhaps eventually a vice-presidency and a place on the executive board. It is far easier for him to win advancement by joining forces with the leadership than by opposing it.

There are union politics at the level of the local union as well, though their complexion is likely to be somewhat different. Since it is the local which is often most directly involved in collective-bargaining negotiations, local politics are likely to center around the union–management relationship to a greater extent than at the national level.

The local election, more frequently than the national election, involves a contest. Competing candidates engage in a rivalry for votes. Once elected, the local official must retain the support of his constituents in order to be returned to office. To win election and reelection, he must convince his fellow workers of his capacity to do for them the things which they would like to have done. The obvious vote catchers are a pay increase, reduced hours, and better working conditions. These become campaign "promises" to attract support, and if the candidate is elected he may feel some compulsion to make good on his promises in collective-bargaining negotiations. In some instances, the promises are impossible of achievement and the result is likely to be a disillusioned electorate or a leader who fights to get as much of the impossible as is possible. These are facts of political life which are familiar to Americans from an early age.

The political nature of unions thus leads to a rather continuous importunacy, affecting what the union will demand in collective bargaining as well as what it is satisfied to accept. The standard method by which the union leader evidences his responsibility to his constituency is by making demands on management, either general (such as a wage increase or vacation plan) or specific to particular members (the settlement of grievances). His appeal for votes customarily runs in terms of what he plans to obtain for the members if elected. A candidate for office or an officeholder must match the promises of his rivals and must not fall too far behind in making good on his promises. He may even eliminate rivals by his effectiveness in demanding and getting more and more.

His responsibility to the membership is gauged primarily in such terms, and it is on this relationship that his authority largely rests.

Although members of management have frequently condemned union leaders as irresponsible because of these "political" maneuvers, such tactics actually reveal the responsibility of the union leaders to their members. Indeed, the same individuals who criticize the unions for such political behavior frequently criticize them too for their lack of democracy. But the greater the degree of membership control over the organization, the more likely it is that union candidates and leaders will resort to campaign appeals designed to allure the electorate.

The union-democracy issue

Are unions democratic? If one listened to many managers, he would think not. At least he would conclude that they are about as democratic as a Chicago ward. If he listened to the unions' own spokesmen, he would conclude that they were the purest expressions of self-government. The truth is a good deal more complex. Part of the difficulty in arriving at it lies in the different meanings which attach to the term "democracy."

Let us first dispense with one red herring. It is no secret that some unions have fallen under gangster domination. Racketeers have made use of union "fronts" in order to extort payments from employers in either of two ways. One is by insisting on the employer's paying "dues" for all his employees under a so-called "sweetheart contract" (an agreement with substandard terms which is the employer's quid pro quo for signing up with the union; the employees may not even know its terms and are likely never to see a union "representative"). The other is by exacting bribery for not calling the "membership" out on strike; hired thugs may serve as the "pickets" if the racket must demonstrate its power to shut down the shop, store, or plant.

The legitimate labor movement is as distressed over the presence of these racketeer elements as are law-enforcement agents and the public. It may try to minimize the prevalence of such rackets, in protection of organized labor's general reputation, but it does not seek to justify their operations. There can be no question that gangster-dominated unions are undemocratic. If we wish to examine the union-democracy issue objectively, we should recognize that rackets in the guise of unions, while a problem, are not part of the democracy issue. They are a law-enforcement problem.

Perhaps the most generally accepted definition of union democracy is that it refers to the control by the union membership of its own affairs, and thus stands opposed to centralization of authority and domination of the membership by an entrenched officialdom ("labor bosses," in the terminology of some critics). We have already seen how authority tends to become centralized in national-union administration through the use of political machines which, in effect, establish one-party rule. Opposition is seldom tolerated when it begins to be effective.[9] If a "rebel" candidate manages to attract a sizable interest on the part of the membership in spite of the overwhelming odds in running against the incumbent, the chances are good that he will be branded as the leader of a "dual-union" movement and charged with splitting the union, destroying its unity, and laying it open to employer attack. A gross example of this kind of action was provided by the 1958 Steelworkers' convention which passed a resolution calling on the national union and affected locals to "purge" from their midst an opposition leader and his associates who had polled a quarter of a million votes in the previous election and who had continued to attack the union's administration. Union history contains a number of other examples of such intolerance of effective opposition.

There are those who believe that this tendency for unions to become self-indulgent bureaucracies is a natural development, traceable in most large-scale voluntary organizations. The political sociologist Robert Michels formulated an "iron law of oligarchy" applicable to such institutions, and some observers see the operation of such a law in labor unions.[10] In this view, as unions become established and secure and grow in size, there is a natural tendency for power to pass from the membership to the leadership, with the former simply passively approving or (less often) disapproving actions initiated by the officials. Democracy withers away.

Functional democracy

This line of thought has been sharply challenged, however. Some who have been closely identified or associated with the labor movement deny that unions have become stabilized or secure. They maintain that, on the contrary, organized labor continues to find itself on the defensive, and that even where it has obtained temporary recognition, its capacity to win benefits for its members depends on its power. The consequence is that while a union does have governmental functions, it must act like a military government, preserving discipline and unity in the face of likely attack or in order to perform its function of effectively representing its membership. And military governments are not commonly models of democracy.

Former Supreme Court Justice Arthur Goldberg espoused such a view when he was chief counsel for the Steelworkers Union. He questioned whether, as a society, we could rightfully demand of unions that their political behavior should conform to the same standards we apply in civil government.[11]

There are industries in this country in which the existence and status of the union is relatively unquestioned, either by the workers or by the employers. And some of the basic assumptions upon which our political democracy rests may perhaps be applied in such situations. But, equally, we have in this country many situations in which almost the contrary is true, where the great struggle is to organize the working force into unions and keep it organized, and where employer opposition is continuous and sometimes successful. And even where the existence and status of a union is unquestioned—as, for example, in the basic steel industry—it is unlike political government in that it cannot legislate by itself on the matters of primary concern to it—wages, hours, and working conditions. It can only make demands and its success in achieving them depends upon agreement of the employer and upon the economic strength of the union, should the employer refuse.

Goldberg's solution was not to require the unions to engage in "competitive politics" or to conform to specified procedures, but to allow them to govern themselves in their own way, subject only to the social constraint of operating within certain broad "limits" designed to safeguard basic membership rights.

The rationale behind Goldberg's view and similar opinions is an interesting and important one. Labor unions, they maintain, were formed to bring democracy into industry. The unions may have considerable influence in the lives of their members (something which critics of union "undemocratic" practices usually stress), but they do not have as much influence as do the employers of their members. They were established in the first instance to protect the interests of their members and to give them some sense of security and independence in the workplace. This function, their only excuse for existence, can be effectively performed only by a strong organization. A strong organization in the collective-bargaining environment (inescapably one of conflict) requires a degree of centralization of authority that is not necessary in nonfighting types of voluntary organizations. Thus, in order to perform its essential function, the union may have to deny some of the trappings of democracy in its own internal governmental processes.

From this point of view, labor unions—whatever their internal processes—bring their members "functional democracy," or what has for a good many years been referred to as "industrial democracy." If the unions were themselves to adopt all the procedures we associate with political democracy—opposition candidates, unlimited debate, partisan tactics, and so on—the result might be to make the unions themselves democratic, but in the process to cripple them or prevent them from achieving that industrial or functional democracy which is what they were established for in the first place. What good is a union, however democratic, if it can do nothing for its members against antagonistic employers or managers who put other interests than those of the workers first?

Stated differently, the absence of a two-party system within most unions is seen as less important than the promotion of a two-party system in industry itself—the employer and the union, each pursuing different interests and, in compromising these differences, serving the interests of both consumers and producers in our society. We do not go further in our political life and demand that the Democratic and Republican parties also promote another two-party system within each of their own organizations, so why should we expect this of either party in an industrial democracy?

This point of view raises the possibility that unions may be considered democratic if their members approve of leadership actions, although they themselves have had little to do with formulating or participating in the policies they represent. When we recall the "two governments" which can be said to characterize labor unions—one, the internal government, concerned principally with the relation between the union and its members, and the other, the external-relations government, which is principally responsible for collective-bargaining relationships with employers —it would appear that the latter is more likely to bear the membership's stamp of approval than the former. Typically, the members have the opportunity to vote, sometimes directly, as in local negotiations, at other times through representatives, as in national bargaining, on the demands which are to be made on employers; they generally must approve the calling of a strike, and are customarily asked to ratify or reject a negotiated agreement. In the handling of grievances, union committeemen usually go out of their way to satisfy their constituents, even to the point of taking weak grievances to arbitration rather than telling a fellow worker that he really doesn't have much of a case. In the collective-bargaining line of union government, then, membership approval of official actions is generally alive and effective. If this is the principal function for which unions exist, is it then so vital that membership sanction of the actions of the internal government is less a reality? This is another way of stating the "functional-democracy" principle.

Indeed, some have maintained that most union members have little interest in the affairs of their unions. As long as the leadership manages to "bring home the bacon," they are content to leave the conduct of union affairs to the officials. It is not democracy but results which union members are after.

Despite the cogency of the functional-democracy argument, it is difficult to avoid an uneasiness that a membership which is concerned only with ends and not means carries dangers to the broader society of which it is a part. How far would it tolerate actions depriving individual members of rights and privileges as long as the leadership "did all right" by the others? Would discriminatory actions against minority groups be allowed to pass without protest as long as the majority fared well? Is not functional democracy the same argument which is used to justify the actions of any autocratic government—the argument that a government is formed for a purpose and not for its own sake, and that, to achieve that purpose in the face of opposition, it is essential to concentrate power and authority in the hands of a militarylike machine? In the kind of society we are trying to build for ourselves, is it not vital that we learn how to achieve objectives benefiting the majority without sacrificing the rights of individuals and minorities?

The issue is not easily resolved. Certainly it is reasonable to assume that there is no necessary pattern of procedures which every organization (or every nation) must adopt in order to earn the label of being a democracy. Diversity may be necessary in the light of differing circumstances. On the other hand, there may be some indispensable characteristics of democracy, some ingredients without which the name means nothing. Protection of the individual's right to express himself freely and the free election of officials would seem to constitute minimum essentials.

Membership apathy

There is a major difficulty with this formulation. It is difficult to "protect" rights which are allowed to fall into disuse. The fact is that, typically, union members exhibit relatively little interest in the government of their unions. In local unions, the attendance at regularly scheduled meetings is normally only a minute fraction of the total membership, perhaps no more than 2 percent and seldom more than 10 percent. Such small turnouts are sometimes regarded as indication of membership apathy in the face of domination by the labor "bosses": why should members put in an appearance simply to be told what their leaders have done or propose to do, while they themselves have little power to influence the affairs of their own organization?

Such a point of view is difficult to defend, however. Labor unions are not alone in drawing only a fractional membership response. The New England town meetings, which are regarded as the epitome of citizen democracy, have frequently fared no better, and even in our presidential elections, in which voter interest and participation are probably at their peak, fewer than two-thirds of the voters ever bother to turn out. As for union meetings, members of the local union are commonly scattered geographically throughout a city. It is asking a good deal to expect them to go to a meeting hall to sit through what is frequently a dull proceeding concerning routine business when the alternative is an easy evening at home.

As President George Meany of the AFL-CIO once remarked:[12]

This may be the price we are paying for the fact that we have a high standard of life, that our people do own automobiles and that they have television sets and radios in the home. . . . Of course, when there is a contract coming up, the boys get out because they have to find out what is going on and what are the prospects. But when things are good and they have a good contract, the membership is prone to stay away. They find something else to do on meeting night. . . . Meetings, of course, are always attended by officers. It is their job to be there. After a while, looking at a half-empty meeting hall, they get the impression that they are the only fellows who are really interested in that union, that the members have no interest in it.

The same phenomenon repeats itself at the national level. Despite the scale of many conventions—running as high as 3,000 delegates—many local unions are often entirely unrepresented. In the United Automobile Workers, for example, a union which is frequently cited as one of the most democratic, only 750 of the 1,250 locals in the union sent delegates to the 1959 national convention. For the most part, the small locals tend to go unrepresented, partly because of the expense of sending a delegate, partly out of a feeling that their voice would not count for much in any event. Thus, in the 1959 UAW convention referred to above, more than half of the local unions with fewer than 150 members failed to send a delegate, as did one-fifth of the local unions with memberships between 150 and 1,050.[13]

We frequently think of the small organization as permitting a purer form of democracy, since its scale of operations allows a greater degree of face-to-face interchange and a more direct involvement of its members in discussion and decision. But it would appear that whatever may be the case in *local* union meetings themselves, the small local fails to contribute to the democratic functioning of the *national* organization, leaving control of the convention to the large locals. This is borne out by the attitude expressed by delegates at the UAW's 1959 meeting: Those from the larger locals (1,050 or more members) tended to look on the convention as a policy-making body, while those from the smaller unions did not, tending to regard it as an instrument for officers to inform the membership about UAW policies.[14]

But if disinterest in the functioning of union government does not necessarily indicate an apathy traceable to bossism, this disinterest may nevertheless make it unrealistic to expect democracy, in the sense of membership participation, in such an organization. Even so, the charge of apathy in unions may itself be exaggerated. Take the matter of small attendance at local meetings. This does not always mean that matters are left to officials to decide as they will. At least in plant locals, a *representative* process may be functioning. In most voluntary organizations, it is a handful of people who do the work. The same individuals who are active in the union are likely also to be either formal leaders (elected shop stewards) or informal ones (in their shop in the plant). Such individuals get to know the sentiment of their fellow workers. During the lunch

hour or in casual talk on the job, they have heard what their fellows think about the company's new job-evaluation plan, about the raw deal that Joe in the milling section got by having a junior promoted over his head, about how a prospective layoff should be handled. By their very nature, it is this handful of shop leaders who are the ones most likely to show up at union meetings. And when they speak or vote, they are likely to express the views not only of themselves but also of their fellows. The "town meeting," which is what the union *ostensibly* remains, has *actually* been converted into an informal, representative "town council." And as long as everything goes smoothly, why should the members as a whole turn out? Can it be considered apathy if in fact they are reasonably satisfied with the way the union is being run? Can it be viewed as "boss domination" if Bill, their steward, comes around the next day to tell them what went on at the hall and what he had to say and how he voted?[15]

This kind of informal representation is more difficult to achieve in the dispersed (craft) locals, where members are scattered and the composition of work crews is impermanent, but here a different kind of grapevine frequently exists. Particularly in longshoring and the building and maritime trades, the union operates as an employment agency in a casual labor market, which means that workers in these trades must visit their union halls and see their key local officials far more often than factory workers do. Also, for a variety of reasons, some of these unions have still not adopted the practice of requiring employers to check off their members' dues, so the member has another reason to see his union officers regularly. Finally, among members of the same construction craft in a local area, there is often a far greater sense of identity and community of interests—and at least as good a grapevine—as can be found among a group of diversified factory workers. For all these reasons, officer–member relations in a geographically dispersed local union are frequently more effective than one would expect.[16]

In the case of small-local representation at national conventions, if the members have a special interest in some issue likely to arise, or wish to raise a matter for consideration, they may arrange to have their views aired by formal resolution or by arrangement with another local union. Normally a belief that the larger locals reflect problems and interests similar to their own may be well founded.

A separation of membership control and leadership?

Despite all such rationalization of memberships nonparticipation, there does seem to remain a problem which cannot be readily dismissed. Just as the corporation has been transformed into an organization where ownership and control are separated, so may it be that labor unions in this country are passing through a phase which may end up in a separation between membership and union control. It may be that the functions of the union will become more routinized, and membership in it more like an act of taking out insurance ("joining" a mutual insurance society), in which no citizenship role is really expected.

The tendency in this direction may become more pronounced if the labor unions pursue a course which is frequently urged on them—that of providing "executive training programs" for their leaders. The argument is often made that the conduct of union affairs increasingly requires a more sophisticated economic understanding, an improved competence in administrative affairs (with which most old-time union officials are impatient), a greater knowledge of the mutual impact of unions and society. Some unions, such as the Steelworkers and the Automobile Workers, have established formal programs ("labor colleges") with these objectives. Whereas union educational programs formerly were focused exclusively on the membership, increasingly they are now being geared to union leaders' needs. But if a union invests in the education of its officials, it is all the less likely that it will promote internal political procedures which subject its trained officials to the hazards of a contested election. The pressures for building a stable bureaucracy will be greater, and probably will be well enough understood by the membership. Unless incumbent officials are delinquent, they are likely to be returned to the offices for which they have been groomed and in which they have gained experience.

If this should be the case, we may also expect that the power of a union over its members, which could be used adversely to individual interests, will be more circumscribed. The limitations may be achieved in various ways. One may be by the development of new institutions by the labor unions themselves, as the Upholsterers Union and the Automobile Workers have developed neutral review boards or boards of appeal to which members may bring complaints against their union.[17] It may, and already has to some extent in the Landrum-Griffin Act, come through legislation. It may also come through some option to the union of instituting its own devices or otherwise subjecting itself to the supervision of a governmental agency such as the NLRB.

Summary and conclusion

Where, then, do we wind up on the democracy issue? The centralization of power in labor unions is real, in national unions more than in local, and in internal governmental affairs more than in collective-bargaining (external relations) activities. It has taken place in large part because labor unions continue to feel insecure and because they are capable of winning gains for their members only through a display of power, both elements leading to a psychology of military government rather than civil government, of an army rather than a polity, of a partisan cause rather than a diversified society. Through its internal discipline, it seeks a strength which enables it to discharge more effectively its principal function of achieving "democracy in industry" for its members. It thus excuses weaknesses in its internal democracy by the achievement of strength in industrial democracy. This rationalization has some validity, but it can be carried to excess and made the basis for the denial of rights which can be considered elemental, such as the right to express one's opinions and to enjoy a free choice of one's leaders.

Membership apathy in union affairs at both the local and national levels is due not so much to a feeling of ineffectiveness against boss domination as to a lack of membership interest. This throws on union leaders the necessity of taking power into their own hands for the effective functioning of the organization. Growth of bureaucratic structures also contributes to increased distance between members and leaders. This factor can be exaggerated, since a kind of informal representation may take place through activist members, but it seems probable that membership interest in union functions declines with time and familiarity, so that the union is looked on less as a society in which one participates than as an agent which is expected to take action on behalf of its members. Membership thus appears to be increasingly divorced from control, in unions as in corporations. Recognition of this fact may be partial explanation for the increased interest in legal limitations on the power of union officials to dominate or control individuals and in imposition of forms of social accountability on union officials.

ADDITIONAL READINGS

Chamberlain, Neil W.: *Sourcebook on Labor,* McGraw-Hill, New York, 1958, chaps. 3 and 4.

Cook, Alice H.: *Union Democracy: Practice and Ideal,* Cornell University, New York State School of Industrial and Labor Relations, Ithaca, N.Y., 1963.

James, Ralph C., and Estelle D. James: *Hoffa and the Teamsters,* Van Nostrand, Princeton, N.J., 1965.

Leiserson, William M.: *American Trade Union Democracy,* Columbia University Press, New York, 1959.

Lipset, Seymour M., M. A. Trow, and J. S. Coleman: *Union Democracy: The Internal Politics of the International Typographical Union,* Free Press, Chicago, Ill., 1956.

Mangum, Garth: *The Operating Engineers,* Harvard University Press, Cambridge, Mass., 1964.

Seidman, Joel, Jack London, Bernard Karsh, and Daisy Tagliacozzo: *The Worker Views His Union,* The University of Chicago Press, Chicago, 1958.

Seidman, Joel, and Daisy Tagliacozzo: "Union Government and Leadership," in N. W. Chamberlain, F. Pierson, and T. Wolfson, *A Decade of Industrial Relations Research, 1946–1956,* Harper, New York, 1958.

U.S. Bureau of Labor Statistics, *Directory of National and International Labor Unions in the United States,* issued biennially. The series contains a wealth of information on the structure of the labor movement, recent developments within unions, and the current size and distribution of union membership.

FOR ANALYSIS AND DISCUSSION

1. Compare the constitutions of any two national unions, one of which has a traditional craft orientation and the other a traditional industry orientation. What basic differences do you discover, if any? What explanation for any such differences can you suggest?

2. Of what value is the national union to the local union? What is the value of the AFL-CIO to a national union?

3. If you were a union member, would you be interested in running for local-union office? Why or why not? If you concede that getting good men is important for union governments no less than other governments, can you devise any ways of encouraging their availability and selection?

4. Explore the hypothesis that there is a growing separation between union membership and union control just as, for a long time, there has been a separation between corporate ownership and corporate control. Is there any reason to fear the effects of one any more than the other?

5. What criteria of democratic government do you consider most relevant to unions? What specific union practices would you consider necessary to satisfy the criteria you have set up? To the best of your knowledge, do most unions follow such practices? If possible, stop in the office of some local union or speak with an official of some local union to see whether the practices in that union appear to conform to your criteria. What reasons can you give for failure of the unions to measure up to any of the criteria you may have established?

6. John Jones had been president of Local 101 for five years. In that time he had seen to it that his members' grievances had been expeditiously

and equitably handled, and he had tried, in negotiations, to obtain wage increases and improved
conditions for them. He had also come to appreciate the company's competitive and financial
problems. It was supplying parts to the major
automobile assemblers, and there were numerous
rivals who would have been glad to take over its
contracts. Its equipment was not obsolete but
neither was it modern; its costs were—management maintained—higher than the average for
the industry.

Management had found John Jones to be more
reasonable than his predecessor, who had taken
the employees out on three strikes in five years.
There had been none in the last five years, under
Jones. The company had tried to make as much
information on its operations available to Jones
as it responsibly could, on the assumption that, if
he were convinced the company was being honest with him in its protestations that generally it
could not afford a wage increase as large as had
been granted by several competitors, he would be
more disposed to agree to a reasonable settlement.
Management's strategy of honesty appeared to
have paid off, and there was a good deal of satisfaction—sometimes expressed before local public
gatherings—with the state of union–management
cooperation in the plant.

The union elections were coming up in about
three months. Much to the surprise of John Jones
and the management, when Bill Smith announced
that he was going to run against Jones for the
presidency, he seemed to stir up a lot of enthusiasm. More and more "Smith" banners were
surreptitiously planted before they were detected
and removed by supervision. "Smith" labels appeared on more and more workers. As the elec-
tioneering became more active, it was evident
that the issue on which Smith was winning most
support was that Jones had been too "soft" with
the company, that he had worked so closely with
management that he had got to thinking like it,
that he was more concerned with whether the
company broke even than whether his members
broke even. Smith promised to change all that.
He would make the tightfisted company directors
pony up with wage increases—at least as much
as the other companies were paying. It was only
fair that workers in this company should get as

much as other workers who were no more skilled
than they, whose products sold for just the same
prices as theirs, and who didn't work any harder
than they worked.

Jones was puzzled. He didn't like the notion of
being defeated in the union election, but it looked
as though that was a distinct possibility. Some of
his friends told him that he was going to have to
talk as tough as Smith. But that would have meant
changing his character. He wasn't the fire-eating
type and he didn't want to appear like a double-
dealer to the management group, whose respect
he prized. On the other hand, if he didn't do
something along the lines his friends were urging,
he was going to find himself an ex-president, his
past five-year record discredited by his defeat,
without a position of prestige which he now
realized was pretty important to him. He won-
dered if he could talk tougher about management's having to improve its efficiency so that
wages could follow the industry pattern, without
at the same time raising false hopes that would
later be held against him both by the members of
his local and by management.

If you had been Jones, what would you have
done?

NOTES

1. U.S. Bureau of Labor Statistics, *Directory of
National and International Labor Unions in the United
States, 1967,* Bulletin 1596, 1968, pp. 69–70. Ironically, the average period between conventions may
now be a little longer under Landrum-Griffin than it
was before. In the mid-1950s, union constitutions
showed the following percentage distribution of convention frequency: 26 (one year), 34 (two years),
11 (three years), 14 (four years), 7 (five years),
and 8 (other or no provisions). See *Handbook of
Union Government, Structure, and Proceedings,* National Industrial Conference Board, New York, 1955,
p. 79. These figures may be misleading, for in earlier
years a few unions did not hold conventions as often
as their constitutions called for. But it is possible that
conventions are held less frequently today, partly because of their higher cost but perhaps also because
Landrum-Griffin now gives union officials a socially
approved time limit of five years, which is actually
longer than most unions had voluntarily adopted before 1959.

2. Myron L. Joseph examines the strengths and
weaknesses of the field representative staff in three
industrial unions in "The Role of the Field Staff

Representative," *Industrial and Labor Relations Review,* vol. 12, pp. 353–369, April, 1959.

3. Data on dues and initiation fees are from *A Report of the Bureau of Labor-Management Reports, Fiscal Year, 1960,* U.S. Department of Labor, 1960, pp. 26–27. Data for later years are less comprehensive but show no major changes since 1960. See Leon Applebaum, "Dues and Fees Structure of Local Unions," *Monthly Labor Review,* vol. 89, pp. 1236–1240, November, 1966, and Edward R. Curtin, *Union Initiation Fees, Dues and Per Capita Tax,* National Industrial Conference Board, New York, 1968.

4. We shall here be concerned only with the more frequently encountered intermediate bodies. There are other more complex structures which make some international unions look like holding companies for subsidiary organizations, which in turn charter other units, including locals.

5. Alice H. Cook has developed the two-governments theme in her very perceptive essay, "Dual Government in Unions: A Tool for Analysis," *Industrial and Labor Relations Review,* vol. 15, pp. 323–349, April, 1962.

6. Sam Romer, "The Area Conferences of the Teamsters Union," *Monthly Labor Review,* vol. 85, pp. 1105–1109, October, 1962; Ralph C. James and Estelle D. James, *Hoffa and the Teamsters,* Van Nostrand, Princeton, N.J., 1965, chaps. 5–8; and "One-Man Rule Ends for Teamsters," *Business Week,* May 20, 1967, pp. 152–153.

7. A forceful example is provided by President Ralph Helstein of the United Packinghouse Workers, in Arnold Weber (ed.), *The Structure of Collective Bargaining,* Free Press, New York, 1961, pp. 151–152:

It has become increasingly evident over the past decade that, at least from the point of view of the union, it is harder to separate the meat packing industry from the food industry as a whole.... In the past few years certain companies known primarily as producers of canned soups have, because of the nature of their product, become heavily involved in what has traditionally been thought of as the meat packing industry and perhaps to an even greater degree in the poultry business. A baking company, national in scope, is today one of the major factors in the production of packaged dinners, as is a wholesaler with national distribution both at the wholesale and retail level. Chain stores, which it has been estimated currently account for over 90 per cent of all meat and groceries sold to the American consumer, are also becoming involved in both the poultry and the meat packing and slaughtering industry.

It is symptomatic of these developments that the UPWA, which originally confined its organization to meat packing and slaughtering, has expanded its activities to include membership in other sectors of the food industry. Currently the UPWA is in such

diversified areas of the food industry as sugar production and refining, canning, poultry, agriculture (factories in the field), and miscellaneous operations involving fish and dairy products among others....

Reference is made to these developments for two reasons: (1) to suggest that the industry is in a state of transition and that no current discussion of the collective bargaining process can realistically overlook this fact, because changes in production and marketing methods inevitably create problems that must be dealt with through the collective bargaining process; and (2) to suggest that in the not-too-distant future the many labor unions presently active in various sections of the food industry will find it essential to re-evaluate their total position and to consider the kinds of mergers that will eventually result in the establishment of a single union in the food industry as a whole.

8. Additional reading on these trends may be found in John T. Dunlop, "Structural Changes in the American Labor Movement and Industrial Relations System," Industrial Relations Research Association (IRRA) *Proceedings,* 1956, pp. 12–32; Mark L. Kahn, "Contemporary Structural Changes in Organized Labor," IRRA *Proceedings,* 1957, pp. 171–179; Lloyd Ulman (ed.), *Challenges to Collective Bargaining,* Prentice-Hall, Englewood Cliffs, N.J., 1967, chap. 1; George H. Hildebrand, "Cloudy Future for Coalition Bargaining," *Harvard Business Review,* November–December, 1968, pp. 114–128; and John T. Dunlop and Neil W. Chamberlain (eds.), *Frontiers of Collective Bargaining,* Harper & Row, New York, 1967, chaps. 1–2.

9. Of all American unions, only the International Typographical Union has institutionalized political opposition by providing for a two-party system. For a full-length treatment of this unusual union, the reader is referred to S. M. Lipset, M. A. Trow, and J. S. Coleman, *Union Democracy: The Internal Politics of the International Typographical Union,* Free Press, Chicago, 1956. An abbreviated version is contained in S. M. Lipset, "Democracy in Private Government: A Case Study of the International Typographical Union," *British Journal of Sociology,* vol. 3, pp. 47–65, March, 1952.

10. Michels' statement is to be found in his *Political Parties,* International Library, New York, 1915, reprinted by The Free Press, Glencoe, Ill., in 1949. An application to unions has been made by Will Herberg, "Bureaucracy and Democracy in Labor Unions," *Antioch Review,* vol. 3, pp. 405–417, Fall, 1943.

11. Arthur J. Goldberg, "A Trade Union Point of View," in Michael Harrington and Paul Jacobs (eds.), *Labor in a Free Society,* University of California Press, Berkeley, 1959, pp. 105–106.

12. George Meany, "Clean Democratic Trade Unions," an address before the Industrial Union Department, AFL-CIO, 1957, pp. 20–21. The musing of

a union staff official is pertinent: "Is it always a question of the leaders autocratically taking control or is it a question of the members withdrawing and leaving the leaders no alternative?"

13. W. A. Faunce, "Size of Locals and Union Democracy," *American Journal of Sociology,* vol. 68, pp. 291–298, November, 1962.

14. The same, p. 294.

15. This thesis has been advanced by Joseph Kovner and Herbert J. Lahne in "Shop Society and the Union," *Industrial and Labor Relations Review,* vol. 7, pp. 3–14, October, 1953.

16. Joel Seidman, Jack London, Bernard Karsh, and Daisy L. Tagliacozzo, *The Worker Views His Union,* The University of Chicago Press, Chicago, 1958, chaps. 3 and 9; and George Strauss, *Unions in the Building Trades, A Case Study,* University of Buffalo Studies, vol. 24, no. 2, June, 1958, chaps. 6–8.

17. The UAW's Public Review Board has the longest history of effective operation, having decided nearly 200 cases from its founding in 1957 through 1968. The decisions of the Board, composed of prominent individuals independent of the union's officialdom, are final and binding upon the union. The Upholsterers' Public Appeals Board appears to be defunct, having limited authority and having decided only one case (in 1956) since its establishment in 1953. In 1965, the Western Pulp and Paper Workers, an independent union of 20,000 members on the West Coast, set up a review board, and in 1967 the American Federation of Teachers also established such a board. See Jack Stieber, Walter E. Oberer, and Michael Harrington, *Democracy and Public Review,* Center for the Study of Democratic Institutions, Santa Barbara, Calif., 1960.

CHAPTER II

**COLLECTIVE BARGAINING I:
THE STRUCTURE AND THE
PROCESS**

As we have already noted, the only reason for the existence of unions lies in the agency role which they perform on behalf of their constituents. To some extent this function can be performed through political activity at local, state, and national levels. Organized labor then takes on the character of a political pressure group seeking advantages for those with whom it is identified. We shall examine this political function later. At the moment, we are concerned with the agency role which has been most characteristic of American unions—that of representative of a particular group of workers in their relations with a particular employer or group of employers. It is a bargaining agent in a bargaining process.

We have already touched on this process at a number of points in previous pages—necessarily so, since the process is so central to union activity. In Chapters 6 and 7, we saw that the history of organized labor in the United States has been an exercise in counterpoint, with the theme of social reform set off against the theme of attempted accommodation with existing business interests, one theme and then the other at times taking ascendancy, but with growing emphasis since the turn of the century on accommodation. The theme of accommodation is played on the instrument of collective bargaining, so that the history of unionism in the United States is largely the history of the growth in importance of the institutions of bargaining. In Chapter 8, we noted the legal devices for structuring the union–

management power relationship along lines considered socially constructive. In Chapter 10, we saw that the union's bargaining activity calls for a government separate in important respects from the government which administers its internal affairs. In the present chapter, we shall take a closer look at the bargaining process itself and how it operates.

The bargaining unit

Collective bargaining begins with the negotiation of an agreement specifying the terms of employment. But terms applying to whom? If the Steelworkers and United States Steel sign an agreement, this tells us very little about who is covered by its provisions. It is not likely to cover the railroad employees on the rail facilities which the company owns and operates in conjunction with its plants; they will be provided for under an agreement or agreements with the railroad brotherhoods. It is not likely to cover certain groups of construction workers, for whom the building-trades unions such as the Carpenters and Bricklayers will bargain. It is not likely to cover some of the company's truck drivers and warehousemen, for whom the Teamsters may act as bargaining agent. It is not likely to cover the clerical employees or salesmen, who may not be represented by any union at all. Just whom it does cover has to be spelled out in the agreement. The *bargaining unit* is simply a short term for the employer and employee groups who are in fact covered by a particular contract.

The legal determination of the bargaining unit, preliminary to a representation election, is a function of the National Labor Relations Board, as was noted in Chapter 8. In performing that function, the Board has elaborated a number of rules as to what constitutes an "appropriate" unit for bargaining purposes—rules which specify what kinds of employees may appropriately be grouped together, and what parts or divisions of a company (or what companies, when more than one is involved) constitute a fitting unit for collective bargaining. There is often a difference, however, between the initial unit which is the basis for a representation election and the actual unit which evolves over time, after the election has taken place. Thus the NLRB may rule that all the production employees in a newly organized plant constitute an appropriate bargaining unit, but if those employees select as their agent the same union which is already representing the workers in the company's other plants, the chances are that a single agreement will cover all the plants of the company, including the new one. The *legal* determination of the bargaining unit in this instance would have been significant only for purposes of the representation election and not for the bargaining process itself. It is the latter, the bargaining process, which concerns us now.

There are surprisingly few statistics available on the incidence of collective bargaining in the United States, for no complete census of bargaining units has ever been made. It is estimated, however, that there are about 140,000 union–management contracts in effect in the country as a whole. Perhaps two-thirds of these agreements cover workers who are employed in the same *plant*; about four-fifths of all agreements are limited to workers of a single *company*. Thus only one-fifth of all bargaining units are multiemployer. These, however, account for at least one-third of all workers under collective agreements.[1]

The fact that bargaining in the United States customarily proceeds on a single-employer basis is especially noteworthy in view of experience in other countries. Abroad, the characteristic pattern is negotiation on an industry or an association basis. These industry agreements are often sup-

plemented by local agreements, but the basic terms are negotiated in a multiemployer unit usually encompassing most of an industry. In some countries there is the further practice of "extending" by governmental authority the terms of an agreement negotiated by "representative" industry and union authorities to all other establishments in that industry, whether or not organized by the same union or not organized at all. Collective bargaining around the world is thus customarily collective on the side of employers as well as employees. The United States is the major exception to this rule. Here, collective bargaining is primarily collective only with respect to employees, and on the employer's side is largely on an individual-firm basis.

The vast number of units are small in size. Probably as many as one-sixth have fewer than 25 employees. Two-thirds cover no more than 200 to 300 employees. Units with more than 20,000 employees constitute no more than ½ percent of all units. It is clear that, despite the publicity attending major negotiations, the United States is predominantly a nation of small bargaining units. This is in line with the emphasis on single-plant and single-employer bargaining.

Although the bulk of the units is small, the bulk of the workers covered is in large units. Although perhaps only one-half of all units have as many as 100 employees, they account for almost 95 percent of all workers covered by agreements. The Bureau of Labor Statistics has twice taken a census of all "major" units covering at least 1,000 workers.[2] The total number of such units in 1961 was 1,733, embracing 8.3 million workers or perhaps not quite half the number under all collective agreements. The nine largest units (those including 100,000 workers or more) together represented almost 23 percent of the total number of workers covered by the 1,733 agreements in 1961. Six of these were in transportation and transportation equipment. The other three were in steel, coal mining, and men's clothing. These nine units accounted, then, for more than 10 percent of all workers under collective-bargaining agreements in the United States.

The fact that wage and employment matters are negotiated unit by unit does not imply that each bargaining unit—discrete though it be—has no relationship to any other. Within recent years there has developed an intricate system of "pattern setting" and "pattern following." There is a well-recognized tendency for the wage increase which is negotiated in one of the major bargaining units in an industry to set a pattern which lesser bargaining units follow. Key bargains are not always followed without deviation, but wage changes in a given industry are likely to conform, within imprecise limits, to what is negotiated by the pattern setter. We shall examine this in greater detail when discussing wage determination.

Changing dimensions of bargaining units

It has rather generally been accepted that the secular trend in the United States is toward larger and larger bargaining units. Over the years there has been some tendency for the unit in one plant to be merged with the units in other plants in the same company; in most large corporations, bargaining at one time proceeded (and in some cases still does proceed) on a separate plant basis before graduating into a companywide negotiation. Similarly, the firm which once bargained by itself may join with other firms in a multiemployer unit—on a purely local, citywide basis if it is engaged in a local trade, such as dry cleaning, or department-store selling, or moving and storage, or hotelling, or on a national-industry basis if operating in a national-product market. That single-plant and single-employer bargaining still predominate does not necessarily negate the presumption that this trend toward larger units is nevertheless at work, effectively whittling away at the parochial character of American industrial relations.

One example of how this expansion in the scope of the unit may take place over time is provided by the meat-packing industry. Two unions, the Amalgamated Meat Cutters and Butcher Workmen (first in the field, and originally affiliated with the AFL) and the United Packinghouse Workers (a CIO-created union from the hectic organizing days of the late thirties) are the principal labor organizations. Although the importance of the firms in the industry has undergone some shift in recent years,

Swift, Armour, Wilson, and Cudahy are still popularly referred to as the "Big Four." Generally, the NLRB-determined appropriate bargaining units in the industry consist of the production and maintenance employees in a single plant of a company. By 1943, however, notwithstanding the plant certifications, each major company was negotiating a master agreement for all its meat-packing and slaughtering plants. The next stage was informal consultation between the two unions, on the one hand, and among the major companies, on the other. The fact that all agreements have common expiration dates facilitated such discussions. In 1959 the pattern-setting company in the industry, followed by the other principal companies, negotiated a joint agreement with both unions, resulting in single-company multiunion contracts but with very comparable terms. Thus, over a period of twenty-five years this industry moved from single-plant units to something approximating an industrywide agreement.[3]

The enlargement of a bargaining unit is almost always designed to incorporate within the framework of one agreement all those individuals—employees and employers alike—who otherwise might undercut each other by setting different wages and prices, thereby making impossible the maintenance of any standard. Basically, the idea behind the larger bargaining unit is the same principle that underlies minimum-wage laws—to create some wage standard below which producers will not be allowed to set their rates as a means of competing. Even without government powers, labor unions can attempt to "take wages out of competition," to use the phrase which they have popularized, by seeking to set the same rate in all their negotiations; they can accomplish the result even more effectively by including all competitors under the same agreement.

Although unions thus tend to favor broader bargaining units than employers do, there are many exceptions to that generalization. It is true, for example, that many employers are resisting coalition bargaining by unions today, but others—such as the meat-packing companies just described—have long seen advantages in coalescing bargaining units. Also, we noted in Chapter 8 that a move to sever a craft group from an industrial unit will often produce a confusing lineup of parties, with the employer joining the industrial union in opposing the smaller unit sought by the craft union.

In dealing with multiplant corporations operating in national-product markets, most industrial unions have pressed hard for a companywide contract, often supplemented by plant agreements dealing with local issues, and employers have long agreed to such contracts in auto, rubber, and several other industries. But some of these unions have lost their earlier enthusiasm for pressing the bargaining unit further to include all of the large corporations in a concentrated industry; instead, they now favor the type of single-employer negotiation which we have seen is actually the more characteristic form in the United States. The reason for this change of heart is not hard to fathom. If the union is left free to concentrate its pressure against that major corporation within the industry which seems most susceptible to agreement on favorable terms, those terms can be made the pattern for the industry. With the pattern set by an industry leader, other firms in that industry will have the burden of proving why they cannot grant terms at least as favorable. If some less prosperous firms can indeed make such a showing, the terms may be shaved somewhat to suit their particular circumstances, but only after tough bargaining.

This pattern-setting procedure has been contrasted by those who espouse it to the multiemployer bargaining situation. In the latter case, employers must first agree among themselves on the terms they will jointly accept before they can strike an agreement with the union. In their group will be included not only the industry's most prosperous companies but also its most struggling firms. The common terms must somehow be made to fit both extremes. The likelihood is, therefore, that the terms finally agreed upon will strike some sort of balance between the most and the least profitable firms—an "average" settlement, which may place some pressure on the marginal employers, but with which they can, with great effort, manage to live. But the terms have been bargained down from what the industry's leading companies could afford to pay. With pattern setting, however, the union picks out the company from which it expects to win the most favorable

settlement and then bargains all other firms *up* to that level or as close to it as possible, with the union guarding against the possibility that any firms to which concessions are granted might engage in unfair competition on the strength of their somewhat lower wage rates.[4]

On the whole, the large national corporations have preferred single-firm bargaining. They have resisted having decisions on wages and other labor costs and conditions made for them by other employers, who may be operating under quite different circumstances or philosophies. They have sought to retain an independence of action and an opportunity to tailor their terms to their own needs on the strength of their own bargaining power. They have been wary lest multifirm bargaining by the "giants" invite government intervention to avoid a strike or to influence a settlement presumed inflationary. Therefore, multiemployer units are generally composed of small companies rather than big corporations.

But just as some labor leaders have undergone a change of heart with respect to the size of the bargaining unit, so have some management people, but in the opposite direction. There is a greater appreciation of the advantages of pooling their power against a national union which might otherwise play one against the other in negotiations. Thus an industrial-relations executive in the steel industry has commented that since 1955, when the steel companies "reluctantly acceded to a union proposal for intercompany negotiations," the industry has found that:[5]

. . . industry-wide bargaining gave management certain advantages. It prevented the union from attempting whipsaw tactics. It gave the smaller companies among the top twelve a larger voice in determining the final settlement than they had had when following the pattern-determining settlements of U.S. Steel. And industry-wide bargaining also helped to balance the economic power of the union.

In industries characterized by numerous small firms, where the classical concept of pure competition is approached, unions are still wedded to multiemployer bargaining as the procedure by which advances in wages can best be made. No single firm—small and struggling against numerous competitors—can afford to improve its terms unless all its business rivals do likewise. By bringing all such small employers together into an association and negotiating a settlement with all simultaneously, the union can make gains which otherwise would be impossible. Moreover, employers in the intensely competitive industries are themselves likely to prefer dealing with a union through employers' associations rather than as individuals. Each employer feels weak and impotent alongside the union; a strike while his rivals continue to operate would put him out of business, but so also would a wage increase not matched by his competitors. The solution to this dilemma is provided by his jointly negotiating with his business competitors, so that all grant the same wage increase and, if necessary, all take a strike together.

There are thus a variety of forces at work affecting the area of the bargaining unit—union efforts to escape competitive pressures on wage rates, small-employer efforts to band together to resist the power of the union, the traditional feeling of independence on the part of most employers, the rise of large corporations which have assumed pattern-setting functions, and industry cohesion to avoid whipsaw tactics. As has been noted, there are no adequate statistics to measure what the net effect has been of these various influences, but the prevalent belief among labor economists is that the trend is toward a continuing enlargement of the scope of the bargaining unit, with industrywide bargaining comparable to the practice in most other countries as the eventual result.

This may indeed be the long-run result, but there is some reason for keeping an open mind on the question. There have been numerous instances in which larger units have been fractionalized, as demonstrated by the continuing flow of craft-severance petitions filed with the NLRB. These changes in the direction of smaller bargaining units—which admittedly may be short run, not affecting a long-run drift toward larger units—provide us with the clue to why the dimensions of bargaining units change. The units expand or are split up as one party or another seeks to manipulate the unit to improve its own bargaining power. If an individual employer splits off from

an association and insists on negotiating his own agreement, it is because he believes that he is in a position to win better terms as an individual than those he would have to accept if he were forced to comply with the association's settlement. If several employers agree among themselves not to make any independent arrangements but to settle only as a unit, their purpose may be to avoid a union's divide-and-rule tactics.

The reason why a bargaining unit expands or contracts can always be traced back to the efforts of one or the other party to win a more advantageous agreement than would be possible in a different unit. At some times this dictates smaller, and at other times larger, units. It therefore seems an equally reasonable hypothesis to lay alongside the view that units generally will expand to become industrywide that, while there will always be some units in the process of expanding (as this suits the interests of union or employers), there will also always be large units in the process of disintegration, with no trend actually developing in either direction.

The *net* effect of expansion and contraction may turn out to be in the direction of larger and larger units. It may prove to be true that units will tend to expand to become coextensive with product markets. But this end result no longer seems quite so certain as it once did.

Negotiating the contract

After the bargaining unit has been defined, there begins the often bewildering process of negotiating the contract that is to govern the union–management relationship over a fixed period—usually for two or three years, though the contract's duration is itself a subject for bargaining. Regardless of the topic, however, why do labor negotiations so often appear to be irrational, with table thumping and threats and absurd demands and frantic, all-night meetings as the strike deadline approaches? Why don't the parties rely more on facts and less on propaganda and power? And particularly, why does society permit bargaining disagreements to be settled by the brute force of a strike?

One of the most perceptive analyses of the bargaining process has been made by Professors

Richard E. Walton and Robert B. McKersie,[6] who point out that labor negotiations actually consist of four systems of activity: distributive bargaining, integrative bargaining, attitudinal structuring, and intraorganizational bargaining. Each of these processes deserves examination, for each makes different demands upon negotiators and each also sheds light on the questions posed above.

By "distributive bargaining," the authors mean that type of negotiation with which most people are familiar—straight-out haggling over how to split up a pie, with one party's gain being the other party's loss. Nearly everyone has engaged in this type of bargaining in buying a used car or in selling a house or in conducting similar activities. In labor negotiations, of course, wages are the classic example of a distributive issue. If anyone knew what a "fair wage" is, we would not need bargaining or even competitive markets; we could establish wages by law and forbid employers to pay less and workers to ask for more. But since no one can measure a fair wage, we leave the issue to the interplay of market forces and, in a very loose sense, the worker's gain is the employer's loss.

These truisms have two implications for negotiators. First, "hard facts" have only a limited value in determining a wage settlement. The union negotiator will admit that wages of $20 an hour would bankrupt the average employer, who in turn will admit that wages of $1 an hour would leave him without any good workers, but such factual outer limits are not of much help in deciding whether workers now averaging $3 an hour should be raised by 10, 20, or 30 cents an hour. Second, given this range of indeterminancy, each negotiator has an incentive to bluff. If the union man really would accept a 15-cent increase rather than call a strike, why not open with a demand for 30 cents and plead and threaten and bluff with the employer in the hope of persuading him that it will take at least 18 or 20 cents to avert a strike? If the bluff succeeds, the union negotiator has done his job well; if it fails, he can still fall back to his true position of 15 cents. Also, for all the union man knows, perhaps the employer has privately determined that he will go as high as 20 cents to avoid a strike, and the union negotia-

tor would consider it foolish to risk opening for less than the employer might eventually be willing to give. But the employer is also thinking in the same terms, so each party often opens with a transparently unrealistic position; each knows what the other is doing, and the art of distributive bargaining is to probe for (and possibly alter) the true position of your opponent while concealing your own for as long as possible.

At the same time, however, the parties may also be engaged in "integrative bargaining," meaning the negotiation of an issue on which both parties may gain, or at least neither one loses. Suppose, for example, that the parties have decided in principle on a job-evaluation system, or retraining for workers who will be technologically displaced, or an extension of the health-insurance plan to cover dental expenses. Once the contentious issues of principle and money are out of the way, both parties may well gain from a cooperative search for the best job-evaluation system or retraining program or dental-insurance policy— one that will fit their particular needs and give maximum results for each dollar they have agreed to spend. For this purpose, quite different tactics are called for: open and frank discussions of possible alternatives, with perhaps joint committees to uncover the facts on these technical issues. Yet, how can you be frank and factual on these issues while still bluffing and storming over the distributive issues?

Third, collective bargaining differs from many other types of negotiation by its strong involvement in "attitudinal structuring," meaning the shaping of such attitudes as trust or distrust, friendliness or hostility, between the parties. Unlike many businessmen and diplomats who negotiate agreements, union and management negotiators often must live with each other and their contracts the year around. It is one thing to bluff and threaten someone with whom you have only a sporadic and strictly commercial relationship; it can be quite a different matter to negotiate with someone today on whom you must depend tomorrow and every other day in performing your job as industrial relations director or union president. This factor can promote restraint (or even collusion) between the negotiators, but it can also have the opposite effect: If friction has developed between these officials in their daily dealings under the old contract, a backlog of bitterness may have developed that can erupt and make a shambles of the negotiations over a new contract.

Further, note that a peculiar metamorphosis is supposed to occur during the bargaining process. On most days of the year, part-time union officials are subordinates taking orders from management on the job, and off the job even full-time union leaders often carry a lower social status than their employer counterparts. Yet, during negotiations the law says these union officials are management's equals and in a showdown they may even prove to be "superior" in the power they bring to bear. One need not be a psychologist to appreciate the strains that can arise from this change or reversal of roles, particularly when a union first organizes a plant, an experience many employers find deeply humiliating.

The internal bargains

Finally, perhaps the most underrated aspect of labor negotiations is the process of "intraorganizational bargaining," by which Walton and McKersie mean the maneuvering to achieve consensus within (rather than between) the labor and management organizations. It is understandable that most people view collective bargaining as a clash between two monoliths, for each party strives to present a solid front to the other and to the public. In fact, however, internal bargaining is very widespread and has a pronounced effect upon bargaining between the parties.

If we think of the union first, this is more readily apparent. A union is composed of a number of individuals of varying skills, ages, ambitions, and other distinguishing characteristics. Because the union is designed to reduce competition among them in their relations with the employer so that workers do not reduce wages and other benefits by bidding against each other for jobs, this does not mean that competition in other forms does not go on among the employees of a company. Indeed, the fact that the union reduces competition among them in certain respects probably intensifies other forms of competition.

There are always groups within a union which believe that their interests are not being given adequate consideration by the organization. The skilled workers may believe that the union pays too much attention to the unskilled; women members may think that their interests are not fairly considered by the men who run the union; in a company with two plants, the local at one may feel that its interests are subordinated to those of the other; and so on. In the election of union officers, these interest groups are in the same kind of bargaining relationship as the voter and the politician in the broader political society. Candidates for union office will try to appeal to factional interests to win votes, and the factions or special-interest groups within the union will seek to use their votes to place in office the men most favorably disposed to their concerns.

Not only are there such differences to be bargained out within the local union, but sometimes differences arise between the local union and the national organization. Suppose, for example, that the local leadership is convinced that management will not grant more than a 5-cents-an-hour increase, but the national union pattern is 15 cents an hour. To permit a settlement at the lower figure may jeopardize what the national union can obtain in other negotiations; to insist on the higher figure may involve the local union in a long and fruitless strike. The competing interests within the union must be resolved, and this resolution comes about through a bargaining process —though not of a formal nature. Bargaining with the employer cannot even begin until this internal bargaining has taken place.

If a unit expands, subsuming more and more worker groups under a single agreement or set of terms, the more likely will it be that members' aspirations will be divergent and competitive rather than common. The larger the unit, the more difficult it becomes to find the common denominator to which all can relate themselves. Groups that believe that their interests are being sacrificed and their aspirations ignored may find greater reward in dissociating themselves from the alliance and negotiating on their own behalf—or at least they may have greater bargaining power in internal-union decision making if they threaten to do so.

In examining union government in the preceding chapter, we observed that special provision must sometimes be made for representation of particular blocs or interest groups within the union. This is especially true with respect to collective bargaining. Craft groups in industrial unions may be given an element of autonomy in deciding the conditions which will apply to them, or they may obtain disproportionate representation in collective bargaining.[7]

Once bargaining begins with the employer, the union negotiator must still be sensitive to these internal pressures. For example, a union often submits a staggering number of initial demands not only for purposes of distributive bargaining— to provide itself with a stock of trading materials, some important and others throw-away items— but also to demonstrate to each group in the union that its particular demands have been voiced to the employer. Also, few political leaders win reelection by appearing to be cozy and comfortable with the opposition, and union leaders are certainly no exception. They can never win everything the members want, but they can at least appear to be tough and aggressive in hammering out a compromise. This militant behavior may even serve a further purpose: For workers who chafe under the daily discipline of their jobs and sometimes yearn for the courage to tell off their foremen, there may be a certain catharsis—healthy or unhealthy, depending on one's view—in seeing their union leaders verbally flay top management itself. For some or all of these reasons, a union leader must negotiate with one eye on management and the other on his constituents.

On the side of the employer, something of the same sort also takes place. In a small firm under owner control, there is, of course, little need to resolve conflicting interests comparable to those facing the union. In businesses of any size, where the management hierarchy is large enough to involve special departmental interests and conflicting judgments, there may well be differences which have to be resolved between, for example, the sales manager and the company treasurer. The sales manager may urge that a settlement be made with the union and a strike avoided at all costs so that the relationship with important customers can be protected, and the company treasurer may insist that any wage increase beyond a given amount would be disastrous to the com-

pany's finances. Similarly, there may be conflicts between those who believe that the best way to deal with the union is to be tough with it and those who think it wisest to try to work out more amicable relations.

Moreover, just as the union must resolve conflicting interests between local and national, so too must the company harmonize the objectives of a local plant and the company as a whole. Plant management may be directed to take a stand on some issue which is either contrary to its own best judgment or not suited to its own needs, for fear that a precedent will be set which the union will seek to use in bargaining with other plants of the same company. Where management bargains through an employers' association, the problem of reconciling differences among the companies that compose the association is directly comparable to that confronting the union in dealing with special-interest blocs within its membership. In ocean shipping, for example, differences often develop between the subsidized and non-subsidized lines; in trucking, between companies running different routes or hauling different commodities; and in construction, between local and national contractors when the latter are only working temporarily in a particular area and thus have no long-run interest in standing firm against a local union.

For the management negotiator who is not the owner of the business, all of this means that he too must please the "constituents" on whom his job depends. Like his union counterpart, he too can never win everything in bargaining that his constituents would like to have, so a show of militancy may also help him to prove that he is not selling out to the other party when he ultimately makes concessions.

In summary, Walton and McKersie's analysis demonstrates that the negotiation process is far more complex than it appears to the casual observer. It is not just a poker game for high stakes or another buyer-seller relationship, although it contains elements of those and other types of economic and political (and theatrical) activities. Nor does it impugn the integrity of labor and management negotiators to point out the ritualistic nature of much of the bargaining process; the players usually know the rules of the game and understand that serious issues are at stake. But because there is seldom a single "right" answer to the economic issues in dispute, and because the union–management relationship also involves a clash of political, psychological, and organizational interests, the negotiation process inevitably bears little resemblance to a dispassionate search for truth. Each of the four subprocesses described above places severe and conflicting pressures upon a negotiator, some pushing him to be candid and cooperative and others tempting him to bluff and browbeat his opposite number. Different negotiators respond to these conflicting pressures in very different ways, and no one has yet discovered a formula for success at the bargaining table.

The function of the strike

How is this elaborate maneuvering ever resolved? If there is no "right" answer to be discovered and if each negotiator has an incentive to conceal his true position on some issues for as long as possible, how do the parties settle anything? The answer lies in the fact that nearly every union contract in this country has a fixed expiration date; the union usually agrees not to strike during the life of a contract but is then free to pursue a policy of "no contract, no work." Negotiations for a new contract thus begin one or two months or more before the current contract expires, frequently drag on in a desultory fashion for a few weeks, and then quicken in pace and movement as the expiration date approaches—for that is the deadline at which all the bluffs are called, all the speeches must end, and either the parties agree on contract terms or both will incur the costs of a strike.

Later chapters will discuss the concept and weapons of bargaining power in some detail, but at this point it is important to understand the crucial role of the strike in the bargaining process. When labor and management disagree over wages or any other issue, how might their disagreement be resolved? One way, of course, is for the employees to quit and look for work elsewhere, but that is hardly what Congress meant when it said that workers could have an equal voice in determining wages and working conditions. Indeed, if this free-market alternative worked satisfactorily,

we would have no reason to permit unions to exist at all. Second, the workers could marshal all the facts at their disposal and plead their case before management. But even the most fair-minded employer is bound to disagree often with his workers' view of the facts of industrial life, and in effect he wins every dispute as long as the workers can only talk, leaving him free to determine wages and working conditions as he sees fit. Third, society could require both parties to submit their dispute to a government agency or court for a binding decision, but such compulsory arbitration is opposed by most management and union officials and by both of the major political parties. There are several reasons for this opposition which we shall explore later, but to illustrate: If the government is to fix wages, why should it not also fix prices and profits and make all the other economic decisions now left in private hands?

That appears to leave only the alternative of permitting workers to cut off their employer's income by means of a strike. No one can claim that the strike is an elegant or a precise weapon, or that it has never been abused. But neither has anyone yet discovered an alternative generally acceptable to the parties which permits workers an *effective* voice in establishing their terms of employment. It is true that the strike can nearly obliterate some employers, but its effectiveness varies greatly from one situation to the next. Often overlooked, for example, is the fact that the strike cuts off the workers' income as well as the employer's, so that a union leader must think twice before recommending that his members walk out rather than accept the employer's last offer.

That also suggests why, contrary to popular belief, the lockout is not usually the employer's equivalent of the strike. If a union strikes only the most vulnerable company in a multiemployer unit, the other companies may lock out their workers to preserve a united front. In the more typical bargaining relationship, however, the employer would gain nothing by triggering a lockout upon the expiration of a contract; that would be tantamount to calling a strike against himself. As long as the union continues to talk instead of strike, he is ahead of the game with his profits and production continuing as before, usually on the terms of the expired contract.[8] The employer's real counter to a strike is, paradoxically, his ability to take a strike—or, stated differently, his ability to force the union, at the strike deadline, to choose between accepting his last offer or calling a strike that will hurt its own members as well as the employer.

For these reasons, the strike weapon has a pronounced impact upon negotiations *even when it is not used*. In the mid-1960s, there were only 4,000 to 5,000 strikes a year in the estimated 140,000 bargaining units in this country (though because of long-term contracts there were fewer than 140,000 negotiations in any one year). But the mere availability of labor's right to strike for its demands, and the countervailing "right" of the employer to take a strike rather than yield to those demands, weigh heavily in the calculations of both parties as the strike deadline approaches. There lies the primary incentive for the parties to back off from their extreme positions and to inch toward a compromise agreement, most often without resort to an actual strike.

New approaches

What has just been described is the orthodox model of labor negotiations. In practice, of course, no two negotiations are ever alike, but in general those are the conventional explanations of what goes on at the bargaining table and why. This process has never suffered from a lack of critics, however, and in recent years there have been two particularly interesting attempts to revamp the negotiating procedure.

One of these is known as "Boulwarism," after its originator, Lemuel Boulware, formerly a vice-president of the General Electric Company. This company had progressive personnel relations in the 1920s, accepted unions without a fight in the 1930s, and had generally good labor relations up to the mid-1940s. GE's management was therefore shocked when its workers launched a bitter, two-month strike in 1946, and the company decided that the orthodox approach to collective bargaining left something to be desired. The alternative it adopted is unique in two respects. First, the company refuses to play the haggling game. Instead of starting low and letting itself be dragged up to the final offer it perhaps had in mind from the start—a tactic that makes the union the hero and the company the villain in the eyes of many workers—GE now makes its first offer a full and final one. Second, in addition to meeting with union representatives, GE conducts an extensive communication program in which it tries to sell its offer directly to the employees and urges them to make their views known to their union officials.

There are several avowed objectives of this policy. By making a good offer from the beginning and explaining it directly to the workers, the company hopes to demonstrate that it "does right voluntarily" by its employees and not because it is forced to do so by the union. Similarly, by refusing to alter its offer to play the bargaining game, or to make the union officers look good, or even to avert a strike, the company hopes to establish the same credibility with its workers that it believes it has with its product customers; that is, it wants to prove that its word can be trusted whether the management is describing its refrigerators or its contract offers.

And, finally, the company asserts that it is attempting to substitute reason for force in the bargaining process by formulating its first and final offer on the basis of all available facts, including the union's proposals, and by making sure that the union members know what they are voting on if their leaders ask them to reject the company's offer. As a company official has stated this:[9]

> General Electric does not believe in changing proposals merely because of the threat, or carrying out, of a strike. This stems not from any intransigence on our part, but rather because we believe that peace and progress is not advanced by rewarding force, and because we believe our proposals should be soundly based on facts.... Bluff, blunder, and force are all out of place in collective bargaining today, if, indeed, they ever had a valid place.

To the many critics of Boulwarism, all of this is rhetoric which conceals a power relationship in which the company holds the upper hand.

In the continuing controversy over Boulwarism,

three facts may best summarize its future prospects. In 1964, after one of the lengthiest NLRB investigations on record, the Board ruled in effect that Boulwarism constitutes bad-faith bargaining. In brief, the Board reasoned that GE's use of a "first, full" offer indicated a take-it-or-leave-it attitude, and that its intensive communication program indicated an attempt to deal with the union through the employees rather than with the employees through their union.[10] This decision has been upheld by the courts and will undoubtedly discourage most other employers who might be tempted to adopt Boulwarism.

Probably more significant is the fact that very few companies adopted this strategy even before the Board decision, although Boulwarism was widely publicized and appeared to be highly successful at GE throughout the 1950s. Finally, the protracted GE strike in 1969 and 1970 produced concessions on the company's part that suggested to some observers that the advantages of Boulwarism were being reevaluated. In these negotiations, a number of unions representing GE employees had organized a coalition which retained its unity throughout the three-month stoppage, a factor which sufficiently strengthened the unions' bargaining position to make a "holding-of-the-line" strategy excessively expensive to the company.

Taken together, these facts suggest that Boulwarism can only flourish in a very special environment—one requiring (depending on your viewpoint) either great skill or great power on the part of management—and it is most unlikely to be the trend of the future in labor negotiations.[11]

Continuous bargaining

The other new bargaining approach has been dubbed "continuous bargaining," to contrast it with conventional deadline bargaining. Instead of postponing meaningful negotiations until the last few weeks or even the last few hours before a strike deadline, this approach calls for the parties to explore particularly difficult bargaining problems in joint meetings over a long period of time, sometimes throughout the life of each contract.[12]

The basic steel industry provides the classic example of both the strengths and weaknesses of continuous bargaining. In the first decade after World War II, this industry was racked by five major strikes and various forms of government intervention up to and including a presidential seizure of the steel mills. Critics charged both parties in the industry with being less interested in genuine bargaining than in establishing a favorable public relations image to bolster them when the White House ultimately stepped in. Steel wages and prices soared, but so did unemployment and foreign and domestic competition. Then in 1959, the parties reached a new height of conflict: Steel management suddenly went on the attack for changes in long-established work rules, the union countered that its members needed more rather than less job security, the ensuing 116-day strike was ended only by a Taft-Hartley injunction, and the final settlement was reached not at the bargaining table but in the home of Richard Nixon, then Vice-President of the United States.

But to everyone's amazement, the next steel contract was quietly settled three months before the previous agreement had expired, and then, to cap the climax, in the next round in 1963, the parties deliberately refused to invoke the formal reopening clause of their agreement and peacefully negotiated a new contract with no deadline at all confronting them. During this same period, the Kaiser Steel Company, which had broken away from the rest of the industry during the 1959 strike, joined union leaders and outside experts in a tripartite committee which, also without a strike, produced a formula to settle the thorny issues of technological change and job security in that company.

What had happened? The complete story may never be known publicly, but certain facts stand out. Collective bargaining was going through a difficult transitional period in many industries, including steel. In the full-employment, inflationary years of the 1940s and early 1950s, collective bargaining often struck observers as being "much like quarreling over who will pay the check when both parties can put it on the same expense account."[13] By the late 1950s all this had changed. Faced with stable prices and more intense foreign and domestic competition, employers fought for lower wage increases and more freedom to cut labor costs by technological and work-rule changes. Unions, faced with growing unemployment among their members in several industries, strongly resisted any whittling away of their traditional job safeguards and, indeed, demanded added protection against the inroads of automation.

At this point, the late James P. Mitchell, then the highly respected Secretary of Labor in the Eisenhower administration, sounded a theme soon to be echoed by many others:

> In 1959 . . . Mitchell warned employers and unions that they must not place too much reliance on "antiquated" collective bargaining processes. Contracts had become too complex to be negotiated in the last month of an expiring contract, with tension, tempers, and timetables creating problems. Mitchell urged continuing bargaining during the life of a contract —a closer working relationship of the employer and union.
>
> At the time, Mitchell was sorely concerned about the basic steel deadlock and developing steel strike of 1959. He saw the impasse as dangerous for the future of collective bargaining.[14]

The disastrous 116-day strike seemed to confirm Mitchell's worst fears but, buried in the final agreement (in which Mr. Mitchell, as well as Mr. Nixon, had a hand) was an apparently innocuous provision calling for the establishment of two committees: the Committee on Local Working Conditions, in which the parties, together with a neutral chairman, were to explore further the major strike issue of work rules; and the Human Relations Research Committee, with a vague mandate to study, in effect, whatever other problems the parties could agree needed joint study. To most observers at the time, this looked like the classic gambit of burying a tough issue by referring it to a committee (or, even worse, two committees). In fact, the parties proved unable even to agree upon a neutral chairman for the first committee, and it quickly expired.

From some source, however, the parties developed the will to make the second committee work. This group, later known simply as the Human Relations Committee, was given considerable credit by some for paving the way to the early settlement of the 1962 contract, but others felt the Kennedy administration had also played a major role in persuading the union to accept its smallest postwar economic gain. But in 1963 there was no government intervention of any kind and no dispute over the key contribution of the committee. In sharp contrast to the headline-seeking negotiations of former years, both sides not only refrained from formally reopening the 1962 contract but even denied, up to the point of final agreement, that they were really bargaining in the 250 or more private committee meetings held during the term of the old contract. Also, the new contract contained a unique "experimental agreement" on four job-security issues to be overseen by the Human Relations Committee, permitting further bargaining on these issues to be undertaken during the term of the contract.

Little is known about the detailed workings of the Human Relations Committee for the good reason that much of its success depended upon little being known by outsiders. Its membership included the same top union and management officials who formed the bargaining teams for the United Steelworkers and the eleven basic steel companies which negotiate together. In addition, several subcommittees were established to investigate particular problem areas, each usually staffed by four or five experts from each side. The management coordinator of the committee described the development of its procedures as follows:[15]

> Candor requires the acknowledgment that at first the steps were quite halting. The parties had been accustomed to discussions in a forum where an admission against interest was deadly; where a position once taken was a position to be steadfastly defended; where a movement in the direction of the other party's views was a concession irretrievably made. If such an atmosphere persisted, then such desirable aims as objective study, pursuit of the facts, better understanding of the parties and experimental and exploratory thinking would be hard to come by.
>
> Therefore, some ground rules emerged and were adopted by common consent. Although they have never been . . . written, they have never been violated by either party. . . . The rules are essentially these:
>
> 1. The approach to study of a particular

problem should be whatever the respective sub-committee could jointly agree upon. Thus, neither party had an unlimited hunting license.

2. There would be no record, whether for use in later formal bargaining, in grievance disputes or for publication. No one on either side was later to be embarrassed by a view he might express either with or without adequate consideration or counsel at the time.

3. Opinions, views and positions expressed by either side could later be denied, withdrawn, revised or amended, and with no allegation of bad faith by the other side.

It was also gravely reported that another rule permitted only one committee member to be angry at a time.

Other examples

A few other union–management relationships have also experimented with continuous bargaining, usually having begun in the late 1950s, as steel did, and also concentrating on the prime bargaining issue of that time: how to compromise management's need for technological innovation with labor's need for job security. The record of these experiments has been mixed. On the one hand, the West Coast longshoring industry and the International Longshoremen's and Warehousemen's Union scored a notable success with this technique even before the steel industry did, engaging in more than three years of negotiation to reach an agreement in 1960 that in effect scrapped various featherbedding rules in exchange for a guaranteed annual wage and other job-security measures. Also, as previously noted, when the Kaiser Steel Company broke away from the rest of its industry in the 1959 strike, its contract with the Steelworkers largely anticipated the Human Relations Committee by establishing a group with the jawbreaking title of Committee to Develop a Long-Range Plan for the Equitable Sharing of the Fruits of Economic Progress (irreverently termed "the Fruits Committee" in union and industry circles). This committee differs by including neutral experts as well as union and management members, and it has been judged a success by most observers.

On the other hand, the railroad industry offers

ample evidence that continuous bargaining is no panacea for troubled labor relations. One of the late Secretary Mitchell's last acts in office was to persuade the railroad employers and unions in 1960 to take the issue of work rules (such as those governing the use of diesel firemen) off the bargaining table—where it was proving just as explosive as, and far more complicated than, in the steel negotiations of the previous year—and attempt to find a solution with the help of neutral experts, plenty of time, and an absence of contract deadlines. After more than two years of fact finding, experts' recommendations, and mediation efforts by seemingly everyone in Washington, this effort failed and the issue was settled only by compulsory arbitration. Also, efforts have proved abortive to promote this approach in the strike-torn newspaper industry in New York City.

The experience of the Armour Automation Committee falls somewhere between these extremes of success and failure. This committee was launched in 1959 by an agreement between the Armour Company and the two major unions in meat-packing. The company agreed to build up a fund of $500,000 to finance the committee (which includes neutral experts) in studying the labor problems arising from the modernization and centralization of the company's operations, experimenting with various solutions to those problems, and recommending action the parties might take in their formal bargaining. Among other things, this committee tried to retrain displaced Armour workers and find jobs for them in other industries, which understandably proved to be difficult in the early 1960s when unemployment was high. The committee nevertheless developed several ideas for cushioning the effects of plant shutdowns, which the parties wrote into their contract, and its retraining efforts also were more successful when the economy itself picked up.

Yet another sobering note has been introduced by the demise of the Human Relations Committee in basic steel. In the 1965 election for the presidency of the Steelworkers' union, the eventual winner, I. W. Abel, strongly attacked the incumbent, David McDonald, for his support of the Human Relations Committee, charging that the committee's effect had been to turn over much of the bargaining to union staff technicians and to freeze out elected officials and the rank and file. It is difficult to assess the impact of Abel's charge on the union membership for, as in any election, there were several factors that contributed to McDonald's defeat. Also, while Abel permitted the committee in basic steel to expire after his election, he did not attack the Kaiser committee, which continues to be active. It is nevertheless clear that any union official who participates in continuous bargaining runs the risk of being charged with becoming too friendly with management. In Walton and McKersie's terms, a union leader may gain his integrative and attitudinal goals by joining in candid, off-the-record meetings with management, but in so doing he may lose his intraorganizational support—and his union job.

In summary, continuous bargaining appears to have a brighter future than Boulwarism as a new approach to negotiating the labor contract, but it is far too soon to declare this strategy to be the wave of the future in collective bargaining. Although it has been vigorously promoted by several prominent individuals and groups, continuous bargaining has been formally adopted in relatively few relationships, and then usually in response to the need in the 1950s to adjust inflation-born contracts to more competitive conditions. Since the resurgence of the economy in the mid-1960s and the easing of both job and product competition, no major relationships have adopted continuous bargaining. In fact, the principal development in recent years—the abandonment of steel's Human Relations Committee—served to spotlight the danger which this strategy may pose to union officials.

It therefore seems likely that the orthodox approach to labor negotiations, in spite of its infirmities, will continue to predominate in the foreseeable future, particularly on the conventional distributive issues such as wages and hours. Continuous bargaining in its purest sense will probably spread only in fits and starts, if at all, depending on whether changing conditions pose a problem too complex to be handled in ordinary deadline bargaining. But between these extremes there already exists a widely employed variation which might be termed "early bargaining." In a compromise between continuous discussions in a permanent committee and the orthodox practice of exploring mutual problems only after formal negotiations begin, early bargaining calls for setting up one or more joint committees to study certain problems for a few weeks or months before negotiations open. The hope is that such committees can map out the factual dimensions of complex issues for the negotiators, even if they do not agree on particular solutions. This eminently pragmatic compromise, tailored to the shifting needs of particular parties, will undoubtedly continue to be used in far more relationships than the more dramatic alternatives of Boulwarism or continuous bargaining. In fact, early bargaining was used as long ago as 1955 by, interestingly enough, General Electric and the IUE.

ADDITIONAL READINGS

Chamberlain, Neil W.: *Sourcebook on Labor,* McGraw-Hill, New York, 1958, chaps. 7 and 8.

Chamberlain, Neil W., and James Kuhn: *Collective Bargaining,* McGraw-Hill, New York, 1965.

Cullen, Donald E.: *Negotiating Labor-Management Contracts,* Bulletin 56, Cornell University, New York State School of Industrial and Labor Relations, Ithaca, N.Y., 1965.

Dunlop, John T., and Neil W. Chamberlain (eds.): *Frontiers of Collective Bargaining,* Harper & Row, New York, 1967, parts I and III.

Stevens, Carl M.: *Strategy and Collective Bargaining Negotiation,* McGraw-Hill, New York, 1963.

Ulman, Lloyd (ed.): *Challenges to Collective Bargaining,* Prentice-Hall, Englewood Cliffs, N.J., 1967, chaps. 1 and 7.

Walton, Richard E., and Robert B. McKersie: *A Behavioral Theory of Labor Negotiations,* McGraw-Hill, New York, 1965.

Weber, Arnold R. (ed.): *The Structure of Collective Bargaining,* Free Press, New York, 1961.

FOR ANALYSIS AND DISCUSSION

1. There is something in the American environment which makes support of small business a popular cause and support of large business suspect. The same attitude seems to apply in some

measure to bargaining units. The small-scale plant unit gains ready approval, while the large unit, particularly a multiemployer or industry unit, is regarded dubiously. How do you account for this attitude? Do you concur in, or disagree with, whatever premises you may find underlying such an attitude?

2. It has been argued in the text that the principal reason why an employer or a union prefers one bargaining unit over another is that the preferred type of unit augments its bargaining power. If this view is valid, how can one explain the numerous situations in which employer and union prefer the *same* bargaining unit?

3. A member of top management once complained that he saw no good reasons why he should have to sit down and discuss his business decisions with men who only knew how to work with their hands, some of whom weren't even particularly good at that. Is there any good reason for his contention?

Contrast this attitude with that of a union official who maintained that the real purpose of collective bargaining was to obtain the consent of the governed. Is this analogy to civil affairs appropriate to the conduct of business?

4. Analyze why the process of *internal* bargaining becomes more difficult with the growth in size of a union. Does a company experience this problem in the same way or to the same extent? Can you develop a relationship between the difficulties of internal bargaining in large organizations, on the one hand, and the effectiveness of multiemployer collective bargaining, on the other? Under what circumstances would you expect that the advantages of multiemployer bargaining would offset the greater difficulties of internal bargaining?

5. Comment on the following extract from General Electric's statement of its collective bargaining policy:

We resolved to prepare for coming negotiations by the steady accumulation of all facts available on matters likely to be discussed.

We would then add to, discard or revise these facts on the basis of any additional or different facts we learned from union or other sources *during* negotiations as well as before.

Then at the appropriate time, and when seemingly all the available significant facts were in and had been fully discussed, we would offer what the facts from all sources seemed to indicate was fully up to all that was right in the balanced best interest of all. This was to be the full truth as we saw it—with nothing held back for future jockeying.

We would stand ready and willing to alter what we had offered immediately upon our getting new or old additional facts—from union or any other source—which would indicate changes that were in the interest of all. . . .

We should and would publicize our offers when made. We would keep our employees and neighbors advised of the course of negotiation—including any changes in our offers in response to union representations or any reason of any other developments. . . .

Our entire program of mutual study and public discussion of the facts—and of honest, forthright, non-artful bargaining—is intended to encourage the development and aid the influence of such honest, direct and responsible union leaders. In contrast, our program is bound to be somewhat discouraging to any who want to go back to the old double-standard or "fleabitten Eastern bazaar" type of bargaining. . . .

It may seem naïve to admit it, but we see no reason why collective bargaining cannot be conducted with both parties accepting and applying practically the same facts and standards toward a common end, and seeking at the same time to be sure emotion and misinformation do not obstruct a settlement that is fair and just for all concerned.

NOTES

1. U.S. Bureau of Labor Statistics, *Directory of National and International Labor Unions in the United States, 1967,* Bulletin no. 1596, pp. 68–69; and Neil W. Chamberlain, "The Structure of Bargaining Units in the United States," *Industrial and Labor Relations Review,* vol. 10, pp. 3–25, October, 1956.

2. "Major Unit Contracts in the United States, 1961," *Monthly Labor Review,* vol. 85, pp. 1136–1144, October, 1962. For the earlier census, see L. C. Chase and E. M. Moore, "Characteristics of Major Collective Bargaining Agreements," *Monthly Labor Review,* vol. 79, pp. 805–811, July, 1956.

3. This development is recounted by Ralph Helstein, president of the United Packinghouse Workers, in Arnold R. Weber (ed.), *The Structure of Collective Bargaining,* Free Press, New York, 1961, pp. 156–165.

4. Another way of making the distinction, in economic terms, is to say that the pattern-setting procedure allows unions the usual advantages of discriminatory pricing (in this case, wage determination). They get as much more from each company as they can, using the key bargain as leverage.

5. William Caples, vice-president of Inland Steel, in Weber, *The Structure of Collective Bargaining,* p. 187. Caples adds, reflecting the union's ambivalence in the matter:

At the same time the USW [United Steelworkers] apparently found that while it wanted just one bargaining representative for labor, it now wasn't so sure that it wanted just one for the companies. For some issues the union felt that it preferred a bargaining condition of monopoly for labor but competition for industry! The union attempted to achieve this state of affairs by requesting the companies to bargain on an individual basis for some issues and on a joint basis for others. The companies maintained that they could not bargain individually as long as all steel labor was bargained for as a unit.

6. *A Behavioral Theory of Labor Negotiations,* McGraw-Hill, New York, 1965.

7. The president of the Packinghouse Workers has commented, with respect to local union participation in major negotiations with the large national corporations:

Usually efforts are made by the local unions to have cross-sectional representation from the various departments and operations in the plants. Such devices for representation have helped to avoid, for the most part, problems of the character that have developed in other industries, where skilled craftsmen felt that they were being denied an effective voice in contract negotiation. When rates of pay or conditions of work in UPWA plants seem unfair or oppressive to a group of workers, such as maintenance or mechanical employees, the local unions will generally name to their bargaining committees a greater representation of people from these classifications. If difficult problems have been encountered by employees in processing departments or in slaughtering departments, this situation will generally be reflected in the fact that the representation from the locals will weigh more heavily on the side of persons from these departments.

See Ralph Helstein in Weber (ed.), *The Structure of Collective Bargaining,* p. 161.

8. The situation would be different if employers sought to *reduce* wages at the expiration of an agreement. Then a lockout might be viewed as an effective bargaining ploy. In the face of union resistance, an employer would in effect be saying, "Agree to my terms or stop working." There has, however, been little occasion for a downward pressure on wages

since the depression days of the 1930s—itself an interesting commentary on the performance of the economy.

9. Philip D. Moore, manager, Employee Relations Service, General Electric Company, "The Shifting Power Balance in the Plant," *Industrial Relations,* vol. 2, p. 102, October, 1962.

Contrast Moore's statement with that by an industrial relations manager of the Bowaters Southern Paper Corporation:

Why can't management simply say, "We are prepared to go this far on wages, and we will go this far on this particular fringe item, but you are going to have to forget the rest of it"? The realities of true collective bargaining are such that no management spokesman could possibly afford to be so blunt at this [early] stage in negotiations. To do so is to commit management prematurely. An ironclad rule of the bargaining table is that an offer once made cannot be retracted without serious consequences. From the union's standpoint a union spokesman couldn't accept such an abruptly given proposal without the militants in his union accusing him of a sellout. Certainly, at this early stage of skirmishing he can't possibly afford to *drop* an item from his program.

See George R. Koons in "Bargaining Table Techniques," *Labor and Management Face the Future,* American Management Association Personnel Series no. 172, 1957, p. 65.

10. General Electric Co., 150 NLRB 192 (1964). For a criticism of this decision, see James A. Gross, Donald E. Cullen, and Kurt L. Hanslowe, "Good Faith in Labor Negotiations: Tests and Remedies," *Cornell Law Review,* vol. 53, pp. 1023–1035, July, 1968.

11. For a sympathetic account of GE's labor policies, see Herbert R. Northrup, *Boulwarism,* University of Michigan, Bureau of Industrial Relations, Ann Arbor, 1964. For a critical account, see Salvatore J. Bella, "Boulwarism and Collective Bargaining at General Electric: A Study in Union-Management Relations," Ph.D. dissertation, Cornell University, 1962 (Ann Arbor: University Microfilms, Inc., 1962).

12. This section on continuous bargaining is taken largely from Donald E. Cullen, *Negotiating Labor-Management Contracts,* Bulletin 56, Cornell University, New York State School of Industrial and Labor Relations, Ithaca, N.Y., 1965, pp. 28–37.

13. John Kenneth Galbraith, "The Impact of Collective Bargaining on the Economy," in *The Emerging Environment of Industrial Relations,* Michigan State University, Labor and Industrial Relations Center, Lansing, 1958, p. 88.

14. "Steel Without Strikes," *Business Week,* June 29, 1963, p. 25.

15. R. Heath Larry, "Steel's Human Relations Committee," *Steelways,* September, 1963, p. 18.

Before we discuss the specific subjects of labor negotiations in the next chapter, it is necessary to tackle two questions that underlie nearly every bargaining issue. First, can a line be drawn between decisions within a firm that should be made by management alone and those that should be made jointly with labor at the bargaining table? Second, what is the significance of the common assertion that collective bargaining is a power relationship?

The first question poses the problem of management rights, always the most fundamental issue in collective bargaining since the first union served its demands upon an employer used to deciding for himself what the employment conditions should be in his own shop. Examine the major subjects in collective bargaining over the years —from wages and hours to the closed shop, technological change, seniority, discipline, subcontracting, and plant location—and you will find that each involves essentially the same dispute: a clash between management's "right" and need to run its business efficiently and profitably, and the "right" and need of workers to have a voice in decisions affecting their jobs.

Thus the question of which subjects the employer should bargain over is not radically different from the question of how to resolve disagreements over the subjects he already agrees are bargainable. Both questions are variations on the same theme: the need of society to compromise

the legitimate interests of both consumers and producers. At the bargaining table, the employer is usually viewed as the consumer's agent, not because he is any more public-spirited than his workers but because his own interests are served by fighting for lower costs and maximum efficiency and innovation—goals which coincide with those of consumers. In their working lives, however, most people also want to participate in shaping their terms of employment, which is why we permit and encourage labor unions to exist. The search for a compromise of these conflicting interests is what the management-rights issue (and indeed collective bargaining) is all about, regardless of the specific subject in dispute.

As for the second question, we shall attempt to provide substance to the concept of "bargaining power" and then argue that this power provides the primary basis for resolving the management-rights argument so crucial to all of collective bargaining.

The expanding scope of bargaining

In the early years of union–management relations, the collective agreement which resulted from the bargaining process was frequently a short document, perhaps no more than a dozen paragraphs, setting forth a scale of wage rates and certain broad principles which were expected to govern the employer-employee relationship. But since people's judgments often differed as to what such broad principles should mean in practice, there was an inescapable tendency to amplify and codify the terms of these agreements. In addition, as unions won a more secure and powerful position in industry, they inevitably sought a voice in more and more of the employer's decisions which affected their members. The result is that the scope of bargaining has expanded decidely over the years.[1]

How far has this expansion gone? Unfortunately, no one can answer that question with any precision. The listing on page 221 provides a useful basis for sorting out the dozens of ways in which one union contract or another has limited management's authority, but it should not be assumed that all contracts cover all of those subjects. We only know that the average contract covers more of these subjects today than ever before, but no one has ever drawn a scientific sample of the hundreds of thousands of clauses contained in all the estimated 140,000 contracts in this country.

It can also be misleading to measure the extent of management "losses" by the thickness of union contracts. It is quite true that in the average General Motors plant, for instance, a manager's relations with his workers are governed by more than *350 pages* of legally binding contract language. Compare the GM manager with some non-union employers who have made no written commitments to their workers about anything, other than a few shop rules telling employees what they cannot do, and it does indeed look as if labor has taken over General Motors. But a closer look at the United Auto Workers contract with GM shows that over a hundred of its pages are devoted to the provisions of ordinary fringe-benefit plans (pensions and health insurance), another hundred pages describe the supplemental unemployment benefit plan (a less common benefit, but one suggested by GM itself in the 1955 negotiations), and most of the remaining pages deal with such ordinary subjects as wages, hours, vacations, discipline, grievance handling, and leaves of absence.

The Auto Workers union, in other words, has nothing to say about the design of next year's Chevrolets or the price of Buicks, or whether GM should locate a new plant in Tennessee or West Germany, or the price the company should pay for steel, the dividends it should declare, the advertising it should buy, the new products it should develop—on these and many similar decisions, management still calls the shots in General Motors and in most other companies.

On the other hand, it is equally misleading to assume that the huge, headline-making unions in industries such as steel and autos have gone furthest in limiting management's authority. Walter Reuther probably exerted less impact on the management function in General Motors than a local business agent often exerts in construction, printing, trucking, longshoring, or the entertainment industries. It is in industries such as those that unions have frequently won a strong voice—not always spelled out in the joint agreement—in decisions on hiring, the size of work crews, the pace of work, the tools and materials to be used, and other controversial matters.

In spite of all these qualifications, the fact remains that unions have made major inroads on what were once thought to be "management prerogatives." In the private sector, the traditional definition of bargainable subjects—wages, hours, and conditions of employment—seems to become more elastic each year as labor and the NLRB insist that employers bargain on everything from food prices in the company cafeteria to subcontracting. And we have seen that the public-sector equivalent of management rights—the presumed sovereignty of the legislature—is steadily crumbling not only under labor's demands to negotiate wages (still a major rights issue in many jurisdictions, including the federal) but also under novel demands such as those by teachers who wish to negotiate the size of classes and the content of the curriculum. Small wonder that the reaction of many employers, private and public, is summed up in the despairing question, "Where will it all end?" In the words of one company official, "The legitimate areas of collective bargaining must be defined. Until that time, management is in the position of an army retreating and regrouping. At some point it will have its back to the wall and there will be no further retreat—without a new economic system, possibly along socialist lines."

A CLASSIFICATION OF UNION CONTRACT CLAUSES

**Establishment and administration
of the agreement**

Bargaining unit and plant supplements

Contract duration and reopening and renegotiation provisions

Union security and the checkoff

Special bargaining committees

Grievance procedures

Arbitration and mediation

Strikes and lockouts

Contract enforcement

Functions, rights, and responsibilities

Management rights clauses

Plant removal

Subcontracting

Union activities on company time and premises

Union–management cooperation

Regulation of technological change

Advance notice and consultation

Wage determination and administration

General provisions

Rate structure and wage differentials

Allowances

Incentive systems and production bonus plans

Production standards and time studies

Job classification and job evaluation

Individual wage adjustments

General wage adjustments during the contract period

Job or income security

Hiring and transfer arrangements

Employment and income guarantees

Reporting and call-in pay

Supplemental unemployment benefit plans

Regulation of overtime, shift work, etc.

Reduction of hours to forestall layoffs

Layoff procedures; seniority; recall

Worksharing in lieu of layoff

Attrition arrangements

Promotion practices

Training and retraining

Relocation allowances

Severance pay and layoff benefit plans

Special funds and study committees

Plant operations

Work and shop rules

Rest periods and other in-plant time allowances

Safety and health

Plant committees

Hours of work and premium pay practices

Shift operations

Hazardous work

Discipline and discharge

Paid and unpaid leave

Vacations and holidays

Sick leave

Funeral and personal leave

Military leave and jury duty

Employee benefit plans

Health and insurance plans

Pension plans

Profit-sharing, stock purchase, and thrift plans

Bonus plans

Special groups

Apprentices and learners

Handicapped and older workers

Women

Veterans

Union representatives

Nondiscrimination clauses

SOURCE: Joseph W. Bloch, "Union Contracts—A New Series of Studies," *Monthly Labor Review,* vol. 87, no. 10, pp. 1184–1185 (October, 1964).

Historical background of the prerogatives issue

In this instance, as with most such questions, historical perspective is helpful to dispassionate analysis. The issue of "management prerogatives" is as old as the master-servant and employer-employee relationships. (Indeed, it can be argued that in its broadest sense it is as old as the parent-child relation.) Wherever one individual exercises authority over another, the exercise of that authority is sure to be called into question, precipitating an argument about the basis for authority. Under what circumstances must the subordinate accept the rule of the superior as final? In the event of conflict of interests, can resolution come through an appeal to rights which the other does not recognize? By whom is the scope of any authority to be defined—by those who assert it or by those over whom it is exercised?

In the United States, management charges that unions were invading the realms of authority properly belonging to management can be found in the earliest records. One sharp expression of this view, and one which is reminiscent of some statements of the last few years, appeared in the editorial columns of the New York *Journal of Commerce* in 1851, at a time when the Typographical Union was making certain "unjustified" demands on the publishers. Wrote the editors:[2]

> Who but a miserable, craven-hearted man would permit himself to be subjected to such rules, extending even to the number of apprentices he may employ, and the manner in which they shall be bound to him, to the kind of work which shall be performed in his own office at particular hours of the day, and to the sex of the persons employed, however separated into different apartments or buildings? For ourselves, we never employed a female as a compositor, and have no great opinion of apprentices, but sooner than be restricted on these points, or any other, by a self-constituted tribunal outside of the office, we would go back to the employment of our boyhood, and dig potatoes, pull flax, and do everything else that a plain, honest farmer may properly do on his own territory. It is marvelous to us how any employer, having the soul of a man within him, can submit to such degradation.

Such belligerent blasts as the above should serve to remind us that recent charges that unions are about to destroy the system of managerial authority are nothing new. The intensity with which the debate raged in the post-World War II period probably stemmed more from the fact that, for the first time, employers as a group faced a strong and entrenched national labor power than from the unprecedented nature of the challenge. The organization of the mass-production industries by

the CIO unions and the equally expansive organization of trades and industries by a competitive AFL had proceeded for barely a half-dozen years before the war intervened and forced union–management relations into a state of deepfreeze for the duration. It was not surprising that when the thaw took place, management should react with quickened displeasure to the immodest demands of unions which were testing the strength that had come to them through growth. Though the issue of worker challenge to managerial control was as old as history, it appeared with the novelty that vastly expanded dimensions always produce.

The lines of conflict were quickly and sharply drawn in a conference which President Truman had assembled in the hope of producing a formula for labor–management harmony. In the National Labor–Management Conference of 1945, a special committee, consisting of high-ranking union and management officials, was set up to attempt to draft some basic statement of principle that would permit a determination of what areas of business decision making fall within the scope of the unions' interests and what areas fall outside that sphere. Agreement proved impossible, however, and the management members of the committee concluded:[3]

> The labor members are convinced that the field of collective bargaining will, in all probability, continue to expand into the field of management. The only possible end of such a philosophy would be joint management of enterprise.

Union members of the committee, on the other hand, wrote:

> It would be extremely unwise to build a fence around the rights and responsibilities of management on the one hand and the unions on the other.... We cannot have one sharply delimited area designated as management prerogatives and another equally sharply defined area of union prerogatives without either side constantly attempting to invade the forbidden territory, thus creating much unnecessary strife.

A little more than two years later, at a time when the United Automobile Workers was seeking to bargain with General Motors on the matter of a pension plan which the company had unilaterally instituted, Charles E. Wilson, then General Motors president, remarked:[4]

> If we consider the ultimate result of this tendency to stretch collective bargaining to comprehend any subject that a union leader may desire to bargain on, we come out with the union leaders really running the economy of the country; but with no legal or public responsibility and with no private employment except as they may permit. . . .
>
> Competition will be stifled and progress in the improvement of industrial processes which reduce the cost and price of the goods produced by industry will be halted.
>
> Only by defining and restricting collective bargaining to its proper sphere can we hope to save what we have come to know as our American system and keep it from evolving into an alien form, imported from East of the Rhine. Until this is done, the border area of collective bargaining will be a constant battleground between employers and unions, as the unions continuously attempt to press the boundary farther and farther into the area of managerial functions.

In fact, the "border area" of collective bargaining has continued to be a battleground to this day, as it has been throughout the history of union–management relations. The subjects in dispute change over the years—from fringe benefits in the 1940s to subcontracting in the 1960s and doubtless a different subject in the 1970s—but the basic conflict persists.

The concept of management

One consequence of this conflict in the early postwar years was a reexamination of the concept of management. If unions were assumed to be trespassing on the management function, what was the nature of that function? From where derived that authority which managers were seeking to preserve? Here were issues of concern to economists, political scientists, and sociologists. And as one probed deeper, the problems proved complex indeed.

One approach frequently found in the literature identified the function of management with decision making. The business firm is the locus of decisions about what line of products or services shall be produced, on what scale, at what prices, by what methods. The function of management is to make such decisions. The attractive simplicity of this approach is deceptive, however, for it fails to tie the function of management with the people of management. The unions, in collective-bargaining conferences, actually participate in making some of these decisions. When, for example, they negotiate clauses which determine the content of particular jobs, or the number of people to be assigned to particular operations, or how certain operations are to be performed, they are helping to make decisions concerning the method of production. Although rare, unions at one time or another, in one place or another, have negotiated clauses dealing with plant location, product prices, sales, and other such matters. If decision making in such areas is identified as the management function, and if unions participate in such decision making, they can and do participate in the management function wherever collective bargaining occurs. How, then, can it be argued that unions should not encroach on the management function when their very purpose is such encroachment—at least if one identifies management with decision making? If management is nothing more than decision making, then others besides those who have traditionally viewed themselves as managers can lay claim to a share in that function.

As a corollary of the above, some members of management were themselves conscious of an inconsistency in their struggle to preserve discretion in business decision making. Among those who sought to bar the unions from encroachment on the management function, there were few who went so far as to argue that the unions should be deprived of all bargaining rights. Most managers were prepared, by this time, to concede that unions could legitimately seek a voice in the matter of wages. But on what basis could decision making on wages be distinguished from decision making in other areas? On the ground that other decisions are more vital? But a firm's wage rates are certainly as important a part of its labor costs as its work loads or speed of operations; on what logic, then, could it concede the unions' participation in the former but refuse it in the latter? In some businesses the wage bill is the largest single item of expenditure. How, then, can its importance, in relation to other areas of company decision making, be minimized?

Can the willingness to give the union a voice on wages be justified on the ground that somehow its interests there are more deeply involved? Who, then, is to determine *how* deeply involved must be the employees' interests before the union, as their agent, is given a right of participation? May not the very jobs of employees be dependent on some strategic managerial decisions involving styling, or capital financing, or purchasing? Is not the continuity of worker income as important as its amount? If so, is the union then entitled to a voice in these matters? These were disturbing questions for management to face in all honesty.

If there are these problems in defining management as decision making, then perhaps management can better be defined as consisting of those who have been accorded a legal basis for exercising the decision-making authority. On this approach, it is not so much the decisions themselves that identify management as the authority with which decisions are made, an authority which is recognized in the law. It is on this ground that management has taken its strongest stand. It has argued that its right to make its own business decisions free from union intervention stems from property rights. As the actual owner or as agent for shareholders, it is free to decide how privately held property shall be used.

Indeed, in the private corporation the law forces on management the responsibility of acting in the single interest of the shareholding owners. This is the test of the lawfulness of the actions of corporate management. If, then, the unions should lay claim to a share in management on behalf of a different interest group (the employees), management would be abnegating the legal basis of its authority by recognizing such a claim. If the management function of decision making were exercised on behalf of two distinct client groups, there would cease to be any clear standard for managerial action, as the law now imposes. To accede to union demands for an enlarged participation in corporate affairs would require management to abdicate an authority, which it derives from a position of trust, to another group exercising it on behalf of competitive interests. Thus management is more than decision making—it is a decision-making power conferred by law. If this legal characteristic of the management function is not recognized, there would be no barrier to the assumption of the decision-making role by anyone who has the power to snatch it from others. Only law—property law—gives definition to management.

There is one major difficulty with this formulation, however. *Property rights confer a control only over things, not over people.* The owner or manager of a plant can, it is true, decide for himself how he would like to employ his physical capital, but he has no power of compelling others to implement his decisions. He can make all the decisions with respect to what and how many products he would like to turn out in his plant and the technological processes he will employ in producing them. But he cannot, on the strength of his ownership of physical assets, force workers to conform to his decisions. He can only seek to induce them to do so.

The inducement generally takes the form of money—a wage or salary paid to the employee in return for his compliance with management's decisions. But there is no reason why those people whose cooperation is needed if the physical assets are to be put to use may not demand something more than money as a condition of their supplying their services. What conditions may they impose? They may insist on any conditions except those which are specifically banned by law. There is nothing which can prevent them from demanding, as the price of their cooperation, that management give them a voice in matters of production, or sales, or location, or even the selection of supervisory personnel. Whether they can win such demands depends, of course, upon the degree of their bargaining power—but it is equally true that management's ability to avoid such demands, if made, depends not on its legal status as owner or agent of private property but on *its* bargaining power.

The price for turning physical assets into a going concern may be concessions on a number of fronts. It then becomes evident that the exercise of the function of management, if that function is viewed as decision making, is not based on property law but rests on broader economic and political considerations. The nature of managerial authority thus remains obscure. The law cannot clarify it.

One further approach has been suggested. The union justifies its claim to a voice in business decisions on the democratic principle that the making of decisions should be shared in by all whom they affect. This is basically the same philosophy that inspired such ringing slogans as "No taxation without representation," which have become hallowed parts of our history. It provides the only rationale for what has come to be known as industrial democracy, a term which, despite its vague content, has certain generally understood connotations.

If this union philosophy offers no comfort or guide to management in determining the framework of its own authority, there is another way of approaching the problem which skirts the issue of authority and builds on expediency. It is an approach which has a genealogy going back at least to Elton Mayo of the Harvard Business School, with the modern human relations school as its more immediate forefather. This new philosophy of pragmatic management starts from the view that decisions are not the cerebration of the top men behind the mahogany desks—at least not only that. Decisions are what get translated into action. And since, in the typical business, a completed action is something which has been participated in by numbers of individuals, decision making is actually a group process. Who decides what shall be the speed of an assembly line? It is not just the engineers, or the production manager who accepts their estimates, or the foreman who tries to put them into effect, but also the workers who may from time to time skip a unit on the line on the plea that they can't keep up with it. The amount produced is what actually comes off the line, and this "decision" has been shared in by everyone in the process from top management down to manual worker. Or, to take another example, who decides who shall be the new supervisor? It is not simply his predecessor, who has moved up one notch, or the general superintendent, or the personnel office, but also the men who will

be asked to work under him, without whose acceptance of his authority he cannot in fact perform the functions assigned to him.

Once it is recognized that decision making is a process shared in by numerous people at various levels of formal authority, all of whom can affect the outcome—the actual decision—in some degree, then it may make sense for management to try to obtain agreement on the part of all involved as to what shall be the objective for which all will strive. To secure such agreement may require some concessions, but the result may be a better outcome—a better decision in fact—than would have evolved without such concession, however much it may be poorer than the result which management on its own would have sought.

The union's philosophy is participation in decision making by all those who are affected by the outcome. Without denying the appeal of that approach, management's own pragmatic philosophy might well be participation in decision making by all those who can affect the outcome. This would at least provide it with some guidance in its negotiations with the union. But however useful such a pragmatic approach may be, it fails to resolve what constitutes the managerial function.

Nature of the management function

There is, however, another approach to this problem. It starts off by rejecting the notion, which has pervaded all the formulations suggested above and which is deeply imbedded in the literature, that management is to be identified with decision making. The difficulty with that view is that everyone in a business firm is concerned with making decisions, at some level of specificity. This approach therefore fails to distinguish a genuinely isolable function. It converts *discretion* into *management* and makes of the custodian's decision to clean out a stock room a function no different from the directors' decision to go into the money market for new capital. But if these two roles are to be distinguished, management must be conceived of as something more than, or other than, simply decision making.

The conception which will be developed here begins with the fact that all individuals have aspirations—not simply an unintegrated bundle of hopes but a picture of the kind of person they want to become and the kind of society in which they would like to live and raise their children. Some aspirations can be achieved by an individual's own efforts, such as cultivating a taste for music, but others obviously require an income for their achievement—the home we want, the education we seek for our children, and so on. For this reason most of us must work. But once we are in a job, we find other values associated with it. We would not work if the job did not pay us an income, but once we find ourselves working for an income, there are some aspects of a job which become part of our aspiration structure and for which we may even sacrifice some of the money which is our prime reason for working in the first place. So work carries with it both pecuniary and nonpecuniary objectives.

If this admittedly oversimplified conception of a person's aspirations has any validity, then each individual in a business enterprise necessarily seeks the attainment of certain of his aspirations through the medium of the business. What the firm does is not a matter of unconcern to him, because what it does affects his chances for realizing his objectives. We can think of the individual as espousing certain policies which he would prefer that the firm adopt because such policies would further his goal realization. The policies and actions which individuals wish from their company differ from individual to individual not only in the sense of diverging from each other but also in the range of the individual's interests. To the man in the shop, the kinds of actions in which he has a personal interest lie primarily in the range of personnel policy. He would like to see policies adopted and decisions made which would increase the satisfaction he gets out of the kind of work he does, which would give him a feeling of having a secure stream of income comparable in amount to that received by his customary associates, and which would create a congenial work society. The average manual worker has no knowledge of, or concern with, a company's depreciation policy, however, since decisions in that area appear to have too remote an impact on him to give him a preference for the firm's using historical cost over current cost as a basis for depreciation reserves, for example.

But for one of the firm's vice-presidents, the firm's depreciation policy may be a matter of real concern, insofar as he has identified his career with the company and fears that the present depreciation policy will affect the firm adversely perhaps five or ten years from now.

So people at various levels in the enterprise have a varying set of preferences for company actions, based on their perception of how such corporate actions affect the realization of their own aspirations. Behind every decision or action or policy statement within a firm stand one or more people without whose personal objectives such decisions or actions or policies would never have come into existence. The only life which an enterprise has is in the people who compose it and whose purposes it must serve if they are to continue as part of it.

We may think of all the individuals within a company, then, as making certain "demands" on that company—demands dealing with its remuneration policy, its sales policy, its production methods, its vacation plan; with who will get the job of executive vice-president or the opening as machinist second-class; with whether a new plant should be opened, and if so, whether in Virginia or California; with whether the company should embark on this new product X or introduce new automatic equipment in shop Y.

Not all members of the enterprise will have preferences on all these items; for all those who feel strongly on any of these matters, however, only one decision can be made. There can be only one remuneration policy, only one person chosen for the job of executive vice-president, plans for a new plant must either be made or dropped, the new product undertaken or not undertaken. In each instance one decision must bind all the members of the enterprise, however divergent their views on what should be done, however differing their "demands" on the company. Each individual with preferences would like to influence the course of the company's conduct in the areas of his preferences, but his influence must be laid against the influence which others with interests in those same areas likewise seek to exert. Out of such conflicting influences must emerge one decision.

Not only is it the case that just one decision can

be made with respect to any issue and that this decision must bind all the participants in the company's operations; it is also the case that each decision must be consistent and compatible with all other decisions. The decision as to the wage and salary structure must be compatible with decisions as to the organizational structure of the firm (the assistant sales manager cannot be paid more than the sales manager); it must be compatible with the company's revenues (more cannot be paid out than is available) and hence with its price policies; it must be consistent with the payments to materials suppliers (so much must not be paid out in wages and salaries that bargains cannot be struck with those who supply the stuffs for processing); it must be consistent with the determination of the dividend level (a proxy fight must not be precipitated by failure to provide some minimum return to the stockholders); and so on. In each of these areas of decisions, certain individuals and groups have preferences as to how the issue should be resolved, but the resolution of each particular issue must somehow be made consistent with decisions being reached on all the other issues on which it impinges or which impinge on it.

How, then, is any decision made, or any action taken, or any policy decided on, in the face of these many conflicting demands which the members of a firm make on one another? The first part of the answer to that question is that *decision is made on the basis of the relative bargaining powers of those whose views and interests clash.* By bargaining power is meant another person's inducement to agree on your terms. Or, to put it another way, your bargaining power is my cost of disagreeing on your terms relative to my cost of agreeing on your terms. This ratio measures the extent of my inducement to accept what you propose. Similarly, my bargaining power is your cost of disagreeing on my terms relative to your cost of agreeing on my terms.

Suppose each of us makes certain proposals to the other. Agreement must be on a single set of terms binding both of us. That agreement will not be forthcoming as long as, for both of us, the cost of agreeing on the other's terms is greater than the cost of disagreeing. But as soon as, for one of us, the cost of agreement drops below the cost of disagreement, we will have a bargain. And relative bargaining powers are subject to manipulation, since—among other things—each person involved can indulge in actions or effect alliances with others that will increase his opponent's cost of disagreement, or he can make concessions which will lower the other's cost of agreement. In either event, he increases the other's inducement to agree and thereby strengthens his own bargaining power and improves his chances of getting what he wants.

Within a company, let us assume that a decision has to be made on whether some new product is to be added to the company's line. For many of the people in the firm, that decision will not be important and they will have no preference. But to the production manager who is charged with manufacturing it, to the sales manager who is charged with selling it, to the treasurer who is concerned about financing, to the executive vice-president who has appraised the likelihood of success and its meaning to the company's future and to his future within the company, the decision will not be a matter of indifference. Each of these people is likely to have his preference, which constitutes his "demands" on the others. If the decision is an important one, cliques are likely to form, with those whose preferences are closely linked banding together to increase their strength. In any event, a bargaining contest will emerge.

What is the cost to group A of agreeing with group B, which wishes to undertake the new product? It means an initial investment that will preclude development of another product in which group A has more confidence; a heavy cost which will tie up the company's liquid assets beyond the safety point for the short run; a chance that the product will not catch on in the way that group B expects it to, weakening the company for the long run (in all respects affecting adversely the company to which the people in group A have tied their future); the possibility that if the product is as good as group B says it is, it will start the company along wholly new lines into which the people of group A will not fit so readily, so that their chances for further advancement in the company may be dimmed.

But what are the costs of disagreeing with

group B? It means danger that some competitor may come out later with a similar product and "clean up," thus reflecting on the soundness of group A's judgment and possibly lessening chances for better positions; the possibility that if the production manager (who is one of group B) does not get this new product, he may quit to take a job with the principal competitor, who is known to be blandishing him with arguments that this company is too conservative for his talents (and the production manager is one of the company's biggest assets, so that his departure would have its impact on the company's future); the further danger that the sales manager (also one of group B) has friends on the board of directors to whom he might complain in roundabout fashion that they, the group A management people, are preventing the company from moving ahead, and so on.

Such bargaining cannot usually proceed directly between the parties concerned, however, particularly when the issue is only one of a very large number of such bargains which are in a continuing state of negotiation—bargains not only between functional groups within the management hierarchy but also between workers and materials suppliers and capital suppliers and stockholders and customers, usually with numerous categories of each of these classes. Each is seeking to fulfill the aspirations of its members through the medium of the corporation and therefore prefers that the corporation take certain actions or make certain decisions rather than others, thus trying to influence corporate conduct to the extent of its bargaining power.

Because of the number of individuals and groups involved, because of the many issues concerning which each has his preferences, because of the requirement that with respect to any issue, only one resolution can be made, applying to all affected, and because of the further requirement that the decision on any issue must be consistent and compatible with the decisions on all other issues—because of all these conditions, it is necessary that there be a coordinator of the bargaining. *This task—the coordination of the bargains of all those who compose the business—is the unique function of management.* It is an inescapable func-

tion within an enterprise, since the various terms demanded by the various component parts of the firm do not somehow coordinate or arrange themselves. It is an isolable function, and one which can be performed only by the managers of a firm and not by those who make demands on the firm. The bargains which are struck constitute the decisions made within the corporation—the decision-making process is seen as a kind of multilateral bargaining process involving those whose aspirations are somehow related to any of the numerous decisions which are constantly being made or remade. But this decision-making process is not the same thing as management, any more than collective bargaining is. Beyond the terms which are demanded, the bargains which are struck, the decisions which are made, is the inevitable necessity of a coordinating authority who must see to it that the numerous bargains or decisions are somehow made consistent with one another. It is that coordinating authority which is here identified as management.

Requirements of the management role

In the exercise of this function, management must fulfill two necessary conditions if the organization is to survive. First, for all of those on whom the ongoing corporation depends, the cost of agreeing on the complex of internally consistent bargains must be less than the cost of disagreeing on that complex. If management fails in this respect, then the organization crumbles or disintegrates as those on whom it depends for certain of its functions leave to go elsewhere. If they can be replaced, no harm is done, but someone must be found who can fulfill each of the necessary functions on which the organization as constituted depends and for whom the cost of agreeing on the existing complex of bargains is less than the cost of disagreeing. This first condition is relevant to organizations of all types, but the second condition applies peculiarly to business (that is, profit-making) organizations. As far as the economic component of bargains is concerned (the money costs), the total outflows of the firm must be matched by its inflows. The latter may include borrowing or use of savings or sale of assets, but from whatever source funds are secured, management must arrange to cover the pecuniary concessions which are part of the network of bargains.

There is nothing in the nature of organization which somehow arranges the demands which its members make on each other so that these two conditions are automatically fulfilled. Unless someone is charged with the specific responsibility of seeing that a complex of bargains (decisions) is arrived at which will maintain the adherence to the organization of all those on whom it depends, and that the necessary money concessions fit within a framework of money flows whereby the total of outflows is covered by the total of inflows, these two conditions of a viable organization cannot possibly be met. None of the parties at interest —the union, the suppliers, the owners, the customers—is in a position to assume this responsibility. It is a responsibility which is unique to management.

Because the complex of bargains does not arrange itself into an internally consistent pattern but must be coordinated, management itself must engage in bargaining with all the parties at interest. It must manipulate the relative bargaining powers so that, somehow, the two conditions necessary for survival of the organization are realized. Faced with incompatible demands from workers, suppliers, and customers, it cannot pit these parties directly against each other but must itself act as the focal bargaining point, testing where bargaining power is relatively weakest and strongest, where concession can be obtained from this one so that it can be offered to that, pressing for an "advantage" here because it knows it must give ground elsewhere.

Coordination as a function has frequently been associated with management, but the coordination which has usually been specified has been the technical coordination associated with division of labor and specialization. That type of technical or productive coordination is obviously important, but it is not sufficient as a basis for organization. The coordinating function which management must perform consists not only in bringing numerous specialized agents into a production process in an engineering sense. Indeed, that is commonly the least of its worries—one that can be delegated

to experts for implementation. But the coordination of which we are speaking here is the coordination of *bargains,* the terms on which the numerous individual specialists are willing to become part of an organization. This is commonly the greatest of management's worries and a function which cannot be delegated.

Managerial objectives

If we were to stop at this point, however, we should be left with a conception of management as a kind of neutral agent, manipulating bargains to achieve a workable organization but without any positive drives of its own. Obviously this would be a false impression in a society whose managers are the epitome of ambition, who have become, worldwide, a symbol for restless energy, who have sometimes been portrayed in fiction as ruthless in their push for expansion and growth.

Managers, too, have their time stream of aspirations. Like others within the enterprise, they too seek the realization of many of their objectives through the medium of the business. Indeed, they are more likely than others to seek their goals by this means. They are, as a group, strongly disposed to climb to positions of power and influence, from which they can use the organization as an instrument of creative expression, as a tool for the accomplishment of significant personal projects. The identification between the corporation and the individual becomes very close, so that the achievements of one are closely interconnected with the achievements of the other. All this does not suggest that management is satisfied with the role of a neutral coordinator.

In the achievement of his goals, the top manager requires a right of individual initiative and the use of funds with which to finance his projects. Neither of these perquisites accrues to him simply by virtue of his position. If they are to be had, they must be won. They can be won only in the course of bargaining, only in the performance of management's unique role of coordinator. As long as management is able to satisfy the demands which all the interested parties make on the corporation sufficiently to ensure their adherence to the organization, all residual discretion and resources accrue to it for use within the framework of the enterprise.

On the American scene, it is not the shareholder, the owner, who is the residual beneficiary of corporate activity as much as it is management in its official capacity. Regardless of legal considerations, conceptually we can treat owners on a plane of equality with all other parties in interest, as a group making demands on the corporation and possessing some degree of bargaining power and certain interests that must be incorporated within the complex of internally consistent bargains in such a manner as to secure its members' continuing adherence to the organizational pattern. But as long as management meets their demands and the demands of all the other participants without bargaining away the whole of its discretion or committing the total of the firm's inflow, the remainder of both is at its own disposal. As long as it has not bargained away (or had reserved in law) the right to initiate a new research program, or to produce a new product which is the result of that research, or to build new plants or expand production, and as long as the firm's revenues provide the resources for such enterprise after the satisfaction of the pecuniary element of all bargains, these things it can do at its own discretion. That in some instances corporate laws *have* restricted its initiative by requiring board or stockholder approval of certain actions, or that in some cases management *has* had to concede such authority in bargaining with board or stockholders, does not reduce the validity of that statement. To the extent that there is no such restraint or that such restraints are only formal or ineffective, management retains the right of initiative, financed by such resources—labeled, with some terminological ambiguity, undistributed profits—as it has been able to retain after the terms of all bargains have been satisfied.

This exercise of control over uncommitted discretion and resources is not, however, the basic managerial function. This essential function is coordinating the bargains of the various participants in the organization, as has been said. But the power of initiation and innovation which comes through residual discretion must surely be the icing which gives piquancy to the cake, the lure which makes all the personal sacrifice of high position somehow seem not too high a price for the end to be gained.

Implications of the analysis

Where, then, does the union stand with respect to management? Does this conceptual approach shed any light on the union's alleged invasion of the management prerogative?

It suggests that there is no barrier except relative bargaining powers to the scope of the subject matter in which the union may interest itself. It can seek to bargain on any matter which is of sufficient importance to its membership to permit it to array a bargaining power adequate to the objective. In seeking to bargain, it is striving to make decisions concerning the conduct of the company. It is seeking a greater measure of control over corporate conduct, and there is nothing to prevent its securing that greater measure of control except the bargaining powers which confront it—which are likely, of course, to be considerable. For the other parties in interest will themselves be trying to influence corporate action to their advantages, and their powers are frequently at least as great as labor's.

Of course, society at large may exert its own "bargaining power" by declaring in law that certain subjects are not bargainable. And we have seen that Congress has done precisely that by declaring that no union—regardless of its power—can negotiate a closed shop or contract terms that discriminate on the basis of race or lack of union membership (except for the union shop). Such restrictions are perfectly consistent with our analysis of the scope of bargaining, for each is based on a reasonable belief that the interplay of private power might thwart the public interest in some *specific* respect, such as perpetuating racial discrimination. That is very different from urging Congress to draw a line between bargaining subjects on the sole ground that some are "inherent prerogatives of management" and others are "inherently bargainable." No such line can be drawn by Congress or anyone else.

Historically, the union's power to win concessions has both ebbed and flowed. In the decade following World War II, managements often acted like beleaguered captains of industrial forts, seeking to stave off incursions by predatory and powerful unions. They were sometimes forced into bargains which gave the impression that the only way to "coordinate" was to concede, and customers and stockholders were given short shrift because they had relatively little countervailing power to bring to bear on management, the coordinator. But the tides of fortune changed about 1958. A combination of circumstances, probably including prolonged unemployment, the growing "threat" of automation, government policies determined more by international than domestic pressures, and the McClellan investigation, contributed to strengthening the consumer and investor vis-à-vis the worker.

Unions ceased to be viewed as Leviathans. Managements were more readily enabled, and in some respects *required* by other pressures, to manipulate relative bargaining powers to restrain union demands. By 1962, observers were speaking of the "hard line" that business was adopting toward unions. But as the economy moved back toward full employment during the later 1960s, the hard line evaporated, wage settlements escalated, and employers again professed to be powerless to stem the onslaught of organized labor.

A second implication of the analysis is that unions, in seeking to extend the range of their decision making within the enterprise, are not trespassing on the management function. Management is the locus of all the bargains, so that those affecting the firm are always struck with it; but in fact the bargaining takes place among all the parties in interest, with management serving as the control point in the process. The management function is to coordinate all the bargains which are being struck, a never-ending process, so that such bargains become internally consistent with one another, so that they create for all those on whom the organization must depend (for the kind of corporate performance on which the bargains are predicated) a cost of agreement lower than the cost of disagreement, and so that the inflows of the firm cover all the outflows. No matter how extensive the range of the union's interests, that function must in its nature always remain unimpaired.

Nearly as much bargaining goes on in a nonunion firm as in one which is unionized. This fact is overlooked in the usual formulation of the management-rights issue, which pictures the employer as completely free to make any and all decisions in his firm until that dark day when a union appears and for the first time forces him to share his authority. A closer look at the nonunion employer, however, reveals that he too can only run his business by ceaselessly striking bargains with suppliers and stockholders and banks and customers and the many divergent groups within his firm —including informal but necessary bargains with his unorganized workers if he is to retain them.

The union, by seeking a greater voice in corporate decisions (that is, bargains), can make life more trying for management by making the coordination process more difficult. Management's manipulation of relative bargaining powers to make the bargains come out consistent may become a little more frenetic. A union's importunate demands may even, conceivably, create a condition where management, despite all the manipulation of which it is capable, cannot achieve consistency in its bargains or cover outflows with inflows, so that the organization must deteriorate or disintegrate. Thus the union may force management to preside over the dying struggles of the organization—just as any other parties in interest, including customers, may do. But it does so not by taking over the management function but by making that function more difficult for management to carry off successfully. This is not, however, any common eventuality. Ordinarily a union makes organizational life more difficult for management just as the presence of shareholders makes life more difficult than it would be if one could have their capital without their presence, but organizational life goes on, under managerial control.

The real fun in managing a business, it would seem, must lie in projecting one's own creative imagination into realms which none of the participating parties dreams of. The real managerial satisfaction must come in conjuring up ways in which this organization—which you have held together by your coordinating abilities—can now be used by you to accomplish objectives beyond the imagination and even beyond the interest of those who form its several parts. It is here that the quality of the firm's management shows through.

Just as in the arts, where the function of the artist is to blend intellect and emotion in a meaningful experience, so in management, where the function is to blend the activities of all those who compose the organization, can this function be discharged with varying qualities of performance. The managers to whom we tend to give the accolade are—as in the case of the artist—those who can accomplish their functions while building into their work some purely personal expression which will be the mark of their uniqueness and vision. This possibility the unions can never remove from management. To the extent that the union's bargains, its participation in decision making, close off one avenue of managerial discretion, there is nothing except the limitations of management's own imagination which can prevent it from opening up new avenues of opportunity for its own creative expression, with the organization as its medium.

Further implications of bargaining power

Up to this point we have argued that bargaining power is the ultimate determinant of the management-rights issue in its narrowest sense of deciding the scope of bargaining. Essentially the same analysis can now be applied to the rights issue in its broader sense. Even on issues that both parties agree are bargainable, such as wages and hours, there exists the basic dispute that was noted at the beginning of this chapter: the clash between management's "right" and need to run its business efficiently and profitably and the "right" and need of workers to have a voice in decisions affecting their jobs (and aspirations). There is no objective answer or solution to this clash of interests at the bargaining table any more than there is a timeless solution to the conflict of buyers and sellers in the product market or of liberals and conservatives in the political arena. A free society is wary of claims to absolute truths in secular matters, and this is nowhere better illustrated than at the bargaining table.

Once it is admitted that no one can objectively define a fair wage or a fair day's work or the one best way to introduce technological change or to hire, promote, lay off, and discipline workers— once it is admitted that neither management nor labor has any "scientific" solutions to these crucial problems, then it becomes obvious why collective bargaining is inevitably a power relationship. Regardless of the subject, the resolution of differences between union and management ultimately rests on the balance of the relative bargaining power of the two parties. This power aspect of industrial relations is fundamental and inescapable, but it also means something more than the exercise of raw force.

Earlier in this chapter, bargaining power was defined as the ability to secure another's agreement on one's own terms. To put it another way, your bargaining power is my willingness to agree on your terms, a willingness which is influenced by a variety of factors. Your bargaining power is thus a reflection not simply of your personal powers to make me agree to your terms but a reflection of all the surrounding circumstances— economic, political, social, psychological—which affect what terms you demand of me and my willingness to agree on your terms irrespective of your personal power.

As was also noted earlier, this concept of bargaining power can be stated more specifically in the form of a ratio: my willingness to agree to your terms depends upon the relative cost to me of disagreeing or agreeing with your terms. If it costs me more to disagree with you than to agree, then I will agree. If it costs me more to agree than to disagree, then I will disagree. And my willingness to agree on your terms represents the extent of your bargaining power.

This deceptively simple concept of bargaining power already suggests several significant considerations. For one thing, if two parties, such as a union and a management, are each making demands on the other, no agreement will be forthcoming unless one of them finds the cost of agreeing on the other's terms is less than the cost of disagreeing. If both consider it costlier to agree then to disagree, a stalemate will obviously develop.

Another consideration—and a vital one—is that one's bargaining power is relative to the demands he makes. We sometimes talk of bargaining power as though it were something absolute; we speak of the United Mine Workers' bargaining power vis-à-vis the mine operators and of the UAW's bargaining power vis-à-vis General Motors. But it is obvious, on reflection, that their bargaining power must be relative to what they are asking, so that it is adequate to secure some demands and inadequate to secure others. The UAW's bargaining power might be strong if it were asking for a 25-cents-an-hour increase but very weak if it were seeking 90 cents an hour. If your bargaining power is based on my costs of disagreeing and agreeing on your terms, then high demands by you make it more costly for me to agree and increase my resistance, whereas modest demands are likely to have the opposite effect.

Assume that a union comes to the bargaining table asking for a 25-cents-an-hour increase, which management refuses outright. Assume too that the union would actually be willing to settle for 10 cents an hour if it had to, rather than resort to strike. If the union's bargaining power is inadequate to secure 25 cents an hour, it will not therefore drop its demand immediately to the 10 cents an hour it is actually prepared to accept. Instead, it will gradually lower its asking price, first perhaps to 20 cents, then 18, then 15, at each point seeking to create the impression that this is as low as it will go, in the hope that at some point it will enter into a zone where management's cost of agreeing on the union's new terms will actually be lower than the cost of a strike in the event of disagreement. As the union drops its demands, its bargaining power—the power to effect agreement on its (lowering) terms—becomes more effective. Its bargaining power (management's willingness to agree on its terms) may become sufficient to obtain a wage increase somewhat above that which it would be willing to accept rather than go on strike.[5]

The above raises, as a third consideration, the importance of bluffing in the bargaining relationship. We have discussed this tactic in the previous chapter, but it is useful to describe it again in the terminology of power. Your bargaining power is based on my estimates of the costs of disagreeing and agreeing on your terms, and my bargaining power similarly is based on your estimates. *But neither of us can know what the other's estimates really are.* Consequently, we are left to guess the other's reactions to our proposals. In the example above, the union must guess at what point man-

agement's cost of disagreeing on the union's terms is sufficiently high that it would rather concede to the union's demands. At that point the union holds firm. If it guesses too high, it will find itself in a strike that it does not want (since it would prefer to settle at 10 cents an hour rather than strike). But if it guesses too low, it will deprive its members of a possible wage gain. In the meantime, management is engaged in the same process of guessing, probing, and bluffing.

As we have seen, there is a good deal more to the negotiating process than the above paragraphs suggest. Even on distributive issues such as wages, the parties seldom come to the bargaining table with their own final offer so firmly fixed. It is part of each party's job of persuasion to convince the other that the costs of agreeing are actually lower and those of disagreeing actually higher than the other may have estimated, thereby moving the other's "final" position. There have been numerous instances in which a union has become convinced, in the course of negotiations, that management could not give what the union genuinely expected to make its "last-ditch" demand and in which managements have been persuaded of the reasonableness of sums which they considered grossly unreasonable on first entering into negotiations. Moreover, the very process of bargaining provides the opportunity for the negotiators on each side to seek clues—in facial expressions, a tone of voice—that will reveal the other's positions and provide firmer ground for the judgments they are forming of the other's estimates of his costs of disagreeing and agreeing.

Another, subtler aspect of negotiations is the mutual understanding which people who repeatedly bargain with each other come to have, leading to a variety of devices to avoid disagreements that neither wants. Among these devices may even be an exchange of confidences by leaders of the respective teams as to what each side "really" must have in order to settle.

Finally, this concept of bargaining power stresses a fact too often overlooked: The power of one party is relative to the power of the other and is not a fixed quantity which a union or an employer has on tap, like money in the bank. Sweeping generalizations are sometimes made about the bargaining power of "labor" and "management" in the economy as a whole, but such statements conceal as much as they reveal. Even a single company like General Motors has different degrees of power at any given moment, depending on whether it is dealing with the United Auto Workers, or one of the smaller unions scattered about its many plants, or its unorganized white-collar workers. Similarly, the UAW itself has less power when facing General Motors than when dealing with a small supplier of auto parts. Nor does the power balance between a particular company and a union remain fixed over time, as demonstrated by the shifting fortunes in nearly any bargaining relationship one cares to examine.

Determinants of bargaining power

There is no yardstick to measure the distribution of power in a specific union–management relationship at a given time. At best, only a rough estimate can be made by analyzing such things as a company's profit record, cost structure, inventory position, and degree of market control; the union's political cohesiveness, extent of organization, relations with other unions, and level of strike benefits; and the general economic and political context, such as the rate of unemployment, attitudes in the local community, or the political complexion of the current administration in Washington.

Unfortunately, the list of factors that *may* affect bargaining power is nearly endless, and even if a complete list could be agreed upon, there is at present no way of knowing how much weight to give each item. In some relationships, the employer's profit outlook is the crucial determinant of the final bargain; in others, it is the extent to which a union has organized its industry; and in yet others, economic, political, and psychological elements are so entangled that the negotiators themselves could not say which carries the greatest weight.

Although we do not have a precise formula by which to describe the determinants of bargaining power, certain points nevertheless stand out. For one thing, facts do have a role in this power relationship. As noted above, since each party must guess at the other's costs of agreeing or disagreeing to a proposal, a negotiator can and does change his opponent's estimates and thus his own

power status—often by sheer bluffing, of course, but also often by presenting facts concerning his own position or the implications of a proposal which his opponent did not know or has honestly overlooked. This certainly does not imply that logic and statistics alone will carry the day at any bargaining table. It does mean, however, that a power relationship is shaped by more than the effectiveness of a picket line.

On the other hand, one of the primary determinants of power in the average buyer-seller relationship—the ability of the parties to shop around for a better deal elsewhere—is largely absent from the union–management relationship. When the parties enter labor negotiations, it is with the realization that *some* agreement must be reached between them. The Excelsior Shoe Company does not have the option to contract with the United Shoe Workers local, which represents its employees, or with some other union; it can deal only with the United Shoe Workers as long as that union represents its employees. And that union does not have the option of obtaining an agreement for its local members from the Excelsior Shoe Company or from some other company; it must reach an agreement with the company where its members are employed. As long as the "marriage" lasts, the parties must deal with each other. Marriages do of course end with divorce or death, and similarly a union may be broken in a strike or its members may desert it; a company may go out of business or, if small enough, replace all its workers if they do go on strike. But these are seldom genuine alternatives to reaching an agreement.

This lack of satisfactory alternatives to agreement in some instances tends to make the parties more reasonable in their bargaining approach to each other. They adopt an attitude of "I have to learn to live with him." One cost of disagreement may be viewed as the threat of continued unpleasantness if either becomes stubborn and demanding in a relationship which cannot be avoided. But dependence on the other can also lead to more intense conflict: in the absence of a genuine alternative, one of the parties may adopt extreme measures to force its will on the other, to whom it is bound. The other party seems more and more offensive if it is regarded as blocking the achievement of one's aspirations and at the same time there is no other place to go, no alternative relationship to substitute. The more detested the other party becomes, the less are the psychological or emotional costs of disagreeing with it. Both of these positions are probably extreme. The former requires a greater sense of brotherliness than a competitive society tends to generate in its economic relationships. The latter reflects a pathological state of mind. The typical situations fall somewhere in between.

Finally, in speaking of the "costs" of agreeing and disagreeing on another's terms, we cannot concentrate solely on monetary costs. Involved too are such intangible matters as principles, prestige, and sentiment. This returns us to the importance of the aspirations that each individual brings with him into his working life—his objectives, goals, drives, and purposes—which we have seen are not limited to his income needs.

It is these aspirations which ultimately determine the costs of agreeing or disagreeing on another's terms, for such costs are, to a large extent, sacrifices of a person's aspirations. On all those issues on which there is disagreement, the conflict arises out of the effect of concession on people's goals. To agree to what someone else wants means giving up something that you want, a something which may involve money but which may also involve principle or prestige or status, both within and outside the organization. For management to give in on some issue may be to limit its authority and prestige in the plant and lower its prestige among fellow managers outside the plant. For the union to concede may weaken its hold on its members, reduce its officers' prestige within the plant, lessen its members' own feeling of pride and status, and decrease its standing among brother union leaders or superiors outside the plant. On the other hand, not to give in on some issue may involve a shutdown, with different attendant damages to aspirations for both union and management. Conceding or refusing to concede, by union to management and by management to union, always has an effect on the aspirations of those involved.

Manipulating bargaining power

Relative bargaining powers do not have to be taken as given. Even if there is no alternative to reaching *some* agreement, one party can still increase his bargaining power by making disagreement on his terms more costly to the other. For this purpose, the union may resort to the strike, picketing, appeals for the support of other unions in the form of strike donations, boycott of the product, and other actions. The company resorts to neutralizing such union action, for example, by shifting its orders among plants or even moving the equipment of the struck plant to another plant which is not unionized, or by seeking legal limitation of the union's picketing, and so on. Its efforts at increasing the union's cost of disagreement on its terms may include threatneing to close the plant altogether, installing machinery to reduce its dependence on labor, mobilizing public opinion against the union, and so on. Some of these weapons have, however, been banned or limited by law.

There is another method of manipulating bargaining power to one's advantage—by decreasing the other's cost of agreement on one's terms. Obviously this can be done by improving one's offer—the union can shave its demands, the company can increase its counterproposals. Because bargaining power is always relative to demands, such an action can be expected to improve one's capacity to settle on his own terms. But because concessions also reduce one's achievement of his goals, unions and managements come to offering them only as a last resort. Before that time, they may seek to lower the other's cost of agreeing to their terms by such devices as:

On the union's part, giving assurances of stimulating greater cooperation by its members, thus potentially reducing the impact of the increased wage bill to management; promising to take a stronger hand in the curbing of wildcat strikes; agreeing that an international representative of the union will work more closely with a local union leader who has been giving management trouble, and so on.

On management's part, promising to consult with the union before undertaking any major changes in production processes; agreeing to talk to an obstreperous foreman who consistently ignores the collective-bargaining agreement as much as he can get away with; talking over the company's economic position with the union leadership at regular quarterly meetings; establishing a "human relations committee" to anticipate problem areas, and so on.

Such devices may be treated by the other party as "concessions," particularly for public relations purposes, but as long as they do not constitute any sacrifice of aspiration by the party who resorts to them, they are actually a means of improving one's bargaining power by lowering the other's cost of agreement while *avoiding* concession. In some instances, they may be only face-saving gestures, but to provide such an escape hatch for a party which has perhaps trapped itself by a bluff that failed is an important way of reducing its cost of agreement on one's own terms.

All of this sounds very Machiavellian, and indeed the notion of manipulating personal relations has today been given a sinister connotation, somehow connected with the notion of George Orwell's autocrats manipulating people, like puppets, for their own benefit. Actually, however, all of us are constantly attempting to manipulate interpersonal relationships in the sense that we consciously strive to arouse the affection and respect of others by a variety of approaches and that we seek to induce others to respond to our wishes or points of view. Once we reassure ourselves that the bargaining-power relationship is not simply a clash of force but that it constitutes an effort by one to induce another to agree to his terms—an inducement which may take the form of promises made as well as pressure applied—we see that *generically* it is similar to many other relationships, from courtship to campaigning for political office.

The study of what has come to be known as "human relations" is specifically designed to help us motivate people to do what we would like to have them do. Unions have sometimes condemned managements for seeking to manipulate the workers, through such human relations techniques, to the company's advantage. But the unions too attempt to manipulate workers—to join unions—and might profitably employ human relations techniques themselves in their efforts to maneuver their relationships with management to their own benefit.

It is not manipulation per se which should be viewed with suspicion, since it is virtually synonymous with societal relations, but rather certain forms of manipulation. We do not approve of the suitor who tries to increase the girl's cost of disagreement by threatening to foreclose her father's mortgage. Nor do we approve of managements that say they will close down their plants sooner than deal with a union, nor of unions which resort to violence on the picket line—in both cases to raise the other's cost of disagreeing on their terms. The problem is made difficult, however, by our inability to draw any clear line of demarcation between admissible forms of pressure and inadmissible ones. Just as in product markets we have not been sure how far competition (which we approve) can go before it becomes cutthroat (which we condemn), so in union–management relations we have been uncertain how far the parties might go (secondary boycott or untrue accusations? discriminatory promotions or refusal to give facts on company performance?) before we treat their pressures as unfair. It is clear that it is not pressure itself that we object to, but only pressure past some point.

What we so frequently forget, however, is that pressures are applied by the parties in the pursuit of their aspirations, and these aspirations are not only for money (profits or wages) but also go back to people's conception of the kind of life they hope to carve out for themselves, of the kind of society in which they would like to live and raise their children. The use of pressure thus involves social values and standards of morality, however inchoate these may be in the minds of most people.

The ethical base of bargaining

The immediate objectives for which the battle is waged—the questions of whether wages shall be raised by 5 or 7 cents an hour, whether work loads are fair, whether promotion shall be by seniority or ability—often seem petty issues in themselves. They acquire a significance, however, as links in a *chain* of aspirations: they are important because they stand as the immediate goals in a continuing struggle to achieve longer-run aspirations which have their roots in philosophical and ethical convictions. The bargaining-power relationship is thus not simply a crude trial of force but a contest of differing moralities.

That such ethical values do indeed characterize individuals and classes of individuals (even if ultimately based on self-interest) is evidenced by the fact that if we were asked to draft a statement of the kind of society American business leaders would prefer and one on the kind of society that American union leaders would prefer, we would expect such statements to differ in important particulars, even if agreeing in others. The respects in which their views agree lessen the conflict between them, since their objectives coincide, and on these points neither is seeking to secure the adherence of the other to a point of view or a basis for action to which he takes exception. But the ways in which their notions of what constitutes "the good society" differ are bound to stimulate conflict, since whatever demands one makes on the other which are predicated on such a philosophy are certain to stir a deep, emotional resistance.

Only in the light of such ethical convictions is it possible to understand the recurring intensity of the conflict between unions and managements. Although for a spell they get along in relative harmony, periods of bitterness and deep conflict continue to erupt. The basis for such acrimony lies in the fact that each party holds strongly to its dreams of the kind of society in which it is to play its part, and the ethical content with which such beliefs are surcharged excuse, in its eyes, the excesses which are committed to serve the cause. Just as the emotional attachment to the Christian creed "excused" the shameful acts of crusade and inquisition, so in the eyes of union and management leaders are some of their actions—inexcusable to others—justified by the cause they serve. If picketing at times injures neutral parties or if it is made the basis for forcing unwilling employees to accept a union which they do not want (so that their employer can continue to conduct his business), the process has been excused on the ground that it is a method of strengthening the labor movement and that the objectives of the movement are good in that they will lead to a better society. If management at times puts the

active union leaders in a position where they can be discreetly fired or passes the word that, in the event of unionization, the shop will move to another state, it can condone such actions on the ground that unions are inimical to society, which progresses by individual strength and a logic of efficiency.

That such convictions may be rooted in rationalization of personal interest is not particularly relevant. The rationalizations are felt strongly enough to motivate. They provide an ethical content to bargaining power, an ethical content which sometimes makes the bargaining relationship bitter. As long as a person feels deeply concerning his values, then every effort to manipulate the power relationship to his advantage—within the limitations of his own code—seems justified by the end it serves.

It would be wrong to suggest, however, that so great a gulf divides unions and managements in this country as to make compromise and mutual accommodation rare. Actually, as we know, the reverse is true. Unions and managements commonly resolve their differences without open conflict, even though with tough bargaining. Differences of economic and political philosophy are not so sharp as to create class cleavages. Businessmen and workers alike are to be found in both of our major political parties. Social-status distinctions are not woven into the fabric of our society. At the same time, we would be disguising reality to adopt the point of view of the "harmony" school of thought, which maintains that the interests and objectives of workers and management are fundamentally alike. There are differences of values and interests which can only be resolved by the exercise of bargaining power.

Thus, in answer to the questions posed at the outset of this chapter, it is futile to search for some ultimate solution to the rights issue in collective bargaining—either by drawing a line around subjects presumably reserved to management in the natural order of things, or by exhorting the parties to discover the "right answer" to the problems on which they now bargain. The basic issue in collective bargaining is not how to define management's rights but how to compromise the rights and interests of *both* management and labor. For that purpose, we have not yet discovered an acceptable substitute for bargaining power.

ADDITIONAL READINGS

Bakke, E. Wight, Clark Kerr, and Charles Anrod: *Unions, Management, and the Public,* 2d ed., Harcourt, Brace & World, New York, 1960, chaps. 7 and 9.

Chamberlain, Neil W.: *Sourcebook on Labor,* McGraw-Hill, New York, 1958, chaps. 13 and 14.

Chamberlain, Neil W.: *The Union Challenge to Management Control,* Harper, New York, 1948.

Chandler, Margaret K.: *Management Rights and Union Interests,* McGraw-Hill, New York, 1964.

Cullen, Donald E., and Marcia L. Greenbaum: *Management Rights and Collective Bargaining: Can Both Survive?,* Bulletin 58, Cornell University, New York State School of Industrial and Labor Relations, Ithaca, N.Y., 1966.

Derber, Milton, W. E. Chalmers, and Milton Edelman: "Union Participation in Plant Decision Making," *Industrial and Labor Relations Review,* vol. 15, pp. 83–101, October, 1961.

FOR ANALYSIS AND DISCUSSION

1. The strategy and tactics of collective bargaining have often been compared to the strategy and tactics of military campaigning. In military operations, surprise is an element of great tactical advantage. But the National Planning Association, which conducted extensive investigations to identify the factors contributing to stable and satisfying collective-bargaining relations, concluded:

> Surprises of any kind are likely to upset negotiations. Each party has greater confidence if it has a thorough understanding of the issues to be raised by the other as well as of the social, political, or economic background of the various demands which are presented. Where the parties had been successful in solving problems and in developing effective communications, each was likely to enter new contract negotiations with a fairly sophisticated awareness of the other's needs and with a reasonably good idea of the probable reactions to any given demand.

Why should the element of surprise be so advantageous in military tactics and so disadvantageous in union–management relations? Or is the National Planning Association too sweeping in its statement? Are there in fact certain circumstances under which surprise in negotiations may add to one's bargaining power?

2. Professor Ryder has suggested that when a union and management reach a stalemate in bargaining, so that a strike seems inevitable, one technique frequently used is that of trying to create for the other a "picture of loss," that is, a realization of the costs to the other of disagreeing on its terms.

Compile a list of the items that might go into the pictures of loss which the union draws for management and which the management draws for the union. How effective do you believe this technique might be?

3. Collective bargaining is often criticized as a process whereby questions involving justice and equity are decided by power and force. Do you concur in this judgment?

4. Some people fear that labor unions will sooner or later take over all management functions, leading the economy ultimately into socialism. Do you agree that this conclusion follows from the unions' efforts to bargain on a wide variety of matters formerly reserved to management's decision and their refusal to "draw a line" demarking the issues on which they will not seek to bargain?

5. Look into your crystal ball and predict the new issues you would expect to find covered in labor agreements twenty years from now. What is the basis for your expectations? If you were a management negotiator, how would you deal with a union's demand to bargain on these issues when they first arise?

NOTES

1. This section is largely taken from Donald E. Cullen and Marcia L. Greenbaum, *Management Rights and Collective Bargaining: Can Both Survive?,* Bulle-

tin 58, Cornell University, New York State School of Industrial and Labor Relations, Ithaca, N.Y., 1966, pp. 36–40.

2. *Journal of Commerce,* Feb. 7, 1851.

3. *The President's National Labor–Management Conference, November 5 to 30, 1945,* U.S. Bureau of Labor Standards Bulletin 77, 1946, pp. 56 and 61.

4. *New York Times,* March 24, 1948.

5. Prof. Alfred Kuhn has taken exception to this concept of bargaining power on the ground that it runs counter to common usage by making bargaining power increase with a scaling down of demands. He comments that this "implies that the worse the terms one is willing to offer, the greater is his bargaining power" (*The Study of Society,* Dorsey-Irwin, Homewood, Ill., 1963, p. 333). But of course this is not the case. To the extent anything as intangible as power is measurable at all, it is measurable only *relative* to a given objective. This does not mean, then, that bargaining power in some *absolute* sense increases as one drops his demands, but only that bargaining power becomes more effective in securing an agreement reflecting as much of one's aspirations as possible.

The "terms" which a party asks from another derive directly from its aspirations. Since the objective of the bargaining process is not to increase one's bargaining power but to achieve his aspirations (terms), one would scarcely begin the process by giving away everything he seeks. In the very nature of the concept, he would reluctantly scale down what he seeks only when, and to the extent, he finds this necessary to make his bargaining power adequate to obtain agreement. To say that one could increase his bargaining power to the maximum by not seeking anything at all is a *reductio ad absurdum.* It assumes that bargaining power is the objective of the bargaining process, and not its instrument.

If the two preceding chapters have accomplished their purpose, we can now examine the specific subjects of collective bargaining as parts of a common pattern. There are, of course, important differences among contract clauses dealing with wages, seniority, technological change, and the many other subjects included in the typical labor agreement. Yet, in one guise or another, each of these subjects presents the same clash of rights and interests and aspirations—summed up in the legitimate drive of management to operate efficiently and profitably, pitted against the equally legitimate drive of labor to share in decisions affecting workers. Also, regardless of the subject on the bargaining table, a negotiator is under the same set of complex pressures from within as well as outside his organization, and he knows there are no "right" and final solutions to any bargaining issue—only an endless series of compromises based upon the relative power of the parties.

To illustrate this common pattern, we shall focus on the issues of technological change, seniority, and discipline, plus the grievance procedure for administering all contract clauses during the life of an agreement. (The issue of union security has already been described in Chapter 9, and the wage-and-hour issues will be examined in later chapters.)

The featherbedding issue

With the possible exception of union security, no single aspect of collective bargaining has gen-erated as much controversy over the years as labor's attempts to regulate technological change. Employers have argued strenuously that new technology creates new jobs as well as new products and lower prices; workers are convinced that technological unemployment is a real and constant threat; to add to the confusion, both parties are right—over the *long run*, new technology has indeed created more and better-paying jobs, just as in the *short run* it has undeniably destroyed the jobs and skills of many workers at a particular time and place. As noted before, agriculture provides the classic example of the costs and benefits of technological change: every industrial society has benefited enormously from the technological revolution in farming, but millions of farmers have been displaced in the process.

As a bargaining subject, however, technological change is far more complicated than this debate over abstract principles and economywide trends. To the employer, excessive labor costs are a threat to his major objective—maintaining or increasing the profitability of his firm; and if he is to keep even with, or ahead of, his competition, he must constantly search out improved methods of production. In some instances, these methods involve the substitution of machines for men. In other instances, they permit greater output with the same number of men by a reorganization of the work flow, by a change in materials used, by a redesigning of the product—all calculated to reduce the labor cost of a unit of output. Or management may seek to improve efficiency simply by eliminating existing practices which are considered costly or unnecessary—"restrictive practices," they are sometimes called, or "featherbedding."

The drive for greater efficiency becomes most pronounced in recessions or when companies are experiencing vigorous competition. In boom times, when there is no difficulty in disposing of total output at good prices, the striving for efficiency is less compulsive. Inevitably, whenever management seeks to improve productive performance in ways that threaten to displace workers from their jobs, or to require their transfer to less desirable positions, or to change their methods of operation so that they produce more in the same amount of time, workers resist. The conflict between the efficiency-driven management and the security-seeking workers sometimes takes on personal overtones, with the latter charging the former with lack of concern for worker welfare and sole interest in dollars of profit.

While the *way* in which management seeks to introduce change may sometimes reflect indifference to employee interests, that it strives for efficiency and profitability as primary objectives does not establish callousness: it reflects only the fact that management's performance of its function sometimes *obliges* it to take actions which run counter to the interests of employees. Management is playing a social role and must read the lines which go with its part. If a union leader were to change sides and take a management job in industry, as has sometimes happened, he would have to conform to the institutional requirements of his new position no less than the man whom he now castigates for doing so. Society *expects* its managers to be efficient and to meet or better their competition.

This institutional imperative is not, however, persuasive to those workers who see their interests adversely affected by management's compulsive drive for efficiency. For a variety of reasons, they attempt to throw roadblocks in the way of management's attempts to change methods of operation. Thus is born the "work-rules controversy" which is not simply a product of unionism but which predates it by many centuries. Unions, however, have highlighted the controversy by formalizing the disputed work rules, often reducing them to written form and incorporating them

in collective agreements. Custom and practice—work rules—are sometimes spelled out in formal requirements such as how many men shall be hired to perform certain tasks in a specified way; they are sometimes protected simply by a general contractual provision that "past practices" shall be continued unless there is a major change in a job's technology; they are sometimes secured by grievance decisions which rule that even without contractual agreement, past practices create enforceable rights and expectations of continuity in the absence of some demonstrable change in the underlying circumstances; and they are sometimes safeguarded solely by the bargaining power of a group of workers or a union which refuses to accept modification of the established way of doing things. This encrustation of rules and a general reluctance to accept new ways of organizing production often frustrate management, which is geared to change in the industrial order and which is constantly on the lookout for new ways of improving performance. So the two forces collide.

They collide not over the issue of whether there should be work rules. No business could operate without them. Unless a company is willing to put up with the inefficiencies of random practice, continued purposeless experimentation, the vagaries of worker motivation, uncertain costs, and safety hazards, there must be rules. The issue is not work rules as such, but what rules are reasonable, who makes them, and under what conditions they should be changed. These are the questions with which operating and personnel managements must grapple as they seek to organize a work force productively and profitably. When managements complain about the restrictive practices or featherbedding rules of unions, they are frequently complaining about practices and rules which once were reasonable and acceptable even in their own judgment, but which time and change have made obsolete.

What is the nature of some of these obsolete rules which require the use of more manpower per unit of output, more men to do a given job, than management thinks efficient? We can identify four major categories:

1. The number of workers in a crew may be larger than needed. Prior to the 1960s, the long-

shore industry provided several examples. On the Atlantic Coast, employers objected that "artificial" work rules had frozen the size of a work gang for unloading a ship at an unnecessary twenty: eight men to work at a hatch, eight men on the dock, and four in the hold. Employers maintained that often half the men on the dock had no work to do. On the West Coast, in many ports a "four-on–four-off" gang was customary: of the eight men whom the union required to be in the hold, four were working while four were resting. Because a longshoreman is paid time and a half for overtime after 6 hours, and usually puts in an 8-hour day, this meant, according to shippers, that a longshoreman in the hold was actually working only 4 hours for 9 hours of pay.

2. Work rules may require hiring workers to perform "unnecessary" functions. There are a number of celebrated examples of this situation. Despite the protestations of the Brotherhood of Locomotive Firemen and Enginemen, several impartial commissions have concluded that the use of a fireman helper on nonsteam locomotives is unneeded and could be discontinued without loss of efficiency or safety,[1] but this has been a hotly disputed issue for many years. Of even longer standing has been the controversy between the Typographical Union and newspaper publishers over the setting of "bogus." This practice, that first came into existence about 1870, obligated a newspaper publisher to reset any type that he might have borrowed, already set, from a neighboring publisher. The issue became acute with the introduction of papier-maché matrices which permitted an advertiser to set up copy just once in type, from which any number of matrices could be made and sent to newspapers, which then could produce a plate simply by taking a metal casting from the matrix, obviating the setting of type by each publisher. The ITU has required newspapers which use such "mats" in local advertising to pay compositors to reset the same copy, even though the reset type would never be used—in fact, it might be set up weeks after the ad had been run. This has been branded as pure make-work; the type is not needed, the employer will not use it, but he must pay to have the work done nonetheless. Similar complaints have been directed to the requirement of standby orchestras

in some kinds of theater productions; the players collect their checks by mail without ever showing up at the theater.

3. Work rules may require workers to perform necessary functions in wasteful ways. Here, perhaps the most frequently cited examples come from the building trades. Painters have placed prohibitions on the use of paint brushes wider than a specified number of inches, or of rollers or spray guns. Glaziers have refused to install preglazed sash, and electricians have sometimes insisted that control panels or switchboards which have been wired at the factory be disconnected and rewired on the construction site. Bricklaying equipment may be boycotted by bricklayers, who insist that the work be done by hand.

4. Work rules sometimes limit the amount of work a worker can do in a given time. The number of pounds which can be hoisted in a sling or lifted out of a ship or the speed of assembly lines may be restricted by practice or written agreement, and at levels which management often believes to be excessively low. Some managers have argued that the conscious effort to "hold back" is more fatiguing to workers than the work itself. It has been said that some unions have lowered production rates to the point where workers must kill time in order not to exceed them.

These various restrictive practices and featherbedding techniques sound antisocial and misguided. They appear to run counter to the accepted American credo of doing one's best, putting in an honest day's effort, and accenting progress. In short, they seem immoral, wrong, dishonest. It is understandable, then, that such rules and practices often provoke managerial wrath rather than an effort at understanding. Yet, when one considers the problem more objectively, he is faced with the fact that if make-work rules and restrictive practices are as widespread as they are claimed to be, and if they are somehow immoral, then management is charging a large segment of the American population with engaging in immoral conduct at the workplace. Clearly there must be other reasons for worker resistance to more efficient job practices than that half the population consists of misguided "chiselers." What really motivates workers' response to technological change?

Justifications offered for the worker's position

The answer to this question is far more complex than many managers realize and involves, among other things, an examination of the social function of work. Here we can do little more than touch on some of the points which are relevant.

1. A job is more than a source of income; it helps to define a person's social status. In our society the position a person, particularly the head of a household, occupies—in his family, in his neighborhood, in his church, in his varied organizational life—depends upon his job as well as upon his income. In general, they are intimately related in that what affects the former affects the latter. The place he has carved out for himself in his society, whether he has only recently entered the labor force or is about to leave it, is—let us exaggerate just a little to emphasize the point— absolutely dependent on his employment, its kind, and its remuneration.

In some European countries, a man is so identified with his trade that he is listed in the telephone directory not alphabetically by his given name but alphabetically by occupation. If the identification is less complete in the United States, it is still real and vital. People are accorded varying degrees of respect depending on what they do. Workers in the skilled trades have a status denied to those who are only semiskilled or unskilled. People in the professions are customarily treated with more esteem than manual workers. The never-ending controversies over occupational wage differentials, wage "inequities," and factor weights in job-evaluation systems are part of the same phenomenon. If performance differences between jobs diminish, distinctions of title and pay are likely to be more jealously guarded. What is at stake is the worker's institutional role which he has built up over the years; to this role attach expectations which people have of him and which he has of other people's attitudes toward him.

Workers are thus required by all that gives dignity to human existence to protect the social role they have constructed for themselves. Now place these people in work situations which are subjected to the fragmentation and disintegration and remolding of technologies and markets. A job need not actually be lost for this to spell catastrophe; social capital is being wiped out even if a worker is only downgraded or if his job is reduced in importance. A man's institutionalized personality, his social substance, is threatened, damaged, or broken, and he presumably is to be comforted by the fact that his personal tragedy is a necessary price of social progress.

In the running controversy over the fireman on the diesel engine, a spokesman for the Pennsylvania Railroad once said that "nearly 4,000 firemen continue to be paid approximately $28 million every year, although their historic mission of shoveling coal has long since ended." Putting oneself in the position of the corporate vice-president who made that statement and whose own institutional role required him to press on every front for efficiency and profitability, that represented an intolerable situation. The very structure of our economic society is premised on the assumption that people in his position will make every effort —for their very survival, *must* make every effort —to do away with such waste. But what about the 4,000 firemen? Each of them was the nucleus of a complex set of social relationships premised on his job as fireman. His institutional role demanded that he safeguard that premise.

Some members of the managerial group might reasonably doubt whether workers' stubborn adherence to a specific work practice which has over time lost its reason for existence is based on anything more subtle than that they have inherited a profitable privilege which they seek to protect by joint coercive effort. To be sure, if it often hard to disentangle the personal effort to maintain social status from the concerted effort to exercise power over others in the protection of special privilege. But this is no less true of other groups than of workers. Business groups which bring political pressure to bear on Congress in defense of tariff protection for their industry and agricultural blocs which resort to similar pressures to obtain special treatment which on purely economic grounds is patently indefensible (including payments for nonproduction and make-work) could hardly charge workers and unions with engaging in conduct which is peculiarly and uniquely anti-social. In all such efforts, the desire to shield one-self from the adverse effects of change leads to an exercise of such bargaining power as can be mustered and, however rationalized, constitutes an understandable defense of socioeconomic status, even though distasteful to those who pay the price.

2. A job—not just in the sense of a place on the payroll, but a particular cluster of activities—is sometimes regarded as a property right. From this point of view, any effort to tamper with or modify the activities composing the job constitutes an interference with property rights, something we have been brought up to consider unethical. Here, the charge of "immorality" is turned by workers against management.

Professor William Gomberg, an industrial engineer with a background in unionism, makes this point:[2]

Many of the work rules define an emerging property right of the worker in his job. For example, a jurisdictional claim of a yard worker that he and he alone can handle a train in the yard and the corresponding claim of a road worker that he and he alone can handle a train on the road stems from a property right of each craft in the particular job area. The equivalent of the worker's property deed is the collective agreement. It would be silly and pointless to deny that work in many cases could be performed more cheaply if these property rights and the penalties for their violation did not exist. However, in a democracy other values than those of productivity receive equivalent attention from the community. . . .
. . . Many automobile public roads and expressways wind a serpentine path between two points. The road is much longer than if a surveyor and engineer were permitted to lay out the most effective path that would afford the traveler the shortest distance at the minimum consumption of gasoline. It is true that society has invented the concept of eminent domain. Its purpose is to prevent the holder of private property from imposing too absolute a restraint on public purpose and public efficiency. However, the exercise of this right of eminent domain is reserved to the government and its

specified agents; then the government can only take over after due process and fair compensation.

3. A job is not just a cluster of activities but a place on a payroll. This, of course, is the opposite of the rationalization for restrictive work rules mentioned above. In this formulation, the important thing about a job is not so much the status attaching to particular duties. This may or may not be present, but it is not relevant to the present point. The consideration here is simply that in a pecuniary society, a person needs a tie to a job in order to obtain the income that keeps him and his family going. He is dependent on a job for a living.

The classic expression of this notion is referred to as the "lump-of-labor" theory. Current among workingmen but branded as a fallacy by most economists, it took the point of view that at any time there was just so much work to go around. Hence, the more rapidly a person finished his job assignments, the sooner he worked himself out of a job. If he could stretch his work load over a longer period of time, he kept his tie to an income that much longer. (Economists pointed out that such a philosophy led to higher costs of production, limiting demand for a product, reducing the amount of work available to the high-price firm, and thus killing the job which the worker was trying to prolong.)

The more modern version of this theory adopts the philosophy that a job is not so much specific services rendered for specific pay received as it is a place on somebody's payroll, almost regardless of the functions performed, as the necessary condition of being tied into our pecuniary society. Payment for services not performed is perfectly compatible with this notion.

The drive to establish supplementary unemployment-compensation programs and pensions and the demand for extended vacations and "sabbatical" leaves are all consonant with this philosophy. None of these programs requires the performance of services; they simply represent claims to a continuing income. Any large organization has numerous jobs which are not essential to its functioning, particularly in the white-collar ranks; the discontinuance of some record keeping, of some forms of "happiness" work in the personnel department, of some jobs filled by pretty receptionists, would not vitally affect the efficiency or profitability of the company. Long-service officials who have outlived their usefulness before reaching retirement and who have been sidetracked or "promoted" to honorific or functionless positions provide other examples. In these instances, as in the case of make-work practices in the production end, any large-scale organization can be expected to carry its "share" of the population on its payroll, as a contribution toward tying every member of society somehow into the pecuniary stream. This thesis is seldom spelled out so starkly, but it is often implied.

4. Work rules should be subject to joint employer-worker agreement and not imposed unilaterally by the employer. The question of how much work shall be performed in a given time, by how many men and in what way, is one to which people have differing answers for differing reasons. Management's answer, based on efficiency considerations, is only one possible response. Whether it can make its position effective depends on whether it has the bargaining power to change present rules and practices as it wants. It has no more right to insist on its view of what the work rules shall be than it has to insist on its view of what the wage-rate structure shall be. Both are subject to a bargained agreement.

This is an argument which is hard to dispute. Though Sen. Robert A. Taft, cosponsor of the Taft-Hartley Act so roundly condemned by labor leaders, at one time considered inclusion of a clause which would outlaw a number of specified make-work practices, he was eventually persuaded of the error of such an approach, as it would have put the government into the business of deciding how many men are needed to perform certain tasks, or of taking the position that whatever an employer decides is somehow "right." (The Taft-Hartley Act instead tried to get at the featherbedding problem by a more general approach, declaring it an unfair labor practice for a union to "attempt to cause an employer to pay . . . for services which are not performed or not to be performed." This has proved to be a dead-letter provision in the law, for even the most restrictive work rules state that workers will or

might provide *some* services—such as setting bogus type—although these services may not be desired by the employer.)

Contract practice

How have the parties bargained out their apparently irreconcilable differences over technological change? Is featherbedding a major problem throughout American industry or only in a handful of situations? There is no quantifiable evidence with which to answer these questions precisely, but a general pattern emerges from a Brookings Institution report, *The Impact of Collective Bargaining on Management*,[3] which is easily the most thorough study made of bargaining practices in the postwar period. Approximately 650 individuals, representing 150 companies, 25 industry associations, and 40 unions, were interviewed in three years of intensive field research. The companies were not selected on any sampling basis but included manufacturing and nonmanufacturing, large companies and small companies, and companies in various sections of the country.

The researchers grouped union policies toward technological change into five categories—willing acceptance, opposition, competition, encouragement, and adjustment. We shall follow this classification in reporting their findings.

Willing acceptance   It may surprise some that "the most usual policy of unions towards technological change" was found to be one where "the union leaves the initiative to the employer and simply acquiesces rather completely in accepting the changes."[4] The most celebrated example of this approach is that of the United Mine Workers during the reign of John L. Lewis, but it is also the approach generally taken by unions in most manufacturing industries over the past thirty years. Even in the much-criticized building industry, many new materials and tools have been accepted peacefully, with the dramatic rise to power of the Operating Engineers linked directly to the introduction of new equipment in heavy and highway construction. In the late 1950s, it is true, the policies of unions in both mining and manufacturing shifted toward that of adjustment, in response to worsening employment situations.

Yet it is worth remembering that the past thirty years have witnessed not only the growth of union power but also the mushrooming of management's research and development activities, the continuation of long-run productivity trends, and the coming of the age of automation. Either unions have been much weaker than their critics have charged, or they have accepted technological change more willingly than is often believed.

Opposition At the other extreme, this study found that "the policy of outright and uncompromising opposition to technological change is not rare, but it is pursued in only a small proportion of cases."[5] Since such opposition often springs from the workers' fear of displacement, some people had expected a withering of restrictive practices during a long period of full employment. Yet in the mid-1950s, the research team still found some painters refusing to use spray guns, some longshoremen refusing to handle cargo on pallets or in certain large containers, teamsters blocking the "piggybacking" of trucks on railroad cars, printers opposing the automatic typesetter, and several other examples of the restrictive work rules described earlier. In fact, the evidence suggests that make-work rules increased markedly from the 1930s to the late 1940s as the rapid growth of both union power and product demand undermined employer resistance, but in subsequent years "there has been on balance a drop in their extent and severity" as more normal competitive conditions goaded managers into a limited counteroffensive.[6]

The most celebrated rollbacks of work rules have occurred in railroads and longshoring, the two industries that used to top many lists of featherbedding practices. As mentioned in Chapter 11, in railroads the work-rules issue proved too explosive to be handled by either conventional or continuous bargaining, and it was eventually ordered to arbitration by act of Congress. The arbitrators' award in 1963 in essence upheld management's contention that firemen are unnecessary on many diesel locomotives and permitted their gradual displacement. (The longshoring experience is described later when discussing adjustment.) Other work rules have undoubtedly changed or even disappeared since the Brookings

study was made, but there surely remain many employers today who are stymied by union pressure from introducing certain technological innovations. Yet note the pattern emerging: Employers who have been completely stripped of their initiative on this issue are in a distinct minority and tend to be concentrated in certain nonmanufacturing industries—often those marked by a high level of job insecurity and intense competition among many small employers. Although there are many exceptions, this suggests a logical tendency for work rules to be most restrictive where labor's bargaining power and fear of job loss are both pronounced.

Adjustment "The essence of the policy of adjustment to technological change is an effort by the union to control the use of the new equipment, process, or materials. . . . Since no two technological changes are alike, implementing the policy of adjustment means negotiating tailor-made agreements on a wide variety of issues such as, who is to do the work; what will be the rate of pay; what is to be done about the displaced workers. . . ?"[7] The authors offer no estimate of the incidence of this policy, but obviously it is the typical bargaining compromise between the approaches of opposition and acceptance. To put it another way, most of the technological changes introduced each year in unionized companies are not bargained over in the usual sense, but on those changes which are bargained, contract clauses are far more likely to qualify than to prohibit management action.

There are innumerable forms of adjustment required by labor agreements. Perhaps the mildest clause is one requiring the employer to give advance notice of major job changes. Examples can be found in the Chicago building-service industry (thirty days' notice of the installation of automatic elevators), several railroad contracts (sixty days for some changes and ninety days in cases requiring a change of an employee's residence), and the Newspaper Guild-*New York Times* contract settling a 1965 strike (six months' notice of major changes). One of the strongest adjustment clauses, on the other hand, guarantees that no present employees of a company will be laid off as a result of technological change, although the employer may reduce the number of available jobs as his present workers die, quit, or retire. Such attrition clauses are particularly widespread in the railroad industry, and other examples are found in longshoring, printing, Kaiser Steel, and local transit. Somewhere between the advance-notice and attrition clauses lie the growing number of severance-pay provisions, some applying to all types of layoffs and some specifically to technological unemployment (such as one covering television technicians displaced by video tape).[8]

West Coast longshoring presents one of the purest examples of the manner in which collective bargaining can transform a conflict of rights and principles into a pragmatic trade between parties who have something to offer each other. In that industry, it will be recalled, the union had long enforced rules prescribing such things as the minimum size of work gangs, the maximum load of cargo slings, and the practice in certain gangs of four men resting and four working at any given time. After more than three years of exploration and negotiation, the International Longshoremen's and Warehousemen's Union and the Pacific Maritime Association concluded a radical agreement in 1960, under which the employers in effect "bought out" these make-work rules:

> The shipowners and stevedoring contractors are freed of restrictions on the introduction of labor-saving devices, relieved of the use of unnecessary men and assured of the elimination of work practices which impede the free flow of cargo or ship turnaround. These guarantees to industry are in exchange for a series of benefits for the workers to protect them against the impact of the machine on their daily work or on their job security.[9]

More specifically, the contract pledged employers to establish a $29 million fund, to be built up over five and one-half years for the purpose of financing early retirement and a guaranteed annual wage for the most senior group of longshoremen. Productivity has risen substantially since the plan took effect, with the surprising result that, instead of large numbers of idle men drawing guaranteed pay, so many chose retirement in the plan's first three years that *no* guaranteed pay benefits were

paid out—and, in fact, it proved necessary to take on 2,600 new workers! The contract was renewed in 1966 with some changes. On the East and Gulf Coast docks, on the other hand, the International Longshoremen's Association fought to retain similar make-work rules until 1965 when, after a 33-day strike, the employers won a relaxation of some rules in return for a form of the guaranteed annual wage.

Competition and encouragement Finally, a few unions have attempted to compete with technological change by such methods as taking a wage cut or advertising the superiority of the old "quality" method over the new, while others have actually taken the initiative in promoting change and efficiency, with the engineering departments of the needle-trade unions the best known example. Neither of these policies is widely followed, but they further illustrate the diversity of bargaining practices on this subject as on most other issues in dispute between labor and management.

To summarize, collective bargaining has not handled technological change to the complete satisfaction of anyone—workers, employers, or economists of any persuasion. Yet its record is far better than suggested by those examples in which workers are summarily replaced by machines or employers are completely handcuffed by union work rules. The facts indicate that workers and unions accept most of the innovations occurring daily in American industry for the simple reason that most of these changes do not threaten many workers. And when such a threat does exist, the typical (though not universal) bargaining solution is one which permits the employer to innovate, but at the price of cushioning the impact of change upon employees.

The nature of seniority

The term "seniority" has crept into the public's vocabulary to a degree that makes definition seem almost superfluous. Actually, it is a more complex phenomenon than many who use the term realize.

Seniority is an employee's length of service in some employment unit. Just as every worker has a chronological age of his own, he also has an employment age—the time he has been on the job. This employment age, his seniority, ranks him in relation to all other workers in the unit. The seniority roster establishes clearly how long each employee has been employed on a job, or in a department, or with a company, whichever is relevant.

In unionized companies, this length-of-service measure is used for a variety of purposes which are usually spelled out in the collective agreement. These several purposes may be grouped into two categories: benefit seniority and competitive-status seniority. Both "discriminate" among employees on the basis of seniority, but in quite different ways. In the first category, benefits are allocated to *all* workers who meet a certain length-of-service standard, but in the second category some workers win a benefit *at the expense of others.* When all workers with ten years' seniority can take three weeks of paid vacation but workers with one year of service can take only one week, that is an example of benefit seniority. Indirectly, of course, there is an element of competition in that arrangement, but not as directly as in the pure case of competitive-status seniority: three out of thirty men must be laid off in a department, and the three who go must be those with the lowest seniority.[10]

The distinction is important because most critics of labor's "abuse" of seniority unwittingly overstate their case. Few people actually object to the widespread use of benefit seniority in labor contracts. To most, it seems fair that the senior employee is preferred over the junior one in the length of their paid vacations and in their eligibility for and size of pensions, severance pay, and sick leave.

Far more controversial, however, is labor's demand for competitive-status seniority. Its most common use is to determine the order of layoffs in the event of lack of work. Customarily, the employees with least seniority are laid off first, and when recalled to work they are called in the inverse order in which laid off, so that the most senior employee among those on layoff is given the first reemployment rights. Thus the worker who is lowest on the seniority roster is the first to be laid off and the last to be recalled.

Seniority is also used in determining promotions among rank-and-file employees, though the weight accorded it varies. In some instances, "strict seniority" is the rule, which means that in the event of an opening, the most senior employee is always given first chance, *provided* that he can do the job. (In some instances, the agreement may even require that the senior employee be given first chance if he can learn to do the job within some specified term, such as thirty days.) In other cases, however, seniority is used as a secondary basis for determining which of several employees deserves the promotion. The employee with greatest ability has first claim on the opening, but in the event that the abilities of several candidates are relatively equal, then the most senior employee takes precedence.

Although it is with respect to layoffs and promotions that seniority has its chief significance, it may also be used to determine who shall be transferred (if the transfer is desirable, the most senior employee has some preference; if it is undesirable, the least senior employee is likely to be designated) and which employees shall have prior choice of vacation time, or shift assignment, or preferred location, or overtime, and so on.

What counts as "service" for purposes of determining seniority depends on the seniority unit, just as what counts as "residence" for purposes of voting depends on the governmental unit—national, state, or local. National residence does not count for local voting, and similarly, plant service does not count toward occupational seniority.

There are, in fact, a number of possible seniority units. In some companies, the seniority unit may be based on craft or occupation—for example, all welders in an automobile plant (whether acetylene, tack, assembly, or other type of welder) may constitute a seniority unit in which they are ranked in the order of length of employment and enjoy certain privileges depending on where they stand in that ranking. The seniority unit may be a department or a division within a company. It may also be plantwide or companywide. Indeed, in some few instances seniority may be exercised on an industrywide basis (as is true of truck drivers in the brewery industry in New York City, for example, and of seamen on the Atlantic and

Gulf Coasts). In general, the seniority unit reflects the nature of a company's operations. If job requirements are fairly uniform and skills interchangeable, then the larger seniority unit is likely to be established. But if there is a wide range of skills required in a variety of occupations, so that the skills of one worker are not readily transferable to another operation, then the seniority unit is likely to be narrower.

Within a unionized plant, every employee who has passed a probationary period of one to six months appears on some seniority roster, being ranked with all other employees in his seniority unit in accordance with his length of employment in that unit. In some instances different seniority units may be used for different purposes, as when occupational seniority may be relied on for promotions and plantwide seniority for layoffs. Also, benefit seniority is usually based on the broadest possible unit, while competitive-status seniority is frequently limited to an occupation, a department, or one of a firm's several plants. In these cases an employee's name would appear on more than one seniority roster.

The rationale of seniority

What are the reasons for this system of giving priority to those workers who have been longest on the job, a system which is widely practiced in the United States, especially in unionized establishments?

Unions have fought for seniority systems as a means of eliminating management favoritism in the designation of employees to be rewarded or penalized. In the first instance the objective was to remove management's power of breaking a union by giving preferred treatment to nonunion employees. Although this remains as one objective, its importance has been lessened by federal legislation which makes unlawful a preferred treatment on the basis of the union membership or nonmembership of a worker. Nevertheless, when it comes to the designation of the man who is to be laid off or promoted, many workers still retain a belief that management judgment will be biased, that the individual who is more subservient to management will be chosen for promotion, that the worker who has shown greater independence of action and thought may be the one selected for layoff.

But seniority also plays another role, particularly in its competitive-status form. It constitutes a system of rules by which workers decide *among themselves* who shall be given preference in certain employment conditions. Even if one imagines that managers were removed from an enterprise and that workers were running the business cooperatively, the decisions about who should be laid off, who transferred, who promoted, who given first choice of vacation time, who allowed shift preference, and so on, must be made. In our hypothetical case the workers would have to decide such questions for themselves. In many plants, seniority is the decision rule which worker groups of former years established (chiefly in the forties) and which has been handed down to the present generation of workers.

Seniority must thus be recognized as an allocative device designed to deal with situations of scarcity—a scarcity of jobs (who gets laid off), or a scarcity of *better* jobs (who gets promoted), or a scarcity of preferred assignments (who gets the day shift, or overtime, or the newest machine), or a scarcity of preferred conditions (who gets first choice of vacation time). This basis for judgment eliminates the troublesome question of deciding that one person is better than another; instead, it rests decision simply on the ground of who has worked here longest, who has built up the greatest equity on a job by virtue of his time investment. In the words of one industrial relations director, "Seniority has set up a system of morality that has no basis in economics that I can find. The only purpose is that it sets up a basis that is objective. You know who goes and who moves, and therefore you do not have to face up to the more obscure problems such as transfer and movement on the basis of skill or ability."

Since seniority actually serves as an allocative device in the presence of scarcity conditions, it is designed to remove an area of competition among workers, thus bolstering union solidarity and supporting the principle of the common rate. If the question of who would be laid off or who promoted were left to be decided by competition among workers, the award might go to whoever was willing to work the hardest or accept the poorest terms for his efforts. Under seniority, the terms of the job remain the same for whoever fills it, and selection of the incumbent is based not on competitive bidding but on the factual basis of relative length of service. But a diminution of competition in one respect may stimulate competition in other respects, and seniority—which diminishes competition among workers for jobs on the basis of who wants or needs the job the most—has stimulated another form of competition among workers. This consists of efforts to manipulate seniority to the advantage of one group over another.

The exercise of seniority rights may be thought of as a file of individuals, whose order in the file depends on length of service, rising or descending on "ladders" of promotion or layoff. One's movement up or down the ladder depends on the seniority arrangement. Let us construct one possible situation. Assume that promotions and layoffs are based on occupational seniority. Within the department, one job is viewed as a natural step to another better-paying, more skilled job, which in turn logically leads to still another "higher" job. This would be one ladder of promotion. Other ladders of promotion, consisting of a succession of jobs each of which prepares the occupant for the next higher job, also are to be found in the department. Sometimes several of such ladders will converge on a given occupation. Figure 13-1 suggests such a pattern. The most senior worker

in the job A1 group will always be the one to advance to job B1 whenever there is an opening in that group.

In the pattern suggested in the diagram, workers in job C1 can exercise their seniority to bid not only for job D1 but also job D2. The logic has been established that C1 training is a natural prerequisite to D2 jobholding. C1 employees thus have two avenues of advancement, as against C3 employees who can only advance to D3. To enlarge their opportunities, the C3 group, through the grievance procedure, may protest that their experience is just as valuable as C1 experience when it comes to holding down a D2 job. They will seek to reconstitute the seniority ladder to increase their promotional opportunities (as indicated by the dotted line in the diagram). If they are a strategic group, they may well be able to carry off this maneuver through pressure on supervisors or on their union officials.

Attitudes toward seniority

The principle of allocating jobs within a firm on the basis of seniority is so widely practiced in our society that it is often not seriously questioned. It has come to be a familiar institutional means for determining, within the relevant seniority unit, who gets what job. Individuals have acquired a stake in the system by having advanced on their own seniority lists, and new entrants to the labor force often take for granted that they too must work themselves up the lists.

It has been suggested that the acceptance of seniority in industry perhaps is rooted in the general belief in the justice of "taking turns." "Today when people peacefully form a queue before a ticket window, for example, they do so ostensibly because of custom and courtesy, but in reality, as Carl Van Doren once remarked, because there is something about taking turns which strikes men as being fundamentally fair."[11] Competitive-status seniority is simply a practice of queueing up for jobs, of standing in a job line on the basis of first come, fire served. Something in the idea of a younger man competing against a worker of longer service, to take his opportunity away from him, impresses many people as unfair, in the same way that most people regard as unfair

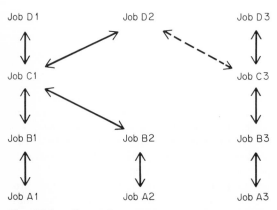

Fig. 13-1. *Promotion patterns under seniority systems.*

the latecomer's easing himself in at the front of a line. Notions of simple justice have thus perhaps influenced the conception and institutionalization of seniority systems.

Nevertheless, several points about the "acceptance" of seniority should be made.

Although seniority was a device rather commonly used even before the spread of labor unions, they have been most responsible for the systematic and widespread adoption of the practice. Despite the fact that our society places value on older people, though perhaps less so than in some other societies, with respect to employment matters age has generally been penalized. The older worker—whatever prestige his age entitled him to in the community—has often been regarded as a liability in industry, a liability that could be dropped or sidetracked for the good of the enterprise, to make way for the infusion of new blood which was necessary to the firm's survival in a competitive society. If regard for the older worker was nothing which the unions invented, what the unions did was to systematize and enforce the procedures under which the older worker's interests were to be given priority.

Seniority is not confined to unionized establishments,[12] but in other instances the criterion of length of service is usually more effectively qualified by such considerations as ability. For this reason, as well as because of the absence of a union to process claims through to arbitration or strike, most unionists would be unwilling to grant that seniority as applied in unorganized establishments creates the enforceable claims that it does in a unionized plant under collective bargaining. Aside from this contention, the increased acceptance of the seniority principle in industry generally, whether or not organized, is in large measure due to the union's exertions on behalf of that principle. The unions have educated the American public—and American management— to a greater acceptance of seniority in employment practices.

But this is not to say that American managers have come to accept seniority in all its possible applications. More willing to apply the seniority rule in layoffs, they would prefer to accord it a secondary position in promotions, putting ability first. The logic of *corporate* efficiency drives them

in the direction of emphasizing ability in *individual* performance. Even though the growth in size of many corporations has forced on them a bureaucratic necessity for developing some decision rule to guide personnel policies, where they are now dealing with thousands of individuals, they remain reluctant to accept seniority as such a rule in the matter of job progression. They have been led to give it greater emphasis than they would themselves prefer because it has been difficult to find as objective a basis for promotion as seniority, and because—driven by unions to justify their personnel actions through the grievance procedure —objective justification has become necessary.

That the seniority rule in promotions runs counter to the managers' efficiency concepts is amply illustrated by the promotion policy which they apply to the management ranks themselves. Length of service obviously plays some part, but it is far from conclusive. A variety of considerations (in part of a "political" nature—whom do you know how well in the levels above you, on "whose team" do you play?) create uncertainty in the selection process, and the justification for the eventual choice—seldom objective—runs not so much to equity for those under consideration as to "the good of the company."[13]

Because of this conflict in values between management, which stresses efficiency, and union which, as agent for the employees, stresses security, the role of seniority, particularly as it relates to promotions, has been a continuing subject of debate. In management's view, if men are laid off and promoted solely on the basis of length of service, both the carrot and the stick have been removed. There is no inducement to the younger worker to exert himself; he knows that he cannot accelerate his advancement but must patiently await his turn. Nor is there any incentive for the older worker to do a better job; he knows that his reward will come automatically with the passage of time. Seniority thus eliminates the purposeful drive of workers to improve their performance in the hope of reward (promotion) or in the expectation of avoiding penalty (layoff). Seniority encourages the dead level of mediocrity. Particularly in a competitive environment (which we profess to seek) is a company's ability to reward superior performance vitally important. To the small-scale producer, the difference between keeping a man who turns out 10 to 15 percent more product per hour rather than an employee who happens to have an extra year of service may be the difference between success and failure in a competitive industry.

Even should the seniority clause call for promotion by seniority only "where ability is equal," the personnel manager argues that this is no solution. The difficulty of defending before an arbitrator, in the terminal stage of the grievance procedure, the judgment that the junior employee had greater ability has frequently led supervisors to avoid a showdown—in which they might well lose —by selecting the senior man even when convinced that he was not so well qualified for the job. The alternative might be a painstaking and costly selection process in order to ensure adequate defense of the man finally chosen, should his promotion be contested by the union because he turned out to be "junior." A personnel man has summed up his reactions as follows:

> We are stuck with a seniority plan for advancement, and we are not happy. We feel that a job is best done by the people best able to do it. If seniority governed jobs up to my level, I would not be here. The result of this system, in my opinion, is that someone who is low seniority-wise, who may be very able, will not be interested in doing more than an average job. So we are a little unhappy. I don't see where much purpose is served if a person moves up just because his number comes up. With respect to layoffs, where we do not resist the seniority provisions, it has become a sort of morale provision. If we attempted to deviate too seriously, we would run into morale problems that would indicate that the game was not worth the effort. We accept it and live with it.

In the view of the union, management's concern for the incentive effect is based more on emotion than fact. On many types of work, differences in worker ability are unimportant, as they can find no expression on the job in any event. This is particularly true where work is machine-paced, as on an assembly line. In such work situations, it makes no difference what motivates a worker; the nature of his assignment requires him to perform certain operations within prescribed time limits, and any difference in ability between two men would make little difference in job performance. Under the circumstances, it makes no sense to judge between them on the basis of some presumed differential ability which has no job significance. The objective test of length of service is actually more relevant. On the other hand, on many highly skilled jobs which are not machine-paced, promotions are simply not an issue. An electrician, for example, is either an apprentice or a journeyman, and for journeymen electricians there are usually no higher jobs to which they can be promoted—except in supervision, and most employers can select anyone they want for a supervisor's job.

Furthermore, even in those instances where skill differences are significant, the abler workman frequently proves to be the one who has been longest on the job. Hence, selection on a basis of seniority is not likely very often to lead to a different choice from the one that management would on its own have made.

In support of this position, a study undertaken by Prof. James J. Healy of the Harvard Business School, a frequent arbitrator in grievance disputes, might be cited. Impressed with the frequency with which, in promotion cases, unions were lined up on the side of the straight length-of-service criterion while management fought for the right to promote a junior employee on the grounds of his greater ability, Healy selected a number of cases in which the union's position had been upheld by an arbitrator's ruling. Going back to the employer a year or so later, Healy inquired how the senior man had made out on the job which management had been reluctant to award him. In a clear majority of cases, the employer was well satisfied with the senior worker's handling of the new job, and in a number of instances confessed doubts that the junior man whom he had preferred would have done any better on the job.[14]

Finally, says the union, if management complains that, because of inability to justify its preference before an arbitrator, it is forced to promote an employee other than the one whom it prefers, this is itself indicative of the shaky basis for its judgment. If management cannot establish the superior ability of one man over another by criteria that make sense to a disinterested third party, the objective test of length of service is likely to be at least as satisfactory as far as job performance is concerned and will certainly be more satisfactory as far as acceptability to the workers themselves is concerned.

Possible technological effects on the seniority principle

This running debate between managers and unions over the appropriate personnel policy in the case of promotions may, however, conceal rather than reveal the underlying realities of a changing industrial situation. Corporations and labor unions both are bureaucracies, and as such tend to develop a body of rules and regulations governing the relations of people in the organization, and these rules sometimes persist long after the conditions which they were intended to regularize have changed. One recent study, undertaken by two California sociologists, suggests that the presumed worker sentiment in favor of seniority as the decision rule governing promotions has little basis in fact.[15] A questionnaire survey of approximately three thousand workers in eight establishments (one Federal government installation, three large unionized corporations, and two large and two small unorganized companies) inquired whether, in promotions, an opening ought to be offered first to the most senior applicant or to the one who had "the best training and experience for the job." Only 8 percent favored the seniority principle, while 91 percent approved the ability criterion (1 percent gave no answer). Union membership made a difference in attitude; 16 percent of those who were then union members preferred the seniority rule in promotions, or about twice the percentage of all workers taken together, but even so, this is a long way from representing a massive sentiment on behalf of advancement on the basis of length of service. Less-skilled and less-educated workers tended to prefer seniority as a basis for promotion, professional and technical workers and college graduates were least in

favor. Only half as many high school graduates as dropouts favored seniority. Longer-service workers understandably were more kindly disposed than short-service employees toward the seniority principle in promotion, but even so, the sentiment was predominantly opposed.

To be sure, this was a single survey, undertaken in California where one would expect to find a higher proportion of more mobile employees (in light of the very substanial postwar immigration), and one might posit that, to some degree, mobility might correlate with ambition and self-confidence so that promotion on the basis of ability would have more appeal to people in this particular sample than might generally be true. Nevertheless, the results cannot be lightly dismissed. They suggest several hypotheses.

It is entirely possible that the present acceptance of seniority in promotion is simply a carryover from the period when such rules were written into agreements, when managements were more suspected of antiunion discrimination and foremen were guilty of more arrant forms of favoritism. With federal labor legislation outlawing discrimination because of union activity, and with grievance procedures protecting workers against foreman abuse, it is at least conceivable that one of the original purposes which seniority served in the case of promotions is no longer present or not present in significant degree. The generation of workers which has come on the scene since the union revival of the thirties confronts a generation of managers who have been brought up on a new labor philosophy which, while stressing efficiency, also makes room for "human relations," fairness of treatment of subordinates, ability to defend one's judgments by logic as much as by authority. The original need for seniority as a protection against managerial abuse has been passing with changes in the industrial environment.

The changing complexion of the labor force may also be having its effect. We have already noticed, in Chapter 2, that the educational level of workers has been steadily rising, and that more and more workers are being employed in white-collar jobs and jobs demanding skills, in contrast to unskilled and semiskilled assignments. The

California study suggests that these characteristics (which presumably impart a greater sense of personal competence) correlate with a greater preference for promotion on the basis of ability rather than length of service.

The lack of sympathy with seniority as the decision rule in promotions which was found in the California survey did not carry over to seniority as the basis for layoffs. Whereas only 8 percent favored length of service as the criterion in promotions, 36 percent approved it in the case of layoffs. Among unionists, while only 16 percent opted for seniority in promotions, 66 percent voted for it in layoffs. Even among more skilled and more highly educated personnel, the greater appeal of seniority in layoffs than in promotions was quite marked. This suggests that the sense of job insecurity which the pace of technological change has engendered may still provide solid support for using length of service as the bureaucratic rule for layoffs, but that the same rapid technological change may suggest the infeasibility of relying primarily on length of service in the promotion process. The longer a person has been in service, the more difficulty will he have in finding other employment, but the less, rather than the more, capable may he be of handling some higher job assignment.

If additional investigations should lend support to these hypotheses, the personnel manager will be confronted with a genuine challenge. In the face of a preference by employees as well as managers for promotions based on ability, what objective measures of ability can be devised that will satisfy the employee's sense of fair play? If, as the California researchers suggest with respect to their respondents, "it seems reasonable to conclude that they would prefer rules that stress evaluation of qualification and performance rather than rules based upon length of service,"[16] what can the personnel manager offer? Granted that a bureaucracy must operate through some set of rules, what rules respecting ability (meeting the values of both management and workers) can effectively substitute for the seniority rule?

If the findings of this study are substantiated, the unions too face a challenge. They have been defending a principle which grows out of their organizational past without testing whether it continues to meet the needs and wants of their present membership. Can they abandon that principle for which they fought (and continue to fight) so vigorously without appearing to be surrendering to management pressure? Can they admit that they, the agents of their members, have been misjudging their members' interests, if that should prove to be the case?

The chances are that the situation does not call for so much of an about-face as these questions may suggest, however. Undoubtedly there are some work environments in which skill differences are minimal and seniority continues to be a valid and perhaps preferable basis for allocating scarce promotional opportunities. In other situations, training and ability may be so vital that there is little room for seniority as a guide to selection. In between, there may be a larger category of situations in which competence is sufficiently important that it commands the support of workers as well as managers, providing that its measure can be appropriately established. This last category may offer an opportunity for union and management officials to work together to find a new solution to this perennial problem.

An appraisal

To sum up, seniority is like most bargaining issues in the resistance it offers to any "scientific" appraisal. There is little or no statistical evidence concerning the effects of seniority on worker motivation, mobility, or performance, so happily everyone can hold a firm opinion about this issue without danger of being proved wrong.

Few people question the principle of "benefit seniority" in determining pension and vacation rights, and even "competitive-status seniority" is widely accepted as an equitable criterion for determining layoffs, recalls, and shift preference. And in translating this principle into practice, the bargaining process has often proved more flexible than expected. On the critical issue of layoffs, for instance, the conventional position of labor in the early years was to seek the widest possible seniority unit, to prevent the inequity of a long-service worker being laid off in one department while short-service men were still working in another department. Management, on the other hand, fought to establish many narrow units to minimize the "bumping" of some workers by others with more seniority—which, during a layoff in a broad unit, can assume chain-effect proportions which are very costly and can result in the loss of key employees. The Brookings study found that over the years both parties moderated their positions and devised many ingenious compromises on this problem, such as allowing widespread bumping among the less skilled jobs but little or no bumping among the more skilled.[17]

Most of the controversy over seniority therefore centers on only one of its several applications in a unionized firm—on promotions. Even there, to debate "seniority versus ability" is to imply that a choice is being made between two equally identifiable qualities, but the fact is that employers often have difficulty in proving that one worker is clearly superior to another bidding for the same job.

That argument cuts both ways. It is true that many of the worker characteristics that management wishes to reward by promotion—initiative, maturity, responsibility, leadership potential—cannot be measured objectively, but neither can the importance of those qualities be denied. Certainly unions do not select their own leaders and staff members solely on the basis of seniority or any other "objective" standard. In fact, the Congress of the United States is one of the few organizations that base promotions (to the powerful posts of committee chairmen) solely on seniority, and that system has few admirers among labor leaders or any other group. Also, as more and more workers produce intangible services rather than physical products, it becomes increasingly unrealistic to demand objective measures of ability. And as we further noted, if the California study proves representative of union members' attitudes elsewhere, the seniority element in promotions would have lost its principal rationale.

For these reasons, we would conclude that seniority has provided a workable basis for balancing the parties' needs in most of the employment decisions to which it has been applied, but its value in the key area of promotions needs reexamination.

Another problem area associated with seniority of recent and growing importance involves the integration of black workers into the labor force. The hard-core unemployed who have been given special training to make them employable, at considerable public and private expense, would be among the first to be laid off in time of economic downturn—a situation characterizing the automobile industry in the winter of 1969–1970. Should such disadvantaged employees be given special rights—some form of superseniority, as a matter of social policy (as World War II GIs were granted special seniority status after their discharge)? A related question affects qualified Negroes who may have been held back from advancement discriminatorily. Should such employees be given special consideration beyond that called for by their seniority status, in partial compensation for past injustice? These are issues which as yet have no resolution.

Discipline and the grievance procedure

On most bargaining subjects, the collective agreement sets out in some detail the rules and rights governing management and the union in their dealings with each other. On seniority, for example, a contract may devote ten or twenty pages to defining precisely how seniority is to be calculated (does it accumulate during layoffs, sick leaves, or military service?), the several seniority units within the overall bargaining unit, and the way in which seniority is to be applied in various situations. Even then, as we have seen, disputes arise over applying this contract language to particular workers, such as deciding whether a junior worker has greater "ability" than a senior worker. In this and all other areas covered by a labor contract, management is initiating action almost daily. And whenever action is initiated, there is always the possibility that it may run counter to the provisions of the agreement. Even with the best of faith, a management may transfer one employee when the union believes the contract calls for the movement of another; it may temporarily assign an employee to work which he believes calls for a higher rate of pay than he usually receives; it may deny a worker a paid holiday to which he believes himself entitled. To handle such matters, there has gradually developed a specific procedure to resolve controversies over the meaning and application of the collective agreement—the grievance procedure.

On the crucial subject of discipline, however, the typical union contract surprisingly says little more than that the employer may discipline for "just cause." Of course, most employers have a list of written or unwritten shop rules forbidding various types of behavior from smoking and horseplay to stealing, gambling, or drinking on the job, but few unions attempt to negotiate changes in these rules at the bargaining table. Instead, they usually prefer to let the employer initiate discipline for whatever reason he chooses and then to challenge through the grievance procedure those decisions they believe to be unfair. Most of the "bargaining" over discipline therefore occurs *during the administration of the labor contract,* as the parties grapple with specific cases and eventually build up a set of disciplinary rules that are relatively permanent and well understood in each relationship.

Thus a grievance procedure is needed for resolving disputes over how any contract clause should apply to particular situations during the life of the agreement, and especially the clause on discipline, which seldom provides any guidance except the principle of "just cause." Regardless of the clause in dispute, however, the basic problem in administering a labor contract is the same: how to protect the workers' rights under the contract and still satisfy the employer's need to respond quickly to the shifting pressures on his firm without endlessly debating the "legality" of every decision before he can act.

To illustrate the compromise that the parties have evolved, suppose the following sequence of events occurs: A foreman notices that some hand tools are mysteriously disappearing from his department; he questions several employees, two of whom hint broadly that a worker named Charlie may be the culprit; at quitting time the foreman spots a suspicious bulge in Charlie's pocket, stops and searches him after he has punched out, discovers the bulge to be a $25 wrench belonging to the company, and demands an explanation; Charlie asserts that he simply forgot to take the wrench out of his pocket at quitting time; and the foreman, unconvinced, fires Charlie on the spot.

At that point, the grievance procedure is triggered. The question to be resolved is *not* whether management has the right to discipline a worker caught stealing, for every union agrees that management has such a right even if it is not mentioned in the contract or posted as a shop rule. But can management prove that this particular worker was stealing company property? And even if it can, was the penalty of discharge—often termed the industrial equivalent of capital punishment—a fair punishment for the crime involved? Those are the questions which cannot be left exclusively to the company to answer, for if management's judgment cannot be questioned, then the "just cause" provision is meaningless. No matter how arbitrary a supervisor might be, a worker could only appeal to the good will of top management. If the management always backed up its foremen—either on the merits of each case or because it did not want to undercut the authority of foremen by publicly reversing their decisions—the workers would have no protection against "unfair discipline," however one defines that term. On the other hand, the union can hardly claim the right to be sole judge of these disputes, for its decisions could just as arbitrarily ignore management's interests. In short, the labor–management contract obviously gives each party an interest in how it is to be applied from day to day, and the grievance process must therefore be a joint affair.

The result is an *appeals* procedure by which any individual who believes that he has been wronged can enter a claim and have it heard. If it is denied at one level, he can appeal it to higher authority through a series of three to six appeals stages. In our hypothetical case, after the foreman has turned down Charlie's appeal to reconsider his decision, Charlie will go to his union steward or committeeman. The steward is a worker's representative at the shop level; his jurisdiction corresponds roughly to that of the foreman, whose union counterpart he is. His primary job is to keep his men active in the union and to represent them whenever they have a grievance.

In this instance he listens to Charlie and gets all the facts; then he talks to the foreman to get his side of the story. Then, if he thinks that maybe Charlie is innocent of the charge and that perhaps the foreman, however well-intentioned, was wrong, he will urge the foreman to reconsider his action. If the foreman persists in his judgment, however, the steward will help Charlie put his grievance in writing. The foreman too will summarize his position in writing, and this docket then is processed to the second step of the procedure. This much of the process is fairly standard in all union–management relationships.

Which union and company officials are designated for the several additional appeals stages varies from situation to situation. In a typical case, however, at the second stage Charlie's complaint might be presented by a chief steward for the union (or by the chairman of the local union's grievance committee) to the company's departmental supervisor. If the latter comes to the conclusion that the foreman was justified in his action, the union might then proceed to a third step, in which the whole grievance committee (numbering perhaps nine men) or the local president might represent Charlie, while the plant personnel manager or the general plant manager might appear for the company. If no settlement is reached here, an international representative of the union might take Charlie's case up with someone from top management, perhaps a vice-president in charge of labor relations.

If the company's reply is still to the effect that Charlie's discharge should stand, and if the union is still persuaded that he is innocent, and with all the bilateral appeals stages now exhausted, the union might take the case to arbitration. Twenty-five years or so ago, a great many managements were reluctant to consent to arbitration of grievances, taking the position that this would make an outsider's judgment superior to management's. In the absence of arbitration, however, the union usually retains the right to strike to enforce its position, since the company's view of how the contract clause should be applied is no more final than the union's view. To eliminate this recurring threat to continuity of production, whereby a walkout in any shop might occur at almost any time, suspending production for an entire plant, arbitration has been increasingly accepted as the final step in the grievance procedure, coupled with the provision that the union give up its right to strike over the grievance.

It is usually understood, moreover, that the arbitrator, whose decision is final and binding on both parties, has the power to "make whole" an employee for any loss he has suffered. In our example, if an arbitrator found that Charlie was completely innocent of the charge of stealing, the employer would be ordered to reinstate him on his job with no loss of seniority for the period during which his case was being appealed *and* to pay him the wages he would have earned during that period. But how does the arbitrator determine guilt or innocence in such cases? Usually he does so by applying the standards of equity and due process that have been fostered in common law and in social usage: A man must know the reason for his discipline, he is presumed innocent until proved guilty, he must be able to confront and cross-examine his accusers (in this case, not only the foreman but also the two workers who hinted at Charlie's guilt, if management uses their accusations to buttress its case), he must be able to present witnesses in his own behalf (perhaps a tool-crib attendant would testify that on other occasions Charlie had inadvertently taken a tool home and returned it the next day). As in many court cases, the decision may rest ultimately on the arbitrator's appraisal of purely circumstantial evidence and the character of witnesses whose testimony cannot be objectively verified. (For example, if Charlie refused to take a lie-detector test requested by management, would his refusal count against him? No, say most arbitrators, following the lead of the courts in judging such tests to be unreliable as legal evidence.) Without knowing the evidence developed at the arbitration hearing, we cannot say how this or any other case would be decided, any more than one can predict the outcome of a court case. In both instances, we rely on the common sense and objectivity of a neutral (judge, jury, or arbitrator) to decide disputes in which any verdict must often be subjective.

Even if an employee is found guilty as charged, the arbitrator usually has the further power to review the penalty levied by management in order to determine whether the punishment fits the crime (or the "criminal"). Did the worker steal a wrench for his own use or a secret product formula to sell to a competitor? Is Charlie a young worker who has repeatedly been disciplined during his two years with this firm, including a one-week layoff for minor pilfering, or is he an employee with twenty years' seniority, a spotless record, and five years to go to retirement? Depending on his assessment of such extenuating circumstances, an arbitrator might either uphold management's discharge of a worker found guilty of an offense or he might modify the penalty—a frequent compromise being to reinstate the worker but to deny him back pay for the period he has been off the job. (Note here a value of seniority that never appears in any contract. Even putting aside notions of fairness, discharge clearly imposes a greater cost—in the loss of competitive and benefit seniority rights—on long-service workers than on others. Arbitrators know this and will often deal more leniently with senior employees in discipline cases, thereby creating another seniority benefit that is never explicitly negotiated by the parties.)

An appraisal

The significance of this grievance procedure can hardly be overstressed. It is one of the truly great accomplishments of American industrial relations. For all its defects—the bypassing of some of the appeals stages, its use by the union as a political device to convince the employees that it is looking out for their interests, the slowness with which it sometimes operates—it constitutes a social invention of great importance. Although a somewhat similar procedure is used in some other countries, it is perhaps safe to say that nowhere else has it reached the high stage of development that it has in the United States, in the sense that it is so widely employed and has achieved so much vitality at the local level. In this country, most unionists and some managements speak of the grievance process as the "heart" of collective bargaining. The negotiation of the agreement occurs perhaps every two years, but the grievance procedure takes care of the gripes and individual problems which are bound to arise in any plant or shop every day.

At times, if workers are asked why they want a union and they reply that they regard it as "good insurance," it is not so much that they think of the union as necessary to get them wage increases, though that is important to them too, but it is the feeling that if they should find themselves on the short end of a management decision sometime, they would have a means at hand by which to seek relief. It is the grievance procedure which takes the arbitrariness out of managerial personnel actions, requiring management to conform to certain mutually accepted standards.

This relationship is often described as a quid pro quo trade between the parties: The no-strike clause grants management the advantage of uninterrupted production during the life of the contract, while the arbitration clause grants the employees and the union the assurance that management's interpretation of the contract is subject to outside review. But the significance of the grievance procedure is even broader than that. In nearly every area of decision making—discipline, work assignments, promotions, layoffs, and others—*it is understood that management can initiate action without securing prior approval from the union.* This may appear to be an obvious management right, but it is by no means the only method for administering a contract. Some unions, for example, have pressed for a clause stating that a discharged worker can continue on his job (and on the payroll) until his guilt or innocence is finally established through the grievance procedure. If management could only "recommend" action and never move until each proposed decision affecting workers had been fought through, if necessary, to arbitration, its operating effectiveness would be hampered far more severely than it now is, when only a tiny proportion of its daily decisions are later reversed in the upper stages of the grievance procedure. At the same time, the power of the arbitrator to remedy most management errors, particularly through back-pay awards which are binding upon the employer, affords workers a strong guarantee of fair treatment.

To repeat, this procedure is far from flawless. As we noted in Chapter 9, the individual worker may be helpless if his union officials refuse to press his grievance for any reason, and even reinstatement and back pay cannot fully compensate for the anxiety and expense incurred by a discharge or layoff that is reversed only after several weeks. And on management's side, we have stressed the difficulty of "proving" to an arbitrator the validity of many decisions—such as the superior ability of a junior employee in a promotion case—which can lead a supervisor to make the safe decision that will not be contested rather than the one he believes to be correct. Compared to the available alternatives, however, the parties have devised a remarkable compromise of their conflicting interests in the administration of discipline and most other clauses in the labor agreement.

Industrial "jurisprudence" in place of arbitrary action

The resemblance between the grievance procedure and a judicial procedure is evident. There is an effort to apply general "law" (the agreement) to specific situations, with an eventual determination—if need be—by an impartial judge. The grievance process has therefore often been called the "compliance process," or the basis for the building of an industrial jurisprudence. Especially has this view been held when the arbitration phase of it is stressed: arbitral decisions are collected and published like judges' opinions, and like judicial decisions they often serve as precedents applying to subsequent situations (despite a common belief among the parties that reliance on such "precedents" is undesirable, since every situation is in some respects different).

In effect, what the grievance process has done, as an integral part of the collective-bargaining relationship, is to require management to rationalize its actions satisfactorily to those who are affected by them—to rationalize its *specific* actions in terms of the overall agreement. Since the foreman has the most direct responsibility for personnel actions affecting the rank and file of workers, it is he who is put on the firing line in collective bargaining as far as personnel administration is concerned. If company policy and union interpretation of the agreement conflict, it is at the foreman's level that the conflict is most likely to manifest itself. No wonder he is often referred to as "the man in the middle."

The extent to which this has modified the nature of the foreman's function and elevated in importance the human relations aspects of his job can be best appreciated by contrasting his present necessity to rationalize his decisions with his pre-union power to impose his will arbitrarily. As an assistant steward remarked: "There's been a lot of difference in the plant since the union got in. Most of it has got to do with the department foreman. . . . They used to work you wherever they wanted to put you. . . . It used to be, before the union, if they didn't like a guy they'd put him on a bad job or a dirty job someplace." And a shift foreman from the same plant commented, "When I went to work out there, in 1928, the foreman hired at the gate. You had to suit the foreman. If the foreman told you you were fired, that was the end of it. You can can a guy now, but you'll have to be ready to back it up."[18]

Power relations in the shop

But the grievance process constitutes more than judicial machinery by which the "rightness" of supervisory actions may be tested. On the union side, the foreman's counterpart is the steward, an elected or appointed representative of the men in the shop, to whom they turn when they have a grievance. Depending on the respective temperaments of the steward and the foreman, and depending too on the climate of union–management relations within the plant,

The foreman may find himself exercising leadership in his shop subject only to a more or less reasonable expectation that he explain any personnel actions which adversely affect the interests of any of his men.

Or he may find himself in a running battle with his steward, a continuing power struggle in which he is subject to repeated nagging and his actions are open to constant challenge.

Or at the extreme, he may even find that the steward has more control over the men than he has himself.

Collective bargaining thus confronts the foreman with a new challenge to his power over his men. Previously, he dealt with them as individuals. Now they are united, cohesive, organized under their own leadership, sometimes militant. To a greater or lesser extent, they seem to conform to their union's slogan, "An injury to one is an injury to all." Their cohesion initially stemmed from a common impulse to protect themselves from the foreman's exercise of power, which was sometimes arbitrary and abusive. But at what point does use of power end and abuse of power begin? At what point, if ever, is there a resolution of the bargaining-power relationship between the foreman and his men regarding his exercise of authority?

It is easy to say that the collective-bargaining agreement defines the limits of permissible discretion by the supervisor and the limits of exercisable rights by his men. This would be the judicial view of the grievance process. The foreman discovers, however, that actions which he might take, even if seemingly within the framework of the bargained agreement, can encounter resistance, overt or covert. If his men show little interest in maintaining a standard speed of operations, if they are slow in getting to their positions in the morning or quick to leave at night, if horseplay becomes more prevalent, if the "no smoking" rule is violated, if they interfere with the production of a nonunion worker, if scrap increases through reduced attentiveness or lack of interest, and so on, any attempted disciplining of the offenders may meet a concerted retaliatory response. The very behavior complained of may spread to others— and can the foreman discipline the whole shop? His men may avoid him and keep their silence in his presence—and can he, their nominal leader, stand to be so boycotted? With a touch of the malicious, the work crew may conform precisely to what he or the rule book requires—precisely and no more—and can he tolerate the subsequent inefficiencies which would inevitably result? Operations can be delayed through complications which, while seemingly adventitious, have never occurred before—and can he punish his men for what he cannot prove was not an accident? At the extreme, there is the possibility of slowdown or wildcat walkout—and does he dare risk so patent a manifestation that he cannot control his own men?

Under the circumstances, a foreman is sometimes subjected to considerable pressure to conform to the will of his organized shop, to relax his discipline, to sheathe his authority, to avoid a contest of power with his men in which he might ultimately have to give ground and lose face.

Even more discouraging may be the lack of support he gets from his superiors. Higher management is in constant touch with the union on numerous matters of varying degrees of importance, and a logrolling and "mutual-accommodation process" (to use a currently fashionable phrase) inevitably develops. When the foreman, strong in the belief that he is in the right, exercises his authority within the framework of the collective agreement, he may find to his distress that top management, in order to get some desired concession from the union or to build up a fund of good will, may give away the foreman's case in the upper stages of the grievance process. Such an exchange might make eminently good sense from top management's point of view, but it leaves the foreman a lonely man.

One should not gain the impression, however, that today's foreman lacks the basis for an effective exercise of authority because of the presence of union organization. His authority has been curbed but he still commands important means of imposing on his men penalties for noncompliance and rewards for cooperation. In making job assignments, personal evaluations of ability where they are relevant for promotion, and recommendations for merit wage increases where they are not automatic, in administering discipline where he can defend the reason for it, he has powers which are integral to his position and which can be employed to good advantage.

Moreover, some foremen have attempted to work out their own additional sources of power. A study of foremen by the Technology Unit at Yale found in one plant several foremen whom management stamped as "good" on the strength of their production records. The union, when asked about the foremen, concurred in management's judgment about these select few—but for a quite different reason: they got along well with their men. These were the foremen, it appeared to the analysts, who chose to regard the framework of company policy as a flexible guide, interpreting it loosely when occasion required, sometimes flouting it in minor particulars. Punishable offenses would be overlooked at the foreman's own discretion. A long lunch hour would be granted on occasion. One of the men would be given the afternoon off for a reason that would have been unacceptable to the personnel office. The operating procedures laid down by the engineering staff would be violated if neither the men nor the foreman saw any common-sense reason for observing them. He might connive with the men in getting a loose piece rate.

This flexibility allowed him to get along more easily with his men—not because he submitted to their importuning out of weakness, but because he manipulated the granting of concessions and favors as a method of rewarding and punishing his men. These were concessions for which his men could not press in the grievance procedure, since they were illegal or extralegal, for which they could not expect the support of their union in any organized demonstration such as slowdown or walkout. They were concessions for which his men had to bargain with him, for which he demanded a quid pro quo in the form of production.

As a consequence, the Yale observers found that such a foreman might, if the occasion really demanded it, push his men at a pace that other foremen could not exact. This was the price for that afternoon off when the foreman knew perfectly well, and his men knew that he knew, that attending a sick wife meant watching a ball game. He could, when shorthanded, pitch in and work alongside his own men in strict violation of the collective agreement, without the union steward's batting an eye. This was the price for letting a morning tardiness after the lodge's annual meeting pass with only a sarcastic remark that brought laughs from the others. By ignoring management regulations to suit his purpose, he could carve out an unintended area of discretionary judgment that gave him power to reward and punish those who looked to him. As a result, he could focus his shop around his leadership. His men liked the result, especially since any abuse of authority or discriminatory action was always subject to check through the grievance procedure and the foreman was aware of that fact and did not push his demands for the production quid pro quo to the point of protest. The union functioned as an effective safeguard, and the foreman functioned as an effective production leader.

In some companies, management has moved to strengthen the foreman's position vis-à-vis the steward in a variety of ways, such as coaching him in grievance handling while allowing him

full discretion in his decisions, or enforcing regulations with respect to the steward's freedom to "roam around the shop" or the amount of time he can spend on grievance handling, or by refusing to take back wildcat strikers, and in general by adopting a "tougher line" regarding contract interpretation. The notion is that "appeasement" (including mutual accommodation) does not pay.[19]

Fractional bargaining

The kind of power relations described above makes the foreman-steward relationship sound like a personal contest. The grievance process, with the steward as the union's first-line representative and the foreman as the company's, is seen as a tug-of-war for leadership in the shop. The steward, on behalf of his men, can make use of it to try to bring a foreman into line in an attempt to win concessions on a variety of small matters affecting individuals in the work group. The bargaining process that goes on within the grievance process may be more than that, however.

We have already noted that the union is not always a homogeneous entity but may be composed of numerous special-interest groups, based on age, occupation, color, sex, and so on. The interests of these groups sometimes diverge, leading to political jockeying in the election of union officers and in the composition of collective-bargaining committees. But even after differing points of view have been resolved with respect to what demands the union should make on management in collective negotiations and an agreement has been negotiated and ratified, some groups within the union whose members occupy particularly strategic positions in the plant may continue to seek special concessions for themselves, using the grievance process for that purpose. Because they are bargaining for only a part of the union membership (or of the employees in the bargaining unit) rather than the whole, we may refer to this as "fractional bargaining."

Such fractional bargaining is different from the steward-foreman power struggle described in the preceding section, where the contest is over how much authority a foreman shall exercise over his men in the day-to-day management of the shop. In fractional bargaining, a whole shop or a special segment of the labor force may join in an effort (again, overt or covert) to win some special concession for the group as a whole, whether on a one-time or continuing basis. In some cases, fractional bargaining pits a segment of the union membership or work force not only against management but also against the union leadership or the rest of the union membership, as they attempt to do better on their own than the group as a whole has done for them, asserting a measure of bargaining autonomy that the collective-bargaining relationship does not contemplate. They may win special privileges on time allowed for "washing up," or the amount of work demanded of them, or even additional base wage rate increases. They may assert claims to jobs during a time of slack which more properly might have been filled by others.

Professor James Kuhn of Columbia University has made a study of this phenomenon in the rubber and electrical-appliance industries. His findings are the most authoritative to date on this little-investigated aspect of the bargaining relationship. One local union official in Akron commented to him:[20]

The grievance process is year 'round, continuous collective bargaining. The contract is like a rubber bag. You probe it this way and that—what you need is leverage. The company does not view all the grievances judiciously, because it cannot. Through its prerogatives and initiative it usually has more leverage than the union. We have to resort to undercover bargaining tactics to get any leverage to penalize the company. You've got to move the situation, and you don't always do it by being nice and talking sweet. I have always felt that the successful leader is the resourceful man who is able to find new ways to put the pressure on, whenever the company is able to block the old.

In this kind of fractional bargaining, work groups—particularly if technologically distinct and strategically situated in the work flow—develop a unit of interest quite independent of the union and sometimes competitive with its larger interests. Kuhn reports:

In some of the plants studied where the representative tried to follow a policy pushed by the local union that ran counter to the group's interest, the members of the work group simply ignored the elected leader and followed an informal spokesman. One such group had taken a line so independent that it became in reality an autonomous unit over which the union had almost no authority.

He describes one such tightly knit group, the tire builders, in these words:[21]

The tire builders form a strong, united work group in the plant and within the union. They maintain tight self-discipline in enforcing work and earning limits and act as one man in slow-downs, a tactic that requires close and careful group control. They choose their elected officials upon the basis of service to the tire builders, not the union. In one local union where an election was coming up, a tire builder remarked that he guessed he wouldn't be voting for the presidential incumbent. "He's not bad, but then he hasn't done anything for the tire builders that I know of." The incumbent received very few votes from the tire builders group in the election that followed.

Small wonder, then, that a local union officer remarked:[22]

It is in the tire building room that I think we have most of the difficulties. The men's solidarity is most pronounced here. The tire builders are a breed apart. They're like miners, and they're definitely worse in going their own way. The pitmen are just as independent. They're famous for their walkouts too. There's been a long history in tire building and in the pits of the men running the department to suit themselves; they take action on their own.

Collaboration in the shop

Normally we are inclined to think of the grievance procedure as a union device, as a protest technique. But the grievance procedure in its bilateral stages can also be viewed as a consultative technique, and the sophisticated foreman can make it a tool for his own use. The union has provided him with a steward, with the intention that he should act as the first-line check on supervision, ensuring that the rights of union members are respected. But there is no reason why the foreman cannot make use of him for his own administrative purposes. The union steward can become a useful tool of management. Let us see how.

The one effective curb which has always been exercised over leaders is the reluctance of their followers to comply with directions. At some point, on some issue, individuals will rebel against even so-called "absolute authority." Even a dictator cannot completely ignore the feelings of his followers. To obtain compliance, it is necessary not to ask too much. In order for authority to remain unchallenged, its exercise must be accepted by those to whom it applies. This simple homily is relevant to authority wherever found, including that of the foreman in his shop. His command may meet with an apathetic response that robs it of its intended effect. His decision may be translated into only partially conforming behavior by those to whom it is entrusted, whose interests may be involved quite differently from the interests of the foreman, and whose actions are designed to protect as best they can their own interests which he has overlooked.

It is difficult for any individual to predict the likely reaction of others to his assertion of authority. All of us have experienced surprise at the hornet's nest we have kicked up by some decision or action of ours. For every such overt display of resistance, we can be sure there are many more covert manifestations about which we know nothing.

Under the circumstances, clues to the probable responses of others become important management aids. If the foreman improves his understanding of how his men are likely to react to his decisions, he can make his decisions more effective. The contemplated action which he finds is likely to make more trouble than he has originally expected can be modified to avoid that consequence. With respect to any change, the singleness of *his* objective may blind him to the multiplicity of effects on *others* and the accompanying protective responses evoked from others which modify or even nullify the results intended by the change. If he is made aware of these conditioning

circumstances, the proposed action can be reformulated to accommodate, at least in some degree, interests which have been neglected. The outcome may be less desirable than had previously been *intended* but far more rewarding than it otherwise would have been *in fact*.

Within the context of this approach to the decision-making process, the union steward can play a dual function. Not only is he the leader of the opposition and the champion of those injured by the exercise of authority; he becomes a consultant with whom the foreman may confer, whose advice he may solicit, whose opinions he may use as a sounding board.

In the hands of an inept foreman, this approach may lead to an abnegation of authority to the steward. At the point where consultation leads to a bifurcation of leadership, with a sharing of authority between foreman and steward, the foreman's effectiveness as a leader of his men suffers. Investigations suggest that shop morale may decline, for many men prefer to work for a foreman who is not afraid to use the authority of his position.

The extent to which this use of the grievance process can be made to work to the joint satisfaction of management and union depends on the characters of foreman and steward. That it is a process which lends itself to abuse at the hands of an ambitious union officer or is ineffective when used by a top-sergeantlike foreman does not mean that it should be generally avoided, however. Few shops run more smoothly than those in which there is a good working relationship between these two. In such instances, the function of the grievance process has been extended to anticipate difficulties and to deal with potential problem areas before they materialize. The bargaining-power relationship between foreman and steward is as inescapable as that between company and union, but in situations where cooperation has been achieved, there is an appreciation that reducing the other's cost of agreement enhances bargaining power.

The grievance procedure is thus a many-splendored thing. It is in part the judicial process of applying the terms of the agreement to particular situations, as it is most frequently pictured. It is also the mechanism through which the first-line representatives of union and management engage in a continuing contest over the exercise of authority in the shop—a contest which may be relatively quiescent at the one extreme, or almost brutal at the other, but which is always present in some degree. The grievance process is also a device which strategic groups within the union can use to engage in fractional bargaining on their own behalf, sometimes challenging the authority of the union in the doing but more often clothing their purpose in "grievances" which have at least the air of legitimacy about them. And finally, the grievance process, in the hands of sophisticated practitioners, can be made an instrument for more effective administration within the shop.

Summary

The bargaining process is an intricate set of relationships between workers and managers and their respective organizations, the union and the company. It involves the negotiation of basic understandings between the two groups, but before this can take place, the several interests on each side of the bargaining table must first arrive at an understanding among themselves. The agreement, once reached, must be applied, and questions as to whether the application conforms to the intent of the agreement may be thrashed out through the grievance process. The grievance process is also an extension of the bargaining process itself on a day-to-day basis, with management and union representatives seeking to win minor individual advantages or more significant concessions applying to special groups within the organization.

Throughout the whole of this complex set of relationships runs the dominant theme of relative bargaining powers, conceived as not merely the exercise of coercion by one group against another but as the effort to induce the other party to agree on one's preferred terms. The "terms" relate to values and philosophies as well as to money and status. The inducement to agree includes benefits proffered as well as threats of imposed costs. There is no straight road to agreement, no appeal to some incontrovertible facts which reveal indisputable solutions. The road is usually devious, twisting, and tiring, with bluff and blunder as its

milestones. It is viewed as worthwhile only because of its destination—agreements rather than imposed decisions.

Finally, how well does the institution of collective bargaining perform in resolving the major conflicts which, in one guise or another, run throughout the labor sector—the clash of producer interests against consumer interests, the desire for security versus the need to maintain incentives, and the difficulty of simultaneously achieving full employment, stable prices, and a free economy?

On the first of these issues, we have argued that collective bargaining on the whole deserves a good grade. Too many criticisms of labor unions compare their impact with an idealized economy that has never existed—one in which sober, hard-working individuals can always find a decent job; employers always treat their workers fairly because it would be irrational and unprofitable for them to do otherwise; and workers and employers together know they can best serve their own interests by serving the consumers' interest. In that kind of world, unions could certainly do nothing but cause trouble. In the real world of imperfect men and markets, however, and particularly in a society which exalts democracy outside the plant gate, it is inevitable that workers will often see a conflict between their interests and those of the employer and the consumer, and many of these workers will demand a voice in resolving that conflict.

Unions and collective bargaining therefore cannot be judged solely by their impact on costs, efficiency, and innovation, for workers hardly join unions to promote those goals, but rather by their success in compromising the legitimate interests of both consumers and worker-producers. We have seen that unions and the bargaining process have failed even that test in several respects: they have not served Negro workers much, if any, better than the rest of society has (thus not even serving all producers' interests equitably); union members sometimes are abused by their own officials; no one can define the "appropriate" size of a bargaining unit; flagrant featherbedding still exists in some relationships; seniority can be pushed too far in deciding promotions; and so on.

But the evidence also suggests that in most bargaining relationships the parties strike roughly reasonable compromises on most issues, whether on the question of "management rights" in general or the more specific issues of technological change, seniority, discipline, and contract administration. Thus, in spite of the undeniable exceptions, our opinion is that collective bargaining has granted most union members a significant degree of dignity and protection in their working lives, while preserving for their employers a large measure of the authority to initiate and innovate that is so crucial to serving consumer goals. (Needless to say, our opinion is not universally shared.)

As for the relationship of collective bargaining to the other two major issues in the labor sector, we must defer judgment at this point. In its narrowest sense, of course, the issue of "security versus incentives" is simply a restatement of the clash between producer and consumer interests. More commonly, however, this issue refers to the controversy over the welfare state, and we have not yet examined the many ways in which private bargaining supplements public measures such as pensions and unemployment insurance. Also, we have not discussed up to this point the impact of collective bargaining on wages, prices, and employment in the economy as a whole. To assess these issues, we will need to examine labor not only in the union hall and at the bargaining table, but also in its several other economic and political roles.

ADDITIONAL READINGS

Dunlop, John T., and Neil W. Chamberlain (eds.): *Frontiers of Collective Bargaining,* Harper & Row, New York, 1967, chaps. 8–10.

Kuhn, James: *Bargaining in Grievance Settlement,* Columbia University Press, New York, 1961.

Phelps, Orme: *Discipline and Discharge in the Unionized Firm,* University of California Press, Berkeley, 1959.

Slichter, Sumner H., James J. Healy, and E. Robert Livernash: *The Impact of Collective Bargaining on Management,* Brookings, Washington, 1960.

Somers, Gerald G., Edward L. Cushman, and Nat Weinberg: *Adjusting to Technological Change,* Harper & Row, New York, 1963.

Weinstein, Paul A. (ed.): *Featherbedding and Technological Change,* Heath, Boston, 1965.

FOR ANALYSIS AND DISCUSSION

1. One of the major differences between unionized and nonunionized firms is that in the former, the employer bears the major burden of proof in disciplinary cases, whereas in the nonunion firm the employee often has that burden. Explain this difference. Do you think unions are justified in thus shifting the burden of proof?

2. Why are there different seniority units within a single bargaining relationship? That is, why don't the parties simply agree that there shall be a single seniority unit, with boundaries identical to those of the bargaining unit?

3. Do you see any difference between the long-run union effort to reduce the hours of work per week and an attempt to reduce the expenditure of effort in whatever hours are worked? For example, would you call a union's demand for a 30- or 35-hour week an example of attempted featherbedding? Why or why not?

4. Under some collective-bargaining agreements, employees displaced by a machine or new process are paid a separation allowance, based upon their length of service. Do you consider this (*a*) a reasonable protection for workers who lose their jobs through no fault of their own, as an incident in society's march of progress, or (*b*) an undesirable penalty upon employers who introduce technological improvements which can benefit all society, even if a few must suffer temporarily in the process? If you agree with (*a*), at what point would you consider that an increase in such "allowances" might make you agree with (*b*)?

5. Assume the following situation:

a. You are the director of industrial relations. A foreman (whom we shall call Able) of fifteen years' service in your company, whose record has been good—not spectacular but distinctly above average—is admittedly difficult to get along with. Able's superiors have been aware that his men find him intolerant, unsympathetic, even obnoxious, but they have glossed over the situation because of his good production record. They view him as putting his mind on getting his job done, and done well, and letting the chips fall where they may, and they cannot regard his behavior as blameworthy.

b. Able's shop has had more grievances going through the appeals stages than any other shop in the company. The personnel office has commented on this to Able's superiors, who, however, have not taken the matter seriously. The fault may be with the men more than with Able. And as long as his production performance is good, what's the problem? His supervisors have casually raised the matter with Able, who has acidly replied that workmen these days try to get away with doing as little as they can and object to every little demand that's made on them. You can't get production by coddling them.

c. The matter comes suddenly to a head one day when one of Able's men, whom he has always felt he had to keep pushing, makes a costly error. Able is furious, accuses the man of carelessness, and dresses him down in most insulting terms. The other men in the shop listen or gather around to see what is going on. Angered by this public abuse, which he considers unwarranted, and stung by some epithet, the man is goaded into lunging at Able. Able fires him on the spot.

d. After a brief pause during which the action sinks in, one of the men mutters in Able's direction, "You're the s.o.b. who ought to be fired and maybe we ought to see that you are." Once the notion of direct action has been mentioned, a wildcat walkout follows almost as if planned. The men line up outside the plant, asserting they won't go back until the discharged man is reinstated and Able is fired. Work elsewhere in the plant is disrupted as men from other shops crowd around the windows to ask questions or yell encouragement or gather in groups to talk it over. It will be only a matter of hours before most of the plant will have to suspend operations, in any event, because of the interruption in the flow of work from the idle shop.

Your president asks your advice. What do you recommend should be done?

NOTES

1. The New York State Public Service Commission, a bipartisan agency, implied this opinion in 1960, in advocating repeal of the so-called "full-crew" law which had been on the state's statute books since 1913. The Presidential Railroad Commission was more specific in its 1962 *Report,* chap. 4. The 1963 Arbitration Board, operating under congressional mandate, came to the same conclusion.

2. William Gomberg, "Some Observations on the Problems of the Relationships between Union and Management in the Transportation Industries," a mimeographed report prepared in connection with the Transportation Study of the U.S. Department of Commerce, 1960.

3. Sumner H. Slichter, James J. Healy, and E. Robert Livernash, *The Impact of Collective Bargaining on Management,* Brookings, Washington, 1960. The description of the Brookings study and other evidence of contract practice is taken largely from Donald E. Cullen and Marcia L. Greenbaum, *Management Rights and Collective Bargaining: Can Both Survive?,* Bulletin 58, Cornell University, New York State School of Industrial and Labor Relations, Ithaca, N.Y., 1966, pp. 49–56.

4. Slichter, Healy, and Livernash, pp. 348–349.

5. The same, p. 350.

6. The same, pp. 333–335.

7. The same, p. 361.

8. The same, pp. 462–489; Rudolph Oswald, "Easing Job Changes by Advance Notice," *AFL-CIO American Federationist,* December, 1965, pp. 13–17; and "Protecting Job Rights Through Attrition Clauses," *AFL-CIO American Federationist,* June, 1965, pp. 13–17.

9. Otto Hagel and Louis Goldblatt, *Men and Machines,* International Longshoremen's and Warehousemen's Union and Pacific Maritime Association, 1963, p. 3. Also see Wayne L. Horvitz, "The ILWU-PMA Mechanization and Modernization Agreement: An Experiment in Industrial Relations," and Lincoln Fairley, "The ILWU-PMA Mechanization and Modernization Agreement: An Evaluation of Experience under the Agreement; The Union's Viewpoint," *Proceedings of the Sixteenth Annual Meeting of Industrial Relations Research Association* (Madison, Wisc., 1964), pp. 22–47.

10. Slichter, Healy, and Livernash, p. 106, make this insightful distinction.

11. Dan H. Mater, *Journal of Business of the University of Chicago,* vol. 14, p. 409, 1941.

12. A study of 110 nonunion firms in 1950 revealed that 96 percent of these firms gave some weight to length of service in layoffs, 83 percent in rehires, 72 percent in promotions, and 62 percent in transfers. *Seniority Practices in Non-unionized Companies,* National Industrial Conference Board, Studies in Personnel Policy, no. 110, New York, 1950.

13. An interesting analysis of managerial promo-

tions has been made by Norman H. Martin and Anselm L. Strauss, "Patterns of Mobility within Industrial Organizations," *Journal of Business,* vol. 29, pp. 101–110, April, 1956.

14. James J. Healy, "The Ability Factor in Labor Relations," *Arbitration Journal,* vol. 10, p. 8, 1955.

15. Philip Selznick and Howard Vollmer, "Rule of Law in Industry: Seniority Rights," *Industrial Relations,* vol. 1, pp. 97–116, May, 1962.

16. The same, p. 116.

17. Slichter, Healy, and Livernash, pp. 157–168.

18. Milton Derber and others, *Labor–Management Relations in Illini City,* The University of Illinois Press, Urbana, 1953, vol. 1, pp. 183–184.

19. Prof. George Strauss describes this "hard-line" approach in "The Shifting Power Balance in the Plant," *Industrial Relations,* vol. 1, pp. 65–96, May, 1962.

20. James Kuhn, *Bargaining in Grievance Settlement,* Columbia University Press, New York, 1961, pp. 78–79.

21. The same, p. 139.

22. The same, pp. 150–151.

We have traced the history of the rise of labor unions in this country and their coalescence into a common cause which is referred to as the labor movement. We have observed how individual unions perform a representative or agency function to obtain immediate benefits on behalf of their memberships, and how the labor movement has recurringly sought more fundamental modifications or reforms in existing social institutions. We have seen that unions, whose rationale lies in their agency and reform roles, inevitably acquire special interests of their own and at times may be led to engage in programs and activities that are designed to perpetuate and benefit the organization itself and the leadership that is in command of it. Finally, we have noted how labor unions bring into question their relationship to their own members (do they extend or curtail their liberties? are they responsive to member interests or do they dominate them?) and their relationship to society as a whole (do they constitute a vital arm of a democratic society or are they a dangerous source of private coercive power?). The relationships of the union to individual rights, on the one hand, and social welfare, on the other, have been themes which have run through the development and evolution of labor law in this country and have colored public attitudes toward unionism.

We shall have more to say about some of these issues in later chapters, but for the time being, we shall take leave of the labor movement and turn our attention to the way in which employers and managers, in their role as organizers of productive activity, look on labor as a factor of production. Before doing so, however, let us try in this section to pull together these many aspects of labor unions and the labor movement, which we have so swiftly covered, by trying to conceptualize —that is, to capture the essence of—this complex phenomenon of the labor movement. Many students of labor have tried to do this over the years, with results that do not always agree. We shall take a look at what some of the major writers on this subject have had to say, and then attempt to extract from their contributions those elements which appear most relevant.

These several efforts to conceptualize the labor movement have usually been referred to under the rubric "theories of the labor movement." Such theories attempt to answer the broad question Why is a labor movement in a given country (usually the United States or England), at a given time, what it is? Or to put it another way, they constitute efforts "to give an ordered explanation, to account for the origin and behavior of labor unionism," to provide "a basis for predicting the conduct and policies that may be followed by the labor movement in the future."[1] The first group of theories which we shall consider emphasizes economic determinants of the union role.

Marx and his followers

Marx, as a kind of ideological deity to his followers, has had so many prophets, each claiming to be the only "true" interpreter of the master, that it is difficult to lump them together. Nevertheless, there are certain elements which most of them have held in common.

As originally conceived, the real enemy of the working class was the capitalist system and the capitalists who controlled it. This concept was not based on the fact that capitalists were inherently evil people but simply that they were caught in the grip of a system which compelled them to take certain actions which ran counter to worker interests. In brief, the accumulation of capital was expected to lead to a falling rate of profit, which could only be offset by such devices as imperialistic expansion, on the one hand, and by increasing exploitation of the wage earners, on the other. The historic inevitability of this pressure would drive capitalists, in the nature of the system of which they were a part, to press down ever lower on wage rates, to extend hours, or to extract more effort, leading to a further and continuous degradation of the working class. These were the "chains" in which the "system" held workers in bondage, but which would—inevitably —be thrown off at some point in time when proletarian misery was too great to tolerate. The timing would differ from country to country, depending on the stage of its economic evolution, on the degree of political (class) consciousness among the working class, and on the strength and will power of the capitalist opposition.

In the nature of this apocalyptic vision, the trade unions had a relatively minor role to play. Their function was chiefly economic, while the real strength lay in political solidarity. Their focus of interest was in their trade, while the future lay with worker-*class* consciousness. Their program was to win gains which, given the nature of historic inevitability, could only be temporary, or to fight off exploitation, again only for the moment. The unions were thus concerned chiefly with the short run, whereas the only meaningful objective was somewhat further off and could be realized only by reorganizing society along totally different lines, rather than by accommodating to present controlling interests.

The chief function which unions could serve in this greater struggle was to act as agents of protest, mobilizing worker unrest, stirring up that consciousness of class on which the future social order depended. Unions were thus tools in a continuing conflict, shock troops which could be expended in the achievement of a greater good. They were useful, and hence to be encouraged. But they were useful not as institutions in their own right, performing a function (like collective bargaining) which could be considered a desirable objective on its own; they were useful only as a short-run instrument for achieving a long-run goal.

In Lenin's view, trade-union consciousness was something that arose spontaneously, the product of the sufferings and indignities of workers in their place of work. It required no imagination and no intellectual understanding; it was evoked by the actions of the capitalists who themselves could not escape from the necessity of grinding down their workers. Trade-union consciousness was thus a natural response to unavoidable pressures. Workers could not help organizing into trade unions to protect themselves from the oppression which the system forced on them, however limited and temporary might be the effects of their resistance. But social democratic consciousness was something else again. It required intelligence and imagination to perceive the political power that could be wielded by the mass of workers when they organized their strength to overthrow the system which was the source of their misery. Thus the Socialist intelligentsia was to be the instructor of the trade unions, guiding their thinking and making their protest actions count.[2]

Marxian Socialists understandably favored industrial unionism over craft unionism. Since their objective was to create class consciousness, they sought to influence not simply those workers who were relatively well off (and least open to revolutionary persuasion) but more especially the larger numbers of unskilled, who could be more effectively mobilized into action and whose numbers counted in the kind of protest actions contemplated. The one true revolutionary labor movement which this country has produced was the Industrial Workers of the World, who counted the AFL craft unionists as much their enemy as they did the employers against whom they struck.[3]

"The day of the skilled worker," says the I.W.W., "has passed." Whether this is true or not, the unskilled are just awakening to their power.... They are capable of great efforts and achievements, greater than those of some groups of more prosperous workers.... The great middle ranks of labor are first to be reckoned with. They are not entirely unskilled, but their skill consists solely in the fact that they are speeded up and specialized in many graduated degrees; they are not set apart by education or experience in a group by themselves. This mass of workers ... will no longer wait for the permission or the cooperation of the skilled before they strike, *and this constitutes nothing less than a revolution in the labor movement.* If the aristocracy of labor will give them no consideration, they are ready, if necessary, to fight the aristocracy.

This concentration on the unskilled and semi-skilled, organized into industrial unions, explains the degree of interest of Communist agents in the early CIO unions. The degree of their penetration in the face of an inexperienced union bureaucracy finally brought CIO leaders to the painful necessity of performing major surgery by expelling eleven affiliates for Communist domination. It also helps to explain the lack of success of Communist infiltration in AFL unions, even though the latter for many years harbored sizable numbers of moderate (Fabian-type) Socialists.

Perhaps the foremost radical Socialist thinker in United States history was Daniel DeLeon, an intellectual who played a role in the Knights of Labor and the IWW both, although always finding himself embroiled in partisan squabbles. De-Leon's view of the place of the union in society captures all the above threads—the emphasis on the industrial organization of the whole working class, the scorn for the skilled "aristocrats" of labor who were willing to sell out for short-run advantage, and the long-run nature of the union mission to which all else must be sacrificed but which did permit temporary benefits as long as they did not interfere with the grand goal.[4]

In the first place, the trades union has a supreme mission. That mission is nothing short of organizing by uniting, and uniting by organizing, the whole working class industrially—not merely those for whom there are jobs, accordingly, not only those who can pay dues. This unification or organization is essential in order to save the eventual and possible victory from bankruptcy, by enabling the working class to assume and conduct production the moment the guns of the public power fall into its hands— or before, if need be, if capitalist political chicanery pollutes the ballot box. . . .

In the second place, the trades union has an immediate mission. The supreme mission of trades unionism is ultimate. That day is not yet. The road thither may be long or short, but it is arduous. At any rate, we are not yet there. Steps in the right direction, so-called "immediate demands," are among the most precarious. They are precarious because they are subject and prone to the lure of the "sop" or the "palliative" that the foes of Labor's redemption are ever ready to dangle before the eyes of the working class, and at which, aided by the labor lieutenants of the capitalist class, the unwary are apt to snap—and be hooked. . . . We have seen that the pure and simple trades union belongs to the latter category, the category of "traps," and we have seen the reason why—it is merely a jobs-securing machine, consequently it inevitably rends the working class in twain, and, on the whole, has the love and affection of the capitalist exploiter.

Another homegrown but more moderate Socialist view of the place of the labor union was offered by Eugene V. Debs, best known for his leadership in the Pullman strike of 1894 and several times Socialist candidate for the United States presidency. Debs saw the labor movement as a bifurcated structure: There was its economic arm, consisting of the trades unions which, while confined to a particular trade or industry, nevertheless mobilized workers in their job interests; there was also the political arm, which the Socialist party constituted and which (potentially) embraced the whole of the working class. The labor union has the limited function of bettering conditions under the prevailing wage system, but the Socialist party has the larger function of capturing political power in order to wipe out the wage system. These efforts are not antithetical but complementary. Every worker ought to be "unionized" on both the economic and political fronts.[5]

In this program, the trades-union and the Socialist Party, the economic and political wings of the labor movement, should not only not be in conflict, but act together in perfect harmony in every struggle whether it be on the one field or the other, in the strike or at the ballot box. The main thing is that in every such struggle the workers shall be united, shall in fact be unionists and no more be guilty of scabbing on their party than on their union, no more think of voting a capitalist ticket on election day and turning the working class over to capitalist robbery and misrule than they would think of voting in the union to turn it over to the capitalists and have it run in the interest of the capitalist class.

The Marxian or Socialist point of view, a philosophy growing out of a theory, has found very little support on the American scene. The deterioration of the living conditions of workers under capitalism, which it foresaw, has so completely failed to materialize that some contemporary Marxian "revisionists" have explicitly abandoned this element of their faith. What does remain is a belief in the inevitable fusion of economic and political power in a propertyless society. The testing of that belief, however, lies in a future which presumably few current Marxian theorists really expect to see for themselves.

Karl Polanyi and the "double movement"

Few people since Karl Marx have painted on so broad a screen as Karl Polanyi, Austrian-born British economist. His book, *The Great Transformation*,[6] is a penetrating analysis of the social forces which, over the last century and a half, have been in the process of remolding social organization, their outcome not yet predictable but the direction clearly discernible. It is far more than a theory of the labor movement, but it too—like Marxian Socialism—seeks to place the labor union in its broader context.

Polanyi sees Western-style labor unions, as well as employers' trade associations, growing out of two economic movements seeking to make peace with each other. One was the system of economic liberalism or market capitalism—all that we associate with the notion of the price system. This had its heyday in England in the half-century from 1830 to 1880. Before it came to flower, merchandising had been limited to the exchange of *goods*. Their method of production had been socially regulated by government and guilds. The rise of specialized, mechanized production made this system of regulated responsibilities impractical. In particular, it required a free *labor* market, permitting merchant-capitalist interests to hire labor as needed and dispense with it when not needed with no continuing responsibilities for its welfare. Thus in the market economy, the factors of production as well as the goods which they produced became subject to free-market pricing and competition. (One is immediately reminded of the labor movement in the United States in the middle years of the nineteenth century, when craftsmen objected to "the wages system" itself as something which forced them to put themselves on the market rather than the goods which they created.)

The misfortune the market system brought with it was not that it lowered economic well-being, as Marx would have it. Economic welfare may indeed have been increased. The real catastrophe was that the market system subordinated all social relationships to the economic relationship, based solely on price. In response to this disruption of the fabric of familial and institutional life, there arose a second movement, which Polanyi refers to as "the social-protection movement"—a spontaneous effort by people in all walks of life to protect their social relationships by erecting limits to the demands which the free competitive market made on them.

The labor unions were a product of this social-protection movement, drawing workers together in the common cause of refusing to allow themselves to be bought as individuals and dismissed as individuals, acting jointly not only to set common terms so that they could not be made to compete against each other, but also erecting defenses to their organized shop societies.

Abetted by social reformers, they won new factory legislation designed to set limits on the extent to which competition among producers would drive down working conditions. Wage-and-hour legislation was sought and eventually secured. But not only workers took part in this spontaneous movement to rear new institutions to protect social relationships. Employers, through their trade associations, sought restraints on all-out competition. They looked to tariffs to safeguard not only their investments but also their social positions based on their economic functions.

Thus social protection, for all interest groups, took the two forms of autonomous self-help organizations (unions and associations) and protective legislation. The consequence of these interventions in the self-regulating market system was, however, to render it unworkable. It could not be tolerated in its pure form because it ignored the social basis of society. But in erecting defenses against its effects, interest groups prevented its effective functioning. There thus arose a kind of institutional deadlock, creating a socioeconomic crisis which could only be resolved by the substitution of new institutions.

Although the outcome may be deferred and although there may not yet be a clear perception of the historical drift, Polanyi believes that a deepening crisis (of which the two world wars are symptoms) will make necessary some radical resolution of the deadlock posed by an economy which still relies on a market system for its economic performance but allows that system to be hobbled by private protective systems—the pockets of private pooled power to which we referred in an earlier chapter. An economic system so handicapped will produce continuing unemployment and maldistribution of its resources. Its operation will become more and more makeshift until the need for fundamental revision—transformation—becomes too pressing to be avoided.

Polanyi sees two major groups competing for the power to end the institutional deadlock by substituting for it a new social organization fashioned to their taste. One is composed of the employers, owners, and managers who are responsible for the conduct of industry and thus wield enormous power, and who gain public backing from a recognition of the importance of their economic functions. The solution such groups seek is some governmental planning machinery based on the philosophy of business efficiency and business authority. One might apply to it the ugly word "fascism," but the term obscures the basic issue by evoking emotional overtones. The principal consideration is that the solution sought by

such groups in order to end the institutional deadlock is one which plays down representative instruments in industry and politics, since these are almost *designed* to permit expression of opposition, which curtails the efficiency and directive authority that constitute the basis of the business solution.

The other major interest group offering a solution is made up of workers and their unions, who draw support from a public of which they constitute a large segment. The solution they propose is a greater measure of social planning. This is viewed as permissive of the expression of private and group interests, even though requiring their coordination through a variety of bargaining or voting procedures. It is, however, destructive of private property rights in business, since it is from these interests that deadlock-creating opposition can be expected.

The first important conclusion for Polanyi is that whichever solution is adopted, it will place greater emphasis on collective decisions. Each recognizes what for him is the "reality" of *society*, in contrast to free-market individualism. As between the two systems, he himself clearly prefers the second, since it is his belief that with its representative institutions, of which labor unions constitute one, there is opportunity to *plan* the strengthening of individual rights and freedoms within a system of social responsibilities. He sees democratic regulation as essential to freedom and not its antithesis: unemployment, for example, is a "brutal restriction on freedom" which can effectively be met only through planning and regulation. The authoritarian solution he rejects, since it totally denies the individualistic values which have come down to us through the past, with their emphasis on the worth of the person, an objective no less important—though also no more important—than social organization.

Insofar as the "liberal" individual identifies freedom with the market system, and the market system is untenable (as the social-protection movement indicates), then the "liberal" is led to conclude that freedom is untenable. The only alternative is nonfreedom, or fascism. What we must come to realize, says Polanyi, is that there can be planning *for* freedom. The false dilemma can be rejected and the true alternatives seen:

regulation and control for freedom (some form of representative socialism), or regulation and control without freedom (some form of authoritarianism).

On this analysis, Polanyi sees unionism as arising out of the need for protection and of moving (against odds) toward some form of socialist planning in which it will continue to play a representative role. Unlike Marx, he does not envision unions as simple tools to an end but as part of the eventual solution, if that solution should be socialism. Unlike Marx, he does not see the socialist solution as inevitable, so that unions may go down swinging.

One may question whether Polanyi is justified in positing as necessary "social" solutions two such extremes as planning without representation and planning without private property. Planning with both representation and private property, even with the latter subject to regulation, would appear as another possibility. Appropriate institutional changes may permit a balance of interests without developing into a deadlock or stalemate. Nevertheless, the Polanyi thesis is a stimulating intellectual challenge.

John R. Commons and the extension of the market

The only student of the labor movement in the United States who can be said to have founded a "school of thought" is John R. Commons, a professor at the University of Wisconsin from 1904 to the Depression years of the thirties. His institutional approach involved a detailed grubbing for the "facts" of the labor market, which he then sorted out and made the basis for his major concepts. He was part statistician, part economist, part sociologist, part historian. He did not develop anything which could properly be labeled a theory of the labor movement, but out of his work emerged certain pieces which, when fitted together, are entitled to be called such.

It is Commons's thesis[7] that the nineteenth-century development of a labor movement in the United States, culminating in the establishment of the AFL in 1886, was due in largest measure to the geographical widening of product markets, bringing more and more producers into competition with one another and forcing workers to combine on an equally extensive geographical basis to resist the adverse consequences of product-market competition.

What does Commons mean by "extension of product markets"? It is an historical process which he generalizes from the detailed study of the shoe-making industry, supplemented by other, less detailed case studies. Down to the end of the eighteenth century, he finds that the production of shoes and other commodities went on in small establishments operated by a producer (a master workman) who himself had very little capital. He bought a limited amount of raw material, which he and a journeyman or two in his employ would work into finished goods "to order" or, in some trades, into a small stock of goods which could be sold on market day—in either case, a sale bringing a quick recovery of the capital investment. These small-scale operations were almost an adjunct to the producer's own household.

The "work force" thus consisted of a very small number of journeymen working right alongside the master, and their "wages" were actually closely related to the price of the goods they produced—so much so that a journeyman would receive, not so much "pay" for an hour or a day of work, but one "price" for a pair of ladies' dress shoes and another "price" for a pair of gentlemen's riding boots, and so on. In a sense, the journeyman could be said to charge the master a price for his work, and the master then turned around and charged the customer a somewhat higher price. The "profit spread" represented a return to the master for investing his limited capital in materials and for taking some slight risk that something might interfere with the final sale.

In this kind of relationship, says Commons, the interests of the journeyman and the master were very similar. Both were interested in obtaining as high a "price" for the product as they could, but both—journeyman and master alike—were acutely aware that excessive prices might drive away trade and injure their reputation. By and large, they operated in small communities isolated from other settlements, so that either they often had something of a local monopoly or, if there were several producers in the area, there were

few enough so that they could effect an understanding among themselves without much difficulty. But social pressures prevented them from
exploiting the customers unduly, even though a
degree of monopoly power also enabled them to
pass along occasional modest price increases when
circumstances seemed to make that necessary or
desirable. Thus there was a system of mutual interests and forbearances—the journeyman refrained from pressing the master for too high a
price for his work, the master forbore asking the
customer too high a price for his product, but
jointly they sought to protect their mutual interests by extracting "reasonable" concessions from
the local market (their neighbors).

But some urban areas were growing. Before the
turn of the century, the Atlantic Coast ports had
become cities of more than 25,000. Some more
enterprising masters had accumulated the additional capital necessary to undertake production
for stock as well as for order. Retail establishments began to spring up. In these, a master
might have a dozen or more journeymen working
under him. His own time would increasingly be
given over to supervising the jobs in process, to
buying materials and selling finished goods. This
merchant function was still performed by the
master producer, but it was a more important part
of his activity than formerly it had been and still
was in the smaller and more isolated communities.

In cities the size of Boston, New York, and
Philadelphia, retail establishments competed with
one another for local trade, and no longer was
there the same easy identification of the interests
of journeymen and masters. In periods of rising
prices, a producer-retailer would be more hesitant
to pass along a price increase to his customers in
order to accommodate the squeeze on his journeymen's standard of living. He was worried whether
his competition would follow. Thus, with the expanding product market in the larger communities, the interests of the journeymen began to diverge from those of the masters. The men in one
shop might meet together in a tavern to discuss
their mutual problem—should they press the master for a price increase, that is, an increase in the
amount they were paid for the various kinds of
work they turned out? But how could they suc-

cessfully pressure their master unless he knew
that the other masters were also going along with
a price increase? So the men from the several
shops in the town pooled their interests and
brought their collective power to bear on all the
masters. Even at this stage, however, the masters
could view the situation with no great alarm, since
if they all passed the increase along to their customers, none would suffer very much. As long as
the workers' demands were "within reason," jour-
neyman-master differences were still not great.
The customers—the public—might feel less protected, however, since in a large town social pressure operated as a restraint on monopoly power
less effectively than in a small community.

The next step in the expansion of product markets came when some of the more ambitious masters began to produce not only for their own
retail shops but also for wholesale. A producer in
Philadelphia would take orders from a general
store in New Orleans or Memphis for so many
pairs of various kinds and sizes of boots, for example. But before long the producer in Philadelphia found that in this kind of wholesale trade, he
was in competition with producers of boots and
shoes in New York, Albany, Pittsburgh, and other
industrial centers, and with less possibility of getting together with his competitors to keep a floor
under the price of his goods. The only thing he
could do was to try to produce his goods as
cheaply, and to price at least as low, as they. If
unsuccessful in these respects, he would be driven
out of the wholesale market to which he aspired.

But in order to keep his costs low, he had to
revise his methods of production. Apparently,
few masters tried to make out by cutting wages
of their journeymen, but they did try to reduce
costs by the method of specialization to which
Adam Smith had drawn special attention. Instead
of a journeyman having the satisfaction of turning out a whole pair of boots, for which he was
paid a price, he might be set to doing only one
part of the production process, for which he
would be paid a piece rate. For the parts of the
operation that called for less skill, an apprentice
could be used. From this time on there developed
considerable resentment among the skilled craftsmen over the use of "green hands" (as the less

skilled and younger workers were known) and women, who were also brought in for simple, repetitive operations. Thus the rise of the whole-sale market, bringing producers from a wider geographical area into competition, had its reper-cussions on the workplace and created, for the first time, a really sharp cleavage between the interests of men and master. The expansion of markets was raising a threat not simply to stand-ards of living but to the status of the artisan.

The producer turned merchant required capital, and as markets continued to expand so did his capital needs. For a time local bankers and com-mission men helped him to meet his financial problems, but there came the time when these sources of finance, coupled with his own preoccu-pation with both producing and selling, placed limits on his growth. At this point the merchant-capitalist takes over. He is primarily a "bargain-ing specialist," in Commons's phrase—one who can secure the capital needed to finance larger-scale operations and purchase the necessary ma-terials for the master workman or producer, who now surrenders his marketing function and be-comes simply the employer-producer or labor contractor. The master makes his profit not on the sale of goods in assorted retail and wholesale markets but by turning over his whole output to the merchant specialist, who disposes of it through a network of brokers and agents. It is the mer-chant specialist who sizes up the potential mar-kets, commands credit, and drives the bargains on the strength of which he derives his profit. He is a transaction specialist, and his transactions in-clude bargains with numbers of employer-pro-ducers who supply him with the goods he sells, and who have to meet his price or lose out to other producers who can. In order to meet his price, they are more than ever under the com-pulsion to keep costs low. The process of restrain-ing wage increases, subdividing the work process, and using less-skilled help is reinforced.

But the merchant-capitalist does not have his markets wholly under his control. His retail and wholesale outlets can, if they wish, buy their goods from other merchants. They can play the offers of other merchant-capitalists against him. In order to retain the network of dealers to whom

he can dispose of his product, the merchant-capitalist sometimes finds it necessary to take a hand himself in reorganizing the production process.

The changes which occurred in consequence of this extension of the area within which product competition took place can be exaggerated, but it is undeniably true that something approaching what Commons referred to as "a cataclysm in the condition of the journeyman" did occur in the first half of the nineteenth century. We have noted in an earlier chapter how this change gave rise to reform movements which were designed to wipe out the hated "wages system" and return to the craftsman his control over the "whole job." It is noteworthy that those who most protested the change were those whose actual or potential loss was the greatest—the *skilled* workers, those who later came to be called the "aristocrats" of labor, whose special status was being eliminated by the industrial reorganization at work. And the mas-ter workmen of the start of the century, whose interest had been in mutual association to support prices at "reasonable" levels (enabling them to pay reasonable "prices" to their journeymen), now had as their primary interest mutual associa-tion to hold down wages against the concerted protest of their outraged journeymen. The latter had no alternative but to seek their own protec-tion through trade-union organization.

The "final" stage in the process came toward the end of the century when the various inde-pendent contractors (or subcontractors) of a merchant-capitalist were brought together in a single corporate structure, combining the financ-ing, production, and distribution functions in one large-scale organization operating on a national scale. Labor unions now came into conflict with corporate giants as well as with the associations of smaller-scale employers to which they had long been accustomed.

Thus Commons sees American labor history in terms of the relentless spread of competition over an ever-widening area until the nation be-came "a single market menaced at every point of its vast expanse by every competitor." Within such a single competitive market, the pressure of retailers and wholesalers on the manufacturer led in turn to pressures on the worker. As competition intensified and the pressures became greater, the need for labor unions accordingly became greater. By the end of the nineteenth century, the process of market expansion had reached its limit (at least, so long as a tariff wall protected American-made goods from competitive pressures from abroad). And simultaneously, American labor had shaken off the false hope of a return to past forms of industrial organization and had established the first permanent trade-union movement in the form of the AFL.

Technological changes aided in this process, to be sure, but Commons does not find them the key to understanding worker protest. Mass-production techniques aided in splintering the skill of once-proud craftsmen, bringing them together in large industrial anthills under the close control and supervision of managers of huge pools of capital, but this technological revolution (though it had begun decades earlier) did not have a significant or widespread impact on workers until *after* the nationwide expansion of product markets and the consequent intensification of competition had already pressed down on their standards. It was the expansion of markets which made mass production possible.

Commons's preoccupation with the expansion of product markets caused him to place less emphasis on a related and concurrent development —the growing competition in the labor market. As means of travel improved, itinerant labor became a more common phenomenon. The problem of the "outsider" entering a community and seeking employment at wages below those which the local craftsmen had already set as their standard confronted workers increasingly as the nineteenth century wore on. On the occasion of local strikes called by printers, carpenters, shoemakers, and similarly skilled trades, it was a common expedient for the struck employers to insert advertisements in the newspapers of other towns announcing that "good jobs" were available. When applicants showed up, they were not always ready to sacrifice the "opportunity" for which they had traveled, perhaps several hundred miles, simply to strengthen the position of workers with whom they had little by way of common interest. As Prof. Lloyd Ulman has so carefully documented,

it was probably as much because of this competition in the labor market as because of product-market pressures that local unions sought to link themselves into national organizations that could work to prevent the undercutting of standards by itinerant labor.[8] Workers no less than products could travel and compete against one another. This pressure on the labor-market side was intensified by the waves of immigrant labor, particularly in the latter part of the nineteenth century, leading to union political pressures for limitations on immigration. This addendum does not undermine Commons's basic thesis, however; the labor movement in the United States arose as a spontaneous worker protest to the effect of competition on working conditions. In this respect, his thinking runs closely parallel to Polanyi's. Labor unions come into existence, in his view, as a means of weakening or controlling the destructive influences of the competitive market system.

But at this point Commons parts company with Polanyi. Once labor unions come into existence, they constitute a power group, like a large corporation or a trade association or a farmers' cooperative.[9] The issue then becomes transformed from one of the rise of an institution to protect its members from a deteriorating situation to one of that institution's use of the bargaining power which comes into its possession. The question is no longer why a labor movement is born but how, having come into existence, it interacts with other power groups in economic society to create a mosaic of transactions which somehow produce and distribute the social income. It is not that power groups sometimes produce deadlocks that impresses Commons; it is that somehow, pragmatically, groups learn to adjust to one another to get society's work accomplished, and that they develop institutions to resolve such deadlocks as arise.

To Commons, society itself is a form of "collective action," not simply a locus for the unstructured relations of numbers of individuals. Within the enveloping framework of laws and customs, collectively established, there are subordinate exercises of collective action—some formal, such as business firms and labor unions. Both with respect to the broad social framework and the subordinate "going concerns," as he calls them, collective action is more than control over individual action. By controlling the actions of some, it makes possible the actions of others; it frees them from coercion and forms of competition which have been branded as "unfair." By controlling the actions of some as through the working rules of organizations and the collective agreements between organizations, it enormously expands the capabilities of others.

Looking more specifically at the economic component of society, Commons finds the economy to be a myriad of going concerns, bound together internally and related externally by a complex of customs and rules governing their interactions, which in fact constitute a flow of transactions. These transactions are basically of three types: (1) bargains among legal equals; (2) determinations by governments affecting the allocation of income and property (these he calls "rationing transactions," and they include, among other things, taxes); and (3) managerial transactions, which are the privileged use of private power and property (primarily in production) *after* bargains and governmental decisions have set the limits to the exercise of such authority.

The mix of the three types of transactions changes with time and place. All three coexist in any society, but the degree to which one or another is dominant affects the complexion of that society. Commons considered the growth in the size of the corporation in the United States as enlarging the sphere of rationing and managerial transactions and reducing the scope of bargaining transactions—a substitution of authority for voluntary agreement. Cross-culturally, he viewed the rise of communism and fascism as emphasizing the command-and-obedience relationships of the authoritative rationing and managerial transactions, in contrast to the liberalistic economics of the West which still left important scope for choice and discretion in bargaining transactions. "But there may be all degrees of combinations, for the three kinds of transactions are interdependent and variable in a world of collective action and perpetual change. . . ."[10]

The economic role of the labor union is obviously affected by the extent to which the bargaining element is given prominence in a society at a given time. If rationing transactions become dominant, its role, as we know it, would undergo change. It would move toward becoming more of a political instrumentality.

Like economists generally, Commons concerns himself with scarcity conditions, both natural and legally created, and the resulting conflict of interests to which they give rise. Competition between individuals and groups takes the form of negotiations over the terms of transfer of scarce goods and services. Property ownership involves the power to withhold goods or services from use by others, a power which can be employed to win concessions as to terms of exchange. This is a mutual power: both buyer and seller, employer and union, are in a position to withhold something the other wants. As long as individuals and groups bring this element of bargaining power to their transactions, the question will inevitably be raised whether their exercise of it is "reasonable."

The line between reasonable and unreasonable exercises of power, says Commons, is not drawn by any broad social philosophy or public principle, at least in the United States, but is hammered out on a case-by-case basis in the resolution of particular disputes. As conflicts of interest emerge and protests are voiced over the unreasonable use of power by some offended person or group, an appropriate authority—a manager, an arbitrator, a government official, the courts—makes a decision on the merits of the complaints, and out of these decisions there gradually cumulates a body of custom and law imposing limitations on the exercise of power. The rights of property, over which the economic contest takes place, become defined over time by an encrustation of working rules, court decisions, and traditions.

Bargaining power, Commons feels, can never be made equal between people or groups. But limits can be set to its exercise. These rights, privileges, powers, and immunities of property can be spelled out by judicial-like decisions, which become precedents and whose total net effect is to move individuals and groups into reasonable relations with one another, thus bringing order out of conflict. Individual and group objectives are satisfied as far as possible and permissible by compromise with other individuals and groups. The basis for agreement is power, restrained "within reason" by a set of working rules.

The working rules can change, the composition of organizations can change, their power base can change, their objectives can change—all in relatively unpredictable ways. One can and must seek to identify and anticipate likely responses to such changes, but the range of possible resulting activity is limited only by the imagination and perseverance of people operating within a framework over which they themselves have some measure of control. No "natural" or "expectable" outcome is discernible. When individuals join with one another to form associations, build cliques within them, split into factions, divide into competing and cooperating societies, contest the rules which should limit or release their behavior—then the possibility is ruled out of *automatic* adjustment of the inevitable conflicts to which scarcity gives rise. Agreement must be contrived, bargained out at many levels, from the agreements between individuals and going concerns right on up to the overall social framework which ties them into a workable system.

Thus Commons sees the origin and rise of labor unions as simply a special (historical) case of the effort of one group or class of individuals in American society to press for working rules which set "reasonable limits" to the competitive pressures from other groups which were weighing down on them. Over time, the pressures and problems take new forms, institutions are altered, and labor-union objectives undergo modification. In the ongoing process, however, one element remains relatively stable: Unions, like other organized groups, seek to exert their power to achieve economic benefits for themselves, and are restrained—just as their business "opposition" is restrained—only by the hammering out, over time, of a body of changing rules which set new "reasonable limits" to the exercise of their power.

Unlike Marx and Polanyi, Commons does not see labor as caught up in any great social transformation which sweeps them irresistibly on to some climax. He admits the presence of a drift toward a greater reliance on authority to determine economic relationships, but the nature and extent of that authority remain within the control of all those who, collectively, establish its working rules—not according to any internal system of logic but pragmatically, over time.

Selig Perlman and workers' scarcity consciousness

Some principal efforts to explain the labor movement rely heavily on sociopsychological properties which are said to characterize workers in their economic environments. Perhaps the most famous "theory of the labor movement" in the literature is that of Selig Perlman, a student and then a colleague of Commons at the University of Wisconsin, who came to this country from a Russian birthplace and originally with a Marxian philosophy. In the course of his collaboration with Commons, he reexamined the Marxian interpretation and found it inapplicable to the American scene. The successful unionists appeared to be those who threw off the Socialist ideological yoke. With this as a clue, Perlman began to fit the parts and pieces of the labor jigsaw puzzle together in a way that produced a different picture. The result appeared in 1928 as *A Theory of the Labor Movement*.[11]

Perlman saw three major forces shaping the course of the labor movement in any country, three "strands" of influence which are interwoven in differing ways with differing results. Each of these forces or influences is identified with a particular class of individuals, and each of these classes is supposedly driven by its own peculiar psychological predispositions. The three groups are the capitalists or entrepreneurs, the manual workers, and the intellectuals.

In any modern industrialized society there is, or at least has been at some stage, an entrepreneurial class which has sized up the opportunities for economic exploitation of a country's resources and has moved to take advantage of them for personal gain. The members of this class have been spurred by a spirit of individualism and by a will to succeed. Failures do not deter them but are regarded simply as hurdles to be surmounted in an obstacle race. They intend to keep for themselves and their heirs what they have wrested from nature and rivals, so that the institution of private property is to them sacred. To them, the notion of social welfare is simply an environment which allows every individual to extend himself to the fullest. From the results of the efforts of innovators and pioneers and risk-takers like themselves will flow a stream of benefits for all to enjoy.

The psychological outlook of this business class is thus an expansive one. It consists, in Perlman's phrase, of an "opportunity consciousness." The prizes to be won beckon, and the means of winning them are never exhausted. Economic life is conceived as an exhilarating adventure—difficult, filled with challenges, always a gamble in which there are necessarily losers to complement winners, but withal, zestful and satisfying. To the *degree* that this view of the world characterizes the business class of a society, to that degree will it possess a will to extend and defend the institutions on which survival of its kind of world depends. It will develop a resistance to reforms. If the sense of opportunity consciousness is strong, the resistance power of capitalism is strong. If the sense of opportunity consciousness is weak or shrivels, the resistance power of the entrepreneurial or business class suffers.

Opposed to the capitalist group are the manualist workers, who must be regarded not as some monolithic and cohesive class but simply as people trying to earn a living for their families in a world which generally gives them a rough time. The workplace is the focus of their interest; as long as they can maintain a tie to it and keep their place in it relative to other workers, their economic survival is more assured. But there are always more claimants for jobs than there are jobs to go around. There are always more aspirants for the *better* jobs. Occasionally, there may be a brief period when there seem to be jobs for all, but more frequently, even at times when employers talk of the "shortage of labor," from the standpoint of the manual worker himself jobs that he could fill or would want to fill look scarce.

In contrast to the businessman's outlook, then, the worker's psychological outlook is typically one of scarcity consciousness. Opportunities are few and competitors for them many. This situation of scarcity is one that he seeks not so much to change as to adjust to. Adjustment takes the form of rules, within a shop or company or trade, for parceling out the limited number of job opportunities and apportioning the better jobs among the claimants. The worker's objective and that of his fellows is some measure of control over the whole relevant collection of job opportunity so that they may administer it themselves in ways that give a greater sense of security to themselves.

This can be done through the formation of a union capable of forcing on the employer a set of rules governing the allocation of work. In effect, the manualists seek to assert a kind of proprietary control over the production process. In essence, they attempt to strike a bargain with their employer in terms which say, "You pay us, as a group, an agreed-upon amount of money for an agreed-upon amount of work, and leave to us to decide who does what, how he does it, what his obligations are to the rest of the group, and how he should be disciplined for failing to live up to those obligations."

This scarcity consciousness which expresses itself through attempted job control eschews any notion of overthrowing the economic or social system and substituting something else for it. For one thing, the manualist worker has no clear idea of any "system" which he might substitute for the one he knows and works under. He seeks only a degree of control—through organization—over the existing system which will permit him to manage scarcity in ways that will give him a sense of security. Perlman refers to this attitude, which he asserts has characterized workers throughout history, as the philosophy of "organic labor" or "organic unionism." The adjective presumably is meant to suggest that wherever labor and unions adopt a more revolutionary or reformist standpoint, it is not because they have changed their mentality but because they have come under the influence of an "outside" point of view that is foreign to their own (organic) nature.

That "foreign" influence stems from Perlman's third set of players in the economic drama—the intellectuals. By this term he does not refer to a university-trained breed of scholars, or even to people whose occupations are principally of a mental nature. It is an inclusive label for all those who are dissatisfied with the existing social system and who would like to substitute for it, or for some of its particulars, a new and "contrived" set of relationships. Intellectuals are reformers, by (Perlman's) definition. They analyze the deficiencies of the present social order, and they devise new social systems which are intended to remedy present evils or weaknesses. Is there a shortage of jobs? Change the system so that jobs become plentiful. Are workers paid inadequate wages? It is because "the system" fails to produce and allocate efficiently; change the system to improve production and distribution both. Perlman's intellectuals operate like social engineers. If the social system or the economic system fails to perform satisfactorily, then devise a new piece of machinery to accomplish what's wanted.

This class of intellectuals is very broad indeed. It includes all the reformist groups whose history in this country we briefly traced in Chapter 6. It embraces all the Marxist factions, with which Perlman himself had been very well acquainted and whom he had most in mind when he wrote. It presumably would include the New Deal brain trusters of Franklin D. Roosevelt's administration and the technocrats who were popular in the thirties. It would blanket in modern-day "democratic economic planners" such as are currently popular in France. Whoever believes that economic relationships can be redesigned on paper and then put into practice is a member of the club.

Perlman has little use for their contribution. Their chief sin is that they tend to lead labor down false paths, away from its own "organic" interests. In a phrase which has been quoted again and again, the intellectuals envisage labor "merely as an 'abstract mass in the grip of an abstract force.' "[12] They see unionism as a tool which can be used to achieve social designs which they are convinced have the logic of social evolution behind them.

These, then, are the three dramatis personae, each with its own psychology—the business or capitalist class with its opportunity consciousness, the manualistic worker class with its scarcity consciousness, and the intellectual class with its reformist orientation. It is the *relative* strength and influence of these three groups which determine the shape of the labor movement in any country. In a country like Russia, says Perlman in one of his studies, the capitalist class was undeveloped and weak, the labor movement was assertive of its organic point of view but subject to domination by the intellectuals, who thus became the strategic

force. The consequence was the overthrow of the capitalist group by a worker group mobilized by the intellectuals and the substitution of a new, "contrived" system. In the United States, by way of contrast, the capitalist mentality was buoyant and its will to resist strong, and the intellectuals could make no lasting inroads on the thinking of the manualist workers, with the consequence that the natural "organic" character of the workers asserted itself in a labor movement (the AFL) which accommodated itself to the going system and sought only the negotiation of collective agreements granting a large measure of job control. In similar fashion, the interplay of the three strands of forces explains the labor movement of any time and place.

No theory of the labor movement has been so widely accepted and yet so roundly criticized as this one. The terminology it created has passed into the literature and will probably remain there. As a theory, it leaves a great deal to be desired, however. One of its chief weaknesses is that the three strands, which presumably are independent, actually constitute a reflection of one another. The resistance power of capitalism is itself dependent on the degree to which the labor movement has accepted it, and this acceptance depends in part on the influence which social thinkers may have had in society at large. The influence of the intellectuals in turn depends in large part on the resistance power of capitalism and on the degree to which labor turns its attention inward on the job. And the extent to which the labor movement is content with limited job control depends in part on the degree of employer opposition it encounters and the extent to which it is responsive to new ideas. Thus what are supposedly three independent variables turn out to be the same can of worms.

Moreover, the marked dichotomy between the opportunity consciousness of the businessman and the scarcity consciousness of the worker is overdone. In this respect, Polanyi's concept of the protective movement characterizing *all* groups in society threatened by competition appears to be more sound. Certainly the formation of businessmen into cartels and trade associations, the passage of legislation aimed at "unfair" competition, the insistence on tariffs, and a variety of other forms of protection which have been sought by business interests are testimony to the presence of at least a tincture of scarcity consciousness on their part.

The unsavory light in which Perlman casts the intellectual is probably a reflection of his own flight from a Marxian background, a revulsion carried to an extreme. Certainly, as we saw earlier, the Marxian approach did see trade unions as tools to be employed to achieve the goal conceived by creative social thinkers such as Marx and Lenin. But social invention is no monopoly of the Marxists. The Constitution of the United States, for example, is an intellectually contrived system of relationships which has worked rather well over the years. Ideas have always profoundly affected societies, and social philosophies have left their mark on civilizations long after their expositors have passed from the scene. There is no evident reason for believing that the acceptance of ideas, even by workingmen, necessarily has a malevolent influence.

Nevertheless, there is one aspect of the Perlman approach which is too important to be dismissed with caustic criticism. If one interprets his organic unionism as being the workers' drive to assure themselves some degree of control over the affairs of the workplace, some means of establishing working rules which allocate the admittedly scarce job opportunities of *any* place of employment (the preferred jobs, the preferred shifts, the preferred assignments) and which remove from an arbitrary authority the power to make such decisions, then it is easy to agree that workers everywhere share such an organic interest. There is a place for worker organizations performing such a function under communism no less than under private enterprise, in the United States Civil Service no less than at General Motors, and informally if not formally.

This insight represents a signal contribution to an understanding of the labor movement. It is entirely conceivable, and some experts do in fact believe, that the future role of labor unions in society at large may be less important than it has been in the recent past. It is at least arguable that labor leaders have had their brief hour to strut upon the public stage in leading roles. But if that should prove to be true, and if the future of labor

unions should be less glamorous and less prestigious than their past, of one thing we may be reasonably sure: They will continue to play the organic role which Perlman assigned to them. They will continue to seek a degree of job control in places of employment that will permit their members, rather than an arbitrary authority, to perform the function of allocating scarce opportunities and structuring preferences.

Frank Tannenbaum and the clustering of workers around their jobs

A professor of history at Columbia University for more than a quarter-century, Frank Tannenbaum was himself a participant-observer in the labor stirrings in New York City in the period immediately following World War I. He has described his writings in the field of labor[13] as a "philosophy" rather than a theory of labor, but they add up to the same attempt to explain the origins and internal logic of unionism as those works we have already considered.

Like Polanyi, Tannenbaum sees unions as arising out of the need of workers to reestablish a sense of society, following the disruptive influence of nineteenth-century competitive individualism. The concomitant effects of industrialization and urbanization broke up the simple rural and familial patterns to which people had been accustomed for centuries and left them "isolated and bewildered in a city crowded with strangers." Trade unions arose as spontaneous expressions of the need for workers to reestablish social ties in the face of this industrial anomie.

This need had itself been a by-product of the rise of the "liberal" or market economy in the late eighteenth and nineteenth centuries, as a result of which work had become converted into a commodity, with the worker necessarily "sold" with his work. The rise of the market economy destroyed the ties of family and community in two ways—by making individuals *dependent* on a money wage for their livelihood, so that they must rely on others even for subsistence, and by making each member of a family or community (even child and wife) *independent* in that he could or must detach himself to earn a separate income. This monetization of the labor supply inevitably stressed the economic role of the individual in contrast to his former attachment to a producing *group* such as family, guild, or village.

The individual, cast adrift from his former and accustomed moorings, sought new associations to replace the old. These he found in his new place of work, where he encountered other similarly rootless individuals. The first unions arose as spontaneous expressions of the need for social ties among these whom the impersonal market process had brought together to perform common functions. "The original organizer of the trade-union movement is the shop, the factory, the mine, and the industry."[14]

But the social ties which the union restored to the worker were of a particular nature. They involved the relationship of man to his work, something which Tannenbaum refers to as an "organic" relationship with moral significance. A man is what he does, and society associates him with his function.[15]

> If there is any meaning that can be derived from the persistent grouping of men about their tools or within their industry, it is that work must fill a social and moral as well as an economic role. The vacuum created between the job and the man has proved intolerable; and it cannot be filled by higher wages, shorter hours, better conditions of labor, music in the shops, or baby clinics. Man has to belong to something real, purposeful, useful, creative; he must belong to his job and his industry, or it must belong to him. There is no way of permanently separating the two. What gnaws at the psychological and moral roots of the contemporary world is that most urban people, workers and owners, belong to nothing real, nothing greater than their own impersonal pecuniary interests. To escape from this profound tragedy of our industrial society is the great issue of our time, for a world in which neither the owner nor the worker is morally identified with his source of income has no principle of continuity. No institution can survive for long in a moral vacuum. For the worker the trade-union has represented an unwitting attempt to escape from this dilemma.

The need for an ethical basis was recognized by the beneficiaries of the individualistic market society. In the liberal economics beginning with Adam Smith, the doctrine of the coincidence between private gain and social good was expounded with great eloquence and logic. Smith's "invisible hand," which led people who were seeking only their own advantage unconsciously to advance the welfare of society as a whole, became perhaps the most widely quoted simile in the economic literature. But the effort to create a morality out of the profit drive was bound to fail, says Tannenbaum. It was founded on the false premise that economic objectives took precedence over social ones, and that the disruption of man's direct ties to his fellow men, as in the family and on the job, was not too high a price to pay for a higher material standard of living.

The individualistic market economy failed too because, having forced the worker into a state of dependence on a money wage, it could give him no assurance that the money wage on which he relied would continue without interruption. Failure of a business, recurring depressions, the arbitrary exercise of power by an employer could deprive him of the money which was now his sole means of survival. The spontaneous clustering of workers in shop or factory into informal trade unions was thus an effort not simply to recover a lost sense of functional community but also to protect its members against the uncertainties and hazards which threatened the survival of both the group and its individual members. To make the job secure was the first objective of worker associations, and then to try to make it yield a higher return. In more recent times, the next logical step to be taken was that of attempting to derive from the job a security of income even in periods of sickness, injury, temporary slack, and old age. Thus unions strive to obtain for their members two types of security—a continuity in the job itself and in the work community of which it is an integral part, a moral objective, and a continuity of money income to meet the worker's material needs and those of his family, an economic objective.

But now a further development begins to emerge from this worker quest for security. The unions which were first formed as local democracies began to find their power inadequate to control the market forces which were the source of their insecurity. Efforts were made to pool local resources into national organizations, but the earliest attempts failed because of the unwillingness of local democracies to subject themselves to more centralized (more remote) authority. But the imperative of creating a power sufficient to curb the adverse effects of market competition which knew no local boundaries eventually led to the establishment of durable national unions. Increasingly these asserted an authority in the determination of policy and the negotiation of collective agreements with employers. The rules which they prescribed for the local unions under their supervision and guidance now served to bind the once-autonomous local unions. To avoid the undercutting of wages and benefits, the national union imposed a "common rule" or standard terms to which the employers of its members must consent—and the small producers who could not meet the terms were either driven from the field or inhibited from even entering.

As Tannenbaum sees it, the unions, in the attempt to protect the job security and money income of their members by imposing standard terms, have thus strengthened the business "monopolies" which they once considered their prime enemies. They have done this by making it increasingly difficult for the small businessman to survive. And similarly, in the effort to provide security and income for their members, the national unions have been led to circumscribe the control of workers over their own working conditions. This result is not due to any personal ambitions or greed on the part of the national-union officers. It is a necessary consequence of the drive for securing the worker in his job and income; it is built into the logic of the attempt (Tannenbaum would say "the need") to subject the modern economy to social objectives.[16]

The essence of the conflict is union power, because without it the union could not survive, and the necessary logic of the situation requires that it always increase it. This conflict over power within the economy has community-wide implications. The search is always for greater security, the method is always increased power for setting up standards of economic life that will stabilize the job and, by implication, the economy. The effects have always been increasing limitation of freedom of action, and an increasing trend toward equality of income. The trade-union and the older range of competitive freedoms are incompatible.

Tannenbaum agrees with Polanyi that "historically, the ideal of a free competitive world, where each man by himself is a representative of the implicit harmony of the whole, has proved a snare and a delusion, and self-defeating."[17] In its place has come a gradual reversal of the movement, which Sir Henry Maine identified as a move from status to contract, that is, from socioeconomic positions defined by rules and customs to positions defined by the voluntary relationship of individual to individual. For many workers (a growing number, Tannenbaum believed in 1951, when he wrote his statement), the union has become a new form of society in which membership has become essential and in many instances inevitable—for example, through union-security provisions. The internal rules and collective agreements of these new societies are eliminating the possibility of contract as a method of establishing voluntary individual relationships and are now defining individual rights and privileges in terms of rules and customs.[18]

One of the long-run and unforeseen byproducts of the individual worker's attempt to achieve "economic security" is the gradual remolding of industrial society on the older order of "estates." The Industrial Revolution destroyed a social system in which each man had his place in a "society" and in which he could fulfill his role as a human being. . . . The industrialism that destroyed a society of status has now re-created it. The last one hundred and fifty years are a strange interlude in the history of man in the Western World, a period in which man was "freed" from one age-old association and, after a lapse, gradually reidentified with another one.

In Tannenbaum's view, the belief that workers would subject themselves to the vagaries and uncertainties of a market economy was a delusion. The insecurity of such a system is intolerable. He sees two alternatives, and it remains a question which will win out. On the one hand, the state may move in to provide the security which the free market destroyed. If or when this happens, Tannenbaum envisages that it will lead to a destruction of all decentralized authority and establish an authoritarian directorship for economy and society alike. The alternative is the development and improvement of the trade-union approach:[19]

If the workers do not succeed in making the industry and the union the vehicle for the provision of essential security, then the state will perform the task. In the process it will destroy the liberties of our time and make man subservient to an all-absorbing Leviathan. If the trade-union succeeds in doing it, it will re-create a society of status, where the rule of the larger community law may survive as a means of protecting the individual against paying too heavy a price for the security he is given by the union.

This protection that the individual needs against his union springs from those deficiencies of union government, examined in Chapter 10, which permit abuse of power by entrenched officials. Tannenbaum regards this as a flaw in the labor-movement case which the community might pressure it into correcting. (Presumably, he would approve the intent, if not the specific provisions, of the Landrum-Griffin legislation.) But beyond this need for unions to seek an improvement in their relationship to their members, Tannenbaum sees an even more basic need, which the unions can fill only through the understanding and cooperation of the business community.

If economic activity and the relationships which compose it require some underlying "morality," as he believes, and if a struggle for profit cannot be construed as such an "ethical" foundation for business activity, then workers—despite their clustering around their functions—will be shut off from the highest fulfillment of their moral quest, which is to relate their work function to social needs. In Tannenbaum's judgment, this result can only be achieved if workers, through their unions, share an increasing responsibility for the management of industry, playing a more integral role in the business decision-making process.

Moreover, he sees one method of moving toward this result which is more or less compatible with the present institutional system. Unions whose pension funds are accumulating large sums can buy into the companies in which their members are employed. It is not necessary for them to seek control but only to acquire some greater stake, so that workers come to look upon the company more as their "own" and not as the fictional property of a group of ever-changing stockholders who have no interest in it other than the profit it returns:[20]

The union, with all its faults, may yet save the corporation and its great efficiencies by incorporating it into its own natural "society," its own cohesive labor force, and by endowing it with the meanings that all real societies possess, meanings that give some substance of idealism to man in his journey between the cradle and the grave.

It is easy to see why Tannenbaum refers to his stimulating statement as a philosophy rather than a theory, though it combines elements of both. Like any bold work, it is subject to criticism. If there has been a persisting drive of workers to cluster around the job, leading to unionism as a substitute for earlier forms of association, one might inquire why this drive has been limited to perhaps one-third of the organizable work force in the United States. Are white-collar workers somehow immune to this need or sense of "vacuum" to be filled, or do they find alternative solutions? Is it possible that the sense of anomie or urban rootlessness, to which contemporary sociologists testify, may be a passing phase of social adjustment leading to new social attitudes or forms of adjustment rather than a return to old statuslike solutions? Can "meaningfulness" be found through other means than work, as, for example, more constructive uses of an increasing amount of leisure?

Is the concept of structured status relationships one which can be maintained in a society as geared to rapid technological and institutional changes as ours—changes which are not solely a product of the "market"? Is it inevitable that the state become a Leviathan when it turns to welfare measures designed to reduce economic insecurity? Are there not variations in governmental procedures and political philosophies which save them from being all of a pattern? Cannot unions, industry, and the state collaborate to improve the nature of economic society, without the unions and the state becoming engaged in a race in which only one can be the winner?

Questions like these raise doubts concerning aspects of Tannenbaum's thesis. What remains, however, after all criticisms have been leveled, is his strong and persuasive emphasis on the need for economic security in modern society as the challenge to which the labor movement constitutes a response.

Kerr, Dunlop, Harbison, Myers, and the industrialization of society

One recent effort to interpret the labor movement also deserves our attention: a collaborative enterprise of four economists—Clark Kerr, John T. Dunlop, Frederick Harbison, and Charles A. Myers. Out of a field investigation of the organization of economies in various stages of economic development they have elaborated a generalized schema which seeks to explain the labor–management relationship in any country at any given time, and its probable development.[21]

The key to their analysis consists of two central concepts—the industrialization process, and the group of men responsible for its introduction to a society, whom they dub an "elite." Preindustrial societies are a mixed lot, representing great cultural diversity. Into these varied social systems there intrudes, at one time or another, that new technology which goes by the general name of "industrialization," involving specific techniques and production requirements.

The effect which industrialization has on the social organization of work depends on the nature of the "elite" group which sponsors it. Five "ideal" types of elite sponsors are identified, each having its own associated strategies for adapting industrialization to its own ends, with each strategy evoking its own form of worker response.

These five elites and their characteristic industrial-social patterns are:

1. The dynastic elite, usually drawn from a landed or commercial aristocracy which seeks to preserve its own position and traditions by taking early control of a process which, if left to others,

would threaten the old order. This aristocratic control naturally involves a sense of managerial (family) prerogative and a paternalistic regard for workers.

2. The middle-class elite, a new group which assaults the old aristocratic order not on any ideological grounds but purely with an expedient and pragmatic intent to use the industrial process as a ladder of personal progress. The emphasis is on the ability of the individual to make good. Control of industry tends to be diffused rather than centralized. Workers are dealt with on a basis of necessary bargains to achieve wanted results.

3. The revolutionary intellectual elite likewise assaults the traditional preindustrial aristocracy but seeks to replace it with a new, patterned system under the centralized control of the state. It sees itself as the agent of the new society, and it sees the workers as instruments for the execution of its program, as those from whom it has a right to exact singleminded loyalty in the service of the revolution which it has initiated.

4. The colonial elite is doubly an "alien"—not only does it introduce an alien system (industrialization) but it does this on behalf of an alien power. Production is organized for the benefit of the mother country, with the consequence that the servant mentality it seeks to impose on workers itself precipitates rebellious, nationalistic worker organizations.

5. The nationalist elite is a charismatic type which sponsors industrialization as part of a mass independence movement. Planned governmental programs involve direction of the labor force in order to support a platform of national unity.

Industrializing elites seldom appear in any pure form, according to these four analysts. They may combine elements of several ideal types, and they change over time. But each of the five types does tend to have its own evolutionary path, so that any two countries whose elites exhibit similarities are likely to follow similar lines of development.

In brief, the dynastic type, if it is ineffective in controlling the industrialization drive, tends to give way to either the revolutionary intellectual or the nationalistic elite; if it is effective, it eventually takes on a middle-class coloration. The colonial type precedes the nationalistic, while the nationalistic elite, if it proves ineffective, is succeeded by the revolutionary intellectuals, and if effective, it, too, in time becomes middle class. The revolutionary intellectuals are only temporary custodians of the industrializing process, a transition to some form of middle-class leadership.

Thus, as time passes, all the initial elites evolve toward the middle-class pattern, which is the only stable type. It changes, to be sure, but never in history has it been displaced, once "in full control of the industrialization process."

In effect, an elite, of whatever type, seeks to adapt the new technologies to its own special ends. At the start, there is interaction between the industrial process, elite control, and cultural constraints. But as industrialization spreads throughout a society, its own universal technical requirements overshadow any distinctive character imparted by its elite sponsors and cultural parts. The elites must adapt themselves to the tiger they are riding, and with each succeeding generation, the controlling elites in all countries tend to become more and more alike, in the middle-class mold. Modern technology spreads over the world like an irresistible glacier, transforming societies by the strength of its own "logic," with the various types of leadership groups in country after country around the world seeking to harness its tremendous powers for their own ends, only themselves to be swept aside or transformed in the process.

The homogeneous industrial society which is the end product of this movement has clearly identifiable forms, according to these economists' thesis: an enveloping system of education geared to technological processes; a highly differentiated labor force structured on occupational rather than class lines; urban dominance of the society; a large role for government by way of regulating and coordinating the economic and power relationships; a pluralistic society predisposed to seek consensus among its various interest groups.

What role for the unions in such a society? They—and professional associations with them—become the instruments by which workers interact with other groups, especially management, just as at present in the United States. Workers every-

where want progress and participation, and while they may, in some less developed countries or in emergency circumstances, be willing to give up participation for progress, over the long haul they want both. Thus unions more or less in the pattern of those in Western society can be expected to spread to other lands. Along with the enterprises of which they are a part and with the government as the overall coordinator, they will elaborate "a great web of rules" which constitute pragmatic solutions to questions of authority and responsibility, status and change.

The illuminations and perceptions of this rather grandiose vision are marred by the heavy emphasis on ideal types, whose real-life counterparts, even if "originally" identifiable, soon get lost in the evolutionary shuffle. Their analytical role is somewhat obscure. Further, the notion of a "mature" or "complete" or "successful" industrialization (not yet achieved in any country), pervades the schema, even though the authors assert there is no "final equilibrium." The picture of a rather idyllic middle-class society modeled on United States lines seems a short-term projection of present institutions, without allowing for the possibility that further technological developments and changes in economic structure may impose a "logic" of a different order.

Nevertheless, this four-author approach is commendable for attempting to conceive of the "labor movement" in broader terms than those of nineteenth-century capitalistic development.

Summary and evaluation

The sweeping canvases on which theorists of the labor movement have painted with broad brush strokes may obscure the immediate relevance of what they have to say. Their hypotheses are not simply academic exercises of no practical value but are aids to understanding what is going on within our own society, from the vantage point of the labor movement.

No effort will be made to point up all the areas of similarity and disagreement among the several theories which have been described, but we can profitably single out several matters for comment. First, the common thread which runs through all these analyses except the last is that labor unions have come into existence as devices to protect their members from the rigors of the competitive market. (The industrialization thesis suggests that in non-Western societies, unions have at times been initiated by governments as instruments of economic policy.) The free-market system is viewed by some (Polanyi, Tannenbaum) as antisocial and doomed, while others (Commons, Perlman) see it as subject to modification over time in ways that may limit market controls without destroying them.

The theorists are in greatest discord with respect to the continuing purpose of unionism. Commons, Perlman, and the Kerr-Dunlop-Harbison-Myers team regard unions as bargaining agents capable of pragmatic adaptations as the needs of their members dictate. Tannenbaum sees them as continuing into the future only as a systematic alternative to the welfare state; if the government intervenes with measures to provide the economic security on which workers insist, the trade-union approach will collapse. Polanyi anticipates that societies will be driven to collective economic planning for survival, and that unions have a future only if the choice comes down on the side of democratic, socialist systems in which unions can play a representative role. The orthodox Marxian view is that unions are only a tool for the accomplishment of a collectivist system, having no independent value.

Without attempting any assessment of the merits of these several approaches for other societies, let us concentrate on the labor movement in the United States. Let us see if it is possible to develop an eclectic view which uses the best of these contributions.

First, when we speak of the labor movement we must recognize that it is composed of many parts—the national unions and their numerous locals being the most important. These parts are in fact discrete special-interest groups, usually concerned with their own job interests and economic advantage. Far from constituting a federation of cohesive and fraternal units, the movement may often be looked on as a collection of internally feuding and antagonistic elements, each seeking its own advantage without respect to the interests of the others. This characteristic—the particularism of decentralized and relatively autonomous special-interest groups—is always present in some degree; it cannot be avoided.

But there is also the whole which the parts compose, the class interest which joins workers of all the particularistic units together in a common effort to secure greater advantage for their class as against other economic classes, and which unites them with respect to the threat of depression or unemployment, or to the challenge of the survival or strength of the constituent unions. Here the *movement*—the unitary interest—shows through.

It is evident from the theories we have examined that unionism tends to *arise* as a particularistic phenomenon—a spontaneous response to the needs of a group of workers, but before long it identifies its common interest with other workers in securing a modification of those aspects of the social and economic system which most threaten their welfare, and at this point the labor *movement* takes shape. But the rise of the movement does not do away with the special interests of the particularistic groups. The two interests—the special and the general—coexist, with one or the other at times becoming dominant. The particularistic or special-interest approach is characterized by job action, collective bargaining, business unionism, operating within the existing institutional framework. The unified movement is more directly concerned with social reform and operates through political channels rather than through job action.

It is probably an accurate generalization that in the United States, the special-interest aspects of unionism have been uppermost ever since the formation of the AFL in 1886, with the brief exception of the five-year period 1935 to 1940, which was marked by the rise of the CIO. While unions have made common cause with respect to certain pieces of legislation, and in recent years have engaged in more joint political activity than formerly, on the whole American unions have been concerned with their own special advantages. Jurisdictional strife has been a continuing phenomenon and for half a century has been largely responsible for the weakness of organizing drives. Competitive unionism and rival leadership, with one trying to outdo the other in gains, have been more common than cooperation.

Why should the particularism of unions so dominate the unitary character of the labor movement in the United States? The answer probably lies in one aspect of labor organizations which the several theories we have examined tend to neglect. Without exception, they treat unions as agents and representatives of workers. When there is recognition that at times unions have exploited the membership, there is (as in Tannenbaum) a belief that this evil can be remedied by making unions more responsive to their memberships. But what is overlooked is, as we noted in Chapter 5, that unions—once they have come into existence—inescapably acquire institutional interests of their own. They look to their own perpetuation, strength, and growth. Their organizational autonomy is buttressed by whatever stresses the importance of the job they are set up to do (collective bargaining), but threatened by whatever stresses the significance of functions which they, by themselves, are incapable of discharging (institutional reform through political action). Unions have vested interests in their own survival and hence can be expected to pursue strongly a continuation of the special-interest, job-action kind of unionism which is their special province. The individual unions of the AFL-CIO do not have much incentive to urge the formation of more effective political instruments, since this would undermine their own functions and threaten their autonomy.

The result is hardly surprising. American unions have become effective bargainers, winning substantial benefits for their own members in separate bargaining units, but the American labor movement has been relatively weak and ineffective in the field of social reform. Such institutional modifications as have come in the last half-century have, almost without exception, been sponsored by nonlabor groups (Perlman's "intellectuals"). At times reform legislation, such as unemployment compensation and old-age pensions, has even been opposed by labor unions which feared it would wean their members away and thus affect the organization's survival and the leadership's status.

It seems quite probable that most American workers prefer the separatist representation of their own special economic interests to any more political representation of their common interests, at least in "normal" times. The philosophy of opportunity consciousness, which Perlman ascribed to businessmen as *individuals,* seems also to characterize workers in *groups.* Each seeks to obtain as much for itself as it can. One might surmise that only a serious crisis, such as war or deep depression, might be sufficient to override the particularist sentiment of American workers and their union agents.

In any event, any theory of the labor movement must take account of the twofold role of labor organizations—as representatives of special interests and as representatives of class interests. The first is largely an economic function within an existing social framework; the second is largely a political function which looks to institutional reform. It is questionable whether both functions can be performed adequately by the same set of organizations. The two roles may actually conflict, at least to the extent that any institutional reforms weaken the collective-bargaining or job-action functions of unions or interfere with the freedom of such independent actions. When that is—or is feared to be—the case, one can expect that the interests of unions in their own survival and of union leaders in their own undiminished status will evoke a weak support of political action and reform and a strong endorsement of free collective bargaining. This is one reason why labor unions in the United States have, quite accurately, been called a conservative influence in our society.

ADDITIONAL READINGS

Industrial Relations Research Association: *Interpreting the Labor Movement,* 1952.

Kerr, Clark, John T. Dunlop, Frederick Harbison, and Charles A. Myers: *Industrialism and Industrial Man,* Harvard University Press, Cambridge, Mass., 1960.

Perlman, Mark: *Labor Union Theories in America,* Harper, New York, 1958.

Perlman, Selig: *A Theory of the Labor Movement,* Macmillan, New York, 1928.

Tannenbaum, Frank: *A Philosophy of Labor,* Knopf, New York, 1951.

Ulman, Lloyd: *The Rise of the National Trade Union,* Harvard University Press, Cambridge, Mass., 1955, part II.

FOR ANALYSIS AND DISCUSSION

1. What points of agreement and disagreement do you find among the "theories" discussed in this chapter?

2. With respect to the several theories examined, try to separate the conceptual and analytical content from the normative and philosophical content. (What *have* been the determinants of the development and behavior of the labor movement? What *should* be the role of the labor movement in society?)

3. What is the nature of the market or price system to which Polanyi refers? Catalog as many manifestations of his "social protection movement" as you can think of. Explain how these "social protections" interfere with the working of the market system.

4. Analyze the legal history of unionism in the United States, as set out in Chapters 8 and 9, from the viewpoint of John R. Commons, to indicate how judicial and legislative policies might be construed as efforts to build a set of working rules imposing reasonable limits on the exercise of private power.

5. Examine the psychological motivations around which Perlman and Tannenbaum construct their respective theories for their validity. How crucial is the psychological factor to their analyses?

6. List the principal characteristics which you think apply to the "industrialization" process on which Kerr, Dunlop, Harbison, and Myers rest their thesis. Do you agree that these "logically" drive all societies in the direction of open, representative, participating unions roughly comparable to those in the U.S.?

NOTES

1. Philip Taft, "Theories of the Labor Movement," in Industrial Relations Research Association, *Interpreting the Labor Movement,* 1952, p. 1.

2. Taft summarizes this Marxist position neatly in the same article, pp. 6–7 and 17–20.

3. William English Walling, "Industrialism or Revolutionary Unionism," *The New Review,* vol. 1, p. 88, Jan. 18, 1913. Italics in the original. Professor Taft has called to our attention that Walling later col-

laborated with some of the top AFL officials whom he here condemns by implication.

4. Daniel DeLeon, *The Burning Question of Trades Unionism: A Lecture at Newark, N.J., on April 21, 1904,* Socialist Party, New York, 1919, pp. 34–35, reproduced in Mark Perlman, *Labor Union Theories in America,* Harper, New York, 1958, p. 79.

5. Eugene V. Debs, *Unionism and Socialism: A Plea for Both,* Terre Haute, Ind., 1904, p. 26, reproduced in Perlman, *Labor Union Theories in America,* p. 98.

6. Karl Polanyi, *The Great Transformation,* Holt, New York, 1944.

7. John R. Commons, "American Shoemakers, 1648–1895: A Sketch of Industrial Evolution," *Quarterly Journal of Economics,* November, 1909, pp. 39–84.

8. Lloyd Ulman, *The Rise of the National Trade Union,* Harvard University Press, Cambridge, Mass., 1955, especially part II.

9. Commons's examination of the bargaining relations and transactions between organized groups was set forth in general terms, applicable to economic society generally, rather than as a theory of the labor movement. The role of the labor movement and the methods of its functioning are simply one instance of the way economic power is manipulated in a free economy. Commons's thinking was set out at exhaustive length in his trilogy, *The Legal Foundations of Capitalism,* Macmillan, New York, 1924, *Institutional Economics,* Macmillan, New York, 1934, and *The Economics of Collective Action,* Macmillan, New York, 1950. A summary analysis of his position is provided in Neil W. Chamberlain, "Institutional Economics of John R. Commons," in C. E. Ayres and others, *Institutional Economics: Veblen, Commons, and Mitchell Reconsidered,* University of California Press, Berkeley, 1963, pp. 63–94.

10. Chamberlain, p. 93.

11. Selig Perlman, *A Theory of the Labor Movement,* Macmillan, New York, 1928.

12. The same, pp. 5–6.

13. Tannenbaum's three major contributions in this area are *The Labor Movement,* Putnam, New York, 1921, "The Social Function of Trade Unionism," in the *Political Science Quarterly,* vol. 62, June, 1947, elaborated in *A Philosophy of Labor,* Knopf, New York, 1951.

14. Tannenbaum, *A Philosophy of Labor,* p. 60.

15. The same, p. 106.

16. The same, p. 136.

17. The same, p. 137.

18. The same, pp. 142–143.

19. The same, pp. 150–151.

20. The same, p. 168.

21. Clark Kerr, John T. Dunlop, Frederick Harbison, and Charles A. Myers, *Industrialism and Industrial Man,* Harvard University Press, Cambridge, Mass., 1960.

PART FOUR

LABOR AS A FACTOR OF PRODUCTION

From the perspective of the household, labor constitutes a source of income, the means by which a family ties itself into a pecuniary economy. The inflow of food, clothing, and creature comforts depends upon an inflow of funds, and for most households the principal source of funds is the jobs of their members.

"Labor" also means the constituency of the labor unions and of the labor movement. Unions represent the interests of their members in the amount of their earnings, the conditions under which they work, and the security they feel in their jobs. Unions also acquire organizational interests in their own survival and introduce a variety of practices which look to their own security and continuity.

Labor as a source of profit

Some of these practices—whether undertaken on behalf of the security of their members in their jobs or of the organization in its own survival—importantly affect the management of a business firm. To the private firm, "labor" is first and foremost an input in a production process. The results of that production process enter into the flow of goods and services coming onto the market, the chief customers for which are the workers and their families. But the process is undertaken, in an enterprise society such as that of the United States, only in the expectation of making a profit. "Labor" is hired only if it is expected to be profitable. If it ceases to make money for the firm, it is dismissed.

From the viewpoint of the firm, then, labor is primarily a factor of production. It is something to be hired, assigned to particular jobs, transferred as needed, structured into appropriate production relationships with other men and machines, and induced to be efficient in its performance—all for the goal of a satisfactory profit. This does not mean that management is not concerned with workers as human beings. Most managers have as much of the "human feel" as other people. It is simply that in their very function, and in the function of a business firm, managers must be concerned first with the economic performance of the organization. If the firm does not make a profit, it will soon cease operations—and cease to provide jobs. Thus the price of staying in business is making an adequate profit, which necessitates treating labor as an input rather than as people. Or, more correctly, it involves treating labor as *both* an input and as people. This imposes a dual obligation on the firm—it must consider both abstract economic values and very real human values. The function of the personnel office is somehow to make these two responsibilities compatible.

The "typical" firm

It is not simple to describe the characteristics of the American firm, but we can say that small-size firms predominate. A great many of these little establishments are family operations, really little more than an extension of the household. Others are members of trade associations and industry groups, sometimes in industries where small firms tend to be characteristic, such as in retail trade, the manufacture of clothing, laundries, and construction. At the other extreme, roughly the top one percent of the business population by themselves account for about half of all business, all assets, and all employees. The big firms, especially in the manufacturing area, are likely to spread across a number of industries and to operate numerous establishments on a nationwide and indeed worldwide front.

Which type of firm is then more representative of American business? The Jones & Co. Hardware Store or General Motors, the Excell TV Sales and Repair Service or General Electric? It all depends on what we mean by representative. But if we wish to identify the business characteristics which *distinguish* the American economy and to locate the principal centers of economic power, there can be no doubt that we would have to concentrate on the relatively small number of large corporations around which so much of total business activity focuses—such as the supply of materials and parts to them by networks of small establishments, and the marketing of their products by hundreds of thousands of wholesale and retail outlets.

The managers

Who are the men who exercise control over these mammoth business organizations which play such an important role in the American economy? We have very little information on their much more numerous small-business counterparts, but there have been several major investigations of the men in command of the giants. Our most authoritative source is a study undertaken in 1952 by two researchers, then at the University of Chicago, who obtained their information from questionnaire responses of 8,300 top-management people in American business.* (More recent but more limited studies support their general conclusions.)

Of the executives in this survey, the average individual entered upon his business career shortly after reaching the age of twenty-one. It took him approxi-

* W. Lloyd Warner and James C. Abeggven, *Occupational Mobility in American Business and Industry,* The University of Minnesota Press, Minneapolis, 1955.

mately twenty-four years to reach his present position. He was now approaching fifty-four. The chances were high that he had never engaged in manual labor. Only 12 percent of the sons of big business executives had had such work experience, and even among the sons of manual laborers, less than one-fourth had worked with their hands. Their entrance into the world of work had been in white-collar and professional jobs for the most part, reflecting their advanced educational training.

It would appear from these and other statistics assembled in this extensive survey that although a significant number of our management leaders have risen from humble origins (perhaps as many as one-fourth), the probabilities are three to one that they come from families with a business or professional orientation, that they have received college training, and that they have never worked with their hands but have pursued careers calling for the manipulation of words and ideas and people.

The world of such business leaders is vastly different from the world of the workers on their payrolls, as well as from the world of the union leaders with whom they sometimes deal either at first- or second-hand. If it is true, as it has been reasonably maintained, that one cannot genuinely understand the sentiments of the men in the shops unless he has worked alongside them, then it must be true that the men at the mahogany desks can never attain full comprehension of the wants and needs of the men for whom they hold themselves responsible—of the men whom the union leader comes to represent.

But the student would be making an egregious error if, somehow, he were to treat this conclusion as critical of management. For it can equally be maintained that the man in the shop, and the union leader who represents him, can never have a clear conception of the duties and desires of the man who runs the business. They live in different societies, in different worlds, though their paths sometimes cross; as men of good will, each has often made earnest efforts to comprehend the structure of the other's living and thinking, with more or less success, but, necessarily, always with more or less failure too.

The statistical findings given here relate primarily to large business firms whose gross annual incomes are measured in millions of dollars. There is no clear indication of their applicability to smaller firms, though it is the judgment of Warner and Abegglen that smaller firms would be less likely to provide opportunities for upward mobility and would be more likely to maintain preferred positions for those in elite groups.

Value structure

In the hierarchy of aspirations characterizing management personnel, goal motivation tends to take the form of specific but ever-changing objectives: consummating a particular deal, developing a new product or process, achieving a larger share of the market, increasing the firm's profit, forcing the growth of the business. Such focused objectives are in contrast to the less driving aspirations of workers for satisfactory "states," such as participation in a stable work group, good relationships with supervisors, opportunities to savor the manualist's pleasure in good workmanship, a standard of living that compares favorably with that of their friends and neighbors. Yet both groups—management, with its driving ambitions, and the work force, with its search for social satisfactions and security—must seek the realization of their desires through the same medium, the business enterprise. Small wonder, then, that conflict is unavoidable. The very actions taken by management to achieve a more profitable concern, to pass competitors in sales, to perfect a product before a rival accomplishes the same thing, and so on, may create changes in the company's operation that threaten the status achieved by the work group. And the actions of the work force, such as setting limits on output, restricting the transfer of men among jobs, rationing opportunities for advancement instead of letting the best man win, and protesting time-and-motion study, create obstacles to management's achieving its goals.

The very vocabularies of the two groups reflect their different orientation. "Efficiency" has a good connotation to management, a bad one to the work group. "Security" implies a static and a stagnant state to management, protection in a desirable way of life to the work group. In management's lexicon, "ability" is something to be rewarded; to the men in the shop, it tends to connote a way of weaseling a long-service man out of his rightful due. While management speaks of "incentives," the union man speaks of "rate busters." To many businessmen, "scientific management" represents an ideal to be achieved; to many workers, a conception of the devil.

In previous chapters we have examined this conflict of interests and values in the shaping of labor legislation and in the negotiation of union–management contracts. In this section, we want to take a closer look at terms such as "efficiency," "productivity," and "labor costs"—terms which understandably dominate the thinking of any employer, unionized or not, in deploying labor within his firm. Then we shall focus on some of the ways in which management, through the personnel function, attempts to meet its dual obligation to treat labor as both an input and as people.

To a worker, the most significant aspect of his job is the money income he derives from it—his earnings. There may be other important elements of satisfaction or dissatisfaction attaching to the work process itself, but despite their importance we can be sure of one thing: He would not be at the job unless it paid him money. He might be willing to put up with poor working conditions or an unreasonable supervisor or an uncongenial work crew or a monotonous operation, at least as long as nothing better was available, but he would not put up for a moment with the discipline of a job that did not pay him money.

His pecuniary earnings come, if he is a manual worker, in the form of an hourly wage rate times the number of hours he works. If he is a white-collar employee, they usually are paid in the form of a "salary"—which is simply a wage rate for a period longer than an hour, usually a week, sometimes a month. An electrician says, "I make $5 an hour." A typist says, "I make $100 a week."

To the employer who pays the wage or salary, however, the important consideration is not simply the rate. The employee may be concerned with income, but the employer is concerned with cost. And costs depend on more than the rate; they depend as much on what is obtained for the rate. An employer would rather pay $5 an hour to someone who could produce 100 units of output than $4 an hour to someone who could produce only 50. The lower rate does not compensate for the fact that what it buys is proportionately even less. This is almost embarrassingly obvious, but we sometimes fail to keep this consideration in sight when the circumstances become a little more complicated.

What the employer is most concerned with in the employment relationship, then, is the labor cost of his output. What the worker is concerned with is income. They are looking at "wages" from different points of view, and this at times leads to friction and at other times facilitates compromise and agreement. In this chapter we shall not attempt to explore how these two points of view may become reconciled, but shall limit ourselves to setting out some of the complexities that are involved in translating a wage rate or salary into a cost of production. We shall be dealing with technical relationships primarily and human relationships only insofar as they are relevant.

Wage rates and occupational classifications

The point of departure for management as well as for workers is the rate or salary for a job. This is compounded of two elements. One is the average wage *level* of the company in comparison with other companies in the same industry or the same community. Is the company a "good payer" or a "poor payer"? On the average, do its rates tend to be 10 cents higher than those of other companies with which it may be compared, or 10 cents lower, or about the same? The wage level is necessarily bargained out with the union in any company which is organized.

But to speak of "average" wage levels is to speak in abstractions. The wage-rate *structure* of a company is the reality with which management and union and workers must deal. By wage-rate structure we mean the way in which the complex of jobs in a business are sorted out and assigned specific wage rates. How much does one position pay in relation to another? Is job A worth 10 cents more or 10 cents less than job B?

The principal basis for distinguishing the worth of one job relative to another is functional. The rate attaches to a cluster of duties which are collectively termed an "occupation" (not in the career sense which we encountered in Chapter 3 but in the sense of a particular assignment). But before examining the wage-rate structure in the firm, let us take a quick look at occupational distinctions in the economy at large, since these set limits to what the firm is free to do.

Occupations are like industries in the respect that the number of occupations which can be separately identified depends on the degree of detail in the occupational descriptions. If the descriptions are precise, the number of "different" occupations can run into the hundreds of thousands. If job descriptions are based on only a few major job characteristics, the number of occupational categories can be reduced to three—skilled, semiskilled, and unskilled. The differences in wage rates between occupational groups are usually referred to as occupational or skill "differentials." They have both an economic and a social significance.

Occupational differentials are economically important for two primary reasons. First, they are intended to offer an inducement to workers to undertake jobs requiring more energy, attentiveness, responsibility, and capability. Jobs make demands on their occupants; the more demanding a job, the greater the inducement which may be necessary to get someone to fill it. If less exacting positions paid just as much as the more difficult occupations, a great many people might be disposed to take things easy. A higher wage rate attaching to the more demanding job may overcome this disposition. In such instances, the additional pay is regarded as compensation for the increased real costs on the job.

In other instances, however, real costs on the more highly remunerated jobs are actually less than on lower-rated employments. There are many who would consider the role of a skilled machinist to be much pleasanter and actually easier (in terms of physical demands) than the role of helper or janitor. The additional real costs connected with being a machinist come not on the job so much as in the preparation for the job—in the years when earnings are passed up while a skill is being mastered, the years when apprenticeship is being served or when the expenses of education are being paid. Once the skill has been acquired, a differential wage advantage may not be necessary to get a worker to practice that skill. Even if wage rates for machinist and custodian were identical, the trained machinist would still prefer to follow his craft. The wage advantage which he receives is designed less to induce him to undertake that job than to induce others—presently without training—to undergo the sacrifices which he has already incurred, for the benefit to be gained in the future.

Both these economic functions of wage differentials are important: to induce workers to accept more exacting assignments, and to induce workers to incur the costs of training and education.

Wage differentials also perform a social function. They help in determining social status within the work group. Although often there are characteristics of the jobs themselves which make certain jobs more prestigious than others, the wage rates attaching to them in part symbolize and in part create the social distinctions in the work group. "From this standpoint, the important thing is not the absolute level of the wage, but its level *relative* to the wage rates of others with whom the worker thinks he should be compared."[1]

Workers have often expressed their feelings on the subject. From a pattern maker: "I'm a very skilled worker doing a very skilled job; yet I get less money than carpenters. . . . And the carpenters are really only hammer jockeys, while I have to be a carpenter, a wood carver, a machinist, an architect, and an artist. I should get more than a carpenter." And from a toolmaker: "Well, sometimes the unskilled workers on piecework can make as much as we do and more. Of course the company tries to offset that. They give us a bonus, but I don't think it's quite fair."

Wage differentials must thus perform the dual economic purposes just mentioned and at the same time satisfy reasonably well the function of mirroring social status. Sometimes these separate functions come into conflict, as when it is necessary to pay high rates to get someone to perform an unpleasant task. Only a person at the lower end of the work hierarchy will take on the job, but at the same time he will earn more than his "superiors" in the work society.

Strains also arise when a traditional wage relationship is upset for any reason. In the public sector, for example, many cities have long paid their police and firemen precisely the same salaries, just as society has accorded them roughly equal status. But in the 1960s, the policeman's job became more difficult (or at least more politically sensitive) under the impact of rising crime rates, the demand for more "law and order," the many demonstrations and riots ranging from the campus to the ghetto, and other forms of social turmoil. As a result, policemen are now insisting that they deserve higher salaries than firemen for reasons of both equity and recruitment, asking who would apply for a police job today if he could get the same money by becoming a fireman? Firemen, on the other hand, argue that their jobs are just as hazardous as those of the police and they are bitterly resisting every attempt to destroy the traditional wage parity between these occupations, for that would mean a serious loss of status for firemen.

The occupational wage structure within the firm

Prior to the advent of a union in a company, determination of wage policy lies within the control of management. Because market forces allow a considerable area of discretion, the occupational wage structure which develops within a firm is not likely to be systematic unless management has consciously sought to introduce system into it.

Historically, many managements (at a time when they were independent of unions) paid each employee a rate which had been agreed upon individually. Consequently, employees with similar skills and engaged in similar operations were seldom paid the same rate; the rate for each would depend upon the time at which he had been hired, who had hired him, how badly he had needed a job, personality characteristics or kinship ties which might dictate favored treatment, and so on. Each rate was a personal rate rather than a rate for an occupation.

These illogical rate relationships frequently led to a sense of injustice on the part of workers, such as is reflected in the workers' comments cited earlier. Once a union had organized such a firm, the management would be faced with protests over discriminatory wage treatment, processed through the grievance procedure. A deluge of grievances alleging "inequities" would then follow. This pattern of events is illustrated in the case of United States Steel:[2]

Some of the first grievances filed by the union following its recognition by U.S.S. in 1936 were concerned with inequities in intraplant wage rates. An agreement signed in 1937 emphasized the need for a study of wage problems in the steel industry; one organization for instance, employing 160,000 men, had more than 25,000 wage rates operating in their plants.

Wages in the main were determined by departmental and plant supervisors without recourse to a central department. Consequently groups of men doing similar work in different parts of the mill were paid varying wage rates. There were also jobs with similar titles in various parts of a mill but with different duties attached to them and no standards by which the work could be classified; there were no fixed wage scales and no established means of determining the equity of any given rate. Considerable discrepancy also existed between different mills.

In an attempt to deal with this situation the 1937 agreement specified that where wage inequities existed they could be taken up for local adjustment and settlement. It soon became apparent that inequities could not be successfully dealt with on a case to case basis. The adjustment of one wage rate merely emphasized the need to adjust related wage rates; and the situation if anything became worse.

Faced with the necessity of rationalizing why one job should pay more, or less, than another, managements were forced into more formal and planned methods of determining wage relationships. Some managements, it is true, had anticipated this development even before unionization of their plants, but the impetus to rationalization of a firm's wage structure has come in great part from union demands for the adjustment of wage inequities.

Obviously, what is needed is some system of *classifying* jobs in some way that permits their *evaluation*. Equally obviously, there is no single one best method of accomplishing this. A variety of systems have been devised. Basically, however, they can be grouped into two broad approaches, which may be referred to as "job ranking" and "factor comparison."

Both begin by identifying each functionally distinct job by precisely drawn job descriptions. These are designed not to spell out in detail every aspect of a job, but to identify its principal functions and the relative frequency with which they are performed. The second step is then to compare all the jobs, as they have been described, to establish their relative value.

In the job-ranking approach, which is used by the large automobile companies, for example, perhaps a dozen well-known jobs with considerable variation in job content are ranked in relation to one another. The ranking may be done by a committee working together, or by evaluators who work independently and then compare results and discuss differences of judgment. The result is a kind of "ladder" of jobs, arranged in order of worth—a short ladder, to be sure, but the various "steps" of which are easily understood and appreciated. Then every other job, as it has been described, is slotted into the ladder at the point where the evaluators judge that it is worth more than one of the "bench-mark" jobs but less than the bench-mark job next highest on the ladder. Then, depending on the wage rate which has been decided on for the upper and lower ends of the ladder (the wage *level,* as determined by where

the company prefers to place itself in terms of community and industry wage levels—something we shall examine in a later chapter), all other jobs can be given rates which conform to their relative position on the ladder.

Variations on this occur. A number of jobs whose descriptions differ may nevertheless be sufficiently similar to be grouped together under a broader job title or classification, thereby reducing the number of wage-rate classes. Workers on an assembly line, for example, perform a variety of specialized tasks in serial fashion, so that their individual job descriptions differ. Yet all of them do perform assembly-line work of roughly comparable difficulty and exactness, making it possible to lump them all together in a classification of "assembler" and to give them all the same rate.

Under this system, the number of classifications in a large company may still be quite large. The number of rates would be vastly reduced in contrast to that in a system of informal, personal rate setting, yet it might still run to as many as a thousand separate classifications, each slotted into the wage-rate ladder at the particular level where it is judged to be roughly equal in value to other jobs on that same level and appropriately more or less relative to the worth of the adjacent bench-mark jobs.

In large-scale establishments where work processes are complex, it becomes increasingly difficult to compare whole jobs, however. There is some tendency to break jobs down into their several aspects. This job is more demanding than that one in terms of physical effort but requires much less concentration. Job X can be learned in a day, but it takes at least a month to get to know the ropes of job Y. Identifying the relevant aspects of jobs, by which they can be compared, in reality establishes the *criteria* for determining their relative worth. What elements of a job contribute to its value? Skill? Responsibility? Effort required? Then how much of each of these is embodied in job A, how much in job B, and so on?

This is the type of job evaluation known as factor comparison (or, in a popular variant, the point system). Its use can be illustrated by the plan introduced into United States Steel to eliminate the chaotic situation previously described.

Since the criteria by which jobs are to be judged

(the job factors) are not all of the same importance, they must be weighted. In the United States Steel plan, twelve job factors are considered in estimating the value of any job:

Job Factor	Maximum weight
Preemployment training	1.0
Employment training and experience	4.0
Mental skill	3.5
Manual skill	2.0
Responsibility for materials	10.0
Responsibility for tools and equipment	4.0
Responsibility for operations	6.5
Responsibility for safety of others	2.0
Mental effort	2.5
Physical effort	2.5
Surroundings	3.0
Hazards	2.0

As many gradations or levels of each of these factors as are believed to be distinguishable are provided for. Thus three levels of preemployment training and experience are defined, nine levels of employment training and experience, six levels of mental skill, five of manual skill, and so on. A judgment is made as to the level of each of the twelve factors which is appropriate to the job being valued, and the numerical weight computed. If there are five levels of manual skill, for example, and the maximum weight for that factor is 2.0, a job which requires very little manual skill (say that of a common laborer or messenger) would be rated at the first level and given a numerical weight of 0.4 for that factor.

Each job is scored for each of the twelve factors, being given a rating or weight for each. The total for all factors is then summed, and this score, when rounded to the nearest whole number, is known as the job class. There is a total of thirty-two job classes, and every hourly rated job falls into one of these thirty-two classes. For each class there is a specific wage rate, and the rate for any individual is the rate of his job class. Instead of thousands of individual rates, there are just thirty-two job-class rates which are applicable to all employees.[3] The rate for any job can be justified in relation to the rate for any other job, by reference to the relative requirements of the two jobs.

In the United States Steel case this job-evaluation plan and the job ratings made under it were agreed upon by company and union. As a result, the union was willing to concede that the rate for a job, once determined, would not be changed unless the job changed so that, on rerating, it fell into a different job class. In most instances when a job-evaluation plan is introduced, however, management makes the ratings on its own. Usually these are subject to initial challenge by the union, but once they have been in effect for a specified time—perhaps thirty days—they are presumed to remain effective without further challenge, unless there is a substantial change in the nature of the job.

Except in those relatively few instances when unions have participated in setting up the job-evaluation plan and in the rating of individual jobs, they have tended to be critical of this method of formalizing the wage structure. Their chief objection is that job evaluation tends to freeze the rate of pay for each job on the basis of some predetermined formula. The application of this formula may create inequities in the process of removing others. As one authority has said:[4]

> Strong social relations are built up around existing wage differentials. One job may be regarded as better than another simply because it has always paid more. The question whether or not it is worth more may be of more importance to the analyst than to the workers. The prestige of a promotion secured after many years of waiting can be destroyed by a reevaluation of jobs. The vividness with which workers recall changes made many years earlier and their persistence in seeking to restore the old relationships if the changes were to their disadvantage again emphasize the strength of custom.

In general, the unions prefer to remain free to negotiate and renegotiate wage rates attaching to classes of jobs rather than to have the rate ground out "mechanically," once and for all, by a process over which they have relatively little control.

Also, it should be noted that job evaluation, like time study and many other tools of "scientific management," is seldom applied to supervisors, managers, or professional workers. Obviously, it is easier to compare routinized and manual jobs than to compare, say, the positions of research chemist and purchasing agent. Yet, it can also be seen why a blue-collar worker may have an ambivalent attitude toward job evaluation: It does help to eliminate wage inequities within manual occupations, but it further highlights the difference between the blue-collar world—in which jobs are assumed to be so standardized that they can be catalogued for comparison—and the white-collar world in which each job is so interesting (that is, so unpredictable and open-ended) that each manager and each professional must, within limits, be judged as an individual and not as a standard unit of input.

Employment costs or labor-related costs

Wage rates and salaries are not the only remuneration workers receive, nor the only costs to which employers obligate themselves when they employ workers. The additional employment costs can be classified in a variety of ways, but the following is perhaps as simple a classification as any.

First, there are the wage rates attaching to the job, as we have already seen. (We shall restrict ourselves to time payment for the moment and discuss piecework payments later.)

Second, there are wage supplements attaching to the worker himself. These typically come in the form of "merit increases" (an extra which is paid over and above some base rate for the job, presumably related to the quality of the worker's performance) or increases based on service (an increment paid either automatically at stated intervals or nonperiodically in the company's discretion "for faithful service").

Third, there are fringe benefits (vacations, holidays, pensions, et cetera) which are matters of managerial discretion or the result of collective bargaining.

Fourth, there are legislatively provided benefits, for which an employer pays, such as social security. These are neither discretionary nor negotiable, but compulsory.

Fifth, there are premium payments in connection with the work process itself, such as overtime payments and shift differentials.

Sixth, there are a variety of indirect costs which an employer incurs simply by being an employer, such as the expenses of running a personnel office, maintaining a nurse on the premises, operating a company cafeteria or recreation room, and so on. A number of these expenses may be impounded in some general accounting category such as "administrative overhead," but they nevertheless represent costs which have been incurred in the company's role as employer.

Few companies know the actual costs of the sum of these items, but they amount to a substantial proportion of the wage bill. Table 15-1 lists the average expenditures in 1,181 companies in 1965 on most of the major types of wage "extras." Although these are often lumped under the heading of fringe benefits, that term has no precise definition. Some people, for example, would not consider paid rest periods a fringe benefit but would include (as Table 15-1 does not) shift differentials and overtime premiums. Also, notice that the table includes no estimates of indirect labor costs such as the expense of maintaining a personnel department or a dispensary.

In spite of these definitional problems, it is probably safe to say that these various wage and salary supplements now total 20 to 30 percent of total labor compensation in the average firm, and by any measure these costs have literally mushroomed over recent years. There are no comparable surveys of employers' expenditures on these supplements in the years before the advent of the welfare state and widespread unionism in the 1930s, but they surely must have averaged well under 5 percent of payroll. Even in the postwar period, one sample of eighty-four companies showed that fringe payments rose from 16 percent of payroll in 1947 to 28 percent in 1965. And though the level of fringe payments varies widely among industries and companies, these benefits are seldom a direct substitute for higher wages. On the contrary, fringe benefits are usually higher in those industries and plants with high average wages and salaries than in those with low wages and salaries.[5]

In summary, "labor cost" means something far more complicated than the average wage or salary multiplied by the number of employees in a firm. Both the employer and the employee are vitally concerned with the way in which job rates are distributed around that average and with the size and content of those supplements to the basic wage which add greatly to the employee's income and security—and to the employer's cost of doing business.

Productivity

It is not simply the aggregate labor cost which is important to a producer, however. As has already been noted, he is equally interested in what he obtains for his expenditure. It is an input-output relationship which concerns him—what he gets out for what he puts in.

Basically, of course, he is concerned with this relationship in money terms—how much income he derives from the sale of his output, how much he has had to spend to obtain that output, and how much is left over (profit). But so many elements enter into determining these pecuniary relationships that it is necessary, for meaningful analysis, to dig below them. His money receipts depend on the quantity of his output times the price he gets per unit. His costs depend on the quantity of inputs (labor, material, equipment) times the price he has to pay for them per unit of output. The quantity of output may be rising relative to the quantity of input, evidencing an increase in productive efficiency, but this effect may be offset by adverse price movements. The price of his product may be falling because of stiffer competition or of changing consumer tastes, or the price of his inputs may be rising, perhaps because of effective union bargaining or of greater demand in the factor markets. Thus, in order to analyze the cause of any change in his profit position, the producer must disentangle the physical input-output relationships in his production process from the price relationships in the markets in which he operates.

The relationship between physical input and physical output is known as "productivity." Productivity is a measure of efficiency. It could, for example, refer to the efficiency of a machine—how many thermal units of heat per ton of fuel consumed, how many miles per gallon of gasoline. It could also refer to a ballplayer's batting average—how many hits he produced for the number of times at bat. It is always the input-output relationship that productivity measures.

Table 15-1 *Fringe Payments in 1965*

Type of payment	Percent of payroll
Total fringe payments	24.7
Legally required payments*	4.9
Old Age, Survivors, and Disability Insurance	2.7
Unemployment insurance	1.4
Workmen's compensation	0.7
Other	0.1
Private welfare plans*	7.7
Pensions	3.7
Health, accident, and life insurance	3.0
Supplemental unemployment benefits	0.1
Separation or termination pay	0.1
Discounts on goods and services purchased by employees	0.2
Employee meals furnished by company	0.3
Other	0.3
Paid leave	7.7
Vacations	4.1
Holidays	2.6
Sick leave	0.7
Military, jury, witness, voting, and personal leave	0.3
Paid rest periods, lunch periods, wash-up time, travel time, clothes-change time, etc.	2.5
Other items (profit-sharing, thrift plans, Christmas bonuses, suggestion awards, etc.)	1.9

* Employer's share only.

SOURCE: Chamber of Commerce of the United States, *Fringe Benefits—1965*, Washington, 1966, p. 9.

This definition should help to clear away one common misconception. Frequently individuals tend to identify productivity with production. Production, however, deals with only one of our variables—output. It does not express a rate, but simply a quantity. Productivity relates two variables—input and output. It always expresses a rate rather than an absolute quantity—so much of one thing per unit of something else.

Indeed, it is entirely possible for production to be rising while productivity is falling, and vice versa. During World War II, for example, when many people were drawn into the labor force who had had no previous training and who had mental and physical characteristics that in normal times would have prevented their being hired, and when plants and factories that otherwise would have been abandoned as uneconomic were called back into production, many firms secured greater output through the application of a vastly augmented input. But even though production was rising, productivity in some instances declined. The augmented factors of production, by sheer number, turned out more goods than before, but because many operations were less efficiently conducted than in normal times, there was less production per unit of input.

On the other hand, in a time of depression, firms are driven to the most economical operations possible just as a matter of survival. Under this circumstance, a drop in production may actually be accompanied by an increase in productivity—less is produced, but what is produced is produced more efficiently. An inverse relationship between production and productivity is not usual, but the fact that it is possible should establish clearly in one's mind not only that they are not the same thing but that they may even not move sympathetically.

When we refer to productivity in economic affairs we are interested in some measure of the input-output relationship in producing goods and services. This gives rise to a variety of technical problems of measurement with which we cannot here be concerned. Suffice it to say that the procedure which has become commonly accepted is to measure industrial productivity as a ratio of output, expressed in constant prices, to man-hours of input. It would be preferable if output too could be expressed in physical units, but since most plants produce a number of products, this is not usually feasible even at the company level, let alone for the economy as a whole. Hence, the practice is normally to take value of output, statistically adjusted to eliminate the effect of price movements, as the most reasonable approximation of physical output.

Why should man-hours be used as a measure of input, when not only labor but also capital, materials, and managerial skills are necessary to production and may even be more responsible

than labor for any improvement in productivity? Actually, productivity could theoretically be measured in terms of any of the inputs, since it is only an expression of output per some unit of input. The difficulty comes in finding an adequate measure of the input factor. It is hard to think of any unit which measures the capital input quite as neatly as the man-hour measures the labor input. But the fact that man-hours are taken as measuring productivity (and the productivity measure is therefore referred to as "labor productivity") carries no implication that any discernible increase in efficiency is due to labor. The term "labor productivity" means only that productivity is being measured in terms of man-hours of labor.

In fact, anything that affects the amount of output and anything that affects the number of man-hours used will have its impact on productivity. Obviously, the quality and the number of the tools which workers use will influence the amount of time they must spend in producing goods. So will the quality of the raw materials on which they work. Management's ability to organize the work process, to take advantage of new methods, to standardize production, and so on, certainly has an important bearing on how much labor is required to turn out a given amount of goods. Other important factors are the amount of capital available to management, government policies that limit the degree of monopoly and encourage competition, the size of business operations, and the level of economic activity as this affects the level of operations in the firm. Even the weather can play its part in determining how much output there will be in terms of a man-hour of activity. This is obvious in farming, but it is also true in some industrial operations where the amount of moisture in the air or degrees of heat and cold affect the materials that are being worked. All these things have their effect on labor productivity.

To be sure, such things as the degree of skill of the workers, their educational and intelligence levels, their health, morale, adaptability, geographic mobility, motivation, and attitudes also vitally affect how much output will be achieved from so many man-hours of input. But, to repeat, when we speak of labor productivity, we do not mean how much production may be imputed to workers in comparison with management or capital, for example, or the extent to which workers are responsible for the level of production; we mean simply to identify the particular unit of input in terms of which we are measuring the ability of an economic organization to produce goods.

Perhaps this point can be made clearer by analogy. One frequent measure of the operating performance of a car is the number of miles it will run on a gallon of gas. If a car gets 8 miles a gallon, we say it has a poorer performance than if it achieves 15 miles a gallon. But none of us would ever argue that, although we *measure* the car's efficiency in terms of gallons of gasoline, it is the gasoline which *determines* the car's efficiency. If the car's performance were poor, we might tinker with the carburetor, or get new spark plugs, or change the points. We *might* also change the kind of gasoline we were using. Any of these things could have an effect on the car's ability to get more miles per gallon of gas. But the use of the particular input, gallons of gasoline, as a measure of the car's performance by no means implies that the gasoline is solely responsible for the car's efficiency. No more do we imply, by using labor units to measure industrial performance, that labor is solely responsible for any change in performance.

Social and private productivity

It is now time that we take note of an important distinction—the distinction between social productivity and private (or company) productivity. So much has been said in recent years about the use of productivity as a standard for noninflationary wage settlements (a topic which we shall examine in considerable detail in a later chapter) that the idea has taken root that the *measure* of productivity for the economy as a whole is somehow equally relevant to the individual company. If labor productivity (total output divided by man-hours) represents the economy's efficiency, then presumably labor productivity in the individual company (its output, measured in constant prices, divided by total man-hours) is equally a measure of corporate efficiency. But this is hardly the case.

From the point of view of society as a whole,

over the long run any increase in the output per man-hour of input is the source of an improved standard of living. There is more to go around. The productive effort of every individual has a higher payoff. It is immaterial how that result has been achieved—by the accumulation of capital, by superior industrial organization and management, by a more highly skilled work force. The simple fact is that output, as measured by man-hours of input, has risen, indicating that the same expenditure of labor can produce a bigger bundle of goods to be divided, or that a bundle of goods of the same size as was previously produced can now be turned out in fewer man-hours so that there is more leisure to be divided. No attribution is intended, as we have noted. No one says that people are entitled to more income because they have worked harder. It is a simple statistical relationship that is involved, an average for the economy as a whole, and an abstraction having no counterpart in real life. A 3 percent increase in productivity does not mean that there now exists 3 percent more of something real called "productivity"; it indicates only that insofar as statisticians can make all the appropriate allowances, on the basis of less than adequate data, on the average the economy seems to be able to turn out 3 percent more goods this year than last, with the same number of man-hours.

But the relevance of this figure to any individual firm is not very great. We can, of course, say that the abstract statistical average was derived from the operations of all the individual firms in the economy, taken together, so that any improvement in productivity in the economy had to have its origins in individual firms. But as desirable as an increase in productivity is to society as a whole, it does not constitute the same objective for the firm. This can be quite simply demonstrated. It would be perfectly possible for many companies to double their output per man-hour if they used company resources without stint to buy the best capital equipment and to continue buying it right up to the point where it added even a minute increment of output per man-hour. The purpose of such a policy would be to seek the maximum output per man-hour possible— the highest level of labor productivity within the company's reach. It would also be a very foolish and profitless policy for any company to follow, since it would ignore the matter of the return on its capital investment, substituting for profit, as its goal, the meaningless "efficiency" ratio of output per man-hour. What would it matter to a company if it achieved the highest labor-productivity ratio in the nation, if it lost even a dollar of profit in the doing?

We thus return to the point made earlier: An employer must be concerned with both the *physical* input-output relationships in his internal operations and the *price* relationships in the markets in which he operates. This conclusion may seem obvious, but consider the arguments that occur when a union urges an employer to increase wages in step with his firm's productivity increases.

On the one hand, some employers attack such a proposal for all the wrong reasons, claiming that if wages go up as fast as the firm's productivity, labor is unfairly capturing *all* the savings from the efficiency increases that probably were stimulated by better management or equipment. Any union negotiator can nail that argument with no trouble. Assume that a firm turned out 100 units of a product last year and 105 units this year, using the same number of man-hours each year. Then, all other things equal, the firm's total revenues as well as productivity have gone up 5 percent and *each factor* of production can get a 5 percent increase in returns without changing its share of total revenues. Also, this 5 percent increase in wages, salaries, dividends, rent, and interest payments will have no effect on the firm's price structure because they are all offset by the productivity increase; hence, *unit* costs end up the same as in the previous year. In this limited sense, unions are right in arguing that some employers have woefully misinterpreted the productivity measure.

On the other hand, note the crucial assumption in the union's argument that all other things are equal in these two years of the firm's life. If the unit price of the firm's output drops for any reason in the second year, then where is that 5 percent bonanza in total revenues to come from? And even if revenues do increase by 5 percent, all of that increase might (or might not) be absorbed by the cost of some new equipment that

enabled productivity to rise or simply by an unexpected jump in the price of materials used by the firm. For that matter, we have seen that labor costs themselves could increase with no change in wage rates—if, for example, Congress imposed a higher tax rate for social security benefits in the second year, as it frequently has done. Finally, how can the employer know how his firm will fare on either the productivity or cost-price fronts *next year,* which is when he will actually be paying any wage increase? Those are the major arguments that will be used by an employer who understands the real but limited utility of the productivity measure at the level of the firm.[6]

But there is one other difference between social and private productivity that deserves mention. In the economy as a whole, inflation can result if the wage level is pushed up faster than productivity, and in this sense everyone benefits if wages and productivity *on the average* increase in step with one another. At the level of the firm, however, a direct tie between wage and productivity increases would produce an exploding wage structure which no union, employer, or economist would want. If productivity could be measured in each firm (which is an heroic assumption), the results would show that at any given time, output per man-hour is increasing very rapidly in some companies, rising less rapidly in others, and even declining in yet others; also, there would be sharp ups and downs in productivity within the same firm over time. Translated into wages, this would mean that some workers' wages would be shooting up at a rate of perhaps 20 or 30 percent at the same time that others were being cut and most were erratically going up or down at rates between these extremes—all with no reference to worker skills or employer ability to pay or any other criterion of equity or of supply and demand.

Finally, this argument comes full circle in the proposal that most negotiated wage increases should indeed be tied to increases in productivity —but to the increases in *social productivity* (the average in the entire economy), not to productivity increases within the firm itself. This proposal of wage guideposts is, however, part of the much larger topic of full employment and inflation which we must defer until a later chapter.

Labor cost[7]

For the individual firm, then, the objective is to produce a projected output at the lowest possible cost, and this entails two subsidiary objectives. One is to operate at a suitable level of efficiency, given existing technology and organization, and the second is to seek technical and organizational improvements that permit even greater efficiency in production.

The first of these objectives—operating at an appropriate level of efficiency—can be sought in a variety of ways. For present purposes, it will be sufficient if we take a summary look at the method which is probably most frequently employed by American business firms of any size. This is a combination of budgetary planning and standard costing.

Most business firms plan ahead for at least a year, and an increasing number plan for longer periods. These plans incorporate "budgets," which constitute expectations of levels of sales of the company's major product lines over the planning period, based on forecasts of gross national product (GNP) and more detailed examination of the company's own markets. Starting with such sales expectations, a company can then construct its production schedules, manning tables, and its materials-purchasing timetable. These will obviously have to be revised as the planning period unfolds, but at any moment of time there exists a set of expectations, incorporating the latest adjustments, on the basis of which production is planned and manpower and materials are scheduled.

To plan sales and output, a company must have expectations as to the quantity and prices of both its products and its factors. The prices of its factors times the amount of each factor directly needed in the production of any item constitute its direct costs; the wages of labor times the amount of labor directly required in turning out a product constitute the direct labor costs for that product. In addition, there are indirect costs (for maintenance, housekeeping activities, and so on) which have to be appropriately allocated, by cost accounting conventions, to the variety of products which are being produced. These indirect costs are incurred in the course of production, and their amount varies with output, but they are directly chargeable not to any one product but to a number of products and over a period of time. Beyond these direct and indirect costs, there are certain fixed costs which run on regardless of the amount of the company's production, but for purposes of current operations it is the costs which vary with output and therefore are controllable that are relevant.

In smaller plants or those which follow less systematized procedures, direct labor costs are usually estimated by each foreman for the particular operations for which he has responsibility, for that quantity of output for which the production schedule calls. These cost estimates may be simply informed judgments, based on last year's or last month's costs adjusted for volume, and revised by his superior and perhaps the controller's office for consistency and accuracy. Sometimes the foreman converts by formula the number of units of product into the hours of labor of various types which are required. Labor costs are then derived by multiplying man-hours by the relevant wage rate. This may be an average of rates or specific rates for specific skills.[8]

Materials estimates follow the same general pattern. Either from knowledge based on experience or from a table of allowances, the foreman calculates the materials required for the projected output, making due provision for scrap and wastage. Frequently the purchasing department will have compiled a catalogue of materials prices, using current prices or forecasting price changes, on the basis of which total materials costs for the unit, for the period, for the volume, and for the product mix can be calculated.

These estimated or budget costs are, in effect, an expectation based on past experience of what the cost of producing a given output should be. But of course circumstances almost always alter the actual outcome from that which is expected. A design change introduces problems which have not been allowed for, materials depart in minor particulars from those which have previously been used and make more of a difference in the rate of output than has been anticipated, accidents occur, with turnover the work force is not so experienced as last year's, the foreman falls ill, and any number of other things can happen which will make costs higher—or lower—than they were. In any event, it would be most surprising if actual cost figures exactly tallied with the expected (budgeted) cost figures. A variance almost always emerges. And then it is incumbent on the foreman, or other responsible supervisor, to analyze why the variance occurred. This is necessary if management wants to prevent costs from getting out of hand or if it is seeking to achieve high-level efficiency.

But no company can ever operate at peak efficiency for any length of time—a certain amount of "accidental" effects can be viewed as "normal." But how much? That is a neat question, made especially difficult because the historical experience on which the foreman bases his cost estimates probably includes some built-in inefficiencies of which he is unaware because he has become so accustomed to them. Or, on the other hand, it may incorporate some run of exceptional performance, the reasons for which he has not analyzed because their exceptional nature has not been apparent to him.

Thus the budget may set certain cost targets for a supervisor to attempt to realize, based on experience, but whether those constitute targets embodying a reasonable level of efficiency is not clear. Cost estimates or collected cost figures do not in themselves provide bench marks or yardsticks by which to judge whether—if actual cost varies from budget—the cause is due to poor estimates in the first place or to poor performance, or to something of both.

Standard costs are intended to provide such a guide. They constitute measures of the cost of producing goods under efficient conditions and are usually prepared by industrial engineers working with operating supervisors. Such measures are thus useful for controlling production standards as well as for making financial estimates. As an early statement explained the purpose, "The procedure is based on the theory that under normal efficient operating conditions the product can be made for a stated sum which can be readily calculated from known conditions, and that any expenses incurred in excess of this sum are un-

necessary—an economic loss, which it is the duty of management to eliminate."[9]

In addition to the predetermination of direct costs, including direct labor costs, in this manner, appropriate standards of indirect costs have been developed through what are called "flexible budgets." The intent behind flexible budgeting is to determine the amount of all semivariable expenses which are appropriate for whatever level of production actually materializes. The planning budget, based on some anticipated sales and production level, in effect constitutes a first approximation, on the basis of which financial needs may be estimated, personnel may be hired, materials ordered, and the plant, in general, "tooled up." But if the actual level of production deviates materially from what was planned, it is helpful if a new budget is readily available to substitute for the original one. This the flexible budget provides. It can be used both for the company as a whole and for a subunit.

In some instances, there is a predetermined, semivariable expense budget prepared for several identified ranges of activity. If capacity is figured at 93,600 units of output or man-hours of direct labor, for example, a budget of all indirect costs associated with that level of production can be prepared in advance. Similarly, a budget can be prepared for 90 percent of capacity or 84,240 units or hours, for 80 percent of capacity or 74,880 units, for 70 percent of capacity or 65,520 units or hours, and so on. More frequently, flexible budgets provide for expenses associated with some range of output (say, the range from 80 to 85 percent of capacity). Under flexible budgeting, whatever output level develops, there is a predetermined budget available to indicate what the appropriate associated expense level is. That becomes the *standard* governing the semivariable cost.

We have already had occasion to note that manufacturing companies are now using more white-collar (usually indirect) labor and less manual (direct) labor in their production processes. This often means that more and more of a company's labor costs are being converted to the semivariable type and included in flexible budgets. The salary costs of such personnel are constant over a range of output; their numbers are cut only when production drops below some predetermined level and increased when production rises above some level. To this extent, labor cost is less variable than it has been in the past, creating additional pressures on management to stabilize its output.

Cost control

Most managements are cost-conscious. They are made so by the pressures of competition and by efforts to achieve profit objectives. The control of costs has become a major area of strategic and tactical planning.

Budgeting and standard-cost procedures provide the firm with one set of instruments for controlling costs. The instruments are not automatic —there is nothing in the budget or in the measured or estimated "efficient" costs per unit or per period which is self-applying. They are nevertheless effective tools since they are quick to reveal departures from what had been planned or expected, permitting prompt inquiry and—where possible—correction of conditions giving rise to poor performance. Such an inquiry is known as "analysis of variance"—variance from standard cost or variance from the budget.

There are three principal categories of cost variances which may arise: (1) materials variances, (2) labor variances, and (3) overhead variances. We shall not be much concerned here with the techniques of analysis which have been developed, but simply note that labor variances are traced either to an expenditure of more labor time for the actual output than standard allowances would call for, or to labor time paid at higher rates than those on which the allowance was based. This last variation may be attributable not only to an increase in rates but also to the labor mix—the use of higher-rated workers than standard performance of the operation requires. Variance analysis revealing adverse conditions does not, of course, carry with it any necessary implications about the proper correctives. Nevertheless, it has become a major business tool for highlighting costs which are out of line.

Nothing about variance analysis, however, contributes to cost improvement *over* standard. If actual performance should equal budget, cost performance would be considered satisfactory. And yet the pressures for cost reduction would remain —not felt quite so ineluctably as if adverse variances had appeared, perhaps, but still inescapable insofar as the forces of competition and the motivation of profit objective drive managements toward continued improvement of performance. Variance analysis is thus inadequate by itself as a cost-control instrument. It is one facet of the strategy and tactics of cost reduction, but it does not represent the whole campaign.

Cost control proceeds by three main routes: forced draft, opportunism, and institutionalized procedures.

The forced-draft approach is used under pressure. In the face of a poor profit position, all budgets may be slashed by some arbitrary percentage, leaving it to the heads of departments and divisions to determine where best to make the cuts. Most managements look with disfavor upon such a blunt approach, but many argue that periodically it serves to eliminate useless expenditures which have a way of creeping into the budget.

Such arbitrary attempts at cost reduction may proceed even when a company is not experiencing the harsh driving force of adversity. In one session of the annual meetings of the National Association of Accountants,[10] "a member explained that maintenance costs had been reduced in his company by (more or less arbitrarily) cutting the maintenance department crew."

> On an experimental basis, one maintenance employee was dropped. Results were observed carefully and it was noted that down-time did not rise and that the general plant remained in good repair. Several months later another member of the crew was let go. Over the past four years, approximately five employees have been removed from the maintenance department in this manner without any observable bad results. It was this company's feeling that this procedure has automatically picked-up those people who were not performing a full day's work and has eliminated (at least partially) the practice of sending excessive crews to do a job. As yet this company has not reached the point at

which rising down-time, poor plant conditions or overtime indicate that maintenance service is suffering.

The opportunistic approach to cost reduction consists simply in a readiness and alertness to profit from any beneficial changes which might be called to management's attention from any source. Chance reading of business literature, attendance at executive-training or trade-association sessions, and conversations with other businessmen are some of the ways in which usable suggestions may filter into a company. The employee-suggestion system, that butt of many a bitter joke, is another such device.

In some companies, cost reduction has increasingly become institutionalized. The procedures and practices vary, but all rely on a systematic study and examination of administration, organization, production, marketing, and finance in a conscious effort to lay bare sources of inefficiency or potentials for reduced cost. In general, these efforts tend to rely on a group of professionals who have become identified as methods engineers or industrial engineers. In some companies, the industrial engineering department has grown into a very sizable undertaking. In other firms, industrial engineering departments are built into each operating division.

Their function is continuously to review the use of materials and the use of production methods to discover economies which may be effected. Beyond this, they are sometimes concerned with redesigning products, plant layouts, inventory procedures, transportation arrangements—all with the objective of maximum economy. Particular attention is paid in some firms to the use of engineers at the time when new models or new products are being introduced.[11]

The use of such staffs, with a directive to determine where costs may be cut throughout the company's operations, builds cost reduction into the company's organizational system. They are driven to achieve results by the pressures on them to justify their organizational existence. This sometimes leads to excesses of misplaced ingenuity, but there can be no doubt that, overall, the effect is favorable on the company's profit objective.

In all these efforts at cost control—whether through the use of predetermined standards built into operating budgets against which actual performance is compared or through an engineering department which is given a general hunting license to see what economies it can flush out—management's objective is not, or not generally, to curb costs by depressing the wage *rate*. Its objective is to economize on the use of labor itself, as long as the cost of doing this is less than the saving. The higher the wage rate, the greater the incentive to reduce the number of man-hours incorporated in units of output.

This management drive to economize on labor clashes with the security drive of workers and unions. Rising productivity means fewer jobs in the firm unless output expands simultaneously and sufficiently. Greater efficiency may mean the reassignment of workers from jobs with which they have identified themselves to other jobs with lower status and lower pay. Is it any wonder that management and its efficiency engineers are viewed as the enemy?

But if management is the enemy, it is not so by choice. It is management's function to be efficient, to cut costs, to make profits, to sell more goods more cheaply, to be as competitive as possible. When workers and unions resist changes initiated by management to accomplish these functions which society has assigned it, sometimes even after it has taken steps and made concessions to reduce the shock of change, it is management's turn to regard the workers and their unions with something less than love.

Time-and-motion studies

To illustrate the major points of this chapter, no better example can be found than incentive-pay systems. Here is the classic expression of the employer's view of labor costs—employee compensation directly linked to employee output via a system that enables these costs to be controlled and predicted. On the other hand, incentive systems also symbolize to many workers and union leaders all that is wrong in management's approach to determining a "fair day's work and pay."

That overstates to some extent the parties' conflict over this issue, for, as noted in Chapter 7, the debate over scientific-management techniques has simmered down considerably since the early 1900s. Many employers do not use incentive-wage systems today, and those who do rarely claim their methods are infallible. Similarly, unions have accepted the need for incentive systems (or at least their inevitability) in many industries and have learned to live with them. There nevertheless remains a basic difference in the parties' viewpoints that makes this issue the source of constant grievances in many relationships.

As in job evaluation, there are numerous ways of conducting time-and-motion studies, the first step in establishing an incentive-wage system (and often a basis for the "standard costs" described previously). But all methods consist essentially of measuring the time a "normal" worker takes to perform some operation as a basis for determining how much work he ought to be able to complete within some time period such as an hour or a day, making allowance for fatigue and personal needs. Professor Adam Abruzzi has made a penetrating analysis of this entire process, and we shall draw heavily on his studies.[12]

Abruzzi first stresses the difference between *estimation* and *evaluation* in time study. The former involves the collection of quantitative data; the latter relates to a determination of the data's significance. The estimation component of time-and-motion study includes selecting a worker for study, selecting a measuring instrument and method, and selecting a recording instrument. The elements of the operation being studied and the number of readings to be taken are defined. Data are customarily summarized in terms of some measure of central tendency such as an arithmetic average.

But after these estimates have been made, there remains the question of their meaning. Abruzzi observes:[13]

... Certain aspects of time study are purely evaluative. This is particularly true of the procedures used for rating worker performance. This is intended to establish what production rates ought to be; it has nothing to do with measurable variables in a scientific sense. Many difficulties indeed flow from this unannounced and unhappy wedding between a meek estimation function and an overbearing evaluation function. ...

Rating procedures are intended to transform observed time study data to a unique value. This value is considered to represent the production rate that ought to be realized by a so-called "normal" worker presumed to have certain idealized performance characteristics. ... The concept of "ought" is basic to all evaluation procedures which means that all specifications, including those derived from rating procedures, must ultimately be based on value judgments on what is desirable. That remains true even though only objective factors or parameters are considered. An evaluation must always be made as to the factors considered relevant in particular situations and how they are to be weighted.

As soon as we enter the realm of values, we are in the presence of conflicting judgments which cannot be resolved by an appeal to fact, even though facts may be relevant. The arguments here are the same as those we encountered in discussing the use of fact in the collective-bargaining process. Differing views of "ought" are entertained by workers and by supervisors, and sometimes differences emerge between first-line supervisors, time-study engineers, and top management as well. These questions of what *ought* to be the rule cannot be settled solely with reference to what *is* the actual performance in a particular case or even an average of cases.

This conclusion may not be immediately evident. One might react: But if it is observed that half a dozen workers on a particular operation are capable of producing an average of so many units of output in a specified time, why should that not be accepted as a standard of what workers generally on that operation should be expected to do? The difficulty lies on several fronts. First, there is the choice of the half-dozen workers. On what grounds can they be considered "representative" or "normal"? The fact that one can measure their output and strike an arithmetical average does not endow the resulting figure with any inherent significance. An average implies a range. Who is to say that the worker who produces the least output is not more representative of workers generally than the other five? Or, for that matter, that the worker who produces at the upper end of the observed results is not more normal?

Push the matter a little further. Any job can be

performed in a variety of ways. Workers on a particular operation may tend toward some degree of standardization in the method of performance, but differences remain, reflecting differences in intelligence, adaptability, and personality. Some workers are clearly more clumsy than others. Some are infinitely more clever and skillful. In selecting those workers who are to be studied, a time-study man is necessarily, whether he admits it or not, selecting also a *method* of performing a job.

Bargaining over performance

Most time-study men indeed not only recognize that fact but incorporate it into their own estimating procedures. They attempt to "standardize" the work process before they measure it. This is where the "motion" part of time-and-motion study enters the picture. An effort is made to establish the particular sequence of motions and the use of equipment which are observed to be the most productive. Very often there is an underlying notion that there exists some one best way of performing any job, which an industrial engineer should be alert to discover.

But this ignores the purposive element in work behavior, as Professor Abruzzi demonstrates. Work is composed of two elements—the routine and standardized, and the unexpected and varying. The former commands little of the worker's attention and interest, and the latter, when it occurs, absorbs his attention. But precisely because there is no interest in the routine and standardized task, workers tend to introduce individualistic patterns into their performance. These may be "routines" in the sense that they are repeated, but they are discretionary with the individual, peculiar to him, and serve to vary what otherwise would be an unvarying succession of "efficient" motions.

It is here that Abruzzi makes some of his most penetrating observations, based on his own experimental work in factories. He finds that "regulation of work" begins with the worker—not in terms of simple restriction of output but in terms of controlling the work process to his needs. Mastery of a job involves in part formal training, in part the absorption from other workers of what they have learned with respect to the job, and in

part the development of the worker's own "stance" toward his job. This last really amounts to a worker's "playing games" with his work environment to discover how far he can go in expressing his own feelings and whims within the compulsions which the work environment places on him.[14]

A realistic regulating program requires that workers be given a certain amount of latitude in planning and developing work activities, if for no other reason than to take advantage of their skill potentials. In immediate terms this means that direct empirical action with regard to man-controlled operations should not be taken just because correlations exist. . . .

. . . Workers regulate their performance levels in terms of individual abilities and purposes . . .

Indeed, it is precisely because purposive behavior is not taken into account, except perhaps in a superficial sense, that the classical "one best way" theory of work fails to have experimental meaning. The "one best way" approach—and this applies to all classical concepts of work and its measurement—would have meaning only if workers could be reduced to completely non-purposive beings, at least at the workplace."

Abruzzi illustrates this conclusion with reference to one of the factories in which he made his observations.[15]

. . . [M]any of the operators in Plant A were highly productive, some of them even having productivity values exceeding 200 per cent. Clearly the common practice of overtly depressing output to protect lenient rates and conditions was not followed in this plant. Yet there is considerable evidence that the workers in the plant did plan and regulate output.

For example, one operator stated that she and her companion operator had decided that each of them would produce an average of six lots of garments daily. Also, they never finished more than three lots in the afternoon although they did produce as many as seven lots on some days. It was explained that, with this production policy, a satisfactory earning level could be achieved without undue exertion.

The mechanics of output regulation is revealed by an incident involving another operator. When preparations were being made for a [time] study, this operator was working on an operation different from the one scheduled for study. She became extremely disturbed when asked to make a change. The department supervisor later said that most operators carefully planned daily work schedules in terms of a definite number of lots on a definite operation. They also paced themselves during the day according to these schedules. They objected vigorously when asked to change operations, claiming that this disturbed their schedules and threw them "off their stride."

These are typical examples of how workers regulate output according to ability and purposes. Regulation, then, is a direct outcome of the stance adopted by individual workers in what might be characterized as a game between them and the work environment. This game is an extension of the much more overt game between workers and time study engineers on production standards. The present game is much more subtle, with the work environment acting as the worker's adversary. Although it is probably not consciously developed, the stance of the worker represents an attempt to arrive at an optimum balance between his requirements and those of the work environment.

This kind of normal worker *regulation* of output does not necessarily entail *restriction* of output. Some employees reported by Abruzzi produced at 200 percent of the base rate. Restriction of output enters as a special case of regulation of output. Whenever workers apprehend that management is trying to tighten up or speed up the operation, to modify their accustomed stance to the work environment, to deprive them of some leniency or latitude in the regulation of their work methods, or to change the existing rules, they are likely to adopt a protective and defensive attitude. This is particularly evident in the shop whenever a time-study man enters to time a job. On such occasions, the worker selected as the one to be timed engages in a variety of deceptive and diverting maneuvers designed to win a favorable rating which will permit retention of the customary latitude on the job. In effect, the time-study man at that point becomes part of the individual's work environment toward which the worker adopts the "gaming" attitude referred to earlier. In effect, the worker plays games with the time-study man.

Some workers derive actual enjoyment from, and acquire considerable skill in, this kind of game.

One might think that this sparring between worker and time-study man would rob the resulting rates of any significance. But these rates—which have an efficiency significance to management—may have a different meaning for workers. They may have no carrot-or-stick effect but may constitute a target for them to shoot at, with a "prize" if they do better, something to relieve the inherent monotony of the job, like a game of darts or bowling. On a straight hourly pay rate ("day rate," as it is frequently referred to), there is no such target, no cigar or kewpie doll or (in actuality) "prize money" if the worker rings the bell or knocks over the milk bottles with three balls or (in actuality) exceeds the job's production rate.

The game would cease to be a game, however, if the rate were imposed. It is precisely because it is a bargained rate, one which has developed out of a matching of wits by worker and time-study man, that the rules of the game (the production rate) are accepted.

Abruzzi emphasizes this inter*play* between workers and time-study men.[16]

> Workers' behavior over time studies can be classified as a component of informal bargaining, with the objective of obtaining favorable standards and rates of pay. This form of bargaining proceeds in two stages. In the first stage workers present a biased impression of the job requirements. In the second stage they protect lenient or "loose" standards and rates, while they protest stringent or "tight" standards and rates by a number of devices, including grievance procedures.

When workers organize and are represented by a union, these protective devices often are supported by formal provisions in the collective agreement, specifying the circumstances under which a job may be retimed or a new job studied and establishing procedures for protesting the findings.

This adversary position of worker and union in the face of time-and-motion study is a direct consequence of the existence of different value systems guiding them in contrast to management. For them, the objective is development and retention of a satisfactory stance with respect to their job. For management, it is efficiency in the face of competition. Since these values conflict, they can only be resolved by compromise based on relative bargaining powers. What purports to be a scientific procedure is thus revealed as simply one ingredient in the process of finding a pragmatic solution to certain work-rules problems:[17]

> There is only one reason why competitive and even contradictory time study procedures —complete with competitive assumptions, definitions, and claims—can coexist. The reason is that time study is essentially a component of the bargaining process. In that framework the actual procedure is of negligible consequence and its assumptions, definitions, and claims are of even less consequence. All that matters is whether the production standards and the earning opportunities provided are considered acceptable regardless of its details.

Thus in the final analysis, even in the restricted area of work rules governing production rates in manufacturing processes, management's reliance on a scientific approach must give way—informally or formally—to compromise. The authority that goes with management is insufficient to lay down enforceable work regulations. These depend on worker acceptance, which must be induced, and inducement must be bargained for.

Incentive-payment plans

Time study may be made the basis for setting standards which employees who are paid a standard hourly rate are expected to realize; this is commonly referred to as "measured day work." Here work measurement or production rating is not expected to have much of an incentive effect, at least in the sense of providing rewards for overfulfillment of norms. Workers are simply placed under the compulsion of achieving a specified level of output as a condition of retaining the particular assignment.

More commonly, however, time study is used as the basis for incentive-payment plans which are intended to elicit from workers an added effort and more output, as we noted above in connection with the contest between the time-study engineer and the time-studied worker. Incentive systems are of several types, but basically reduce to two: piece-rate plans and production bonuses. The former pays a specified sum per piece, so that total earnings are directly related to number of pieces produced. The latter provides for an extra payment for output in excess of a set "norm" or "base." In both, there is usually some guarantee of a minimum hourly rate, intended to provide for situations where output falls below normal through no fault of the employee. Incentive plans may be on an individual or a group basis. They generally apply to direct-labor operations but are sometimes extended to indirect labor as well.

Surveys by the Bureau of Labor Statistics indicate that somewhat more than one-fourth of production workers in the United States are paid on an incentive basis.[18] This number seems to have remained relatively constant over most of the postwar period. Among experts in the field there is a prevailing belief, however, that incentive plans will disappear at an increasing rate with the spread of automated processes. As the number of units of output becomes less and less dependent on the motivated response of employees, the rationale for paying workers "by the numbers" will evaporate. The number of pieces produced will bear little relationship to worker effort. The advanced technologies will take over routine operations, and workers will be paid for controlling processes rather than for engaging repetitiously in a sequence of more or less efficient motions. It is sometimes said that payment by the piece treats workers as "mechanical" producers, and when machines take over the present mechanical functions of work, the payment methods associated with those processes (such as piecework) will cease to have meaning. The role of workers will be upgraded from being machine substitutes to being machine controllers. This presumably is something different from being a machine tender, which puts the worker in the role of being an adjunct to a machine rather than its master, but whether he is tender or controller, the effect on incentive-pay plans is likely to be the same. They will be rendered obsolete.

This prevision, like all prophecies, is necessarily

speculative. While one cannot accurately predict the speed and nature of technological change, there does appear to be good reason to anticipate an accelerating rate of introduction of wholly integrated automatic-production processes, and if so, the effect on incentive systems is likely to be as predicted.

In the meantime, however, they remain an important part of the American wage structure. In spite of the valid criticisms of time-and-motion studies, production often does increase when an incentive system is introduced. Many workers do like the opportunity to earn more by producing more, and many employers do find incentives useful in controlling and predicting their labor costs, particularly in industries like clothing in which production schedules are irregular and output is not machine-paced. The point, in short, is not that incentive-pay systems are so "unscientific" as to be useless, but rather that these systems are like any other management tool: they can be helpful in the employer's legitimate drive for lower labor cost, but they certainly do not answer the perennial question of what constitutes a fair work load or paycheck.

Summary

In management's unremitting efforts to control labor costs, we have seen that far more is involved than keeping a lid on wages. There is no easy translation of average wages into labor cost. For one thing, the *structure* of wage rates around any average is often changing and always controversial. For another thing, employment costs involve a good deal more than the rate or salary for a job. They include a congeries of premiums and benefits and administrative charges which add up to a substantial proportion of the wage bill itself.

In addition, labor costs are determined not only by how much is paid out to workers but also by how much management obtains from the performance of those workers. This input-output relationship is a concept applicable to the economy at large as well as to the firm, but there are important differences between social and private productivity. In a much simplified sense, an economy prospers in direct ratio to its increases in output per man-hour, and these productivity in-

creases in turn determine the pace of average wage increases. For the individual company, however, the objective cannot be to raise physical productivity regardless of cost, nor can the wages of workers be determined solely by the productivity of their particular firm. Instead, an employer's success depends (among other things) on lowering the *cost* of any given level of output, and to do that, he must constantly weigh the benefits of productivity increases against the costs of achieving those increases.

In attempting to control both sides of their cost equation—compensation and efficiency—employers have adopted a variety of techniques, from job evaluation and time study to budgets and standard costing. In addition, management is constantly searching for new equipment and improved processes to reduce its operating costs. But this drive, which is built into management's role in our competitive society, often conflicts with the objectives of workers. As a class, workers certainly benefit from lower production costs in the form of better goods at lower prices, but in any individual company the search for lower costs poses a potential threat to many workers—to their jobs, their income security, their status, and their individuality. The resulting conflict is not irreconcilable, but neither can it be resolved simply by exhorting management to be less cost-conscious or labor to be less security-minded.

ADDITIONAL READINGS

Abruzzi, Adam: *Work, Workers and Work Measurement,* Columbia University Press, New York, 1956.

Chamberlain, Neil W.: *Sourcebook on Labor,* McGraw-Hill, New York, 1958, chap. 18.

Chamberlain, Neil W.: *The Firm: Micro-economic Planning and Action,* McGraw-Hill, New York, 1962, chap. 8.

Gomberg, William: *A Trade Union Analysis of Time Study,* 2d ed., Prentice-Hall, Englewood Cliffs, N.J., 1955.

Kendrick, John W., and Daniel Creamer: *Measuring Company Productivity: Handbook with Case Studies,* National Industrial Conference Board, New York, 1961.

Pigors, Paul, and Charles A. Myers: *Personnel*

Administration, 5th ed., McGraw-Hill, New York, 1965, chaps. 21–23.

Slichter, S. H., J. J. Healy, and E. R. Livernash: *The Impact of Collective Bargaining on Management,* Brookings, Washington, 1960, chaps. 17–20.

FOR ANALYSIS AND DISCUSSION

1. One union leader commented: "Job evaluation is nothing but scientific hogwash. Frequently the employer's interest in putting it in is simply to mystify the worker. You can't weigh and measure human beings as you do wheat or coal. The margins of error in evaluations are terrific and the results are no better than those based on just pure common sense."

A businessman remarked: "Job evaluation is the only way by which you can logically organize a business where you have a great many workers in a complex setup—to understand the responsibility of each and be sure that all are adequately and fairly paid in relation to other workers. It prevents the overlapping of jobs and satisfies the employee that he is being paid for the effort he puts in."

Comment on each of these two views.

2. Construct a job-evaluation system for professional occupations, and then rate (*a*) a high school teacher, (*b*) a college instructor, (*c*) a football coach, and (*d*) a nurse in the student infirmary. Does your system work? If not, what are the difficulties?

3. Does it make any difference to management whether its labor costs come in the form of straight wages or fringe benefits, or other employment costs?

4. To what extent is the management of companies like General Motors or American Telephone and Telegraph under a pressure to reduce costs? What control do they have over the rate of introduction of improved methods of production? Is it in society's interests that they should exercise whatever control they have to slow down or accelerate the rate of improvement in productive efficiency? Whichever your answer, do you mean to say that they should slow down or accelerate without limit (that is, as much as possible)? If

not, within what limits (how much slower or faster)?

5. In the August, 1956, issue of its publication, *Ammunition,* the United Automobile Workers printed an article under the challenging title "Time Study Is Spinach," in which the following paragraphs appeared:

> The language of time study is the language of Madison Avenue, with the hard sell and soft sell blended. In the same honeyed breath, you are told that time study is both scientific and fair.
>
> At this point, the worker who has had eight hours of sleep puts on his thinking cap and asks himself what's so fair about science? What's fair about H-bombs? What's fair about the diagnosis that tells a man he has cancer and six months to live? What's fair about chemistry? What's fair about mathematics?
>
> But time study is "fair." Yet, if time study is fair, then it isn't scientific. And if it's scientific, then it isn't fair. If it's scientific, why should it have to justify its presence in the shop by the added slogan—"it's fair"? That's the Madison Avenue touch. It's fair. It's mild. It's smooth. Take a time study every day, work harder, die younger, be scientific.
>
> At this point, the worker jams his thinking cap into his back pocket, calls his Union committeeman, and collective bargaining sets in on that plus or minus five per cent of error that almost any engineer, in the privacy of his heart, will admit is inherent in any time study.

Comment on the above statement.

NOTES

1. Lloyd G. Reynolds and J. Shister, *Job Horizons,* Harper, New York, 1949, p. 85. The two quotations in the text are taken from this book.

2. British Trades Union Congress, *Trade Unions and Productivity,* undated but issued about 1951, pp. 38–39.

3. In some systems, instead of a single rate for a job class, a rate range may be provided. All jobs in the job class fall within that range, but the specific rate within the range that any individual receives is based on such considerations as length of service and individual merit.

4. E. R. Livernash, in W. S. Woytinsky and Asso-

ciates, *Employment and Wages in the United States,* Twentieth Century Fund, New York, 1953, p. 431.

5. For 1947–1965 comparisons, see *Fringe Benefits —1965,* Chamber of Commerce of the United States, Washington, 1966, p. 27. For the relation of wage and fringe levels, see Arnold Strasser, "The Changing Structure of Compensation," *Monthly Labor Review,* September, 1966, p. 955.

6. See the National Industrial Conference Board Executive Report, "Productivity Gains, Despite Obstacles," in the *Business Record,* October, 1957, pp. 461–467, for a fascinating compilation of executives' opinions—some erroneous and some very sophisticated—concerning the productivity concept.

Thus some of the respondents obviously interpreted labor productivity as referring to production increases for which workers were responsible, using such phrases as "the productivity of our operators," and many used only man-hours of production workers despite the heavy shift from blue-collar to clerical positions. But one executive voiced grave doubts about the labor-productivity concept in the face of changing product mix, another because of the difficulty of constructing adequate price indexes to deflate sales figures, another because of fluctuations in volume of output, several because of the lack of relationship of changes in man-hours to other factor costs, and some because of the use of direct labor only in the man-hours input figures.

For a typical union view, note this statement from the United Steelworkers, *Why a Steel Price Increase in 1957?,* Pittsburgh, 1958, p. 23:

Increases in productivity mean simply that unit labor requirements decline—that each ton of steel is produced with less hours of labor. Even if the cost of each hour of labor is increased by wage rate increases directly *proportionate* to rising productivity, these increases can be *absorbed* out of the gains in productivity without reducing the other shares of the product such as Profits.

7. Most of the material in this and the following sections has been drawn from Neil W. Chamberlain, *The Firm: Micro-economic Planning and Action,* McGraw-Hill, New York, 1962, chap. 8.

8. A complicating problem is presented in years when collective agreements fall open for negotiation. To budget labor costs on prevailing rates, when it is expected that a new rate will be bargained, introduces distortion into the figures. To use an estimate of what the new rate will be, however, tips management's hand if the information gets out, as it might easily do if foremen are involved in the budgeting process. Practice varies on this point. "It is the policy of the company to prepare the original budget each year without consideration of the wage increase that may be granted in the renewal of the union agreement. The original budget is revised after the union agreement has been signed and the new labor cost has been estimated." A steel company reports that it budgets on the ostensible basis of existing rates, but disguised allowances for probable wage increases can be built into the figures by the use of unspecified contingency reserves, disregarding offsetting productivity increases, or by assuming that subsequent price increases will offset wage increases. Another company reports that it figures on the basis of "our guess as to the amount of the annual wage increase." Another writes in its administrative manual, "No attempt should be made to predict and include in Plans the inflationary or deflationary movements in general wage or price levels. However, expected increases or decreases in labor rates, costs of materials, etc., for the budget year should be recognized."

9. George Rea, *An Introduction to Predetermined Costs,* National Association of Cost Accountants Official Publications, vol. 5, no. 7, p. 4, Dec. 15, 1923.

10. "Control of Maintenance Costs," *N.A.C.A. Bulletin,* sec. 3, p. 158, September, 1956.

11. A. D. H. Kaplan, J. B. Dirlam, and R. F. Lanzillotti, writing of General Motors in *Pricing in Big Business,* Brookings, Washington, 1958, p. 52, remark:

Coincidentally with the evolution of a new model, the engineering, manufacturing, and procurement departments are continually called into consultation in an effort to find out what can be anticipated in the way of unit cost for the suggested style and other alterations. Pressure is on these departments to devise methods of cutting costs on both new and old constituents of the model, to provide leeway for introduction of new features.

12. Abruzzi's first analysis, *Work Measurement,* Columbia University Press, New York, 1952, was elaborated in *Work, Workers and Work Measurement,* Columbia University Press, New York, 1956.

13. Abruzzi, *Work, Workers and Work Measurement,* p. 26, pp. 44–45. He repeats, on p. 31, "Since the rating component of time study performs an evaluation function, it cannot possibly be a scientific process."

14. The same, pp. 116, 142, and 249–250.

15. The same, pp. 113–114.

16. The same, p. 19.

17. The same, p. 25.

18. L. Earl Lewis, "Extent of Incentive Pay in Manufacturing," *Monthly Labor Review,* May, 1960, pp. 460–463; and George L. Stelluto, "Report on Incentive Pay in Manufacturing Industries," *Monthly Labor Review,* July, 1969, pp. 49–53.

Personnel policy

Personnel policy is a matter of concern to management for a number of reasons. First, good personnel policy is necessary for business efficiency. In the selection and training of workers, in the promotion system, in the methods of rewards and punishment, in the incentives provided to stimulate initiative and effort may lie the difference between good performance and poor. Second, the spread of unionism has forced management into a sharper scrutiny and a rationalization of its personnel policies. If there is a union in the plant, the union will itself constitute the spur to management's continual reexamination of its relations with its employees. In a plant in which there is no union, management may hope that the quality of its personnel program will keep a union out of the plant. Third, the government's increasing intervention in the personnel relation—through social security programs, wage-and-hour laws, government-contract administration, labor relations regulation, and so on—has, like unionism, stimulated management to a closer study and greater systematization of its employee policies. And fourth, most management people—at least most management people with whom the authors have had any contact—have a genuine interest in the welfare of their employees. Although there is sometimes a gulf between interest and good practice, there has been a marked improvement in the moral qualities of the employer–employee relationship within the last few decades, particularly within the large corporation.

For all these reasons personnel policy is today recognized as a necessary and even vital phase of any company's operations. But what is included within the scope of "personnel policy"?

Personnel relations can be defined (as it was by one vice-president in charge of personnel relations) as including all phases of human relationships within a business. It would thus include all relations between management and employees, relations among employees, and relations among management people. Such a definition might appear too broad, at first glance; it would seem to encompass such matters as a foreman's giving a routine order to one of his men or even the way the men order their food from the girls who work in the company cafeteria. But such matters are part of the system of relations among people within the organization, and if one thinks of the functions of personnel policy rather than of some particular administrator or office, it becomes apparent that relations between a foreman and his men, for example, constitute an important area for the *practice* of such personnel policies as the company seeks to carry out.

The same personnel officer who supplied the definition cited above has also provided a statement[1] of the two basic objectives which should lie behind any employee relations program:

1. To facilitate the economic function of business by helping to produce a better product or service at lower cost through effective use of human resources.

2. To assist in providing a completely satisfying work experience for those who are active participants in the enterprise.

If these objectives are to be realized, experience has indicated that some individual must be designated to do something about them. Thus comes into being the office of director of personnel relations or industrial relations director or vice-president in charge of personnel. Obviously, he is not the one who carries out personnel policy—or at least not the only one. As we have just seen, right down to the foreman in the shop, indeed right down to the most menial worker, anyone who has anything to do with others is responsible for carrying out the company's personnel policy.

What, then, is the personnel director's job? It is a mélange of many things. It consists of helping to formulate policy, helping to enforce policy, acting as advisor and assistant to members of management in their dealings with employees, dealing with employees on behalf of other members of management (as in hiring or disciplining), conducting special programs or services for the benefit of the employees, keeping records. The specific areas in which he performs this variety of functions can be catalogued—perhaps not completely—as follows:

The hiring and recruitment of employees, including the finding, interviewing, skill- or aptitude-testing (in those companies where testing procedures are used), and consulting with the operating personnel who are to supervise whoever is hired

Wages, including a continual review of the wage structure (by job analysis or job evaluation, where such systems are used), participation in the setting of incentive rates, supervision of the merit-rating procedures and results, and a consideration of the appropriateness of wage levels in view of rates prevailing elsewhere

Working conditions, including general housekeeping but especially emphasizing safety and health

Training, including the induction of new employees and a review of job training and supervisory training

Transfers and promotions, including general review of the balancing of seniority and ability and the adequate training of individuals for purposes of replacement and flexibility

Hours and overtime, not actually determining schedules but reviewing methods of scheduling and allocation of overtime work

Extracurricular employee activities, such as supervising a program of athletics, operating a plant library, assuming responsibility for social activities, overseeing operation of the cafeteria

Benefit programs, including the representation of management in the operation of pension funds, insurance programs, health insurance, et cetera

Employee information, including the editing of any employee publication and the dissemination of company policies among the work force

Relations with the union, including preparation for collective bargaining and general supervision of employee grievances

The fact that in this listing the last-named function, union–management relations, is only one of many items conveys a misleading impression as to its importance. Collective bargaining and grievance handling, the primary points of contact between union and management, have their influence on wages, working conditions, discipline, transfers and promotions, hours and overtime, and benefit programs—all vital parts of personnel administration. Indeed, maintaining a satisfactory working relationship with the union while at the same time seeking to carry out management's own policies occupies much of the time of a personnel staff and provides them with some of their thorniest problems (many of which we have discussed in previous chapters).

Even setting aside union relations, a single chapter cannot possibly do justice to all of the other personnel activities listed above. We shall therefore focus on only a few issues and programs —the staff role of the personnel office, its recruitment and management-development activities, and its goal of increasing both morale and efficiency within the firm. In fact, this last responsibility is central to the appraisal of every personnel function. Can management realistically treat labor as both a factor of production and as people, or are economic and humanistic goals basically incompatible? Or, stated more simply, is there any relationship between worker happiness and worker efficiency?

The staff function

Most firms in the United States are too small to have any specialized personnel office, and too small to need one. The approximately 1 million companies employing from 4 to 99 persons are likely to handle their employee relations problems either on an informal basis or through employers' associations. Not until one reaches the approximately 38,000 firms employing 100 employees or more (out of a total business population of about 4.5 million firms) is it likely that the personnel function is sufficiently well defined to have its own full-time functionary.

The organizational procedures for handling personnel problems are varied. To some extent they simply reflect the same kind of organizational variety that one would expect to find if he were examining how companies handle their sales or public relations or capital investment or research programs. But to some extent, they also reflect varying degrees of experience and maturity in the conduct of personnel relations. Until two or three decades ago, many companies paid little attention to this phase of business operations, either taking it for granted or assuming that it required no special competence.

Where a full-time personnel officer is employed, the range of his discretion depends in part upon the size of the company. In firms of perhaps fewer than 250 employees, the likelihood is that he will decide virtually all questions of policy only after informal discussion with the president. In larger companies, there appears to be a practice of dividing personnel decisions into the two categories of major and minor policies. There is usually no sharp line of demarcation between the two categories, but the criteria for distinguishing one from the other are typically three: (1) the amount of money involved, (2) the number of employees involved, and (3) the significance of the expected effect on union–management relations.[2]

In companies of medium size (those with a median number of 6,000 employees in a sample of eighty-four companies), the probabilities are that the personnel director will handle all minor issues on his own authority but will discuss major policies with one or two superior officers in the company—perhaps the president, the executive vice-president, or a vice-president in charge of industrial relations if the personnel director does not himself have such status.

In larger companies (those, in the same sample, with a median number of 10,000 employees and with a range overlapping that of the medium-sized group), the reporting procedure is somewhat more formalized. While the personnel or industrial relations director may assume personal responsibility for minor policy decisions, major issues are referred to a designated committee of the corporation's officers, such as a committee of the top operating officials, a planning committee, a special labor or employee relations committee, the executive committee or special subcommittee of the board of directors, or the board of directors as a whole.

A company that operates more than one plant usually has a plant personnel office which, in conjunction with the plant's operating people, makes policy and decides issues involving relations with employees and the union at that plant. The headquarters personnel office of such a company would normally serve in an advisory capacity to the plant office. If a uniform, companywide policy is desired on some personnel matter, it would take the form of a directive from the company's top management to the several plant managers. The headquarters personnel office would normally have no formal authority to force policy on the operating plant management.

Indeed, the personnel office in theory has no authority to enforce policies against anyone. As a staff department, its duties are presumably to advise those in the line organization and to carry out certain administrative duties under the direction of line authority. It is the line officials, those charged with the responsibility of making decisions concerning the actual operation of the business, who alone can put into effect such policies as the personnel office may recommend, perhaps with modification. In practice, this traditional distinction is so muddied as to be robbed of any real usefulness: the plant manager may look upon the company personnel director as an agent of headquarters and treat his suggestions as orders; foremen may come to believe that the personnel office actually has a greater voice in sustaining or reversing such of their actions as have been protested by the union than does the department head to whom they nominally report in the line structure. With respect to certain kinds of personnel actions—some disciplinary matters, merit rating for purposes of pay increases, job evaluations or time-and-motion study—a foreman very often prefers that the personnel office or its agent take the responsibility; in these cases, he willingly relinquishes his "line" authority to a "staff" officer. In other instances, such as the transfer of employees between two departments or two plants, the personnel office acts as broker, since two line units are involved, and under such circumstances may have more to say about the action than those with whom authority supposedly lies.

This confusion of organizational lines of authority has been increased by the need for specialized knowledge. Wherever specialization occurs so that some are in possession of knowledge on which others must rely, those having such knowledge acquire a kind of authority which does not appear on any organizational chart. The nonspecialist manager at any level within the organization—from first line to top line—finds it difficult to do anything but accept the judgment of experts in fields such as engineering, finance, law, and personnel, despite the fact that these are all staff functions. He may, of course, contest their judgments by substituting the judgments of other experts, or he may arbitrarily disregard their advice and act on the basis of intuition, hunch, or prejudice. But more and more the line manager realizes that any such attempted assertion of his official authority is fraught with danger; he is bucking the informed opinion of someone who has specialized in a branch of knowledge with which he himself has at best only a superficial acquaintance. He comes to appreciate that while it may be wise to question the judgments which are tendered him to make sure that the expert has exercised his expertise in a responsible manner, it is usually equally wise to rely on the expert's conclusion. There are obviously circumstances when the generalist has to take choice into his own

hands regardless of technical advice, or when the technical advisor can provide him with only part of the picture and the operating officer has to add other elements of information in order to arrive at a decision. Nevertheless, special knowledge does possess an authority of its own, so that the old distinction between line and staff as a distinction between adviser and decision maker is less and less valid.

In recognition of this fact, some organizational theorists today use the term "lateral relationships" to refer to situations formerly encompassed by the old line and staff categories. In lateral relationships, the usual organizational lines of authority are missing, and the person who actually possesses authority with respect to the issue under discussion is ambiguous and perhaps unimportant. Experts are likely to be involved in lateral relationships, since they possess no formal authority to impose decisions but have an authority of knowledge which those who carry the line insignia may not choose to dispute. The personnel office thus is typically involved in a multitude of lateral relationships.[3] At the same time, while the personnel officer may exercise a degree of authority not traditionally comprehended within a staff function, it is still basically true that the top operating management sets the tone of the company's approach to personnel policy. The personnel office applies its engineering, psychological, legal, and economic expertise within a "corporate philosophy" that has to be supplied by those who are responsible for coordinating all the parts of the complex organization to achieve the objectives they have set.

It is this responsibility for coordinating *all* the parts of the organization—not only the *functional departments* like production, sales, and finance, but also the *interest groups* like stockholders, customers, and employees—which almost of necessity gives top management a different perspective toward personnel and industrial relations policy from that held by the personnel office. In particular, top management's attitude toward the union is likely to be more resistant and critical. From where management sits, the various interests composing the corporation must all be given satisfaction, and it cannot look on employees and union as having some special claim to satisfaction. From where the personnel director sits, he can discharge his function effectively only if he succeeds in creating a reasonably good working relationship with employees and their agent. From where top management sits, efficiency is the principal key to achieving its objectives. From where the personnel director sits, efficiency must sometimes be sacrificed—or at least be sought more indirectly than line managers desire—in order to meet the divergent value structure of workers and union and to achieve that effective working relationship which he seeks.

Since the personnel director is involved in day-to-day relations with the union and its officers, he gets to know them personally and to understand what kind of people they are. If he construes his job as one requiring him to effect a good working relationship with the union on behalf of the labor force, this job orientation is likely to lead him in the direction of accepting compromise. The president of the company can sit in his office and tell the personnel director, emphasizing with fist thumping on the desk, that he will never give in to the union on such and such a matter, but the personnel director must be concerned with whether or not he can reach an understanding on any other basis. Knowing the union leaders, he can better assess what issues they will be willing to trade off against others and on what issues they will refuse to concede. If his president is unyielding and the union too is adamant, how can agreement be forthcoming?

If, then, the personnel or industrial relations director sees his job as one requiring him to assist in effecting agreement, he will be driven to perform a quasi-mediation function. Many directors will quite freely admit that developing a conciliatory attitude in top management is as much, and as difficult, a part of their task as is developing such an attitude in the union leaders. Top-line management still retains all the formal authority to make the final decisions; the personnel director can only suggest, but it becomes part of his function to persuade a top management which is already inclined to be critical of the union that it should be a little more reasonable. The personnel director is thus frequently in an ambiguous position. He must argue on behalf of the management in his negotiations with the union, but he must

argue on behalf of the union in his negotiations with top management.

This does not mean, however, that the typical personnel man is a "bleeding heart" who always knuckles under to the workers. In fact, precisely because the top line manager is under pressure from many sources to keep production going (to meet customers' deadlines, to pay expected dividends, and so on), he may yield to union pressure although his personnel staff advises him not to. On this point, the Brookings study of labor relations in 150 companies is most revealing:[4]

Criticism of labor relations staffs for lack of interest in efficiency is rarely valid. Actually staff employees, by suggesting policies and by striving for reasonably consistent application of policy, are commonly giving more thought to the goal of long-term efficiency than is the line. It [is] the labor relations job ... sometimes to "stiffen the back" of the line, and at other times to "restrain the line."

... Time after time labor relations officials recounted instances where they felt that the line, under pressure for production and quick resolution of problems, wanted to make concessions detrimental to long-term efficiency, to get the question resolved quickly and not interfere with production.

Just as interesting are situations where the line is tempted to take advantage of a particular situation. In one company a particular plant was regularly exceeding production schedules. The plant manager always started the production lines above the scheduled and engineered level. Frequently neither the workers nor the union objected. If, as happened from time to time, the union and workers put up a fairly stiff objection to the work pace, he cut the lines back to the engineered level. The vice-president of the company for production shrugged the problem off with the comment that at least that was the kind of one they could live with for the time being. But the question is how long they will be able to report that they do not have a militant local at that plant.

In that particular case, who is better serving the company's interest in greater efficiency—the plant manager who is rolling up production records today, or the personnel manager who protests that tomorrow that speed-up policy will backfire if the workers and union rebel and fight every production standard, whether reasonable or not? That is often the real difference between the line and staff views of "efficiency." No personnel man ever argues that efficiency is unimportant, and indeed he maintains that good personnel relations improve efficiency *in the long run*. In his view, if short-run gains are bought by conceding either too much or too little to labor, the firm will eventually lose more than it has saved in labor costs. The line manager is aware of this possibility, of course, but he is under such constant pressure to produce results that he may be skeptical of advice to forgo a temporary advantage today to avert labor problems that might (or might not) arise tomorrow. If you were the plant manager in the above case, for example, would you alter your approach when it obviously has the support of your corporate superior (the vice-president for production)?

Recruitment and selection

These practices and problems of the personnel manager can be illustrated by examining his role in the hiring of new employees. This personnel function also reveals the very different views of the labor market held by employers and workers. In Chapters 3 and 4, we saw that, to the young worker seeking his first job or to the experienced worker who has lost his old job, the job hunt can be a frustrating experience where "who you know" often seems more important than what you know, where it is hard to discover which employers are even in the market for workers, and where job hunters always outnumber job openings. To the employer, on the other hand, there is always a shortage of *good* workers and no matter how vigorous his recruitment efforts or how attractive his wages and benefits, it often seems that the unemployed are too lazy to apply for a job or too poor in quality to be hired.

In the conventional theory of line-and-staff relationships, recruitment proceeds as follows: Line supervision determines the number and quality of new workers needed, the personnel office screens all applicants to find those who meet the firm's standards, and the line supervisor makes the final selection among the eligibles because he is the one ultimately responsible for the new worker's performance. Sometimes the process actually works that way, particularly in the hiring of key employees, but often the personnel office also makes the hiring decision in fact if not in name. The reasons for this have already been suggested. On the one hand, a busy supervisor simply may not want to bother with interviewing several candidates for each routine job he must fill and will gladly let the employment interviewer make the decision. On the other hand, if the personnel manager tells a dissatisfied supervisor that he has scoured the market and turned up only four applicants for a job, three of whom failed a battery of tests required for that job, on what ground could the supervisor reject a "recommendation" that he hire the fourth and only applicant referred to him?

But there are more difficult and subtle problems than that inherent in the employment process. First of all, the term "hiring standards" implies that the content of each job dictates the quality of the worker whom the firm must hire if it is to maintain an efficient work force. In practice, however, these standards are rubber yardsticks which must and do change as labor-market conditions change. When business is good and many companies are expanding, competition for workers is very keen and hiring standards tend to fall, particularly in the less prosperous companies which must take what they can get. In slack periods, of course, the reverse is true and each company can afford to be more selective. A classic illustration of this process is the rise and fall of hiring standards for engineers during the postwar period, reflecting (among other things) the swings and shifts in government defense activities.

This elasticity of hiring standards has several implications. During the period between 1955 and 1965, for example, many economists and labor leaders feared that automation was increasing the severity of "structural unemployment," meaning a growing mismatch between the education and skills possessed by the unemployed and those required by the new technology. In retrospect, much of the excessive unemployment of that period was clearly due to the weakness of aggregate demand, which in turn permitted employers to require workers to have high school diplomas in order to pump gas or in other ways to raise hiring standards so sharply that it indeed appeared as if millions of workers had suddenly been rendered obsolete. When the economy boomed in the middle and late 1960s, however, employers discovered again (as they had in World War II and other times of labor shortage) that many of the workers who were "unemployable" one day could usefully be employed the next. This is not to deny the existence of structural unemployment, a problem we shall examine in a later chapter, but to point out that its magnitude can easily be exaggerated if one forgets how employers adjust their hiring standards upward in a loose labor market.

This need to respond to changes in available labor supply also creates problems within the firm. If the personnel manager does not lower hiring standards quickly enough in a tight market, he intensifies the shortage problem facing his firm, but if he overreacts, he may lower the quality of the work force more than necessary. Even if he guesses correctly, problems can later arise in the promotion process. Workers of mediocre ability, taken on when the labor market was tight, may block the advance of workers of superior ability who came in during a subsequent period of labor slack. Finally, it should be noted that recruitment is only one illustration of the fact that *no personnel standard or technique can be applied without regard to external market forces.* For example, if a job-evaluation system says that the equitable wage differential between two jobs should be 10 percent but the market says a 20 percent differential is needed to fill the higher job, the evaluation system will have to give way. Similarly, discipline and incentive-wage standards are often tightened in a loose market and relaxed during periods of labor shortage.

Hiring promotable workers

Another recruitment problem springs from the fact that hiring a worker involves more than simply filling a vacant slot. It is not just a job which is being filled, but a probable succession of jobs. This is due to the fact that most positions above what are known as "intake jobs" are filled by promotion from within. In some companies, this is a matter of management policy. It is considered good practice to stimulate employee performance by holding out the prospect of advancement as a reward for meritorious service. In other companies, the matter is no longer discretionary with management but is written into the collective agreement. Whatever the source of the policy, the effect on the hiring process is the same: The personnel office weighs the candidate not simply against the requirements of a particular job (usually at the low end of the job scale, where most intake jobs are to be found) but also considers him in terms of his longer-run future with the company, whether he has the capacities to advance in the job hierarchy and to make a contribution of increasing value all the while.

In a study of more than eighty manufacturing companies in the Trenton, New Jersey, area, Prof. Richard Lester of Princeton found this to be the prevailing philosophy and practice:[5]

All or most of the manual jobs up the occupational ladder are filled by promotion from within, in four-fifths of the companies interviewed. In this group, roughly one-quarter of the companies fill all of the jobs above the bottom grade by in-plant promotion, another quarter staff practically all such jobs by promotion, and half promote into more than 50 per cent of the jobs up the line. With two exceptions, all the companies employing 500 or more workers fill most or all of the plant jobs above the bottom grade by means of promotion from within.

... In many of the companies interviewed, practically all classifications except the starting jobs are closed to initial placement for workers without seniority, so that nine-tenths or more of the firm's present plant work force were hired at the bottom of the job hierarchy despite their previous work experience.

There are exceptions to this general policy. In some companies most jobs are roughly on the same level of skill and pay, so that there is no inducement for workers to move between jobs when the transfer carries no benefit (and may even involve some loss, if pay is on a piecework basis and a new routine must be learned before one earns as much as he has been getting on a familiar process). Here new hires may start in a broad variety of jobs, but the prospect of advancement is missing in them all. The other major exception is in the firms with more rapidly changing technologies, where particular openings may call for a type of training or knowledge not provided by prior experience in the company, so that the job's requirements can only be met by hiring from the outside. The same consideration is present, however, as in hiring for the less glamorous "intake" positions: What is the likely long-run contribution which the applicant can make to the company?

The importance of that question can perhaps best be realized if one conceives of a company as putting at the disposal of every worker on its payroll a piece—some share—of a complex and often expensive organization, which a worker can either debase or increase in value. This implies that a company puts in the hands of each worker not simply a capital investment averaging somewhere between $6,000 and $20,000, but also *some* responsibility for the effectiveness of the organization itself—an intangible value but no less significant. To the extent that a worker becomes disgruntled, noncooperative, or lackadaisical, he contributes to the deterioration of the organization. To the extent that he lacks imagination, capacity for growth, and adaptability, he acts as a deterrent to its betterment. Thus the personnel office, in recruiting, is concerned not solely with seeing that some specific job gets done in the present but also with ensuring that the company places its future in the hands of those who will most contribute to it.

This concern for an employee's outlook and personality characteristics is one reason for the widespread use of psychological tests in the hiring process. Despite the debunking of this practice by such writers as William H. Whyte, Jr. (*The Organization Man*), Martin L. Gross (*The Brain Watchers*), and Vance Packard (*The Pyramid Climbers*), various surveys suggest that more than half of all companies having personnel offices make use of such test procedures for salaried personnel, and almost half use them in the hiring of hourly rated employees. The tests themselves may be suspect, but the pressures leading to their use are understandable.

As for the use of tests in general—performance and aptitude as well as psychological tests—their role remains nearly as controversial today as when they were first adopted by industry in the 1920s, but a few generalizations can safely be made. First, tests can certainly be useful in appraising many manual skills. In filling a typist's job, for example, no one would challenge the utility of a test of typing speed and accuracy. But at the other extreme, how does one test the innovative potential of a fledgling chemist? Second, most tests can better predict failure than success. If an applicant for either a typist's or a chemist's job flunks every relevant test of knowledge, performance, and aptitude by a wide margin, that applicant usually would not perform as well on the job as an applicant who passed all the selection tests. Among those who pass, however, a few will also fail on the job, many will be only average employees, a few will be outstanding—and rarely will these differences be predictable from their test scores. Either we know too little about what it takes to be outstanding on certain jobs or, even when we think we know, we seldom can measure or predict intangibles such as motivation, creativity, or leadership ability. Third, it follows that in hiring for nearly any series of jobs at any level, tests alone are not an adequate basis for selection and usually must be supplemented by interviewing each applicant, examining his education and previous experience, checking his references, and so on.

The academic world offers several obvious parallels to these selection problems in industry. Among high school students competing for admission to college, those with poor course grades and low scores on the "college boards" are clearly greater academic risks than those with high grades and scores. Among those chosen, however, every reader probably knows some students performing far below their intellectual capacity and others doing far better than their early test scores would predict. This process is repeated in the scramble for graduate school, in which references and work experience and interviews often play a role but selection is primarily based on undergraduate grades and the scores achieved on various standard tests—again for good reason but with mixed results in predicting student performance. Finally, the graduate student who wishes to enter teaching learns that colleges have much the same recruitment goal as industrial firms: to hire at an intake job (instructor or assistant professor) someone with the potential to merit eventual promotion from within to a series of higher-rated jobs (associate and full professor). And colleges have just as much trouble predicting the teaching potential of someone who has never taught as industry has in predicting the managerial potential of someone who has never managed.

In short, it is difficult enough to "grade" individuals on what they know and are able to do at a given time, but it is even harder to predict what they will learn and do in the future. Yet, that is what the personnel manager must attempt to do in recruiting and selecting new employees.

Hiring disadvantaged workers

As a final example of recruitment problems, the hiring of disadvantaged workers presents a unique test of the possible clash between equity and efficiency. The conventional activities of the recruiter certainly pose no such clash, for the firm that lands the best (most promotable) workers presumably profits from their higher productivity. Now we encounter the problem of whether and how the firm should adjust to job seekers who, by normal hiring standards, may not qualify even for an intake job, much less for future promotion.

"Disadvantaged workers" is a term much like "underprivileged children" or "underdeveloped countries"—impossible to define with precision or without overtones of condescension. We shall use it here to refer primarily to Negro workers who have trouble meeting normal hiring standards because of poor education or training or work experience or simply outright discrimination. By any definition, of course, not all disadvantaged workers are Negroes nor are all Negroes disadvantaged in the labor market. Also, it is difficult to distinguish between disadvantages which are the products of racial discrimination and those which are not. If a Negro fails to pass an employment test because of the poor education he received in a segregated school, for example, is he any less a victim of discrimination than the Negro who passes the test but is rejected solely because of his color? In spite of these definitional problems, many Negro job seekers are clearly examples of the "disadvantaged worker" who is

challenging conventional selection techniques in American industry (and society) today.

As many employers have been quick to point out, their hiring practices have usually reflected the attitudes of society at large concerning minority groups (and thus, it might be added, have reinforced those attitudes). Only a generation or two ago, racial discrimination was regarded as so natural and inevitable that few people besides "reformers" even asked why employers refused to hire Negroes in many industries or occupations. If the question did arise, a frequent answer was that the employer himself was not prejudiced but, alas, he could not say as much for his white workers or customers who would rebel if he hired Negroes. The tight labor markets of World War II enabled Negroes to make major employment gains in some high-wage manufacturing industries, but still, few companies hired Negroes for any white-collar job or promoted Negro production workers to skilled or supervisory jobs, regardless of their qualifications. In that period, most employers were obviously *not* gearing their hiring standards to obtain the most efficient workers available, but were seeking only the most efficient among the majority group in the labor force. Indeed, it was often at the management level— where education and tolerance were presumably greatest—that the "WASP syndrome" was most pronounced (that is, reserving the best jobs for white Anglo-Saxon Protestants).

Then, in the the late 1940s and the 1950s, pressure mounted on employers to be strictly objective and "color-blind" in their hiring—to judge Negro and white job applicants by precisely the same standards, favoring neither one nor the other. This was the major thrust of the fair employment practices laws passed in several Northern states in this period, the efforts of every postwar president to secure nondiscriminatory practices by firms holding federal contracts, and finally the ultimate achievement that had appeared impossible only a few years before—the Civil Rights Act of 1964 which declares, among other things, that it is unlawful for almost every employer in interstate commerce to do the following:[6]

(1) to fail or refuse to hire or to discharge any individual, or otherwise to discriminate

against any individual with respect to his compensation, terms, conditions, or privileges of employment, because of such individual's race, color, religion, sex, or national origin; or

(2) to limit, segregate, or classify his employees in any way which would deprive or tend to deprive any individual of employment opportunities or otherwise adversely affect his status as an employee, because of such individual's race, color, religion, sex, or national origin.

But events had moved more swiftly than Congress, and employers had scarcely digested this new law before they were propelled into the third stage of this evolution of hiring standards: the demand that they be *more than neutral* in their hiring and instead seek out and give special aid to workers who, often through no fault of their own, cannot meet normal hiring standards. The reader will again recognize the parallel with developments in the academic world, where the battle in the 1950s to eliminate blatant segregation in Southern public schools expanded in the 1960s into demands that Northern colleges, private and public, do more than admit Negroes with the same college-board scores required of whites. And in both arenas, the rationale behind these demands is the same—not that the world owes Negroes a living (or an education), but that it is hypocritical to pretend that if only discrimination were wiped out today, whites and Negroes could compete on even terms tomorrow. After generations of discrimination in education, housing, and most other areas, it is argued, the average Negro now begins his working life so poorly equipped, compared to the average white, that he cannot instantly compete on equal terms if employers do no more than drop color from their list of hiring standards. Given a chance to get up to the white's starting line in most respects, however, the Negro will take his chances.

We are not going to resolve this civil rights revolution in a page or two, but it is important to examine how employers are responding to these rapid shifts in the social and legal environment in which they recruit. No one knows, of course, the number of employers who are flouting the Civil Rights Act either openly or through the subterfuge of "tokenism," but surely there must be thousands who are hoping to cling to the old order as long as possible. Impressionistic evidence suggests, however, that a number of the nation's largest and most visible companies are making an honest attempt to comply with the law and that many, in fact, have moved into "phase three" and are experimenting with new hiring techniques that go beyond the neutrality required by law. The motives of these employers are probably mixed—ranging from idealism and a sense of social responsibility to a fear of lawsuits, boycotts, and unfavorable publicity—but whatever the reason, it is a hopeful sign that these pattern-setting firms are reacting to the Civil Rights Act far more constructively than they did to the equally radical Wagner Act in another day. We shall therefore concentrate on those employers who have taken some initiative in meeting the problems of Negro job seekers, not because they are yet typical of American industry but because their experiences herald the changes that are certain to come eventually throughout most of the labor sector.

New employment policies

For any firm to alter its hiring stance toward disadvantaged workers, a crucial first step is *the active involvement of top management*. It is not enough for a company's chief executives to be men of good will who generously contribute their time and money to community organizations that promote better race relations. If the company has long practiced discrimination in its hiring, either actively or passively, a spate of liberal speeches by the company's president will seldom change the practices of the personnel staff and of the supervisors who do the actual recruitment and selection. Before they change, these individuals require concrete assurance and direction that top management really means to practice privately what it is suddenly preaching publicly.

For example, when the auto industry embarked on a program to hire the hard-core unemployed following the Detroit riots of 1967, Henry Ford II explicitly committed his company in a strong letter to some 10,000 Ford executives and supervisors, and in Chrysler, both the board chairman and the company president called some twenty top executives together and told them each man would be held personally responsible for the success of the program in his division. That is the language which executives and supervisors understand. Also, management frequently institutes some system of auditing a new employment program, to check on how many disadvantaged workers are actually being hired, trained, promoted, and so on—which also represents a change from the fair-employment goals of earlier years, when companies were urged to eliminate all reference to race in their personnel records. In short, many employers are relearning an elementary rule of personnel administration: "Nothing gets done without top management backing, without passing the word, and without a followup organization."[7]

The second step in such a program requires the employer *to take the initiative in recruiting disadvantaged workers.* Given the urgent needs of these workers, why don't they swarm to any firm that announces its willingness to hire them? If they are not lazy and shiftless, why should an employer practically have to beg them to apply for jobs? Again the academic parallel is instructive. For many years the most prestigious colleges in the North prided themselves on their nondiscriminatory admission standards, and yet relatively few Negroes applied to these colleges. This was partly because of inadequate academic preparation but partly, too, because few Negroes believed they would really be welcome in the world of white fraternities and football weekends that constituted the college image projected by books, movies, and often the colleges' own recruitment material. When these colleges determined to expand their Negro enrollment in the 1960s, they found it necessary to do more than repeat their pledge of nondiscrimination, and so began the competition among college recruiters for promising Negro students. Much the same process has occurred in the labor sector. If a firm has for many years practiced active discrimination in its hiring or has applied employment tests that screen out all but the most exceptional ghetto residents, it is not surprising that the disadvantaged worker is skeptical of that firm's press release that, beginning today, things will be different. After all, if experience proves that even lower-level managers

inside the firm need convincing, why should the unemployed Negro be more trusting?

In addition, it will be recalled that the grapevine is often more important than formal channels in matching up jobs and job seekers. The employer leans heavily on at-the-gate applications and recommendations by present employees to fill job openings, and the unemployed worker depends on his employed relatives and friends for leads to the "employment gates" at which he should show up. But if a firm is trying to tap a new source of labor supply, the grapevine may be of no value. How do white workers living in Burbank spread the word to Negroes in Watts that their company is now serious about integrating its work force?

For these reasons, an employer who wants results from a "fair-employment policy" must open up new channels of recruitment and to some extent take the job to the worker. A study of twenty companies that adopted aggressive programs in this area reported:[8]

> A number of companies attempted to form close personal relationships with key members of the Negro community—ministers, teachers, scout leaders, directors of settlement houses, welfare workers, and recreational workers, for example. Such contacts yielded many applicants who could not be reached through traditional job referral channels, especially for nonprofessional and nontechnical jobs. . . .
> . . . The companies most often used specialized Negro agencies for recruitment—for example, the Urban League's regional skill banks, which serve both Negro job applicants and companies seeking Negro workers The companies also made intensive use of predominantly Negro high schools and southern Negro colleges as sources of recruitment. *Direct applications were less important sources of Negro than of white workers.*

Even in the auto industry, which had long hired many thousands of Negroes, employers recognized that a program to recruit the hard-core unemployed required new approaches. These workers did not answer the usual want ads for unskilled auto workers, but they did respond when Ford sent its interviewers directly into Negro neighborhoods with the authority to hire men on the spot. Or, as the board chairman of American Motors observed: "We concluded that a company couldn't live up to the spirit of an equal-opportunity employment policy simply by sitting on its nondiscrimination clauses. We felt we had to seek out qualified Negro applicants actively, and to let people know that we were doing just this."[9]

It is the third step in this process—*selecting which applicants are to be hired*—that generates the most controversy. After active recruitment has turned up many workers who would not normally bother to apply to a particular firm, should the personnel manager then apply his usual selection standards? If he does, these new recruitment procedures do not threaten the firm's goal of efficiency; in fact, that goal is better served because the firm can now select workers from a larger-than-usual pool of applicants. But if few or none of these disadvantaged workers can meet the firm's usual selection standards, should those standards be changed or lowered in any way? That is the crux of this problem today, and neither employers nor neutral experts can agree on its solution.

We have seen how difficult it is to predict the future performance of a worker even when his ability to perform an intake job can be measured. In appraising disadvantaged workers, however, no one is yet sure how to measure their ability at the intake level, much less their potential for the future. As President Lyndon Johnson once observed:[10]

Men and women of all races are born with the same range of abilities. But ability is not just the product of birth. Ability is stretched or stunted by the family you live with, and the neighborhood you live in, by the school you go to, and the poverty or richness of your surroundings. It is the product of a hundred unseen forces playing upon the ... infant, the child, and finally the man.

The practical implication of this fact for the selection process is that employment tests and other hiring criteria may be so geared to white, middle-class values and experience and education that they are largely irrelevant in appraising Negro (and also many white) members of the hard-core unemployed. For example, one employer hired fifteen Negro workers for assembly jobs without the usual battery of tests, but then administered those tests after the workers had been on the job for six months. "In spite of the fact that each one had received a satisfactory rating on the job, not one of the fifteen received a passable test score!"[11]

Or consider the hurdles that faced a worker applying for a blue-collar job in the auto industry until the mid-1960s:[12]

Typically, a person going to an employment office of any one of the Big Three—General Motors, Ford, Chrysler—would fill out an application. About a week later (the time lapse giving a firm the opportunity to investigate the applicant's statements), he might receive a card telling him to report again to the employment office—or he might *not* hear from the company again. . . .

. . . The man who had progressed this far would take a written "Industrial Personnel Test." In effect, the tests tended to discriminate against the untutored—that is, the hard core. Part I, typically, consisted of perhaps 50 multiple-choice questions to test a man's accuracy with words. Part II contained about 20 arithmetic questions: "Town X is 30 miles north of Town Y. Town Y is 15 miles north of Town Z. How far is Town Z from Town X?"

. . . After this test, applicants were sent home with the advice that "we'll call you if we need you." It would take another week for those who had passed to hear from the firm; those who failed were never told why. And even a man who was called to report for work still faced a physical examination in which he might be turned down after all.

In sharp contrast, the selection process operated as follows when Ford interviewers went into Detroit ghetto areas: Each applicant filled out, alone or with help, a simple 5-by-8 card that asked for basic information on schooling, military and work experience, and arrests (but applicants had been told that a police record was not an automatic bar to employment); each was interviewed for about half an hour; those who passed were given a medical examination; and those who passed that exam were hired immediately and were on the job within the next two or three days, where they performed neither better nor worse than most other employees.

Few employers have gone that far, however. For one thing, the auto firms themselves stressed that they faced an acute labor shortage when they initiated their new hiring program in Detroit, so their employment standards would have dropped in any event. But in a loose labor market with many job seekers well qualified by the "old" standards, can an employer be expected to make special provision for the hard-core unemployed? For another thing, an assembly-line job is easier to fill than an opening for an electrician, a skilled printer, or an engineer. Obviously these and many other jobs require more rigorous selection standards than a half-hour interview and a medical exam. But what test or other standard can ever compensate accurately for the "hundred unseen forces" that operate so differently in the worlds of whites and blacks?

Although no one has the answer to these questions, it is clear that the selection process in American industry will never again be quite the same as in the past. Most employers still insist that it would be neither efficient nor fair to lower their hiring standards to favor disadvantaged workers, but that is not always the question at issue. Many disadvantaged workers can perform well on many jobs, but to find them, the employer may have to adopt hiring standards that are *different but not necessarily lower* than his previous standards—and that is exactly what many employers are now searching for. It is true, for example, that testing will continue to be used for many jobs and also that there is no such thing as a culture-free test that measures equally well the intelligence or job aptitude of a Chinese peasant, a Negro sharecropper, and the president of IBM. The fact remains that many employers are now taking a hard look at their selection tests from a new perspective and are discovering that they can eliminate at least the most blatant sources of cultural bias in some tests, or that they can achieve the same predictive results with other and simpler tests for the disadvantaged or sometimes even with no tests whatever, as illustrated above.

The high school diploma is another screening device that is being reappraised, as study after study shows that it does not predict better performance on many of the jobs for which it has been required in recent years.

The requirement of a high school diploma has in fact become a kind of shibboleth in personnel practice, often applied without thought as to its usefulness in selecting workers able to perform the jobs that are to be filled. ... The result has been that large numbers of Americans who do not complete their high school educations find it increasingly more difficult to get jobs where such an education is demanded but not always necessary for proper job performance.... [Also, dropouts are not necessarily inferior in ability.] Often the reason for failing to complete high school is economic, or due to problems at home. One report ... covering over 21,000 dropouts found that 11 percent of them were students of very high ability. A number of other studies indicate that general intelligence is not important in identifying potential dropouts.
... To the extent employers believed that possession of a diploma *might* increase the odds in favor of good job performance [regardless of job requirements], they were warranted in indulging in the luxury of insisting on such standards when the national rate of unemployment varied between 5 and 7 percent between 1958 and 1964 and the employer could indulge his whims by picking and choosing from a pool of unemployed.

But insistence on diplomas for all workers makes no sense among employers now [in 1968] complaining about labor shortages. The real fact is that the use of the diploma as a work permit, frequently supplemented by tests that actually disregard job requirements and abilities of the applicant, shuts the door to many capable workers. For a variety of reasons, a larger proportion of minority group youngsters than white youngsters lack high school diplomas, and this has become one of the major factors helping to explain, but not excuse, the shockingly high rate of unemployment among nonwhite teenagers.[13]

The fourth and final step in hiring disadvantaged workers involves *special placement procedures* to help those selected to learn their jobs and adjust to a work environment that is often strange to persons accustomed to long periods of unemployment interspersed with occasional handyman jobs. Employers vary widely in their approach to this step, with some feeling that as little fuss as possible should be made over these new workers. Others have established special training programs for these workers (often with federal aid), "buddy systems" on the job or in the worker's home neighborhood (that is, an experienced worker shows the new man the ropes on the job or simply helps him get to work regularly and punctually for perhaps the first time in years), informal discussion sessions with foremen, special training for supervisors, and orientation programs for white workers when Negroes are to be employed for the first time.

On the last point, experience shows that resistance from white workers (and customers) is usually far less than expected, particularly when management is firm in asserting that company policy is henceforth to be nondiscriminatory. Apparently, few whites are prepared to quit their jobs rather than work with Negroes, although

Table 16-1 suggests that resistance may take more subtle forms. It is well known that many workers pick up much of their skill through informal channels on the job—tips from foremen and senior employees, temporary assignments in other jobs, and so on—rather than in formal training classes. In the twenty companies covered by Table 16-1, management had followed most of the steps just described in preparing to hire more Negro workers and assumed that, once established on the job, they were sharing equally in informal training. Clearly this was not the case.

More than any other feature of the work situation [in these companies], the lack of exposure to informal job learning was described with bitterness and frustration by the unskilled Negro employees, who saw it as a reflection of interpersonal relations at work. The fact that management spokesmen were unaware that Negroes were virtually excluded from informal job learning suggests that such de facto discrimination may be well insulated from earnest attempts to equalize opportunities. It might yield to a plan of job rotation. . . .[14]

Table 16-1 *On-the-Job Learning Opportunities for Unskilled Workers in Twenty Companies, by Race**

Question and answer	Percent of workers giving specified answer	
	Whites	Negroes
On your present job, are you restricted to one kind of work, or do you have opportunities to learn other skills?		
Restricted to one job	63	94
Have opportunities to learn other skills	37	6
Do you often get a chance to work at a job that involves more responsibility than your own?		
Yes	27	7
No	73	93
Do you often get a chance to trade jobs or to fill in on jobs that give you an opportunity to become familiar with work that is different from your own?		
Yes	34	7
No	66	93

* Based on responses from 57 white and 170 Negro employees on unskilled blue-collar jobs in 20 companies.

SOURCE: U.S. Department of Labor, Manpower/Automation Research Monograph no. 9, *Finding Jobs for Negroes: A Kit of Ideas for Management*, 1968, p. 13.

An appraisal

On balance, does the hiring of disadvantaged workers require that labor costs must be increased as the price of eliminating racial discrimination in the labor market? To answer that question for the economy as a whole involves a type of social accounting that we have not even touched upon. It is easy to see that labor costs would increase if private industry were suddenly ordered to hire all the workers now unemployed, regardless of each firm's needs or each worker's qualifications, but no one proposes such a draconian law. The question instead is what the costs and benefits would be of a vast number of interlocking programs, ranging from improving the general health, education, and housing of disadvantaged groups to offering better work-training programs, government aid to employers willing to hire the disadvantaged, and perhaps government jobs to workers considered unemployable by private industry. If we thus spent billions to improve the quality of the labor supply and to shore up the demand for labor, would this cost be more than offset by improved efficiency throughout the economy (to say nothing of the noneconomic benefits)? Many economists would answer "yes," but this is a question that needs more exploration in later chapters.

At the level of the individual firm, the answer also depends upon the question asked. Are there limits beyond which it would be very costly for an employer to continue hiring disadvantaged workers? Of course. Does this mean that any liberalization of hiring policy toward these workers must cost the firm more than a conventional, pre-1960 policy? Not at all. If an employer does no more than drop the color bar from his hiring standards, his firm's efficiency can hardly suffer from enlarging the pool of job applicants who meet all his other standards. And more important, some employers have demonstrated that the "disadvantages" of many Negro job seekers exist in the eye of the beholder instead of in the workers themselves. When these workers are recruited, selected, and placed with care and imagination, they frequently prove to be as efficient as the average employee hired by conventional techniques. To repeat, this does not mean that any disadvantaged worker can perform any job as well as anyone

else can. It does mean, however, that any conflict in the hiring process between equity and efficiency is less irreconcilable than was assumed only a few years ago.

Management development

As a final example of personnel techniques, management development is interesting for several reasons: It is one of the newest areas of personnel management; it illustrates the problems of applying standards to the growing number of unstandardized, white-collar jobs; and it also reveals the difficulty that personnel managers have in proving the effectiveness of most of their programs, whether designed for blue-collar or white-collar workers.

Employers long operated on the assumption that only blue-collar workers needed on-the-job training and that supervisors and managers were born, not made. In the 1940s, the rise of unions and the research findings of industrial sociologists led many companies to initiate training programs for their foremen, particularly in human relations skills, and of course the proportion of managers with business school and other college training has been rising steadily. Only in the last decade or two, however, have many companies attempted to systematize the training and development of executives after they have been hired.

> According to a recent [estimate] ..., U. S. companies, in an effort to fight the increasing problem of management obsolescence, put some 500,000 executives through on-the-job training courses, management seminars, and formal academic programs during 1966 alone—nearly twice the number put through such programs in 1961. In 1953 only four universities offered programs specifically conceived and directed for executives, whereas today [1967] more than forty universities offer advanced management training programs, ranging in duration from several weeks to several months.[15]

To establish a management-development program, a company must first determine its current and future needs at the executive level. An "inventory" of present managers may reveal, for example, that several key executives are of about the same age and thus due to retire at about the same time, which could create serious problems if their potential replacements are not spotted at an early date and groomed to move up. The ideal inventory will also indicate which managers need more training to perform better on their present jobs, which show the most promise for promotion, and the kind and number of executives needed to anticipate future moves into new products or methods.

But even an ideal inventory of executive talent will not answer the question of precisely what or how a manager should be taught in any development program. American companies (and government agencies) employ a wide variety of techniques in training their executives and, as in most educational programs, there is no consensus on the "one best way" of teaching. For example, *on-the-job* development techniques range from informal coaching, in which a manager consciously uses his daily contacts with subordinates to test and expand their ability and not just to give them orders, to highly structured programs, in which junior executives are rotated among different jobs and departments, or placed on task forces studying special problems which are often interdepartmental in nature, or assigned as assistants to top executives for a period or as understudies to the managers they are to replace. Also included in this category is the performance appraisal, in which a manager's effectiveness is periodically rated by his superior. Many companies use this technique today, sometimes just to determine who merits a promotion or salary increase but often for training purposes as well. In that case, the rater must discuss his appraisal with the subordinate in an interview intended to help the latter improve his performance—an interview which, if mishandled, can be a painful experience for both participants.

Off-the-job development programs exhibit an even greater diversity, with their only common element being that they are conducted away from the trainee's immediate job setting. This may mean a series of weekly classes presented by the personnel staff during working hours, or a two-day conference sponsored by a professional association and open to managers from any company, or a university program requiring trainees to live

on campus and attend special classes for several weeks. The methods used in these various programs include the lecture, group discussion, case study, role playing, business games (in which mathematical models and computers may be used to simulate a competitive problem which changes as the players, each representing a different firm, receive feedback on the results of their decisions), and the "in-basket" technique (in which each trainee must deal in a specified time with the memoranda and other materials an executive in a hypothetical firm finds in his in-basket on a particular day).

> The material covered in . . . [off-the-job] programs ranges from the most esoteric to the most mundane. At each extreme, moreover, the material is considered practical by some executives. The study of ancient Greek literature and modern music, for instance, has been justified on the grounds that it would broaden a middle manager's background so that he would be able to see his business problems in a larger social perspective. At the other end of the scale, courses in the writing of memos and reports are said to provide training in an essential management skill.
>
> Within this wide range, however, most management subjects that are offered can be grouped into four major categories: general or specific management skills; economics and business conditions; human relations and supervision; and other related material. General management and economics are used typically for upper-middle managers and higher; specific management skills and, particularly, supervisory skills are used typically for lower-level managers.[16]

Easily the most controversial development technique today is "sensitivity training," which involves no formal subject matter whatever. Instead, individuals who are usually strangers to one another live together for perhaps two weeks in a place remote from their homes, meeting for several hours each day in a group which has no agenda, no leaders, no lecturers, and in which the trainees may not use their business titles. To men who are used to working toward given goals within established superior-subordinate relationships, this can be a frustrating and even painful experience as the group thrashes out what it should talk about, how it should make decisions, and who should be its leaders. The purpose is to help participants become more "sensitive" to their personal strengths and weaknesses (for mutual criticism is often extensive) and to the motives which underlie other people's behavior. Critics charge that this technique is a dangerous flirtation with group psychotherapy that can damage some personalities, but many managers who have gone through sensitivity training claim that it has been of great value to them.[17]

In appraising management-development programs, most authorities agree upon three points. First, although every personnel program needs the support of top management to some extent, this support is particularly crucial to the success of management training. Many supervisors and junior executives have learned new techniques and attitudes in training programs and then discovered, upon returning to their jobs, that their bosses are still operating with the old techniques and attitudes. Faced with a conflict between, for example, an authoritarian boss and a training program extolling democratic styles of leadership, the prudent man will understandably tend to follow the example of his boss. Thus, the personnel manager may have the delicate task of persuading high-level executives that their own behavior and attitudes must change—that is, that they too need more training—if any program is to succeed in changing the behavior and attitudes of their subordinates.

Second, it is far more difficult to define the *goals* of training at the managerial level than at the blue-collar level. Experts will differ over the best method for training a machinist or electrician, but they can agree on the knowledge and skills that any apprentice in those occupations should eventually learn in one way or another. But just how does a manager manage, and in particular, what does a successful manager do or know better than his less successful colleagues? There are plenty of definitions of management, such as "getting things done through other people" or "planning, organizing, and controlling," but these are not very helpful in setting up a specific training program. It is for this reason that the subject matter varies so widely among development programs, from memo writing to Greek

literature (and why the debate continues over whether a liberal arts or business school education is better preparation for a career in management). If no one can put his finger on why some senior executives are more effective than others, then how can anyone be sure what subjects should be taught to junior executives?

Finally, it also is difficult to *evaluate* any management-development program. In part, this is simply an extension of the preceding point: It is obviously difficult to measure whether a training program achieves its goals when no one can define those goals with any precision. Train some men in how to run a lathe and you can easily determine whether the course was successful, but how do you test the success of ten classes on "economics for management" or two weeks of "sensitivity training"?

But this evaluation problem plagues nearly all personnel programs, whether aimed at the blue-collar or white-collar worker. Within certain limits, a management can often predict the returns it will receive from investing in a new type of equipment or material or production process— or at least it can determine after the fact whether its investment did or did not pay off. In most personnel programs, however, the company cannot calculate its returns on a given expenditure *either before or after* it has spent its money. There are simply too many variables involved in the average personnel problem to permit a precise evaluation of any single remedy. Why does a particular company suffer from a high rate of turnover or absenteeism or grievances or wildcat strikes, or why is efficiency low in some departments and high in others? These and other personnel problems seldom spring from a single cause but instead result from some combination of top management's policies, foreman attitudes, the firm's technology and wage level, the state of the economy, the political situation within a union, and many other possible causes, only some of which are within the company's control and even fewer of which are measurable in their impact. Given this ambiguity, how can anyone determine the extent to which a new fringe benefit reduces turnover, a job-evaluation system minimizes grievances, or a management-development program improves the quality of executive decisions?

None of this is meant to belittle the solid achievements of personnel management. After all, we encounter the same difficulties in tackling social problems outside the plant, none of which has a simple cause or solution. Also, personnel experts are fully aware of these difficulties and are working to refine their program goals and evaluation techniques. The fact remains that in many organizations the personnel function is not quite as "respectable" as the line or certain staff functions such as engineering, and a major reason is the inability of the personnel manager to prove his value in dollars and cents.

Morale and productivity

For a variety of reasons, then, personnel managers have long been concerned with the relationship between worker morale and worker efficiency. On the one hand, personnel management traces part of its heritage to the scientific-management movement but, as we have seen, it is difficult to demonstrate the profitability of any specific personnel program. It would therefore be comforting if management could assume that any program that increases worker morale will indirectly increase worker efficiency, even though this payoff could not be measured with any precision. On the other hand, many companies initiated personnel programs in the 1920s and 1930s on the explicit assumption that "a happy worker is a good worker," which, freely translated, meant a belief that satisfied workers were not likely to join a union and impose costly and inefficient practices upon management. It is easy to poke fun at these assumptions by questioning whether a company bowling team and the anticipation of a gold watch after thirty years' service are really going to make a worker happy with a dreary job at low wages. Yet, it *is* sensible to expect that low morale leads to low worker effort, and nearly every management—not just those who are paternalistic or antiunion—bases many of its labor policies on an assumed linkage between morale and productivity.

Unfortunately, this linkage has proved to be far more complex than many managers once believed. To oversimplify considerably, in the early years of industrialization, workers were thought to be motivated primarily by money and fear (of discipline or unemployment); beginning in the 1930s, the rise of unions and the new field of industrial sociology stimulated a sharp swing in management thinking toward a stress on the noneconomic bases of workers' behavior—their desire for equity, participation, two-way communication, and other aspects of good "human relations"; and today there is a healthy state of confusion as both managers and scholars have come to recognize that worker motivation is just too complicated to sum up in any simple theory, either economic or noneconomic in nature.

But first let us put this problem in perspective. The *principal* determinants of productivity in a company or an economy are factors such as the quantity of capital equipment and the quality of the work force, not the nature of manager-worker relations. (That is, whether employers in India treat their employees brutally or decently over the next decade, the efficiency of the Indian economy will obviously lag far behind that of the American economy for other reasons.) On the other hand, significant differences in worker efficiency often exist among departments or plants within the same company and among companies within the same industry—that is, differences which cannot be easily explained by differences in technology or the quality of the labor force or similar external forces. It is these variations in worker performance that personnel managers are expected to know and do something about.

What determines morale?

In an excellent survey of the voluminous research done in this area, Prof. Victor H. Vroom points out that even the meaning of "morale" is difficult to pin down, to say nothing of its causes and effects.[18]

... [Morale] has been used to refer to such widely different properties of individuals as their satisfaction with their membership in an organization and their willingness to exert effort to attain organizational goals. It has also been used as a descriptive property of social systems ranging in size from the face-to-face work group to a whole nation. Even here the definitions vary from a "group persistence in the pursuit of collective purposes" ... to "a

shared feeling of like among group members."
. . . [Also,] workers can be found who report
that they are very satisfied with their supervisors, indifferent toward company policies,
and very dissatisfied with their wages. Which
one, or combination of these, represents their
level of job satisfaction?

Given this uncertainty over the *meaning* of
morale (or job satisfaction or job attitudes), it is
not surprising that the experts disagree over the
causes of high or low morale. Several studies, it
is true, have shown a statistical association between high morale (defined in various ways) and
the following factors: supervision which is em-
ployee-oriented rather than production-oriented
(that is, supervisors who are considerate of their
subordinates' desires as contrasted to those who
view their workers primarily as means to the
end of high production); supervision which permits workers to participate in making decisions;
the worker's membership in a congenial work
group; job content (morale tending to be higher
on jobs with a high skill content, few repetitive
tasks, and a work pace controlled by the worker
rather than by a machine); high relative rather
than absolute wages (the key, that is, being
whether the worker believes he is earning as
much as, or more than, workers of equal skill, not
whether he is matching some fixed income goals);
and good opportunities for promotion. On the
other hand, Vroom shows that other studies have
found no relationship between morale and some
of the factors just cited, and even the studies
supporting these relationships do not agree on
how important any one or all of those factors are
in shaping morale. In short, "there is a great deal
of variance in job satisfaction that remains to be
explained."[19]

A particularly interesting attempt to bridge
these inconsistencies is Prof. Frederick Herzberg's
theory that job satisfaction and job dissatisfaction
are not two sides of the same coin but instead
represent separate and distinct experiences. Herzberg suggests that if something is wrong in the
context of a job—such as company policies, supervision, peer relations, working conditions, and
perhaps even wages—the difficulty can indeed
produce dissatisfaction for all the usual reasons,
but improving the job environment can only pre-

*vent dissatisfaction and will not in itself produce
a happy or highly motivated worker.* In Herzberg's view, it is the *job content* which contributes
to positive satisfaction—the opportunities the job
offers for a sense of achievement, recognition, responsibility, growth, and advancement—although,
again, the absence of these content factors will
not necessarily produce active dissatisfaction. Several studies have supported this theory when
tested on professional and managerial employees,
but its validity has not been established with respect to blue-collar workers. Assembly-line workers in an auto plant, for example, have exhibited
very different attitudes, reporting that the content
of their jobs (repetitive and machine-paced) is
their chief aggravation and that pay and job
security are their chief sources of work satisfaction.[20]

As yet another reason why thirty-five years of
research have failed to produce a consensus on
this subject, Vroom reminds us that both individuals and situations vary greatly. For example,
some individuals may always welcome authoritarian supervision, others always prefer democratic leadership, and yet others may prefer one
type of supervision in some job situations and
another type in other situations. "Job satisfaction
must be assumed to be the result of the operation
of both situational and personality variables," but
few investigators have tried to cope with both
variables in the same study.[21]

Effects on Worker Performance

Even if we knew precisely what causes high and
low morale, the question would remain of whether
an improvement in morale leads to an improvement in job performance. If a hard-driving, tyran-
nical boss is replaced by someone more considerate of people's feelings, for example, will the
workers love the company more but produce less,
or do workers respond to better treatment by
working harder?

Several studies have shown that job satisfaction
is negatively correlated with turnover, as one
would expect—that is, dissatisfied workers are
more likely to quit than satisfied workers are—
and there is some evidence of the same relationship between morale and absenteeism. To the ex-

tent these relationships hold, higher morale does indeed pay off to an employer. *But on the critical question of whether morale is linked to productivity, the evidence is at best inconclusive.* Vroom compared the results of twenty studies that correlated some measure of morale with some measure of worker performance (such as the quantity or quality of work produced), and he found that the reported correlations between morale and performance ranged all the way from .86 to −.31, with the median for all twenty studies being a weak .14.

Does this prove that workers will perform in the same way regardless of how they are treated? No, but these studies do show how little we know about the causes and effects of worker attitudes toward their jobs. Note again, for instance, the different meanings given to the concept of morale. If it means something like *esprit de corps,* then high morale among a group of workers may well lead them to cooperate in setting new production records—or in maintaining informal production standards at a low level out of fear of unemployment or to beat an incentive system or to back up union demands or for a number of other reasons. Team spirit is high in both cases, but the effects on efficiency can obviously vary according to many different circumstances. On the other hand, if the worker has little control over his work pace, as on an assembly line, how can his output vary with his morale, no matter how defined? Some studies have suggested that both morale and efficiency can be increased by rotating low-skilled workers among jobs or by enlarging their jobs to include several tasks to maintain interest, but clearly there is some point beyond which job enlargement will be less efficient than the division of labor which characterizes all modern industry. Finally, even when morale and performance are found to be closely correlated, which is the cause and which the effect? Many managers have assumed that if a worker becomes more satisfied with his wages or supervision or peer relations, he will improve his job performance. But many psychologists now stress the importance of the reverse relationship: The chance to perform well on an interesting and responsible job produces worker satisfaction. As Herzberg argues:

You cannot love an engineer into creativity. The love may make him more comfortable, less hostile, but it is the challenge of the *task* that is the means for unleashing his talents.[22]

This last argument raises the provocative possibility that the Protestant Ethic will return in modern dress, with "human relations" of less importance to worker morale than the knowledge that a challenging job has been met and surmounted. It also poses for the personnel manager the problem of how to introduce interest and challenge into the many uninteresting and unchallenging jobs found in every organization.[23]

Conclusions

To return to the central question of this chapter, can management realistically treat labor as both a factor of production and as people, or are economic and humanistic goals basically incompatible? Men have been arguing for generations over that question in one form or another, and perhaps the most that can be said today is that we better understand why it is unanswerable in any definitive way.

For one thing, the question assumes a clear-cut distinction between "economic" and "noneconomic" motives and behavior, but we have seen that this distinction is often difficult to draw in the real world. Does economic behavior mean that an employer's lust for profits drives him to treat workers as machines instead of men? That type of behavior has certainly occurred throughout industrial history, but it offers at best only a partial answer to our problem. For example, the profit motive cannot explain why government agencies, labor unions, schools, churches, and similar organizations have frequently treated their employees as shabbily as any capitalistic organization has done. And even within a profit-making firm, a personnel manager can argue persuasively today that it is "good economics" to deal fairly with unions, hire disadvantaged workers, treat employees with respect and consideration, train workers for better jobs at company expense, make dull jobs more interesting, develop a sensitivity among executives for modern music or the feelings of other people—all in the name of greater efficiency or lower costs over the long run. Similarly, whether you agree with those managers and psychologists who believe that higher morale produces greater efficiency, or with those who maintain that the chance to do well on a challenging job produces high morale, the thrust of both theories is that economic and noneconomic goals can actually be interdependent to some degree. In short, an employer's choice of personnel policies is far more complex than deciding whether he wants to make money or to be nice to people.

As another reason why this question cannot be answered with finality, we have seen how stubbornly it resists statistical testing. After years of careful research, we still cannot predict with certainty how various workers will react—in either their attitudes or their performance—to a change in wages, supervision, job content, or other variables in the work situation, and we cannot even measure the precise impact of many personnel programs after they have been in effect for months or years. This is hardly surprising, for neither can we predict or evaluate with much precision in any other area of human relationships. Who can prove statistically that one political system is better than another in producing happy or effective or creative individuals, or that one style of courtship or teaching students or rearing children is always more effective than another? In comparing the behavior of individuals or groups, the researcher can never hold all things equal except the one or two variables that he is testing, which means that the motives of both managers and workers must continue to be a subject of speculation as well as scientific inquiry.

But employers cannot wait forever for the academicians to thrash out all these conceptual and statistical problems. They must make decisions on personnel problems each and every day, and clearly the trend in these decisions has been for some time toward a more "liberal" approach—toward training foremen and managers in more democratic methods of supervision, devising effective grievance systems, systematizing wage and salary decisions, minimizing racial discrimination in recruitment and selection, cushioning the impact of technological change, treating collective bargaining as an operating problem rather than an ideological confrontation, and so on.

It is obvious that laws and unions and tight labor markets have all pushed employers in this direction regardless of their original inclinations, but it is also obvious that this trend has permanently changed norms and expectations in the world of work. The college-trained executive of today may not be able to prove statistically the value of high morale or a particular personnel program, but his model of "good management" certainly includes an attention to personnel relations that would have been incomprehensible to an earlier generation of executives, just as most workers today, in or out of unions, expect far better treatment on the job than their fathers would have considered normal and reasonable. Cause and effect and motivations all become hopelessly intertwined, but this trend toward more "progressive" personnel management is unmistakable and probably irreversible.

ADDITIONAL READINGS

Dubin, Robert: *Human Relations in Administration,* 3d ed., Prentice-Hall, Englewood Cliffs, N.J., 1968.

Pigors, Paul, and Charles A. Myers: *Personnel Administration,* 5th ed., McGraw-Hill, New York, 1965.

Sayles, Leonard R., and George Strauss: *Human Behavior in Organizations,* Prentice-Hall, Englewood Cliffs, N.J., 1966.

Tannenbaum, Arnold S.: *Social Psychology of the Work Organization,* Wadsworth, Belmont, Calif., 1966.

Vetter, Eric W.: *Manpower Planning for High Talent Personnel,* University of Michigan, Bureau of Industrial Relations, Ann Arbor, 1967.

Vroom, Victor H.: *Work and Motivation,* Wiley, New York, 1964.

FOR ANALYSIS AND DISCUSSION

1. Are unions a reflection of management's failures? More specifically, can management, by adopting good personnel policies and paying careful attention to their implementation, create a set of working conditions sufficiently satisfactory to its employees to eliminate the need for a union in the plant?

2. There are numerous proposals for improving the employment opportunities of disadvantaged workers: Pursue expansionary fiscal and monetary policies to avoid recessions and keep the economy as a whole booming; vigorously enforce civil rights legislation in the hiring process; appeal to the social conscience of employers; subsidize employers who hire and train disadvantaged workers; expand government training programs (such as the Manpower and Development Training Act and the Job Corps) to give these workers the skills necessary to compete in the labor market; and undertake public works projects for those unable to meet the hiring standards of private industry. On the basis of the evidence we have covered up to this point (plus your own knowledge and values), which one or more of these proposals do you believe we should push hardest in order to meet the problems of disadvantaged workers? Explain your choice.

3. Relate the problems of morale and performance to your own experience as a student. First, define what you mean by student morale (high and low) and student performance (good and poor). Second, list the major variables that you believe affect most students' *attitudes,* positively or negatively, toward their college and their class work (such as teaching, housing, and social life). Third, list the variables (other than whatever is meant by "native intelligence") that you believe affect students' *performance.* Fourth, rate yourself and, through an interview, one other student on the morale and performance scales you have just constructed.

Based on this admittedly inadequate sample, do you find any relationship between the morale and performance of students? And do you expect to find the same relationship (or lack of it) between your own attitudes and performance on the job you hope to land after graduation, or are academic and work environments completely different in this respect?

4. When a college graduate who is trained as a scientist is recruited to work in an industrial laboratory, he is often a more difficult "personnel problem" than his classmate with a liberal arts or business administration training who is recruited into the general-management side of the same company. Why might scientists have more trouble

in adapting to organizational life than most other college graduates?

5. In an article entitled "Management Personnel Philosophy and Activities in a Collective Bargaining Era" (*Annual Proceedings of the Industrial Relations Research Association, 1953*), Sol Barkin, then a trade-union official, argued:

> The American trade union movement has responded more truly to the basic forces in our cultural development in matters of personnel and industrial relations philosophy and practice than has management as a group. The latter has generally continued in line with the more autocratic attitudes, made more acceptable to the public and salable to the unsuspecting by the current use of "humanistic" language and the incorporation of a number of psychological techniques aimed at implanting a deep feeling of enterprise-consciousness among employees. This philosophy and the practices and procedures which flow from it are all designed to leave management's position supreme.

Paraphrase this statement. Then analyze it to see to what extent you may agree and to what extent you may disagree with it.

NOTES

1. "Digest of Discussion on Personnel Organization and Administration," by Howard Dirks, vice-president in charge of personnel relations, Carrier Corporation, NAM Institute on Industrial Relations, Boca Raton, Fla., Jan. 6–10, 1947. An extensive examination of personnel policy, both overall and with respect to specific aspects of company activity, is provided by the National Industrial Conference Board, *Statement of Personnel Policy,* Studies in Personnel Policy no. 169, 1959.

2. This and subsequent information on the organizational aspects of personnel practice have been drawn from Helen Baker's *Management Procedures in the Determination of Industrial Relations Policy.* Princeton University, Industrial Relations Section, Princeton, N.J., 1948.

3. Charles A. Myers and John G. Turnbull discuss the ambiguity of the personnel officer's relations in "Line and Staff in Industrial Relations," *Harvard Business Review,* July–August, 1956, pp. 113–124.

4. Sumner H. Slichter, James J. Healy, and E. Robert Livernash, *The Impact of Collective Bargaining on Management,* Brookings, Washington, 1960, pp. 892, 893–894.

5. Richard A. Lester, *Hiring Practices and Labor*

Competition, Princeton University, Industrial Relations Section, Princeton, N.J., 1954, pp. 32, 33–34.

6. Section 703(a) of the Civil Rights Act of 1964.

7. *Finding Jobs for Negroes: A Kit of Ideas for Management,* U.S. Department of Labor, Manpower/ Automation Research Monograph no. 9, 1968, p. 1. This monograph summarizes a research study, *The Negro and Equal Employment Opportunities: A Review of Management Experiences in Twenty Companies,* conducted by Prof. Louis A. Ferman for the U.S. Department of Labor.

8. *Finding Jobs for Negroes . . . ,* p. 9. Italics added.

9. "The Negro as an Employee," *The Conference Board Record,* September, 1965, p. 45. For the Ford experience, see Gertrude Samuels, "Help Wanted: The Hard-Core Unemployed," *The New York Times Magazine,* Jan. 28, 1968, pp. 27, 42–50.

10. Lyndon B. Johnson, in an address at Howard University in June, 1965.

11. *Finding Jobs for Negroes . . . ,* p. 8.

12. Samuels, "Help Wanted: The Hard-Core Unemployed," p. 44.

13. "Credentials and Common Sense: Jobs for People Without Diplomas," U.S. Department of Labor, Manpower Report no. 13, December, 1968, pp. 2, 5–6.

14. *Finding Jobs for Negroes . . . ,* p. 12.

15. Robert J. House, *Management Development: Design, Evaluation, and Implementation,* University of Michigan, Bureau of Industrial Relations, Ann Arbor, 1967, p. 9.

16. National Industrial Conference Board, *Developing Managerial Competence: Changing Concepts, Emerging Practices,* Studies in Personnel Policy no. 189, New York, 1964, p. 72.

17. The same, pp. 90–94.

18. Victor H. Vroom, *Work and Motivation,* Wiley, New York, 1964, pp. 4–5 and 101.

19. The same, p. 173.

20. The same, pp. 126–129. Also, Frederick Herzberg, et al., *The Motivation to Work,* New York, 1959, and F. Herzberg, "The New Industrial Psychology," *Industrial and Labor Relations Review,* April, 1965, pp. 364–376.

21. Vroom, p. 173.

22. Herzberg, "The New Industrial Psychology," p. 371.

23. Instead of trying to trace the relationship of management policies to morale and then to worker performance, many studies have omitted morale and focused directly on the relationship between performance and variables such as supervisory style, wages, job content, and the nature of the work group —to test, that is, how these factors affect worker performance regardless of whether they also affect worker morale. For a review of the mixed results of these studies, see Vroom, chap. 8.

PART FIVE

LABOR AS A MARKET

Approximately 75 million men and women in the civilian labor force, most of them working in more than 4 million private business establishments, are drawing wages and salaries for the services they perform. What determines how much each of them receives? We can hardly conceive of 75 million different rates flying off in all directions, each one pursuing its independent course without reference to any other rate that workers in the labor force are receiving. What is it, then, that gives structure to the multitude of individual rates? What is it that relates wages to each other? This is the problem to which wage theory addresses itself.

All theory is necessarily an abstraction from reality. Every event is unique in some respect (if only in regard to time or place), and a generalization designed to explain a *class* of cases can therefore deal only with certain characteristics presumably held in common, even though the cases differ in other—for the particular purpose, presumably nonmaterial—respects. Moreover, however we try to come to grips with "reality," there is no way in which we can tell whether a theory in fact describes reality. Starting with certain concepts, we deduce what would happen, given certain conditions. We then compare our deduced conclusions with what we observe in the real world. If what we deduced *would be* the outcome actually *is* the outcome in enough instances to establish some level of confidence in the theory, we say the theory is "workable" or "satisfactory"—*based on the results we achieve from it*. But we can never know whether a theory actually describes "reality," since we have no way of apprehending that directly.

The first systematic attempt to analyze wages is to be found in the competitive price analysis, whose two principal progenitors were Adam Smith and Jeremy Bentham—the former a social philosopher, the latter a student of government. That analysis has been continually refined and has come down to us as a thoroughly worked-out theoretical doctrine. It is no secret that the competitive price analysis today is much criticized, but it is also true that there are economists who continue to support it as fundamentally sound, and even those who criticize it accept some of its tenets. It has shown amazing vitality and continues to play an active part in our economic thinking. If not acceptable in its entirety as a *system,* it contains enough insights to warrant our using it as a point of departure. It is used in that way here.

The competitive price analysis employs five basic concepts, four of which are supposed to be approximations of reality, the fifth being purely a simplification to facilitate deductive reasoning. The basic concepts are these:

1. In economic matters, people act rationally to maximize their satisfactions as consumers. Consumption of goods and services is viewed as the economic benefit or pleasure which people seek, while work is a necessary pain or cost which they undergo for the sake of obtaining goods and services. Maximization means obtaining as much of consumption goods per unit of effort as is possible. People may not always accomplish this objective, but they strive for it, and it is believed that an analysis based on that principle will be more likely to describe reality than would one founded on some other motivational assumption.

2. In Western society, typically, there is choice—by consumers, among a rather large number of products which serve as acceptable substitutes for each other; by the factors of production, among a large number of possible employers; by producers, among a larger number of factors which are alternatives to one another. Because there is always a range of substitute products or services to which the consumer may turn, no one producer has any control over the market. Similarly, there are numerous workers of all skills and abilities in the labor market, so that no worker can set a price on his labor higher than that which other workers of similar skill are demanding.

The effect of organizations—or labor unions and large corporations—is treated rather cavalierly in the competitive analysis. They are ignored, or regarded as incapable of thwarting the underlying and more powerful economic pressures of competition, or if they are conceded to have the power to interfere with competition, they are viewed as susceptible to public control so that competitive conditions can be restored.

3. A high degree of mobility characterizes both goods and services. Transportation facilities permit cheap and rapid movement of people and things. On the part of workers, there is a sufficient willingness to move around to permit their transfer over time from areas of labor surplus to areas of labor shortage. This mobility of products and factors prevents price and wage distortions from arising on a geographical basis.

4. There is easy and full dissemination of information throughout the economy. Thus consumers have a good knowledge of products being offered, their qualities, and their comparative prices. Similarly, producers are aware of consumers' wants and of the availability of the various factors. Workers have information concerning job offerings and relative wage rates. Movement of goods and factors occurs in response to such knowledge, as both consumers and producers seek to maximize their economic advantage.

5. The above four assumptions are really conceptions of Western Society. They are not perfectly or universally valid statements of social conduct, to be sure, but

it is believed that they are so close an approximation of reality that logical conclusions deduced from such conceptions are likely to be correct. There is a fifth concept employed in the competitive price analysis of which this is not true. The construct of a static society is introduced not because it is believed that society is static, but to facilitate deductive reasoning. It is a way of holding constant variables which admittedly are continually changing, a device which is employed to permit conclusive reasoning. By a static society we mean one in which population, consumer tastes, and technology remain constant. If these assumptions were to be abandoned in favor of the assumption of continuing change in these variables, deductive reasoning would become complex and (often) less conclusive. As long as these variables are held constant, then the effects of maximizing behavior, of available substitutes, of mobility, and of information have time to work themselves out along the lines which the competitive theory deduces. Even when we admit change in these important variables over time, the results of static reasoning can be viewed as *tendencies*—never fully realized *because* of changes but always constituting a strong influence in the indicated direction.

Moreover, some conclusion as to the effect of change in one of these three variables may be obtained by the device of comparative statics. Thus a situation may be analyzed, assuming population, tastes, and technology to be given. Then a change in population (or tastes or technology) may be assumed and the situation analyzed under these changed circumstances. The two results may then be compared to see the effect of the change. This is not the same thing as dynamic reasoning, which admits *continuing* change to the analysis, but it is much easier to work with.

The fact that the competitive price analysis is based (in part) on this concept of a static society does not necessarily rob it of acceptability. If it can reveal central tendencies, if it can predict with a higher degree of probable accuracy than other theories (or chance), this is as much as can be asked. There are grounds for concluding that purely competitive theory is inadequate even on this basis, but even so we cannot avoid dealing with its concepts.

Before we plunge into the details of the theory, a few preliminary remarks are in order. We are viewing wages in a rather simplified way. Wages are considered the "price" of labor, whether we think of them as the hourly *rate* or average hourly earnings or a weekly or annual salary. But this is something different from the cost of labor per unit of product, as we noted in Chapter 15, since the latter takes into account the efficiency with which labor is employed (all the elements entering into its productivity), as well as all the nonwage expenditures associated with the employment of labor. ("Fringe benefits," for example, are not specifically considered, although we have seen that these various wage and salary supplements today comprise 20 to 30 percent of total labor compensation in the average firm.)

If wages are viewed as a price, this is a price which is established in a *market*. Households offer labor, and firms hire it, thus creating the supply and demand sides of a labor market. But what do we mean by a market? Technically, it is the area within which our assumptions as to substitutability and mobility of the factors, and information concerning them, apply. But this creates problems for us, since normally one does not expect to find an area within which the competitive assumptions are wholly valid, and outside of which they are wholly invalid. Mobility, for example, is in part a continuous function of distance and transportation facilities, so that one might expect it to be high in local areas, somewhat reduced within a larger region, lower still within the national economy, and even weaker on an international plane.

Obviously, we cannot confine our analysis of wage determination to a local area, as though each local area were discrete and autonomous, unrelated to all other local areas in the United States. But equally obviously, we cannot treat the whole of the United States as though it were a local area. There are in fact a *number* of local markets which are interconnected in ways which transmit pressures and influences from one to the other, but with "impulses" of varying degrees of intensity. This beclouds the competitive analysis, as we shall see, and constitutes one of the elements which require modification.

Although we start by analyzing labor as a factor which has a price set in a market by supply and demand considerations, this does not imply that these are necessarily sufficient for an explanation of how wages are determined. Whether supply and demand considerations are enough to explain the structure of wages is one of the questions in issue. But at least we begin with these old, familiar conceptual friends.

CHAPTER 17

SUPPLY AND DEMAND OF THE LABOR FACTOR

From the time of Adam Smith down to the present, the competitive model has never suffered from a lack of criticism. In viewing the operation of product markets, for example, skeptics have challenged the model to explain the boom-and-bust cycles which have plagued most Western countries since the Industrial Revolution, or the power of the giant corporation to influence prices, or the role of modern advertising in manipulating consumer demand.

It is in the labor sector, however, where many critics have concentrated their strongest attacks upon orthodox economic theory. To some people, it seems almost immoral to argue that a worker's income is or should be determined by essentially the same impersonal forces which determine the price of a bushel of wheat or a ton of steel. In the classic expression of this view, "Labor is not a commodity." To other critics, the competitive model is suspect because it has so often been used by the rich to condemn laws desired by the poor. (And, it is noted, despite warnings that the welfare state would undermine incentives, our economy has grown spectacularly since the social revolution of the 1930s.) Still other critics have charged that labor markets violate every basic concept of competitive theory: unlike the consumer in a supermarket, the worker on a job has severely limited choice and knowledge, cannot easily "switch brands" of employer, and obviously tries to maximize more than his economic interests.

How valid are all these criticisms? This question is important not only to the professional economist but to anyone concerned with whether labor unions are too strong or too weak, whether minimum-wage laws do more harm than good, whether we are doing too much or too little for the hard-core unemployed. On these and similar issues of public policy, anyone holding a strong opinion (as most of us do) is in effect passing judgment on the competitive model. Those who condemn the growth of union power and welfare legislation are implicitly saying that market forces can better serve the interests of consumers and producers alike, while those who champion union and government "intervention" are saying that labor markets do not work as well in fact as in theory.

In appraising this controversy, we shall argue that competitive forces do indeed play a major role in the labor market—but not the all-embracing one pictured in orthodox theory. The hard question, in other words, is not whether the competitive model should be totally scrapped, but in what respects it needs to be modified or supplemented when applied to labor markets.

The short-run supply of labor to the economy

Let us start with the simplified competitive analysis. As we know, consumption is treated as a *good,* and work is regarded as a *cost.* This is the pleasure-pain nexus of economic activity which Bentham and the utilitarian school made so well known. The rational individual, seeking to maximize his satisfactions, balances the pain of work against the pleasure of consumption. Where these are equal, he has achieved his most preferred position: any further work would create more pain than pleasure, and any less work would decrease his pleasure more than his pain. This reasoning also leads to the familiar, upward-sloping supply curve, which assumes that at a given time a high wage level calls forth a larger supply of labor than does a low wage level.

Clearly there is much validity to this view of why people work. Few if any individuals would stay on their present jobs if offered no wages whatever; most workers in this country prefer a full-time job of about forty hours a week to a part-time job that offers less "pain of work" but also provides less "pleasure of consumption"; many workers will put in more than forty hours in return for premium pay. In these and other ways, it makes sense to picture the short-run supply of labor as being determined by individuals calculating how to maximize their economic satisfactions through the existing structure of wages.

But there are deficiencies to this view of labor supply, some of which have been accommodated by the competitive model and some of which have not. In Parts One and Two of this text, for example, we stressed that it is the family household, not the individual, which makes many of the key decisions affecting the labor market. This fact does not invalidate the model, but it does complicate it.

When the family determines how much of the time of its members will be sold, it must reckon with the alternative uses of that time. Paid employment and the goods that it will buy must compete with unpaid uses of time for schooling, leisure, household chores, and other family activities—*all of which are substitutes for one another.* Stated differently, the opportunity cost of leisure time is the goods that could have been obtained by selling that time to an employer, just as the opportunity cost of selling time to an employer is the leisure forfeited, or the education that could have been obtained by going to school instead of working, or the maternal care of a young child.

Thus, whether a son should continue with his schooling rather than go to work, or a mother should take on part-time employment, or a father should get a second job—decisions of this sort affect the entire family and typically are talked out at home rather than made by the one individual most directly involved.

We can therefore restate the maximizing assumption to say that a household will sell the time (labor) of all its members up to the point where the value of the unpaid uses of the remaining time is as great as the value of the consumer goods that could be obtained from the sale of that additional time. That is, the value of nonworking time and its uses is equated with the value of income and its uses *at the margin:* at the point where any increase in either, at the expense of the other, would represent a less desirable state of affairs.

What determines the scale of values that a family attaches to the various uses of its time? The easy answer is that these values are determined by "a mixture of economic and cultural factors." In our society, for example, very little of our children's time will be placed on the labor market because most families (and society as a whole, through child-labor laws) have decided for several reasons—and not just economic self-interest—that time spent in school and play is of more value than the few dollars a child could earn. Cultural forces also account in large part for the fact that the father is more likely than the mother to sell time in the labor market. Whatever the source and nature of these values, it can be argued that they are relatively fixed in the short run and that the family will still allocate its time in a maximizing fashion, that is, in a way that equalizes the marginal value (however determined) of an hour of paid employment and an hour of unpaid use of time, for each of its members.

Now, however, the competitive model becomes a more uncertain tool for prediction as the linkage becomes more complex between individuals and wage rates. For example, assume that for some reason all wage rates increase significantly tomorrow, while prices and most other economic (and cultural) variables remain relatively constant. In the short run, would the number of married women seeking employment increase, decrease, or stay about the same? We know that more than one-third of all married women are now in the labor force, and that this proportion has been rising throughout the twentieth century, just as wage rates have been rising in the same period—which suggests that a further increase in wages would call forth larger numbers of these workers. But we also know from earlier chapters that the growing participation rates of women have resulted from many factors other than wage changes, such as the feminist "emancipation" movement, the rural-urban shift, the decline in family size, the growing ease of household maintenance, and the desire to use increased education to satisfy nonmonetary aspirations—all of which suggests that the participation rate of married women may well continue to rise over the long run, but that it would not change much in response to a short-run jump in wage rates if these many cultural factors remain constant. Or, if one assumes that married women work primarily to supplement their family's income, one could argue plausibly that a sharp increase in all wage rates would induce a *drop* in the number of working wives, since many families' needs could then be met by the higher income earned by the husbands alone. Thus, depending on the values you believe the family places on the alternative uses of the wife's time, the maximizing assumption will obligingly support nearly any prediction you care to make about the effect of a wage increase upon this important source of labor supply.

A similar problem complicates the prediction of how the male head of the household would react to a sharp wage increase. As we have seen, leisure or any other unpaid use of time is competitive with consumer goods, since each is an opportunity cost to the other. Leisure must therefore be treated as a good, as something which—like food, clothing, and entertainment—is wanted and for which a price must be paid (the price here being the forfeited earnings). At a higher wage, a household head may indeed offer more hours of work, since each hour will now buy his family more goods—*or he may decide to offer fewer hours of work*, since they will now buy him the same amount of consumer goods plus more leisure. Or family heads might not immediately

change their working patterns at all in response to a wage increase, since certain cultural forces—such as society's expectation that the head of a family will work "full time"—would remain relatively fixed in the short run. Again the competitive model is of little help to the forecaster, for it will support any of these predictions according to the values one assumes that families attach to income versus leisure.

Finally, how will the labor supply react to a sharp recession or depression, during which wage rates may drop and certainly total income will decline in many families as one or more members lose their jobs or are cut back to part-time work? The conventional supply curve assumes that less labor is offered at low than at high wage rates, and one can easily imagine a married woman, for example, being less willing to trade her time at home for a low-paying than a high-paying job. A modern variant of this view is the "discouraged worker": Not that people prefer to work fewer hours when wage rates fall, but that some individuals become so discouraged after prolonged unemployment that they stop looking for work and drop completely out of the labor force, thereby reducing the short-run supply of labor. But an opposing view is that of the "additional worker": When the father loses his job, that is precisely the time when the mother and perhaps the oldest children will most likely be driven into the labor market to sustain family income, thereby *increasing* the short-run supply of labor during a recession or depression. Again, depending on your assumptions, any or all of these worker reactions can be called maximizing behavior.

Clearly the competitive model is an uncertain guide in these matters, and only experience can determine which of these plausible alternatives best describes the actual behavior of the labor supply. As so often happens, however, the "hard facts" of past experience are difficult to analyze and have been interpreted in different ways by different experts. As Prof. Jacob Mincer has noted:[1]

After three decades of research and occasionally animated controversy, the short-run behavior of the labor force is still not well understood. We are not clear about the causes of monthly movements of as many as three million people in and out of the labor force, nor do we fully understand the huge seasonal swing in the labor force and the year-to-year variation in the seasonal [swing].

Reviewing the responses of participation rates to unemployment during the postwar period, for example, Mincer stresses the diversity of responses within the labor force: the primary labor force (males twenty-five to sixty-four years old) has been cyclically insensitive, meaning that the proportion of this group working or seeking work has remained relatively constant in good times and bad; secondary (all other) workers *as a group* have responded as the discouraged-worker thesis (and conventional supply curve) would predict, with participation rates following the rise and fall of labor demand; but some subgroups of secondary workers have behaved quite differently, such as nonwhite females who responded as the additional-worker thesis would predict and exhibited peaks of participation *inverse* to the business cycle.[2] On balance, then, the total labor force (relative to population) did tend to expand and contract during the postwar period in response to short-run changes in demand, much as conventional theory would have predicted, although the divergent responses of particular groups could not have been predicted with certainty.

And that, of course, is the point we have been making—not that the competitive model is useless, but that its weaknesses should be recognized as well as its strengths.

The long-run supply of labor

Let us turn very briefly from the total supply of labor in the short run to the possible effect of changes in wage rates on the size of the labor force in the long run, where even more difficult problems are encountered. We saw in Chapter 2 that a bewildering number of crosscurrents have been at work in the labor force since the late 1800s, such as the shifts from blue-collar toward white-collar occupations and from the farm to the factory and then toward the service sector, the decline in the participation rates of young and old men, and the rising participation rate of women. Yet, in spite of these many diverse trends and the huge increase that has occurred in real wages, *the total participation rate—the percentage of the working-age population who are working or looking for work—has remained nearly constant from 1890 to today.*

More specifically, Clarence Long has estimated that, of the population in this country who were fourteen years of age and older, those in the labor force constituted 54 percent in 1890, 53.4 percent in 1950, and in intervening census years fluctuated only between 52.2 and 55.7 percent. Based on different definitions and survey methods, annual data for the postwar period show the same stability: as a percent of the noninstitutional population sixteen or more years of age, the labor force in this country did fluctuate, as Mincer and others have noted, but only within a range of 58.9 to 61.0 percent from 1947 through 1968. Also, participation rates have been stable through most of this century in Great Britain, Canada, New Zealand, and Germany.[3]

What explains this remarkable stability in the long-run supply of labor? In particular, has it just been a coincidence that the increasing participation rates of women have almost precisely offset the declining participation rates of young and old men? Long himself hypothesized that these trends have been systematically related. The changing technological, industrial, and occupational characteristics of the economy meant that employers could obtain the new services that they were coming to need more readily from mature women, who were increasingly well educated, than from the less-trained youths and (to put it crudely) more obsolete older males. At the same time, recognizing that other influences were encouraging boys to protract their education and older men to retire at an earlier age, Long suggested that these voluntary departures of many young and old males left a kind of vacuum which was filled by the women, who were increasingly available for work as a result of the "automation" of household work and the declining size of families. Thus, he surmised, women have *pushed* some young and old males *out* of the labor force and the voluntary departure of other boys and older men has *pulled* more women *into* the labor force. As for the relative stability of long-run participation rates among men aged twenty-five to sixty-four, Long reminds us that, in spite of the increasing numbers of working wives, *most* families have always had only one member (usually the male head) in the labor market. When these families wanted to purchase more leisure with their rising income over the years, they could hardly withdraw completely from the labor force—but they could and did demand that working hours be reduced from the high levels at the turn of the century.[4]

Whether or not you find Long's hypothesis persuasive, note that there is nothing in the competitive model that would have led anyone to predict in 1890 that the labor force would still be the same size (relative to population) in 1970, in spite of the dramatic changes that have occurred in income, technology, and cultural norms. In fact, quite a different prediction was offered in the heyday of the classical economics school. Then, it was assumed that at higher wage rates, marriages would occur earlier and families would be larger, and with an increasing population, the expanded labor supply would force wages back to a lower subsistence or basic standard-of-living level. On the other hand, low wage rates would prevent marriages and fail to support large families, so that birthrates would decline and death-rates rise until, with a smaller labor supply, the price of labor would be forced upward to some level which would just sustain, at the basic standard of living, the actual amount of population increase. The long-run supply of labor would thus adjust to a basic minimum wage (culturally determined, to be sure), rising whenever wages rose above that minimum, declining whenever wages fell below the minimum. It was because of this conclusion that wages could not deviate far from some basic minimum that economics understandably became known as "the dismal science."

At a later day, however, as knowledge of birth-control practices grew more widespread, Western economists came to assume that such population movements characterized only peoples in primitive economies. In the Western world, where birth control placed in the hands of married couples the decision of whether to spend income on a large family, or a small family, or on themselves alone, the result was less evident. The possibility was presented that at higher wage levels the rate of population increase might fall off. It was no

clearer, however, as to what rates of population increase might be associated with different rates of wage increase. It did not follow that, because the birthrate had dropped as a matter of historical record during a period in which labor incomes were rising, if labor incomes rose further the birthrate would decline further. Here again, in the long run, we are faced with a problem of consumption preferences—stated bluntly, a choice between commodities or leisure or children. Labor-supply schedules thus offer a number of variant possibilities, and the mechanics of the pricing process for factors may be affected by the nature of the supply curve which we are assuming.

The supply of labor to the firm

In addition to the question of the response of total labor supply to wage rates, there is the further question as to how a given labor force will distribute itself among the firms which are offering employment. Here the competitive answer is relatively simple. Workers' preferences for jobs depend on comparative wage rates when all other conditions of the job are considered similar. On the maximizing assumption that workers will prefer more rather than less, higher rates at one firm will attract workers from lower rates at another firm—*ceteris paribus*. The assumption that workers on the whole tend to be mobile permits their movement between firms, and the assumption that information about job availability and wage rates is generally known is all that is needed to reshuffle workers among jobs so that they always move to the highest-paying employments for which they are fitted.

It was never imagined that the money or consumer-goods motivation of individuals or households operated as an exclusive force. Most economists have followed Adam Smith in recognizing that job conditions do vary in the sense that certain kinds of work require more training, or involve costs of transportation, or entail special hardships or discomforts or a sacrifice of desirable social relationships. We can presumably allow for these differential job conditions, however, by saying that the relative net economic advantages will determine which jobs workers will take—the comparison of the total utilities and disutilities of the jobs being considered. Workers then can be said to choose among alternative employments on the basis of the maximum net economic advantage.

Despite such qualification, however, the competitive analysis tends to reason *as though* the money-maximization motive were operating unalloyed. "It is very doubtful that laborers or owners of other productive agents sacrifice money return for other considerations to any large extent on the whole."[5] The near-necessity for adopting this point of view if one is to apply competitive reasoning lies in the fact that otherwise prediction and validation are impossible. It is relatively easy to test a prediction that workers earning $2 an hour will move whenever possible toward jobs paying more than $2 an hour, but how do you test or use a prediction that job changes will be dictated by wage differentials *plus* the many non-monetary motives of different workers and *plus* the many nonwage conditions of different jobs? By that global definition, you can "explain" every decision to move or not to move after it has been taken, but you can only guess the direction of future moves.

The fact that individual workers do indeed have different job preferences, as we noted in Chapter 4, and that these affect their willingness to move to jobs paying more, is one major difficulty with the competitive assumptions. It permits a range of job rates to exist in a labor market without their necessarily affecting the supply of labor to a given firm, or at least affecting the supply in a predictable way. Firms offering low rates may attract workers for a variety of reasons which workers find sufficient—proximity to home, the presence of a relative or friends, the work atmosphere, the unavailability of acceptable alternative employment, and so on. Thus the supply of labor to the firm is not necessarily governed by the wage rates attaching to its jobs.

The preference of workers for particular kinds of jobs or job characteristics is especially noticeable once we think of "labor" not simply as manual workers at hourly rates but also as salaried people in clerical, technical, and professional jobs. The fact that a grade school teacher might earn more as a barmaid or a secretary does not necessarily cause her to look for employment in those capacities. Researchers who spoke with employees of banking and insurance firms in the Boston area reported:[6]

> The girls we interviewed place a high value on their working surroundings and on the status of the work they do and the organization they work for. Most of them seem to have consciously rejected factory work, selling (where many of them had had experience on part-time jobs), or even in some cases office work for a manufacturing concern. Thus, they have narrowed their range of job choice tremendously.

We shall have occasion to examine this aspect of the labor market more fully when we consider the demand of the firm for labor: supply and demand—how workers will react to wage offers, what wage offers a firm will make—are obviously both affected by the fact that jobs can be differentiated in other ways than wage rates. Meanwhile, let us take a look at several other respects in which labor markets appear to depart from competitive markets on the supply side.

Mobility Numerous surveys have established that there is a wide range in the wages paid to workers employed on similar jobs. It is difficult, of course, to establish that the jobs performed by any two workers are precisely the same, but there are some types of jobs for which the requirements are sufficiently standardized to permit rough comparisons. At issue, of course, is the competitive assumption that worker mobility will tend to equalize wages on comparable jobs.

In the country as a whole, as might be expected, there are very large wage differentials for comparable work. Among blue-collar workers in 1966–1967, for example, janitors averaged as little as $1.40 an hour in Raleigh, North Carolina, and as much as $2.64 in Detroit, just as tool- and diemakers' wages ranged from $2.96 an hour in Portland, Maine, to $4.29 in San Francisco. Among clerical occupations, a typical example is class A switchboard operators, whose weekly wages in 1966–1967 averaged only $74 in Boise City, Idaho, but $117 in Detroit. College graduates starting out in a profession are highly mobile, and yet in 1966, in the country as a whole, monthly salaries ranged from $450 to $1,050 for trainee attorneys doing routine legal work, from

$475 to $825 at the beginning level of engineering work (with a bachelor's degree), and from $400 to $800 at the beginning level for chemists. And even among those specialists in market behavior, the professional economists, annual salaries in 1964 varied from $7,000 to $10,500 for those with a Ph.D. degree and less than two years' experience.[7]

No one, however, can realistically expect wage uniformity throughout a country as huge as our own (although one might expect regional differentials to be smaller than they are). But wage differences are also pronounced even *within geographic regions.* In the six New England states, for example, the hourly earnings of janitors in 1966–1967 varied by as much as 30 percent, from $1.61 in Manchester, New Hampshire, to $2.13 in Worcester, Massachusetts. During the same period in the South, tool- and diemakers averaged only $3.15 an hour in Chattanooga, Tennessee, but $4.07 in Louisville, Kentucky, also a range of 30 percent. And in the mid-Atlantic region, the

average weekly earnings of class B switchboard operators were $60.50 in York, Pennsylvania, and $88 in New York City—a range of nearly 50 percent.

Finally and most significantly, wages often vary greatly on comparable jobs even *within local labor markets,* where workers can most easily shift among employers. In the ten occupations shown in Table 17-1, for example, earnings among the "middle 50 percent" of Los Angeles workers differed in 1968 by as little as 4 percent (among tool- and diemakers) and by as much as 38 percent (among laborers). When the very lowest and very highest earnings are compared within each occupation, this outside range is no smaller than 45 percent (again, toolmakers) and is as large as 190 percent (for female payroll clerks). There are few comparable surveys of professional workers' salaries by local area (except for the industrial nurses shown in Table 17-1), but it is suggestive that among assistant professors employed in the Los Angeles area in the 1968–1969 aca-

Table 17-1 *Distribution of Earnings in Selected Occupations in the Los Angeles Metropolitan Area, March 1968*

Occupation	Straight-time hourly earnings*		
	Median	*Middle range†*	*Outside range‡*
Electricians, maintenance	$4.09	$3.79–$4.31	$3.25–$5.30
Mechanics, automotive (maintenance)	4.11	3.83– 4.17	2.85– 4.50
Tool- and diemakers	4.11	4.02– 4.19	3.25– 4.70
Janitors, porters, and cleaners	2.33	2.13– 2.66	1.60– 3.50
Laborers, materials handling	3.31	2.68– 3.70	1.65– 4.10
	Straight-time weekly earnings*		
Clerks, payroll (men)	$136.00	$124.50–$157.50	$ 92.50–$195.00
Clerks, payroll (women)	113.50	99.00– 130.50	72.50– 210.00 (and over)
Secretaries, class A	150.50	140.00– 161.00	102.50– 210.00 (and over)
Draftsmen, class A	170.50	161.00– 180.50	127.50– 210.00 (and over)
Nurses, industrial	145.00	134.00– 153.00	102.50– 175.00

* Earnings exclusive of premium pay for overtime and for work on weekends, holidays, and late shifts.
† A fourth of the workers surveyed earn less than the lower of these two rates and a fourth earn more than the higher rate.
‡ The lowest and highest rates received by the workers surveyed.
SOURCE: U.S. Bureau of Labor Statistics, Bulletin 1575-64, *Area Wage Survey: The Los Angeles— Long Beach and Anaheim—Santa Ana—Garden Grove, California Metropolitan Area, March 1968.*

demic year, average salaries ranged from about $5,800 at Pasadena College to about $12,000 at the Claremont Graduate School.[8]

Do these local wage differentials persist over long periods, or are they only short-run market signals which are eventually flattened out by worker mobility? Unfortunately, we do not have comprehensive data on local wage structures prior to the 1940s, but most wage analysts would probably agree that the truck drivers' rates presented in Table 17-2 are roughly representative of the trend of other local differentials over time. Indeed, the fact that these are union rates might even understate the "natural" dispersion of drivers' wages in the Chicago labor market, since unions frequently strive for "equal pay for equal work" (which is, ironically, also the competitive ideal). In any event, it is plain that substantial wage differentials have persisted for many years for roughly the same skill in the same city. These differentials are certainly not static: some rates have moved up in relative standing (such as general freight) as others have dropped back (such as breweries), and the difference between the highest and lowest rates shrank from 131 percent in 1938 to 77 percent in 1967. Yet, driver rates in the florist and scrap-iron categories remain at

Table 17-2 *Union Wage Scales for Motortruck Drivers in Selected Industries in Chicago, 1938 and 1967*

	Rate per hour	
Industry	June 1, 1938	July 1, 1967
Florists (trucks of less than 2 tons)	$ .54	$2.46
General freight (less than 2 tons)	.68	3.48
Scrap iron and metal	.74	3.12
Department stores	.77	3.59
Oil and gasoline	.88	3.66
Bakery (cracker)	.89	3.70
Armored car	.90	3.26
Newspapers	.91	3.35
Milk (wholesale)	.96	4.06
Brewery	1.00	3.19
Coal (6-wheel trucks)	1.00	3.78
Construction (6-wheel trucks)	1.25	4.35

SOURCE: U.S. Bureau of Labor Statistics, *Union Wages and Hours: Motortruck Drivers*, Bulletins no. 676 (Table 7) and no. 1591 (Table 9).

the bottom of the heap after twenty-nine years, rates in construction, coal, and milk remain near the top, and a 77 percent spread after three decades is still a far cry from wage uniformity.

It is hard to see how differentials of these magnitudes for comparable jobs could arise and persist over the years if there is the ready mobility of workers which is assumed in the competitive analysis. One would expect that workers in the low-wage areas and industries and companies would have moved to the high-rate employers, tending to narrow if not eliminate the differentials for comparable jobs.[9] The reasons why this has not happened have been described at some length in Chapter 4 and may be summarized as follows:

1. About 10 percent of all American workers change their jobs each year, and about half of these move their families to a different labor market, which adds up to an impressive volume of mobility.

2. But wages are not the only factor in a worker's decision to leave or stay on a job. He also considers the intrinsic nature of the job (whether it is boring or interesting work, safe or hazardous, clean or dirty) and its social setting (the congeniality of the work group and the nature of supervision). In addition, his decision may be influenced by his seniority and pension rights; his family's resistance to being uprooted from familiar associations of church, schools, and friends; the family's preference of climate; whether he owns his home; the existence of racial barriers; and so on.

3. Even when a worker wants, or is forced, to change jobs, he often has poor information about where job openings exist and the wage and nonwage aspects of these vacancies. Employment agencies and other formal channels do not fill this gap, so the worker frequently depends on the grapevine of family and friends.

4. As a result, there appears to be only a weak tendency for job changers to move from lower- to higher-paying jobs. (See Table 4-3 in Chapter 4.)

Yet another reason for the persistence of wage differentials is the "job-vacancy thesis," which says that many job moves are dictated less by wage comparisons than by the mere availability of work. A worker who has been unemployed a long time, for example, may take nearly any job he can get, rather than hold out for a better wage than he received on his last job. And particularly among secondary workers, the decision to enter or leave the labor market may hinge primarily on the availability of work. In many small towns and rural areas, for instance, a wife may be lucky to hold down any job, and the notion of prospecting for a better job is rather fanciful. In such situations, it can even be said that a firm which employs primarily women can in effect *create* its own labor supply by moving into the area. By the simple fact of providing job opportunities for married women who wish to work, it can add to the labor force of the area overnight. If a firm leaves such an area, just the reverse may occur as previously employed wives withdraw from the labor force. In these instances it is not the wage rate that attracts or repels the firm's supply of labor except within quite broad limits, but it is primarily the availability of work.[10]

Again, these criticisms of the competitive model should not be pressed too far. A great deal of worker mobility does occur throughout the labor sector and this mobility does provide some check on wage differentials. Wages for tool- and die-makers, for example, do vary greatly but not randomly: nowhere in this country can you hire this skill for as little as $1 an hour and nowhere do you have to pay as much as $10 an hour, and rates for this job within a particular market, such as Los Angeles, will tend to cluster around an average that is obviously higher than the average rate for less skilled jobs. The fact remains, however, that worker mobility erodes wage differentials with far less effectiveness in real labor markets than in competitive theory.

The quality of labor   Can the difference in wages paid on similar *jobs* be explained by the differing ability of the *workers* on those jobs? Surely not all tool- and diemakers are equally proficient in their craft, nor are all janitors, truck drivers, lawyers, or economists. And if wage differentials within an occupation simply reflect differences in worker "quality," wouldn't this fact serve to validate the competitive model?

There are two difficulties with that proposition. On the theoretical side, an allowance for individual differences leads to a diffusion or multiplication of supply schedules which reduces the value of this analytical tool. On the practical side, we have so few measures of labor quality that it is difficult to test the influence of this factor on wages. Each of these problems deserves examination.

Labor as a factor of production is necessarily abstracted from those who supply it and measured in some unit which is considered appropriate. An hour of work has probably been the unit most frequently employed, on the ground that this is more precise than days or weeks, since these are not composed of any standard number of hours. On one axis, then, we have hours of work, and on the other axis we have hourly rates or hourly earnings. Figure 17-1 diagrams the usual supply curves of labor. In a labor market, or in a large firm which constitutes an important part of the total labor market, it is presumed that at any given moment more hours of work will be forthcoming only at higher rates of pay, as in the (*a*) curve (although, as we have noted, over time an income effect may lead workers to offer fewer hours of work as higher wages give them larger incomes and permit them to "buy back" some of their time as leisure). For the individual small firm in a local labor market, the supply curve is presumed to be virtually horizontal, as in the (*b*) figure. Its operations are sufficiently minute so that any expansion or contraction in the size of its work force will involve no more than a few workers and these it can expect to obtain at the prevailing market wage rate, whatever that may be, without having to offer higher earnings as inducement. The hours of work may come from individuals already employed (as long as overtime rates are not in effect) or from new entrants to the labor force. The employer is hiring hours of labor and the person to whom they attach is of no consequence. (We should be clear, however, that supply curves such as those in Figure 17-1 are for a particular grade or kind of worker; they do not pretend to lump skilled and unskilled workers together, for example.)

But obviously this can be so only if all the individuals who are offering hours of work are rea-

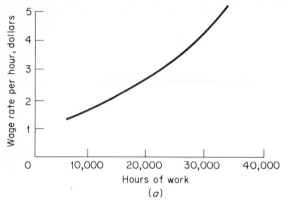

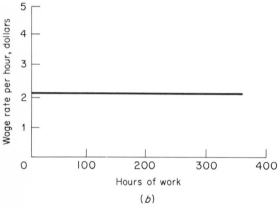

Fig. 17-1. *Supply schedule of labor (a) in a labor market and (b) to an individual firm.*

sonably alike in their capabilities—substitutable and interchangeable for one another without loss or gain in efficiency. This is one of the assumptions of the competitive analysis. If one did not make such an assumption, then he would have to be concerned with the fact that all workers (of a given grade or kind) are not alike in ability, so that "hours of labor" would not be a homogeneous category. It would be exactly the same if the unit of measure of the other axis, "wage rate per hour," were called "currency," and if it were assumed that it made no difference to the person supplying hours of labor whether the numbers on the axis referred to dollars, marks, pounds, francs, or yen. Obviously, since one unit of these various currencies has varying value, a worker would be very much interested in whether he

is being paid in dollars or drachma or dinars. Similarly, if the unit of an hour of labor does not always have the same value but depends on the characteristics of the worker from whom it comes, an employer would be very much concerned about what he is buying. If all switchboard operators are not alike in efficiency, then it is questionable what the supply curve for the services of switchboard operators means.

There are several ways in which theorists have sought to meet this problem. The favorite device is to recognize that the problem is real and that "hours" is not an appropriate measure of labor supply. What should appear on the horizontal axis is something such as "units of efficiency." On this basis, to take an example from Table 17-1, the janitor in Los Angeles who received $3.20 an hour in 1968 is assumed to have been twice as good at his job as the janitor who received only $1.60 in the same market. By assigning two units of efficiency to the first man and one unit to the second, you can justify their wage differential and preserve the integrity of the single supply curve for this category of labor.

That appears to be logical, but do labor markets actually work that way? Do the best janitors, secretaries, and physicists in fact earn the "top dollar" in their respective fields, and do the poorest workers earn the least? Here we encounter our second problem in handling differences in labor quality, namely, that no one has really been able to devise a "unit of efficiency" which is sufficiently objective that totals can be summed for a labor market and an employer can tell how many such units an applicant possesses. Personnel tests do attempt to screen job applicants on an ability basis, but no economist would accept the use of such tests as a satisfactory instrument for determining the number of units of efficiency floating around the local labor market.

A closer approximation probably comes through the use of piece-rate systems, as we noted in Chapter 15. If an employer pays for results, he automatically separates the sheep from the goats. The employee who produces fifty pieces an hour is worth twice as much as the person who produces twenty-five pieces, and he is paid twice as much. But again there are problems. Since business firms produce various goods and services, it would be difficult to arrive at some common measure of production which could serve as the unit of account on the horizontal axis. "Piece" means something different to a shoe manufacturer from what it does to a telephone company.

One way around this dilemma might be to compute, by some kind of time-study procedure, the "normal" output per hour for any kind of work, and attach the wage rate to this figure. Then, with an incentive system, anyone who produces more than the normal output would be remunerated accordingly, since that person has supplied a larger number of efficiency units. But this solution also has obvious drawbacks, for there are many kinds of jobs for which no "normal output" can be figured. What is the normal output of an engineer, an English teacher, a secretary, or a policeman? And even for those manual workers whose output can be measured, how do you correct for the largely unpredictable effects of motivation—for the fact, that is, that the same worker's performance may vary from day to day, or from boss to boss, or from work crew to work crew, depending on his psychological outlook? In short, individuals do indeed vary in their ability and performance on the same kind of work, but it is exceedingly difficult to measure these quality differentials in a way that would permit comparisons with wage differentials throughout a labor market.

In fact, surprisingly few studies have even attempted to test this aspect of the competitive model. From those which have, findings such as the following have emerged:

Among professional economists throughout the country, about one-half of the total variation in their 1966 salaries can be "explained" by seven factors: academic degree (other things equal, Ph.D.'s earn more than those with a master's degree, and so on); work activity (management or administrative duties pay more than research which pays more than teaching); type of employer (industry pays more than government which pays more than educational institutions); years of experience; age; economic specialty (for example, labor economists earn more than economic historians); and sex (women earn less than men, even when the other six factors are held constant).[11]

In the country as a whole in 1949, the median wage and salary income of employed women was only 58 percent of that of men, but when account is taken of the male-female differences in occupation, working hours, age, turnover, absenteeism, and work experience, the sex-income ratio rises from 58 to about 88 percent.[12]

In the country as a whole in 1959, incomes within given occupations were higher in concentrated than in unconcentrated industries, that is, higher in industries with a few large companies (such as autos) than in those with many small companies (such as clothing). But all this difference in earnings can be statistically accounted for by the "personal characteristics" of those employed in concentrated industries, such as education, race, age, residence (urban versus rural, North versus South, and so on), family size, generation (whether second- or later-generation American), and mobility (whether moved residence since 1955). Thus, it is argued, "the monopolistic industries do get superior 'quality' for the [higher] incomes they offer."[13]

Clearly, then, there *is* some tendency for wages to vary with worker ability within a given occupation, and for this reason wage data such as those in Tables 17-1 and 17-2 undoubtedly do overstate the differences in wages among workers of truly equal skill or efficiency. It must be equally clear, however, that *there remains a substantial amount of wage variance that cannot be explained by differences in labor quality*—or at least that has not been explained by the measures of quality used to date. Of the several measures used in the above studies, education appears to be the least debatable, but it explains none of the male-female earnings differential on similar jobs; in fact, because working women have a higher average education than their male counterparts, a correction for this factor slightly widens the sex-income differential.[14] And even when education correlates directly with earnings within an occupation (as it usually does), questions can be raised about the accuracy of this factor as an index of quality: The high school graduate is not always a brighter or better worker than the dropout, nor is the holder of a Ph.D. always a better teacher than the person with a master's degree, although it is often convenient for employers to make such assumptions in the absence of a better measure of worker quality.

In spite of these qualifications, there are obviously good reasons for accepting differences in education as one measure of worker ability. But consider some of the other "personal characteristics" that correlated with wages in the third study above. The fact that Negroes in a given occupation earned less in 1959 than whites with the same years of education may have been partly due to the inferior quality of education received by many Negroes, but one suspects there was also some plain, old-fashioned discrimination behind that wage differentiation. Or why should income from the same occupation have been higher for those individuals who (other things equal) lived in cities of over rather than under 250,000 population, or in the North rather than the South, or with a middle-sized family rather than a very large or very small family, or who were second-generation Americans rather than third-generation or later? Everyone can think of some possible explanations for each of those findings, but it is as difficult to believe that they reflect only differences in worker quality as it is to think of measures that might be more accurate.

We can, of course, treat this problem of labor quality as sufficiently insoluble to ignore, and assume that whatever nonhomogeneity is involved in the measure of labor supply is probably not "important" enough to worry about. But if we take that easy way out, we cannot then explain away wage variations on comparable jobs by asserting that they really represent differences in worker quality. On the other hand, we can assume that wages do vary with worker quality and that the supply schedule of labor is a meaningful concept if expressed in efficiency units rather than hours. But then, because of our poor measures of labor quality, we must admit that the theorist cannot validate this model and that it provides the employer with only a fuzzy guide in making his hiring and wage decisions. To repeat, the most reasonable conclusion is that the conventional supply curve is a useful but not infallible tool of analysis, just as quality differences explain some but not all the wage differentials found on comparable jobs in every labor market.

The effect of unions on labor supply   The competitive analysis is dominantly a theory of individualistic economic behavior, as we have already noted. It makes no effort to examine economic organizations for their own special characteristics. Instead, it treats organizations as though they too were animated by the same drives as individuals, possessing only a different degree of market power. The fact that unions, for example, are agents for the household merely means that they act as managers of the supply of labor to the labor market as a whole and to the firms which operate in it. They sometimes are able to restrict the number of entrants to skilled trades by imposing apprenticeship regulations and limiting the number of apprentices. They seek to establish a common wage rate which all employers are obliged to pay, or at least some minimum rate. They sometimes impose work rules affecting the number of workers an employer must hire or the amount of work he can expect for his wage payments.

In competitive theory, the extent to which unions are successful in these attempts depends on their ability to control market forces. If they succeed in reducing the supply of labor of a particular skill, then they will be able to win higher rates for such workers. It may also mean that the workers who are precluded from entering the restricted trade are forced into other occupations, whose wage rates are thereby lowered. The union has acted like any monopolist, and its success, like that of any monopolist, is governed by the nature of its control over the competitive market.

By and large, economists who stress competition as a controlling force tend to regard unions as something of an economic nuisance but not very important. They would look on the union as they would on an agent for an actor or an orchestra or a writer—the object of the agent is to get as good a price for his client as possible. But as with the booking agent, basically the price is determined by the quality of the client. A good agent might get a little more than the client would on his own, and save him the chore of bargaining, but the agent can hardly set aside market forces.

We shall not at this point attempt any assessment of the influence of a union on the wage rates which it obtains for its members nor examine whether it can secure higher rates only by affecting the supply of labor to market and firm. It will be easier to analyze those issues after we consider the role of the employer as a buyer of labor services, the demand side of the labor market. For the present, it is enough to note that even in these limited terms the union makes a difference. By the added power which organization brings, it is capable of affecting the supply of labor. When workers come together and agree on the terms for which they will be willing to supply their services, there is a reasonable assumption that the result will be different (even though a question remains as to how much different) from what it would have been if they had individually competed against one another.

The supply of labor reconsidered

The effect of these several qualifications on the competitive analysis is not to destroy the usefulness of the latter but to put it in better perspective. To some extent competitive wage-and-price theory has suffered from attempts at excessive precision. In an effort to build a tight closed-loop analysis (often referred to as a "model," reflecting the objective of engineering exactitude), economic analysis has tended to lose sight of the variety which is not only possible but inescapable in social structures. It is true that there must be some system in order to hold a society and its institutions together, but the system may be loose and the resulting behavioral patterns more complex because of that fact. One must still look for central tendencies and dominant themes around which the variations are woven, but it would be a mistake to conceive of the symphony as consisting only of its major themes.

Thus we can accept as meaningful and significant the tenet that people are interested in the amount they are paid for their services, and that there is some tendency for people to be drawn to employments which pay them more. The fact that our culture is consumption-oriented means that additional income is highly valued by most people

and most households. "Keeping up with the Joneses" calls for as much (or almost as much) money as the Joneses have. But this motivation does not operate in an exclusive manner. People want income, and the more the better, but they do have preferences about the way they earn it—what they do, with whom they work, where, the attitude of the supervisor, the permissiveness of the work environment, the opportunity for obtaining a variety of satisfactions out of the job itself—and these preferences have their impact on the desire for income.

This interest in the nature of one's work is as important to keep in sight as the income obtained from it. For one thing, it means that there is not a single supply schedule for labor of a particular grade or type in a local market. We might realistically think of the existence of a number of labor-supply schedules in a locality—perhaps, indeed, a schedule for every firm in the market. The quantity of labor services that will be offered to any firm depends on more than its wage rate.

But the fact that there may be a number of labor-supply schedules in a market, or even one for each firm, does not mean that they are wholly independent of one another. To some extent the supply schedules interlock. The wage rate that workers expect from one firm does bear some relationship to the wage rates similar kinds of workers obtain from other firms, and if expectations are too grossly frustrated, the supply of labor to that firm will be affected. The supply of job applicants may not wholly dry up, but their quality may deteriorate. All the better workers will not necessarily leave the firm to go elsewhere, since they may have special reasons holding them, but its labor turnover is likely to be high whenever the labor market turns advantageous to job seekers. The chances will rise that its employees will be pushed to look for other work by dissatisfaction with their present wage scale.[15]

Thus, even though there may not be a single labor-supply schedule within a local market, the number of supply schedules will be interdependent. Different wages for the same kind of work can prevail without exciting worker movement, but at some point workers' tolerances for differentials may be stretched so thin that a firm, in order to hold the workers it needs, will have to lessen the gap. At *some* differential, worker gravitation from low-paying firms to high-paying firms will increase.

The same thing can be said of the interrelationship of local labor markets. Wage differentials for the same type of work may exist between labor markets in the same region without effecting a redistribution of workers sufficient to create a single labor schedule for the whole area. Indeed, the differentials within a region are almost certain to be greater than the differentials within a local labor market. The degree of interdependence becomes somewhat more attenuated with distance, as more of an inducement is needed to overcome inertia. But some relationship must nevertheless exist between the labor-supply schedules in one local market and those in another, or worker inertia will tend to be overcome sufficiently to reestablish the necessary relationship. The rates for switchboard operators in York, Pennsylvania, and New York City cannot get too far out of line without inducing girls in York, who would on the whole prefer to remain there, to take their chances on the unknown working conditions in Manhattan rather than continue to put up with "starvation wages."

The same effect occurs between regions. Again, the interdependence is attenuated. The differential may have to be greater to stimulate worker movement from one region to another. But rates in the South for a particular kind of labor cannot be set without any relation to what that same kind of labor is earning in the West or the North Central states. Some differentials can exist and persist, and often of a rather substantial amount, but beyond some point a differential becomes too great for a firm or a locality or a region to maintain the labor supply on which it has been able to rely in the past.

Thus we can think of "labor supply"—how much work will be offered at a given rate—as consisting of a large number of loosely related schedules rather than a single integrated schedule. The looseness of the relationship *and* the presence of a relationship are both important. The lack of any precise relationship is further underscored by the fact that what is being supplied for a given wage rate is not clear. What the worker is selling to an employer may not be exactly a pig in a poke but it is an enigmatic effort. The fact that many workers choose to market their services through unions likewise adds to the uncertainty—not only because of the differential market powers which various unions are able to acquire but also because organization permits workers to exercise variable controls over their performance on the job, the "work" which they are supplying. It is all very much more complicated than the competitive analysis with which we started.

The individual firm's demand for labor

We turn now to the demand side of the labor market and, as in the consideration of supply, we shall begin with the competitive analysis. As in the case of supply, we shall find that competitive theory provides a too tightly integrated demand analysis to be wholly acceptable, but at the same time it offers insights we cannot do without.

The producer in almost any line of business is faced with the problem of the particular combination of factors (their kind and quality) which he will employ. Within limits, factors are substitutable for one another. One kind of labor may be substituted for another kind of labor, or capital equipment may take the place of labor, or more land may be the equivalent of less land plus fertilizer, and so on. The units of each kind of factor are assumed to be homogeneous; that is, they are reasonably equivalent as far as their relevant properties are concerned. The producer is faced, then, with the problem of how much of each kind of factor he will hire.

This problem for the producer is like the problem consumers face in balancing quantities of various goods in such a manner as to achieve the greatest possible satisfaction. Two considerations are present for both consumer and producer:

1. Technical considerations—for consumers, preference ratings among various types of goods and services; for producers, productivity ratings as derived from production functions, that is, how much of a marginal physical product a factor unit gives rise to in the various possible technological combinations in which it can be used. This physi-

cal product is converted into value terms by reference to the product price.

2. The exchange ratio—for consumers, the price ratios of commodities; for producers, the price ratios of factors. Both these elements are necessary to the solution of factor demand no less than consumer demand.

The problem of the producer's demand for the factors of production is simply one aspect of the general maximizing problem. In product pricing the businessman reaches his point of maximum advantage at the output where marginal cost equals marginal revenue. Short of this point he can get, let us say, a dollar of additional revenue for another 90 cents of production costs, so he would gain by producing more. Past this point his production costs per unit would be higher—say $1.05—than the dollar he would get in return, and there is obviously no percentage in taking a loss by producing more. But at the point where an additional dollar of cost produces an additional dollar of revenue, he knows he has done as well as he can. More or less would be disadvantageous.

This basic principle likewise governs his demand for the factors of production, but with a technical variation. The marginal cost and marginal revenue of a product are computed on the basis of a unit of that *product*. But any decision as to employment of factors must be made in terms of units of the *factor*. Hence we convert the maximizing problem from one of "how much of the cost and how much of the revenue of the marginal unit of product must be attributed to each factor" into the problem of "how much cost and how much revenue does the marginal unit of each factor give rise to." Essentially, we are interested in weighing the marginal cost of a unit of labor against the marginal revenue earned by that same unit, as well as against the marginal costs and marginal revenues of the other factors, such as capital and natural resources.

The marginal cost attributable to a given quantity of some factor is easily enough ascertained for the individual firm. To the single firm under competitive conditions, factor prices, no less than product prices, must be taken as given. The marginal cost of hiring an extra unit of a factor is simply the market price of that factor. The firm's marginal cost of hiring eight units of some factor instead of seven units is just the price of one unit of that factor in the market—a price which is given to the individual firm. We thus have the rule that the marginal cost of a factor is the market price of that factor.

The marginal revenue (or marginal productivity in value terms) attributable to the factor may be determined as follows. The addition to output resulting from the hiring of an additional unit is that factor's marginal product expressed in units of the good being produced. By multiplying this marginal physical product (MPP) by the market price of the good (P), we arrive at the value of the marginal product. (Since demand, to the individual seller under competitive conditions, is perfectly elastic, the sale of additional units involves no lesser revenue on previous units of output, so that no deduction need be made from the value of the marginal product in order to arrive at the net addition to revenue.) We may call this net addition to revenue which is attributable to the marginal factor unit the marginal value product (MVP). Symbolically, MPP $\times P$ = MVP.

Thus having derived marginal factor cost and marginal value product, we are in a position to relate these to solve the producer's maximizing problem. We shall approach it in two stages: (1) When a unit of one factor is to be preferred to a unit of another factor (this involves a preference for one kind of factor over another kind), and (2) how many units of any given factor it is profitable to employ (this involves a preference for one amount of the same factor rather than another amount).

First, as to preference for kinds of factors. The producer will prefer to hire a unit of one factor rather than a unit of another factor whenever the former will make a greater *proportionate* contribution to marginal revenue than will the latter. He will thus be satisfied with his combination of different kinds of factors when their *relative* contributions are equal. The contribution, however, is a proportionate or relative one—proportionate or relative to the marginal cost (or price) of the factor which makes it. We can convert this proposition into the general rule that a maximizing producer will hire the various factors of production in such combination that their marginal value products are all equally proportional to their prices. Using a small-letter subscript to refer to a particular kind of factor, we can say that the equilibrium position for the producer in the combination of factors must include the condition that $MVP_a/P_a = MVP_b/P_b = MVP_c/P_c$, etc.

Suppose unit labor costs should be $8 while the marginal value product of labor was $20, and unit capital costs were $15 with a marginal value product of $25. Our ratios would then be $20/8 > 25/15$, revealing that the producer would not be operating with the most profitable combination of labor and capital. The marginal dollar spent on labor adds $2.50 to total revenue, while the marginal dollar spent on capital yields only $1.67. Labor is thus more profitable than capital at the margin. To reach his maximizing position, the producer could substitute labor for capital, within the framework of his production function.

According to the law of variable proportions (or, essentially the same thing, the principle of diminishing returns), the marginal physical product of a factor must eventually decline if other factors are not increased in equal proportions. The same conclusion is applicable to the marginal *value* product of a factor, since this is only marginal physical product times a constant price. We can be sure, then, that with fixed plant the marginal value product of a variable factor will move inversely with the number of units of the variable factor employed. The greater the number of factor units, the smaller the marginal value product. The fewer the factor units, the larger the marginal value product. Consequently, by adding units of labor (whose marginal value product will be falling) and by subtracting units of capital (whose marginal value product will thus be rising), the above two ratios can be brought into balance.

Let us say that the producer, by substituting labor for capital, will arrive at a position where

$$\frac{\text{Labor's MVP of \$16}}{\text{Price of labor of \$8}} = \frac{\text{capital's MVP of \$30}}{\text{price of capital of \$15}}$$

At this point the proportionate marginal contribution of labor would be exactly equal to that of capital. The proportions of the various factors would thus be in balance and provide no inducement for the businessman to substitute capital for

labor or labor for capital. It is through such substitution of factors for one another that the condition of equiproportionate marginal contribution of the factors is achieved.

The possibility of achieving this particular condition of equilibrium in the firm is dependent on the time period that we assume. In the short run, we have certain factors whose quantity is fixed (buildings, blast furnaces, and the like) and which consequently have no marginal product; for them we could calculate an average value product but not a marginal value product. The fixed factors are, by definition, immune from the possibilities of substituting for other factors or being substituted for by other factors and hence are not subject to the maximization process described above for achieving optimum factoral combination. In the short run it is only the variable factors (such as labor, raw materials, or light tools and equipment) to which a marginal value product can be attributed and which may be substituted for each other. The achievement of equiproportionate marginal contributions of the factors is thus, in the short run, limited only to the variable factors. In the long run, however, all factors become variable, and the various kinds of factors may be combined in such a manner that all, without exception, render proportionately equal profit-maximizing services.

One consequence of this condition for profit maximization is readily apparent. As the price of factors changes, the producer's relative preference for them must likewise change. If, in the previous case, where the relative ratios were

$$\frac{\text{MVP}}{p} = \frac{\overset{\textit{Labor}}{16}}{8} = \frac{\overset{\textit{Capital}}{30}}{15}$$

we should now introduce a doubling of the price for capital, so that

$$\frac{\text{MVP}}{p} = \frac{\overset{\textit{Labor}}{16}}{8} = \frac{\overset{\textit{Capital}}{30}}{30}$$

the producer would find it to his advantage to increase his hiring of labor and decrease his hiring of capital. As more units of labor were added, the marginal value product of labor would decline; as fewer units of capital were employed, the marginal value product of capital would rise. At some combination of the factors, the two ratios would be brought into balance, leading to some result such as

$$\text{MVP} = \overset{Labor}{\frac{12}{8}} = \overset{Capital}{\frac{45}{30}}$$

A little reflection will suggest, however, that the condition of equiproportionate marginal contribution of the various factors is not a sufficient condition for a maximizing position. None of the combinations of factors listed above leads to maximum producer advantage, even in the short run. So far, we have been concerned only with the question of the proportions in which different kinds of factors must be combined for maximum economic gain. We must now turn to the companion question of the number of units of each factor which should be hired

In the supply of commodities and in the pricing of products, the maximizing objective leads producers to the rule that each unit of output must add no more to cost than to revenue, but production must be extended as long as each unit of output adds more to revenue than to cost. Equilibrium is reached at the point where marginal revenue (MR) equals marginal cost (MC). With respect to the producer's demand for factors, the objective of maximization must lead to a parallel principle. In the individual firm, for which the price of factors is given, additional units of the factor will be hired as long as their contribution to revenue (MVP) is greater than their addition to cost. Just as a condition of equilibrium in the supply of commodities is that MR = MC for the individual producer, so we find that, by breaking each of these elements—marginal revenue and marginal cost—down into its constituent parts, we arrive at a similar condition of equilibrium in the demand for factors. Marginal revenue can be broken down into the constituent marginal value products of the respective factors, that is, the revenue which each gives rise to. Marginal cost can be dissected into the constituent marginal costs of each of the factors (which, as we have seen, is their price). Our maximizing rule for determining the number of units of any factor which should be hired, then, is that MVP = factor price.

As long as the marginal value product of a factor is greater than its price, the maximizing producer will continue to hire additional units of the factor. As we know, marginal value product must fall as the number of factor units increases. At the point where the falling marginal value product is just equal to the constant factor price, the producer has realized his maximum gain from the employment of that particular factor. If he continues hiring units, marginal value product will dip below price: more will be added to cost than to revenue. Only where MVP = factor price will the producer obtain his maximum advantage.

Again it should be noted that in the short run only variable factors give rise to a marginal value product. Here, variation in the quantity of fixed factors is impossible, by definition. It is only in the long run, then, that this condition of equilibrium can be achieved for all factors.

If the marginal value product of *each* particular factor is just equal to its supply price, the previous condition of equiproportionate marginal contribution of *all* factors will necessarily be maintained. With a price of $8 for labor and of $30 for capital, as in our previous example, we should find that units of capital and labor would be hired up to the point where

$$\frac{\text{MVP}}{p} = \overset{Labor}{\frac{8}{8}} = \overset{Capital}{\frac{30}{30}} = 1$$

We are now in a position to construct a factor-demand schedule for the individual firm. This schedule will indicate the demand for one factor (all units of which are considered homogeneous) when the prices of all other factors are held constant, when the price of the product is likewise assumed to remain constant, and when the production function (state of technology) is given. Table 17-3 provides the technical data. The only relevant range is one over which marginal product, in both physical and the value terms, is diminishing, since short of that the producer has no problem—each additional unit of output creates more value than the previous one, and he will obviously go on hiring labor, for example (at the same wage rate), at least as long as that relationship between MVP and factor price holds good.

Table 17-3 *Data for Derivation of a Firm's Demand Schedule for a Factor*

(1) Number of factor units	(2) Marginal physical product (given)	(3) Price of the good (given)	(4) Marginal value product (col. 2 × col. 3)
3	15	$1	$15
4	12	1	12
5	10	1	10
6	9	1	9
7	8	1	8
8	7	1	7

Using the data from Table 17-3, we could construct Figure 17-2, which plots the MVP at varying levels of employment. Now, since a firm will hire factor units (say, labor) up to the point where their price (wage) is *equal* to MVP, we can substitute "wage rate" for MVP on the vertical axis. The result is the individual firm's demand schedule for labor. Thus, at a factor price of $15 the producer is willing to hire three units of the factor, since the marginal value product of the third unit is equal to $15. He will not hire a fourth, however, since the marginal revenue contribution of the fourth unit is only $12. Not unless the price of the factor falls to $12 will the producer be willing to add a fourth unit to his expenses.

Factor demand in industry and economy

To arrive at the market or industry demand for a factor of production, we would, as a first approximation, simply sum the demand schedules of the individual firms. We must recognize, however, that such a collective demand schedule for a factor would be based on the assumption of a constant product price. That assumption is, of course, entirely appropriate in the case of a single producer (under pure competition) abstracted from the industry as a whole, since no matter what his output, it constitutes so small a part of the total that price is unaffected. He may add more factor units and thus increase his output, or reduce his hiring of factor units and thus decrease his output,

without having any impact on the product price. But the same assumption cannot be so easily accepted when the industry as a whole is concerned.

We know that for the individual firm in equilibrium, marginal physical productivity × product price = factor price. We also know that as more units of a factor are employed, the marginal physical productivity will decline. If, then, the price of the factor should fall, the individual producer would expand his employment of the factor up to the point where the lowered marginal physical productivity times product price equaled the new lower factor price. But if all firms in the industry took the same action, as they would, this would mean an increase in total output for the industry, with a consequent downward pressure on the price of the product, the demand curve for which has not changed. As product price fell, the

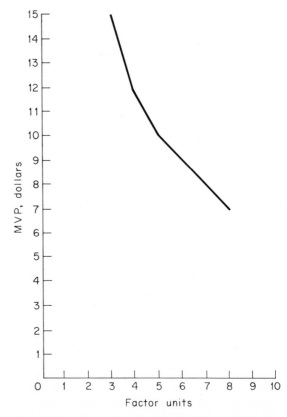

Fig. 17-2. *Demand schedule for labor of the individual firm.*

marginal value product of the factor would necessarily also fall (since product price is one of its components). With falling MVP, the number of additional units of the factor which each producer would be willing to hire at the new lower factor price would be reduced. The market-demand schedule for a factor must therefore take into account whatever impact on product price is caused by variation in industry output as factor hirings increase or decrease.

We have now explored the forces giving rise to producers' demand for factors, under conditions of pure competition, and have seen that equilibrium in the hiring of factors is established in the long run, when all factors are adaptable, by effecting the condition that the marginal value product of each factor be equal to its price. By talking about the *price of a single product,* we have concentrated our attention upon an industry, in abstraction from the rest of the economy. We should recognize this important distinction between community and factor demand, however: The *industry* is defined in terms of the product in a market, and not in terms of the factors which it uses. *Factor* demand cuts across industry lines, so that a change in the price of a factor affects many if not all industries.

Thus in an industry which is expanding to meet rising consumer demand (say, for a new product), one might expect that its MVP would be considerably above the wage rate it is paying. As it sought to recruit additional workers, it would find it *necessary* to raise its wage offer to pull workers away from their present jobs, and *feasible* to pay more than the going wage, owing to its high MVP. Since the industry as a whole would be undergoing an expansion phase, the workers it needs could not be obtained in sufficient numbers at current rates, and the heavy consumer demand for its product would make it profitable to pay what is necessary to induce the needed number of job applicants.

But, equally, as workers moved from other employments in response to this changed demand from one industry, the reduced outputs in the companies they left would result (via the principle of variable proportions or diminishing returns) in higher MVPs in those companies, permitting the payment of higher wage rates and thus

stemming the movement away from present jobs to the expanding industry. The movement would presumably come to an end when the rising MVPs in the old companies were made equal to the falling MVP in the expanding industry. At that point wage rates on old and new jobs would be equal. The labor force would have been redistributed in such a way as to permit production of the new product in an amount and at a price which satisfied the wants of consumers in relation to the other goods and services they were buying. The expansion of an industry would have affected wage rates for all industries employing the same type of labor.

Modifications of the competitive-demand analysis

The competitive analysis assumes that employers bid among themselves for the services of workers. Their competing demand forces up the price of labor until it is equal to the MVP to which its employment gives rise. As long as any employer can obtain a higher MVP from labor than the prevailing wage, he will hire more workers (if he can get them) or, if necessary, increase the wage rate he is offering up to the point where it is equal to his MVP. It is not labor's MVP which sets the wage—that is determined by the interaction of bids and offers in the labor market, supply and demand factors both—but labor's MVP sets a limit to the bidding which employers will engage in for labor's services.

Out of this competition among employers for workers, a single integrated demand schedule would be expected to emerge in a labor market. Any given wage rate for a particular grade or type of labor would be equivalent to the MVP of all firms (at the level of production representing their maximum advantage). Thus at every point on a labor-demand curve, the MVP of the workers involved would be equal in all their various uses. If for any producer the MVP of that kind of labor were higher than the wage rate, he would continue to bid for labor until MVP and wage rate were equal. If his MVP were less than the wage rate, he would dismiss some of his labor until MVP (rising, in view of the law of variable proportions) was equal to the rate. Thus, in a competitive labor market, the MVPs of all firms would be equal to one another when the bidding for labor services was all through, and equal to a prevailing wage rate.

But as we know, typically within a local labor market there is a range of wage rates for the same kind of labor, and the range is wider in a larger geographical area. We have already explored some of the reasons for such wage differences on the supply side of the labor market. Any explanation for wage differentials which traces to the demand side of the labor market must run in terms of (1) reasons why firms operate at levels of output where their MVPs are not equal; hence they are willing and able to pay more or less than other firms, depending on whether their MVP is more or less; and (2) reasons why firms may not follow a purely maximizing behavior. They may pay more than other firms, or more than they have to in a given labor market, for what appear to be noneconomic reasons. We shall consider these possibilities briefly.

Product differentiation with lumpy production
These two characteristics of the average business firm could be considered separately, but we may as well treat them together. Under competitive conditions rival products are assumed to be perfectly substitutable for each other. Thus each of the large number of competing producers can sell his whole output at a market price, but he cannot sell any at a higher price; consumers would simply turn to a rival producer and buy the product for less. Moreover, output in a firm can be expanded or contracted in very small amounts, even by a single unit if need be. Thus if supply or demand conditions for products or factors alter, all firms can readily adjust their output to a new equilibrium position.

But actual conditions depart from both these assumptions. Typically, firms differentiate their products by introducing qualitative features, both functional and stylistic, in an effort to attract customers by virtue of particular and even unique qualities (of form, location, complementary services, and so on) and to create a continuing brand or firm loyalty. This means that products of a given class are no longer perfect substitutes for one another, so that product-price differentials

can emerge and persist, based on consumer preference for one brand over another. This also means that a firm cannot necessarily sell its whole output at the same (market) price. Each firm in a sense becomes a little industry of its own, and as such can sell more of its specialized product only by lowering its price. (It can, alternatively, perhaps sell more at the same price but only by increasing its advertising and marketing expenditures.) Thus, the marginal return it receives at larger outputs is not the number of additional units times a constant price; it is the number of additional units times the lower price which makes their sale possible, less the reduced amount on all the previous units which now must be sold at the lower price too.

It would still be possible for any firm, even with a differentiated product, to continue to push its output to the point where its MVP (taking the above consideration into account) would be equal to the wage rate. But to do this would require that it be *technically* possible for the firm to vary its output by such small amounts that it could reach precisely that level of production where the MVP, now declining not only because of the law of variable proportions but also because of a downward-sloping demand curve, would come to equivalence with the unit cost of labor. But technical conditions often do not permit such minute adjustments in output. Capital equipment is not infinitely divisible, so that to expand output requires bringing into operation another machine, or bank of machines, or even another plant; manpower cannot always be scheduled in very small quantities (a second crew or even a second shift may have to be hired and not just a few hours more scheduled, and indirect labor as well as direct labor added if the existing level of output is at the limit of the range for which it is adequate). Thus a firm may have to decide whether it will increase its output by some "lumpy" amount such as 5 or 10 percent rather than by infinitely small variations. Marketing arrangements may further complicate the situation, as disposal of a larger output may require adding to the number of sales outlets or selling in bulk amounts or increasing the sales force—all actions which would not be profitable for only small additions to output.

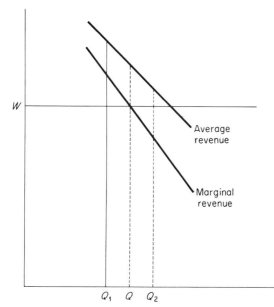

W

Average
revenue

Marginal
revenue

Q_1 Q Q_2

Fig. 17-3. *Imperfect adjustment of labor demand and supply due to imperfect adjustment of product demand and supply.*

But to increase output by the amount necessary to justify these additional capital, manpower, and marketing outlays might require dropping the price of the product by an amount which brings MVP below the wage rate. The firm, because of its sloping demand curve and lumpiness of production, cannot set its output precisely at the point where MVP equals the cost of a unit of labor. It must operate either above or below that point.

Figure 17-3 illustrates the problem. With sloping average and marginal revenue curves (owing to product differentiation) and a given wage rate W, the firm is currently producing at output Q_1. ("Average revenue" is, of course, the unit price of the product.) Here, however, its marginal labor cost (W) is less than its marginal return, so that an expansion of output is indicated. The preferred point of production would be Q, where W and MR are equal. But technical conditions do not permit its producing precisely at that point. If it increases output, it must go to Q_2. At Q_2, however, its marginal return is below the wage rate. Whether it decides to stay with its pres-

ent output or expand, then, its marginal value product cannot be brought to equality with the wage rate.

If the firm faces a rising supply curve for labor, perhaps due to poor working conditions or inconvenient location, so that it can expand its output only at a higher wage rate, which would have to be extended to its present employees as well as the new ones, its problem of equating MVP and the wage rate will be compounded.

A variation on this situation is sometimes referred to as the "kinked" demand curve, illustrated in Figure 17-4. Here, owing to some circumstance of the product market, the demand for a product is not a smooth function of price. Demand may be quite elastic up to some level of output, but inelastic at that point over a considerable price range so that only a sharp break in price can lead to an increase in sales. This might be the case for products which have established "price classes" for themselves, such as clothing and automobiles. Beyond output Q, small price variations will have relatively little impact on consumer demand. It would take a really substantial price cut to induce a larger volume. In this event, at an output in the neighborhood of Q a wage rate anywhere between a and b could be made com-

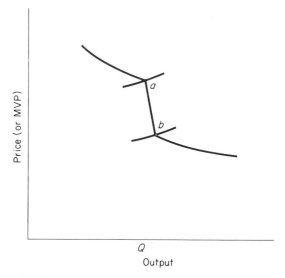

Price (or MVP)

a

b

Q
Output

Fig. 17-4. *Wage latitude with a "kinked" demand curve.*

364 LABOR AS A MARKET

patible with the requirement that it be equal to the firm's MVP, introducing a considerable range of latitude.

Oligopoly pricing Product differentiation can take in small firms and is not incompatible with price competition, even though it introduces other nonprice elements of competition as well. The number of firms supplying rival products may be sufficiently large that there is no possibility for them to try to reach an understanding among themselves as to the "appropriate" price level for their products. A wide range of prices may exist for products which are functionally similar but differentially appealing. In the case of oligopoly, this does not hold true. The number of rival sellers is small, and often the product may be quite homogeneous (iron or steel or aluminum or oil, for example). Any price reduction by one, to increase sales, will have an immediate impact on its few rivals, usually inviting a retaliatory price cut. As the firms come to understand this situation over time, it does not require formal agreement for them to limit their price rivalry. They will likely emphasize nonprice variables such as good service, reliable supply, and product differences where possible, but will refrain from price cutting for fear of involving themselves in a price war from which all will suffer.

Oligopolistic sellers typically view themselves as facing a demand curve which is inelastic downward, since price cuts designed to increase sales will simply evoke comparable reductions from rivals, leaving them all with roughly the same market as before. At the same time, there is no confidence on the part of any oligopolistic firm that price increases, designed to add to income, will be matched by its competitors, so that such increases can be expected to drive customers to its rivals—a conception of upward price elasticity. (This conception of their demand curves by oligopolists is similar to the demand curve pictured in Figure 17-4, with price and output intersecting at point *a*. From this point, a price reduction brings little added business but a major loss of revenue, while a price increase brings a major loss of business and little added revenue.)

Since the several oligopolistic rivals all hold the same view that a price reduction will be matched

and a price increase is not likely to be followed, there is a strong tendency for them to hold prices constant. This is not a constant price in the same sense that a competitive price is constant at a market level, however; it is a constant price due to a learned behavior on their part, requiring no formal agreement but having the same effect as a price understanding.[16] It does not mean that they can all sell as much of their output as they wish at the maintained price level. On the contrary, a considerable part of plant capacity may lie idle. This price inhibition means that oligopolistic firms are often not able to push output to the point where a falling MPP (with a constant maintained price) brings MVP into equality with the wage rate. Hence such firms could operate indefinitely with their MVP above the prevailing wage.

Subsidized inefficiency The fact that a firm's demand for labor is effective only at a wage rate below that being paid by other firms does not necessarily drive it from the market. For a variety of reasons which we have already considered in examining labor supply, a firm may face a specialized supply of labor, and at times may even be able to "create" its own supply. Such a semi-independent labor supply may be content to work at wages which in effect subsidize the inefficiencies of the producer. In particular situations, a firm may be satisfied with the "rejects" of the labor market—workers of inferior skill or with personality quirks or peculiar time schedules, who might have great difficulty in finding employment elsewhere. In these cases the lower wage rate may be equal to the firm's MVP, but both are below "prevailing rates." We shall have more to say about this later.

Hiring prejudices and preferences In contrast to those firms which may not be fussy about the kind of workers they hire as long as they can get them cheaply enough, there are those firms which pay more than they have to or more than the market would require in order to get workers of a preferred type. The most obvious example is the discriminatory hiring treatment of Negroes. Although a maximizing firm should presumably be interested only in what functional contribution a pair of hands or a brain makes to its operations and its profits, in some instances social prejudices get in the way of maximizing economic gain. An employer will pay more for a pair of hands because they are white. He voluntarily pays more than he has to in order to indulge a social preference. (On the other hand, an employer willing to hire Negro workers is likely to obtain his labor more cheaply.)

Attempts have been made to explain such prejudicial or preferential hiring within the framework of competitive analysis. One economist has suggested that if an employer is willing to pay extra to avoid social contact with a particular class of labor, he is paying for what is to him a utility or satisfaction, just as he might pay more than he has to for housing simply because he prefers to live in a particular neighborhood. The bias may be labeled a "taste for discrimination," and it is said that the employer pays not only a wage rate equal to labor's MVP but a surplus charge to indulge his taste for discrimination.[17] There are several objections which one might enter to such a formulation, but the most relevant one at the moment is that such an effort to retain the "purity" of competitive analysis, by subsuming exceptions within the rules by a taxonomic exercise, has only the result of robbing the competitive analysis of any usefulness or even meaning. In the same way, we could explain away worker immobility (even though the competitive analysis rests on a mobility assumption) by saying that some workers have a "taste for immobility," which is measured by the amount of the wage return they are willing to forgo by remaining where they are. On such an approach, all departures from predicted results can be made to appear as logically consistent with the theory. Propositions cannot be disproved because any contrary result constitutes an equally satisfactory proof of the proposition. It seems far more satisfying to recognize that labor demand does not operate precisely as one would expect if he were operating on the maximizing assumption of competitive theory.

A somewhat different case is provided by those firms which pride themselves on paying "at the top of the market" while other employers in the same labor market are paying less for comparable skills. They may regard themselves as socially conscious employers who are trying to set a good example to fellow employers, or they may derive special satisfaction from the climate of good feeling which above-average working conditions produce (indulging "a taste for happy employees"?), or they may believe that they are thereby acquiring workers of higher ability. We have already examined the difficulties attending the analysis of differential rates of pay for workers of differential quality. Unquestionably, differences of ability among workers do exist and may give rise to differential MVPs in firms, but it is difficult to measure such differences and to accommodate them within an integrated demand schedule.

One theorist has suggested that a worker's MVP must be regarded as whatever the management of that company thinks it is. The marginal product is not an objective quantity but something which exists in the mind of the businessman. The MVP of any factor being whatever the employer conceives it to be, he will hire or fire, make substitutions among factors (capital for labor), or set his wage scale in accordance with whatever subjective views he may have of the consequences. Thus, as long as he *believes* that by paying above-average wages he is obtaining an above-average MVP, his action is in accord with competitive principles.[18] On this approach, MVP would vary from employer to employer and would render impossible any meaningful comparison of wage rates based on objective considerations, since differential rates might simply reflect subjective differences in producers' evaluation of labor's MVP. We can accept as valid the proposition that businessmen's judgments are important data in economic life, but this should not be made a means of explaining away incompatibilities and inconsistencies in competitive theory as though they were in fact only part of the system.

The demand for labor reconsidered

As in the case of labor supply, the analysis of the demand for labor under conditions of competition is subject to several significant qualifications. The rivalry of employers for the services of workers does not lead to a single integrated demand function for a particular grade or type of labor even within a local market. There are employers who are willing and able to pay more than others, either because they believe they are thereby acquiring higher-grade labor ("you get what you pay for") or because of some personal satisfaction deriving from the reputation for being a good employer or from a congenial work environment or because of personal prejudices which segregate the labor market in which they choose to operate from a more general labor market. There are other employers who are unable to pay as much as others but who nevertheless find that their demand for labor remains effective either because immobile workers subsidize their inefficiencies or because they are content with workers whom other firms reject, not necessarily on grounds having to do with their work capacity.

The demand schedules attaching to particular firms do not, then, sum into some single demand schedule for the market. Instead, multiple demand schedules emerge. Just as for labor supply, these are interlocked even though not integrated. The rates offered by one firm are not entirely independent of the rates offered by other firms. The wage one firm offers cannot deviate too far from that offered by others, on the low side, without the firm's losing its work force or some substantial part of it, or, on the high side, without involving it in cost conditions which may threaten its continuing growth and profitability (what it can afford now it may not be able to afford later).

As with labor supply, so with labor demand is it true that interdependency is greater in local labor markets and more attenuated with distance. There is in fact a kind of galaxy of labor-demand schedules, inclusive of clusters and constellations whose component parts are closely related to each other and produce readily discernible configurations, and other, more remote and semiautonomous schedules whose relationship to the total system is weaker and less evident.

Competitive clearing of the market

In the competitive analysis we assume a "market" within which workers compete directly for jobs and employers bid against one another for labor services. The assumptions of maximizing behavior, ready substitutability of units of any given grade of labor for each other (and, within limits, of all factors for each other), the ready mobility of factors, the availability of information concerning jobs and factors and rates—all lead to a single integrated supply schedule in which more labor is assumed to be forthcoming only at higher rates, and a single integrated demand schedule in which more labor services will be purchased only at falling rates. In the short run, these two schedules intersect at a single point, which is the equilibrium rate, as indicated in Figure 17-5(a). All the firms whose schedules have indicated their willingness to buy so many units of labor at that rate will be able to hire all the workers whose sched-

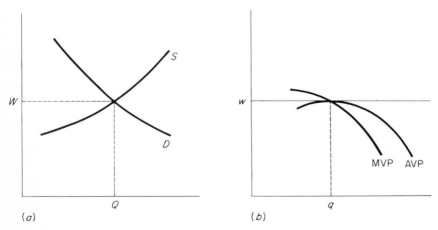

Fig. 17-5. *Equilibrium of labor supply and demand in a market (a) and in a firm (b).*

ules have indicated their willingness to supply the same number of units. There are no unsatisfied buyers or sellers of labor. In each firm, production will take place to the point where MVP is equal to the market-set wage rate, indicated by q in Figure 17-5(b).

In the long run, we should have to deal with a supply curve the exact shape of which is indeterminable without further assumptions (since it is based on population and labor-force projections) and a demand curve which reflects the producer's demand for the factor in both its fixed and variable uses. The intersection of these market curves determines the equilibrium price. At that price, firms will hire the factor up to the point where its MVP in *all* uses equals its price.

The numerous units of a factor—workers of a particular skill, for example, like electricians or machinists or semiskilled operatives—are distributed across industries producing many types of products. This serves as the link by which a competitive economy assures that its factors of production are employed in those uses which are most desired by consumers. The marginal value products of the various factors (whose prices are set economywide) must be equal in all industries where they are employed, and equal to the common factor price, for general equilibrium to obtain. Wherever the factor price is less than MVP, producers will seek additional units of that factor, bidding for it until its price is equal to MVP.

If employers figure they can get $5 in revenue from the output produced by $4 worth of a given kind of labor, their maximizing drive is unsatisfied. They will continue to bid for workers, trying to lure them away from other employers and from other industries or employments, causing wages to rise, and they will continue to turn out more goods, causing the unit value of their product to drop. Not until MVP and the wage rate meet—perhaps at a figure of $4.50, perhaps at $4.60 (depending on technical considerations of consumer preferences and production functions)—will employers let up on their demand for labor, having extracted the fullest profit advantage possible. Since this process goes on in all industries, and factor prices are common to all industries, equilibrium necessitates that the MVP of a factor be the same throughout the economy and equal to the factor price.[19]

General equilibrium

It is perhaps worth taking a moment to elaborate a bit on this larger economic setting in which competitive wage determination is presumed to take place, and which to many economists gives the competitive analysis its broader significance and greater appeal, despite its evident weaknesses.

Wages are the price for the services of only one factor, labor. There are numerous other prices in the economy too—prices for other factors and prices for products. In competitive theory, these prices are all intimately and sensitively linked together into a *system* of prices. A change in any one price then sets off repercussions on other prices, as the system is disturbed and tries to readjust itself.

There is one major principle governing these attempts at adjustment or readjustment, the principle of maximization, which dictates the substitution of any factor for another when this is advantageous, or of one product for another. If prices are linked together to provide the most advantageous possible employment of all factors in the most advantageous possible production of goods, then a change in any factor or product price motivates producers and consumers to readjust their purchases of factor services and of goods in order to reestablish maximum advantage under the new, changed circumstances. Whenever all producers, factors, and consumers are in situations which they cannot improve by any further adjustment under the existing circumstances, we say that there is general equilibrium.

To suggest the general equilibrium outcome—of which wages are a part—we may make use of an algebraic formula as simple in fact as it is complex in appearance. While indeed oversimplified as an expression of general equilibrium,[20] it does emphasize (if we recall the underlying competitive assumptions) the compatibility of the manifold interdependent relationships. We make use of the following symbols:

MPP = marginal physical productivity
P = price of product
p = price of factor
Small-letter subscripts (a, b, etc.) = factors, all units of each factor being homogeneous.
Capital-letter subscripts (A, B, etc.) = products, all units of each product being homogeneous.

$$\frac{\mathrm{MPP}_{a(A)} \times P_A}{p_a} = \frac{\mathrm{MPP}_{b(A)} \times P_A}{p_b}$$

$$= \ldots \frac{\mathrm{MPP}_{n(A)} \times P_A}{p_n}$$

$$= \frac{\mathrm{MPP}_{a(B)} \times P_B}{p_a} = \frac{\mathrm{MPP}_{b(B)} \times P_B}{p_b}$$

$$= \ldots \frac{\mathrm{MPP}_{n(B)} \times P_B}{p_n}$$

$$= \frac{\mathrm{MPP}_{a(N)} \times P_N}{p_a} = \frac{\mathrm{MPP}_{b(N)} \times P_N}{p_b}$$

$$= \ldots \frac{\mathrm{MPP}_{n(N)} \times P_N}{p_n} = 1$$

As we know, the marginal physical product (MPP) of factor *a* in the production of product A times the price of product A is simply the marginal value product (MVP) of *a* in the production of A. And all (but what an all!) which the foregoing complex formula asserts is that the MVP of factor *a* will be the same in all its uses and equal to its price, and the MVP of all other factors will also be the same in all their uses and equal to their prices, and the ratio between MVP and price will thus be the same (namely, unity) for all factors, in all their uses.

Should the price of any product or factor be affected, a series of chain reactions is set in motion. A change in one product price will cause a movement of factors into or out of that line of production, creating a compensating change in marginal physical productivity, since, it is assumed, MPP varies inversely with the number of factors. If more units of a factor are drawn to one line of employment, lowering its MPP, they must be drawn away from other lines of employment and thereby raise the MPP in those lines. The change in product prices thus effects a reallocation of the factors of production. Similarly, a change in the price of one factor will set up repercussions. Under our competitive assumptions, all markets are so closely related that a shock in any one must touch off effects in other markets.

Actually, when we consider the matter, we are driven to the conclusion that all prices—of products and factors both—must be settled *simultaneously* to achieve equilibrium. How much will be charged for products depends on factor prices, and factor prices are in turn dependent on product prices. The conception of the simultaneous

solution of an almost infinite series of equations as the basis for general equilibrium is generally attributed to the French economist Leon Walras. There is an equation for each product price and each factor price, that is, an equation for each unknown, so that the problem becomes mathematically determinate.

This mathematical approach to general equilibrium argues most unequivocally the mutual determinacy of all prices—both product and factor—in the system; we are enabled to see how no one price can be fixed without a simultaneous determination of all other prices. Nevertheless, the degree of abstraction of this theoretical system has militated against its acceptance. There is nothing in this conception of a simultaneous setting of all prices that seems to approximate central tendencies in our society.[21]

There is no need for being puristic about the matter, however. We need only consider that with any price change of product or factor, consumers and producers effect a rearrangement of their expenditures in order to restore the position of maximum advantage which has been disturbed. Starting from a set of prices which are given as of any moment of time, then, such adjustment comes by substituting one good or factor for another good or factor until the most satisfactory balance is achieved for any given income level. The process of substitution will, it is true, result in "prices chasing each other." If we start with a single price change, that change will set off other price changes which in turn will have their ramifications, and so on, in a never-ending succession of price fluctuations. Each change is intended as a closer approximation to that perfect balance which is the ultimate goal never quite realized. The *possibility* of realization is indeed present; the mathematical theory demonstrates the potential determinacy of the system. But there is nothing in such a demonstration to establish that the achievement of equilibrium through successive approximations is likely, or other than accidental. The mathematical theory thus shows possibility but not process.

In terms of the effective working of the price system, however, the actual achievement of general equilibrium is viewed as less significant than the tendency toward such equilibrium, a tendency which is logically demonstrable under the principle of substitution for maximization. Admittedly, there are short-run deviations from the ideal outcome; there are swings of business activity indicative of imperfect adjustment of prices to each other. But the competitive price analysis is largely unconcerned with such short-run phenomena. It seeks to explain the persistent, underlying pattern of economic relationships—the main economic drift.

The significance for employment and wage theory of this analysis is readily apparent. First, the system provides for full employment of all factors, if we define full employment as a sufficiency of employment opportunities for all factors offering themselves at the market-determined price for their services. (Those factors unwilling to work at the freely determined rate of remuneration would, by this definition, not be regarded as unemployed.) Such a conclusion follows inevitably from the assumptions of the system. The equilibrium market price for factors may be determined *only* by completely registering the voluntary supply of factors at each price over a range of prices. If, then, some workers are unable to find jobs at the going wage rate under free competition, this is simply indicative of the fact that the going rate is not an equilibrium price and that market pressures will yet drive it toward equilibrium. The unemployed workers will offer their services for less than the going rate, and employers will of course stand ready to hire them as long as the lowered wage rate equals the (diminishing) marginal value product. Since all units of a factor are homogeneous, workers already employed must likewise accept the lowered wage rate. Thus the rate is forced to an equilibrium position, at which level all those who wish to work at that rate will find employment.

Second, the factors of production are directed into given lines of employment, in accordance with collective consumer preferences. Factual remuneration is tied directly to consumer valuations as expressed in product prices. Changes in product prices affect factor payments. Since product prices thus reflect relative consumer preferences, factor remuneration is highest in the production of those goods most desired by consumers. The drive to maximize pecuniary return can then be counted upon to channel factors into the em-

ployments offering the greatest returns. Ideal output is the outcome—ideal output defined as the most effective use of resources for purposes of meeting society's collective consumer preferences.

Third, all goods are being produced at minimum cost. In the long-run equilibrium position, all firms must be of optimum size and so producing at the lowest average cost. In no case is factor remuneration (including profit for the entrepreneur) more than is just necessary to hold that factor in its employment. All technical and economic possibilities for cheaper production have been fully exploited. The stock of consumption goods is as great as known production functions and rational maximization will permit.

Finally, the allocation of the output of society (in the form of income) among all its members proceeds on the basis of the contribution which each makes. Each individual receives the value of the product which is attributable to him. This distribution of income can be altered only by giving to some factor an amount greater than his contribution, while giving to another factor an amount less than his contribution. The individual's income (or command over consumption goods) is thus governed by the standard of how much he has contributed to society's stock of consumption goods.

It can be readily appreciated from the several "significances" of this theory, as listed above, that it is often highly regarded and warmly defended, not because it constitutes a good explanation of the process of wage setting in a competitive economy, but because it embodies values which are highly regarded. The acceptability of the theory then, unfortunately, is made to hinge not on whether it is reliable but on whether it is desirable.

Competitive equilibrium reconsidered

The general equilibrium analysis summarized all too briefly here depends for its validity on the deduction, arrived at from its set of assumptions, of completely integrated and wholly interdependent supply and demand curves for all factors, including labor. We have seen that because of weaknesses in certain of the assumptions (a maximizing drive which takes precedence over all, ready mobility, and homogeneity of all the factors of a particular grade or kind) supply and demand for labor are not integrated into single schedules, intersecting to establish a single wage rate for that grade of labor. Instead, there are numbers of supply and demand schedules even in a local labor market, establishing a range of wage rates even for the same grade or type of labor. Wages thus do not tend toward equality, as the competitive analysis would have it. We have already noted several reasons why this result emerges, and need only summarize some of the more pertinent considerations here.

The existence of job preference places in the hands of the employer a certain degree of control over workers. Since other jobs to which they might turn are not, for many of them, equally acceptable alternatives, wage differentials can exist between his and other firms without evoking worker movement. His wage scale may be 5 or 10 or even 25 percent below that of other companies in the community, for workers in similar occupational categories, yet his work force may not stand ready to move to those rival employers when openings develop because they are located in less convenient parts of town, because it would mean becoming juniors of a new work group, because they could not expect that special consideration which comes from long association with a company, which they now enjoy in their present employment, and for other reasons. Wage differentials for similar occupations can thus emerge and persist in a labor market.

Technically speaking, the employer under such circumstances enjoys a certain element of monopsonistic power. In certain respects he constitutes a unique market for the sale of services by factors, just as through product differentiation he constitutes, in certain respects, a unique supplier of his product. A monopsonist—literally, a single buyer—is often associated with exploitation, in an invidious sense, but monopsony is used here in a specialized sense which is characteristic of most firms, just as monopoly in the specialized sense of product differentiation is characteristic of most firms. In this specialized sense, it is in itself no basis for condemnation, but something which is built into the social system which an employer could not avoid if he would. The manner in which

monopsonistic power is used, however, is something about which people can legitimately hold contrasting views.

Competition in the labor market is not eliminated by monopsonistic conditions, any more than competition in product markets is eliminated by product differentiation. But the basis for competition becomes more than price or wage rates—it is quality differences as well. Just as firms have incurred expense in differentiating their product from other products, so have firms incurred expense in trying to establish work conditions that give them a favorable competitive position in the labor market. Just as in product competition, so in the labor market is it true that unique advantages cannot always be overcome by rival firms. New firms may have as much difficulty in drawing employees away from other firms, at comparable wage rates, as new firms have of luring customers from familiar branded products selling at about the same price. Or new firms in the labor market may be able to attract only a relatively low-grade labor force, workers of skills and personal characteristics such that other employers will not hire them at the wage scale prevailing in their plants. There is thus the possibility that above-average profit can be earned even over long periods, if new firms do not prove themselves successful competitors for the labor supply.

Monopsonistic advantage does not place unfettered control over wage rates in the hands of any employer. The shape of his labor-supply curve is dependent on the attachment of his workers to their place of employment and on the reputation which the firm enjoys among the labor force in the community at large. The firm's wage policy is itself one important determinant of its reputation as an employer. If the employer should reduce wages or fail to raise them because he is confident that his employees would remain with him, the effect of such a policy would be to weaken the very attachment on which the employer counted, shifting the labor-supply curve to his disadvantage. The curve might become flatter from the point of current employment backward and steeper from that point forward, indicating relatively less power on the part of the employer to hold his existing labor force and relatively increased cost in adding to it. Employers, recognizing this possibility, sometimes pay wage rates higher than their competitive position in the labor market would appear to necessitate.

Just as workers have job preferences, employers often have worker preferences and will pay more or less depending on the kind of worker that satisfies them. Often these preferences are in the nature of prejudices (of race, nationality background, sex, education, appearance) without necessary relation to work ability.

With varying compulsions on workers and firms, there are good reasons for wage rates to differ, even for workers of comparable skills, and for differences to persist over time. The competitive conclusion that wages tend to equality has not been borne out by the facts.

A second outcome which the competitive price analysis would lead us to expect is a self-equilibrating economy that would maintain continuous full employment. Whenever unemployment emerged, so that the supply of workers exceeded the demand for workers at the going wage rate, competition among workers for jobs would lead to a reduction in the wage rate. The new lower rate would then fall below the marginal value product of labor in its various employments, inducing employers to add to their work forces until, via the law of diminishing returns, MVP would be equal to the new wage rate. Only at that point would the employer achieve his position of maximum profit. Continuous full employment is thus presumed to be achieved by the adjustment of the wage rate.

The fact is, however, that periods of unemployment have been at least as characteristic of the United States economy as periods of full employment. It was the English economist John Maynard Keynes who was chiefly responsible for disseminating a theoretical explanation for the unreliability of the competitive price analysis in this respect. Although a restatement of his argument lies beyond our present purpose, and although the main lines of his argument generally run in other terms, it is possible to summarize briefly the essence of his statement in terms which the analysis of this chapter has made familiar to us.

As has been said, the competitive analysis assumes that full employment can always be maintained because the wage rate automatically adjusts

to secure that result. The wage rate rises or falls to the point where it equals the MVP of all workers who are seeking jobs at that rate. This analysis, however, assumes that as wages rise and fall, to make the proper adjustments, MVP remains relatively stable in the economy. MVP, it will be recalled, is the product of the marginal physical product (MPP) times the price (P) of the product. We may assume that in the immediate situation the technology of production does not change sufficiently to alter MPP. But if MVP is to remain stable, we must also assume that the price of the product remains stable, which is to say that demand for the product is unaffected by—among other things—the adjustments which are being made in the wage rate. If the rate is to adjust upward or downward to equate with MVP at a level of full employment, then MVP cannot itself be affected by the movements of the wage rate in such a way as to prevent that result. On the contrary, it must be assumed to remain relatively independent of wage adjustments.

It was just this assumption that Keynes questioned. If wages must be reduced to prevent unemployment from emerging or persisting, he argued, such a reduction in wages will curtail the purchasing power of workers. The prices of the products they buy will therefore decline. Producers will become pessimistic in the face of declining sales and hence will cease to make capital investments, so that their purchases of capital goods will likewise fall off. With the prices of both consumer and producer goods declining, labor's MVP (compounded of MPP *and* prices) will also fall. Thus the cut in the wage rate (which was designed to bring wages into line with MVP) actually causes MVP itself to decline. If wages are cut again in an effort to equate them with the now lower MVP, this action once again has the effect of reducing MVP. MVP thus chases wages downward.

At some point, however, wages are brought into alignment with MVP, but not in the way pictured by the competitive analysis. At some point workers will themselves resist any further cuts in their wages. It is true that the wage cuts to which they have been consenting are not so drastic as appears on the surface, because prices too have been falling, so that real wages have not suffered so much as money wages. But workers have a certain psychological feeling about money wages as such that leads them to call a halt to further declines, regardless of what is happening to prices. If wage rates have been $2 an hour, workers would resent having those money rates cut to 50 cents an hour even though the prices of all products were cut proportionately so that their standard of living would not suffer. The amount of the money wage rate is itself important. Keynes referred to this as the "money illusion."[22]

At the point where workers call a halt to further declines in money wage rates, that number of workers will be employed whose MVP is equal to this rate. Other workers will remain unemployed but will not act as a depressant on the wage rate, since they are unwilling to offer their services for anything less than those employed are earning. It is at this point that occurs, then, in Keynes's terminology, equilibrium at less than full employment. There is no inducement for employers to hire more workers, nor is there any reason for them to hire fewer. They are in their positions of maximum advantage, under the circumstances. But unemployment exists and may persist.

In this respect too—its expectation of continuing full employment—just as in its expectation that wage rates for comparable kinds of work tend toward equality, the competitive analysis has shown its deficiencies. We have not, however, been flogging a dead horse (though it must be admitted that at times it has come pretty close to that). Whatever its weaknesses, the competitive analysis has provided us with some basic conceptual threads which we shall want to follow as we continue our explorations in the labyrinth of wage determination—admittedly one of the messiest components of economic theory. In particular, we shall want to keep in mind its emphasis on the relatedness of product prices and workers' wages, and of relative wage rates. That relatedness, we find, is less exact than has often been assumed, but the job we face is to try to discover relatedness in whatever form it exists. We continue to face the question with which we began this section: What is it that keeps the millions of wage rates for millions of workers in countless varieties of jobs in a myriad of labor markets around the country from flying off in all directions? What—if anything—supplies cohesion?

ADDITIONAL READINGS

Cartter, Allan M.: *Theory of Wages and Employment,* Irwin, Homewood, Ill., 1959.

Dunlop, John T. (ed.): *The Theory of Wage Determination,* Macmillan, New York, 1957.

Gordon, Robert A., and Margaret S. Gordon (eds.): *Prosperity and Unemployment,* Wiley, New York, 1966, parts II-V.

National Bureau of Economic Research: *Aspects of Labor Economics,* Princeton University Press, Princeton, N.J., 1962 (particularly the papers by Jacob Mincer, George P. Shultz, Armen A. Alchian and Reuben A. Kessell, and Melvin W. Reder).

Reynolds, Lloyd G., and Cynthia H. Taft: *The Evolution of Wage Structure,* Yale University Press, New Haven, Conn., 1956.

Taylor, George W., and Frank C. Pierson (eds.): *New Concepts in Wage Determination,* McGraw-Hill, New York, 1957.

FOR ANALYSIS AND DISCUSSION

1. In what ways are the "automatic mechanisms" of the marketplace supposed to eliminate wage differentials between workers of comparable ability and ensure full employment?

2. Explain how the individual firm helps to determine the going wages of labor in the short run, under pure competition, and how it then determines the actual amount of labor it will hire at the wages so determined.

3. "An increase in the demand for labor raises wages."

"An increase in wages curtails the demand for labor."

Reconcile this pair of statements within the framework of competitive analysis.

4. It has sometimes been argued that if factoral returns are based on marginal productivity, this constitutes an ethical justification for whatever wages workers receive.

It has sometimes been argued in rebuttal that the value of the services a worker renders is based on effective consumer demand, the pattern of which is determined by the existing distribution of incomes, which has no ethical justification.

What validity, if any, do you see in either of these positions?

5. In your community, inquire of employers what their rates are for such jobs as common labor and maintenance electrician. What range of rates do you find? See if you can obtain explanations from employers for any differentials which you discover between their rates and those of other firms.

6. Professor Simon Rottenberg has defended the theory of competitive wage determination in an article, "On Choice in Labor Markets," *Industrial and Labor Relations Review*, vol. 9, pp. 183–199, 1956. He has argued, among other things, that the existence of differential wage rates does not disprove the competitive analysis.

The apparent persistence of wage differentials in similar employments in a labor market does not necessarily mean that calculated comparison does not occur. What seem to be similar employments may not be similar at all in the worker's perception of them, and there also may be errors in observation. What appears to be "the same kind of work" may really be different when account is taken of all the qualities considered by workers in making occupational choices. Some of these are surely so subtle that they escape detection. . . .

If there are persistent price differentials in truly similar employments, it may only be because adjustment is not quickly brought about. McCulloch said on this point:

"It often happens that, owing to an attachment to the trade, or the locality in which they have been bred, or the difficulty of learning other trades, individuals will continue, for a lengthened period, to practice their peculiar trades, or will remain in the same district, when other trades in that district and the same trades in other districts, yield better wages to those engaged in them. But how slowly soever, wages, taking everything into account, are sure to be equalized in the end."

a. If you accept the above argument, do wage differentials have any value as a test of validity of competitive theory?

b. What meaning do you see in the statement that wages "are sure to be equalized in the end"?

7. Keynes maintained that a situation of general unemployment could not be corrected by wage cutting. Is his argument equally applicable to situations of particular unemployment (that is, cases where workers are laid off from a given company or industry although employment remains relatively stable elsewhere)?

NOTES

1. Jacob Mincer, "Labor-Force Participation and Unemployment: A Review of Recent Evidence," in Robert A. Gordon and Margaret S. Gordon (eds.), *Prosperity and Unemployment,* Wiley, New York, 1966, p. 73.

2. The same, pp. 92–100.

3. Clarence D. Long, *The Labor Force under Changing Income and Employment,* Princeton University Press, Princeton, N.J., 1958, chap. 12 and appendix A. For 1947–1968 data, U.S. Department of Labor, *Statistics on Manpower, A Supplement to the Manpower Report of the President,* March, 1969, p. 1.

4. Long, chap. 13.

5. Frank H. Knight, as quoted in George Stigler, *The Theory of Price,* Macmillan, 1946, p. 109. R. G. Tugwell commented: "One great justification . . . for the distributive categories of rent, interest, profit and wages lies in the fact that each furnishes an incentive to distinct individuals to do a distinct thing. . . ." "Human Nature in Economic Theory," *Journal of Political Economy,* vol. 30, p. 336, 1932.

6. George P. Shultz, Irwin L. Herrnstadt, and Elbridge S. Puckett, "Wage Determination in a Nonunion Labor Market," Industrial Relations Research Association, *Proceedings,* 1957, p. 12.

7. Blue-collar and clerical workers' data are for July, 1966, through June, 1967, from U.S. Bureau of Labor Statistics, Bulletin 1530-87, *Wages and Related Benefits: Part I: 85 Metropolitan Areas, 1966–67,* 1967, Tables A-1 and 5. Data for professional workers (except economists) are from U.S. Bureau of Labor Statistics, Bulletin 1535, *National Survey of Professional, Administrative, Technical, and Clerical Pay, February–March 1966,* 1966, Table 4. Data for economists from "The Structure of Economists' Employment and Salaries, 1964," *American Economic Review Supplement,* December, 1965, p. 45.

8. "The Threat of Inflationary Erosion: The Annual Report on the Economic Status of the Profession, 1968–69," *AAUP Bulletin,* June, 1969, pp. 206 and 220–221.

9. Why such movement would tend to eliminate wage differentials will be more evident when we come to examine the demand side of the market. Briefly, it involves the law of diminishing returns. With fixed capital equipment in the short run, a movement of workers from one plant to another would presumably tend to raise marginal physical product in the first plant and lower it in the second. Since wages are geared to marginal product, this would tend to pull

them up in the low-wage sector and gradually depress them in the high-wage sector, until the two became approximately equal.

10. Richard C. Wilcock and Irvin Sobel document this point in *Small City Job Markets,* University of Illinois, Institute of Labor and Industrial Relations, Urbana, 1958.

11. N. Arnold Tolles and Emanuel Melichar, "Studies of the Structure of Economists' Salaries and Income," *American Economic Review Supplement,* December, 1968, pp. 70–115. This study did not purport to be a test of the competitive model or a measure of labor quality, but its findings are obviously relevant to these issues.

12. Henry Sanborn, "Pay Differences Between Men and Women," *Industrial and Labor Relations Review,* July, 1964, pp. 534–550.

13. Leonard W. Weiss, "Concentration and Labor Earnings," *American Economic Review,* March, 1966, p. 115.

14. Sanborn, p. 534.

15. It has been shown, for example, that quit rates in fifty-two industries varied inversely with average annual earnings (corrected for skill mix) in 1963, and this relationship was even stronger in 1966 when unemployment was lower and alternative job opportunities were therefore more numerous. The quit rate also varied inversely among these industries in relation to the percentage increase in earnings over the last three years, the extent of unionization, the percentage of male Negro workers, and the skill mix. For an interpretation of these findings, see Vladimir Stoikov and Robert L. Raimon, "Determinants of Differences in the Quit Rate Among Industries," *American Economic Review,* December, 1968, pp. 1283–1298.

16. Prof. William Fellner refers to this as a quasi agreement in *Competition among the Few,* Knopf, New York, 1949.

17. Gary S. Becker, *The Economics of Discrimination,* The University of Chicago Press, Chicago, 1957.

18. Fritz Machlup, "Marginal Analysis and Empirical Research," *American Economic Review,* vol. 36, pp. 519–554, 1946.

19. In addition, a factor's *average* value product must equal its price if there is to be long-run equilibrium—otherwise some firms would be incurring losses and leaving the market or, alternatively, some firms would be making above-normal profits and thus inducing the entry of new firms. The average revenue of a product (its price) is the sum of the average value products of the factors, just as the average cost of a product is the sum of the prices of the factors which produce it. Consequently, as long as the average value product of any factor is greater than its price, new producers will find it advantageous to un-

dertake employment of that factor. As long as the average value product of any factor is less than its price, producers will find it advantageous to forgo employment of that factor in the long run. Equilibrium is reached only when the average value product of a factor, no less than its marginal value product, equals its price, since long-run maximization would result in greater demand for, or greater supply of, any factor at any other price. Thus, under long-run equilibrium, factor price = marginal value product = average value product.

20. It is only the elaborated statement of factor pricing and allocation.

21. Certain conceptual devices or analogies have been employed to make the notion more palatable. The English economist Edgeworth developed the notion of "recontracting," in which all bargains struck at any time, under given conditions, are only tentative; as bargaining between buyers and sellers continues back and forth, the "consensus" of the market is ultimately arrived at with respect to each factor and product, so that the set of prices at which supply and demand would be brought into balance is discernible, and here all bargains are made firm. The Swedish economist Cassel likened the process to a gigantic auction which, however, has the peculiar feature of requiring the simultaneous auctioning of all goods and factors, since buyers are able to determine how much they will spend on any one item only in the light of the alternatives prevailing at the moment of expenditure.

22. An interesting rationalization of this position was made by Prof. Henry C. Emery a quarter century before Keynes wrote his *General Theory of Employment, Interest, and Money,* Harcourt, Brace & World, New York, 1936. In an article, "Hards Times and the Standard Wage," in the *Yale Review,* vol. 17, pp. 251–267, 1908, Emery wrote of the trade unionists' philosophy:

What they dread most of all is a reduction of wages, not so much because they unreasonably refuse to make any sacrifices when the whole community is suffering, but because they believe, and they think they know from experience, that a reduction of wages once made is very difficult to restore. . . . When the manufacturer cannot pay standard wages and run full time at a profit, let him curtail his production, let some men be discharged, but let the level of wages continue intact. Then, when the readjustment comes, there will be no need of a fight, but, automatically, as the demand for products increases, the capitalist's self-interest will send him again in search of more labor.

CHAPTER 18

THE DETERMINATION OF WAGES

In the previous chapter we examined the rudiments of the competitive theory of wage determination and some of the weaknesses in that theory. In particular we noted the reason for not expecting a single supply curve for labor in a local market, integrated through the maximizing mobility of workers, and a single demand curve for labor, integrated through the maximizing production drive of firms. On the contrary, we found reasons to expect a number of interlocking supply and demand curves.

Before we proceed to put together some of the pieces we have left lying around, out of which we hope to construct a system of wage relationships, let us briefly pursue two further lines of thought which should prove helpful to our task. We have already had occasion to refer to the fact that competitive analysis tends to overlook organized economic activity such as unionism. It deals with people only as individuals. We shall want to add unionism to the ingredients which we propose to mix and blend into the wage-determining process, and have a look at how unions affect worker and employer attitudes toward wages.

We have so far operated within the framework which the competitive economic theorists have set for us—basically a pecuniary-oriented supply and demand analysis. If we have found weaknesses in their system, these have only resulted in modification of the basic supply-demand analysis which they have provided. Before attempting

to resolve our problem of what gives cohesion to the system of wage rates, we shall do well to pay a little attention to an alternative (or at least a supplementary) approach, based not on the competitive maximizing behavior of people as abstract economic factors but on the concept of people normalizing their status role in a social system.

Thus, we are still focusing on the *structure* or *dispersion* of wages in the American economy. In the long view, of course, the dominant wage trend has been the phenomenal increase in the *average* level of real wages over the past century, due to improved technology, a better educated work force, and similar factors. But we have seen that there is a wide dispersion of wages around that average at any given time, a fact leading to endless controversy between workers and employers and also among economic theorists. It is this dispersion around the average wage level which we shall explore further in this chapter—particularly the dispersion among jobs within the same occupation. Then, in the next chapter, we shall examine (among other things) the wage differences among workers in different occupations.

We shall be covering so much ground in this chapter that it may be helpful to provide a brief map of the terrain before we begin to explore it. These are the issues we shall be examining:

1. The economic nature of union wage pressures
2. "Political" wage influences

3. Economics and politics both
4. The union impact on relative wages
5. The social basis for wage relationships
6. Intrafirm wage differentials
7. Interfirm wage differentials within local markets
8. Wage relationships among local labor markets
9. The initiation and transmission of wage changes
10. Tendencies to wage relatedness and dispersion

Economic nature of union wage pressures

In postwar research, explanations of union influences on wage relationships have tended to fall into two general categories: (1) those which emphasize the same market determinants of the wage structure we have already examined, but with greater interest in how unions may manipulate these determinants to their advantage, and (2) those which, without denying an underlying market influence, stress that unions introduce a new element. Because they are necessarily "political" institutions, they have to satisfy the needs of constituents, officials, and the ongoing organization itself, with consequences that make the wage system something different from what it would be if market forces alone were operating. For shorthand purposes, these are commonly referred to as the "economic" and the "political" interpretations of union wage behavior, though exponents of each view maintain that they do not intend to exclude the other approach as invalid— it is principally a matter of emphasis. Nevertheless, it is convenient to treat these as alternative explanations in order to sharpen the emphasis which each intends.

The economic approach is perhaps the most traditional. It starts from the familiar point of departure that unions, as economic agents, must be maximizing something. There has been no great confidence in what this something actually is, since, although wages are inevitably the objective, they may be conceived in a variety of ways. Unions might seek to maximize the total wage bill in the unit which they represent, or the

wage bill for members retaining employment plus unemployment compensation or other out-of-work benefits to those laid off, and so on. One of the most widely discussed economic explanations for union wage behavior has been that unions seek to maximize the total wage bill for all those whom it regards as members, whether or not employed.[1]

In any event, there is no sophisticated exponent of the view that unions try to maximize wage rates themselves, since the economist's model of how a trade union behaves gives an important place to conscious consideration of the employment effects of bargained wage rates. Wage demands may be restrained and wage cuts accepted because of realization that otherwise the jobs of some members will be lost.

The emphasis on maximization does not imply that union officials engage in a careful, rational, marginal calculation of the effects of wage costs on labor demand. It suggests only that economic forces inevitably induce conforming behavior, that this is the thread of consistency that runs through union wage decisions (even though deviants can be found, even though union leaders could not rationalize their actions), that this conception of union behavior leads to reliable deductive conclusions—the ultimate test of any conception. It conforms to the "pork chops" character commonly associated with American unions; the strident cry of the trade-union leadership for "more, always more" is indicative of maximization, in at least a common-sense meaning of that term.

Maximization is not confined to any particular time dimension. Unions presumably are capable of taking into account long-run effects of current wage changes; they may give up a wage increase now in exchange for some nonpecuniary consideration which is expected to augment their strength and facilitate their winning even larger increases in the future; they may accept a lower present increase in return for a long-term contract which precludes important wage adjustments over its lifetime because of an expectation that, within that period, their relative bargaining position is likely to deteriorate as a result of adverse economic circumstances.[2]

The wage gains which any union can secure for its members are limited by the same basic economic conditions which largely determine the wage rates of unorganized workers. It is the product markets in which employing firms operate that ultimately decide their wage-paying ability. Unions can act as pressure devices to try to extract from an employer more than he would voluntarily pay. And to the extent that he is a monopsonist in his labor market, the union may be able to raise wages, without endangering the employment of its members, simply by forcing the firm to pay labor's marginal value product.

This possibility is demonstrated by Figure 18-1. Here the employer is operating under conditions of a rising labor-supply curve, indicated by AC (average cost), since for our purposes we may treat costs as consisting wholly of wages. That is, in order to obtain additional workers he must pay a higher wage. The result is that the cost of additional employees is not simply the addition to the wage bill of the amounts paid to them, but the increase in the wage rate of workers already on the payroll who must now be paid the same higher wage rate. For this reason, marginal cost rises by an amount greater than average cost. If we also assume that the firm is producing a differentiated product, as is likely to be the case, marginal revenue will similarly be falling by more than average revenue as output increases. Since the firm will maximize profit by operating at the point where marginal cost equals marginal revenue, we may expect an output equal to Q. At that output the employer must pay a wage rate of W. Labor would technically be considered exploited at this wage rate, since it is not receiving an amount equal to its marginal value product (MR). We should remind ourselves that exploitation in this sense involves no critical judgment on the employer, but is something built into the situation. Now suppose that a union organizes the employees and is successful in raising the wage rate to W_u. The employer will still maximize profit by operating at the point where marginal cost equals marginal revenue. He will thus continue to employ the same number of workers as at the old, lower rate. All that has happened is that the union has succeeded in capturing for its members some of the firm's excess profits, that is, profits over and above those necessary to keep the employer in business. His workers are no longer

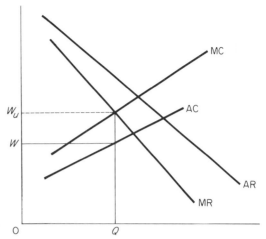

Fig. 18-1. *Labor "exploitation" in imperfect product and labor markets.*

exploited, in the technical sense, since now their wage rate equals their marginal value product (MR).

Even with a more elastic labor supply, or beyond the point where the monopsonist has had to forgo the gains from operating in his exclusive labor market, the union's pressure may be able to extract further modest wage gains. These may be the result of what has come to be known as the shock effect. In most business operations there is some waste and slack, particularly after a period of prosperity (which permits waste) or in the face of high corporate-profits taxes (which lessen the cost of waste). Under the spur of union demands, a firm may be able to provide for a higher wage bill out of increased efficiency and reduced waste. In marginal terms, an increase in efficiency means an increase in the marginal physical and (other things equal) value productivity of labor, thus shifting the entire MR curve to the right and justifying a higher wage for the same number of workers.

But after these expedients have been resorted to, the rate of wages for unionized, just as for unorganized, workers depends on the state of the firm's product markets. The firm is a maximizer and will hire only as many workers as can produce a profit for it. Further wage increases will simply mean that the margin to which the producer pushes his operations will come at a smaller output; at a higher wage rate and hence higher marginal cost, he cannot afford to carry production (subject as it is to diminishing returns) quite so far. Or if he tries to recoup his added costs through a higher price for his product, he will lose some of his customers, and again output will fall off, reducing the number of jobs available to union members. As long as demand for the product remains what it has been, the union's power to pressure wage gains for its members is limited by the realization that such gains will also create unemployment among them. According to this view, with every wage rate there is an associated rate of employment—not precise, to be sure, but a fairly narrow range. And a union which is seeking to maximize the total income of its members cannot fail to consider the employment effect of its wage policies.

If it is the product markets which thus largely limit the wage potential of the unions, the unions are not entirely helpless, however. Their organization permits them to seek some measure of control over the product markets themselves—striving to limit competition or to turn it to their own advantage in a variety of ways. They have been the stimulus to, or participant in, industry advertising programs to increase consumer demand, as in the dress trade. They have joined with management in seeking governmental support of their industry's special interests—the Flint Glass Workers (along with numerous other unions) petitioning for higher tariffs, the Teamsters supporting the trucking industry in its continuing fight to escape restrictive state regulation, the railroad brotherhoods and the Mine Workers joining with those industries in opposing the St. Lawrence Seaway—successfully for a time, unsuccessfully in the end, the Shipbuilding Workers calling for expanded congressional subsidies in the construction of merchant ships, the Jewelry Workers seeking an end to excise taxes on the products of their industry, the Brewery Workers fighting against "excessive and discriminatory excise taxes levied against distilled spirits," and so on. Such lobbying activities, a list of which could run to many pages, were all designed to increase demand for the industry's product or to limit competition from substitute products.

In some industries, primarily those in local competition, the union has been able to enforce price controls, so that all competitors can raise wages and prices simultaneously without fear of losing business to one another. In particular communities, for example, organized barbers have been able to secure compliance of shops with an understood structure of minimum prices, and the same has been true of unions in certain other local fields, such as dry cleaning.

The scope of the bargaining unit has something to do with the power of a union to manipulate market conditions to its advantage. In general, the more fully this unit comprehends the product market, the more feasible it is for the union to limit the effects of competition *among* producers of the particular product. The same wage change which is effected in one case is effected in the case of rivals, so that the individual firm need not fear the competitive disadvantage of making a more favorable wage concession than its rivals.[3]

The union is not totally helpless in the face of market forces, then, but, at least under certain circumstances, can manipulate market conditions to its advantage. But the possibilities of manipulation should not be exaggerated; fundamentally, the union must itself adjust to product-market conditions which it can affect in only a limited sense. Its power to gain wage increases is conditioned by its own recognition of the impact of wage changes on employment, particularly in times of economic adversity in its industry.

It is the employer's state of profitability—growing out of his competitive position in the product markets—that largely determines his cost of disagreeing and his cost of agreeing on the union's demands, thus defining his bargaining power. And it is the wage-employment effect—again largely a consequence of the place of the firm in the product markets—that is the major determinant of the union's cost of disagreeing and its cost of agreeing on the employer's terms, similarly identifying its bargaining power. It is the product markets, interlinked with their demand elasticities (for both firms and industries), which provide the explanation of what unions are able to do for their members. The unionized sector of the economy differs from the unorganized sector, in this respect, only in the enhanced, but still limited, possibilities open to it of manipulating market relationships to its advantage.

What of the key-bargain phenomenon, the practice of pattern setting and pattern following in rounds of wage movements? Is the economic approach to wage determination consistent with such a manifestation of power influences? Those who subscribe to this approach find no incompatibility. The key bargain sets up an expectation in those who look to it for a pattern, but whether it will in fact be followed depends upon the economics of each particular company's situation. Departures occur where it is infeasible to follow the pattern; the wage-employment effect dictates that some unions accept less than the key bargain if they are not to sacrifice the jobs of some of their members, if they are not to wind up with a total wage bill less than would result from the employment of a larger number of members at a somewhat lower rate.

Key bargaining is thus, to a considerable extent, illusory. At best it has the effect of putting pressure on an employer to pay as close to the pattern as is possible within the framework of his market position. He may even forgo profit or incur loss on a very short-run basis to keep wage rates as close as possible to the rates of those whom he regards as his principal competitors. But he cannot go on following wage patterns, year in and year out, unless his market position allows.

"Political" wage influences

The foregoing economic interpretation of the nature of union pressures on wages has not gone unchallenged. Others have contended that there are "political" forces generated by labor unions which have an independent effect on wage determination, and a sufficiently important effect that to disregard it would be almost as much in error as to disregard the constraining market influences.

The politically oriented approach starts from the notion that workers tend to judge how satisfactory a wage increase (or decrease) is by reference to the treatment accorded other workers with whom they compare themselves. A wage raise given by another company may be contrasted with what one's own employer has done; the rate of a craft may be compared with that of a related craft; and so on.

Certain of these comparisons are so important to the particular group of workers in question that they may be thought of as incumbent on them—if the comparison is adverse it compels action to correct the situation. These may be called "coercive comparisons."[4] If the Jones Machine Tool Company of Weehawken, organized by the International Association of Machinists, gives its employees a raise of 20 cents an hour, the employees of the Smith Machine Tool Company, in the same town and organized by the same union, will be mighty restless until their employer gives them an increase of like magnitude. So also will be the employees of the Brown Lock Company, operating in a different product market but organized by the same union, and employees of the Black Machine Parts Company, operating in a related product market but organized by the UAW. If their expectations of what constitutes an equitable relationship remain violated, such employees will be driven to seek remedial action. The union, with collective bargaining, is their means of remedy. And officers of their unions know that they will be judged by their success in winning wage awards comparable to those won by other unions and superior to those of still other unions. The pressure is thus on the union's negotiators to make good—or to fail in reelection to their union offices. This is a political, not an economic, pressure on wage policy.[5]

Wage pressures thus emanate from the important pattern-setting units and are coercive on other pattern-following units since, for political reasons, they are compelled to seek the same objective. But how coercive can a wage change won by the one union be on another union if the economic circumstances of the two firms or industries are significantly different? The "equitable" increase, even if it can be forced in the face of adverse market conditions, may prove self-defeating by forcing a price increase that limits sales and reduces employment. While some members might gain a higher income, others would lose their jobs. Does not this employment effect of a wage change reduce, if not invalidate, the coerciveness of comparisons, as the market approach to wage determination claims? Not usually, according to this political interpretation. It is asserted, as "essentially an empirical finding based on fairly wide observation," that "the union is not automatically or mechanically concerned with the 'quantity of labor sold,' " and "union leaders are not normally in any position to consider the 'employment effect' of their wage decisions even if they were so inclined, for the reason that they do not have the means to predict it."[6]

> There is no assurance that labor costs will decline even if wage rates are cut; that total costs will fall even if labor costs decline; that selling prices will be reduced even if total costs fall; or that sales and employment will increase even if selling costs are reduced. Therefore [in an often quoted phrase], the real employment effect of the wage bargain is lost in a sea of external forces. The volume of employment associated with a given wage rate is unpredictable before the fact, and the effect of a given rate upon employment is undecipherable after the fact. . . . The typical wage bargain is necessarily made without consideration of its employment effect.

The problem of local-union leadership is to strike wage terms which satisfy the various factions within the local union that their particular interests have been adequately represented, which please the general local-union membership, which are acceptable to the international authorities, which are appealing to potential members, and which advance the prestige of the union and its leaders in the city central. The requirements may be easily restated in terms of national bargains.

While these "orbits" of wage comparison may be regarded as chiefly binding on union wage policy, they cannot be neglected by employers. They necessarily become important determinants of company wage policy if the company would avoid labor unrest. Examples are readily available of how employers have bowed to the necessity of granting a wage increase of sufficient magnitude to satisfy their union's "political" needs, thereby avoiding the danger of lowered morale, work

stoppages, and some of the agitation connected with campaigns for office within the union and organizational raids by rival unions. In general, those who adopt this political approach to the determination of wages are convinced that market competition in the American economy is not so rigorous as to preclude such noneconomic adjustments to the wage bill.

Nonunion segments of the economy are less susceptible to these political influences, to be sure, but they are far from immune. Unorganized employers must be conscious of the comparisons which are coercive upon their own employees if the latter are to remain nonunion, and they must respond to their employees' concepts of comparative equity before union organizers appear on the scene and appeal to those same concepts. Thus the thread of group-oriented political behavior runs throughout the economy and is accommodated by an economy in which the impersonal authority of price competition in product markets has been sufficiently muted to permit such adjustments.

Economics and politics both

Although these two approaches, the economic and the political, originally appeared as contending interpretations of union wage influence, the to-be-expected synthesis soon became apparent. Since neither political nor economic influence can be denied its reality, the question turns on the relative roles of these two sets of forces.

The evidence is gratifyingly clear on this question, even though it does not permit any precise formulation. *On the one hand, there is a similarity among many key bargains in the labor sector which cannot be explained by economic factors alone.* Professor John E. Maher has demonstrated this in his study of nineteen major bargaining relationships scattered through eleven different industries, such as auto, steel, copper, aircraft, meat-packing, and shipbuilding.[7] In totaling the major wage changes (including cost-of-living adjustments) that were negotiated in these key contracts from 1946 through 1957, Maher found that increases in seventeen of the nineteen relationships fell within the narrow band of $1.10 to $1.33 over the twelve-year period. Also, he found "an even greater regularity prevailed" during several shorter intervals within this period, and the cost of fringe benefits increased by about the same amount in most of these relationships. These industries are not completely independent of one another, of course, for many occupy some of the same labor markets and all were subject to the inflationary and full-employment pressures that marked much of the period from 1946 through 1957. Yet, in the absence of unions, no one would have expected wages and fringe benefits to increase uniformly over twelve years in shipyards on the Pacific Coast, copper mines in Montana, meat-packing plants in Chicago, and steel mills in Pittsburgh. Thus, there clearly are "orbits of coercive comparison" among bargaining relationships in which the parties have considerable discretion in setting wages, and political forces are crucial to an understanding of wage movements in these situations.

On the other hand, other union settlements often deviate from these key bargains for economic reasons. The popular notion of union wage policy, in which the contract won from the richest company is ruthlessly imposed on all other employers, simply does not square with the facts in most industries. The classic demonstration of this is the study by Prof. George Seltzer of United Steelworkers' contracts during the period from 1946 through 1950.[8] Even among the settlements made by this powerful union during a boom period, Seltzer found several types of deviations from the bargains struck with the leader, the United States Steel Corporation. Among the 250 firms in basic steel, the key pattern was followed very closely by the other fully integrated companies (Bethlehem, Republic, and so on) but less closely by the semi-integrated firms and still less closely by the nonintegrated firms (those producing finished steel but no pig iron or ingots)—and outside of basic steel, in steel-fabricating and non-steel firms organized by this union, the pattern influence was even weaker. In the Chicago area in 1947, for example, the key wage pattern was matched by only 40 percent of the 130 Steelworkers' contracts outside of basic steel. Seltzer also found that conformity to the United States Steel pattern was strongest in 1946 and declined as the economy cooled off in subsequent years, and that

the pattern was followed more closely on wage-rate increases than on fringe benefits and minimum-rate levels. Subsequent studies of bargaining in several other industries have confirmed Seltzer's point that unions often use a national pattern as a goal from which deviations will be made to cope with local differences in employers' ability to pay, labor-market conditions, and other threats to the jobs of union members.[9]

It is tempting to generalize from these studies that union wage behavior conforms to the political model at the national, "big-bargain" level and to the economic model at the local, small-unit level, but there are too many exceptions. Consider the curious case of the United Mine Workers, for example, which was clearly a national wage leader in the postwar years. Maher deliberately omitted this union from his study of national wage patterns from 1946 to 1957, confessing that "after an exhaustive study of wage movements in coal, I have reached the conclusion that the only approximate explanation of the enormously large wage increases in coal is John L. Lewis."[10] Lewis was indeed a rare union leader, for he professed to be unconcerned that his wage demands contributed to the rapid mechanization of the mines and the consequent dwindling of miners' jobs, arguing that mining was such a dirty and dangerous occupation that he would be happy to see it ultimately disappear. In recent years, however, as employment continued to plummet and nonunion competition became more severe in coal mining, Lewis's successors have apparently tolerated widespread "chiseling" of contract terms—that is, in order to save jobs they have permitted many small producers to pay less than the wage-and-fringe scale called for in the national agreement.[11] How, then, can one classify this union's wage behavior over the last thirty years as either "economic" or "political"?

Or how would one classify the Teamsters, in which bargaining for many years was highly decentralized, with negotiations in Atlanta bearing little relation to negotiations in New York or San Francisco—but which now, after Hoffa's successful drive for national bargaining, is narrowing not only the differentials among over-the-road (intercity) drivers but also the regional differentials among some types of intracity drivers? Or, finally, look again at Table 17-2 in the previous chapter, which shows that Teamster rates in Chicago vary sharply by industry, suggesting again that unions adjust their local wage demands to differing economic contexts, but which also implies that the high Teamster rates in construction are influenced by political comparisons with the high-wage building trades.

In short, both political and economic forces shape union wage behavior and there is no precise guide to what this mixture will be in a particular time or place. The element of coercive comparisons clearly makes the wage structure something different from what it would be if shaped by economic forces alone, but those economic forces just as clearly set limits to every union's political tendencies. Where a union adjusts its demands to a firm's adverse competitive position, it usually adopts over time a new pattern, a new comparison, which may be related to the old (a 5-cent differential from the key bargain, for example) or may be an entirely new pattern based on a comparison with another firm in similar economic circumstances. Thus, the parties in every bargaining relationship refer to some pattern or another, but this does not mean that political comparisons always override market forces. Similarly, it is probably true that political influences are more significant during prosperous times than they are during depressed periods, in protected more than in competitive product markets, and in competely rather than in partially unionized industries, but it is even more certain that *both* political and economic influences are present in *every* bargaining relationship at any time.[12]

Once this is realized, the contention between these two approaches loses much of its interest and the more important question emerges of how the two forces interact, that is, how unions pursue their political goals within a market context. As we attempt to fit unions into our broad problem of what provides system to the millions of wage rates found in the labor sector, we shall therefore need to remember both that unions are politically motivated institutions which must be conscious of how well they perform for their members, and that they are constrained in their political drives by conditions in product and labor markets.

The union impact on relative wages

We have concentrated up to this point on the motives of union wage behavior and the evidence on how wages differ within and among the jurisdictions of various unions. But none of these facts tells us *by how much unions have actually raised the wages of their members* over the wages of other workers and have thus contributed to the wage differentials found in every labor market. Economists have wrestled with this question for years, and in so doing have received little help from the participants in wage decisions. Union leaders naturally claim that collective bargaining has greatly increased their members' wages, although in the next breath they often deny that unions have much impact on costs or prices. And many employers are also ambivalent on this question, sometimes arguing that unions can do little or nothing for workers ("you can't repeal the laws of supply and demand") and at other times painting unions as invincible monopolies winning huge gains for their members at the expense of everybody else.

Why is this question so difficult to resolve? A few quick examples will show why it is often hard to prove that unions raise wages at all, to say nothing of measuring the precise gain. The fact that unionized auto workers earn more today than nonunion farm workers obviously demonstrates nothing about the effectiveness of unionism, since there are many differences in the skill mix and geographic location of these two groups. So we need two groups of workers who are identical in all respects except union membership—but there are no nonunion auto workers. Let us therefore compare wages in the same city for identical jobs in different industries: the rates of janitors, say, in Ford's River Rouge plant and in nonunion firms in Detroit. But Ford is in a far more profitable industry than most employers, so how can we be sure that it would not pay higher rates even in the absence of a union?

To avoid these problems with point-in-time comparisons, let us test whether wages have increased *over time* at a faster pace in the auto industry than in farming and other nonunion industries. Now, however, we must somehow correct for the fact that the demand for farm labor was falling precipitously during the years when employment was rising rapidly in autos, so that auto wages should have risen faster even without the help of a union—but how much faster? And even when nonunion wages are found to rise as fast as union wages, how do you correct for the possibility that some nonunion employers matched union wage increases in order to fend off labor organizers—or just to compete for workers in unionized labor markets?

Until quite recently, the safest generalization that could be made about a generation of economists' attempts to crack this problem was that the evidence was "mixed," if not downright confusing. Some studies showed unions had a strong impact on relative wages and others showed only a minor impact; some showed the impact varied with the length of organization (strongest in the first years after a group organizes) and others showed the impact varied with the industry or the business cycle; and no one could do more than guess at the net influence of all unions on the wage structure of the American economy. We still do not have all the answers to this problem, but Prof. H. Gregg Lewis has recently provided far more consistent and precise estimates of union wage impact than we have ever had before. In *Unionism and Relative Wages in the United States*,[13] which has quickly become the definitive work on this subject, Lewis analyzed twenty earlier studies of union wage impact, frequently adjusting the original findings in light of more recent data or for other reasons; combined and added to these studies by means of sophisticated statistical techniques; and applied these findings to estimate the overall effect of unions on wage differentials at different periods of time. We cannot reproduce the complex techniques used by Lewis to meet the many measurement problems described above, but we can summarize his major conclusions.

First, Table 18-1 presents the most widely quoted of Lewis's estimates, indicating that the average effect of unionism has been to raise union wages above nonunion wages by as little as zero to 5 percent between 1945 and 1949 and by as much as 25 percent or more from 1931 to 1933. These findings appear nonsensical at first glance, showing unionism to have been far more effective in the depths of the Depression, when unemployment was high and unions had organized less than

Table 18-1 *Average Relative Wage Effect of Unionism in Selected Periods*

Period	Average extent of unionism in the economy* (percent)	Average wage effect: union labor relative to nonunion labor† (percent)
1923–1929	7 to 8	15 to 20
1931–1933	7 to 8	greater than 25
1939–1941	18 to 20	10 to 20
1945–1949	24 to 27	0 to 5
1957–1958	27	10 to 15

* Number of union members as a percent of number of persons engaged in the civilian economy.
† The percentage difference between union and nonunion wages attributable to unionism alone.
SOURCE: H. Gregg Lewis, *Unionism and Relative Wages in the United States*, The University of Chicago Press, Chicago, 1963, Table 50, p. 193.

10 percent of the labor force, than in the early postwar years of full employment when strike activity reached an all-time high and collective bargaining had spread throughout the basic industries. To explain this apparent paradox, Lewis follows other economists in positing a "wage-rigidity effect" in collective bargaining: During periods of sharp deflation such as from 1931 through 1933, nonunion wages drop because of excess labor supply but unions fiercely resist wage cuts because they fear it would be difficult to win back higher rates at a later time. In a sharp inflation such as that between 1945 and 1949, on the other hand, nonunion wages rise quickly in response to labor shortages, but now *employers* of union labor fear the future consequences of a bad contract and strongly resist unusually large wage increases (for, if the economy cools off next month or next year, they cannot cut wages back as easily as nonunion employers can); also, union contracts with a fixed term of a year or more can force union rates to lag in responding to a rapid increase in demand. It will be interesting to see whether future studies show the same drop in union wage impact during the inflation of the late 1960s, when the wages of many nonunion workers certainly increased rapidly but many more union contracts contained cost-of-living escalation

clauses than in the period from 1945 through 1949. In any event, no one has come up with a better explanation of the almost countercyclical effect of unions on relative wages, and it should be noted that Lewis's estimate of a 10 to 15 percent union impact in the late 1950s has been roughly confirmed by later studies using more detailed data from the 1960 census.[14]

Second, Lewis confirmed the findings of many others that union wage impact varies among industries. During the late 1950s, for instance, he estimated that the union impact ranged as high as 50 percent in bituminous coal and 30 percent among airline pilots and as low as zero percent in the men's clothing industry,[15] although the overall average for that period was 10 to 15 percent. What are the reasons for this variation? That is, among industries equally well organized, why do wages still vary for the same occupation at a given time, or why do average wages increase over time more rapidly in some of these industries than in others? Lewis did not offer any answer to this question, finding the results of other studies "quite inconclusive" on this point and believing that much more research is needed before we can determine how the wage impact of unions is affected by interindustry differences in profitability, productivity, employment trends, the ratio of labor to total costs, and similar factors suggested by one conflicting study or another. To illustrate the confusion: Some early studies showed that union wages rose faster in concentrated industries like autos than in competitive industries like clothing; Lewis questioned whether there really is such a systematic relationship between concentration and union effectiveness, in light of unionism's pronounced wage impact in competitive industries like mining and construction; and Prof. Leonard W. Weiss has recently demonstrated that, on the basis of 1959 data, there is a systematic but *negative* relationship, with unionization seeming to add "about 9 percent to annual earnings when concentration is low and 4 percent when it is high."[16]

Still, it is worth remembering that unions sometimes reduce competition in industries that would otherwise be fiercely competitive, thereby permitting their influence to have greater effect. For this and other reasons, concentration ratios (the percent of an industry's output accounted for by, for example, the four largest companies) are not always a reliable measure of competition in industries such as mining, construction, longshoring, and trucking. Thus, despite a lack of conclusive evidence, we believe that a negative correlation does exist between the extent of competition and the size of wage increases within an industry, and that union members do benefit from limitations on competition—whether those limitations are imposed by technology and other market forces, or by employer collusion, or by the unions themselves through collective bargaining.[17]

Third, Lewis calculated that unions have increased the dispersion of average wages among industries, although not by very much. Note that this finding does not automatically follow from the first two; if the most effective unions were in those industries in which the average wages of all workers are low because of an unfavorable skill mix, for example, the union effect could have been to compress the interindustry wage structure. Instead, Lewis estimated that "unionism may have made the relative inequality of average wages among industries . . . about 6 to 10 percent higher than it otherwise would have been" in the late 1950s, and had an even smaller effect in earlier years.[18] Reinforcing this conclusion is a more recent study indicating that the wage gains of unionized blue-collar workers do not spill over to inflate the salaries of nonproduction workers; that is, contrary to popular belief, white-collar salaries are not systematically higher in industries in which unions have raised blue-collar wages.[19]

Fourth, with respect to wage differentials among all individual workers (that is, allowing for the effect of unions on skill, sex, and other differentials *within* unionized industries as well as on the union–nonunion differential *among* industries), Lewis estimated that "the impact of unionism on relative wage inequality among all workers has been small—under 6 percent" in the late 1950s, with available evidence unclear as to whether this net effect has been in the direction of widening or narrowing total wage dispersion.[20]

Fifth, Lewis estimated in a later paper that the relative employment effects of unionism have been roughly the same as its relative wage effects.[21] If correct, this means that in the late 1950s, for example, the higher wages in union industries served to reduce employment in those industries by an average of 10 to 15 percent below the levels that would have prevailed in the absence of unionism.

Assuming that most of Lewis's estimates are accurate, do they add up to a proof that the wage impact of unions has been of major or minor significance? Judgments will naturally differ on this point, depending on (among other things) whether one has expected the union impact to be huge or trivial. Professor Albert Rees has provided an interesting perspective by estimating the loss in real output in the economy as a whole caused by collective bargaining, using Lewis's outside estimates of a 15 percent wage-and-employment effect in the union sector during the late 1950s:

> Under certain conventional assumptions, it can be shown that the loss of real output is approximately equal to one-half the product of the wage effect and the employment effect.... I have used this formula to make a rough estimate for 1957, the last nonrecession year covered in Lewis' estimates. This estimated loss [from the wage and employment effects of unionism] turns out to be approximately 600 million dollars. Since gross national product in 1957 was 443 billion dollars, the loss is approximately 0.14 percent of national output. This welfare loss is of the same general magnitude as that estimated earlier by Arnold Harberger for enterprise monopoly (0.1 percent).[22]

Finally, mention should be made of Prof. Robert M. Macdonald's provocative attack upon the idea that anyone can measure the wage effects of unions by comparing behavior in union and nonunion labor markets. He argues that such a comparison assumes that these two types of labor markets are functional alternatives when in fact they are not. Most observers agree that the nonwage effects of unions—such as protecting workers against the abuse of managerial authority, providing them with political representation, and promoting other aspects of "industrial democracy" —are important reasons why workers accept our present economic and political system, and history suggests that if workers are denied this protection through unions, they will attempt to change the system and pursue their interests through political

or other channels. Industry might be nationalized or wages dictated by government or layoffs and discipline decided by labor courts, but whatever the form, an outlet would be found for the needs that have led to the rise of a union movement in every industrial, democratic society. Thus, Macdonald says, you cannot really measure how wages would differ in the absence of unionism in our present economy, because our entire society would be radically different without unionism.[23]

Despite the cogency of Macdonald's argument, estimates such as Lewis's of the union impact on relative wages can be valuable, provided one treats them as a partial explanation of the present wage structure and not as a basis for predicting what would happen to wages if only unions would go away tomorrow. For our purposes, the prime conclusion to draw from these several studies is that unionism does indeed increase the wages of many workers significantly above the rates paid to other workers on similar jobs, *but this union impact falls far short of explaining all the large and persistent differentials that exist throughout the labor sector,* both within and outside of the unionized industries. We therefore need to examine other wage determinants, beginning with one—social status—which, like unionism, does not fit neatly into the competitive model.

The social basis for wage relationships[24]

The concept of status is a familiar one to the sociologist but less so to the economist. By status we shall simply mean a position in society, customarily but not always joined to some functional role, which relates a person to those around him in terms of the deference and obligations which are owed to him and which he owes to others. Status places a person in his society; it defines his social position. Frequently it involves a hierarchical set of relationships—where a person stands in an authority structure. Status runs through the organizational units of which a society is composed and through society as a whole. Family relationships involve status position—of husband vis-à-vis wife, or parent with respect to children. So too are status relationships present in economic organization. There are people who give and people who carry out orders, and in a large business firm these people are organized into a complex structure which is charted in ladderlike layers, with upper rungs on the organization chart representing higher-status positions.

Status relates not simply to one's position in a chain of command, however. It also involves prestige considerations. Some economic functions are considered high status, such as those of the doctor, the engineer, the judge. Other jobs are looked on as low status, such as rubbish collection, custodial care, delivery service. Here prestige attaches not to one's place in an organization but to his place in society generally.

Status also attaches to classes of people. Although for some purposes Western society accords high social status to women, in most economic pursuits they are regarded as inferior to men. Minority groups, on a racial or nationality basis, are customarily relegated to lower status positions than people of comparable ability who come from the dominant group in our society. Certain occupations may not even be open to them, as we noted in Chapter 3.

Without attempting any exhaustive examination of the economic effects of status, let us simply note that, by and large, high social status tends to attach to positions involving authority and assumed to require higher levels of education. Generally these are also the positions involving higher levels of remuneration. Economists have tended to explain this correlation on the ground that people having the ability to hold down positions of responsibility or to acquire advanced knowledge are relatively rarer and hence, on a straight scarcity basis, can be expected to command higher rates of return. Economists have also maintained that the costs (real and money) involved in acquiring specialized training and education would be incurred only if the positions calling for such skill or knowledge carried pay scales compensating for the investment which the individual has had to make to fit himself for them.

This rationalization is partially but not wholly persuasive. Wage and salary relationships tend to assume a hierarchical order without regard to supply and demand considerations. Full professors receive more than instructors, although their abilities and contributions are not always as great.

Deans commonly receive more than professors, and usually not because there is any shortage of candidates for the position or because the position demands any extraordinary skills. Within a corporation there are often numerous contenders for an opening which all view as a promotion, but the job is not auctioned off to the lowest bidder even if they are all considered relatively equal in ability. The fact that it stands in a hierarchy of jobs requires that the rate bear some "appropriate" relationship to jobs below and above it in the hierarchy. In some companies, the differential between "levels" of authority is precisely defined in terms of some percentage increment—hardly a convincing demonstration of market-mediated supply and demand effects.

The jobs which are viewed as "dirty" or disagreeable or self-demeaning—the low-status jobs—tend to carry low rates, and often are difficult to fill. On traditional economic reasoning one would expect that these jobs should contain compensating advantages (of pay or working conditions) which would make their "net advantage" equal to alternative employments, but this is seldom the case. If economic considerations alone were involved, there should be nothing at all peculiar about paying a garbage collector or a ditch digger as much as an accountant or a mechanic if the number of those willing to perform the former functions were in sufficiently short supply. Yet most of us (and accountants and mechanics in particular) would regard this as somehow inappropriate.

Occasionally we are made aware of this "discrepancy" between social and economic considerations, as when a newspaper carries a feature story of the high school history teacher who quit to become a truck driver because there was more money in it. Some may argue that the teacher has been "false" to his "calling." Most would feel that appropriate social relationships have somehow been reversed, that a truck driver is not "entitled" to as much as the teacher who is performing the vital service of educating the next generation. We say there is something wrong with a society which permits such an "inversion of values," when all that has happened is that supply and demand considerations—which presumably we approve as a basis for wage determination—have in this instance performed their intended function. It is our social-status values, not our economic values, which have been offended.

The sense of propriety which we seek to attach to social-status distinctions which are made the basis for income differentials is bolstered by a variety of terminological devices. We tend to dignify the high-status positions with the label of "profession," in contrast to the term of "job" or "occupation" for lower-status functions, though people have long argued over what identifies a profession as such. (Formal instruction and licensing provisions are frequently cited as primary characteristics, but we are less inclined to speak of the "profession" of barbering than the profession of medicine. A social-status distinction is probably at least in part the root.) Similarly, we tend to consider jobs carrying salaries as more prestigious than those carrying a wage rate. "The term 'wage-earning' is not normally applied to posts located at the upper end of the social scale; and it is exceptional (though not, perhaps, in quite the same degree) for predominantly manual occupations to be described as salaried."[25] This subtle terminological difference carries with it a status distinction which is entirely unrelated to economic function, and (as in the case of the label of profession) somehow serves to justify or rationalize a higher income for the positions to which the more prestigious term applies.

That income tends to correlate with social status or prestige has sometimes been called circular reasoning. It is said that prestige is accorded a position because it carries a high income, rather than vice versa, so that status itself has no special wage-determining power. Status follows the market. That highly paid jobs are esteemed in a society which, like our own, is pecuniary-minded is obvious, but this does not mean that the reverse may not be equally true for the same reason: in a pecuniary society, jobs which carry special social status have higher incomes attached to them. The "market" recognizes and rewards status.

Comparisons of rates for one position relative to rates for other positions run throughout our society. They are not necessarily the comparisons which "job shoppers" make before deciding whether to leave one job for another, even though in particular cases they may lead to satisfaction or dissatisfaction with one's present position and have some bearing on whether he stays or moves. More commonly they are the comparisons of "moralists": am I getting a "fair" wage relative to John Jones? Is it equitable for someone whose work calls for less education or training to earn more than I do? The comparisons frequently thus involve a sense of "social order" or "social rightness" or "social equity." The medieval notion of the "just wage," which had strong canonical roots of a quasi-religious nature, has never been wholly eradicated even in our market-oriented society. These are basically the same kinds of comparisons which we just encountered in discussing the "political" influence of labor unions on wages, except that here whatever organizational pressures occur are usually of a different "hierarchical" sort.

Especially to the extent that mobility is limited (for whatever reasons) and job opportunities are not equal (again, for whatever reasons), comparisons between rates may be made the basis for adjustment of rates without reliance on actual or potential job movement to establish appropriate differentials. The economist's concern that this would almost surely lead to a "misallocation" of resources may be justified on the principle of maximum consumer advantage, but a society may be willing to sacrifice *maximum* consumption as a sole or sufficient criterion.

In any event, in our effort to explore what it is that provides cohesion and system to the wage-determining process, we shall want to consider the role of status considerations.

Intrafirm wage differentials

To illustrate the interaction of these three types of wage determinants—supply and demand, unionism, and social status—we shall first examine why wages vary among people working for the same employer in the same labor market. Most of these intrafirm differentials are obviously related to differences in occupation or skill level, such as the earnings range from janitor to electrician to engineer to company president, and neither the competitive model nor institutional theory expects these very different jobs to receive equal wages. We shall therefore investigate this occupational wage structure more fully in the next chapter, introducing it here only to provide the necessary context for our discussion of why wages differ on *similar jobs*: first, within the same firm and then, in the next sections, between firms in the same local labor market and finally between different labor markets.

Supply and demand effects   To begin with, we can reasonably expect that the wage rates attaching to different skill functions must reflect some supply and demand elements. The number of workers capable of performing given functions relative to the market value of those functions to employers or customers cannot fail to have a substantial bearing on how much people are paid for what they do. In a gadget-centered economy, mechanics are probably always scarcer, in relation to the demands for their services, than are salesclerks, for example. It takes more time to create a satisfactory mechanic than it does to train an adequate salesman in a department store. Moreover, the number of potential clerks is greater than the number of potential mechanics, since women can be drawn on for the former (though here we have a social element intruding, in the form of expectations as to what work is "appropriate" for females). The marginal value product of a mechanic is probably greater, if for no other reason than that his services can be employed more fully and effectively. A salesperson has to be kept on the payroll against the possibility that customers may show up, and if they do not (or if fewer customers buy than the clerk's salary has been predicated on), there is little or no return to the employer for the wage expenditure. Sales cannot be "stockpiled" so that a customer who comes in today can be waited on tomorrow. A mechanic, however, need be hired only for work which is actually scheduled, and if none is available, he may be laid off in the knowledge that any orders which materialize can be held for later completion. Obviously, the value product of these two types of workers is based on other considerations, but at least these examples give the flavor of the kinds of circumstances which create differential supply and demand conditions giving rise to differential wage rates.

Over time, such influences as changing levels of education in the population at large may affect the supply side—people who can follow or give written instructions are no longer in as short supply as they once were, for example. Changing tastes and especially changing technologies may affect the demand side—the value contribution of a musician is typically less today than a few generations ago, in part because orchestras are less frequently employed for social occasions but even more because recordings and television make possible the mass distribution of the performance of a single artist or orchestra. In industry, for many centuries technological change has been viewed by skilled workers as a threat to the skills which give their work a differential value. Thus the skill mix which is available on the supply side and the skill mix which is wanted on the demand side are inevitably major determinants of relative wage rates, and these are themselves predominantly technologically determined.

The supply of workers of a particular skill may be artificially limited to increase their scarcity value. Apprenticeship rules and licensing requirements, presumably intended to assure the public of some minimum level of competence in the trade or profession, may be stricter than necessary and may be used as instruments for excluding unwanted competitors. Such restriction will be especially effective where the service provided is one difficult to do without, such as plumbing and doctoring. The marginal-value contribution to the customer or patient in these instances is high enough to accommodate a quite substantial wage or fee if the supply can be checked sufficiently to sustain it. Demand, we say, is relatively inelastic.

Tidying up after the market   Obviously, supply-demand elements such as these will have their effect on the structure of rates in a labor market, but if relied on exclusively, they would leave a rather untidy mélange of wage rates. If a company employing even a few hundred employees relies on some sixth sense of what the "market" prescribes for a given kind of job as the basis for its own internal rate structure, or even if it follows the more pragmatic policy of filling vacancies or retaining workers by paying what is necessary to draw them or hold them, it is bound to wind up with a patchwork quilt of job rates, one for each employee. The problem is further complicated by the fact that frequently a company has a particular assortment of jobs not exactly duplicated in any other company in the local market (or any other labor market, for that matter).

It was this lack of logic in company wage structures which, in the face of union pressures, led to the spread of job-evaluation systems, as we noted in Chapter 15. On the basis of certain job "factors" such as skill and training and responsibility, jobs can be rated in relation to each other, point values assigned to rank them, and wage rates attached to them. This attempt at systematizing the internal occupational-wage structure probably reflects a good many of the influences operating on the supply and demand sides of the local labor market, but to the extent there is some conflict between market and job-evaluation rates, these can be adjusted informally by a simple process of juggling as needed. Thus, typically employers do not rely on "raw" market pressures to determine the wage rate attaching to the jobs in their companies, but improve on "nature" with such artful devices as job evaluation.

Status and custom   But there is more to the occupational-rate structure than supply and demand considerations, however manipulated through restrictive devices on the supply side or mediated by job evaluation on the demand side. As we noted earlier, social custom plays its part as well. Within a firm or within society generally, certain kinds of functions are viewed as more important than others, and a ranking by traditional status may be as influential in wage or salary determination as an evaluation on a simple supply-demand basis. It is easy to see how this can be true with respect to categories of employments whose value contributions may even be difficult to measure, such as an office receptionist, or a customs inspector, or a policeman, or a truant officer, or a doorman at a hotel. In these and many more instances, there is no ready way of referring to the market for an unequivocal answer as to their "worth." To a considerable extent the levels of remuneration have become established by custom, and the supply-demand influences which admittedly are still relevant and influential have themselves become influenced by the expectations created by customary levels of earnings.

Even within the framework of a single firm's job-evaluation system, the same phenomenon is apparent. Certain positions have a status attaching to them which demands their placement somewhere within a given segment of the wage spectrum. The fact that there are a number of job "factors" which have to be rated before a job can be evaluated, and that such rating is necessarily subjective, helps to accommodate these status requirements.[26]

Scholarly studies show, for example, that most job factors, such as degree of education, really don't have to be considered at all. Yet these factors are still given a standing in job evaluation, and one of the principal reasons is that recognition can be accorded to characteristics considered socially desirable, such again as degree of education.

Job evaluation is basically a method of making job and wage comparisons according to a system that produces results which are acceptable to those to whom applied, combining equitable comparisons with market considerations.

In sum, the spread of rates among workers of different occupations at the nonmanagerial and nonprofessional levels is partly—probably largely—based on market pressures, even though these normally cannot be identified so clearly as to establish anything which resembles an equilibrium rate for a given occupation. An employer cannot, in any event, rely on these fluctuating and vaguely defined influences to establish an appropriate occupational rate structure within his own company, particularly if he must deal with a union. Job-evaluation systems, some very "refined" and others quite simple, seek to establish rate relationships according to criteria which are reasonably acceptable and which are sufficiently flexible to permit adjustment when and where needed.

"The sense of the appropriate"   There are some kinds of employments whose relative values are more difficult to measure by supply and demand considerations, and which typically are not included within job-evaluation systems. What kind of point system would be required to include both the president and the custodian at Bethlehem Steel, for example? How would one evaluate the amount of education, skill, responsibility, and

working conditions attaching to the job of advertising manager in comparison with that of a tool- and diemaker? Within the medical order, what is the value of a general practitioner in relation to a surgeon, or a brain surgeon compared with a heart specialist? How much is a state senator worth in contrast to a United States senator? There are obviously some "orders" or professions where the same considerations do not apply, or do not apply so forceably, as they do to the rank and file of jobs. What is the "market" for lawyers when their fees for services often are not stated in advance and price competition is considered unethical?

The answers to questions such as these would involve introducing considerations of prestige and social status which, attaching as they do to certain positions and occupations, affect the level of earnings along with any market influences. To some extent, remuneration for positions like these is governed by social conceptions of standards of living which should attach to them, just as the salary of a union president is usually justified, depending on the union, on the quite different grounds either that it should be comparable to the earnings of the members he represents or of the management people with whom he deals.

Differentials on similar jobs It is often difficult to draw a sharp line between *inter*occupational and *intra*occupational wage differences within the same firm. A maintenance electrician's job is clearly more skilled than a janitor's, but how does one account for the wide range of wages found among the dozens of "semiskilled" jobs in the average factory? Surely an assembler-A job does not carry a higher rate than an assembler-B job because they are in different "occupations," as that term is usually used. And the same question may be raised about the salary differences among white-collar jobs such as "secretaries, class I, II, or III," or assistant and full director of personnel relations, or any number of other junior versus senior positions within the "management" occupation.

We have obviously encountered again the problem of differences in quality within the labor supply. As we noted in the last chapter, everyone agrees in principle that quality differences exist among individuals and justify some wage differentials even within the same occupation in the same firm, but in practice these quality differences are often hard to measure. Thus, some employers in the past cited "quality differences" for paying lower rates to women or Negroes than to white males on the same job, a practice now illegal, and today some probably achieve the same result by paying equal rates but hiring only "superior" women or Negroes, particularly in managerial and professional positions long reserved for white males. Even in the absence of deliberate discrimination, however, employers must use various shortcuts as a substitute for precise measures of quality differences: the public school teacher with a master's degree automatically earns more than his colleague with a bachelor's degree and equal experience; the long-service employee usually earns more than the short-service worker on the same job at both the white-collar and blue-collar levels; earnings under an incentive system may vary by as much as 50 percent among workers on the same job, reflecting not only differences in ability or effort but often deficiencies in the incentive system itself.

It is ironic that one of the major criticisms of unions is that, under the banner of "equal pay for equal work," they often attempt to impose on the firm the very wage uniformity that competitive theory seems to call for. The problem, of course, is again that of differences in individual ability. To the extent that unions eliminate differentials based solely on sex, race, or favoritism by supervisors (all of which have certainly existed in many nonunion firms), they can hardly be faulted on either economic or social grounds. But to the extent that unions require equal pay for workers of unequal ability on the same job, or demand equal increases at a given time for all workers on every type of job in an industrial bargaining unit, or fight to retain traditional differentials between various craft units regardless of changing supply and demand conditions—to the extent these and similar policies are pursued, unions undoubtedly do change the shape of the intrafirm wage structure in ways that are "noncompetitive." On balance, unions probably do narrow intrafirm differentials on comparable jobs, even though it is impossible to say by how much.

To summarize, supply and demand conditions determine the *general shape* of each firm's internal wage structure, but these market forces seldom operate with the vigor implied by the competitive model. The product market may sometimes tell a buyer precisely what he must pay to obtain a bushel of wheat or a share of stock, but the labor market rarely tells the employer the precise rates he must pay to every occupation, job, and individual within his firm. And because the labor market operates only imperfectly, a range of discretion exists within which the forces of status and custom and unionism also contribute to shaping the internal wage structure.

Interfirm wage differentials within local markets

In any local labor market some firms are known as high-paying and others as low-paying, and the wage spread between them may be considerable. Why is this?

Table 18-2 indicates one major reason: All the firms in the same *labor* market do not operate in the same *product* market. Because some industries employ a higher proportion of skilled workers than others, the all-worker average wage will naturally be higher in printing firms, for example, than in firms manufacturing toys. Moreover, while technological change affects the kind of labor an industry requires, there is no indication that over time this has led to a reduction (or leveling up) of the skill composition of all industries toward some common level. This is difficult to demonstrate statistically for particular cities because of the paucity of long-run wage data at the local level, although Table 18-2 shows that the same industries tended to be at the top and bottom of the manufacturing wage structure in New York City over a seventeen-year span and that this structure was, if anything, even more widely dispersed in 1967 than in 1950. Long-run data are available, however, on the interindustry wage structure in the country as a whole, and studies

Table 18-2 *Average Hourly Earnings of Production Workers in Selected Manufacturing Industries, New York City, 1950 and 1967**

Industry	1950 Earnings	1950 Rank	1967 Earnings	1967 Rank
All manufacturing industries	$1.57	—	$2.82	—
Printing and publishing	2.08	1	4.16	1
Apparel	1.67	2	2.64	11
Machinery, except electrical	1.62	3	3.20	3
Instruments (optical, scientific, etc.)	1.56	4	2.86	7
Transportation equipment (cars, ships, etc.)	1.51	5	3.03	4
Furniture and fixtures	1.49	6	2.65	10
Chemicals	1.47	7	2.94	6
Fabricated metal products	1.43	8	2.73	8
Food and kindred products	1.42	9½	3.25	2
Leather products	1.42	9½	2.23	14
Stone, clay, and glass products	1.40	11	2.99	5
Textile mill products	1.36	12	2.70	9
Electrical equipment and supplies	1.34	13	2.49	13
Paper and allied products	1.32	14	2.60	12
Toys and sporting goods	1.20	15	1.94	15

* Some industry definitions are not precisely the same for both 1950 and 1967, but all are at least roughly comparable.

SOURCES: U.S. Bureau of Labor Statistics, *Employment, Earnings, and Wages in New York City, 1950–60*, and *Employment and Earnings Statistics for States and Areas, 1939–67*.

have confirmed that this structure changes very slowly over time and exhibits no marked trend toward either contraction or expansion.[27]

This is scarcely surprising. Just as we expect intrafirm differentials between occupations, we also expect interfirm differences in *average* wages because of differences in skill mix. What is more interesting and difficult to explain is why wage rates for *similar* jobs do not tend to be uniform among firms within the same local labor market, as economic theory would lead us to expect. As Tables 17-1 and 17-2 in the previous chapter demonstrate, these local wage differentials on comparable jobs are often very wide and can apparently prevail for many years. This is the same sort of relationship we noted earlier when we found that union rates for similar jobs vary because of the industries in which those jobs are located. Now we are asking why the industry should make a difference in how much a given job is worth, even if a union is not present.

Interplay of industry and occupation   As a first consideration, firms in industries requiring the use of expensive and perhaps specialized labor are likely to find that their high wage rates tend to rub off on other workers on their payroll whose counterparts are also to be found in other firms with characteristically lower wage levels. All, or at least many, firms in an area are likely to make use of certain occupational types, both skilled and unskilled (from maintenance electrician and machinist down to sweeper and elevator operator). But when these common occupational types are hired by firms in industries with high-level wage scales, they tend to earn more than when they are employed in low-paying industries. For one thing, a job-evaluation system within a single company typically does not provide a point spread which would encompass its own above-average rates and the lower rates of average or below-average firms. The necessity to maintain some relationship within their own wage-rate structure transcends any pressure to maintain a relationship with the labor market as a whole, for the particular grade of labor.[28]

> ... [I]n a small city one inquires of a high-paying firm what they pay an industrial nurse

and why. The explanation is given that the job is evaluated and comes out at x dollars. Upon further discussion, we find that the personnel man feels that, in truth, the evaluation is definitely on the low side; but, after all, they're paying 25 per cent more than the local hospitals. In a low-paying firm, we find that they pay the switchboard operator the identical rate paid by the telephone company. We ask whether that isn't high in terms of their other office jobs. The answer is yes, but they always hire a trained operator; the rate is really quite independent of other office rates; and it causes no "trouble." Consider an over-the-road trucking rate in a low-paying mill. Do they meet the trucking-firm rate? No, but they aren't organized yet and they do have the rate up so high that they would hate to have to argue it with some of their skilled production workers. In fact, they're not at all sure that they shouldn't sell their trucks and contract the work.

A firm is not just in an industry nor is it just in a local labor market. It is necessarily in both. It is an employer of occupational groups or skill levels which cut across industry lines—some skilled, such as machinists, some unskilled or semiskilled, such as messenger boys and salesclerks. It responds to both its industry and labor-market setting. The rate it pays for the "standard" occupational types will reflect both its own high or low industry level and the rates which other local firms are paying for similar kinds of labor. Some central pull or tendency may be provided by supply and demand considerations in the local labor market, but there are also tendencies toward dispersion which are provided by differential industry effects. Thus a spectrum of *occupational wage rates* as well as of *firm wage levels* will be created within the locality.

Ability to pay   But this is by no means the whole of the story. The evidence strongly suggests that, in addition to the influence of an industry's occupational mix on the wage rates which it pays, the firm's own profitability has its effect. Differential wage levels among firms in a local labor market even for comparable grades of labor appear to be due in large part to differential ability to pay. The firms which are known for their high wage levels in a community are likely to be the ones which are able to pay well. The poor payers are the less profitable firms.

Several influences determine whether a firm is profitable or not. One of these is, again, the industry or product market within which it operates. Actually we should use the plural—industries or product markets—since most goods-producing firms straddle more than one. If a company has the good fortune or good management to be part of an expanding industry, presumably reflecting a marginal value product above prevailing wage rates, or if it is part of an oligopolistic industry which is shielded from price rivalry by difficulties of entry to the business (such as large-scale capital needs or control over scarce raw materials or command of choice location), or if it has a product mix which protects it from the harshest effects of recessions, or if its products are differentiated in such a way as to enjoy special consumer favor, its rate of return on investment will be above average and so too will its pay scales. Profitability thus tends to be correlated with a firm's position in the wage spectrum.

A firm's profitability is affected not only by the product markets it creates or in which it operates, however. The technological processes it employs are also of prime importance. The capital-intensive firms tend to be more profitable, reflecting the use of more up-to-date equipment producing at lower cost per unit. The machinist who has modern machinery to work with will be more productive than the machinist who has to make do with obsolete tools. The automated plant is not necessarily, but probably, more profitable than the firm which still relies heavily on manual coordination of its production processes. To some extent this involves profit "circularity": the higher the profit, the more feasible is it for a firm to invest in advanced technology, and the more profitable are its operations likely to be.

Finally, differential ability to pay is likely to be a function of differences in managerial ability and organizational structure. Managerial competence is inevitably reflected in the manipulation of the firm's product line, and its currency with technological progress is a further manifestation of its alertness to potential sources of profit improvement. One further organizational factor which affects the ability of a plant to pay above-

average wages in a local labor market is likely to be whether it is a unit or a subsidiary of a larger corporation. The relationship between size and profitability is a much too complicated question to explore here, but suffice it to say that size has its advantages. If it is problematical whether the larger firm is always the more profitable, it is beyond question that smallness shows a low correlation with profitability. By and large, the plant of a major corporation tends to be among the firms at the top of the wage scale in a local labor market.

All industries do not, of course, produce products. Some, especially those with local markets, produce services. Normally service industries are labor-intensive in nature, frequently tend to be associated with lower-status jobs, are often subject to considerable competition or sharing of the market, and, because small in scale, are operated by people of lesser managerial skill. They are sometimes little more than family affairs. Except for the few large-scale chain operations, or prestige establishments in the major cities, or professional offices, they are likely to be relatively low-profit and low-wage businesses.

Willingness to pay There is still a missing piece in the argument, however. Simply because some firms are able to pay higher wages than others is no reason why they should. If it is possible for them to obtain workers at the same lower rates as other firms in the area, why should they pay more? One answer comes readily to mind. A strong union, backed by the leadership and treasury of its national office, may force higher rates on them. Above-average profits whet the appetite of workers for above-average wages. Why should they too not share in the good fortune? After all, they contributed to the result. Whether or not the appetite is warranted or the logic is valid, the more important consideration is that the very existence of a high rate of return increases the bargaining power of the union vis-à-vis the company. Management's cost of agreement with the union is made relatively lower—it can "afford" to meet the union's terms without hardship—and the cost of disagreement is made relatively higher, since to take a strike would lose it its superior earnings and perhaps jeopardize its relationships with customers, on which those earnings are based. Thus, the simple fact that a company is profitable strengthens the union's bargaining power and increases the likelihood of its obtaining wage concessions that others are unable to secure.[29]

But aside from paying more under pressure, a profitable firm may voluntarily choose to pay more. There are some advantages to a high-wage policy. If management can afford the luxury of being a "good" employer, it thereby creates a more congenial climate within which it can itself function. (It can, if it wishes, more readily indulge its "taste for discrimination.") Such a policy also simplifies the recruitment of workers, assuring the firm of a continuing supply during a tight labor market and permitting it to be choosier about whom it hires. As we noted earlier, depending on the effectiveness of the personnel office, to some extent high wages may be self-compensating by allowing a firm to hire the more productive workers. And the policy also has a nice public relations value. There are therefore obvious advantages to paying above the market. Less profitable firms might like to purchase these benefits, but they simply are unable to afford them.[30]

The local wage escalator The wage differentials which emerge from the varying ability to pay on the part of firms spread themselves over a spectrum, from high to low. Each firm in the local labor market finds its place on that spectrum in terms of whether it is recognized as a "good" or "fair" or "poor" payer of its workers. Over the years, a firm's position on the spectrum may shift, but in general the shift will not be great. The quality of workers it has assembled, the reputation it has to live up to, the union, if it has one—all will impose on the firm a compulsion to maintain its place on the scale. Thus, as the general level of wages in the community moves up or down over the years, the particular wage scales of the firms in the community tend to move up and down in a rough relationship; the impression is conveyed of a kind of escalator, on which each firm finds its place at some level, with all moving up and down together, shifting places slightly but usually not markedly. "Over the course of time these differences in plant wage levels become recognized and customary. Individual managements

do not strive to eliminate them and achieve absolute equality with other plants. They strive rather to protect their established position in the wage hierarchy of the area."[31]

We have spoken of firms and plants as occupying positions on the wage escalator, but in some instances room must also be made for employers' associations, as in the construction industry. Where a firm or plant or employers' group stands on the escalator depends largely on its profitability, which to an important extent is a reflection of the industries or product markets in which it operates. But which *types* of workers are affected by a firm's position on the escalator depends chiefly on its technology. Which types of workers are affected by the local escalator *as a whole,* and how they are affected, depends on the labor market's industrial composition—the product markets represented chiefly determining the height to which the escalator climbs, and the technologies represented determining which workers are most wanted on the escalator.

A firm's position on the local escalator involves not simply a firm's wage level but also its general reputation as an employer—the fairness of its treatment of employees, the generosity of its fringe benefits, its physical accommodations. If an incentive plan is involved, the level of the "norm" and how much over "norm" one can make with a given effort affect its standing. While these qualities tend to go together, the fact that more than simple wage-rate levels are involved in attracting and holding workers creates a measure of fuzziness in the concepts of wages and labor markets and escalator. Comparisons become somewhat more difficult, and there is room for some workers to respond to some aspects which make up a firm's standing rather than to others. New institutional arrangements further complicate the picture. The assortment of fringe benefits has become immensely more complex and, in total amount, more important than it was even ten or fifteen years ago. Some firms have moved toward instituting an annual wage, and others, profit-sharing or bonus schemes. Such developments rob the "local labor market" of some of its cohesiveness by rendering comparisons more obscure. As we earlier had occasion to note, the local labor market tends to become segmented, with particular kinds of skills and workers with particular wants or tastes gravitating toward the local employers who are looking for workers of the same characteristics. It is almost like a mass courtship, with particular workers and particular firms marrying and producing a family of supply and demand schedules, all more or less related.

In any event, actual or potential mobility between firms does not seem to be the sole means for maintaining firms in their approximate relationships on the escalator. There are social pressures within the community—expectancies generated by time—which also serve to keep employers "in line." A firm which began to drop back on the escalator would lose local favor and violate employee expectations, with possible morale, if not recruitment, problems. A firm which forged ahead would encounter fewer problems, but might create some pressures on the traditional leaders to do better. Positions do change over time, obviously, with changes in a firm's product position and technical needs, or with changes in management, but by and large the firms become sorted out on the basis of the factors we have noted, and tend to move up and down (mostly up) on the escalator together.

Although the conception of the local wage escalator is generally valid, at least one reservation is worth noting. We have seen that there has been a marked rise in the importance of the service sector in recent years, especially in such fields as education, health services, and local government. This shift from goods to services represents an evolutionary development in our economy. Gross national income and per capita income have been rising, people's wants have been modified, and the jobs catering to these wants have multiplied. Increasing urbanization has also strengthened the demand for certain public services and has altered job requirements. The pace of this change has meant that some of these newer jobs (or even traditional jobs like those of teachers and police, which have become newly important) have no well-established place on the escalator. They are still jockeying for position, as we had occasion to note in discussing the growing importance of unions of public employees. In this respect the "sorting process" is still working itself out.

Wage relationships among local labor markets

Just as there are high-wage and low-wage firms within a single labor market, there are also high-wage and low-wage communities within the national labor market and even within the same region. But, as we observed in the previous chapter, local labor markets are only partially autonomous; their wage levels and employment opportunities *are* related to some degree. We can deal briefly with these conflicting influences toward uniformity and dispersion among intermarket differentials, since we have already touched on most of them in appraising intrafirm and interfirm differentials.

The effect of industry composition The single most important determinant of a local labor market's wage level is its industry composition. The influence of this factor is obvious in some respects, but less so in others.

It is no surprise to learn, for example, that the all-worker average wage is likely to be higher in Gary, Indiana, dominated by the high-wage steel industry, than in Nashua, New Hampshire, dominated by the low-wage textile and shoe industries. To some extent, this is just a matter of simple arithmetic: In the same way that a local firm's average wage level will vary directly with its *skill mix,* so a local market's wage level will vary directly with its *industry mix.* The implications of this fact are not always appreciated, however, as illustrated by the case of New York City, which is simultaneously labeled "high cost" by employers and "low wage" by some union officials. Table 18-3 shows that both labels are correct in the sense that employers can point to the majority of industries in which wages are decidedly higher in New York City than elsewhere, and unionists can show that the average wage of *all* factory workers is no higher in this city of very high living costs than it is in the rest of the country.

The explanation, of course, lies in the industry mix of this labor market. The top-wage industries of primary metals (such as steel), transportation equipment (autos and aircraft), and petroleum refining employed 18 percent of all factory workers in the country as a whole in 1967, but employed only 5 percent of the factory workers in

Table 18-3 *Employment and Average Hourly Earnings of Production and Related Workers by Major Industry Group, United States and New York City, Annual Averages, 1967*

Major industry group	United States Employment Number (in thousands)	United States Employment Percent	United States Average hourly earnings	New York City Employment Number (in thousands)	New York City Employment Percent	New York City Average hourly earnings	New York City share of United States employment
All manufacturing industries	14,300	100.0	$2.83	849.7	100.0	$2.82	5.9
Durable goods							
Ordnance and accessories	175.6	1.2	$3.17	2.3	0.3	n.a.	1.3
Lumber and wood products, except furniture	519.5	3.6	2.36	5.7	0.7	$2.82	1.1
Furniture and fixtures	374.7	2.6	2.33	17.6	2.1	2.65	4.7
Stone, clay, and glass products	500.3	3.5	2.82	8.7	1.0	2.99	1.7
Primary metal industries	1,057.1	7.4	3.34	14.3	2.9	n.a.	1.4
Fabricated metal products	1,051.9	7.4	2.98	36.8	4.3	2.73	3.5
Machinery	1,367.1	9.6	3.19	29.8	3.5	3.20	2.2
Electrical equipment and supplies	1,318.3	9.2	2.77	51.8	6.1	2.49	3.9
Transportation equipment	1,370.8	9.6	3.44	9.9	1.2	3.03	0.7
Instruments and related products	279.8	2.0	2.85	22.6	2.7	2.86	8.1
Miscellaneous manufacturing industries	338.5	2.4	2.35	69.9	8.2	2.33	20.7
Nondurable goods							
Food and kindred products	1,185.6	8.6	2.64	62.0	7.3	3.25	5.2
Tobacco manufactures	74.6	0.5	2.27	2.9	0.3	n.a.	3.9
Textile mill products	848.8	5.9	2.06	35.8	4.2	2.70	4.2
Apparel and related products	1,240.0	8.7	2.03	233.4	27.5	2.64	18.8
Paper and allied products	527.9	3.7	2.87	27.2	3.2	2.60	5.2
Printing, publishing, & allied industries	661.6	4.6	3.28	125.8	14.8	4.16	19.0
Chemicals and allied products	592.5	4.1	3.10	42.3	5.0	2.94	7.1
Petroleum refining & related industries	114.6	0.8	3.58	7.7	0.9	n.a.	6.7
Rubber & miscellaneous plastics products	396.6	2.8	2.75	11.7	1.4	2.18	3.0
Leather & leather products	304.1	2.1	2.07	31.4	3.7	2.23	10.3

NOTE: Because of rounding, sums of individual items may not equal totals.

SOURCES: U.S. Bureau of Labor Statistics, *Employment and Earnings Statistics for the United States, 1909–1968,* and *Employment and Earnings Statistics for States and Areas, 1939–1967.*

New York City. On the other hand, the three industries at the bottom of the national wage scale (textiles, apparel, and leather) employed only 17 percent of all factory workers in the country but accounted for 35 percent of New York's factory employment. Thus, New York wages are high for the industries in which it specializes, but unfortunately it specializes, with only a few exceptions, in low-wage industries. The opposite effect of industry mix can be seen in cities such as Pittsburgh, Detroit, and Birmingham, in which a concentration of high-wage industries produces a high level of average earnings.[32]

But our primary concern is why wages differ between local markets for the *same* type of job, as the previous chapter demonstrated that they do to a marked degree. Here the effects of a market's industry mix may be direct or indirect. We know that wages for a given occupation tend to be higher in industries that are profitable, concentrated, strongly unionized, technologically advanced, or rapidly expanding than in industries without one or more of those characteristics. Other things equal, then, a community with a large proportion of the first type of industry will exhibit a higher wage average for the same occupation than a community with a low proportion of these industries—which is one of the several causes of the wage variance for similar skills between the North and the South and urban and rural labor markets.

In addition, the dominant industries indirectly affect the wage decisions of other employers in an area. Both the garage mechanic and the school janitor will probably earn more in a steel town than a textile town, largely because of simple supply-demand influences but also because of the social process of equitable comparisons. That is, just as the firm that pays above-average rates to its skilled workers will often pay above-average rates to its unskilled workers, so the wage levels of the dominant industries in a local market will (to a lesser extent) rub off on the wages of other industries in the same market.

Mobility and immobility of workers All occupations and skill levels may thus be contagiously infected by the low-wage virus of a low-wage area or be blessed with above-average earnings by their association with a high-wage area. Such interarea differentials are likely to persist over time only in the face of some degree of immobility between local labor markets. We have already noted the familiar resistances to worker movement which indeed tend to give definition and identity to a local labor market in contrast to its blending imperceptibly into some larger and more amorphous geographical entity. How else would a local labor market be defined except in terms of an area where worker movement is less likely to be out of the area than within it?

Indeed, some areas (especially, it seems, those based on natural resources which are declining in local availability or general use) tend to develop a residue of immobile workers who persist in their immobility despite prolonged unemployment and who somehow manage to subsist, even to a second and third generation. This has been true, for example, of the Appalachian coal fields, and to some extent of the North Central cut-over timberlands and copper-mining areas. In these instances, remoteness, social isolation, and a community of misery may breed both a reluctance to venture beyond familiar social patterns and an absence of the social pressures to mobility that usually come from unfavorable comparisons with one's neighbors.

The *persistence* of interarea differentials for the same type of work, attributable primarily to worker immobility, does not exclude the possibility of *short-run* influences on labor supply-demand relationships which affect the amount of the differential. Rates may move up or down in one area because the demand for workers (of a particular type of skill or of all types) changes without any immediate parallel change in the supply of workers, or because the supply of workers (of a particular type or of all types) changes in relation to the demand for them. The large influx of Puerto Ricans to the New York metropolitan area is an example of this effect. Here it is not the immobility of workers which acts as a depressant on rates but their very mobility: the Puerto Ricans who landed on the mainland were ipso facto more mobile than the ones who remained behind on their island.

Over time some of these more mobile types may move on to other areas where rates for their services are above those in New York, or firms employing workers may move to New York to take advantage of low-wage rates there. But mobility—both of workers and firms—depends on other influences than relative wage rates, and there is no evidence that it operates so systematically as to remove interarea wage differentials traceable to the industrial complex, even though such wage differentials get pulled and hauled in the process.

Forces relating labor markets If the industry mix and worker immobility are long-run forces making for dispersion of wage levels among local labor markets, reinforced by short-run imbalances in labor supply-demand relationships affecting areas differentially, there are other forces which have the effect of narrowing interarea differentials. These are the influences which, while not strong enough to establish economywide equality of wage rates for a given occupation or skill level, nevertheless are instrumental in establishing *some* relationship among the local wage-rate structures, providing a cohesive force that gives some sense of system to the national wage-rate structure.

First, there is worker mobility itself. *All* workers are not so immobile as to resist the pull of higher rates in other areas. In fact, the evidence reviewed in Chapter 4 indicates that each year about 5 percent of all heads of families change residence from one local labor market to another. Particularly among skilled manual, technical, and professional workers is there an orientation toward one's occupation in contrast to one's employer, a career identification which evokes a greater responsiveness to career possibilities in areas other than the one of immediate residence. This tendency to mobility, to the extent it does exist, requires local employers to meet the competition of other areas, and to some degree the upward pull on rates for the affected skills becomes reflected even on the less skilled and less mobile by the process of "appropriate relationships" and "equitable comparisons," which we have previously noted.

Firms no less than workers may be mobile. An expanding company may choose to locate its new plants in a low-wage area, with its added demand raising the level for the local market. Large national corporations which locate plants in new areas are more likely to establish themselves at the upper end of the local wage escalator, thereby raising the average wage level for the area.

National labor unions have also been influential in reducing interarea differentials. To some extent this is done through a conscious effort to "level up" the rates of low-wage areas in order to protect higher rates which have been won elsewhere; employers whose labor costs are relatively higher than those of competitors are likely to pressure the labor union with which they have a collective contract to bring the rest of the industry into line, to reduce their competitive disadvantage. To some degree unions have succeeded in winning agreement from national corporations to reduce or eliminate interplant (intrafirm) differentials, thereby exerting an upward pull in any low-wage areas in which plants are located.

Less commonly recognized, however, is that union pressure to remove interarea wage differentials may sometimes be achieved through concessions made to employers on the productivity front. As we noted in Chapter 15, what concerns employers is not wage rates as such but labor costs. If unions are willing to "tighten up" on loose incentive standards or to reduce the amount of unproductive but remunerated time or to cooperate with management in other ways, wage rates may be brought into line with those in other areas without adding to labor costs. In his investigation of the Automobile Workers bargaining program, Prof. Harold Levinson found that "the union was more willing to provide relief to individual firms through adjustments in productivity rather than hourly compensation since the former technique could not be as easily known to outsiders and, hence, involved less possibility of adverse secondary effects."[33]

To a minor extent national legislative minimum-wage provisions provide a floor under wage levels and thus reduce the possible interarea wage range. Perhaps more effective in this respect are the administrative Walsh-Healey minimum-wage determinations on government contracts, which we shall examine in a subsequent chapter. Finally, we may note that the cost of living tends to be higher in high-wage areas and lower in low-wage areas, so that real-wage differences are usually not so great as money wages would suggest. We would expect this from the contagious effect which the wage levels of the dominant industry or industries have on the local labor market generally.

Importance of the industry influence If we review the various influences affecting the relationships among local labor markets, we are struck by the overwhelming role played by the industry or product market tie. Interarea wage levels differ predominantly because of differing industrial composition. Those industries which tend to employ high-wage workers, and are dominant in an area, give a high-wage coloration to the whole area. Dominant low-wage industries convey some of their more baneful effects to the labor market in which they are located. One might expect differences for the same occupations or skill levels to be brought closer to equality over time by the migration of low-paid workers to high-paying areas, or of high-wage firms to low-wage areas. Some of this equilibrating movement of workers and firms does in fact take place, but not enough by itself to effect a tight relationship among areas. There is never a long enough period over which movement can take place without being affected by other intervening influences to produce the equilibrium result which a straight supply and demand analysis would project.

Despite the massive migration that has occurred from the farm to the city, for example, the ratio of farm wage rates to average hourly earnings in manufacturing has actually *dropped* slightly, from 43 percent in 1929 to 40 percent in 1968.[34] It is true that farm rates increased fivefold over that period and, all other things equal, the farm-factory wage gap should have been greatly narrowed if not eliminated. But other things did not remain equal to the 1929 status quo, and as productivity, employment, profits, and unionization expanded in manufacturing, factory wages rose even faster than farm wages over the last forty years.

And yet some system of interarea wage relationships is established even without actual movement, or with only minimal movement. The buildup of wage pressures in one area manages to be conveyed to other areas not simply with respect to the strategic and mobile occupations; through the relationship of those occupations to a firm's whole internal structure of wage rates, they have their effect more broadly within the firm, and through the relationship of that firm to other firms in the area via the local wage escalator, the influence is felt beyond the firm and through the community. This transmission of effects is likely to be related to the industry composition of the local labor markets: the strategic and mobile occupations are, at any time, likely to be more related to certain industries than to others, and hence more influential on the internal wage structures of firms in those industries.

But one need not rely solely on such sympathetic and perhaps more speculative wage movements, via the process of wage comparisons, to establish the industry nexus for interarea wage relationships. The influence of the national corporation and the national union is of major importance: The wage policy of the larger corporation will be influential on the numerous plants which compose it, and the wage policy of the national union will be felt in all firms with which it bargains. Moreover, to the extent that profitability affects wage levels on the local escalator, and at the same time reflects which industries (which product markets) are riding high or doing poorly, then areas which are influenced by approximately the same mix of industries will be subject to approximately the same wage influences. These local labor markets will show roughly comparable levels. The industry nexus thus relates some areas more closely to others; the wage relationship is stronger between two areas in both of which steel is the dominant influence than between two labor markets in one of which steel is dominant and in the other, perhaps furniture or shoes.

Since industries themselves have varying degrees of relatedness, depending on how closely their products serve as substitutes or complements for one another, these product-market (industry) influences produce a family of effects on local labor markets. As one industry prospers, the industries for whose products its own goods are substitutes will be adversely affected, while those for which it produces complementary products (as the automobile industry for tire, battery, and accessory industries) will simultaneously prosper.

These *relative* profitabilities, based on product-market relationships, spread through the economy and affect the wage range and wage levels in local markets, and in a systematic rather than a random way. Such changes in industry profitability, arising through shifts in product markets, may be stimulated by changes in consumer tastes (including the acceptance of new products), changes in technology (affecting product prices with their attached demand elasticities), and changes in income. Thus even without mobility of factors and firms, interarea wage levels—never reduced to equality and never in equilibrium—are pushed and pulled into some rough pattern.

The initiation and transmission of wage changes

Changes in wage rates have their origins in the *differential* profitability of firms operating in various product markets, as we have seen, and in the *general* profitability of business, depending on the balance of forces making for general prosperity or depression. The fruits of increased productivity in the firm (*value* productivity, which may be attributable to higher prices for the same output or a larger output at the same or possibly even lower prices, as well as to improved efficiency in production processes) are passed along to workers in the form of increased wages. Indeed, there has been some tendency for firms to negotiate longer-term collective agreements with their unions, three years being a frequent period of effectiveness, with prior stipulation of wage increases which will take effect at various stages in the life of the agreement, thus committing the firm to share a prospective greater profitability even before it has taken place. For example, when Profs. Otto Eckstein and Thomas Wilson investigated the wage changes in key manufacturing industries (such as auto, rubber, and steel) from 1948 to 1960—asking not why they moved together, as we know they did, but why all these key wages increased more in some years than in others—they could explain most of these wage changes by variation in the profit rates and unemployment rates within these key industries *during each of the five bargaining rounds in this period.* In other words, wage increases in these industries did not vary in

size with each year's changes in profitability and unemployment, but instead with "the economic conditions prevailing and expected at the time of negotiations."[35]

Whether because of the prosperity of particular industries or of business generally, wages can be expected to move upward sympathetically with profits. (Profit-sharing schemes simply systematize the wage-profit relationship.) This tandem effect is not attributable to unionism, or not only to unionism; as we have seen, it could and would occur even in the absence of unions. Unions, however, reinforce the effect, giving it sharper definition and sometimes (though not always) faster acceleration. The wage bargains which they strike with the principal national producers—General Motors in automobiles, General Electric in the electrical-equipment field, Swift in meat-packing, United States Steel in the steel industry, and so on—become the patterns which the national unions seek to enforce in all their bargains. Each of these corporate giants of the industry has numerous plants throughout the country, in as many as a hundred communities, to which the central wage bargain applies.

Following the key bargain, the union brings pressure upon the other national companies in their respective industries—on Ford and Chrysler in automobiles, on Westinghouse in electrical equipment, on Armour and Wilson in meat-packing, on the "little steel" companies—to conform to the same terms. These larger companies, too, have their numerous plants spread throughout the country, to which the negotiated terms apply.

Next come negotiations with the smaller, more local, more specialized firms. A representative of the national union usually sits in on all such conferences, stiffening the resolution of the local negotiating team to hold out for the amount of the key bargain. Deviations must frequently be made in line with these lesser companies' ability to pay, but the key bargain sets the expectation and provides the comparison which is coercive on the local union and, through it, on the local management. Thus the influence of bargains in a particular industry is spread to a large number of communities via the influence of the national union, which acts as a transmission belt.

In these communities, then, wage changes occur in local plants of one of the national companies or in a local unionized company to which the pattern has been applied. Particularly in local plants of national corporations are these employers likely to be important wage leaders in their communities. The consequence is to upset the relationships among firms on the local wage escalator. Previously existing relationships are distorted as the firms in which changes have been made move—in a time of prosperity—up the ladder. There then occur the pressures within other local firms to make some wage adjustment to preserve the rough historical relationship on the local escalator.

The struggle to maintain position on the local wage escalator is imposed by the consequences of failing to maintain step. If other companies are paying more, workers in a given company will regard it as only fair that their employer should likewise raise wages.[36]

One employer explained the problem in this way: "It isn't so much that people leave you. It's mainly that they start muttering around the shop. The word comes back very fast—'Gee, did you hear about so-and-so? They gave a ten-cent increase.' Pretty soon the word goes all over the shop—'We are going to get an increase too.' The pressure builds up inside the shop, and unless the increase comes through, you have trouble on morale and production."

The wage changes granted as a result of such pressure will not be uniform, and hence positions on the local wage escalator may shift to some extent, but there is strong incentive to preserve approximately the same relative wage standing in the community. With leads and lags, companies move up (and sometimes down) the wage ladder by the process of nudging each other. The same relative positions are not consistently maintained —primarily because of shifts in ability to pay— but there is enough consistency to provide a pattern to wage movements.

Wage "drift" The apparent pattern of negotiated wage rates or wage changes at times grows a little fuzzier on closer inspection, however. This is due to a phenomenon which has become identified as

the wage "glide" or "slide," depending on whether business is in an advancing or a receding phase. If business is booming, firms may find that their workers become more mobile. As we noted in an earlier chapter, labor turnover tends to be higher in good times, declining in depression. In order to keep employees on the job, employers may raise their pay beyond the level specified by collective agreement, or accelerate a merit increase, or upgrade them to better-paying positions.

In slack times the reverse may occur. Although kickbacks of wages are now less common than they once were, a firm may be lax in meeting its "fringe obligations" in time of stress (as notably in the bituminous coal industry, where many firms have reneged on royalty payments to the union's health and welfare fund), or merit increases may be delayed, or employees may be downgraded to jobs paying less. The *official* rate structure in both periods remains intact, but the *actual* wage payments glide upward in prosperity or slide downward in recession. If one adds in the productivity effects as well (the extent to which efficiency may be relaxed in good times and tightened in bad), the glide-and-slide effect is even stronger with respect to labor costs than are wage rates.

These "unofficial" wage movements are not attributable to union pressure. Indeed, they are frequently initiated by managements either in response to their reading of the pressures being generated by the state of the labor market, or in response to their estimation of the profitability forthcoming from the state of the product market.[37] At such times, the same influences which determine the official rate structure are responsible for the actual distribution of wage rates within the firm and between firms, except that labor unions are less likely to be involved and groups of workers may engage in fractional bargaining on their own. The pattern of wage rates is thus likely to remain, but with a little more variability than first inspection might suggest.

Tendencies to wage relatedness and dispersion

Another way of describing the simultaneous tendencies toward wage dispersion and wage relatedness within and between labor markets makes use of the bargaining-power concept which was developed in Chapter 12. We employ the ratios:

$$\text{The union's BP} = \frac{\text{management's cost of disagreeing on the union's terms}}{\text{management's cost of agreeing on the union's terms}}$$

$$\text{Management's BP} = \frac{\text{the union's cost of disagreeing on management's terms}}{\text{the union's cost of agreeing on management's terms}}$$

Coercive comparisons—the wage increases which have been won elsewhere—affect the aspirations of the workers in a given company and thus increase their cost of agreeing on anything less than the pattern which has been set for them. The higher wage demand also means that it will be more costly for management to agree on the union's terms, since the union is more likely to make a firm stand on a rate somewhat higher than would have been the case in the absence of the pattern.

But the economic parameters to the bargain likewise affect its terms. How much management will be willing to concede depends on the state of its product market and on its own technical efficiency. These factors also help to determine its cost of agreeing on the unions demand. And management's disposition to be stiff or lenient (depending on the economic circumstances) affects the union's cost of disagreeing with management, since it affects whether the union will have to put up a long and costly strike before it can win its demands—if then.

The amount of the wage pattern, and the state of the product markets, and the technological efficiency—these three factors which so importantly affect the determination of the wage rate in a particular company—have characteristics which are in some degree present in all firms throughout the economy and characteristics which in some degree are unique to the particular firm or industry. In a time of prosperity, the market position of most firms is conducive to making a profit—most firms share in the boom, and in this sense they are all similarly affected. But some share in the boom more than others, and thus firms differ from each other in their profitability. In the same fashion,

major technological change is a force which tends to affect most industry. Industrial research spreads its benefits across the economy as a whole and thus is likely to reduce costs in all firms. But some industries benefit from technological advancement more than others and in this way reap peculiar advantages. Consequently, when a wage movement begins in the economy, it tends eventually to include most workers, so that the pay envelopes of most employees are a little fatter. But some pay envelopes become fatter by a little more than others.

The respects in which all firms are similarly affected thus explain what gives structure and relatedness to the system of wage payments, why wage rates do not go flying off in all directions without relationship to one another. But the ways in which firms are uniquely affected by changing conditions explain why wage diversity arises. Circumstances alter the structure of wage rates, setting up divergences from central tendencies.

Our traditional economic theory is right in asserting that such divergences cannot go too far without setting up corrective tendencies. The workers who are grossly underpaid (in relation to rates in other firms) will leave to go somewhere else, or cannot be replaced when they retire. The firm whose wage rates are so high as to leave no profit will suspend operations or transfer its plant elsewhere. We recognize now, however, the likelihood of a greater degree of continuing diversity than classical theory allowed for.

Let us pursue this point a bit further because of its importance. If differential profitabilities in large part determine where firms stand on the local wage escalator and how closely they can follow the general wage changes which are imported to their communities primarily by industry transmission belts, we face an intriguing question, to which we have already given partial answer but which it is useful to confront now directly.

Why is it that over time all less efficient firms are not eliminated by the more efficient firms? Why is it that differential abilities to pay (profitability) can apparently persist? Why is it that the wage escalator is not telescoped by a weeding out of the inefficient firms, with the result that the surviving firms, of roughly comparable profitability, pay near-uniform rates for comparable kinds of work? It is no answer to say, for example, that some industries decline and others rise, or that some firms innovate and others do not. These are only symptoms. Presumably an ability to foresee and meet such changing conditions is one of the tests of good management, so that if, over time, only the better managements survive, we should expect them to handle the problems which decline or inertia only symptomatize.

There are several possible explanations.

First, economic theory has stressed the tendency of prices of substitutable products to move toward uniformity. Even with product differentiation, we have thought in terms of product markets in which firms have only a limited control over the prices they charge. But it appears that in most product markets, price escalators—cousin to the wage escalator—can and do emerge.[38]

Such a price escalator is one circumstance permitting the survival of less efficient firms. The fact that the less competent manager cannot match the price of his abler rivals does not mean that he is finished. There is no simple test of survival based on the ability to compete in a market of substitutable products of near-uniform price. Instead, the weaker firm can establish itself somewhere on the price escalator, in line with the kind and degree of competence which its management does possess. This may mean that it becomes a high-price quality firm with a limited market, for example. Or that, at the other end, it survives as a low-price, low-quality producer, again for a restricted trade. Obviously, the profit potential will be affected by the choice of position on the escalator, but the firm will survive—less profitable, less able to pay wage rates comparable to its more effective rivals, but it will survive. As long as it can maintain its relative position on the price escalator and continue to meet the needs of its limited market, the life of the firm can go on.

Second, the ability of less efficient firms to survive is abetted by the possibility of their locating on the lower end of the wage escalator. Since this aspect has already been discussed, nothing more need be said here. It is true that we face the further question of how a low-wage firm can continue to command the necessary labor supply over time, and we shall consider that question shortly.

Third, the survival of less competent manage-ments is also made possible by their willingness to accept lower rates of return for both themselves and their firms. If a firm has to shave prices to maintain its customers, and inch up on wages to maintain a labor force, the result—in the absence of other action—will be a squeezing of profits and a limiting of management salaries. If management (and the owners whom it represents) is willing to accept the lower rate of return, the firm can continue to survive. We are then left with the question of how a low-margin firm can continue to command managerial services and capital over time. This is analogous to the question raised previously concerning its ability to continue to secure needed labor at low rates, and we may consider both of these questions jointly.

Why is it that if a firm can provide only comparatively low wages to its employees, and comparatively low salaries to its management, and comparatively low profit rates to its owners, these three groups do not abandon it for greener pastures? Again there are several possible and reasonable explanations.

1. Where would such individuals go? It is not true that the more efficient firms always stand ready to receive more workers, more supervisors, more managers, more equity capital. And if we assume that we are talking about the less efficient half of any group of competitors, a substantial amount of movement might be necessary to effect the reallocation.

If such movement does not take place in the present, however, can it not take place over time, with the less efficient firms simply dying off as they find themselves unable to recruit new workers, and management personnel, and capital? This is a more likely eventuality, but it is by no means a certain one. For as long as a firm, even an inefficient one, is in the market for people's services, there are often people to be had who have difficulty in placing their services elsewhere. They may be misfits, but they are not necessarily inefficient for that reason, at least no less efficient than the people they replace. And there are offsetting compensations to such people, too. Because the firm is not in a position to be choosy, it offers a more permissive atmosphere in which to work. Rules are less strictly enforced, idiosyncrasies tolerated. New capital is likely to be a more serious matter, but even here it is surprising how long old machines can be maintained and, when scrapped, replaced with secondhand equipment. Or a spell of good times may finance new machinery which will carry the company through another extension of its life.

2. Although we have heard a good deal about the diminution, with age and length of service, of mobility-mindedness on the part of workers, there has been relatively little said on this score with respect to management. But the same considerations apply. Management which has been associated with a particular enterprise for a number of years and has reached or passed its prime does not readily sacrifice the security of what is known for the insecurity of a new position in which it will have to prove itself all over again. Moreover, its job opportunities may well be limited simply by reason of the fact that it has been associated with a second-rate operation. The easiest and safest solution is to stay where one is. The incentive not to move is very great.

Nevertheless, most economists would argue that although inefficiency is never eliminated, the *tendency* lies in that direction. This presumably would have as one consequence the tendency of wage differentials to narrow as the discrepancies in ability to pay on the part of firms in the local labor market likewise were reduced.

Such examinations as have thus far been undertaken, however, reveal no tendency for interfirm wage differentials to be reduced over time. The range of the local wage escalator fluctuates, but it exhibits no trend toward narrowing. Again we can discern a number of possible reasons why this should be so.

1. If less efficient firms drop out, their place at the low end of the efficiency spectrum may be taken by the new entries, inexperienced and lacking business connections.

2. Efficiencies are not fixed. A corporation whose top management retires and is replaced by a new management may find itself operating under direction which is more, or less, capable than that of its predecessor management; it may become marginal or even submarginal under the successor management, thus providing a continuing population for the low end of the efficiency continuum. On the other hand, the efficiency even of a previously efficient firm may be increased, pushing the upper end of the efficiency band still higher, so that even if firms at the low end drop out, the range of the efficiency band remains as wide as before: the whole band has simply shifted upward, in absolute terms. The mortality of individuals guarantees that there will be such shifting up and down the ability continuum, whether or not the corporation itself enjoys "immortality."

3. The supply of top efficiency is obviously limited: there is not enough of the highest quality to manage and operate all the nation's enterprises. The less efficient people must always be drawn in just to carry on the normal business of the economy. They will generally receive lesser awards in contrast to the more efficient, and it is likely that their operations will be less rewarding to those who work for them, but not necessarily less rewarding than they could find elsewhere. When one stops to think of it, there is no real reason why one should expect that the band of profitability of firms should narrow over time, if it reflects relative abilities on the part of management. Superior earnings—which economists have labeled "rents"—are a prevalent phenomenon. Firms of lesser profitability probably tend to draw as managers people of lesser levels of ability, so that there is some sorting out of management people of varying abilities by the profit rates associated with certain industries or firms, just as there is some sorting out of workers of varying abilities by the wage levels associated with particular firms.

4. It is true that the more efficient firms might expand at the expense of the lesser, but this carries its own problems. There is no guarantee that the firm's efficiency will remain as high after expansion as before. Doubling the size of an enterprise may in fact drop it from the ranks of the more profitable to those of the less profitable, in relative terms, even though the absolute size of the profit figure increases. Moreover, the larger firm needs more middle managers and more supervisors. These are likely to be people who are no more capable than the managers of the smaller businesses whom they replace, so that internally the expanding firm may actually be retro-

gressing in the direction of ordinary performance. It expands because of the quality of its leadership, but in the expansion that leadership may be diluted by having to rely on subordinates of lesser efficiency.

Finally, to some extent it *is* true that the less efficient firms do die out. We know, for example, the high attrition rate of new operations, where inexperienced management prevents the survival of a business for even the first few years of its life. The same kind of attrition undoubtedly characterizes firms which have weathered the storms of adolescence and youth, even some which have reached the mature years; for such firms, continued survival is a never-ending Darwinian struggle, and each year some of this number fall prey to their more efficient rivals. There is understandably virtually no statistical information on such attrition, since it would be difficult to determine the cause and to attribute the degree of efficiency or inefficiency present in each case. That it does occur seems indisputable, but it does not occur to all firms. There is no ground for believing that even in the long run all inefficiency in business is replaced by efficiency. There thus appears to be no necessary, or even likely, narrowing of the range of profitability and ability to pay within the product markets, and of wages within the labor markets.

Such an approach to understanding the behavior of wages obviously must lead into important questions relative to the effectiveness of business operation itself. It is quite a distance removed from the more polarized "economic" and "political" approaches with which we began this chapter. It raises interesting questions concerning the kinds of managerial ability which are most important to business success and how such requirements differ from one industry to another, or differ with the size of firms, or differ with the scope of the markets in which they operate, and so on. These very practical questions have their direct relevance to economic theory and, more narrowly, wage theory.

In general, we can say that the significance of this kind of approach lies in the greater degree of permissiveness and tolerance which it sees in the economic system. The economy is characterized by a tendency toward diversity as well as toward uniformity. We need to know more about the interaction of these two tendencies; we need to know the limits of each and how each controls the other. What is becoming clear is that the world in which wages are determined is a world filled with interesting variables, including rivalries in product markets and a sorting out of producers into a price spectrum in which most of their number can live and let live, and including coercive comparisons and a sorting of firms onto a wage escalator on which they move up and down together without much trampling on each other. It is a world in which managerial skill becomes a key factor, though it expresses itself in a variety of ways, and in which deviation and conformance are mutually restrained and restraining forces.

ADDITIONAL READINGS

Chamberlain, Neil W.: *Sourcebook on Labor,* McGraw-Hill, New York, 1958, chap. 18.

Dunlop, John T.: *Wage Determination under Trade Unions,* Macmillan, New York, 1944.

Levinson, Harold M.: *Determining Forces in Collective Wage Bargaining,* Wiley, New York, 1966.

Lewis, H. Gregg: *Unionism and Relative Wages in the United States, An Empirical Inquiry,* The University of Chicago Press, Chicago, 1963.

Pierson, Frank C.: *Unions in Postwar America, An Economic Assessment,* Random House, New York, 1967.

Ross, Arthur: *Trade Union Wage Policy,* University of California Press, Berkeley, 1948.

Wootton, Barbara: *The Social Foundations of Wage Policy,* G. Allen, London, 1955.

FOR ANALYSIS AND DISCUSSION

1. Identify as many influences as you can think of in determining the earnings levels of a college graduate accepted as trainee by a large corporation and a high school graduate accepted as a skilled manual worker by a plant of the same company.

2. Suppose that you were called in as a member of an arbitration board charged with deciding

a wage dispute in a large corporation such as United States Steel, or General Motors, or Westinghouse. On what would you base your decision?

3. A cartoon by Whitney Darrow, in the *New Yorker,* showed a group of management people sitting around a conference table, obviously discussing policy, with one crusty old gentleman asserting vigorously, "It boils down to this—we haven't had a strike in ten years, so we must have been overpaying them all along."

How much validity would you concede to his remark?

4. An assistant industrial relations director once wrote in a personal letter:

> Sometimes I despair of the efforts put forth by the leaders and intellectuals propounding labor philosophy when I see our respective sides clutch their cudgels and file into the conference room. Reason is a very minute part of the process. As a friend of mine once said about law, "If you don't know the facts, argue the law, and if you don't know the law, pound like hell on the table." You should see our tables!

Assuming this to be an accurate description of what this one man observed, and assuming it to be characteristic of most collective negotiations, what forces give any kind of rationality to the wage structure of the nation?

5. Suppose that you are the president of a thirty-year-old company producing plastic products, facing such severe competition that next year's orders are never assured—they depend on how good a product you turn out and at how low a price, as compared with the quality and price of your competitors. You recognize that your wage rates, and probably your working conditions, are below those of comparable plants both in the industry and in the community, and for some time you have been worried that your employees would join a union to try to improve their circumstances. You yourself would like to do more for your employees if you could, but you are afraid to do so for fear that increased costs would put you at a competitive disadvantage.

Your company has assets of about $10 million and is owned by a relatively small group of stockholders in the region—perhaps 500. You yourself have a small stock holding, but your principal income comes from your salary.

A union is formed—as you had feared—and comes in with demands for wage increases and improvement of working conditions. How would you meet these demands?

6. Suppose that you are elected president of a union which has just been formed at the above company. In the NLRB election, 250 out of 350 employees voted for the union, which is a local of the Chemical Workers Union. It seems pretty clear that the reasons so many wanted a union were:

Wages are lower than in comparable plants.

Management is considering installing some new machinery, which is likely to eliminate the need for some jobs.

Management wants a time study of all jobs to see if work loads should be increased.

Management has been bringing in some younger men and apparently has been using them as "pacesetters," promising them promotions over the heads of older employees whose productivity is not so high.

Employees have been called in on "rush" jobs on Saturdays and Sundays and then given compensating time off in the middle of the week, at the convenience of the company.

Management has discharged several employees for "insubordination" when they objected to foremen's orders which they thought were unfair.

Older employees are being told to "think about" retiring, although the company has no definite pension plan, each case being considered individually at the time of retirement.

There are no paid vacations, but the company closes down for two weeks during the summer (without pay).

July 4, Labor Day, Christmas, and New Year's Day are the only paid holidays.

As president of the union, what demands would you advocate making on the company?

NOTES

1. John T. Dunlop, *Wage Determination under Trade Unions,* Macmillan, New York, 1944, chap. 3.

2. This flexibility in the time horizon over which union gains are said to be maximized leads to a considerable ambiguity, however. Nearly any union behavior can be rationalized as maximizing: whether a union does or does not trade a union shop for a wage gain, whether it goes for a large wage increase now or takes the long view and moderates its demands to save jobs. This point is made by Melvin W. Reder, in "The Theory of Union Wage Policy," *Review of Economics and Statistics,* vol. 34, p. 35, February, 1952.

3. We should not attribute to large-scale bargaining a uniform impact on all firms, however. For one thing, the same wage increase can lead to a variety of cost increases, depending on the cost functions of the individual firms, and, in all likelihood, to non-uniform price increases. If product homogeneity is sufficiently great not to permit the latter, at least there will be differential effects on profits. If, despite product heterogeneity, the oligopolistic nature of the industry unit encourages price leadership so that price increases can be made uniform or held within a narrow range, where products are differentiated they may face differential elasticity effects. (The distinctive product of one firm may suffer more or less than the competing—but distinctive—products of rival firms, since demand conditions for each are unique in one or more respects.) Hence the competitive effects of a given wage change on employment within particular firms may remain.

Even granting that a marketwide unit lessens the competitive impact of a union-induced wage change, this is a long way from contending that large-scale bargaining releases unions from dependence on product markets for their basic gains. The larger unit is powerless to protect itself, collectively, from the effects of a wage change on demand for the industry's product, and, assuming the individual firms composing the unit are attempting to maximize profit, cutbacks in output and employment may occur not because any one firm is disadvantageously affected in relation to other members of the same industry, but because the whole industry may be disadvantageously affected in relation to other industries (that is, to substitute products). What is the effect of a wage-induced increase in the price of coal on the demand for coal as compared to oil or natural gas? What impact does an upward movement in the wage-cost-price relationship in steel have on the relative demands for steel and plastics? Thus the wage employment relation may still act as an inhibiting force on the union's demands even within the larger unit, though with an influence somewhat reduced from what it would have been within a single-company unit.

4. The terminology is that of Arthur Ross, whose *Trade Union Wage Policy,* University of California Press, Berkeley, 1948, offers the most systematic presentation of the political approach to wage determination.

5. In the recent past in the United States the significance of coercive comparison ran even deeper. Because of the existence of the two rival federations, the AFL and CIO, each with national affiliates seeking to win jurisdiction in the same industries, coercive comparison led to rivalry involving not simply the tenure of union office, but the very life of the union. If an AFL union in the automobile-parts industry did better in its negotiations than a CIO union in the same industry, this might be made the basis for a campaign to persuade the membership of the latter to switch affiliation to the former.

With the merger of the two federations in 1955, some of the urgency of interunion rivalry was reduced. Nevertheless, there remain powerful political motives for continuing such rivalry. The superior performance can be the basis for winning greater influence within the merged federation itself—the successful leader adds to his prestige—and for extending one's organization, not necessarily at the expense of other unions' *existing* memberships but of their *potential* memberships.

Perhaps as important, there are still major unions outside the federation, notably the Teamsters, which stand ready to accept under their banner any group of workers which applies.

6. Arthur Ross, "The Tie between Wages and Employment," *Industrial and Labor Relations Review,* vol. 4, pp. 99–100, October, 1950. In the same reference Ross admits four major exceptions to his general statement:

> Clear and predictable wage-cost-employment relationships are likely to be found under the following circumstances: (1) Compensation is based on piece rates rather than hourly rates (piece rates are more closely linked with unit labor cost.) (2) Labor cost is a fairly substantial proportion of total cost. (3) The product market is highly competitive. (4) Part of the industry is nonunion and, therefore, wages cannot be standardized throughout the market.

It is Ross's belief, however, that such exceptions "are not now so numerous as they once were."

7. John E. Maher, "The Wage Pattern in the United States, 1946–1957," *Industrial and Labor Relations Review,* vol. 15, pp. 3–20, October, 1961.

8. George Seltzer, "Pattern Bargaining and the United Steelworkers," *Journal of Political Economy,* vol. 59, pp. 319–331, August, 1951.

9. For an excellent summary of these and related studies, see David H. Greenberg, "Deviations From Wage-Fringe Standards," *Industrial and Labor Relations Review,* vol. 21, pp. 197–209, January, 1968.

10. Maher, p. 5, n. 6.

11. Greenberg, pp. 202–203.

12. For a persuasive analysis of this debate, see Reder, "The Theory of Union Wage Policy," pp. 34–45.

13. H. Gregg Lewis, *Unionism and Relative Wages in the United States,* The University of Chicago Press, Chicago, 1963.

14. See Leonard W. Weiss, "Concentration and Labor Earnings," *American Economic Review,* March, 1966, pp. 115–116, in which the author terms as a probable understatement his finding of a union wage effect of 6 to 8 percent in 1959. For a similar finding for the same year, see Robert L. Raimon and Vladimir Stoikov, "The Effect of Blue-Collar Unionism on White-Collar Earnings," *Industrial and Labor Relations Review,* vol. 22, pp. 362–363, April, 1969.

15. Lewis, pp. 184–186.

16. Weiss, p. 105; and Lewis, chaps. 3 and 4 and pp. 284–285.

17. Professor Harold M. Levinson has adopted essentially the same position, arguing that the basic element of union strength is protection against nonunion entrants into the product market, which is indeed provided by concentration (or oligopoly) in the manufacturing sector but by an alternative characteristic of production—"the spatial limitations of the physical area within which new entrants can effectively produce"—in nonmanufacturing industries such as construction and longshoring in which unions have been successful. See Harold M. Levinson, "Unionism, Concentration, and Wage Changes: Toward a Unified Theory," *Industrial and Labor Relations Review,* vol. 20, pp. 198–205, January, 1967.

18. Lewis, p. 292.

19. Raimon and Stoikov, pp. 358–374.

20. Lewis, p. 295.

21. H. Gregg Lewis, "Relative Employment Effects of Unionism," *Proceedings of the Sixteenth Annual Meeting, Industrial Relations Research Association,* Madison, Wisc., December, 1963, pp. 104–115.

22. Albert Rees, "The Effects of Unions on Resource Allocation," *The Journal of Law and Economics,* vol. VI, pp. 70–71, October, 1963. The reference in the last sentence of this quotation is to Arnold Harberger, "Monopoly and Resource Allocation," *American Economic Review,* May, 1954, p. 77.

23. Robert M. Macdonald, "An Evaluation of the Economic Analysis of Unionism," *Industrial and Labor Relations Review,* vol. 19, pp. 335–347, April, 1966.

24. Barbara Wootton has developed this theme most fully in her *Social Foundations of Wage Policy,* G. Allen, London, 1955.

25. The same, p. 39.

26. Adam Abruzzi, "The Quest for Certainty," *Journal of Industrial Engineering,* vol. 9, p. 458, September–October, 1958. It is interesting to note that among the number of job factors usually included in job-evaluation systems are hazardous conditions, unfavorable work surroundings, and other such "low-status" job elements. These are the kinds of factors which economists presume to require offsetting compensation in order to create a "net advantage" equal to jobs not possessing such undesirable characteristics, but which typically are found to vary directly, not inversely, with pay. A job-evaluation system permits taking account of these without giving them overriding consideration (the relative weight is typically higher for factors such as skill and responsibility), thus giving at least some sense of equitable treatment.

27. Lewis, pp. 286–287, and Donald E. Cullen, "The Interindustry Wage Structure, 1899–1950," *American Economic Review,* vol. 46, pp. 353–369, June, 1956.

28. E. Robert Livernash, "The Internal Wage Structure," in G. W. Taylor and F. C. Pierson (eds.), *New Concepts in Wage Determination,* McGraw-Hill, New York, 1957, chap. 6. This is a most perceptive discussion of internal influences on the wage-setting process.

29. In the case of some local industries with which unions bargain on an industry (employers' association) basis, the individual firms are divided into classes by some criterion roughly corresponding to profitability. Hotels and restaurants are commonly classified in this way. The result is to permit the union to bargain for wage rates for segments of the local industry, broken down according to ability to pay, gaining more from those in the above-average categories, accepting less from those in the below-average groups.

30. Do high-wage firms get their money's worth by attracting higher-quality workers, as the competitive model predicts? The general impression of some researchers has been that these firms do secure better workers, but that this quality difference is not so great as the wage difference between firms. Weiss has now challenged that impression by his study of interindustry differentials in annual earnings within fourteen occupations in 1959, which concluded that earnings were significantly higher for most occupations in concentrated industries than in unconcentrated industries, but all of this earnings differential could be statistically explained by differences in worker "quality" (education, race, age, etc.)—in short, monopolistic industries do get their money's worth for the higher wages they pay. (Weiss, pp. 96–117.) In Chapter 17 we questioned whether all of the worker characteristics used in this study (such as race) really reflect differences in worker quality, but no one has compared wage and quality differences at the local-market level as rigorously as Weiss has done at the national level.

31. The concept of the local wage escalator was developed by Lloyd Reynolds in *The Structure of Labor Markets,* Harper, New York, 1951. The quotation is from pp. 157–158.

32. For an informative study of this subject, see *Employment, Earnings, and Wages in New York City, 1950–60,* U.S. Bureau of Labor Statistics, Middle Atlantic Regional Office, June, 1962.

33. Harold M. Levinson, "Pattern Bargaining by the United Automobile Workers," *Labor Law Journal,* September, 1958, p. 672. Also see Greenberg, "Deviations from Wage-Fringe Standards," pp. 200–203.

34. Council of Economic Advisers, *Economic Report of the President, 1969,* Washington, 1969, p. 261. For a discussion of the farm-factory wage differential, see Melvin W. Reder, "Wage Differentials: Theory and Measurement," in National Bureau of Economic Research, *Aspects of Labor Economics,* Princeton University Press, Princeton, N.J., 1962, pp. 260–268.

35. Otto Eckstein and Thomas A. Wilson, "The Determination of Money Wages in American Industry," *The Quarterly Journal of Economics,* vol. 76, p. 387, August, 1962.

36. Reynolds, p. 160.

37. E. H. Phelps Brown provides an excellent discussion of this phenomenon in "Wage Drift," *Economica,* November, 1962, pp. 339–356.

38. A price escalator is principally due to product differentiation, location, and advertising, but there are other reasons. On the demand side, there are likely to be such considerations as differential assurances of good quality or performance that come from the reputation of the company; on the supply side, the willingness of firms to bid for particular kinds of jobs, the degree of convenience in working jobs of a particular kind or size into normal production schedules, cost differentials with differing markup practices, the size of the market the firm plans to tap (which may in part be based on the time horizon of the particular firm), and the acceptability of given profit levels.

The labor market, as part of the market *system,* is intended to perform two primary functions: (1) It allocates workers to those jobs and occupations where they can make the greatest contribution to the satisfaction of economic wants, and (2) it rewards them for their services, just as other factors of production are rewarded for their contributions, thus distributing the national income among claimants according to a general principle.

The extent to which the labor market successfully performs the allocation function depends upon the degree of mobility of the factors of production, the completeness of the information which workers have concerning alternatives, and the presumed pull of a maximizing motivation. We have already noted in Chapter 17 that if these assumptions of the competitive system were all borne out in fact, the result would be the full employment of all resources in ways most conducive to the satisfaction of consumer wants. We have also had occasion to note that markets do not operate in quite so perfect a fashion, and hence large-scale unemployment can and does recur.

The existence of extensive unemployment is testimony to the fact that relative wage rates do not motivate worker responses so that "labor" (treated as an abstract factor of production) flows readily to whatever use promises it a greater return. Presumably an unemployed worker would be willing to accept any job rather than no job, if he were maximizing his consumer advantage; in reality, few workers would react in such a manner. They tend to think in terms of customary or expected payments for particular kinds of work and are unwilling to accept jobs paying much below those standards. They frequently regard themselves as "belonging" to some profession or occupation and are unwilling to take just any employment as long as it carries a pecuniary return. Society does not even *permit* workers to take jobs paying less than a specified hourly rate, in most instances.

As we have seen, higher rates do not necessarily lure workers from present jobs, for a variety of reasons, and on the other hand, workers are sometimes willing to move to a new job with no advance in earnings: to some degree, job opportunities themselves act as an allocative device, without respect to differential wage rates attaching to them.

Using the competitive system as a norm or ideal, economists have sometimes considered the above phenomena as evidencing a "malfunctioning" of the labor market. Their proposed solution to unemployment and unequal rates of earnings would run principally in terms of eliminating the impediments to mobility and knowledge. There is a good deal to be said for such an approach, but it is questionable whether it constitutes an adequate answer. In any event, some of the issues raised by the fact that not all workers are "allocated" to appropriate employments, whether or not this can be attributed to a malfunctioning of the market, are resolvable only on the political front, by the adoption of public policies. In the next chapter we shall turn to a consideration of political activity by organized labor, and in subsequent chapters, to some of the public policies which have been adopted.

The way in which the labor force of the United States is in fact allocated among employments (or consigned to unemployment) has already been described statistically in Part Two. A census of the labor force reveals not simply the "supply" characteristics of the labor market (how many men and women of what qualifications are offering what kinds of services to what industries) but also, as of the census date, the effects of the labor market's operation. The fact that these people are employed as they are, on the date when the census tally is taken, is the end result of the market process—the interaction of the supply and demand sides of the market. There is thus no need for us to repeat here the statistical data relating to the allocation of labor among occupations and industries in the United States.

We have not, however, similarly explored the distribution of national income in our society, and we shall do that now. We shall first investigate the *functional* distribution of income among the three major factors—land, labor, and capital—which combine to produce the output that is the basis of all income. Which factor receives the lion's share of the income pie? Have labor unions and the welfare state squeezed corporate profits, as employers often complain, or are union leaders correct in charging that the profit share has expanded at the expense of wages? How, in other words, have these functional income shares changed over the years?

But most people today are more interested in the *personal* distribution of income—the differences between the rich and the poor or, more precisely, how families and individuals compare to one another in the income they receive from *all* sources, whether in wages, welfare benefits, stock dividends, or some other form. In Chapter 1 we presented evidence that confirmed the general belief that our society is easily the richest in the world today, as measured by the income of the average family or individual, but we also showed that this high average masks a wide gap between those at the top of the income structure and those at the bottom. We now need to examine this problem more closely. Is income distributed more equally today than in the past? How do we compare with other countries in this respect? Who are the poor and why are they poor?

Our focus is thus much broader than in the previous chapters in this section, in which we concentrated on wage differentials within a given occupation. Here we shall explore income differentials among the factors of production, treating all of labor as a whole, and differentials among families and individuals regardless of (or partly because of) their differences in occupation. Our central concern, however, remains the same: to appraise the effectiveness of the market system in allocating workers and distributing income.

The functional distribution of income

Anyone venturing into the subject of factor shares should be warned at the outset that there is even less agreement among economists on this subject than on wage differentials within the same occupation. One can interpret the available data as showing that labor's share of national income either has been increasing or, with certain adjustments, has been essentially stable over the long run. Regardless of which interpretation is adopted, economists still disagree over whether or not competitive theory explains the behavior of labor's share and whether that share should ideally be larger or smaller. We cannot resolve all these longstanding disputes but we can indicate the major areas of agreement and disagreement.

Let us first examine what the data *seem* to show about this type of income distribution. National income may be meaningfully disaggregated into the three major components of employee compensation, the income of unincorporated enterprises (sometimes referred to as entrepreneurial income, with its two main subcategories of farm and nonfarm enterprises), and property income (with its principal subclassifications of corporate profits, interest, and rent). (Included in the rent category is the imputed value of owner-occupied dwellings, but not the rental income of businesses owning property, since this is subsumed under profit.)

Prof. Irving Kravis has put together from several sources estimates for overlapping decades for the period of 1900 to1957, as given in Table 19-1. The most striking fact is that within this period the income of employees rose from 55 percent of total national income to 67 percent. Over the same period, entrepreneurial income (that is, the income of unincorporated enterprises) declined rather steadily from approximately 24 to 15 percent. Property shares as a total fell less precipitately—only from 21.4 to 19 percent—but the components of this classification deserve some attention. During the period profits doubled, while interest was cut in half and rental income declined to a little more than one-third its original proportion in the national income.

Other economists have estimated factor shares for as far back as 1850, and most of these studies suggest that the growth in labor's share had been going on considerably prior to the turn of the century. On the other hand, Prof. Stanley Lebergott has persuasively challenged all of these historical studies by demonstrating that the flimsy data available for the years prior to the 1920s, when analyzed with different but equally plausible assumptions and techniques, will show little growth in labor's share.[1] We need not pursue that particular debate, however, because, fortunately,

much better data are available for all of the period since 1929, the year in which the U.S. Department of Commerce began its national income series. These data are presented in Table 19-2, and they clearly show that labor's share of national income has, with some ups and downs, risen from 59 to 72 percent between 1929 and 1968. What, then, is all the argument about?

In the first place, just as we have seen that industry mix can largely determine the wage level of a local area, so a change in the *industry mix of the economy* can affect the income share going to wages and salaries. More specifically, we know that the proportion of the labor force working in agriculture has dropped sharply over the years, so that millions of people who in earlier years would have worked on a farm now work in a factory or a store or at a desk. But agriculture is an industry in which the farmer is viewed as the proprietor of an unincorporated enterprise, so that the erstwhile farmer —by taking a job for wages—has decreased the amount of national income which might be credited to capital and has increased the total attributed to labor in the form of wages and salaries. And this shift occurs even if yesterday's farmer is today's factory manager instead of a blue-collar worker, for the salaries of all corporation executives are counted in Table 19-2 as em-

Table 19-1 *Distributive Shares in National Income, 1900–1957 (Averages of percentage shares for individual years)*

	Distributive shares					
Period	Employee compensation (1)	Entrepreneurial income (2)	Corporate profits (3)	Interest (4)	Rent (5)	Total (6)
1900–1909	55.0	23.6	6.8	5.5	9.1	100
1905–1914	55.2	22.9	6.9	5.8	9.1	100
1910–1919	53.2	24.2	9.7	5.2	7.7	100
1915–1924	57.2	21.0	8.9	5.3	7.6	100
1920–1929	60.5	17.6	8.2	6.2	7.6	100
1925–1934	63.0	15.8	6.4	8.1	6.6	100
1930–1939	66.8	15.0	4.9	8.2	5.0	100
1929–1938	66.6	15.5	4.3	8.9	4.6	100
1934–1943	65.1	16.5	9.1	6.0	3.3	100
1939–1948	64.6	17.2	11.9	3.1	3.3	100
1944–1953	65.6	16.4	12.6	2.1	3.4	100
1949–1957	67.1	13.9	12.8	2.7	3.4	100

SOURCE: Irving B. Kravis, *American Economic Review*, December, 1959, p. 919.

Table 19-2 *The Distribution of National Income among the Factors of Production, 1929–1968*

		Percentages of national income							
	*Total national income** (billions)*	*Compensation of employees*			*Unincorporated enterprises*				
Year		*Total*	*Wages and salaries*	*Supplements to wages and salaries†*	*Nonfarm*	*Farm*	*Rent*	*Corporate profits*	*Net interest*
1929	86.8	58.9	58.1	0.8	10.3	7.1	6.2	12.1	5.4
1930	75.4	62.1	61.3	0.9	10.1	5.7	6.3	9.3	6.5
1931	59.7	66.6	65.5	1.0	9.7	5.7	6.4	3.3	8.3
1932	42.8	72.7	71.3	1.4	8.4	4.9	6.3	(−)3.0	10.7
1933	40.3	73.2	72.0	1.2	8.2	6.4	5.0	(−)3.0	10.2
1934	49.5	69.3	68.1	1.2	9.5	6.1	3.4	3.4	8.3
1935	57.2	65.2	64.2	1.0	9.6	9.2	3.0	5.9	7.1
1936	65.0	66.0	64.5	1.5	10.3	6.6	2.7	8.6	5.8
1937	73.6	65.0	62.6	2.4	9.8	8.1	2.8	9.2	5.0
1938	67.4	66.8	63.8	3.0	10.2	6.5	3.9	7.3	5.3
1939	72.6	66.2	63.2	3.0	10.2	6.1	3.7	8.7	4.8
1940	81.1	64.2	61.4	2.8	10.6	5.5	3.6	12.1	4.0
1941	104.2	62.2	59.6	2.6	10.6	6.1	3.4	14.6	3.1
1942	137.1	62.2	59.9	2.3	10.5	7.1	3.3	14.8	2.2
1943	170.3	64.3	62.1	2.2	10.0	6.9	3.0	14.3	1.5
1944	182.6	66.4	63.9	2.5	10.0	6.4	3.0	13.0	1.2
1945	181.5	67.8	64.7	3.1	10.6	6.7	3.1	10.6	1.2
1946	181.9	64.8	61.6	3.2	11.9	8.2	3.6	10.6	0.8
1947	199.0	64.8	61.8	3.0	10.2	7.6	3.6	12.9	0.9
1948	224.2	63.0	60.4	2.6	10.1	7.8	3.6	14.7	0.8
1949	217.5	64.8	61.8	3.0	10.4	5.8	3.9	14.2	0.9
1950	241.1	64.1	60.9	3.2	10.0	5.6	3.9	15.6	0.8
1951	278.0	65.0	61.5	3.5	9.4	5.7	3.7	15.4	0.8
1952	291.4	67.0	63.5	3.5	9.3	5.1	3.9	13.7	0.9
1953	304.7	68.6	65.0	3.6	9.0	4.3	4.2	13.0	0.9
1954	303.1	68.6	64.8	3.8	9.1	4.1	4.5	12.5	1.2
1955	331.0	67.8	63.8	4.0	9.2	3.4	4.2	14.2	1.2
1956	350.8	69.3	64.9	4.3	8.9	3.2	4.1	13.1	1.3
1957	366.1	69.9	65.2	4.7	9.0	3.1	4.0	12.4	1.5
1958	367.8	70.1	65.2	4.9	9.0	3.6	4.2	11.2	1.8
1959	400.0	69.8	64.6	5.2	8.8	2.8	3.9	12.9	1.8
1960	414.5	71.0	65.3	5.7	8.3	2.9	3.8	12.0	2.0
1961	427.3	70.8	65.1	5.7	8.3	3.0	3.7	11.8	2.3
1962	457.7	70.7	64.7	6.0	8.1	2.8	3.6	12.2	2.5
1963	481.9	70.8	64.6	6.2	7.9	2.7	3.5	12.2	2.9
1964	518.1	70.6	64.4	6.2	7.8	2.3	3.5	12.8	3.0
1965	564.3	69.8	63.6	6.2	7.5	2.6	3.4	13.5	3.2
1966	620.8	70.2	63.6	6.6	7.2	2.6	3.2	13.5	3.3
1967	652.9	71.7	64.8	6.9	7.1	2.2	3.1	12.3	3.6
1968	712.8	72.0	65.0	7.0	6.7	2.1	2.9	12.5	3.7

* National income is the total net income earned in production. It differs from gross national product mainly in that it excludes depreciation charges and other allowances for business and institutional consumption of durable capital goods, and indirect business taxes.

† Employer contributions for social insurance and to private pension, health, and welfare funds; compensation for injuries; directors' fees; pay of the military reserve; and a few other minor items.

SOURCE: Computed from data in *Economic Report of the President, 1969*, Table B-12, p. 241.

ployee compensation and not as entrepreneurial income. Further, we know that the labor-intensive service sector—that is, industries such as retail trade, health services, and particularly government in which wages and salaries often form a high proportion of total costs—has been expanding steadily. Thus, a major reason for the increase in labor's share of national income has been simply this shift in the industry mix of the economy —and *not* that the labor factor has actually been receiving more for its contribution through average wages that were rising faster than profits and other shares.

Stated differently, some increase in labor's share of national income would be expected merely because the proportion of the labor force classified as "labor" (that is, workers receiving wages and salaries) has gone up: from 64 percent in 1900 to 70 percent in 1929 and 84 percent in 1968. In fact, Prof. Harold Levinson has calculated that as much as *90 percent* of the increase in the share of wages and salaries between 1929 and 1947 resulted from these shifts in the relative importance of industries with differing factor proportions.[2] And several more recent studies have also demonstrated that when factor shares are compared within reasonably homogeneous sectors such as private, nonfarm corporations, labor's share has been relatively stable, or at least it has increased less than the data in Table 19-2 suggest.[3]

A second difficulty in interpreting the apparent rise in labor's share lies in the puzzle of *entrepreneurial income*. Table 19-2 shows that the bulk of the increase in labor's share has been at the expense of the share going to unincorporated enterprises, which has dropped (for farm and nonfarm enterprises combined) from 17.4 to 8.8 percent between 1929 and 1968—or by 8.6 percentage points, compared to the increase of 13.1 points in labor's share. But what does that really mean? Everyone agrees that farmers, store owners, doctors, lawyers, and the other owners of unincorporated enterprises receive simultaneously two types of income: a return on their hours of labor (that is, the wage or salary that they could earn if they worked for someone else) and a return on their capital (the profit or interest their capital might earn if invested in some firm other than their own). Unfortunately, this distinction is

far easier to draw in theory than in fact, and no one actually knows how this entrepreneurial income, amounting to $63 billion in 1968, should be divided between the shares of labor and capital —which is the reason, of course, why this type of income is always reported separately instead of being allocated (as the income of corporations is) among wages, profits, and other categories. And closely allied to this problem is that of the *government sector,* in which it is virtually impossible to compute any returns to capital in the form of profits, interest, or rent. In fact, the output of government operations is measured solely by the input of labor, with the result that the large growth in the public sector since 1929 shows up in Table 19-2 exclusively as an addition to labor's share. This is a compromise that statisticians must make in the absence of any better measure, but obviously the public payroll does not measure the total contribution to national output and income made by government operations in construction, education, health, law, and other fields.

In the face of these severe data problems, can anyone say with certainty how labor's share of national income has behaved over the years? Probably not. Indeed, Lebergott has concluded that "nothing useful can be learned by dealing with relative shares ... for the economy as a whole" or for any sector in which entrepreneurial income plays a significant part.[4] But economists continue to be fascinated by this problem, and if you are willing to settle for their cautious estimates instead of precise proof, it can be said that the prevailing opinion is that *labor's share of national income, when corrected for changes in industry mix, has remained roughly stable over the long run in the United States and several other industrialized countries.*[5]

There is also agreement that labor and profit shares often tend to move in opposite directions with short-run swings in the business cycle. Table 19-2 shows this most clearly for the depression years of the 1930s, when profits literally disappeared for a short period and the wage share rose simply by default, in spite of lower wages and mass unemployment. The opposite tendency can be discerned during the boom years of 1946 to 1948, when labor's share dropped as the profit share increased, and to a lesser extent during the "boomlet" of the middle 1960s. It is also generally agreed that government policy largely explains the decline in interest and rental shares since 1929. To accommodate the Treasury's problem of financing the national debt, swollen by wartime expenditures, the Federal Reserve maintained an easy-money policy during the 1940s which kept interest rates at a low level, and for a variety of reasons these rates did not rebound to their 1929 levels until the tight-money period of the late 1960s. In the case of rental income, the low depression levels of the mid-thirties were continued by rent controls imposed first by the Federal government as a wartime measure and later remanded to the states and cities. These rent ceilings have now largely disappeared (although New York City is a major exception), but meanwhile other factors have operated to keep the rental share far below its level of 1929.

The union impact

Finally, for those who believe that labor's share has remained relatively constant within homogeneous sectors of the economy, it follows that labor unions have not increased that share through collective bargaining. And that, in fact, is the conclusion reached by most of the studies directed toward this question.[6]

Several reasons have been advanced to explain this relative lack of impact of collective bargaining on income distribution. It has been said that in a free-enterprise economy, management may meet union demands by a variety of expedients— price increases, improved techniques, product redesign, and so on—that leave the property shares unaffected. It has been argued that only if unions sought to operate outside of such a free-enterprise framework, limiting managerial discretion either by political means or by themselves restricting its adaptability to their demands, would they be able to capture some portion of the income going to other groups.[7] As yet, American unions have shown little disposition to move along these lines.

But this argument should not be pushed too far. Even within the present political and economic structures, unions can have some impact on income distribution through political channels or through a combination of bargaining and po-

litical pressures. Note in Table 19-2, for example, the steep rise since 1929 in wage supplements, consisting primarily of employers' contributions to both public and private pension, health, and welfare funds. If labor's total (adjusted) share of national income has not risen over the last forty years, then this huge increase in wage supplements presumably means that union bargaining and political pressure have still served to redistribute employee compensation away from immediate wages toward pensions and similar types of income protection—a shift which many (though not all) workers would consider a distinct gain. And if labor's total income share *has* actually increased beyond that accounted for by industry shifts in employment—a possibility not to be entirely discounted[8]—then a major source of that increase might well have been this rise in wage supplements which, in some respects, are more difficult than wages for the employer to evade. (If wages rise too rapidly, the employer may lay off some workers or eventually replace some with new equipment, but he cannot evade a pension obligation to workers already retired. On the other hand, he still might try to pass on higher pension costs to consumers to the same extent he would pass on a wage increase, so the net difference between the impact of a pension plan and a wage raise cannot be assessed with any certainty.) Also, since the profit figures and other data in Table 19-2 represent income shares *before* taxes, unions have had a redistributive effect to the degree that they have provided important political support for the graduated income tax and various welfare measures that have reallocated income between the rich and the poor *after* taxes.

On balance, however, the evidence seems to indicate—in spite of these several statistical flaws, the short-run variations, and the indirect effects of unions—that the shares of national income going to labor and capital as a "reward" for their contribution to production have remained surprisingly stable over the long run when corrected for changes in the industry mix of the economy.

Theoretical and policy implications

Assuming that labor's share has remained constant over the long run, the question remains of *why* this should have happened. The shift in industry mix is a sound statistical reason for explaining away the apparent rise in labor's share, but it offers no conceptual clue as to why labor and capital should still be receiving the same proportions of pretax income after forty years or more of drastic changes in the supply of and demand for these factors and in the technology and techniques with which employers put these factors together. In fact, wouldn't competitive theory predict that income shares would fluctuate continually as labor and capital were combined in different ratios at different times?

As Professor Lebergott has dryly observed, rational regularities pervade economic theory but they appear so seldom in empirical records that economists "are quite unprepared on the rare occasions when a rigid constancy is reported."

> The share of wages in the national income seems to be such a constant, and a particularly dubious one—for it appears not only to lack a basis in theory, but even to be in conflict with it. Not surprisingly some of the most distinguished economists have been bemused by this. Keynes, with Anglo-Saxon understatement, spoke of the constancy as "a bit of a miracle." Schumpeter decided that it was "a mystery"— as did Joan Robinson. Solow has found that the miracle "may be an optical illusion," but still ranks it as "an interesting problem." And Reder's recent review of the problem concludes that we are still in the dark.[9]

In the face of this confusion within the ranks of the experts, we will only sketch in the major hypotheses that have been advanced and declare the issue still unresolved. In economists' jargon, there are currently two competing theories—the neo-marginalist and the post-Keynesian—as to why the shares of labor and capital have apparently remained stable over the long run. (Very little attention has been devoted to the rental share going to land as the third factor of production.) The first theory is essentially our old friend, marginal productivity analysis, aggregated or generalized from the level of the individual firm to that of the economy as a whole. On the debatable assumption that the elasticity of substitution between labor and capital is near unity over the long run—that is, each can be freely substituted for the other—then it follows that

> ... if the employment of one factor changes proportionately to the other, its reward per unit shall change in the reverse proportion relatively to the other, so that its relative share in distribution (the quantity employed multiplied by its relative unit price) shall remain unchanged.[10]

In other and oversimplified terms, if unions or minimum-wage laws or some other force should drive up wage rates "too fast" (above the marginal productivity of labor), employers will substitute capital to roughly the point at which fewer workers at higher rates are totaling no more in wages (relative to capital) than a larger number of workers would receive at a lower rate. Thus the labor share can vary only within relatively narrow limits before triggering countervailing reactions by employers throughout the economy.

The post-Keynesians argue that macrodistribution is something more than the summing up of production decisions made within millions of individual firms. They start instead from effective demand as the generator of income, which in turn depends upon the investment-savings relationship. Two assumptions are made: In a steadily growing economy, capital and output tend to grow at the same rate (an assumption for which there is some statistical support), and the propensities to save out of wages and profits are stable through time (a more debatable proposition). Given these assumptions, over the long run the proportion of total output devoted to investment will be constant, the rate of profit on this investment will be stable, and hence the share of profit in total income will be stable. Thus,

> ... the constancy of the relative shares is turned into a long-run condition of equilibrium for balanced growth, since the constancy of the profit share is implied in the constancy of the investment rate. ... [F]or given propensities to save, the same state of equilibrium will persist as long as the capital-output ratio keeps constant, whereas, for given production functions, the neo-classical theory would make the state of equilibrium depend on the flexibility of the relationship between capital and labour—that is,

on a high elasticity of substitution between factors.[11]

Stated differently, the neo-marginalists tend to stress the role of supply in fixing the share of wages, with profits as something of a residual, while the post-Keynesians emphasize the role of demand in fixing the share of profits, with wages in effect being a residual.

This debate is reminiscent in one respect of the puzzle we reviewed in Chapter 17 concerning another "rigid constancy," namely, the long-run stability of the labor force as a proportion of the total population. Just as we noted there that few if any economists in 1900 would have predicted that the labor-force participation rate would remain constant over the next seventy years, it is equally unlikely that either neo-marginalists or post-Keynesians would—in the absence of the historical record—predict a stable split of income between capital and labor. This is not to suggest that any theory that encounters an unexpected fact must be wrong, but it is a reminder that economic analysis is still far from an exact science. On the issue of trends in income shares (as well as the question of participation rates over the long run), we believe that no theoretical model has yet proved its case.

Finally, is labor's share of national income too high or too low in relation to society's goals? Given the disagreement over why labor's share is now around 70 to 75 percent of income, there is understandably little agreement as to what would happen if tomorrow the government somehow pushed up that share to 85 percent or pushed it down to 65 percent. Economists can speculate endlessly on the impact of such a change on purchasing power, investment incentives, employment, and other variables. Both schools of thought described here, however, would probably agree that the underlying forces determining income shares—whatever those forces may be—have proved to be so powerfully constant over the years that they would defeat any government effort to impose a sharply different pattern of distribution in an otherwise unregulated economy. And as for the difficulty of applying standards of social justice to this type of income distribution, most economists would probably agree with

the following paraphrased remarks of Prof. Armen Alchian:

> Professor Alchian asserted that it would have been delightful to have been born into an economy in which labour's share was only one per cent while the capitalist owner[s] of non-human goods got 99 per cent. This could mean that people did almost no work and lived off a highly automated economy. Or it might mean that . . . most people were very poor with one person possibly owning the "capital." Obviously the situation depended on the distribution of ownership of various forms of wealth and not basically on the human/non-human division of income.[12]

For this reason, most people are less concerned with the distribution of income between two abstract factors called labor and capital than with the subject of the next section: how income is distributed among the millions of families and individuals in society, whether they are called capitalists or workers or just people.

The personal distribution of income

Before describing the inequality in personal income that plagues this country, we should again place this problem in perspective:

> The most obvious fact about American income is that it is the highest in the world and rising rapidly. In terms of gross national product per capita—or any other measure of the average availability of goods and services—the United States far outranks its nearest competitors, Canada and the countries of northern Europe. . . .
>
> After adjusting for price level increases and population increases, it is estimated that personal income per capita in constant dollars was four times greater in 1966 than at the turn of the century. In other words, those of us living today have four times as much in the way of goods and services as did those living in 1900.
>
> The signs of affluence are everywhere. Americans own more than 60 million automobiles; 95 percent of American households own at least one television set, 25 percent own at least two; and over 60 percent of American families own their own homes.[13]

These facts do not excuse the persistence of poverty in the United States, and indeed they emphasize the tragedy of this problem. No one can expect an impoverished nation like India to wipe out poverty overnight, but how can the richest country in the world plead inability to provide a decent income for all its own citizens? It is nevertheless important, in appraising possible remedies to this problem, to avoid throwing out the baby with the bath water: an economy that has outperformed all others in most respects can still have grave weaknesses that need correction, but obviously it can also have many strengths worth preserving.

But our purpose in this chapter is not to examine remedies but to describe the problem itself. Just how unfair is the distribution of income among American families? The short answer is that this is still a value judgment, in spite of the mass of income statistics now available. As we pointed out in Chapter 1, few people really want or expect an absolute equality of income throughout our society, and in fact no "advanced" society anywhere has ever approached this norm of absolute equality. Further, the income of most people classified as poor in this country would be considered a handsome income in many other parts of the world—and even in our own country a few generations ago. Given this absence of any fixed standards, how can we decide how much of the income variation we have today is normal and desirable in any society—to provide incentive and reward superior performance and indicate consumer preferences—and how much is inexcusable discrimination by the haves against the have-nots?

One test that is commonly used is *whether income inequality has at least diminished over time,* even though no one expects it to have disappeared. This test is partly justified by our political ideals, in that we expect an open society to erode gross inequities such as those believed to have existed in the days of robber barons and sweatshop labor. But competitive theory would also predict a narrowing of income differentials over the long run—not to the point of uniformity predicted for wages within a given occupation and market, but certainly to some extent as the suppliers of labor, land, and capital had time to move toward the early sources of higher wages, profit, and other income.

Table 19-3 demonstrates that there has in fact been some reduction in the inequality of income distribution since 1929, but *most of that reduction had occurred by 1947 and there have been only minor changes since that year.* Unfortunately, there is no continuous series of distribution data for the years since 1929, since the earliest series was terminated in 1962 and the current Census Bureau series did not begin until 1947. But the data for overlapping years in Table 19-3 confirm the picture of relative stability since 1947, as do independent studies by the Survey Research Center of the University of Michigan.[14] Also, note that the income figures in the upper series in this table include an allowance for the home-grown food consumed by farm families and both series include all transfer payments, such as welfare assistance, public and private pension benefits, veterans' benefits, and unemployment insurance payments. As for the years before 1929, the most reliable study shows no change in the share of income received by the top 1 percent of the population between 1913 and 1929 and actually a slight increase in the share of the top 5 percent from 1917 to 1929.[15]

Why did income differentials shrink from 1929 to 1947 and then level out? Most of the reasons are related to trends in the economy that we have already examined. We know from Table 19-2, for example, that the share of national income going to wages and salaries increased from 1929 to 1947; the shares going to interest and rent dropped; and while the profit share first dropped and then returned to its 1929 level, the high corporate-income taxes imposed during and after the war years meant that a smaller proportion of profits was then available for distribution as stock dividends, the only portion of corporate profits that appears in the family-income data in Table 19-3. These shifts away from property income tended to narrow income differentials because, as one would expect, upper-income families receive a larger share of their income from property (and a smaller share from wages and salaries) than do lower-income families.

This trend has not completely halted since 1947 but it seems to have slowed down as corporate-

Table 19-3 *Two Measures of the Distribution of Family Income in Various Years, 1929–1968*

Measures of distribution	Percent of total family income* received							
	1929	*1935–1936*	*1941*	*1947*	*1957*	*1962*	*1967*	*1968*
Fifths of consumer units:†								
Lowest	{12.5}	4.1	4.1	5.0	4.7	4.6		
Second		9.2	9.5	11.0	11.1	10.9		
Third	13.8	14.1	15.3	16.0	16.3	16.3		
Fourth	19.3	20.9	22.3	22.0	22.4	22.7		
Highest	54.4	51.7	48.8	46.0	45.5	45.5		
Top 5 percent	30.0	26.5	24.0	20.9	20.2	19.6		
Fifths of families:								
Lowest				5.0	5.0	5.1	5.4	5.7
Highest				43.0	40.5	41.7	41.2	40.6
Top 5 percent				17.2	15.7	16.3	15.3	14.0

* In both sections of the table, family income includes wage and salary receipts, other labor income, proprietors' and rental income, dividends, personal interest income, and transfer payments. In the upper section, certain imputed items are also included in income, such as wages in kind, the value of food and fuel produced and consumed on farms, the net rental value of owner-occupied homes, and imputed interest.
† Consumer units consist of both families and unattached individuals.

SOURCES: Data on consumer units from U.S. Bureau of the Census, *Income Distribution in the United States*, by Herman P. Miller (1960 Census Monograph), 1966, Table I-10. Data on families from U.S. Bureau of the Census, *Current Population Reports*, Series P-60, no. 66, 1969, Table 8.

tax rates were eased, as the interest share slowly rose, and as the rental share dropped more slowly. Also, we know that the labor force has been shifting out of low-income farm and unskilled jobs toward higher-paying industries and occupations, though perhaps the continued growth in the service sector in recent years—where wages are frequently lower than in the nonfarm-goods industries—has softened the equalizing impact of the farm-to-factory shift. Finally, the income differential between occupations (between skilled and unskilled labor, for example, or between professional and clerical workers) narrowed during the period between 1929 and 1947 but has been stable in the years since then, for reasons we shall examine shortly.[16] (The data in Table 19-3 show that some shift occurred in income shares in the late 1960s, but it is too early to tell whether this shift represents a new trend or only a temporary deviation from the postwar pattern of stability.)

Table 19-3 might therefore suggest that since 1947 the pattern of income distribution has achieved its market equilibrium and that we have solved the problem of what constitutes the "natural" or acceptable degree of income inequality in our society. That is very unlikely, however. As we noted in our discussion of wage differentials in Chapters 17 and 18, the constant change that is the hallmark of a modern economy prevents competitive forces from ever working themselves out to that ultimate equilibrium which theory posits. This does not deny the importance of market forces in shaping our present pattern of income distribution, but it is a warning against assuming that any economic pattern, even one persisting for twenty years, is a long-run equilibrium position. More specifically, the fact that government policy has had a major impact on the trend of every component of family income—profits, interest, rent, transfer payments and, more indirectly, wages and salaries—means that a change in government policy can produce a change in income distribution at any time.

And that brings us to a second test of the equity of income differences: *a comparison of income distribution before and after taxes.* After all, who cares (except the rich) if the corporation president receives $200,000 a year in salary and dividends and his blue-collar employees average only $6,000, if the government then relieves the top man of 90 percent of his income to provide public schools, unemployment insurance, pensions, police protection, and so on for the blue-collar worker and his family? Table 19-3 certainly gives a very confused picture of the net effect of government tax and spending policies; "personal income" is reported there as the sum received from all sources *before* payment of income taxes, but stock dividends are affected at their source by corporation taxes, net rental income is influenced by property taxes, and transfer payments are primarily paid out by the government from its tax receipts.

Figure 19-1 presents a recent attempt to measure how both the burden of taxes and the benefits

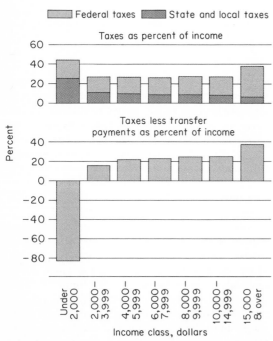

Fig. 19-1. *Taxes and transfer payments as percent of income (excluding transfers), by income class, 1965.*

SOURCE: Economic Report of the President, *1969,* p. 161.

of government spending are spread among various income classes. To anyone who fears that we are taxing away the incentive to rise from rags to riches, it may be comforting to learn that upper-income families do not pay out a much larger share of their earnings for taxes than most other people do, and indeed pay a smaller proportion than the lowest-income families do. The explanation lies primarily in the regressive nature of state and local taxes—particularly sales, excise, and property taxes—and also the effect of the social security payroll tax. But even the federal income tax is not as progressive as commonly assumed, partly because upper-income families benefit more than others from certain features of the tax law (unkindly labeled "tax dodges" by their critics) such as the zero tax rate on interest income from municipal bonds, the special rate for capital gains, and the deductions allowed for executives' expense accounts. On the other hand, Figure 19-1 shows that the poor receive nearly as much, and sometimes more, from transfer payments than from all other sources. That is, the average family that earned only $1,000 in wage income in 1965 paid out about $400 in taxes but received about $1,200 in transfer payments (such as unemployment insurance, pension benefits, or welfare assistance), meaning a net gain from government sources of $800 (or 80 percent of the family's "income excluding transfers").

But even that is a very incomplete picture of the net effect of government policies. On the side of tax burdens, Figure 19-1 omits the effect of the corporate-income tax, part of which reduces the income of those receiving stock dividends and part of which is shifted forward to consumers; on the side of government spending, it omits all those "nonwelfare" expenditures that form the overwhelming bulk of public spending, such as national defense, education, highways, and police and fire protection. The mere enumeration of these programs suggests the staggering problems facing anyone who tries to allocate their benefits among various income groups. The ghetto resident often has a different assessment from that of the suburbanite of the benefits of their respective schools and police forces; the superhighway brings profit and enjoyment to some and misery and dislocation to others; and who would care to divide the cost of the war in Vietnam between the hawks and the doves? The Tax Foundation, a private, nonprofit organization, has nevertheless tackled this insuperable problem by the following ingenious method:

The incidence of expenditure benefits is assumed to be entirely on the immediate recipients of transfer payments (e.g., veterans benefits may be assumed to benefit veterans exclusively), or persons easily identified as direct beneficiaries of other expenditures (e.g., a substantial portion of highway expenditures may be assumed to benefit motorists in proportion to their automobile expenditures).

However, for [other] expenditures ... we have resorted to two alternative assumptions.

The first is that the benefits of such general purpose expenditures may be allocated on a per family basis. . . .

The second basis ... was family income. That is to say, families are assumed to benefit from general government expenditures, such as those for defense, international affairs, police and fire protection, and general administration, in proportion to the size of their incomes.[17]

Figure 19-2 shows the results when these assumptions are applied to all government spending in 1961, so that half of the defense budget for that year, for example, is allocated on the basis of the number of families in each income class and the other half on the basis of family money income (the family with a $20,000 income is as-

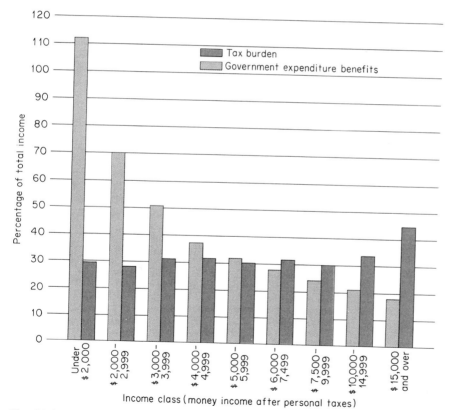

Fig. 19-2. *Estimated total tax burden and expenditure benefits as a percent of total income by income class (all families), 1961.*

SOURCE: Tax Burdens and Government Expenditures by Income Class, 1961 and 1965, *Tax Foundation, Inc., New York, 1967, p. 13.*

signed twice as much as the family with a $10,000 income). Also, half of the burden of the corporate-income tax was assumed to be shifted forward to consumers and half was assumed to fall on stockholders. The result is surprisingly similar to the pattern shown in Figure 19-1, in that the lowest-income families show a net gain from government sources equivalent to about 80 percent of their private income, the top-income families show a net loss (but only of 27 percent here, compared to nearly 40 percent shown in Figure 19-1), and the other income groups are distributed smoothly between these extremes. The principal difference is that Figure 19-2 shows several middle-income groups receiving more in government services than they do in Figure 19-1, which makes sense because families in this income range receive relatively little in transfer payments (the only offset to taxes measured in the first chart) but they benefit a great deal from government expenditures on education, highways, health, fire and police protection, and so on.

Even granting the sweeping assumptions underlying Figure 19-2, however, some people would still argue that the government's net impact on income distribution is far less progressive than it appears. None of the data so far presented adequately allows for the tax advantages open to upper-income families with respect to company expense accounts, use of company transportation and other types of facilities, full or partial compensation by business for medical and educational expenses, capital gains, depreciation and depletion allowances, and deferring or sharing income by means of pensions, trusts, and deferred-compensation contracts. In total dollars, it is probably true that "our so-called welfare state spends more, and more willingly, on the nonpoor than on the poor."[18] No one knows, however, whether this is also true in relative terms—that is, how radically Figures 19-1 and 19-2 would change if they made full allowance for these hidden tax benefits for the wealthy. Some estimates have been made of the distributive effect of a few of those tax benefits, but it is probably impossible to measure the effect of most of them.[19]

On balance, then, the best available estimates are that government policy probably does have a "progressive" impact on the distribution of income when the tax burden is compared, however crudely, with the tax benefits accruing to each income class. The central point remains, however: Even if we could surmount all the measurement problems mentioned above and could compute precisely the net tax advantage or disadvantage of every family in the United States, *the equity of this adjusted income pattern would still be a matter of judgment.* Government tax and spending policies change constantly and a precise measure of their effect today would not prove what they "should" be tomorrow.

Other measures

A third test of income equality is the behavior of the Negro-white differential. For most people today, no elaborate justification is required of the proposition that the historic difference in income between Negro and white families should be shrinking if our political and economic systems are working properly. Table 19-4 shows that this differential has in fact narrowed since 1947, as median nonwhite income (corrected for price changes) had more than doubled by 1968 and median white income had risen by only 82 percent. On the other hand, the income of the average Negro family was still only 63 percent of the income of the average white family in 1968 and, though not shown in this table, Negro families with two earners still averaged less income in 1968 than white families with only one earner, and Negro men still earned less than white men at every educational level, with the greatest disparity among those with a college education.[20]

Finally, an international comparison of income differentials should be revealing. If we do not have any fixed standards for judging the equity of our income structure, we might grade ourselves "on the curve" by seeing how we compare with other countries in this respect. In a fascinating study,[21] some of the results of which are presented in Table 19-5, Prof. Simon Kuznets has shown that income is distributed about as equally (or unequally) in this country as in other industrialized nations. Note that the shares of the low-income group are surprisingly similar in underdeveloped and developed countries, while there is a sharp difference in the shares of the top-income group,

Table 19-4 *Distribution of Family Income in Selected Years, 1947–1968, by Color of Family Head*

Total money income,* 1968 dollars	1947	1957	1968
White Families			
Percent	100.0	100.0	100.0
Under $3,000	22.8	16.6	8.9
$3,000 to $4,999	28.4	17.1	11.0
$5,000 to $6,999	23.1	23.8	14.3
$7,000 to $9,999	15.0	25.2	24.0
$10,000 to $14,999	10.7	12.8	26.1
$15,000 and over		4.6	15.7
Median income, dollars	4,916	6,379	8,936
Index (1947 = 100)	100	130	182
Nonwhite Families			
Percent	100.0	100.0	100.0
Under $3,000	60.0	44.9	22.8
$3,000 to $4,999	23.4	23.8	21.9
$5,000 to $6,999	8.7	16.3	16.5
$7,000 to $9,999	5.4	10.7	17.7
$10,000 to $14,999	2.6	3.7	14.7
$15,000 and over		0.5	6.3
Median income, dollars	2,514	3,421	5,590
Index (1947 = 100)	100	136	222

* Income (before taxes) received from wages and salaries, self-employment, dividends, interest, net rents, private pensions, and government transfer payments.

SOURCE: U.S. Bureau of the Census, *Current Population Reports*, Series P-60, no. 66, 1969, Table 5.

indicating that one of the prime effects of industrialization is to increase the share of the "middle classes." Also, in most of the developed countries for which long-run data are available, income differences narrowed in about the same sequence as in this country, being relatively large and stable in the early years of the century and narrowing sometime in the period from 1920 to 1945. In fact, in the early 1900s income distribution in today's developed countries was roughly similar to that found in many underdeveloped countries today, although per capita incomes were even then much higher in countries like the United States than they are today in countries like India. As for the redistributive impact of government taxes and

benefits (as in Figure 19-2), Kuznets compared the few studies available and found that the net impact of government policy was apparently more "progressive" (a narrowing of differentials) in Norway and Great Britain than in the United States in 1949 and 1950, but less progressive in El Salvador and Guatemala. On balance, however, the dominant impression is that differences in economic development largely override differences in political systems in determining a country's pattern of income distribution.

To recapitulate, we have applied four tests to the pattern of income distribution in this country in an effort to appraise its equity. These tests showed that money-income differentials did narrow from 1929 to 1947 but have since remained stable; that the net effect of government taxing and spending policies is impossible to measure precisely but has probably narrowed "real" income differentials substantially (that is, has spread the access to goods and services more evenly after taxes than before); that the Negro-white differential has significantly narrowed since 1947, although the remaining gap is still huge; and that the United States compares favorably to most

Table 19-5 *Distribution of Income among Families or Spending Units in Selected Countries*

Country	Year	Percent of total income before taxes	
		Top 5 percent	Lowest fifth
United States	1950	20	5
Sweden	1948	20	3
Denmark	1952	20	3
Great Britain	1951–1952	21	5
Puerto Rico	1953	23	6
West Germany	1950	24	4
Italy	1948	24	6
Netherlands	1950	25	4
India	1950	33	8
Mexico	1950	40	6
Colombia	1953	42	n.a.
Kenya	1949	51	n.a.
Southern Rhodesia	1946	65	n.a.

SOURCE: Simon Kuznets, "Quantitative Aspects of the Economic Growth of Nations," *Economic Development and Cultural Change*, vol. 11, January 1963, Table 3, p. 13.

other countries with respect to the distribution of family income before taxes. None of these tests, however, tells us just how fair or economically sound our present pattern of income distribution is, and by the same token none of them proves that we cannot or should not alter that pattern if society desires to do so.

Occupational differences in income

In discussing the distribution of income among the factors of production and between rich and poor families, it is easy to gain the impression that most income differences arise between the owners of capital and the suppliers of labor. But the preceding chapters demonstrated that there are also substantial differentials among wage and salary workers: even in the rates paid for the same job in the same locality, but particularly among the wage levels of various industries, primarily because of differences in the mix of skills or occupations, for example, in printing and construction, as compared to agriculture or textiles. It is to these income differences between occupations that we now turn.

Table 19-6 shows, as one would expect, that there are enormous differences in the average wage or salary income of various occupations, ranging among men in 1967 from $1,432 for farm workers to $9,357 for executives, and among women for an incredible $488 for farm workers to $5,225 for professional workers. These annual earnings data are more meaningful than weekly or hourly wage averages to the extent that the annual figures reflect occupational differences in involuntary unemployment; to the extent that they also reflect differences in voluntary decisions by many workers to work only part-time or part of the year, the annual data can be misleading. But even when comparisons are limited to male, full-time workers in 1967 (those who worked fifty weeks or more on a full-time job), data not included in Table 19-6 show that average wages varied from $2,489 for farm workers to $9,817 for managers.

In assessing these large differentials among workers, we again encounter the problem of "how much is too much?" Neither competitive theory nor democratic ideals call for the farm

worker to receive the same pay as the corporation president, but neither of those standards tells us whether the pay gap between these workers should be $1,000 or $100,000. Both our political and economic ideals would call for some narrowing of occupational differentials over the long run, however, as successive generations of workers had the time and (ideally) an equal opportunity to respond to differences in occupational earnings. Has this narrowing actually occurred?

As usual, data for the long run are highly imperfect but they appear to show the following pattern: *Occupational differentials narrowed substantially over the first half of this century but have been fairly stable during the last twenty years.* Unfortunately, we do not have earnings figures for white-collar occupations prior to 1939, so for earlier years this generalization rests entirely upon studies of the difference in hourly earnings between skilled and unskilled manual workers. These studies show that the "skill margin" in manufacturing industries shrank from 107 percent in 1907 to 37 percent in 1953 and remained the same in 1956; in other words, skilled factory workers averaged twice as much per hour as unskilled workers in 1907 but earned only about one-third more in the mid-fifties. Shifting to the annual earnings data for all occupations in Table 19-6, we see a confirmation of the trend toward narrower differentials from 1939 to 1950, for average earnings then increased more rapidly in most of the lower-paid occupations than in most of the higher-paid occupations. Since 1950, however, this trend has halted and occupational differentials may even have widened to some degree as the higher-paid occupations advanced at least as much, and in some cases more, than the lower-paid occupations. The results are mixed where comparisons are made of earnings trends in more detailed occupations and in specific industries, but by and large there is a post-1950 pattern of stability.[22]

It is difficult to isolate the reasons for this recent stability of the occupational wage structure or to determine whether this is a temporary or permanent halt in the long-run trend toward narrower differentials. Consider the possible role of unions, for example. During the 1940s many of the large industrial unions successfully pressed for

Table 19-6 *Median Wage or Salary Income, by Major Occupation Group and Sex, 1939–1967*

Occupation and sex	Median wage or salary income, all workers, 1967	Percentage change		
		1939–1950	*1950–1960*	*1960–1967*
Professional, technical, and kindred workers:				
Men	$8,882	114	64	40
Women	5,225	121	71	35
Managers, officials, and nonfarm proprietors:				
Men	9,357	95	65	36
Women	4,724	89	68	35
Clerical workers:				
Men	6,193	111	60	29
Women	3,719	114	47	22
Sales workers:				
Men	6,644	147	51	40
Women	1,870	81	18	38
Craftsmen, foremen and kindred workers:				
Men	7,142	160	60	31
Women*	3,717			
Operatives:				
Men	5,702	172	56	30
Women	3,088	178	47	30
Private household workers:				
Men*				
Women	512	51	6	8
Service workers:				
Men	4,251	176	37	35
Women	1,904	82	59	33
Farm laborers and foremen:				
Men	1,432	219	(−)9	60
Women*	488			29
Nonfarm laborers:				
Men	3,764	175	38	47
Women*	2,395			

* Data not available for indicated years.

SOURCES: U.S. Bureau of the Census, *Income Distribution in the United States*, by Herman P. Miller (1960 Census Monograph), 1966, Table III-6; and U.S. Bureau of the Census, *Current Population Reports*, Series P-60, no. 60, 1969, Table 18.

wage increases to be given in the form of flat cents-per-hour increases to all members of the bargaining unit, skilled and unskilled, which naturally served to narrow the percentage difference between skilled and unskilled rates. During the 1950s and particularly the 1960s, skilled workers in several unions rebelled against this policy and forced their bargaining representatives to secure either percentage increases or sizable "skill bonuses" to be added to the flat-rate increases. Also, the construction unions, which account for a large share of all skilled workers in the country, have won extraordinary increases during the 1960s. Yet, even if this shift in union impact has been of major importance (and it is hard to measure), this explains at best only why skilled manual workers have maintained their position relative to semiskilled and unskilled workers. It sheds no light on why white-collar workers also did relatively better from 1950 to 1967 than from 1939 to 1950. We know, of course, that certain types of white-collar workers have been in great demand in recent years, such as government administrators and teachers and nurses and research scientists and engineers—but we also know that many types of service workers have been in demand, including policemen, cooks, and hospital attendants, and that earnings in that occupational group did not increase as rapidly between 1950 and 1967 as between 1939 and 1950.

Thus the chief explanation for this recent stability of occupational differentials probably lies in the relative looseness of labor markets during much of the period between 1950 and 1967. For reasons we shall examine shortly, occupational differentials seem to narrow during major booms and widen during depressions. The 1940s certainly qualified as a boom period and, while the period between 1950 and 1967 was obviously far from being a depression, there were recurrent recessions from the end of the Korean War to the mid-sixties which qualified those years as an intermediate or "stabilizing" period in this context. If that explanation is valid, however, then this type of wage differential should have begun narrowing again in the tighter labor markets of the late 1960s, but data are not yet available to test this hypothesis.

Let us therefore suspend judgment on the recent behavior of occupational differentials and explore the reasons why these differentials have narrowed over the long run, why they vary during prosperous and depressed periods, and what the long-term implications are of these trends.

The long-run trend

There are two principal reasons why occupational differentials have narrowed over the long run, much as the competitive model would predict.

First, there has been within this century a political tendency to greater equalitarianism. Broad social movements with political programs have laid emphasis on improving the conditions of the underprivileged. In the United States, for example, this has taken such forms as old-age pensions, unemployment insurance, minimum-wage regula-

tion, workmen's compensation. The graduated income tax has made its contribution to reducing the spread between incomes. It would be surprising if this tendency had not had the effect of disseminating, quite generally in our society, notions of the desirability of raising the level of the low-paid relative to others.

The consequence would be to place greater reliance on the prestige characteristics of skilled jobs to ensure adequate recruitment and to encourage a reduction of wage differentials down to the point at which recruitment was hampered. This is possible since occupational differentials are not set with such precision, nor is the supply of labor to particular occupations so elastic, that a decline in the relative advantage will necessarily have an adverse effect on the supply of skilled labor, particularly if absolute differentials are actually widening, as has been the case. The unions constitute simply one of the carriers of this equalitarian ideology; their flat increases reflect the prevailing philosophy that those who earn least should be helped to raise their standards relative to those of others. It is this philosophy rather than the unions' policy which is responsible, in part, for the result.

Second, economic factors have been at work to reduce skill differentials. In the early years of a country's industrialization, the supply of needed labor skills is generally inadequate. The new jobs in the developing industries require special training, and except for a few transplanted foreigners who bring their skills to the new location, there are few who have had such training. Hence the wage advantage for skilled labor is likely to be great. But with the passage of time, the supply of skills increases, and the differential declines.

This increasing supply of skilled personnel is largely the product of an improving educational system. More and more boys and girls are taught to read and write and work with figures, and to apply their learning to vocational pursuits. Thus is built up a labor force in which the capacity for skilled work is increasingly present. Concomitantly, the process of increasing technological specialization has permitted the fractionalizing of jobs, so that tasks which, when grouped together, require broad training, when broken into individual operations can be mastered by people with lesser skills. Thus the requirements of a number of jobs are reduced while the capacities of a number of workers are increased. The result is a lessening of the relative value of skills in the labor market.

Short-run variations in skill differentials

The secular tendency for skill differentials to narrow is superimposed on cyclical variations in the relative rates for skilled and unskilled workers. As we have noted, there is some tendency for the skill margin to shrink during major booms. Prof. M. W. Reder has suggested a theoretical explanation for this observed behavior.[23]

An employer can meet variations in the relative scarcity of workers in either of two ways. He can bid up the price of workers whose skills are in short supply, a practice which would widen the skill differentials. He can also accept workers who are somewhat inferior in ability to those whom he has previously hired for the jobs in question, but who nevertheless can perform the duties expected of them, even though not quite so expertly. The advantage of this latter practice is that he is saved the necessity of having to grant the same higher rate to workers with the wanted skills who are already on his payroll.

Consequently, when labor in general becomes tight in a period of full employment, instead of searching for additional skilled workers and paying higher rates for them in competition with other employers, most employers follow a policy of filling the vacancies at the skilled level by promoting from within. The educational level of most employees—the capacity for taking on more skilled work—makes this upgrading of workers feasible. As one set of workers is moved up to higher-rated jobs, the jobs which they leave vacant are filled by the skill group just below them. And so on, as workers throughout the firm are moved up the job ladder to meet the shortages of labor at all levels. Only when the least-skilled workers have been advanced to the next level will it be necessary for the employer to fill vacancies from without. And the vacancies which he will be filling will be those calling for unskilled labor.

Thus in the labor market, as employers generally follow the practice just suggested, the greatest competition for new hires is likely to center on the unskilled. Obviously this analysis has been somewhat exaggerated for purposes of exposition, and the search for skills which an employer cannot supply from within his existing force creates competition for skilled labor as well, but it is the differential pressure which is important. Because most jobs demanding skill can be filled by upgrading workers already in the work force, the greatest pressure comes on the intake positions, where skill is not needed. These positions, in such boom times, can for a while be filled by resorting to workers who might normally not expect to be employed—older people who may have once retired, younger people who have not planned to enter the labor force so soon, handicapped people, the long-term unemployed, housewives. But if the boom continues, even these reserves may be insufficient.

When the supply of the unskilled is exhausted, but more are still needed because those formerly at that level have been moved up, rates for these unskilled positions tend to be bid up in relation to the rates for the skilled jobs. The skilled rates can remain comparatively stable as long as the positions can be filled from within. The pressure on rates is greatest at the bottom of the skill hierarchy—unskilled rates move upward, and the differential is narrowed. Such a major boom has historically been associated with war, and we do find that in the periods of the First and Second World Wars, relative wages did in fact tend to move as this theoretical model would suggest.[24]

A classical economist might very well question why labor *reserves* (older workers, younger workers, housewives, and so on) should ever come into existence in the first place. If such people would prefer to work, so that they constitute part of the normal labor supply, why would not wage rates tend to adjust downward to the level at which they would prove employable in normal times? Reder argues that this will not happen, because— for people with such a low marginal value as employees—wage rates would have to drop so low to make it worthwhile for an employer to hire them that the public would not tolerate such "antisocial" wage levels. At any moment, he argues, there is a "social minimum" wage, which is the lowest average hourly rate at which society permits employers to hire workers. The labor reserve is composed of all those whose marginal value product falls below the social minimum. In times of prosperity, however, with increasing demand and rising prices and a developing shortage of labor, the marginal value product even of these "reserves" rises above the social minimum, and they are pulled into the labor force to take the places of those who have moved out of unskilled jobs, to substitute for those whose capabilities permit them to take on more skilled work.

If the skill differential narrows in times of prosperity for the reasons that Reder has suggested, is this process reversed in periods of recession? As superfluous workers are downgraded, does the excess supply tend to concentrate on the lowest job level, as laid-off workers seek reemployment, with the consequence that the skill differential now widens? Evidence on this score is not wholly persuasive, but it does appear that there is some tendency for differentials to expand. It likewise appears that former skill differentials are not likely to be wholly restored, since the social minimum is itself likely to be rising (in keeping with the prevailing political philosophy of improving the lot of the less fortunate and in keeping with the generally higher level of productivity). As the social minimum rises, it prevents the gap between skilled and unskilled rates from widening as much as it otherwise might.

Although Reder's theory is presented as an explanation of short-run (cyclical) variation in occupational differentials, it has its long-run implications. Over time, with recurring booms, the skill margin is narrowed, and this is possible because of the economic considerations which we examined before: a rising level of public education, coupled with technological specialization, permits the upgrading of workers into more skilled positions as labor demand increases and puts an upward pressure on unskilled rates where replacements are less available. Moreover, over time, with recurring recessions, the old skill margins are less likely to be restored; the gap between skilled and unskilled rates which narrowed in boom time remains narrowed (even though by not quite so much as in the preceding boom). And this phenomenon arises because of the political consideration which we noted before—an equali-

tarianism which, in seeking to benefit the underprivileged, has continued to raise the minimum rate at which they may be employed. The longrun effect is thus to shrink the margin of advantage for skilled labor.

In this process labor unions play some part by helping to shape the social philosophy which underlies the social minimum wage. But we are hardly warranted in ascribing to unions the continuous reshaping of differential rates for skill groups. More fundamental influences on the supply of and demand for the different grades of labor are at work.

Long-run effects of declining skill differentials

Skill differentials, it should be recalled from Chapter 15, perform both economic and social functions. They provide an incentive for workers to undertake the training for, and responsibilities of, more difficult assignments, and they constitute a basis for, and reflection of, social distinction. Has the narrowing of occupational differentials over time adversely affected the performance of these functions?

The evidence is mixed as to the economic function, but on the whole it does not appear that the recruitment of workers for the skilled trades and professions has thus far been greatly affected. There is more evidence that the social function of providing a basis for, as well as reflecting, status distinctions within the work society has been handicapped. Workers who have been accustomed to regard themselves—and to be regarded—as aristocrats in the world of labor have seen the distinction between themselves and others, as measured by relative rates, chipped away. This has not happened without protest.

It is this resistance to the loss of social status in the work group, as measured by relative wage rates, which seems to pose limits to the decline in the skill margin as much as, if not more than, any effect which narrowing differentials have had upon recruitment of skilled labor. There appears to be a point beyond which the erosion of skill differentials creates problems for unions as well as managements. The protest of craftsmen has in recent years led to some adjustments in collectively bargained rate structures designed to protect their skill margins.

There is presently some difference of opinion as to whether the secular increase in the supply of trained labor will serve to compress occupational differentials still further, or whether the growing demand for highly skilled labor will outrun the supply, leading to a reopening of wage rates in favor of the skilled.[25] But whatever the correct judgment may be concerning this purely economic influence on skill differentials in the future, there is evidently some limit of a social nature which seems likely to slow the process.

If occupational differentials reflect the same tendency as we discerned in examining the personal distribution of income derived from all sources, and the distribution of wage income among all workers generally and among workers disaggregated by industry, one might expect that the trend toward further equalization, observable down to World War II, has been arrested. It may even be in the process of being slightly reversed. If that is the case, then skill differentials are likely to exhibit greater stability than in the first half of the century, and perhaps even show some tendency to widen.

But the issue is likely to be a good deal more complicated. Because of their increasing numbers, the value of those who are better educated and more highly trained, in general, may continue to diminish somewhat, even if only slightly, relative to less well-trained people *who find jobs*. But the proportion of the less well-trained people in the *employed* labor force may decline as many become excluded by a social minimum wage higher than any value productivity they can offer, so that skill differentials *relative to this entire group* may rise markedly.

Poverty in the midst of affluence

We have seen that the average level of income is far higher in this than in other countries, that this average has quadrupled in real terms since 1900, that the distribution of income around that average is about the same as in other Western, industrialized countries, and that family and occupational differentials are narrower today than they were a generation or two ago. In the face of those facts, it may be hard to understand how the government in 1968 could officially classify as "poor" over twenty-five million individuals, or 13 percent of the entire population.

In fact, one of the government experts chiefly responsible for the poverty measure now in use has said:

> For deciding who is poor, prayers are more relevant than calculation because poverty, like beauty, lies in the eye of the beholder. Poverty is a value judgment; it is not something one can verify or demonstrate, except by inference and suggestion, even with a measure of error. To say who is poor is to use all sorts of value judgments.[26]

For example, should the lowest 10 or 20 percent of income receivers automatically be termed poor people, with the implication that they deserve government aid? That is surely an arbitrary approach, for one can think of several reasons—such as the width or narrowness of income differentials, the various reasons for low income, or the state of the economy—why this measure might be too stringent in some times and places and too generous in others. Then why not simply total the number of people on the welfare rolls at any time? But some critics would charge that there are many slackers and chiselers on welfare, others would object that many needy people are too proud to "go on relief," and all would agree that welfare standards vary greatly from state to state, so that the same low-income family would qualify for welfare assistance in some places and not in others. As for international comparisons, no one can seriously argue that an American is poor only when his income sinks to the level of $50 or $100 a year found in the poorest countries of the world.

Given these many problems, the poverty measures developed by the Social Security Administration in the mid-1960s are far more persuasive than most alternatives:

> We have developed two poverty thresholds, corresponding to what we call the "poor" and the "near-poor."... The threshold is defined as an attempt to "specify the minimum money income that could support an average family of given composition *at the lowest level consistent*

with the standards of living prevailing in this country. It is based on the amount needed by families of different size and type to purchase a nutritionally adequate diet on the assumption that no more than a third of the family income is used for food." The two thresholds were developed from food consumption surveys by the Department of Agriculture . . . [which] revealed that the average expenditure for food by all families was about one-third of income. . . .

The amount allocated to food . . . was cut to the minimum that the Agriculture Department said could still provide American families with an adequate diet. We used the low cost plan to characterize the near poor and for the poor an ever lower one, the economy food plan, which postulated 70 cents a person for food each day [in 1963], assuming all foods would be prepared at home. The Agriculture Department estimates that only about 10 percent of persons spending that amount or less actually were able to get a nutritionally adequate diet.[27]

Nearly all current studies and discussions of poverty in the United States use the *lower* of these two measures: the cost of the economy food plan in 1963, plus twice that amount for all other needs, with this total then adjusted for other years to reflect changes in the Consumer Price Index since 1963. (More precisely, this is the poverty standard for nonfarm families of three or more persons. A slightly higher standard is used for smaller families and persons living alone, to reflect the relatively higher fixed expenses of these smaller households, and a lower standard is used for farm households—85 percent of the corre-

sponding nonfarm levels—to compensate for the fact that these households grow some of the food they consume.)

Table 19-7 presents this poverty standard for the year 1968. It is hard to characterize as overly generous a measure that categorizes any nonfarm family as poor that in 1968 had *less income* than that necessary to spend about 80 cents a day on food for each person (adjusting for price increases since 1963) and $1.60 a day per person for housing, clothing, medical care, transportation, and all other expenses. We shall therefore use this measure in the discussion that follows, recognizing that any definition of poverty is arbitrary but that this is easily the best available.

Who are the poor?

After years of being relatively ignored, the poor have recently been counted, categorized, and cross-classified to an exhaustive degree. We are still not sure how to eliminate poverty, but we can at least puncture some of the myths about who is poor and why.

Table 19-8 presents some of the key characteristics of those families classified as poor by the poverty measure we have just described. Although the number of poor families has declined significantly since 1959, poverty clearly remains a major problem in this country when *one of every ten families* still fell in that category in the prosperous year of 1968. (Note that Table 19-8 does not include unrelated individuals and that it counts each family, regardless of size, as one

Table 19-7 *Income Thresholds at the Poverty Level, 1968*

Number of family members	Total	Nonfarm			Farm		
		Total	Male head	Female head	Total	Male head	Female head
1 member	$1,742	$1,748	$1,827	$1,700	$1,487	$1,523	$1,441
2 members	2,242	2,262	2,272	2,202	1,904	1,910	1,812
3 members	2,754	2,774	2,788	2,678	2,352	2,359	2,258
4 members	3,531	3,553	3,555	3,536	3,034	3,031	3,018
5 members	4,158	4,188	4,191	4,142	3,577	3,578	3,565
6 members	4,664	4,706	4,709	4,670	4,021	4,021	4,020
7 or more members	5,722	5,789	5,804	5,638	4,916	4,919	4,847

NOTE: Income figures refer to pretax money income from all sources, including transfer payments.

SOURCE: U.S. Bureau of the Census, *Current Population Reports*, Series P-60, no. 68, 1969, p. 11.

household. When the poverty measure is calculated in terms of individuals living alone or in families, it yields the estimate cited earlier: 25.4 million men, women, and children, or 13 percent of the population, were counted as poor in 1968.)

Consider first the myth that most poor people are black, or that most black people are poor. The fact is that 72 percent of all poor families in 1968 were white (as were 82 percent of all unrelated individuals classified as poor). On the other hand, while most Negroes are not poor, Table 19-8 shows that the *incidence* of poverty is certainly far higher among nonwhites: 28 percent of all nonwhite families were poor in 1968, compared to only 8 percent of white families. We need not repeat here the several direct and indirect ways in which racial discrimination has operated—in education, training, hiring, voting, and so on—to produce this dismal result.

Or consider the myth that the solution to poverty is not more handouts but more jobs and economic growth. Table 19-8 reveals that *nearly one of every four* poor families in 1968 was headed by someone sixty-five years of age or over. How would more jobs help this group? Also, though not shown precisely in this table, another 30 percent of poor families in 1968 were headed by a woman younger than sixty-five (that is, families in which the male spouse was not present because of death, divorce, separation, or desertion). Some of these mothers now have outside jobs but would prefer to stay home with their children; some would like an outside job but cannot arrange for child care; some neither have nor want an outside job. More jobs (and child-care centers) might help some of these women escape poverty, but clearly that is a limited remedy which no one suggests should somehow be forced on mothers who prefer to stay at home.

Further, note that a large number of the poor already have jobs: 57 percent of all poor family heads worked for some period during 1968 and (not shown in Table 19-8) 27 percent actually worked full time, that is, at least 35 hours a week for fifty weeks or more.[28] If that seems surprising, remember that a worker receiving the legal minimum of $1.60 an hour and working a full 2,000-hour year would earn only $3,200, which is less than the poverty standard for any nonfarm family

with four or more members. As several authorities have noted, many of the poor need not more but better jobs. Finally, among the 2.1 million heads of poor families who did not work in 1968, over 600,000 were ill, injured, blind, or disabled. "More jobs, not more charity" or "Get the able-bodied off relief" may be stirring political slogans, but clearly they are not the sole answer to poverty.

On the other hand, neither is the counter-myth that economic growth is of no help at all because the poor are so handicapped—socially, educationally, physically—that they cannot compete for jobs, or will not be allowed to compete, or will only be given poverty-level jobs. Table 19-8 shows that there has been a significant drop in the incidence of poverty, from 18.5 percent of families in 1959 to 10 percent in 1968. Some of this improvement can be credited to more and better manpower and antipoverty programs and to higher social security and other transfer payments, but most of the credit goes to the economic growth that occurred between the recession years of 1959 to 1961 and the prosperity of the late 1960s. As the Council of Economic Advisers has summed up the evidence:

> Virtually all the progress in reducing poverty over the past 20 years has occurred during periods of general prosperity. In three periods of sustained economic expansion—1949–53, 1954–56, and 1961 to the present [1969]—the annual decline in the number of individuals in poverty averaged two million or more a year. In contrast, during recessions the number of poor people has increased. The brief recession of 1954 wiped out half of the gains of the preceding 4-year expansion, and several successive years of sluggish economic performance in the late 1950's increased the number of persons in poverty to about the level of 7 years earlier.[29]

Yet another myth about the poor is that nearly all of them are concentrated in urban ghettos in the North. Actually, only about one-half of the poor live in metropolitan areas anywhere in the country, and nearly one-half of all poor families live in the South. Also, the *incidence* of poverty is much higher in rural areas—23 percent of all rural families were poor in 1967, with heavy concentrations in the South and Appalachia, compared to 19 percent of families in towns and small

Table 19-8 Selected Characteristics of Families below the Poverty Level in 1968 and 1959 (Numbers in thousands. Negro data for 1959 from the 1-in-1,000 sample of the 1960 Census)

Selected characteristics	1968				1959			
	Number below poverty level	Percent below poverty level*	Percent distribution		Number below poverty level	Percent below poverty level*	Percent distribution	
			Below poverty level	Above poverty level			Below poverty level	Above poverty level
Sex and race of head:								
Total	5,047	10.0	100.0	100.0	8,320	18.5	100.0	100.0
Male head	3,292	7.3	65.2	91.9	6,404	15.8	77.0	93.0
Female head	1,755	32.3	34.8	8.1	1,916	42.6	23.0	7.0
White	3,616	8.0	71.6	92.0	6,185	15.2	74.3	94.3
Male head	2,595	6.3	51.4	85.3	4,952	13.3	59.5	88.0
Female head	1,021	25.2	20.2	6.7	1,233	34.8	14.8	6.3
Negro and other races	1,431	28.2	28.4	8.0	2,135	50.4	25.7	5.7
Male head	697	18.9	13.8	6.6	1,452	44.2	17.5	5.0
Female head	734	52.9	14.5	1.4	683	72.0	8.2	0.7
Negro	1,366	29.4	27.1	7.2	1,860	48.1	22.4	5.5
Male head	660	19.9	13.1	5.8	1,309	43.3	15.7	4.7
Female head	706	53.2	14.0	1.4	551	65.4	6.6	0.8
Residence:								
Total	5,047	10.0	100.0	100.0	8,320	18.5	100.0	100.0
Nonfarm	4,553	9.5	90.2	95.3	6,624	16.1	79.6	94.3
Farm	494	18.8	9.8	4.7	1,696	44.6	20.4	5.7
Age of head:								
Total	5,047	10.0	100.0	100.0	8,320	18.5	100.0	100.0
14 to 24 years	437	13.2	8.7	6.3	622	26.9	7.5	4.6
25 to 54 years	2,731	8.6	54.1	64.2	4,752	16.0	57.1	68.0
55 to 64 years	678	8.2	13.4	16.6	1,086	15.9	13.1	15.6
65 years and over	1,201	17.0	23.8	12.9	1,860	30.0	22.4	11.8
Size of family:								
Total	5,047	10.0	100.0	100.0	8,320	18.5	100.0	100.0
2 persons	1,831	10.5	36.3	34.2	2,850	19.6	34.2	31.7
3 and 4 persons	1,431	7.1	28.4	41.2	2,420	12.8	29.1	44.9

	A	B	C	D	E	F	G	H
5 and 6 persons	991	10.2	19.6	19.3	1,793	20.2	21.6	9.3
7 persons or more	794	24.7	15.7	5.3	1,257	45.6	15.1	4.1
Number of family members under 18:†								
Total	5,047	10.0	100.0	100.0	8,320	18.5	100.0	100.0
No members	1,700	8.0	33.7	42.9	2,877	15.9	34.6	41.3
1 and 2 members	1,465	8.0	29.0	37.2	2,458	14.2	29.5	40.4
3 and 4 members	1,119	13.2	22.2	16.1	1,854	24.5	22.3	15.6
5 or more members	763	30.7	15.1	3.8	1,131	53.0	13.6	2.7
Number of earners:								
Total	5,047	10.0	100.0	100.0	8,320	18.5	100.0	100.0
No earners	1,666	40.2	33.0	5.5	1,981	59.1	23.8	3.7
1 earner	2,096	10.8	41.5	37.9	4,030	18.7	48.4	47.6
2 earners	936	4.7	18.6	41.5	1,659	10.6	20.0	38.0
3 earners or more	349	4.8	6.9	15.2	650	14.2	7.8	10.7
Employment status of head:								
Total	5,047	10.0	100.0	100.0	8,320	18.5	100.0	100.0
Employed	2,410	6.0	47.7	83.1	4,536	12.8	54.5	84.3
Unemployed	146	19.3	2.9	1.3	559	33.7	6.7	3.0
In Armed Forces or not in labor force	2,491	26.0	49.4	15.6	3,225	40.8	38.8	12.7
Work experience and occupation group of longest job of head:								
Total	5,047	10.0	100.0	100.0	8,320	18.5	100.0	100.0
Worked	2,880	6.7	57.1	87.8	5,620	14.6	67.6	89.2
Professional and managerial workers	322	2.6	6.4	26.3	471	5.0	5.7	24.6
Clerical and sales workers	210	3.7	4.1	11.9	284	5.7	3.4	12.7
Craftsmen and foremen	327	3.7	6.5	18.6	558	7.2	6.7	19.6
Operatives and kindred workers	534	6.4	10.6	17.3	1,064	14.1	12.8	17.6
Service workers incl. private household	526	16.5	10.4	5.8	732	25.3	8.8	5.9
Nonfarm laborers	332	15.3	6.6	4.0	701	29.4	8.4	4.6
Farmers and farm laborers	629	26.3	12.5	3.9	1,810	54.1	21.8	4.2
Did not work	2,107	30.9	41.7	10.4	2,538	45.2	30.5	8.4
In Armed Forces	60	6.7	1.2	1.8	162	15.5	1.9	2.4

* Poor families as a percent of all families in the category described under "Selected characteristics."
† Other than head or wife.

SOURCE: U.S. Bureau of the Census, *Current Population Reports*, Series P-60, no. 68, 1969, p. 4.

cities, 16 percent in the major cities, and 9 percent in metropolitan suburbs.[30] The reasons for rural poverty are far too complex to summarize here, although we have touched upon some of them in discussing the barriers that impede migration between regions and occupations. The point is nevertheless clear that, while poverty is a critical problem in the central city today, it is also very much of a rural and small-town problem.

Thus the facts refuse, as usual, to conform to any tidy stereotype. Far more whites than blacks are poor, although a higher proportion of blacks are poor; "more jobs" is not the answer for the one-half or more of the poor who are too old, too sick, or too burdened with maternal responsibilities to take a job, but it can be the best answer for millions of other poor people; poverty is obviously a major problem in every urban ghetto, but it is also, if less obviously, a problem throughout the country.

The poverty cycle

Data such as those in Table 19-8 do not, however, get directly at an aspect of poverty that troubles many people, namely, the extent to which many persons may be poor because they lack the ambition or talent to be anything else. Aside from the aged and disabled, that is, aren't poor people really different in many ways from the rest of us, as indicated by their frequently inferior records at school and at work and in their often disorganized lives at home? In many ways this is quite true, but does that prove that "low-quality" workers produce poverty or that poverty produces "low-quality" workers? We cannot adequately cover this dimension of poverty here, but some excerpts from an analysis by Elizabeth Herzog make the principal point:

> For example, some psychological attributes often attributed to the culture of poverty are intertwined with the effects of hunger and malnutrition in such a way that they operate both as cause and as effect. The most familiar effects of extreme malnutrition are loss of weight, weakness, and anemia. . . . Other symptoms . . . are "depression, loss of ambition, apathy, lethargy, impotence, and a sensation of being old." Obviously, some characteristics that nutritional experts attribute to diet deficiency are

the same ones often ascribed to the culture of poverty. . . .

> Poor school performance by children of the slums is often attributed to the low esteem in which book learning is held by the culture of poverty . . . [but the fact that] inadequate diet can contribute to poor school performance has been established by systematic studies. . . . Poor school performance is also promoted by lack of sleep, a deficiency . . . often the result of overcrowded housing. [Also], a number of studies have made it clear . . . that the educational aspirations of very low-income parents for their children are often as high as, or higher than, those of the affluent.

> According to [several] reports, middle class standards of sex and family life do not rank as high on the value pyramid of the poor as on that of the prosperous. But they are preferred as luxuries one would gladly be able to afford —just as certain business men prefer certain forms of honesty, while considering them unrealistic for practice in daily life. . . .

> The exigencies that prompt the poor to depart from preferred norms . . . include, among many things, early marriage, lack of education, employment problems, and welfare regulations. The man who is not a provider loses status in the eyes of the community, his family, and himself. He may leave because of this or because his family cannot obtain public assistance while he is present. . . .

> The vicious cycle is aggravated by the fact that the poor have larger families than the nonpoor. Not because large families are their choice . . . [but because] the nonpoor have greater access to means of limiting the family and of averting extramarital pregnancy.[31]

Thus, the poor are indeed different from the nonpoor and the basic difference is, after all, that they have less money—which creates and perpetuates so many of the "cultural" or "quality" characteristics that impair their earning capacity that no one can isolate the original cause of this dismal cycle.

The poverty gap

We shall defer to later chapters the many existing and proposed programs designed to combat poverty: minimum-wage laws, health and unemployment insurance, public and private pensions, welfare assistance, the negative income tax, and so on. At this point, it is sufficient to drive home the paradox of continuing poverty in our affluent society by describing the "poverty gap." This is a measure of the difference between the actual incomes of the poor and the incomes necessary to place them above the poverty line, and in 1968 it amounted to $9.8 billion.[32] That is, if that sum of money had been added to the 1968 incomes of the five million families described in Table 19-8 (plus the five million unrelated individuals who were poor in 1968), no one in the United States would have fallen below the poverty lines described in Table 19-7.

That is a large sum of money, of course, and the poverty-gap measure is itself a statistical artifact in the sense that it makes no allowance for what would happen to incentives, cultural norms, and other variables if $10 billion were immediately distributed to the poor. Since total national income in that year was $714 billion, however, it is important to recognize that the endless debate over poverty remedies is essentially one of how best to transfer *less than 2 percent of national income* from the haves to the have-nots.

Conclusion

In Chapters 17 through 19, we have explored the ways in which the labor market allocates the supply of labor to meet the shifting demands of consumers and how the market rewards workers for their contribution to production. In addition, we have compared this performance of the labor market with the prime tool of economic analysis—the competitive model—to determine how useful this tool actually is in understanding and predicting developments in the labor market.

Our theme throughout has been that competitive theory is both an indispensable and imprecise guide to analysis of the labor sector. On the plus side, there is no other single theory in economics or the other social sciences which better explains the major trends of the past in wages and employment or which offers a better basis for predicting future trends. It is true that both the worker and the employer are considerably more complex than the walking cash registers pictured by the maximizing assumption, and yet without that assumption much of the activity in labor markets makes

no sense whatever: the shift from the farm to the factory and from South to North, the relationship (definite if rough) between the wages of workers of the same skill and also among the wages paid to different skills, the employer's reactions to wages that are "too high" and the worker's reaction to those that are "too low," the narrowing of occupational differentials over the years, the impact of economic growth on the number of poor households, and so on.

But we have also seen that the operation of real labor markets is seldom as neat as theory portrays: all things other than money differentials are never equal; incomplete knowledge, unequal opportunity, and noneconomic preferences intrude; and even if this world were populated exclusively by "economic men" (a depressing prospect), change is so constant in a modern economy that market forces never have time to work themselves out to that final equilibrium implicit in competitive theory. As a result, within the broad limits set by competitive forces, the labor sector is shot through with income variations that competitive theory cannot explain or predict with any precision—differences in wages even for the same skill in the same locality, differences that persist for decades on end (as between farm and factory wages), and differences between the rich and the poor that surely exceed whatever inequality of income one believes is either efficient or inevitable. In fact, we have seen that when uniformity does appear in real labor markets, it is often a source of consternation to those most wedded to competitive precepts: many employers denounce unions for trying to obtain the same wage for all workers performing the same job, and theorists are stumped by the long-run uniformity of the labor-force participation rate and of labor's share of national income (adjusted for employment shifts).

It would be satisfying to be able to conclude that competitive theory is either valid or invalid in the analysis of labor markets, but unfortunately the facts support only this qualified appraisal that the competitive model is a useful but fallible tool —which is the best, after all, that can be said of any theory in the social sciences.

Finally, we have tried to demonstrate in these chapters that these theoretical issues involve more than an intramural scrimmage among academicians. If labor markets truly mirrored the competitive model, there would be little excuse for allowing these markets to be influenced by the "anticompetitive" forces of big business, big labor, or big government. For the beauty of a competitive economy, if it worked to perfection, is that it would strike the most efficient and, in a sense, the most democratic balance possible between the competing interests of consumers and producers—and do this without any group coercing another. Probably no one, of course, any longer believes that such social and economic justice would automatically follow upon the dismantling of General Motors, the AFL-CIO, and the Department of Health, Education, and Welfare. There nevertheless remain honest and bitter divisions of opinion over the best way to remedy the poverty and other faults which plague the labor sector, and most of these quarrels are basically over whether we should rely upon the efficacy of impersonal market forces to do the job or whether we should turn for help to the limited power of labor unions or the ultimate power of the government.

ADDITIONAL READINGS

Marchal, Jean and Bernard Ducros (eds.): *The Distribution of National Income,* Macmillan and St. Martin's, New York, 1968.

Miller, Herman P.: *Rich Man, Poor Man,* Thomas Y. Crowell, New York, 1964.

National Bureau of Economic Research: *The Behavior of Income Shares,* Princeton University Press, Princeton, N.J., 1962.

"Perspectives on Poverty," *Monthly Labor Review,* vol. 93, pp. 32–62, February, 1969. A series of five articles.

President's Economic Report (most recent year).

U.S. Bureau of the Census: *Current Population Reports,* Series P-60, *Consumer Income.* A series of reports containing the most recent data on the distribution of personal income.

FOR ANALYSIS AND DISCUSSION

1. Prof. Barbara Wootton has argued that the notion of functional "shares" of national income is not a very realistic one. In her book, *The Social Foundations of Wage Policy* (G. Allen, London, 1955), p. 174, she has said:

> The whole concept of an undifferentiated national income, subsequently divisible into the respective "shares" of labour, capital, and other "factors of production," which is the traditional mode of economic analysis, is highly artificial.... For wage questions are, in practice, not handled *in general;* the complete picture is the result, and mostly the undesigned and unintended result, of innumerable decisions scattered throughout the parts.... We have to realize that wage determinations are in fact made, and will continue to be made, at the level of the individual trade or profession.... In this matter it is not the whole which determines the parts; it is the parts which govern the whole.

This point of view seems to call into question any analytical usefulness to a breakdown of national income by wages, profits, interest, and so on. Can you see any value in aggregative data of this sort?

2. Why has there been so much interest over the years in income inequality? How far would you wish to push for an equalization of income, or at least for a leveling of peaks and a raising of the valleys of income? What positive and negative values do you associate with (*a*) absolute income equality, and (*b*) extreme disparities of income? What actions, if any, do you think ought to be taken to redistribute income?

3. Herman Miller of the Bureau of the Census has commented: "Standards of poverty are culturally determined. They can be arbitrarily defined for a given time and place. But they vary from time to place, and they differ from time to time in any one place." ("New Definition of Our 'Poor,'" *New York Times Magazine,* April 21, 1963, p. 11.)

How would you go about constructing a meaningful definition of what constitutes an "adequate" standard of living (*a*) as of the present, for the United States, and (*b*) over time, for the United States?

4. A few years ago a Midwest company manufacturing machine tools advertised:

If You Want Higher Wages, Make Sure of Higher Profits

The only essential difference between a starving coolie and a prosperous American workman with his own home and car is *tools*. The coolie actually works longer and harder, but *tools* let the American produce and enjoy more than fifty times as much.

The tools cost money.

The money to buy them comes out of corporations' profits.

No profits, no tools. No tools, no high wages for workers; the worker then can get paid only for his muscle, like the coolie. And higher profits are needed to pay the higher prices of better machines; only better and better machines can keep wages going up and up, for a man can be paid only out of what he produces.

To attack company profits is to say you want to be on a par with a coolie.

To promote company profits is to say you want continued prosperity.

Following the reasoning in this advertisement, would you conclude that the American economy would have been better off, over the last thirty or forty years, if the share of profits in the national income had increased, instead of the share of employee compensation (unadjusted for employment shifts)?

5. The previous chapter reported the findings of studies showing that unions have raised the wages of their members above the levels they would have attained without unions, but this chapter reports the findings of studies that show that unions have not increased the share of national income going to labor. Are these studies consistent with one another?

NOTES

1. Stanley Lebergott, "Factor Shares in the Long Term: Some Theoretical and Statistical Aspects," in *The Behavior of Income Shares, Selected Theoretical and Empirical Issues,* A Report of the National Bureau of Economic Research, Princeton University Press, Princeton, N.J., 1964, pp. 67–79.

2. Harold M. Levinson, *Unionism, Wage Trends, and Income Distribution,* 1914–1947, The University of Michigan Press, Ann Arbor, 1951, p. 96.

3. For a recent summary of other studies, see Bernard F. Haley, "Changes in the Distribution of Income in the United States," in Jean Marchal and

Bernard Ducros (eds.), *The Distribution of National Income,* Macmillan and St. Martin's, New York, 1968, pp. 21–28.

4. Lebergott, p. 83.

5. See the several papers in the National Bureau of Economic Research Report, *The Behavior of Income Shares,* and in Marchal and Ducros (eds.), *The Distribution of National Income.* The editors of the latter volume note (on p. xxvi) that a secular increase in labor's share does seem to appear in the data for several countries in recent years, including the United States, but this "was not usually regarded as a matter for explanation by [the] distribution models" debated at this international conference of economists concerned with income distribution. The major concern, that is, was in explaining the assumed constancy in the shares of labor and capital.

6. This is the conclusion of Walter S. Measday in "Labor's Share in the National Income," *Quarterly Review of Economics and Business,* vol. 2, p. 31, August, 1962, and substantially the view of Clark Kerr, in "Labor's Income Share and the Labor Movement," in G. W. Taylor and F. C. Pierson (eds.), *New Concepts in Wage Determination,* McGraw-Hill, New York, 1957, p. 296. Levinson, in the study cited in note 2, credits union bargaining power as having played some part in the increased share of labor in national income, but secondary to a number of other considerations. (*Unionism, Wage Trends, and Income Distribution, 1914–1947,* p. 109.)

Most statistical studies designed to test directly the question of whether unionized workers have been able to appropriate a larger share of their industry's total income than have unorganized workers have concluded in the negative. The statistical procedures, it is true, do not always invite confidence. A favorite procedure has been to divide industries into two large categories of those which were predominantly organized and those predominantly unorganized over a period of time (say from 1920 to 1960) and then to observe the relative movement of labor's share in both groups. This approach has been followed by Prof. Edward Budd in *Employment, Growth, and Price Levels,* Hearings, part 8, pp. 2519–2525, and Allan M. Cartter, *Theory of Wages and Employment,* Irwin, Homewood, Ill., 1959, pp. 167–170. The nonunion group evidently fares better than the unionized group in skimming off a higher proportion of income accruing to the industry. The difficulty with this approach, as the investigators themselves fully appreciate, is that it tells nothing about causation. There is no way of knowing whether the organized industries would have taken off a larger or a smaller share if they had been unorganized, and vice versa. A somewhat different procedure, followed by Norman Simler with generally similar findings, is not free of this difficulty either. (*The Impact of Unionism on Wage Income Ratios in the Manufacturing Sector of the Economy,* University of Minnesota, Minneapolis, 1961.)

Despite the inescapable inconclusiveness of these investigations, it is hard to dispute Cartter's cautious judgment (p. 171) that "trade unions have not in fact had an *observably* important effect on the income share going to labor in general, nor their share in the organized employment sectors."

7. Clark Kerr, *Papers and Proceedings of the 66th Annual Meeting, American Economic Association,* May, 1954, pp. 279–292, and in Taylor and Pierson (eds.), pp. 295–298.

8. See note 5 above.

9. Lebergott, p. 53. Original sources cited therein.

10. Marchal and Ducros (eds.), "Introduction," p. xv. Also see (in pp. 476–501 of the same source) M. Bronfenbrenner, "Neo-Classical Macro-Distribution Theory."

11. Marchal and Ducros (eds.), p. xviii. However, evidence suggesting that capital requirements per unit of output are declining in the United States has been provided by Bert G. Hickman in *Investment Demand and U.S. Economic Growth* (Brookings, Washington, 1965).

12. Marchal and Ducros (eds.), "Discussion," p. 611.

13. *Toward a Social Report,* U.S. Department of Health, Education, and Welfare, 1969, p. 42.

14. Haley, "Changes in the Distribution of Income in the United States," p. 6.

15. Simon Kuznets, *Shares of Upper Income Groups in Income and Savings,* National Bureau of Economic Research, New York, 1953.

16. For a detailed analysis of these and other reasons for the difference in income patterns before and after 1947, see Haley, pp. 6–21.

17. *Tax Burdens and Benefits of Government Expenditures by Income Class, 1961 and 1965,* Tax Foundation, Inc., New York, 1967, pp. 9–10.

18. Dorothy K. Newman, "Changing Attitudes About the Poor," *Monthly Labor Review,* vol. 93, p. 33, February, 1969.

19. On the one hand, see Allan Cartter, "Income Shares of Upper Income Groups in Great Britain and the United States," *American Economic Review,* vol. 44, pp. 875–883, 1954 (if undistributed earnings and corporate-profits taxes are imputed to the family income of stockholders, this erases most of the apparent decline from 1939 to 1948 in the share of the top 5 percent). On the other hand, see Selma F. Goldsmith et al., "Size Distribution of Income Since the Mid-Thirties," *Review of Economics and Statistics,* February, 1954, p. 20 (an allowance similar to Cartter's actually intensifies the loss in the share of the top 5 percent between 1929 and 1935–36, but then no further decline occurs between the mid-thirties and 1950); and Maurice Liebenberg and Jeannette M. Fitzwilliams, "Size Distribution of Personal Income, 1957–60," *Survey of Current Business,* May, 1961,

p. 14 (the addition of capital gains increases the share of the top 5 percent by less than a percentage point).

20. U.S. Bureau of the Census, *Current Population Reports,* Series P-60, no. 66, 1969, Tables 18 and 41.

21. Simon Kuznets, "Quantitative Aspects of the Economic Growth of Nations," *Economic Development and Cultural Change,* vol. 11, pp. 1–80, January, 1963. For other international comparisons, see Irving B. Kravis, "International Differences in the Distribution of Income," *Review of Economics and Statistics,* vol. 42, pp. 408–416, November, 1960; and John H. Chandler, "An International Comparison," *Monthly Labor Review,* vol. 93, pp. 55–62, February, 1969.

22. For a summary of the Bureau of Labor Statistics studies of hourly earnings since 1907, together with an exhaustive analysis of occupational differences in annual earnings between 1939 and 1960, see U.S. Bureau of the Census, *Income Distribution in the United States,* by Herman P. Miller (1960 Census Monograph), 1966, chaps. 3–5.

23. Melvin W. Reder, "The Theory of Occupational Wage Differentials," *American Economic Review,* vol. 45, pp. 833–852, 1955.

24. Other observers have argued that in periods of prosperity, when opportunities increase for workers to advance into jobs providing greater satisfaction, employers are forced to pay more to secure workers for the more disagreeable types of employment characteristic of unskilled labor.

25. Professor Reder inclines toward the former point of view, thus expecting a continued narrowing of rates, in "Wage Differentials: Theory and Measurement," *Aspects of Labor Economics,* National Bureau of Economic Research, Princeton University Press, Princeton, N.J., 1962, pp. 266–267. Taking the opposing view is Prof. Richard Perlman, in "Forces Widening Occupational Differentials," *Review of Economics and Statistics,* May, 1958, pp. 107–115.

26. Mollie Orshansky, "How Poverty Is Measured," *Monthly Labor Review,* vol. 93, p. 37, February, 1969.

27. The same, p. 38 (emphasis added). Other sources are cited in the original article. The Department of Agriculture describes its economy food plan as one designed for "emergency or temporary use when funds are low."

28. U.S. Bureau of the Census, *Current Population Reports,* Series P-60, no. 66, Tables 18 and 41.

29. *Economic Report of the President, 1969,* pp. 155–156.

30. The same, p. 153; and Mollie Orshansky, "The Shape of Poverty in 1966," *Social Security Bulletin,* March, 1968, p. 12.

31. Elizabeth Herzog, "Facts and Fictions About the Poor," *Monthly Labor Review,* vol. 93, excerpts from pp. 45–47, February, 1969.

32. U.S. Bureau of the Census, *Current Population Reports,* Series P-60, no. 66, p. 6.

PART SIX

LABOR AS A PRESSURE GROUP

"Organized labor" is organized for more than bargaining with employers; it is also organized for political action. As we noted in Chapter 6, although the making of demands on employers constituted the first concerted activity of workers in this country, it was only with the communitywide organization of workers (in Philadelphia, in 1827) that the labor movement can be said to have come into existence, and this community action was chiefly of a political nature. Neither the economic nor the political aspects of union activity have ever been wholly absent since that time. There has, however, been a continuing contest over the weight which should be accorded one or the other. In some reformist quarters, right down to the end of the last century the proper objective of organized worker activity was thought to be the overthrow of the very wages system which was the only rationale for collective bargaining. In the Perlman thesis, it was only when American unions learned the folly of the former philosophy and placed their bets on the latter that they achieved stability and made advances.

Labor's political action serves a number of purposes.

First, it may constitute a spearhead for institutional reform. As such it is expressive of a labor *movement*.

The view presented in Chapter 14 was that direct economic action by unions, through collective bargaining, represents the particular interests of separate groups, with the union acting as the *agent* of the affected employees. In some respects it may even be said to set workers against workers, since the economic gains of one strategic union may have to be paid for by weaker groups in the form of higher prices for goods and services. In contrast, the labor *movement* looks to institutional changes that transcend such specialized and temporary interests and that are concerned with longer-run social interests. Here unions perform something other than a pure agency function. This form of political activity—as a radical social movement, "radical" in the sense of seeking institutional modification—has been noticeably lacking in the United States.

Admittedly, this makes too sharp a distinction between the two forms of action.

Even in their *separatist* collective-bargaining activities unions can produce institutional reform. Collective bargaining itself can be said to be an institutional reform secured only through the labor movement. It may also be viewed as the instrument by means of which other social changes have been initiated and then spread through the economy. The recognition by employers of the union right to protest disciplinary actions and to obtain redress for inequitable treatment, for example, constituted a reform of major magnitude. But after we have recognized this important degree of coincidence between the two, it remains true that the emphasis on economic bargaining in a corporate bargaining unit has highlighted the specialized interests of particular groups of workers rather than any unitary interests which have to be sought in a larger political unit.

Managements have preferred to fight their battles with labor principally in the business rather than the political arena, since it is there that managements have greater experience and enjoy greater control in a social setting which they have largely helped to fashion. The unions, after their nineteenth-century spasmodic and quixotic efforts, have on the whole been content to follow management's preference—perhaps out of a necessity arising from what Perlman dubbed the "resistance power of capitalism." In conforming to management's preference for keeping the contest in the business rather than the political arena, unions have developed a leadership strain suited to this type of action. They have thus conformed to their environment, and in doing so have emphasized the separatist aspects of labor unions, the special interests of special groups.

A second function of organized political action by labor is to secure its own protection. We traced the story in Chapters 8 and 9 and need only remind ourselves here that unions have had to fight first for their legal existence and then for certain legal privileges, which not only managements in particular but also society in general were long reluctant to accord them. On this front the unions can act and have acted as a cohesive force, out of the need for self-preservation.

This is a different kind of political activity from the first (social movement) category. It is concerned only with the survival of unions as such, rather than with whether—survival once assured—they will operate principally on an economic or a political stage. Indeed, most efforts at securing union rights have been in terms of the economic (collective-bargaining) function which is attuned to the special interests of separate groups—a kind of "group individualism." In this category of political activity, the chief legislative landmarks—the Clayton Act, the Wagner Act, the Taft-Hartley Act, the Landrum-Griffin Act—have all dealt with union rights as such, with the privileges of unions as agents for workers in a contest with employers at their place of business. There was no thought of seizing social initiative, except possibly in a few minds for a few brief months in the depression years of 1937 to 1938.

Third, political action by organized labor may be directed toward immediate goals involving worker welfare, such as a law against garnishment of a worker's tools, or a minimum-wage law, or a more progressive income tax. Most of such measures can be viewed as protective of labor's interests within the existing institutional structure. Some minor modifications may be sought and achieved—a static social framework is not possible—but there is no thought of any radical transition to a new economic order.

It is the second and third types of political activity which have most characterized American unions in the twentieth century. Until the Depression of the thirties, there was even some reluctance to engage in the third category of efforts to gain protective legislation. As we shall see, some of the most influential labor leaders preferred a policy of noninvolvement with government except in self-defense. Since the thirties, there has been a marked change in this respect, and now organized labor makes an active political effort to secure specific pieces of legislation—in the federal, state, and local spheres—favorable to its members' interests. It has become an effective special-interest or pressure group among other special-interest groups. In the following chapter we shall explore its methods and accomplishments in this third category of political activity.

As we have seen, workers and their unions, on the one hand, and management, on the other hand, are motivated by aspirations having varying degrees of intensity and immediacy. The achievement of these aspirations depends on the bargaining power which can be mustered in support of them. Bargaining power is not something which must be taken as given but is an instrument which the individual or group can seek to manipulate to its advantage. It can do this by anything which increases its bargaining opponent's cost of disagreement on its terms or which lowers the cost of agreement. This calls for limiting the alternatives which are available to satisfy the other party (removing them or making them less desirable) or for increasing the desirability of the relationship which is being offered.

There are two spheres in which unions and managements operate to achieve their objectives —the private and the public. We have come to think of the private sphere as synonymous with economic relationships and the public sphere with political relationships.

Thus unions and managements seek their objectives both in the collective-bargaining relationship and through political action. As we shall see in later chapters, to some extent this has meant that the parties may pursue an objective by one of these routes and, on finding this gambit unsuccessful, may seek it by the other route with greater success. This tandem relationship was clearly described by the legal counsel for the Automobile Workers in a Supreme Court case involving union political activity.[1]

> For a hundred years, if Your Honors please, we have been engaged in political activity. Our own union Constitution, from its first day, urges it. One cannot draw a line between bargaining and politics. Bargaining is supplemented by legislation and legislation is supplemented by bargaining.
> Now, you cannot split legislation from bargaining. At the bargaining table we get Blue Cross and Blue Shield and at the Congress we ask for national health insurance to supplement it.
> In Congress we get unemployment compensation, and at the bargaining table we supplement it with supplementary unemployment payment. This is as one, what you have here, the bargaining and the legislative process.

Aspects of the political process

The political process itself can best be conceived as a bargaining procedure, with three distinct but related aspects. We shall be able to treat these here in only summary fashion.

The first has to do with the relationship between the special-interest group and the politician. The objective of labor and management in resorting to political activity is to influence the exercise of governmental power on their respective behalves. But since governments are composed of men, this requires, as a first step, an effort to place in office men who are favorably disposed to their specific causes. The familiar political slogan, "Reward our friends and defeat our enemies," given formal expression by the first AFL president, Samuel Gompers, has guided not only labor but management as well.

Politicians who are running for office are seeking votes. Unions and managements have, in varying degree, the power to supply votes—if not directly, then through the grant of money which the politician can spend in his campaign to win votes. Unions and managements—which we can identify as "interest groups"—are seeking the adoption of government policies favorable to their own interests. Politicians, once in office, have in varying degree the power to secure adoption of the policies sought by their supporters. Thus both the politician and the interest groups have something which the other wants. Consequently, they are placed in a kind of bargaining relationship in which the interest groups make their support of the politician conditional upon his favorable attitude toward them, and the politician makes his support of the interest groups conditional upon their backing him.

The interest groups may be concerned with the politician's attitude toward some specific piece of legislation or with his attitude toward their interests in general. The politician may be concerned with getting from union or management a public endorsement, or the leadership's active campaigning on his behalf, or a financial contribution, or all of these. The extent of the favors being sought will determine how much has to be offered to effect a political bargain.

The bargain effected between politician and interest group may take several forms. It can be explicit—a deal the terms of which are clearly understood by both parties. In exchange for the union's support, the politician agrees to introduce and work on behalf of this particular measure in which the union is interested. Such explicit bargains are probably much less common than is popularly supposed, however. More frequent are the implicit bargains, where the acceptance of a union's campaign help is "understood" to commit the politician to a favorable attitude with respect to labor's interest, or where a politician's adoption of views acceptable to management is "understood" to mean that management will support

him. Failure by either party to live up to such implicit commitments would be regarded as double-dealing by the other. Finally, there are the conjectural bargains, where neither politician nor interest group is sure of the other's support but believes that such support is likely to pay off. There is no commitment, either expressed or implied, by either party, but there is a relationship of faith.

The relationship between politician and interest group is, of course, much more complex than this simplified picture suggests. For one thing, unions and managements have interests broader than those involved in industrial relations. Management, for example, is likely to be concerned with tax policy, government attitude relative to the terms of government contracts, tariff policy, and so on. Unions are likely to be interested in full-employment measures, education and housing, extension of social security, and so on. To some extent, a politician may be expected to have a position acceptable to the interest group on the whole range of its concern, but this is by no means always the case. Where there is some divergence from the union line or the management line, then these groups must calculate whether they prefer to support a candidate who is "right" on certain issues but "wrong" on others or another potential candidate who has a different set of views.

Similarly, the politician is engaged in political bargaining not only with unions and managements but with a variety of other interest groups—professional societies, farmers, veterans, church groups, and so on. The views which he espouses to win the votes of one group—say labor—may lose him not only management votes but also the support of the American Legion and of farm constituents. He must therefore calculate what is likely to be the net effect, in terms of votes, of supporting an interest group like the unions or employers to the degree on which they are insisting as the price of a political bargain.

All this sounds very devious to most people, and the political process in the United States is usually regarded with cynicism and distaste. Nevertheless, it is hard to see how a representative political system could effectively function in any other way. Like the exercise of bargaining power in private economic life, it is not the use of bargaining power per se in political life that is to be condemned, but its use in ways which might be considered excessive. Most people would agree that groups have a right to use their votes and their campaign efforts to sway the views of those seeking office and that politicians have a right to expect the campaign support of those to whose cause they are friendly. But most people would also agree that bribery is out of place in political life. At what point, however, can one say that the gift of money as a campaign contribution passes beyond the bounds of legitimate support and enters into the realm of bribery? As in the case of the exercise of bargaining power in other aspects of social relationships, we attempt to define by law and social pressure the shadowy line demarking the acceptable from the unacceptable forms of political action. The attempt is never wholly successful, but it is all that we can do.

This skeletonized conception of the political process of vote getting is not intended to suggest that a politician is a man without scruples or ideals who will pick up votes wherever he can find them in greatest number by making the necessary concessions, offering his political powers when in office to that group which makes the highest bid. It is as true of politicians as of people in economic pursuits that they have their own ethical persuasions, their own convictions of the kind of society in which they would like to live and play their part. These convictions affect their readiness to accept the terms which interest groups offer them; like aspirations in all bargaining relationships, the politician's aspirations are one of two major determinants of the costs of agreeing and disagreeing on the other's terms. The other determinant, it will be recalled, is the alternatives which are available—what other groups can take the place of this one if its terms are refused.

We have said that there are three aspects to political bargaining, the first of which is the relationship between the interest group and the politician. But no politician can, *unaided*, make good on his bargains (and thus maintain faith with his supporters, an important consideration if he contemplates politics as a career). If he has been elected to an administrative office such as that of

mayor, governor, or president, he requires the support of a council or legislature to effect his aims and those of his constituents. If he has been elected to a council or legislature, he must have the support of fellow councilmen or legislators to translate his policies into law.

Since those with whom he must work can hardly be expected to share all his views, his ability to win government support for his constituents depends on his ability to win the support of enough of his fellow politicians for causes in which they may not be interested or to which they may even be opposed. At the same time, his fellow politicians are seeking his vote for measures in which they or their constituents are specially interested. There results, then, as can readily be expected, a series of attempted bargains, in which one may trade off support for another's projects in exchange for support of his own. Again, as in the relationship between interest group and politician, the terms of such bargains may be explicit, implicit, or conjectural.

This familiar process has been called logrolling and, like most elements of the political process, has been viewed with disfavor. But again it may be remarked that this process is an inescapable part of deciding most general issues as well as special-interest matters. The winning of the support of others to one's cause is the essence of the political art. Particularly when a legislative body is large, as in the two houses of Congress, and an issue is close, it can scarcely be expected that parties will refrain from seeking to manipulate the end result—to put together a majority favorable to their cause. We generally tend to regard the effort as shrewd and skillful if it succeeds in a matter to which we are favorably disposed, and as sinister and malignant if it wins out in a cause to which we are opposed. But as long as people have aspirations which mean anything to them and as long as they must rely on the support of others to achieve those aspirations, such bargaining will go on.

If the bargaining relationship between politician and interest groups constitutes one aspect of the political process and if the bargaining process that goes on among the politicians themselves constitutes a second phase of the process, there remains a third and equally important step. This is the bargaining relationship between the government and those to whom its actions apply.

To put the matter in another way, we may realistically view government as the source of a coercive power over others within the society, which by laws and orders may require conformance to policies which it has duly enacted. But such powers of government, as has been suggested here, are necessarily exercised by men who have made certain political bargains and alliances in order to win or remain in office and who seek to use the powers of government to fulfill their own aspirations (including their ethical convictions) as well as their political bargains. The exercise of governmental powers for such objectives must be expected, however, to run counter to the interests and aspirations (including the ethical persuasions) of others within the society, such as those whose candidates were defeated. The men in government are thus faced with the problem of how far they can go in implementing their own interests and convictions and those of their supporters without encountering a determined resistance from their opponents. Although the coercive powers of government are great, they are never—even in a totalitarian state—sufficient to overcome all opposition. Passive resistance and an underground rearguard action, open defiance of law or stealthy breaking of it, are always weapons available to a determined opposition. The United States provides one of the obvious examples of the effectiveness of such resistance in the case of its prohibition attempt during the interwar period. The slow pace of racial integration in the last decade or two—both North and South—is another.

If a law is to be effective, then, the cost of complying with its terms must be lower than the costs, such as fine or imprisonment, which the coercive powers of government can impose on those who refuse to accept it. Here the costs of agreement and disagreement on the terms of the law are measured by such things as the degree of personal sacrifice demanded, the intensity of moral beliefs, the enforceability of the law, the extent of the resistance, and so on. In the field of union–management relations, as in other fields, a law cannot be made wholly effective against the determined opposition of those whose interests are attacked. Thus, despite legal provisions against strikes by government employees, such strikes continue to occur. Thus, despite the provisions making it unlawful for an employer to interfere with his employees in their right to form a union, such interference is common in small Southern towns. A government is always faced with the question of how far it dare go in fulfilling the aims of those in office before it encounters an opposition which endangers any gains at all. This too is a kind of bargaining relationship, usually of the conjectural variety. There have, however, been times when explicit bargains have been made between the government and those to whom a law was intended to apply, to establish the terms which would prove on the one hand enforceable, and on the other hand acceptable. This has been particularly true in federal farm legislation, where proposed measures are sometimes submitted to a referendum of the farmers themselves for approval or rejection.

Labor's political activity

Within this conceptual framework let us consider the nature of the political activity of unions and managements.

The history of labor's political efforts prior to the New Deal administrations beginning in 1933 can be summarized very briefly. In the years when unions were first making their appearance in this country, workingmen's parties were organized on a city basis, campaigning for specific reforms such as protection of a worker's tools against seizure for debt, improved public education, and voting reforms. The high tide of such activity occurred in Philadelphia in 1829, when a workingmen's party won virtual control of the city government. But these local political forays were as ephemeral as the unions themselves in those early days.

In the second half of the century, government appeared to ally itself more and more with employer interests. Strikes were broken by political as well as judicial intervention. Temporary alliances between workers and farmers to stem the growing power of the "trusts," culminating in passage of the Sherman Antitrust Act in 1890, seemed to have relatively little effect. The Fourteenth Amendment to the Constitution was interpreted by the Supreme Court to immunize corporations, as legal persons, against effective government regulation, at the same time that the injunction was being used more and more repressively against the unions. To the radical reformers of a past era these events simply signaled the need for more active political effort. The year 1886 proved to be one of almost spectacular ferment at platform and poll. Local contests—the biggest being Henry George's labor-supported candidacy for the New York City mayoralty—evoked tremendous worker enthusiasm. A national movement for the 8-hour day took on the tenor of a revival campaign. It was as though bottled-up frustrations were exploding. But after they had burst forth, the results were indeed disheartening. The 8-hour movement proved a debacle. George was defeated. The Knights of Labor, deeply committed to political reformism, was further discredited.

It was in this climate of disillusionment that Samuel Gompers was confirmed in the rightness of the collective-bargaining approach of the craft unions, which he was championing in the newly formed AFL. He imposed on the rising new organization his own conviction that unions should rely on their own strength, seeking no favors from government or those in political office.

Unfortunately for labor, this one-way policy could not be made effective against the government, which continued to concern itself with labor's activities. The Sherman Act was applied against the unions, becoming a serious threat to their effective operation. In 1906 Samuel Gompers admitted that noninvolvement was a failure and urged upon the AFL the policy of rewarding labor's political friends and defeating its political enemies. The AFL departed from this nonpartisan position in only one election year, 1924, when it joined with the railroad brotherhoods in the third-party candidacy of Sen. Robert LaFollette. The dismal results of that venture only served to underscore the desirability of not linking labor's political activity to a chosen party, but of retaining the flexibility of choosing labor-oriented candidates from any (that is, either) party. This remains the official policy of the AFL-CIO.

Despite this change in attitude, the AFL adhered to a view that reliance on its own strength for the improvement of labor's conditions was preferable to reliance on a government whose purposes could not be trusted. Its political activity was primarily, though not exclusively, devoted to seeking removal of some of the legal disabilities which unions suffered. Its greatest triumph in this pre-1933 period was the inclusion in the 1914 Clayton Act, largely at its instigation, of sections designed to limit the application to unions of the Sherman Antitrust Act. The union's distrust of government was not diminished, however, by the fact that in less than five years the Supreme Court had so construed the Clayton Act as to render these sections virtually meaningless, reimposing on labor the restraining hand of the Sherman Act.

The independent railroad brotherhoods were somewhat more successful in their political bargaining during this period. In 1916 they secured, under the threat of a nationwide rail strike as the cost to Congress of disagreeing on their terms, an 8-hour day on the railroads. And in 1926 a Railway Labor Act was passed granting to the railroad unions rights of organization and representation which other unions had to wait another seven to nine years to obtain, ultimately securing them through the labor boards of the National Industrial Recovery Act and the National Labor Relations Act.

The labor movement generally was slow to follow the lead which the railroad unions provided, however. Still struggling under the tenet that the unions' own voluntaristic efforts were preferable to government welfare programs, the AFL was surprisingly lacking in enthusiastic support of the Wagner Act and the Social Security Act, both coming in 1935. It was the CIO, which broke away from the parent body in that year, that undertook the invigoration of labor's political activity. In 1936 under the guidance of John L. Lewis, who regarded campaign contributions as a quid pro quo for benefits to be received, the CIO made labor's first substantial contribution to a national political campaign with a gift of $770,000 to the Democratic National Committee. Since that time no campaign has taken place in which the labor movement has failed to play an active role.

In part, this slow adjustment to changed conditions by the AFL leadership in the period of the thirties was attributable to the fact that our society was itself in the process of modifying its thinking as to what kinds of activity are appropriate for a government to engage in. The old concept of government as a policeman, preserving order but not otherwise interfering in private affairs, had been shown to be untenable in the face of the deepest depression our country has ever known. But it was this philosophy of the government as constable that had in part turned the \AFL in the direction of voluntarism. Why weary oneself fighting to secure adoption of minimum-wage and maximum-hour laws, or child-labor laws, and so on, if these were only to be nullified by a Supreme Court who ruled them to be outside the government's sphere of interest? The new philosophy of the government as responsible for the people's welfare in circumstances where they could not be expected to provide for their own well-being made political efforts by the unions potentially more rewarding. But it took time for the potentialities to sink into the thinking of the old leadership.

Efforts have been made since that time, certainly with management's backing in this game of seeking to manipulate relative political bargaining powers to one's advantage, to restrict the unions' political action. Most of these limitations applied equally to managements, as in the case of the 1940 Hatch Act which put a ceiling of $5,000 on individual cash contributions to campaign funds and limited the total expenditures by any single campaign committee. (The result was simply a greater diversification of campaign activities, with numerous committees being set up by each party, each one capable of spending up to the legal limit.) The Smith-Connolly Act of 1943 went a good deal further by prohibiting altogether contributions by labor unions to candidates in national elections. It said nothing about contributions to the funds of candidates seeking *nomination,* however, leading to the pattern of labor political-action committees' collecting funds from the unions to attempt to swing the nomination of friendly candidates, and then—in compliance with the law—collecting smaller contributions directly from union members to be used in the election campaigns. Nor did the law prohibit direct political expenditures by the unions themselves, in contrast to contributions to candidates. That is, a union could legally buy newspaper space to

endorse a candidate, but it could not give union funds to the candidate himself.

Political expenditures as well as contributions by unions, not only in elections but also in primaries and conventions involving federal offices, were then prohibited in 1947 in the Taft-Hartley Act, matching a similar prohibition on corporate contributions. Some states have followed the national law with legislation applying to state elections and primaries. As yet, however, none of these laws affects the right of an organization, established by labor but not functioning as a union, to collect voluntary contributions directly from union members and the public, usually in small sums, most commonly $1 per person. Under the CIO, the Political Action Committee (PAC) performed this function; for the AFL it was Labor's League for Political Education (LLPE). In the merged AFL-CIO, the Committee on Political Education (COPE) has replaced the former two.

The Supreme Court has also ruled that direct expenditures in the form of political advocacy in regular union publications are permissible, hinting that any ban on such activity would probably run afoul of the First Amendment's free-speech guarantee.[2] Moreover, the federal law does not apply to any except federal elections, leaving union expenditures for local campaigns unaffected in the absence of state laws, and it also does not touch the lobbying activities of unions on behalf of specific pieces of legislation.

This problem of labor's political spending raises again the difficult issue of balancing majority and minority rights, much as the right-to-work debate does. On the one hand, there is the view that unions are primarily instruments for bargaining with employers and it is repugnant to democratic ideals to allow union officials to spend members' dues (particularly when collected under the duress of a union-security clause) in support of political causes and candidates that some members oppose. On the other hand, it is argued that the activities of federal, state, and local governments have as much impact as collective bargaining, if not more, on the welfare of workers and, so long as a majority of a union's members want their leaders to support a particular cause or candidate, the minority should go along as in any democratic organization.

A compromise of great appeal is the British practice of "contracting out," that is, having each union label the portion of its dues to be used for political purposes rather than for negotiating and administering the contract, and then permitting any member who so wishes to pay only the "bargaining fee" and to exempt himself (to "contract out") from paying the political assessment by some formal notification to the union. In fact, the Supreme Court has come close to deciding that this type of system is all that is allowable in this country. In a 1961 case involving six workers covered by the Railway Labor Act, the Court ruled that if a worker is compelled by a union-shop contract to pay dues and if he objects to the nature of his union's political spending, he may file a formal protest which will entitle him to a refund of the "political" portion of his dues.[3]

But however funds are or should be raised, how do unions actually operate in the field of politics? In several ways. In election years, for example, union officials confer with the leadership of the two political parties on the acceptability of potential candidates and on the desirability of certain provisions in the party's platform. Although for more than three decades the top leadership of the labor movement has been found in the Democratic camp, there are always certain influential union chiefs who serve as Republican labor advisers.

The union's influence on party decisions stems from the belief that labor's endorsement will mean additional votes. The bargaining goes on over what concessions must be made by the party to win the union's approbation and support. This support largely takes the form of (1) getting out the vote—making sure that all union members are registered and that they get to the polls on election day; (2) political education, in the form of identifying labor's friends and enemies; and (3) various forms of campaigning, including the dissemination of pamphlets, sponsorship of radio and television programs, conduct of public rallies, and so on.

Between elections, labor continues its political bargaining by lobbying on behalf of specific measures. At both the state and federal levels, for example, the AFL-CIO has legislative representatives to keep an eye on the measures which labor backs

and opposes. At critical times, pressures on congressmen may be mobilized through constituent unions.

How effective is labor's political action?

In recent years the question has been repeatedly asked, What influence do the unions really have on the voting of their members? If their bargaining power with the parties rests primarily on the influence which they have with their memberships, can they in fact "deliver the vote"?

Particularly since the 1950 election in Ohio, when Sen. Robert Taft, coauthor of the Taft-Hartley Act, won by an immense majority despite the active opposition of the unions in that highly unionized state, it has frequently been argued that there is no such thing as a "labor vote," that union members will not be bound by any ties with political parties which are effected by their officials, and hence that the political parties may very well ignore the unions without suffering any significant penalty. Others, a little more cautious, agree that the ability of union leaders to influence their members' voting has perhaps been overrated in the past but nevertheless does have its effect. What can be said about this issue?

The matter can be approached through a series of propositions.

1. Union members have more or less common economic aspirations but also a multiplicity of other values. Among the 18 million members in the labor movement in the United States can be found all forms of religion, a variety of views with respect to this country's proper role in world affairs, differing sectional interests, conflicting ideas of the proper spheres of government, and so on. But their economic aims are largely the same.

2. In times when their economic aims are being met reasonably well, they can afford to allow their other prejudices and interests to have political expression. They may well ignore the candidate whom their union has endorsed because he happens to be a Catholic and they are Protestant, or because he favors the United Nations and they are isolationist, or because he is for integration

and they are for segregation, or because their brother-in-law is working for the other party's candidate and they'll do him a favor, or just because they don't like his looks. Thus the votes of union members are dispersed rather than concentrated.

3. At times when their economic interests appear to be threatened, however, particularly in time of spreading unemployment, then economic interests dominate other interests, and they coalesce politically. This can happen too if there is a prevalent enough belief among workers that they are sharing considerably less than proportionately in the benefits of a period of sustained prosperity. At such times, there is a tendency for union votes to be concentrated on their common economic interest, rather than dispersed on their other multiple values.

4. Some party will usually appeal for the labor vote by promising to support its interests. In times of relative adversity, it is this party that will be the recipient of the bloc of worker (not just union) votes. In times of prosperity, it is likely to gain a considerable portion of worker votes, but by no means can it count on a worker vote solid enough to ensure election. In recent times this role of labor's supporter has been played by the Democratic party.

5. Under such circumstances the influence of union leaders lies (a) in focusing the members' interest and intent, (b) in arousing their enthusiasm, and (c) in making sure that they vote. The union leaders do not control their members' votes and, except in times of stress, they are only one of a number of influences determining how member votes are cast—not an insignificant influence, but nevertheless only one influence to be laid alongside many others. But in times of economic adversity, as so interpreted by workers generally, union leaders can effectively marshal the vote. They do deliver it not in the sense of controlling it but in the sense that they see that it is counted. They can rely on their members' common economic interest and perception to ensure that their votes are cast the "right" way.

These propositions are stated categorically for purposes of clarity. Actually, even in economic matters workers do not think and feel politically as one. To the extent that unemployment and poverty are concentrated in certain classes, industries, or geographical sectors, this lessens the *general* impact of economic adversity and may disperse labor's vote. There is, however, greater unity of outlook in this area than in most others, so that the statements made can be looked upon as having a high degree of probability.

This approach is somewhat similar to the motivational approach underlying economic-indifference analysis, namely, that which is least satisfied is most stressed. The economic interest dominates a worker's political thinking when he becomes relatively more unhappy about it than about other interests. It is then that his union, his economic agent, mobilizes his sentiment and makes him politically more effective than he would be without the union. In more prosperous times, he can afford the luxury of voting for a candidate who is personally more attractive than another or who appeals to him on some noneconomic issue.

One corollary of the above line of reasoning is that the surest antidote to a cohesive labor vote is a prosperous economy. In the congressional elections of 1966, for example, only 52 percent of the candidates endorsed by the AFL-CIO won election, compared to 65 percent in the recession year of 1962. For those fascinated by the shifting sands of politics, the following analysis of the 1966 vote, written one week after the election, makes interesting reading today:

When, as now, prosperity is general and there is no specific labor issue, unionists have shown that they are more responsive to voices other than their leaders'. Last week, all over the country, analysis of the votes showed that they reacted more for moderation in civil rights—as householders who didn't want a Negro next door—or out of vague dissatisfaction over Vietnam [an issue on which the AFL-CIO strongly backed President Johnson] and other Administration policies, or as taxpayers concerned over rising taxes and spending, or as consumers irritated by rising prices. . . .

In California, unions endorsed Pat Brown for governor, but shop stewards worked hard for eventual winner Ronald Reagan. . . . In Michigan, UAW spokesmen conceded privately that they had little hope of beating Governor George Romney [who easily won reelection]. . . .

In Illinois, Republican Charles Percy got labor votes in industrial areas that are normally strongly Democratic. . . . Even more unexpected were the labor votes that helped in the House victory of Robert Taft, Jr. . . .

For all the effort, labor can count only one real victory over the [civil rights] backlash. In the Maryland gubernatorial race, with harsh civil rights overtones, labor supported and helped elect a liberal Republican, Spiro T. Agnew.[4]

Political influence

But there is more to the story than this. We earlier noted that the political process is composed of a network of bargains. The capacity of labor unions to deliver the vote, even in the limited sense suggested above, is not a measure of their political influence. While politicians and parties may be mindful of their commitments to union sympathizers and supporters and even attempt to support their special interests, the bargaining process, as we know, continues within a city council or a state legislature or the United States Congress. A majority must be put together in order to secure the actions which an interest group seeks, whether it be labor or business.

It is the uncertainty of how this legislative and administrative process will turn out which renders suspect any sweeping judgments as to the degree of political power residing in particular segments of the community. The 1958 congressional elections are instructive in this respect. Less than a month before they occurred, the chairman of the board of General Electric asserted that the AFL-CIO constituted the "most aggressive and successful force in politics." He spoke of their influence in the preceding session of Congress. "No bill was passed that they opposed," he said. "But now they seek—and most observers seem to believe they will gain in the coming election—the added eleven Senators and forty-one Representatives that will give the union officials an absolute majority and the power to pass or repeal legislation at will."[5]

The voting trend in 1958 was as this business spokesman had anticipated, and the new Congress reassembled with a larger proportion of labor-backed Democratic congressmen and senators. We may assume that the sharp rise in unemployment

that year coalesced the labor vote along the lines we have just analyzed. Immediately following the election, an outstanding analyst of the contemporary labor scene commented as follows, in a private gathering:

. . . [W]hat is labor going to do in terms of government policy as a result of the substantial number of people who owe their election to labor's organizational support? My own guess is that the incoming Congress will not give labor a great deal. As a matter of fact, that seemed to me rather apparent when the Federation got around to holding its first Executive Council meeting after the election. It seemed to me that labor didn't have any very clearly defined goals. At the first council meeting, of course, the immediate announcement was that labor would expect repeal of 14(b) of Taft-Hartley, would knock out right-to-work laws, and that labor would like to see something along the lines of the Kennedy-Ives bill, or perhaps a somewhat less potent version of that bill. Reuther pointed out that labor ought to have some kind of affirmative program, and so at this point they reached into the bottom drawer and came out with a rather tired old program: for expanded housing, expanded education, higher minimum wages. It was clear that there had been a dearth of original thinking of what labor would do with its victory in the event that it won. . . .

This prediction was more than justified. Not only was labor without an affirmative program to press for; ironically, in the light of the previous business warning as to labor's forthcoming political omnipotence, it was unable not only to secure amendment to the Taft-Hartley Act but even to prevent passage of the Landrum-Griffin Act, causing union spokesmen to comment bitterly that they could not afford many more such election successes. A UAW resolution in the convention of 1959 stated: "The Democratic victories in November 1958 were turned into Republican victories in 1959 on one vital bill after another through the clever use of negative Presidential vetoes and sharp revival of the Dixie-GOP coalition." The same resolution went on to explain, in an effort to save something from the ruins of the previous year's hopes, that most Northern Democrats whom the unions had supported had remained loyal to their supporters and had voted against the Landrum-Griffin measure, and that only the solid Southern Democrat–Republican combination had managed to put across the hated bill. But this only underscores the tenuousness of imputing some monolithic political power to either labor or business simply by assigning this senator or that congressman to one camp or the other, on one basis or another, and then tallying the score. There remains the hard and uncertain task of putting together a legislative majority on any given issue, usually with administration support, and that is a process scarcely susceptible to statistical prediction.

The irony of the 1958 elections was completed by labor's raising scare warnings—comparable to those of the GE spokesman—that "big business" was mobilizing its manpower and money to ensure control of the 1960 results. "If the people's interest is not to face a severe defeat in 1960, organized labor and its liberal allies must organize themselves better than ever. . . ."[6]

Party alignments

The political process in the United States has customarily operated through a two-party system. Third parties have made their appearance in many elections, it is true, but usually as protest votes rather than as responsible political organizations with any expectation of victory or continuity. Because neither party in such a system can hope for success unless it appeals to a general constituency, we have never developed in this country parties that have been identified as labor- or business-dominated. Nevertheless, it is true that in recent years the Democratic party has been regarded as more congenial to labor's interests and the Republican party to business interests. Despite such alignments we cannot regard these in any sense as "class parties," since they must appeal to broad constituencies if they are to win any election, as both parties have continued to do. More than the parties developing class orientations, the interest groups (workers and business) have developed party orientations.

Richard Centers, in his interesting study *Psychology of Social Classes,* found that business and professional people were oriented toward the Republican party, that small business was almost evenly split between the two parties, and that workers were oriented toward the Democratic party. Worker orientation was strongest in the manual group (perhaps 60 percent Democratic to 25 percent Republican), but even white-collar workers showed this disposition (50 percent Democratic to 35 percent Republican).[7] Similarly, Professor Newcomer, in surveying the characteristics of top management (presidents and board charimen) of 428 of America's largest corporations in utilities, railroads, and industry, found that 76 percent considered themselves Republican (as opposed to 20 percent Democratic).[8] Other studies have confirmed these political alignments of unions and workers, on the one hand, and business and managements, on the other.[9]

While some have expressed concern at this development as suggesting class cleavage,[10] there appears to be little cause for alarm. As long as we continue to operate within the framework of a two-party system, each of the parties must seek a broad support, which means eschewing extreme positions. The independent vote acts as an important, moderating force in this regard. Experience has shown that in periods of prosperity people can be induced to cross party lines, and at any time there are always some "liberal" Republicans who attract many labor votes—such as President Eisenhower, Governor Nelson Rockefeller, and Mayor John Lindsay—and some "conservative" Democrats who attract many nonlabor votes, such as Senator Frank Lausche, Governor George Wallace, and Mayor Richard Daley. Also, new issues come along—the war in Vietnam, racial integration, law and order—on which interests are split on lines other than manualist–nonmanualist. The cleavages are shifting. As long as issues of comparative economic welfare are not persistently dominant, as long as we can make use of our improved knowledge of economic processes to maintain a state of continuing or increasing prosperity, we need not worry about the rigidification of political life along class lines.

Further, despite the public pronouncements of officials of unions which are primarily oriented toward national product markets, union officialdom is by no means single-minded in its political loyalties. Those officials who are predominantly oriented to local markets have often learned to make peace with whatever party is in local office in order to ensure the continuity of policies and favors which are important to their members. The building-trades locals in particular are often quite apolitical as long as their interest in zoning ordinances and building codes is recognized by both parties. They are unlikely to jeopardize a good local working relationship with the Republican party, for example, by encouraging their membership to vote a national Democratic ticket simply because of its "official" labor endorsement.

A labor party?

What, then, of a labor party? This question is raised whenever labor's political role is discussed. This too is a matter of shifting outlook. Whenever unions feel that they are being treated too cavalierly by the existing political parties, and particularly by the one in which they feel most at home, the specter of a third (labor) party is raised to frighten the politicians. It is designed to increase their cost of disagreement on the unions' political terms.

It may be that at some future time a labor party will come into existence. It appears that there is a lingering sentiment among some workers that leads them to harbor such a hope, in the same way that some people continue to dream that someday they will go into business for themselves. But among most union leaders in recent years, the sentiment has been against independent political activity by labor. Even so militant a unionist as the late Walter Reuther, who once identified himself with the labor-party adherents, later set his face in the other direction and maintained that such a course would be folly.

The leadership is aware of the difficulties that independent political action would bring it. First, union officials realize that they cannot deliver the vote in the sense of controlling it. Hence, in times of prosperity, when the union membership exercises its prerogative of voting for a Democrat or a Republican, the infant labor party would suffer a loss of prestige that might be fatal. Even in times of adversity, there might be greater confidence of the union members in an old and experienced political party, like the Democratic, which, even if not supporting their interests as vigorously as the leadership would like, would give greater promise of winning the election and hence of doing *something* about labor's demands.

Second, the leadership is aware of the common fate of third parties in the United States. The older parties, or one of them, adopt the new party's platform, so that the reason for its existence withers away. Again, there would be a loss of prestige from which it would suffer in future political bargaining. Third, for any party in the United States to be successful requires a broad base. It must appeal to the independent vote if it is to win. But this would weaken the partisanship which would be a labor party's principal reason for existence.

Fourth, there is a danger that union leaders would be diverted from their job at the collective-bargaining table, where they have made their greatest gains. Their energies would be drawn off into political activities, to the detriment of their economic program in negotiations with employers. Fifth, there is the persistent question of whether they could not gain almost as much and perhaps more, and escape all the cited difficulties, by acting as an effective pressure group within one of the established political parties.

The net effect of these considerations is to create a situation in which the labor unions are quite unlikely to instigate an independent labor party, unless so rebuffed in their political bargaining by both major parties that they have no other alternative. At the moment, this appears unlikely.

Recent trends and attitudes

Two postwar developments within organized labor deserve particular mention. The first is the rapid growth of unionism among government employees who do not have the legal right to strike. It is true that in New York City many groups of government workers have struck in recent years, as have postal workers, teachers, and some other public employees across the country, but *most* unions of federal, state, and local government employees have observed the ban on strikes in the public sector. How, then, do these unions bargain over economic issues with employers that are political bodies—without the economic weapon of the strike? At the beginning of this chapter, we stressed the difference between collective bargaining and political action as channels through which most unions and employers seek their objectives, but what happens when these channels merge into one and the same process in the public sector?

Unfortunately, few people other than the participants really know. We have many studies of the bargaining process in private industry but almost none analyzing that process in the public sector. Unions in that sector often engage in vigorous lobbying with legislators, of course, and indeed that is the only way most unions at the federal level can influence the pay scale of their members (which is set by congressional statute), but is that collective bargaining? And in "labor towns" like New York City, there are often dark hints that bargaining simply consists of back-room deals in which the mayor promises fat wage increases to city workers in return for their support at the polls. Some of this undoubtedly does occur, but it is likely that the process more often involves an honest manipulation of bargaining power (in political form) in a way similar to that described at the outset of this chapter, with wages and other contract issues at stake instead of the usual objects of political action.

A second postwar development of significance is the emergence of the average union worker as a solid member of the middle class. In January, 1967, for example, 46 percent of union families reported that their incomes ranged from $7,500 to $15,000 a year, and another 32 percent were in the range of $5,000 to $7,500 a year. Also, nearly 50 percent of all union members then lived in the suburbs (and nearly 75 percent of the members under forty years of age), and one-half of all members rated television as their most reliable source of information.[11] Can these workers be much interested in the political goals of union leaders, many of whom are still echoing the war cries of the New Deal days?

Figure 20-1 shows that most members are indeed still interested in the "liberal" political goals of their unions, though with some interesting variations. (Although the data in Figure 20-1 were collected by a poll commissioned by the AFL-CIO, the poll itself was conducted by a reputable and independent organization and is as accurate as most opinion surveys.) It is evident that most union members support by a wide margin most of the major legislative goals of organized labor in recent years, with the two ex-

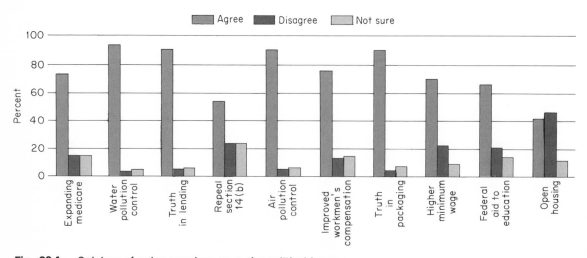

Fig. 20-1. *Opinions of union members on major political issues.*

SOURCE: *Alexander E. Barkan, "The Union Member: Profile and Attitudes," The American Federationist, August, 1967, p. 4.*

ceptions of right-to-work laws (only 54 percent favoring repeal of section 14(b) of Taft-Hartley) and open housing (only 43 percent in favor, with 46 percent opposed). Most members also favored the reelection of President Johnson at that time, before he withdrew from the race.

Members polled were [also] asked this question: "What are the big problems on your mind —the things that bother you and should be getting attention?" The issues clearly uppermost in their minds were those involving jobs and economic security, the war in Vietnam, and civil rights.

Fifty-three percent of all members listed economic problems ranging from the cost of living and taxes to the employment picture and wages. Forty-two percent listed the war in Vietnam, with the largest percentage of these supporting the President's policies there. More than 33 percent listed civil rights as a major issue. While most members supported civil rights progress in voting and public accommodations, support for open housing was slightly below the 50 percent point. . . .

Finally . . . [the pollsters] found that suburban living naturally has directed members' attention to suburban problems, often in higher priority than national issues. Members in the suburbs share their neighbors' concern about local tax assessments, zoning, sewage and garbage disposal, street repairs, transportation and school bond issues. It is not that they change from liberal Jekylls to conservative Hydes the moment they cross the city line into the suburbs; it is that in many cases their roster of interests is shuffled and becomes more locally oriented.[12]

The AFL-CIO spokesman quoted above naturally found the results of this poll encouraging, although admitting that support was generally weakest among the younger members who are forming a growing proportion of the union movement. (As he also pointed out, however, labor is not the only institution having trouble in satisfying its younger members these days.)

The results also make sense in several ways. After all, the median income of all families in 1967 was $7,800, so that in a relative sense (often the most meaningful, for these purposes) most union members were still not in a position to stop worrying about economic security. The union member who expects to send his children to college today may feel almost as strongly about the need for federal aid to education as the laborers of the early 1800s felt about the need for public schools. Also, other studies have shown that individuals at the very bottom of the income ladder are seldom active political radicals but instead exhibit political inertia and indifference, feeling they can have little influence over life or governments. It is therefore often the workers with more income, education, and information who are more active politically in pursuit of their interests.[13]

On the other hand, opinion surveys of a single group are always difficult to interpret in the absence of some control group. It is hard to imagine, for instance, that most corporation executives in 1967 were not also concerned with the cost of living, taxes, Vietnam, and civil rights—and who in America is not in favor, at least in principle, of controlling water and air pollution? Also, one can seldom judge the relative intensity of feeling about an array of issues in an opinion survey, or predict a person's actions from his responses to such a poll. In fact, note that this poll was taken only two months after the 1966 congressional elections described above, in which many union members voted "wrong" from the AFL-CIO's viewpoint.

Thus, the poll results shown in Figure 19-1 are valuable for indicating that most union members, in spite of their present affluence, continue to support most of the political goals of organized labor. But this poll does not invalidate our previous conclusion that when the union member steps in a voting booth, he can be as unpredictable as any other American voter—and, ironically, he is most unpredictable when the economy has achieved the very prosperity sought by many of labor's political programs.

Conclusion

Let us return to the point of our departure. Unions and managements live in a world where economic and political activity have their mutual effect upon the industrial relationship. Each operates in both these spheres; each seeks to manipulate economic and political processes to improve its own bargaining power in the achievement of its goals. The political bargaining leads to the passage of laws and the administration of agencies which help to create the socioeconomic climate within which the private collective-bargaining relationship takes place. Political bargaining is also a means of achieving certain objectives which cannot be attained through the private relationship. There are, indeed, some who believe that, in time, more and more of the important issues now confronting unions and managements will be transferred from the private economic-bargaining sphere to the realm of public political bargaining. Whether or not this proves to be true, there can be no doubt of the importance to both parties of these two major fields of action.

ADDITIONAL READINGS

Bakke, E. Wight, Clark Kerr, and Charles Anrod: *Unions, Management, and the Public,* Harcourt, Brace & World, New York, 1960, chap. 8.

Chamberlain, Neil W.: *Sourcebook on Labor,* McGraw-Hill, New York, 1958, chap. 6.

Heard, Alexander: *The Costs of Democracy,* The University of North Carolina Press, Chapel Hill, 1960, especially chap. 7.

Kornhauser, Arthur, Albert J. Mayer, and Harold L. Sheppard: *When Labor Votes,* University Books, New York, 1956.

Rehmus, Charles M., and Doris B. McLaughlin (eds.): *Labor and American Politics, A Book of Readings,* The University of Michigan Press, Ann Arbor, 1967.

Seidman, Joel, Jack London, Bernard Karsh, and Daisy L. Tagliacozzo: *The Worker Views His Union,* The University of Chicago Press, Chicago, 1958, chap. 10.

FOR ANALYSIS AND DISCUSSION

1. A fear of union political activity is often expressed. What is the basis of that fear? Is there any justification for it?

2. Two conflicting points of view as to the politicoeconomic role of unions have been expressed:

a. Unions, as powerful social agents, must engage in broader economic planning and assume greater responsibility for social blueprinting. As worker organizations acquire power, they assume commensurate responsibilities. It is not enough for them simply to accommodate themselves to other forces in society; they themselves should be a force in the achievement of more clearly defined social goals. Labor groups cannot marshal their power for wage gains, fringe benefits, better housing, and so forth, without assuming the responsibility for determining where such programs fit into the larger framework. Asking unions to take responsibility for inflationary controls is, for example, really a comment that unions should restrain their bargaining strength in the light of certain, more broadly conceived social objectives. It is to a more explicit identification of such objectives that unions should pay more attention.

b. Any such approach as that suggested in (*a*) will more sharply define class interests and draw ideological lines. The strength of American society is in its freedom from rigid social groupings, carried over into political life. If unions simply act as one pressure group among other pressure groups, in a way that does not conflict sharply with public interests, then they can achieve most of their objectives without assuming larger responsibilities. Pragmatic and piecemeal change is more characteristic of the American scene than is more comprehensive social planning; the unions will do well to continue an approach which is congenial to American political philosophy. It may be less dramatic, but in arousing less opposition it is almost sure to be more rewarding to those who follow it.

Which of these two approaches would you prefer that the American labor movement follow? Which do you think would be better for unionists?

3. Which group—labor or management—is politically the more active and influential? Marshal as much evidence as possible in support of your view.

4. In a study of Teamsters Local 688, St. Louis, Missouri, Prof. Arnold Rose of the University of Minnesota came up with the indications, shown in Table 20-1, of the type of political action favored by union members.

Recognizing that this is only one small bit of evidence, would you take the above results as

Table 20-1

Question	Percentage of members				
	Saying "yes"	Saying "no"	Saying "don't know"	Giving no answer	Total*
Should the union engage in politics in any of the followings ways:					
Tell members which candidates are friendly to labor	77.3	20.4		2.3	100.0
Advise members how to vote	35.0	62.2		2.8	100.0
Help to start a Labor party sometime in the future	44.9	44.4	1.3	9.4	100.0
Get union members to run for political office	69.1	25.3		5.6	100.0
Encourage union members to go to the polls	92.1	5.1		2.8	100.0
Collect a dollar from each union member to help friendly candidates	53.7	40.6		5.7	100.0
Spend union funds to get laws friendly to labor	71.7	23.5	0.2	4.6	100.0

* The number of cases in each total is 392—the total sample.

SOURCE: A. Rose, *Union Solidarity*, The University of Minnesota Press, Minneapolis, 1952, p. 84.

suggesting—however tenuously—that there is a "labor vote"? Why, or why not?

5. If workers constitute the interest group which encompasses the largest proportion of the total population, why would not candidates who are willing to make the greatest concessions to labor invariably win?

6. The following is Recommendation no. 2 of the President's Commission on Campaign Costs, chaired by Prof. Alexander Heard of the University of North Carolina, submitted in April, 1962:

Tax Incentives for Contributors

In 1960, $8,200,000,000 were donated in the United States in voluntary contributions for charitable, health, welfare, religious, and educational purposes. These contributions were deductible for income tax purposes.

In the same year, the total spent for all nomination and election activities, at all political levels, approximated $165,000,000 or $175,000,000. This sum was supplied by about 10,000,000 givers. These contributors should be encouraged to give more to political campaigns, and others should be encouraged to join them, by providing tax benefits that recognize the propriety and importance of political giving.

Our recommendations of tax incentives for political contributions take two forms: a credit against tax due or a deduction from taxable income. We recommend these tax incentives because of the administrative complexities in-herent in combining the two. Our purpose is to encourage taxpayers to give as much or as little as they want to the recipients of their choice. No payment would be made to the taxpayer, should the tax due be less than the credit claimed.

As a credit, we propose one-half of the total contributions to specified committees up to a maximum credit of $10 per year. (A husband and wife filing a joint return could claim up to $20.) As an alternative, we recommend deduction of contributions to such committees up to a maximum total deduction of $1,000 per year per tax return.

The recommended credit is intended to encourage large numbers of small gifts. The bulk of Presidential campaign funds available to both parties is now supplied by a relatively small group of contributors giving sums ranging from a few hundred to several thousands of dollars. We are recommending, however, that no deduction be granted for contributions above $1,000 per return. We hope that this incentive to medium-sized gifts, coupled with the incentive to small gifts, will stimulate the massive giving needed by the parties. If it does not, other forms of governmental subsidy may be inevitable.

Comment on the desirability of the above proposal from the viewpoint of (*a*) a disinterested member of the public, (*b*) a union official, and (*c*) the president of a major corporation.

NOTES

1. Pages 82 and 84 of the official transcript in *U.S. v. UAW,* 352 U.S. 567 (1957), cited in John F. Lane, "Political Expenditures by Labor Unions," *Labor Law Journal,* October, 1958, p. 725.

2. *U.S. v. Congress of Industrial Organizations,* 335 U.S. 106 (1948).

3. *International Association of Machinists v. Street,* 367 U.S. 740 (1961). Also see *Brotherhood of Railway Clerks v. Allen,* 373 U.S. 113 (1963).

4. "Unions Fail to Deliver the Goods," *Business Week*, Nov. 19, 1966, pp. 103 and 106.

5. Ralph J. Cordiner, as reported in the *New York Times,* Oct. 19, 1958.

6. UAW Resolution no. 31, 1959 convention.

7. Richard Centers, *Psychology of Social Classes,* Princeton University Press, Princeton, N.J., 1949, chap. 5.

8. Mabel Newcomer, *The Big Business Executive,* Columbia University Press, New York, 1955, p. 49.

9. In what is perhaps the most intensive examination of union efforts in a presidential election (*When Labor Votes,* University Books, New York, 1956), Profs. Arthur Kornhauser, Albert J. Mayer, and Harold L. Sheppard found that a sample of UAW members resident in Detroit were 67 percent Democratic against 7 percent Republican. The University of Michigan Survey Research Center likewise found a strong business orientation toward the Republican party, with workers leaning toward the Democratic party. (Angus Campbell, G. Gurin, and W. E. Miller, *The Voter Decides,* Harper, New York, 1954.)

10. Thus Centers remarks (*Psychology of Social Classes,* p. 66):

> There exists some fairly convincing evidence in the data obtained from this survey that the political alignments of our population are shifting steadily in a direction of cleavage along stratification lines.... The suggestion is that in the future more and more manual workers will align themselves with a liberal party—as the Democratic Party has sometimes been —and more and more of non-manual persons will cling to the conservative views of such a party as the Republicans.

11. Alexander E. Barkan, "The Union Member: Profile and Attitudes," *The American Federationist,* August, 1967, pp. 1 and 5.

12. The same, pp. 3–4.

13. Kornhauser, Mayer, and Sheppard, "When Labor Votes," in Rehmus and McLaughlin (eds.), *Labor and American Politics, A Book of Readings,* The University of Michigan Press, Ann Arbor, 1967, pp. 413–415.

PART SEVEN

LABOR AS THE SUBJECT
OF SOCIAL PROTECTION

The emergence of the "welfare state" in this country is a fascinating story of battles fought against overwhelming odds in the courts and legislatures and sometimes the streets of the nation, the eventual triumph of ideas once branded as revolutionary—and the morning-after feeling that somewhere something went wrong. For today we have attained nearly every policy goal of the liberals of the 1930s, together with an economy performing beyond the wildest dreams of yesterday's conservatives, and yet our domestic problems seem to persist and even multiply.

But in our preoccupation with how far we now must travel to meet almost anyone's definition of a "just society," it is easy to forget how far we have already come. It was only thirty-five or forty years ago when the average American worker—though well paid as always, by the standards of other countries—could nevertheless be refused a job for any reason that crossed an employer's mind, from the worker's race and religion to his union sympathies; once on the job, his specific pay rate depended partly on the uncertain workings of market forces and partly on the whims of his foreman, and he could be fired at a moment's notice, again for any reason whatever; and when he could not work because of sickness, an accident, or just old age, it was usually up to him, his family, and the local welfare and charity organizations to figure out how he could make ends meet. By most economic tests of performance, this system worked well; by today's standards of equity, it bred needless misery and degradation for millions of workers.

In contrast, the average worker today (though there are exceptions, as we shall see) can call upon a government employment service for help in locating a job; he cannot legally be refused a job (for which he is otherwise qualified) because of his age, sex, race, religion, or union sympathies; once hired, he cannot be fired or otherwise discriminated against for any of the reasons just described, and he must be paid no less than the minimum wage established by law; if injured on the job, he receives workmen's compensation; if unemployed through no fault of his own, he receives unemployment insurance; when he retires, he receives a government-administered pension; and when he dies, his widow receives a burial benefit and a monthly survivor's benefit.

If this does not add up to the complete "womb-to-tomb" security desired by some and feared by others, it nevertheless is an impressive array of social programs for a country often considered the epitome of heartless capitalism. In fact, about the only major types of welfare programs found in countries like Sweden and Great Britain, but not here, are family allowances (so much for each child) and national health insurance, and these gaps have been narrowed by our huge (if much criticized) program of Aid to Families with Dependent Children, plus Medicare for the aged and Medicaid for the needy. Further, despite dire prophecies that such a social revolution would destroy work incentives and perhaps the entire free-enterprise system, our economy has never performed better than since 1940. In short, we seem to have had the best of both worlds: a stronger economy and a more humane society.

As every day's newspapers remind us, however, poverty and dissension and injustice have not disappeared according to plan. In part, this can be explained by facts such as the relative nature of any poverty definition, the inevitability of some dissension in any free society falling short of utopia, and the role of the civil rights movement in exposing injustices that have always existed but were largely ignored even by most reformers in earlier days. But there is more to the story than that. After all, over two out of every three Americans classified as poor are white, not black, and we have seen that the official poverty definition, relative as it may be, is certainly not so generous that we can ignore the needs of over twenty million people whose incomes fall below those modest guidelines.

In retrospect, it is clear that the thrust of the New Deal's social program was far more conservative than generally realized at the time. That is, the major programs of the 1930s aimed at protecting the dignity and income of people *who were in the labor market*—by providing more jobs, union and minimum-wage protection on the job, unemployment insurance between jobs, and old-age pensions built up by contributions during a person's working life. Those were the great needs to be met during the 1930s, and it was implicitly assumed that other social needs would almost automatically be met if only the industrial worker were adequately protected in the job market. And to a very large extent, the factory worker—the epitome of the underprivileged class through most of our industrial history—has now won his social revolution, only to expose the needs of many others who cannot compete in the labor market because of age, disability, or family responsibilities (female heads of households). Welfare-state advocates had expected "relief" benefits, based on the humiliating needs test, to fall over the years as benefits expanded under social security and other social insurance programs which pay benefits as a matter of right, not need. Instead, benefits paid out under *both* types of programs have soared.

We have considerably oversimplified matters, of course. On the one hand, there are many people actively in the labor market who still earn only a poverty-level income and, on the other hand, many of the aged poor are covered by Social

Security and could escape poverty if benefits were liberalized. Yet, it remains generally true that, as many conservatives exaggerated the beneficence of an unregulated economy, so did many liberals oversell the virtues of the 1935 model of the welfare state.

As a result, many of the debates of that era are now recurring. Of the three themes we have pointed up throughout this book, the one most obviously at issue here is the controversy over the mixture of *security and incentives* that should prevail in the labor sector. Although the general public may now have accepted minimum-wage laws, for example, we shall see that the experts remain sharply divided over their merits, with many critics asserting that such laws create some of the very problems of unemployment and poverty that we are trying to solve. And everyone is familiar with the charge that guaranteeing an above-poverty income to every family would destroy the incentive to work of both those who are now in the poverty group and those who now stay just above the poverty line through hard and continuous work that would no longer seem worth the effort.

But our other two major issues are also relevant here. In discussing the clash of *producer and consumer interests* up to this point, we have stressed that both of these interests are usually found within every family: the worker who seeks higher wages and more security as a producer also wants the benefits of competition in his role as a consumer. In this area, however, the clash is even sharper, as many feel the poor produce nothing and only consume at the expense of the working nonpoor. As for our third theme—the difficulty every industrial society faces in securing simultaneously the advantages of *full employment, stable prices, and a minimum of government controls*—the relevance is plain. How can we urge the poor to seek out jobs at the same time that we are trying to keep the lid on prices by closely checking demand forces, thereby running the risk of increasing the number of unemployed and poor, as in the 1950s, which in turn encourages the clamor for more government intervention, as in the 1960s?

We shall see, however, that all is not gloom and doom and it is possible that we are entering a new and constructive phase in this ancient battle over labor's need for social protection. On the one hand, most conservatives now accept the fact that the welfare state is here to stay and that many of its programs are worthwhile and effective. For example, few if any conservative spokesmen now suggest that we should entirely scrap old-age pensions or unemployment insurance or workmen's compensation, although they may quarrel over the precise content or the administration of these laws. Also, it was Prof. Milton Friedman, widely regarded as the leading conservative economist in this country, who was one of the earliest and most vigorous proponents of the negative income tax, and it was a Republican President, Richard Nixon, who proposed national standards to strengthen and unify many relief programs that have long been in the domain of states' rights. On the other hand, among liberals who once regarded any attack upon the welfare system as a sign of reactionary prejudice against the poor, there is now a widespread recognition that the social problems of the 1970s need remedies far different from those which solved many of the problems of the 1930s.

On the issue of minimum-wage laws, however, the battle lines have hardly changed in over fifty years, and so we shall begin with that issue in order to present in its starkest form the controversy that still persists over the proper role of the government in protecting workers from the rigors of a competitive market system.

In 1966 the heads of nearly two million families held down full-time jobs that brought in so little money that their families were officially termed poor.[1] Clearly, there is still a poverty problem among many people in the labor force as well as among those outside. As we noted in Chapter 19, this is not so surprising when you realize that a worker earning the federal minimum wage of $1.60 an hour, and working a full 2,000-hour year, would make only $3,200—compared to the income of $3,335 needed by a nonfarm family of only four members in order to escape the poverty classification in 1967. Why don't we solve this problem of the working poor by simply raising the wage floor from $1.60 to $2.60 or $3.60 an hour?

There were another 573,000 poor families in 1966 whose head worked part of the year but was unemployed the rest of the year. To solve this type of poverty, why don't we spread the work, that is, induce or require employers to work their present labor force only 32 or 35 hours a week instead of the usual 40, and hire the unemployed to make up the difference in output?

Those are the principal issues to which this chapter is directed. To illustrate the conflict that they still engender, consider the recent remarks of two very able men concerning the Fair Labor Standards Act, the federal wage-and-hour law. First, W. Willard Wirtz, the Secretary of Labor in the Kennedy and Johnson administrations:

The 1961 and 1966 amendments to the Fair Labor Standards Act actually went a long way toward the development of a philosophy of that Act consistent with its relevance to the attack on poverty. Increases in the minimum wage level ... to the $1.60 level ... brought it roughly in line for the first time with at least the low side of what is considered a minimal decent subsistence income.... The extension of coverage [of the act] to an additional 3½ million workers in 1961 and then, particularly, the inclusion of another 10½ million people by the action taken in 1966 reflected the Congress' recognition that the human needs of the principal contributors to the economy were entitled to at least as much consideration as the conveniences of the enterprises involved. There was clear indication that the self-interest pressure groups which have been responsible for the large scale exemptions and exclusions from the coverage of the Act will have an increasingly difficult time in the future in pressing their claims against the broader national interest in seeing to it that a day's work gives whoever does it a day's decent living.[2]

On the other hand, Prof. Milton Friedman of the University of Chicago:

The fact is ... the minimum wage rate is a major cause of Negro teenage unemployment. Of all the laws on the statute books of this country, I believe the minimum wage law probably does the Negroes the most harm. It is not intended to be an anti-Negro law but, in fact, it is. ...

The real tragedy of minimum wage laws is that they are supported by well-meaning groups who want to reduce poverty. But the people who are hurt most by higher minimums are the most poverty-stricken.[3]

The case for minimum-wage laws

We shall first examine the arguments favoring minimum-wage legislation and the history and current status of such laws, and then we shall appraise the attacks made on these laws. Of the several justifications offered for statutory minimums, four have been given particular emphasis.

First, it is said that in the absence of legal wage minimums, unscrupulous employers who are in a favorable bargaining position will hire workers at sweatshop wages. The cost advantage which they derive at the expense of the workers whom they employ permits them a competitive edge over their business rivals. The latter are therefore driven to cut wages of their own employees, in simple self-defense. Thus, without some legal floor to wage rates, wage levels will tend to be set by those employers who have the greatest bargaining advantage over their workers and who are ruthless enough to use it. Regardless of how other employers may feel about such practices, they are driven to depress the wage rates of their own employees as the price of business survival. Competition among business firms, it is argued, should proceed not on the basis of which employers can squeeze their employees the most, but on the basis of relative managerial efficiency. "Take wages out of competition" is the slogan which has been used to popularize this notion.

The second major justification for minimum-wage legislation lies in what is presumed to be the role it plays in restraining the downward drift of depressions. As expenditures fall off, and in the absence of a lower limit to wages, employers will seek to stimulate sales by cutting prices; with mounting unemployment, they will be able to accomplish this through reducing the wage rates of their employees. This is a phenomenon which is not chargeable to only a few "scoundrels" in some sweatshop industry, but which may emerge in all sectors of the economy. But with declining wage rates, workers have less to spend, so sales continue to fall off, prices and wages decline further, and so on, in a downward spiral which results in a "demoralization of market prices."[4] Minimum wages prevent this effect by calling a stop to the downward movement of wages—and through them, of prices—at some fixed level.

A third argument is based on the positive benefit which may come from added wages in the pockets of workers. If employers are forced to redistribute income in favor of employees, by bringing wages up to some legislated minimum, this added purchasing power in the hands of low-income groups—who may be expected to spend it promptly—will increase the demand for mass-production goods and services and act as a forward thrust to the economy.

Fourth, low wages, it is said, constitute a kind of subsidy to the employer who pays them. Workers cannot maintain their families on a satisfactory standard of health and decency if they are paid substandard wages. The consequence is that the community must maintain free health clinics, provide relief in times of emergency, establish houses of correction for those whose waywardness has its roots in poverty-bred slum conditions, and so on. These costs are borne by society at least in part because some employers exploit their labor, the contention runs. Thus society is subsidizing those employers' low-cost operations. If a wage floor is established, raising the wages of the lowest-paid wage-earning group, these social costs can be reduced, since those workers will now be better able to provide for themselves.

These arguments on behalf of minimum-wage legislation have not gone unchallenged, as we shall see.

Legislation in the United States

Prior to the 1930s the Federal government had been unconcerned with the wages paid employees except for those few who were actually engaged on government projects. In the separate states, some action had been attempted, it is true, but it had not been notably successful. By the early 1920s, about one-third of the states had passed laws regulating the wages paid to women and children. It should be noted that it was only women and children who were affected. This was on the premise that these groups were less capable of fending for themselves and hence the state might legitimately assert a protecting role. In the case of men, the prevailing philosophy of self-reliance precluded such an attitude. A man could be expected to stand on his own two feet. Women and children—well, they were in another category. They could use a little protection.

Even this limited protective role was struck down in 1923, however, by action of the United States Supreme Court, which held such laws to be unconstitutional as a deprivation of the liberty of the individual to take whatever job he chooses, on such conditions as are acceptable to him.[5]

It has been said that legislation of the kind under review is required in the interest of social justice, for whose ends freedom of contract may lawfully be subjected to restraint. The liberty of the individual to do as he pleases, even in innocent matters, is not absolute. It must frequently yield to the common good, and the line beyond which the power of interference may not be pressed is neither definite nor unalterable but may be made to move, within limits not well defined, with changing need and circumstance. Any attempt to fix a rigid boundary would be unwise as well as futile. But, nevertheless, there are limits to the power, and when these have been passed, it becomes the plain duty of the courts in the proper exercise of their authority to so declare. To sustain the individual freedom of action contemplated by the Constitution, is not to strike down the common good but to exalt it; for surely the good of society as a whole cannot be better served than by the preservation against arbitrary restraint of the liberties of its constituent members.

This same constitutional conservatism led in 1935 to the invalidation by the Supreme Court of the National Industrial Recovery Act, under which the government's first efforts at the general establishment of minimum wages had been attempted as part of the recovery drive. Codes of fair competition had been drafted for each industry, with each code providing for minimum wages and maximum hours, and it was this regulation of business by code that was ruled to be contrary to the intent of the Constitution. Prevented from relying on this method for seeking to redistribute income in favor of wage earners and in the hope of stimulating mass purchasing power and thus

production and employment, Congress executed an end run around the Court by resorting to its powers of specifying the wages to be paid by employers doing business with the government. It had already utilized that power in adopting the Davis-Bacon Act in 1931, which still requires that private contractors working on any federally financed construction project must pay hourly rates at least as high as the rates prevailing for each skill in the locality surrounding the public construction site. Then, in 1936, Congress extended much the same principle to other industries through the Walsh-Healey (Public Contracts) Act of that year, which permits the Secretary of Labor to fix the minimum wages which must be paid in the manufacture or supply of all goods purchased by the Federal government under contracts amounting to $10,000 or more. We shall return to these prevailing-wage laws later, but at this point their relevance is that they did not have to be justified by the debatable constitutional powers of Congress to regulate private industry, for they rested on the clear right of the government as a buyer to insist upon stated contractual conditions.

One year later, in 1937, the Supreme Court was called upon to review its 1923 decision declaring state minimum-wage laws to be unconstitutional. The law in question was again one applying to women and minors, this time in the state of Washington, and in its decision—as in several other decisions of this period—the Court evidenced a change in its thinking. In tune with the temper of the times, it placed greater weight on the need for social legislation and accepted the powers of the Federal government to control private discretion in the interest of public welfare.[6]

In each case the violation alleged by those attacking minimum wage regulation for women is deprivation of freedom of contract. What is this freedom? The Constitution does not speak of freedom of contract. It speaks of liberty and prohibits the deprivation of liberty without due process of law. In prohibiting that deprivation the Constitution does not recognize an absolute and uncontrollable liberty. Liberty in each of its phases has its history and connotation. But the liberty safeguarded is liberty in a social organization which requires the protection of law against the evils which menace the health, safety, morals, and welfare of the people. Liberty under the Constitution is thus necessarily subject to the restraints of due process, and regulation which is reasonable in relation to its subject and is adopted in the interests of the community is due process. . . .

What can be closer to the public interest than the health of women and their protection from unscrupulous and overreaching employers? And if the protection of women is a legitimate end of the exercise of state power, how can it be said that the requirement of the payment of a minimum wage fairly fixed in order to meet the very necessities of existence is not an admissible means to that end? The legislature of the State was clearly entitled to consider the situation of women in employment, the fact that they are in the class receiving the least pay, that their bargaining power is relatively weak, and that they are the ready victims of those who would take advantage of their necessitous circumstances.

With the encouragement provided by this decision, other states have passed minimum-wage legislation. At the present time, thirty-six states, plus Puerto Rico and the District of Columbia, have "effective" wage laws (that is, laws that are actively enforced and are amended to keep their rates up to date). Most of these laws now apply to both men and women but are limited to industries primarily engaged in intrastate commerce. Also, the minimum rates and specific industries covered vary considerably from state to state.

The most important wage law in the United States is therefore the *Fair Labor Standards Act* (FLSA) at the federal level, first adopted by Congress in 1938 in the wake of the Supreme Court's "conversion" and subsequently amended several times. As Figure 21-1 shows, the legal minimum rate began at 25 cents an hour in 1938 and has since moved up to $1.60 an hour. It can also be seen that, with many jumps and lags, the statutory minimum has tended to be about 50 percent of the average wage of all blue-collar factory workers. There is no particular magic in that comparison, for obviously the ratio would be lower if the FLSA rate were compared only to construction wages (37 percent in 1968) and far higher if compared to agricultural wages (132 percent in

1968). As we have noted before, however, until recently the factory worker has been the prime object of most labor legislation and for that reason, plus the fact that wage data have always been more comprehensive for manufacturing than for most other industries, this type of comparison has become traditional in assessing the adequacy of FLSA rates. (Actually, a newly constructed wage series has shown that straight-time earnings in manufacturing are roughly representative of average gross earnings in the entire nonagricultural private sector.[7]) Also, anyone can argue that the ratio "should be" higher or lower than 50 percent, but apparently congressmen as well as labor negotiators like to cling to an established wage pattern.

Table 21-1 shows that the federal minimum wage now applies to 78 percent of all nonsupervisory workers in private industry, and another 7 percent are covered by state wage laws. But these totals are misleading in certain respects. First, rates of less than $1.60 an hour are permitted to be paid to learners, apprentices, and handicapped persons; to workers in firms and industries covered for the first time by the 1967 extension of the act (where application of the full minimum was delayed until 1971); and to workers covered only by the several state laws which permit lower rates. Second, from the viewpoint of proponents of minimum-wage laws, the coverage of the federal law is perverse, being most extensive in the high-wage, strongly unionized industries (manufacturing, mining, transportation, and construction) and most limited in the low-wage, weakly organized industries (farming, trade, and services) in which wage supports are presumably most needed. Also, within these low-wage industries, the act applies primarily to the largest farms and stores and other enterprises, where again the need for wage protection is assumed to be less urgent than in the smaller operations.

But even with these qualifications, the coverage of the act today is far more extensive than it was before the amendments of 1961 and 1966 added 14 million workers in industries previously exempt. As late as 1960, that is, the FLSA covered only about 55 percent of the nonsupervisory workers in private industry, and in the low-wage sectors it covered only 19 percent in services, 3 percent in retail trade, and less than 1 percent

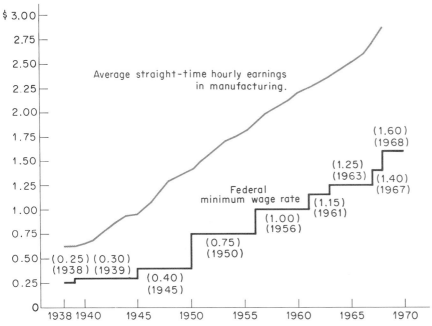

Fig. 21-1. *The federal statutory minimum-wage rate and average straight-time hourly earnings in manufacturing, 1938–1968. Note: Wage data for manufacturing include overtime earnings for 1938–40, but exclude such earnings for 1941–1968. The original FLSA provided that tripartite industry committees could recommend a 40-cent minimum prior to the scheduled date of 1945 and, because of the wartime increase in wages, this rate was adopted early in several industries. For the 1960s, the rates shown are those for previously covered workers; the lower rates for workers newly covered by the extension of the act in 1961 were $1 (1961), $1.15 (1964), and $1.25 (1965), and the rates for those newly covered in 1967 were $1 in that year, plus 15 cents more each year until the rate reached $1.60 in 1971.*

SOURCE: *U.S. Department of Labor.*

in agriculture. In contrast to the expansion in coverage of other New Deal legislation, such as old-age pensions and unemployment insurance, the proportion of the labor force covered by the FLSA was no larger in 1960 than in 1938 and was perhaps even a trifle smaller—which is another reflection of the fact that the minimum wage has remained the most controversial and strongly resisted of the welfare measures that came out of the 1930s.

Finally, this act also established the now familiar practice of paying "time-and-a-half for overtime," that is, the requirement that 150 per-cent of the base rate must be paid for all work in

covered employment beyond 40 hours in one week and, by amendment in 1965, beyond 8 hours in any one day. We shall return to these provisions in our discussion later of the regulation of working hours. Another amendment, effective in 1964, requires employers to pay women the same rate as paid to men for similar work.

Attitude of unions toward minimum-wage legislation

Since minimum-wage legislation in the United States has always sought to cover only the lowest-paid workers, at least in principle if not in fact,

Table 21-1 *Employees Covered by Federal and State Minimum-Wage Laws, by Industry, February 1, 1969*

Industry	Total nonsupervisory employees* (in thousands)	Percent covered by the FLSA†	Percent covered by state laws only‡	Percent not covered by the FLSA or state laws†
Total private sector	53,506	78	7	15
Agriculture, forestry, and fisheries	1,327	46	5	49
Mining	558	99	—§	—§
Construction	3,312	99	—§	—§
Manufacturing	18,081	97	1	2
Transportation, communication, and utilities	4,026	98	1	1
Wholesale trade	3,392	76	2	22
Retail trade	9,574	58	20	22
Finance, insurance, real estate	2,963	75	4	21
Services (except domestic service)	7,893	71	15	14
Domestic service	2,380	0	0	100

	Total employees¶ (in thousands)		
Government sector	12,548	22	n.a.	n.a.

* Excludes executive, administrative, and professional employees.
† FLSA refers to the Fair Labor Standards Act.
‡ Data are only for those states having minimum-wage laws or orders enacted or revised from 1962 to December 1, 1968. A few other states have wage laws on their books, but these are assumed to be inactive or outdated.
¶ Includes all employees, as estimated by the Bureau of Labor Statistics. Data for nonsupervisory employees only are not available for the public sector.
§ Less than 1 percent.
SOURCE: Computed from U.S. Department of Labor, Wage and Hour and Public Contracts Divisions, *Minimum Wage and Maximum Hours Standards Under the Fair Labor Standards Act, 1969*, 1969, Table 1, p. 29.

and since unions in collective-bargaining agreements commonly are able to establish minimum hiring rates superior to those provided for by Congress, there is reason to question whether unions have any occasion to be interested in such legislation. Indeed, although unionists are now among the most vocal supporters of wage minimums, for reasons which we shall shortly examine, in earlier years there was some ambivalence in their attitude. Some among their number feared that if workers came to rely on the government for their protection, the interest in and efforts at self-advancement through unions would

suffer. They argued that if the government would protect workers' right to organize into unions, there would be no need for further governmental protection in the form of minimum-wage laws. "The one force necessary to maintain wages is the organization of workers into unions where they can exercise their economic strength."[8]

By 1937, when the Fair Labor Standards measure had come up for discussion before the committees on labor of both houses of Congress, William Green, as president of the American Federation of Labor, endorsed the measure. But he made clear in his testimony that he regarded minimum-wage regulation and collective bargaining as alternatives. The latter made the former unnecessary:[9]

> Let collective bargaining be extended and expanded until, through the collective bargaining process, we establish minimum rates in practically every industry and then, as that is extended, let the Government recede. Let collective bargaining be expanded and Government interference, if I may put it that way, Government regulation recede.

With the passage of time, however, unions have abandoned any notion that government minimum-wage laws are antithetical or an alternative to collective bargaining. In a very few cases, such as the one or two unions struggling to organize farm workers, an increase in the federal minimum can mean a direct increase in the low wages of nearly all of their members. More important, however, is the indirect advantage to unions with wage scales beginning at, or slightly above, the legal minimum, such as those in the garment industry. If firm A, unorganized, has been paying a legal minimum of $1.25 an hour, and firm X, under union contract, has been paying a minimum of $1.60, when the legal minimum rises to $1.60 the union will bring pressure on firm X to increase its rates by another 35 cents in order to preserve its "historical differential" over firm A.[10] Or, if all workers in firm X have been averaging $1.60 an hour but unskilled workers have been getting only $1.25, an increase in the federal minimum will have a "ratcheting" or "tandem" effect as the union demands that all other rates inside the firm increase proportionally to preserve normal occupational differentials. (This process will occur to some extent in nonunion firms as well.)

Also, the federal minimum wage can be an important weapon in the battle between states and regions to win or preserve jobs. Both the textile and clothing industries in the North have seen many firms and jobs move South, with the result that Northern employers and unions in these industries often join forces to urge an increase in the FLSA minimum rate—hoping that this will narrow the North–South wage gap and reduce the South's competitive advantage in both labor and product markets.

For these reasons unions now seek, almost continuously, to increase the amount of the minimum and to extend the act's coverage to groups now exempt from its provisions.

Economic effects of minimum-wage legislation

We have noted the intended consequences of minimum-wage legislation—to move low-income workers closer to a decent standard of living, to compensate for the weak bargaining power of workers who are relatively immobile, to eliminate competition which is based on depressed wage rates, to act as a protection against the downward spiral of wages and prices in times of recession, and to serve as a stimulus to the economy by augmenting purchasing power in the hands of a low-income group who can be counted on to spend what they earn. There are a number of economists, however, who question whether minimum-wage legislation will achieve the objectives intended. There are several grounds on which such legislation is criticized.

It will be recalled that in the theory of economic competition, which includes competitive wage determination, the wages of an employee can be assumed to equal his marginal value product. A maximizing producer will hire employees up to the point where the additional value of the total output is equal to the additional cost added to the total wage bill. It would certainly not pay a producer to hire more employees when the value they contribute is less than the wages which must be paid them.

In actuality, of course, there are circumstances under which an employee may not be receiving his marginal value product. Lack of alternative employment opportunities (as in a one-company town) may permit an employer to pay his workers less than their true market value. But in those situations where workers are in fact receiving wage payments roughly equal to their marginal value, minimum-wage legislation can be expected to have adverse consequences for those very people whom it is designed to help. Some workers may be paid little because their marginal value product is little, not because they are being exploited by an employer under circumstances which permit him to evade paying the market value of their labor. If, then, minimum-wage legislation "artificially" raises the price of labor, wages of these low-paid workers will exceed their marginal value product. Since business does not operate as a charity, the employer will not continue to hire workers who cost more than they contribute, whose employment involves a loss. Such workers will be laid off. The low-income receiver, whom the minimum-wage legislation was designed to benefit, finds himself without any income at all. He cannot find another job in any of the other industries which are subject to the minimum-wage provisions, since it can be assumed that in these, too, his contribution will be less than his cost. He is driven into industries not subject to such legislation, where he and others like him compete for the limited number of jobs, depressing wage rates in those industries. Even if he is fortunate enough to obtain employment, it will be at a wage rate lower than he has formerly received.

There is another way in which jobs of those employees whom minimum-wage legislation is intended to benefit may be jeopardized. If wage rates are forced above the level of their marginal value product, employers may seek to offset the added costs by substituting capital equipment for labor. Machinery and automatic equipment that may not have been economical to install when the cost of hand operations was lower may be economical now that wages are raised. It becomes cheaper to operate with machines than with men. So those whose incomes were expected to rise in conformity with the legal wage rate find, instead, that their total income has been lost in the process. Again, if they are fortunate enough to find another job, it is likely to be in an industry not subject to minimum-wage provisions, and at rates lower than they formerly earned. Legislators, however well-intentioned, have succeeded only in making victims of their intended beneficiaries. So goes the argument.

There is an alternative method by which some producers may seek to bring the new higher minimum rate into line with the marginal value product of their workers. Marginal value product, it will be recalled, is equal to marginal physical product times the price of the product ($MVP = MPP \times P$). If wages rise, conceivably marginal value product may also be made to rise. The substitution of capital for labor, mentioned in the preceding paragraph, is actually one way in which the marginal value of the workers retained is increased. With fewer workers employed on more capital equipment, the marginal physical product of these workers is pushed up. But the same result can be achieved if the producer is in a position to raise the price of his product. If P rises, so too must MVP. If the demand for the firm's goods is relatively inelastic so that output can be reasonably well maintained, the higher wage rate will result less in unemployment than in higher prices. The cost of increasing the wages of the low-paid workers is borne by the consuming public.

The extent to which any one firm is free to increase the prices of its products depends upon a number of considerations, among which are the demand conditions confronting it and its cost position relative to the cost positions of its competitors. If a large part of the industry is unaffected by the minimum-wage legislation, the few firms which are affected cannot very well raise prices without running the danger of losing at least some of their business. But in industries where the impact of such legislation is rather widely felt, it may prove feasible for the firms in that industry generally to raise prices. The upward pressure on costs and prices may be pyramided as one industry transmits the effects to another industry for which it serves as a supplier, and so on and on. The public pays—including other low-income receivers, some of whom may not themselves have benefited from the legislation and may indeed be worse off than its beneficiaries.

There is a third adverse economic effect which has been charged to minimum-wage legislation. It has been claimed that a minimum rate which is applicable to the whole economy prevents the areas with surplus labor from attracting industry by the lure of low wage rates. There are only two cures for a labor surplus and low wages: an expanded demand for labor, which must be achieved by providing industry with an incentive to settle in that area, or an emigration of labor, reducing the labor supply, which must be achieved by providing workers with an inducement to leave the area. The incentive for firms to move in and workers to move out is the same—a wage level which is low relative to other areas. As labor demand comes into balance with labor supply, wage rates will rise to the levels prevailing elsewhere. But a minimum-wage law, establishing a wage floor throughout the economy, reduces wage differentials and, with them, some of the inducement for capital to enter and labor to leave.

These are the principal arguments raised against efforts to put a legal floor under wages—that the result will be (1) unemployment for those workers whose value to employers is less than the legal minimum, (2) higher product prices in the industries which are most affected, and (3) a slowing down of the process of industrialization in areas where there are more workers than well-paying jobs.

Supporters of wage regulation have their answers to these arguments. The rebuttals run as follows:

Granted that in some instances workers may be laid off because their contribution is less than the legislated wage, these cases are fewer in number than the situations where workers are not receiving their full marginal value product either because the employer enjoys a monopsonistic position and hence can get his workers at bargain rates or because some workers are relatively immobile, for a variety of reasons. Under pressure of the law, employers must pay a wage more commensurate with the value they receive from their employees. Since minimum-wage rates are usually set at a level which is low in comparison with average hourly earnings, there is relatively little danger that the legal rate will have the unemployment effect which is attributed to it. Where a worker's output is low due to some physical handicap, he may be certified as handicapped and exempted from the law's coverage.

By and large, the firms which are most adversely affected by having to pay a higher wage rate under compulsion of the law are the less efficient firms. Minimum-wage legislation puts pressure on them to tighten up their operations—to improve their quality controls, reduce scrap, make better use of their labor, put more effort into selling, improve product design, and so on.

Higher wage rates may also pressure backward managements into making more use of mechanized processes; such substitution of capital equipment for labor may result in displacement of workers, it is true, but this does not necessarily mean their unemployment if the economy as a whole is operating at a high level. Such technological progress is in fact to be welcomed.[11]

If some price increases are necessary in order to pay decent wages to those who work on the products involved, this is a consequence which society should be prepared to accept. If goods can be obtained cheaply only at the expense of the workers who produce them, consumers are themselves exploiting those whose bargaining power is weak.[12]

> There is no more justification for the production of a 5-cent artificial flower or a 50-cent pair of work trousers in the present state of technology and the industrial arts, than there would be for a 10-cent haircut or a $200 new automobile. Such prices of goods and services would mean that the persons employed in their production would have to be paid wages on which it would be impossible to exist at all.

In summary, the arguments over minimum-wage laws are essentially the same as those over the union effect on wages. If laws (or unions) can really raise wages above market levels without hurting anybody, ask the critics, why don't we make everybody rich by simply legislating a wage floor of $10 or $20 or $30 an hour? When stated in those extremes, everyone can see that the price and employment effects would be disastrous, so why does anybody doubt that the same thing happens—only on a smaller scale—when the artificial wage floor is $1.60 or $2 an hour (or when unions raise wages only 10 percent instead of 100 percent over market levels)?

And the answer from the other side is also the same, whether collective bargaining or the minimum wage is at issue: market forces certainly do impose limits beyond which wages cannot be driven at any given time without all the repercussions predicted by orthodox theory, but those restraining limits are not as narrow and predictable as the competitive model implies—as proven by the prevalence of large wage differentials for the same skill even in nonunion markets. Given these glaring imperfections in the "natural" market forces, it is argued, there are both room and need for some intervention by the government (and unions) in the wage-setting process.

The hazards of measurement

In view of this similarity of the basic issues, it is not surprising that studies of the impact of minimum-wage laws encounter most of the same research problems which plague the union-impact studies described in Chapter 18. The basic obstacle remains the fact that "all other things" refuse to stay constant in the real world, making it very difficult for the researcher to isolate the effect of a wage law (or collective bargaining) from the effects of all the other forces that constantly influence wages, employment, and prices.

No one seriously argues, for example, that the sole reason wages today are higher than in 1938 is the lifting of the FLSA rate over this period from 25 cents to $1.60. Even if the period of comparison is narrowed to one or two years, however, there remain serious hazards in interpreting the law's effect. The 25-cent minimum of 1938 and the 30- to 40-cent range of 1939 were followed by the beginning of the defense and war boom in 1940; the 75-cent minimum took effect just six months before the Korean invasion and the subsequent inflation from 1950 to 1952; the $1 minimum became effective as the economy was expanding in 1956 prior to its relapse into the recession beginning in 1957; and all of the increases in the 1960s occurred during one of the longest periods of expansion in the history of the country. What would have been the law's effect if the economy had instead been stable or declining during each of those periods?

In an effort to minimize the effects of these economywide changes, several studies have made before-and-after comparisons limited to a few weeks or months bridging the introduction of a new minimum, but these studies may be unintentionally biased in either direction. On the one hand, they may underestimate the negative effects of a minimum by not including long-range adjustments such as the introduction of laborsaving machinery (which can rarely be done overnight),

the raising of hiring standards in filling future vacancies left by normal turnover, or even the complete shutdown of some plants which managed to survive the first few months of a new minimum but could not last indefinitely. On the other hand, "quickie" studies may magnify negative effects, since some managements, fearing the worst, produce furiously for inventory in the weeks just before a new minimum takes effect and then sharply reduce their level of operations in the period immediately following; or some employers may not discover for some time all of the ways in which they can absorb a wage increase without adverse employment or price effects; or if the plants least affected ultimately capture the sales volume lost by those hardest hit, an initial contraction or shutdown by low-wage plants may later be tempered or offset by employment expansion in high-wage plants.

This, then, is the central dilemma in attempting to measure the actual effects of minimum-wage laws: The shorter the period examined, the greater is the danger of ignoring important long-run effects, but the longer the period, the greater is the difficulty of correcting for the effects of all the other economic forces constantly at work. This poses formidable problems of interpretation for even the most dispassionate observer. For instance, many studies have attempted to hold "all other things equal" by including in their sample only plants which were continuously in existence both before and after a legal minimum was applied. This approach obviously excludes plants wiped out by such a law and has been justifiably criticized as based on a logic which, for example, by examining the health of identical soldiers before and after a war, could show that no soldier had been fatally wounded.[13] On the other hand, this approach also excludes new plants which may have come into an affected industry, and even a complete count of the plants both opened and shut down during the relevant period would have to be carefully compared to the high rate of plant turnover which often characterizes low-wage industries at all times.

Finally, the difficulty of assessing the impact of a national minimum wage "is aggravated by the relatively low minimums that have been set under the FLSA. In even the most affected low-wage industries, to have raised all workers to the minimum would have required only a 5 to 15 percent increase in payrolls and a 1 to 3 percent increase in total cost."[14] Of course, the cost impact was far higher for some individual firms, but it was even lower for the average industry covered by the law and so low for the entire economy that the law's effect on such things as inflation and mass purchasing power probably cannot be measured at all.

We have dwelled on these research problems to explain why anyone will be frustrated who is looking for definitive proof that minimum-wage laws are "good" or "bad." It is true, for example, that the U.S. Department of Labor invariably concludes that its studies prove that the FLSA has benefited millions and harmed few, while nearly every study by "private" economists in recent years has maintained that such laws have precisely the disemployment effects predicted by marginal theory. It is tempting to shrug off this conflict as evidence of bias: the Labor Department has a vested interest in placating the labor unions that press for higher minimums, and the academician has a vested interest in proving that the real world conforms to his classroom models. But that type of thinking underestimates the competence of the economists found on both sides of this issue and, as we have seen, it also underestimates the research hazards facing every analyst in this area.

The Labor Department studies

Turning first to the studies by the Department of Labor, we find that they have been issued regularly since 1955, when Congress first directed the Secretary of Labor to supply it annually with data on the effects and adequacy of the FLSA. The result has been a massive accumulation of data which, in their scope, precision, and depth, surpass any information we (or probably any other country) have ever had on the impact of a wage law. Appraising these data for 1968, the Secretary of Labor concluded:

Employment in the areas affected by the extension of coverage [to 10½ million workers in 1966] has increased, and there is no evidence of any restraining effect of the broader coverage on employment opportunity. The increased minimum wage levels set in 1966 have not contributed to the current inflationary spiral to an extent which permits reasonable questioning of their net value in strengthening both the position of low-paid workers in particular and the economy in general.[15]

This appraisal rested on four types of evidence. First, a *general appraisal of the economy* showed large benefits and no adverse effects from the act. Wage surveys indicated that a total of 7.3 million workers should have received wage increases when the FLSA rates were increased on February 1, 1968, for that was the number of covered workers earning less than the new rates just prior to this increase. And obviously not many of these 7 million workers lost their jobs, because total employment rose by about 1.5 million persons in 1968, total unemployment dropped by nearly 200,000, and the unemployment rate reached its lowest level since 1953. The general price level did increase in the first six months of 1968, of course, but by less than it had in the same period in 1967 and by little more than in the first six months of 1966, indicating that the inflationary trend of these years was caused by other factors.

Second, *field investigations of reported distress situations* showed few adverse effects of the 1968 amendments. Certain Labor Department personnel scattered throughout the United States were instructed to be on the alert for all reported instances of adverse conditions attributed to the impact of the higher FLSA rates and to forward these reports to Washington. Only sixty-three reports were received alleging that a plant shutdown or layoff would occur, or had occurred, because of the impact of the act, and follow-up investigations revealed that more than half of these actions never took place (some employers had apparently been overly pessimistic) and fewer than 300 workers lost their jobs in the remaining situations, in which there were usually factors other than the FLSA contributing to the firm's economic difficulties.

Third, *area studies* showed no consistently adverse effects. Wage and employment trends were analyzed in four widely scattered cities (in Wisconsin, Arkansas, New Hampshire, and North

Carolina). As one example of the findings: Among industries in which the minimum rose from $1.40 to $1.60 in February, 1968, non-supervisory employment rose from June, 1967, to June, 1968, in three of the four cities, increasing the most in the city with the *highest* proportion of covered workers who had earned under $1.60 and rising least in the city with the *lowest* proportion of these "direct-impact" workers.

Fourth, *studies of low-wage industries* also demonstrate that higher wage minimums have not had serious disemployment effects. These studies have covered a wide range of industries over the years, but we shall center on those analyzing the initial impact of the FLSA on agriculture. It will be recalled that farm workers were not covered by the FLSA until February 1, 1967, when a minimum of $1 an hour was imposed on the largest farms (those using more than 500 man-days of hired labor in any calendar quarter of the preceding year), with the rate rising to $1.15 in 1968 and $1.30 in 1969. If ever there is going to be a clear-cut test of marginal theory in the labor market, this would seem to be the ideal place for it: Farm employment has been declining for years, the industry is highly competitive, employers are willing and able to mechanize many of their operations, and wages are so low that *39 percent* of the workers on covered farms were receiving less than $1 an hour when that rate became the legal minimum (and 58 percent were under that rate in the South). Here is a high-impact industry by any definition, and yet the Labor Department found the following:

> Average hourly earnings of hired farmworkers on all farms in the United States increased by 28 cents over the 2-year period between May 1965 and May 1967. . . .
>
> There is evidence that employment on farms continued its long-run decline in 1967. However, the decline was far greater on noncovered farms than on covered farms. Between May 1965, 1 year and 8 months before the effective date of the minimum wage, and the end of May 1967, 4 months after, employment dropped 31 percent on noncovered farms and 11 percent on covered farms.
>
> Employment on southern noncovered farms declined 37 percent over the 2-year period,

approximately the same as on southern farms which are subject to the minimum wage. In the West, employment on covered farms increased 55 percent . . . while it declined 32 percent on noncovered farms.

> The rate of decline in hired farmworker employment was lower in the first 9 months of 1967 than it has been in similar periods in recent years.[16]

And after the rate went to $1.15 on February 1, 1968, the findings were equally surprising:

> Nationwide, average hourly earnings of all hired farmworkers increased from $1.28 to $1.47 . . . between May 1967 and May 1968. On covered farms the increase (16 percent) was twice as great as on noncovered farms.
>
> On covered farms, hired farmworker employment increased 36 percent during the [one-year] period spanning the effective date of the $1.15 Federal minimum wage. During this same period employment on noncovered farms decreased by 9 percent. . . .
>
> In the South, where the effect of the Federal minimum was greatest, covered employment increased one-fifth between May 1967 and May 1968, while there was a slight decline in employment on noncovered farms.[17]

As the Labor Department acknowledges, these trends can be partly or entirely attributed to the long-run trend toward larger commercial farms and to the record crops in 1967 and 1968. But that is precisely its point: Employment and unemployment trends are primarily determined by forces other than the effect of minimum-wage laws.

The critics' attack

We do not mean to imply that the dispute over the effects of minimum-wage laws is strictly a contest of government versus nongovernment economists. A few of the former have stated that some employment displacement is an inevitable cost of an effective minimum, and some "private" economists have argued that such displacement is trivial.[18] Yet, most of the nongovernment studies in recent years have been strongly critical of the Labor Department's position.

Some of these studies use much the same techniques and data employed in the government studies but emerge with very different conclusions. One of the first and best, by George Macesich and Charles Stewart,[19] reexamined the Labor Department data on the impact of the $1 minimum (effective in 1956) from 1955 to 1957, from which the Department had concluded that the disemployment effects were insignificant. These authors stressed that the most precise of the Department's several measures of employment effect was a special survey of eleven low-wage industries classified by regional location and by wage levels prior to the new minimum, and that these industry segments consistently showed the wage-employment relationship predicted by the competitive model. For example, among fertilizer plants in the Southeast, employment dropped by 9 percent from 1955 to 1957 in the high-impact (lowest-wage) plants, dropped by only 3 percent in the medium-impact plants, and actually rose by 4 percent in the low-impact plants (those requiring less than a 1 percent increase in payrolls to meet the $1 minimum), and the same pattern occurred in most of the other ten industries.

Also, Macesich and Stewart pointed to another Labor Department study of eight low-wage industries which showed that 45 percent of the firms surveyed spent more on machinery and equipment in the year after the new minimum took effect than they had in the year before; about 20 percent reported making changes in plant layout or work procedures; and a minority also raised production standards or made some change in product lines— all as competitive theory would predict. Finally, the authors cited other Labor Department figures that showed the rate of violations of the act had jumped after the new rate took effect, with investigators discovering 77,000 workers receiving less than the new minimum in fiscal 1957 and estimating that another 230,000 violations went undetected—another employer "adjustment" to the minimum that is, like the other facts, consistent with competitive expectations. Professor John Peterson has achieved much the same results in his reexamination of the pre-1950 experience of three low-wage industries covered by the FLSA and of three groups of workers covered by state wage laws: When the data were refined to focus

on firms making similar products under roughly similar conditions, employment changes tended to be inversely related to the wage increases imposed by a minimum-wage law.[20]

There is also a group of studies in which the adverse effects of legal minimums are inferred less directly than in the industry-impact studies. Professors Milton Friedman and Yale Brozen, for example, argue that the relationship shown in Figure 21-2 demonstrates that the FLSA is a major reason for the fact that unemployment rates have recently been much higher among Negro teen-agers than among white teen-agers. The graph indicates that this difference is not an historical inevitability, for the rates were similar

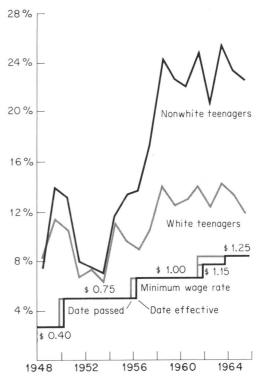

Fig. 21-2. *Unemployment rates for male teenagers (ages 14–19), by race, compared with increases in the federal minimum wage.*

SOURCE: *The Minimum Wage Rate: Who Really Pays?, an interview with Yale Brozen and Milton Friedman, The Free Society Association, Washington, 1966, p. 12.*

in 1948 and the early 1950s, nor did the gap grow slowly as one would expect if it had resulted from increasing discrimination, more rural-urban migration, or a growing demand for skilled labor. Instead, a small gap appeared at the time the FLSA minimum rose from 40 to 75 cents in 1950, closed during the boom period of the Korean War, and then suddenly opened wide in 1956 and 1957, when the minimum jumped by one-third, from 75 cents to $1, and has remained large ever since. Because Negro youths have a lower level of education on the average than white youths, argue Friedman and Brozen, they are "less productive" in an economic sense, are not able to earn as high a wage as white youths in the absence of a minimum, and thus are more likely not to be hired at all when the FLSA minimum is pushed too high and too fast.

These authors also show that roughly the same pattern has occurred in the unemployment rate of all teen-age males (regardless of color) compared to the rate for adult males. Some gap here is predictable because teen-agers are generally "less productive" than adult males, but that gap also widened sharply after the minimum went to $1 and it has remained large in the years since. Critics argue that Friedman and Brozen have overstated their case: It is true that the unemployment gap between white and Negro teen-agers did widen after two increases in the FLSA minimum (1950 and 1956), but it did not widen after two other increases (1961 and 1963) and the gap between teen-age and adult males actually narrowed after the 1950 increase and did not change after the 1961 and 1963 increases. These critics suggest that the experience from 1956 to 1958 was significant not because of the FLSA increase but because the economy was then sliding into a prolonged period of recession in which disadvantaged workers always fare poorly.[21]

Three other "indirect" studies may be summarized as follows:

1. Bimonthly unemployment estimates are available for 150 major labor market areas in this country (areas containing at least one city with a population of 50,000 or more). Over the period from 1950 to 1965, unemployment was consistently higher in those markets covered by a *state* minimum-wage law than in those not covered by a state law. (The average rate of unemployment in the first group was 5.2 percent over the entire period, compared to 4.6 percent in the second group, and the first group's average rate was higher on seventy-eight out of the ninety-five bimonthly reporting dates during this period. These differences are statistically significant and in the direction predicted by the competitive model.) Also, within the group covered by a state minimum, unemployment tended to be higher under laws with a broad coverage (including men) than under laws with a narrow coverage (only women and minors); and when one of these states raised its minimum, unemployment in that state tended to rise relative to the rates of unemployment in other states.[22]

2. Among *all* manufacturing industries during the period from 1947 to 1954, spanning the increase in the FLSA minimum from 40 to 75 cents, nonwage inputs (such as new plant and equipment) tended to increase most in high-wage industries and least in low-wage industries. Among nineteen low-wage industries most vulnerable to the new minimum, however, this relationship was reversed: the lower the wage before the new minimum took effect, the *greater* the subsequent increase in nonwage inputs, as the competitive model would predict. This same relationship held during the years from 1954 to 1958, spanning the introduction of the $1 minimum in 1956, and also held *within* most of the low-wage industries when size of firm was held constant. For example, among textile firms of the same size but paying different wages in 1947, nonlabor inputs went up fastest in the lower-paying firms most vulnerable to the higher minimum.[23]

3. Competitive theory predicts that an increase in the statutory minimum wage will disemploy some workers in covered industries who will seek jobs in uncovered industries and relatively depress wages in the latter sector. Domestic service is an uncovered occupation (see Table 21-1) in which employment usually moves countercyclically, as workers move out to better jobs during good times and move into household work during depressed periods. *This pattern is broken, however, whenever the FLSA minimum rises:* the number of household workers always increases in the months

after the minimum wage goes up, even though these increases have always occurred during up-swings in the economy. This has probably served to keep the wages of household workers lower than they would have been in the absence of the FLSA.[24]

Thus, the thrust of these studies is that a mini-mum-wage law does have the effects predicted by marginal analysis: workers who would otherwise have jobs are laid off or not hired; employers step up the introduction of new equipment, raise hir-ing and production standards, and in other ways strive to increase the marginal value productivity of their labor force to match a higher wage mini-mum; and these effects are most pronounced among low-wage firms and among the lowest-paid and lowest-skilled workers—the very ones the law is designed to aid.

An appraisal

In the face of all this conflicting evidence, Sar Levitan may well be right when he observes, "In the final analysis, the economist's conclusions [about the merits of minimum-wage laws] will depend upon what he believes deep down in his heart to be true; and whatever his conclusions, it is likely that he will find some relevant supporting facts."[25]

And, indeed, which of the tons of available facts are the most relevant? The proponent of minimum wages points to the millions of workers who receive a wage increase without losing their jobs, and the critic stresses that there are never-theless losses and that they occur in the pattern predicted by competitive theory. Obviously both are right: there are gains *and* losses from any effective minimum, and the problem is how these balance out. Unfortunately, many studies seem pointed toward proving that these laws produce *only* gains or *only* losses (depending on the study) rather than weighing both effects.

Even when a rare effort is made to present both sides of the picture, however, the balancing of the results is a hazardous task. Consider, for exam-ple, a study that Levitan calls "possibly the most thorough attempt to evaluate the impact of mini-mum wage legislation," namely, an analysis by

the New York State Department of Labor of the effects on retail trade when a state minimum was increased in 1958. This study found that weekly payrolls in retailing in that state increased by $328,000 (about one percent) and that 73,000 workers received increases averaging 14 cents an hour as a result of the new minimum. On the other hand, store owners reacted by cutting hours and customer service, laying off 1,000 employees (many of them part-time workers), and not re-placing another 500 workers when they quit—resulting in a weekly payroll savings of $79,000.[26] Who won in that trade-off? At first glance, it ap-pears that the law benefited far more workers than it hurt, but how do you weigh the possible price increases to consumers (which were not measured), or the possible cost to the community if the laid-off workers had to be helped with un-employment insurance or welfare benefits, or the cost of the "silent firings"—the workers who, as Friedman and Brozen contend, might have been hired over the next few years by these stores but who are now not "worth" the higher wage they would have to be paid?

Our own opinion is that to date the gains from minimum-wage laws have probably outweighed their costs, but not by much, and such laws are decidedly not a significant solution to the poverty problem. On the plus side of these laws, their critics have proved that some losses do occur in a predictable pattern, but they have *not* proved that these losses add up to a complete offset to the wage gains of millions of workers covered by such laws. Part of the critics' problem, of course, is that it is much harder to trace long-run and diffused effects in prices, mechanization, "silent firings," and the like than it is to show, for exam-ple, that seven million covered workers were re-ceiving less than the new rates which took effect in February, 1968, and there was then no jump in unemployment during the next one or six or twelve months. But surely more is involved here than measurement problems. Everything we know about labor markets tells us that competitive forces do not operate with the inexorable and pin-point precision suggested by the typical supply and demand graph. It is therefore entirely credible that minimum-wage laws can improve the wages of many workers without the "invisible hand" of the market exacting a penny's worth of tribute for every penny of gain.

Yet, we have also tried to show the absurdity of arguing that because competitive forces work imperfectly in the labor market, this proves they do not work at all. You cannot cure poverty in either India or the United States by passing a law decreeing that everyone who works must be paid $300 an hour or even $3 an hour today, for market forces would sabotage this "solution" as surely as night follows day. In fact, those market forces probably work with more severity and predictability in the very sector where workers most need help—in the low-wage but often highly competitive industries—than in high-wage industries like auto and steel. Although the critics cannot quantify the adverse effects of wage minimums, it is significant that they can identify any losses at all, for we have seen that federal and state minimums to date have been set at subsistence levels or below, and have seldom required as much as a 15 percent increase in any industry's payroll costs (which means an even smaller increase in total costs). If losses appear even at this low level of effectiveness, any minimum set much above the poverty level seems doomed to exact a very high cost in unemployment or price increases. Finally, it must always be remembered that a large segment of poor people are not even in the labor market and thus cannot be helped by any minimum wage.

It is for those reasons that we believe—but, like everybody else, cannot prove—that the benefits from minimum-wage laws have probably outweighed their costs in the past, largely because their rates have not been pushed to high levels, and that by the same token their effectiveness in combating poverty has been and will continue to be very limited.

Prevailing-wage laws

There are several other wage laws that utilize a quite different approach in setting wage standards for government employees or for workers in private firms doing business with the government. In general, these laws do not specify a fixed rate as the FLSA does, but instead provide that the wages of the covered employees shall at least equal the rates paid for similar work by private industry. Thus the minimums set by these laws are often determined by an administrative agency and can vary among areas and industries and from year to year.

We have already mentioned two of these laws, the Davis-Bacon and Walsh-Healey Acts. Under the former, the Secretary of Labor is given the authority to determine the prevailing (or average) rates paid in the area surrounding each federal construction project for every manual occupation —from electricians and plumbers to laborers and apprentices—and to require that those occupational rates be the minimum paid on the federal site by all private contractors. Several states have similar laws covering state and local public construction. Many employers and economists have strongly attacked these laws, charging that the federal and state labor departments administering them nearly always decide that the union scale is the prevailing wage, that construction workers are the last group who need government wage protection these days, and that these laws are an important cause of the inflationary wage and price increases in this key industry.

The defenders of these laws argue that it is only fair for the government to meet the prevailing wage standards of private industry instead of encouraging cutthroat competition, that the union scale *is* usually the prevailing wage among the large groups of skilled workers needed on huge projects in remote areas or on any project in unionized cities, and that nonunion rates have been declared prevailing where the facts warrant. Unfortunately no independent study has been made of Davis-Bacon, and so this controversy— unlike that over the FLSA—continues without the burden of too many facts.[27]

The Walsh-Healey Act applies the same principle to most Federal government procurement contracts (for supplies, equipment, and so on) amounting to more than $10,000, except that it requires that only the prevailing *minimum* rate in a locality be paid for the type of work for which the contract is let—that is, only the average rate paid for the least skilled jobs involved, not for every occupation as under Davis-Bacon. Also different is the fact that many critics charge this law with being too weak rather than too strong in its effects. There is one major exception, a 1956 determination by the Secretary of Labor that the relevant "locality" in bituminous coal was the entire industry, which meant that the United Mine Workers' scale was declared prevailing and nonunion mines were severely handicapped in bidding for government contracts. Professors Carrol Christenson and Richard Myren have found, however, that Walsh-Healey determinations in most other industries have been very close to the lowest rate actually being paid—with the result that the act has been administered "fairly" but has not had much, if any, effect on wages. "Perhaps the most important effect of the determinations has been to concentrate government orders in those firms that were already paying wages according to the determination or could easily adjust to doing so."[28] They therefore recommend that the act either be revamped or (their apparent preference) that it be repealed and the FLSA be relied upon exclusively for minimum-wage protection.

The prevailing-wage principle is also an important standard in determining the wages of employees hired directly by the Federal government. Since the passage of the Federal Salary Reform Act of 1962, the government has been generally committed to a goal of paying its civil service employees (primarily white-collar workers) salaries comparable to those paid for similar work in private industry. This goal has not been completely attained, for Congress still determines the specific salary schedule for these employees and weighs several factors in so doing, from the political "clout" of various employee groups to the real or imagined need for the government to set an example for private industry in restraining wage increases for anti-inflationary purposes. And among the nearly one-third of all federal employees who are not covered by civil service classifications—the blue-collar workers in federal defense installations, parks, custodial and maintenance and cafeteria operations, and so on—wages have long been determined not by Congress but by a series of wage boards, sometimes including union representatives, which operate exclusively on the principle of determining and matching the wage rates paid by private industry for comparable work. Of all these prevailing-wage laws

affecting millions of government and private workers, however, only the Walsh-Healey Act has received any serious study.[29]

Limitations on the hours of work

Minimum-wage laws in recent years have often been coupled with maximum-hours provisions, as in both the Walsh-Healey and Fair Labor Standards Acts. The term "maximum hours" is technically a misnomer, since there is generally no proscription on an employee's working any number of hours a day or days per week he may choose (although some state laws limit the number of hours an employer may work women and minors). The federal acts simply require payment of one and one-half times the hourly rate (the worker's regular hourly rate, not the statutory minimum) for all hours in excess of 8 per day or 40 per week. They therefore seek to shorten hours of work by means of penalty rather than prohibition.

The drive by workers to reduce hours of work has a long history—but still not so long as we sometimes carelessly assume. The expectation that work would extend from "sunup to sundown" seems to have persisted into the nineteenth century, and it was only about the 1830s that a determined effort was made by workers, loosely organized as they were at that time along lines as much political as economic, to break through the age-old custom and set a limit of 10 hours a day. What have been the reasons—the relative preference for goods and leisure—behind the drive for shorter hours which has continued almost without cessation since that time?

The fatigue effect of long hours Historically, workers and unions have sought to lower the hours of work for three principal reasons. The first of these is that long hours of work produce fatigue. When 60 hours was standard, workers were cumulatively worn out by their jobs. While wartime emergency situations requiring accelerated production have established that for short spells people can work with good efficiency for as long as 72 hours in a week, it is impossible to sustain that pace for protracted periods. Putting workers on regular schedules of 10 and 12 hours a day in time saps their vitality, reduces their productivity on the job, increases absenteeism, and subjects them to greater risk of ill health.

In view of this long-term effect of excessive work on health, it is not surprising that a reduction in the hours of work may actually lead to an increase in output. An individual who puts in 12 hours a day may have to pace himself to prevent exhaustion before the end of his shift, and he cannot afford to put into his operations the energy which he could muster on a 10- or 8-hour shift. The result may be that he is able to produce more, rather than less, in the shorter period—at least after a sufficient time has elapsed for him to rebuild his energies. It is the same as the differential performance of a machine that is well maintained and one that is overused without proper maintenance.

Even if total output cannot be maintained within the shorter period, labor costs may be held constant with only minor adjustment in the take-home pay. A worker making 50 cents an hour for 60 hours of work and producing 120 units in that time would show a labor cost per unit of 25 cents. At 55 cents an hour for 50 hours of work, with output declining to 110 units, the company would still maintain a labor cost per unit of 25 cents. Its employee would have "bought back" ten hours of leisure at a cost of only $2.50, that is, at just half the price which he was previously being paid for those same hours. Under such circumstances no one would lose, and worker and society both would gain.

Even though a reduction in hours of work might lead to a decline in output, there have been those, including some employers, who were ready to accept this consequence as socially justifiable when hours were longer than they are now. The statement of one Southern cotton manufacturer in 1918, in reply to an industry questionnaire, harks back to a period when child labor was still practiced: "In view of the fact that a plant such as ours works a number of hands who have not yet fully developed physically, we are of the opinion that the change from 66 to 60 hours per week was a good one, but wish to state that when we reduced the hours 9% we reduced our production in like proportion."[30] One can scarcely argue that society does not benefit, in terms of a healthier citizenry, when the hours of work of youngsters "who have not yet fully developed physically" are reduced below 66 per week.

Even with respect to fully matured adults, it is reasonable to assume that social welfare was advanced, for example, in the physical fitness of the steel workers, when the hours of steel-industry employees at the blast furnaces were reduced from 84 hours a week, which was the standard workweek for 75 percent of such employees in 1910 and for 29 percent as recently as 1920.[31]

There is obviously some point past which a further reduction in hours not only produces a decrease in total output and—with wages maintained—leads to an increase in labor cost, but also has no further beneficial physical effect on the individual. There are many who believe that this may be true of the 8-hour day, 40-hour week, although it is difficult to establish this very satisfactorily.[32]

The cultural value of shorter hours   A second objective behind the century-long drive to reduce hours of work has been the desire by workers to have enough leisure time to enjoy the fruits of civilization. When workingmen must spend all their energies in earning a living, the opportunities to cultivate senses and tastes and intellect are denied. If the underpinning of a democracy is an informed citizenry, people require sufficient time to read, discuss, and to participate in civic affairs.

This line of thought was made popular in the 1860s by a labor leader by the name of Ira Steward, who expressed his philosophy of how workers might achieve a rising standard of living with the slogan: "Whether you work by the piece or work by the day, decreasing the hours increases the pay." Behind this jingle lay the view that workers who enjoy greater leisure will cultivate higher tastes, the satisfaction of which requires more income, to achieve which they will put more pressure on their employers for higher rates, forcing a diversion from profits to wages. The stimulation of wants will create the drive leading to their satisfaction. This belief persists in the labor movement and has recently enjoyed a wider circulation.

This point of view was challenged by an historic upper-class fear that if workers were allowed free time, they would use it only for idleness and vice. Daniel Defoe had earlier expressed this opinion in *The True-born Englishman,* where appears the couplet:

> Good drunken company is their delight
> And what they get by day, they spend by night.

The American *Voice of Industry* published a similar opinion in 1846: "The morals of the operatives will necessarily suffer if longer absent from the wholesome discipline of factory life, and leaving them thus to their will and liberty, without a warrant that this spare time will be well employed."[33] Such concerns are still voiced by some who believe that workers "misuse" their leisure time or have more time than they know what to do with.

One may reasonably believe that some amount of disciplined work is desirable in the normal person's life, but the view that time spent away from assembly-line operations or clerking is of less value than those occupations in forming a person's character and intellect is difficult to defend. Widespread participation of workers in the cultural and political life of their communities is evidence that the fruits of leisure are not something which can be appreciated only by a limited few occupying professional or managerial positions. Many labor unions are today playing an active role in channeling the nonworking time of members into rewarding uses—not focused around the union hall as much as around the organized travel tour or adult-education courses in the public schools. The higher levels of education which have been characteristic of younger generations of workers over the years also give reason to believe that this objective behind the drive for shorter hours of work has been not just a rationalization of unworthy motives (*vide* Defoe and the *Voice of Industry*) but a by-product of our own changing culture.

"Sharing the work" through shorter hours   A third objective, of more recent vintage than the foregoing two, has been to spread available work among the labor force to avoid unemployment. In former years this was dubbed "the lump of labor fallacy" by economists, as we had occasion to note in Chapter 13, since it rested on a rather

simple belief that work could be stretched out and made to last longer, or could be parceled out among a larger number of operatives, thus maintaining employment—without regard to the impact on labor cost and a subsequent feedback effect on sales, production, and jobs. A current belief still asserts that when some men work long hours, other men are deprived of opportunity to work at all, so that shorter hours can be made a means of spreading the available work among those who depend on work for existence. The underlying argument in support of this position has become more sophisticated, however.

The most significant aspect of the post-World War II shorter-hours movement is that it is premised solely on this line of argument. No claim has been made that hours are too long for physical endurance or social enjoyment. The position of labor spokesmen has rested exclusively on expectations of the future state of the labor market. At least some of them believe that productivity will increase at a faster rate than in the past, owing to automation. If a 2 to 3 percent increase per annum has been customary in the past, they anticipate a 5 to 6 percent per annum increase in the future. With an expected increase in the rate of growth of the labor force, based upon census projections, this means that every year several million new job opportunities must be created to maintain full employment.[34]

Because unions have developed some skepticism that the Federal government will move promptly or effectively to meet this need for new jobs, they have turned to an expedient over which they have greater control—spreading the work through a collectively bargained reduction in the workweek. The increase in productivity which they foresee will presumably permit a reduction in the hours of work without any loss in earnings, and a reduction in the hours of work will require the employment of more workers, presumably all who wish to work.

It is this aspect of the shorter-hours movement that is attacked most strongly today by employers and many economists. Their argument is simple but potent. If unions should ask for a reduction in weekly hours from 40 to 32 with hourly rates staying the same, it is quite possible that some of the poor and unemployed could then be put to work (waiving problems of training, work schedules, and the like). But unions term this a "sharing of the misery" and always demand that *weekly pay remain the same* on a shorter workweek, meaning that *hourly rates must increase sharply*—by 14.3 percent if hours are lowered from 40 to 35 with no cut in weekly pay, and by 25 percent if hours are reduced from 40 to 32 per week. Put in these terms, the shorter-hours debate is reduced to the familiar argument over the effects of a wage increase. Surely most employers faced with a huge wage increase of 15 to 25 percent will think of laying off workers (and raising prices), not hiring more. And even if some rare employer could completely offset such a large wage increase by an equivalent boost in his plant's productivity, why would he then want to hire more workers?

Unions can argue, of course, that a reduction in hours might be phased in gradually, perhaps shortening the workweek by an hour or so each year, and we shall shortly examine such compromises. At this point, however, note that, by labor's own reasoning, this gradual approach would not contribute much if anything toward solving an immediate problem of unemployment. The lure of shorter hours as an antidote to unemployment has always been the implicit assumption that employers would feel compelled to turn out the same volume of goods tomorrow as they do today, so a large cut in the hours of those now employed would somehow force employers immediately to hire many more workers to maintain output. Once it is acknowledged that this assumption is fallacious and that hours can be cut only gradually, this proposal loses whatever appeal it had as a short-run method for creating jobs.[35]

At least one major union, the UAW, has partially recognized the force of this objection and, instead of seeking a flat reduction in hours, it has proposed that the workweek be reduced below 40 hours only when unemployment rises above some specified minimum, and then weekly pay would be maintained through payments from an "equalization fund" financed by an employer payroll tax. Thus, the costs would be spread over the entire business cycle and all employers. When any employer reduced the workweek to, say, 35 hours in his firm in accordance with a governmental rec-

ommendation, he would be reimbursed from the fund for the added cost of continuing to pay his workers for a 40-hour week. Although this is an ingenious proposal that might well induce many employers to avoid making unemployment worse during a slump, it is difficult to see how it would encourage them to hire additional workers unless the workweek were cut back far more severely than the drop in product demand that had already occurred. In that event, the necessary payments could be very large—and the administrative complexities fearsome.

The income effect of shorter hours Supplementing these three historical reasons behind the workers' drive for shorter hours, a fourth has been added in recent years. With the use of a scheduled or "normal" workweek to represent not the desirable or preferred working time but the period within which a standard wage rate would apply, additional hours would be paid for at premium rates. Indeed, in some companies and industries where employees have won a collective demand for a reduced workweek of, say, 35 hours, they have at the same time sought, and sometimes won, a *guarantee* of an additional 5 hours at overtime pay. Here there is no effort to disguise the fact that it is premium pay and not leisure or work sharing which is wanted. Similarly, in many companies overtime has been so much prized by workers that it has had to be allocated by some rationing device such as seniority. The pressure for shorter hours in these instances has been converted into an indirect pressure for higher income.[36]

There is some documentation for the proposition that numbers of workers—how many one can only guess—have shown more interest in selling additional time than in buying some back. In the words of a union research director who made a survey of the situation in his union:[37]

Aside from the workers' desire for their paid holidays and paid vacations, there is no evidence in recent experience that workers want shorter daily or weekly hours. The evidence is all on the other side. Hundreds of local and international officials have testified that the most numerous and persistent grievances are disputes over the sharing of overtime work. The issue usually is not that someone has been made to work, but that he has been deprived of a chance to make overtime pay. Workers are eager to increase their income, not to work fewer hours.

Reduced hours have a further income appeal of a similar nature. For those workers who prefer more pay to more leisure, a shorter normal working week makes possible supplementary employment. Even with the 40-hour week, it is surprising how many workers are engaged in a second job (usually part-time)—clerking in a local store on weekends, selling insurance at night, filling in on odd jobs such as taking inventory in some plant other than their own, and so on. As hours fall below 40, the number of two-job workers increases and the number of hours they put in on the second job rises. The outstanding illustration of this phenomenon occurs in the Akron rubber industry where, as a carry-over from Depression days, a 36-hour week (6 days of 6 hours) is normal. There the union has estimated that the number of rubber workers employed at secondary work has sometimes run as high as 75 percent, while the number who in recent years have held a *full-time* second job has been about 10 percent of the total. Sometimes a man will put in 6 hours on a shift in one rubber company and follow it with a full 6-hour shift at a second rubber company.

Although that situation is rather extreme, surveys begun in 1956 have consistently shown that about 5 percent of all employed persons are "moonlighters"—those who hold two or more jobs at the same time.[38] In addition, a shorter workweek can mean increased income to a *household*, even if not to an individual worker, for a wife may be able to take on a job of 32 hours, for example, when one of 40 hours would be too demanding, in addition to her household chores.

Projecting past trends

A more general argument in favor of shorter hours, which can buttress the case for any of the specific objectives just described, is that working hours have declined greatly in the past without adverse effects and therefore they can and will continue to decline in the future. For example,

workers in nonagricultural industries averaged 62 hours per week in the early 1890s and only about 38 hours per week in the late 1960s, so why shouldn't this trend continue in the coming years?

In many respects this is a perfectly valid argument, and most experts agree that the workweek will probably be much shorter in the next generation or two. But that is not the same thing as saying that the workweek will or should decline next year by some "historically inevitable" percentage, for past reductions in hours have not followed a smooth continuum. Within manufacturing, for example, blue-collar workers had achieved a 40-hour week by 1940 and, except for the heavy overtime work of the war years, they have continued to average about 40 hours per week ever since. (To be precise, since 1945 factory workers never averaged less than 39.1 hours or more than 41.3 hours per week in any year through 1968.) Weekly hours have also remained stable through the postwar years in mining, have perhaps dropped fractionally in construction, and have dropped substantially only in retail trade—from 43 hours in 1939 to 41 in 1945 and 35 in 1968.

Thus, while the "average" member of the labor force undoubtedly works fewer hours per week now than twenty or thirty years ago, this is primarily due to the occupational and industry shifts we have stressed so often: The proportion of white-collar workers in the labor force has been growing, and on the average these workers (at the clerical level, for example) have a shorter workweek than blue-collar workers have, and the workweek is also shorter in many of the expanding service industries (such as retailing, the finance, insurance, and real estate groups, and in many parts of government) than in agriculture, mining, and manufacturing. Some postwar reduction in hours has occurred within individual industries, it is true. Unions have won shorter workweeks in the needle trades, for instance, and in the printing industry and some parts of construction—with the most spectacular gain being that of the electricians' union in New York City, which won a 25-hour workweek in 1962 (plus guaranteed overtime). Yet, the 40-hour standard has proved remarkably durable over the past thirty years, and the standard of a 5-day week has hardly been questioned since its adoption in the

1920s and 1930s. In 1969, however, the Industrial Union Department of the AFL-CIO did come out for a 4-day week to offset the effects of automation.

Thus, no one questions the fact that we *can* have a shorter workweek in the near future, but past trends are no guide to determining *when* and by *how much* working hours will decline. The economy's increases in productivity can be taken in the form of higher real consumption or more leisure or some mixture of the two. It has been estimated that in this century we have so far accepted our economic gains in the proportions of about 60 percent in real goods and 40 percent in increased leisure, but there is no particular reason why we should continue that same ratio in the future. The decision will depend upon how millions of families balance their preferences for both more goods and more leisure, and we have seen why some people believe that, in the years since 1940, American families have leaned heavily toward more goods rather than more leisure.

Appraisal

The foregoing criticisms of the short-hours movement are persuasive in some respects and overstated in others. As a remedy for unemployment, the shorter workweek is no more effective than minimum-wage laws are in attacking poverty. In both cases the "dismal science" must be given its due: Employers simply cannot be expected to stand still when their hourly wage bill suddenly escalates by 15 or 25 percent or more, the increase necessary to eliminate poverty-level wages through the FLSA or to cut the workweek from 40 to 35 hours or less in one fell swoop (and still maintain weekly pay). At those impact levels, the market is a harsh taskmaster and employers would react just as competitive theory predicts—by plant shutdowns, layoffs, higher prices, more substitution of machinery for men, and all the rest.

But neither this argument, nor those concerning the apparent preference of workers for income over leisure, means that organized labor's drive for more leisure has been stalled in recent years. We have talked so far only about a shorter workday or workweek, but leisure also comes in other forms. The same ex-union officer who was quoted earlier to the effect that workers now compete for overtime assignments, suggesting a preference for income instead of a shorter day, has commented on the rapid spread of another form of leisure— holidays and vacations—for which workers appear to be ready to sacrifice income.[39]

The unions in the mass production industries have introduced an important innovation in shorter hours of work. Beginning in 1940, the practice appeared of granting paid holidays and paid vacations and certain other provisions for time off without loss of pay. At first, the provisions were quite modest, but their popularity and their general acceptance by the community resulted in their gaining momentum until they are now characteristic of all industry as well as greatly improved. Each year, unions negotiate new benefits of this kind, increasing the number of paid holidays, increasing the vacation period for long-service workers, and granting at least 1- or 2-week vacations to relatively new employees. There appears to be no sign of a letup in this development.

The success of this drive apparently reflects a deep-seated desire on the part of most workers for a new kind of leisure. In this sense, the movement is philosophically close to the thinking and agitating of the 1830's when leisure was an objective of the shorter hours movement. During the early years of the vacation movement, there were some efforts on the part of workers, and employers, too, to convert the vacation into additional income. But this effort has largely been eliminated, so that workers are taking their vacations and using them as they were intended.

The importance of this development can hardly be overemphasized. Instead of making a dramatic choice between holding the line at a 40-hour week or risking a plunge to 35 or 32 hours, the bargaining process has quietly produced the pragmatic compromise of shortening the *work year* in small steps which employers can absorb. And these small steps add up to impressive gains for employees. Each week of paid vacation, for example, is equivalent, over the course of a year, to a cut of 0.77 hours per workweek (with no cut in pay), and each paid holiday averages out to a cut of 0.154 hours per week. Thus, a worker who receives three weeks of paid vacation and nine paid holidays per year—not particularly unusual today —is in effect averaging *36.3 hours of work per week for 40 hours' pay.* Add in various items such as paid sick leave, supplemental unemployment benefits, call-in pay, and (to stretch things) paid rest and lunch breaks, and it is clear that many union (and nonunion) workers have already won the 35-hour week, although they are still reported in most statistics as working a 40-hour week.

In addition, unions and governments and market forces have all combined to reduce the length of *working life* through postponed entry into the labor force (child-labor laws, the trends away from agriculture and toward more education, and so on), and through public and private pension plans which permit retirement at sixty-five years of age or earlier.

American workers are therefore continuing to gain added leisure in spite of the apparent stability of the workweek, and in forms that invite imaginative experiments. The academic world, for example, no longer has a monopoly on sabbatical leaves, for in 1963 the Steelworkers secured such leaves in most of their major contracts, which now provide for three months of paid vacation every five years for high-seniority workers. Long leaves of this sort would help to make possible the broadening experience of foreign travel for the average American workman. (Already unions are chartering all-expense tours to Europe for their members.) Perhaps even more important, they make possible "educational leaves" which could assist workers in advancing their competence in the face of rapid technological, scientific, and organizational changes.

While workers at present income levels may prefer more income to more leisure (at least of the shortened-workday variety), with rising income the choice is likely to be less decisive. With increasing income, the marginal rate of substitution of income for leisure changes, so that an hour's pay is more willingly given up for an hour's free time. This *future* predictable shift in the relative attractiveness of leisure and the goods which more income will buy is perhaps more relevant than the unions realize. They may conceivably be bargaining for the right objective for the wrong reason. Objectives such as a shorter workweek are not achieved without a preparatory buildup. The

Automobile Workers and Steelworkers spent ten years fighting for the guaranteed annual wage before winning the first installment on it. Thus, without fully realizing it, the unions may be more forward-looking than their critics. Shorter hours for the purpose of sharing limited work opportunities may be a poor tactic, a counsel of despair, but shorter hours, with leisure bunched so that it can be used more flexibly and productively, may nevertheless prove to be a sound objective.

Finally, the price in real income which must be paid for an increase in leisure may not be so great as some calculations would suggest. This for two reasons.

First, the translation of added free time into income renounced is based on a static assumption that the added free time does not have modifying consequences. It concentrates on the immediate loss without considering the possibility of long-run gain. But the ways in which increased leisure is used may stimulate in workers an intellectual development, a mental alertness, a less inhibited and parochial outlook, all of which over time may actually increase the productive powers of those so responding to an extent not otherwise possible. From this approach, leisure, if employed well, may be regarded as a capital investment. "The improvement of human resources and their utilization through hygiene, education, recreation, and the heightened exercise of imagination make a contribution to economic growth which is commonly underestimated if not ignored."[40] Paid educational leaves are one example of this.

There is a second reason why per capita national income may not fall so far as expected, as a result of a reduction in the normal hours of work. It lies in the probability that some who now exclude themselves from the labor force because they cannot devote so many hours to a job (housewives, for example) will find it more feasible to put in a briefer week of work. The number of man-hours of labor which the economy would lose by reducing the length of its standard workweek would thus be partially offset by the additional hours of labor which it would gain from those whom the reduced workweek would draw into the labor force.

For the above reasons, one would be comparatively safe in predicting that shorter working hours—perhaps chiefly in other forms than a shorter scheduled working week—are in the cards. But there is one large proviso which must be entered. The unknown component is the pressure which may be brought to bear on this country by underdeveloped nations to provide them with the resources to industrialize and improve their standards of living. It is entirely conceivable that such pressure may be as difficult to resist as the similar internal pressure which has led to a redistribution of national wealth via a graduated income tax. It may be difficult for this country, and others which enjoy high standards of living, to appropriate for themselves the whole fruits of their efforts without inciting strong external demands for a similar redistribution of wealth on an international basis. The possibility of reducing the hours of work for Americans may have to give way before unavoidable pressure to use our manpower to relieve continuing want and misery overseas.[41]

Western society has for the first time in the history of the world achieved mass leisure for its peoples and widespread enjoyment of the cultural satisfactions of life which only leisure can make possible. But it may not be feasible for them to increase the material distance between themselves and the underdeveloped world without unleashing that unrest and protest which have always been a threat to the position of the privileged few among the underprivileged many.

Conclusion

From a minimum wage to relieve the bargaining disadvantage of exploited workers to a society which has achieved mass leisure—the distance we have covered in this chapter—is quite a jump. To end on a note that ours is a privileged society perhaps having to use its productive potential for the benefit of those less privileged may seem a long way from the examination of wages-and-hours legislation as a form of public assistance or protection to our own disadvantaged groups.

We should remind ourselves, however, of the findings of Chapter 19—that we do have in our midst very sizable numbers of people who exist on the ragged edges of subsistence as we have culturally defined that term. Their "subsistence" may look luxurious to the poor of the under-

developed economies, but alongside standards of living to which we have become accustomed, their level of existence arouses an understandable and commendable desire on our part to assist them through social legislation. By and large, the labor movement—with a lag—has used its power as a political pressure group to further such legislation.

The disadvantaged groups, such as the unskilled and uneducated, women who are the principal support for a family without a male head, older workers, and nonwhite workers, are often among those who are unorganized, or if organized have limited bargaining power. They are thus peculiarly subject to exploitation, and the forces of competition may tend to force employers, sometimes against their own desires, to follow the pattern set by the most ruthless or the most desperate of their rivals. We have covered all this before. We need only remind ourselves that minimum-wage legislation, even if it cannot eliminate poverty, may serve the limited and useful task of setting a floor—perhaps a rather low floor—to wage competition and labor exploitation. The numbers who are actually benefited by having their wages raised may not be large, and there are no doubt others who suffer by losing employment altogether, but on balance the effort to establish *some* socially approved minimum level of payment seems justified. Its actual level is wide open to debate.

That some compromise is just barely possible on this issue is illustrated by some further remarks of former Secretary of Labor Wirtz and Professor Friedman, whom we quoted at the outset of this chapter as examples of the polar differences in opinion concerning minimum-wage laws. In recommending universal coverage by the FLSA and a $2 minimum in 1969, Wirtz noted:[42]

There is ample precedent for a subsidy arrangement here—to cover whatever "uneconomic" factor might be involved in the payment of a decent subsistence wage by *all* enterprises. This is a basic element in the JOBS work-training program, with the Federal Government paying employers the extra cost of training new employees whose disadvantages make their hiring and training more expensive than would normally be the case. . . .

In certain extreme situations—such as the employment of handicapped persons by sheltered workshops (or other employers)—a subsidy provision would make clear good sense. . . . [The handicapped worker] ought to receive *what he needs for what he does*—with provision that the workshop be compensated for the extra costs over and above what that person's work brings in.

And Professor Friedman:

And suppose society feels . . . [a worker's income] should be higher than he is able to earn. In my opinion, it would be far better to supplement his income in some fashion than it is first to make him unemployed and then to give him the whole sum. We should at least let him earn what he can. . . . Then he has the self-respect and dignity of holding a job, of contributing to his own support.[43]

These men are still far apart on what to do about the FLSA, and yet Wirtz recognizes the dangers that might arise if the minimum wage were set at a "decent" level, Friedman admits that an unregulated labor market may pay some people less than society considers a decent minimum, and both agree that it would be best to make up the "uneconomic" difference in a way that will not cost these workers their jobs and self-respect. Minimum-wage laws in their present form will not do that job—nor will simply eliminating these laws do the job.[44] The search today therefore is for a mechanism by which the "social minimum" implicit in laws like the FLSA can be reached through governmental and market powers that supplement, rather than offset, one another. We have not yet discovered that ideal mechanism to help the working poor, although the following chapters will show that public and private sectors have often cooperated to meet the problems of the sick, the aged, and the unemployed.

As for the public and private attempts to regulate working hours, we have seen that these too have compiled a mixed record. The application of penalty rates to working hours past some socially approved maximum has not created jobs for the unemployed, but it has had the unexpected effect of providing those already employed with an effective device for augmenting their income. Also, while unions have been largely stymied in their recent efforts to obtain a direct reduction in the workweek, they have helped to achieve a substantial reduction in the work year and work life of most members of the labor force. This gradual and indirect shortening of working hours is far less dramatic than the historic battles for the 10-hour and 8-hour days, but for millions of workers the growth of paid holidays and vacations has been one of the major triumphs of collective bargaining.

ADDITIONAL READINGS

Chamberlain, Neil W.: *Sourcebook on Labor,* McGraw-Hill, New York, 1958, chap. 20.

Christenson, Carrol L., and Richard A. Myren: *Wage Policy under the Walsh-Healey Public Contracts Act: A Critical Review,* Indiana University Press, Bloomington, 1966.

Cullen, Donald E.: *Minimum Wage Laws,* Cornell University, New York State School of Industrial and Labor Relations, Ithaca, N.Y., Bulletin 43, 1961.

Dankert, Clyde E.: "Shorter Hours—in Theory and Practice," *Industrial and Labor Relations Review,* April, 1962, pp. 307–322.

Greenbaum, Marcia L.: *The Shorter Workweek,* Cornell University, New York State School of Industrial and Labor Relations, Ithaca, N.Y., Bulletin 50, 1963.

Levitan, Sar A.: "Minimum Wages—A Tool to Fight Poverty," *Labor Law Journal,* vol. 17, pp. 53–60, 1966.

U.S. Department of Labor, Wage and Hour and Public Contracts Divisions, *Minimum Wages and Maximum Hours under the Fair Labor Standards Act,* annual reports submitted to Congress.

FOR ANALYSIS AND DISCUSSION

1. Samuel Gompers, the first president of the American Federation of Labor, is revered by the labor movement as its founding father. In May, 1914, Gompers testified in New York before the United States Commission on Industrial Relations, and an amended and modified version of his testimony was later published by the AFL in pamphlet form under the title *The American Labor Movement: Its Makeup, Achievements and*

Aspirations. On page 14 of that pamphlet, Gompers said:

> The A. F. of L. is not in favor of fixing, by legal enactment, certain minimum wages. The attempts of the government to establish wages at which workmen may work, according to the teachings of history, will result in a long era of industrial slavery. . . .
>
> There is now a current movement to increase wages by a proposal to determine a minimum wage by political authorities. It is a maxim in law that once a court is given jurisdiction over an individual it has the power, the field, and authority to exercise that jurisdiction. "I fear the Greeks even when they bear gifts." An attempt to entrap the American workmen into a species of slavery, under guise of an offer of this character is resented by the men and women of the American trade union movement.

What possible fear of "the Greeks" (the government) could Gompers have had, and was he justified "according to the teachings of history" in holding that fear? And how does it happen that George Meany, the current president of the AFL-CIO in 1970, does not share that fear?

2. List and illustrate some of the difficulties in trying to derive conclusions from statistical evidence as to the effect of minimum-wage rates on employment.

3. Analyze the feasibility and desirability of a minimum wage tied to the consumer price index.

4. The U.S. Chamber of Commerce has maintained that the FLSA time-and-a-half requirement should be made to apply to the *minimum* wage rather than the *regular* wage. Employers would thus "not be compelled *by law* to pay fantastic wages for overtime which have no social justification whatsoever in terms of the objectives of the wage-hour law or any other socially-desired objectives."

Analyze this argument.

5. Some people have argued that the effective utilization of leisure time is one of the most important social issues we must face in the future. Why should the use of time be any matter for concern? Is there danger that workers, with more leisure time, will spend it at the local bar or bowling alley, or glued to a TV screen? How

would you prefer that Americans spend their leisure time?

6. Union leaders have sometimes been accused of plumping for shorter hours in order to prevent their unions from shrinking in numbers. What is the basis for such a charge?

NOTES

1. U.S. Bureau of the Census, *Current Population Reports,* Series P-60, no. 54, 1968, Table 13, p. 30.

2. U.S. Department of Labor, Wage and Hour and Public Contracts Divisions, *Minimum Wage and Maximum Hours Standards Under the Fair Labor Standards Act, 1969,* 1969, pp. 3–4.

3. *The Minimum Wage Rate: Who Really Pays?* An interview with Yale Brozen and Milton Friedman. The Free Society Association, Washington, 1966, pp. 11 and 26–27.

4. The phrase is that of Paul Douglas and Joseph Hackman in "The Fair Labor Standards Act of 1938," *Political Science Quarterly,* vol. 53, p. 491, 1938. This article and another in the succeeding issue provide an interesting examination of the background and legislative history of the first federal legislation in the minimum-wage field.

5. *Adkins v. Children's Hospital,* 261 U.S. 525 (1923).

6. *West Coast Hotel Co. v. Parrish,* 300 U.S. 379 (1937).

7. See any recent issue of the *Monthly Labor Review* for both of these wage measures.

8. AFL *Weekly News Service,* April 29, 1933.

9. Fair Labor Standards Act of 1937, *Joint Hearings before the Committee on Education and Labor, United States Senate; and the Committee on Labor, House of Representatives;* 75th Cong., 1st Sess., 1937, part 1, p. 217. Green did suggest, however, that collectively bargained rates "prevailing in a substantial and fairly representative portion of the class, craft, industry, trade, business, or division or unit thereof" should be made the legal minimum for the whole of the class, craft, industry, etc. (The same, p. 222.) It is difficult to see how such "extension of the agreement," a practice which has been used in some other countries, can be reconciled with a withdrawal of government from wage fixing as collective bargaining expands.

10. Thus, at the 29th convention of the ILGWU, President Dubinsky reported (*Daily Proceedings,* May 11, 1956, p. 71):

> The recommendation of the GEB [General Executive Board] and what the committee here recommends is, that when agreements are made or renewed in future, the minimum rate for any worker shall be set at no less than 15 cents above

the federal minimum, or $1.15. As long as the federal minimum will stay at $1, our minimum will be $1.15. I know that the employers sitting on the platform are not opposing this because they represent an old established industry and they have higher minimums in any case. But I do know that we will have difficulties in parts of the South and in parts of the Midwest, and in other sections of the country where open shops and nonunion shops will fight to continue at the $1 minimum. In those cases the $1 minimum is not only a minimum; it is also the average and in some cases even the maximum. When we have a $1.15 minimum it means the average worker earns more and the efficient worker earns much more. We realize it will be difficult in many cases to obtain this goal. But I consider this as a goal towards which we should strive and which we must win . . . I am confident that we will succeed, but we must make a serious, conscientious effort. Even if we have to strike in some instances to establish it. We should have the courage and determination to do it.

11. An examination of the arguments of those who favor or oppose minimum-wage legislation makes it painfully apparent that argumentation more frequently proceeds from a conception of where personal interest lies than from consistent economic logic. The people who are prone to maintain that technological unemployment is unimportant, because the technological progress which causes it leads to an expansion of job opportunities which will absorb those displaced, are also likely to contend that minimum wages harm those whom they are designed to help by displacing them with capital equipment or by inducing concern in the use of labor. And those who usually claim that technological unemployment works heavy hardship are the same people who argue that if higher minimum rates lead to the displacement of workers by technological changes, this is not serious because those displaced can be absorbed elsewhere in a "dynamic" economy.

12. *Economic Factors in Statutory Minimum Wages,* analysis prepared by the Legislative Reference Service of the Library of Congress, 80th Cong., 2d Sess., Senate Document 146, 1948, p. 34. Those who rely on this argument must, of course, be prepared to accept the unemployment of some of those employed in the production of cheap goods. As prices rise, sales fall off, and presumably those displaced are not in a position to find as profitable an employment elsewhere.

13. George J. Stigler, "Professor Lester and the Marginalists," *American Economic Review,* vol. 37, p. 157, March, 1947.

14. John M. Peterson, "Employment Effects of Minimum Wages, 1938–50," *Journal of Political Economy,* vol. 65, p. 414, October, 1957. That this has held true for later increases in the FLSA rate is shown by the estimates that the initial application of

the 1966 amendments (raising the rate for previously covered workers from $1.25 to $1.40 in 1967 and setting a rate of $1 for newly covered workers) directly affected no more than 11.5 percent of covered workers (i.e., the proportion who were previously earning less than the new rates), and raising all these workers' pay to the new rates (assuming no disemployment effect) required an increase of only 0.5 percent in the total payrolls of all previously covered workers and only 0.8 percent in the total wage bill of all newly covered workers. U.S. Department of Labor, Wage and Hour and Public Contracts Divisions, *Maximum Wage and Hour Standards under the Fair Labor Standards Act, 1967,* 1967, Table 8, p. 26.

15. U.S. Department of Labor, *Maximum Wage and Hours Standards . . ., 1969,* p. 1.

16. U.S. Department of Labor, Wage and Hour and Public Contracts Divisions, *Hired Farmworkers, A study of the effects of the $1.00 minimum wage under the Fair Labor Standards Act,* 1968, pp. 1–2.

17. U.S. Department of Labor, Wage and Hour and Public Contracts Divisions, *Hired Farmworkers, A study of the effects of the $1.15 minimum wage under the Fair Labor Standards Act,* 1969, pp. 1–2. These studies make no reference to the possible effect of the FLSA minimum on farm prices, but other sources show that most farm prices actually dropped in 1967 and then rose in 1968. Given the inflationary trend throughout the economy in those years, it would be difficult to assess what effect, if any, the FLSA rates alone had on farm prices.

18. Compare, for example, H. M. Douty, "Some Effects of the $1.00 Minimum Wage in the United States," *Economica,* vol. 27, pp. 137–147, May, 1960, and Paul A. Brinker, "The $1 Minimum Wage Impact on 15 Oklahoma Industries," *Monthly Labor Review,* vol. 80, pp. 1092–1095, September, 1957.

19. George Macesich and Charles T. Stewart, Jr., "Recent Department of Labor Studies of Minimum Wage Effects," *The Southern Economic Journal,* vol. 26, pp. 281–290, April, 1960.

20. John M. Peterson, "Employment Effects of Minimum Wages, 1938–50," *The Journal of Political Economy,* vol. 65, pp. 412–430, October, 1957; and "Employment Effects of State Minimum Wages for Women: Three Historical Cases Re-examined," *Industrial and Labor Relations Review,* vol. 12, pp. 406–422, April, 1959. Also see "Comment" by Richard A. Lester and "Reply" by Peterson in *Industrial and Labor Relations Review,* vol. 13, pp. 254–273, January, 1960.

21. Brozen and Friedman, *The Minimum Wage Rate: Who Really Pays?,* pp. 10–17. For a critique, see Jacob J. Kaufman and Terry G. Foran, "The Minimum Wage and Poverty," in Sar A. Levitan, W. J. Cohen, and R. J. Lampman (eds.), *Towards Freedom From Want,* Industrial Relations Research Association, Madison, Wisc., 1968, pp. 205–211.

22. Colin D. Campbell and Rosemary G. Camp-

bell, "State Minimum Wage Laws as a Cause of Unemployment," *The Southern Economic Journal,* vol. 35, pp. 323–332, April, 1969. It should be noted that the average rates of unemployment cited for each *group* of markets are weighted by the size of the labor force in each of the markets within that group. Researchers have long disagreed over whether employment weights should be used in studies like this, with some arguing that it is useful to know what happens among the largest number of workers and others arguing that, for testing the competitive model, a small labor market is just as "important" as a large market and should carry equal weight.

23. David E. Kaun, "Minimum Wages, Factor Substitution and the Marginal Producer," *The Quarterly Journal of Economics,* vol. 79, pp. 478–486, August, 1965. Kaun's measure of nonwage inputs is value added minus wages divided by man-hours; he uses wages per man-hour in 1947 and 1954 as a measure of the vulnerability of a firm or industry to the FLSA minimum.

24. Yale Brozen, "Minimum Wage Rates and Household Workers," *The Journal of Law and Economics,* vol. 5, pp. 103–109, October, 1962.

25. Sar A. Levitan, "Minimum Wages—A Tool to Fight Poverty," *Labor Law Journal,* vol. 17, p. 58, January, 1966.

26. The same, p. 58, summarizing a study by the New York State Department of Labor, *Economic Effects of Minimum Wages: The New York Retail Trade Order of 1957–1958* (Publication B-148), 1964.

27. For some information on this law, see *Hearings on Administration of the Bacon-Davis Act Before the Special Subcommittee on Labor of the House Committee on Education and Labor,* 3 parts, 87th Congress, 2nd Session, 1962.

28. Carroll L. Christenson and Richard A. Myren, *Wage Policy under the Walsh-Healey Public Contracts Act: A Critical Review,* Indiana University Press, Bloomington, 1966, p. 224. Also see Herbert C. Morton, *Public Contracts and Private Wages: Experience under the Walsh-Healey Act,* Brookings, Washington, 1965.

29. For a comparison of salaries in private industry and under civil service classifications, see the annual publication of the U.S. Bureau of Labor Statistics, *National Survey of Professional, Administrative, Technical, and Clerical Pay.* For a description of recent changes in the "wage-board" system, see Harry A. Donoian, "A New Approach to Setting the Pay of Federal Blue-Collar Workers," *Monthly Labor Review,* vol. 92, pp. 30–34, April, 1969.

30. National Industrial Conference Board, *Hours of Work as Related to Output and Health of Workers: Cotton Manufacturing,* Research Report no. 4, New York, March, 1918, p. 30.

31. *The Twelve-Hour Shift in Industry,* by the Committee on Work-periods in Continuous Industry of the Federated American Engineering Societies, Dutton, New York, 1922, p. 226.

32. For a summary of the various studies that have sought to establish a relationship between output and less than a 40-hour week, see Herbert R. Northrup and Herbert R. Brinberg, *Economics of the Work Week,* National Industrial Conference Board, Studies in Business Economics no. 24, New York, 1950, pp. 26–31.

33. Quoted by Norman Ware in *The Industrial Worker, 1840–1860,* Houghton Mifflin, Boston, 1924, p. 127.

34. The union argument has been stated in *Shorter Hours: Tool to Combat Unemployment,* AFL-CIO, Washington, 1963.

35. Professor Howard G. Foster has shown, however, that in some circumstances shorter hours can "create" more jobs. For example, if *both* productivity and total sales (demand) in a firm increased by 5 percent in one year, and if a union had won a 5 percent cut in weekly hours (with no cut in weekly pay) at the beginning of that year, the employer could increase his work force by up to 5 percent without increasing his unit labor costs or depressing his product market. This would be of little help in a recession, when the demand for most products may be stable or declining, but the argument illustrates that a work-sharing proposal can sometimes be practical. See Foster, "Unemployment and Shorter Hours," *Labor Law Journal,* vol. 17, pp. 211–225, April, 1966.

36. The desire by some workers for overtime hours obviously conflicts with the interest of union officials in shorter hours to spread the work. This is another instance where membership and organizational objectives may diverge. In 1963, union officials lobbied in Congress for higher penalty rates on overtime to induce employers to take on additional workers rather than give extra work to employees already on the payroll—an objective patently in conflict with the preference for more work and more income on the part of some of their members.

37. George Brooks, former research director, International Brotherhood of Pulp, Sulphite and Paper Mill Workers, speaking at the 1956 AFL-CIO Conference on Shorter Hours of Work, reported in the *Monthly Labor Review,* vol. 79, p. 1273, 1956.

38. "Multiple Jobholders in May 1965," *Monthly Labor Review,* May 1966, pp. 17–22.

The president of one large manufacturing company remarked, in 1957, that his company had given its toolmakers a standard 54-hour week, with overtime for all hours past 40, "because we could not get effective tool workers without doing this. They were holding another job and making expensive mistakes as a result. We work them 54 hours so they will be too tired to take another job. The overtime we pay on a 54-hour week is nowhere near the cost of inefficient toolmakers."

39. George Brooks, *Monthly Labor Review,* vol. 79, pp. 1272–1273, 1956.

40. Nelson N. Foote, in a discussion of "The Shortening Work Week as a Component of Economic Growth," *Papers and Proceedings of the 68th Annual Meeting of the American Economic Association, 1956,* p. 227.

41. This possibility is discussed in Neil W. Chamberlain, *The West in a World without War,* McGraw-Hill, New York, 1963, chaps. 3 and 4.

42. U.S. Department of Labor, *Minimum Wage and Maximum Hours Standards . . . , 1969,* p. 4.

43. Brozen and Friedman, *The Minimum Wage Rate: Who Really Pays?,* p. 32.

44. Levitan, "Minimum Wages . . . ," p. 57, makes this point well:

. . . reliance upon the elimination of minimum wages as a means of increasing employment would require the acceptance of radical changes in our society's values and a sharp curtailment of our welfare system. For as long as society continues to provide the basic needs of most of the destitute, it can hardly be expected that the unemployed would accept jobs which provide little more income than benefits paid under the welfare system. And in most states even low earnings would disqualify a worker from receiving public assistance, thus destroying the incentive to accept a job below current minimum wage rates. We must conclude, therefore, that the elimination of minimum wage statutes is at best a doubtful panacea for the reduction of unemployment.

Our competitive economic system has outperformed other economies in many respects, but neither our system nor any other has achieved a true equality of economic opportunity. We have seen the difficulties in solving this problem through the mechanism of the market itself. The freedom to change jobs has benefited millions of workers, but the barriers to mobility facing millions of others have stripped them of a meaningful choice of job and occupation; labor unions have democratized the workplace, but their economic gains are severely limited by market forces; the government can establish a minimum wage, but it cannot prevent the dismissal of workers thought to be worth less than that minimum; and competitive forces do nothing for the millions who are in need precisely because they are cut off from the market, being too young or too old or too sick to work.

We shall therefore concentrate, in this and the following chapters of Part Seven, on how our society meets the needs of those without any job income for one reason or another. This income loss may be temporary but unpredictable, resulting from sickness or injury or a slump in the economy, or it may be predictable but permanent, resulting from old age, or it may be due to causes too complex to categorize—such as the many other causes of poverty ranging from poor education to racial discrimination and broken families. Whatever the cause, the problem is the same: No family can long exist in a modern society without

cash income, which means for most people a wage or salary earned on a job. When that "cash nexus" is snapped for even a few weeks or months, the average family is in deep trouble. It is that simple fact which has led to the proliferation of income-maintenance programs that we shall examine in these chapters—workmen's compensation, health insurance, unemployment insurance, old-age pensions, and a host of welfare and antipoverty programs.

An overview

Before plunging into the details of these many programs, however, it is important to gain an overall view of the scope of "welfare-state" activities in this country, which some critics believe have gone much too far and others believe are woefully inadequate.

Statistics rarely settle political arguments like this, but the data in Table 22-1 may at least puncture the more extreme myths about welfare spending in this country. On the one hand, conservatives are obviously correct in charging that social welfare spending has mushroomed in both absolute and relative terms, having risen more than twice as fast as the gross national product (GNP) since 1945. Also, note the persistence of "public-aid" spending, which was supposed to fade away as social insurance programs expanded—that is, as we provided income maintenance for the aged and unemployed and others as a matter of right,

Table 22-1 *Social Welfare Expenditures under Public Programs as Percent of Gross National Product, Selected Years, 1890-1967*

Fiscal year	Gross national product (in billions)	Social welfare expenditures as percent of GNP							Total health and medical care expenditures as percent of GNP[h]
		Total[a]	Social insurance[b]	Public aid[c]	Health and medical programs[d]	Veterans' programs[e]	Education[f]	Other social welfare[g]	
1889-1890[i]	$13.0	2.4		0.3	0.1	0.9	1.1		n.a.
1912-1913[i]	39.9	2.5		0.3	0.4	0.5	1.3		n.a.
1928-1929	101.0	3.9	0.3	0.1	0.3	0.7	2.4	0.1	0.5
1932-1933	56.8	7.9	0.6	1.2	0.7	1.4	3.7	0.2	1.0
1935-1936	77.4	13.2	0.6	4.0	0.6	4.9	2.9	0.1	0.8
1938-1939	87.6	10.5	1.3	4.8	0.7	0.7	2.9	0.1	0.8
1940-1941	112.1	8.0	1.2	3.1	0.6	0.5	2.3	0.1	0.8
1945-1946	210.3	6.1	1.7	0.5	0.9	1.1	1.6	0.1	1.1
1950-1951	310.4	7.7	1.5	0.8	0.9	1.9	2.4	0.1	1.2
1955-1956	409.5	8.6	2.6	0.8	0.8	1.2	3.0	0.2	1.1
1960-1961	506.5	11.5	4.4	0.9	1.0	1.1	3.8	0.3	1.4
1965-1966	715.2	12.3	4.5	1.0	1.0	0.9	4.6	0.3	1.5
1966-1967	763.1	13.1	4.9	1.2	1.1	0.9	4.7	0.4	2.1

[a] Includes public housing, not shown separately.

[b] Benefit payments under those public programs that provide income maintenance and other benefits without a means test: OASDHI (old-age, survivors', disability, and health insurance), unemployment insurance, workmen's compensation, state temporary disability insurance, and railroad and public employee retirement systems.

[c] Programs that provide payments in cash, kind, and services to needy individuals and families as determined by a means or income test. Includes public assistance (aid to specific categories of the needy—the aged, blind, disabled, families with dependent children, and the medically indigent—plus general relief to needy persons who do not qualify under the categorical programs) and other public aid (the work-relief programs of the 1930s and the recent antipoverty programs that provide work experience and training for disadvantaged persons).

[d] Includes public health programs, medical research, the construction of hospitals and other medical facilities, and some hospital and medical care (such as that provided in federal, state, and local hospitals and to military personnel). For other medical expenditures, see note [h].

[e] Veterans' pensions; compensation for service-connected disabilities; survivors' benefits; educational allowances; low-cost life insurance.

[f] All expenditures for the support, maintenance, and operation of local, state, and federal educational institutions.

[g] Programs that do not readily fit into other classifications, such as vocational rehabilitation, school meals, child welfare (foster care, day care, etc.), and some of the antipoverty programs (Community Action, VISTA).

[h] Combines expenditures for "Health and medical programs" and for medical services provided in connection with social insurance, public aid, and veterans', vocational rehabilitation, and antipoverty programs.

[i] In fiscal 1889-1890 and 1912-1913, social insurance expenditures totaled less than 0.05 percent of GNP, and "other social welfare" payments are included under "public aid."

SOURCE: U.S. Department of Health, Education, and Welfare, Social Security Administration, *Social Welfare Expenditures Under Public Programs in the United States, 1929-1966*, p. 192.

"handouts" based on a means test were expected to largely disappear. Instead, benefits under *both* types of programs have grown since 1945, and in the prosperous year of 1967 we were spending as large a share of GNP on public aid as we did in the depths of the Depression in 1932 and 1933, when there were practically no social insurance programs. Thus there is some basis for the charge that welfare expenditures seem to grow ever larger even in a prosperous economy.

On the other hand, many liberals are obviously correct in arguing that the economy has never performed better than during the evolution of the welfare state. If the growth in welfare spending has really undermined incentives and efficiency, as often charged, it is hard to see how the GNP managed to triple in size (measured in constant dollars) between 1940 and 1967.

Also, since 1929 welfare spending has grown fastest in the areas of social insurance and education, which are generally less controversial than "public-aid" and health programs. Within the social insurance area, for example, nearly 80 percent of all benefits are paid out under the various pension programs which are self-supporting—that is, the money dispensed has been contributed by workers and employers through payroll taxes, rather than by "the rich supporting the poor," and few conservatives any longer attack these pension programs. As for spending on education, obviously no one expects the public school system to be scrapped in spite of the continuing battles over racial integration, and in addition, over 80 percent of this spending is by state and local governments and not by the "Washington bureaucracy." Table 22-1 shows that these two areas of social insurance and education account for nearly three-quarters of all social welfare expenditures today. It is true that spending on public aid, probably the most criticized of all these programs, has not dwindled as expected, but this category accounts for less than 10 percent of all health, education, and welfare spending by government today.

Other data (not included in Table 22-1) show that these social welfare expenditures, as a percentage of total government spending for all purposes, have not increased as much as some critics imply. This percentage stood at 37 in fiscal year 1929 and had risen to only 43 in fiscal 1967. As for the *distribution* of this spending among the various levels of government, there has indeed been a shift "toward Washington": the Federal government accounted for only 20 percent of social welfare spending in 1929, with state and local governments accounting for the other 80 percent, but in 1967 the federal share was 54 percent. Most of this shift had occurred by the mid-1940s, when the federal share had already reached 50 percent, and it has never been lower than 44 percent in the years since.[1]

But none of these facts tells us whether our society is spending too much or too little on social welfare programs. There simply are no hard-and-

fast standards of adequacy in this area, just as we have no fixed standard for measuring the equity of income distribution. Neither classical nor Keynesian economic theory has much to say on this subject, nor can any political scientist or social worker identify the ideal proportion of GNP that we should be spending on social welfare.

We can compare our welfare spending to that of other countries, of course, but this comparison only reinforces preconceived ideas. When countries are ranked by the percentage of GNP spent on government health, education, and welfare programs, the United States lags considerably behind most other developed countries, spending (in these relative terms) only one-half to three-quarters as much as Canada, France, Great Britain, West Germany, Austria, Belgium, Norway, Sweden, and Denmark.[2] To those who already believe that income-security programs are inadequate in this country, this international comparison demonstrates that we can improve those programs as other countries have done without collapsing into bankruptcy or communism. But to critics of the welfare state, the significant fact is that the standard of living remains higher in this country than in those which lean more on government assistance and less on private markets than we do.

Another criterion of welfare spending might be some form of cost-benefit analysis. Conservatives too often seem to assume that every dollar spent on public welfare programs means one dollar less for the taxpayer to spend on his private needs. But if we abolished all welfare programs tomorrow, we would still have to do more for the aged, sick, and unemployed than give them lectures on self-reliance. Elderly people now receiving government pensions and Medicare benefits, for example, would have to be supported by their children or private charity, and other people without income would also have to be supported from private sources in one way or another. Public welfare programs can also increase private wealth in many ways: a healthy and well-trained worker is more productive than the worker who cannot afford proper medical care or education; maintaining income for the unemployed props up purchasing power during recessions and promotes mobility during good times; reducing poverty reduces the costs of crime and other by-products of poverty. In short, the benefits derived from our current welfare expenditures may well outweigh their costs by a wide margin even when judged on purely economic grounds, to say nothing of their contribution to the intangible goal of "social justice."

Unfortunately, however, no one can accurately measure the net benefits of any type of government spending, whether for building missiles or delivering the mail or attacking poverty and injustice. Surely there is some point beyond which the costs of public assistance outweigh its benefits, but where is that point? For example, if tomorrow the government should provide every family with free education, free medical care, free housing, and a guaranteed income of $10,000 a year, most experts would confidently predict a severe impairment of work incentives and serious repercussions throughout the economy. But if you ask for the net gain or loss that would accrue from spending just another 2 or 3 percent of GNP to improve our existing programs of income maintenance, no expert can give you more than an informed guess—and these guesses will vary widely depending on the programs you propose to strengthen and the political views of the experts you consult.

Thus, while it is the authors' opinion that our society should do more than it has to meet the income needs of many disadvantaged groups, neither we nor anyone else can "prove" that welfare expenditures in the United States are now too low or too high or about right. The welfare state must still be appraised today as it always has been: not by the abstract approach of comparing total welfare spending to GNP or spending in other countries, but on a program-by-program basis, with experts and laymen alike making imprecise judgments as to whether a particular type of income loss (such as from sickness or unemployment) can best be met through private initiative or government assistance or—the most frequent decision—through some combination of private and public efforts. We shall supply facts and figures to aid this process of judgment, but in the final analysis each person's political and social values will be at least as decisive.

Health care in the United States

Few welfare issues stir up voters' passions more than the role of government in providing medical services. The New Deal revolution of the 1930s largely avoided this subject. Various attempts to launch a system of national health insurance in the 1940s never got off the ground, in spite of official backing by President Truman, and Medicare and Medicaid were adopted in 1965 only after several years of bitter debate inside and outside of Congress. The American Medical Association has led the fight against government involvement in health care, charging that "socialized medicine" would impair the doctor-patient relationship and the general quality of health care. Many liberals scoff at these charges and argue that our affluent society can and should provide every citizen with adequate health care just as we now guarantee everyone a basic education, treating both as rights to be met outside of the competitive market system and regardless of individual differences in ability to pay.

Much of this controversy reflects different assessments of how well we are now meeting our health needs. There is no simple basis for making such an assessment, of course, but a recent report by the Department of Health, Education, and Welfare summarizes many of the major strengths and weaknesses of our present system of health care.[3]

On the one hand, we have clearly made tremendous strides in providing better medical care to most Americans. At the turn of the century, for example, the average life expectancy at birth in the United States was 49.2 years, but by 1966 it had risen to 70.1 years. Taking public and private expenditures together, we spend a larger share of GNP on health services than any other country— 6.5 percent in fiscal 1968, or $53 billion. We also spend more than any other country on biomedical research and we probably lead the world in biomedical science and technology.

Yet, for all these advances, life expectancy is longer in at least fifteen other nations than in the United States. In 1950 we ranked fifth among the countries with the lowest infant mortality rates, but we had dropped to fourteenth by 1964; we rank only sixth in maternal mortality rates; and we also compare poorly in death rates from tuberculosis and pneumonia. It is also significant that large differences in health status exist among regions and groups within the United States:

There is a difference of about 5 years in life expectancy at birth between those States with the best records and those with the worst. Moreover, the infant mortality rate is twice as great in the poorest State as in the best State, and the maternal mortality rate was four times as great. . . .

There is a major disparity between the life expectancy of Negroes and whites at almost every age. Negro infant mortality has been about four-fifths greater than that of whites. Though infant mortality for whites was 20.6 per 1000 live births in 1966, for nonwhites it was 38.7 per 1000. Negro maternal mortality has been about *four* times as great as the white rate. . . .

Furthermore, the available information indicates that illness causing limited activity is significantly higher for persons with low incomes, both black and white. For example, for males in the working age group 45–64, those with incomes of less than $2,000 have three and one-half times as many disability days as those in the over $7,000 income group.

Why do these disparities persist in the face of our large expenditures on health care? With respect to other countries, part of the answer may lie in our style of life—we drink and eat and smoke and drive more than many other peoples —and in the competitive pressures that may contribute to our higher rates of ulcers, hypertension, and similar illnesses. But these factors probably do not explain all the international differences in health status cited above, and they certainly do not explain the differences among regions and groups within this country. Three other factors are major causes of these remaining differences.

First, the use and probably the availability of medical services in the United States vary with income and color.

The lower a person's income is, the less often he sees a doctor. Whether we look at data on visits to physicians per year, or the interval since the last visit, or the use of a specialist's services, we see a clear, positive relationship between higher income and greater use of physicians' services. At the same time, there is more illness to be treated among low income than high income people.

The use of dentists also varies markedly with income. More than 20 percent of people in families with incomes under $3,000 have *never* visited a dentist, as compared to 7.2 percent of those in families with incomes over $10,000. . . .

A person's race is also related to the likelihood that he will obtain medical care, even after adjusting for differences in income. Negroes at every income level use medical services less than whites. . . . This suggests that cultural and educational factors may also influence the use of health services, and that fewer health services may be available and accessible to Negroes.

Second, medical care is more available in some geographic areas than in others.

For example, Mississippi has less than one-half as many physicians in relation to its population as New York. . . . Rural areas tend to have fewer doctors in relation to population than metropolitan areas (about 55 percent as many) whereas inner city ghetto areas have fewer doctors than middle class neighborhoods in the same cities. In general, States with low doctor/population ratios tend to have high infant and mortality rates, a relatively high incidence of infectious disease, and a shorter than average life expectancy.

Third, the escalating cost of medical services intensifies the uneven distribution of health care in this country:

From 1946 to 1967, all consumer prices increased 2.6 percent annually while medical care prices increased at an annual rate of 3.9 percent. Moreover, in recent years the rise in medical care prices has accelerated. They increased at an annual rate of 6.5 percent during 1965–1967.

Hospital daily service charges have been increasing faster than other medical care prices. They rose at an annual rate of 8.3 percent from 1946 to 1967. . . . During the two-year period 1965–1967, hospital charges rose about 16 percent per year. Physicians' charges increased at an average annual rate of 7.0 percent during the same two-year period.

The relatively rapid rise in medical care prices and increases in demand for services have resulted in an increase in the percentages of personal disposable income devoted to medical care (from 4.1% in 1950 to 5.9% in 1966). Even so, the public probably consumes fewer medical services than they would if prices had risen less rapidly.

Putting all these facts together, it is clear that the distribution of medical care in this country is governed not simply by the health needs of the population but also by economic and social forces. Since nearly everyone else likes to maximize his income, it is difficult to criticize the doctor who prefers to set up practice in Westchester rather than in Harlem or Mississippi, just as it is difficult to criticize the nonprofit hospital that must keep raising its daily charges merely to keep abreast of the rising costs of medical equipment and personnel. On the other side of the coin, many doctors and hospitals provide their services free of charge or at reduced rates to those unable to pay their full fees.

In spite of this help and various types of public assistance, however, *low-income families still spend a higher percentage of their income for medical care than higher-income families do*— even though they use doctors and dentists less than more affluent families do. Waiving any social inequities of this situation, it has been estimated that 6.2 million man-years were lost through illness in 1963, and 4.6 million of these would have been economically productive. Obviously no system of health care can eliminate all illness, but some of this economic loss to both workers and consumers could have been prevented if medical facilities had been equally available to everyone regardless of income, race, or area of residence.

Who pays the bill?

It is therefore tempting to view the issues in this area as a clash between "free-enterprise medicine" and "socialized medicine," as if we faced the option of continuing an individual doctor-patient relationship based on free choice and ability to pay or switching to a system in which the government tries to provide free health services for everyone. But that dichotomy is far too simple

to describe either current practice or the policy choices now open to us in the health field. Consider these little known facts:

Of all the money spent on health care in this country, *over one half already comes from "third-party" sources,* and less than one half is in the form of direct payments from the individual patient to a doctor, dentist, hospital, or drug store. More specifically, of total expenditures on personal health care in 1967, government payments alone accounted for 32 percent (medical benefits under Medicare, workmen's compensation, and various public assistance programs; medical care for veterans and present members of the armed forces; state mental hospitals; city general hospitals; and so on); another 22 percent was in the form of private health insurance payments, usually under group plans such as Blue Cross which were originally opposed by the AMA because they interposed a third party between the patient and his doctor; and another 1.7 percent of health spending came from philanthropic and other third parties.[4]

When a worker is sick or injured, he not only incurs the cost of doctor and hospital bills but he also suffers a loss of job income. To meet this problem, four out of every five wage and salary workers are now covered by workmen's compensation laws which require their employers to make good some portion of the wage loss (as well as paying the medical bills) arising from work-connected injuries or illness. In addition, two out of three wage and salary workers have some form of income protection in the event of non-work connected sickness or injury: through insurance plans required by law in four states and in the railroad industry, or through insurance or sick-leave plans adopted voluntarily by employers or required by union contracts.[5]

Thus, Americans have attacked the problem of paying for health care in the same pragmatic fashion they have approached most problems in the labor sector—relying partly on market forces, partly on collective bargaining, and partly on government aid and regulation. It is therefore pointless to debate the merits of "socialized medicine" as an abstract proposition. Given the fact that government programs already pay one-third of all medical costs in this country (and also cover some of the income loss caused by sickness and accidents), the practical question here—as with most social issues—is not whether you are for or against government intervention, but rather which of several possible blends of private and public action you prefer.

Compensation for job accidents

The Industrial Revolution exacted a fearful toll in work-connected deaths, injuries, and illnesses. As late as 1907, for example, 4,534 workers were killed in railroading alone in this country, and another 2,534 men were killed that year in bituminous mines.[6] Under common law, an injured worker could sue his employer for damages in the civil courts, but to collect he had to prove that the injury was due to the negligence of the employer.

> The employer, however, could block recovery by availing himself of three common-law defenses: (1) assumption of risk—the injured man could not recover [damages] if it was proved that his injury was due to an ordinary hazard of his employment [and was thus a known risk that the worker assumed when he took the job]; (2) fellow-servant rule—the employee could not recover if a fellow worker could be proved to have caused the injury by negligence on his part; and (3) contributory negligence—any contribution to the accident by negligence on the part of the employee, regardless of the fault of the employer, would preclude recovery by the employee.[7]

Given these sweeping defenses, plus the inability of most workers to underwrite a protracted court battle, employers seldom had to pay damages under the common law. Workers were killed or crippled by industrial mishaps for which they were not responsible in any meaningful sense, and yet they or their survivors were often thrown on charity. There was no hint of worker shiftlessness, such as the unemployed were often charged with, but only the sudden catastrophe which could strike at any man and jeopardize his economic security and that of his family for life.

The manifest injustice of this situation became a matter of public protest, and in the late 1800s several states adopted "employers' liability acts," which generally sought to shift the burden of proof of responsibility from the injured worker to the employer. These laws often applied only to particularly hazardous industries, however, and all still required the injured worker to institute suit. Recoveries were always uncertain and even if the worker ultimately won his case, the award was often inadequate, long delayed, and reduced in value by as much as 30 to 50 percent for legal costs.[8]

But much more important was the fact that the employers' liability acts still did not come to grips with the essence of the problem. In retaining the common-law approach to job accidents— which stressed that someone was *responsible* for each accident—these laws failed to recognize that modern industry had become so complex and hazardous and impersonal that accidents daily occurred which could not be traced to *anyone's* specific negligence but which were an almost inevitable concomitant of production. Was it really a worker's "fault" when he allowed his attention to wander just long enough for his hand to be crushed in moving machinery—or was it as much the "fault" of a production process that exposed him to such a risk, day after day? And even when it could be "proved" that the worker had been "at fault," the rise of mechanization often made the consequences of an accident much more costly than they would have been under handicraft production.

For these reasons, a new approach to the accident problem was pioneered in Europe: the principle of accident compensation *without respect to responsibility*. First in Germany in 1883 and then in England in 1897, this principle was incorporated in workmen's compensation laws, as they came to be known, which quickly spread to other European countries and eventually to the United States.

> Workmen's compensation laws were intended to replace the uncertainties of litigation at common law or under employers' liability laws with the promise of a fixed schedule of benefits payable to compensate occupationally injured workers and their families for wage loss and medical expenses, regardless of fault. *Industrial*

injuries were regarded as part of the productive process, and their costs were held to be a proper charge against the expense of production.

The first effective workmen's compensation law in the United States was enacted in 1908, when Congress adopted a program for certain Federal civilian employees engaged in hazardous work. Similar laws were enacted by 10 States in 1911; by 1920, all but six States had such laws.[9]

Current compensation laws

Today these laws are on the books of every state, but they vary considerably in their coverage. Some laws exempt small firms from coverage (ranging from those with fewer than two employees in some states up to firms with fewer than fifteen employees in one state); many laws exclude farm and domestic workers and employees in various nonprofit and government sectors; some states limit coverage to "hazardous" occupations (though often defined liberally to cover most occupations today); and nearly half of these laws are elective for many of the employers covered—meaning that the employer may accept or reject coverage by the law, but if he rejects it (which relatively few do), he loses the common-law defenses against suits by his workers. As a result, the proportion of wage and salary workers covered by these laws varies from less than 70 percent in several states (primarily in the South and Midwest) to over 85 percent in others (primarily in the North). In the nation as a whole, these laws now cover 80 percent of all employed wage and salary workers.[10]

With respect to financing, every compensation law is based on the principle that the employer alone must bear the costs of industrial injuries, since these costs are now considered an "expense of production." Some or all of these costs will be passed forward to the consumer, of course, but it is also expected that employers will attempt to minimize these costs as they would any other—which means that employers now have a direct incentive to improve job safety, for they can lower their compensation costs by preventing accidents. The actual method of financing these costs varies widely, and this further reflects our society's reluctance to attack a social problem through exclusive reliance upon either private industry or the government:

Employers in most jurisdictions are permitted to carry insurance against work accidents with commercial insurance companies or to qualify as self-insurers by giving proof of ability to carry their own risk. In seven jurisdictions, however, they must insure with an exclusive State insurance fund (under two of these laws, they may instead self-insure), and in 12 there is a State fund that is "competitive" with private insurance carriers. Federal employees are provided protection through a federally financed and operated system.[11]

Finally, benefits also vary widely under the different laws. In 1966, for example, the Alabama law required employers to provide or pay for the medical care of injured workers but only up to a maximum period of two years and in any case at a cost of no more than $2,400; in New York State in the same year, there were no dollar or time limits on the employer's responsibility to provide medical care. If a worker were killed on the job in Alabama in 1966, his survivors received cash benefits for a maximum of 300 weeks or $15,200; in New York, death benefits continued to be paid to the widow until her death or remarriage and to her children until they reached eighteen years of age. And for the most common type of industrial accident—involving "temporary total disability" (the employee is unable to work while recovering, but he is expected to recover fully)—all state laws require the employer to pay some part of the injured worker's lost wages, but in 1968 the maximum cash benefit actually required was as high as $150 per week in Arizona and as low as $35 per week in Louisiana, Mississippi, and Texas.[12]

Appraisal of workmen's compensation

Thus, starting from a time when an injured worker could obtain some indemnity only through expensive and time-consuming litigation, if at all, four of every five employees today have (at least in principle) a *right* to compensation for injuries sustained on their jobs—automatically and without question as to responsibility for the accident. How well are these laws actually working in practice?

Over 14,000 people are still killed on their jobs each year and over 2 million workers are still injured each year. Obviously no program can compensate these workers and their families for all the tragic costs of job injuries, but Table 22-2 shows that workmen's compensation laws are making a substantial contribution toward meeting the monetary costs involved. Benefit payments under these laws now total more than $2 billion each year, with one-third of these benefits paying for medical care and the other two-thirds compensating for the wage loss of injured or deceased workers—a ratio that has remained relatively stable throughout the postwar period. Also, the total cost of workmen's compensation to employers continues to average only 1 percent of covered payrolls (and therefore averages even less than 1 percent of total costs).

Further, Table 22-2 shows that the injury rate in manufacturing has declined since the 1940s, and other data (not shown here) indicate that the safety record in most American industries has improved greatly over the past fifty years.[13] (These injury rates vary greatly by industry, of course. For example, mining, construction, and longshoring are far more hazardous than the average fac-

tory job, while many service industries and government jobs are less hazardous.) Although it cannot be proved, workmen's compensation has probably been partially responsible for this improved safety record in American industry. To be sure, even without the incentive of improved accident insurance rates, managers were coming to realize the economic, social, and public relations benefits of a better safety record than that at the turn of the century. Workmen's compensation laws nevertheless helped to focus attention on the problem and created an additional economic advantage to lowering the accident rate.

But in spite of these achievements, workmen's compensation laws have fallen short of their goal in several respects. *First, the coverage of these laws remains inadequate.* Although the principle of workmen's compensation has been accepted in most states for half a century or more (and in all states since 1949, when Mississippi became the last to adopt such a law), one employee in five still lacks the protection of these laws. There is no good reason why a worker should be excluded from coverage because he happens to work on a farm instead of in a factory, or because he works in a small firm instead of a large one. Nor is there

Table 22-2 *Selected Statistics Relevant to Workmen's Compensation Laws in Selected Years, 1940–1967*

Year	Total	Benefit payments (in millions) Medical and hospitalization payments	Compensation for wage loss	Benefits as percent of payroll in covered employment	Total cost to employers as percent of payroll in covered employment*	Injury frequency rate in manufacturing†
1940	$ 256	$ 95	$ 161	0.72	1.19	15.3
1946	434	140	294	0.54	0.91	19.9
1948	534	175	359	0.51	0.96	17.2
1950	615	200	415	0.54	0.89	14.7
1955	916	325	591	0.55	0.91	12.1
1960	1,295	435	860	0.59	0.93	12.0
1964	1,705	565	1,140	0.62	1.00	12.7
1967	2,134	725	1,409	0.63	1.07	n.a.

* Total cost includes benefit costs plus the overhead costs that employers pay to insure or self-insure the risk of work injury. Included in overhead are such expenses as payroll auditing, claims investigation, legal services, and general administration, plus (in insurance provided by commercial carriers) commissions and brokerage fees, taxes, and profit.
† Average number of disabling work injuries per million employee-hours worked.
SOURCES: *Social Security Bulletin*, October, 1966, pp. 9–20, and January, 1969, pp. 34–37.

any excuse for the "elective" laws which permit an employer to choose not to carry insurance for this purpose. Even though such employers are stripped of the old common-law defenses when sued, how many workers can afford (or would dare) to sue their employer over every injury that disabled them for "only" a few days or weeks—the most common type of job accident? And in case of a permanent impairment or death, the worker or his survivors might eventually win a favorable verdict from a court, only to discover that the employer without insurance is unable to pay any large award.

Coverage is also incomplete with respect to occupational diseases, in contrast to the full coverage of physical injuries incurred on the job. Although many laws now cover all types of occupational disease, nearly twenty states still restrict coverage to certain diseases specified in their laws. (And even the meaning of "full coverage" is the subject of much litigation, for it is quite possible—though difficult to prove—that job pressures can contribute to illnesses such as nervous breakdown, heart attack, and even alcoholism.[14])

Second, workmen's compensation benefits are inadequate by nearly any standard. It is true that benefit payments now total over $2 billion per year, but this aggregate figure becomes less impressive upon close examination.

For example, once a state accepts the basic principle of workmen's compensation, how can it justify limiting the medical benefits available to an injured worker? It is hard to imagine why a worker would want to roll up unnecessary medical bills, even if he could find a doctor or hospital willing to connive in doing so. Yet, nearly one-fourth of the states still limit medical benefits for job injuries and nearly one-half limit benefits for occupational diseases, by means of an upper limit on the monetary amount or on the period of time for which the cost of medical care will be covered.

Or how can one justify the fact that three-quarters of the states place dollar or time limits on the payments to the survivors of a worker killed on his job, and nearly one-half limit payments to a worker permanently and totally disabled? These maximums range in various states from about 300 to 500 weeks and from $12,000 to $35,000, but plainly none of these ceilings is adequate for all cases. Assume, for example, a worker who was permanently and totally disabled on his job in 1963, when he was forty years old, had a wife and a child of eight, and was earning the average wage in his state. Under the compensation laws then in effect, how would the benefits this worker would receive over the next twenty-five years compare to the earnings he could expect to have received if he had worked until age sixty-five, even assuming he never received a wage increase? The dismal answer is that compensation benefits would replace *less than 15 percent* of this worker's income loss in eighteen states, and less than 50 percent in another twenty-four states.[15]

But perhaps the most criticism has been directed at the cash benefits provided for temporary total disability, for this type of injury strikes at about two million workers a year and, though "temporary," can mean a loss of job income for several weeks or months. Most state laws base these cash benefits on a percentage of the worker's weekly wages at the time of his accident, usually 60, 65, or 66⅔ percent. There is no particular magic to those figures, and one could easily argue that a worker is entitled to 100 percent indemnity of his wage loss. The proportion of two-thirds has nevertheless been adopted from the earliest days as a compromise between the worker's needs and the employer's fear that a high guarantee would encourage malingering. *The fact is, however, that few states even meet their avowed standard of replacing two-thirds of the worker's income loss,* for nearly every state places dollar maximums on these weekly benefits which reduce them to less than the statutory percentage for many of the workers covered. Figure 22-1 shows that in 1965 only twelve programs, with slightly more than 25 percent of covered workers, had weekly maximums that equaled 55 percent or more of the average weekly wage in their jurisdictions.

Consequently, in 1965 only five programs (including the system for Federal employees) with 7 percent of the covered workers had weekly maximums that were high enough to permit the statutory percentage to be effective for workers with average wages (though not for many workers with higher-than-average wages)....

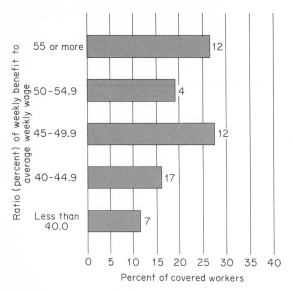

Fig. 22-1. *Distribution of covered workers and of jurisdictions, by ratio of actual weekly compensation benefits payable for temporary total disability to weekly wages, for a single worker with average weekly wage, 1965. (Figures to the right of bars represent the number of jurisdictions—fifty states plus the District of Columbia and the system for federal employees.)*

SOURCE: *Alfred M. Skolnik, Social Security Bulletin, October, 1966, p. 13.*

In 1965 for the Nation as a whole the weekly rate of compensation, weighted by coverage, for a single worker with average wages was estimated at $52.98 or 49.6 percent of the nationwide average weekly wage.[16]

The need for federal standards

Several other weaknesses plague workmen's compensation laws today, in addition to the inadequacy of their coverage and their benefits.[17] Without detailing all these deficiencies, enough has been said to demonstrate that *perhaps the most fundamental weakness remaining in our compensation laws is their great variation from state to state.*

It would be bad enough, that is, if workers on farms or in small plants were uniformly excluded from the coverage of every compensation law, but it is particularly inequitable that such workers are protected in one state and not in another. And why should a worker with a particular type of job injury receive full medical care in one state and limited care in another, or a worker at a particular wage level receive cash benefits of only $35 a week in one state and $150 in another? Or why should the loss of an eye be worth a maximum of $16,800 in Arizona but only $3,000 in Mississippi? No one can scientifically calculate a formula for fairly compensating all injured workers, but surely these gross differences in benefits make no sense whatever, depending primarily on where the worker happens to live rather than on the nature of his injury, the amount of his lost income, or other measures of his need.

There were good reasons for beginning the workmen's compensation system at the state rather than the federal level. In the years around World War I, the Congress was not interested in initiating national programs of social insurance and, even if it had been, the Supreme Court was then holding to a very narrow view of the Federal government's authority to regulate interstate commerce. In addition, the reformers of that day hoped that the states would be "laboratories for social experimentation," with different states trying different approaches to the new problems of industrialization and benefiting from one another's experience.

But that hope has been dashed by a combination of market and political forces. Each state understandably wants to retain the industry and jobs it already has and to attract a share of the new jobs created by our growing economy. The resulting competition among states benefits both consumers and producers in many ways, but it also tempts each state to hold down the costs of its workmen's compensation program—in the case of poor states, so they can attract employers from other states; in the case of rich states, so they can keep the industry they now have. Thus, instead of the states competing in innovative solutions to the common problem of job accidents, there has been an inevitable tendency for them to compete in restricting costs—which usually means restricting coverage and benefits.

Table 22-2 shows, however, that workmen's

compensation costs only average about 1 percent of total payroll costs for covered employers. This ratio is higher in some states than in others, of course, but in a study of twenty-eight states for which detailed and comparable data were available, Prof. John Burton found that the *maximum* interstate differential in compensation premiums was only equivalent to 1.5 percent of payroll and 0.3 percent of total costs in 1965. Since this variation is too small to influence the plant-location decisions of many employers, why do state legislators worry about it? Burton concluded:

> Unfortunately, this appears to be an arena where emotion will triumph over fact. There is considerable uncertainty about the factual costs of workmen's compensation, and state legislators cannot be expected to be experts on the question. . . . Furthermore, it is likely that a state legislature which is contemplating an improvement in a workmen's compensation statute . . . will be faced with claims from some employers that the higher costs will force interstate movements; and it will be virtually impossible for the legislators to know whether the employers are serious or just bluffing. And to add to the confusion, there are states which have even abetted the illusion of the runaway employer by advertising about the low cost of workmen's compensation in their states. . . .
> When the sum of these inhibiting factors is considered, it seems likely that most states will be dissuaded from reforms of their workmen's compensation statutes because of the specter of the vanishing employer—even if the apparition is a product of fancy and not fact.[18]

For these reasons, the AFL-CIO has urged that the state system of workmen's compensation be scrapped in favor of a single federal statute, or at least (as the Johnson administration proposed) Congress should fix minimum standards that all state compensation laws would have to meet. The authors share this opinion that federal action of some kind is necessary to improve the protection offered by this program. Since every state has accepted the principle of workmen's compensation as necessary and desirable, competition among the states to restrict the program's benefits and coverage serves no useful purpose.

In fact, the Federal government has taken a few small steps into this field. In a series of amendments beginning in 1956, Congress has extended the Social Security Act (now known as OASDHI—the national old-age, survivors, disability, and health insurance program) to provide monthly cash benefits for certain severely disabled workers. As of 1969, workers were eligible who had suffered a total disability expected to last more than one year and who had worked in covered employment for at least five of the ten years prior to their accident. Monthly payments are equal to the amount the worker would receive if he were retiring at sixty-five, and these benefits may be added to workmen's compensation payments up to the point where both payments total 80 percent of the worker's average monthly wage before he became disabled. This program is financed by a tax of 0.95 percent on every covered worker's annual earnings up to $7,800, with half of the tax paid by the worker and half by his employer.

The Federal Coal Mine Health and Safety Act of 1969 is a temporary program for the relief of miners suffering from "black lung" disease. In signing this measure, President Nixon expressed his reservations concerning its terms, voicing his belief that "workmen's compensation has been and should be a State responsibility." Thus, in spite of the several failures of state compensation laws, the Federal government has shown little desire to break the tradition of state supremacy in this area of welfare legislation.

The problem of nonoccupational accidents and illness

Workmen's compensation laws apply only to diseases or injuries sustained "in the course of employment." Thus, even if these laws were greatly improved in their coverage and benefits, they would still fail to meet a large portion of the average family's cost of health care.

In the first place, it is often difficult to distinguish between occupational and nonoccupational disability. As we mentioned before, doctors disagree over the relationship between the physical and mental demands of various jobs and the onset of such common illnesses as heart attack and nervous breakdown. A similar problem has now emerged concerning the effects of radiation on workers exposed to this risk, for these effects may not show up except over a long period and may also result in part from exposure off the job— such as from x-rays, contaminated food, and even the atmosphere. If all these borderline cases were decided in favor of the worker, employers would understandably object and might also take "evasive action" detrimental to many workers (for example, some employers already shy away from hiring anyone with a record of heart trouble). On the other hand, if these cases are decided against the worker, he must bear the full cost of medical care and lost income.

Second, even the most liberal workmen's compensation law imaginable would not cover the many injuries and illnesses that are in no way related to a worker's job. Yet, to the worker and his family, the consequences are the same whether he loses his hand in a job accident or while fixing his power mower at home, whether he is killed in a mine explosion or in an auto accident, whether he contracts an occupational disease such as silicosis or lung cancer from too many cigarettes. In short, the death or disability of a worker always creates the same two problems—loss of income and the cost of medical care—whether it occurs on or off the job.

Also, workmen's compensation laws naturally cover only the worker's own disabilities and not those of his family, although his wife or children may incur medical bills just as crippling to the family income as those incurred by the worker himself. Finally, these laws offer no protection to those without a job—the unemployed and those not in the labor force, such as the aged worker who has retired and the widow or divorcée with dependent children and no outside job.

For these reasons, it has always been plain that workmen's compensation laws can offer protection against only a fraction of the total losses imposed by accidents and illness. Until quite recently, however, the family was expected to cope by itself with the cost of nonoccupational health problems. After all, why should the employer pay for a sickness or an accident having nothing to do with the worker's job, or why should some taxpayers provide income protection and medical care to others—unless, of course, the sick and injured are

paupers who qualify for charity? Illness and injury were viewed as part of life's risks, and it was feared that any attempt to provide complete security against those risks would only encourage the lazy and improvident to malinger at the expense of the honest and thrifty members of society.

This attitude is still held by many Americans today, as evidenced by the fact that we are the only major Western society without a national health insurance system. But developments in collective bargaining and welfare legislation over the past thirty years clearly signal the emergence of a radically different attitude: whether or not a worker's disability is job-connected, his loss of cash income is often a catastrophe but seldom anyone's fault; the average family should not be driven into bankruptcy before it can qualify for help in meeting its medical bills; and given the high cost and unpredictability of these two risks, protection should be sought through collective action rather than reliance upon individual thrift.

As with most social problems, Americans have not made a dramatic, either/or choice between these opposing philosophies. The following pages will demonstrate, however, that *the trend is plainly toward collective action to meet the costs of nonoccupational injuries and illness.*

Income-loss protection [19]

As we noted before, two of every three employees now have some form of protection against income loss in the event of nonoccupational sickness. Figure 22-2 shows that most covered workers are protected by voluntary plans, although government-mandated programs also cover one in every five employees.

Government programs Four states, Puerto Rico —and the railroad industry—have social insurance programs which provide workers with partial compensation for the wage loss caused by temporary nonoccupational disability. The only federal law of this nature is the Railroad Unemployment Insurance Act, which was first amended in 1946 to provide this type of benefit and which today covers about 700,000 workers in railroading. About 14 million workers in other private

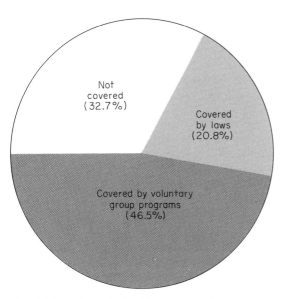

Fig. 22-2. *The extent of income-maintenance protection against short-term sickness, by percentage of all employees covered, December, 1967.*

SOURCE: *Daniel N. Price, Social Security Bulletin, January, 1969, p. 24.*

industries are covered by such laws in California, New Jersey, New York, and Rhode Island—each adopted in the 1940s—and by a similar law in Puerto Rico which took effect in 1969.

In general, all of these public programs—known as temporary disability insurance laws—aim to replace about one-half of the weekly wage loss of a sick worker for a period of up to twenty-six weeks. Like workmen's compensation laws, however, these disability programs vary greatly from one jurisdiction to another. In 1968, for example, the maximum weekly benefit ranged from $50 in Rhode Island to $80 in California; in two states, the workers paid the entire cost of the program through a payroll tax of 1 percent, but both employers and employees were taxed to finance the other programs; only one state (California) covered farm workers; and two plans operated exclusively through government channels and the others permitted employers to self-insure or to buy protection from private insurance companies.

Voluntary group programs There are two major types of income-maintenance programs that have been adopted voluntarily by many employers, either on their own initiative or as a result of collective bargaining. One type is *group sickness and accident insurance,* which usually returns one-half to two-thirds of the wages of a temporarily disabled worker, often after a waiting period of one week and for a maximum of thirteen to twenty-six weeks. These plans are therefore very similar to those required by the laws described above, except the private plans are adopted voluntarily and each is limited to the workers of one company or bargaining unit.

The other type of voluntary program is *paid sick leave,* which commonly provides for the continuation of full wages for five to fifteen days a year in the event of illness. Some of these plans vary the maximum benefit period with seniority and some permit unused leave days to be accumulated from year to year up to some maximum limit.

Each of these programs tends to be strong in ways in which the other is weak. On the one hand, sick leave provides much better income protection for the most frequent types of illness—those lasting only a few days—and these plans are also easier and cheaper to administer than an insurance program. On the other hand, employees are more likely to abuse a sick-leave plan, for some may view their annual-leave allotment as a right to take time off for nearly any reason, and insurance programs also provide better protection against the lengthy illness that can be most crippling to a family's finances.

Appraisal of income-maintenance programs Taking together all public and private programs, a total of $3.8 billion dollars was paid out in 1967 in partial compensation for the income loss caused by short-term, nonoccupational accidents and illness. Rather surprisingly, sick leave accounted for 55 percent of these total benefits. (This is largely explained by the prevalence of sick-leave plans in the public sector, for over 85 percent of all full-time government workers have this protection.) The balance of these payments came from voluntary group insurance (17 percent), private individual insurance for the self-employed and others (14 percent), and plans required by the disability insurance laws in four states and the railroad industry (13 percent).

How adequate were these benefits to the needs involved? Table 22-3 shows that benefit payments offset only 30 percent of the income losses caused by nonoccupational, short-term sickness in 1967. (There are no estimates of income protection against long-term disability.) The average worker therefore continues to bear the brunt of this heavy and unpredictable cost. And even the protection that is available is distributed unevenly in favor of the high-wage worker: sick-leave plans predominate among white-collar and government workers who already have a relatively high and secure income the year around; group insurance is undoubtedly more widespread among union workers than nonunion; and the few laws on the books (except in Puerto Rico) are concentrated in high-wage states and the high-wage railroad industry.

On the other hand, given the small number of jurisdictions in which there are laws requiring this type of protection, an income-replacement ratio of 30 percent is unexpectedly high. Also, note that this ratio nearly doubled in the short period from 1948 to 1967, *and most of these benefits are provided through the worker's place of employment.* Most employers of an earlier generation saw no reason why they should be responsible in any way for the wage loss suffered by workers who were disabled off the job, but the rapid growth of this type of income protection illustrates again how radically the employer-employee relationship has been changing in this country—due to a mixture of union pressure, new laws, changing employer attitudes, and labor-force shifts toward the white-collar and service sectors.

Protection against the costs of medical care: private health insurance

We have seen that our society has long accepted the principle that a worker disabled on his job is entitled (as a right and not as charity) to protection against the twin costs of medical care and lost income. We have also seen that since the 1940s a handful of jurisdictions have provided some protection against the loss of income caused by nonoccupational accidents and illness. *Until the 1960s, however, no federal or state law provided insurance against the medical bills resulting from a worker's nonoccupational sickness or the sickness of any member of his family.*

As a result, most families long viewed medical care as an expensive luxury. Many called a doctor only for dire emergencies, and a lengthy stay in a hospital often spelled financial disaster. It is true that many doctors scaled their fees to their patients' ability to pay and charity wards were available in many public hospitals, but most Americans—and not just the rich—have always viewed the acceptance of charity as an admission of failure.

This picture has changed dramatically over the past thirty years, primarily because of the amazing growth of private health insurance. As Figure 22-3 shows, in 1940 less than 10 percent of the population were insured against hospital expenses (meaning primarily room and meal charges), but coverage shot up to 50 percent by 1950 and had

Table 22-3 *Protection Provided against Income Loss from Nonoccupational Short-term Sickness,* Selected Years, 1948–1967*

Year	Income loss† (millions)	Protection provided‡ (millions)	Protection as percent of loss
1948	$4,568	$ 757	16.6
1950	4,795	939	19.6
1960	8,555	2,422	28.3
1967	12,583	3,751	29.8

* Non-work-connected disability lasting not more than six months, and the first six months of long-term disability.

† For wage and salary workers, annual payrolls multiplied by estimated (from surveys) average workdays lost per year due to short-term sickness (7.0 for workers in private industry, 7.5 for state and local government, 8.0 for Federal government) and divided by estimated workdays in year (260 for federal employees, 255 for all others). For self-employed persons, annual farm and nonfarm proprietors' income multiplied by 7 and divided by 300.

‡ Total benefits provided through formal sick-leave plans, group sickness and accident insurance plans (both voluntary and those required by law), and individual insurance policies.

SOURCE: Daniel N. Price, *Social Security Bulletin,* January, 1969, pp. 22 and 32.

reached 83 percent by 1967. It can be seen that coverage of surgical costs and of in-hospital medical expenses (visits by physicians inside the hospital) has also mushroomed since 1940. A variety of forces have contributed to this expansion of health insurance but labor unions have clearly led the way, making this one of the major accomplishments of collective bargaining.

Despite its tremendous growth, private health insurance offers only limited protection to the average family. Plans such as Blue Cross and Blue Shield apply chiefly to the hospital expenses described in Figure 22-3, and even here there are usually limits on the doctor's fees and daily room charges that will be paid and limits on the time period for which coverage is provided. More important is the limited protection most families have against medical expenses incurred outside of hospitals. At the beginning of 1968, for example, less than one-half of the population had any insurance coverage of the following types of health costs: doctors' visits in the office or home (40 percent had some coverage); prescribed drugs outside the hospital (36 percent); nursing-home care (10 percent); and dental care (2 percent). Only 40 percent were covered under "major medical policies" that offer protection against catastrophic illnesses—those which may result in medical bills of $5,000 or $10,000 or more, far exceeding the limits of the typical insurance plan.[20]

Furthermore, private health insurance does not adequately cover those who most need it. In 1967, hospital insurance covered 90 percent of those persons with family income of $10,000 or more, but only 35 percent of those with less than $3,000 of family income. And in 1965, before Medicare took effect, hospital insurance covered 81 percent of those under sixty-five years of age and only 64 percent of those sixty-five and over—although the aged are sick more frequently and often have lower incomes than people in their prime years.

This uneven coverage is partially the result of competition among commercial health insurance carriers, which offer favorable terms to groups (or their employers) of an age and income composition that lowers the probability of illness. This practice enables commercial carriers to siphon off many of the preferred risks and leaves nonprofit

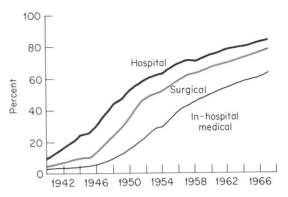

Fig. 22-3. *Percent of civilian population with specified type of health insurance coverage, 1940–1967.*

SOURCE: *Louis S. Reed and Willine Carr,* Social Security Bulletin, *February, 1969, p. 8.*

plans such as Blue Cross, which long operated with flat rates for all members, with a disproportionate number of poor-risk insurees. This in turn increases the costs and rates of the nonprofit companies and, in many cases, has forced them also to adopt experience rating, which discriminates against the aged, those with chronic conditions, and other "poor risks."[21] Consequently, the best and cheapest insurance coverage is usually available *through the employment relationship*—under group plans for white-collar employees or for blue-collar workers in unionized firms. This is of little help to the aged who have retired or to low-income workers who are frequently unemployed and who, even when working, are often found on nonunion, blue-collar jobs in the service or farming sectors.

What is the net effect of these several strengths and weaknesses of private health insurance? Perhaps the best measure of adequacy is the proportion of all personal health-care expenditures met by private insurance, which had reached 9 percent by 1950, peaked at 25 percent in 1965 (the last year before Medicare and Medicaid began), and stood at 22 percent in 1967. Clearly the average family has far better protection against unpredictable medical expenses today than a generation ago, particularly against the soaring costs of hospitalization. Just as clearly, voluntary programs still cover only a small share of the total costs of health care—which explains why there is continuing pressure for the government to play a larger role in this field.

Protection against the costs of medical care: government programs

As we noted before, the government is already involved in meeting the costs of medical care in this country to a far greater extent than is commonly realized. During the years 1950 to 1965, for example, as the controversy grew over whether some form of federal health insurance was desirable, payments under government programs were even then accounting for 20 to 25 percent of annual expenditures for personal health care. These payments were made through a large number of relatively noncontroversial programs—such as the operation of federal, state, county, and city hospitals, the provision of health care for veterans and current members of the armed forces, school health programs, and workmen's compensation—as well as welfare programs for the poor based on need rather than on social insurance principles.

In spite of these many exceptions, there has long been strong opposition, led by the American Medical Association, to the *principle* of government intervention in this field. As the costs of medical care spiraled during the postwar years, however, and as the evidence mounted that private health insurance was not an adequate solution, support grew for some public program to assist at least the aged and the poor to meet their medical bills. As one observer summed up the outcome:

> The struggle over government health insurance raged back and forth across the country for more than a generation, it cost the A.M.A. and its affiliates and allies something on the order of fifty million dollars, it gave the Association a reputation that would not be envied by the Teamsters, and it left political wreckage that may not be cleared away for more than another generation. The long war finally ended in the summer of 1965 with enactment of the bill that is commonly known as Medicare—making the United States the last industrialized

nation in the West to adopt a compulsory health-insurance program.[22]

Medicare Part of the 1965 law was designed solely to help the aged meet their costs of medical care. This was done through amending the Social Security Act to set up two related contributory health insurance plans for virtually all persons aged sixty-five and over: a basic *compulsory* program of hospital insurance and a *voluntary* program of supplementary medical insurance.

The basic program is a form of social insurance, meaning that workers (and their employers) contribute during their working lives to a self-supporting government fund from which they are entitled to draw benefits upon reaching sixty-five as a matter of right, without having to prove financial need. More specifically, every person subject to the Social Security Act—which now covers about nine out of every ten persons working for a living—is taxed 0.6 percent of the first $7,800 of his earnings each year to pay for Medicare, and his employer must pay a matching amount, making a total payroll tax of 1.2 percent to underwrite this program. For self-employed persons, the tax rate is also 0.6 percent.

Upon reaching age sixty-five, the covered worker (and his wife) is entitled to the following benefits: *inpatient hospital services* for up to ninety days of each spell of illness (the patient must pay the first $40 of his total bill for the first sixty days and $10 a day for each of the next thirty days, for services including semi-private accommodations, drugs, operating room, and most other hospital charges except doctor bills); *posthospital extended care* in a nursing home or the convalescent section of a hospital for up to 100 days of each spell of illness (after the first twenty days, the patient must pay $5 a day); and *posthospital home health services,* by visiting nurses or therapists, of up to 100 home visits a year following the patient's release from a hospital or nursing home.

Note that doctors' bills are not covered by the mandatory Medicare program, but protection against that expense can be purchased on a voluntary basis under the second part of Medicare—supplementary medical insurance. Except for certain aliens and "subversives," *any* person sixty-five and over may enroll in this program, and not just those covered by the Social Security Act. Those who enroll pay a relatively low monthly premium ($5.30 in 1971, but this is subject to revision to keep up with rising costs), and this premium is matched by an equal amount from federal general revenues.

This voluntary insurance covers 80 percent of the "reasonable" charges for nearly all physicians' and surgeons' services, after the patient pays the first $50 of these charges in any one year. Various home health services and outpatient hospital services are also covered, in addition to those insured under the compulsory program.

In 1969, these two Medicare programs paid out a total of $5.7 billion in benefits—$4.2 billion under the compulsory hospital insurance program and $1.5 billion under voluntary medical insurance.

Medicaid   In the din of the battle over Medicare, few people in 1965 recognized the significance of the program now known as Medicaid, initiated under another section of the same bill which established Medicare. For the first time in our history, Medicaid provides direct government aid in meeting the medical expenses of persons who are neither aged nor clearly destitute nor injured on their jobs, and this aid is financed out of general tax revenue rather than by payroll taxes. In the years since 1965, it is this program—and not Medicare—which has become the center of bitter controversy.

Like many other welfare laws in the past, Medicaid offers federal matching funds to states that voluntarily adopt a certain type of aid to the needy. But Medicaid differs in two respects. First, it has established a single and uniform approach to this particular welfare problem. Before 1965, there was one federal-state program to meet the medical bills of welfare recipients who were blind, another for the aged, another for the disabled, and so on. The Medicaid law replaced this "categorical" approach with a single program of medical assistance covering nearly all welfare recipients and most types of hospital and physicians' services. Each state's plan must meet certain require-

ments, such as the provision for a specified range of medical services and excluding any eligibility rule based on age or length of residence in the state. When a plan meets these requirements, the Federal government pays from 50 to 83 percent of its cost, depending on the per capita income of the state.

Second, and far more controversial, *the Medicaid law introduced a new measure of need which has far-reaching implications.* To be eligible for any type of welfare program (or public assistance, as distinct from social insurance), a person must qualify by a means test. This test varies from one jurisdiction and program to another, but in essence it always requires the welfare recipient to prove that he does not have sufficient income (or means) to support himself or his family. This is the test used to establish eligibility for the Medicaid program described above. In addition, however, this law offers the states the option of extending the same kind of medical assistance, with the same federal aid, to a new group called the "medically indigent"—persons who are able to provide their own maintenance (and who therefore are not "poor" by the usual needs test) but whose income and resources are not sufficient to meet all of their medical care costs.

In effect, Congress has declared for the first time that medical expenses are an economic risk against which the near-poor of any age deserve protection, without first having to bankrupt themselves to qualify for the usual welfare aid.

> To determine financial eligibility of the medically indigent groups, States are required to specify the amount of income each family may retain before an "excess" is considered to be available for payment of medical bills. Although these amounts, which vary by size of family, are sometimes referred to as maximum income limitations, families with larger incomes are eligible for help with their medical bills to the extent that payments of these bills would leave them with less than the specified amount for daily living expenses. . . .
>
> Only income which is actually available may be considered in determining need and any resources of the individual must be reasonably evaluated. Most States disregard the value of owner-occupied homes as a financial resource

and exempt reasonable amounts of liquid assets in the determination of eligibility.

In December 1967, maximum income eligibility levels for families of four ranged [among various States] from $2,448 to $6,000, with an average requirement of $3,470.[23]

Unfortunately, the costs of Medicaid quickly exceeded all expectations. Payments to "medical vendors" (primarily doctors and hospitals) totaled $1.2 billion in 1966, the first year Medicaid was in effect, more than doubled to $2.5 billion in 1967, and soared to nearly $4 billion in 1968. This naturally alarmed many taxpayers, and Congress moved as early as 1967 to limit costs by lowering the income-eligibility levels. By 1970, a state could receive federal matching funds under Medicaid only for families or individuals whose income was no more than one-third higher than the income considered adequate for persons on welfare in that state.[24]

What accounted for the skyrocketing of Medicaid costs? To some extent, this cost increase was simply a bookkeeping mirage: because not all states adopted Medicaid plans in the first year of its operation, costs naturally increased as other states (now numbering over forty) came under the program and transferred to its account the medical payments previously made under categorical programs such as Aid to the Blind. Also, the continuing rise in the "unit cost" of all medical services accounts for some of the increasing costs of the Medicaid program.

But those factors do not seem to explain all of the rise in Medicaid's costs, and there is heated debate over what the other causes might be. Many people believe that fraud has been widespread—some charging that patients have bilked the program, some claiming that doctors have charged excessive fees and prescribed unnecessary services, and some criticizing state and local governments for lax auditing of both patients and doctors.[25] Others believe that some states defined "medical indigence" far more liberally than Congress intended. For example, when New York State first set an income-eligibility limit of $6,000 for a family of four (and up to $9,400 for a family of eight with one wage earner), it was estimated that 40 to 45 percent of New York's population became potentially eligible for Medicaid. (New York's limits were later cut back—to $5,000 for a family of four, for instance.) And yet other people believe that Medicaid's costs reflect the extent to which previous welfare programs failed to meet the legitimate needs of the poor and near-poor, creating a backlog of health problems that would be costly to solve in the first years of any genuine program of medical assistance.

For better or worse, Medicaid and Medicare have now established the principle that our society should help to meet the medical expenses not only of the poor and those injured on their jobs, but of other persons as well. Medicare applies no needs test whatever to the elderly, and yet employers must pay one-half of the cost of the compulsory hospital insurance and the general taxpayer must pay one-half of the cost of the voluntary medical insurance. Medicaid does apply a needs test, but its concept of "medical indigence" provides protection for millions of families with income above the usual welfare standards, and this protection is also paid for out of general tax revenues and not directly by the patient. Arguments will doubtlessly continue over the costs and administration of these programs, but the principle they represent—a radical innovation in the American context—is probably here to stay.[26]

Conclusions

Although the United States does not have a comprehensive system of national health insurance like that found in many countries, Americans have erected many partial defenses against the economic costs of accidents and illness. To meet the *income loss* caused by worker disability, every state has a workmen's compensation law which makes up some of the wage loss resulting from job-connected injuries, a few jurisdictions have temporary disability laws covering nonoccupational sickness, and several million workers have income-maintenance protection from private group insurance or sick-leave plans. To meet the *costs of medical treatment,* most workers injured on their jobs can again call upon a workmen's compensation program, and in the event of a nonoccupational illness, nearly all of the elderly now have the protection of Medicare, the poor and the near-poor have Medicaid, and millions of other families have private health insurance.

Unfortunately, no one can measure the overall adequacy of this bewildering network of public and private programs. We have seen that these programs differ widely in their goals, their financing, and their administration; each has its own strengths and weaknesses; and there simply is no calculus available to add up these disparate costs and benefits.

Most important, there is no objective basis for evaluating any health plan's mixture of *security and incentives*—the key issue underlying most debates over the welfare state. On the one hand, our society is clearly moving away from the "competitive model" of health care, under which a person's ability to pay is the determinant of the quantity and quality of medical services he receives. Even in 1965, the year before Medicare and Medicaid took effect, payments under government programs accounted for 21 percent of all expenditures for personal health care in this country—and by 1967 this proportion had jumped to 33 percent.

Also, several government programs already incorporate the features most criticized by opponents of "socialized medicine." Few patients have a free choice of doctors in state mental hospitals or the welfare wards of city hospitals or in the armed services or even under many workmen's compensation laws (most of which still permit the employer or insurance company to select the doctor who will initially treat an injured worker). Some of these programs also employ doctors on a full-time, salaried basis, which means these doctors seldom have a free choice of patients. And every public program has an element of compulsion and breaks the fee-for-service link between the individual patient and his doctor—the employer must pay all the costs of workmen's compensation; every person covered by the Social Security Act must pay the Medicare tax, whether or not he wants to; the general taxpayer must foot half the cost of Medicare's voluntary insurance and all of the bills under Medicaid.

On the other hand, probably most Americans remain hostile to the idea of total security. Most people appear to believe that if our society should guarantee every person that he would never lose a dollar of income because of sickness, and that he would never have to pay another medical bill (except indirectly through taxation), important incentives would be dulled or destroyed. It is feared that workers would take a week off whenever they had a hangnail; hypochondriacs would clog every hospital and doctor's office; the doctors themselves would have little incentive to be efficient; repressive controls would arise in a vain effort to check fraud and malingering; and the costs of such a program would be astronomical.

For all these reasons, we have stressed that the crucial question in the field of health care today is not, as some propagandists would have it, whether one favors security *or* efficiency, compulsion *or* individual choice, private *or* socialized medicine. The hard question is, instead, how to strike the best balance between these simplistic extremes, both of which our society has plainly rejected. On that question, which requires a value judgment as well as cold facts, there is no consensus among either experts or laymen.

Some believe that national health insurance would be the best solution for the health-care problems of the entire population, for essentially the same reasons that Medicare—which in fact is compulsory health insurance—proved necessary to meet the problems of the aged. That is, many persons under sixty-five also find the costs of illness so large and unpredictable that they need to share this risk through some form of insurance; the non-aged also find that private insurance is helpful but cannot do the entire job, particularly for those most in need of protection; and both the young and the old deserve reasonable medical care as a right, not as a consumer good available to the higher bidder or a handout available to the poor.

Further, it is argued that "socialized medicine" is a scare term which, taken literally, means a system under which all doctors are on government salary and all patients and doctors are subject to government dictation. As Medicare demonstrates, however, a system of national health insurance does not have to go to those lengths to be effective. Even the much-maligned British system of health care allows considerable freedom of choice for both patients and doctors, and is far more popular with both of those groups than critics in this country admit.[27] Finally, there are some very pragmatic pressures at work here. In 1969, for example, a majority of state governors urged the establishment of a national, compulsory health insurance program—an astonishing move dictated less by liberal ideology than a desire to relieve the states of the burgeoning costs of Medicaid.[28]

Needless to say, these arguments fail to convince many people, who feel that public programs now adequately cover those most in need of medical assistance—the poor, the aged, and the worker injured on his job—and that private health insurance offers good protection for other, middle-income groups. Also, while no one knows what the cost would be of a comprehensive national insurance scheme, experience under Medicaid and most other welfare plans suggests that these costs might well escalate beyond original expectations. And if we cover everyone's medical bills today, how can we refuse tomorrow's demand that we also insure everyone against the other cost of illness—that of income loss? Where will it all end?

Our own opinion is that further government action is both inevitable and desirable in this field. This action will probably not take the form of a sweeping, universal system of health care, but will instead continue the present trend of improving the programs we now have, occasionally adding another to meet the need of a specific group, and relying on private supplements to public programs. Whether this approach is termed creeping socialism or Yankee pragmatism, its thrust will be the same—a growing proportion of the labor force will gain protection against the worst economic effects of injuries and illness.

ADDITIONAL READINGS

Andersen, Ronald, and Odin W. Anderson: *A Decade of Health Services: Social Survey Trends in Use and Expenditure,* The University of Chicago Press, Chicago, 1967.

Bowen, William G., and F. H. Harbison, R. A. Lester, and H. M. Somers (eds.): *The American System of Social Insurance: Its Philosophy, Impact, and Future Development,* McGraw-Hill, New York, 1968, chaps. 1–3, 5, and 7.

Brinker, Paul A.: *Economic Insecurity and Social Security,* Appleton-Century-Crofts, New York, 1968, chaps. 7–11.

Cheit, Earl F.: *Injury and Recovery in the Course of Employment,* Wiley, New York, 1961.

Levitan, Sar A., W. J. Cohen, and R. J. Lampman (eds.): *Towards Freedom from Want,* Industrial Relations Research Association, Madison, Wisc., 1968, pp. 3–87.

MacIntyre, Duncan M.: *Voluntary Health Insurance and Rate Making,* Cornell University Press, Ithaca, N.Y., 1962.

Somers, Herman M., and Anne R. Somers: *Doctors, Patients, and Health Insurance,* Brookings, Washington, 1961.

Somers, Herman M., and Anne R. Somers: *Workmen's Compensation,* Wiley, New York, 1954.

FOR ANALYSIS AND DISCUSSION

1. Are there any limits which you would impose on the principle of compensation for occupational disabilities without respect to responsibility for them?

2. How would you estimate the value to a worker of a lost arm or a lost eye?

3. Suppose you were a member of a state legislature faced with a bill seeking to remove present maximum limits to workmen's compensation benefits so that these would be equal to 60 to 66⅔ percent of a worker's usual (or lost) earnings, which is set forth as the legislative intent. What arguments would influence you for and against the measure? How would you resolve the issue?

4. List the major questions to which you would want answers if you were considering the desirability of a national health insurance system. Make sure your questions are objective; that is, the answers to them might lead you to either an affirmative or negative conclusion. Then see if you can find data on which to base answers to your questions, and decide for yourself whether you would favor such a system. If "yes," along what lines would you fashion it? If "no," would you make any provision for the health needs of those in low-income groups beyond the laws we now have?

5. How far would you be willing to carry the

principle of a "minimum social standard" for people's needs? In what areas would you want to apply the principle, and how would you decide the minimum standard?

NOTES

1. U.S. Department of Health, Education, and Welfare, Social Security Administration, *Social Welfare Expenditures Under Public Programs in the United States, 1929–1966,* Research Report no. 25, 1968, pp. 191 and 194.

2. Among twenty countries classified as "developed" on the basis of per capita income, the United States ranked eighteenth with respect to "social security benefit expenditures" (most of the programs included in Table 22–1 except education) as a percent of GNP in fiscal 1963. The percentage was between 10 and 15 for most developed countries in that year, 6.2 for the U.S., and lower only in Israel and Venezuela. (Most underdeveloped countries spend a far lower share of GNP on social security programs; in India in 1963, for example, the share was 1.6 percent.) See Walter Galenson, "Social Security and Economic Development: A Quantitative Approach," *Industrial and Labor Relations Review,* vol. 21, pp. 559–569, July, 1968, and occasional studies by the International Labour Organization entitled *The Cost of Social Security.*

Precisely comparable data are not available for education, but the U.S. ranked sixth among the same twenty developed countries with respect to public education expenditures as a percent of national income in 1965. Most developed countries spent between 3 and 6 percent of income on public education in that year, with the U.S. figure being 5. (Computed from *United Nations Statistical Yearbook,* 1967 and 1968, various pages.)

Taken together, these data indicate that when the U.S. was spending 10 to 12 percent of GNP on health, education, and welfare programs from 1963 to 1965, most other developed countries were spending about 15 to 20 percent. For the only two Communist countries included in this comparison, the percentage was about 20 for Czechoslovakia (the same as for Austria and Belgium) and about 16 for the Soviet Union (the same as for Canada).

3. U.S. Department of Health, Education, and Welfare, *Toward A Social Report,* 1969, chap. 1, pp. 1–13. Unless otherwise noted, all the data and quotations in this section of the text are from this source.

4. Data from Dorothy P. Rice and Barbara S. Cooper, "National Health Expenditures, 1950–1967," *Social Security Bulletin,* January, 1969, pp. 15–16.

5. Data from "Workmen's Compensation Payments and Costs, 1967," and Daniel N. Price, "Income-Loss Protection against Illness, 1948–67," both in the *Social Security Bulletin,* January, 1969, pp. 21–37.

6. Herman M. Somers and Anne R. Somers, *Workmen's Compensation,* Brookings, Washington, 1961, p. 9, with citations.

7. Alfred M. Skolnik, "Twenty-Five Years of Workmen's Compensation Statistics," *Social Security Bulletin,* October, 1966, p. 4.

8. Somers and Somers, pp. 22–25, and U.S. Department of Labor, *The Growth of Labor Law in the United States,* 1962, p. 159.

9. Skolnik, p. 4. Italics added.

10. The same, pp. 4–9.

11. U.S. Department of Health, Education, and Welfare, Social Security Administraton, *Social Security Programs in the United States,* 1968, p. 64.

12. The same, pp. 66–69; and Lawrence Smedley, "The Failure of Workmen's Compensation Laws," *AFL-CIO American Federationist,* March, 1966, p. 18.

13. For work-injury data going back to the 1920s, see U.S. Bureau of the Census, *Historical Statistics of the United States, Colonial Times to 1957,* 1960, p. 100. The U.S. Bureau of Labor Statistics ceased publication of national work-injury data in mid-1966, although it will provide unpublished estimates for later years upon request. Estimates in the text of recent experience are based on *Monthly Labor Review, 1964–65 Statistical Supplement,* pp. 181–192; *Injury Rates by Industry, 1964 and 1965,* BLS Report no. 342; and *Economic Report of the President, 1969,* p. 19. Annual reports by the New York State Department of Labor provide more recent and detailed data, but limited to that state alone.

14. Harrison M. Trice and James A. Belasco, *Emotional Health and Employer Responsibility,* Cornell University, New York State School of Industrial and Labor Relations, Bulletin 57, 1966, pp. 3–16.

15. Skolnik, p. 17, with citation.

16. The same, pp. 12 and 14. Since workmen's compensation benefits are not subject to federal income or social security taxes, they can be a larger percentage of actual "take-home" pay than shown in the text. For a worker earning an average wage in 1965, benefits averaged (in the country as a whole) 61 percent of his weekly take-home pay if he had no dependents, and 73 percent if he were married, had two dependent children, and worked in one of the sixteen jurisdictions with dependents' allowances.

On the other hand, in more than two-thirds of all jurisdictions there are no dependents' allowances and there the married man with two children would have averaged only 54 percent of take-home pay in 1965 benefits, and even less if he earned above-average wages. Also, this income-restitution ratio is reduced further by the fact that most states require a seven-day waiting period before filing for benefits, and benefits are usually retroactive only if the disability extends beyond three or four weeks.

17. For example, by 1967, only thirty-one compensation laws contained special provisions for rehabilitation in the form of retraining and other help for injured workers in finding suitable work, and not all of these provided maintenance benefits to cover the worker's additional expenses during the rehabilitation period (such as travel, tuition, and the cost of living away from home). Also, litigation is excessive under most laws; the waiting period is often too long; most laws provide that the employer or insurance company shall choose the doctor, while many authorities recommend that the injured worker should have this choice; and the ratio of benefits paid to total expenses is far higher under exclusive state funds than under private insurance companies.

18. John F. Burton, Jr., *Interstate Variations in Employers' Costs of Workmen's Compensation,* W. E. Upjohn Institute for Employment Research, Kalamazoo, Michigan, 1966, pp. 74–75. See chapters 2 and 3 for Burton's cost measures, which are more precise than those given in our Table 22–2.

19. This section is based upon Price, "Income-Loss Protection against Illness, 1948–67," pp. 21–34; and Social Security Administration, *Social Security Programs in the United States,* 1968, pp. 76–85 and 103–107.

20. Data in this section are from Louis S. Reed and Willine Carr, "Private Health Insurance in the United States, 1967," *Social Security Bulletin,* February, 1969, pp. 3–22.

21. Herman M. Somers and Anne R. Somers, "The Interrelationship of Public and Private Health and Medical Care Programs," *Labor Law Journal,* July, 1959, p. 470.

22. Richard Harris, *A Sacred Trust,* New American Library, New York, 1966, p. 3. This book is a highly critical history of the AMA's long campaign against government health insurance.

23. Social Security Administration, *Social Security Programs . . . ,* 1968, pp. 92–93.

24. More precisely, the 1967 amendments to the Medicaid law specified that, starting July, 1968, states would be limited in setting income levels for federal matching purposes to 150 percent of the payment level under the program of Aid to Families with Dependent Children. This percentage dropped to 140 in 1969 and 133⅓ thereafter.

25. For example, some 2,700 doctors collected $25,000 or more each in Medicaid fees in 1968, which some critics find excessive. In one state with annual Medicaid expenditures of about $100 million, seventy employees reviewed claims in 1969, but another state with the same level of expenditures employed only seven persons for auditing. A federal audit of Medicaid in New York City in 1969—where the program then covered 1 million welfare recipients and 650,000 low-income families not on welfare—claimed considerable "potential fraud" existed because of the city's inadequate controls. *New York Times,* Aug. 23 and Aug. 26, 1969 (both page 1).

26. How did a program as controversial as Medicaid slip through Congress with little fanfare in 1965? At least part of the answer probably lies in the fact that, to meet the rising concern over the medical needs of the aged, Congress had adopted in 1960 a program of federal grants aimed at helping the medically indigent aged 65 and over—that is, the elderly who had more than a welfare-level income but who could not easily pay their medical expenses. This program (the Kerr-Mills Act) provided federal supplements out of general revenues to those states which elected to put up money of their own to provide such assistance to the near-poor aged.

Although this voluntary program was not effective enough to stave off the demands for a Medicare-type program for the aged, it nevertheless established the principle of federal aid in meeting the medical expenses of a group other than the poor on welfare. And once that principle is adopted, why should it be applied only to the elderly? If it is good public policy to help a seventy-year-old retiree meet his medical bills without first bankrupting himself, why shouldn't the same concern be shown for the forty-year-old worker with an income just above the poverty level? In this sense, Medicaid was simply an extension of prior public policy, and not quite the abrupt innovation it appears to be. It is clear, however, that the 1965 Congress did not expect Medicaid to assume the proportions it has.

27. For a description and highly favorable appraisal of the British system, see Almont Lindsey, *Socialized Medicine in England and Wales: The National Health Service, 1948–1961,* The University of North Carolina Press, Chapel Hill, 1962. The British Medical Association opposed the Health Service when it was first enacted in 1946, but by 1956 a survey of British doctors reported that over two-thirds indicated that if they had a chance to go back ten years, they would vote in favor of establishing the Service (p. 460). In the same year, 90 percent of all people polled gave the Service a favorable rating (p. 473). And in 1962, the British Medical Journal editorially dismissed as "vulgar, cheap and nonsense" attacks by the American Medical Association on the English system as the epitome of the evils of socialized medicine (*New York Times,* July 14, 1962, p. 32).

28. *New York Times,* Sept. 3, 1969, p. 1.

Under conditions of economic interdependence, no household is able to provide for all its wants. Any interruption to its inflow of earnings constitutes a threat to its way of life. Such an interruption may come from a number of sources—sickness and accident, as we have noted in the preceding chapter, and old age, as we shall see in the next chapter; but the threat of which workers tend to be most aware is unemployment. Even under conditions of high-level employment, from 2.5 to 4 percent of the civilian labor force are likely to be without work against their will.

Extent of unemployment

Table 23-1 provides figures on the number of unemployed and the percentage of the civilian labor force which they represent, over the period 1929 to 1970. In the darkest days of the Great Depression, it will be noted, one out of four workers was jobless. Throughout the entire decade 1931 to 1940 the unemployment rate did not fall much below 15 percent of the labor force. Unemployment then plummeted during World War II, as government spending stimulated demand and the armed services drained off ten million men from the supply of civilian labor. The early postwar years generated less unemployment than had been expected, but since 1949 the unemployment rate has consistently hovered between 4 and 6.8 percent except during the Korean War (1951–1953) and the years following the 1965 buildup in Vietnam.

There is much disagreement, among experts as well as laymen, over the causes of these fluctuations in unemployment levels, the remedies needed to achieve full employment, and the best way of helping individuals who are jobless. Before tackling those subjects, however, we need to know more about the data in Table 23-1, for some people believe those figures exaggerate the extent of unemployment and others believe they minimize the problem.

Since it is a huge task to take a complete census of the population even once every decade, monthly and annual statistics on the labor force must depend upon a sample designed to represent (with a predictable margin of error) the population as a whole. Currently this sample consists of about 50,000 households scattered throughout the country. Interviewers trained by the Bureau of the Census visit each of the sample households every month, obtaining information about the employment status of each member of the household sixteen years of age and over. These survey data are then "blown up" into estimates for the labor force as a whole, using the following distinctions between the employed and the unemployed:

Employed persons comprise (a) all those who during the survey week did any work at all as paid employees, or in their own business, profession, or farm, or who worked 15 hours or more as unpaid workers in an enterprise operated by a member of the family, and (b) all those who were not working but who had jobs or businesses from which they were temporarily

Table 23-1 *Unemployment in the United States, 1929-1970**

Year	Number of persons (in thousands)	Percent of civilian labor force
1929	1,550	3.2
1930	4,340	8.7
1931	8,020	15.9
1932	12,060	23.6
1933	12,830	24.9
1934	11,340	21.7
1935	10,610	20.1
1936	9,030	16.9
1937	7,700	14.3
1938	10,390	19.0
1939	9,480	17.2
1940	8,120	14.6
1941	5,560	9.9
1942	2,660	4.7
1943	1,070	1.9
1944	670	1.2
1945	1,040	1.9
1946	2,270	3.9
1947	2,311	3.9
1948	2,276	3.8
1949	3,637	5.9
1950	3,288	5.3
1951	2,055	3.3
1952	1,883	3.0
1953	1,834	2.9
1954	3,532	5.5
1955	2,852	4.4
1956	2,750	4.1
1957	2,859	4.3
1958	4,602	6.8
1959	3,740	5.5
1960	3,852	5.5
1961	4,714	6.7
1962	3,911	5.5
1963	4,070	5.7
1964	3,786	5.2
1965	3,366	4.5
1966	2,875	3.8
1967	2,975	3.8
1968	2,817	3.6
1969	2,831	3.5
1970	4,008	4.9

* Data for years prior to 1947 are for all persons fourteen years of age and over in the civilian labor force; from 1947 on, for all persons sixteen years of age and over This difference is insignificant for most purposes; the two measures yield nearly identical unemployment rates.
SOURCE: U.S. Bureau of Labor Statistics.

absent because of illness, bad weather, vacation, labor-management dispute, or personal reasons, whether or not they were paid by their employers for the time off, and whether or not they were seeking other jobs.

Unemployed persons comprise all persons who did not work during the survey week, who made specific efforts to find a job within the past 4 weeks, and who were available for work during the survey week (except for temporary illness). Also included as unemployed are those who did not work at all, were available for work, and (a) were waiting to be called back to a job from which they had been laid off; or (b) were waiting to report to a new wage or salary job within 30 days.[1]

Few observers question the statistical soundness of the household sample, but many employers and others doubt that the above measures present a true picture of unemployment. The issue here is usually one of assessing either the *motivation* or the *need* of those who say they are available for work but cannot find a job. For example, should society really worry about the skilled machinist on layoff who is too proud to take a job as a janitor? Or the "slacker" who goes through the motions of job hunting but secretly prefers to do nothing as long as his welfare check or unemployment insurance keeps rolling in? Or the wife or teen-ager who is casually looking around for some extra income, even though the male head of the family is working full time at top wages?

On the other hand, we presented evidence in Chapter 1 showing several ways in which gross unemployment data, such as those in Table 23-1, actually understate the problem of joblessness. We saw, for instance, that in addition to the 2.8 million persons counted as unemployed in 1969, another 2 million were *underemployed* in the average month of that year. These were people who wanted full-time jobs but were only working an average of about 20 hours a week because of economic reasons over which they had no control —they could not find a regular full-time job or they had one but were on partial layoff because of a sales slump or material shortages or similar reasons. Also, while Table 23-1 shows a monthly *average* of 2.8 million unemployed in 1969, the constant turnover within the labor force meant that a *total* of about 11 million persons were jobless at some time or other during that year. About one-half of these workers were unemployed for fewer than five weeks, but nearly one-fourth were out of work for fifteen or more weeks. Finally, Table 1-2 in Chapter 1 shows that the burden of unemployment falls disproportionately on the Negro, the young, and the unskilled.

The point should be clear: Unemployment is a highly complex problem which cannot be summarized by any one statistic. The figures in Table 23-1 are not biased in either direction but are simply incomplete, as any single measure of joblessness must be. Even to the individual worker, who may be supremely disinterested in these quarrels over statistics, unemployment can have different meanings at different times. It is one thing for him to lose a few days of pay when he voluntarily quits one job to move to another with better prospects, but it can be quite another matter when he is on involuntary layoff and can find no other work. Also, a spell of even two or three weeks without work can strain the finances of many families, but if unemployment stretches out for as long as fifteen weeks or more—as it did for 2.5 million persons even in the prosperous year of 1969—it can generate fear and despair as well as severe economic pressures.

Thus, nearly every unemployed worker faces the immediate problem of how to finance the operation of his household, and many face the additional problem of whether they should change their occupation or industry or home base, if they are to find work again. *These are the two central problems which will occupy our attention in this chapter—how best to maintain the income and improve the employability of the people without work.*

Types of unemployment

Obviously there are many kinds of unemployment (we shall here distinguish four) with different causes and requiring different cures.

1. Seasonal unemployment stems from weather (affecting agriculture and construction, for example, and dependent industries, such as food processing), from annual style and model changes which necessitate a production lull during the changeover (as in automobile manufacturing), and from customary buying patterns such as are associated with holidays (Christmas and Easter, most notably). All these are factors creating shifts in the demand for labor over the calendar. In addition, one major supply factor affects the seasonality of unemployment—the large numbers of students who are let loose for summer vacation, not all of whom are able to find jobs. Thus for workers under twenty-five, unemployment reaches its peak in June, when it may be as much as 60 percent above the annual average for that age group. For the same workers, unemployment is at its seasonal low in October, with the resumption of school, when it drops back to approximately 75 percent of the annual average for workers in that age bracket. For men over twenty-five in the labor force, the seasonal low point of employment comes in February, reflecting layoffs in outdoor jobs, and for women in January, as a result of reductions in clerical and sales forces following the holiday period.

Of course the decline in trade, construction, agricultural, and some manufacturing activity in accordance with a seasonal pattern does not always trail an equal amount of unemployment in its wake. Numbers of workers, particularly housewives and students, enter the labor market only at the time of peak activity and leave it as soon as they are no longer needed. Employment thus rises and falls with the seasonal activity, but when employment ceases numbers of people move out of the labor force rather than into unemployment. Even so, the seasonality of economic activity is responsible for a significant amount of unemployment, sometimes as much as a fourth of the total, averaged over the year.

2. Frictional unemployment refers to joblessness, usually of a short-run nature, which is due to the movement of people between jobs; this is an unavoidable (and to a degree, desirable) aspect of any labor market. No worker is frozen into a job, nor is he guaranteed a job. There is normally a churning around of people looking for jobs and employers looking for people, even in prosperous times—we could even say *especially* in good times. Since such adjustments are seldom

made with precise timing, so that a worker leaves one job at 5 P.M. Friday and starts another one at 8 A.M. Monday, there is often a period of unemployment separating the transition. The labor market, we say, is not frictionless, and loss of paid time represents the "frictions" which are inherent in its functioning.

In a single month as many as a million or a million and a half persons can expect to be separated from their jobs, voluntarily or involuntarily, and to become unemployed. At the same time, about the same number of people who have been unemployed will start new jobs or resume old jobs. The *total* of unemployed may not change much at all, either up or down, but it will for the most part consist of a different group of people. Although some of last month's unemployed will remain unemployed this month and perhaps next month as well (the long-term unemployed), they will be offset by those who are without a job only for a few days. Not all, but a considerable part of, the unemployment at any given time thus is short run—perhaps only a few weeks in duration —and may be viewed as virtually unavoidable.

In recognition of the inescapable nature of some frictional unemployment, even proponents of full-employment programs have usually defined full employment as a situation not where all workers have jobs, but where the number of workers seeking jobs is matched by the number of job openings for which workers are being sought. Unfortunately, there is no agreement on the precise rate of unemployment that would still exist during a period of "full employment." Some argue that experience in World War II shows that we could drive unemployment down to about 2 percent if we really tried; others argue that the postwar years show that demand matches supply in most labor markets when unemployment is about 4 percent, since inflationary pressures have developed when the rate has dropped much below that level; and yet others argue that the target rate will differ from one period to another, depending on the shifting structure of employers' demands and workers' skills. The key fact, however, is that everyone agrees there would be *some* frictional unemployment—around 3 percent of the labor force—under any realistic definition of full employment.

As with some of our other unemployment categories, we shall find that the frictionally unemployed are not a very clearly demarked group. This can perhaps best be seen if we inquire a little more closely into the characteristics of those who compose it. We can subdivide frictional unemployment into four rather different subtypes: (*a*) transitional unemployment; (*b*) voluntary unemployment; (*c*) entry unemployment, and (*d*) terminal unemployment. There are some who would also include seasonal unemployment as a subtype, but we have treated that independently.

a Transitional unemployment is attributable to the misfortunes or miscalculations of individual firms, quite randomly. This company finds its sales falling off and is forced to curtail production at the same time that competitors may be doing quite nicely; or that company must close down a plant perhaps because of a shift in its markets, or go out of business, perhaps as a result of mismanagement. Business for profit means risk taking, and risk taking means the possibility of setbacks and failure. Unemployment due to such tides in the affairs of business is unavoidable. It is termed transitional because of the expectation that workers who are left jobless by the failures of some firms will soon find other jobs with firms which are enjoying success.

Figure 23-1 graphically illustrates how a single company's ups and downs affect employees, in this case, even *within* a large corporation. It diagrams the percentage change in employment in fifteen of General Electric's largest plant locations as well as in the company as a whole, the electrical-manufacturing industry, the durable-goods sector of the economy, of which electrical manufacturing is a component, and the total economy over the period 1955 to 1960. While overall employment in General Electric rose more than 10 percent, and in the electrical-manufacturing industry by almost 20 percent, and in the durable-goods sector by about 4 percent, and in the economy as a whole by about 5 percent, eight GE plants registered declines, three of them by as much as 30 percent and another two by more than 20 percent. Thus while job opportunities were increasing elsewhere, workers in these plant locations were faced with declining employment.

Most blue-collar workers have experienced lay-offs at some time during their working career because of lack of business in the company where they were employed. One study indicates that skilled and semiskilled workers have become quite adept in calculating for themselves the likelihood of a prompt recall and the consequent relative advantage of "waiting out" a spell of unemployment with the expectation of going back to the old, familiar job on which they enjoy seniority, or of prospecting for a new job. In either event, they are "transitionally" unemployed.[2]

b The voluntary unemployed are the individuals who on their own initiative leave a job because they are unhappy with it or hope to find something better. Table 23-2 shows that 15 percent of all those unemployed in 1968 were in this category. Although this rate appears to be relatively constant regardless of age, sex, and color, this appearance is misleading in one respect. If we focus on those workers who held jobs just before becoming unemployed (that is, if we compare only the second and third columns in the table), the proportion of voluntary unemployment is decidedly smaller among adult men than among either teen-agers or adult women. This makes sense, for the head of a family will probably be more reluctant than a "secondary earner" to quit one job without having another lined up.

We also noted in Chapter 4 that the quit rate closely follows the ups and downs of the business cycle, indicating that workers are naturally less likely to quit their jobs when other openings are scarce than when they are plentiful. Further,

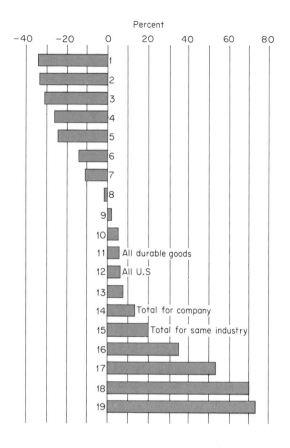

Fig. 23-1. *Percent change in total employment in fifteen plant locations of one company, 1955–1960.* SOURCE: *G.E. Relations Newsletter, Aug. 12, 1960.*

Table 23-2 *Reasons for Unemployment, 1968, Percent Distribution*

Age, sex, and color	Total unemployed	Lost last job	Left last job	Reentered labor force	Never worked before
Total	100.0	38.0	15.3	32.3	14.4
Both sexes, 16 to 19 years	100.0	15.5	11.6	33.5	39.4
Male, 20 years and over	100.0	60.4	16.8	20.7	2.2
Female, 20 years and over	100.0	34.7	17.0	42.9	5.6
White	100.0	38.1	15.5	32.3	14.1
Nonwhite	100.0	37.4	14.5	33.2	15.9

SOURCE: *Manpower Report of the President, Statistical Supplement, 1969*, p. 19.

Table 4-2 in Chapter 4 shows that although white-collar workers change employers less frequently than blue-collar workers do, the former are *more* likely to quit than to be laid off—and they are *less* likely than blue-collar workers to be unemployed between jobs. In this sense, the right to quit is a more meaningful and less costly option for the average white-collar worker than for most blue-collar workers.

This category of frictional unemployment is troubling on other counts as well. The right to quit is often hailed as an essential feature of a free society—whether one quits because of a domineering boss or the distasteful nature of a job or the chance to earn more money elsewhere. Our competitive market system also encourages voluntary mobility, on the assumption that workers will tend to move toward expanding sectors of the economy and will thereby serve consumer interests as well as their own. In practice, however, few people consider the worker who has quit his job to be an "unemployment problem" in the same sense as is the worker on involuntary layoff. Our society (like others) is wary of making it "too easy" to quit, fearing this would dull the incentive to work, and we shall see that unemployment insurance laws reflect this wariness.

c Entry unemployment occurs during the period before new entrants in the labor market find their first job or before those reentering the labor force find "reemployment." Government data draw the following arbitrary distinction between these groups:

New entrants are persons who never worked at a full-time job lasting two weeks or longer.

Reentrants are persons who previously worked at a full-time job lasting two weeks or longer but who were out of the labor force prior to beginning to look for work.

As in all categories of unemployment, both new entrants and reentrants must be actively seeking work to be counted as unemployed.

Table 23-2 shows the surprising importance of this type of unemployment, which accounted for nearly one-half of all joblessness in 1968. This proportion fluctuates, of course, with changes in both the demand for and supply of labor. We do

not have comparable statistics for earlier periods, but during the worst years of the 1930s, for example, the great majority of the unemployed undoubtedly had "lost last job," few had voluntarily "left last job," and entry unemployment—while it certainly existed—was far less important than today. In the late 1960s, in contrast, boom conditions served to raise the quit rate and lower the incidence of layoffs among adult males, the "baby boom" of the 1940s showed up in the form of millions of youths looking for their first jobs, and (for reasons discussed in Chapters 1 and 2) a growing number of wives reentered the labor force after their children had reached school age.

To pin down this type of unemployment more precisely, note in Table 23-2 that the largest number of adult women unemployed in 1968 were re-entering the labor force after a period of absence, and the majority of unemployed teen-agers were, as one would expect, either new entrants or reentrants (the latter group often having worked summers between school years). Stated more meaningfully (although not shown directly in this table), *teen-agers and adult women accounted for 83 percent of all entry unemployment in 1968.*

d At the other end of the working career may occur terminal unemployment. The older worker who is laid off may be unable to find a new job, so that a final spell of unemployment fades into retirement. Marginal workers, such as those who are physically or mentally handicapped, or housewives who are not well adapted to industrial or commercial employment, may temporarily enter the labor force during a period of labor shortage when employers are willing to hire them in the absence of more suitable help; as the labor shortage eases, such workers are retired into the "labor reserve." They may for a time consider themselves, and be considered by others, unemployed, although the likelihood of reemployment is negligible. They can scarcely be regarded as transitionally unemployed, since they are not actually in transition to another job, even though for a time they may believe (or hope) that they are.

3. Cyclical unemployment is perhaps the most familiar form of all. It is illustrated by the rise and fall of the unemployment rate in Table 23-1.

As a recession or depression spreads across the nation, the mounting rolls of the unemployed are attributable not to seasonal factors which will shortly be self-corrected nor to the random and temporary effects of frictional unemployment; the effects are general, affecting almost all industries and a high proportion of all firms, and of indefinite duration, running on perhaps for twenty months before economic prospects for the nation begin to brighten. As more and more firms start to rebuild depleted inventories and find it necessary to replace or add to old equipment, as people's spirits begin to revive so that they spend more on consumer goods, and as government fiscal and monetary programs swing toward stimulation of the economy, then the employment rolls rise, and—usually a little more slowly—the unemployment rolls shrink.[3] The prosperity phase is under way, and the cycle begins once again.

A business cycle may be of long or short duration, and sometimes short cycles are superimposed on long cycles with disastrous results. It is very unlikely, however, that we shall again suffer a massive depression like that of the 1930s, for the "Keynesian revolution" in economic thought has apparently convinced most conservatives as well as liberals that the government can and should avert any major collapse of the economy. We were nevertheless plagued by four recessions in the short period from 1949 to 1965, indicating that cyclical unemployment remains a persistent threat in our economy.[4]

4. Structural unemployment—the last major category of joblessness—arises from major imbalances in the supply of and demand for particular kinds of labor. This term applies to the "hard-core unemployed" who are not just temporarily jobless as they change employers, nor are they out of work because of a seasonal lag in a particular industry or a major slump in the economy as a whole. Instead, these are workers who are not hired to fill current job openings because they have the "wrong" education or skill or color or age or area of residence. In other words, the *structure* rather than the *level* of demand does not match supply in many labor markets, and the impact of this imbalance falls heavily on particular groups of workers.

This is a relatively new concept of unemployment which arose in response to certain postwar developments. Table 23-1 shows that since 1948 the unemployment rate has consistently been above 4 percent, except during the years of the Korean and Vietnam wars, and each postwar recession has left a larger residue of unemployment than its predecessor. It was also during the 1950s and early 1960s that the term "depressed areas" came into wide usage to describe regions such as the Appalachian coal fields, in which unemployment and poverty remained acute despite the prosperity of the country as a whole. And it was during this period when concern mounted over the "dropout," as teen-age unemployment became a major social problem; when more people became aware of the growing importance of the "shift to services," as blue-collar employment lagged; and when the civil rights movement forced attention upon the far higher rate of unemployment among blacks than among whites.

What had happened? To many observers, it seemed that a second Industrial Revolution had hit the American economy and sharply raised hiring standards beyond the reach of many workers. For example, technological change has always created some frictional unemployment in our economy, but now it is feared that automation has upgraded many job requirements so radically that the displaced worker can no longer adjust by simply picking up a little more job experience or by moving to another area or employer. We also know that the shift toward white-collar jobs began before the turn of the century, but it has now reached such proportions—claiming nearly one-half of all jobs in 1970—that even the high school diploma is no guarantee of success today. To oversimplify this argument, it was painful but possible for the farm hand to shift to factory work a few decades ago, but it is nearly impossible for the assembly-line worker to shift to either repairing or programming computers today.

Many economists challenge this interpretation of postwar developments, but the concept of structural unemployment has nevertheless gained wide acceptance. For example, most of the manpower-training programs adopted in the 1960s rest on the assumption that there is a hard core of unemployment which is not of fleeting duration—not due, that is, to normal market frictions or a temporary seasonal or cyclical slump—but instead springs from the fact that certain workers find themselves without the skills demanded on most jobs today.

Theory versus practice

We have defined four major types of unemployment—seasonal, frictional, cyclical, and structural—to show that this problem is more complex than some critics imply. For instance, you can hardly write off all the unemployed as loafers unless you can somehow explain why the proportion of loafers in the labor force varies from month to month and year to year, between one region and another, and among different occupational and age groups. At the other extreme, you cannot condemn all unemployment as a social evil unless you are prepared to ignore the political values implicit in the right to quit and the economic value of frictional unemployment, which largely results from the ceaseless change in any economy with a rising standard of living.

Unfortunately, it is far easier to identify these various types of unemployment in theory than in practice. Take, for example, a particular migrant farm worker who is found to be unemployed during a given week. He might, of course, fit into the category of seasonal unemployment, but again he might not. If he has just finished the harvest season in one state and is now moving northward where the same or a different crop will be ready for harvesting next week, is he seasonally unemployed, or is this a normal "friction" of casual labor markets, like farming and construction, in which many workers expect to move from one employer to another employer even during the busy season?

Or, if the economy is depressed and there is more competition than usual for unskilled farm work, is this worker a victim of cyclical unemployment? He *might* be structurally unemployed, for technology has destroyed innumerable jobs in farming and this worker may be unable to find steady work elsewhere because of his poor education and job training (though it is hard to say when technological displacement ceases to be temporary and frictional and becomes semipermanent and structural). Finally, this migrant worker

may well be either a Negro or a Mexican American and thus more vulnerable to *every* type of involuntary unemployment to the extent that discrimination alone explains the tendency for minority groups always to be among the last hired and the first laid off.

This classification problem involves more than the semantic quibbling of a few experts. The point is that it is impossible to frame an intelligent public policy to help "the unemployed" as an undifferentiated group. Deficit spending by the Federal government can produce jobs when the problem is cyclical unemployment, but such spending can easily produce nothing but inflation when frictional or structural unemployment is the problem. Similarly, the action needed to combat racial discrimination in hiring is obviously not the same as that needed to flatten the seasonal swings in construction or to retrain workers whose skills have become obsolete.

More specifically, the new concept of structural unemployment has evoked a sharp debate among economists and policy makers. We described above the major reasons for the view that the unemployment record of the postwar years cannot be explained by the conventional categories of unemployment. That view has been challenged on several grounds:

1. We do not have detailed statistics for the prewar years, but everything we know about labor markets suggests that unemployment rates have *always* been highest among the young, the uneducated, and the unskilled—regardless of whether the unemployment has been frictional, seasonal, or cyclical. This fact does not minimize the problems of these groups, but it does mean that the "structuralists" must do more than point to this pattern to prove their case. They must instead present some evidence for believing that typical pattern has become more pronounced in the postwar years.

2. The specter of a second Industrial Revolution has yet to materialize. Machines were wiping out jobs and skills long before the age of automation and there is little evidence that this type of frictional unemployment is more common today than in the past. Chapter 1 showed that there has not been any large jump in the productivity of the

economy as a whole, nor have the several case studies of automation shown that it sharply upgrades the occupational structure.[5]

3. There is also nothing new about depressed areas and sectoral shifts as either the cause or effect of unemployment. Much of the rural South has been a depressed area since Civil War days, and the postwar shift toward the service sector is no more radical than the prewar shift from farm to factory. Again, the point is that these unemployment problems are real but not necessarily new or different.

4. A more plausible explanation is that aggregate demand consistently fell short of the level necessary to achieve full employment during most of the postwar years. Particularly during the 1950s, it is argued, the Federal Reserve Board and the Eisenhower administration were so apprehensive of inflation that they slammed on the monetary and fiscal brakes too hard and too often, producing recessions in 1954 and 1958 and largely precipitating another which hit bottom in 1961. Thus, the excessive unemployment of the postwar period—above the normal frictional and seasonal levels—is regarded as being primarily cyclical in nature.

This debate was at the heart of the economic problems facing Congress and the Kennedy administration in the early 1960s. The new President had pledged to "get the country moving again," but even his own advisers were divided over how best to achieve that goal. If the unemployment problem were primarily structural in origin, it would do little good and much inflationary harm to stimulate aggregate demand. The remedy should be to upgrade the labor supply through manpower training and similar programs, not to increase further the demand for skills that the jobless did not have. On the other hand, if that unemployment were cyclical in origin, it would do little good to train the unemployed for openings that did not exist.

Lessons from the 1960s

Both the Kennedy and Johnson administrations resolved this apparent dilemma in a highly practical fashion, namely, by adopting *both* types of

unemployment remedies! To stimulate demand, monetary policy was eased and several fiscal measures were initiated, such as tax credits for investment, liberalized depreciation allowances, and particularly the tax cut of 1964. Also, while the Vietnam buildup beginning in mid-1965 obviously occurred for other reasons, it nevertheless accounted in large part for the increase in federal deficit spending from $6 billion in 1964 to $25 billion in 1968.

Most economists now seem to agree that it was primarily this increase in aggregate demand which lowered the unemployment rate from 6.7 percent in 1961 to 3.6 percent in 1968. Also, while this overall rate was declining by 46 percent, unemployment dropped even faster among certain "hard-core" groups—by 66 percent among adult Negro males and by 51 percent among nonfarm laborers. Further, the number of depressed areas (defined as major labor markets with over 6 percent unemployment) dropped from 101 in 1961 to only 6 in 1968. All of this strongly suggests that the chief cause of unemployment between the Korean and Vietnam war periods was not the structure but the level of demand.

As we have noted before, however, economists can seldom nail down an hypothesis with finality in the real world, where "all other things" never remain equal. In this case, during the years when the Kennedy and Johnson administrations were stimulating aggregate demand, they were simultaneously launching an unprecedented barrage of programs designed to upgrade the labor force: the Manpower Development and Training Act of 1962, the Vocational Educational Acts of 1963 and 1968, the Economic Opportunity Act of 1964, the Elementary and Secondary Education Act of 1965, the Higher Education Acts of 1963 and 1965, and several others. Also, the Area Redevelopment Act of 1961 provided financial and technical assistance to depressed areas, and the Civil Rights Act of 1964 outlawed discriminatory employment practices. No one can measure the contribution of these many "structuralist" programs to the reduction of unemployment during the 1960s, but surely they must have had some positive effect.

The debate between these two schools of thought therefore continues today, although on a much muted scale. There is now a fairly general agreement that fiscal and monetary policies are the key to reducing unemployment to a level of about 5 percent.

There is also general agreement, however, that if inflationary pressures are to be escaped, specialized manpower training and similar programs are needed to cope with the "next" 1 or 2 percent of unemployment. It is significant, for example, that as the *overall* unemployment rate was dropping by 46 percent from 1961 to 1968 (that is, from 6.7 to 3.6 percent), the rate among *teen-agers* (16 to 19 years old) dropped by much less —declining by 29 percent among white teen-agers during this period, and by only 10 percent among nonwhite teen-agers. In fact, as Table 1-2 in Chapter 1 shows, the unemployment rate among Negro teen-agers remained at the shocking level of 24 percent even in the prosperous year of 1969. Also, severe inflationary pressures developed when unemployment was pushed below 4 percent in the late 1960s, and at least some of these wage-price pressures could be reduced in the future by improving the ability of workers to react quickly to the job vacancies that develop as the economy approaches full employment. (In Chapter 28 we shall return to this crucial question of why our economy—like most others—has such difficulty in reaching full employment except during periods of war.)

Finally, the concept of structural unemployment serves an important *social* purpose, regardless of its historical validity. We have long known in a general way that the risk of unemployment is spread unevenly through the work force. It has only been since the 1950s, however, that the civil rights movement, the great debate over poverty in the midst of affluence, and other forces have combined to make us fully aware of the extent to which joblessness is concentrated among the young, the unskilled, the less educated, the black, and those in depressed areas. This new awareness of the inequitable impact of *all* unemployment— whether seasonal, cyclical, or frictional—led in turn to the "manpower revolution" of the 1960s, during which the Federal government greatly expanded its efforts to provide better education and training to disadvantaged groups. In this sense, it does not much matter whether there has

been a change in the actual structure of unemployment or only in the public's awareness of that structure. In either event, the concept of structural unemployment helps to focus attention on a dimension of this problem that was too long neglected.[6]

Maintaining the household-income stream

We have said that one of the two major problems attending unemployment is that of somehow maintaining an adequate flow of income into the household. When unemployment strikes, most of a family's normal inflow of funds automatically dries up. Until a new job is landed, some other source of funds for necessary expenditures must be found. The first resort is often such savings as may have been accumulated. Credit from stores or other forms of borrowing is also a crutch. Reliance on help from relatives is another possibility.

A survey undertaken by researchers from Columbia University in 1957, involving interviews with a sample of unemployed in the Albany–Schenectady–Troy area of New York State, reveals some of the adjustments of this type which were made and it is probably still generally valid in its conclusions.[7] Changes in the net-asset position of the survey group were especially revealing. In over half of all cases, and in three-fifths of the one-earner family units, the household's asset position deteriorated. "That is, either they spent cash on hand, drew on savings, cashed life insurance policies and/or securities, borrowed cash, or were involved in some combination of these activities. . . ."

But for many of the families interviewed, savings and credit were not enough. About a third of them had to call on friends or relatives for assistance. This was true for all except eight of the sixty-two families whose normal annual incomes were under $4,000. Even these measures did not of course permit them to maintain their former standard of living. "In short, although the net asset positions of practically all these lower income families deteriorated, very few were able to get along by calling on past and future earnings."

Similar findings were reported in a study of 223 workers with long-term unemployment in the Lansing area. In addition to drawing on savings and borrowing, 15 percent of the households represented had depended on aid from relatives, and 25 percent had sent a second family member (usually the wife) into the labor force to supplement dwindling resources.[8]

The private resources of households (including assistance from friends) are seldom sufficient to see them through a spell of unemployment that lasts very long. In such instances public assistance may be unavoidable.

Public *relief* to the unemployed needy was more important in the past than it is today, for reasons which we shall explore shortly. (Even so, in August, 1970, almost one milion persons were receiving public assistance in New York City alone.) Through most of the decade of the thirties it remained a principal support of the jobless, along with public works programs designed to create jobs for those without them. It is not always easy to picture the character of such programs, particularly during the depths of the Great Depression of the thirties. The flavor of public relief at that time is provided by this paragraph from a 1935 report by a citizens' committee appointed by the mayor of New York.[9]

> By the middle of December [1934], 123 depots had been set up throughout New York City from which families secured their coal. Each family was allowed 200 pounds a week and had to call for it at the nearest depot twice a week. At the depots it was given out in four twenty-five pound paper bags. These bags broke frequently in wet weather. Many families had to walk long distances to reach the depots. The coal was carried home in improvised wagons of every description, varying from ex-baby carriages to grocery boxes attached to children's skates.

The unemployment compensation program

Today, in place of relief, public assistance primarily takes the form of unemployment compensation (sometimes referred to as insurance), which is paid out to eligible employees without applying the hated "means test" but as a matter of right. Charitable relief is generally reserved for individuals who are not covered by the unemployment compensation program, which came into existence under the Social Security Act of 1935. Congressional fears that the act's provisions might be held unconstitutional by a Supreme Court which had been generally unsympathetic to social legislation, as well as the fact that one state—Wisconsin—had already established its own state system and other states were contemplating the same action, led to setting up the program under the administration of the separate states and the District of Columbia. The Federal government limited itself to establishing certain overall standards to which the states were required to adhere, but very great latitude was allowed the states in determining the substantive details of their respective programs.

The method by which the Federal government ensures compliance with its minimum standards is through its taxing power. It imposes on most employers of four or more workers a tax now amounting to 3.1 percent of the first $3,000 earned by each covered employee. But the employer is allowed to offset against this tax any amount up to 2.7 percent of the taxable payroll which is paid to a state unemployment compensation fund meeting federal standards. (This portion of the tax is used solely for paying benefits; the other 0.4 percent is used for paying federal and state administrative expenses.) A state therefore has nothing to gain by refusing to "join up," since all covered employers would still have to pay the federal tax, and it has much to lose, for all of this tax revenue would flow out of the state and local workers would not be eligible for any benefits. Given this "choice," every state naturally has elected to establish an unemployment insurance program.

Actually, few employers pay their state fund as much as 2.7 percent of taxable payroll, since the federal law permits each state to establish "experience rating" in determining the tax liability of employers. This system permits each employer's tax rate to vary on the basis of his firm's employment experience, the idea being to offer an incentive to the employer to reduce unemployment by stabilizing the size of his work force. In 1967, for example, unemployment tax rates ranged "from a low of nothing for some employers in some States to a high of 5.4 percent for some employers in one State."[10] For the *average* covered employer, however, experience rating has long operated to reduce his tax rate well below the nominal level of 2.7 percent. Thus, the actual contribution rate under all state programs amounted to only 1.4 percent of all taxable payrolls in the decade following World War II, and averaged only 1.6 percent in 1967. Also, the $3,000 ceiling on taxable wages reduces even further the employer tax as a percent of *total* payrolls.

Coverage and eligibility

Figure 23-2 shows that unemployment insurance covers nearly four out of every five employed wage and salary workers in the country. The federal act specifically excludes the categories shown as not covered (and also excludes the self-employed), although each state is free to take in any of those categories on its own initiative. In fact, about one-half of the states have extended coverage to private firms with fewer than four employees and to state and local government agencies (in which case their employees are counted among the covered in Figure 23-2). Spe-

cial laws also cover railroad workers, federal civilian employees, and persons leaving the armed services.

On the other hand, Figure 23-2 seriously overstates the coverage of unemployment insurance in one respect: It counts as "not covered" only *those employed in uncovered firms.* It does not include those workers seeking their first job or reentering the labor force after a long period of absence, and no unemployment insurance law covers this important category of "entry unemployment." To be eligible for benefits, that is, a worker must always have earned a certain minimum amount within some specified period of time—such as $800 in the year preceding his claim. The terms of this requirement vary from state to state, but the purpose is always to test the claimant's attachment to the labor force so that benefits will be reserved for genuine workers and not be wasted on those just looking for a handout. This is a laudable goal, of course, but the peculiar result is that under these laws a worker is considered unemployed only if he recently held a job, even

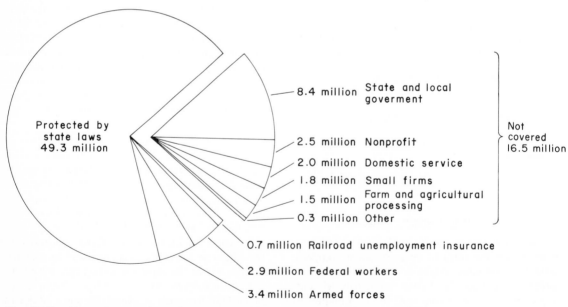

Fig. 23-2. *Unemployment insurance coverage of wage and salary workers, 1967.*
SOURCE: Unemployment Insurance Review, *October–November, 1968.*

though Table 23-2 shows that definition included only about one-half of those actually unemployed in 1968.

Other eligibility rules reflect this same dilemma: how to make benefits available to the majority of workers who "deserve" them while denying benefits to those who do not "deserve" them, without applying a means test or psychoanalyzing each claimant to determine whether he "honestly" wants to work. No one can resolve this dilemma to the satisfaction of both liberal and conservative critics, but the following describes the general pattern of compromises that has emerged over the years:[11]

All States require that for a claimant to receive benefits he must be able to work and must be available for work.... One evidence of ability to work is the filing of claims and registration for work at a public employment office. Most State agencies also require that the unemployed worker make a job-seeking effort independent of the agency's effort in order to qualify for benefits....

The major causes of disqualification for benefits are voluntary separations from work without good cause; discharge for misconduct connected with the work; refusal, without good cause, to apply for or accept suitable work; and unemployment due to a labor dispute. In all jurisdictions, disqualification serves at least to delay a worker's receipt of benefits. The disqualification may be for a specific period [such as seven weeks] ..., or for the entire period of unemployment following the disqualifying act. Some States not only postpone the payment of benefits but also reduce the amount due to the claimant.

It can be seen that the "model" claimant is the good worker who has lost his job through no fault of his own (his employer went bankrupt or moved South or hit a seasonal sales slump), who is looking hard for another job, and who deserves something better than charity to prop up his family's income for the few weeks before he finds other work. But how do you handle the many cases that do not fit that model?

For example, what is a "good cause" for quitting? No one wants to reward the person who quits only because he would rather draw unemployment insurance than work, but what about the wife who quits to follow her husband to another city where he has found work? Or the Negro who says his foreman used racial epithets? Or the secretary who claims her boss often chased her around the office? And even if you think these are "good causes" for quitting, how do you determine the facts in disputed cases, knowing that some workers may bend the truth to win benefits and some employers may do the same to keep down their experience rating?

An equally controversial rule is that permitting claimants to refuse "unsuitable work." The rationale of this rule is that no one would really benefit by disqualifying (as an extreme example) a laboratory technician on temporary layoff in Chicago for refusing to take a farm job in Nebraska, even if that were the only work then available. Both society and the individual could lose through such dissipation of a worker's skill, and the original employer could lose experienced workers whom he had intended to recall. It would also be unfair to disqualify this technician for refusing any job in his own specialty regardless of the wage, for an unscrupulous employer could then beat the market by offering a technician's job at a janitor's rate and this worker would have to accept—or lose his unemployment benefits. But, again, where do you draw the line? Should an unemployed actor be free to refuse any job outside of the theater? Can a union carpenter refuse a nonunion job paying one-half the union scale? Is a job unsuitable if it requires two hours of commuting time?

To handle these and many similar questions, the federal law requires every state to set up an appeals procedure similar in intent to the grievance machinery used to interpret union–management contracts. Any worker whose claim for unemployment benefits is denied (or any employer who thinks benefits should not have been granted to one of his former employees) may appeal through administrative channels—usually first to an impartial referee or tribunal and then to a board of review—and these administrative decisions may in turn be appealed to the courts.

Finally, even if a worker passes all of these

coverage and eligibility tests, he is by no means insured against every day he is out of work. On the one hand, all but four laws require a waiting period, usually of one week, before unemployment benefits can begin, and only a few states then pay benefits retroactively for that waiting period. Once benefits begin, on the other hand, every state also limits the period over which they can be paid even to a fully qualified claimant. In 1968 this ceiling varied from twenty-two weeks in South Carolina to thirty-nine weeks in Oklahoma, with most states having a maximum duration of twenty-six weeks of benefits. Further, most states vary this maximum payment period according to the weeks worked or wages earned by a claimant in the base period before he became unemployed, so in the same state some workers may be cut off after nine or ten weeks while others receive benefits for twenty or thirty weeks.

In spite of this mountain of rules and regulations governing eligibility, there is always a brisk market for editorials and articles attacking the scandalous fraud in the unemployment compensation program.

> Actually, the amount of fraud in the sense of willful misrepresentation is small. . . . The states spend millions of dollars each year in investigating suspected claims. In fiscal year 1964, only 12 out of every 1,000 beneficiaries were found to have made fraudulent claims that resulted in "overpayment" of benefits. Of every $100 paid out in benefits during the year, only 31 cents was an overpayment resulting from fraud and 64 percent of these overpayments . . . were recovered from the claimants by the state agencies.[12]

Many alleged abuses of unemployment insurance are in fact either run-of-the-mill cases, in which the critic disagrees with how a legislature wrote the basic law, or borderline cases of interpretation (such as the questions raised above about "good cause" and "suitable work"), in which the critic disagrees with the verdict reached after extensive argument before administrative tribunals and the courts. Any legislative or judicial decision is fair game for criticism on its merits, of course, but dark hints about fraud and scandal are something very different.[13]

The net effect of all these exclusions and restrictions is that fewer than one-half of those unemployed at any given time are actually receiving unemployment compensation. In 1969, for example, total unemployment averaged 2.8 million persons each month, but those drawing unemployment benefits averaged only 1 million each month —or 36 percent of the total jobless. That proportion rises during recessions, as many experienced workers are laid off and the share of entry and voluntary unemployment drops, but even then coverage seldom approaches 50 percent. Figure 23-3 shows this relationship for the years from 1960 to 1969.

In July, 1969, President Nixon proposed that unemployment insurance coverage be extended to an additional 4.8 million workers (primarily those in firms with fewer than four employees, on large farms, and in nonprofit organizations); that workers be eligible for benefits while enrolled in training programs designed to increase their employability (twenty-five states deny benefits to such workers on the theory that they are not "available for work"); that a minimum of fifteen weeks of employment in the base period be required as a condition of benefit eligibility, but no flat dollar amount be permitted as the only yardstick (the latter measure discriminates against the low-wage worker, for he must work for a longer period to be eligible); and that the maximum benefit period be automatically extended for up to thirteen more weeks in all states whenever the national unemployment rate among those covered by insurance equals or exceeds 4.5 percent for three consecutive months (benefit periods were extended temporarily during the 1958 and 1961 recessions, but this proposal would build an automatic "trigger" into the law to meet long-term unemployment during slumps).[14]

A significant number of the jobless would still remain without unemployment compensation even if Congress adopted all of the Nixon proposals, but those changes would at least help to close the gap in coverage. It is true that this gap cannot be eliminated completely in the foreseeable future, given our desire to preserve work incentives by denying or delaying benefits to new entrants, voluntary quits, those who refuse suitable jobs, and similar groups. Proposals such as President Nixon's

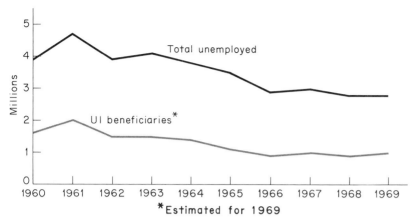

Fig. 23-3. *Total unemployment and average weekly number of beneficiaries under all state unemployment insurance programs, 1960–1969.*
SOURCE: Social Security Bulletin, *January, 1970, p. 63.*

nevertheless show that we can improve our dismal record of offering insurance protection to fewer than one-half of the unemployed.

Adequacy of benefits

The salient facts about unemployment compensation benefits bear a striking resemblance to those characteristics of workmen's compensation benefits which we examined in the previous chapter.

First, both types of laws proclaim (directly or indirectly) an ideal standard of benefits. It will be recalled that most workmen's compensation laws aim to replace two-thirds of the income lost by a worker injured on the job. In the case of unemployment insurance, the goal of most state laws is to replace only one-half of the worker's income loss. This difference in goals probably reflects the suspicion that few workers would deliberately invite injury in order to collect benefits, but many of the able-bodied might welcome or needlessly continue their unemployment if benefits were too generous. This reasoning is certainly plausible, but it could as easily support the conclusion that income restitution should be 100 percent for the disabled and 70 or 80 percent for the able-bodied unemployed, rather than the present standards of 66 and 50 percent. The fact is that no one knows how high this benefit-to-wage ratio can be pushed before it seriously impairs work incentives, al-

though 50 percent seems to us a conservative estimate.

Second, many of the insured unemployed do not receive even this low standard of 50 percent of their previous wages, just as many injured workers fail to receive the two-thirds standard under workmen's compensation. The reason is the same in both cases: Most states have established dollar maximums on weekly benefits and have failed to increase those maximums in step with the increase in wages. For example, in 1939, when unemployment payments began, the average beneficiary received 43 percent of the average weekly wage among covered workers, but by the late 1960s this proportion had declined to about 35 percent. As a result, *in 1969 at least two out of every five claimants received unemployment benefits that equaled less than one-half their previous weekly wages.*[15]

Third, benefits vary greatly among the states, under unemployment insurance as under workmen's compensation laws. In January, 1968, the maximum unemployment benefit was around $40 to $50 per week in most states, but this maximum ranged from $30 in Mississippi to $65 in California and $90 in Connecticut (one of nine states granting extra benefits to those with dependents). Again, no one can define the "ideal" benefit a jobless worker should receive, but neither can differences in living costs or other factors justify this huge variation in benefits from one state to another.

Finally, the inadequacy and variability of benefits under both types of laws spring largely from the same cause—competition among the states to retain or attract industry by minimizing the tax burden on employers. At first glance, the unemployment insurance system would seem to have neutralized this competitive factor by imposing a uniform federal tax on all covered employers in all states. (Under workmen's compensation, it will be recalled, each state controls the benefits and costs of its own program, without any regulation by the Federal government.) Two developments, however, have undermined the effectiveness of this federal tax standard:

1. Congress has failed to raise the taxable wage base beyond its original level of the first $3,000 of a covered worker's annual wages. That limit was reasonable in 1939, when it encompassed 98 percent of all wages paid to covered workers, but by 1969, after average wages had increased almost fivefold, this limit of $3,000 meant that the unemployment insurance tax was levied on less than 50 percent of all wages paid to covered workers. Not only is this inequitable (high-wage employers now pay a smaller tax, as a percent of total payroll, than low-wage employers do), but this low tax base also limits the funds available for benefits. Any state can raise the tax base beyond $3,000 within its own borders, and several have done so, but this action always raises the fear that some employers will move to "cheaper" states where only the low federal standard prevails.

2. Experience rating has apparently degenerated into a competitive weapon. Each state has wide latitude in setting the rules under which employers are permitted to pay less than the full federal tax of 3.1 percent (or, more precisely, less than the 2.7 percent which the states can collect to finance benefit payments). Instead of using this discretion to encourage *individual* employers to stabilize employment, many states seem to have used experience rating to lower the tax liability of *nearly all employers* in order to compete in the interstate scramble for new industry. Thus, benefits could be significantly improved today even within the limits of the $3,000 tax base if the states were to

collect the full 2.7 percent tax from most employers—but, as we have seen, in 1967 the average employer had to pay only 1.6 percent of his taxable payroll to his state system.

It is easy to see why many experts doubt that differences in unemployment insurance costs really induce employers to move from one state to another. Since these costs average less than 2 percent of taxable payrolls, they average even less of total payrolls and less yet of total costs, and state variations around that average are within such a narrow range (from about 0.8 to 2.8 of taxable wages) that most employers would need a microscope to estimate the effect on their profit margins of one state's unemployment tax compared to another's.[16] As with workmen's compensation, however, many employers and state legislators *believe* that interstate differentials in this tax are important and that belief largely accounts for the states' reluctance to raise benefits.

To meet this problem of inadequate benefits, President Nixon proposed in 1969 that the taxable wage base be raised from $3,000 to $6,000 over a five-year period, and he urged each state to raise its benefit maximum to two-thirds of the average wage in the state, a move which he estimated would permit at least 80 percent of insured workers to obtain benefits, if unemployed, equal to 50 percent of their previous wages.[17]

The problem of incentives

We have concentrated up to this point on the ways in which unemployment insurance tries to meet the legitimate income needs of the jobless while at the same time preserving their incentive to work—by applying several tests of eligibility and by controlling the ratio of benefits to wages. This absorption with the problem of worker incentives is understandable, but it has diverted attention from the equally serious problem of *employer incentives*.

As Prof. Richard A. Lester has cogently argued,[18] our present system of unemployment insurance is based largely on obsolete economic doctrines. Experience rating rests on the astonishing assumption that, to some significant extent, employers cause unemployment and therefore, given the incentive of a tax break, they will cure unemployment. That concept of employer blame makes about as much sense in this context as the worker-blame concept did in dealing with job accidents a century ago. Can anyone still believe that cyclical unemployment, like that in the 1930s, is caused by heartless or thoughtless employers instead of by a collapse in aggregate demand which the individual firm is powerless to stop? Or consider the "transitional unemployment" which occurs in any dynamic economy. Does anyone imagine that some employers deliberately guess wrong in predicting shifts in technology or consumer tastes, or that they would have better foresight if their payroll tax were shaved a point or two?

As for entry and structural employment, Lester points out that experience rating can actually penalize the employer who makes an effort to hire the young, the poorly educated, and other "hard-core" types, for his tax may go up because turnover is often high among these workers and, if laid off for any reason, they have trouble finding other jobs. An incentive is thus given to hire only "good" workers and to meet fluctuations in demand by scheduling longer or shorter workweeks for a stable work force, not by taking on the risk of new entrants or disadvantaged workers.

This leaves seasonal unemployment as the major category of joblessness that might plausibly be dented by experience rating. As a simple example, the employer who sells fuel oil in the winter is given an incentive to sell air conditioners in the summer and thereby avoid laying off his workers. But how many farmers or building contractors or retailers could actually smooth out the huge seasonal swings in their business even if they tried, and how many would bother to try such a risky and expensive move just to gain a minor tax advantage? Also, Lester argues that insurance is intended to cover unpredictable risks, and it can therefore be abused when applied to regular and predictable events such as seasonal layoffs. For example, "seasonal employers, as in northern seashore hotels or in fruit and vegetable canning factories, are able to offer low wages if they can couple 15 or 17 weeks of work with eligibility to draw 10 to 26 weeks of unemployment benefits in off-season periods."[19]

For all these reasons, no one is very happy with the way in which the unemployment insurance system handles the crucial problem of incentives. A strong case can be made for the complete abolition of experience rating, for neither theory nor practice supports the assumption that this tax incentive for employers can significantly reduce unemployment; instead, it too often gives employers and states an incentive to restrict benefits and coverage. As a practical matter, however, experience rating has become such an established part of unemployment insurance that its critics can hope only for some reforms, such as requiring a minimum tax of 1 percent on all employers.

As for the attempts to preserve workers' incentives, we can see no way in which to eliminate the controversy surrounding this issue. Everyone agrees that *some* controls are needed over eligibility and benefit levels in order to prevent abuses of the program, but no one can measure workers' motivations with enough precision to prove that one set of controls is any better than another in balancing equity and incentives. The inevitable result is that almost any control will be damned as too harsh by labor or as too lax by management. As for ourselves, we find it hard to believe that the present system of unemployment insurance is sapping the moral fiber of many Americans, when fewer than one-half of the unemployed usually do not qualify for any benefits and those who do qualify often receive less than one-half of their previous wage.

The manpower revolution of the 1960s

During most of the period since the mid-1930s, governmental attacks on unemployment have concentrated on two fronts: maintaining the income of the jobless through unemployment insurance, and creating new jobs through fiscal and monetary measures aimed at stimulating the growth of the economy as a whole. In the 1960s, however, the Federal government added a new weapon to its armory—an active manpower policy—which is still in its developmental stage but which promises to be a permanent fixture in our struggle to solve the unemployment problem.

The major thrust of this new policy is toward increasing the employability of those workers who are always the most prone to unemployment—

because of their poor education, lack of skills or work experience, residence in a depressed area, membership in a racial minority, or similar problems which will not fade away even if we greatly improve the unemployment insurance system or step up our rate of economic growth. As noted before, this policy was the result of growing concern over structural unemployment during the period from 1955 to 1965, a concern bolstered by the demands of the civil rights movement and the discovery that poverty still existed in the midst of affluence. Also, even among those economists who reject the structural thesis, there is now general agreement that an active manpower policy can help to reduce inflationary pressures at full employment by improving the ability of the labor force to react quickly to shifts in demand.

Like most innovations in public policy, this "manpower revolution" of the 1960s can easily be interpreted as only an evolution of prior practice rather than a sharp break with the past. Certainly our system of compulsory education in public schools has long constituted, among other things, a government manpower policy of overwhelming importance in supplying the skilled labor force needed by a modern economy. Further, federal aid to occupational training dates back as far as 1862, when the Morrill Act provided land grants for agricultural colleges; the federal-state system of vocational education in secondary schools began in 1917; the present United States Employment Service was created in 1933 to improve the matching of workers and jobs; and the GI Bill of Rights in 1944 provided training and education to millions of war veterans. In these and other ways, all levels of government have obviously been engaged for many years in increasing the employability of their citizens.

A change nevertheless did occur in the 1960s, as much in attitudes as in specific programs. Most of the older programs aimed to provide a general education for very large groups (all young people in the public schools, all veterans under the GI Bill), or were oriented toward providing workers for particular industries (such as agriculture), or directly helped the unemployed only during a major depression (through the Civilian Conservation Corps and other temporary programs in the 1930s). The "new look" today in manpower plan-

ning is the attempt to get at the special problems of the most disadvantaged workers and the recognition that this effort requires a varied attack, federal direction, and a continuation through prosperous as well as depressed times.

Table 23-3 summarizes most of the new manpower programs that emerged during the 1960s (plus three older programs—vocational education, vocational rehabilitation, and the Employment Service). These programs are too numerous and complex to be appraised here in any detail; also, any description would be rapidly outdated because of the changes still occurring every year in this field. We shall therefore review the programs of the 1960s only to the extent necessary to illustrate the three goals of current manpower policy—to develop workers' abilities, to create jobs making the most of those abilities, and to match workers and jobs.[20]

Developing workers' abilities

One of the first questions always asked about current manpower policy is why there are so many different programs. Wouldn't it be more efficient to have one comprehensive program under which a single agency determines the skills needed to fill current job openings and then offers training in those skills to the unemployed?

The easy explanation for this proliferation of activities is that government programs are often shaped by political compromise. For example, the problem quickly arose in the 1960s of whether the training of disadvantaged workers should be directed primarily by the Department of Labor with its expertise in labor affairs, or by the Department of Health, Education, and Welfare with its expertise in both general and vocational education, or by the Office of Economic Opportunity, the agency specially created to lead the "war on poverty" in new and imaginative ways. Neither Congress nor any administration has yet solved that problem, with the result that all three agencies have a "piece of the action" and an incentive to promote new programs.

But even a single and highly efficient agency could not meet present manpower goals with only one or two programs. The whole point of this new approach is that different workers are unemployed (or underemployed) for different reasons, and therefore the same program will not suffice for the teen-age dropout, the displaced farmer, and the widow on relief. This is a major reason for the large number of manpower programs shown in Table 23-3—some aimed at youth (such as the Jobs Corps), some at illiterate adults (Adult Basic Education), some at urban residents (JOBS), some at rural residents (Operation Mainstream), and so on.

Another reason is the difficulty of defining the jobs for which the unemployed should be trained. It sounds eminently sensible to say that people should be trained only for occupations in which there is a shortage of workers, but we know that demand is strongest at the top of the occupational structure—for more doctors and nurses, for example, or at least for more skilled craftsmen—while the hard-core unemployed are clustered at the bottom, usually without either the formal education or the work experience needed to begin to qualify for most shortage occupations. This dilemma faced the administrators of the Manpower Development and Training Act of 1962 (MDTA). In order to get quick results and prove the validity of this new approach to unemployment, these administrators tended to pick only the most promising "students" among the unemployed and to train them for only the most promising occupations, with the result that the workers most in need of training often found themselves unable to qualify for the early MDTA programs.

There is probably no complete escape from this dilemma, and certainly none in any program restricted solely to the hard-core unemployed. Three solutions have been attempted, all of which have required adding more programs:

1. It was decided in 1966 that henceforth 65 percent of the total MDTA effort would be directed to training the disadvantaged and only 35 percent devoted to meeting the need for trained personnel in occupations with skill shortages. The continuation of the latter type of training was justified not only by the desire to fill skill shortages, but also by the realization that helping better-prepared workers move up the occupational ladder can create openings on the lower rungs that the unemployed can handle. Thus, training is of-

fered to some workers already employed, as well as to those unemployed.

2. There was a frank acknowledgment that many job shortages at the professional level could not be met by better training of either the unemployed or those currently employed, and therefore other programs were needed to train high-level manpower. These programs (not included in Table 23-3) include the establishment of the National Teacher Corps in 1965, activities under the Education Professions Development Act of 1967, the Nurse Training Act of 1964, and the Health Manpower Act of 1968, and a host of college fellowship and traineeship programs designed to add to the supply of scientists, engineers, teachers, and medical personnel.

3. Although there were several reasons for the increased federal support of general education during the 1960s, certainly one was the growing awareness that the lasting solution to most structural unemployment must begin long before a person looks for his first job. It is very difficult to retrain a worker forty-five years old with a fifth-grade education, but we now try to help his children escape the same fate through programs such as Operation Head Start; the Elementary and Secondary Education Act of 1965 (special assistance to school districts with high concentrations of poor children); the Vocational Education Acts of 1963 and 1968 (more financial support and the freedom to offer training in any nonprofessional occupation, instead of the prior emphasis on agriculture and home economics); Projects Upward Bound and Talent Search (to find and help disadvantaged youths who, with some assistance, can qualify for college); and several programs providing colleges with more facilities and college students with more grants, jobs, and loans.

Finally, manpower programs have grown in number and complexity because experience has shown that the needs of the hard-core unemployed are more varied than once assumed. For a worker with little schooling and a history of intermittent employment on odd jobs, it is often either a traumatic or a boring experience to be placed in a classroom setting in which he is instructed on how to be a welder or a punch-press operator. If he is assigned to a specific job in a specific company,

Table 23-3 *Summary of Federally Supported Manpower Programs, 1969*

Program	Persons serviced in recent fiscal year*	Services provided	Eligibility criteria	Worker allowances
Manpower Development and Training Act:				
Institutional training	140,000	Remedial and skill training and basic education, provided in public schools or skill centers and in private schools	Mostly unemployed workers, but some up-grading of the employed	For youths, $20 per week. For adults, $10 above average weekly unemployment benefits in state, plus $5 for each of up to four dependents
On-the-job training	125,000	Subsidies to employers to cover training costs	Same	None (worker receives wage from employer)
Neighborhood Youth Corps	467,400	Work experience, plus some counseling and education	14 to 21 years of age, family income below poverty level	For those in school, $1.25 per hour for a maximum of 15 hours per week. For those out of school, $1.25 to $1.60 an hour for a maximum of 32 hours per week
Job Corps	64,600	Skill training, conservation work, and basic education. Trainees live away from home in rural conservation or urban residential centers	School dropouts up to 21 years of age, family income below poverty level	$30 to $50 per month plus $50 a month adjustment allowance, half of which can be allotted for family support with matching by Job Corps
JOBS (Job Opportunities in the Business Sector)	84,000	Subsidies to employers to cover training and supportive services (counseling, remedial education, health services, etc.)	The hard-core unemployed in the fifty largest urban areas	None (worker receives wage from employer)
New Careers	4,300	Training for subprofessional jobs in public and private nonprofit agencies (schools, hospitals, etc.)	Disadvantaged adults	Employment at minimum wage
Operation Mainstream	12,600	Work experience in community beautification and improvement activities, plus some training and supportive services	Disadvantaged adults, primarily in small towns and rural areas	Employment at minimum federal or prevailing local wage
Special Impact	2,600	Inducements to private business to generate new jobs in specific slum areas (such as Bedford-	None specified, but slum residents are intended beneficiaries	None specified

Stuyvesant, New York City).
Subsidies to cover training and
supportive services

Program	Number	Services	Eligibility	Allowances
Work Incentive Program	n.a.	Work experience, skill training, basic education, and supportive services (including day-care services for children of working mothers)	All employable persons 16 years of age and over in families receiving Aid to Families with Dependent Children	$30 per month added to welfare benefits as a training incentive
Adult Basic Education	411,000	Rudimentary education	Persons over 18 years of age with educational accomplishment below the level of eighth grade	None (but classes are free of charge)
Manpower activities of the Community Action Program	n.a.	Any service enhancing employment and employability of the poor	Income below poverty level	Determined by specific project
Concentrated Employment Program	16,000	Designed to combine other programs into a comprehensive system of all manpower services—direct placement, training, education, and supportive services—and to concentrate the impact of these programs on specific urban and rural poverty areas	Disadvantaged workers unemployed in the areas designated	Determined by specific program
United States Employment Service (USES)	5,815,000	Recruitment, counseling, testing, placement, employer services, and limited labor-market research	All workers, but primarily those unemployed	None
Vocational education	7,048,000	Formal job training and prevocational training in the public schools	State-determined; primarily full-time students but also part-time training of employed adults	For a small number of poor youths, $45 per month not to exceed $350 per year
Vocational rehabilitation	174,000	Medical and psychiatric assistance, prosthetic devices, skill training, education, and other services needed to enhance employability	Physically, mentally, or "socially" handicapped	In a few special projects, $25 per week plus $10 for each of up to four dependents

* These figures are only a rough indicator of the level of operation of the various programs at a point in time, and are not a measure of either cost or effectiveness. For the first eleven programs (all initiated in the 1960s), the data refer to the number of first-time enrollments in fiscal 1968 or, in the case of the JOBS program, the number of workers hired from June through September, 1968. Data for the older programs are for 1967—for USES, the number of nonfarm placements; for vocational education, the number of students enrolled; and for vocational rehabilitation, the number of persons rehabilitated.

SOURCES: *Manpower Report of the President, 1969*, pp. 82 and 140, and "National Manpower Policy Task Force Report," *Daily Labor Report*, January 7, 1969, no. 4, p. F-19.

however, he will frequently have more incentive to learn—for now that he is doing a man's job and not just going back to school, he can better see the reason for learning to do the job one way instead of another, and he can also see that there is a job available if he can master it. Yet, this worker may still fail, not for lack of intelligence or incentive but because he does not read well enough to comprehend written job orders, or he and his family have health or housing or transportation problems that prevent his being as dependable as other workers, or he simply has never developed the work habits that others take for granted after years of persevering on a job that is often unexciting and working with bosses and fellow employees who are often less than congenial.

It is for these reasons that there has been a shift in MDTA programs away from institutional training (in which seven of every eight trainees were enrolled in 1964) toward on-the-job training (nearly one-half of all trainees in 1968), more programs have been added under which employers are encouraged to hire the disadvantaged first and train them later (such as JOBS and New Careers), other programs have been set up to provide trainees with work experience though not with permanent jobs (such as the Neighborhood Youth Corps), and several programs have added "supportive services" (counseling, remedial education, health services) to the usual training in job skills.

Creating jobs

The second goal of an active manpower policy is to create jobs on which unemployed workers can use the skills they already have or are acquiring in a training program. The government's major method of job creation is, of course, the use of fiscal and monetary policies to promote economic growth, but we have seen that these broad-gauge policies do not eliminate the pockets of structural unemployment that exist even in the midst of general prosperity. The problem is how to generate more jobs that the hard-core unemployed can fill while avoiding the type of make-work, leaf-raking jobs that infuriate the affluent and humiliate the poor.

As in the case of the new training programs, the attempt to create meaningful jobs for the disadvantaged is still in the experimental stage in which the problems far outnumber the solutions. One approach has been to stimulate the growth of jobs in depressed areas through the Area Redevelopment Act of 1961 and the Appalachian Regional Development and the Public Works and Economic Development Acts of 1965. These laws have focused primarily on attracting private business into depressed regions such as Appalachia and the Ozarks by providing federal support to improve each area's economic base (for example, by improving roads and water and sewage and educational facilities) and by offering business loans, planning grants, and technical assistance to communities trying to attract new industry into these regions.

In effect, these programs are attempting to duplicate the success of the Tennessee Valley Authority which, since its creation in the 1930s, has transformed an impoverished region through methods ranging from flood control to the provision of cheap power for local industry. Also, since we know there are many barriers to worker mobility, it makes sense to try to bring some jobs to where the workers are, instead of depending solely on workers moving to where the jobs are. Yet, progress has been slow and uneven under these programs, partly because of inadequate funding and partly because of continuing disagreements over the best method of promoting regional development.

The Model Cities Program represents roughly the same approach to the problem of unemployment in city ghettos. This program involves much more than an attempt to create jobs, for its goal is to change the entire character of slum neighborhoods by improving their housing, community facilities, and social services, but the program also calls for neighborhood residents to be given preference in the construction activities and, if they lack the required skills, to be given on-the-job training. Although authorized in 1966, this program was still bogged down in 1970 in disputes over political control and over the reluctance of the construction unions to yield jurisdiction over the jobs involved.

Yet another approach has been taken through those programs described in Table 23-3 as offering work experience. These programs do double duty: As noted in the previous section, they provide the training in work habits needed by many of the unemployed who are not ready for competitive employment, and they also provide temporary jobs and income for these workers. During the summer of 1968, for example, the Neighborhood Youth Corps provided paid jobs for 364,000 young people on projects such as working with children in Head Start programs and in summer recreation programs, or in improving and maintaining school buildings, parks, and recreation facilities. Other programs in this category include the Job Corps, New Careers, Operation Mainstream, and Work Incentive.

Finally, there is general agreement that something should be done to reduce the incidence of seasonal unemployment, although again no one can claim much progress on this front. In 1968, for example, President Johnson directed the head of each federal agency to recognize that the government is a major buyer of construction and to attempt to let contracts and schedule projects in a way that would facilitate year-round work in that industry. One difficulty in doing this is that most agencies live from one fiscal year to the next, seldom knowing until the budget deadline how much money Congress will allot to this or that project, which makes long-range planning nearly impossible. Also, there is probably a fear that winter construction will be more costly and therefore result in fewer roads, airports, houses, and dams being built out of each year's appropriation.

Matching workers and jobs

In principle, there is nothing new or controversial about the third goal of an active manpower policy —to improve the ways in which workers and jobs are brought together. Both labor and management support this goal, our market system offers innumerable incentives to bring workers and jobs together, and the U.S. Employment Service has existed since 1933 to promote this matching process. In this and earlier chapters, however, we have seen that in practice this process works well for most but not all workers, with the result that some unemployment always exists among workers with the ability to fill existing job openings but without the knowledge of, or access to, those openings. Thus, what is new and controversial in

this field of manpower planning is not the goal of matching jobs and workers but the methods now used to reach that goal.

Certainly the most controversial of these new methods is the attempt to eliminate those racial barriers that have so long prevented some members of minority groups from working at jobs they could fill if ability were the sole criterion. The Civil Rights Act of 1964 forbids both employers and labor unions to discriminate against any individual because of race, color, religion, sex, or national origin, and in 1965 President Johnson issued an Executive order requiring firms doing business with the Federal government to go even further and take "affirmative action" to recruit and train members of minority groups. (In addition, the Age Discrimination in Employment Act of 1967 forbids discrimination against older workers because of their age.) We reviewed in Chapter 16 some of the problems and progress in ensuring "equal employment opportunity," noting that this goal has certainly not been reached, but at least some movement is under way—too much for some people, too little for others.

Also controversial to some degree is the attempt to promote mobility by subsidizing workers in moving from one geographic area to another. Sweden and a few other countries have well-established programs for this purpose, but in this country there is still the suspicion that the unemployed worker who stays in one place is just too lazy to move elsewhere—an attitude which ignores all the evidence that many workers, and particularly the disadvantaged, know little about job opportunities outside their home area and have neither the money nor the contacts to move about as freely as professionals and managers do. It was not until 1965 that Congress authorized experimental programs of relocation assistance under the MDTA, and by late 1968 these provisions had helped only about 13,000 workers and their families to move to new jobs. In another attack on geographical barriers to mobility, the Department of Transportation has been experimenting with projects to subsidize bus lines from slum areas to the industrial suburbs of several cities, to enable slum residents without cars or money for normal public transportation to get more easily and quickly to where the jobs are.

A very different problem is the need for child

day care to help those mothers who want and need regular employment outside of the home. Under the stimulus of several different federal and state programs, the number of children cared for in licensed day-care facilities rose from 185,000 in 1962 to nearly 500,000 in 1968.

Finally, the public Employment Service has undergone radical changes in recent years.

Before 1962, the Employment Service functioned primarily as a labor exchange and as administrator of the work tests for unemployment insurance claimants. In its strictly placement functions, the agency was limited by the types and numbers of jobs offered by employers and listed voluntarily with the local office, and by the workers and unemployment insurance applicants who found their own way to the office. Today, with the new tools which the legislation of the 1960's gives to the Employment Service, its role is no longer passive. . . .

Local employment offices have become the chief manpower agencies in their communities —responsible for reaching unemployed and disadvantaged workers, identifying their needs, referring them to training projects and other services to increase their employability, locating job openings for which they are suited, and providing continued counseling on the job to help them adjust to the new environment. . . .

To handle its greatly expanded functions, the Federal-State Employment Service system has had a 33-percent rise in budgeted positions between June 1963 and June 1968 [and the number of local offices has increased by nearly one-fourth, to 2,147]. The additional personnel have staffed new local offices in or near slum neighborhoods; new services to rural residents; and new and expanded services to disadvantaged youth, older workers, veterans, and other special groups.[21]

An evaluation of manpower policy

In appraising the manpower revolution of the 1960s, any judgment must be largely subjective. Most of the programs are still so new and experimental in nature that neither their friends nor their critics have much evidence to draw upon.

Also, we have few criteria by which to appraise any evidence that is available. For example, we know that from 1963 to mid-1968 about 700,000 individuals enrolled in MDTA institutional programs, about 450,000 completed their training course, 90 percent of those obtained jobs during the first year after training, and most said their jobs were related to their training. Those figures are encouraging, but no one knows how many of these trainees might have found as good or better jobs during the economic expansion from 1963 to 1968 even in the absence of MDTA. And how can anyone estimate the tangible or intangible benefits and costs of programs such as the Civil Rights Act?

There is nevertheless one criticism of current manpower policy on which everyone agrees: The multiplicity of programs and agencies involved has resulted in a confusion of responsibility and much overlapping and duplication of effort. In 1966, for example, one study found there were fifteen to thirty separate manpower programs in each of the major urban areas, all supported by federal funds. In 1967, funds for adult basic education could be sought from ten different program sources, skill training from ten, supportive services from nine, work experience from five— and most of these programs varied in eligibility rules, application procedures, expiration dates, and other ways guaranteed to bewilder any worker or local official in search of help for the unemployed.[22] Repeated attacks have been made on this problem, such as the Concentrated Employment Program described in Table 23-3, but clearly much remains to be done.

In spite of these severe problems of administration and appraisal, the manpower programs of the 1960s demonstrated that something could and should be done for the hard-core unemployed beyond the promotion of general prosperity and the provision of welfare or unemployment insurance benefits. No final solutions have emerged from these experiments, but the commitment to continue the search appears to be here to stay.

Private programs

It would be wrong to leave the impression that only the government is making any effort to minimize the risk and cost of unemployment. In addition to the several public programs which require the cooperation of private industry to provide on-the-job training, training and income-maintenance programs have been undertaken by employers alone or by employers and unions together.

Private plans to provide income to the unemployed include severance pay, early retirement (allowing older workers threatened by unemployment to retire before the normal age of sixty-five and draw reduced pensions), the guaranteed weekly wage (to discourage underemployment in the form of short workweeks, a few union contracts guarantee four or five days' pay in any week in which a worker is scheduled for any work at all), the guaranteed annual wage (still rare among blue-collar workers), and supplemental unemployment benefits (under union contracts covering 2.5 million workers in auto, steel, and a few other industries, laid-off workers receive weekly cash payments to supplement their unemployment insurance benefits). Like unemployment insurance itself, all of these private programs benefit only workers with employment experience and do not reach new entrants to the labor force or many of the hard-core unemployed, but they provide an important measure of income security to millions of other workers.

As for improving workers' employability, we noted in Chapter 16 that training is a prime function of personnel management in most companies of any size today. Most of this training effort is undertaken out of employer self-interest and is directed toward the "good workers" who already have jobs, but many of those workers would be vulnerable to unemployment in the future without the training they are now receiving under company auspices. Similarly, while many union apprenticeship programs deserve criticism for their length, rigidity, nepotism, and other restrictive features, the fact remains that these programs annually turn out thousands of well-trained graduates.

Thus, our society attempts to cope with unemployment as it does with every other labor problem—through a combination of both private and public programs.

Conclusions

When it comes to giving a final grade on the adequacy of society's provision for the unemployed, we might pass it, but scarcely with flying colors. There has been notable progress in the last three decades or so. We have instituted an unemployment compensation program which is based on the philosophy, both realistic and humane, that unemployment usually occurs through no fault of the individual, but is a by-product of a complex economy—just as industrial accidents are—and that households whose income flow is shut off by unemployment—just as by accidents—should have some continuous income to keep them financially afloat. But having adopted that sensible philosophy, we have been hesitant to make it effective by maintaining and improving the benefit scale, and have even allowed it to deteriorate. We have come increasingly to recognize that there are identifiable groups who are especially disadvantaged and who need special assistance, but our remedial measures have been rather halfhearted.

Probably this lack of enthusiasm in making provision for the unemployed is traceable to a lingering, puritanical fear of "coddling" individuals who should learn to stand on their own feet. That fear is a poor basis for a modern manpower policy.

The fact is that the kinds of self-reliance which are needed change. Few of us would be particularly successful at surviving the conditions of the distant past. A knowledge of physics and economics is certainly more intimately related to a person's survival in today's world than is the lore of a woodsman, important as that once was. Similarly, though the capability of carving out a job for oneself in the economic jungle of a young economy was once essential to survival, our improved arts of organization and economics have now put us a stage or two beyond that primitive state. Governmental programs to give assistance when people are temporarily jobless and to reduce special disabilities associated with particular groups in our society, followed up by broad programs to mobilize the improved talents of the members of these groups in productive channels, can scarcely be thought of as debilitating to their character unless we have lost all sense of perspective. Character can as readily be tempered *on* a job as in repeatedly or protractedly seeking one.

ADDITIONAL READINGS

Becker, Joseph M.: *Guaranteed Income for the Unemployed: The Story of SUB*, Johns Hopkins, Baltimore, 1968.

Chamberlain, Neil W.: *Sourcebook on Labor,* McGraw-Hill, New York, 1959, chap. 23.

Ferguson, Robert H.: *Unemployment: Its Scope, Measurement, and Effect on Poverty,* Bulletin, Cornell University, New York State School of Industrial and Labor Relations, Ithaca, N.Y., 1971.

Haber, William, and Merrill G. Murray: *Unemployment Insurance in the American Economy,* Irwin, Homewood, Ill., 1966.

Manpower Report of the President, published annually.

Weber, Arnold R., F. H. Cassell, and W. L. Ginsburg (eds.): *Public-Private Manpower Policies,* Industrial Relations Research Association, Madison, Wisc., 1969.

FOR ANALYSIS AND DISCUSSION

1. No one—not even the people who have devised it—is wholly satisfied with the definition of the unemployed now used by the Bureau of the Census. Analyze what you consider its chief weaknesses, and then see if you can come up with a better definition.

2. Recognizing that society cannot do everything at once, in what order would you want to tackle the problems of unemployment? Which ones do you consider most urgent, and why?

3. It is sometimes argued that any further extension of income guarantees would make workers "soft," sap their initiative, and dull the incentive to get ahead. On the other hand, it has been said that appropriate income guarantees reduce the fears which now prompt workers to institute restrictive practices and to foster make-work programs and would thus release worker initiative to do a better job. Do you agree with either of these points of view?

4. Should society assure every person some minimum level of income just because he is a member of society? What conditions, if any, would you want to attach to such a guarantee if you come out for it? How would you handle the problem of substandard living conditions if you are opposed to a guarantee?

5. Should depressed areas be given special governmental assistance? How would you justify such help to other communities which, while not qualifying for aid, were barely staying out of the "depressed" category and which argued that with a little outside assistance they could avoid falling into it?

NOTES

1. For a more detailed description of these definitions and of the household survey, see U.S. Bureau of Labor Statistics, *How the Government Measures Unemployment,* Report no. 312, June, 1967.

2. Gladys L. Palmer and others, *The Reluctant Job Changer,* University of Pennsylvania Press, Philadelphia, 1962, p. 154.

3. Employment and unemployment do not represent two parts which compose a stable whole. The "whole" is of course the labor force, and this changes, too, under a variety of pressures which we noted in Chapter 17. Employment may rise and unemployment may go up at the same time, strange as that may seem, owing to a net increase in the size of the labor force, which is distributed between both categories. Frequently, employment increases while unemployment remains relatively stable; more workers have been hired, but there have been as many new entrants to the labor force.

4. Although a great deal of sophisticated business-cycle analysis has taken place since his time, particularly under the sponsorship of the National Bureau of Economic Research, perhaps the most famous exposition of business cycles is that of Prof. Joseph A. Schumpeter, set forth at length in his two-volume work, *Business Cycles,* McGraw-Hill, New York, 1939. On p. 169, he sets forth his schema, based upon three recurring cycles of different length and origin—the Kitchin cycles of about forty months, the Juglar cycles, averaging nine to ten years, and the Kondratieff long waves of about fifty years. Peaks and troughs are exaggerated when two or three of these cycles coincide.

5. U.S. Department of Labor, *Manpower Report of the President, 1969,* pp. 155–156.

6. For a good exposition of the "anti-structuralist" case, see Albert Rees, "Economic Expansion and Persisting Unemployment: An Overview," in R. A. Gordon and M. S. Gordon (eds.), *Prosperity and Unemployment,* Wiley, New York, 1966, pp. 327–348. For evidence of increasing structural unemployment among youth and nonwhites between 1947 and 1963, see Vladimir Stoikov, "Increasing Structural Unemployment Re-examined," *Industrial and Labor Relations Review,* vol. 19, pp. 368–376, October, 1965.

7. *Benefits, Incomes and Expenditures of Unemployed Workers,* New York State Department of Labor, 1957 (mimeographed). The materials here drawn on come from pp. 47–52. The families in this survey were all receiving unemployment compensation from the state, so that the private household

adjustments which were necessary were reduced to that extent. Families not eligible for such compensation would have had to resort to even greater expediencies.

8. W. Stanley Devino, "U.I. Claimants Exhausting Benefits during 1957–58," *Monthly Labor Review,* March, 1960, p. 247.

9. *Report of Mayor LaGuardia's Committee on Unemployment Relief,* New York City, 1935, p. 19.

10. U.S. Department of Health, Education, and Welfare, Social Security Administration, *Social Security Programs in the United States,* 1968, p. 59.

11. The same, p. 51.

12. William Haber and Merrill G. Murray, *Unemployment Insurance in the American Economy,* Irwin, Homewood, Ill., 1966, p. 137.

13. For the "prosecution" side of this debate, see Kenneth O. Gilmore, "The Scandal of Unemployment Compensation," *Reader's Digest,* April, 1960, pp. 37–43; and (anonymous) "The Scandal in Unemployment Insurance," *Atlantic Monthly,* February, 1964, pp. 84–86. For the "defense," see "Analysis of Reader's Digest Article, 'The Scandal of Unemployment Insurance,' " in William Haber and Wilbur J. Cohen, *Social Security: Programs, Problems, and Policies,* Irwin, Homewood, Ill., 1960, pp. 309–322; and Raymond Munts, "A New Role for Unemployment Insurance," *The American Federationist,* June, 1965, pp. 5–12.

14. Bureau of National Affairs, *Daily Labor Report,* July 8, 1969, no. 130, pp. AA-1 through 5. President Nixon also proposed that coverage be narrowed in one respect, namely, that benefits be denied to workers on strike. Actually, only two states now pay benefits to strikers—New York (after a seven-week waiting period) and Rhode Island (after six weeks). Although such benefits can be justified in principle (when workers are truly available for other work after this long period), in practice they have often been used as supplemental strike benefits, which clearly violates the intention of unemployment insurance.

15. The same, p. AA-3. Note that these two measures of benefit adequacy are quite different. The second is more precise, for it compares the benefits and wages of *individual* claimants, but this measure is not available for earlier years. The first measure, comparing *average* benefits and *average* wages in covered employment, can be misleading for a single year. Since low-wage workers probably suffer a dis-

proportionate amount of unemployment, one would expect this benefit-wage ratio to be less than 50 percent even if there were no dollar maximums on benefits. It is therefore the *decline* in this ratio over the years that suggests the failure to maintain the 50 percent standard, for there is little reason to believe that low-wage workers form a growing proportion of the insured unemployed.

Also, both measures overstate benefit adequacy in one important respect. When allowance is made for initial waiting periods on nearly all claims, penalty periods of delayed benefits for quits and some other categories, and the ceiling (usually twenty-six weeks) on the benefit eligibility of all claimants, it is plain that unemployment insurance covers less than one-half of the *total* wage loss even of those who actually receive full, 50 percent benefits during their weeks of eligibility. Finally, when allowance is also made for those workers who are not eligible to receive any benefits, it is estimated that unemployment insurance benefits meet only about 20 percent of the total wage loss from unemployment in a typical year. (Richard A. Lester, "The Uses of Unemployment Insurance," in William G. Bowen and others, eds., *The American System of Social Insurance,* McGraw-Hill, New York, 1968, p. 172.)

16. Paschal C. Zecca, "Interstate Impact of UI Taxes on Plant Location Decisions," *Unemployment Insurance Review,* May, 1968, pp. 6–16.

17. *Daily Labor Report,* July 8, 1969, pp. AA–1 through 5.

18. Lester, pp. 165–172.

19. The same, p. 169.

20. For an excellent and detailed review of manpower trends and policies during the 1960s, see the *Manpower Report of the President, 1969,* which is the primary source of most of this chapter's material on this subject.

21. The same, pp. 11–12 and 125–126. Also see Leonard P. Adams, *The Public Employment Service in Transition, 1933–1968: Evolution of a Placement Service into a Manpower Agency,* Cornell University, New York State School of Industrial and Labor Relations, Ithaca, N.Y., 1969.

22. *Manpower Report of the President, 1969,* p. 129; and Sar A. Levitan and Garth L. Mangum, *Making Sense of Federal Manpower Policy,* Policy Paper no. 2, The University of Michigan and Wayne State University, The Institute of Labor and Industrial Relations, 1967, p. 14.

Prior to 1935, limited industrial groups—such as on the railroads and in the Federal government itself—had benefited from public pension systems, but otherwise only a relatively small number of workers had been provided for through private pension plans established by a union or a company. In that year the Social Security Act was passed by Congress, providing a federal system of pensions for retired workers, along with the federal-state unemployment compensation program which we examined in the preceding chapter.

Economic circumstances of the aged

The need for public assistance to older workers is now clearly recognized. Once out of work, some are *forced* into premature retirement. They draw unemployment compensation for as long as they are eligible, but then, as the months pass without any prospect of reemployment, they may be finally driven to admit that they are not likely to work again. They must face the problem of how to eke out a living without any earnings.

Other workers who may not have had to cope with unemployment eventually face the increasingly prevalent business policy of requiring the retirement of employees at age sixty-five. Some companies permit their people to continue to sixty-eight at management's discretion, with retirement obligatory then. While these are "ripe" ages and many workers are ready to give up active employment by the time they have reached them,

there are many others who still feel full of bounce and who would like to continue in their familiar work environment and associations a good deal longer. In these cases compulsory retirement at sixty-five or even sixty-eight means not only a substantial loss of income but also a loss of purpose.

Along with the deterioration of the economic status of the older worker goes a deterioration of social status. Whereas, in an earlier, more rural culture, older people enjoyed a respected and sometimes even governing role in a household which included not only themselves but their children and their children's children, today grandparents are likely to live apart in a relatively lonely existence, regarded as people whose views are to be humored rather than respected. Once retired, they cease to have any real social status, no role in a household which includes others but which they regard as their own. Approximately half of all people over sixty-five live away from any members of their own family, as single individuals.

Finally, in addition to deterioration of economic and social position, the older person's physical condition is likely to be impaired, if not by the time of retirement, within some few years afterward. In Chapter 22 we noted the greater incidence of illness among the aged and the financial difficulties they face in providing for their medical needs.

The three great problems which older people

face, then, are loss of social status, loss of health, and loss of income. Society has so far done nothing about the first of these, and it did not move in effectively on the health problem until 1965 and the adoption of Medicare, reviewed in Chapter 22. To meet the income problem, however, we have been building for many years a system of old-age pensions, both public and private, which is today the most comprehensive—and many believe the most successful—of all the welfare-state programs initiated in the 1930s.

The aged population

Before considering the details of public and private pension programs, let us first get some measure of the number of people involved.[1]

Figure 24-1 shows the "population explosion" that has occurred among the aged. In 1900, only one person out of twenty-five was sixty-five years of age or older, but today nearly one of every ten is in that age group. In absolute numbers, 20 million Americans were sixty-five or over in 1970 —a number equal to the combined populations of twenty states.

We also know that the number of the aged will continue to grow in the future—to 23 million by 1980 and to 25 million by 1985. In fact, by the year 2000 the aged population is expected to be more than twice as large as it was in 1960.

Behind these figures, of course, lies a remarkable growth in life expectancy. The average American born in 1900 could expect to reach only his forty-seventh birthday, but those born today have a life expectancy of seventy years and those born tomorrow will undoubtedly have an even longer life span. This trend represents great progress in many ways, but it also means that everyone's chances have vastly increased of reaching an age when he can no longer earn an income but must depend on some other source of support.

Also, while we often think of the aged in terms of elderly couples struggling to make ends meet, the truth is that about one-half of the aged are "nonmarried"—the widowed, the divorced, the separated, and the never married. A large majority of these nonmarried persons are women, because women tend to outlive their husbands and because widowers are more likely than widows to

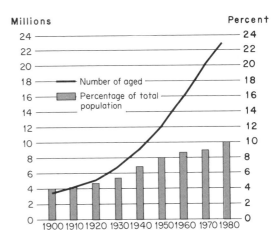

Fig. 24-1. *Population 65 years of age and over in the United States, 1900–1980.*

SOURCE: *U.S. Senate, Aged and Aging in U.S., 1959, p. 21; and Economic Report of the President, 1969, p. 251.*

remarry. This means that any adequate retirement program must include benefits for survivors as well as wage earners, since many women have not been wage earners themselves and hence have no independent claim for a pension.

The income position of people after retirement is thus of importance to considerable numbers of people directly, aside from relatives who are affected indirectly. Let us now try to get some notion of what their income position is.

When a person retires from his regular employment, the possible sources of his income are some continuing part-time earnings; his own savings and income on any investments; his social security pension; a private pension or annuity; contributions from family or friends; and public assistance if all these should prove insufficient to his needs. We shall be interested in the relative magnitudes of income received from these several sources and in how the "mix" of retired people's income has changed over the years.

Eligibility for social security benefits

We have already noted that in 1935 the Social Security Act provided a system of old-age benefits to wage earners. Congress added dependents' and survivors' benefits in 1939 and, as we noted in Chapter 22, it extended coverage to the permanently and totally disabled in 1956 and added Medicare in 1965. All of these provisions are now commonly referred to as the national old-age survivors, disability, and health insurance (OASDHI) program.

As a result of several amendments over the years, the OASDHI program today approaches universal coverage, in sharp contrast to the minimum-wage, workmen's compensation, and unemployment insurance programs.

> During a typical week, more than 9 out of 10 persons who work in paid employment or self-employment are covered or eligible for coverage under [this] program, compared with less than 6 out of 10 when the program began. . . . Except for special provisions that are applicable to only a few kinds of work, coverage is on a compulsory basis. Unlike some of the social security systems of other countries, the American program covers all kinds of workers, whether wage earners, salaried employees, self-employed persons, farm workers, or farm operators, including those workers with high earnings.
>
> The majority of workers excluded from coverage . . . fall in three major categories: (1) workers covered under Federal civilian staff retirement systems, (2) household workers and farm workers who do not earn enough or work long enough to meet certain minimum requirements [for example, earning at least $150 in a year from one farm employer], and (3) persons with very low net earnings from self-employment [less than $400 a year].[2]

In addition, more than 70 percent of all employees of state and local governments have been brought under coverage of OASDHI through voluntary agreements between the states and the Federal government, and railroad workers have a separate federal program. Adding together the coverage of the basic OASDHI program and the special programs for railroad and government employees, it is estimated that *95 percent of the working population now have retirement protection through public programs.*

Because the OASDHI program is a system of social insurance, benefits are paid as a statutory right and there is no direct test of financial need. There are, however, two other tests of eligibility. The first, a measure of attachment to the work force, is designed to screen out persons (other than dependents or survivors) who have seldom or never worked for a living:

> The period of time a person must have spent in covered work to be insured for benefits is measured in "quarters of coverage." A person paid $50 or more in covered nonfarm wages in a calendar quarter is credited with a quarter of coverage. . . .
>
> For most types of benefits, the worker must be "fully insured." In general, a fully insured person is one who has at least as many quarters of coverage (acquired at any time) as the number of years elapsing after 1950 (or year of attainment of age 21, if later) and up to the year of attainment of age 65 (62 for women), disability, or death, whichever happens first. A worker with 40 quarters of coverage is fully insured for life and needs no further employment to qualify for retirement or survivor benefits. . . .
>
> If a worker dies before acquiring a fully insured status, certain survivor benefits may be paid if he is "currently insured." An individual is currently insured if he has acquired six quarters of coverage within the 13-calendar-quarter period ending with the quarter in which he died.[3]

The second eligibility criterion is called a retirement test and consists of a dollar limit on the amount of earnings one may have and still be considered retired.

> Beginning in 1968, a beneficiary whose earnings do not exceed $1,680 a year can get benefits for all 12 months of the year. If he earns above $1,680 in a year, $1 in benefits is withheld for each $2 of earnings between $1,680 and $2,880 and $1 in benefits is withheld for each $1 of earnings above $2,880. Benefits are payable, though, regardless of annual earnings, for any month in which the beneficiary earns $140 or less in wages and does not render substantial services in self-employment. Benefits are also payable to beneficiaries when they reach age 72 regardless of their earnings. The

age 72 provision recognizes that some people go on working and paying contributions to the end of their lives and might otherwise never get any monthly benefits.[4]

This retirement test is justified on the ground that the basic purpose of a pension program is to maintain the income of workers who have retired, not to provide extra income to those still working beyond age sixty-five. Also, on a more pragmatic level, the elimination of this retirement test would significantly increase benefit disbursements and hence the cost of maintaining a given level of benefits.[5] Many critics view this eligibility criterion as an indirect type of means test for the aged, and there is constant pressure to eliminate, or at least to liberalize, the dollar ceilings.

Types of benefits

A fully insured person who passes the retirement test draws monthly benefits according to a formula based on his average monthly earnings up to $650. Since that is the wage on which workers and employers currently pay their social security taxes, benefits are thus related to past earnings and contributions—the high-wage worker usually receives larger benefits than the low-wage worker who has contributed less in tax payments. In this sense, the OASDHI program parallels private insurance.

But the relationship between wages and benefits is not strictly proportional, for the benefit formula has always been weighted in favor of low-wage workers in two ways. In 1969, for example, the law provided that the "primary" benefit (the monthly amount payable to a worker at age sixty-five) would be equal to about 71 percent of the first $110 of his average monthly earnings plus only 24 to 28 percent of the next $540. Second, the law fixes a flat minimum for primary benefits—$55 per month in 1969—which favors those whose past earnings would otherwise entitle them to less than that minimum. Also, while the provision of additional benefits for a retired worker's dependents can help both high-wage and low-wage workers, this criterion of family size further dilutes the relationship between benefits and past earnings or contributions. In these and other ways, the OASDHI program departs from private-

insurance principles and qualifies as "social insurance."

Under certain circumstances, persons may draw early benefits. For example, a worker may retire at age sixty-two rather than at sixty-five and draw a pension which is permanently reduced to 80 percent of the regular primary benefit. This provision is advantageous for the older worker who becomes unemployed for any reason and, because of his age, has difficulty in finding another job. Also, a worker who becomes permanently and totally disabled at any age is eligible for full benefits, provided that he is fully insured and has worked in covered employment for at least five of the ten years before the onset of his disability.

In addition to his primary benefit, the pensioner receives supplemental allowances for his dependents. This category generally refers to a wife sixty-two or over and children under eighteen, although certain others are also included. The benefit for each dependent is usually 50 percent of the insured's primary benefit, up to a maximum family benefit fixed by the law. In 1969, this family maximum was $82.50 per month for a worker receiving the minimum primary benefit of $55, and ranged up to $434 for those receiving the highest primary benefit.

Survivor benefits are a third important category. If the household's breadwinner is fully insured and dies before retirement, his survivors are entitled to benefits ranging from 75 percent of the primary benefit for dependent children to 82.5 percent for a widow aged sixty-two or over. As noted earlier, the law also takes into account that a household head may die before he becomes "fully insured," in which case he needs only to have been "currently insured" for benefits to be paid to his dependent children and also to his widow, regardless of her age, if she is caring for a dependent child. Finally, the law provides a lump-sum funeral benefit equal to the lesser of $255 or three times the deceased worker's primary benefit.

Trends in benefits

We have seen that the benefits actually received under this program depend on a number of variables, such as a worker's past earnings, the size of his family, and the frequent changes made by Congress in the program's coverage, eligibility tests, and benefit formula. To show how aged and disabled workers have actually fared under this program over the years, Table 24-1 shows the average benefits received by different groups during the period since 1940 and compares these benefits to the trend in consumer prices and factory wages over the same period.

This table partially belies the common belief that inflation always hurts the retired person who is assumed to be on a fixed income. Even though consumer prices more than doubled from 1940 to 1967, average benefits increased nearly fourfold over the same period as Congress repeatedly liberalized benefits and as workers earned higher wages during their working life.[6] On the other hand, inflation does exact a toll in the years between the periodic increases in benefits. For instance, Congress made no change at all in the benefit formula from 1939 through 1949 in spite of the severe inflation of that period, so that Table 24-1 is misleading in showing only the increases belatedly instituted in 1950. Congress has reacted more promptly to price changes since 1950, but there is always a lag of at least two or three years between benefit adjustments. This has led President Nixon, among others, to propose that a cost-of-living escalator be added to the law to adjust future benefits automatically to price changes.

Table 24-1 also shows that benefits have lagged in relation to wages since 1940. The weekly factory wage is an imperfect measure of the earnings of all those covered by the Social Security Act, but other measures, such as per capita disposable income, show the same trend: old-age benefits have increased less rapidly than workers' earnings over the years. Stated differently, there has been a deterioration in the relationship between a worker's income before retirement and his social security income after retirement.

It must be remembered, however, that relatively few workers were actually receiving pensions during the early years of the program. Specifically, only 0.7 percent of the aged were drawing OASDHI benefits in 1940, but by 1967 this proportion had mushroomed to 83 percent. Even more impressive is the fact that "as of 1966, for those who became 65 the previous year, 92 percent ... were eligible for social security insurance and *97 percent were eligible for either social security, civil service retirement, or railroad retirement [benefits].*"[7]

None of these comparisons tells us how well the aged are actually faring in relation to their income needs today. We shall return to this crucial question after we investigate the financing of OASDHI and the nature of other public and private sources of income for the aged.

Financing the system

Both the costs and benefits of the OASDHI program are truly staggering, far surpassing those of any other welfare or social insurance program. In an average month during 1968, for example, only

Table 24-1 *A Comparison of OASDHI Benefits, Consumer Prices, and Factory Wages in Selected Years, 1940–1967*

	1940	1950	1960	1967
Average monthly benefit paid under OASDHI to:				
Retired worker without dependents	$22.10	$42.20	$ 69.90	$ 81.70
Retired worker and aged wife	36.40	71.70	123.90	144.20
Aged widow	20.30	36.50	57.70	75.20
Disabled worker without dependents			87.90	96.20
Average gross weekly earnings of factory production workers	24.96	58.32	89.72	114.90
Consumer price index [1957–1959 = 100]	48.8	83.8	103.1	116.3

SOURCE: *Social Security Bulletin*, Annual Statistical Supplement, 1967, p. 97, and U.S. Department of Labor.

Table 24-2 *Tax Rate Schedule for OASDHI*

Year	Tax paid by each covered employee and his employer, as percent of first $7,800 of employee's earnings	Combined employer-employee rate, as percent of first $7,800 of earnings	Tax paid by the self-employed, as percent of first $7,800 of net earnings of $400 or more
1968	4.40	8.80	6.40
1969–1970	4.80	9.60	6.90
1971–1972	5.20	10.40	7.50
1973–1975	5.65	11.30	7.65
1976–1979	5.70	11.40	7.70
1980–1986	5.80	11.60	7.80
1987 and after	5.90	11.80	7.90

SOURCE: Social Security Administration.

1 million workers were drawing unemployment compensation but cash benefits under OASDHI covered *24 million persons*—12 million retired workers, 1 million disabled, 5 million dependents, and 6 million survivors. For 1968 as a whole, the states paid out a total of $2 billion in unemployment benefits but cash benefits under OASDHI totaled $25 billion that year.

Where does the money come from to finance these huge outlays? General tax revenues underwrite a small portion of total costs, covering special programs such as noncontributory wage credits granted for military service and benefits for certain people attaining seventy-two years of age who had worked outside of covered employment in the system's early years. *On the whole, however, the OASDHI program is self-supporting,* with benefits paid for by the social security taxes levied on all covered employees, employers, and self-employed people. These tax payments go into federally administered trust funds—one for disability insurance and the other for old-age and survivors insurance—which can use the money received only to pay benefits and operating expenses. (The Social Security Administration, incidentally, is one federal agency with an excellent reputation for efficiency, based on its record of keeping down the administrative expenses of this complex operation to about 2 percent of contribution income.)

Table 24-2 sets forth the current and future schedule of payroll taxes that support the OASDHI program. Note that the covered worker and his employer each pay the same rate of tax on the first $7,800 of the worker's earnings, and this combined tax will total over 10 percent in the 1970s and will reach nearly 12 percent in the 1980s. At the program's inception in the 1930s, the worker and his employer were each taxed only one percent of the worker's first $3,000 of earnings, but it was recognized from the outset that these rates would have to increase over the years to keep step with the increase in the number of eligible retirees, and other increases became necessary to pay for new benefits such as Medicare. Also note that Congress had raised the OASDHI tax base to $7,800 by 1968, in contrast to its failure to raise the tax base for unemployment insurance above its original level of $3,000. (The employer's unemployment insurance tax, authorized by a different section of the Social Security Act, is paid in addition to the OASDHI tax, not as part of it.)

In discussing benefits earlier, we mentioned that the OASDHI program is similar in some respects to private insurance and different in others. The same is true of this program's financing. On the one hand, most people under OASDHI must contribute money during their working lives in order to qualify for benefits upon retirement, just as under a private pension or annuity plan, and the federal trust funds accumulate a reserve against future liabilities, as private insurance companies do. Thus, contrary to a widespread impression, OASDHI is not a "pay-as-you-go" program, able to meet current liabilities only out of current contributions or annual appropriations from Congress.

On the other hand, this program is not funded

on the "full reserve" basis required of private insurance companies. To protect policy holders against the risk that a private insurance company might go bankrupt and be unable to pay claims, such a company must keep its reserves at a level sufficient to meet all of its future pension liabilities even if it should go out of business today. To apply that principle to the social security system, however, would ignore the fact that the government is not going to go out of business and it would also mean the accumulation of a gigantic government reserve (with uncertain economic effects) and the imposition of higher payroll taxes to meet any given level of benefits. Consequently, OASDHI has always been funded on a "fully self-supporting" system which falls somewhere between full-reserve and pay-as-you-go financing. In fiscal 1969, for example, the program collected about $30 billion, paid out $26 billion in benefits, and had a reserve of $32 billion (enough to meet one year's benefit claims).

All of this means that the average person on a social security pension has not fully paid his own way, as he often supposes. In 1960, in fact, many persons then on the rolls had contributed less than 1 percent of the value of the benefits they ultimately received, and the maximum proportion of benefits paid by an individual's own contributions was only about 10 percent.[8] Adding the employer's contribution would double those figures, of course, and probably the individual's own contributions form a higher proportion of his benefits today, since more beneficiaries have now worked more years in covered employment. Yet, that still leaves a large share of current benefit payments that are not covered by past contributions and therefore must be paid out of the current contributions of those now at work. *In other words, those who are now retired are having their own contributions of past years greatly supplemented by the current contributions of active workers.*

It is that fact which leads many critics to charge that the OASDHI program is not fiscally sound. How can today's active workers be sure of drawing pensions in the future when most of their current "premium payments" are not set aside for their later use but are spent to support those who are already retired? This returns us to the difference between public and private insurance programs. Because the government is not going to go bankrupt in the foreseeable future, and because there will always be more active workers paying into the pension fund than retired workers drawing from it, the OASDHI program can continue indefinitely on its present basis—guaranteeing future benefits not by accumulating huge reserves but by pledging the continued stability of the government itself. Stated differently, it is true that the OASDHI program could not meet its commitments if the Federal government actually collapsed at some point, but in that catastrophic event most other public *and* private commitments would also not be met.

One might still ask whether it is fair for workers today to have to pay higher contribution rates than workers in the past have paid—or whether it is fair for this generation of workers to vote themselves higher benefits for which the next generation will have to pay in large part. Again, the key point is that this is a system of *social* insurance under which there is no expectation that returns should be precisely proportioned to what one has paid in himself. The intent is rather that society as a whole shall help to take care of the needs of its older people out of its present production of goods and services, setting aside, as it were, claims to a limited amount of those goods and services for the benefit of those who are no longer able to work. The size of that allocation is a political decision that is justifiably open to debate, but the debaters should not assume that social and private insurance can be judged by identical standards of equity.

There is no denying the fact, however, that the OASDHI program is expensive. Even though its financing system safely permits a lower contribution rate than a full-reserve system would require, we have seen that the combined employer-employee tax rate has climbed from its original level of 2 percent of the first $3,000 of earnings to about 10 percent of the first $7,800 of earnings, and that this rate must approach 12 percent in the 1980s to pay the current level of benefits to the much larger number of workers who will have retired by then. If benefits are further liberalized, as many people believe they should be, the contribution rate must go even higher if the system is to continue to be self-supporting. We shall return to this problem of costs after we examine the other sources of income available to retired people.

Old-age assistance

It would be logically preferable to consider public assistance to older people only after we had considered such additional sources of income as private pensions, income from assets, and so on, but since the old-age assistance program (OAA) is an integral part of the Social Security Act, we may as well turn to it now.

Prior to passage of the 1935 act, such old-age assistance as was provided came from the states. Actually, only a few had established any kind of systematic program for giving financial assistance to the needy aged. Private charity and "poor houses" were still called on to provide such aid to the indigent as might be offered. When the federal social security program was being fashioned, it was recognized that there would always be some people who would fail to qualify for pensions or whose social security would prove inadequate for subsistence, so provision was made for them through a program of old-age assistance. The administration of this part of the act is through the states, but the Federal government establishes certain administrative standards with which states must comply in order to qualify for federal grants to assist in the financing. States are free to determine the amount of any assistance they give, but federal participation is based on the size of the payments which they make.[9]

Of the several differences between the OAA and OASDHI programs, three deserve emphasis:

1. OASDHI benefits are paid as a right, but OAA benefits are paid only to those aged persons who can prove they are in financial need. The first is social insurance, the second a welfare program.

2. OASDHI is financed by employer and employee contributions, OAA from general tax revenues.

3. An OASDHI beneficiary will receive the same benefit no matter where he lives, but OAA benefits vary widely from state to state. In June, 1969, for example, OAA money payments aver-

aged $70 per month for all the states, but ranged from a high of $116 in New Hampshire to a low of $39 in Mississippi. This variation, it will be recalled, is characteristic of all income-maintenance programs administered by the states, such as unemployment insurance and workmen's compensation.

While it was expected in the 1930s that there would always be needy aged, it was also expected that their number would steadily dwindle as more and more people met the qualifications for OASDHI over time. That prediction has been modestly fulfilled, as Figure 24-2 shows, but the dwindling has not occurred so rapidly as had been hoped. Notice that the number of OAA recipients, in fact, began to move upward about 1945, with rising prices and static pension levels. In 1950, when OASDHI benefits were increased, the number of OAA recipients again began to decline and has continued to do so rather steadily. This is not attributable solely to more adequate pension levels, of course. As we shall see, the number of private pension programs increased rapidly about this time, too.

Despite the decline in the number of those receiving assistance, approximately one out of every ten persons sixty-five years or older, or a total of two million, is on the OAA rolls. It is interesting to note that about one-half of these are receiving assistance in addition to a social security pension, in view of the inadequacy of the latter to take care of their needs. After all, a retired widower who qualifies only for the minimum pension can scarcely be expected to live on $55 a month.

Private pension programs

We have been speaking about the federal system of old-age pensions and assistance. Since 1949 there has also developed in the United States a large number of private pension plans, instituted by individual companies or employers' associations, usually in response to the demands of labor unions. Company pension plans had been in existence at least since 1875, and a few unions had earlier negotiated for pensions. The most notable instance of a pre-1949 collectively bargained system was in the coal industry, where a

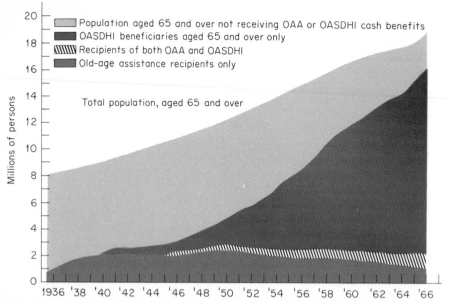

Fig. 24-2. *Population aged 65 and over and social security programs for the aged, 1936–1966.*

SOURCE: *Social Security Administration.*

1946 agreement financed a variety of welfare benefits through an arrangement whereby coal producers paid a royalty of so many cents per ton into a welfare and retirement fund. Generally, however, employers resisted union demands on this front not only because of the cost factor but because they were inclined to look on pensions as something which were granted at their own discretion. Such an attitude was conducive to using pensions, when they were given at all, as a reward for long and faithful service, in an unsystematic way that lent itself to favoritism and discrimination.

The Supreme Court's Inland Steel decision in 1949 sustained the National Labor Relations Board in its view that pensions were a bargainable issue. From this time on, employer resistance crumbled and the private plans mushroomed. Pensions came to be regarded as a "condition of employment," like wages and hours. They have increasingly been referred to as a form of deferred wages, although this construction has remained somewhat ambiguous since under some

conditions workers can lose their pension rights.

The number of workers covered by private plans has nearly tripled since 1950, from 9.8 million in that year to 27.6 million workers in 1967, so that today nearly one-half of all wage and salary employees in private industry are working under such plans. The number of workers who have retired and are drawing private pensions has increased even more rapidly, from only 450,000 in 1950 to 3.4 million in 1967, but that means *only about 18 percent of persons* aged sixty-five and over were receiving private pensions in 1967. That proportion will increase, of course, as more and more workers covered since 1950 reach retirement age.[10]

It is difficult to compare the size of benefits under public and private pension programs, but the available data suggest that private benefits are often less generous. In 1967, for example, "average outlays per beneficiary" under private plans were $1,271 for the year or about $100 per month. In the same year, OASDHI benefits averaged $85 per month for retired workers alone, plus $44 for dependent spouses and $33 for dependent children. In addition, social security benefits rose more rapidly than private pension payments between 1950 and 1967, and thus were less eroded by the price increases of that period. (These comparisons are not meant to imply that private pensions should ideally equal or exceed public pensions. These two systems complement rather than compete with one another, for the great majority of those who are drawing private pensions are also drawing social security benefits.)

As one would expect, private pension plans vary considerably in their terms. Under some plans, the firm pays the whole of the cost; under others, the employees contribute as well. Under some, the firm is obligated to fund its pension program; under others, it operates on a pay-as-you-go basis. Under an increasing number of plans, accumulated claims are vested in the employee—that is, he gains an equity in the sums paid on his account by the employer too; under other plans, there is no vesting, and an employee who leaves the firm recovers only what he himself has contributed. Under some, the retirement of an employee is compulsory at a specified age, usually sixty-five; under others, retirement is compulsory unless the employer voluntarily permits continued employment; under still others, nothing is said on this point and the unions have maintained that a man should be allowed to continue on the job as long as he wishes and is able to perform his duties.

Eligibility provisions vary greatly. In some, short-service employees are given a modest benefit; in others, there is a minimum requirement of ten years of service with the employer; in still others, a higher minimum, such as twenty-five years, is required. Provisions may or may not be made for early retirement where the required service is accumulated before the normal retirement age, or for payment of disability pensions. Some plans allow for medical benefits after retirement.

The benefit formulas under which the amount of the pension is determined differ markedly. The commonest type provides that benefits vary both with the worker's length of service and with his earnings. The second most prevalent type of formula is one in which benefits vary only with

length of service. The third general type, much less frequently found, provides a flat benefit to all workers who have completed some specified period of service upon reaching the normal retirement age. Under some agreements, the amount of the federal old-age pension is deductible from the employer's liability; under others, only some portion of the federal pension—perhaps one-half—may be offset against the firm's guarantee; under still others, and this seems to be the present trend, the federal pension is wholly independent of the private pension. The bargained arrangements for such old-age insurance differ in many more respects.[11]

Private versus public plans

There is rather widespread agreement that it would have been preferable had such private pension systems never materialized and that the benefits under the federal plan had been increased instead. It is said that with the practice of collectively bargaining for a private plan, the question of how much a retired worker gets, in addition to any social security benefit, depends upon the bargaining power of his union. The matter of retirement benefits should be settled, the argument runs, on some fairer and more equitable basis, so that the older employee who retires from the textile industry, and whose need is as great as that of the employee retiring from the automobile industry, will not be forced to scrape along on a much smaller allowance simply because his union and industry competitively were not in a position to pass the costs of a larger pension on to the consuming public.

For several reasons, however, this is a rather superficial view. In the first place, the unions had been seeking an increase in federal pensions prior to 1949 but had made no progress in their political negotiations. As we have seen, although the act was passed in 1935, and although the country had experienced rising price levels through the war period, at the time when the unions began their push for private pensions in 1946 the scale of benefits in effect was roughly the same as at the act's inception. In the postwar period, it would have been impossible for a retired worker to live on the primary benefit which was still pegged at

Depression levels. In the absence of legislative action to improve pensions—a course over which the unions had no direct influence—the unions resorted to collective bargaining for supplementation of the federal benefit, a course of action over which they did have control.

It was not until the unions had bargained pensions into their collective-bargaining agreements, with some of the major agreements providing that federal benefits could be offset against company guarantees, that corporate managements began to speak out in support of improving the scale of federal payments, which would lessen their own liabilities.[12] The unions, through their device of collective bargaining in the private sphere, were thus one of the primary influences in securing legislative action on public pensions at a time when the social security principle appeared to be in jeopardy, owing to grossly inadequate benefits. To argue, then, that it would have been preferable to improve federal pensions instead of resorting to private programs is actually only to sing a lament over a lost opportunity, for the emphasis on private programs came only because federal payments continued to remain so meager.

There is a second reason why it is difficult to accept the view that it is somehow inequitable for the workers in one industry to use their bargaining power to obtain a pension program superior to that which can be secured by workers in another industry—unless, indeed, we are prepared to scrap the whole concept of collective bargaining. As long as we rely on bargaining in a competitive economy for the determination of the terms of employment, there will always be discrepancies in the benefits which one group of workers obtains over another group. Is it inequitable for workers in steel to bargain for a basic wage rate of $3 an hour while workers in restaurants may obtain only $1.50? Not many of us would answer "yes." But other economic benefits are simply part of the pattern of remuneration, and if workers in an industry choose to take more of their remuneration in the form of pension payments, it is difficult to see why that should be considered objectionable. Inequality of return is rooted in the economics of competition and is recognized in the economics of collective bargaining. If that inequality assumes the form of old-age

insurance as well as wages, vacations, sick-leave provisions, and so on, it constitutes no greater a departure from the principle of equality than that we have long accustomed ourselves to.

This is not to argue that private pensions are good because unequal, but only that they should not be labeled bad for that reason. There is good reason to prefer an adequate public pension system to a poor public system with private supplementation. One advantage of the former over the latter is that it acts as no inhibitor of labor mobility; no worker need avoid a shift of jobs because he does not want to lose his stake in a nonvested pension in the company where he is then employed. A second advantage lies in its providing something of a subsidy to retired workers whose earned incomes have been low during their working lives, which is beyond the possibility of most private business. But such a preference for a public system need not carry as corollary a regret that the private programs ever materialized.

Other sources of income

Many aged people have income from sources other than OASDHI, OAA, or private pension plans. Some still work on a full-time or part-time job after they are sixty-five; some receive income from stocks and bonds; some receive help from their children. Figure 24-3 shows the relative importance of these several sources of income in 1962, the latest year for which we have such information.[13]

The enormous importance of government income-maintenance programs comes through clearly in this chart, which shows that nearly one-half of all income of the aged in 1962 came from social insurance, veterans', and public assistance programs. In fact, among those sixty-five or more years of age in that year, nearly 90 percent of the couples and 80 percent of the nonmarried individuals had some income from one or more of those public programs. Private pension benefits then provided only 3 percent of the total income of the aged and were going to only 16 percent of the couples and 5 percent of the nonmarried individuals sixty-five or more years old.

On the other hand, one-half of aged couples were still earning a wage or salary from some job

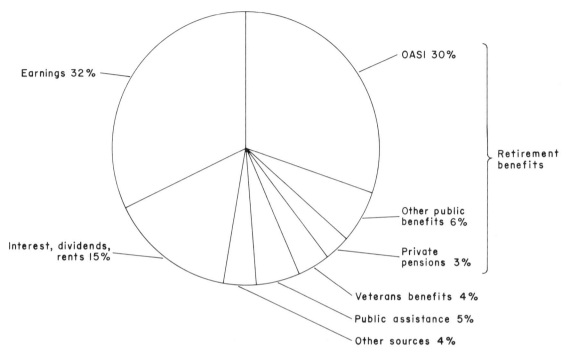

Fig. 24-3. *Shares of aggregate money income, by source, of persons aged 65 and over, 1962 (including their spouses). (Percentages do not total 100 because of rounding.)*

SOURCE: *Lenore A. Epstein,* Social Security Bulletin, *March, 1964, p. 4.*

in 1962 and two-thirds were receiving some interest, dividend, or rental income. Among nonmarried individuals (two-thirds of whom were women), however, only 24 percent had any job earnings and 50 percent had interest or similar income.

Taking together the income from all these sources, the median income for an aged couple was $2,875 in 1962. For the nonmarried—the widowed, the divorced, the separated, and the never married who together make up about half the aged population—median income was only $1,130 in that year.

Finally, what of the assets of the aged, such as the value of their stocks and bonds, their savings accounts, and their equity in a business, farm, real estate, or home? In 1962, the median value of all

these assets of aged couples was $11,180—and only $3,000 when the equity in their nonfarm homes was excluded. Nonmarried men and women averaged less than one-third these amounts.

Averages can be as misleading here as anywhere else, of course, and allowance must be made for the fact that the aged include both the very rich and the very poor. Among aged couples in 1962, for example, 5 percent had an income of over $10,000 a year and 35 percent had assets of $15,000 or more, while at the other extreme 5 percent had an income of less than $1,000 and 10 percent had no assets at all. In this respect, the aged are like the unemployed and the sick and injured—some need further help and some do not, which is a major reason why any government aid to these groups is always attacked by some critics as too generous and by others as too stingy. How, then, can we determine whether all these data on the income of the aged add up, on balance, to a passing or failing grade for our present policies?

Adequacy of income

To answer that question, we return to the poverty measure described in Chapter 19. As we stressed in that chapter, there is no timeless and "scientific" definition of poverty, but easily the best available is that developed in the 1960s by the Social Security Administration. Tables 19-7 and 19-8 in that chapter show the following:

1. In 1968, the poverty income line for a two-person family was $1,904 in annual money income for those living on farms and $2,262 for nonfarm couples. For an individual living alone, the comparable figures were $1,487 and $1,748. These standards are hardly lavish, ranging from $29 a week for the individual on a farm to $44 a week for a nonfarm couple. (By way of comparison, anyone working at the FLSA minimum of $1.60 an hour earns $64 for a 40-hour week.)

2. Yet, of all households headed by an aged person, *nearly one-third (31 percent) had less income in 1968 than the meager amounts specified* —17 percent of the families (primarily couples) headed by a person sixty-five or over and (though not shown in those tables) a shocking 49 percent of the many aged individuals who were living alone.

By this minimum test, it is clear that our present public and private programs for maintaining the income of the aged are not doing an adequate job. It is true that without these programs the aged would be far worse off than they are. In 1967, for example, nearly six million more aged persons would have been classified as poor if they had not been receiving OASDHI benefits that pushed their income above the poverty line. It is also true, however, that in the same year another six million persons were receiving OASDHI benefits that were so low that the recipients were still counted among the poor.[14]

Improving economic security for the aged

Although most people agree that public and private pension programs need improvement, there is little agreement over just how this should be done. Let us first consider some of the problems of improving the OASDHI program.

In principle, everyone favors raising social security benefits to a level sufficient to wipe out poverty among the aged, but this is easier said than done. On the one hand, costs might be minimized by raising only the minimum benefit above the poverty level and leaving higher benefits untouched. If that had been done in 1967, by raising the minimum benefit from $44 to $125 a month (or $1,500 a year), benefit payments in the next year would have risen by $10.2 billion—*but about $4.8 billion of that increase would have gone to nonpoor beneficiaries.*[15] That is because a number of those receiving low OASDHI benefits are also receiving other income from part-time jobs, private pensions, and the other sources we described earlier. Also, raising only the minimum benefits— and by that large a jump—would dilute much further the relationship between benefits and past earnings, which is already weighted in favor of the low-wage worker, and this would move the OASDHI program toward being a welfare system based on a means test instead of a social insurance program.

On the other hand, if *all* benefits were raised by the amount necessary to bring minimum benefits above the poverty level, this move would naturally increase costs even faster than if the minimum alone were raised, and an even larger proportion of this benefit increase would go to the nonpoor aged. Yet, who would argue that the aged above the poverty line should have their benefits frozen in order to help the poor, when such a freeze would actually mean a cut in "real" benefits because of the eroding effects of inflation? In short, it is very expensive to combat poverty through any program of social insurance which, by definition, grants benefits as a right to the poor and nonpoor alike. (Congress compromised on this problem in 1967, raising most benefits 13 percent but increasing the minimum by 25 percent, from $44 to $55 per month.)

And where will the money come from to pay for increased benefits, when the combined employer-employee tax rate is already over 10 per-cent of covered payroll and is scheduled to go even higher to pay for the present schedule of benefits? How high can payroll taxes be pushed before triggering serious repercussions? The only honest answer is that no one knows. Some critics of the welfare state are excessively naive about this question and refuse to recognize that most of each year's social security contributions do not disappear into some secret vault in Washington, but instead are paid out as benefits to the aged who return them rather promptly to the stream of purchasing power which provides jobs for those still working. These payroll taxes are nevertheless a form of forced savings, and there is some point beyond which active workers resist having their income reduced to pay for insurance against the future. Just where that point of resistance may be —whether at 20 or 40 or 60 percent of current income—is anybody's guess. Similarly, since no one is quite sure who pays for the employer's share of OASDHI taxes (that is, whether he passes this tax along to the consumer, deducts it in effect from wages, or accepts a lower profit re-turn), we cannot predict with certainty the effect of further increases in his tax burden. About all we can say is that there is no evidence that the present OASDHI tax schedule has produced off-setting reactions from either workers or employers.

Many experts have long argued that adequate social security benefits can only come when the system is supported by government contributions from general tax revenues in addition to the con-tributions from employer and employee payroll taxes. This proposal is defended on several grounds: payroll taxes are more regressive than general income taxes (low-income workers usu-ally pay the social security tax on all their earn-ings but high-income workers pay on only the first $7,800 of their salaries and nothing on their dividend or interest income); without OASDHI, the government would have to pay more in OAA benefits to the needy aged, so it is only fair that it pay part of the cost of the pension program; fur-ther increases in payroll taxes may encounter more political resistance than increases in income taxes; and several other countries have adopted tripartite financing without damaging their social security systems.

Defenders of the present system of financing claim that the regressive impact of the payroll tax is offset by the fact that the benefit formula favors low-income over high-income workers, and they also fear that introducing government contribu-tions would weaken cost controls over the pro-gram. "There could be the tendency to vote changes in the program without regard to the cost considerations on the grounds that the necessary financing can always be obtained from general revenues."[16] These arguments have so far proved persuasive with Congress and, as noted earlier, it has contributed general revenues to OASDHI only for limited purposes, such as paying the cost of noncontributory wage credits for certain military service.

We have also mentioned two other changes often proposed for OASDHI: that an escalator clause be added to ensure that benefits would in-crease automatically with increases in the cost of living, and that the retirement test be liberalized to permit the aged to earn higher incomes without sacrificing any of their pension benefits. Although support appears to be growing for an escalator provision, some people fear that its adoption would relax the pressure for more basic benefit reform (and others wonder whether many con-gressmen will ever vote for an escalator that would deprive them of the chance to claim credit for every boost in benefits). As for liberalizing the retirement test, that could indeed help many of the aged but probably few among those counted as poor. After all, a beneficiary can now earn up to $1,680 a year with no reduction in OASDHI benefits, and up to $2,880 before he loses $1 in benefits for each additional $1 in job earnings. Even if Congress completely abolished these limits on job earnings, what significant difference could it make to most of the 3 million aged widows re-ceiving an average benefit of only $87 per month in 1969, or to the 1.3 million disabled workers or the 2.5 million men aged seventy-five or over then on the rolls? Surely few members of these groups are now turning down high-paying jobs because of the retirement test.

For all these reasons, the future course of the OASDHI program is not entirely clear. It has helped millions of workers to retire in dignity over the last thirty years and, having now achieved nearly universal coverage and having added the vital protection of Medicare, the program will doubtlessly be the major source of income security for most of the aged for many years to come. It has nevertheless failed to stave off poverty for a substantial minority of the aged—particularly workers with a history of irregular and low-wage employment and widows entitled only to meager survivor benefits. Concerning these groups, there is a growing debate over whether we should radically revamp the OASDHI program or search for new and better welfare programs designed specifically for the poor of any age. We shall return to this problem in the next chapter.

In the field of private pensions, the problems are nearly as numerous and the solutions equally difficult to find. Benefit levels have steadily increased and many workers now retiring can obtain a fairly comfortable income from their combined social security and private pension benefits if they have worked twenty-five or thirty years for a company with a private plan. But what of the workers who retired ten or fifteen years ago from the same company? Granting them the same benefit increases negotiated for present workers would sharply raise the cost of any increase to the company and would lower the increases that could be obtained for present workers. Unlike social security, the tendency under private plans has been to leave pensions of persons already retired as they were at the time of retirement. Nor have the private plans done much more than social security to protect future benefits against the inroads of inflation, although a few plans have experimented with escalator clauses and several invest a high proportion of their reserves in common stocks as a hedge against inflation. Perhaps the most hopeful development among private plans has been the continuous spread and liberalization of vesting provisions, which guarantee the worker a right to his accrued benefits after a certain period of service with a company (such as fifteen years) even if the worker then leaves that company and works elsewhere before his retirement.

There is now a greater awareness of the income needs of older people than there has ever been before, and this awareness is likely to grow with the increasing number of persons (and voters) over sixty-five. The problem of meeting these income needs has proved to be even more difficult than the framers of the Social Security Act anticipated in the 1930s, but at least there is now an acceptance of the fact that this is a problem which society as a whole must solve, and not just the aged alone.

ADDITIONAL READINGS

Bowen, William G., and Frederick H. Harbison, Richard A. Lester, and Herman M. Somers (eds.): *The Princeton Symposium on the American System of Social Insurance,* McGraw-Hill, New York, 1968.

Brinker, Paul A.: *Economic Insecurity and Social Security,* Appleton-Century-Crofts, New York, 1968, chaps. 2–6.

Chamberlain, Neil W.: *Sourcebook on Labor,* McGraw-Hill, New York, 1958, chap. 22.

Levitan, Sar A., William J. Cohen, and Robert J. Lampman (eds.): *Towards Freedom from Want,* Industrial Relations Research Association, Madison, Wisc., 1968, pp. 3–87.

McGill, Dan M.: *Fundamentals of Private Pensions,* 2d ed., Irwin, Homewood, Ill., 1964.

Slavick, Fred: *Compulsory and Flexible Retirement in the American Economy,* Cornell University, New York State School of Industrial and Labor Relations, Ithaca, N.Y., 1966.

Social Security Bulletin, the official monthly publication of the Social Security Administration.

FOR ANALYSIS AND DISCUSSION

1. It might be argued that the ideal social security system toward which we should be working is one which guarantees every person the same standard of living after retirement which he had achieved prior to retirement. Appraise this argument.

2. A minority report of the House Ways and Means Committee, signed by Rep. Carl T. Curtis of Nebraska, contained the following statement:

> This concept of "the higher the wage the higher the benefit" has generally been rationalized on the grounds that a greater "wage loss" is suffered when a higher-paid worker dies or retires than when a lower-paid worker

does. But I feel that this concept results in mal-distribution of social insurance funds, and ignores the important fact that the higher-paid worker should be expected to accumulate far greater resources than the lower-paid, with which to supplement his social insurance benefits. In fact, this concept is so inconsistent with the social insurance objective set forth above, that the reverse concept of "the lower the wage the higher the benefit" would be more nearly correct.

It is my belief that benefits should be uniform in amount, and independent of previous wage history. A system providing uniform benefits would recognize the fact that since the amounts available for social security are necessarily limited in total, it is far better to divide up these amounts without discrimination, than to pinch one man's benefit in order to deal more generously with another man's.

Comment on this point of view.

3. In a talk before the 44th Annual Meeting of the United States Chamber of Commerce in 1956, Ray D. Murphy, chairman of the board of the Equitable Life Assurance Society, made the following comment:

I am not in favor of abolishing the Social Security Act. I do believe however that what changes are made in the Act will have much to do with the future economic condition of this country. The Act has been repeatedly amended to increase the benefits. It is a tempting political opportunity when election time approaches—and for an obvious reason. When benefits are liberalized, a large number of our older citizens get an immediate or nearly immediate increase in income. Naturally, they like it. That ultimately means, however, an increase in Social Security taxes upon active workers; but the full impact of these taxes is largely postponed. In fact, the future tax increase, even if it is to be substantial, probably escapes the attention of most people. They will become conscious of it only when the increased taxes are taken out of their pay envelopes. That illustrates the political attractiveness of recurring increases in benefits.

a. Do you share Murphy's fear of political influences on the social security program? Spell

out how such influences would be felt and what counteracting influences they might encounter.

b. If there is such danger of political pressure to increase benefits, how do you account for the fact that benefits are not higher than they are now, and that unions were unable to gain a more sympathetic congressional hearing for their pleas to increase benefits in the period immediately following World War II?

4. One problem which the pension development has created is to enlarge the number of nonproductive members of our society. There is a noticeable tendency for companies which have instituted private pension plans to write some kind of provision for compulsory retirement (usually at age sixty-five) into their terms. In general, an employer prefers compulsory retirement because of the expectation that younger men will be more efficient, because of the fear that failure to create promotional vacancies for younger men to move into may mean the loss of more ambitious workers, and because of the danger that if retirement were made optional, it would be embarrassing and difficult to force the retirement of older men if they became senile or otherwise a problem, as long as others their own age continue to work.

On the other hand, we are becoming more appreciative of the psychological effects of forcing premature retirement. Some doctors are now concerned over the prospect of large numbers of still reasonably healthy and alert people having nothing of any consequence to occupy their minds and energies.

Do you see any ways in which these conflicting pressures can be reconciled?

5. The increasing attention paid by workers and unions to fringe benefits, particularly to those providing pensions, health and life insurance, supplementary unemployment benefits, and so on, has prompted some to raise a question as to whether workers are not excessively security-conscious. On this matter, the late Prof. Arthur Ross once commented (in *Labor Law Journal*, August, 1956, page 481):

Fears are often expressed that the current emphasis on economic security signalizes a serious deterioration of moral fiber, but I tend to doubt it. It has always been regarded as a virtue for a man to buy a great deal of life insurance, even at the cost of current impoverishment, so that some third cousin can be made wealthy when he dies. My insurance agent never tires of stressing the moral advantage of holding as much insurance as possible. Why then should it be an ominous development if the same man gets his employer to buy life insurance for him with part of his earnings? It has always been said that a provident man will not spend all his income but will set something aside for a rainy day. Why is it a moral problem if he and his fellow employees take advantage of the insurance principle to guard against illness or unemployment?

Do you agree with Ross that a double standard is being applied when workers are criticized for seeking to provide against economic contingencies by bargaining for such protective benefits?

NOTES

1. In addition to the sources noted in Figure 24-1, the data in this section are drawn from Lenore A. Epstein, "Income of the Aged in 1962: First Findings of the 1963 Survey of the Aged," *Social Security Bulletin,* March, 1964, pp. 3–24, and "Text of President Johnson's Special Message on Aid for the Elderly," *New York Times,* Jan. 24, 1967, p. 16.

2. U.S. Department of Health, Education, and Welfare, Social Security Administration, *Social Security Programs in the United States,* 1968, pp. 22–23.

3. The same, pp. 24–25 and 28. This source also describes the different eligibility tests for farm workers, the self-employed, and workers covered only recently by the law.

4. The same, p. 28.

5. In 1964, the chief actuary of the Social Security Administration estimated that the elimination of the earnings test would have then increased benefit disbursements by $2 billion in the first full year and would have required a permanent increase of one percent in the combined employer-employee tax rate. Robert J. Myers, "Earnings Test Under Old-Age, Survivors, and Disability Insurance: Basis, Background, and Experience," *Social Security Bulletin,* May, 1964, p. 12.

6. A more precise comparison is that a beneficiary who came on the rolls in 1940 with a benefit equal to the average for that year and who was still drawing benefits at the end of 1967 would have then been receiving a benefit with purchasing power about 23 percent greater than that of his first benefit. *Social Security Programs in the United States,* p. 9.

7. Paul A. Brinker, *Economic Insecurity and So-*cial Security, Appleton-Century-Crofts, New York, 1968, p. 60. Emphasis added.

8. Robert J. Myers, in *Retirement Income of the Aging,* Hearings before the Senate Special Committee on Aging, 87th Cong., 1st Sess., 1961, p. 19. For an excellent discussion of most of the financing issues concerning OASDHI, see William G. Bowen and others (eds.), *The Princeton Symposium on the American System of Social Insurance,* McGraw-Hill, New York, 1968, chaps. 3 and 4 (papers by Otto Eckstein and Robert J. Myers).

9. For states that have a Medicaid program, the federal share of OAA payments is 31/37ths of the first $37 of a maximum average monthly payment of $75 per recipient, plus a proportion (varying between 50 and 65 percent, depending on the state's annual per capita income) of the next $38 of such payment. For states without a Medicaid program, a variation of this formula is used.

10. Coverage and benefit data in this section are from Walter W. Kolodrubetz, "Employee-Benefit Plans, 1950–67," *Social Security Bulletin,* April, 1969, pp. 3–20.

11. For recent information on trends and variations in private plans, see Donald M. Landay and Harry E. Davis, "Growth and Vesting Changes in Private Pension Plans," *Monthly Labor Review,* May, 1968, pp. 29–35; and Harry E. Davis, "Negotiated Retirement Plans—A Decade of Benefit Improvements," *Monthly Labor Review,* May, 1969, pp. 11–15.

12. Once federal benefit levels had been raised, however, unions generally sought to convert provisions which offset governmental payments against private guarantees into provisions which made private payments wholly supplementary to OASDHI benefits, and they have been largely successful in doing so.

13. For the detailed results of this study, see Lenore A. Epstein, "Income of the Aged in 1962: First Findings of the 1963 Survey of the Aged," *Social Security Bulletin,* March, 1964, pp. 3–24; "Assets of the Aged in 1962," *Social Security Bulletin,* November, 1964, pp. 3–13; and Erdman Palmore, "Differences in Sources and Size of Income . . . ," *Social Security Bulletin,* May, 1965, pp. 3–8. More recent data should soon be available from similar studies of the aged being conducted by the Social Security Administration in 1969.

14. Brinker, pp. 75–76.

15. Wilbur J. Cohen, "Economic Security for the Aged, Sick and Disabled: Some Issues and Implications," in Sar A. Levitan and others (eds.), *Towards Freedom from Want,* Industrial Relations Research Association, Madison, Wisc., 1968, p. 73.

16. Robert J. Myers, "The Past and Future of Old-Age, Survivors, and Disability Insurance," in Bowen and others (eds.), *The Princeton Symposium . . . ,* p. 99.

CHAPTER 25

POVERTY AMID PLENTY: THE AMERICAN PARADOX

The title of this chapter is taken from a report issued in late 1969 by a Presidential commission that spent twenty-two months studying the poor in America and the programs designed to help them.[1] Now that we have examined the facts concerning average incomes in this country (in Chapter 19) and the range of current welfare-state activities (in Chapters 21 to 24), we can see the force of this commission's central theme: It is not only tragic but paradoxical that poverty is still a major problem in this of all countries.

If the best antidote for poverty is a healthy economy, as conservatives have long insisted, then poverty should have largely disappeared in a country where gross national product has now topped $1,000 billion and the income of the average family will soon reach $10,000 per year. Or if the solution to poverty lies in government protection for those who are disadvantaged in the competitive struggle, as liberals have long argued, this country can now claim nearly every type of social legislation demanded by reformers in the past. Today we have laws designed to protect union activity and to ban racial discrimination by employers, laws to raise the minimum wage of those who are working and to provide a minimum income for those who are not working because of old age, injury, a recession, or for many other reasons, laws that offer training to those without job skills, and laws that provide medical care for the aged and for workers injured on the job.

Yet, neither the free market nor the welfare state has solved the poverty problem in the United States. It is true, of course, that both institutions have been of enormous benefit to *most* Americans and also that poverty is a relative concept which we apply to many Americans today who would be considered well off in a different time or place. Even allowing for these and similar qualifications, however, it is fair to say that poverty remains a far greater problem today than either conservatives or liberals would have predicted a generation ago, given the great advances we have made in both the productivity of our economy and the scope of our social legislation.

To recapitulate some of the grim evidence of our failure to solve this problem:

The standard measure of poverty categorized as poor any nonfarm family of three or more persons who had less income than $2.40 per person per day in 1968. Roughly similar criteria applied to smaller families and to individuals living alone.

By that Spartan measure, 25 million men, women, and children were living in poverty in 1968—that is, 13 percent of the entire population, and 10 percent of all families.

In New York City alone, 1 million persons were receiving welfare checks in the prosperous year of 1969. That is, all these persons had qualified for assistance based on need, above and beyond whatever income they had from wages or social insurance benefits.

Even in Westchester County, the New York

suburban area that has long been a synonym for wealth, 4 percent of the population were on welfare in 1970 and one-half of the county's budget—nearly $100 million—went to welfare spending in that year.[2]

What went wrong? And if neither economic growth nor social insurance can solve this problem, why not simply guarantee every American family the annual income it needs to live decently, through a negative income tax or a similar plan? Or would such a guarantee backfire and actually *increase* the number of low-income families, by destroying the incentive to work of many of those whose incomes are now above the poverty line?

Those are the questions to be explored in this chapter.

Public assistance in the past

Before we tackle those questions, it is important to describe the government program most often associated with aid to the poor. The official name for this program is "public assistance," but the public knows it as "welfare" or "relief." Whatever the name used, *this program provides assistance only to people who can prove they do not have enough income to meet their subsistence needs.* This is in sharp distinction to the social insurance programs described in previous chapters, under which eligible persons receive unemployment compensation or social security pensions or other benefits *as a right,* with no questions asked about their financial need.

Like so many of our laws, public assistance in this country was strongly influenced by English precedents. In a series of "Actes for the Releife of the Poore" adopted in the period from 1597 to 1662, Parliament established an English Poor Law which lasted, with few changes, until its repeal under a Labour government in 1948. The basic principles of this Poor Law were that relatives of the needy had primary responsibility to support them, and in the event this support was not adequate, the responsibility passed to *local* government units which were mandated to levy taxes to finance relief of the poor. Also, different categories of the poor were supposed to receive differ-

ent treatment: the sick and aged were to be placed in charitable hospitals; the employable poor were to be put to work, preferably in "workhouses"; and the shiftless were to be put to work in "houses of correction."

These principles passed intact over the Atlantic, appearing first in the Poor Laws or Pauper Laws adopted by the American colonies and then continuing to form the basis of public assistance in this country down to the 1930s and, to some extent, down to this day. Moreover, practice in both countries often departed even from those harsh principles set down in Elizabethan days:

> Like their counterparts in the mother country, local overseers of the poor ... in America usually were as much concerned with "keeping down the [tax] rates" as in restoring "paupers" to a condition of self-support. Given preoccupation with costs rather than cures, the three-institution system foreseen by the Poor Law usually went by the boards as too expensive. ... By the late nineteenth century, many American local governmental units were operating one catch-all institution, the poor farm, the almshouse, the poorhouse, or as it was often known in the vernacular, the "pogey." Here were committed, indiscriminately, the elderly lady in reduced circumstances and the old drunk, the child for whom no other facilities were available and the village imbecile, the unemployed laborer with his wife and children, the insane man ... and the tramp.[3]

Some liberalization of this system began to occur around the turn of the century, particularly in the larger cities where private charities and the social work movement made important contributions, but through most of our history the symbol of public policy toward the poor has been that grim image of the county poorhouse. Add to this the strength of the Protestant Ethic in America—the belief that a man's success in supporting himself and his family is a measure of his moral worth—and one can see why most Americans have always thought of "going on welfare" as a shameful act.

Public assistance today

The cataclysmic Depression of the 1930s wrought two major changes in these attitudes and programs. First, poverty became a national as well as a local problem. Given their limited sources of revenue, few cities or counties or even states could cope with the massive destitution that marked those years of crisis. Federal action of some kind became an imperative and the Poor Law Principle of local responsibility was permanently breached (though not abolished, we shall see).

Second, the welfare state was born, with its emphasis on social insurance as a more humane and effective method of providing economic security. With the economy in a shambles and as many as 25 percent of all workers unemployed, it became impossible to maintain the pretense that the poor had only themselves to blame for their plight. As we have seen in previous chapters, the fact was finally accepted that most Americans—not just the shiftless—faced the hazards of unemployment, old age, the premature death of the family breadwinner, sickness, and disability, and the decision was made to offer some protection against these hazards as an earned right rather than as public charity.

The result was the Social Security Act of 1935, which not only established unemployment insurance and old-age pensions but also put the Federal Government in the field of public assistance. The reasoning behind this odd merger was that social insurance would eventually provide income security for most workers against most hazards, but a few exceptional categories of persons would still need other assistance—such as aged individuals who were already retired by 1935 and thus could not build up the work credits needed for a social security pension.

More specifically, the Social Security Act authorized federal grants to states which provided assistance to three categories of people in need. These programs, plus a fourth initiated in 1950, are as follows:

(1) *Old-Age Assistance (OAA)* To provide cash assistance to needy persons who are age 65 or over.

(2) *Aid to the Blind (AB)* For the needy blind. Most states define blindness in terms of inability to earn a livelihood rather than complete blind-

ness. Twenty-nine states have no age limit for AB; the remainder have minimum age requirements, usually of sixteen or eighteen years.

(3) *Aid to Families with Dependent Children (AFDC)* The most controversial of the assistance programs and the one with the fastest-growing caseload. AFDC originally provided aid to needy children whose dependency was based solely on the incapacity or death of a parent or a parent's continued absence from the home. Since 1950, payments have included an allowance to meet the needs of the parent or relative who is caring for the child. In the 1960s, Congress extended this program, at the option of each state, to include needy families with an *unemployed* (but not incapacitated) father in the home, but only twenty-five states adopted this option.

(4) *Aid to the Permanently and Totally Disabled (APTD)* Begun in 1950, this program provides cash payments to needy persons who are at least eighteen years old and have a physical or mental impairment that is expected to continue indefinitely and that substantially prevents the person from engaging in any useful occupation either as a wage earner or homemaker.[4]

The cost of these four programs (plus the cost of Medicaid, which since 1966 has provided the medical care for those covered by these programs) is shared by the Federal, state, and local governments under a formula which calls for federal funds to cover about one-half of the costs, with the exact proportion varying inversely by the per capita income in each state. Although a state's program must meet certain administrative guidelines to qualify for federal matching, *each state has considerable latitude in deciding who is eligible for assistance and the amount of assistance payments.* For example, it is perfectly legal for one state to determine that AFDC benefits should be $200 a month for a family of four and another state to determine that a similar family needs only $100 a month; in both cases, the Federal government will pay one-half of the costs. In this important respect, public assistance is still shaped at state and local levels.

But what of the poor who do not fall into any

of the four categories described above? For these persons, there is a fifth catchall type of welfare program—*General Assistance (GA)*—which is entirely the responsibility of state and local governments.

General assistance is aid furnished by States or localities to needy individuals or families who do not qualify for help under the federally aided assistance programs or—in a few States—to persons not getting enough help from such programs to meet their needs. This type of aid often is the only resource for many temporarily or permanently unemployable persons and for persons out of work who cannot qualify for unemployment insurance or whose benefits under that program are inadequate or have been exhausted. However, about a third of the States will not pay general assistance to a family with an employable person in the household except in defined emergency situations. State and local GA programs are generally more limited than the federally aided assistance programs as to the duration and the amount of assistance paid. In some States, only emergency or short-term assistance is given; in other States, aid is restricted to defined special situations. In addition, a very few States limit the length of time an eligible person can get general assistance.... Money payments only are made in about one-half of the State programs; the remaining use either vendor payments [to the seller of food or housing or medical services, rather than to the family itself] or both cash and vendor payments.[5]

Table 25-1 presents data on the recipients and payments under these five welfare programs in selected years. It will be recalled that the hope and expectation of reformers in the 1930s was that welfare programs would largely wither away as the economy returned to full employment and as social insurance programs took over the burden of providing income security against the major economic hazards. We have now had thirty years of relatively continuous prosperity, cash payments under the various social insurance programs (such as old-age and survivors' insurance, workmen's compensation, and unemployment insurance) have risen from $4 billion in 1940 to $42 billion in 1968—and yet Table 25-1 shows that welfare spending has also climbed and now totals well over $5 billion a year, and we know too that all of this spending and general prosperity have still not eliminated poverty. It is therefore time to take up the question "What went wrong?"

The failure of free markets

Since we have explored this question in detail in other chapters, we shall only summarize here the reasons why poverty has not been abolished by the automatic workings of the free market even after three decades of nearly continuous economic growth.

First, every modern economy—whether capitalist, socialist, or communist in nature—generates constant threats to the economic security of even the best of workers and during even the best of years. A shift in consumer tastes, a relocation of a plant to a lower-cost area, a new machine which displaces an old craft, an accident on or off the job—any of these or similar events can abruptly shut off that flow of cash income which is indispensable for subsistence in a nonagricultural economy. It is true that many workers adjusted to these ceaseless changes without government help over the past thirty years, but many others faced such severe obstacles to geographic or occupational mobility that their income inevitably fell to poverty levels—some temporarily, some permanently.

Second, when a modern economy can threaten the income security of a "good" worker, it obviously poses an even graver threat to the millions who do not start the competitive race on an even footing—because they are black or have a poor education or live in a depressed area or are otherwise "disadvantaged." The past thirty years have shown that these problems of discrimination and structural unemployment have far deeper roots than most people suspected in the 1930s, and the free market by itself works with painful slowness in eradicating these major sources of poverty.

Third, although the American economy has grown phenomenally since the 1930s and we have not suffered another major depression, we have failed (as have all other countries) to solve the riddle of how a free market can achieve simultaneously the benefits of full employment and stable prices. We shall return to this problem in

Table 25-1 *Public Assistance Recipients and Payments, by Program, 1940–1968*

Program	1940	1950	1960	1968
Number of recipients, December (thousands):*				
OAA	2,070	2,786	2,305	2,028
AB	73	97	107	81
AFDC:				
Families	372	651	803	1,522
Recipients†	1,222	2,233	3,073	6,086
Children	895	1,661	2,370	4,555
APTD‡		69	369	703
GA (recipients)	3,618	866	1,244	827
Average monthly payment, December:§				
OAA	$20.25	$43.05	$58.90	$69.55
AB	25.35	46.00	67.45	92.15
AFDC:				
Per family	32.40	71.45	108.35	168.15
Per recipient†	9.85	20.85	28.35	42.05
APTD‡		44.10	56.15	82.60
GA (per recipient)	8.30	22.25	24.85	44.75
Total money payments for year (millions)§	$1,020	$2,354	$3,262	$5,660
OAA	473	1,454	1,626	1,673
AB	22	53	86	88
AFDC	133	547	994	2,823
APTD‡		8	236	656
GA	392	293	320	420

* Includes only those receiving cash assistance payments; excludes those receiving only medical care.
† Beginning 1950, includes as recipients the children and one or both (since 1962) parents, or one caretaker relative other than a parent, in families in which the requirements of such adults were considered in determining the amount of assistance.
‡ Program initiated October, 1950.
§ Excludes vendor payments for medical care. In 1968, medical vendor payments under Medicaid, GA, and all other assistance programs totaled $4.1 billion.

SOURCE: *Social Security Bulletin*, January, 1970, pp. 65–66.

Chapter 28, but it should be noted here that the poor have lost in both ways: when unemployment has been low but prices have risen, as from 1945 to 1948 and the late 1960s, it is the low-income family which is least likely to have a hedge against inflation in the form of stocks or a union contract with an escalator clause; and when "fiscal restraint" drives up the unemployment rate in order to combat inflation, as in the 1950s and in 1969 and 1970, it is the low-wage worker who often is the first to be laid off. Thus, while neither unemployment nor inflation has reached epidemic proportions during these years, we have always had enough of one or the other to push many low-income families below the poverty line.

Finally, the free market can do little by itself for the many who are poor precisely because they are outside of the market—the sick and disabled, the very young and the very old, the mothers without husbands and without day-care facilities for their children. Table 19-8 in Chapter 19 shows that nearly one-half of the heads of all poor families are not even in the labor force, and while some of these may be the shiftless louts of conservative lore, most could not take a job if they were offered one.

All of this does not add up to the conclusion that American capitalism has been an abysmal failure. On the contrary, our system of free markets has performed extremely well for most Americans since 1940. It is nevertheless important to recognize the limitations of private markets, and because a significant amount of poverty has persisted throughout the longest period of sustained prosperity in our history, it is clear that any "war on poverty" must continue to rely upon government programs to supplement the workings of the private economy.

The failure of social insurance

But which government programs can we rely upon? The welfare state was constructed in the 1930s, and elaborated upon in later years, for the precise purpose of giving workers more income security than the market system alone provides. How has poverty resisted the combined effects of minimum-wage laws, unemployment insurance, workmen's compensation, old-age and survivors' insurance, disability insurance, and Medicare, not to mention the vast growth of collectively bargained plans providing health insurance, pensions, and a variety of other income guarantees?

One answer to that question, we have seen, is that few if any of these social insurance programs have been carried through in practice to the extent intended by their proponents. State legislatures grandly proclaimed their intention to reimburse one-half or two-thirds of the wage loss suffered by injured and jobless workers, and then attached so many exclusions and exceptions that benefits often fell short of avowed standards; 20 percent of all workers are still not covered by any workmen's compensation law; and 50 percent or more of those unemployed at any given time are not receiving any unemployment compensation. Old-age and survivors' insurance has come closer than any other program to achieving universal coverage and political popularity, and yet its benefits are so low that 10 percent of all recipients also need OAA payments to make ends meet and nearly one-third of all households headed by an aged person still had poverty-level incomes in 1968. Only four states have disability insurance

to provide income to a worker disabled off the job, and Medicare benefits are only for the aged.

But even if all of these programs had miraculously achieved universal coverage and the funding necessary to pay adequate benefits since their inception, *they would still not have reached many of the poor who are marginal members or nonmembers of the labor force.* The basic rationale of social insurance is that benefits are rights which are earned, not charity doled out to supplicants, but that means that eligibility for any benefits is always based on an employment relationship (of either the individual or the family head) and the size of benefits varies primarily with past earnings rather than current needs. This logic leads to the denial of benefits to the person looking for his first job, the divorced or deserted mother with no employment credits, and those too handicapped to work. It also leads to inadequate benefits for many workers with large families but a record of low-wage and intermittent employment—a fairly common pattern among low-income groups. (Collectively bargained fringe benefits also are tied to the employment relationship, of course, and reach far fewer of the employed than government programs do.)

Finally, there is the often overlooked problem of the worker who is employed the year around and still does not earn enough to support his family adequately—which describes 27 percent of all heads of poor families in 1968. The only nonwelfare program of the 1930s designed to help this group is the minimum-wage law, and in Chapter 21 we described our reasons for believing that a minimum rate pushed to the level necessary to make a serious dent in poverty—which has not yet been attempted—would trigger disemployment or price reactions that would largely nullify any income gains.

To parallel our conclusions about the free market, these criticisms of social insurance do not constitute a blanket indictment of the welfare state. The billions of dollars paid out by these several income-maintenance programs have undoubtedly provided increased security and dignity to a great many workers and their families, and there is no convincing evidence that these programs have seriously impaired work incentives.

In retrospect, however, it seems plain that the architects of the welfare state—like their more conservative contemporaries—underestimated the complexity and severity of the poverty problem.

The failure of public assistance

As the final step in our examination of how poverty has managed to persist so stubbornly over recent decades, we return to public assistance programs. Although the principle of public charity was distasteful to both conservatives and liberals in the 1930s (if for different reasons), both recognized that assistance had to be provided for groups such as the blind, the disabled, and children in broken homes. Also, we have seen that spending under these welfare programs has more than quintupled since 1940. Why, then, did these programs fail in their mission to fill the poverty gap left by the operation of the private economy and social insurance?

The basic criticisms of public assistance are the same as those leveled at unemployment insurance and workmen's compensation: the states set benefit standards that are barely adequate and then often refuse to meet their own standards, with the result that benefits are low in the average state and vary wildly from one state to another. In addition, eligibility is hedged about with so many restrictions that many of the poor cannot qualify for any assistance at all.

The arbitrary nature of welfare programs begins with the determination of the income level that is needed to sustain a poor individual or family. We know that there is no objective measure of where this poverty line should be drawn, but the variations in this standard are so extreme among states, and even among different programs in the same state, as to defy all understanding.

The amount States set as needed for an AFDC family of four ranged from $144 in North Carolina to $332 in New Jersey and $419 in Alaska in 1968. For an aged woman living alone, the "need" [under OAA] ranged from $82 in South Carolina to . . . $262 in Alaska in the same year. The average budgeted need [among all states] for a family of four on AFDC was $238 in April of 1968,

or slightly below $60 per month per person. For a single elderly person the average budgeted need at the same time came to $124. Thus, it is clear that budget standards vary considerably for individuals, depending on the program for which they are eligible [and the state in which they happen to live.][6]

Many states' standards obviously fall far below the Federal government's definition of poverty lines which we reviewed at the beginning of this chapter. For example, North Carolina's monthly standard of $144 for a family of four works out to only $1.20 per day per person, or one-half the federal standard of $2.40. *Yet, twenty-six states make payments that fall short of their own minimum standards in AFDC and sixteen do the same under OAA,* through applying "reduction formulas" and imposing legislative ceilings on benefit payments. Thus, in 1968 Alabama had a budget standard of $177 per month for a family of four on AFDC but actually paid such a family (without other income) only $89 per month—or 74 cents per person per day.[7]

Further, even these meager benefits are denied to many of the poor who run afoul of one or another of the many rules determining eligibility. For instance, until the Supreme Court declared residence requirements to be unconstitutional in 1969, most states required welfare applicants to have lived in a particular state for some period of time—from one up to five years—before they were eligible for assistance from that state. Or consider the rule under which many states have denied assistance to families with an able-bodied father in the home.[8] Although designed to induce the employable to find a job instead of "loafing" on welfare, the effect of this rule has been to force many fathers—either unable to find a job or with a job paying too little to meet their needs—to make the ugly choice of staying with a family they cannot support or deserting their family so the mother and children can become eligible for assistance.

Finally, there remains the controversial *means or needs test* which is at the heart of every welfare program. In principle, there is little objectionable about such a test. The income tax, for example, is really a type of means test, and no reformer has proposed that anyone should be able to drop into a government office and pick up a few thousand dollars with no questions asked. In welfare practice, however, the means test has gained an odious reputation because administrators and caseworkers have so often been forced (or have chosen) to act not as trusted counselors aiding individuals to escape from poverty, but as policemen making sure that the poor are actually as poor as they claim and that they are not violating some taxpayer's notion of morality.

It is hard to imagine how rules such as the following can be administered without demeaning both the social worker and the welfare recipient:

All states permit a recipient to own his own home, but about a third disqualify a person if the value of his home exceeds a specified amount and 31 states may take liens on the homes of recipients so as to recover later the amounts spent on assistance. Thus, some families may have to sell their home before qualifying for welfare.

All states permit a recipient to own some personal property other than a home, but only up to some limit such as $300–$500 for a single person. Thus, a family may have to cash in its life insurance policies to qualify for assistance.

Many states have required that a woman maintain a "suitable home" to be eligible for AFDC, a provision which has encouraged official scrutiny of morals. For example, until it was overturned by the courts in the 1960's, several states enforced a "man in the house" rule which denied AFDC benefits to children when a man not legally responsible for their care lived with the family. And in 1960 Louisiana dropped about 23,000 children from its AFDC rolls under a state law passed to deny benefits to unmarried mothers who continued to have illegitimate children. Equally incredible, the proposal has been advanced (but not adopted) for the compulsory sterilization of AFDC mothers with illegitimate children.

Over half of the states require adult children to contribute to the support of needy parents, and many take vigorous steps to enforce this filial responsibility.

Earned income is treated in all sorts of ways, from dollar-for-dollar reduction of benefits to permitting recipients to earn up to some amount with no reduction in benefits. Whatever the formula, the social worker can find himself checking whether a teenager in a welfare family is picking up a few dollars on a part-time job and, if he is, whether the family's relief grant should be cut accordingly.[9]

It should now be clear why public assistance did not close the poverty gap left by the private economy and social insurance over recent years. Despite the growth in welfare costs, the result of the many restrictions and exclusions cited above has been that *fewer than one-half of the poor received aid from any of the five public assistance programs in 1968,* and those who did receive aid usually found that benefits were so low that their income remained at a poverty level.[10]

Have incentives been dulled?

Before turning to the new remedies proposed for the poverty problem, we should consider the widely held opinion that poverty has persisted since the 1930s not primarily for the reasons we have set forth, but because the welfare state has so dulled the incentive to work that public policy has perpetuated the very problem it set out to solve in the days of the New Deal. As Professor MacIntyre has summarized the debate over this issue:

There seem to be two opposing and irreconcilable views about public assistance and its effect on motivation and work incentives. One holds that men are naturally indolent and that relief, especially too much relief, encourages idleness and rewards lack of enterprise. The other view . . . holds that men generally prefer work and the status that work confers, that hope is the real source of incentive, and that poverty-engendered apathy and sickness are the real underminers of . . . [the] propensity and will to work.[11]

Facts and figures can seldom settle an argument like that, which involves a clash not only of political philosophies but of strongly held views concerning the nature of man. As for the authors' own view, we see no reason to assume that the poor are invariably the salt of the earth or to deny that some welfare recipients prefer charity to work—but neither can we believe that the latter fact explains a major portion of the poverty that exists today, when we know that one-quarter of all heads of poor families worked full time throughout 1968 and over one-half of all poor families were then headed by a person who was age 65 or over, or sick or disabled, or a mother with dependent children.

Nor can we believe that many of the poor are really content to live in the squalor revealed by a 1967 survey of AFDC families (by far the largest category of welfare recipients):

- 17 percent of these families had children who sometimes stayed home from school due to lack of shoes or clothes;
- 23 percent had no private use of a flush toilet or of a bathroom with shower or tub;
- 24 percent had no hot and cold running water;
- 25 percent did not have enough furniture so that everyone could sit down together for meals;
- 30 percent did not have a bed for each family member; and
- 46 percent had no milk for the children at some time in the six months before the survey because of lack of money.[12]

But as we noted, neither these nor any similar statistics can really settle the argument over whether the welfare state has dulled the incentive to work. It is unclear how one would directly measure the strength of work incentives even today, and certainly no one has measured fluctuations in the will to work over the past thirty or forty years. The parties to this debate must therefore rely upon inferences drawn from other developments since the 1930s, and that leaves much room for honest disagreement. To us, the evidence seems clear that the persistence of most poverty in this country has not been due to any "coddling of the poor," but other observers read the same evidence quite differently.

Proposed remedies

We have attempted, up to this point, to summarize the great debate over poverty that took place in this country throughout the 1960s. When poverty was "rediscovered" during those years,

an agonizing reappraisal began of many cherished beliefs and policies. How could the free enterpriser any longer argue that a healthy economy is the best antidote to poverty, when three decades of unprecedented growth had left over 10 percent of the population in dire need? And how could the champions of the welfare state explain the continued growth in welfare rolls after three decades of social insurance? And if poverty could not be solved by economic growth, social insurance, or public assistance, what other remedies were left?

That debate continues to the present day, of course, and we cannot possibly do justice to all the views and proposals it has elicited. But we can illustrate the radical shift in attitudes that has occurred during this debate by describing two of the proposed remedies for poverty which are now receiving serious attention—the negative income tax and the government as the employer of last resort.

The negative income tax

One of the most astonishing social and political developments of recent years has been the speed with which a radically new idea—that the Federal government should make direct cash payments to the poor to assure them a guaranteed annual income—has attracted strong support from all across the political spectrum.

The principle of the negative income tax was largely unknown in the United States before 1962, for example, and it was then broached not by a visionary planner from the left but by Prof. Milton Friedman, often regarded as the leading conservative economist in the country.[13] By 1966, a Presidential commission of labor, management, and public representatives, originally set up to look into the problems posed by automation, was urging Congress to "give serious study to a 'minimum income allowance' or 'negative income tax' program."[14] In 1968, President Johnson appointed another tripartite commission, charged specifically with examining all types of income-maintenance programs including those guaranteeing minimum incomes—a move which could have created a storm of controversy in any previous administration—and this commission strongly recommended the creation of a "universal income supplement program financed and administered by the Federal Government, making payments based on income needs to all members of the population."[15] And in 1969, President Nixon proposed a fundamental overhaul of the welfare system and the substitution of a program under which a family of four would have a federal guarantee of an income of not less than $1,600 a year.[16]

Although we shall concentrate on the negative income tax, there are several other types of income guarantees. Old-age and survivors' insurance is one type, for example; the Nixon proposal for liberalizing public assistance is another; and a third is the system of children's allowances found in Canada and in every European country.[17] What distinguishes the negative income tax from other income guarantees?

In all versions of the negative income tax, ... what is actually proposed is to pay subsidies to poor households through the medium of the federal personal income tax, using the Internal Revenue Service and the Treasury as the institutional agencies for such purpose. ... To distribute transfers in this novel way means that subsidies would become the counterpart of taxes. If a given tax reporting unit has an income below the zero-tax point on its appropriate tax schedule, it would get a subsidy. If its income lies above this limit, it will continue to pay a tax. ...

What is "negative" in the calculation of the subsidy is neither the payment itself nor the rate at which it is determined. Rather, the negative element is the amount by which household income before subsidy falls short of some chosen upper income limit, say the zero-tax point, for example.[18]

To add to the confusion, several people have proposed different versions of the negative income tax, but the common elements of most plans are contained in the version recommended in 1969 by the President's Commission on Income Maintenance Programs. Table 25-2 presents the essence of the Commission's proposal, which is that *(1) each household with no other income should be granted an annual allowance of $750 for each of the first two adults in a family and $450 for each additional member, and (2) these benefits should decline by 50 cents for each dollar of other income.*[19]

Thus, under this plan a family of four with no other income would receive a federal allowance of $2,400 per year; if the father (or mother) landed a job bringing in $1,000 a year, this family's allowance would drop by $500 (one-half

Table 25-2 *Federal Payments to Households under a Proposed Income Guarantee*

Household size	Annual amount of other income*									
	$0	$500	$1,000	$1,500	$2,000	$3,000	$4,000	$5,000	$6,000	$7,000
	Annual amount of federal payment (dollars)									
One person	$ 750	$ 500	$ 250	0						
Two (one parent, one child)	1,200	950	700	$ 450	$ 200	0				
Two (couple)	1,500	1,250	1,000	750	500	0				
Three (one parent, two children)	1,650	1,400	1,150	900	650	$ 150	0			
Three (two parents, one child)	1,950	1,700	1,450	1,200	950	450	0			
Four persons†	2,400	2,150	1,900	1,650	1,400	900	$ 400	0		
Five persons†	2,850	2,600	2,350	2,100	1,850	1,350	850	$ 350	0	
Six persons†	3,300	3,050	2,800	2,550	2,300	1,800	1,300	800	$ 300	0
Seven persons†	3,750	3,500	3,250	3,000	2,750	2,250	1,750	1,250	750	$ 250

* Includes income from all sources other than income-tested public assistance and veterans' pensions.
† Assumed to include two adults. One-adult families of the same size would receive $300 less.

SOURCE: *Poverty Amid Plenty: The American Paradox,* Report of the President's Commission on Income Maintenance Programs (preliminary copy), 1969, p. 389.

of "other income") to $1,900; if the job paid $2,000 a year, this family's allowance would drop to $1,400 a year; and so on. Stated differently, this plan would provide cash assistance of some amount for all families of four with incomes up to $4,800 per year.

The great appeal of the negative income tax is its offer of a quick and simple way to plug many of the gaps in our present system of dealing with the poor. We know that both the free market and social insurance largely miss the poor who are outside of the labor force and many of those who are in it but are looking for their first job, or are temporarily disabled, or have exhausted their unemployment or workmen's compensation benefits, or are working at wages inadequate for their family needs. The negative income tax would provide cash assistance to all those groups.

In addition, this plan could obliterate the need for most of the present welfare programs by reaching all of the poor now served by those programs plus the many others now excluded by one rule or another, and it could do all this through a more efficient and less demeaning needs test— the filing of income returns to be audited by the Internal Revenue Service, just as returns for most of the nonpoor are now audited by that agency. Finally, the President's Commission argued that its proposal would serve the interests of equity by providing equal benefits for families with equal income needs (in contrast to the great variation among states in the benefits now paid under most welfare and some social insurance programs), and this plan would preserve work incentives by always yielding a higher income to those who work than to those who do not (among households of the same size) and workers who earn more would always receive higher total incomes than workers who earn less.

Some criticisms

The proponents of the negative income tax mount a highly impressive case, but few of them would claim that this is an instant cure for poverty.

For one thing, there is the always sticky problem of costs. A comparison of Table 25-2 and Table 19-7 in Chapter 19 will show that the benefit levels proposed by the President's Commission

for families with little or no other income are well below the income lines defining poverty, and the Commission estimated in fact that (until improved) its plan would eliminate only one-half of the poverty-income gap. Yet, even that modest beginning would increase net federal budget costs by an estimated $7 billion in 1971, and to have set the payment levels at the poverty line immediately would have cost an estimated $27 billion.

The point is that an effective plan of this type will necessarily cost more than suggested by the concept of the poverty gap—that is, the difference between the actual incomes of the poor and the incomes necessary to place them above the poverty line. If incentives are to be preserved, a program cannot simply promise to pay a family of four, say, the difference between its current income and its poverty line of $3,500 (as of 1968), for that would invite all families below that income level to stop working and also the workers in many families with income up to $4,000 or $5,000. It is for that reason that all versions of the negative income tax include some provision such as that deducting only 50 cents from benefits for every dollar of other income— which means that some benefits will be paid to families with total incomes well *above* the poverty line and the plan's total cost will accordingly increase well above the amount of the poverty gap. One can still argue that it is worth $27 billion a year, or even much more, to eliminate the blight of poverty, but opposition will obviously mount with the size of the bill.

And will a negative income tax really preserve the incentive to work, even with the partial offset for other income? On this crucial point, the Commission justifiably argued that no one yet knows the answer. There is general agreement that the "100 percent tax" on earned income levied under some welfare programs—that is, benefits reduced one dollar for every dollar earned by the recipient—is the worst possible way to preserve incentive. At the other extreme, a "zero tax" would presumably offer the maximum incentive but would also increase enormously the costs of any program by raising the level up to which earnings could be supplemented. The Commission's compromise on a 50 percent rate seems reasonable, as does its argument that the general level of benefits in Table 25-2 is so low that few families would be tempted to forgo an opportunity to earn more. The fact remains that no one can predict with assurance what effect a plan like this would have on the motivations and behavior of the millions of individuals it would cover.[20]

Finally, even if a negative income tax worked to perfection, it would only ameliorate, but not really solve, many of the basic problems of the poor, such as racial discrimination, broken homes, a lack of job skills, and poor schools and housing and health care. Also, many proponents of this plan warn that it should not be used as an excuse for failing to broaden the coverage and improve the benefit level of the social insurance programs which are of benefit to many of the poor and non-poor alike.

In short, the negative income tax is not a cheap and instant solution to all the problems of the poor—but it does hold great promise as an improvement upon (not a substitute for) our present system of income maintenance, and its advocates have played a major role in moving American society to consider for the first time the idea of guaranteeing an annual income to every individual or family.

Employer of last resort

When all is said and done, the negative income tax strikes some critics as only a glamorized form of public assistance which does not provide employment or dignity for the poor who would prefer to earn their own living. For this and other reasons, some support has developed for a proposal that the government should act as an "employer of last resort" and provide jobs for those who cannot find any in the private sector.

In 1970, for example, the AFL-CIO strongly endorsed a congressional bill that provided such a job program at an estimated cost of $5 billion for the first year. In the words of a union spokesman:

> For those who remain unemployed or seriously underemployed, a federally-financed public-service employment program is the only logical answer. . . . Such a program would create jobs and it would provide badly needed public services in hospitals, schools, parks, recreation

centers and other public and private non-profit facilities. Linked with training and guidance, such a program would make it possible for these workers to move into regular employment.

> Private employers, no matter how lofty their goals and how hard they work to achieve them, cannot realistically do more than make a dent in the ranks of the hard-core unemployed.[21]

This proposal has not received much systematic analysis in either Congress or the professional literature, but some clues can be gleaned from our experience with work-relief programs in the 1930s.

One set of problems emerges if the primary purpose of such a program is to provide jobs for all the poor who want or need them. Since many of the poor have few job skills, the quickest and easiest way to put them to work is on projects of marginal importance and with a low skill content —which gave rise to the image of the indolent leaf-raker in a public park as the epitome of the much-maligned Works Progress Administration (WPA) during the New Deal era. And what wage should these workers receive? One estimate is that if the Federal government had served as employer of last resort in 1969 and paid only the legal minimum wage, the program would have employed about 9 million workers at an annual cost of $16 billion.[22] Further, we know that the legal minimum of $1.60 an hour is not enough to lift many families out of poverty, but raising the rate to an "adequate" level (and should this vary by the size of each worker's family?) would raise total costs considerably, bring cries of anguish from private employers paying less, and pose problems such as whether a worker could quit a lower-paying job in private industry for a higher-paying one on this public program.

On the other hand, a different set of problems emerges if a major aim of the program is to accomplish socially useful tasks—such as the Public Works Administration (PWA) attempted to do in the 1930s by building dams and roads and public buildings, or as many would like the government to do today by attacking pollution and the many shortages in education, housing, and medical care. There are limits on how much help can be expected from the unskilled poor in tackling these problems, for most public programs in these fields rely heavily upon the skills of construction workers, teachers, nurses, engineers, and other highly trained personnel. Also, when an agency has only so many dollars to build hospitals or attack smog, it wants to show maximum results and not "waste" its funds on hiring and training the hard-core unemployed.

Thus, while we certainly have many unmet social needs and many unemployed poor, it can be exceedingly difficult and expensive to match one with the other. *Also, it cannot be repeated too often that perhaps one-half or more of today's poor are cut off from the labor market,* and these people would gain little if any benefit from an increase in job opportunities.

All of this probably overstates the case against the proposal that the government act as the employer of last resort. If such a program were applied with vigor and imagination, it undoubtedly could provide meaningful jobs for some thousands of the hard-core unemployed and that would indeed be a worthwhile gain. Many problems must be solved, however, before this proposal can offer an escape from poverty for any large proportion of even the employable poor.

Conclusions

It is clear that the American paradox—of poverty persisting in the midst of affluence—is going to be with us for many years. Entering the 1970s, this paradox had resisted resolution through three decades of unparalleled growth in the output of the private economy, the scope of social insurance, and the cost of public assistance, and any problem that formidable is not going to succumb without a long and hard fight.

What have we learned from the failures of the past thirty years? At the risk of piling paradox upon paradox, it seems fair to say that the major lesson has been that poverty is both more and less complex than most people assumed in the past. It is more complex in the sense just mentioned: we know now that poverty will not automatically disappear through either a bigger and better GNP or a bigger and better Social Security Act, the favorite remedies of the right and left in the 1930s. Both the free market and social insurance

have performed wonders for most Americans, but both have failed the poor for the reasons described in this chapter.

By the same token, we know now that any effective "war on poverty" must be fought on dozens of fronts—against racial discrimination, the shortage of decent housing, inadequate health care, broken families, poor schools, barriers to job and occupational mobility, the problems of depressed areas, the many ramifications of the farm problem, and so on. Although most of these have been recognized for generations as problems afflicting the poor, we can now see more clearly that they are all *causes* as well as effects of poverty. Thus, even if the negative income tax or some other plan managed to raise the income of everyone above the poverty threshold tomorrow, there would be a continuing need for government action against most of those causes of economic (and social) inequality.

On the other hand, poverty now appears to be *less* complex than once assumed, in the sense that we are beginning to accept the elementary fact that the poor need more money to become nonpoor. As we have remarked, the rush to embrace the principle of a guaranteed annual income has been nothing short of remarkable. After all those years in which conservatives warned that labor's passion for security was threatening the American way of life and liberals denounced the means test as an affront to human dignity, important figures in both camps have now rallied behind the negative income tax or other plans to assure a minimum income to all who can prove they need it, including the working poor and the able-bodied unemployed.

It is true that these new plans attempt to preserve work incentives and eliminate the most demeaning features of the needs test, but nevertheless their chief mission is to guarantee an income to everyone who needs it—in sharp contrast to our past preoccupation with guaranteeing that no one gets help who does not "deserve" it. This revolution in attitudes could not have occurred without the experience of the past thirty years, during which economic growth and the 1935 model of the welfare state had every chance to solve the poverty problem and failed to do so for a substantial minority of the population.

Thus, while the end of poverty is not yet in sight, there are reasonable grounds for hope—not only because of the ingenuity of new proposals such as the negative income tax, but because of the new attitudes toward poverty that lie behind those proposals.

ADDITIONAL READINGS

Green, Christopher: *Negative Taxes and the Poverty Program,* Brookings, Washington, 1967.

Hildebrand, George H.: *Poverty, Income Maintenance, and the Negative Income Tax,* ILR Paperback no. 1, Cornell University, New York State School of Industrial and Labor Relations, Ithaca, N.Y., 1967.

Levitan, Sar A., Wilbur J. Cohen, and Robert J. Lampman (eds.): *Towards Freedom from Want,* Industrial Relations Research Association, Madison, Wisc., 1968.

Poverty Amid Plenty: The American Paradox, Report of the President's Commission on Income Maintenance Programs, 1970.

Turnbull, John G.: *The Changing Faces of Economic Insecurity,* The University of Minnesota Press, Minneapolis, 1966.

Vadakin, James C.: *Children, Poverty, and Family Allowances,* Basic Books, New York, 1968.

FOR ANALYSIS AND DISCUSSION

1. One criticism of the Federal government's measure of poverty is that its income lines reflect the living standards and expectations of the 1960s, when they were first developed, and therefore define as poor many people with incomes that would have been considered well above the poverty level in earlier years. For that reason, it can be argued, these income lines overstate the severity of the poverty problem today.

On the other hand, the President's Commission on Income Maintenance Programs criticized the concept of a poverty line that remains fixed for even a decade. It pointed out that the current poverty measure remained essentially unchanged through the 1960s, except for adjustments to reflect increases in prices, with the result that during the period from 1959 to 1968—when the median income of all nonfarm families of four rose by 57 percent—there was only a 20 percent rise in the poverty line defining which of those families were poor. Thus, the Commission argued, the gap between the living standards of the poor and the more affluent actually increased during that period, and in that sense the government's poverty measure understates the severity of the problem today.

Which argument do you find more persuasive, and why?

2. It has often been proposed that the United States follow the lead of Canada and all European countries and adopt a family-allowance plan as an aid in the fight against poverty. For example, Prof. James Vadakin has urged that the following plan be adopted:[23]

1. Benefits would be paid at the rate of $10 per month for each and every child in the family under the age of eighteen years, with all families eligible regardless of income or employment status.

2. Satisfactory school attendance would be a condition for receipt of benefits for children of school age.

3. The program would be financed from general tax revenues of the Federal government. Benefit payments would be included as taxable income under the Internal Revenue Code, and exemptions for children under the federal income tax law as now constituted would continue. On this basis, the gross cost of the program in 1968 would have been $8.6 billion, from which $1.3 billion would have been recovered through the income tax, leaving a net annual cost of $7.3 billion.

Appraise the strengths and weaknesses of this proposal.

3. The Federal government administers two programs designed to give low-income households an opportunity to supplement their diet. The Commodity Distribution Program provides for the direct distribution of surplus farm products, or items using such products, such as flour, rice, canned meat and vegetables, dried peas, butter, and raisins. The Food Stamp Program sells stamps at a discount to low-income families, who use the stamps to purchase food at their grocery stores.

About one-fourth of the poor benefited from one or the other of these programs in 1969, at a cost to the government of over $400,000,000.

Do you think this type of public assistance is more or less preferable than cash grants to the poor?

4. Many arguments over anti-poverty policy come down to each person's view of the poor. Nearly everyone agrees that some people are poor for reasons clearly beyond their control, such as physical disability; some are poor because they are lazy; and some are poor for a mixture of those or other reasons. There is still much disagreement, however, over which of those three groups predominates among the poor.

State your own opinion on this crucial question and defend it with whatever evidence you can find.

NOTES

1. *Poverty Amid Plenty: The American Paradox,* Report of the President's Commission on Income Maintenance Programs, Nov. 12, 1969.

2. National data are given in more detail in Chapter 19; New York City and Westchester data are from the *New York Times,* Nov. 19, 1969, pp. 49 and 95.

3. Duncan M. MacIntyre, *Public Assistance: Too Much or Too Little?,* Bulletin 53–1, Cornell University, New York State School of Industrial and Labor Relations, Ithaca, N.Y., 1964, p. 11.

4. Most of this section describing public assistance programs has been drawn from U.S. Social Security Administration, *Social Security Programs in the United States,* 1968, pp. 85–97.

5. The same, pp. 93–94.

6. *Poverty Amid Plenty: The American Paradox* (preliminary copy), p. 290.

7. The same, p. 292.

8. As noted earlier in the text, AFDC benefits were originally restricted to needy children whose dependency was based on the incapacity or death of a parent or a parent's continued absence from the home, and only twenty-five states later availed themselves of the option (first offered by Congress in 1961) to extend AFDC to needy families with an unemployed father. Also, no state may grant AFDC aid to any family whose father is employed, regardless of how low his income or how large his family. Further, about a third of the states will not pay GA to a family with an employable person in the home except in certain emergency situations.

9. Based on MacIntyre, pp. 26–51 and 73–76; and *Poverty Amid Plenty,* pp. 286–289.

10. The estimate of coverage is derived as follows: Table 25–1 shows that in December, 1968, the number of welfare recipients totaled 9.7 million individuals, a number equivalent to 38 percent of the 25.4 million persons classified as poor in 1968 by the application of the Federal government's poverty index (*Current Population Reports,* Series P-60, no. 68). That figure probably understates the proportion receiving aid during the year as a whole, since there is undoubtedly some turnover from month to month in welfare recipients, but the President's Commission on Income Maintenance Programs also states that "less than two-fifths of the poor" receive any public assistance (*Poverty Amid Plenty,* p. 286).

Why have welfare costs and rolls (particularly under AFDC) risen so dramatically, even though not enough to close the poverty gap? The President's Commission suggests several reasons: eligibility requirements have been broadened by Congress and the courts; states have increased their budget standards (although often too little and too late); the proportion of poor families applying for welfare has increased (often under the encouragement of the federal poverty program and the recently organized welfare rights groups); welfare administrators have used their broad discretionary powers to accept a larger proportion of applicants (either as a conscious policy or in response to the changed political climate); continuing urbanization has brought more poor people to the city, where a cash income is often more crucial to survival than it is on a farm; and there may be a tendency for poor families headed by women to be larger in size today than before. (The same, pp. 301–302.)

11. MacIntyre, p. 71.

12. *Poverty Amid Plenty,* pp. 297–298.

13. Milton Friedman, *Capitalism and Freedom,* University of Chicago Press, Chicago, 1962, pp. 191–195.

14. National Commission on Technology, Automation, and Economic Progress; Report, vol. 1, *Technology and the American Economy,* Washington, 1966, p. 40.

15. *Poverty Amid Plenty,* p. 17.

16. The key part of the Nixon proposal was the elimination of the AFDC program and its bar to aid to the working poor and, in many states, to families with an unemployed father (see note 8 above). For the first time, the Federal government would set an income floor under public assistance payments—a family of four whose head was unemployed would receive a minimum of $1,600 a year (higher than 1969 benefit levels in twenty states) and families with earnings up to $3,920 would be eligible for lesser supplements. It was estimated that these changes would at least double the number of persons eligible for public assistance. The quid pro quo for this increased assistance was that able-bodied adults would be required to take job training or employ-

ment when offered them or would have their funds cut off (but not those funds going to their wives and children, which would be administered by a trustee or welfare agency).

17. Children's or family allowances are typically monthly payments by a government or employer to *all* families with dependent children, with the size of payments varying by the number and often the age of children but not by the income of the family.

18. George H. Hildebrand, *Poverty, Income Maintenance, and the Negative Income Tax,* ILR Paperback no. 1, Cornell University, New York State School of Industrial and Labor Relations, Ithaca, N.Y., 1967, pp. 9–10.

19. *Poverty Amid Plenty,* pp. 17–23, 120–131, and 387–410.

20. A research project begun in 1968 may eventually provide the first solid evidence on this issue of incentives. With the support of a government grant and under the direction of Prof. Harold Watts, this study contracted to provide about 500 working-poor families in New Jersey with guaranteed incomes (of various amounts and with various marginal rates) for a period of three years, in return for which the families are required to provide information on their work experience. In a preliminary report issued on the first ten months' results, the researchers had found little or no evidence that work effort had declined among those receiving income payments as compared to a control group receiving none. *Business Week,* Feb. 28, 1970, pp. 80–82.

21. Andrew J. Biemiller, Legislative Director of the AFL-CIO, as quoted in Bureau of National Affairs, *Daily Labor Report,* March 17, 1970, p. A–10.

22. *Poverty Amid Plenty,* p. 372.

23. James C. Vadakin, *Children, Poverty, and Family Allowances,* Basic Books, New York, 1968, chap. 7.

PART EIGHT

LABOR IN RELATION TO THE PERFORMANCE OF THE ECONOMY

Not only is labor, in the form of households, the subject of legislative protection by a society which is concerned with the welfare of its weaker and more disadvantaged members. But labor, through its union agents, also constitutes pools of private power which can create problems for society.

There are a number of ways in which it may do this, and we cannot explore them all in these pages. We shall select only the most important of its influences. These include its impact on the public by virtue of its resort to the strike as a bargaining weapon; its effect on price and production decisions by virtue of monopolistic powers which it enjoys; its pressures to secure "full employment" and the possible inflationary consequences; its effect on industrial productivity and the resulting competitiveness, or lack of it, of American goods in world markets.

Because we are focusing on labor in this book, the concern with the problems which unions make for the economy almost inevitably introduces a certain bias. We are not singling out the behavior of labor groups because it is especially provocative or puzzling with respect to the impact on economic performance, but only because it is relevant to our field of inquiry.

Collective bargaining is a process of voluntary agreement. Agreement comes when one or both of the parties would rather accept the other's terms than face the consequences. In line with the definition of bargaining power which we developed earlier, we may say that a bargain is struck whenever, for one party, the cost of agreeing is less than the cost of disagreeing.

Strike strategy

A stoppage of operations is the chief consequence of disagreement which both of the parties would prefer to avoid if possible. Both suffer—the workers through loss of pay and management through loss of sales and customers. Whether we look on the union as precipitating a strike because unsatisfied with the management's offer, or on management as responsible for the strike by refusing to concede the union's demands, a strike constitutes a declaration that each side would rather suffer the losses involved than settle on the other's terms. It is only at the point where either union or management concludes that the loss to it from a strike would be greater than the "cost" of surrendering on the other's conditions that an agreement evolves.

To be sure, the interplay of relative bargaining powers involves a great deal more than the union's threat of striking or management's threat of taking a strike. We have surveyed some of the elements making up the costs of agreement and

the costs of disagreement of the two parties in Chapter 12. Here, however, we are concerned solely with the use of the strike and its impact on the public, not with the broader issues of bargaining power and collective bargaining. All that we need to remind ourselves at this point is that we prize collective bargaining because it constitutes the expression of free decision making by private parties—the determination by employees, their union representatives, managers, and owners of the terms on which they will cooperate. But collective bargaining also implies conflict; it could not exist without conflict. To bargain means to try to resolve a *difference of opinion*—otherwise there would be nothing to bargain about. How does one go about inducing someone else to agree with him? By making disagreement more costly than agreement, or agreement less costly than disagreement.

In other forms of commercial bargaining, if disagreement persists the consequence may simply be no bargain, or the parties may make bargains with other people. But in the labor–management field we face something different. As long as the union and the company continue in existence, some bargain *has* to be reached, eventually. It may be on management's terms, with the employees going back to their jobs without having gained a thing. Or it may be on the union's terms, with management having to concede everything demanded. More commonly it will be after some give and take on both sides. But *some* agreement is almost inevitable.[1] This fact leads each party to put maximum pressure on the other, so that when the agreement is reached, as it inevitably will be, it will be as much to the party's liking as possible. No one likes to continue a relationship on somebody else's terms.

By and large, the strike has been eliminated as an instrument of bargaining power in that class of disputes known as grievances, as we had occasion to note in Chapter 13. These are differences of opinion usually relating to the interpretation or application of an existing agreement, or a dispute involving the interests of some individual or group of individuals rather than the whole bargaining unit. In most union–management relationships, these disputes are finally referred to arbitration if they cannot be settled between the parties directly.[2] Standards usually exist, in the agreement or in prior grievance decisions, to which such disputes may be referred, and the stakes involved are usually small. In this chapter, when we refer to strikes we shall be talking about disputes not over grievances but over the terms of a contract itself, where commonly no procedure exists for resolving the disagreement except the play of relative bargaining powers.

Without attempting to catalog all the devices to which the parties resort to make their strike strategies effective, we can briefly take note of a few. On the union's part, it may start with a "strike-authorization" vote taken by the local membership, which performs two functions. First, it demonstrates to the union's national office that the local members are really behind the strike, and second, if an overwhelming majority of members vote in favor of permitting union officers to call a strike—as they almost invariably do—this decision is an indication to management of membership solidarity.

Picket lines likewise serve two functions. For one thing, they constitute visible reminders to the membership and the public that the dispute is still active and also serve as a means of involving the members in the active conduct of the strike, thus keeping their support lively. For another, they are a means of enlisting the support of other unions whose members may refuse to cross the picket line —to deliver merchandise, to make repairs, to buy goods, thus putting more pressure on management.

Unions also try to make their strikes more effective by the payment of benefits to strikers, partially offsetting the income lost. A 1967 survey disclosed that 70 of 113 national unions had specific provisions for the payment of strike benefits. These were either flat benefits (the average weekly amount was $25) or benefits related to earnings, need, or dependents. In a few unions these benefits sometimes reach substantial amounts. Locomotive engineers receive $100 a month plus $30 for the wife and $25 for each child under eighteen. Typographers with dependents are paid 60 percent of the day-work scale. These benefits are financed out of a strike fund which is accumulated by paying into it some part of the members' regular dues. Even in those unions which have no explicit provisions, benefits are usually paid, though on a basis of need rather than a scheduled amount. This bolstering of the strikers' income position helps to keep a strike going.[3]

On the management side, smaller firms often try to recruit new employees to take the place of strikers, or encourage a back-to-work movement by keeping the plant doors open and operating with as many employees as continue to show up. Large corporations typically close down, since the job of replacing a sizable work force is usually unmanageable. In 1960, however, General Electric managed to keep its plants working even in the face of a strike of one-third of its employees who were represented by the International Union of Electrical Workers—in part because of defection within the union.

In some instances, management has tried to stimulate the recruiting of striker replacements, and at the same time to break the spirit of the strikers, by offering superseniority to those accepting employment, but in general this has been ruled out of bounds by the NLRB or by private grievance arbitration decisions. More effective has been the continuance of operations by relying on supervisors and office workers to man the jobs abandoned by the strikers. As industrial processes have become automated this has become more feasible. In earlier years, a strike of telephone operators was looked upon as a community calamity, but now automatic dial equipment continues to provide service more or less indefinitely. Some managements have said that one inducement to invest in improved automatic equipment is not only the usual expected rate of return but also the fact that it gives them strike insurance.

But managements have also sought insurance in a more literal sense. By paying a premium either to an insurance company or to an industry pool, a company acquires the right to receive benefits in time of strike, compensating it for some of its lost income. In the New York City newspaper strike of 1962, publishers recouped from 30 to 50 percent of fixed costs under insurance policies which allowed them $11,000 a day after the first week of the strike, and $22,000 on Sundays, up to a maximum of $550,000 a year for a single paper and $2,225,000 for all the papers in one city or under one collective agreement. In a twenty-five-day strike in 1960, the Long Island Railroad received about $1.3 million from the strike insurance plan in that industry. And under a "mutual-aid" plan adopted by the major airlines, four lines that were struck by the machinists in 1966 received $44 million in payments from four lines that were not struck. Those three industries—newspapers, railroads, and airlines—have pioneered the strike-insurance movement, perhaps because all three face multiple and rival unions and all sell products or services that cannot be stockpiled in the event of a strike. Other industries have also flirted with the idea of strike insurance, with construction being the latest to try it.[4]

Strike stakes and violence

The very essence of a strike is that its outcome is uncertain, or else it would never have been undertaken. If union and management could predict the result it would of course pay them to settle on those terms at once and avoid all the costs attending a strike. But a strike is a gamble which may or may not pay off, and union members and managements are necessarily gamblers when they decide to call or take a strike. It is this very uncertainty of the outcome, coupled with the fact that men's livelihoods are at stake when a company starts recruiting replacements, that sometimes precipitates a degree of bitterness that turns into violence. This is less true now than formerly. In pre-Wagner Act days, when manage-

ments were free to attack unions with virtually no holds barred, violence was a common accompaniment of strike actions. Today it is much less frequent, in large part because so many managements simply stop operating and try to wait the union out—thus threatening to break the strike but not the union, to deprive the men of the gains which they seek but not of their jobs.

Indeed, at times managements have gone so far as to provide comfort shelters and hot coffee to the men who have closed down their plants, thus drawing the emotional sting from their actions. But when companies try to replace strikers with new hires, as does happen, the bitterness and violence of earlier years reassert themselves. In the early stages of the UAW-Kohler dispute in Sheboygan, Wisconsin, in the fifties, before it hardened into a contest of grim determination after the passage of several years, paint bombs were splashed through the windows of strikers and nonstrikers, tires were slashed, unionist fathers stopped speaking to nonunionist sons. "The village of Kohler armed itself with tear gas and machine guns, while the Governor threatened to send in the National Guard." One nonstriking worker was beaten to death.[5]

Effects on the public

A strike is likely to injure not only the party against whom it is directed but the public as well. Indeed, at times the "innocent" public seems to be regarded by the parties only as a weapon or bludgeon to be used to force surrender; each side proclaims its sympathy for the public, which is being abused by the *other's* adamant refusal of concession, and seeks to align public support for its own position by expressing sympathetic concern for public welfare.

There are two ways in which public welfare may become involved. It may be adversely affected by the terms of the settlement which ends the strike. Particularly with respect to an increase in wage rates which seems to necessitate an increase in the price of a product or service, it often appears that the two parties are so concerned with reaching terms on which they can both agree that they ignore the cost to the public. If workers in a strategic position exact high rates from their employer, it may be other workers in less advantageous positions who wind up paying those rates in the form of higher prices. Other issues than wages sometimes have a substantive impact on the public—sometimes involving even foreign relations and matters of state—but the price effect is the most common.

We shall defer consideration of this kind of public involvement until later chapters, where we shall explicitly examine whether unions exercise monopoly powers and, if they do, whether they should, and what standards may be developed on the basis of which the fairness of the terms of settlement may be judged. For the moment we shall concern ourselves exclusively with the second of the two ways in which the public is affected by a strike—the inconvenience caused by the disruption of services or production.

Any strike obviously has an effect—or potential effect—on the household consumers of the product involved, and it is this that we frequently have in mind when we speak of the impact of strikes. But in addition to this "consumption effect" there is also an "income effect." Employment may be curtailed in the firms which normally supply goods and services to the struck plant, as well as in businesses which use the struck product in their own productive operation and which have difficulty switching quickly to another source of supply. Local merchants and landlords, *any* producer of consumer goods and services, even churches and community budgets may be adversely affected by the reduction in the stream of expenditures due to the strike itself and the impact on other employment.

Whether these effects appear and the degree to which they appear depend on a number of factors, chief among which are (1) the necessitous character of the struck good or service, (2) the stock of the good available, and (3) the extent to which satisfactory substitutes for the struck good are available. These three elements determine a strike's severity. We could spend a good deal of time elaborating and refining these three factors, but a general understanding is enough for our purposes.

Some goods or services are simply more vital than others, either to consumers or producers or both. Local transit services are obviously more important to most people than bowling alleys.

Steel mills are more dependent on rail transportation than on garbage disposal.

But even if a product is important to households or businesses, a strike which interrupts its output is less serious if there is an inventory of that product on which to draw while the strike is in effect. A steel strike has a limited impact on steel-using firms for at least several weeks, because the stocks of steel already on hand can keep production processes going.

Finally, whether a strike affects the public depends also on whether there are adequate substitutes for the product or service involved. A theater strike imposes little hardship, since people can turn to television or concerts for entertainment. A rail strike is serious because there are no adequate alternative means of transportation for many kinds of haulage.

Both the stock effect and the substitutability effect are likely to be more serious in the case of services than of products. It is usually more difficult to maintain an inventory of services, and they are likely to be specialized and localized so that substitutes cannot readily be diverted or imported from elsewhere.

It will be noted that two considerations have been left out of the picture which normally, and rightfully, are given a good deal of weight in assessing a strike's impact—its duration and its scope. A short strike will obviously harm the public less than a long strike, and a strike which is confined to only one of a number of producers of a particular product or service will work less injury than a strike which blankets in all producers. Duration and scope are, of course, vitally important in determining the impact of a strike on the public, but they are significant only to the extent that they affect the three principal variables identified above. The length of a strike has an important bearing on the adequacy of stocks, for example, and the scope of a strike affects both the stock and the substitutes.

Industry strike patterns

How these three variables affect the public may be suggested by noting briefly the characteristic impact of strikes in three industries: coal, steel, and railroads.

Strikes in the coal mines were once among the

most frequent and troublesome types of stoppages. Union–management collaboration, in part
induced by the economic adversity of the industry, has now virtually eliminated all except small
and unofficial walkouts.

Bituminous coal stoppages between 1939 and
1950 revealed an impact generally greater on producers than on consumers, despite substantial
household dependence on coal in wintertime.
Consumers were normally protected by coal supplies already on hand, which could be stretched
by rationing if necessary. Only in a prolonged
strike, such as that of 1949 and 1950, which
lasted, off and on, for 145 days, did the hardship
on household consumers outweigh the hardship
on producers. In short coal strikes, the effect fell
almost entirely on suppliers of services to the industry, chiefly the coal-hauling railroads.

In the case of steel strikes, the "need" effect on
consumers is so negligible that it may be ignored.
Steel-using producers bear the brunt of the impact. With average stocks on hand, distributed (as
they usually are) in uneven fashion, the influence
on them begins to make itself felt after one or two
weeks and then mounts rapidly. After four weeks,
as steel stocks become depleted, these effects become more and more telling. They widen (blanket
in more firms) and deepen (reduce output more
drastically), and involve as well the suppliers of
such firms. In recent years, however, steel users
have somewhat softened the impact of a strike
by building up inventories in anticipation, thus
reducing the effect of strikes on stockpiles.

Strikes on the railroads show a different pattern. It appears that the first day of a rail stoppage weighs more heavily on travelers than on
shippers. But this initial hardship on consumers
remains relatively constant as the strike continues,
while the losses to producers mount rapidly. An
expansion in the scope of the strike, involving
more lines, or an increase in its duration intensifies the impact on producers more than proportionately: the improvisations to keep production
going in the face of a few nondeliveries cannot be
extended to cover many nondeliveries. Unless a
strike continues for long, however, it will not
seriously involve companies supplying goods or
services either to the railroads themselves or to
other rail-using industries.

The pattern of strike effects may be expected to
be quite different in other industries from the patterns in these three.

Governmental intervention in strikes

The right to strike has been defended by employers, as by unions, as a necessary instrument
to the making of a *private* determination of the
terms and conditions of employment. Restriction
of the right to strike carries with it a threat that
determination of the terms of employment may be
made by some outside authority; thus in wartime,
when work stoppages cannot be tolerated because
of the urgency of obtaining maximum production,
curbs on strikes *must* be accompanied by the
establishment of a tribunal (a War Labor Board
or a Wage Stabilization Board) empowered to
make final determination of wages and other matters in dispute between unions and managements.
To avoid the threat of such authoritative imposition of terms on the parties in normal times, both
have therefore defended the general principle of
freedom to strike. Since in the United States there
is a strong predilection for private decision as
against public determination, this attitude of
unions and managements has found general support.

When a strike involves a product or service
which is essential, however, and stocks of it are
inadequate or nonexistent, and there are no acceptable substitutes, then the principle of freedom
to strike confronts the principle of government
responsibility for public welfare. It is no longer
only an issue of whether the parties should be left
free to work things out for themselves, but also of
whether the public should be subjected to injury
in order to make that possible. There is no easy
reconciliation of these two opposing objectives of
private decision making and public welfare.

The most frequent and effective way of attempting such a reconciliation is through the
process of mediation. Mediation is often invoked
even when public hardship is not significantly involved on the theory that everyone would be better off if union and management could be helped
to reach agreement without a strike.

The Taft-Hartley Act provides for an independent federal mediation service (previously in
existence as a division of the Labor Department),
the function of which is to assist unions and man-

agements in the resolution of disputes. When two parties have reached an impasse, an independent third party—the mediator—may be able to bring them together by ascertaining from each, in confidence, the concessions which it might be disposed to make in order to arrive at agreement. On the strength of such confidences, the mediator may be able to propose—quite unofficially and informally—terms of settlement to which both parties are willing to agree, even though they had previously been afraid to make concession for fear it would be interpreted as a sign of weakness. He has no power to compel their acceptance of any terms, however. He can persuade and cajole, but he cannot order or dictate.

Mediation is the most effective device yet developed to head off strikes and still permit collective bargaining to function by allowing the parties to exercise their respective bargaining powers, including the union's "dare" to an employer to concede what it asks or face a shutdown. Mediation allows the challenge to be made and resisted, so that the parties can experience the full uneasiness which comes from having to decide whether to gamble with a strike or, alternatively, to settle on the other's terms or whatever compromise can be extracted. But if the decision to gamble is made or is on the point of being made, then the mediator enters and tries to make sure that the parties have explored every possible basis for agreement, and have given careful consideration to the costs associated with possible agreement now, as opposed to the costs of strike and some *eventual* agreement.

Every year mediation helps to achieve agreement in thousands of situations. A cadre of experts has been developed who are skilled in exposing the areas of basic disagreement, in pinpointing the potential for agreement, and then in encouraging the parties to stretch just a little more until they reach each other in the figurative handclasp that seals the bargain. The federal mediation service has encouraged a degree of specialization by its staff so that it has men who are especially knowledgeable about the economics and technology of particular industries.

Mediation is not all of a pattern. It varies in its timing and in its compulsion. It may be invoked before a strike occurs, indeed, in some instances

even before an impasse has been reached. In these cases of so-called "preventive mediation," the outside conciliator may sit with the parties beginning with the early bargaining sessions, in part to develop an inside knowledge of the background of negotiations in the event his services should be required, in part just to remind the parties by his presence that public interests are involved which they are not free to ignore, and in part because at critical stages he may be able to venture suggestions or perform services which will be useful in reaching agreement. In some instances, mediators may be invited in by the parties, their services being requested in the same way that the patient seeks a doctor. In other situations, a government may intervene on its own initiative in a last-ditch effort to effect an agreement.

The fact that there is nothing in the procedure which requires or compels agreement is both its strength and its weakness. The voluntary nature of agreement reached through mediation means that the parties come to it more willingly, but also that it is relatively ineffective in the face of intransigence on the part of either union or management. In the words of one union leader:

> Sometimes mediation helps. If the parties don't understand each other, mediation helps them to get some of the misunderstandings out of the way and get a better clarification of the areas of dispute. But if the parties are merely holding back for the purpose of maintaining the strongest bargaining position, then conciliation won't change that, because the problem there is not misunderstanding. They understand each other too well.

If mediation fails, most strikes can be allowed to occur—with some regret that they should be necessary but with no compulsion on governmental authorities to intervene more actively. After all, collective bargaining assumes that the parties will *normally* be free to bring pressure to bear on each other, including the pressure of a strike called by the union and "invited" by the employer. But the situation is quite different where public interest is significantly involved. In such cases, at some point during the strike, pressures begin to mount for some kind of action to "protect" the public. Irritation with the parties is expressed more and more frequently and finds its way into newspaper editorials, as in this one from the *St. Petersburg Times* of July 28, 1963, during a telephone stoppage:

> General Telephone Co. has 3,500 workers, some 2,800 of whom are on strike.
> In a single day last week, 58,000 telephones operated by General were out of service.
> Hospitals, doctors, police, fire protection and national defense officials, newspapers, radio and television status have had their communications cut off.
> But because this results from a labor-management dispute, the parties to the disagreement seem to feel perfectly free to kick around the rights and interests of a million other citizens.

Such expressions of unrest and impatience do not go unnoticed by governmental officials, whether municipal, state, or national. If a public-plaguing strike continues very long, the pressure on a political administration to intervene in the situation becomes irresistible.

By and large, a government's right to intervene depends on statutory authority. Even the President of the United States cannot simply order the parties to call off their private war or to submit their controversy to some third party for impartial judgment. He has no authority to override the legal rights of a citizen. This lack of independent power to intervene has often puzzled foreigners, who cannot understand why the Chief Executive can only scold even when the nation he leads is subjected to hardship or public interests are jeopardized. But in the absence of specific legislation granting him authority to act, such is the case, at least in peacetime.

We must turn, then, to an examination of the authority to act, in the face of strikes adversely affecting the public, which legislative bodies have granted political executives—specifically, which state legislatures have granted to governors, or Congress to the President. Such strikes or threatened strikes are frequently termed "emergency disputes" because of their public impact.

First, let us consider the means available to the Federal government. There are two relevant statutes; one applies to disputes generally and is contained in the Labor-Management Relations Act (Taft-Hartley Act) of 1947; the other is specific to the railroad industry and is contained in the Railway Labor Act, originally passed in 1926, and since amended.

Public-interest disputes

If the public is to be protected from especially injurious work stoppages, the government must have more authority than the mediation process permits. Consequently, another section of the Taft-Hartley Law gives the Federal government the power of temporarily terminating a strike. This provision was written into the act largely as a consequence of an unprecedented wave of strikes, many of them large-scale, which broke over the nation at the end of World War II.

The Taft-Hartley procedure leaves it to the discretion of the President to determine whether "a threatened or actual strike or lockout will, if permitted to occur or to continue, imperil the national health and safety." In the event of such determination, the President appoints an investigating committee which reports the "facts" concerning the strike but which is expressly forbidden by the act to recommend any basis for settlement. On the strength of such a report, the President may direct the Attorney General to obtain a court injunction forestalling the strike. This remains effective for sixty days. If no settlement has occurred within that time, the employees are polled on whether they are willing to accept the employer's last offer. Twenty more days are allowed for this. If the vote is negative, the Attorney General has no alternative but to request dissolution of the injunction after a total of eighty days, and the President washes his hands of the matter by referring the dispute to Congress for further action.

Experience under the emergency-strike provision of the Taft-Hartley Act has been mixed. During its first twenty years, through 1967, it was invoked twenty-eight times. In some instances the parties reached agreement after a board of inquiry had been appointed but before it rendered a report. In some instances a settlement was reached during the eighty-day period of the injunction. In other cases, after the employees had rejected the employer's "last offer" and the injunction had expired, a settlement was negotiated on terms more favorable to the strikers than the so-called "last offer." In seven cases the strike was renewed after the injunction had been dissolved. This spotty record under the Taft-Hartley procedures, along with the reluctance of both Democratic and Republican administrations to invoke it (though for different reasons), is explainable on several grounds. First, as we have seen, the procedure provides for temporary restraint of the strike but not for its settlement. The procedures may be exhausted and the strike, however injurious to the public, may then continue. Thus it puts the interests of the parties above those of the public in the final showdown.

Second, the courts have construed that the act's enforceable provisions run against the "official" union only. One union (the United Mine Workers) and its officers were fined large sums for refusing to order their members to return to work after an injunction had been issued, but the same union was held immune from penalty when its officers asked the members to recognize the government's injunction and go back to their jobs but the members refused. If the union cannot be identified with the membership, this opens the way to concerted action under the informal leadership of nonofficial "field generals," thereby avoiding even the postponement of a strike.

Third, the provision of the act that forbids the investigating board to make a recommendation for settlement actually robs the board of all function. The President appoints such a board of inquiry only because he believes the dispute is serious, and he does not need their documentation to bolster that belief. The ban on recommendations was presumably inserted to prevent such boards being used as de facto commissions of compulsory arbitration. A recommended settlement by a public board is actually a blame-placing device: it does not rely on the public's being particularly conscious of, or concerned about, the terms of settlement proposed; but it does count on its being hostile to whichever party continues the strike by refusing to agree to the recommendation. There is thus a presumption—however much it may be denied—that the parties *ought* to accept any recommendation which is made by a board of inquiry, and it was this presumption which some members of Congress found unpalatable, since it smacked of coercion. But if this coercive quality is sacrificed, then the chances of settlement are reduced, and the chance is increased that the dispute will be left to the parties to fight out by attrition. Since the act has provided no substitute for the public recommendation, there is good reason for believing that termination of the government's injunction might be expected, more frequently than was contemplated, to result in a resumption of the postponed strike.

The special procedure applying to disputes on the railroads has often been held up as a model of what governmental strike intervention should be. Actually, it is very similar to the Taft-Hartley procedure except that the fact-finding board which the President appoints after mediation efforts have failed is allowed to return a recommended settlement, which of course the parties are not obligated to accept. A strike at the end of the sixty-day period provided for in the act (thirty days for the board to conduct hearings and render a report and a subsequent thirty-day period for the parties to consider its findings) is perfectly legal.

As in the case of the Taft-Hartley emergency-strike provision, experience with the Railway Labor Act procedure has been mixed. Prior to World War II its use was restricted to major disputes and it successfully prevented any major railway strike from occurring. Subsequently, however, the act's strike procedure was invoked in a large number of instances, including minor disputes, and has proved singularly unsuccessful in achieving the desired result. Instead, the parties—especially the railroad brotherhoods—have felt increasingly free to disregard the fact-finding board's recommendations whenever these were not to their satisfaction. On these occasions, the President has sometimes personally intervened to avoid the threatened strike, or has appointed a new commission to review the original board's recommendations, usually resulting in terms more favorable to the reluctant party. Thus the brotherhoods have been conditioned to rejecting fact-finding reports as provided for under the Railway Labor Act, on the assumption that the government will not allow a strike to occur but instead will make further concessions to avoid it.

This "trading up" of terms was particularly marked in the case of the dispute which came to a head in 1963 involving the issue of "job rules," particularly the requirement of a fireman on diesel engines and the specification of the size of train-service crews, under the terms of existing agreements. Special panels had made recommendations for resolving the dispute, including a blue-ribbon Presidential Railroad Commission which spent two years examining the issues involved as well as a fact-finding board appointed under the Railway Labor Act. Failing agreement between the parties on the basis of any of the recommendations made by these public bodies, and with the brotherhoods refusing voluntary arbitration, the only method left for dealing with what was generally regarded as a threat to national safety was for Congress to pass special legislation providing for compulsory arbitration.

Then, in a 1967 wage dispute between six shop-craft unions and most of the major rail lines, this bizarre sequence of events occurred: The unions rejected the fact-finding board's recommendations; at the President's request, Congress passed a special law extending the normal no-strike period for another twenty days; the President appointed a special mediation panel whose recommendations were rejected by the unions; Congress passed another law extending the no-strike period, this time for forty-seven days; at the end of that time, the union struck for two days and Congress passed a third law, ordering the men back to work and setting up a third board to decide the issues. (Although the administration delicately termed this last step "mediation to finality," few observers could discern how it differed from compulsory arbitration.)

Thus the emergency-strike procedures on the railroads, once held up as a model, proved to be ineffective in the final analysis because they too, like the Taft-Hartley Act, failed to provide for settlement. At best, they postpone a strike and provide recommendations which may or may not be a basis for further negotiation.

State procedures for dealing with strikes

Strikes in public utilities, or on bus lines, or involving milk delivery or similar local services

which are "necessitous" in nature and which cannot be stockpiled, and which have no adequate substitutes, may be looked on as "emergencies" warranting further governmental action. But because they are internal to the state they do not fall within the provisions of the Taft-Hartley emergency-disputes procedures, which relate only to *national* effects of strikes.

A great many states—and a few municipalities as well—have created mediation boards which are available to assist unions and managements generally in coming to terms with each other. The value of these efforts is not open to question. But, just as in the case of national disputes, mediation constitutes no protection of the public if it fails to elicit a basis for agreement.

Some twenty-eight states have fact-finding provisions on their statute books, but many of these are inactive and most call only for report and recommendations, which may be persuasive to the parties but which also may not be.[6] Because fact finding constitutes no assurance to the public that its interests will be safeguarded in disputes affecting services of particular importance to it, some states have passed laws providing for compulsory arbitration in public-interest disputes or for state seizure of struck utilities. The first such legislation goes back to 1920, when Kansas established a Court of Industrial Relations empowered to settle disputes affected with the public interest. This act was struck down by the Supreme Court a few years later, however, as a deprivation of the rights of private property without due process of law. There followed a period of twenty-five years during which little effort was made to meet the constitutional objection. But in 1947 as a consequence, like the Taft-Hartley Act, of the wave of strikes which swept over the nation and involved local utilities as well as national industries, eleven states passed laws providing for compulsory arbitration or seizure.

Again, however, the Supreme Court intervened. In 1951 it overturned the Wisconsin act which provided for compulsory arbitration as part of a comprehensive system of industrial relations. This time the objection was to a conflict between the state law and federal legislation in the form of the Taft-Hartley Act, which expressly protected the right to strike. Several other states whose laws provided for binding arbitration subsequently either suffered the same fate as Wisconsin or allowed their legislation to lapse into disuse. But states whose disputes legislation provided for state seizure of a utility which was either on strike or subject to strike threat maintained their legislation in the belief that it contained no conflict with the federal law. For seizure presumably converted the workers into employees of the state, and the Taft-Hartley Act does not apply to public employees.

Missouri was one of the states having a seizure law, passed in 1947. It provided, as a first step, for a board of inquiry which would make a recommendation for settlement. If the parties rejected the recommended settlement and resorted to a strike, the governor was authorized to seize the utility if he found that public health or safety was jeopardized. Between 1950 and 1961 there were nine instances in which seizure was invoked. But the ninth case, involving the Kansas City Transit Company, was brought before the United States Supreme Court, and once again that Court found grounds for rendering a state strike-control law invalid. It ruled that the purported "seizure" was a fiction, and that the utility, when seized, continued operations very much as in the past, without active state management of its affairs. Looking beyond the fiction, the Court concluded that the Missouri law, like the Wisconsin act, was in conflict with federal protection of the right of private employees to strike.

Several other state seizure laws remain alive, even though inactive and their status now in doubt. The question of their validity presumably hinges on whether they constitute a proper exercise of the police power of the state and whether seizure by the state is real rather than illusory. Two of these acts will be described briefly.

Maryland legislation—the Public Utilities Disputes Act—was passed in 1956, as a consequence of unsuccessful efforts to mediate a thirty-seven-day strike in Baltimore's public transit system. The act provides for the governor's declaration of a state of emergency as the result of a strike, followed by seizure of the property in question. This is followed by a fifteen-day period of mediation, which the parties may extend to sixty days if they wish. Failing agreement, a three-man arbitration board may hold hearings and determine "the rates of pay, wages, hours and terms and conditions of employment" for the period of state operation. Seizure ends when the parties have reached agreement between themselves.[7]

The Virginia law, passed in 1947 and amended in 1952, employs the seizure device but eschews compulsory arbitration. Whenever the governor ascertains that there is a threat of substantial interruption in the services of a public utility, he may take possession of it. An administrator is appointed, which in practice has been the state corporation commission. Striking employees are free to refuse to work, as individuals, in which case they lose their employee status and the state is free to recruit replacements. The terms of employment remain as they were, and the state retains 15 percent of profits to compensate for its administrative costs. A utility may refuse to turn over its property to the state on the ground that no subsantial curtailment of services will actually result, in which case the issue may be tried in the courts. The property reverts to its private owners whenever an agreement is reached with the union.[8] The act was invoked on eleven occasions prior to 1953, but has not been used since then.

The validity of state initiative to outlaw strikes in specific situations is thus in doubt, though a congressional amendment to the federal labor law could readily authorize state action. Even without that permission, it is possible for states to curb strikes in some strategic areas, notably hospitals, whose employees are not covered by the Taft-Hartley Act. In 1963, for example, New York State passed legislation specifically protecting hospital employees in the right to unionize and bargain collectively but substituting compulsory arbitration for the right to strike.

Adequacy of strike controls

A number of neutral observers, such as mediators and labor relations experts in the universities, believe that all the fuss about the need for limiting strikes affecting the public interest is overdone. It is their opinion that for a variety of reasons the public exaggerates the importance of "the strike problem."

The absolute number of strikes in the United

States always sounds large. As Table 26-1 shows, in several years during the postwar period the number approached and even exceeded 5,000. The number of workers involved ranges between 1 and 3 million. Lost working time "normally" runs around 20 million man-days and in a year like 1959, when there was a major steel strike, was close to 70 million man-days, admittedly a lot of time.

But instead of looking at these absolute figures, let us relate them to others that provide some perspective. There are at least 150,000 labor contracts in the United States and perhaps one-half to two-thirds fall open each year; in the renegotia-

tion of nearly every one of these (particularly in the private sector, where most contracts are found), a strike might occur—but it actually happens in only about one out of twenty negotiations (5,000 strikes, of which several were still over grievances, out of 75,000 to 100,000 negotiations in 1968, for example.) Also, the 2.7 million strikers in 1968 represented less than 4 percent of the total number of people employed that year, and the total number of man-days they spent on strike added up—as Table 26-1 shows—to only 0.28 percent of total working time. In fact, since the expansion of the labor movement in the 1930s, strike idleness has surpassed 1 percent of

Table 26-1 *Work Stoppages in the United States, Selected Years, 1900–1968*

	Work stoppages			Man-days idle during year	
Year	Number	Average duration (calendar days)*	Number of workers involved (thousands)	Number (thousands)†	Percent of estimated total working time‡
1900	1,839	n.a.	568	n.a.	n.a.
1917	4,450		1,227		
1920	3,411		1,463		
1930	637	22.3	183	3,320	0.05
1937	4,740	20.3	1,860	28,400	0.43
1944	4,956	5.6	2,120	8,720	0.09
1946	4,985	24.2	4,600	116,000	1.43
1948	3,419	21.8	1,960	34,100	0.28
1950	4,843	19.2	2,410	38,800	0.33
1952	5,117	19.6	3,540	59,100	0.48
1955	4,320	18.5	2,650	28,200	0.22
1957	3,673	19.2	1,390	16,500	0.12
1959	3,708	24.6	1,880	69,000	0.50
1962	3,614	24.6	1,230	18,600	0.13
1965	3,963	25.0	1,550	22,300	0.15
1966	4,405	22.2	1,960	25,400	0.15
1967	4,595	22.8	2,870	42,100	0.25
1968	5,045	n.a.	2,650	49,000	0.28

* Figures are simple averages; each stoppage is given equal weight regardless of its size.
† Idleness at the establishments directly involved in a stoppage; figures do not include idleness at firms indirectly affected by a stoppage.
‡ "Estimated total working time" is computed by multiplying the average number of employed workers by the number of days worked by most employees in a given year. For the years prior to 1948, figures refer to total working time in the private, nonfarm sector; from 1948 to the present, figures refer to the total economy (including farm and government employment). The difference between the two measures is negligible, usually 0.1 percent or less for a given year.
SOURCE: U.S. Bureau of Labor Statistics.

total working time only in 1946 during the great wave of postwar strikes that led directly to the passage of the Taft-Hartley Act in 1947.

Moreover, the economic loss from strikes is far less than from other causes about which the public is less excited. In 1962, for example, about twice as many man-days were lost through industrial accidents as through strikes, and about *fifty* times more were lost through unemployment in that year.

If we concentrate our attention not on strikes in general but on the so-called "critical" or "emergency" strikes, there is some evidence that when the public begins to be seriously hurt, the pressures on the parties to settle become irresistible. Public officials, responding to generalized sentiment, find many direct and indirect ways of bringing their influence to bear. Professor Robert Livernash, who made an investigation of strikes in the basic steel industry, concluded: "History in steel indicates that once strikes really begin to be seriously felt over wide segments of the economy, pressure from those affected will in most instances bring about a settlement."[9] A union official once remarked, "There is concern all through the movement regarding public disapproval of strikes, and this of course is part of the pressure on the leader to find solutions to issues by means other than strikes." Thus there tends to be some public control over strikes "built in," as it were, without formal legislation or compulsion.

Related to this is the view that the public tends to squeal before it is hurt. Obviously no one likes to be inconvenienced, and the city dweller who has to find some other way to get to work because the buses are on strike, or the householder who continues to fear that an electric or telephone walkout may shut off his service even though supervisors have been able to keep operations close to normal so far during the strike, or the housewife who objects to driving to some central milk depot to pick up her milk during a drivers' strike, all have an understandable sense of grievance and annoyance. But none of them actually gets hurt; no one's security or health is really endangered.

Usually a striking union makes provision for the continuation of service in those instances where there is some special urgency—such as seeing to it that hospitals are provided for. Two

writers go so far as to conclude: "It would be difficult indeed to find a single instance in which a state strike control law has been invoked where great peril was actually threatening a community, although some cases involving gas or electric power could possibly have created such peril if allowed to continue."[10] Other authorities have made the same comment about national disputes. Henry Mayer, an attorney who frequently represents labor unions, said flatly at a Yale University conference in 1960, "There has been no such thing as a national emergency strike, that is, one which truly affected the health and safety of the public (judicial and presidential decisions to the contrary notwithstanding)."

In addition to public pressures on the parties when the strike begins to pinch (even if it still involves no peril), there are other pressures on the party to settle. Within the union, for example, the national office—which is shelling out strike benefits to local strikers—will want to make sure that everything possible is being done to resolve the dispute. Other local unions, whose members may experience layoffs because of the direct or indirect repercussions of the strike, will likewise bring their influence to bear on the striking union to be reasonable in its negotiations.[11]

On the side of the employer, his customers will want to assure themselves that he is making an earnest effort to settle on terms which they regard as fair if they are to give him support by making temporary arrangements to obtain their needs from other firms, rather than switch permanently to a firm which has shown it is less strike-prone. In industries where strike-insurance pools have been established, firms contributing to the insurance fund will want to know that it is not being drawn down by some member of the pool who has not yet learned how to handle its labor relations effectively. Thus, in the airlines industry, the president of United Air Lines was reported as saying that his company was contemplating withdrawing from that industry's mutual strike-aid program because the actions of some participating airlines had led to costly and "senseless" stoppages. "When you see the policies of some carriers so opposed to your own, then it's time to take action to protect your interests."[12]

There are observable tendencies for the strike

to be used less than formerly. The most comprehensive examination of this diminished reliance on the strike as an instrument of bargaining power has been made by Prof. Arthur Ross. It was his conclusion that over time the volume of strike activity will continue to decline, in part because the parties will become more sophisticated in the conduct of their relations, in part because political activity is a more effective means of accomplishing objectives which have become of increasing importance. While Professor Ross did not precisely expect the strike to "wither away" in the United States, as it has to a considerable extent in Northern Europe, he did expect lessened incidence.[13]

There are other reasons why one should expect diminution of strike activity. Formerly a primary method of obtaining an employer's recognition of a union was by striking his plant; representation elections have now made this procedure obsolete. Previously grievances no less than contract terms were settled by a play of relative bargaining powers that included final resort to the strike, but grievance arbitration has largely eliminated that role for work stoppages.

Looking back over the history of industrial relations in this country, one can spot industries where once strikes were endemic—the apparel industries in earlier years, bituminous coal during the forties, steel in the fifties—but where good relations now seem to obtain and strikes give every indication of subsiding (though such an expectation could quickly enough be shattered). The "bad boys" of industrial relations now appear to be found principally in the transportation industries—rail, air, maritime, and trucking, but history suggests that in time these industries too will learn to resolve their differences. The growth of automation, which makes strikes less effective than formerly, puts pressure on the unions to find alternative methods of reaching agreement with managements.

Finally, there is a prevalent view that even if strikes carry injury to the public, attempts to outlaw them will be even more injurious to society's basic interests. The cure will be worse than the disease or its symptoms. This conviction is based on the fear that once the pattern is set for the government to intervene to settle a strike, the

parties will cease to bargain with each other in good faith but will only make such offers and counteroffers as can be expected to help their case when the government takes over. Concessions will be avoided, in the expectation that an arbitration tribunal will take a party's last offer as its *minimum* concession, and in trying to "strike a balance" will ask both the union and the employer to give way still further. Thus concession and compromise, which are obviously essential to effective bargaining, will be avoided because they undermine the party's case before an arbitration board or a fact-finding commission.

The two processes are essentially different. Collective bargaining requires mutual accommodation, an effort by the parties to find common middle ground. Arbitration requires making as strong a case as possible and then digging in and holding that position. To impose arbitration thus frustrates bargaining. If the parties anticipate that their case may eventually find its way to the arbitrator, as any case might, they will tend to start building their case from the start, and in so doing will make arbitration inevitable. Thus the very existence of compulsory settlement procedures tends to jeopardize collective bargaining, which we have prized as contributing to free, private decision making, which is essential to any democratic society.

These are powerful arguments indeed against any additional attempts to strengthen procedures for curbing strikes. Even if present legislation is of doubtful reliance in protecting the public from inconvenience and injury resulting from strikes, as long as no genuine danger to national health or safety results, there are good grounds for putting up with the "nuisance" and treating it as a concomitant of the kind of freewheeling, individualistic society we tend to prefer. And if health or safety is threatened, then special steps can be taken as needed. This, at least, is one line of argument, and a rather persuasive one. But there *are* arguments on the other side as well, and we turn now to them.

Inadequacy of strike controls

Without denying the validity of much of the foregoing argument, some people (among them the authors) believe that the argument is overdone. Moreover, there are considerations which those who oppose any further interference with the right to strike ignore but which carry considerable weight of their own.

First, with respect to some of the points made above, there are telling rebuttals. It is perfectly true that the loss of man-days due to strikes is infinitesimal relative to total man-days worked or relative to days lost through injuries or sickness or unemployment. But these comparisons are irrelevant. The fact that strikes are concentrated as to industry, location, and time is the significant consideration. Even if there were just half a dozen strikes in the year, and these involved even fewer workers and resulted in even less time lost than now, nevertheless those six strikes could be serious occurrences if coming in strategic industries. Comparisons with total time lost or with sickness or with unemployment are beside the point.

The same consideration is relevant to the presumed decline in strike incidence. The fact that fewer strikes may occur now, at least relative to the potential number of strikes, carries no corollary to the effect that those strikes which do occur may not be injurious. Few people would argue that the police and firemen of a community should be privileged to engage in strikes on behalf of their demands. We feel that the continuity of their service is essential to community welfare. The fact that the number of strikes in the community at large may be relatively fewer than in earlier years does not make us more tolerant of strikes by police and firemen. But the same consideration has equal relevance to other essential services. Because strike incidence is lower now than in earlier years does not make a critical strike, when it does occur, less critical.

Again, it may be true that industries like coal, which were strike-prone in earlier years, have learned how to avoid interruptions in service. This does not necessarily imply, however, that other industries will not take their place as the problem children of the nation or community. There has hardly been a period during which some industry or set of industries has not presented a peculiar industrial relations problem. At the present, as we have noted, the transportation complex fills this spot. It may be that unions and managements in railroads and trucking, on the sea and docks, and in the air will eventually "mature" their relationships, but even should this devoutly wished development occur, we can be reasonably sure that in the absence of new procedures for resolving disputes, other industries will take their place as leaders of the strike parade.

While strikes may be viewed as the price society must necessarily pay for the privilege of decentralizing decision making in economic matters so that workers share in decisions under which they must live, it is also possible that at least some strikes are an *unnecessary* price which the public is paying for less efficient and less responsible negotiation than it has reason to expect from the parties. It may be the price the public is being asked to pay for a willful exercise of private power which, rather than being sanctified as pure democracy, should be called to account for its disregard of the rights of others. While we wish to preserve the system of private decision making, it does not follow that the private decision makers should feel at liberty to trample heedlessly on the reasonable expectations of the society of which they are an integral part.

There are two aspects to this line of thought. One involves the preservation of archaic collective-bargaining systems, the "industrial organization" of the process. This is a problem which confronts some other countries (England, for example) even more than us, but it is present in the United States to a degree which cannot be ignored. An industry which is fragmented into a number of bargaining units and separate collective agreements may find itself (and the public along with it) subjected to numerous, recurring strike threats, as one after another of the unions with which the company or industry deals presents itself and makes its demands. Instead of an agreement which settles the terms for an industrial unit as a whole, in a "federal" sort of way, we operate as though grass-roots democracy (small-scale bargaining units) must be given free expression. Yet we do not follow such a philosophy in community affairs generally. Although local option and states' rights are perennial issues, they have not prevented us from assigning specified major issues affecting all our people to the national government. In industry, it is entirely feasible to give local units the opportunity to make decisions for themselves in matters which are of primary concern to them, but it is anarchic to allow numbers of small groups to retain the power to shut down a whole industry or major segments of it.

In discussing the problems of the maritime industry, for example, the *New York Times* has called attention to "an inexcusable multiplicity of unions any one of which can cripple the industry, personal feuding among maritime labor leaders, and a tendency of unions to whipsaw the industry helplessly by setting contract termination dates at different times for different unions."[14] We may properly think of this as immature or primitive industrial relations organization in this industry. It does not appear unreasonable for society as a whole to pressure the parties into rationalizing their relationships in ways which, while preserving private decision making, make sure that it takes place in intelligent organizational patterns.

The second aspect of this matter of irresponsibility in collective bargaining lies in an attitude on the part of some unions and managements that, because the law gives them a freedom of action which includes the right of stoppage, then negotiation is a personal matter which they may carry on in their own idiosyncratic fashion, like actors on a stage or players at a casino. Society watches while they perform, but society should not interfere with the performance. It may applaud or hiss but it should not stop the show or game.

Examples of this attitude come readily to hand. Even as warm a friend of labor as Sen. Wayne Morse of Oregon denounced the leaders of the railroad brotherhoods in scathing terms for their irresponsible conduct in the work-rules issue which stretched over a period of years. Repeatedly they rejected a basis for settlement (both substantive and procedural) worked out by objective panels and commissions and accepted by railroad managements, until the only alternative to a nationwide rail strike was congressional provision for compulsory arbitration in 1963.

In the course of the New York City newspaper strike of 1962 and 1963, the United States Secretary of Labor, the Governor of New York State, and the Mayor of New York City appointed a three-man "Board of Public Responsibility." Among its conclusions were the following:[15]

... The printers' strike which occasioned the shutdown of all the newspapers was not a move of last resort to which the printers were driven after a full exploration of the possibility of settlement. It was a deliberate design formed by the printers' representatives as the opening gambit in negotiations. Undoubtedly the aim was to secure contract benefits markedly better than the benefits which could be expected in the normal course of bargaining and the course adopted was born of conviction that negotiations to the desired end could not be effective and would not be worth undertaking until after a strike of long duration, which would probably put some papers out of business and bring the rest to their knees.

Then, after reviewing the importance of newspapers to the economy of the local community as well as to the political activity of a democratic society, particularly in times of important public issues, it added: "Deliberately to plan such a prolonged shutdown and to resort to the maneuvers appropriate to the consummation of such a plan, we hold to be a clear breach of this duty to the public, and a matter of grave consequence."

The board continued, by way of indictment of the procedures followed by the printers' representatives:

... There has been a complete failure of the bargaining process in this matter from the moment that the printers stated their terms until the present time. Indeed, it must be said that there has been no real bargaining. A strike was called as a preliminary to bargaining; bargaining was intended to be postponed for a long period until the strike had taken its toll, and bargaining has not been resumed at any time up to the start of the hearings before the Board.

It is not only the unions which at times have used power willfully. Managements too on some occasions have imposed unwarranted hardship and inconvenience on communities by intransigent attitudes and policies at variance with the society of which they are a part, using their corporations as devices to express personal prejudice. There is a proper distinction to be made between complete freedom to express opinions in a democratic society and a limited freedom to employ public-created and public-sanctioned organizations to impose those opinions on others.

The view that collective bargaining and arbitration are two essentially different processes, even conflicting with each other, is probably exaggerated. We commonly refer to the increasing sophistication of the collective-bargaining process, but at the same time we tend to think of arbitration in its primitive, split-the-difference form. Arbitration too, with practice, can and to some extent has become more sophisticated. As a result, an arbitration board, in making its award, can take into account the degree of genuine bargaining between the parties prior to the eventual referral to arbitration, thus at least partially nullifying the stratagem of a party's adopting a rigid position because it anticipates arbitration. An arbitration board, by questioning and analysis, can often come so close to what the parties would themselves have ultimately decided, if they had been allowed to go to strike, that its decision may be no more compulsory on the parties than the compulsion of the strike itself.

We think of arbitration as an *imposed* settlement—imposed by an outsider who is forced to behave like a little Caesar, and we contrast this with collective bargaining as producing a voluntary settlement, mutually acceptable to the parties. But these are stereotypes the reexamination of which is overdue. A settlement which is "voluntarily" accepted by one party because the other has "beaten" it into submission may be no more voluntary and no less imposed than a decision rendered by some neutral (not a Caesar) who is genuinely trying to be *responsive* to the needs and interests of both the parties.

Professor Galbraith has popularized the notion of the "affluent society." Without necessarily accepting that term as applicable throughout society generally, we can agree that the income position of workers has improved materially in recent years. Documentation was provided in Chapter 19. Workers at higher wage levels are able to save more. Through dues payments to the unions, strike funds can be accumulated out of which benefits are paid to supplement savings in time of stoppage. In two or three states strikers are entitled to draw unemployment compensation after a somewhat longer waiting period than usual—

seven weeks in New York, for example. The net effect is that strikers are now often enabled to withstand a stoppage of longer duration without serious economic hardship. During the New York newspaper strike of 1962 and 1963, for example, as the strike passed its seventh week the average journeyman was drawing strike benefits and unemployment compensation which added up to almost as much as his normal take-home pay. What pressure was there on him to settle?

On the other hand, employers in some industries have turned to strike-insurance funds, as we previously noted, similarly softening the economic impact of a stoppage. In other instances, a strike may even be welcome as a means of working off accumulated inventory, as in the 1959 steel dispute, or inventories may be built up in anticipation. Thus the economic pressure on the struck employer to come to terms with the union may be materially muted. The strike can go on longer without as much hardship as formerly to either strikers or management. It is only the public whose position is worsened. Affluence and strategy have made it possible—perhaps even necessary—for the parties to wait each other out longer. Table 26-1 indicates the increase in the average duration of strikes over the past decade. But as strikes become cheaper for the parties, they become costlier to the public. Is the public supposed to be totally unconcerned about this development, treating it as simply part of the private game of the parties?

The view that history and experience have established that strikes are really not so injurious to the public as it imagines they are going to be in anticipation, and that therefore the public should stop crying before it is hurt, and that government officials can afford to temporize with public protest, adopts an attitude more Spartan than present-day economic life warrants. It seems hardly necessary that the public should *actually* be subjected to peril before it is decided that a strike should be curbed. The test of threat to public health or safety seems an excessively harsh standard to apply to a society which has built up reasonable expectations about the continuity of services and supply. If the public must be injured before the private parties are compelled to adjust their differences, this amounts to placing private interests before public ones. This is indeed a peculiar conception of what democracy implies.

There is another reason why it is misleading to argue that because past strikes have not brought chaos and disaster, this proves there is little need for the government to step into future strikes. This reasoning might be persuasive *if* there had been no government intervention in the past. If, for example, "free collective bargaining" had been the practice in steel over the past thirty years and no emergency strikes had resulted, then one could indeed argue that the government should stay out of future steel disputes. As everyone knows, however, the government has repeatedly and vigorously—if not always skillfully—intervened in past steel strikes, as well as in most coal, maritime, longshoring, railroad, and other critical disputes. Injunctions, seizures, White House pressure, and even compulsory arbitration have all been used to stop strikes in these industries. How, then, do you prove that the government should stop intervening in future strikes by arguing that no emergencies had developed when the government intervened in the past?

We therefore believe that, in certain critical situations, the strike has become an anachronistic device. In a society which has become increasingly articulated, and which relies—or struggles to rely —more heavily on rational social processes to complement its rationalized production processes, it is time to search for reasonable alternatives to the strike—if not generally, at least in situations that may be especially annoying (not necessarily imperiling) to the public. As the president of the British Trades Union Congress remarked in its 1959 conference, there is need for a new approach to industrial problems, and even the strike may have to be abandoned as a method of solving industrial difficulties—providing some suitable alternative to it is found. Although defending the general role of the strike in union–management relations, the special panel convened by the Committee for Economic Development concluded:[16]

Opinions as to how emergency labor disputes should be handled have been changing in recent years. Time and changed conditions have influenced these views. It is now clear that the state of world affairs, political as well as economic, calls for reassurance to the American people that irresponsibility in the conduct of labor-management affairs in vital industries or at unusually hazardous times will find our government able to defend the public interest.

One difficulty with the view that the strike as presently practiced should not be subjected to further limitations, in the interests of private decision making, lies precisely in that it weakens our search for a preferable substitute. There is something primitive about grown men walking the pavements carrying signs bearing epithets directed at people with whom they expect to resume a working relationship, and engaging in efforts to inflict sufficient economic injury on the opposing group until it yells "uncle." Yet there are people who quite literally glory in the strike as a "democratic" device. It is, of course, democratic to allow individuals to decide for whom they will work and on what terms, and it is, of course, democratic to allow work groups to join in deciding their conditions of employment. But to go on from there to assert that *therefore* the strike is a *sine qua non* of democratic society is a *non sequitur*. If we can find a more suitable instrument by which people can help decide the conditions under which they work, we will be improving and refining, not deteriorating, the democratic process.

The number of people employed in the public sector has increased remarkably in recent years, as we noted in Chapter 2, and typically the right to strike is denied to such employees. Are we thereby disintegrating our democracy by forbidding them the right to affect the terms of their employment? Logically we would have to respond "yes," if we believe that democracy implies participation in framing the conditions under which one works. But we do not propose to remedy this situation, even though we have come to recognize it more clearly, by granting public employees the right to strike. If any remedy is made, it will have to be through a substitute for the strike. If for the growing number of public employees, then why not for others as well?

The form of strike controls

If we are looking for some means of preventing strikes from occurring when they would be espe-

cially detrimental to public welfare, we should begin by itemizing the requirements of the alternative means of inducing a settlement. These are
two. First, the outcome must be uncertain. Neither
party should be able to guess what the results of
the government's intervention will be. The gamble
which is basic to the strike must be present also
in the substitute for the strike. If it were not,
whichever side could be *certain* of a more favorable result by refusing agreement and forcing the
issue to some third-party resolution would do so.
The consequence would be to put an end to
genuine collective bargaining, as opponents of
strike controls fear. Second, if we are interested
in preserving the system of collective bargaining,
in the sense of a method by which the employees
through their union can negotiate with management the terms and conditions under which they
shall work, then we must leave both union and
management with some effective bargaining *power*.
Bargaining cannot operate without bargaining
power, and this means that each party must have
some means of making disagreement on its terms
costly to the other party. Agreement will come
only when, for one or the other, the cost of agreeing on the other's terms is less than the cost of
disagreeing.

Each side will, of course, retain in its hands the
power to affect the cost of *agreement*—by the
size of the demands it makes and by its offer of
cooperation to reduce the other's cost of concession. But the power to make disagreement costly
requires social sanction. Society has ruled out
violence, and the secondary boycott which entraps
neutral employers, and the firing of employees for
union activity, and other devices which it regards
as too crude to be permitted. It has continued to
sanction the strike, however, and this remains the
most effective means which each party has at its
disposal to impose on the other a cost of disagreeing on its demands. The union can threaten
to call a strike, and the company can threaten to
take a strike, so that either can invoke the stoppage rather than concede the other's terms. If the
right to strike is now to be withdrawn, even if
only in a limited number of instances which are
considered especially inconveniencing to the public, some alternative means must be placed in the
parties' hands if collective bargaining is to be

maintained as the primary reliance. Otherwise,
there would be no reason for either party to concede what the other wants. With no cost of disagreement, the cost of agreeing on the other's
terms would always be higher, and hence there
would never be a negotiated settlement.

With these two requirements in mind, let us
consider what kinds of strike controls might be
effective.

An arsenal of weapons

The approach which has been most frequently
suggested, and which probably has the greatest
support among those who believe that some limitation of the strike in public-interest disputes is
needed, usually goes by the name of "the arsenal
of weapons." It proceeds on the premise that if
some single method of government intervention is
provided for, the uncertainty element is reduced.
The parties can judge from experience with that
method whether one of them is likely to get better
terms from intervention than from a negotiated
settlement. Intervention will be forced by whichever party expects to benefit from it. Use of an
arsenal of weapons rather than a single weapon
seeks to prevent that result.

Let us confine our attention to national disputes
and see how this approach might work. Whenever
the President determined that public welfare was
likely to be seriously affected by a strike or threatened strike, he could invoke any of a number of
actions. Since each of these actions would affect
the parties in different ways, some favorable and
some unfavorable, and the parties could never be
sure which way would be employed, they would
be left facing uncertainty. If they did not resolve
their own dispute, they could reasonably well
predict that the government would intervene, but
they could not predict how, nor how they would
be affected. Hence they would be under some inducement to reach agreement on their own terms.
Like the strike, government intervention would
be a gamble. As Walter Reuther once remarked:

> At the point where there is a great deal of
> uncertainty as to what the Government will do
> when it intervenes, you will get a greater sense
> of urgency at the bargaining table to settle than
> you will when the parties know in advance

what is going to happen, because it is already predetermined. We think that any steps that are predetermined by law tend to minimize the pressure at the bargaining table, and anything that minimizes the pressure makes for inability to get together.

As another consideration, if a single procedure is adopted, it is likely to be used either too frequently or not frequently enough. If it is a weapon which is sufficiently innocuous that the government feels free to employ it even in less important situations, it is likely to be invoked without discretion. If it is a weapon of such power that the government feels privileged to use it only in the most extreme circumstances, it will probably, like massive retaliation generally, lie unused even in situations which call for some government action. The advantage of the arsenal of weapons is that the government is free to employ whichever of a number of devices is most suited to the particular occasion.

Mediation   What are some of the weapons available for the government's strike-control arsenal? First, we should certainly include mediation— whether by the regular federal mediation service or by outsiders called in for that purpose. We have already discussed the functioning of mediation and will say no more about it here. But, as we know, mediation does not ensure a settlement, so we move on to other "heavier" weapons if they should be needed.[17]

Injunction   The injunction is already part of the federal strike-prevention machinery. It differs from other devices in that it is solely within the power of the courts to dispense, and the administrative arm of government must apply to the courts for its grant. The traditional basis for a court's award is that some irreparable injury would be committed if an act—here a strike— were not forestalled; under Taft-Hartley a finding that the strike threatens national health or safety substitutes for the irreparable injury.

An injunction may be of indefinite duration or, as in Taft-Hartley, of specified duration, there of eighty days. In either event, the only thing an injunction accomplishes is to force delay of strike action; it does nothing to encourage or assure

settlement. If settlement is the objective, then the injunction must be coupled with some other device. As a short-run means of preventing strikes, the injunction is without equal. As an instrument for settling the dispute which gives rise to the strike threat, the injunction alone is virtually useless.

As generally employed in labor disputes, the injunction is basically inequitable. It is always on the side of the party which favors preservation of the status quo, and it is always against the interests of the party seeking change. In the post-World War II period, it has usually been the union which has been pressing for new advantage; hence, it has been the unions which have been most vociferous in condemning the Taft-Hartley injunction procedure.[18] But in a severe enough depression to induce employers to seek wage cuts, or in time of a particular company's or industry's economic adversity so that it seeks relief from an existing collective agreement, it would be the union which would benefit from retention of the status quo. Thus it was the railroad brotherhoods which in 1962 petitioned the courts—unsuccessfully—to enjoin railroad management from instituting new work rules which would have eliminated the jobs of many of their members. But aside from any question of equity, it is to be emphasized that the injunction provides no settlement but only delay. It is not a remedy but a relief.

Seizure   Seizure and operation of a strikebound company or one threatened with strike is another weapon which the government might invoke. In this case either of two procedures might be followed. Existing conditions might be retained indefinitely, so that, as with the injunction, the action would redound to the benefit of the party seeking maintenance of the status quo. Alternatively, the government, as operator of the property, might be empowered to make such limited changes in terms and conditions as it might deem appropriate. In either event, some pressure would be felt by the parties to come to agreement—the union because it presumably would gain less than it sought, and the management in order to regain possession of its property. Presumably the parties would be kept in greatest uncertainty by legislation authorizing the government either to freeze terms or to make changes in them, as it deemed desirable.

Neither injunction nor seizure provides for actual settlement of a dispute. Eventually, then, if the parties prove adamant in their refusal to come to agreement, there is no recourse except to provide a settlement for them—some version of compulsory arbitration. Otherwise a strike would be precipitated as soon as the injunction was lifted or the firm restored to its private owners. But the kinds of arbitration which might be invoked are many and varied. An arsenal of weapons could authorize at least several.

Fact finding   Fact finding might be included as one of these, although it is, unfortunately, not often conceived as such. The term itself is anomalous, since the finding of facts is the least important part of the device. What is really meant is an advisory recommendation by a board whose prestige is such that its opinion cannot be lightly disregarded by the parties. But if the opinion is advisory only, what assurance is there that it will be accepted?

As long as it is not made compulsory on the parties, it can be used as a species of voluntary arbitration. By prior sounding out, the government can invite assurances from the parties that— barring an egregiously outrageous decision—they will be willing to be bound by the recommendations of such a board. The proviso gives them confidence that they will not be stuck with an impossible award, while their assurance relieves the government of the danger that rejection of the board's award will force a move to more drastic means of compelling agreement or capitulation to the recalcitrant party. Without such an understanding it is doubtful that fact finding should be attempted.

The desirability of providing the government with a battery of weapons, rather than a single procedure which is known in advance, is well illustrated in the case of fact finding. If this is substantially the only device which is made available to the government, as is virtually true under both the Railway Labor and Taft-Hartley Acts, and if its use is made compulsory once a strike has been found to threaten a national emergency, two undesirable consequences follow. Its use is

forced even in situations where it is known in advance that the board's findings will be rejected by the parties, so that the device itself becomes discredited. And second, if the parties realize that the board's services will necessarily be invoked before a strike is permitted, bargaining will be undermined and the process of voluntary agreement short-circuited.[19]

Compulsory arbitration   If there is no assurance that the parties will accept a fact-finding recommendation, there is one other alternative to actual compulsory arbitration. To some extent the specter of compulsory arbitration would encourage the parties to arrive at their own agreement, since neither unions nor managements ordinarily welcome outside intervention. In general, the possibility of compulsory arbitration could be expected to act as a leveler of relative bargaining powers in the negotiation process. One might reasonably expect that the weaker party would welcome an arbitral determination more, since it would always hope that an outside settlement might be more influenced by rational argument and analysis than by power. If that is indeed the case, then the stronger party might be induced to make concessions to the weaker simply to forestall outside intervention. This would not be a wholly undesirable result.

In any event, compulsory arbitration might be made the instrument for encouraging the parties to develop disputes machinery of their own, as in the construction industry. There, a national appeals board has been established, to which all disputes over work jurisdiction in the industry, whether local, regional, or national, may be taken for decision, either advisory or compulsory, but with the expectation that in either event the disputants will normally abide by the ruling. Pan American World Airways has entered into an agreement providing for binding arbitration over new contract terms with three unions with which it negotiates. The government could encourage similar action in other industries by holding out the possibility, as one of its weapons in the arsenal, that it might compel binding arbitration unless the parties themselves set in motion their own disputes machinery to forestall a stoppage and assure a settlement. The election of this alternative might be regarded by the parties as preserving the voluntary nature of their relation, but they might not have so opted except for the alternative of a government board. This might even be construed as simply one variation on the basic theme of compulsory arbitration.

That "basic theme" would consist of a board appointed by the government and empowered to conduct hearings and to render a decision which would be binding on the parties. Such a board would be composed either of representatives of union, management, and the public (hence referred to as tripartite) or solely of neutral experts. If this is the basic theme, the variations relate either to the powers of the board or to its composition.

One interesting variation of the first type was tried briefly and without much success under the German Weimar Republic, but it continues to possess a certain appealing logic. Under this procedure, the arbitration panel is limited to a choice of confirming either the union position or the management position, but it may not adopt any compromise terms. The obvious intent is to drive the parties toward reasonable bargaining offers which will make voluntary settlement more likely, since with an unreasonable position an arbitration award—if it comes to that—is certain to go to the other party. In some circumstances this procedure could, of course, result in an unreasonable award which might discredit the system, but it is possible to imagine situations in which a rumored intent to invoke this particular type of arbitration might be effective on an intransigent party.[20]

If what is wanted is an element of uncertainty that encourages the bargainers to arrive at their own settlement, several second-type variations of the compulsory-arbitration theme (that is, involving the composition of the board) can be added to the arsenal. One might be to impanel a citizens' arbitration board at random, as is done with the selection of juries; people's names could be drawn from a telephone directory, for example, so that a board of five might be composed of a housewife, a taxi driver, an engineer, a retired school teacher, and a proprietor of a hardware store. This would be arbitration by *inexperts,* by a "jury" of average citizens. Or alternatively an arbitration board of three or five might be drawn at random from a preselected list of perhaps a hundred "experts,"

including not only neutrals but also corporation industrial relations executives and union officials. In this approach, the randomly chosen board might conceivably be composed of two union officials and a professor of labor economics, or possibly a lawyer, a professional arbitrator, and a vice-president of United States Steel. In both cases, the parties would have to decide in advance whether they wanted to take a chance with a board whose composition might not be to their liking.

Imposing a cost of disagreement

The government's arsenal of weapons, any of which could be invoked to prevent a strike, might thus include mediation, the injunction, seizure, fact finding, the parties' own voluntary arbitration as an alternative to compulsory arbitration, and several varieties of the latter. The decision as to which weapons were to be included, and the conditions under which they might be invoked, and the manner in which they could be employed (the standards which the government or its agents would have to follow) would be up to Congress. There is one basic difficulty with this approach, however. While it would effectively satisfy the uncertainty prerequisite, it would fail to meet the second condition which we said any strike-control procedure should meet—that it permit each of the parties to inflict, as well as bear, a cost of disagreeing on the other's terms.

For either party, if it was seeking some change in terms, a refusal to agree to the other's position would be virtually costless. It might not get all that it sought, but it would probably get something out of an arbitration award, and at practically no expense to itself. A union could seek an increase in wages or an employer could demand an easing of work rules, and when the other party refused to concede, could threaten to call or force a strike. And as long as it was reasonably certain that the government would invoke its strike-prevention authority (because the situation was quite clearly one affecting public convenience or health or safety), it could be sure that its case would be heard before an impartial body. The worst that could possibly happen would be that the arbitration board would turn down its demand altogether, but it would stand a good chance that the board would give it something of what it sought. Thus, at the worst, there would be no cost to making the effort, and at the best, it might get what it wanted without any of the inconvenience or expense attending a strike. This would have the effect, then, of undercutting collective bargaining. In any industry affected by the public interest, whichever party was seeking a change would press a dispute to the point of strike threat, and when the strike-control procedure was invoked—under precisely the kind of circumstances for which it was designed—the party would present its arguments to the board and hope for the best.

To be sure, the other bargainer might have made some concession in the course of negotiations, so that the party making the demands might be *uncertain* whether it would get any more from an arbitration board, but this would mean that a union or management, whenever confronted with demands by the other, would always have to make enough of a concession to create that uncertainty. This would put a premium on importunacy—ask and it shall be given—again undermining the legitimate use of collective bargaining.

In short, because compulsory arbitration involves the party making demands in virtually no cost of disagreeing, while imposing on the other party a cost of disagreeing (namely, the probability of an award giving away something it now enjoys), it *creates* a situation conducive to unsettled disputes; it helps to cause the very "emergencies" which it is intended to curb.

If the public needs stronger measures to deal with strikes adversely affecting its interests, what is needed is some procedure which—like the strike itself—imposes costs on *both* parties when it is invoked, so that *each* faces a cost of disagreeing with the other, whether the other is asking something or refusing something.

One method of achieving this result has been termed by some a "statutory" or "nonstoppage" strike and by others a "semistrike."[21] At the time when negotiations between union and management have broken down and a stoppage of work would normally occur, and in those cases where it has been determined that public hardship would result, a governmental order would direct the employees to remain on their jobs, unless as individuals they chose to resign. It would direct management to continue production. The interest of the public would thus be preserved.

But to encourage the parties to effect agreement, and to permit them to impose on each other the same kind of penalties that a strike would have permitted, each would be limited to earning less than it would normally have received. By threatening to stand a strike or to call a strike, each of the parties indicates its willingness to subject itself to some loss in order to impose a loss on the other. But instead of the "total" loss which a shutdown would impose, each is penalized by, say, half the loss while continuing operations. The exact formula is immaterial, but let us say that this result would be achieved if the workers were given only 50 percent of normal wages while the company's returns were reduced to out-of-pocket expenses plus one-half of fixed costs. Thus both parties would get something more than they would have if they had shut down operations—they would earn some return for their continued production. But each would sustain some loss, proportionately equal to what the loss would have been under a stoppage, as a means of bringing pressure to bear on each other.

With operations continuing and with partial losses bearing on the parties, the contest of economic endurance would be on. It would continue until one or the other or both of the parties agreed to concessions that made settlement possible. At this point the statutory strike would be ended, and the parties would revert to full earnings under a new agreement.

The logic of this approach retains its appeal, but it has fatal weaknesses which almost ensure that it will not be used. The "formula" which would be needed to balance losses would be too complex or subtle for the average worker to accept as *obviously* fair, so that the equity of the relative bargaining powers would always be open to question. Further, there would probably be resistance in many quarters to the notion of workers continuing on their jobs without being fully paid, or of a company's contributing its production facilities without full recompense for the use of its property.

In light of these criticisms (which, while damaging, are not directed to the logic of the proposal), a much simpler but perhaps even more effective approach might be tried. Since the problem of compulsory arbitration arises from the fact that it is virtually costless, the evident solution is to make compulsory arbitration costly. First, the parties, by failing to settle their own problems, subject themselves to the public's protection of *its* rights through compulsory arbitration—they are *required* to submit their dispute to a neutral board. But at the same time, the public makes the board's services very expensive, about as expensive as a strike might be if it were allowed. Thus the parties have as much of an inducement to resolve their own disagreement as they would in the normal collective-bargaining situation.

The "cost" of arbitration would in effect be a fine, but it need not be labeled as such. The justification for putting a high price on the board's services could simply be that so much is at stake that every conceivable expense should be amply provided for. The cost might range from perhaps $25,000 to $100,000 a day for each party. The same charge could be made to each party, if that were thought preferable, or a sliding scale could be introduced which would base the union's cost on the number of members involved in the strike and the company's cost on its assets, with some maximum in both cases. If a major strike in steel, involving several hundred thousand employees and billions in corporate assets, should be judged to affect adversely the public's interests, for example, we might assume that the compulsory-arbitration procedure would be invoked, and that the costs of the board's services might be set at the maximum limit (say $100,000 a day), so that a thirty-day arbitration proceeding would cost each party $3 million.

Once arbitration was begun, the length of the proceedings would depend on the parties. Each would want to take enough time to present an effective case, but it would be restrained from taking more time than needed by the cost of each day's proceedings. At the same time, just as a strike might be prolonged by one party to bring greater pressure on the other, it is possible that one of the parties might purposely drag out the hearings in order to impose constantly mounting costs on the other party. Neither side would be permitted to bring the hearings to a close independently—except by reaching agreement with the other, again just as in the case of a strike.

In this kind of procedure, the workers would stay on the job and receive full pay for their work, and the company would continue to produce and receive full return for what it sold. There would be no subtle formulas—everyone could understand a price of so many thousand dollars a day for the services of a government agency. Thus this approach would accomplish what the statutory strike attempts, and much more simply and acceptably. At the same time it would meet the two requirements for an effective strike-control procedure: it would create uncertainty as to the outcome, and it would leave each of the parties with bargaining power which it could bring to bear on the other, so that the basic collective-bargaining process would not be undermined by resorting to this "emergency" device.

In 1970 President Nixon proposed several radical changes in the laws governing national emergency strikes. He asked Congress, first, to scrap the much-criticized emergency provisions of the Railway Labor Act and to place railroad and airline bargaining under the Taft-Hartley Act. Further, he proposed that the Taft-Hartley provisions be amended to give the President three new options, any one of which he could select after an eighty-day injunction had failed to head off a shutdown in transportation—that is, in the rail, air, maritime, or trucking industries. In that event, the President could extend the cooling-off period for up to another thirty days, or require partial operation of the industry for a period of up to six months, or impose that type of compulsory arbitration under which a special panel would choose between the final written positions of the parties in a dispute.

In the authors' opinion, the Nixon proposals offer a constructive attempt to meet the weaknesses of existing strike controls, but they were promptly attacked by both labor and some segments of management and their fate in Congress was still uncertain when this was written.

Strikes by government employees

In Chapter 8 we described the ways in which the laws governing union activity in the public sector have long differed from those regulating union activity in private industry. This gap has narrowed in many jurisdictions and on many issues in recent years, as the Federal and several state and local governments have belatedly moved to assure government workers most of the same basic rights to join a union without reprisal, and to negotiate with their employers, which private-industry workers have enjoyed for thirty-five years. On the crucial subject of the right to strike, however, the gap between the private and public sectors remains nearly as large as ever. The Taft-Hartley Act called for the immediate discharge of any federal employee who engaged in a strike, and this provision was replaced in 1955 by an even tougher statute (Public Law 330) which declares strike activity by a federal employee to be a felony, punishable by loss of job, a fine of up to $1,000, and a jail sentence of up to one year. As for strikes by state and local government workers, these are usually prohibited by state law or enjoinable under common law. In 1970, however, Hawaii and Pennsylvania adopted laws permitting certain public employees to engage in strikes that do not endanger the "health, safety, or welfare of the public."

But as every newspaper reader knows, there has been an increasing number of strikes by government workers in recent years. And how do you prosecute 200,000 postal workers for violating a strike ban, or 50,000 teachers in New York City, or the many police and firemen who are experimenting with near-strike techniques such as mass sick calls (known as the "blue flu," when large numbers of policemen are suddenly too sick to report for work) or refusals to perform anything but emergency duties (no writing of traffic tickets or making fire inspections of buildings)? And even if you figure out how to enforce these strike bans, how can collective bargaining be meaningful when the public employer knows that he cannot be hurt by refusing to accede to any union demand, however reasonable?

It is no longer enough to tell a teacher or policeman that he has a "higher obligation" of some sort than the carpenter or steelworker has, or to talk vaguely of the sovereignty of the public employer who, because he represents "the people" instead of mercenary stockholders, can presum-

ably do no wrong in hiring, firing, and paying his workers. It was for these reasons that we said, in Chapter 8, that the most critical labor problem in the public sector today is not just how to ban the strike but rather how to devise an effective substitute for the strike—the same problem, in other words, which exists in the key private industries.

To appreciate the problems involved in the public sector, one need only examine the alternatives tried by New York State, presumably one of the most progressive jurisdictions with respect to labor law. That state's "baby Wagner Act," like its national model, specifically excluded public employees when it was passed in the 1930s, and few people gave this exclusion a second thought. In 1946 and 1947, however, there was a strike by teachers in Buffalo and "disturbances" among other government employees in Rochester and New York City, which prompted the legislature to enact the Condon-Wadlin Act of 1947. This statute not only formalized the common-law ban on strikes in the public sector but also declared that any state or local government worker who did strike would be considered to have quit his job and would be rehired only on condition that for three years thereafter he could not be paid at a higher rate than he had received when he went on strike, and that for five years he would not have any civil service tenure rights and would be treated as a probationary employee.

This "get-tough law" largely accomplished its aim in communities outside of New York City, where unions were weak and strikes were few, but it became increasingly impossible to administer in the city itself—partly because it provided no alternative method of settling labor disputes in the public sector but concentrated solely on penalizing strikers, and partly because its penalties were too harsh to be enforced on large and powerful groups.

Condon-Wadlin's unworkability was dramatically emphasized in the aftermath of the twelve-day strike of New York City Transit Authority [subway] employees at the beginning of 1966. The strike was finally settled on the basis of a substantial wage increase. When a taxpayer's suit presaged the only order the trial court could render under the law—an injunction against the payment of the increase—frantic efforts were necessary on the part of the

New York legislature to prevent a second strike; the Transit workers were hastily granted a legislative exemption from the law. For reasons of parity, other groups of public employees who had previously violated the law by striking, and hence were subject to its sanctions, were similarly exempted.[22]

In the midst of all this, Gov. Nelson Rockefeller appointed a group of experts, headed by Prof. George Taylor of the University of Pennsylvania, to recommend changes in the law. The group's proposals (with certain modifications) were enacted into law in 1967. The Taylor Act, as it is known, adopted a far more positive approach than its ill-fated predecessor: It explicitly declares that state and local government employees in New York State have the right to join unions of their choice; requires public employers to recognize and negotiate with unions chosen by their employees; provides that, in case of an impasse in negotiations, mediation must be resorted to and, if that fails, the parties must submit their case to neutral fact-finders who will issue public recommendations (though the appropriate legislative body still makes the final decision); and establishes a Public Employment Relations Board to administer and enforce these provisions.

The Taylor Act still prohibits strikes in the public sector, but it attempted to make the strike penalties more effective and enforceable by directing them primarily toward the offending union as an organization rather than toward its individual members. Specifically, the Public Employment Relations Board was empowered to strip a union (which had struck) of its cherished check-off privileges for a period of up to eighteen months; the appropriate executive and law officials were directed to seek an injunction against any actual or threatened violation of the strike ban; and if this injunction were violated, the court could fine and imprison union officials for up to thirty days and could fine the union itself an amount equal to one week's membership dues (up to a maximum of $10,000) for each day of a strike in violation of an injunction. As for the individual striker, the act was deliberately vague, saying only that he was "subject to the disciplinary penalties provided by law for misconduct"—meaning that a striker covered by the Civil Service Law, for example,

might be reprimanded, suspended, fined, fired, or ignored, depending on the choice of his superior and subject to the usual appeals machinery covering disciplinary actions against civil servants.

This law was justifiably hailed as a large step forward in this area of labor relations, and it has performed very well on several counts. Representation elections have been held among thousands of state and local government employees, negotiations have been initiated in many jurisdictions (particularly in public schools throughout the state) in which labor unions had never existed before, and relatively few strikes have occurred. In the very special and highly visible world of New York City, however, strikes by teachers and other government workers continued to occur, in spite of the jailing of some union leaders and the fining of their organizations, and pressure mounted to put sharper teeth in the Taylor Act's strike penalties. It was pointed out, for example, that a fine of $10,000 a day on the New York City teachers' union worked out to only 20 cents a day for its 50,000 members. And so, only two short years after its passage, the Taylor Act was amended in one more effort to solve this intractable problem of how to make a strike ban both equitable and effective. The amendments of 1969 lifted the $10,000 ceiling on the fine to be levied on a union for each day of a strike, leaving the amount to the discretion of the court; lifted the eighteen-month ceiling on the period a striking union can lose its check-off rights; *and also imposed a penalty on the individual striker of the mandatory loss of two days' pay for each day he is on strike*—one day's pay for being absent and one day's pay as a penalty.

It is easy to be philosophical about this problem (this is just the shakedown phase of public-sector bargaining, and matters will work out after the parties gain some maturity in negotiating) or to be fatalistic (it is impossible to prohibit strikes by any technique short of police-state methods, and they are not worth the price even if they would work). Also, as we noted in Chapter 8, many experts have argued persuasively that society should distinguish between essential and nonessential services within the public as well as the private sector, and apply any strike ban only to groups like police and firemen and not to every librarian and cafeteria worker on the public payroll. This would be a sensible (if difficult) move to take, but the knotty question would remain: whether you declare 10 or 100 percent of government employees to be essential, how do you construct a strike ban that is both equitable and effective?

For reasons that should by now be clear, our opinion is that compulsory arbitration of these public-sector disputes is both necessary and desirable. There is no reason why society should tolerate stoppages of essential government services (however defined), nor is there any reason why government employees should be deprived of a voice in determining their working conditions. Negotiations culminating, if necessary, in a binding arbitration award may not be the same process as "free collective bargaining" culminating in a strike, but surely the former is preferable to the present attempt of most government employers to avoid *both* the strike and arbitration, leaving unions the choice of either striking illegally or using political weapons to gain their ends. Most of the strike substitutes that have been tried to date—such as fact finding and mediation—leave the final decision in the hands of the public employer, which is neither equitable nor calculated to inspire the respect from employees that a strike substitute must have.

There is a widespread impression that no government body can constitutionally agree to be bound by a system of compulsory arbitration, on the ground that this would be an improper delegation of legislative responsibility and authority. Yet, by 1971, four states had adopted compulsory arbitration laws to resolve disputes involving police and firemen—Wyoming, Pennsylvania, Rhode Island, and Michigan—and the constitutionality of these statutes had been upheld whenever challenged in state courts.[23] In some other states, such as New York and Hawaii, the relevant laws authorize the voluntary arbitration of public-sector disputes, a method which would seem to require the same delegation of legislative authority as compulsory arbitration. At the federal level, the Nixon executive order of 1969 permits the arbitration of certain types of contract disputes involving federal employees, and the Postal Reform Act of 1970 explicitly requires the arbitration of deadlocked negotiations between the new U.S. Postal Service and its employees. All of this

demonstrates that a strong case can be made for the legality (and political feasibility) of compulsory arbitration in the public sector.

Two caveats must be entered, however. First, it would be difficult to introduce a power element into arbitration in the public sector, for there is no other public institution to which a government would or should be forced to pay the high arbitration "fees" we have suggested for private-industry arbitration. (The same problem would appear to preclude the use of the "nonstoppage strike" in the public sector.) One possibility would be a procedure suggested previously, that an arbitration board be empowered *only* to accept what it concludes is the more reasonable of the positions of the two opposing parties. In doing so it could take into account the whole record of negotiation. There is admitted danger if a law were constituted so rigidly—what would a board do if confronted by two unreasonable positions, the endorsement of either of which would be sure to lead to trouble? But some variation on such a procedure may prove workable.

Second, it must be obvious that no strike substitute can guarantee perfect compliance in either the public or private sector. An aroused group of union members can strike in defiance of a "compulsory award" just as easily as they can against a fact finder's "recommendations," and no penalties devised by any dictatorship, much less any tolerated by a democracy, have completely abolished strikes and produced universal harmony in the labor market. But then, what law does achieve perfect compliance? We have no painless formula for ensuring that compulsory arbitration would prove acceptable. Like any law, it must carry some distasteful penalties for violation and, if it should prove to be one of those rare "Prohibition-type" laws that simply cannot be enforced, it should naturally be dropped. We think it is far too soon, however, to conclude that there is no substitute for the strike in critical public and private industries.

Conclusions

Even though strikes are admittedly a rather primitive exercise of economic power, it must be admitted that the same thing can be said about the pursuit of self-interest in many other parts of our free enterprise system—the companies that abandon communities in order to make more money elsewhere, the employers who pollute the environment because it's cheaper to operate that way, the investors who prefer the profit returns from cigarette companies over the dubious pleasure of contributing to cancer research, and so on. Up to a point, this freedom to pursue self-interest is what makes our economic and political systems work, and work well.

We therefore should not look on all strikes as a breakdown of collective bargaining or some form of sickness in the union–management relationship. Collective bargaining is an important ingredient in our democratic system, and collective bargaining requires the play of relative bargaining *power* between the parties, and as collective bargaining is practiced today, the strike as an alternative to agreement is still an essential element of bargaining power. Conceivably we may find some alternative means by which each party may impose on the other a cost of disagreement, but as yet we have no satisfactory general substitute for the strike. Even the special procedures discussed here could scarcely supersede the strike in all union–management relationships.

Most of the several thousand strikes which occur annually may be mildly annoying to the public, but they are not much more than that. Household consumers are usually protected by the fact that the product involved is not vital or, if it is, stocks are adequate and substitutes satisfactory. Producers and suppliers may be adversely affected, experiencing a loss of income from a curtailment of their own operations in consequence of the strike; but some portion, at times a substantial proportion, of these losses may be recovered by makeup operations following the strike.

There are occasional and recurring stoppages, however, which have a sufficiently damaging effect on the economy and the public to warrant governmental intervention to protect public interests. Although some experts have made out a strong case that present procedures, perhaps with only minor amendment, are adequate to meet most emergencies, there are at least equally good grounds for concluding that a more effective procedure for curbing serious strikes is needed.

But all this discussion of strikes and strike controls should not create the impression that strikes are usual in collective bargaining—as we have seen, they occur in relatively few instances; or that all strikes are necessarily bad—as we have seen, strikes at least at the present time are, *generally* speaking, an essential element in collective bargaining, which is a precious process to those who prize the right of people to participate in determining the conditions under which they work. It is only for the exceptions that preventive measures are needed.

ADDITIONAL READINGS

Blackman, John L., Jr.: *Presidential Seizure in Labor Disputes,* Harvard University Press, Cambridge, Mass., 1967.

Chamberlain, Neil W.: *Social Responsibility and Strikes,* Harper, New York, 1953.

———: *Sourcebook on Labor,* McGraw-Hill, New York, 1958, chap. 17.

"Collective Bargaining in the Public Sector," *Monthly Labor Review,* vol. 92, pp. 60–69, July, 1969. A summary of six papers.

Cullen, Donald E.: *National Emergency Strikes,* ILR Paperback no. 7, Cornell University, New York State School of Industrial and Labor Relations, Ithaca, N.Y., 1968.

Ross, Arthur, and Paul T. Hartman: *Changing Patterns of Industrial Conflict,* Wiley, New York, 1960.

FOR ANALYSIS AND DISCUSSION

1. During Senate hearings on proposed revisions to the Taft-Hartley Act, Sen. Paul Douglas of Illinois made the following comment:

> One of the most puzzling things we have to deal with, and in a sense one of the most unfair things, is that those who disturb an existing situation are inevitably labeled in the public mind as the troublemakers; whereas the maintenance of an unjust status quo may be the real trouble. And those who hold onto an unjust set of conditions may be the ones who are really causing the trouble, not those who protest against it and are willing to go out on strike.
>
> That, I think, is one of the great disadvantages under which unions work. Inevitably when you come to the showdown, in order

to present their case they are forced either to strike or to threaten to strike, and that involves either an interruption or a threat to interrupt production, which no one including the union likes, I assure you.

These remarks raise the question of how one goes about evaluating "responsibility" for a strike. Can you suggest some basis for determining whether it is the union or management which is "responsible" for a strike?

2. Henry Mayer, an attorney who has represented unions for many years, commented in a letter to the *New York Times* during the period when strike controls were most actively being promoted:

> Equality of power around the bargaining table, which is the sine qua non of permanent industrial peace, could only be achieved when each side tests out the other's strength, particularly after the gage of battle has been flung. It may be unfortunate, but it is true, that only through the strike can labor demonstrate the strength that is latent within it, at least to satisfy its adversaries in the arena of economic conflict.
>
> Injury to the public, while regrettable, is as much a necessary by-product in industrial warfare as it is in wars among nations. About twenty years ago the New York Court of Appeals in the case of *Exchange Bakery v. Rifkin,* in discussing the impact and legality of strikes, said: "Resulting injury is incidental and must be endured."

Do you agree?

3. In contrast to Mr. Mayer's statement above, the late Professor Selekman of the Harvard Business School wrote as follows in his book, *Labor Relations and Human Relations* (which is rewarding reading for any student):

> No Government can tolerate the recurrent paralysis of widespread industrial conflict. Certainly power constitutes an important determinant in the dealings between management and unions. But as collective bargaining attains acceptance and maturity, it cannot much longer be enough for public policy—and collective dealings—to mirror the old concept of two power groups striking a fair bargain, as a neutral government seeks only to protect a true

equality in the balance of bargaining strength. We cannot continue recurrently to redress the balance, placing the weight of government protections now on the side of labor, as in the Wagner Act, and then on the side of management, as in the Taft-Hartley Act, while the big protagonists on both sides grow steadily bigger for battling it out. Rather must the protagonists develop their own alternatives for battling it out, or expect to find the government intervening on an ever-widening scale to restrict the fighting.

Comment on this point of view.

4. What actions might the parties themselves take to improve their collective-bargaining procedures, which might make resort to the strike less necessary?

5. Someone once facetiously suggested that if what is wanted is some way by which each of the parties can bring pressure on the other to agree to the terms it offers, then one substitute for the economic strike might be the hunger strike. When an impasse is reached, let union and management officials be confined to quarters and given no food until they reach agreement. It is conceivable that the pangs of hunger might drive them to an understanding more quickly even than a shutdown of the plant. Of course, one stubborn group may be able to hold out longer than the other, forcing the hungrier side to make greater concessions in order to conclude a settlement.

As silly as this may sound, it may not be a great deal sillier than our present strike practice, and at the same time it would protect the public by assuring that strikes would be short. And if what is wanted is the emotional involvement and subsequent emotional release of the workers (as has sometimes been argued), certainly each side could become emotionally involved in the welfare of its starving negotiators.

Interesting possibilities for strategic gambits would also be present. Should the parties, for example, send to the bargaining table their best-fed people in the expectation that they could last the longest? Or should they send in an emaciated and saintly type (a Gandhi) to represent them, bringing pressure on the other side to settle, as he wastes away, for fear of the public opprobrium if they should be the cause of his demise?

In what significant respects, if any, would such an instrument of bargaining power be less desirable or less effective than the economic strike as we know it?

NOTES

1. This is particularly true when a union is certified as the collective-bargaining representative, so that management has a legal duty to bargain with it. Of course, a union may disintegrate in the face of a prolonged strike, and workers might then return without a formal collective agreement, but this happens rarely enough to be covered by our qualification that some agreement is *almost* inevitable.

2. Nevertheless, in the United States in 1965, almost one-third of all strikes arose during the term of an agreement. A number of them were with respect to issues, such as speed of operations, on which unions had specifically reserved their right to strike in the event no agreement could be reached. Others involved "wildcat" strikes—unofficial actions not sanctioned by the union but precipitated by workers who took things into their own hands. Some were the result of jurisdictional disputes between workers. In total, they accounted for only one-eighth of all time lost due to strikes, which indicates their relative brevity.

3. National Industrial Conference Board, *Union Initiation Fees, Dues and Per Capita Tax; National Union Strike Benefits,* by Edward R. Curtin, NICB Survey, New York, 1968, pp. 29–42.

4. "Contractors Try Strike Insurance," *Business Week,* April 5, 1969, p. 56. Also see two excellent articles by Vernon M. Briggs, Jr.: "The Strike Insurance Plan of the Railroad Industry," *Industrial Relations,* vol. 6, pp. 205–212, February, 1967; and "The Mutual Aid Pact of the Airline Industry," *Industrial and Labor Relations Review,* vol. 19, pp. 3–20, October, 1965.

5. *New York Times,* Sept. 30, 1962.

6. Provisions of these laws are summarized in Herbert Northrup and Gordon Bloom, *Government and Labor,* Irwin, Homewood, Ill., 1963, pp. 382–386. The Minnesota act provides perhaps the best-known and most effective of these fact-finding devices. Since 1939, when it came into effect, some 300 tripartite commissions have been appointed under its terms—most of them during the first ten years of the act. On the whole it has achieved a rather impressive record. In approximately 87 percent of the cases coming before it, peaceful settlement was achieved in one way or another. This was not always through acceptance of board recommendations. In fact, in the period 1947 to 1960, almost half of such recommendations were rejected by the parties. The intervention of the tripartite commission thus may have been helpful chiefly in delaying strike action

and giving mediators further time to work with the parties and in subjecting the parties to greater public exposure and pressure to settle matters themselves. A summary and evaluation of the Minnesota experience is given by Joseph Lazar, Vincent Lombardi, and George Seltzer in "The Tripartite Commission in Public Interest Labor Disputes in Minnesota, 1940–1960," *Labor Law Journal,* May, 1963, pp. 419–433.

7. A careful discussion of the act, the circumstances under which it came into existence, and its probable constitutionality is contained in Seymour H. Lehrer, "The Maryland Public Utilities Disputes Act," *Labor Law Journal,* vol. 7, pp. 607–617, 1956. There is some ambiguity in the act as to the period for which the arbitration decision remains in effect. Although the original act specified that the terms were to remain operative only during the period of state seizure, an amendment five days later specified that they might remain effective not longer than one year following termination of seizure, but did not remove the prior provision.

8. Robert R. France has provided a good account of this legislation in "Seizure in Emergency Labor Disputes in Virginia," *Industrial and Labor Relations Review,* vol. 7, pp. 347–366, 1954.

9. E. Robert Livernash, *Collective Bargaining in the Basic Steel Industry,* U.S. Department of Labor, 1961, p. 49.

10. Northrup and Bloom, *Government and Labor,* p. 449.

11. Richard Liebes of the Building Service Employees Union describes a system in San Francisco whereby a union planning strike action must justify its position before the executive committee of the San Francisco Labor Council. The latter explores the reasonableness of the union's position and may itself initiate action looking toward resolving the dispute. Other unions that might be affected can make their views known. At times the Council has ruled against authorizing a union's strike when its demands appeared "out of line." In that event, if a strike is nonetheless instituted, it will not be respected by other unions. (*Labor Law Journal,* October, 1958, p. 799.)

12. *Business Week,* May 4, 1963, p. 54.

13. Arthur M. Ross and Paul T. Hartman, *Changing Patterns of Industrial Conflict,* Wiley, New York, 1960.

14. *New York Times,* April 19, 1962.

15. *New Haven Register,* Jan. 13, 1963.

16. Council for Economic Development, *The Public Interest in National Labor Policy,* New York, 1961, p. 104.

17. Much of the material which follows has been drawn from Neil W. Chamberlain, "The Problem of Strikes," in *Proceedings of the New York University Thirteenth Annual Conference on Labor,* Matthew Bender, Albany, N.Y., 1960, pp. 427–445.

18. Walter Reuther, the most articulate of all the

labor spokesmen, whose testimony before congressional committees has supplied a vast store of quotable quotes, has commented on how delay created by an injunction can be parlayed into advantage:

We used to say back in General Motors that 1 penny [of a wage offer] was worth $6 million. Well, if you can withhold a few pennies for a few months, that runs into many, many millions of dollars. Therefore, the 80-day injunction thing may delay a settlement for a period, retroactive wage increases may not be granted, and the company can save many millions of dollars by the simple process of delay.

Pressed on the question of whether retroactivity provided for by law wasn't a sufficient answer to this problem, Reuther replied:

The ability of a group of workers to make a good bargain as of one calendar date may not be the same thing at a later calendar date. You may not be able to overcome that by any retroactive adjustment. . . . If you say you go back to the period before the 80 days begin, you can't recreate the thing. There may be situations in the industry where the seasonal aspect of the production cycle may have a great bearing upon the ability of workers to get what they consider to be a satisfactory agreement. Eighty days later, maybe the pressure in the industry has tapered off a great deal and the employer can coast for a while.

19. In the words of one union official:

If the Government sets up a fact-finding board, and supposing the company was really willing to give 10 cents, . . . they figure, Well, the fact-finding board will start with 10 cents, and will compromise the thing [starting] with the 10 cents [and moving] toward the union position. But if you don't put any figure on the table, then the fact-finding board will start with zero and maybe they will compromise at 10 cents instead of 10 cents plus. So there is every incentive not to bargain; there is every incentive not to lay anything on the table.

20. This proposal has been explored in detail by Carl Stevens in "Is Compulsory Arbitration Compatible with Bargaining?," *Industrial Relations,* vol. 5, pp. 45–47, February, 1966.

21. This procedure was advocated by one of the authors in Neil W. Chamberlain, *Social Responsibility and Strikes,* Harper, New York, 1953. For a later version, and a review of the relevant literature, see Stephen H. Sosnick, "Non-Stoppage Strikes: A New Approach," *Industrial and Labor Relations Review,* vol. 18, pp. 73–80, October, 1964.

22. Walter E. Oberer, Kurt L. Hanslowe, and Robert E. Doherty, *The Taylor Act,* Bulletin 59, Cornell University, New York State School of Industrial and Labor Relations, Ithaca, N.Y., 1968, p. vi.

23. The Wyoming law was the first adopted (in 1965) and applies only to fire fighters; the other three apply to both police and firemen. For details, see Paul D. Staudohar, "Compulsory Arbitration of Interests Disputes in the Protective Services," *Labor Law Journal,* vol. 21, pp. 708–715, 1970.

CHAPTER 27

**THE MONOPOLY
POWERS OF UNIONS**

Anglo-Saxon legal tradition has generally opposed the exercise of monopoly power by private organizations or groups. Monopoly power may be broadly construed as economic privilege which is conferred by some control over the supply of a good or service, thus restricting the offerings to consumers. Cartels designed to exclude would-be competitors or to limit the output of some product are examples of business monopoly.

Almost from their inception, labor unions in this country have been charged with the exercise of monopoly power and hence with engaging in actions which, if not actually illicit, are suspect. Chapter 8 recounted how the early nineteenth-century courts regarded unions as illegal combinations, in part because they sought to push up wages by excluding from a firm's labor market all workers except those who joined the organization or, at a minimum, conformed to the terms which it set. A shoemaker's union would determine, for example, that wages should be increased by specified amounts for various types of operations, and its members would swear not to work for any master who would not pay those rates and not to work alongside any employee who agreed to accept less. If their union included most of the shoemakers in a locality, the employers faced the prospect either of paying the rate demanded or of standing a strike. This was a monopolistic control over the supply of labor in that industry which courts for some time refused to consider lawful.

There is no need to repeat here the story, told

in that earlier chapter, of how the views of judges with respect to the legality of labor unions were modified over the years. Nevertheless, despite an increasing willingness to accept the right of workers to organize unions to seek an improvement in their wages and working conditions, there has never been a time when labor unions were not under some cloud, both of law and public opinion, for an alleged use of monopoly power to exploit others for their own gain. In this chapter we shall examine the nature and the validity of those charges.

Before doing so, however, we may stipulate one fact. Any union of the employees of a company which bargains for wage increases is in a strict sense exercising some degree of monopoly power. By eliminating competition among the individual employees so that all work at some agreed-upon rate or else none works, and by trying to prevent "scabs"—as they are opprobriously called—from taking over the jobs left vacant, a union of the employees of an establishment is exercising some degree of control over the supply of labor to that firm. That kind of monopoly power is now rather widely accepted and seldom condemned. If a single union (rather than a number of individuals) confronts the employer in bargaining over wage rates, it is no more monopolistic than a single employer confronting his employees. The allegations of union abuse of monopoly power which are currently relevant all involve something more than this.

Monopoly effects on the labor market

It is argued that the existence of national unions, enforcing common wage policies on their constituent local unions, and the practice of industry-wide (multiemployer) bargaining lead to artificial limitations on the availability of jobs to workers. Wage rates for certain occupations and in certain industries are pushed up. On the assumption that firms are operating in the range of diminishing marginal productivity, this limits the number of workers that may profitably be employed and hence reduces the number of jobs available. If firms were bargaining individually, the chances are that the union of their employees would become more aware of this effect and might not force wages to a level that would result in sacrificing the jobs of some of their members. But where local unions are bound to accede to the policy of the national union, which may refuse to approve an agreement that does not follow some pattern, or where local unions are blanketed in a multiemployer bargain from which they are not allowed to deviate, they cannot make the concessions which may be necessary to preserve the jobs of their members. National-union wage policies thus exclude certain workers from union-controlled labor markets and force them into less desirable forms of employment.

The same consequence may come about in another way. Firms which are competitors in the same product market might, individually, be reluctant to grant a wage increase that would necessitate raising prices, placing themselves at a disadvantage vis-à-vis their business rivals. If, however, all these competitors were bound together in the same multiemployer bargaining unit so that all were forced to make the same wage concession, they would be less unwilling to grant the union's demands, since they would have some reasonable assurance that all of their number would seek to recoup the added cost through higher prices, with none being placed at a competitive disadvantage relative to the others.[1] The price increases would, however, restrict sales and production, and hence employment. Some workers would be pushed out into other industries (whether those on the present payroll or those who would otherwise have been hired some time in the future makes no difference).

The effect of pattern following, enforced by the national union, or of multiemployer bargaining is thus a reduction in employment in the industry or occupation affected. The workers who cannot now be profitably employed in that industry or occupation are forced into other occupations or industries, depressing wage rates there. The higher rates won by the union have thus been at the expense of other workers. This result is possible because the union has extended its control over the supply of labor services beyond the individual firm to embrace an entire industry or at least a number of competitive firms.

It is true that there are not many instances where firms operating in national product markets bargain on an industry basis (although substantially the same effect is obtained through the device of the national union's enforcing wage patterns on lesser units). But there are numerous instances of firms operating in local product markets (for the most part supplying services such as local transportation, home construction, laundry and dry cleaning, barber and beauty services, restaurants and hotels) which do bargain on an industry basis, with the same consequence of distorting the wage structure and lessening the employment opportunities for other workers in the local market.[2]

Industrywide bargaining, by imposing wage uniformity throughout the union's jurisdiction or throughout an industry, removes the natural competition among localities and areas for employment on the basis of comparative wage rates. Firms which might locate in small towns, or in the South where wage rates are lower, have less inducement to do so when wage rates are standard.

Just as industrywide bargaining imposes a common wage increase on all firms regardless of the willingness of the employees of certain of those firms to take less to preserve their jobs by making their companies more competitive, so it imposes a standard wage increase even on regions with a labor surplus, regardless of the willingness of the unemployed in those areas to take less for the privilege of working. At lower wage rates, capital might be induced to migrate to the labor-surplus areas, providing employment. At standard wage rates, the incentive is weakened, if not eliminated. Wage differentials are an important influence in attracting mobile capital, and have—like competition generally—a socially desirable function, in this case the development of less industrialized areas. Industrywide bargaining removes this form of area competition.

Unions, the allegation runs, have attempted directly to monopolize work opportunities for their memberships, to the detriment of other workers who are not members. Perhaps the most familiar practice cited in support of this charge is the jurisdictional strike, in which one union strikes an employer in an effort to force him to award employment to its members rather than to nonunion workers or to the members of another union. In many instances, it is further argued, the strike is not actually necessary in order to achieve the effect desired: simple threat of strike may be enough. Thus many an employer would never dream of letting one of his production employees drive a truck, even as a temporary expedient, for fear of retaliation from the powerful teamsters' union. Or a firm might be afraid to keep its regular employees at work painting the plant or equipment, even if they would otherwise be idled, for fear of a reaction from the building-trades unions. In many such instances, the employer could actually save on his expenses if he could, even occasionally, make use of his regular work force, but he is often precluded from doing so by the claim of certain unions to jurisdiction over such work, backed up by economic coercion or even violence. Thus one group of workers makes good its claim to job opportunities at the expense of another group of workers.

Another practice having the same effect is union resistance to technological changes which would deprive their members of work. Building-trades craftsmen, for example, have opposed such developments as preglazed window sash, ready-mixed concrete, prefabricated radiator enclosures, and quarry-finished stone. In doing so, they seek to preserve employment rights for themselves at the expense of job opportunities for those employed in the new process.[3]

Monopoly effects in product markets

Obviously some of the practices which have been mentioned as affecting labor markets have their repercussion on product markets. Wage increases —which may have the effect of reducing employment opportunities for nonunion workers—may also lead to price increases affecting consumers of the products involved. If jurisdictional disputes and opposition to technological advances increase costs and prices, here too the consumer of the products involved will bear the ultimate impact. Again, resistance to the use of a new product which it is feared will lessen employment (the use of spray guns in painting, for instance) has an adverse impact on the producer of the new product and acts as a deterrent to innovation. These effects in product markets are incidental to actions taken in the labor market, however. But there are other union practices which involve direct intervention in, and attempted control over, product markets as a means of winning employment advantages for members of a certain union.

Occasionally, though not often, unions have sought to control the price of the good or service which they produce. In some instances they have pressured for lower prices: at one time, laundry drivers in New York City threatened to strike over a price increase which they feared would lessen business and reduce employment; from time to time journeymen barbers have taken issue with master barbers over the price of haircuts, sometimes maintaining that the price should be raised to permit an increase in the wage rate, but on other occasions arguing that the price should be dropped to encourage trade and permit an increase in actual earnings. Similar ambivalence has characterized milk drivers in the past. At one time the union in Columbus, Ohio, was preventing a differential price between store and door, from fear that an increase in the home-delivery price might drive customers to pick up their own milk at the store, while simultaneously in Chicago the milk drivers' union was refusing to permit any decrease in a premium price for delivered milk, for fear that this would lead to a wage cut.

Most commonly, however, complaints of the unions' control over product prices have focused on their effort to increase prices to expand their own earnings. At one time a New York Teamsters' local joined with a number of employers' associations to establish a "stabilization committee," with authority to fix the prices which would be charged for the moving and storage of goods. In addition, the collective agreement fixed a scale of wages for the union employees and provided that certain "unfair practices" were to be eliminated from the industry. Among these was one described as "quoting or obtaining or attempting to secure a price for any service which shall be less than the sum of the wages necessary under ... the agreement and of reasonable items of expenses and overhead entering into the cost of operation." In such an arrangement, control over prices is obviously linked with power to increase wage rates. This kind of concerted union–management price-wage action is banned by the courts when it comes to their attention, but it may be effective on a sub rosa basis, with an unwritten understanding.

In other cases a union may be able in effect to "tax" a product or service, with the same consequence as a higher price. The Teamsters Union, for example, in 1962 imposed on Western truckers a $5 payment for each van hauled "piggyback" by rail, barge, or plane.[4] In this instance its bargaining power in its own labor market was used to affect costs and prices in another product market just as though railroads themselves had raised their haulage rates by $5 a van.

Unions have sometimes intervened in product markets by restricting access to such markets by competitive firms, which might drive down prices and wages. If a product market can be preserved to a limited group of firms, those firms will be empowered to charge higher prices and to pay their employees higher rates.

Secondary boycotts frequently fall in this category. Nonunion competition threatens a union's ability to maintain a higher wage scale in the establishments it has organized. It can meet this problem by trying to organize the remaining firms. If, however, it should run into strong employer resistance or if employees in those plants were not interested in joining, the union might then seek to bring pressure on the customers or the suppliers of the nonunion firms to cease doing business with them. If successful, it will have limited the access of those firms to their markets, restricting trade to those firms which are unionized.

In fact, we saw in Chapter 8 that a union may even boycott firms organized by other locals of

the same union. That was one of the issues in the Allen-Bradley case, in which the Supreme Court in 1944 condemned the agreement in New York City under which Local 3 of the International Brotherhood of Electrical Workers promised it would not furnish electricians to any building contractor who installed electrical fixtures made outside of the city (even those made by members of other IBEW locals), and in return the local contractors' and manufacturers' associations agreed to employ only Local 3 members—an arrangement which permitted union employers to obtain higher prices and union members higher wages by shutting off outside competition.[5]

And we also reviewed, in that chapter, two 1965 cases in which unions were alleged to have combined with some employers against other employers and the consumer. In the Pennington case, the charge was that in 1950 the United Mine Workers and the major employers' association in bituminous coal had embarked upon a long-term conspiracy to eliminate marginal producers by agreeing that the large companies could mechanize without union opposition in return for liberal wage and fringe-benefit settlements which, in turn, the union would impose on small producers who could not afford to mechanize, thus driving them out of business. In the Jewel Tea case, the target was a multiemployer contract with a clause prohibiting unionized food stores in the Chicago area to sell meat after 6 P.M. on any day, which the union said was aimed at preventing night work by butchers but which, according to the Jewel Tea chain, was directed toward protecting stores without self-service meat departments from the competition of those with such departments.

Other allegations that the unions have acted to restrain competition and to exert monopoly powers unfairly on their members' behalf have been made, but the above constitute the principal indictments. These may be summarized as (1) excluding some workers from unionized labor markets by (a) raising wages on an industry basis to the point where it is uneconomic for certain firms to hire as many workers as formerly; (b) raising wages on an industry basis with a consequent rise in the industry's prices, curtailing output and employment; (c) raising wages on an industry basis, lessening the inducement for capital to migrate to labor-surplus areas and offer job opportunities there because of lower wage rates; (d) resorting to strike and boycott to gain employment for their own members at the expense of other workers; and (2) manipulating product markets by (a) securing control over prices, raising them to increase wages for their members, and (b) excluding other firms from product markets to maintain work opportunities for their own members in the firms already there.

Market curbs on union monopoly powers

Even the most ardent defender of labor unions would have to admit that sometimes they engage in the foregoing practices. He might argue whether these actions take place on the scale which some critics claim, and no basis for settling that argument exists since it would require some information not available and some not accessible. He might also maintain that even if such practices do occur, they carry more benefit to the workers involved than harm to the consumers affected, and are therefore warranted. We shall have a look at that question later. But he might also claim that the degree of monopoly power charged to unions is greatly exaggerated, and that, aside from any legal limitations on union efforts to monopolize economic gains for their members to the disadvantage of other workers and consumers, there are competitive limitations on their exercise of monopoly power. He might point to three.

1. What economists refer to as the price elasticity of demand constitutes an inescapable limitation even on monopoly power. By this is meant simply that as prices rise, demand tends to decline by some measurable amount. For products having good substitutes, the decline in demand would likely be precipitate; if one steel producer had to raise its prices relative to other steel firms because the union had pushed up its costs, it would probably lose a good many sales to competitors, and its employees would consequently lose jobs. Knowledge of that likelihood would act as a restraint on the union.

It might try to wriggle loose from such a restraint by putting all steel companies under a single industrywide agreement. In this situation it could push up wage rates for all, and if steel com-

panies then had to raise their prices they would all do so, so that none of them would act as a low-price competitive threat to the others. The union would here seem to have escaped from the bonds of price elasticity. And, in fact, it would at least have made those bonds a little looser, but it would not be able to shake them off altogether. The substitutes for the products of the price-raising companies would now be less acceptable than formerly; no longer would steel from company A be a low-price substitute for steel from company B, since both A and B had raised their prices. But there would be other more distant substitutes, such as aluminum and plastics. If the union pushed up the price of steel by raising labor costs, at some point price elasticity would have its effect—more slowly and less drastically than in the first case of close substitutes, but still, in time and to a lesser degree, it would have its impact. At some price for steel, customers would rather use a steel substitute. Another kind of substitution would be steel from abroad. At some price for domestic steel, customers would turn to imported steel. Thus even in the case of industrywide bargaining, price elasticity retains some limitation on union monopoly power.

The potency of this competitive check can also be seen within the transportation field. The railroad unions have kept their jurisdiction solidly organized for several decades and have won liberal wage settlements and many stringent job-security provisions, some of which qualify as featherbedding by any definition. Yet, all this has not prevented employment in railroading from plummeting by 50 percent from 1947 to 1967, as railroads have steadily lost ground to other forms of transportation for a variety of reasons (some connected to union impact, others not). The same situation prevails in ocean shipping, in which neither powerful unions nor a wide array of government subsidies has been able to sustain employment in the face of the far lower labor costs of foreign shipping companies.

2. Coal miners in Illinois, if they work for lower wages, are in effect competing with coal miners in West Virginia, and coal production would begin to shift to Illinois and away from West Virginia as the Illinois companies sold their output at lower prices or made higher profits.

There would be pressure on West Virginia miners to accept a pay cut in order to regain jobs, but this might simply lead Illinois miners to agree to a still lower rate to avoid losing the work which they had originally taken away from West Virginia. To avoid this wage competition among workers, unions resort to the practice of establishing a common rate applying to the same kind of work everywhere, when they have the bargaining power to secure such a result. No longer can employers play workers in one location against workers elsewhere. They have to rely on their own managerial efficiency to compete effectively.

This practice of the common rate (whether set by industrywide bargaining or by a pattern which the national union imposes on all its locals) would seem to give unions the power to push wage rates up with little restraint. But in addition to the restraint imposed by price elasticity at the point where rising costs affect prices, a further restraint arises from the fact that not all firms in an industry are equally efficient. At the same time that some firms are making handsome profits, other firms are barely staying alive. The union thus faces the problem that if it pushes wages higher, it may drive these marginal firms out of business and lose jobs for its members. Of course, it may pick up additional jobs at the more efficient firms that expand their production to meet the demand formerly provided for by the defunct firms, but precisely because these firms are more efficient they will not create an equal number of jobs. Even more important, because they are likely to be located in different sites, they will not provide jobs for the same people who have lost theirs. So inevitably unions are driven to worry about whether the rates which they seek to make common throughout an industry are economically manageable for, say, the weakest half of the industry.

If they make a bad guess and set the pattern rate too high, they may find it more and more difficult to enforce the rate even when it is agreed to. When marginal firms are on the point of going under, their employees may agree to a sub rosa reduction in wages just to keep their jobs. Other firms may simply fail to observe the terms set forth in the written agreement, and if their number is large, it will be difficult for the national

union to institute all the arbitration or legal proceedings which would be required to make the terms effective.

We have seen that the bituminous coal industry is an outstanding example of this kind of situation. The United Mine Workers for years cooperated with the larger firms which were introducing technological improvements that vastly increased the productivity of the mines. This was considered essential to keep coal prices competitive with oil and gas, to which coal was losing its markets. It allowed the payment of very good wages indeed, but it also reduced the number of miners needed. Moreover, the small and struggling mine operators who were not financially or technically able to take advantage of the technological advances found themselves saddled with high rates of pay, making profitable operation much more difficult. One after another of them ceased observing the terms of the union contract, and others in effect "reorganized" on a nonunion basis. Because of the level of unemployment in the mine fields, there has been no difficulty in obtaining miners to work at less than the high union rate.

The result has been a continuing increase in the size of the nonunion sector. As recently as the early fifties, the industry was almost wholly organized. A decade later, it was estimated that more than a fourth of the industry was operating nonunion.[6] The union has not yet given way on the maintenance of the wage scale it has set—but neither has it been able to enforce that scale against a significant portion of the industry.

3. Whatever monopoly power a union possesses, it can exploit only *through* some business unit. Except in the rare situations where workers sell their services directly to household consumers, they draw their wages from an employer and are able to gain higher wages only through him. This means that in order for a union to exert its monopoly power, a business unit or an industry must itself possess some monopoly power in its product market, which the union can exploit to its advantage. Union monopoly thus depends on business monopoly. It is true that unions can sometimes cooperate with firms to create a monopoly situation which the employers by themselves could not succeed in doing, so that in some situations it can be said that business monopoly depends on

union monopoly. But in whichever direction causation runs, nevertheless unions cannot continue to employ monopoly advantage unless they do it through business units.

This is no place to stop to explore the factors which provide business firms with market power and the influences which limit the degree or persistence of that power. But we can profitably take note of the proposition put forward by Prof. Joseph A. Schumpeter that there is one kind of competition from which no firm, however large or strategically situated, can keep itself forever immune—*the competition that comes from innovations*, whether in the form of new products or new processes.[7] Such innovations may come from other firms within an industry or from other industries. Inventiveness and ingenuity and initiative in one quarter or another almost certainly assure that while monopolistic power in some product market may confer short-run protection, it cannot give permanent security from competitive products or competitive technologies.

This threat of the effect of innovation on the value of a company's assets drives most large corporations into making heavy investments in research. They strive to come up with a new product or process before a competitor does, in order to protect their corporate position, but in taking such a course of action they are inevitably undermining the present basis for their own temporary monopoly power by making their own existing products or production processes obsolete. This was a process which Schumpeter termed "creative destruction," the destroying of old values by creating new ones.

If the company is successful in its research and development program, it may be able to maintain a highly profitable operation over a protracted period of time. But this is possible not so much because it preserves old monopolies as because it manages to create new ones in the form of a constant stream of innovational advantages over competitors, each of which will be short-lived and will give way to some new product or process, pioneered by either the same firm or another.

Most of us think of industrial research in terms of the huge manufacturing corporations that spend billions on developing new and better drugs and computers and jet planes and television sets, and

it is true that unions in those industries rarely attempt to stop this kind of competition, for they know that any of these companies (and its employees) is doomed if it fails in the race to innovate. But even in industries with small firms and strong unions and a history of restrictive work practices, innovation cannot be kept at bay indefinitely. There has been far more change in construction, for example, than is commonly realized: the painters have lost their fight against the roller and spray gun, carpenters everywhere employ power tools, new materials have largely displaced brick in exterior walls and plaster in interior walls, the do-it-yourself tools and materials have cut into the small-job market, and the widespread use of cranes and rollers and other large power equipment has made the Operating Engineers the fastest-growing union in the building trades. As a curious result, union strength is increasingly concentrated in the most efficient sectors of this industry—the large-scale construction of commercial buildings and public works, which are easily organized and efficient enough to afford union labor—and union strength is apparently dwindling in the home-building and maintenance sector in which featherbedding was believed to exact its highest toll.

In the entertainment field, too, unions have seen their positions eroded by innovation. The powerful musicians' union could not stop the substitution of recorded for live performances, nor could the restrictive practices of several unions on the Broadway stage and in Hollywood movie production stop the rise of radio and television (which benefited yet other unions).

In the short run, then, a union can exploit the monopoly position of the business firm with which it has a bargaining relationship, but its capacity to continue to exploit depends on the capability of the firm to maintain a profitable position. Industries rise and decline, and individual companies experience their own independent ups and downs of fortune, and a union has little to do with such movements. It can profit from them at times, and must suffer from them at other times, but it has no separate monopoly power of its own which enables it to keep alive and profitable a company or industry which is giving way to competition from innovations. Monopoly exploitation cannot have much more chance of indefinite prolongation by unions than by the businesses with which the unions deal.

This limitation on the monopoly power of unions was noted by the special study committee convened by the Committee for Economic Development.[8]

> We are impressed with the restraints imposed on powerful unions or employers by open product markets, in which new products compete with old, in which trade among nations challenges the position of entrenched producers in the home country, in which the ingenuity of men in declining industries may recapture business long since lost. The large firm is forced to produce the small car; plastics are substituted for steel as steel prices rise; the development of "piggy-backing" by the railroads challenges the trucking industry and the Teamsters Union. Thus, truly open product markets are a check of great significance on the power of unions and employers in the labor market.

Thus alongside the roster of monopoly practices in labor and product markets which are attributed to the unions, we can lay the opposing constraints which the competitive market imposes on unions. Price elasticity of demand, the difficulty of embracing all the firms in a product market under a common wage scale, and the ineluctable pressure of innovations from outside a firm or industry all serve to limit the monopoly power of unions. If we can assume as well that union leaders and members do have somewhat more regard for the employment effects of wage bargains than Ross has argued (see Chapter 18), we can expect the resulting decline in sales and output to temper their demands. Even should this not be the case, and should the union stubbornly insist on more regardless of employment effects, we may be sure that *managements* are not so unmindful of declining markets. Their costs of agreeing on the union's continuing wage demands will rise, thereby increasing their bargaining power relative to the union. And whether the union's demands are tempered by management or by others really makes no difference as far as the result is concerned.

The general effectiveness of these several restraints is suggested by the statistical findings, reported in Chapter 18, as to the limited influence of labor unions on relative wage rates. Nevertheless, such market forces by themselves are not always sufficient to contain union power, any more than product market competition is strong and persistent enough to rule out all business monopoly. Just as law has been invoked to deal with the latter, so too has legislation been passed to deal with labor-union power. In addition to existing legislation, a number of other measures have been proposed to curb the practices noted earlier in this chapter.

Legal control of monopoly powers

For almost half a century the principal federal restraint on monopolistic practices of labor unions was the Sherman Antitrust Act of 1890. Within the states reliance was placed either on legislative or common-law doctrines having the same effect. In earlier chapters we have traced the changing judicial interpretations of these doctrines, and we shall refrain from indulging in historical recall at this point. Let us satisfy ourselves with a brief summary of present legal coverage.

Any effort on the part of a union to fix the prices of the products on which its members work is precluded by the Supreme Court's interpretation of the Sherman Antitrust Act. In *Apex Hosiery Co. v. Leader,* 310 U.S. 469 (1940), the Court maintained that union restraints on competition which would be held unlawful under the act included efforts "to raise or fix the market price." Although the Sherman Act is applicable only to interstate commerce, a number of states have similar legislation covering intrastate commerce. Thus the agreement between Teamsters and Warehousemen to regulate the costs of moving and storage, referred to earlier, was found unlawful by the New York State courts.[9] Although the New York antitrust law contains a provision specifically exempting labor unions from its coverage, the court maintained that this exception protects unions in their lawful endeavors but does not protect them in fixing prices under the guise of increasing wages or regulating working conditions.

In principle, union attempts to exclude rivals from a market also fall under the ban of the Sherman Act if the union seeks this end in concert with the employers whom it would also benefit, but this principle has proved to be difficult to apply in practice. In the 1944 Allen-Bradley case, the facts and intent were clear in the three-cornered agreement between Local 3 of the IBEW and the New York electrical contractors' and manufacturers' associations, and the Supreme Court branded that type of agreement a violation of the antitrust law. In the Pennington and Jewel Tea cases in 1965, however, the intent was much less clear behind the UMW's attempt to win uniform wage standards throughout the coal industry and the Meatcutters' attempt to ban night work by its members in the Chicago area—both with the support of some employers against the opposition of others. As we saw in Chapter 8, the Supreme Court split in every direction on these two cases and no one is quite certain whether these types of agreements may in the future be regarded as conspiracies or as a legitimate use of a union's monopoly power.

The use of the secondary boycott, a device which has been employed to prevent nonunion competition with unionized shops, has now been virtually outlawed by the Taft-Hartley and Landrum-Griffin Acts. A union may not now seek to induce its members, or the employees of another firm, not to handle nonunion goods (or the goods of a firm which it has for some reason blacklisted). The jurisdictional strike, which has been used in an effort to monopolize jobs for members of a given union, has also been made an unfair labor practice under the Taft-Hartley Act. As Prof. Frederic Meyers has pointed out, even with the Supreme Court's present, very limited application of *antitrust* legislation to labor activities, the Court's rulings plus the restraining provisions of our labor–management legislation itself now outlaw virtually everything that was forbidden in the heyday of Sherman Act cases directed against the unions.[10] Nevertheless, there are those who believe that existing controls are not sufficient to curb the unions' powers to limit competition in their own interests, and they have advocated additional legislative restraints. While commonly these suggestions emanate from businessmen, they frequently are based upon an allegation that the unions' actions are injurious to other workers and

to consumers. This approach should be no cause for surprise or cynicism, since, as has been previously noted, commonly people seek to advance their own interests by convincing others that public interest is on their side. Among the various suggestions that have been made are the following:

1. Certain union practices which constitute unwarranted restraints on competition should be specifically made illegal. A statutory line would be drawn between legitimate and illegitimate union activities. The United States Chamber of Commerce, which advocates this approach, has recommended that among the illegal practices should be included industrywide bargaining when it assumes monopolistic proportions (a condition which, as with business monopoly, would lie within the province of the federal courts to determine on a case-by-case basis); featherbedding practices; the suppression of technological improvements; and consumer boycotts of nonunion goods.

The Attorney General's National Committee to Study the Antitrust Laws, in its report of 1955, also recommended this approach. With respect to restrictive legislation, the Committee concluded:

> It should cover only specific union activities which have as their direct object direct control of the market, such as fixing the kind or amount of products which may be used, produced or sold, their market price, the geographical area in which they may be sold, or the number of firms which may engage in their production or distribution.... Unlike the present Labor-Management Relations Act, the Government should have the power to proceed, on its own initiative, without formal complaints from others. A coerced employer, for example, might find it advantageous to acquiesce rather than complain.

2. Since a number of the monopoly charges raised against unions relate to the assumed or potential consequences of industrywide bargaining, another approach would outlaw this kind of bargaining. Generally, advocates of this policy have taken the position that the same union should not be allowed to represent employees of competing companies unless the latter are located within the same labor-market area, which has sometimes

been defined as "a single metropolitan or other geographical area, within which a majority of employees who are regularly employed at such places reside, which area shall not include any places of employment which are separated by a distance of more than one hundred miles."[11] Such restriction would presumably rule out multiemployer bargaining everywhere except at the local level.

Others have sought to go further by limiting collective bargaining to the employees of a single firm. Professor Edward H. Chamberlin of Harvard has lent the weight of his authority to this type of restriction. "I suggest as a good general rule that no employer should have brought against him pressures exerted by anyone other than his own employees."[12]

3. There are those who, while agreeing that the basis of the alleged union abuses lies in the imposition of common terms on a number of employers, believe that simple outlawry of industrywide bargaining would be inadequate to meet the problem. These people feel that even in the absence of a multiemployer bargaining unit, the power of the national union to approve or disapprove of contracts negotiated by local unions gives it the means to achieve the same results as industrywide bargaining. Thus the National Association of Manufacturers has advocated that "the problem should be attacked at its roots" by reducing national unions to the status of trade associations, which could service local unions by acting as a clearinghouse for data and an interpreter of relevant legislation and even a promoter of certain policies but which would have no power to enforce their views or will upon the constituent local unions.[13]

These proposals have not gone unopposed. Particularly on the issue of the desirability of banning multiemployer bargaining has there been dissent, even from employers. It has been pointed out that even if bargaining units were fragmented and the national union converted into an innocuous office of reports, it would prove virtually impossible to prevent "conscious parallel action" on the part of interested local unions. It has also been urged that multiemployer bargaining has sometimes improved the employer's position and that in the case of pattern bargaining (which is regarded as a kind of informal, industrywide bargaining relationship), unions have frequently deviated from the pattern because of the special circumstances of individual employers. It has been argued that even if the same wage increase is negotiated with competing employers, this is not likely to lead to identical increases in labor costs (since these would be affected by the wage systems of the several firms, by the state of their technological development, by their product mixes, and other such variables) and hence need not be expected to result in identical price increases. Consequently, employers bargaining jointly would not all be equally willing to concede the unions' demands in the expectation that they could all recover the added cost through price advances, since prices might have to advance more for some employers than for others.

A much more vigorous opposition to these proposals which would restrict the actions of the unions has been based on the proposition that they tend to concentrate on the maintenance of competition as an objective of public policy to the exclusion of the improvement in the conditions of labor as another and equally important objective of public policy. We turn now to this argument.

Dual objectives of public policy

In the United States, concern with the preservation of economic competition is traditional. It is to be found in common-law precedents and in a nineteenth-century popular mistrust of "big business" which reached its culmination in the Sherman Act in 1890. Public concern with improving the lot of workers stems from a somewhat later date. In the period of the country's adolescence, the stage of the economy's raw growth, working conditions were tolerated which later came to be condemned. With increasing national wealth and a greater familiarity with the use of democratic political machinery, it was to be expected that more attention would be paid to the condition and rights of workers. The twentieth century saw the recognition of the principle that workers should be allowed to form combinations to improve their position. Whatever the judicial view, unions were not popularly regarded as monopolistic organizations to be regulated in the same way as business. Indeed, they have frequently been considered as checks on business power. If unions were in their very nature a limitation of competition among workers, this was not regarded as the same sort of evil as a limitation of competition among business firms.[14]

The force of this reasoning emerges most clearly when unions are compared to giant corporations. If many thousands of stockholders can legitimately pool their interests to operate as a single economic entity called General Motors, then thousands of auto workers should also be permitted to pool their interests in a single organization called the United Auto Workers. This is the familiar justification of permitting workers some bargaining (monopoly) power in order to balance the bargaining (monopsony) power of large employers. The *dilemma* posed by this reasoning, however, emerges when one seeks to justify union monopoly power in industries populated by small and highly competitive firms, as in coal, construction, clothing, textiles, trucking, retailing, and many others—where wages and working conditions are often inferior to those in the monopolistic and profitable industries like auto and steel. Here worker organization is directed not against the individual employer but, instead, against the rigors of competitive market forces. Yet, those market forces are what the free-enterprise system is deliberately designed to encourage in order to maximize consumer choice and satisfactions. In other words, we encounter again one of the basic themes of this book: *most of the hard policy problems in the labor sector entail a balancing between the conflicting interests of consumers and producers.*

The point is that neither of these goals of our society—preserving competition in product markets or improving the welfare of workers in the labor market—can be said to be always paramount to the other. But efforts to bring labor unions under the limitations of antitrust legislation attempt to do just that—to make one public objective, competition, prior in importance to another public objective, worker welfare. Legislation which has been introduced into Congress from time to time[15] has sought to declare "that it shall

be unlawful for any labor organization or for the officers, representatives, or members thereof to enter into any contract, combination in the form of trust or otherwise, or conspiracy in restraint of commerce."

The difficulty with such legislation is that the preservation of competition in the product markets and the support of workers' efforts to improve their conditions in the labor market are policies which sometimes conflict.[16] Competition and labor-union activity are not always compatible. Since neither objective takes precedence over the other, how shall the conflict be resolved?

Several examples may help to point up the nature of the dilemma. One of the union practices complained of has been the exclusion of certain rivals from product markets. In the New York City ladies' garment industry, this complaint has been specifically directed to the union's successful efforts to limit by collective agreement the number of contractors with whom a clothing manufacturer can do business. Such a provision obviously limits the access of contractors to the market for their services and necessarily restricts the freedom of manufacturers to choose from among contractors. From time to time the Federal Trade Commission or the Department of Justice has argued that such an arrangement unlawfully restrains competition in the industry.

That the union limitation on the number of contractors is a restraint of competition would be the last thing that the union would deny. Its intent to accomplish a reduction in their number was publicly announced. The union told its side of the story in a pamphlet, *Why This Strike?*, which it circulated in 1936, the year it succeeded in securing this objective.

> The basic elements in the Jobber-Contracting System are immediately apparent to the eye. The jobber styles, cuts and sells the garments, he buys the silk and maintains showrooms for "his" line. He is the chief beneficiary of the industry. But when it comes to hiring workers and paying wages ... oh no! ... let the contractor do it.
>
> The next step is for the jobber to have a lot of contractors; the more the merrier. They bid against each other for work. They assume the speculative seasonal risks. They maintain ma-

chines and pay overhead. If they try to hold out for a just price, the jobber tells him there is another contractor waiting, and there is. . . .

Let us look at how the Jobber-Contracting System operates by peering into the books of a certain large jobber. In one year he had 55 contractors working for him. Twelve of these were regularly employed and produced 85% of his production. The other 43 received 15% of his production and the signal honor of being used as a club to beat down prices for all. Lest this seem an extreme example, a group of 81 jobbers was studied. Here it was found that 37% of the contractors handled 78% of the work, while the other 63% handled 22%. The picture is always the same. . . . Jobbers concentrating their production in a small number of contracting shops and using a large number as a competitive whip to depress prices. . . .

While the Union focuses its efforts and attention on the tens of thousands of workers who suffer under the system, a candid industrial viewpoint cannot avoid seeing the penalties paid by the contractors. Under the pressure of competitive bidding, he may agree to make a garment at a very low price. He may invest many hours in his business. He may draw little pay for himself and dissipate the hard earned dollars borrowed from relatives and friends. He may do all these things, and yet go broke because he tries to stack up against jobber manipulation. As the Governor's Advisory Commission reported, *the competition in the market in securing orders throws upon the contractors a cruel pressure out of all proportions to their powers of resistance.*

Yes, the contractor is more sinned against than sinning, but the sinned-against all too often turn sinner and the dressmakers pay. Every time a jobber hits a contractor, the workers bleed.

The Union announces simply and straightforwardly that the insanity of the unrestrained Jobber-Contractor System cannot be permitted to continue unchecked.

Here is an obvious conflict between the two public objectives of maintaining competition and improving working conditions. Few people would deny the evils inherent in unrestrained competition which has the effect of pressing down "unreasonably" the wages of a number of men and women seeking employment. Indeed, Congress itself recognized the problem involved by specifically exempting the clothing industry from the anti-hot-cargo provision of the Landrum-Griffin Act, thus permitting the unions in that industry to enter into agreements exempting their members from the necessity of working on materials made under "unfair" conditions. But what is unreasonable or unfair? How far should the union be allowed to seek the improvement of its members' welfare before it is deemed to have infringed on the other public aim of maintaining competition?

Even the union's intervention in pricing practices—an action which is usually regarded as the quintessence of abuse of monopoly power—has similarly been defended as necessary to the preservation of equitable working conditions, where competition has turned cutthroat. Thus in such industries as dry cleaning, which involve little capital to enter and where competition for customers has been keen, unions have seen the price of cleaning a garment driven down to such low levels, as one small outfit competes against the others simply for survival, that wages have had to follow prices downward, to permit continued operation. Under such circumstances, unions have sometimes been persuaded that a necessary condition for the improvement of wage levels was the prior maintenance of an "adequate" price level. At times, therefore, they have sought to enforce a "fair" price policy on competing firms by resort to picketing, boycotts, and even occasionally violence. Sometimes the employers in such an industry have welcomed the union as the only influence which will introduce some needed control over excessive competition. But if the union is capable of enforcing a policy of higher prices in the interests of its members, how much may it additionally charge the public for these services, for the benefit of its members, before it is judged to be greedy?

Again, unions have sometimes sought to impose limitations on technological changes in processes which might affect the employment of their members. Such restraints injure the interests of consumers, who otherwise would benefit from a superior product or a lower price. To what extent should we permit the union to exercise such power as it has to prevent or to retard these advantages from accruing to consumers, because the livelihood of its members is involved?

Again, we sympathize with the neutral employer who is involved in a secondary boycott as a union attempts to organize a nonunion employer. But the union points out that the existence of such nonunion firms, undercutting the terms which it has won elsewhere, constitutes a threat to the standards it is seeking to establish, so that it is entitled to resort to the expedient of the secondary boycott in its own protection. Which take priority —the interests of the neutral employer and his customers or the interests of the union workers trying to improve their conditions?

Pragmatic compromise

Such dilemmas are not easily resolved. They go right to the heart of the problem which was posed by the late Prof. John Maurice Clark. We recognize the need for preserving a large measure of competition, since competition is the most effective means of preventing an abuse of power. But unrestrained competition has its own deficiencies. Among other things, it prevents people from pursuing some objectives which can only be secured on a collective basis. In the absence of the union, for example, individual worker would compete against individual worker, with a demoralizing effect in time of unemployment and with the even more important consequence that at all times it would be difficult for the average individual employee to have an effective voice concerning his conditions of employment. Indeed, Professor Clark went so far as to call unions the workers' "alternative to serfdom."[17]

The only way in which a union can bargain effectively for its members, however, is by exercising some restraint on competition, which means asserting a monopoly power. *Once we accept unions, we accept the desirability of admitting some degree of monopoly power in our system of economic relationships.* What Professor Clark has suggested is that we need to work out not only a system of "workable competition" but also a system of "workable monopoly," in which both of these elements play their desirable roles and both are prevented from being abused.

This point of view differs markedly from that expressed by the school of economists typified by Prof. Henry Simons, who once wrote, in a widely cited article, that monopoly power had no use save abuse, and had sharply criticized unions as the most effective monopolies in modern economic society.[18] The Clark approach, which would appear to be more expressive of public attitudes, is that monopoly powers (even though not referred to as such) can have socially valuable functions; we must, however, prevent such powers from being used to excess.[19]

If this approach is accepted, then it seems clear that no *principle* has yet been defined to guide us in reconciling the public objective of maintaining competition in the product markets with the public objective of supporting workers' efforts to improve their conditions. The two objections must be rendered compatible—they cannot be made consistent—on a pragmatic basis. It is foolish to deny that the unions exercise monopoly powers in the interests of their own members. It is equally unwise to assume that all such restraints on competition are socially undesirable—or that they are all socially desirable. It is a matter of judgment, not of principle, as to where the line should be drawn between the licit and the illicit.

ADDITIONAL READINGS

Applicability of Antitrust Legislation to Labor Unions: Selected Excerpts and Bibliography, prepared by the Legislative Reference Service, Library of Congress, House of Representatives Committee on Education and Labor, 87th Cong., 1st Sess., 1961.

Bradley, Philip D. (ed.): *The Public Stake in Union Power,* University of Virginia Press, Charlottesville, Va., 1959.

Chamberlain, Neil W.: *Sourcebook on Labor,* McGraw-Hill, New York, 1958, chap. 19.

Hildebrand, George H.: "Collective Bargaining and the Antitrust Laws," in Joseph Shister, Benjamin Aaron, and Clyde Summers (eds.), *Public Policy and Collective Bargaining,* Harper, New York, 1962, pp. 152–181.

Lewis, H. Gregg: "The Labor-Monopoly Problem: A Positive Program," *Journal of Political Economy,* August, 1951, pp. 277–287.

Mason, Edward S.: "Labor Monopoly and All

That," *Proceedings of the Industrial Relations Research Association,* Madison, Wisc., 1955, pp. 188–208, with discussion, pp. 209–232.

U.S. Department of Justice: *Final Report of the Attorney General's National Committee to Study the Antitrust Laws,* 1955, pp. 293–306.

FOR ANALYSIS AND DISCUSSION

1. Appraise the criticism sometimes made of unions or union leaders that they ignore the consumer's interests.

2. Boycotts of nonunion products have sometimes been condemned on the ground that no union should have the power to influence directly a consumer's (or producer's) choice of products. How would you weigh this contention against the unionists' rebuttal that no employer should have the power to force his employees to work on materials produced under conditions which threaten their own interests?

3. Unions have often sought to exclude from American markets foreign-made goods made with labor paid very low rates. The Ladies' Garment Workers have agitated against the importation of Japanese blouses, the Flint Glass Workers have tried to put limits on the bringing in of glass made in Belgium and other countries, and so on. In these efforts they customarily are aligned on the side of employers. How does this attempt to exclude from domestic markets foreign products made at low wage rates differ in principle from efforts to block the marketing of United States products made at wage rates which are considered in some sense inferior or substandard? Is neither one—or are both—justified?

4. The following paragraphs appeared in the February, 1956, issue of *Labor's Economic Review,* published by the AFL-CIO, an issue devoted to an examination of "The 'Labor Monopoly' Myth":

> When workers join unions the result is markedly different from the effect of combinations of businessmen who ruthlessly rig prices in the product market.
>
> Corporate monopolies are unscrupulous in purpose and illegal in practice; they aim only to increase profits and enrich the few at the expense of the consuming public.

Unions, on the other hand, have emerged to serve the many—not a privileged minority. Today they are the champion of the millions who wish only to earn a decent livelihood and can do so only by combining the meager strength of each in a common cause for the common good. It is just that simple.

Analyze the above statement to establish what points of agreement or disagreement you may have with it.

5. Construct a list of union practices which you believe should be outlawed as monopolistic. Then try to establish the ways in which such practices may protect or benefit the workers involved. Review your original list of proscribed union activities and justify why, in each case, you believe that the consumer's interest transcends the worker's interest in importance.

NOTES

1. In examining postwar price increases, Simon H. Whitney, director of the Bureau of Economics of the Federal Trade Commission, remarked:

> Why, then, have prices since the war shown this new tendency to keep moving upward? . . . One new factor is national collective bargaining, which works in favor of collective, presumably not illegal, price action. With costs of all companies advancing simultaneously, complete independence in setting prices is hard to conceive—especially with products as homogeneous as steel.

See Testimony before the Senate Antitrust and Monopoly Subcommittee of the Judiciary Committee, March 13, 1959.

2. Thus a *New York Times* editorial of July 3, 1963, commenting acidly on the "greedy" demands of building-trades unions, was based on the foregoing line of argument.

> These crafts already enjoy wage scales double or triple those of most New York factory workers. . . . When mass unemployment replaces the overtime work their members are now feasting on [due to the construction demands of the 1964 New York World's Fair], these unions will, of course, be using their substantial political connections to bombard Governor Rockefeller, Mayor Wagner and Chairman Buckley of the House Public Works Committee with demands for massive construction projects to take up the slack. The community will then have the pleasure of paying the inflated new

wages for work designed to relieve the joblessness these wages have helped to create. . . .

3. Featherbedding is also sometimes mentioned as an example of a union's monopoly practice. This involves a union's forcing an employer to hire extra workers whom he does not need or want. It is difficult to see, however, how this is a "monopolistic" practice any different from union pressures for a wage increase. It adds to costs, to be sure, but so does a wage increase, or shorter hours, or fringe benefits. Nor does it restrict work opportunities for others—in fact, such union demands are frequently referred to as *"make-work"* practices. It seems probable that there is some moralistic basis for singling out feather-bedding for special attention—a belief that it is not "right" for workers to be paid for useless labor or even for work not performed at all. But in the present context, it is not apparent how featherbedding differs in any respect from any other demand involving additional labor cost which a union makes on an employer.

4. The obvious link between truck-labor and rail-service markets was emphasized in the explanation of a Teamster spokesman that "whenever a truck trailer is transferred to a flat car, a barge, or an airplane, truck drivers lose some work because of the shift to another form of transportation. He said the payments were designed merely to compensate for that. . . ." *New York Times,* Sept. 20, 1962.

5. Professor Ulman's researches into the origins of national unions have disclosed similar exclusionary agreements going back a good many years, especially in the building trades. He cites one example from the plumbing trade in Troy, N.Y., where a 1900 agreement specified:

That the party of the first part hereby agrees not to employ any plumber, steam and gas fitter who is not a member of Local Union No. 61, of the Plumbers, Gas and Steam Fitters, of Troy and vicinity, while the said Local Union No. 61 can furnish from among their members good, competent men. . . .

In consideration of the above agreement on the part of the party of the first part the party of the second part agrees . . . that the party of the second part also bind themselves and agree that no member of Local Union No. 61 shall accept employment to perform any work pertaining to plumbing, steam or gas fitting from any party or parties in the city of Troy or its vicinity who are not members of the Master Plumbers, Steam and Gas Fitters' Association of Troy and vicinity.

Ulman notes that such agreements were usually more effective when they could also be extended to control the supply of materials from outside the local union's jurisdiction, thus reserving to its members not only the work of installation and servicing but also of manufacturing—as in the IBEW Local 3 case. (Lloyd Ulman, *The Rise of the National Union,* Harvard University Press, Cambridge, Mass., 1955, p. 147.)

6. *Business Week,* Nov. 3, 1962, pp. 49–51. There is some question whether the union may not be repeating its mistake of the twenties when, again under John L. Lewis, it wrested a wage scale from the operators which it found impossible to make effective. The result then was to reduce the union to a state of impotence. To be sure, there are important differences between then and now, notably that large mines now are cooperating wholeheartedly with the union. Even so, the union is admittedly beleaguered.

7. The argument is set forth in Joseph M. Schumpeter, *Capitalism, Socialism, and Democracy,* 3d ed., Harper, New York, 1950.

8. *The Public Interest in National Labor Policy,* p. 138.

9. *Manhattan Storage and Warehouse Co. v. Movers and Warehousemen's Assn.,* 28 N.Y. Supp. (2d) 594 (1941).

10. Frederic Meyers, "Unions, Anti-Trust Laws, and Inflation," *California Management Review,* 1959, p. 37.

11. As in Senate bill 133, introduced by Sen. Joseph Ball in the 80th Cong.

12. "Can Union Power Be Curbed?" *Atlantic Monthly,* June, 1959, p. 49. George Romney, when president of American Motors Corporation, combined both of these limitations in a proposal made before a Senate subcommittee. He would have permitted local unions representing plants of a single company to join together for collective-bargaining purposes, regardless of the numbers involved. Local unions in companies with fewer than 10,000 employees could also join together for bargaining purposes, but only within prescribed geographical limits. The combination of local affiliates of more than one national union to deal with a single company, or with a number of employers of fewer than 10,000 employees within a given geographical area, would be forbidden. (*Administered Prices,* part 6 (Automobiles), Hearings before the Senate Subcommittee on Antitrust and Monopoly, 85th Cong., 2d Sess., 1958, p. 2961.)

13. In his proposal, mentioned in note 12, Romney contemplated "completely autonomous, independent [local] unions, . . . having the right to affiliate with their national unions in activities outside of the direct collective-bargaining area and the use of joint economic power in the same way that an employer can join a national trade association or a national industrial organization . . . Executives and staffs of international unions could provide economic research, reporting, technical, public relations, and advisory services to their autonomous union members." See the same, pp. 2964–2965.

14. This point of view was expressed by the Supreme Court, when it broke with tradition in *Apex Hosiery Co. v. Leader,* 310 U.S. 469 (1940):

A combination of employees necessarily restrains competition among themselves in the sale of their service to the employer; yet such a combination was not considered an illegal restraint of trade at common law when the Sherman Act was adopted, either because it was not thought to be unreasonable or because it was not deemed a "restraint of trade." Since the enactment of the declaration in Section 6 of the Clayton Act that "the labor of a human being is not a commodity or article of commerce ... nor shall such [labor] organizations, or the members thereof, be held or construed to be illegal combinations or conspiracies in the restraint of trade under the antitrust laws," it would seem plain that restraints on the sale of the employee's services to the employer, however much they curtail the competition among employees, are not in themselves combinations or conspiracies in restraint of trade or commerce under the Sherman Act....

Furthermore, successful union activity, as for example consummation of a wage agreement with employers, may have some influence on price competition by eliminating that part of such competition which is based on differences in labor standards. Since, in order to render a labor combination effective, it must eliminate the competition from non-union made goods, ... an elimination of price competition based on differences in labor standards is the objective of any national labor organization. But this effect on competition has not been considered to be the kind of curtailment of price competition prohibited by the Sherman Act."

15. Such as Senate bill 123, in the 80th Cong.

16. It is true that classical economists maintained that these two objectives were not only compatible with each other, but that the second was a logical derivative of the first. Only in a freely competitive society—competitive in labor as well as product markets—could each individual secure his highest reward and could the best interests of society as a whole be ensured. But even the twentieth-century spiritual heirs of the nineteenth-century classicists have now departed from that view.

In an economy operating under competitive forces, there may be numerous ways in which marginal private cost is less than marginal social cost. The speed-up system, unhealthy or unsanitary working conditions giving rise to disease and early disability or mortality, and technological changes which proceed without consideration of their impact on affected workers are obvious instances where the employer may bear little of the costs of injury which others have incurred in the process of working for him. These costs will, however, fall on society at large through expenditures for relief and general welfare purposes. Such situations may be susceptible to control only through concerted action over the competitive area. Indeed, this has been the basis for factory legislation, which has been resorted to because—implicitly—it has been assumed that the social cost of the actions of producers was higher than the costs which those producers were privately bearing, and consequently higher than the value of the marginal product. But the areas in which such control is socially desirable may be equally well or better encompassed through concerted union–management action, perhaps on an individual firm, perhaps on a multifirm basis. In this case it is the union's action which operates to secure society's optimum advantage, rather than the competitive mechanism, by placing on the production of certain goods and services a price tag which is more commensurate with their real cost.

17. J. M. Clark, *Alternative to Serfdom,* Harper, New York, 1948.

18. Henry Simons, "Some Reflections on Syndicalism," *Journal of Political Economy,* vol. 52, pp. 1–25, 1944.

19. This view complements, in the labor market and with respect to producers (whether workers or managements), the similar argument which Prof. Edward H. Chamberlin has made with respect to product markets. Product differentiation confers on producers a monopoly advantage by distinguishing the offerings of one producer from all other producers. This is one of the foundation stones for the theory of monopolistic competition, which Professor Chamberlin has pioneered. But consumers want differentiated products, since this widens the possibility of their quality choices. This means that not all monopoly in the product markets is to be condemned. Limitations on the effectiveness of price competition may be accepted as socially desirable. Our product markets are at their best when they combine elements of both competition and monopoly.

Perhaps the most basic economic problem that has plagued every democratic, industrialized nation during the postwar period is how to achieve the "magic trilogy" of full employment, stable prices, and free markets—the last meaning a minimum of government controls over such matters as wages, prices, and collective bargaining. This chapter explores the reasons why no country, including the United States, has yet solved that problem.

The difficulty, it should be stressed, lies not in identifying the *goals* we seek, but in providing the *means* for achieving them all simultaneously. In this and most other Western countries, you would be hard pressed to find anyone—labor or management, liberal or conservative—who would deny the desirability of any of these three goals of economic policy. But what if we can only achieve any two of these goals at the cost of the third? Which one should we sacrifice—full employment, stable prices, or free markets? No government cares to make that agonizing choice if it can possibly avoid it, and yet many people fear that is precisely the choice we face in the years ahead.

Figure 28-1 illustrates the problem in a general way. If you wish to abolish inflation, economists know a sure-fire remedy: Run the unemployment rate up to 10 or 15 percent of the labor force and leave it there, and you can be sure of stopping any wage-price spiral in its tracks. It can be seen that the massive unemployment of the 1930s even managed to drive prices downward, but obviously at a cost no one would choose to pay

again. Smaller doses of unemployment may stabilize prices for a time (as in 1949, the mid-1950s, and the early 1960s), but this is not certain (note the increase of both prices and unemployment in the late 1950s). In any event, an unemployment rate of "only" 4 to 7 percent still means real deprivation to many people ready and willing to work, and it does not meet the usual definition of full employment.

On the other hand, economists also know a guaranteed way of achieving full employment: Aggressively stimulate demand through large and rapid increases in the federal deficit and in the supply of money. This is not fanciful theorizing but observable fact, for that is precisely what happened when we entered World War II and saw the national debt soar and the unemployment rate drop to the vanishing point. As Figure 28-1 shows, unemployment also dropped during the periods of the Korean and Vietnam wars. On the other hand, those wartime deficits generated tremendous inflationary forces, leading to the imposition of wage and price controls during World War II and the Korean War and—in the absence of controls—the large wage and price increases of the Vietnam period. Thus we can easily obtain full employment, but at the risk of inviting either inflation or government controls.

By the same reasoning, the third goal—free markets—can be realized by simply refusing to institute controls over wages, prices, and strikes, but what will be the impact of that course of action upon the other two goals? Given the

Fig. 28-1. *Consumer prices and unemployment rates, 1929–1969.*
SOURCE: *U.S. Bureau of Labor Statistics.*

existence of many large-scale firms and unions, several experts fear that the closer the economy approaches full employment, the greater the probability that one of these parties will press its market power a little too hard, leading the other party to retaliate in order to catch up and thereby touching off the familiar wage-price spiral—or, if taxing and monetary policies check any price rise, a recession will be triggered as demand proves inadequate to meet the inflated price and wage levels.

If all this seems excessively gloomy, search Figure 28-1 for any period of even three or four years since 1929 during which prices remained stable, unemployment averaged 3 percent or less,

and wage and price controls were absent. Unfortunately, you will not find such a blissful period in the recent history of this or any other major industrial society. (The period between 1951 and 1956 may appear to be an exception, but Korean War controls were not lifted until 1953 and unemployment then averaged over 4.5 percent from 1954 to 1956.) Who is the culprit responsible for this—labor monopolies, big business, or the faulty policies of government?

In tackling that question, we shall first examine how full employment and stable prices became dominant goals of economic policy, then the various theories as to why these goals have been difficult to achieve in the postwar period without government controls, and finally the debate over what course we should follow to escape from this dilemma in the 1970s.

The goal of full employment

Understandably, it was the Great Depression of the 1930s, which at its worst left one-fourth of the nation's workers without jobs and the remainder wondering how long they would retain theirs, that first focused attention on the desirability of government action to ensure employment opportunities for all who wished to work. Government policies of the period aimed in that direction without so precisely spelling out their goal.

The New Deal leadership of the early thirties felt its way falteringly toward its eventual conception of the proper economic role of government. Roosevelt's initial premise that sound economics demanded a balanced federal budget—at a time when millions were jobless—should then have delighted, and would now dismay, even the most conservative economists. But under the pressure of the ineluctable need to do something to relieve the dire straits of a substantial proportion of the population, the New Deal administration stumbled along to the halfhearted acceptance of deficit financing as a valid instrument of public policy. If private enterprise could not provide jobs for all, the government would itself spend to put people to work.

A second major influence came in 1936, when John Maynard Keynes published his famous *General Theory of Employment, Interest and Money,* which provided a theoretical framework for full-employment policy. Keynes challenged traditional doctrine which (to the extent it concerned itself with depressions at all) viewed price dislocations as the principal cause of unemployment. He built a convincing argument that unemployment could emerge and persist whenever the amounts which individuals were willing to invest balanced the sums which individuals were willing to save at some level of aggregate expenditures less than was necessary to put everyone to work. Such a state of affairs might easily come about because different people were doing the saving and spending. If some people attempted to save more, while

other people made no effort to invest an equivalent additional amount, then national income would decline. It would continue to fall until it reached a level out of which people were saving no more than others were ready to invest. And at that level, unemployment could be substantial and could persist—unless government did something. Government could meet the situation by itself undertaking an investment program. It might also try to encourage private expenditures by a variety of measures, such as reducing taxes, insuring loans, lowering interest rates.

Keynesian theory was important in providing an acceptable rationale for governmental full-employment policies; moreover, it offered a theoretical framework within which governments might initiate more comprehensive planning to forestall the emergence of unemployment.

Finally, the sharp contrast provided by over-full employment during World War II and the dismal unemployment of the preceding decade led numerous people to question why, if an economy could be mobilized for maximum production for the destructive purposes of war, it could not also be mobilized for the constructive purposes of peace.

These three influences—the Great Depression of the thirties, Keynesian economics, and wartime planning for full production—set the stage for a movement throughout the Western world to ensure that the ravages of unemployment would not again sweep over the several economies following the ravages of war. By 1945 public sentiment had been effectively mobilized behind programs of governmental economic planning for full employment.

It was this element of economic planning which elicited a sharp conservative protest and precipitated a lively philosophical debate in the decade of the forties. From conservative economists came the charge that economic planning could not proceed without a centralization of authority that spelled a loss of people's liberties. Governmental authorities would determine when and to what extent public-works programs were needed and, if conducted on any large-scale basis, such public investment would preempt more and more of the private field, drying up private investment as businessmen feared to take on the government as a competitor. As the government assumed more responsibility for investment, it would inevitably be drawn into regulating wages and prices and deciding what should be produced and who should produce it. This is the charge of "creeping socialism"—the belief that partial and indirect controls inexorably expand into total and direct control by government, and the allied belief that periodic bouts of unemployment may be a necessary price of economic and political freedom.

In rebuttal to this Spartan view, proponents of a full-employment policy argued that political freedom is an empty abstraction to the man without a job and that no society which fails to provide jobs for its citizens can long retain its democratic basis. Moreover, it was argued, a free society seldom has to choose between total controls and no controls; we have placed some limits on every political freedom—of speech, press, assembly, religion—without going the route of total control, and we can do the same in partially regulating economic activities.[1]

As so often happens, the sharp contention between these camps led to something of a compromise position, the best example of which is the Employment Act of 1946. This was originally presented as a bill entitled the Full Employment Act, but congressional hearings revealed a concern by some over delegating power to any administration to achieve something so dangerously vague and novel as full employment. The final bill therefore pledged the government only "to promote *maximum* employment, production and purchasing power," and then only "in a manner calculated to foster and promote free competitive enterprise." The seed had nevertheless been planted and every postwar administration, Democratic or Republican, has pledged itself to attempt to achieve full employment. The Eisenhower administration, for example, ran up budget deficits to stem unemployment during the recessions of 1954 and 1958, just as the Kennedy and Johnson administrations did in the early 1960s.

The goal of stable prices

Yet, the ink was scarcely dry on the Employment Act of 1946 when inflation displaced unemployment as the chief domestic problem. This was not only an aggravation to consumers but a source of embarrassment to professional economists, most of whom had not anticipated the Depression of the 1930s and now failed to predict the inflation of the late 1940s. In fact, most economists had expected the end of the war to bring mounting unemployment, for that is what had happened after other major wars in our history.

In looking for an explanation of this surprising turn of events, many people naturally picked labor unions as the villain of the piece. It will be remembered that union membership had mushroomed from less than 3 million in 1933 to 15 million in 1946, and strike activity also hit an all-time peak in 1946 as 116,000,000 man-days were lost in 5,000 stoppages. Compared to the recognition struggles of the 1930s and the relatively modest gains made under wage and strike controls during the war, unions now appeared insatiable and unstoppable: a round of 18½-cent increases in 1946 was followed by a round of 15-cent increases in 1947 and 11 to 13 cents in 1948, accompanied by an expansion of escalator clauses, paid holidays and vacations, pensions, health and welfare funds, and union-security clauses. Unions claimed they were simply trying to catch up to the price spiral, but employers and many economists thought collective bargaining was a prime cause of that spiral.

In retrospect, that view has now been rejected by most experts. The most important new element in the 1940s, compared to previous postwar periods, was the fact that rationing and price and wage controls were far more effective in World War II than in previous wars. As a result, the wild inflation of previous wars did not occur during the years from 1941 to 1945 and consumers were able (and almost forced) to save a considerable portion of their relatively high earnings from wartime jobs—savings which were released in a rush when rationing and price controls were lifted after 1945 and families could bid at will for the relatively few cars and refrigerators and other consumer goods available as the economy converted to peacetime production. This was the source of the strong demand that surprised everyone expecting the usual postwar slump. Stated differently, the postwar inflation was basically an old-fashioned example of "too many

dollars chasing too few goods"; if unions intensified or prolonged that inflation, it was not by very
much. Also, the price increases from 1950 to
1953 are attributed primarily to the stresses of
the Korean War, not to either labor or management policies.[2]

This view is consistent with the studies of
union-wage impact in specific industries which we
examined in Chapter 18. It will be recalled that
Prof. H. Gregg Lewis, after appraising all of the
published studies of this question, concluded that
between 1945 and 1949 unions raised their members' wages by only zero to 5 percent above what
they would have been in the absence of unions.
We also reviewed there the reasons for that unexpected result: During a rapid inflation, the fixed
term of union contracts may actually make wages
lag more than they would in a nonunion setting,
and employers resist unusually large increases because they know union rates will be harder to cut
back in a subsequent deflation than nonunion rates
would be.

But the inflation problem did not end with the
Korean War. Examine Figure 28-1 again and
you will see a disturbing pattern for the years
from 1956 through 1965: *prices inched up in
every year, usually by 1 or 2 percent, although
unemployment was never lower than 4 percent
in any of those years and was usually above 5
percent.*

This is the "new inflation" that puzzles economists and frustrates policy makers. Generally
speaking, Keynesian theory can explain and prescribe the remedies for massive unemployment
on the scale of the 1930s, and classical theory
can explain and prescribe for a massive inflation
such as that occurring between 1945 and 1948.
But neither theory easily explains an economy
running a low fever, in which prices creep up
persistently in the face of unemployment rates
which hang somewhere between full employment
and serious recession levels. To policy makers, the
dilemma is painfully clear: If prices drift up by
1 to 2 percent when unemployment averages 5 to
6 percent, what will happen to prices if unemployment is pushed down to 3 percent or less, the
usual goal of those demanding full employment?
Everyone is in favor of providing jobs for the
hard-core unemployed, but everyone is also in

favor of stabilizing prices so they will not eat
away at the income of the aged and other low-
income families, and indeed the income of all
families. Can we provide jobs for the poor only
by driving up prices for everyone?

In assigning blame for this strange state of
affairs, some believe that the steel industry in
1958 provides the classic example of what is
wrong. The United Steelworkers and the major
companies had signed a three-year agreement in
1956, a prosperous year, calling for a wage hike
in 1958, which turned out to be a poor year. The
companies therefore asked the USW to waive the
increase promised for 1958 in order to promote
economic recovery by holding down costs and
prices, but the union retorted that the increase
was necessary to promote recovery by boosting
purchasing power. The union members thus obtained a wage increase, although hundreds of
thousands of steelworkers were on layoff, and the
companies promptly raised prices, although the
mills were operating at 50 percent or less of capacity—and in the economy as a whole, as the
apparent result of these and similar decisions, consumer prices rose by nearly 3 percent in a year
when unemployment averaged 6.8 percent. Critics
differ in assigning blame for such incidents to big
business or big labor or both, but everyone agrees
that something is amiss when wages and prices
continue to climb during years when there are
excess inventories, excess workers, and excess
plant capacity—everything *except* excess demand.

We shall return to this argument shortly, but let
us first finish our examination of the postwar
record. As Figure 28-1 shows, from 1961 to 1965
unemployment had been whittled down from
6.7 to 4.5 percent (but slowly, for fear of provoking inflation) and prices had drifted upward by a
little over 1 percent a year. Then, in mid-1965,
the Vietnam buildup began in earnest; production
and employment climbed and so did government
deficits (to $25 billion in 1968); unemployment
dropped below 4 percent for the first time since
the Korean War, and prices jumped by 15 percent
from 1965 to 1969. Essentially this was the experience of 1945 to 1948 all over again, though
on a somewhat smaller scale (prices then went up
by one third). This time few if any economists
claimed that unions were the major cause of a

war-induced inflation, although some believe that they made matters worse. Also, note that even in the midst of this latest boom, unemployment still had not reached the 3 percent level usually associated with full employment, and hard-core unemployment was still a problem in 1969.

In summary, consumer prices doubled from 1929 to 1969 but two-thirds or more of that increase—that occurring from 1940 to 1953 and 1965 to 1969—is largely if not completely attributable to war-connected forces of the classic type summed up as "too many dollars chasing too few goods." This does not belittle the importance of the "new inflation" of the period from 1956 to 1965 but rather demonstrates how subtle both the inflation and unemployment problems have become. Instead of the great debates of the past, in which some people blamed big business for the 15 to 25 percent unemployment rates of the 1930s and others blamed unions for the 33 percent price increase between 1945 and 1948, we now worry over whether pressing the unemployment rate down just another point or two to 3 percent will cause prices to rise by 4 or 5 percent a year.

But if that appears to be a trivial problem, note that the difference between 4 and 3 percent unemployment is 800,000 jobs today, many of which could be filled by those now unemployed if demand were a little higher and hiring standards a little lower. And also remember that we expect productivity increases of only about 3 percent a year, meaning that the average family's real income is expected to go up by only that much each year even if we have stable prices and full employment. If, instead, prices go up by 4 or 5 percent in a year, the average family will slip backward in its standard of living—unless it wins wage increases of 8 or 10 percent a year to stay ahead of inflation, which then may trigger off even larger price and wage increases.

Explanations of the new inflation

Most attempts to isolate the cause of the new inflation center upon one or more of the following: the power of some unions to win wages above the level dictated by market forces alone; the power of some companies to set prices above com-

petitive levels; the inability of market forces to adjust quickly to shifts in the *structure* of demand among various sectors of the economy (as opposed to changes in the *volume* of demand in the economy); and society's determination not only to avoid inflation, which has always been a goal of economic policy, but also the postwar commitment to achieve full (or at least "maximum") employment. But different analysts mix these ingredients together in quite different ways.

Among the people who regard unions as the major source of trouble are those who believe that we will suffer alternating bouts of inflation (caused by union pressure on wage costs) and unemployment (as the only force effective enough to curb union power). As a succinct statement of this position, the following analysis by Prof. Gottfried Haberler, although written in 1951, still bears repeating today:[3]

> 1. There is under any given set of circumstances a certain limit beyond which the money-wage level cannot be pushed without either a rise in prices or the appearance of unemployment.
> 2. Our society will not tolerate an indefinite rise in prices. Sooner or later, steps will be taken through monetary or fiscal policy, or direct control, to counteract further price rises.
> 3. Labor unions are not satisfied with wage increases on this side of the critical limit; they tend to push beyond it.
> Conclusion: Unemployment is inevitable.

Haberler estimates that the "critical limit" will be reached when prices have risen by 5 to 10 percent a year for only "a year or two." Because he believes that unions have the power to force increases of this magnitude, he sees only one alternative to recurring unemployment. If people want price stability and yet will not tolerate unemployment, they must curb the power of unions.

This version has been largely replaced in recent years by a more sophisticated analysis, based on a statistical examination of the relationship between unemployment and price changes. Instead of anticipating alternating periods of inflation and unemployment, this newer approach sees a political compromise being struck between the exponents of full employment and the opponents of inflation. The compromise takes the form of a higher tolerance for unemployment on the one side and of price rises on the other, but with a restraining hand on excesses of either.

This thesis gained impetus from studies undertaken by Prof. A. W. Phillips of the London School of Economics, an electronics engineer who became interested in economics when a prisoner during World War II. Plotting wage changes against unemployment in the United Kingdom over a period extending from 1861 to 1957, he found a rather consistent relationship between the two emerging from his data.[4] Wage increases were no more than equal to the general increase in productivity, with prices remaining stable, when the rate of unemployment was at about 2½ percent of the labor force. Unemployment rates below that level led to an upward movement in wages (and presumably prices). If wages were held stable, with productivity increases being channeled through price reductions, the unemployment rate had to rise to approximately 5½ percent. The policy implication which many read into these findings was that there had to be a certain "trade-off" between unemployment and wage-level (price-level) changes. Less of one led to more of the other.[5]

These figures were for England, but Profs. Paul Samuelson and Robert Solow made a comparable though admittedly somewhat more casual study for the United States. They found that the bulk of their observations seemed to accord closely with Phillips's data for Britain. But beginning in 1946 the pattern changed. They found a "strong suggestion" that, whereas in the earlier years wage increases could be kept to approximately the 2 to 3 percent rate of increase in productivity when the level of unemployment was about 3 percent, in the post-World War II period it took an unemployment rate almost double the earlier one to hold wage increases to the same level. And to keep money wages absolutely stable, it would take an unemployment rate of perhaps 8 percent.

Their conclusions were succinctly stated as follows:[6]

1. In order to have wages increase at no more than the 2½ per cent per annum charac-

teristic of our productivity growth, the American economy would seem on the basis of twentieth-century and postwar experience to have to undergo something like 5 to 6 per cent of the civilian labor force's being unemployed. That much unemployment would appear to be the cost of price stability in the years immediately ahead.

2. In order to achieve the nonperfectionist's goal of high enough output to give us no more than 3 per cent unemployment, the price index might have to rise by as much as 4 to 5 per cent per year. That much price rise would seem to be the necessary cost of high employment and production in the years immediately ahead.

All this is shown in our price-level modification of the Phillips curve [Figure 28-2]. The point A, corresponding to price stability, is seen to involve about 5½ percent unemployment; whereas the point B, corresponding to 3 per cent unemployment, is seen to involve a price rise of about 4½ percent per annum. We rather

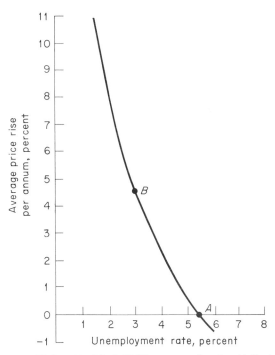

Fig. 28-2. *Modified Phillips curve for the United States.*

SOURCE: American Economic Review, *May, 1960,* p. 192.

expect that the tug of war of politics will end us up in the next few years somewhere in between these selected points. We shall probably have some price rise and some excess unemployment.

Samuelson and Solow were hesitant to ascribe the shift in what has become known as "the Phillips curve," which apparently occurred in the forties and fifties, to either a full-employment policy or the rise of big unions. Other economists have been less hesitant to make the judgment that unions are probably the responsible factor.

Sources of monopoly power

Even if one accepts these findings, they leave questions to be answered. If, even in the face of substantial unemployment and weak demand, wages and prices can rise, this clearly implies that there are forces present which are not responsive to market—that is, competitive—pressures. We have been accustomed to labeling such forces "monopolistic." From what sources do they arise?

Some people believe that labor unions constitute such a monopoly influence. Since we have already devoted a whole chapter to examining the ways in which unions may exercise control over prices and production, let us simply note that one method to which craft unions in particular have resorted has been the restriction on entry by other workers to jobs over which the unions assert jurisdiction. With fewer workers capable of performing certain functions, or available to an employer, there is less competition in the labor market. Even if wages are bargained upward, and prices move up with them, there may be little a customer can do except pay the bill. This is as true of plumbers as of doctors. In both instances there appears to be a high price inelasticity of consumer demand, so that by restricting the number of licensed plumbers and doctors, the practitioners in those fields are in a better position to "set their own wage rates."

But clearly this kind of power is less available to an industrial union, with its membership composed of semiskilled and unskilled as well as skilled workers, most of whom learn their skills on the job and can easily be replaced. Unions in the mass-production industries, far from seeking to restrict the supply of labor, often attempt to force their management to hire more men on a given job than the management thinks necessary. What monopoly power is there here?

The answer is at least as clear as in the craft-union case: business-monopoly power. We have already had occasion to learn that, with few exceptions, whatever monopoly gains accrue to unions and their members must be derived *through* the business firm.[7] In the case of the large corporations, any would-be competitor who might be attracted by high profit rates would quickly forget his dream when he began to consider how much it would cost him to build a plant and get into production and establish retail outlets and service units, and the risks attending such an effort even if he could find the capital. If a group of men began looking enviously at the profit which General Motors makes, how feasible would it be for them to enter the automotive field and skim off some of that profit for themselves?

The division of a market among a few large giants, with a scattering of smaller establishments on the fringes often doing quite well for themselves as long as they are satisfied with staying small, is a made-to-order situation for a union. Once it is able to organize the major producers (and that has now been done), it can use its bargaining power to raise wages, and the corporations with which it bargains can use their market power to pass costs along in the form of higher prices, without fear that nonunion competition will make them regret their action.

To be sure, as we noted in the chapter on labor monopoly, there are some restraints on both union and business power, but as we noted there too, these restraints are less than perfect. As long as the company possesses some power over its market position, the union can exploit that to its advantage—but it is the business firm's monopoly power which is the key. The labor union does have a monopoly position of its own, in the form of an NLRB certification as exclusive bargaining agent, so that there is no danger that an unwilling employer can dismiss it and do business with another union ready to sign an agreement costing less. So the labor union is entrenched as bargaining agent, and the corportion is entrenched in its product-market fields, and the two—with sidelong glances at what is happening to prices of substitute products, and how the public is reacting, and what the government is likely to do—can make a bargain raising wages and prices, even though there are unemployed workers who would be willing to work for less and unemployed plant capacity which could earn a profit on sales at lower prices.

Thus, when a businessman points an accusing finger at the labor union as the cause of inflation, he very often conveniently overlooks that it is a power position of his own firm which gives the union its power. If his business were faced with stiffer competition, he would be less willing to grant the wage increases being demanded. His cost of agreeing on the union's terms would include the loss of a larger share of the market than now is the case, so that he would resist the union more vigorously, forcing it to reconsider its demands before being plunged into a costly strike. The relative bargaining powers of the two parties would be shifted to the company's advantage and the union's disadvantage.

It would be a mistake to exaggerate the monopoly power of even the largest corporate giant; even General Motors is subject to the rigors and uncertainties of competition from other automobile producers and other forms of transportation. We need only note the ineluctable fact that the rigors and uncertainties of competition are less for General Motors than they are for the average small firm, and that the Auto Workers benefit from that fact.

All of this is again consistent with the studies of union-wage impact which we reviewed in Chapter 18. These studies minimized the wage effects of unions in the sharp inflation of the 1940s, but showed a stronger impact (estimated by Lewis to be about 15 percent) in the late 1950s.

From particular to general inflation

If wages and prices rise without respect to the underlying demand situation in one industry, such as steel, we may think of that as a situation of *particular* inflation. It happens in one industry, and by itself can hardly be said to create a condition of general inflation. If one argues that it is labor unions and business firms, both enjoying some measure of monopoly power, which are among the principal agents forcing up the price level, does this imply a belief that enough business firms enjoy sufficient monopoly power (or have it conferred on them by the unions with which they bargain) so that, when all of them advance wages and prices, they thereby produce a general increase in the price level? The answer is hardly so simple.

In order to understand the conclusions which some of the experts have reached, we must first go back to the relationship between incomes and productivity, which we touched on briefly in Chapter 15 and which will play an important part in the analysis which follows. Productivity presumably tells us how much more goods we can produce and distribute because of increasing efficiency. If there is no change in the functional distribution of income, so that wages, profits, interest, and rent all retain their same relative positions, then all can increase by the amount which productivity increases, and prices will remain stable. If the total bundle of goods which we produce increases by 3 percent, owing to better methods of production, then everybody can have 3 percent more income without any change in prices. It is because some get more than this—perhaps in higher profits, perhaps in higher wages—that others must either get less or prices must rise.

There are two schools of thought about the role which unions play in this process. From one point of view, they initiate the inflationary pressures, while from another point of view, they supplement inflationary pressures which have their origin elsewhere.

Unions as initiators of cost inflation Suppose that productivity in the steel industry has risen by 10 percent. The Steelworkers bargain with the industry for a wage increase, and, under a threat of strike, management gives the union a wage increase of 10 percent. (This, of course, does not exhaust the productivity gains, since all factor costs, as well as profits, can be increased by an amount equal to the gain in total productivity.) Suppose further that the industry exercises restraint and does not raise its prices; after all, it does have a rising profit as a result of its higher productivity.

Nevertheless, despite the fact that steel prices have not risen, the Steelworkers can be charged with initiating inflationary pressures. The fact that their wages have increased by 10 percent puts pressure on other unions and even unorganized workers to seek as much and on other employers to grant as much.[8] Even assuming that some unions and workers will be disappointed and some employers will be stubborn, we can realistically assume that the size of the wage increases granted will be larger than if the Steelworkers had settled for less. But in these other industries, and particularly in the service sector, productivity will not be rising by anything like 10 percent. Overall, the economy has tended to experience an increase in productivity averaging about 2.4 percent. In those industries which have enjoyed productivity gains somewhere in the neighborhood of this average, the above-average increases stimulated by the Steelworkers will necessarily force price increases. Thus even though the steel industry may not itself have raised prices, it and the steel union are responsible for the general inflationary pressures which arise even in nonunion sectors of the economy. To the extent that steel raises its prices, of course, the inflationary effect will be all the greater.

In this process the Steelworkers may gain an initial advantage for their members, but their very position as a pattern setter contributes to the short-run nature of that advantage, at least in its full amount. As other sectors of the economy follow suit, with a lag, the Steelworkers' advantage dwindles. They have contributed to a general upward movement in prices without much shift in the proportionate distribution of real goods in favor of their members. No wonder that many Steelworkers in the Pittsburgh area expressed their disillusionment with the real-income effects of bargained money-wage gains when questioned by Duquesne University interviewers in 1959 and 1960.

A group of six economists from five different countries, commissioned by the Organization for European Economic Cooperation, placed heavy emphasis on this mechanism by which unions, and the corporations with which they bargain, generate price-raising pressures. Pointing to, among other things, the tendency for "key bargains" to spread

their influence right across the economy, regardless of the state of demand in the different industries and sectors, it concluded: "All members of the Group are agreed that excessive wage increases secured through negotiations have been a significant factor in the upward movement of prices. . . ."[9]

It scarcely needs adding that one corollary of this analysis is this: The stronger, more powerful, and more visible are the pattern-setting unions, and the greater the market power exercised by the corporations with which they deal, the higher is the wage increase likely to be which is transmitted to other sectors of the economy, including those which are unorganized.

Unions as boosters of inflationary pressures originating elsewhere The most effective statement of this thesis has been made by Prof. Charles L. Schultze, on the strength of a detailed examination of the period 1955 to 1957 in the United States.[10] His conclusion was that a sudden shift in the *composition* of total demand, so that prices rise in one or more sectors of the economy where the new demand pressures are felt, can lead to a general inflationary situation. The general inflation stems not from an overall excess of demand, nor does it stem solely from a cost push by powerful unions. It originates as an excess demand in a particular sector, with prices and wages rising there, and then is transmitted via sympathetic or imitative wage and price movements elsewhere in the economy.

This effect is aggravated by the fact that there is little tendency for wages and prices to decline even in those industries experiencing a drop in demand. There is a strong resistance by workers and unions to any wage cutting, and employers are reluctant to reduce prices because of the adverse consumer reaction if they have to be raised again later. This policy of downward price rigidity is reinforced by the increasing proportion of overhead costs in many operations.[11] With wages and prices stable even in sectors where demand is weak, and rising in those sectors where demand is ebullient and in others to which these latter transmit their influence, the net effect is an upward movement.

Since we may expect the composition of demand to shift from time to time, we can anticipate a secularly rising price level. From 1955 to 1957, the period which Schultze examined, it was the investment goods sector which was the beneficiary of a sudden demand thrust and which communicated its higher wages and prices to other sectors. At another time quite a different sector may be the initiator. Thus Prof. James Duesenberry has suggested that the increasing demand for services and the difficulty which the service trades often experience in recruiting labor probably drove wages up faster in that sector in the period after Korea.[12] The rising cost of services increased the cost of living in the manufacturing and other organized sectors, where—regardless of the state of demand for their own products—unions pressured for higher wages and were accorded them. Here again, but this time in a consumer sector, a shift in demand could be said to have initiated price increases which were given a further boost by workers and unions in other industries.

The Council of Economic Advisers has argued that the same type of sectoral imbalance touched off the inflation of the late 1960s sooner than one would have expected from the rise in total demand as such. When the Vietnam buildup began in mid-1965, unemployment averaged about 4.5 percent and by the end of 1966 it had dropped to only 3.8 percent, suggesting that labor markets were not tight in general. But the sharp rise in demand for defense products (coming on top of an investment boom in new plant and equipment that had begun earlier) imposed special pressures on the metals and machinery industries, and employment in durable-goods manufacturing, which had remained relatively stable since 1954, now rose by one million workers in eighteen months. Since that is a high-wage sector, other employers had to raise wages to attract or retain workers; service prices rose even faster than before and food prices went up for unrelated reasons. Unions had little to do with kicking off these price increases because few major contracts were open in 1966, but the wage settlements made in that year increased in size as union members naturally sought to keep ahead of the rising cost of living —and employers just as naturally sought to pass on increased costs. This does not vitiate our earlier conclusion that the inflation of the late

1960s was *primarily* an "old-style" inflation induced by government spending on the Vietnam war, but the events of 1965 and 1966 illustrate again how sectoral imbalances can lead to wage and price increases even when there is slackness in product and labor markets in general.[13]

Regardless of how one views the mechanism by which particular wage and price increases are generalized to the rest of the economy, it is clear that market or monopoly power is involved. *Both* unions and business firms are part of the process, although they may gain little lasting advantage from their efforts and although, once the process is started, it is virtually impossible to determine whether wages are pushing or chasing prices upward. Even if demand factors play a significant role in starting inflation, it is sometimes the subsequent actions of unions and corporations occupying strategic market positions or enjoying some degree of immunity from competition which keeps the ball rolling by spreading the effects to the rest of the economy. In the light of this fact, efforts to cope with the "new inflation" require some sort of policy which affects the decisions and actions of these institutions.

It is worth dwelling for a moment on this point to make it quite clear. In times of general excess demand, when there is an absolute shortage of all kinds of goods relative to the number of customers waiting with money in their hands, no one doubts that demand is the causal agent in the inflation which is certain to develop. No economist disputes that in such circumstances the monetary authorities have a vital role to play in restricting the amount of credit made available, and fiscal authorities have an equally vital role in sopping up, through higher taxes or through the sale of government bonds, money which otherwise would be spent on goods. This is the old-fashioned inflation about which everyone knows. It occurs principally in connection with war and its aftermath.

The question posed by the new inflation is quite different. As we have seen, it can arise in one sector of the economy and spread contagiously to the rest of the economy, and this may happen at times when there are plenty of most goods available, a surplus of most kinds of workers, and idle plant facilities. Excess demand may still be a factor, but, if it is, it is an excess demand which does not affect the whole economy but is confined to some part of it—the service industries or the investment-goods sector, for example. And one of the major reasons why it can and does spread from one sector to other sectors is that pressures arise to match the wage increases given in the prospering part of the economy, and that such pressures can be accommodated in many instances because (1) competition is not so severe that firms are unable to inch up on their prices, and (2) with numbers of firms raising wages and prices, the Federal government can be counted on to "validate" these increases through fiscal and monetary measures designed to stave off any threat of large-scale unemployment.

Remedies for new inflation

The solutions that have been offered to this problem of the new inflation can be grouped under six headings: employ orthodox fiscal and monetary measures; eliminate the bottlenecks that lead to sectoral imbalances; break up union and corporate monopolies; impose wage and price controls; accept a small amount of inflation or unemployment as preferable to the alternatives; or call for voluntary restraint by labor and management.

Orthodox fiscal and monetary controls There are both logic and political appeal to the argument that creeping inflation can be controlled by the same weapons that everyone agrees will control rampant inflation: Congress can manipulate taxes and public spending so that the government takes out of the economy as much or more purchasing power than it puts into the economy (that is, run a balanced federal budget or a budget surplus), and the Federal Reserve Board can keep a tight check on credit and other forms of money supply.

The logic of this proposal rests on the reasonable assumption that unions and corporations want to maximize their wage and profit gains. If these parties learn through painful experience that the government will *not* jump in to validate excessive wage and price increases, but will instead hold the price line and let employment and profits decline temporarily, then simple self-interest will lead labor and management to curb their market power and we can eventually achieve both full

employment and stable prices. The political appeal of this proposal is that everyone accepts this indirect type of control as a legitimate function of government which does not require any bureaucrat to tell any private citizen what he must or must not do.

The principal difficulty with this approach is that it hasn't worked. Fiscal and monetary controls have long been the chief economic weapons used in every Western country, and properly so, for only these measures can control the *major* swings in the business cycle. No critic disputes this elementary fact. *But these controls alone have not been able to take any country that "last mile,"* in which the final one or two percent of hard-core unemployment is eliminated without pushing up prices. In this country both Republican and Democratic administrations have tried to pull off this trick without using other controls, and both have failed.

The defenders of this approach charge that it has failed only because past administrations (and Congresses) have lacked the technical skill or the political courage necessary to make it work. Its critics believe the problem is more basic, however. First, they argue that fiscal and monetary weapons are too blunt for the task at hand. As Professor Galbraith has put it, to expect orthodox controls to keep the economy at full employment while avoiding inflation "is roughly equivalent to asking a reluctant surgeon to do a lobotomy with a spade."[14] These controls can obliterate a major inflation or depression, but they cannot "fine tune" a complex economy in which their effects must be filtered through the saving and spending decisions of millions of buyers and sellers. Thus, while it may be comforting to think of some wizards in Washington adjusting interest and tax rates by a point or two and thereby reducing unemployment and prices by another one-half percent, such precision is just not possible.

Second, fiscal and monetary weapons have an inequitable impact even when they are effective. We saw in Chapter 19 that federal taxes are not as progressive as commonly thought, and that state and local taxes (primarily sales and property taxes) are decidedly regressive. As for monetary policy, it often requires making credit funds so scarce that it depresses industries particularly sensitive to changes in interest rates (such as construction, which nosedives during any "credit crunch" because prospective homeowners cannot afford the higher mortgage charges), while having little effect upon large corporations which can draw upon depreciation funds and undistributed profits or which, if forced to borrow from banks, will receive preference over small businesses because they are better credit risks. If the wage and price policies of large corporations are a major source of the new inflation, this is an inefficient way of getting at them.

Third, monetary controls have lost some of their flexibility because of our recent problems in maintaining a favorable balance of payments in our dealings with other countries. This is an enormously complicated subject to which we cannot do justice here, but a few facts will illustrate the problem.

Contrary to popular belief, the United States has consistently run a favorable balance of trade throughout the postwar period in the buying and selling of goods and services. That is, we have sold more goods and services (in dollar volume) to other countries than we have bought from them. This favorable balance has dwindled since the 1940s, as other countries have recovered from the war and become more efficient competitors in international markets, but not until 1968 did the value of our imports equal the value of our exports in any postwar year. On the other hand, our heavy expenditures abroad for military and economic assistance to other countries generate very little offsetting inflow, and it is principally this factor which has produced a deficit in our *total* financial transactions with the rest of the world in nearly every year since 1950. This in turn has meant that foreign holders of dollar balances could and to some extent did demand gold in exchange for their dollars, leading to the halving of our gold reserves from 1950 to 1970 and the increasing worry about maintaining confidence in the dollar—and a loss of confidence could mean devaluation of the dollar, sharp cuts in foreign aid and overseas military commitments, restrictions on imports and on travel and investment abroad by Americans, and a loss of jobs dependent on foreign trade.

At the same time this gold drain was develop-

ing, we know that unemployment in the range of 4 to 7 percent was a persistent problem in this country. Normally one tool that would be used to encourage a higher level of economic activity would be a low interest rate. By making it cheaper for businessmen to borrow funds and for people to buy homes and appliances, we would encourage investment and consumption and hope to create additional jobs. But now our balance-of-payments difficulty gets in the way. There is always a substantial amount of "short-term money" moving around the world in response to changing interest rates. If rates in this country were to be lowered to create jobs, this might drive many foreign holders of dollars, who have been leaving their funds in this country to earn interest, to exchange those dollars for other currencies—and for gold—in order to transfer them to more profitable investments elsewhere. This could lead to a very sharp increase in the drain on our gold stocks.

Thus, critics charge, monetary policy has a bias in attacking the price-employment dilemma: there are always good reasons for raising interest rates to check prices and attract or hold foreign investments in this country, but it always looks risky to lower interest rates to counter a drop in employment. For this and the other reasons spelled out above, many economists have concluded that orthodox fiscal and monetary measures, while invaluable up to a point, cannot bridge that final critical gap that separates us from our goal of full employment with stable prices.

Eliminate bottlenecks in the economy   Another approach that would avoid direct controls grows out of the belief that there is not just one economywide cause of the problem summed up in the Phillips curve, but instead, a series of different problems causing bottlenecks in different sectors of the economy. Prof. John Dunlop has proposed this approach:[15]

> The major activities of the government in such a bottleneck program would be as follows:
> (a) The identification . . . of the major priority bottlenecks in the economy. . . .
> (b) The development of detailed private and public policies in the bottleneck sectors to mitigate inflationary pressures by increasing sup-

plies and constricting demands. This policy development would require close collaboration of labor, managements, and operating government agencies at the federal and state levels. . . .

(c) The range of policies developed for each bottleneck sector would involve continuing interchange of discussion, statistics and appraisal of the outlook by private parties and government representatives. . . . It is clear that the appropriate and practical policy is highly variable and specialized to a sector.

Dunlop suggested that the high-priority sectors would be some branches of transportation, medical and hospital services, construction, local government services, certain professional services, and automobile manufacturing. These are the sources of much of the increase in living costs during recent years, and yet many of them are not included in the usual discussions deploring the inflationary effects of big business and big labor. Also, it is obvious that the programs necessary to increase the supply of doctors, nurses, and hospital facilities are not the same as those needed to restrain the market power of large firms in the auto industry or to increase the bargaining power of small firms in the construction industry or to untangle the many problems of the railroad industry. In short, there is no single law or economic policy that can be adopted in Washington to correct all the imbalances in supply and demand—many quite unrelated to monopoly power—which are driving up prices in these and other problem sectors. But until those imbalances are corrected, Dunlop argues, it will probably be impossible to move that "last mile" toward full employment and stable prices.

Others have urged that this is another good reason for improving the operation of labor markets in general and for upgrading the labor supply. As matters now stand, it is argued, increasing demand to full-employment levels creates labor shortages and inflationary pressures because the last one or two percent of the unemployed cannot move smoothly into the jobs newly opened. There are many ways of correcting this situation, most of which we have touched upon in previous chapters: improve vocational education for those still in school; offer training programs for the hard-core unemployed; improve the job-information

and placement activities of the public Employment Service; bring jobs into depressed areas or help workers move out of those areas when jobs are available elsewhere; reduce seasonal unemployment; eliminate discrimination against women and members of minority groups; and improve unemployment insurance, workmen's compensation, and vocational rehabilitation programs. As the workers who are now "marginal" gain more skill and mobility and adaptability, and as the mechanisms for matching job vacancies and unemployed workers are improved, the labor market is less likely to develop inflationary bottlenecks as the economy moves from 5 to 4 to 3 percent unemployment.

It would be hard to find anyone who would challenge the desirability of most of these structural reforms. To oversimplify, liberals have long pressed for many of these reforms as a matter of equity and conservatives have long argued that the best way to meet most economic problems is to improve, rather than regulate, the operation of competitive markets. The question today, however, is whether these programs are enough to solve the price-employment equation—that is, enough to move the Phillips curve down to the point where full employment and stable prices coincide. Everyone is in favor of eliminating racial discrimination and the shortage of doctors and barriers to mobility and the many problems (labor and nonlabor) of the construction and transportation industries, but public and private groups have been wrestling with all of these bottlenecks for years. One can argue that not enough has been done, and that is certainly true, but it seems unlikely that enough will have been done ten or twenty years from now either, if by "enough" one means the elimination of most of the bottlenecks now existing in the economy plus those bound to develop in the future. Meanwhile, what do we do about the wage-price-employment issue this year and next?

Break up union and business monopolies Moving to more direct action, many people have reasoned that if monopoly power is a prime cause of the "new inflation," then the obvious remedy is to eliminate that monopoly power whether found in the form of giant unions or giant corporations.

We have already discussed the flaws in this approach with respect to labor unions in Chapter 27, where we stressed that every union by definition is a monopoly and that the hard question is whether to allow labor a little more or a little less monopoly power, recognizing that this power yields many benefits as well as many costs.

Exactly the same reasoning applies to corporate monopoly. General Motors and IBM and Du Pont do not fit the competitive model much better than the Teamsters and the UAW do. Yet, how could we obtain the benefits of low-cost mass production and the development of new products by industrial research if we replaced each large corporation by thousands of small firms? As Galbraith observed several years ago, the industries usually cited as the epitome of our dynamic economy— autos, steel, chemicals, computers, aerospace, and so on—are often those which depart farthest from the competitive model, and our "problem industries" are frequently those which are most competitive in structure, such as agriculture, coal mining, cotton textiles, and residential construction.[16]

We are therefore not going to turn the clock back to the days of agrarian democracy in order to fight inflation or any other problem on the horizon. We shall doubtlessly continue to control specific abuses of monopoly power as we have in the past—through amending our labor and antitrust laws in one particular or another—but not through a massive restructuring of corporations and labor unions.

Wage and price controls If indirect controls won't work and if corporate and labor monopolies cannot be broken up, why not impose direct wage and price controls? Professor Galbraith is one of the few economists to argue that this is indeed the best answer available:[17]

> Given full employment or any close approach to it, wages and prices are subject to large discretionary movements. The only preventative is some public restraint on this discretion.
> This might not be so very difficult to arrange. In the conventional wisdom the only possible system of control is one that controls all prices and all wages. . . . [But controls] need not cover all industries. No problem exists where there are no unions and where employers obviously have no discretionary power over prices. . . . Where, on the basis of past behavior, prices and wages do interact to bring persistent price advances, wage increases that are held to require a price increase might be subject to ratification by a public tribunal or one on which representatives of management, labor and the public participated. . . . Wage increases not alleged to require price increases would not be subject to such ratification. Wage advances so granted and those found to be within the capacity of the industry to absorb could not thereafter, without showing of cause, be offset by price increases.

Galbraith stresses that these selective controls could not choke off a genuine, old-style inflation, but that is not the problem at issue. Direct controls will have done their job if they prevent the pattern setters in the economy from triggering a wage-price spiral when supply and demand are roughly balanced at full employment. Nor, Galbraith argues, are these controls a subversion of competitive forces; if market decisions in the key sectors were truly determined by competitive forces, the parties could not have obtained the wage and price increases they did in steel and other industries in 1958, for example, causing consumer prices to rise by nearly 3 percent in a year when the unemployment rate approached 7 percent.

The arguments against direct controls are well known and have been recently summarized by the Council of Economic Advisers:[18]

> Mandatory price and wage controls are no answer. Such controls freeze the market mechanism which guides the economy in responding to the changing pattern and volume of demand; they distort decisions on production and employment; they require a huge and cumbersome bureaucracy; they impose a heavy and costly burden on business; they perpetrate inevitable injustices. They are incompatible with a free enterprise economy and must be regarded as a last resort appropriate only in an extreme emergency such as all-out war.

It should also be noted that Galbraith's proposal does not come to grips with one of the stickiest problems of the new inflation: the need for price *cuts* in some industries. For reasons we have described, if price increases are inevitable in the competitive and low-productivity service sector, these must be offset by price reductions in high-productivity industries to ensure overall price stability. It is hard enough to judge whether General Electric can absorb a given wage increase without raising prices, as Galbraith proposes, but it is even harder for a public panel to order GE simultaneously to raise wages and cut prices—harder to do politically and harder to justify statistically. As for the relevance of Galbraith's proposal to the compulsory arbitration plans discussed in Chapter 26, there are both similarities and differences. Both types of controls would apply to essentially the same bargaining relationships, for those in which emergency strikes are most likely to occur are also those in which the parties' wage and price decisions usually have the greatest inflationary potential. But to anyone wishing to eliminate emergency strikes by methods retaining some of the uncertainty and power conflict inherent in collective bargaining, wage and price ceilings would probably be too rigid and confining.

Regardless of these nuances, however, the fact remains that on this issue most economists agree with most political leaders: Direct wage and price controls are a last resort, and there must be a better answer to the problems of the new inflation.

Accept some unemployment or inflation as preferable to the alternatives If some of the remedies described above strike you as too weak to do the job required and others as too harsh to be acceptable, you are faced with the question posed at the beginning of this chapter: Which one of the three major goals of economic policy should be sacrificed to achieve the other two? By opting for wage and price controls, Galbraith has declared his belief that full employment and stable prices have higher priority than maintaining markets free of government controls. It is possible to defend either of the other two options, however.

No one, of course, argues openly any more that a little unemployment is a good thing, either for building a worker's character or for promoting a healthy economy. But one need not be a reactionary to argue that, if a choice must be made, the fact that 1 percent or so of the labor force cannot find jobs (in addition to the 2 or 3 percent who are normally or frictionally unemployed at any time) hurts far fewer people than the number benefited by the maintenance of stable prices and our system of private decision making. Through the negative income tax or some other system, the majority can and should take care of the tiny minority made jobless by this choice, but how can society make restitution to the many millions who will be damaged in other ways if we choose either inflation or government controls? In fact, there are strong grounds for believing that this has been the choice that the majority of Americans and their political representatives have in effect made during the past twenty years—a decision never stated baldly in either party's platform or announced by any administration in office, but a decision reflected in the unemployment statistics for most of the years since the end of the Korean War.

On the other hand, a case can be made that a little inflation is a small price to pay for the many economic and social benefits of full employment and a minimum of government controls. The late Prof. Sumner Slichter, a highly respected economist, startled many of his colleagues by advocating this choice in the late 1950s.[19] A price creep of 1 or 2 percent a year will not inevitably escalate into a galloping inflation, Slichter argued, pointing to our own postwar experience in which just the opposite occurred: the large price increases of the 1940s were succeeded by the moderate increases of the 1950s. Nor will a creeping inflation discourage investment and innovation, as often charged (the great burst in industrial research and development and the age of automation have both come about during the inflationary years since 1940.) Nor will a moderate inflation necessarily ruin people once thought of as fixed-income groups (Congress has increased social security pensions by more than the increase in prices; teachers' salaries have risen considerably and so have those of many other white-collar and civil-service workers). Thus, Slichter concluded, a creeping inflation causes less harm than is popularly supposed, and if we must choose among economic goals, stable prices should be jettisoned for the advantages of full employment and free markets.

Taken in the abstract, these arguments are equally plausible on economic grounds, and one's political values will primarily dictate which choice is more appealing. Both arguments, however, appear to underestimate the severity of the dilemma we are in. One argument assumes we can buy full employment for an annual price creep of only 1 or 2 percent, and the other assumes we can buy stable prices for only an extra 1 percent or so of unemployment. But the dismal record of the years between the Korean and Vietnam Wars was marked by a persistence of *both* a little inflation and more than a little unemployment. That is, prices were already creeping upward by 1 or 2 percent a year when unemployment was steadily averaging 4 or 5 percent. Samuelson and Solow's estimate of the price-employment trade-off still looks all too reasonable: Price stability may require about 5½ percent unemployment each year —a minor but perpetual recession, and full employment may cost price increases of about 4½ percent each year—a perpetual and not-so minor inflation.

When the costs rise that high, neither of these choices looks promising.

Voluntary restraint

The remaining policy proposed as an answer to the new inflation calls for the government to persuade union and business leaders in critical industries to exercise voluntary restraint in making their wage and price decisions. We have placed this policy last, in part because it depends upon productivity as its major guideline, which is a measure and a concept requiring some discussion.

But there is another reason for taking up this proposal only after reviewing the others: A policy of seeking voluntary restraint makes absolutely no sense unless nothing better is available. After all of our stress upon the market power of certain unions and firms, and the extent to which our entire economic system assumes and encourages the pursuit of self-interest, it appears almost comical to suggest that government officials can stop inflation by asking union and management leaders to be good boys and take less in wages and profits than they can get. Isn't this akin to asking the foxes to guard the chickens? Yet, since the new inflation became apparent in the 1950s, every administration, Republican and Democratic, has done just this. The Kennedy and Johnson ad-

ministrations carried the policy furthest, with the wage and price guideposts to be described shortly, but officials of both the Eisenhower and Nixon administrations also issued pleas for voluntary restraint by labor and management—as the governments of several other Western countries have done in the postwar period.

The reason for this curious behavior is implicit in our discussion of the weaknesses of all the other remedies. Every democratic society wants to capture all three goals of full employment, stable prices, and free markets, but if none of the methods described above will do that, what is left? This has always been the major if negative defense of voluntary restraint. As we shall see, nearly anyone can think of at least five or ten good reasons why voluntary restraint won't work —to which the answer of its proponents has invariably been, "What alternative would work any better?" That may appear to be a shaky basis for a government policy, but it also reflects the intractable nature of the wage-price-employment issue.

Stated more positively, this policy assumes that several major unions and companies have more discretion in their wage and price policies than the competitive model assumes; that these parties can cause inflationary pressures as markets tighten but are still short of full utilization; that neither of these parties wants inflation or government control or underemployment; and therefore government officials can and should educate the parties on the implications of their decisions and show them that voluntary restraint in the short run will promote their own interests, as well as society's, in the long run. Or stated in terms of bargaining power, this policy assumes that the parties in key negotiations should include the costs of inflation or controls in their calculation of the costs of agreement and disagreement, but they will not do this without considerable urging from representatives of the public, backed up by the force of public opinion.

Productivity as a wage-price standard

In evaluating the policy of voluntary restraint, it is necessary to take a long look at the productivity principle upon which it rests. In fact, nearly any type of "national wage policy," whether voluntary or mandatory, sooner or later turns to this criterion. It is not enough to tell unions and employers to be "restrained" or "responsible" in their decisions; some guide must be offered as a substitute for pure bargaining power, and the guide usually adopted is that wage and price changes should be related to the basic source of income gains, namely, the rate of increase in productivity.

Using productivity as a standard of appropriate wage increases, as thus advocated, does not envision relating wage increases to productivity gains in individual firms. It is the *national* average productivity change, over time, which is related to the wage changes in any given firm. To be sure, firms experiencing above-average productivity increases might fatten the pay envelope by a little more than those firms having only average productivity increases, and firms with below-average productivity might be a little less generous, but these differences could be expected to cancel out.

If wages in individual firms *were* to vary directly with productivity changes in those firms, the result would be to disorganize the whole structure of wage rates. Figure 28-3 indicates percentage changes in productivity in twenty-three industries over the period 1947 to 1960. If wages had been tied directly to these productivity movements, the hourly earnings of workers in the synthetic-fibers industry would have risen by more than 225 percent, while rates in the glass-container industry would have barely moved. Three other industries would have granted wage increases of more than 100 percent, twelve industries would have given advances of between 50 and 100 percent, while workers in another six industries would have received increases of between 15 and 50 percent. The resulting disparities in wage rates would have led to interindustry worker movements and to worker discontent that would have disrupted the labor market. Workers of comparable skills would be paid widely varying rates depending on the industry to which they were attached. Further disparities would be introduced by interfirm variations in productivity within an industry. Although interindustry and interfirm differentials exist now, they are not of the magnitudes which are suggested above. Differentials of such magnitudes could scarcely be maintained.

To be sure, union leaders frequently employ arguments relating the wage advances in a company to the productivity gains in that same company,[20] but this is chiefly for bargaining purposes. No such comparison is intended by those who advocate productivity as a guide to wage policy.

Perhaps the most authoritative statement of what *is* intended has been provided by the President's Council of Economic Advisors (CEA), which in 1962 elaborated what it labeled "Guideposts for Noninflationary Wage and Price Behavior." The meat of its statement was contained in the following paragraphs:[21]

> The general guide for noninflationary wage behavior is that the rate of increase in wage rates (including fringe benefits) in each industry be equal to the trend rate of over-all productivity increase. General acceptance of this guide would maintain stability of labor cost per unit of output for the economy as a whole—though not of course for individual industries.
>
> The general guide for noninflationary price behavior calls for price reduction if the industry's rate of productivity increase exceeds the over-all rate—for this would mean declining unit labor costs; it calls for an appropriate increase in price if the opposite relationship prevails; and it calls for stable prices if the two rates of productivity increase are equal.
>
> These are advanced as general guideposts. To reconcile them with objectives of equity and efficiency, specific modifications must be made to adapt them to the circumstances of particular industries. If all of these modifications are made, each in the specific circumstances to which it applies, they are consistent with stability of the general price level. Public judgments about the effects on the price level of particular wage or price decisions should take into account the modifications as well as the general guides. The most important modifications are the following:
>
> 1. Wage rate increases would exceed the general guide rate in an industry which would otherwise be unable to attract sufficient labor; or in which wage rates are exceptionally low compared with the range of wages earned elsewhere by similar labor, because the bargaining position of workers has been weak in particular local labor markets.

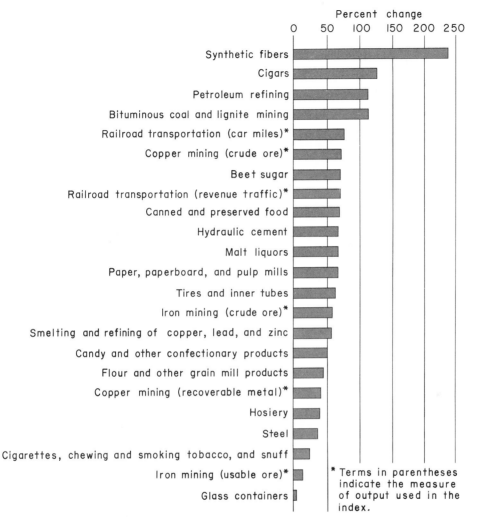

Percent change

| | 0 | 50 | 100 | 150 | 200 | 250 |

Synthetic fibers
Cigars
Petroleum refining
Bituminous coal and lignite mining
Railroad transportation (car miles)*
Copper mining (crude ore)*
Beet sugar
Railroad transportation (revenue traffic)*
Canned and preserved food
Hydraulic cement
Malt liquors
Paper, paperboard, and pulp mills
Tires and inner tubes
Iron mining (crude ore)*
Smelting and refining of copper, lead, and zinc
Candy and other confectionary products
Flour and other grain mill products
Copper mining (recoverable metal)*
Hosiery
Steel
Cigarettes, chewing and smoking tobacco, and snuff
Iron mining (usable ore)*
Glass containers

* Terms in parentheses
indicate the measure
of output used in the
index.

Fig. 28-3. *Output per man-hour of production workers, for selected industries, 1947–1960.*

SOURCE: *U.S. Department of Labor,* Manpower Report of the President, *March, 1963.*

2. Wage rate increases would fall short of the general guide rate in an industry which could not provide jobs for its entire labor force even in times of generally full employment; or in which wage rates are exceptionally high compared with the range of wages earned elsewhere by similar labor, because the bargaining position of workers has been especially strong.

3. Prices would rise more rapidly, or fall more slowly, than indicated by the general guide rate in an industry in which the level of profits was insufficient to attract the capital required to finance a needed expansion in capacity; or in which costs other than labor costs had risen.

4. Prices would rise more slowly, or fall more rapidly, than indicated by the general

guide in an industry in which the relation of productive capacity to full employment demand shows the desirability of an outflow of capital from the industry; or in which costs other than labor costs have fallen; or in which excessive market power has resulted in rates of profit substantially higher than those earned elsewhere on investments of comparable risk.

To avoid any implication that it was seeking to freeze existing patterns of income distribution, the Council added:

> Finally, it must be reiterated that collective bargaining within an industry over the division of the proceeds between labor and nonlabor income is not necessarily disruptive of over-all price stability. The relative shares can change within the bounds of noninflationary price behavior. But when a disagreement between management and labor is resolved by passing the bill to the rest of the economy, the bill is paid in depreciated currency to the ultimate advantage of no one.

Weaknesses of productivity as a guidepost

Although these guideposts may appear eminently fair and rational, they have been attacked from every side—by labor, management, and economists—as being conceptually fuzzy and impossible to administer either fairly or effectively. We shall first review the conceptual difficulties with this approach, many of which the Council of Economic Advisers in the Kennedy and Johnson administrations acknowledged but felt not to be disabling. (The Nixon administration has disavowed the precise guideposts of its predecessors although, as noted before, its spokesmen have called for voluntary restraint without attaching a specific figure or meaning to that term. The following references to the CEA are therefore to the Council in the Kennedy-Johnson years.)

The application of productivity tends to ignore the *market* forces which are the principal determinants of individual wage rates. A company or industry whose markets are declining may be forced to increase its efficiency, but the resulting increase in productivity may only permit survival rather than the raising of wages. The railroad in-

dustry, or at least particular segments of it, is an example of this. Again, the state of the labor market—whether particular kinds of labor are in short or surplus supply—will importantly affect wages regardless of productivity. The CEA guides recognize that such an influence will shift wage changes away from the productivity standard, but they give no indication as to why the *average* of all such shifts should be expected to approximate the national average rate of increase in productivity.

One of the principal students of the subject has said:[22]

> Prices of materials, costs of capital goods, wages in other industries, conditions of demand for the product, the supply of labor, and the cost of living (by no means an exhaustive list) are, generally speaking, on a par with productivity as determinants of wages and prices. In a particular situation, one of these—sometimes productivity itself—may be the key variable. But no one of them is to be considered of prime importance as a matter of course.

There are difficulties in the measurement of productivity which cannot lightly be ignored. It is not only that figures on productivity for the economy or for particular industries are subject to challenge on the ground that data on inputs and outputs are imprecise and incomplete. There are important conceptual problems and alternatives in deciding what it is that should be measured.

Professor Fabricant illustrates the variety of measures which might be employed, leading to different results, by raising the very specific question What was the average rate of growth in the nation's productivity over the period 1947–57? Presumably one would require an answer to that question in order to apply productivity as a wage guide. But, says Fabricant, the National Bureau of Economic Research has made an exhaustive study of that question with the following results: The rate of productivity increase was 3.4 percent a year if we measure it in terms of real gross national product per man-hour in the private goods and service producing economy. It was 3.1 percent if we weight man-hours in terms of changes in their quality (skilled man-hours weighing more than unskilled man-hours). It was 2.3 percent if we measure the same output in terms of weighted man-hours and tangible capital combined. It was 2 percent if we measure the productivity rate for the whole economy, including the government sector. He adds, "This is not an exhaustive list of all the 'answers' even from this single source; and, of course, inclusion of the concepts and calculations of other statisticians would add to the variety."[23]

But which of even these four measures, ranging from 2 to 3.4 percent, should be used as a standard for wage determination? Is there any likelihood that employers would not opt for the former figure, and unions for the latter, and *then* seek to rationalize why there should be a further shift down or up from this level? With each bringing experts to its defense?

To tie individual wage rates to productivity increases implies that existing wage rates are somehow equitable. There are no standards, however, by which it can be argued that the rates which one group of workers are now receiving are "fair" relative to the rates which other workers are getting, or that the general level of wage rates is "fair" relative to the return to other factors.

Here again the Council of Economic Advisers has admitted the justice of this criticism, but argued that if a redistribution of income is to take place, it should take place within the firm or industry, without effect on prices. As one observer commented, however, this places an intolerable burden on the parties to collective bargaining. It makes a man who restrains himself from pressing a bad case seem good, and a man who fails to restrain himself from pressing a good case seem bad. Thus it turns the moral position of leaders "upside down" and their institutional position "inside out." The duty of leaders of industry and labor is to face the community in the name of their members. This policy urges them to face their members in the name of the community.[24]

Further, there is no reason why redistribution should take place, if it takes place at all, only between labor and property. It might equally come between various components of the labor force. Such a redistribution cannot occur within the framework of a single bargain, but evolves from some groups extracting differential advantage from their strategic situations while others

suffer from deteriorated economic positions. This is what now occurs as an end result of all bargains struck in the economy. Some workers gain more than others. It is hard to see how such *competitive* bargains, with their redistributive effects, can be mutually contained within the present fragmented bargaining framework. If there is an intent somehow to limit the exercise of group advantage for fear that it will have an inflationary spillover to other bargains and to the rest of the economy, some *coordination* among the bargains seems inescapable. But this would involve taking positions on distributive justice, the *equity* of competing wage claims.

The time dimension poses a conceptual question. In some lean years workers may get no wage increase at all, and occasionally must even face a wage reduction. But this means one of three things. If the *annual* average wage increase is limited by the *annual* long-run productivity increase, as has usually been suggested, then the *long-term* average wage improvement will fall behind productivity advances, since increases will not be paid in some years. This will hardly prove acceptable to unions. Or else it is intended that managements continue to pay wage increases equal to the long-run average productivity advance year in and year out, in lean years as well as in fat years. This would hardly prove acceptable to employers. Or finally, it may imply that wage increases passed up in the lean years shall be caught up with in the good years. But such a policy is likely to sponsor inflationary pressures precisely at the time it is seeking to avoid them.

The three uses of the productivity concept

Underlying all the problems we have considered in connection with the use of the productivity concept as a wage standard is the fact that we use the term in three quite different senses. A confusion of these three *different* concepts, which results from trying to combine them into a single concept, is really at the base of our difficulty.

Productivity is generally used in an *efficiency* sense, as we had occasion to note in Chapter 15. It is a measure of outputs relative to inputs. Thus it can be used to determine whether a process or a firm or an industry or the economy is making better use of the resources which it employs. It is directly related to the economist's notion of the "production function"—the combination of factors leading to an output of real goods. By combining inputs in different proportions or by varying their quality, the rate of output can be changed. An increase in the amount of capital or the quality of capital used with labor or an improvement in the skill level of workers will have beneficial effects on productivity in this efficiency sense.

In the case of the individual firm, this does not mean maximizing output per man-hour but minimizing total cost per unit of output. This directly involves the problem of capital investment. Employers would seek to maximize output per man-hour, as an efficiency objective, only in the event that they employed labor inputs alone and made no use of capital inputs. That obviously does not describe the average firm in a modern economy. As capital becomes a more and more important part of the production process, output per man-hour as a measure of efficiency becomes less and less appropriate. Efficiency depends on the outputs obtained from the use of *all* inputs.

But there is another sense in which productivity can be employed, which relates actual output to *available* resources, whether or not they are actually employed. Thus it takes account of the extent to which plant facilities and men may be idle. Let us call this, for want of a better term, *effectiveness* in the use of resources. Effectiveness would be measured by the extent to which total output increased with an increase in employment and declined with a decline in employment, with no change in the production techniques or functions. It would be extremely difficult to measure this operationally, since usually efficiency and effectiveness are changing simultaneously and cannot be separately measured. But the distinction can perhaps be made most clear by example.

Let us assume that in the civilian sector this year 70 million people are at work and 5 million are unemployed. We could presumably obtain a measure of the efficiency of the 70 million employed people, in combination with the capital they used, in the production operations in which they were actually engaged. This would be a ratio of inputs to outputs. Now suppose that next year

70 million are still employed. With more entrants coming into the labor force than are retiring, the number of unemployed increases to 5.5 million. The 70 million still employed might be more efficient than last year, in an input-output sense. They might be performing their jobs better, or they might be working with more or better capital equipment. But with more manpower resources now available, but being wasted, we could hardly characterize the entire economy as being more productive—at least in this second meaning of the term (effectiveness). It is more *efficient* in the sense that it is getting more output from those who are employed, but it is less *effective* in that it is losing a greater potential output.

There is an incongruity in speaking of rising productivity at a time of increasing unemployment which is too apparent to be glossed over. The difficulty is overcome only when we recognize that the efficiency of *employed* resources can increase at the same time that the effective use of *available* resources declines. But this distinction underscores the inappropriateness of relying on the efficiency concept as a basis for income allocation, without taking account of the effectiveness with which the economy (and indeed individual business units in the economy) are operating. If we think of average national productivity as constituting a basis for average wage increases, year in and year out, this means that we would in effect be endorsing the granting of higher wages in a period of business recession. It would of course be true that the availability of idle resources makes *possible* an increase in output at such a time, which would then be available for distribution, but it would be hard to think of a less desirable mechanism than rising wages to put idle resources to work at such a time. A tax reduction or heavier government expenditures or both would certainly be preferable, since they would impose no added cost burden on employers in a period when they could least support it.

Similarly, at a time when old-fashioned inflationary forces were at work (that is, when there was general excess demand), a policy which blessed *any* increase in wages might be quite unsound. Increases even no greater than the increase in productivity, in the efficiency sense, would at best fail to stem the inflationary pressures and more probably would accelerate them. The fact is, wages are a method of allocating income which is functionally related to the cost-price-profit aspect of economic activity; any presumption of a logical, consistent, or desirable policy relationship between wages and productivity is not only fallacious but can also be mischievous.

This brings us to the third use which is made of the productivity concept, the one which has just been criticized. Productivity is considered a standard for the allocation of real income. More accurately, it is regarded as a method of distributing that increment of GNP which is available for private consumption and investment. Its claimed advantage is that it is a method of avoiding the *over*allocation of that increment, which would send prices rising. If every employed factor, on the average, received a percentage increase in income equal to the percentage increase in the incremental GNP, there would be no overallocation. If productivity (of *employed* resources, necessarily) rises by 3 percent, all employed workers and other factors of production could get 3 percent more, and this would just allocate the increase in GNP attributable to the rise in productivity.

But this of course is purely an arithmetical exercise and not a policy. There is a big gap, conceptually and operationally, between measuring the change in efficiency of employed resources in the economy at large and using that measure as a basis for income distribution. Any attempt to leap that gap must assume that the firm is a kind of neutral transmission belt or administrative agency for the economy, and that the abstract arithmetical average of the fruits of efficiency can be readily passed along by the two million or so firms having at least one employee, acting as society's agent. But this leap from the aggregate to the individual is not logically permissible. Whether any firm can or will pass along an equivalent wage increase depends on its cost-price-profit position, as we have noted. To assume that somehow each firm can or will act as agent in distributing an average economywide rate of productivity gain has no conceptual foundation. The national *average efficiency* literally has no relevance to *individual wage* behavior. There is a confusion here between an abstract measure of

possible distribution and the actual institutional processes by which distribution takes place. There is no sense in which the one can be said to be a meaningful "guide" to the other.

In summary, critics charge that it is this failure to distinguish between productivity in these three quite different senses that leads to the mistaken belief that productivity can be a useful guide to individual wage and price decisions. Productivity as a measure of economic *efficiency,* in the input-output sense, and productivity as a measure of economic *effectiveness,* in the sense of degree of use of available resources, have little to do with productivity as a measure of *distribution,* except as the efficient and effective use of resources operates on the demand for labor, the cost of production, the price of the product, and the firm's product. And, say the critics, there is no formula or rule-of-thumb that can tie all these together into a workable anti-inflationary policy.

A different approach to productivity

Before examining the defense offered to the above charges, let us complete the case for the prosecution. It is true that many critics have been content to ridicule the productivity guidelines without offering any better alternative, but a few have pressed the logic of their attack one step further and urged that, *instead of concentrating on restricting wage increases to productivity, it would make more sense to concentrate on increasing productivity gains more than wages.*

If this could be done, then we could continue to rely on competition and collective bargaining to distribute the national income, concerning ourselves only with attacking and removing impediments to competition and abuses of power where these pass beyond the bounds of "reasonableness." In general, a checkrein on market power would probably not require any massive or novel measures but simply a more effective application of present techniques and devices. Nor would there be any point in trying to establish in some definitive sense whether unions were more or less responsible than business (or consumers) for inflation. In one situation or at one time it might be one party, in some other sector or period, another. It is unlikely always to be the same "offender."

This proposal is similar in many ways to that described above for eliminating bottlenecks in the economy. Both would aim to remove the obstacles preventing many employers from operating as efficiently as they might, and both would try to upgrade the quality of the work force and to improve the operation of the labor market.

But there are also differences in these proposals. The "bottleneck policy" tends to assume that competitive forces will automatically balance full employment and stable prices if only certain roadblocks are removed which now prevent labor and product markets from operating as they should. The "productivity policy" says that society should not only eliminate bottlenecks in the market but should actively promote a higher rate of productivity increase in order to ease the wage-price tensions under full employment.

For example, it is not enough to train those workers now unemployed so they can meet the current hiring needs of industry. A more important contribution would be the strengthening of the entire educational system. We shall not review here the work that has been done to determine a rate of return on capital invested in education, a subject still fraught with difficulties even greater than those involved in calculating a rate of return on other more conventional capital investments.[25] We may take it on faith that whatever that rate may be on any *individual's* expenditure, in total it constitutes the fundamental basis on which any *economy* rests. The educational process trains researchers who in turn give rise to new knowledge and innovations which ultimately become embodied in physical capital stock. In a dynamic sense, it is impossible to disentangle the benefits of education to the individual from the benefits of the educational process to society as a whole.

This is not to suggest that we treat education as having only economic values, nor does it mean that every student should major in industrial arts in high school and business administration or engineering in college. The point is that nearly every type of education enormously expands the economic capacity *as well as* the cultural values of a society, and any attempt to expand productivity should concentrate as much on improving education as on building bigger and better computers and steel mills. Improvement is certainly

needed not only in our basic educational system, as evidenced by the dropout problem in our high schools and the many dissatisfactions being voiced by students at the college level, but also in the vocational training we now offer for those aiming at a specific occupation, in the retraining programs geared to those whose skills have become obsolete, and—the newest frontier—continuing education, which involves a person in formal study throughout his lifetime, always building on previously acquired knowledge.

Also, economists are now paying more attention to a fact that employers have long known—that research and development pay high returns. Recent studies have confirmed that technical change may be a good deal more important in raising productivity than physical capital formation itself, except as the physical capital embodies the technical change.[26] That is, another billion dollars' worth of the same plant and equipment we now have will often not raise productivity as much as will another billion dollars invested in research aimed at finding a better way of doing what we want to do. Thus government and business should search for ways (such as subsidies or tax incentives) of stimulating not simply capital investment but, even more important, basic research and its practical application.

Finally, instead of the negative approach to union–management relations—trying to reduce strike losses or the average level of wage settlements—the productivity approach would encourage programs of union–management cooperation. These are programs which divide gains from improved efficiency with workers whose own suggestions, recommendations, and cooperation have been partly responsible for the increased productivity, while at the same time guaranteeing workers against loss of job or income.[27] It is true that a few such programs have been around for a long time without showing much tendency to spread. There are numerous reasons for this, such as the fear of employers that union involvement in production matters may lead to a further invasion of management's prerogatives, and the fear of unions that a successful profit-sharing program may lessen the interest and militancy of workers in their union. The fact remains that unions constitute a potential tool for mobilizing the contribution that workers can make to increasing efficiency, and it might be profitable to spend as much time trying to develop this positive side of unionism as we now spend deploring and suppressing the wage demands of unions.

Basic to all these proposals for increasing productivity is the belief that *high-level economic performance is less of an inflationary threat in its own right than it is a counterinflationary force.* In this view, we can stimulate the economy in ways which simultaneously reduce unemployment and inflationary pressures, by putting people back to work in those capacities which are most likely to result in higher rates of productivity increases. It is not enough to give the unemployed a relief check or a job raking leaves. We need to put people to work to provide them with income and security, but we also need them working on highly productive jobs to turn out the goods and services to match the money that people spend, thereby helping to keep prices stable.

In defense of voluntary restraint

There is thus a staggering list of indictments against the guidepost policy, and yet others could be added. This policy nevertheless has its defenders, and it is time to hear their side of these issues.

First, in response to the charge that talking never stopped an inflation and we need stronger weapons, the answer is that given before. It is true that the major weapons in any government's anti-inflation arsenal are its taxing, spending, and monetary powers, just as those are its major tools for promoting full employment. In this larger context, voluntary guideposts are a relatively minor weapon and were never meant to be anything more. The fact remains, however, that the major, orthodox weapons have not proved capable of taking us that last critical mile as the economy nears full employment and the first signs of creeping inflation appear. The same reasoning explains the demise of the guideposts in the late 1960s. No one ever claimed they could stop a classic, excess-demand inflation; they are designed strictly for use in periods of near-full or full employment when total demand and supply are roughly in balance.

Second, in response to the charge that different productivity measures yield different answers and all are imprecise, the answer is that this is true but *relatively* unimportant. The fact that no one can measure productivity in the government sector—accounting for 15 percent of total employment and nearly 25 percent of gross national product—obviously means that any economywide measure of productivity is impossible. For productivity gains in the private sector alone, however, the range of estimates is usually from about 2.5 to 3.5 percent per year. Although that is a wide range of error to a statistician, it is not crippling to a policy of voluntary restraint. The important point is that most economists agree that the private economy now averages productivity gains of "about 3 percent" a year—not 1 or 5 or 8 percent. We seldom have more precise statistics on which to base any economic policy.

Third, the proposal that we raise productivity faster than wages, instead of restricting wages to the present rate of efficiency gains, contains several flaws. It seems plausible that an increase in output should be counterinflationary, but this argument ignores the fact that you must pay a wage to a previously unemployed worker when you find him a job, and you must pay more to other factors of production as you use them more intensively—and thus you have added to both output *and* consumer demand. You have also added to the market power of large firms and unions by tightening labor and product markets. Certainly there is nothing in the record to support the assumption that a fully employed economy is less inflationary than an underemployed economy; the whole thrust of the Phillips-curve findings is precisely to the contrary.

Also, even if we could raise productivity gains from 3 percent to 4 or 5 percent a year at full employment, what is to prevent unions and employers from raising their wage and profit sights to 7 or 8 percent a year? There is again nothing in the recent record to support the assumption that, if left to themselves, these parties would meekly accept less than the traffic will bear. The record instead suggests that an increase in the rate of productivity (while certainly of value for many other reasons) would simply result in the same wage-price-employment tensions occurring over how to divide up 5 percent instead of 3 percent gains.

Fourth, it is frequently charged that a guidepost policy, if it works at all, is inequitable because it brings pressure (from the White House and public opinion) upon only the few "visible" companies and unions. The defense admits this is true, but reminds critics that the whole point of this policy is to induce restraint by those parties who have the most discretion in their market decisions. By and large (though not completely), these are in fact the big, visible companies and bargaining units—the leaders who influence to some extent the decisions that many of the small, "invisible" parties will take.

Fifth, did voluntary restraint accomplish anything in the years when it was most energetically promoted? Prof. George Perry has tackled this question by comparing wage changes in manufacturing before and after 1962, when the guideposts were instituted. In an earlier study, Perry had evolved a formula which explained the wage changes that actually occurred in manufacturing from 1947 to 1960—"explained" in the sense that the wage change in any one year was shown to be statistically predictable from the movement of wages in the previous year and the movement of consumer prices, profits, and unemployment during the year in question. When Perry applied that formula to the same variables for the period between 1962 and 1966, he obtained a measure of how factory wages would have changed in the "guidepost period" if they had behaved as they did between 1947 and 1960. By comparing these predicted changes to the actual changes in factory wages, he found that wages increased *less rapidly* under the guideposts than would have been predicted from their previous behavior. Perry also showed that this slowdown was more pronounced in the "visible" manufacturing industries (such as steel and rubber), where the guidepost pressure was most pronounced, than in the "invisible" group (leather, paper, and so on), and this difference was not explained by differences in employment growth between these two groups. As Perry concluded:[28]

We cannot prove that only guideposts could have caused the wage behavior observed . . .

[but] on the present evidence, I feel one must now try to disprove the impact of guideposts rather than the other way around.

Finally, even the most fervent advocates of voluntary restraint admit that the guideposts suffered serious defeats even before they became a casualty of the Vietnam conflict, but assert that most of these setbacks would probably have occurred under any other policy. Most important, the guideposts seldom if ever won any "positive" victories. If they worked at all, they succeeded only in holding prices constant and wage gains to about 3 percent in certain key industries, but they never induced a price *cut* in industries like autos, where profits and productivity called for more than holding prices constant, nor did they induce lower-than-3-percent wage settlements in industries like longshoring, in which labor was in surplus and hourly rates were already high. As noted before, however, even direct wage and price controls would have trouble handling this critical problem of how to obtain price cuts in the industrial sector to offset the inevitable price increases in the service sector, and apparently fiscal and monetary controls cannot accomplish this without running the unemployment rate up to very high levels.

Another clear defeat was in the construction industry, where major union settlements soared above 6 percent as early as 1965 and continued to go up from there. Again, no one quite knows what to do about this particular wage-price problem. It makes no sense to call for breaking up big labor or big management here, for the industry is highly decentralized already and negotiates in literally thousands of small bargaining units; the Taft-Hartley and Landrum-Griffin Acts both tried to reduce the power of the building trades in several ways, but to little avail; direct controls would be difficult to administer because of the decentralization of the industry; and monetary controls throw home building into a tailspin but that is not where union strength is concentrated. Ironically, the major remedy often suggested for this industry is *more centralization* of collective bargaining—so that employers can better stand together, national officials can better control local militants, and government officials can exercise leverage on a few key bargains.

Another approach

Arthur Ross, the late Commissioner of Labor Statistics, has appraised these and other aspects of voluntary restraint and suggested that it is time to think of a "second generation" of wage-price restraints that will profit from the strengths and weaknesses of the experience under the original guideposts.

It is not enough, Ross argued, for government economists to compute the long-run trend in productivity and then exhort and belabor the private parties to adhere to this standard. That standard is important and cannot be ignored, but it is equally important to allow for other facts: the private parties want and deserve some voice in determining any wage and price restraints under which they are supposed to live; there are inevitably short-run contingencies that require deviations from the long-run goal; and it is unlikely that industrial prices can be cut in the face of the demand prevailing at full employment. Ross therefore urged that the principal interest groups (such as industry, labor, and agriculture) meet annually with government officials to review the outlook for the coming year and attempt to reconcile long-run objectives and short-run needs.

Suppose the cost of living has gone up 3.5 percent? Suppose that raw material prices have shot up through the ceiling on world markets? ... Suppose a massive effort to rehabilitate urban slums is launched? Suppose that a medium-sized war breaks out? ... It would be impossible to ignore the impact of these developments on price and wage policy in the private sector.

Therefore, the terms of price and wage restraint should take the form of specific conclusions emerging from the annual economic review between the private-sector interest groups and the governmental authorities. The statement of conclusions should be the government's responsibility rather than a negotiated tripartite agreement.

Similarly there should be a quarterly post-review of results, an appraisal of how they line up against the objectives for the year.[29]

It is easy to think of objections to this proposal. Some people would view annual meetings like this with great suspicion, believing that they would represent one more step toward centralized control of the economy. Others would argue that such meetings are a poor way of accomplishing anything, for labor leaders would make their usual speeches demanding that industry absorb all costs from their swollen profits, employers would as usual pretend that competitive forces would take care of everything if only labor monopoly and government meddling were eliminated, and government officials would as always be afraid to offend anyone by saying what needs to be said. But the critical question will not go away: If you don't like this or some other anti-inflation policy, what better alternative can you suggest? As Ross concluded:[30]

The skeptics have laid their fingers on the soft spots of the first-generation guideposts. It is hard to find a labor economist (unless he has writer's block) who hasn't written at least one article pointing out that the various exceptions to the guideposts are vague from an operational standpoint, that you can't control the building trades unions, that it is inequitable to put so much pressure on the basic metal industries, that the American labor movement is decentralized and can't control the behavior of its constituent unions, and so on. These are important points; they have been made. . . .

Let us stop belaboring the obvious and have some new thinking on wage-price policies.

Conclusion

If the reader finds himself thoroughly bewildered at this point, seeing perils lurking in every remedy that has been proposed to cope with the new inflation, he may now count himself an expert on this subject. Economists have a penchant for disagreeing among themselves on most issues, of course, but there are few subjects on which their disagreement is more complete than on what to do about the wage-price-employment problem. The authors themselves reflect this disagreement, for one of us favors the approach of maximizing productivity and the other favors voluntary restraint or, if that fails, selective price and wage controls.

There is substantial agreement on two points, however. First, this problem gives every indication of being with us for some time. It is difficult to see any long-run or underlying forces at work that will gradually take care of matters if we just sit tight and do nothing for a few years. Although we shall never know for sure, it is likely that a sustained period of full employment would generate some inflationary tensions even in an economy without large firms and unions, for the slightest imbalance in one sector or another seems capable of tipping the price scales in an economy operating at maximum capacity. When this fragile balance is further subjected to the clash of union and corporate power, plus the many other factors preventing the labor market from operating as smoothly as competitive theory assumes, it is surprising that we come as close as we do to capturing the "magic trilogy" of full employment, stable prices, and free markets. Yet this prize continues to elude all industrial societies, and at this point no one can see why the problem might be easier to solve tomorrow than it is today.

Second, although it is trite to say there are no easy answers to most social and economic problems, the importance of this truth can hardly be overemphasized in appraising the price-employment dilemma. As we have seen, there are grave risks or weaknesses in every one of the remedies that have been proposed. It is all too easy to be an "expert" on this subject and poke holes in other people's solutions, whether offered by the man in the street or by the President's Council of Economic Advisers. It is far harder to come up with a better answer which no one has thought of before. To put the matter bluntly, this problem has so far stumped the experts: not only have they failed to come up with an easy answer, but they cannot agree even on any hard answers.

Thus, barring the appearance of another Keynes with a bold new approach, we shall probably continue for some time the same pragmatic approach we have followed in the recent past, namely, borrowing bits and pieces from all of the "solutions," stirring them together in proportions varying with the administration in office and the mood of the country, and hoping that the problem can be kept within tolerable bounds. Specifically, it looks now as if we shall continue to rely on fiscal and monetary controls to curb any major outbreaks of inflation or unemployment; continue manpower training and other programs to im-

prove the operation of the labor market; continue to wrestle with bottlenecks in the health, construction, transportation, and other industries; continue to amend our labor and antitrust laws to check specific abuses of monopoly power; continue to exhort union and management officials to exercise restraint; perhaps resort to direct controls on rare occasions (as in two railroad disputes in the 1960s)—and, most significantly, *we shall probably continue to accept both a little inflation and a little unemployment rather than incur the cost of eliminating either.*

If this eclectic approach appears to be an unexciting or unimaginative response to one of the critical issues of our time, bear in mind the motto of the pragmatist: Show me something that will work better.

ADDITIONAL READINGS

Chamberlain, Neil W.: *Private and Public Planning,* McGraw-Hill, New York, 1965.

Economic Report of the President, published annually.

Galbraith, John Kenneth: *The New Industrial State,* Houghton Mifflin, Boston, 1967.

Reder, Melvin W.: "The Public Interest in Wage Settlements," in John T. Dunlop and Neil W. Chamberlain (eds.), *Frontiers of Collective Bargaining,* Harper & Row, New York, 1967, pp. 155–177.

Rothbaum, Melvin: "Wage-Price Policy and Alternatives," in Lloyd Ulman (ed.), *Challenges to Collective Bargaining,* Prentice-Hall, Englewood Cliffs, N.J., 1967, pp. 134–154.

Shultz, George P., and Robert Z. Aliber (eds.): *Guidelines, Informal Controls, and the Market Place,* The University of Chicago Press, Chicago, 1966.

FOR ANALYSIS AND DISCUSSION

1. What is the meaning of the Keynesian term "equilibrium at less than full employment"?

2. Read from any of the books referred to in this chapter and others that appear relevant, and draft an outline for a paper designed to answer the question: Does full-employment planning endanger personal liberties?

3. Arthur Krock of the *New York Times* commented in 1957: "Unless the Government steps in with controls repugnant to the American system and spirit—and too late for them to attain the result that is their only justification—it would appear that the only strong inflationary check at this economic juncture can come from some great industry." Krock suggested that, as an "act of managerial statesmanship," some large corporation with a product in nationwide distribution announce "that it would make no further price increase for a certain period, regardless of additional costs and effect on profits, in the hope that labor would follow this example." He expressed the hope that not only labor but "farmers, Government and the rest of the population would respond to that kind of leadership."

Analyze the likelihood of success of such an action.

4. In 1957, when inflation threatened, the life insurance companies placed advertisements in newspapers urging people to save 5 cents out of every dollar, as a means of combating the inflationary threat. What results do you believe would have followed if the public had heeded the advice given? Specifically, if you believe that unions are the active inflationary agents on the cost side, would this have been an effective antidote?

5. Business spokesmen have said:

When an industrywide union, exercising monopoly control over the labor supply of an industry, demands wage increases which discount productivity gains far in advance, possible price reductions of mass-produced products are prevented and buying power is shifted unfairly from the public as a whole to the favored few who happen to work in the industry in question.

Union representatives have said:

It is high time that the insatiable seeking for ever-higher profits by some of our business leaders gives way to some concern for consumers and investors and for the general health of the American economy.

Suppose a friend asks you which of these positions is right. How would you analyze the issue for him?

6. E. S. Redford, in the Joint Economic Committee Study Paper no. 10, *Potential Public Policies to Deal with Inflation Caused by Market Power,* 1959, wrote:

The administrative difficulties to be faced in public effort to prevent the use of market power to produce inflationary increases in prices and wages would be tremendous. Over what industries, companies, or products would surveillance be necessary? Could the public effort be successful without surveillance over a wide range of American industry? Could public effort be pinpointed at the strategic centers from which new inflationary pressures would arise? Could public attention be brought to these centers in time to prevent the beginning of new inflationary chain effects? What type of public action would be needed? Would notice of prospective price and wage increases be necessary? If so, would exceptions to the requirements for notice be required to meet special situations in industry? What follow-up action would be taken after receipt of notice? Could the consideration of filings and the making of fact studies or holding of hearings be completed in the brief period within which judgment would be required? Would factfinding, report on hearings, and advisory recommendations carry real weight with the companies or unions seeking increases? What standards could be used in determining whether to investigate or hold hearings, what to pinpoint in factfinding or hearing reports, what recommendations to make? How could public participation be organized so as to produce confidence in reports but at the same time to produce enough support from the Government to carry weight with the parties affected? Could public authority be exercised with aggressive and continuing attention to public interests or would organs of administration become sluggish and weak in motivation? Would a continuing type of control, similar to utility control, be desirable for a few sectors of the economy? If so, for which sectors? Could agencies for administration of such controls maintain the independence and vigor needed for success?

Take any three of the questions Redford raises and answer them as fully as you can.

7. Write a paraphrase (something in your own words) setting out the three different meanings attached to the concept of "productivity."

NOTES

1. The vigor of this debate over government planning is suggested by the titles of the major books on this issue that appeared between 1944 and 1948: William Beveridge, *Full Employment in a Free Society,* Norton, New York, 1945; Henry A. Wallace, *Sixty Million Jobs,* Simon & Schuster, New York, 1945; Friedrich A. Hayek, *Road to Serfdom,* The University of Chicago Press, Chicago, 1944; Herman Finer, *Road to Reaction,* Little, Brown, Boston, 1945; John Maurice Clark, *Alternative to Serfdom,* Knopf, New York, 1948; Barbara Wootton, *Freedom under Planning,* The University of North Carolina Press, Chapel Hill, 1945; and John Jewkes, *Ordeal by Planning,* Macmillan, New York, 1948.

2. For the definitive expression of this analysis of the inflation of the 1940s, see Walter A. Morton, "Trade Unionism, Full Employment, and Inflation," *American Economic Review,* vol. 40, pp. 13–19, 1950.

3. Gottfried Haberler, "Wage Policy, Employment, and Economic Stability," in D. McC. Wright (ed.), *The Impact of the Union,* Harcourt, Brace & World, New York, 1951, p. 39.

4. A. W. Phillips, "The Relation between Unemployment and the Rate of Change of Money Wage Rates in the United Kingdom, 1861–1957," *Economica,* November, 1958, pp. 283–299. Phillips made allowance for the effect of major changes in import prices on the cost of living, as well as for differential rates of wage changes at a given level of unemployment depending on whether the economy was going up or down. Calculations were made for three sequential periods, but the results were very much the same for all three.

5. One might also conclude that the classical view, that gains in productivity should be transmitted through price reductions so that all might benefit, was clearly unrealistic. If there was an inflationary danger in wages rising in excess of productivity, there was likewise a deflationary danger if they rose less than that.

6. Paul A. Samuelson and Robert M. Solow, "Problem of Achieving and Maintaining a Stable Price Level," *American Economic Review,* vol. 70, pp. 192–193, May, 1960. Their analysis was confined to the "normal" periods from the turn of the century to World War I, and the decade of the twenties. Prof. William G. Bowen has undertaken a similar but more elaborate investigation, with the more pessimistic conclusion that the unemployment rate must be at least 9 percent if the rate of increase in wages is to be held to the rate of increase in productivity

of about 2½ percent. He too finds a difference between the pre-World War II and post-World War II periods. (*Wage Behavior in the Postwar Period: An Empirical Analysis,* Princeton University Industrial Relations Section, Princeton, N.J., 1960.)

7. In some instances the union may have to create the monopoly position *for* the employers in an industry, as when it polices the barber shops or dry-cleaning establishments in a community to make sure that they charge "union scale." In these cases, the "scale" is the price which the employer charges the public, and by charging it the employer is able to pay the wages the union demands. (In 1963 a rival for the presidency of the Barbers union campaigned on the platform that what the membership needed was a $3 haircut. He was campaigning for a price and not a wage.) But in order to prevent low-wage competitors from entering the field and spoiling the market, a union may have to control the labor market to make it impossible for nonunion employers to get the workers they need. This line of reasoning would also apply to the construction industry, in which wage and price pressures have been of great concern in recent years.

8. For a good statement of the strength of the kind of equitable comparisons which Ross analyzed and on which Mrs. Wootton rested much of her "social theory of wages" (described in chaps. 17 and 18), see H. A. Clegg, "The Scope of Fair Wage Comparisons," *Journal of Industrial Economics,* July, 1961.

9. William Fellner and others, *The Problem of Rising Prices,* Organization for European Economic Cooperation, 1961, pp. 51 and 55.

10. Charles L. Schultze, *Recent Inflation in the United States,* Study Paper no. 1 of the Joint Economic Committee's Study of Employment, Growth, and Price Levels, 86th Congress, 1st Session, 1959.

11. Ruth Mack has an excellent discussion of this point in "Inflation and Quasi-elective Changes in Costs," *Review of Economics and Statistics,* August, 1959.

12. James S. Duesenberry, "Underlying Factors in the Postwar Inflation," in *Wages, Prices, Profits and Productivity,* The American Assembly, Columbia University, New York, 1959, pp. 82–84.

13. *Economic Report of the President, 1967,* Chap. 2.

14. John Kenneth Galbraith, *The Affluent Society,* Houghton Mifflin, Boston, 1958 (Mentor Books), p. 236.

15. John T. Dunlop, "Guideposts, Wages, and Collective Bargaining," in George P. Schultz and Robert Z. Aliber (eds.), *Guideposts, Informal Controls, and the Market Place,* The University of Chicago Press, Chicago, 1966, p. 94.

16. John Kenneth Galbraith, *American Capitalism: The Concept of Countervailing Power,* Houghton Mifflin, Boston, 1952, pp. 84–94.

17. Galbraith, *The Affluent Society*, p. 238. Also see Galbraith, *The New Industrial State*, Houghton Mifflin, Boston, 1967, chap. 22.

18. *Economic Report of the President, 1969*, p. 120.

19. Sumner H. Slichter, "Economics and Collective Bargaining," in *Economics and the Policy Maker: Brookings Lectures, 1958–1959*, Brookings, Washington, 1959; and Slichter, "On the Side of Inflation," *Harvard Business Review*, vol. 35, pp. 15 ff., 1957.

20. Perhaps as good a statement as any of the "informed" union view is that offered by Otis Brubaker, research director of the United Steelworkers ("The Collective Bargaining Relationship in the United States and Its Relationship to Productivity and Technological Change," a paper prepared for a trade-union seminar sponsored by the Organization for European Economic Cooperation, 1957, mimeographed):

Unions have generally conceded that, by far the most important movements in productivity which must be considered in collective bargaining, are the Economy-wide changes. All sorts of undesirable distortions would flow from any close linking of wages with productivity trends on a specific industry or company basis. Unions cannot, however, ignore productivity changes in industry and company productivity. For instance, if an industry is rapidly increasing its productivity—even though Economy-wide productivity is not increasing—that industry's profits will rise rapidly and its employees are entitled to, and most certainly will insist on, some sort of sharing in these increased profits. Certainly, where conditions are reversed and industry's productivity is not increasing and its profit margins have been cut to the bone or have disappeared, wage increases quickly become impossible unless the industry is somehow able to raise its prices. Thus, it is important in collective bargaining to examine the productivity figures of particular industries since they do exert an influence, if only a limited and limiting one, on collective bargaining. At the typical small company, single plant level, productivity trends are of little significance to collective bargaining except as they are reflected in the profits of the enterprise and that profit becomes itself a separate matter of collective bargaining.

21. *Economic Report of the President together with the Annual Report of the Council of Economic Advisers*, 1962, p. 189. The quoted paragraphs were set in a context indicating appreciation of many of the difficulties attending the use of productivity as a standard, but the nub of the policy advocated came down to what is reproduced here.

22. Solomon Fabricant, "Productivity Measurement," in *New York University Third Annual Conference on Labor*, 1950, p. 76.

23. Solomon Fabricant, "Which Productivity? Perspective on a Current Question," *Monthly Labor Review*, June, 1962, p. 609. The National Bureau study to which he refers is John W. Kendrick, *Productivity Trends in the United States*, Princeton University Press, Princeton, N.J., 1961, chap. 3 and appendix 4.

One other question of concept and measurement which is currently occupying a great deal of attention concerns the desirability of including the man-hours of *all* workers in the denominator of the productivity ratio, and not simply of production workers, as has usually been done. The latter estimates overstate the increase in productivity which can be distributed in the form of higher wages without increasing unit labor costs, since they ignore the very substantial growth in the number of nonproduction workers, and its consequence that total payrolls per unit of output have been rising more rapidly than unit wage cost figured only on "productive labor."

One other question which can only be mentioned concerns the impact of quality changes on the measurement of output. Some authorities, such as Prof. Richard Ruggles, contend that failure to allow for the improvement in goods and services builds an upward bias into the price index and understates the increase in productivity. (Statement, with Dr. Nancy Ruggles, before the Joint Economic Committee, *Relation of Prices to Economic Stability and Growth: Compendium*, 1958, pp. 298–299.) But if one thinks of productivity in terms of a measurement of output available for distribution, then it would be necessary to impose the limitation that unless the quality change means that people get the same utility at lower cost, or unless it satisfies wants with fewer units of the product and hence lower total cost, the quality change does not affect the amount of real income available for distribution. But if quality changes do have price or quantity effects, then productivity as a measure of the total real income available for distribution has increased. Milton Gilbert also discussed this issue in "The Problem of Quality Changes and Index Numbers," *Monthly Labor Review*, September, 1961, pp. 992–997.

24. Letter from M. G. Ionides of Ripley, Surrey, to the London *Economist*, Aug. 3, 1957, p. 378. The writer was referring to a very comparable policy of "voluntary restraint" which had previously been introduced by Sir Stafford Cripps.

25. See Theodore W. Schultz, "Investment in Human Capital," *American Economic Review*, vol. 51, March, 1961, and "Reflections on Investment in Man," *Journal of Political Economy*, vol. 70, October, 1962, supplement. Also, Gary S. Becker, "Investment in Human Capital: A Theoretical Analysis," *Journal of Political Economy*, vol. 70, pp. 9–49, October, 1962, supplement.

26. See, for example, Benton Massell, "Capital Formation and Technological Change in United States

Manufacturing," *Review of Economics and Statistics,* vol. 42, May, 1960.

27. For a good history and analysis of these plans, see Sumner H. Slichter, James J. Healy, and E. R. Livernash, *The Impact of Collective Bargaining on Management,* Brookings, Washington, 1960, chap. 28.

28. George L. Perry, "Wages and the Guideposts," *American Economic Review,* vol. 57, pp. 903–904, September, 1967. Perry found that his equation for the years 1947 to 1960 (and also an equation for 1953 to 1960) overpredicted actual wage changes in fifteen of the seventeen calendar quarters from 1962 through the first quarter of 1966. Com-

paring wage changes between 1954 and 1957 with those between 1963 and 1966, two roughly comparable periods, he found that annual wage increases in visible industries slowed down from 5 percent in the mid-1950s to 2.9 percent in the mid-1960s, but in invisible industries the slowdown was only from 4.3 to 3.8 percent.

29. Arthur M. Ross, "Second-Generation Wage-Price Restraints," *Proceedings of the Nineteeth Annual Meeting of the Industrial Relations Research Association, 1966,* pp. 11–12.

30. The same, p. 12.

Three themes have run through most of the subjects we have discussed, so let us organize our view of the future around them: (1) the inevitable conflict and compromises between people in their roles as consumers and people in their roles as producers; (2) the incompatibility between maximum production efficiency (of interest both to society as a whole and to the individual producer) and the assured continuity of income and status to employees; and (3) the difficulties of simultaneously pursuing the social goals of full employment and price stability while avoiding "excessive" government intervention in economic decisions. These are problems which can never be resolved; at best, we can deal more intelligently with them by understanding them better.

One major difficulty in approaching these as three separate issues is their close interrelatedness. For example, the general problem in the producers–consumers confrontation may be phrased as how to give workers effective control over their jobs without at the same time giving them the opportunity to exploit those who use or rely on their output. But from only a slightly different point of view, this also can be phrased as how to accord workers a degree of security in their incomes and status without unduly impairing the efficiency of the production process, on which society as a whole and the individual firm in particular depend for their welfare and even their survival—the second of our themes. And since job control and the degree of influence over wages

and prices change with the state of the economy —that is, its closeness to full employment—the first two themes are necessarily played against a background accompaniment provided by our third theme, a theme which at times becomes dominant as well as dissonant. Hence we will find it fruitful to consider these three issues jointly.

The size of the decision unit

If one sees the problem as principally one of making private power subordinate to public power, or private interests conform to public welfare, he is tempted to urge that private *units* (whether business firms or labor unions or bargaining units) be broken into smaller size, more susceptible to control by the market force of competition; or alternatively, that more authority be lodged with government to impose its decisions (on wages and prices, for example) on the private parties whenever they seem to be abusing their power.

But this is far too simplistic an approach. For one thing, it ignores the problem—increasingly complex in our time—of how to give people more effective control over their own affairs. It cannot always be done by confining their scope of organization and action to a local level. For example, as the firm moves from single-plant to multiplant operations, and as the rate of product and process obsolescence increases, the modern large corporation sometimes finds it advisable to dispose of a plant altogether rather than attempt to update it or somehow to integrate it into changing product lines. This means that the seniority rights which workers have built up over the years suddenly lose all value, since typically seniority is applied on a plant-unit basis, under agreements worked out between local union and management. If this problem is to be met, it can only be met within a different and more appropriate unit, such as the company as a whole. Instead of restricting seniority rights to the local plant, seniority may be made companywide under certain circumstances and following certain rules. This transfers the seniority problem from plant to headquarters. The local people may resent being deprived of the authority to reach their own decisions on seniority matters, but they are helpless in the face of the organizational changes which have given to the home office the power to invalidate their seniority decisions by closing their plant altogether. If seniority decisions are to be effective, at least under such circumstances, the local unit must defer to the central unit. Local members can participate in the central decisions by such devices as helping to frame guidelines for their negotiators or sending observers to the central bargaining conference, but the degree of their involvement has been diluted. Nevertheless, in order for them to have any effective say at all in the matter, the only recourse is to participate in the larger unit. Anyone who insists that workers' actions be confined to the plant where they work is obviously limiting the degree of their control over the matters which affect them. This is the basis for the recent union interest in concerted or coalition bargaining.

But this too creates its further problems. As the economy becomes larger and more complex and interrelated, decisions taken at any point potentially affect the welfare of people everywhere. But obviously the individual cannot participate, however indirectly, in all the major decisions constantly being made throughout the economy. Who knows what decision affecting his job and status some computer may be this moment rattling off, in the company where he works or in some other, without his having a thing to say about it? Who knows what bargain may be in process of being struck between industry and union chiefs, at some distant location, that reduces him to being a pawn in a transaction? How *can* one know? Thus the Western philosophical belief that we as individuals should have some influence over the social systems of which we are a part is being severely challenged as the growing scale and complexity of our social organisms render them more and more impersonal, seeming to dwarf the individual and to rob him of his individuality, to reduce the frontiers of his discretion to interpersonal relationships or idiosyncratic behavior.

One consequence of this sense of alienation from the decision-making centers has been to revive people's interest in their local affairs—the local community, the local union—where they can achieve some sense of direct involvement. Hence national unions have been faced with a resurgence of local activism, sometimes quite rebellious, in the form of rejection of negotiated agreements, direct action by dissident factions, election and policy challenges. But now we come full circle, since local control—as we have just noted—is ineffective where the real seat of decision making is somewhere else. The dilemma is a real and critical one: How can workers help to shape their own lives, when the scale and complexity of economic activity act to remove effective decision making to more distant centers? How does collective bargaining fit into the developing picture?

The corporate planning process

Let us begin exploring this question by first examining the corporate decision-making system, of which collective bargaining is a part. This will provide us with a valuable perspective from which to view not only the particular problem we have posed for ourselves but the setting in which it occurs.

Decisions do not get made in isolation. Every decision is necessarily a product of decisions which were previously made and is affected by anticipation of future decisions to which it is expected to lead. Thus a decision is always made within a matrix of other decisions, partly determined by them and partly determining them.

In the business world, which is also the worker's world, this interrelatedness of decisions has been recognized in the corporate planning and budgeting processes, which attempt to bring together into a comprehensive and meaningful mosaic all the separate decisions which must be made with respect to all the parts of the company's activities. The process of business planning, whether for the coming year or a longer time span, relates each part of the organization to the total operation. The amount of information which must be digested into the plan and budget is enormous.

A very large number of decisions, estimates, and schedules relating to production, marketing, and finance must be related in what amounts to a detailed simulation of all activities of the firm which have a bearing on its profit position. This is a rationalization of the planned performance of each individual unit in the light of the expected performance of all other units in the organization over the same period.

While the corporate officials responsible for sales, production, research or engineering, and general administration will have inspected the estimates of the units for which they are responsible before passing them to higher authority, their decisions must be reviewed from the standpoint of their consistency with the company's total scale of operations and their compatibility with the overall company-profit target. This frequently brings decision makers in various units into conflict and invites bargaining and negotiation among them.

There are differences of outlook arising out of differences in responsibility. Sales and production may both argue for budgeting more inventory, the former to ensure prompt deliveries and the latter to stabilize production schedules and the work force, whereas finance may maintain that too much capital is already tied up in unproductive investment in idle stocks of goods, some of which are going obsolete, to add to the cost.

Conflicts at budget time can also arise over questions of equity. A product manager expresses his pique that his product is charged with the proportion of the advertising appropriation that its gross sales bear to total sales, but the advertising program has rarely so much as mentioned the product. A division manager is bitter because his

operation is expected to "turn itself inside out" to realize a 20 percent return on investment, while another division is permitted to "loaf along" with only a 12 percent return.

Such conflicts reveal that the budget or the plan is inescapably a political document as well as a financial one, a product of bargains effected on the strength of relative power positions no less than a product of accountants and industrial engineers.

Where does the worker and where does the union fit into such a process?

The philosophy behind business planning is that, desirably, it should involve everyone in the business who has the capacity to affect the outcome, whose role will help to determine whether in fact the plan is realized. From this standpoint the decisions on production rates are made not in some engineer's office, for example, but by the engineer in consultation with the foreman, and after the foreman has had a chance to review experience with at least some of his key men.

This philosophy is seldom fully carried out in practice. To the extent that it is not, the plan or budget becomes another instrument for imposing authority. Quotas of production or sales are set without much regard for those who are expected to fulfill them. Theoretically, planning the budget is a means of incorporating everyone into the decision-making process. Practically, it is often a system whereby some people set targets which are then used to measure the effectiveness of others. If production processes are mechanized and automated, the individual's discretionary role in the production process is still further reduced; he becomes an adjunct to the mechanized process, and any opportunity for meaningful participation in "planning" his relationship to the whole is virtually nullified.

Where workers play little direct part in corporate decision-making processes, as is typically the case, the union, simply by its presence, helps to assure that their interests are taken into account by those who *are* making the decisions. Workers are not equipped either to participate or to bargain effectively in the corporate planning-budgeting program itself, as individuals or as groups. The best they can do is to attempt, through their representative, the union, to make sure that the corporate planners adopt decisions which are consonant with previously expressed worker interests. Thus collective bargaining neither provides employees with any mechanism for significantly affecting the actual decisions which go into the company's plans, nor does it interfere with that planning process. It simply provides, through its periodically negotiated contracts and their elaboration in the grievance procedure, data which the corporate managers must take into account as they steer the firm into the future.

Adapting to change

A company's plans and budgets relate to its immediate present, when it is concerned with whether it is making a profit on its current operations, and to its long-range future, when it is concerned whether activities are under way which will result in future operations maintaining the profitability of the firm. Once plans and budgets are made, it must then maintain a close scrutiny of how those plans are faring, and whether there are departures from the budget. If the sales which it had expected this month have not materialized, why not? Their failure to do so may lessen the inflow of funds which had been counted on for use in some other corporate activity. They may also suggest that certain products in the company's line are losing favor with the public, jeopardizing its future plans. If costs are higher than expected, they require explanation. Unless purely a temporary phenomenon, the higher cost may carry a threat to the firm's competitive efficiency and profitability. What progress is being made in the planned extension of the company's marketing organization to the Southwest—or to the Far East? Is it on schedule? Has the redesign of a particular product proceeded as planned for its introduction next year? Is R & D making satisfactory headway on product X, which is intended to replace product Y two years from now? Has a site been purchased for the new plant which is to be started in three years in Colorado?

The company analyzes all departures from the budget plan in order to take corrective action as needed. In some instances the deviation from plan can be righted by further application of effort or by removing some impediment to efficiency. In other instances the variance is more intractable, and special action is called for. The plan itself must be changed. In the short run, the principal adjustments which are possible are in controlling production and costs in line with sales. In the longer run, the principal strategic variables with which it must work are new products, new and improved technological systems, and improved organization (referring not only to structure but also to quality of personnel).

How does all this relate to labor? Very importantly. More and more, the pace of *change* has quickened in the business world—change in product lines, markets, production processes, financing, and organization. These must be planned for as best a firm can, but plans are inescapably imperfect. The unexpected is always occurring and bringing with it either misfortune or opportunity. Both must be dealt with promptly in order to preserve and if possible enhance the value of the assets which the company is managing.

This importance of adaptability and flexibility is greater today than it was twenty-five or fifty years ago. For a company to remain profitable and viable, it must be constantly prepared to meet and deal with change. And this is increasingly incompatible with the emphasis on maintaining work practices, customs, and traditions which are the values workers typically seek to preserve. They want to retain them in part because they feel at ease with the familiar—it is a way of life—and in part because the familiar seems to promise security. As long as they can continue with a job they have mastered, performing a function which is integral to a process, protected by seniority, they have greater assurance of the weekly paycheck which is needed to balance the household's budget. And if in addition there is a two-year or three-year contract which spells out rights, and an arbitration procedure which promises their enforcement, and an industrial "common law" which takes note of customs and precedents, so much the better.

But this stress on stability and security by workers and by the unions which are their agents has two weaknesses. First, it is incompatible with the company's need for prompt adaptation to change and thus may jeopardize the profitability and even survival of the company on which the employees are counting for job security. And second, it is in part illusory. It may be powerful enough to retain customary jobs and practices in the present, but it is not powerful enough to retain them in the future, for there is nothing to prevent a company from closing down a whole plant or process or suspending the manufacture of a product as it shifts into new products, new markets, new processes in its continuing preoccupation with metamorphosizing assets, transforming their shape and function and location with the passage of time.

The traditional fixed-term bargaining procedures thus embody disadvantages for both workers and management, but if the authors were to make an impressionistic judgment, it would be that the disadvantage is greater for workers than for management. Managements have learned to cope with all sorts of obstacles in the planning process, and to make their plans taking such obstacles into account. Obviously they would prefer more flexibility if they could get it, but the inflexibilities of collective bargaining are, on the whole, a relatively small price to pay for the freedom to plan corporate operations, with the union's role confined to policing the conditions set out in a fixed-term contract. The employees, on the other hand, are left without any mechanism for affecting the major corporate decisions which will determine their future. They settle for a measure of ostensible future security and present benefits, without any effective participation in the real decision-making process.

For most employees, that may seem a satisfactory bargain. But if the events of the last few years have more than transient significance, we may expect that in time younger and better educated workers, taking their places in corporate life, will be less satisfied with such a version of "industrial democracy." For this reason, the authors believe that the future will see an increasing dissatisfaction with the episodic nature and limited scope of present collective-bargaining forms, and growing pressures for their modification into more effective instruments of participation in the continuing decision-making process. We do not anticipate anything approximating "joint management," but we do expect more sophisticated methods by which employee representatives will make their influence felt in corporate planning. Developments on the campuses and in the communities may be harbingers of what is ahead in business.

Decision making in the economy

If the decisions taken within the business firm are interrelated, and if, to be made effective, they must somehow be coordinated with one another, the same thing is true within the economy as a whole. Private decisions reached within each of the sectors of an economy inevitably have their impact on the rest of the economy, and for that reason sometimes become the subject of public policy. This is true of such matters as the degree of market power which unions and businesses will be allowed to exercise, whether wage increases in key units may set "targets" for others to shoot at which, when added together, have an inflationary effect, whether inducements may not be provided for the development of manpower or the management of capital which, while leaving final decision to private individuals, will encourage them in certain directions. All these issues involve recognition of the relationship of the parts of the economy to the whole, the element of interdependence among decisions, and the consequence that decisions somehow must be coordinated—sometimes not only by the market but also by other more formal means. Just as the sales department of a corporation is not privileged to make decisions without respect to what the production or finance ends of the business intend, so we may reasonably say that the steel industry and the Automobile Workers Union and the electrical-appliance industry and the railroad brotherhoods are not privileged to make decisions without respect to their impact on others.

In addition to this need for some degree of coordination of the units in the private sector to achieve a mosaic of interrelated interests, there are certain functions which only the public sector can perform. Different people would want to phrase this in different ways, but in general there would be agreement that if we relied on the private sphere to provide free scope for people's initiatives and abilities, we would rely on the public sector to expand people's capacities to contribute to the overall result through such devices as improved educational programs, reduction in discrimination, improvement in public health, elimination of slum conditions, encouragement of mobility, and so on. More controversially, some would add that the public sector should provide opportunities for people to *use* their capacities when the private sector fails to do so. In any event, the activities of the private and public sectors must also be coordinated.

The problem of economywide coordination was strikingly expressed by Charles Malik, a philosopher as well as Minister of Foreign Affairs for his home state of Lebanon, in an address before the fiftieth anniversary celebration of the Harvard Business School.[1]

> The Western businessman carries out his planning with four considerations in mind: the inner, autonomous laws of development of his own particular skill; the possibilities of the market; the requirements of competition with other branches of the same skill; and the requirements of competition with other sectors of the economy. In all this there is of course a principle of coordination at work. But it works in an atmosphere of freedom without imposition from the State.

> The challenge of coordination consists of whether the requirements of the whole—and "the whole" in a fast-shrinking world must mean more than the whole of the nation; it must mean and it will increasingly mean the whole of the world—should not be actively kept in mind, whether or not it is the government that thus "actively keeps them in mind" or some independent agency in which all businesses voluntarily participate.

It is precisely this question of to what extent, how, and by whom the requirements of coordination of the separate sectors of the economy shall be accomplished that is puzzling the Western economies now. A variety of experiments in "democratic planning" have been undertaken in Western Europe. How business and labor should be involved in these efforts at coordinating the interrelated decisions of the economy poses a problem somewhat comparable to the involvement in corporate planning of those who are affected by the decisions made. Unless they are involved,

at least through some form of representation, the consequence of planning may be imposed decisions—coordination by authority. On the other hand, if a plan for the economy were to have the tightness of a corporate budget, it would require every firm to conform to its provisions. This would rob managements (and unions too) of discretion and freedom to innovate. Efforts to coordinate the economy must be looser and less authoritative than corporate efforts at planning if we are to preserve Western values.

Most notably, France has been attempting to meet this problem via a network of committees representing many sectors of the economy, on all of which sit representatives of industry, labor, and the government. Their aim is to arrive at some degree of consensus as to a possible and desirable level of production in the economy as a whole and what this implies for each industrial sector, without committing anyone to a specific performance. Other countries in Western Europe have attempted different solutions.

In the United States nothing so systematic has been attempted, but if we dig a bit below the surface we become aware that there are agencies at work which seek to influence and thus to relate in a more meaningful pattern the innumerable independent but interrelated decisions which are continuingly being made in the economy. In part this comes about through formal devices such as the monetary and credit policies of the Federal Reserve System, fiscal devices of the Federal government, the work of numerous regulatory agencies and departments, and in part by informal influence exercised by governmental officials from the President on down.

Perhaps because of this lack of any comprehensive or systematic coordination, there has not been much question of business or labor "representation." Only in wartime, when a system of controls was imposed on the economy, have the major interest groups been involved in policies aimed at coordinating the economy's activities. In peacetime the question of coordination has been so little discussed that the issue of representation has not been relevant, with perhaps the single exception of the short-lived National Recovery Administration in President Franklin D. Roosevelt's first term of office.

It is an open question how seriously the AFL-CIO, or most foreign labor movements, for that matter, wish to become entangled in the making of overall economic policy, however. In our discussion of the labor movement in Chapters 10 and 14, we made a distinction between the interests of the individual national unions and the labor movement as a whole. The former dominate the latter in the United States. If labor representatives, however chosen, were to agree on some policy for more effective "coordination" of the economy and that policy were to curb the activities of strong national unions, it is doubtful whether the independent unions would conform to the requirements of the policy.

Labor unions, by their very nature, are primarily agencies of protest and opposition. We may speak of the representation of labor's interests and of labor's desire to participate in making the decisions which affect its membership, but beneath the verbal symbols the fact remains that organized labor is basically an opposition force, formed to take issue with those in authority, reacting to the exercise of initiative by those who exercise the managerial function both in business and government.

Employment and income security

In recent years a number of men in public life—in government, business, and labor—have asked that the definition of national goals be formalized and more systematic procedures established for realizing them. Whatever may develop on this front, at least since the Employment Act of 1946 full employment has formally been such a national goal. Unfortunately, it is a goal of such elusive content that it does not effectively serve as a guide to policy. With what rate of unemployment is full employment consonant? How far shall full employment be pursued in the face of rising price levels? We explored these issues in an earlier chapter.

We have no acceptable answers to these questions, and the result is that we have been adrift in the sea of economic and social policy. It is a suitable subject for a Swift to satirize when responsible government officials, as in 1970, eagerly hope for an *upturn* in the unemployment figures

and for other signs that economic growth has been *halted*. We seek economic adversity, as a means of stifling inflationary pressures. Of course we are all aware of the Phillips-curve dilemma—the "trade-off" between employment and prices. But when the labor force is increasing, and capital assets continue to multiply, surely there is enough real growth potential in the economy that we need not look to unemployment and below-capacity operations for "relief."

Obviously we need a new perspective on the workings of our complex and interrelated economy. Clearly it calls for better management than we have been giving it. Whether this will require a larger role for government is perhaps still obscure—the chances are that it will, but that we can still preserve a very high degree of decentralized and private decision making. The principal point, however, is that because we do not have clear solutions to our problems, it is time that we begin looking for them. Old methods are not good enough.

The provision of some reasonably satisfactory employment and income security for every citizen, on conditions which are not demeaning, is quite apparently one general economic goal toward which we are striving. Beyond this we seek a level of affluence that will permit a continuing improvement in—to use the already commonplace phrase—the quality of life. These objectives are not to be won simply by "trying harder." They require some reorganization and redirection of our economic activity.

Conclusion

Whatever devices may be developed for the more effective performance of our economy, it does seem evident that the necessity for coordinating its parts will require more decisions at levels beyond the individual firm. Opportunities for employees to affect directly the decisions affecting them will shrink even more than at present—which brings us back to the question with which we began this chapter. How can employees help to shape their own economic activities when the centers of decision making become more remote? Clearly, this is a question without an answer.

Perhaps—however one may regard the possibility—one "resolution" may come with employee acceptance of the general economic environment as a given, like the physical environment, something taken for granted unless a rude shock indicates the need to press for change. This would be a distinct possibility if our control of the economy were to improve to the point where it would provide a relatively satisfactory environment. Within this "given" framework, organized employees could then participate vigorously in molding the local conditions, experiencing whatever satisfactions of involvement that this might provide them.

But the limitations of this approach are brought home by the abrupt manner in which we have had to learn, within the last few years, that even the physical environment cannot be taken for granted. Have we any more reason to assume that the economic environment can be taken on faith, allowing each local unit to plan its own optimistic future? The answer is too obvious to belabor.

Is there an implication, then, that the "big" economic decisions have outgrown the democratic process, and must be concentrated in the hands of a few technical experts at the hub of the system? Some fear, or argue, that this is the case. The only alternative, they say, is an economic system that limps and wheezes and sputters, and in the process fails to provide adequately for those who come under it.

There are others who believe that the way out lies in returning to small units of decision making, breaking down the large corporations and the large unions into their constituent parts, which become independent, autonomous units. Aside from the political improbability of such an approach, consistency would appear to require that large political units—nations themselves—should then be subjected to similar treatment, so that we would repose greater authority and genuine power with the states, for example, rather than with the Federal government. The likelihood that any nation would render itself so impotent seems remote, to put it mildly. The tendencies are all in the opposite direction, as we noted, toward larger units of decision making.

The problem we confront, then, of how to make collective bargaining a genuinely representative institution, allowing those who come under it to participate effectively in the decisions affecting them, is obviously part of a much broader problem—the instruments and philosophy of government itself in a changing society. This is a problem which has occupied the great thinkers from the time of Plato, to which no definitive answer can be given.

Of one thing we may be sure. World society is now in a stage of political ferment, induced less by ideological confrontations than by such major historical phenomena as the rise of nationalism from the ashes of colonialism, the diminished authority of the white Western Christian powers, the dramatic increase in world population, the surge in urbanization, astounding advances in scientific knowledge and technology. In the face of such sweeping developments, social institutions do not remain static. It may seem a long jump from events of such order to the probable future of collective bargaining, but every set of human relationships operates within a larger context, which in turn is enmeshed in a still larger context. These world movements importantly affect the American society and economy, and in turn the form and functioning of our corporate structures, and necessarily then the processes through which working individuals seek some voice in their economic affairs. How long can we expect the processes of today to persist unchanged?

ADDITIONAL READINGS

Berle, A. A.: *Power,* Harcourt, Brace & World, New York, 1969.

Dunlop, John T., and Neil W. Chamberlain: *Frontiers of Collective Bargaining,* Harper & Row, New York, 1967.

Gross, Bertram (ed.): *A New Society?,* Basic Books, New York, 1968.

Harrington, Michael: *The Accidental Century,* Penguin Books, Baltimore, 1965.

Shonfield, Andrew: *Modern Capitalism,* Oxford, London, 1965.

FOR ANALYSIS AND DISCUSSION

1. Do you see any parallel between student and minority demands for involvement in decisions affecting them, and the position of employees of

a company? Are students and blacks catching up with what workers won in the thirties, or are they pointing the way toward what workers may be demanding in the future?

2. Where does the union fit into the corporate planning process, if at all? To what extent must industrial relations issues be explicitly considered by management in constructing a meaningful operating plan? What industrial relations issues would be most important to consider, if any are explored?

3. Do you foresee increasing pressures for effective coordination of the various parts of the economy, whether or not this leads to any formal measures for public economic planning? From what quarters would you expect such pressures to arise? To what extent and in what ways do you think they should be accommodated? What roles would you assign to business and to labor in whatever procedures you are willing to recommend?

4. Over the years various people have constructed blueprints of what they consider a "good society." (Two of the most widely discussed of such blueprints in recent decades have been Walter Lippmann's *The Good Society* and Peter Drucker's *The New Society*, which you might find stimulating reading.) What would be the outlines of "the good society" as you would draw them now? How would these compare with the shape of society today? Of society twenty years ago? How likely is it that you will maintain these same views ten years from now? What, if anything, might change them?

5. A team of researchers who examined the position of low-income groups in the United States concluded: "The economic growth of a country is in large measure a function of purposeful movement by individuals to better jobs, new and better ways of doing things, use of new products, and the ancillary tendencies to plan for the future, accumulate capital, work hard, and provide education for children." (James Morgan and others, *Income and Welfare in the United States,* McGraw-Hill, New York, 1962, p. 447.)

In the light of your study of the labor market and its institutions, suggest ways in which these functions might be improved.

NOTES

1. Charles Malik, "The Businessman and the Challenge of Communism," published in *Management's Mission in a New Society,* McGraw-Hill, New York, 1959.

INDEX

Biemiller, Andrew J., 574
Bill of Rights under Landrum-Griffin Act, 162–164
Blackman, John L., 603
Blacks (*see* Negroes)
Blau, Peter, 41–43, 46, 47, 49
Blind, Aid to the, 561
Bloch, Joseph W., 221
Bloom, Gordon, 153, 605n.
Blue-collar workers, 24–26
  job mobility, 58, 61
Bluffing in bargaining, 233
"Bogus" typesetting, 242
Boulwarism, 212–213, 216
Bowen, Howard R., 12, 15
Bowen, William G., 512, 652n.
Boycott:
  Danbury Hatters case, 128–129
  secondary, 610
  under Taft-Hartley Act, 145–147
Bradley, Philip D., 619
Brewery Workers, 82
Briggs, Vernon M., Jr., 605n.
Brinberg, Herbert R., 490n.
Brinker, Paul A., 489n., 512, 558n.
Brisbane, Albert, 102
British Health Service, 514n.
Bronfenbrenner, Martin, 438n.
Brookings Institution, 245, 255
Brooks, George, 490n., 491n.
Brown, David G., 63, 64n.
Brozen, Yale, 475–476
Brubaker, Otis, 653n.
Budd, Edward, 437
Budgeting in the firm, 305–307
Burton, John, 503
Business agent, 181–182
Business unionism, 100–101

Campbell, Angus, 458n.
Campbell, Colin D., 489n.
Campbell, Rosemary G., 489n.
Caples, William, 218n.
Carleton, R. O., 47
Carol, Arthur, 36
Carpenters, Brotherhood of, 82
Carper, James W., 49
Carr, Willine, 507
Cassell, Frank H., 540
Cassell, Gustav, 374n.
Cartter, Allan M., 372, 437n., 438n.
Centers, Richard, 452
Centralization of authority in unions, 81–82, 85–86

Certification, effect of union, 142–143
Chalmers, W. E., 238
Chamberlain, Neil W., 88, 216, 313, 603, 650
Chamberlin, Edward H., 616, 622n.
Chandler, John H., 438n.
Chandler, Margaret K., 238
Chase, L. C., 217
Cheit, Earl F., 512
Chemical Workers Union, 82
Christensen, Thomas G. S., 178n.
Christenson, Carol, 479, 487
Christie, Robert, 89n.
Chrysler Corp., 326, 327
Cigar Makers Union, 95, 99, 100
Circular flow, 5
City central, 186
Civil conspiracy, doctrine of, 126–127
Civil Rights Act of 1964, 154n., 324–325
  application to unions, 168
Civil rights movements, 113–114
Clark, John M., 154n., 619, 652n.
Clayton Act, 129
Clegg, H. A., 652n.
Closed shop, 158
  in conspiracy trials, 125–126
  (*See also* Union security)
Coal:
  collective bargaining in, 611–612
  strikes, 580–581, 584
  (*See also* Mine Workers, United)
Coalition bargaining, 191
Coercive comparisons, 379, 402
Cohen, Wilbur J., 512, 538n., 541n.
Coleman, J. S., 199, 201n.
Collective agreement:
  rise of, 101
  scope, 219–221
  (*See also* Contract)
Collective bargaining:
  appraisal, 264–265
  defined in law, 134
  effect on corporate flexibility, 658–659
  encouragement of, 134
  ethical basis, 236–238
  fractional, 261–262
  individual rights under, 170–171
  opposed to scientific management, 107
  origins, 92–93
  relative advantages of, 659

Collective bargaining:
  requirements of, 142–143
  subject matter, 134–135, 219–223, 230–232
  supplemented by legislation, 443
  Walton-McKersie analysis, 208–211
  workers' rationale for, 73
Comparative wage rates, 347–348
Commitment, occupational, 38
Committee on Political Education, 448
Common law on unions, 125
Commons, John R., 273–278, 287
Commonwealth v. Hunt, 126
Communism in unions, 100, 116
Competition:
  impact on workers, 271–278, 281–282, 617–618
  union limitations on, 378
  (*See also* Monopoly powers, union)
  workable, 619
Competitive analysis, 339–341, 343ff.
  evaluated, 355–356, 365–366, 369–372, 435–436
Condon-Wadlin Act, 600–601
Congress of Industrial Organizations, 112–113
Conspiracy doctrine, 125–126
Constructive discharge, 160
Consumer interests, 2, 61–62, 340, 369, 461, 617, 655
Continuous bargaining, 213–216
Contract:
  clauses, 221
  interpretation, 255–256
  ratification, 171
Contract-bar rule, 157–158
Contracting out, 449
Conventions, union, 182–183
  attendance, 196–197
Cook, Alice H., 199
Cooper, Barbara S., 513n.
Coordination:
  as management function, 228–229
  need for, 659–660
Coronado cases, 129
Corruption in unions, 165, 175
Cost of agreement, 227–228, 235
Cost of disagreement, 227–228, 234–235
Cost variances, 307